Name	WWW Address (http://)	Remarks

D0471104

Part III. Offshore Markets

Name	WWW Address (http://)	Remarks
Euromoney Magazine	www.euromoney.com	Eurocurrency and Eurobond activity
Euroclear	www.euroclear.com	
Standard & Poor's sovereign ratings	www.standardpoor.com/ratings/sovereigns/index.htm	

Part IV. Derivatives: Futures, Options, and Swaps

Name	WWW Address (http://)	Remarks
Chicago Mercantile Exchange	www.cme.com	Description of contracts, trading, data
EUREX	www.eurexchange.com	Description of contracts, trading, data
London International Financial Futures Exchange	www.liffe.com	Description of contracts, trading, data
MATIF	www.matif.fr	Description of contracts, trading, data
Singapore Exchange Derivatives Trading	www.singaporeexchange.com/sgxdt.htm	Description of contracts, trading, data
Futures Industry Association & Futures Industry Institute	www.fiafii.org	Data and links to all futures and options exchanges
The GLOBEX Alliance	www.globexalliance.com	Electronic, off-floor trading
International Swap Dealers Association	www.isda.com	Information about swap market practices
The Options Clearing Corporation	www.optionsclearing.com	All about the clearing house

Part V. International Asset Portfolios

Name	WWW Address (http://)	Remarks
International Finance Corporation	www.ifc.org	World Bank arm for private sector investing
S&P/IFC Emerging Markets Database	www.spglobal.com/ssindexmainemdb.html	Primary source for emerging market data
International Federation of Stock Exchanges	www.fibv.com	Links to national stock exchanges
The Bank of New York Global Investing	www.bankofny.com/adr	Listing of all ADRs
BradyNet Home Page	www.bradynet.com	Facts and figures on Brady bonds

Part VI. International Asset Portfolios and Financial Risk Management

Name	WWW Address (http://)	Remarks
RiskMetrics	www.riskmetrics.com	Publications and information about Riskmetrics' VAR system
International Association of Financial Engineers	iafe.org	Research and tools for financial risk management
International Treasurer	www.intltreasurer.com	Journal of global treasury and financial risk management

Part VII. Regulatory Issues

Name	WWW Address (http://)	Remarks
Bank for International Settlements	www.bis.org	International banking regulation, market surveys, capital adequacy regulations
U.S. Securities and Exchange Commission	www.sec.gov	
Financial Accounting Standards Board	www.fasb.org	Association responsible for U.S. accounting standards
International Organization of Securities Commissions	www.iosco.org	Association of national SECs
International Accounting Standards Committee	www.iasc.org.uk	Association responsible for international accounting standards

Other Addresses

Name	WWW Address (http://)	Remarks
International Business Resources on the Web	ciber.bus.msu.edu/busres/Static/Statistical–Data–Sources.htm	Statistical data around the world
Financial Data Finder	www.cob.ohio-state.edu/~fin/osudata.htm	Data providers from A-Z
Richard Levich, Stern School of Business	www.stern.nyu.edu/~rlevich	Address e-mail to rlevich@stern.nyu.edu

INTERNATIONAL FINANCIAL MARKETS

THE MCGRAW-HILL/IRWIN SERIES IN FINANCE, INSURANCE, AND REAL ESTATE

Stephen A. Ross
Franco Modigliani Professor of Finance and Economics
Sloan School of Management
Massachusetts Institute of Technology
Consulting Editor

FINANCIAL MANAGEMENT

Benninga and Sarig
Corporate Finance: *A Valuation Approach*

Block and Hirt
Foundations of Financial Management
Ninth Edition

Brealey and Myers
Principles of Corporate Finance
Sixth Edition

Brealey, Myers, and Marcus
Fundamentals of Corporate Finance
Third Edition

Brooks
FinGame Online 3.0

Bruner
Case Studies in Finance: *Managing for Corporate Value Creation*
Third Edition

Chew
The New Corporate Finance: *Where Theory Meets Practice*
Third Edition

Graduate Management Admissions Council, Robert F. Bruner, Kenneth Eades, and Robert Harris
Essentials of Finance: *With an Accounting Review*
Fully interactive CD-ROM derived from Finance Interactive 1997 Pre-MBA Edition
Finance Interactive: Pre-MBA Series 2000
Second Edition

Grinblatt and Titman
Financial Markets and Corporate Strategy

Helfert
Techniques of Financial Analysis: *A Guide to Value Creation*
Tenth Edition

Higgins
Analysis for Financial Management
Sixth Edition

Hite
A Programmed Learning Guide to Finance

Kester, Fruhan, Piper, and Ruback
Case Problems in Finance
Eleventh Edition

Nunnally and Plath
Cases in Finance
Second Edition

Ross, Westerfield, and Jaffe
Corporate Finance
Fifth Edition

Ross, Westerfield, and Jordan
Essentials of Corporate Finance
Third Edition

Ross, Westerfield, and Jordan
Fundamentals of Corporate Finance
Fifth Edition

Smith
The Modern Theory of Corporate Finance
Second Edition

White
Financial Analysis with an Electronic Calculator
Fourth Edition

INVESTMENTS

Bodie, Kane, and Marcus
Essentials of Investments
Fourth Edition

Bodie, Kane, and Marcus
Investments
Fourth Edition

Cohen, Zinbarg, and Zeikel
Investment Analysis and Portfolio Management
Fifth Edition

Corrado and Jordan
Fundamentals of Investments: *Valuation and Management*

Farrell
Portfolio Management: *Theory and Applications*
Second Edition

Hirt and Block
Fundamentals of Investment Management
Sixth Edition

Jarrow
Modelling Fixed Income Securities and Interest Rate Options

Shimko
The Innovative Investor
Excel Version

FINANCIAL INSTITUTIONS AND MARKETS

Cornett and Saunders
Fundamentals of Financial Institutions Management

Rose
Commercial Bank Management
Fourth Edition

Rose
Money and Capital Markets: *Financial Institutions and Instruments in a Global Marketplace*
Seventh Edition

Rose and Kolari
Financial Institutions: *Understanding and Managing Financial Services*
Fifth Edition

Santomero and Babbel
Financial Markets, Instruments, and Institutions
Second Edition

Saunders
Financial Institutions Management: *A Modern Perspective*
Third Edition

INTERNATIONAL FINANCE

Eun and Resnick
International Financial Management
Second Edition

Kester and Luehrman
Case Problems in International Finance
Second Edition

Levi
International Finance
Third Edition

Levich
International Financial Markets: *Prices and Policies*
Second Edition

REAL ESTATE

Brueggeman and Fisher
Real Estate Finance and Investments
Tenth Edition

Corgel, Smith, and Ling
Real Estate Perspectives: *An Introduction to Real Estate*
Fourth Edition

Lusht
Real Estate Valuation: *Principles and Applications*

FINANCIAL PLANNING AND INSURANCE

Allen, Melone, Rosenbloom, and VanDerhei
Pension Planning: *Pension, Profit-Sharing, and Other Deferred Compensation Plans*
Eighth Edition

Crawford
Life and Health Insurance Law
Eighth Edition (LOMA)

Harrington and Niehaus
Risk Management and Insurance

Hirsch
Casualty Claim Practice
Sixth Edition

Kapoor, Dlabay, and Hughes
Personal Finance
Fifth Edition

Skipper
International Risk and Insurance: *An Environmental-Managerial Approach*

Williams, Smith, and Young
Risk Management and Insurance
Eighth Edition

Second Edition

INTERNATIONAL FINANCIAL MARKETS

Prices and Policies

Richard M. Levich
New York University

McGraw-Hill Irwin

Boston Burr Ridge, IL Dubuque, IA Madison, WI New York
San Francisco St. Louis Bangkok Bogotá Caracas Kuala Lumpur
Lisbon London Madrid Mexico City Milan Montreal New Delhi
Santiago Seoul Singapore Sydney Taipei Toronto

McGraw-Hill Higher Education

A Division of The **McGraw-Hill** *Companies*

INTERNATIONAL FINANCIAL MARKETS: PRICES AND POLICIES

Published by McGraw-Hill/Irwin, an imprint of The McGraw-Hill Companies, Inc. 1221 Avenue of the Americas, New York, NY, 10020. Copyright © 2001, 1998, by The McGraw-Hill Companies, Inc. All rights reserved. No part of this publication may be reproduced or distributed in any form or by any means, or stored in a database or retrieval system, without the prior written consent of The McGraw-Hill Companies, Inc., including, but not limited to, in any network or other electronic storage or transmission, or broadcast for distance learning. Some ancillaries, including electronic and print components, may not be available to customers outside the United States.

This book is printed on acid-free paper.

3 4 5 6 7 8 9 0 CCW/CCW 0 9 8 7 6 5 4

ISBN 0-07-233865-2

Vice president and editor in chief: *Robin J. Zwettler*
Executive editor: *John E. Biernat*
Sponsoring Editor: *Stephen Patterson/Michelle Janicek*
Marketing manager: *Rhonda Seelinger*
Project manager: *Christina Thornton-Villagomez*
Production supervisor: *Rose Hepburn*
Designer: *Artemio Ortiz*
Supplement coordinator: *Matthew Perry*
Media technology producer: *Mark Molsky*
Cover design: *Kiera Cunningham*
Cover image: © *Photo Disc*
Compositor: *GAC Indianapolis*
Typeface: *10/12 Times Roman*
Printer: *R. R. Donnelley & Sons Company*

Library of Congress Cataloging-in-Publication Data

Levich, Richard M.
    International financial markets / Richard M. Levich.— 2nd ed.
      p. cm. — (The McGraw-Hill/Irwin series in finance, insurance, and real estate)
    Includes bibliographical references and indexes.
    ISBN 0-07-233865-2 (alk. paper)
    1. International finance. 2. Investments, Foreign. 3. Securities—Prices. I. Title. II. Series.

HG3881 .L46 2001
332'.042—dc21

00-064751

www.mhhe.com

To my parents, for a lifetime of encouragement.

Richard M. Levich is a professor of Finance and International Business at New York University's Leonard N. Stern School of Business. From 1984 to 1988 he served as the chairman of the International Business Program at the Stern School. He is also a research associate with the National Bureau of Economic Research in Cambridge, Massachusetts, and he currently serves as editor of *The Journal of International Financial Management and Accounting.*

Professor Levich has been a visiting faculty member at many distinguished universities in the United States and abroad, including Yale University, the University of Chicago, *Ecole des Hautes Etudes Commerciales* in France, the Australian Graduate School of Management at the University of New South Wales, and City University Business School in London. Professor Levich has lectured in many executive education programs including the Wharton Executive MBA Program, Kiel (Germany) World Institute, International Center for Money and Banking (Geneva), J. P. Morgan, Chase Manhattan Bank, and Bankers Trust. He has been a consultant or visiting scholar at the Federal Reserve Board of Governors, the International Monetary Fund and the World Bank.

Professor Levich has published more than 50 articles on various topics dealing with international finance, and is the author or editor of 12 books including *The International Money Market: An Assessment of Alternative Forecasting Techniques and Market Efficiency* (JAI Press, 1979), *Exchange Risk and Exposure: Current Developments in International Financial Management* (Lexington Books, 1980), *ECU: The European Currency Unit* (Euromoney Publications, 1987), *The ECU Market: Current Developments and Future Prospects* (Lexington Books, 1987), *The Capital Market Effects of International Accounting Diversity* (Dow Jones–Irwin, 1990) co-authored with Frederick Choi, and *Exchange Rates and Corporate Performance* (Irwin Professional Publishing, 1994). In 1997, Professor Levich received a CDC Award for Excellence in Applied Portfolio Theory from the *Caisse des Dépôts Group,* France.

Professor Levich received his Ph.D. from the University of Chicago.

The purpose of *International Financial Markets* is to analyze the key financial markets and instruments that facilitate trade and investment activity on a global scale. The scope of inquiry spans two areas—first, the economic determinants of prices, price changes, and price relationships in the major financial markets; and second, the policy issues that result for private enterprises and public policymakers.

Within the first objective, I bring together the current theories of pricing financial instruments in an international context. I develop the economic determinants of financial prices, discuss the limitations and implications of these models, and assess the empirical evidence related to some of their theoretical predictions. Under the second objective, I outline the decisions facing private individuals and enterprises and public policymakers. For private individuals and enterprises, I analyze how decisions regarding capital financing, investing, and risk management should be approached given our discussion of the markets. For public policymakers, the decisions facing monetary authorities, fiscal and tax authorities, banking and financial market regulators, and accounting standard setting bodies are also examined, again within the context of the economics of markets and the incentives facing private individuals and enterprises.

Through this book, I hope that readers will see both the breadth of innovative financial instruments and the linkages that tie these products and markets together. My aim is to clarify the economic underpinnings of various financial markets, and the economic incentives facing private individuals and enterprises who trade in or are affected by these markets. My goal is to demonstrate how various strategic and policy decisions often depend on a particular economic model or a particular empirical view of the world. I hope to present sufficient empirical evidence to explain why some public policy issues and prescriptive strategies offered to firms appear settled, while others remain in dispute. Finally, I hope the reader will gain fresh insights on a central problem facing public policymakers—whether national financial policies and regulations ought to be harmonized or, instead, tailored to each country's individual environment and interests.

The Underlying Philosophy

The primary theme of *International Financial Markets* is that despite the burgeoning of financial products and expanding network of national market linkages, a small number of concepts guide the *pricing* of securities in international financial markets and guide the selection of *policies* by both private market participants and official market regulators. The key concept is that the seemingly distinct components of a national financial market and the seemingly distinct national financial markets themselves are really part of an integrated international financial market where prices tend to be set efficiently so as to reflect available information and to eliminate unusual profit opportunities. The key mechanism is arbitrage and arbitragelike transactions that bind together spot and forward exchange rates, onshore and offshore money markets, forward rates and option prices, forward rates and swap rates, and other financial contracts.

Pricing efficiency and market integration imply a set of linkages for various financial market products both within and between national financial markets, and a consistency in market pricing. Whether at *the level of corporate financial officers* who wish to maximize investment returns, minimize funding costs, or establish acceptable levels of exposure to risks, or at *the level of national market regulators* who seek to promote the growth and ensure the safety and soundness of their own institutions—it follows that policies must be set giving full allowance to the market forces of efficient pricing and integration. Private individuals will naturally try to exploit the breadth of international markets to overcome the regulatory burden placed on local markets or the general inadequacy of local markets. Given the scope of financial alternatives open to private individuals, I show that the ability of national market regulators to set policies that deviate far from the norm is constrained.

Another implication of this perspective is that participants in international financial markets are subject to both opportunities and constraints. Countries and companies that seek to raise capital see international investors as an immense source of funds. However, investors in these markets are perpetually monitoring conditions in financial markets around the world. The market acts as a source of discipline, directing capital toward issuers and instruments that offer unusually high returns, and withdrawing funds from countries and firms where expected returns are low on a risk-adjusted, inflation-adjusted, and currency-adjusted basis. Thus, markets hold the power to reward good performance by macroeconomic policymakers and corporate managers, while penalizing poor performance. The market's judgments are revealed daily in foreign exchange rates, short-term and long-term interest rates, and equity prices—both in the cash markets and in derivative markets. In this sense, the opening of international capital markets offers both a liberalizing opportunity and a disciplining constraint.

Organization of the Text

Part I of the book begins with an overview of the changes that have occurred in international financial markets since the 1960s. I highlight the policy issues that face individuals, firms, and governments and the central role that foreign exchange plays for all countries. In Chapter 2, I review the history of international financial systems over the last century and document recent price behavior in international financial markets.

The heart of the book is contained in the next four parts, which divide the international financial markets into four major groups: (1) foreign exchange, (2) offshore markets, (3) derivative securities, and (4) international asset portfolios. Under each category, my objective is to describe the institutional setting and economics of pricing in these markets, and then to outline the policy issues affecting both private individuals and public policymakers.

Part II contains six chapters concerned with the foreign exchange market. Chapter 3 looks at the structure and institutional aspects of these markets. I discuss the competitive pressures that affect the foreign exchange market and how this affects the use of the market by private firms and the management of trading activity. The parity conditions in international finance, which are now a standard part of any text in this field, are introduced in Chapters 4 and 5. In reviewing these parity conditions, I emphasize the empirical evidence regarding parity, the factors that lead to systematic (rather than transitory) departures from parity, and the policy rules that might be triggered in response to deviations from parity. In Chapter 6, I address the economic determinants of exchange rates. A vast literature on this topic has evolved over the last 25 years. I review the main themes of this research and highlight the policy questions that remain for private firms and public policymakers.

Closely related to the efforts at exchange rate modeling are the themes of market efficiency and exchange rate forecasting that are the topics of Chapters 7 and 8. I review the theory and evidence on foreign exchange market efficiency and forecasting, giving attention also to policy issues such as whether private individuals should attempt to forecast exchange rates and speculate in currency markets, and whether public officials should intervene to improve the efficiency of markets and reduce the risks facing private enterprises.

In Part III, our attention turns to the Euromarkets, the offshore markets for financial instruments that began their development in the early 1960s. In Chapter 9, I focus on the short-term bank deposits and loans of the Eurocurrency markets. I examine the pricing of Eurocurrency instruments and the geographic spread of the market. The policy matters in this market concern the relative regulatory burden in offshore markets versus onshore markets, and the risks of Eurocurrency deposits. The longer-term end of the offshore markets, the Eurobond market, is the subject of Chapter 10. Again, the determinants of Eurobond prices and Eurobond activity are examined. Effective utilization of the market by issuers and investors is discussed, along with policies to regulate the Eurobond market or affect its competitiveness with traditional onshore bond markets.

The expanding market for new financial derivative products encompassing futures, options, and swaps is the topic of Part IV. The institutional features and pricing relationships for futures, options, and swaps are analyzed in Chapters 11, 12, and 13, respectively. In each case, I consider the economic underpinnings of the market and the adequacy of existing pricing models to explain actual market prices. And in each chapter, I review the general techniques for using futures, options, and swaps in financial risk management. Public policy issues here concern the regulation of these new financial instruments and their impact on the traditional spot, or cash, markets.

In Part V, I look at developments in international asset portfolios. In Chapter 14, I examine the dimensions of international bond markets. A central theme is the calculation of returns on bond investments, both on an unhedged and currency-hedged basis. Evidence on the diversification potential of international bond portfolios is presented, supplemented by the evidence for currency-hedged bond portfolios. A similar analysis for international equity portfolios is presented in Chapter 15. I discuss the dimensions of these markets and the range of investment vehicles available to investors. I also review the findings on the pricing of equities in an international context as well as the evidence on international portfolio diversification. The issues of concern to private agents here include the tendency of investors to show a "home country bias" and overweight domestic securities in their portfolios and whether investors can continue to count on diversification gains in the future as international markets become more integrated. On the public policy side, I consider the case for harmonization of listing requirements, trading and settlement requirements, and accounting practices.

In Part VI (Chapter 16), I examine the measurement and management of risk in international financial positions. I consider the corporate manager's situation, in which risk is derived from the firm's financial positions as well as the firm's operating activities. And I also analyze similar risk measurement and management issues for purely financial portfolios. While various techniques for measuring these exposures (such as regression analysis, scenario analysis, and the recently developed value-at-risk method) are discussed, I emphasize that all of these methods rely on assumptions that may limit the accuracy of these risk measurements.

The book concludes with Part VII (Chapter 17), which explores how regulators may give direction to international financial markets, a critical issue as markets have become global, footloose, huge, and, some would say, beyond the power of regulatory authorities. I examine the pros and cons of competitive versus coordinated and harmonized approaches to regulating national financial markets. Finally, I investigate whether central bank intervention can be effective in containing foreign exchange rate behavior.

As the reader will note, entire books could be (and have been) written about each of the topics covered in the 17 chapters of this book. My coverage is necessarily selective, concerned primarily with what can be said about the economic setting of markets and the pricing of international financial instruments, and on what conclusions one can draw for private enterprises that must act in these markets and for public policymakers who either directly regulate or indirectly influence them.

Intended Audience

This textbook is designed for a one-semester course in international financial markets or international financial management either in a finance department of a business school or an economics department. The text is appropriate for students in an MBA program, master's degree program, or advanced undergraduate course. Students should have had an introduction to the basic principles of international economics (the theory of comparative advantage, balance of payments issues, and so forth) as well as a course in financial markets or investments that covers the basics of cash flow valuation, asset pricing models, and financial market efficiency.

The text contains discussion of numerous empirical studies and numerous graphs and tables that represent the results of those studies. Students should be familiar with the basics of hypothesis testing and regression analysis in order to interpret these empirical results.

Pedagogic Approach

Each chapter typically includes a discussion of the historical origins of a market and/or the present institutional organization of the market. The institutional setting is an important part of understanding how a market "works" and why the market might not behave in the precise way predicted by a stylized economic model.

Not surprisingly, each chapter also contains theoretical material to establish some baseline predictions about how prices in a market are determined, how they should behave over time, and how they may respond to macroeconomic events. I take the view that theory can be practical, as it often points the way to pricing a new product, to hedging the risk in an existing product, or to structuring a particular investment policy or borrowing strategy. However, all theories require testing. The chapters present the results of empirical studies so the reader can assess some of the important empirical regularities in international finance and see what puzzles remain to be resolved.

Graphs are used extensively throughout the text to convey the material in a visual way that complements the text. I use figures often to show the institutional organization of a market, to explain the pattern of cash flows associated with a single financial contract or a set of contracts, or to explain the results of an empirical study or financial strategy or risk management technique. Hopefully, the use of graphs and real-life data makes the topics and the theories seem more vivid.

The text also contains numerous boxed examples. Some boxes show the details of a financial calculation. Other boxes report examples from recent newspaper stories, again illustrating the practical implications of theory and empirical findings in the chapters.

New Features of the Second Edition

Final copy for the first edition of *International Financial Markets* was completed in the spring of 1997. Since then, a remarkable series of events has occurred, once again bringing international financial markets into the spotlight.

Financial Crisis and Contagion

In July 1997, the Bank of Thailand allowed its currency, the baht, to float. In actuality, the baht sank, depreciating by 25 percent in the first month and presaging the Asian financial crisis that deepened over the next year as Indonesia, South Korea, Malaysia, and other countries succumbed to market pressures. These Asian countries experienced deep currency depreciation, loss of reserves, declines in stock prices, and severe economic slowdown. In June 1998, the macroeconomic perfor-

mance of the Russian economy came under closer scrutiny. Concerns increased about the sustainability of the ruble exchange rate, the deteriorating quality of Russian debts, and the viability of free capital movements between the ruble and hard currencies. In August 1998, the Russian government devalued the ruble, then allowed it to float, defaulted on its own national debt (denominated in rubles), and imposed capital controls on access to US$. The Russian crisis touched off a flight to higher-quality and more liquid securities (U.S. Treasury assets in particular) and away from assets in many Latin American and other emerging markets, which were viewed as more risky and less liquid. The extreme price movements and loss of liquidity in certain markets resulted in substantial losses for many investors, especially those that were highly leveraged. In September 1998, Long-Term Capital Management (LTCM), a well-regarded hedge fund with two Nobel laureates in economics among the company founders, reported losing nearly 90 percent of its capital. The collapse of LTCM showed that the problems of excessive risk-taking (leverage), lack of transparency, and spillovers were not confined to distant countries with poorly developed capital markets and weak legal institutions.

Monetary Union and the International Monetary System

On December 31, 1998, we said goodbye to the deutsche mark, French franc, Italian lira, and eight other European currencies. January 1999 marked the beginning of the euro as the currency of the European Economic and Monetary Union (EMU). The euro and the EMU were in the planning stages for years and discussed in the first edition of *International Financial Markets,* but many academic economists (particularly American economists) thought that EMU would be postponed or abandoned at the last minute for some economic or political reason. Yet EMU went forward as planned, marking a watershed event for international financial markets. Prior to EMU, concepts such as purchasing power parity (PPP) could be applied at the country level, for example, the United States and Germany. Now with the EMU, Germany's position is that of a single state within an economic region, similar to the position of California within the United States. The appropriate "country" unit for many international financial comparisons will be the EMU. However, meaningful analyses of some relationships (such as PPP) may be impossible because of limited historical experience with EMU.

The arrival of EMU raises other issues for the study of international financial markets. Traditionally, each market was synonymous with a nation, so it was sensible to analyze, for example, the German, French, and Italian capital markets. Now with a single currency and free capital movements among EMU countries, it is less meaningful to focus on these national markets as distinct from an *EMU capital market*. However, some barriers remain (such as language, taxation, banking regulations, and accounting) that may cause financial markets in Europe to be more segmented than they are in the United States.

In the United States, we seldom speak of a "New York capital market" and a "California capital market." For most purposes, it is not meaningful that Citigroup and the New York Stock Exchange are headquartered in New York while Wells Fargo Bank and the Pacific Stock Exchange are headquartered in San Francisco. However, in Europe at this time, there are still reasons to focus on German versus French or Italian capital markets. For example, it is still meaningful to discuss the German government bond market as distinct from the Spanish government bond market. While both issuers use the euro, they have differing credit risks and, as sovereign nations, they have the implicit right to withdraw from the EMU. Similarly, it may still be meaningful to describe equity markets in Europe by reference to the Frankfurt, Paris, and Milan exchanges. However, recent events have shown that institutions are changing rapidly, and mergers may give way to one or more pan-European stock exchanges.[1]

The launch of the EMU also has implications for the international monetary system. For some time, the economic summits among the G-7 nations (the United States, Germany, Japan, France, the United Kingdom, Canada, and Italy) have been viewed as a G-3 event (meaning the United States, Germany, and Japan). But now the third "nation" is the EMU. The G-7 summits bring together the political leaders (presidents and prime ministers) and economic officials (treasury secretaries and finance ministers) of the seven nations. But

the EMU is an economic union, *not* a political union. Who should speak for the economic interests of the EMU at international assemblies (like the G-7, the International Monetary Fund, and others) is unclear.

New Questions and Concerns

The recent financial crises in Asia, Russia, and Latin America have ignited two strands of debate about the international monetary system. The first regards the causes of the crises, and whether any sort of early-warning system could have predicted the start of each crisis and the spillover effects on other countries. Were the crises a rational result of "bad fundamentals," or was irrational behavior part of the story? Did private investors underestimate the risk of emerging capital markets? Did some countries error by adopting pegged exchange rates, or holding on to their pegs too rigidly for too long?

The second issue concerns the handling of the crises by international agencies, and whether fundamental changes to the international monetary system are called for. Did international agencies contribute to a "moral hazard" by their handling of earlier crises and readiness to lend funds in the event of crisis? What positive steps could the International Monetary Fund take to lessen the likelihood of crisis? Should emerging markets place controls on capital inflows to limit the likelihood of crisis? Should the G-3 consider a return to pegged rates or target zones as a way to stabilize the international financial environment?

In the second edition of *International Financial markets,* Chapter 2 includes an overview of events surrounding the recent international financial crises. We update our discussion of the euro and EMU in Chapters 2 and 3. We also expand the discussion of currency boards in Chapter 2 and note the factors weighing on the possible use of the US$ as the official currency of Argentina. In Chapters 4 and 5, we give more attention to the validity of key parity relationships for emerging markets. We give greater emphasis to forecasting emerging market currencies in Chapter 8. In Chapters 14 and 15, we discuss the impact of the euro and EMU on international bond and equity markets. Throughout the second edition, tables and figures have been updated to show the most recent levels of trading activity and the current institutional features of each market. Each chapter begins with a set of "Learning Objectives" to aid the reader in focusing on the most important themes of each chapter.

---

[1]One such entity is EURONEXT, representing a merger of the Amsterdam, Brussels, and Paris bourses announced in March 2000 and expected to begin operating in 2001. Another is iX, reflecting a merger of the London Stock Exchange and the Deutsche Börse announced in May 2000, but rescinded by September.

A Word on Currency Symbols and Examples Used in This Edition

In order to improve the readability of this text, we will use traditional publishing symbols $, £, and ¥ to represent U.S. dollars, British pounds, and Japanese yen, respectively. Because many countries have named their currency "the dollar," we will attempt to avoid confusion by using A$, C$, NZ$, S$, and US$ to represent the Australian, Canadian, New Zealand, Singaporean, and U.S. dollars, respectively. The symbol € is used to represent the euro, the new currency of the European Economic and Monetary Union. Much like stock traders, foreign exchange traders use trading symbols to represent currencies—USD for the US$, GBP for the British pound, AUD for the Australian dollar, EUR for the euro, and so forth.[2]

_____

[2]For a list of currency trading symbols prepared by the International Organization for Standardization (ISO), readers may visit the ISO website at <www.iso.ch>. Or visit the British Standards Institution site at <www.bsi.org.uk/bsi/products/standards/products/currency.xhtml>.

When this edition appears in print, each EMU country will be in the unusual position of having two local currencies—the euro and its former, national currency, which many now refer to as a "legacy currency." Thus, when a German goes to the local grocery store, he carries physical DM (because physical euros will not be in circulation until 2002) and he is likely to see prices quoted in DM. When he goes to the stock exchange, however, he will see prices of shares quoted only in €. Nearly all security prices (including equities, bonds, futures, and options) were converted to euro prices on January 1, 1999. And when our representative German opens his bank statement, he will very likely see his bank balance reported in both DM terms and in €. For example, a DM10,000 bank balance is equivalent to €5,112.92 (using the conversion factors in Table 2.2). In this edition of _International Financial Markets,_ we will present real and hypothetical examples using the new €, but where appropriate we will also make reference to the former national European currencies.

Richard M. Levich

Many people assisted in the preparation of this book. I am grateful to David Benway, Sari Carp, Gayle De-long, Alexis Hongre, Simi Kedia, and Anthony Morris for their work in assembling data for exhibits and writing questions and exercises for the text. Candace Chase meticulously read the entire manuscript, and Deloris Lewis provided effective secretarial support. I extend thanks to Ronald McKinnon for allowing me to use many exhibits from his article "The Rules of the Game" as the centerpiece for Chapter 2, and to Michael Rosenberg and Joe Prendergast for their help in obtaining market data. Throughout the text, there are references to many colleagues and teachers whose writing has affected me and this book: Robert Aliber, John Bilson, James Bodurtha, Robert Cumby, Rudiger Dornbusch, Jeffrey Frankel, Jacob Frenkel, Kenneth Froot, Richard Herring, Philippe Jorion, Richard Lyons, Michael Mussa, Lee Thomas, and Ingo Walter. And I offer special thanks to the Rockefeller Foundation for allowing me to stay at the Bellagio Study and Conference Center in Bellagio, Italy, to complete early sections of the first edition of this book.

In addition, I would like to thank the following people for reviewing the manuscript in its various stages: Alan Alford, Northeastern University; Rita Biswas, State University of New York–Albany; Ian Davidson, University of Warwick; Diane Denis, Purdue University; Chitru Fernando, Tulane University; Julapa Jagtiani, Baruch College; Coleman Kendall, University of Illinois–Chicago; Sarkis Khoury, University of California–Riverside; Dennis Logue, Dartmouth College; Arvind Mahajan, Texas A&M University; Kenneth Martin, New Mexico State University; Dileep Mehta, Georgia State University; Shazhad Mian, Emory University; Chandra Mishra, Oregon State University; Michael Palmer, University of Colorado; Geoffrey Poitras, Simon Fraser University; Bluford Putnam, CDC Investment Corporation; S. Ghon Rhee, University of Rhode Island; Raul Susmel, University of Houston; and Clas Wihlborg, Göteborg University. Harvey Poniachek contributed many suggestions to add clarity to the second edition.

I also thank the staff at McGraw-Hill/Irwin for their assistance throughout this project including my editors, Beth Bortz, Wendi Sweetland, Jim Keefe, and Maureen Harrington, all of whom have unfortunately moved on to other careers, and to Jean Lou Hess who supervised the production process and struggled to make every page of the first edition reflect the author's wishes. I extend thanks to Eric Gates and Michelle Janicek for their editorial work in preparing for the second edition. I am also grateful to Christina Thornton-Villagomez for her cheerful energy in speeding the second edition along on a tight production schedule. I owe a special debt to Michael Junior, who dogged me for years to write this book.

Last of all, I thank the many students who, over the years, read earlier drafts of the chapters and contributed their suggestions on how to improve the manuscript.

B R I E F   C O N T E N T S

PART I

INTRODUCTION AND OVERVIEW

1 Introduction to the Study of International Financial Markets 2
2 An Overview of International Monetary Systems and Recent Developments in International Financial Markets 23

PART II

FOREIGN EXCHANGE MARKETS

3 Market Structure and Institutions 78
4 International Parity Conditions: Purchasing Power Parity 111
5 International Parity Conditions: Interest Rate Parity and the Fisher Parities 142
6 Spot Exchange Rate Determination 183
7 Foreign Exchange Market Efficiency 227
8 Exchange Rate Forecasting 260

PART III

OFFSHORE FINANCIAL MARKETS

9 The Eurocurrency Market 296
10 The Eurobond Market 333

PART IV

DERIVATIVE SECURITY MARKETS: FUTURES, OPTIONS, AND SWAPS

11 Currency and Interest Rate Futures 374
12 Currency and Interest Rate Options 418
13 Currency and Interest Rate Swaps 475

PART V

INTERNATIONAL ASSET PORTFOLIOS

14 Bond Portfolios 518
15 Equity Portfolios 554

PART VI

INTERNATIONAL ASSET PORTFOLIOS AND FINANCIAL RISK MANAGEMENT

16 Measuring and Managing the Risk in International Financial Positions 600

PART VII

REGULATORY ISSUES

17 Giving Direction to International Financial Markets: Regulation and Intervention in the Competitive Marketplace 644

Appendix A 677
Appendix B 680
Appendix C 683
Author Index 687
Subject Index 691

CONTENTS

PART I

INTRODUCTION AND OVERVIEW

1 Introduction to the Study of International Financial Markets 2

The Changing Financial Landscape 4
  The Expanding Menu of Financial Choices 5
  Greater Volatility as a Feature of Financial Markets 5
  Increased Competition within and among Financial Markets 6
  Financial Crises and Contagion among International Financial Markets 7
Box 1.1: Accidents along the International Financial Superhighway 8
Major Themes 10
  Prices in International Financial Markets 10
  Policy Issues in International Financial Markets 12
Box 1.2: "London, Tokyo Said Crucial to Market in U.S. Treasurys" 15
Challenges in the Study of International Financial Markets and the Practice of International Financial Management 15
  The Importance of Foreign Exchange outside the United States 15
Box 1.3: "Germany Will Issue Short-Term Bills, Sign of Pressure from Euro-Currency" 16

The Importance of Foreign Exchange in the United States 17
The Study of International Financial Markets: More Demanding 20
The Practice of International Financial Management: More Demanding 20
A Road Map for the Remainder of the Book 20
  Summary of Major Topics 20
  Typical Chapter Outline 21

2 An Overview of International Monetary Systems and Recent Developments in International Financial Markets 23

International Monetary Arrangements in Theory and Practice 25
  The International Gold Standard, 1879–1913 26
Box 2.1: Rules of the Game: The International Gold Standard, 1879–1913 27
  The Spirit of the Bretton Woods Agreement, 1945 28
Box 2.2: Rules of the Game: The Spirit of the Bretton Woods Agreement in 1945 29
  The Fixed-Rate Dollar Standard, 1950–1970 30
Box 2.3: Rules of the Game: The Fixed-Rate Dollar Standard, 1950–1970 31
  The Floating-Rate Dollar Standard, 1973–1984 33
Box 2.4: Rules of the Game: The Floating-Rate Dollar Standard, 1973–1984 35

The Plaza-Louvre Intervention Accords and the Floating-Rate Dollar Standard, 1985–1996   35

Box 2.5: Rules of the Game: The Plaza-Louvre Intervention Accords and the Floating-Rate Dollar Standard, 1985–1996   36

The Spirit of the European Monetary System, 1979   37

Box 2.6: Rules of the Game: The Spirit of the European Monetary System, 1979   40

The European Monetary System as a "Greater DM" Area, 1979–1998   40

Box 2.7: Rules of the Game: The European Monetary System as a "Greater DM" Area, 1979–1992   41

The Spirit of the European Economic and Monetary Union, 1999   42

Box 2.8: Rules of the Game: The Spirit of the EMU, 1999   43

Recent Behavior of Prices in International Financial Markets   45

Exchange Rate Developments   45

Box 2.9: A Primer on Foreign Exchange Market Math and Terminology   47

Interest Rate Developments   57

Summary of Recent Developments   65

Policy Matters—Private Enterprises   65

The Conduct of Business under Pegged and Floating Exchange Rates   65

Greater Exchange Rate Variability under Floating   65

Costs of Exchange Rate Variability   66

Policy Matters—Public Policymakers   66

Exchange Rate Policies in Emerging Markets   67

Beyond Currency Boards to Full Dollarization   68

Concerns About EMU   70

Summary   73

PART II

FOREIGN EXCHANGE MARKETS

3   Market Structure and Institutions   78

Importance of Foreign Exchange Market Trading   79

Origins of the Market   79

Volume of Foreign Exchange Trading   80

Foreign Exchange Trading Profits   81

Explaining the Profitability of Foreign Exchange Trading   83

Box 3.1: How to Succeed at Intervention by Really Signaling   85

Foreign Exchange Market Products and Activities   85

Spot and Forward Contracts   85

Foreign Exchange Swaps   87

Types of Trading Activities: Speculation and Arbitrage   87

The Relationship between Spot and Forward Contracts   90

Box 3.2: Example of Reuters Screen Page: Citibank Long-Dated Forward Rates, February 22, 1985   92

The Foreign Exchange Market Setting   95

Comparing the Foreign Exchange Market with Other Markets   95

Tracking Foreign Exchange Transactions   97

Box 3.3: Why Can't Everyone Have Direct Access to the Interbank Foreign Exchange Market?   100

Counterparties and Concentration in the Foreign Exchange Market   101

Policy Matters—Private Enterprises   103

A Close-Up View on Foreign Exchange Trading   103

Controls over Foreign Exchange Trading   105

Valuing Foreign Exchange Trading Profits   106

Policy Matters—Public Policymakers   106

Summary   107

4   International Parity Conditions: Purchasing Power Parity   111

The Usefulness of Parity Conditions in International Financial Markets   112

An Overview of International Parity Conditions in a Perfect Capital Market   113

Purchasing Power Parity in a Perfect Capital Market   114

The Law of One Price   114

Absolute Purchasing Power Parity   115

Relative Purchasing Power Parity   115

Box 4.1: Absolute PPP Comparisons with Alternative Market Baskets and Alternative Inflation Scenarios   116

The Real Exchange Rate and Purchasing
Power Parity   119
Relaxing the Perfect Capital Market
Assumptions   121
Transaction Costs   121
Taxes   122
Uncertainty   122
Empirical Evidence on Prices and Exchange
Rates   123
Empirical Methods, or How to Test a Parity
Condition   123
Evidence on the Law of One Price   123
Relative PPP: Evidence on Recent Quarterly
Data   124
Relative PPP: Evidence from
Hyperinflationary Economies   128
Relative PPP: Evidence from Long-Run
Data   129
Empirical Tests of PPP: Is the Real
Exchange Rate Constant?   131
Empirical Tests of PPP: The Final
Word   132
Policy Matters—Private Enterprises   132
The Role of Parity Conditions for Management
Decisions   132
Purchasing Power Parity and Managerial
Decisions   133
Box 4.2: Gray Markets and the Law of One
Price   134
Purchasing Power Parity and Product
Pricing Decisions   134
Policy Matters—Public Policymakers   136
Summary   138
Appendix 4.1   PPP, Continuous
Compounding, and Logarithmic Returns   139

**5   International Parity Conditions:
Interest Rate Parity and the
Fisher Parities   142**

The Usefulness of the Parity Conditions in
International Financial Markets: A Reprise
143
Interest Rate Parity: The Relationship between
Interest Rates, Spot Rates, and Forward
Rates   144
Interest Rate Parity in a Perfect Capital
Market   144
Relaxing the Perfect Capital Market
Assumptions   148

Empirical Evidence on Interest Rate
Parity   152
The Fisher Parities   155
The Fisher Effect   155
The International Fisher Effect   156
Box 5.1: Deviations from Uncovered Interest
Parity, or How Exchange Rate Changes
Can Substantially Raise (or Lower) the
Cost (or Return) on Your Funds   158
Relaxing the Perfect Capital Market
Assumptions   160
Empirical Evidence on the International
Fisher Effect   160
The Forward Rate Unbiased Condition   163
Interpreting a Forward Rate Bias   164
Empirical Evidence on the Forward Rate
Unbiased Condition   164
Tests Using the Level of Spot and Forward
Exchange Rates   164
Tests Using Forward Premiums and
Exchange Rate Changes   166
Policy Matters—Private Enterprises   167
Application 1: Interest Rate Parity and One-
Way Arbitrage   170
Box 5.2: An Example of One-Way Arbitrage
Profits When There Are No Round-Trip
Arbitrage Profits   171
Application 2: Credit Risk and Forward
Contracts—To Buy or to Make?   172
Application 3: Interest Rate Parity and the
Country Risk Premium   172
Application 4: Are Deviations from
the International Fisher Effect
Predictable?   173
Application 5: Are Deviations from
the International Fisher Effect
Excessive?   173
Application 6: International Fisher Effect
and Diversification Possibilities   174
Application 7: International Fisher Effect,
Long-Term Bonds, and Exchange Rate
Predictions   175
Policy Matters—Public Policymakers   176
Summary   177
Appendix 5.1   Interest Rate Parity, the
Fisher Parities, Continuous Compounding, and
Logarithmic Returns   178
Appendix 5.2   Transaction Costs and the
Neutral Band Surrounding the Traditional
Interest Rate Parity Line   179

6   Spot Exchange Rate Determination   183

News and Foreign Exchange Rates: An Introduction   184
   Exchange Rates and News Stories: Three Illustrations   186
Box 6.1: The Reaction of the Spot Exchange Rate to News Announcements on Macroeconomic and Political Events   187
   News and Foreign Exchange Rates: A Summary   191
Flow versus Stock Models of the Exchange Rate   192
Box 6.2: Foreign Exchange Rate Behavior: Major Concepts   193
   An Overview of the Flow Approach   193
   An Overview of the Stock Approach   194
   Combining Flow and Stock Concepts of the Exchange Rate   196
Asset Models of the Spot Exchange Rate   196
   The Monetary Approach   197
   The Portfolio-Balance Approach   203
Empirical Evidence on Exchange Rate Models   205
   In-Sample Results   205
   Postsample Results   210
   The Role of News   212
Policy Matters—Private Enterprises   216
Policy Matters—Public Policymakers   217
Summary   219
Appendix 6.1   The Implications of Flow and Stock Equilibrium on the Foreign Exchange Rate   219
Appendix 6.2   Demonstration That the Present Exchange Rate Reflects All Future Exogenous Macroeconomic Values   223
Appendix 6.3   The Monetary Model of Exchange Rate Determination with Traded and Nontraded Goods   224

7   Foreign Exchange Market Efficiency   227

Theory of Market Efficiency   229
   Defining the Equilibrium Benchmark   229
   Pictures of Efficient Markets   230

Box 7.1: Exchange Rate Levels and Changes Generated Using the Random-Walk (No-Drift) Model   232
   Interpreting Efficient Market Studies   233
   Defining the Available Information Set   234
   Extensions of Efficient Market Theory   236
Empirical Evidence on Exchange Market Efficiency   237
   Market Efficiency with Certainty and Risk-Free Investment   237
   Market Efficiency with Uncertainty and Risky Investment   238
Box 7.2: Tracking Positions and Profits in a Technical Trading Rule: A Numerical Example   241
Policy Matters—Private Enterprises   252
Policy Matters—Public Policymakers   254
Summary   256

8   Exchange Rate Forecasting   260

Resolving Controversies in Exchange Rate Forecasting   262
   The Forecasting Approach and the Market Setting   262
   Forecast Performance Evaluation: Accurate versus Useful Forecasts   271
Box 8.1: The Difference between Forecasting a Random Walk and an "Almost Random" Walk   272
   Assessing the Economic Value of Currency Forecasts   275
Box 8.2: Evaluating a Forecasting Track Record Using the Percentage Correct Method   276
Forecasting Methods: Some Specific Examples   278
   Short-Run Forecasts: Trends versus Random Walk   278
   Long-Run Forecasts: Reversion to the Mean?   282
   Composite Forecasts: Theory and Examples   283
Policy Issues and Special Forecasting Problems   287
   Consumers of Exchange Rate Forecasts   287
   Producers of Exchange Rate Forecasts   288
   Special Problems in Exchange Rate Forecasting   288
Summary   290

PART III

OFFSHORE FINANCIAL MARKETS

9 The Eurocurrency Market 296

Box 9.1: Did You Request the Eurorate or the
    Euro Eurorate? 297
Historical Overview 299
    The Origins of Supply and Demand for
        Offshore Banking 299
    Onshore Banking Regulations Boost the
        Offshore Market 300
    The Offshore Markets Endure 300
    Growth of the Eurocurrency Market 301
Box 9.2: Creating Eurodollars 302
Pricing of Eurocurrency Deposits and
    Loans 305
    Pricing in the Case of One Currency and
        Two Financial Centers 305
Box 9.3: Costs of Collecting Deposits and
    Servicing Loans 307
    Can Offshore and Onshore Markets
        Coexist? 308
    The Impact of Capital Controls and
        Taxes 310
    Market Share and Pricing in Competing
        Offshore Centers 311
    The General Case with Many Currencies
        and Many Financial Centers 313
Policy Matters—Private Enterprises 314
    Concerns of Depositors 314
Box 9.4: Risk in Cross-Border Transactions:
    The Wells Fargo–Citibank Case 316
    Concerns of Borrowers 318
Policy Matters—Public Policymakers 321
    Offshore Markets and Macroeconomic
        Stability 321
    Could the Offshore Markets Expand
        Indefinitely? 322
    Approaches to Regulating Offshore
        Markets 322
Box 9.5: Japanese Banking Woes: The Daiwa
    Banking Scandal and the Japan
    Premium 324
    Competing for Markets: U.S. Policy
        Initiatives 325
    Offshore Markets: European Policy
        Concerns 328
Summary 329

10 The Eurobond Market 333

Box 10.1: Eurobonds Are Not the Same as
    Bonds Denominated in Euros 335
Historical Overview and Dimensions of the
    Eurobond Market 335
    A First Stimulus to the Eurobond Market:
        The IET 335
    A Second Round of Stimulus to the
        Eurobond Market 336
    The Eurobond Market Endures 336
Regulatory and Institutional Characteristics of
    the Market 340
    Regulatory Bodies and Disclosure
        Practices 340
    Issuing Costs, Ratings, and Exchange
        Listings 341
    Queuing, Currency of Denomination, and
        Speed of Offering 342
    Summing Up: The Pros and Cons of
        Onshore and Offshore Markets 343
Issuing Practices and Competitive Conditions
    in the Eurobond Market 344
    A Brief Sketch of Eurobond
        Underwriting 345
    Tensions and Incentives within a Eurobond
        Syndicate 346
The Gray Market 347
Box 10.2: "Excessive Competition" in the
    Eurobond Market 348
Box 10.3: Examples of Gray Market Prices in
    the Eurobond Market 350
    Evidence of Competition among Eurobond
        Lead Managers 350
    Another Innovation: Global Bonds 354
Pricing Eurobonds 355
    Market Segmentation and the Pricing of
        Eurobonds 355
    Eurobonds and Secrecy 356
    Eurodollar Bond Prices: Some
        Examples 357
    Onshore–Offshore Arbitrage
        Opportunities 359
    Eurodollar Bond Prices: A General
        Model 359
Policy Matters—Private Enterprises 361
    Onshore–Offshore Arbitrage Once Again:
        Exxon Capital Corporation 361
    Using the Eurobond Market to Enhance the
        Value of the Firm 363

Policy Matters—Public Policymakers   364
Box 10.4: Recent Cases of Scarcity Value in the
   Eurobond Market   365
  The U.S. Competitive Response   365
  European Union and the Eurobond
   Market   368
Summary   370

PART IV

**DERIVATIVE SECURITY MARKETS: FUTURES,
OPTIONS, AND SWAPS**

**11   Currency and Interest Rate
   Futures   374**

Distinctions between Futures and Forwards:
   Institutions and Terminology   377
  Dispersed versus Centralized
   Trading   377
  Customized versus Standardized
   Transactions   377
  Variable Counterparty Risks versus the
   Clearinghouse   378
  Cash Settlement and Delivery versus
   Marking-to-Market Convention   379
Box 11.1: Rogue Trading Sinks Baring
   Brothers—But Not the Futures
   Market   380
Description of Futures Contracts   384
  Contract Specifications   386
  Payoff Profiles for Futures and Forward
   Contracts   391
Futures Pricing and Forward Pricing   395
  Forward Pricing and the Cost-of-Carry
   Model   395
Box 11.2: Hedging the Interest Rate Risk in
   Planned Investment and Planned
   Borrowing   396
  Futures Pricing and the Marking-to-Market
   Convention   398
  The Term Structure of Forward Rates   399
  A Risk Premium in Forwards?   402
Box 11.3: Using Futures Contracts for
   Transferring and Sharing Risks   404
Policy Matters—Private Enterprises   404
  Deciding on Futures versus Forwards   406
  New Futures Contracts and Trading
   Arrangements   406

Policy Matters—Public Policymakers   410
  Futures Prices and Cash Market
   Volatility   410
  Transaction Costs and Transaction
   Taxes   411
Summary   412
Appendix 11.1   Synthetic Interest Rate
Futures   413

**12   Currency and Interest Rate
   Options   418**

First Principles: Terminology and
   Institutions   420
  Types of Contracts   420
  Location and Scale of Trading   422
  Contract Specifications   425
Option Pricing: An Introduction   431
  Spot Currency Options: Prices at
   Maturity   432
  Interest Rate Futures Options: Prices at
   Maturity   434
Box 12.1: Practical Applications of Currency
   and Interest Rate Options   436
  Option Prices Prior to Maturity   440
Option Pricing: Formal Models   442
  Pricing Spot Currency Options   442
  Pricing Currency and Interest Rate Futures
   Options   451
Box 12.2: A Link between Put Prices, Call
   Prices, and Market Sentiment   452
Empirical Evidence on Option Prices   455
  Arbitrage Boundary Conditions   455
  Pricing Efficiency and Pricing
   Biases   456
Policy Matters—Private Enterprises   457
  Can Option Pricing and Trading Be Made an
   Exact Science?   457
  Is Volatility Constant or Does Volatility
   Vary?   460
Box 12.3: What Does Implied Volatility
   Predict?   463
  Other Shortcomings of Option Pricing
   Models   463
Policy Matters—Public Policymakers   464
  Options Markets and Price Volatility in
   Underlying Markets   464
  Capital Requirements for Option
   Traders   465
Summary   465

Appendix 12.1   Determination of the Replicating Portfolio in the Two-Period Binomial Model   466
Appendix 12.2   Boundary Conditions, Early Exercise, and Option Prices   467
Appendix 12.3   Introduction to Exotic Options   469

13 Currency and Interest Rate Swaps   475

Origins and Underpinnings of the Swap Market   477
   The Role of Capital Controls   477
   Factors Favoring the Rise of Swaps   478
   Swaps Outstanding, the Volume of Transactions, and Gross Exposure   479
The Basic Cash Flows of a Swap Transaction   481
   Currency Swap   482
Box 13.1: A Summary of the IBM/World Bank Currency Swap   484
   Interest Rate Swap   485
Box 13.2: Comparing Genuine Fixed-Rate and Synthetic Fixed-Rate Financing: A Detailed Example   488
Risks in Swaps   488
   Swap Risks for the Hedger   489
   Swap Risks for the Speculator   490
   Measuring the Risks of Swaps   492
   Using Simulation to Estimate the Risks of Swaps   493
Box 13.3: Interest Rate Volatility and the Potential for Gain and Loss in an Interest Rate Swap Contract   494
The Pricing of Swaps   498
   Price Quoting Conventions in the Swap Market   498
   The Fundamental Determinants of Swap Prices   501
Policy Matters—Private Enterprises   502
   Applications of Swaps: Capturing Arbitrage Opportunities, Reducing Risks, Enhancing Sales   502
   Pricing Interest Rate Swaps: The Source of Gains   503
   Applications of Swaps: Magnifying Risk and Return   504
   Formation of AAA-Rated Subsidiaries   505
Policy Matters—Public Policymakers   506

   A Large-Scale Default Hits the Swap Market   506
   BIS Capital Requirements for Swap Transactions   506
   Netting Agreements and the Risk Exposure of Swap Transactions   508
Summary   510
Appendix 13.1   Valuing the Cash Flows in an Interest Rate Swap   511

PART V

INTERNATIONAL ASSET PORTFOLIOS

14 Bond Portfolios   518

Dimensions of National Bond Markets   522
   Bonds Outstanding by Market Location   523
   Bonds Outstanding by Market Segment   524
Return and Risk in National Bond Markets   525
   Calculating Unhedged Returns in US$ Terms   525
   Calculating Currency-Hedged Returns in US$ Terms   527
Box 14.1: Calculation of Prices and Returns for a Five-Year Swiss Bond on an Unhedged Investment   528
Empirical Evidence on Return and Risk in Global Bond Markets   529
Box 14.2: Calculation of Prices and Returns for a Five-Year Swiss Bond on a Currency-Hedged Investment   530
   Returns on Unhedged Bonds   530
   Returns on Currency-Hedged Bonds   532
   The Efficient Frontier and Gains to International Bond Portfolios   534
Policy Matters—Private Investors and Institutions   534
   Currency-Hedged Bonds: Is There a Free Lunch?   535
   Active versus Passive Currency-Hedging Strategies   537
   Problems in Implementing an International Bond Portfolio   542
Box 14.3: Have Global Bond Funds Delivered?   543

Box 14.4: To Hedge or Not to Hedge—A
Global Bond Portfolio   544
The Impact of the EMU on International
Bond Markets   545
Policy Matters—Public Policymakers   547
The Impact of European Monetary
Union   547
Brady Bonds and Emerging Market Debt
Issues   548
Summary   549
Appendix 14.1   Global Asset
Allocation   550

15   Equity Portfolios   554

Size and Institutional Features of Global Equity
Markets   557
Market Capitalization Measures   557
Box 15.1: How Large Is the Japanese Stock
Market?   559
Institutional Aspects of Global Equity
Markets   560
International Investment Vehicles   564
Direct Purchase of Foreign Shares   564
Box 15.2: The Russian ADRs Are Coming . . .
The Russian ADRs Are Coming!   565
American Depositary Receipts   565
Closed-End and Open-End Mutual
Funds   566
Box 15.3: ADRs: US$ Securities with
Substantial Foreign Exchange Risk   568
Risk and Return in International Equity
Markets   571
Calculating the Unhedged Returns on
Foreign Equity in US$ Terms   571
Portfolio Risk in Domestic and International
Stocks   572
Pricing Determinants   576
Empirical Evidence on Pricing   579
Policy Matters—Private Investors   583
Factors Favoring Overweighting Foreign
Markets in Portfolios   584
Factors Favoring Overweighting Home
Markets in Portfolios   584
Is Investment in MNCs a Close Substitute
for International Investment?   585
Can Investors Create "Homemade"
International Diversification?   586
Can Investors Count on International
Diversification Gains in the Future?   586

Are Emerging Markets Integrated with
World Capital Markets?   587
Policy Matters—Public Policymakers   589
Equity Market Trading
Arrangements   590
Diversity in Accounting Principles and
Disclosure Practices   591
Summary   593

PART VI

INTERNATIONAL ASSET PORTFOLIOS AND FINANCIAL RISK MANAGEMENT

16   Measuring and Managing the Risk in International Financial Positions   600

The Corporate Treasurer's Financial Risk
Management Problem   603
The Market Value of the Firm and Channels
of Risk   603
Accounting Measures of Foreign Exchange
Exposure   607
Exposure of the Balance Sheet: Translation
Exposure   607
Exposure of the Income Statement:
Transaction Exposure   609
U.S. Accounting Conventions: Reporting
Accounting Gains and Losses   610
Economic Logic of Accounting
Conventions   613
Economic Measures of Foreign Exchange
Exposure   613
The Regression Approach: The Basic
Model   613
The Regression Approach: An
Application   614
The Regression Approach: Three
Extensions   616
The Scenario Approach   617
The Scenario Approach: Some
Extensions   618
Empirical Evidence on Firm Profits, Share
Prices, and Exchange Rates   619
Arguments for Hedging Risks at the Corporate
Level   621
Box 16.1: Why Debt Holders Prefer Hedging
and Equity Holders Do Not   622

Financial Strategies toward Risk
   Management   625
   The Currency Profile and Suitable Financial
      Hedging Instruments   625
Box 16.2: How Hedging May Prevent Future
   Windfall Gains and Windfall Losses   627
Box 16.3: Gold Bugs: The Costs of a Flawed
   Hedging Program   628
Policy Issues—International Financial
   Managers   630
   Problems in Estimating Economic
      Exposure   630
Box 16.4: Failed Marriages: When Hedging
   Becomes Speculation   631
   Picking an Appropriate Hedge Ratio   632
   The International Investor's Currency Risk
      Management Problem   632
   The Value-at-Risk Approach   633
Box 16.5: An Example of the Value-at-Risk
   Approach for Hedging Exchange Rate
   Exposure   634
Policy Issues—Public Policymakers   636
   Disclosure of Financial Exposure   636
   Financial Derivatives and Corporate
      Hedging Policies   637
Summary   637
Appendix 16.1   A Scenario Analysis of
Economic Exposure to Foreign Exchange
Risk   638

Financial Market Participants and
   Competitive Behavior   645
Competition among Regulators   647
The Net Regulatory Burden and Structural
   Arbitrage   649
Coordinated versus Competitive Approaches
   to International Financial Regulation   650
Box 17.1: Can We See the Invisible
   Hand?   651
   A New Twist to Financial Supervision   652
   Credit Ratings, Capital Requirements, and
      the BIS   653
Box 17.2: Estimating Value-at-Risk Using the
   BIS Guidelines versus the J. P. Morgan
   RiskMetrics™ Approach   654
Foreign Exchange Market Intervention   656
   Intervention as a Policy Instrument   656
   The Objectives of Central Bank
      Intervention   658
   The Mechanics of Intervention   661
   Empirical Evidence on Intervention   664
   The Effectiveness of Central Bank
      Intervention   667
   Security Transaction Taxes: Should We
      Throw Sand in the Gears of Financial
      Markets?   671
Concluding Thoughts   672

Appendix A   Purchasing Power Parity Calculations:
United States and Germany   677

Appendix B   Interest Rate Parity Calculations: $, £, and
DM Eurorates   680

Appendix C   International Fisher Effect Calculations:
United States and Germany   683

Author Index   687

Subject Index   691

PART VII

REGULATORY ISSUES

**17   Giving Direction to International
Financial Markets: Regulation
and Intervention in the
Competitive Marketplace   644**

Regulation of Financial Markets in an Open
   Economy   645

INTERNATIONAL
FINANCIAL MARKETS

I INTRODUCTION AND OVERVIEW

1 Introduction to the Study of International Financial Markets 2

2 An Overview of International Monetary Systems and Recent Developments in International Financial Markets 23

1 INTRODUCTION TO THE STUDY OF INTERNATIONAL FINANCIAL MARKETS

"International finance is a game with two sets of players: the politicians and bureaucrats in national governments, and the presidents and treasurers of giant, large, medium, and small firms."

Robert Z. Aliber (1987)

Learning Objectives

After reading this chapter, students should

1. Understand the ways in which international financial markets have changed since the early 1970s.

2. Know that this text emphasizes *prices* in international financial markets—meaning the determinants of prices, the relationship among market prices, the behavior of price changes, and the efficiency of markets in setting prices.

3. Understand the connection between our knowledge about prices in international financial markets and the *policies* that are appropriate for private investors, corporate treasurers, and public policymakers.

4. Realize that international elements play an important role for the financial markets and well-being of all countries, including the United States.

5. Appreciate that the world has many currencies, financial markets, and financial instruments—and that the job facing market players is to determine whether all prices are set in a consistent fashion and, if not, how to take advantage of the situation.

International financial markets offer a dramatic setting. Prices are in constant flux. New products are developed along with new trading techniques and market locations. And policies of both private market participants and public officials evolve to address the risks and opportunities that accompany this competitive market setting.

The list of financial products and the prices at which they trade represent the outcomes of a complex process. The process brings together public policymakers and private firms and individuals. Public policymakers set the broad regulatory framework within which financial markets develop. They also determine more specific policy choices such as the stance of monetary and fiscal policies, the timing of exchange market intervention, and market regulations. Private firms and individuals react, making choices about which markets, currencies, and instruments to use for borrowing, investing, and risk management purposes. These choices determine market prices. Often, in an effort to avoid regulatory or economic costs, or to manage financial risks more effectively, these private agents may develop a new product, a new marketplace, or a new institutional practice. And then the process begins again, with fresh regulatory policies and further decisions by private firms and individuals.

This book is about the major markets and instruments that are classified as "international." For sure, this includes the foreign exchange market and products *derived from* foreign exchange, such as foreign currency futures, forwards, options, and swaps. In addition, "international" includes foreign money markets that are essential to the study of foreign exchange, Eurocurrency and Eurobond markets that cross international boundaries, and foreign bond and equity markets that are in the opportunity set of international investors.

In the opening quotation, Robert Aliber describes international finance as a game between public policymakers and private market participants. In this view, international finance is similar to a sporting contest that matches the intellect and nerve of the various players. National policymakers are charged with managing their home economies, yet they often make international commitments. Given these dual objectives, inconsistencies in national policies are commonplace, creating a situation where exchange rate changes are inevitable. And exchange rate changes create both risks and opportunities for firms and individuals in the private sector. Exchange rate volatility, along with volatility in other financial prices, has fostered the development of new markets and instruments that may either reduce or enhance one's exposure to these volatile conditions.

Differences in regulatory policies across countries (and sometimes across markets within a country) are another aspect of the game. Regulatory differences offer their own incentives for private market participants. Some regulatory differences have been valuable because they have encouraged financial innovations that improve risk sharing (the ability of a market to transfer risk from those who hold more than their desired exposure to certain risks to those who hold less), improve financial efficiency (the ability of a financial market to set prices as a reflection of available information), and lower the cost of financial intermediation (the ability to quickly match borrowers and lenders or buyers and sellers in a market). Despite these benefits, some differences in regulation are feared because those markets with too little regulation may jeopardize the safety and soundness of the financial system, putting all market participants at risk.

In analyzing international financial markets and instruments, our aim is twofold: first, to examine the determinants of prices in these markets and, second, to understand the policy choices facing public policymakers as well as private firms and individuals who operate in the markets. Most readers of a book on international financial markets expect to learn "how markets work." Our emphasis in this book is on *prices* and *policies*. Our goal is a better understanding of how prices are formed in the market and how the policies of individuals, corporations, government officials, and market regulators are formulated conditional on the behavior of market prices. Understanding these aspects of prices and policies should convey a vivid sense of how the international financial markets "work."

In the remainder of this chapter, we first review some of the major changes that have affected international financial markets and the trends that are in progress. We then discuss the major themes of the book—prices and policies—in more detail. A discussion of the importance of international financial markets and international financial management follows. The chapter ends with an overview of the book and an outline of a typical chapter.

The Changing Financial Landscape[1]

Over the last three decades, financial markets around the world have been transformed. Some changes have been gradual. The United States and the U.S. dollar (US$) were once undisputed as the dominant country and the dominant currency in world financial markets, but now they play a much smaller role. London and Tokyo as well as Frankfurt, Singapore, and the so-called emerging markets are gaining ground on New York as important centers of primary securities issues and secondary market trading. Throughout much of the last 25 years, the deutsche mark (DM) and the Japanese yen (¥) gained favor at the expense of the US$ as a numeraire for denominating financial contracts and merchandise trade. In 1999, the European Economic and Monetary Union (EMU) introduced its new common currency, the euro, which poses a further threat to the central role of the US$ in international markets. Offsetting this trend, some countries (Argentina, for example) have discussed abandoning their national currency (the peso) and adopting the US$ in its place.

Bank loans, straight debt, and common equity shares were once the dominant financial products. Now these products are being supplanted by commercial paper, financial futures, options, and swaps. Commercial banks and stock exchanges were once the dominant institutions. Now they are being challenged by investment banks, securities firms, and futures and options exchanges. The onshore market (under the control of domestic regulators) was once the dominant venue for new issues and trading activity. But in many cases, the onshore market has been overtaken by the offshore markets (also referred to as the Euromarkets) that are subject to considerably less regulation.

Other changes were more abrupt. In the early 1970s, the Bretton Woods Agreement on pegged exchange rates collapsed. The fall of Bretton Woods ushered in a period of floating exchange rates and more autonomous national economic policies.

By the end of the 1980s, however, the major industrial countries had taken steps to coordinate economic policies, placing target ranges on currency values. On the regulatory front, various international agreements—to harmonize capital requirements for banks, to establish securities trading and underwriting standards, to remove barriers to capital flows across Europe, and even to harmonize national accounting principles and disclosure requirements—were either completed or under serious discussion in the mid-1990s.

But in the latter half of the 1990s, another abrupt change occurred—the sudden collapse of pegged rates in many countries including Mexico (1994), Thailand (1997), Korea (1997), Russia (1998), and Brazil (1999), among others. These shocks and the ensuing financial crises that hit Latin American, Asia, Russia, and other countries raised fundamental questions about the operation of international financial markets. Were the macroeconomic and financial market policies of these countries well founded? Were these crises predictable and, if so, avoidable? Were the responses by international agencies, such as the International Monetary Fund and the World Bank, and central banks appropriate or part of the problem (by providing a safety net to lenders, thereby making crises more likely)? Were investment managers and corporate treasurers taking adequate steps to measure and manage their financial and operational risks?

This transformation of financial markets raises many issues for private market participants and public policymakers. We consider four aspects of this transformation—the wider array of financial products, the increase in price volatility, the greater intensity of

---

[1]In this section, we use a number of technical terms and expressions—floating exchange rates, swaps, options—which are defined and discussed in greater detail in later chapters.

competition across financial markets and the increased incidence of financial crises and contagion among international financial markets.

The Expanding Menu of Financial Choices

The menu of choices facing private investors, corporate issuers, and governments in the 1960s was, in retrospect, fairly limited. Corporate issuers relied on bank financing, investment-grade bonds, or common equity shares that were issued, most often, in their local domestic market and denominated in their domestic currency. Forward contracts could be used to hedge unanticipated exchange rate changes. Futures contracts for major agricultural and industrial commodities permitted hedging of specific risks in these industries.

The menu of financial choices in the 1990s has become long and complex. A firm wanting a fixed-rate, US$ loan has many alternative means to achieve this basic form of financing. For example, the firm could begin with a bond denominated in pounds, yen, or euros, either in fixed-rate or floating-rate terms issued either in the domestic or off-shore market, and combine this bond with a swap to produce the desired fixed-rate US$ loan. "Financial engineering" of this sort has become routine. Corporate issuers and private investors have at their disposal innumerable futures and option contracts (on currencies, commodities, securities, interest rates, and indexes) to acquire or lay off risks associated with economywide shocks (such as a general rise in interest rates) or with firm-specific events (such as a change in the firm's credit rating). Beyond these "plain vanilla" contracts, we find their "exotic" offspring such as options on swaps (swaptions), options whose prices depend on where prices *have been* prior to maturity (path-dependent options) and options *on* options. In an environment of volatile exchange rates, interest rates, and securities prices, the demand for new financial instruments and hedging vehicles has soared.

The surging volume of activity on new markets is testimony to the importance of these new financial products. In the early 1960s, the Eurocurrency and Eurobond markets were of negligible size. In 1999, the gross size of the Eurocurrency market surpassed $9.5 trillion (more than double the size of the U.S. money supply as measured by M2) and the volume of Eurobonds issued reached $1.1 trillion (similar to the volume of new issues in the U.S. corporate bond market). Equally important, Eurocurrency interest rates (the London Interbank Offer Rate, or LIBOR) have become key reference rates for the cost of funds for most corporate and sovereign loans.

The 1970s witnessed the introduction of futures and options on equities and other financial instruments. By 1990, the notional value of trading in futures and options on equities surpassed the underlying cash markets by a factor of 5–10. The first interest rate and currency swaps were completed in the early 1980s. By 1999, the notional value of swaps outstanding exceeded $45 trillion, and swaps had gained an important place in the menu of capital market products.

Greater Volatility as a Feature of Financial Markets

Over the past three decades, financial markets have experienced unusually large price swings. Whether measured in nominal or real (inflation-adjusted) terms, prices of most financial variables—exchange rates, interest rates, and share prices—and the prices of key commodities reached extreme values in the 1970s and 1980s. Not only did the levels of financial prices take on extreme values, but also the speed and volatility of price movements accelerated. For example, the US$ traded at 3.47 DM/$ in February 1985 compared with 1.75 DM/$ in 1979 *and* 1989; and the Japanese stock market index hit 39,000 in December 1989 compared with 15,000 in 1987 *and* 1992.

Volatility on this magnitude led to increased demands for financial forecasting. But the difficulty of financial forecasting led to a greater emphasis on risk management. New derivative instruments (such as futures, options, and swaps) can be used to protect a portfolio against certain kinds of price shocks. But these new instruments themselves may carry their own risks, such as:

- **Counterparty risk:** The risk that a counterparty will default on a financial obligation.
- **Liquidity risk:** The risk that a financial position cannot be sold quickly at prevailing prices.
- **Delivery risk:** The risk that a buyer will not deliver payment of funds after a seller has delivered securities or foreign currencies that were purchased.
- **Rollover risk:** The risk of being closed out from a financial market and unable to renew (or roll over) a short-term contract.

Each of these risks must be taken into consideration. As some managers and shareholders learned to their apparent surprise, these same derivative securities carry price risk and may be used for speculation that exposes the counterparties to substantial losses when prices do not move as expected.

The surge in derivative transactions with their attendant risks has fostered concern that the **system of payments** among financial counterparties is more at risk. **Systemic risk** refers to the possibility that a default by one counterparty somewhere in the world could provoke a ripple or cascade effect, jeopardizing the integrity of the international banking and financial system. While a growing number of firms have lost substantial amounts in connection with derivatives transactions (pushing some firms into bankruptcy), the financial system for trading contracts and for delivery and settlement of payments has held firm. Some of the more sizable financial debacles of recent years are listed in Box 1.1.

Increased Competition within and among Financial Markets

Finally, the last three decades have brought a higher degree of competition in numerous respects. Countries are competing with one another so that financial activities (such as underwriting, trading, fund management, or simply back-office administrative work) can be performed within their borders. Within a country, equity exchanges compete with one another and futures exchanges compete with equity exchanges and with interbank or over-the-counter trading arrangements. Also within a country, institutions such as commercial banks, investment banks, securities firms, and insurance firms compete with one another for similar lines of business. Even regulators are competing as the Securities and Exchange Commission (SEC) and the Commodity Futures Trading Commission (CFTC) vie for control over the same contracts. Through the Bank for International Settlements (BIS), however, an agreement to fix capital-adequacy requirements for certain bank products acts to restrict competition among bank regulators while leaving competitive matters in doubt when similar products are offered by nonbanking firms.

The transformation of financial markets places new demands on regulators. The product line of banks, for example, has expanded to include large amounts of contingent and off-balance-sheet exposures that were not covered by earlier regulations. The boundaries between banks, securities markets, and futures exchanges has been blurred, creating confusion regarding regulatory procedures and responsibilities. The removal of barriers to the movement of capital and the expanded capabilities in telecommunications have strengthened the linkages across national financial markets. Creation of a level international playing field suggests the need for consistent and equitable regulation of national financial markets. However, the short history of many of these products and the complexity of the risks involved, especially when the products are held in portfolios, makes it difficult to assess the risks of these new products and activities and to describe the characteristics of prudent regulation.

The final point embodies the central problem facing market regulators. As international financial markets become more integrated and homogeneous, it is logical to expect that competitive forces will drive financial market regulations toward uniformity. However, because the risks involved are complex, it is difficult for a regulatory body to determine what these uniform standards ought to be. Therefore, uniform ("one size fits all") international financial regulations are likely to be too strict or too liberal. By definition, agreement on international financial regulations stifles international competition among regulators and retards the pace of regulatory adjustments in response to new financial products and environmental change. The central problem facing regulators is whether national financial policies and regulations ought to be harmonized or left free to adjust to each country's individual environment and interests.

Financial Crises and Contagion among International Financial Markets

Another important aspect in the transformation of international financial markets comes from the speed, severity, and scope of market reactions. As we will discuss further in this chapter, policymakers who try to stimulate growth through either expansionary monetary or fiscal policy must face an external constraint imposed by a pegged exchange rate or a limit on how much can be borrowed from foreigners. Throughout most of the post–World War II period, imbalances resulting from differences in national economic policies or macroeconomic performance were slow to develop. Capital mobility was limited, and there was less opportunity for capital flight. At some point, the overstretched country would devalue (by 10 percent, 20 percent, or so) and the cycle would start again—with no great headlines, no great drop in national income, and no knock-on effects to neighboring countries.

Over the last 10 years, the nature of international financial adjustment has changed. With the increase in size and mobility of capital internationally, a substantial amount of national debts may be to foreigners, denominated in foreign currencies ($, ¥, or DM), and in practice these debts are often short-term. As long as foreigners feel confident about the macroeconomic performance of a country, existing short-term debts are rolled over and new capital flows may follow thus furthering the expansion.

However, any event that shakes confidence (a corporate failure, a bank failure, a commodity price drop, a political speech, or a scandal) could halt the flow of capital and jeopardize the rollover of debt on existing terms. A scenario of this sort triggers a demand for international reserves, which are in limited supply at the central bank. Once the supply of international reserves is threatened, the country's central bank may be forced to step aside, allowing the currency to depreciate without any assurance of where the next stable anchor will be. We can call this a *currency crisis*. Because bank debts are in foreign currencies, the devaluation worsens bank balance sheets and banks may be forced to stop lending or call in existing loans to raise cash. Domestic banks are likely to fail (i.e., a banking crisis is likely) if these steps are unsuccessful. Thus, the domestic economy may weaken severely following the currency crisis. If other countries have pursued similar macroeconomic strategies, or face similar macroeconomic conditions,

---

Box 1.1

Accidents along the International Financial Superhighway

Automobiles are considered safe, if driven at prudent speeds by trained drivers. But automobiles can be deadly when the driver is inexperienced, driving too fast for conditions, or drunk behind the wheel.

So too with financial instruments and derivative securities. These are generally considered safe and a useful addition to the financial marketplace. But inexperienced or badly informed users, and users who take positions too large relative to their financial capital and market volatility, can easily get into trouble.

In the last 10 years, a growing list of market participants have experienced substantial losses stemming from transactions involving financial instruments and derivative securities. These cases have involved participants from all sectors of the market—from the United States, Japan, and Germany; from large and small private companies and

public institutions; from corporations, banks, and institutional investors. The surprising element is that all of these incidents involve institutions and people with access to expertise who should have known the riskiness of their strategies. In many cases, the losses were associated with a single "rogue trader" who managed to conceal losses from colleagues and superiors (usually by being responsible for recording and settling his own trading book) for years.

Extending the automobile analogy, a single bad driver often involves other safe drivers in accidents. In financial markets today, regulators are concerned that excessive risk taking or lack of adequate safeguards in the use of financial derivatives could impact not only the immediate firms but also their counterparties, customers, and other market participants far removed from the accident scene.

Sector	Organization (Country)	Date	Approximate Losses	Contracts	Description
Corporate	Procter & Gamble (United States)	April 1994	$102 million	Interest rate swap	Out-of-court settlement with Bankers Trust
	Gibson Greetings (United States)	September 1994	$20 million	Interest rate swap	Out-of-court settlement with Bankers Trust
	Showa Shell (Japan)	February 1993	$1.54 billion	Foreign exchange (FX)	Affiliate of Royal Dutch/Shell Group conceals FX losses for years
	Metallgesellschaft (Germany)	December 1993	$1.3 billion	Oil futures	Firm hedges long-term oil commitments, but cannot meet short-run cash requirements; forces parent into bankruptcy
	Allied Lyons (United Kingdom)	March 1991	$265 million	Foreign exchange options	FX "hedging" grows well beyond scale of company cash flows, and without board's knowledge

or if foreign lenders feel they are overexposed to similar risks in other countries, or if trade flows link countries in a region, the process may repeat itself in other countries. The recurrence of crises in other countries is commonly called *contagion.*

Sector	Organization (Country)	Date	Approximate Losses	Contracts	Description
Financial Firms	Long-Term Capital Management (United States)	October 1998	$4 billion	Leveraged spread and convergence trades	Russian and Latin American crises trigger flight to quality, spreads widen, liquidity dries up
	Credit Suisse First Boston (Switzerland, United States)	August 1998	$270 million	Forward ruble/$ FX contracts	Russian government freezes access to $. CSFB counterparty fails to deliver $.
	Barings Bank (United Kingdom)	February 1995	$1.4 billion	Nikkei index futures	Rogue trader incurs heavy losses on large positions and quick market turnaround; forces parent into bankruptcy
	Daiwa Bank (Japan)	September 1995	$1.1 billion	U.S. government securities	Rogue trader conceals trading losses for years
	Sumitomo Corporation (Japan)	June 1996	$1.8 billion	Copper futures	Rogue trader conceals trading losses for years
Public Agencies	State of Wisconsin Investment Board (United States)	March 1995	$95 million	Interest rate swaps	Mexican peso–US$ interest rate swap suffers losses when peso devalues and interest rate spread widens
	Orange County (United States)	December 1994	$1.7 billion	U.S. government securities and interest rate derivatives	County treasurer takes position expecting interest rates to fall; rates rise
	British Councils (United Kingdom)	1986–1988	$900 million	Interest rate swaps	Local governments enter into losing swaps; House of Lords rules that governments lacked authority to enter into swaps

Note: FX is "foreign exchange."
Source: Various newspaper and company reports.

In the 1990s, we saw currency and banking crises unfold in Mexico (1995) followed by a "Tequila effect," or contagion, into Latin America. We then saw the process repeated in Thailand (1997), with the crisis spreading across Malaysia, Indonesia, Korea, and other Asian countries. And repeated again in Russia (1998), with the crisis reverting back on Latin American countries. These events underscore the impact that a vast pool of capital may have when it is mobile across borders and denominated in a foreign currency. International financial markets impose a powerful disciplining force—rewarding good policies and outcomes, and penalizing poor policies and outcomes—much the same as stock market investors reward and penalize companies for good and bad performance. This new international investment climate raises important questions for the pricing of foreign securities and for investor and macroeconomic policies.

Major Themes

The purpose of this book is to analyze the key segments of the international financial markets with an emphasis on *prices* and *policies*.

Prices in International Financial Markets

A focus on prices includes several distinct areas:

- The determinants of prices.
- The relationship among various financial market prices.
- The pattern and distribution of price changes over time.
- The efficiency of markets where prices are determined.

We examine these aspects of prices both from a theoretical perspective and as an empirical matter based on actual market prices. For the time being, we discuss each of these themes in somewhat loose terms. As the reader will quickly see, understanding the aspects of market *prices* could have immediate consequences for how financial *policies* or *strategies* are selected.

Price Determinants.   Our analysis of the determinants of prices aims to provide an understanding of the fundamental factors that influence financial market prices and the channels through which this influence is felt. We develop models of foreign exchange rates, analyzed in Part II, that relate spot and forward exchange rates to fundamental macroeconomic variables. Then we examine empirically how well these models describe actual exchange rate patterns. In Part IV, we show how prices of derivative securities, including futures, options, and swaps, depend on the prices of underlying financial assets. And again, at least for futures and options, we present empirical evidence showing how well actual derivative prices conform to the predictions of the models.

Price Relationships.   Another element of our focus on market prices is on the relationship *among* market prices. We will develop numerous **parity conditions** that link the price of one financial instrument with the price of another instrument or package of instruments. A parity condition relies on **arbitrage,** the process of buying one package of financial instruments and simultaneously selling another with the expectation of earning a risk-free profit. Arbitrage is a critical activity in financial markets, because we assume that arbitrage occurs quickly to capture a profit opportunity whenever a true parity condition is violated. Some of the key parity conditions we examine include:

1. **Covered interest parity**—the equilibrium relationship between spot and forward exchange rates and money market interest rates.

2. **Put-call-forward parity**—the relationship between put option prices, call option prices, and forward exchange prices.
3. **Currency swap parity**—the relationship between a fixed-rate US$ bond and a floating-rate bond in another currency combined with swaps to emulate a fixed-rate US$ bond.

As we will demonstrate many times, a parity relationship can be used to anticipate what the nth price will be based on knowledge of the other $N - 1$ prices. But if the Nth price is not as expected, an arbitrage profit opportunity may be present. In most cases, we will see that market prices conform closely with arbitrage pricing principles.

Although not as strong as a parity relationship, we will often be interested in the *correlation* between prices of financial instruments. The correlation between prices of U.S. and German government bonds, or between U.S. and French equity shares, plays a role as an indicator of potential diversification gains for investors. The correlation between prices of futures instruments and underlying corporate assets is also of interest as an indicator of the potential hedging effectiveness of these instruments for corporate or investor hedging strategies.

Another important price relationship is that between today's forward rate (for foreign exchange or an interest-bearing instrument) and the future spot rate of the underlying instrument. This price relationship tells us how well the forward rate anticipates future movements in the spot rate, and whether there are any systematic differences in the returns for those who continuously hedge a price risk (at today's forward rate) compared with those who do not hedge (and take their chances on the uncertain future spot rate).

Price Changes.   Our analysis of prices naturally includes a deep interest in price changes, or rates of return as they are also known. On the theoretical side, we want to understand how prices in one market will change in response to economic events at home or abroad. And we want to understand how price changes in one market respond to price changes in another market.

On the empirical side, various statistical properties of price changes are of paramount concern. The presence or absence of a time pattern of price changes is first on our agenda. If a time pattern is present, there is a predictable component to market prices. Whether or not asset prices follow a "random walk" is a long-standing debate among financial economists. We will present evidence that short-run (day-to-day) changes in exchange rates have not been completely random, which offers the hope of using past trends to forecast the future.

The statistical distribution of price changes is another important element. Are price changes normally distributed? If so, then standard deviation (σ) is an appropriate measure of volatility. Or are price changes non-normally distributed? If so, then standard deviation is not an appropriate measure of risk because markets are subject to wider price swings. And when volatility (σ) is an appropriate measure of the riskiness of price changes, is it fairly constant from period to period or does volatility fluctuate? Again, we will review evidence implying wider, non-normal price swings in exchange rates.

Pricing Efficiency.   Last but by no means least, we focus on prices to gauge whether market prices fully reflect available information—in other words, whether markets are **efficient.** If markets are efficient in this sense, then there are no bargain (underpriced) securities and no rip-offs (overpriced securities). When efficiency prevails, market prices respond quickly to assimilate the information content of news announcements.

In some sense, the efficiency paradigm views prices as the "output" of a financial market. Financial markets are working efficiently when market prices move quickly to reflect fair value. Reaching a judgment on whether a market is efficient or not is a critical part of understanding how a market "works" and whether it "works well."

Policy Issues in International Financial Markets

An analysis of prices in international financial markets would be incomplete without discussing how these findings affect market participants directly and other segments of the economy indirectly. In this text, we take the view that our empirical findings about the behavior of market prices have logical policy implications. It is convenient to consider the policy implications separately for two broad groups:

1. Private individuals and managers of private enterprises, for whom their own self-interest (measured by utility maximization) or value maximization (measured by security prices) are the decision criteria, and

2. Public policymakers, for whom broader measures of welfare maximization are typically invoked for decision making.

In this text, we use the word *policy* to indicate a wide range of strategies and actions facing various decision makers. As we will discover, our findings about the determinants of market prices, price relationships, price behavior, and pricing efficiency often have direct implications for the overall strategy adopted by private individuals and public policymakers as well as their specific, individual actions.

Policy Issues for Individuals and Private Enterprises in International Financial Markets.   An array of policy issues follow immediately from our initial analysis of market prices. Individuals and private enterprises often want to know more about the determinants of prices—not out of academic curiosity, but because of practical considerations. Market participants must set a policy or strategy for forecasting future financial prices. They want to know what models or techniques might be useful. Is it possible to forecast exchange rates, interest rates, bond prices, and equity prices? If so, with what measures of accuracy or success?

Market participants clearly need to know about the determinants of prices, because traders or market makers are continuously called upon to offer price quotations as news about underlying economic and political conditions develops. Which data or news items are most relevant? How should traders adjust prices as economic news is released? Market participants also need to be fully aware of parity relationships among the various international financial prices. These parity relationships constrain the prices that a dealer can offer or that a customer would expect to pay.

Our findings on market efficiency will definitely color the policies of any market participant. A market that displays efficiency calls for policies to minimize trading and transaction costs because the likelihood that active strategies and risk taking will be rewarded is small. Efficient markets call for hedging policies that lower an investor's exposure to diversifiable risks because these risks carry no expected return in an efficient market.

A *lack* of efficiency also has immediate, but very different, policy implications. Inefficiency leads to a policy of tilting borrowing and investment decisions more heavily into particular markets or currencies or instruments at particular times with the expectation of making unusual gains.

Corporate treasurers are naturally interested in strategies regarding short-term and long-term borrowing in international markets. Are there individual currencies or more complex strategies that have in the past, and might in the future, offer lower-cost funds? And individuals and institutional investors are interested in policies toward investing in international markets. Are there individual currencies or portfolio strategies that have in the past, and might in the future, offer higher returns? Clearly, risk-return trade-offs play a part in selecting among available borrowing and investing policies.

Given the volatility of financial prices over the last decade, many market participants have focused their attention on managing or containing risks as much as on seeking extra returns. What techniques are most appropriate for measuring financial and economic risks in international markets, and what strategies are likely to be effective in managing these risks? Formulating general policies and specific strategies toward risk management is an essential part of operating amid volatile financial markets.

Policy Issues for Public Policymakers in International Financial Markets.   The perspective of public policy officials is necessarily broader than that of private individuals or firms. Policymakers are concerned about the overall operation of a market and whether there are externalities (unintended side effects) that positively or negatively affect other markets. An underlying presumption in public policy issues is that (1) actions taken by public policymakers can affect the markets, and (2) the benefits of these actions outweigh the costs in some national (or global) welfare calculation. In a broad sense, policymakers monitor market conditions to determine whether intervention is indicated to correct a market failure or a failure of (excessive or deficient) present public policies. Our analysis of price behavior and market practices leads directly to an assessment of public policy issues in international financial markets.

One conspicuous public policy is direct intervention in the foreign exchange market. Policy objectives differ across countries. Countries with a floating exchange rate are most concerned about extreme currency valuations (either overvalued or undervalued) relative to a benchmark, and about excessive volatility (again, relative to a benchmark of what is normal or acceptable). These statements specifically imply that policymakers require a benchmark in order to conclude that a market failure of mispriced or excessively volatile exchange rates has occurred.

The impact of central bank intervention is one of the hotly contested issues in international financial markets. At one extreme, some economists believe that currency markets are prone to excesses, and that central bank intervention is both necessary and desirable to "calm disorderly markets." Successful intervention, they argue, produces a positive externality by promoting a stable exchange market that encourages beneficial trade and financial flows. At the opposite extreme, other economists contend that currency markets are efficient, so that central bank intervention is at best unnecessary and often a factor that produces negative externalities, such as increased price uncertainty and trading losses at the expense of national taxpayers.

Since central bank intervention and unusual exchange market activity often occur at the same time, it is difficult to disentangle which is cause and which is effect.[2] In either case, it is clear that central bank intervention signals a risky time for market participants.

For countries adopting a pegged exchange rate system, two policy decisions are common. The first involves the pegging partner, and the second entails the central rate and conditions for changing or adjusting the central rate.

Consider the case of the British pound sterling, which was freely floating in September 1990. In October 1990, policymakers in the United Kingdom made the decision

---

[2]The fire department is present at nearly all fires, but it is seldom responsible for starting any of them.

to join sterling to the European Exchange Rate Mechanism (ERM). The decision to join the ERM and the selection of the initial central parity rate (2.95 DM/£) as well as the limits of fluctuation around the central rate (6.0 percent) were in part guided by the economic analysis of the fundamental determinants of exchange rates and conditions for exchange rate stability. By September 1992, economic conditions and the apparent policy calculations had changed. The Bank of England withdrew sterling from the ERM (it quickly depreciated from 2.7816 DM/£ to 2.6160 DM/£) and allowed it to float against all currencies.

Regulation of national financial markets is another prominent public policy. Regulation is pervasive in financial markets, but some of the main categories affect:

- Banks: Reserve requirements, capital adequacy requirements, information disclosure on interest paid to depositors, controls on banking and underwriting activities.
- Markets: Exchange listing requirements, margin requirements, permitted securities, price limit movements.
- Firms: Accounting principles for calculation of income, exposure to exchange risk, and so forth; accounting rules for disclosure of geographic activity, business segment activity.
- Taxation: On ordinary income, capital gains; withholding taxes, taxes on payments to foreigners; transaction taxes, stamp duties, or fees on exchanges of securities.

Regulation is intended to promote beneficial externalities and reduce negative externalities that may accompany an unfettered and unregulated market structure. For example, issuers of securities that trade in public markets in the United States are required to meet minimum information disclosure requirements. These rules are intended to redress the asymmetry between issuers of securities and investors, and promote investor protection. Rules that require common accounting policies may provide a positive externality by making accounting statements comparable across firms. Other regulations—such as capital requirements for banks that hold risky financial positions, or margin requirements for individuals with risky financial positions—may produce a positive externality by lowering the likelihood of default and contagion among market participants in the event of a sudden sharp change in market prices.

While regulation is intended to promote good outcomes, it is important to bear in mind that regulations impose a cost on market participants. These costs include administrative compliance or monitoring costs, but there are also direct financial costs, such as those associated with capital requirements and reserve holdings. Specifically, a bank that holds capital reserves earning the U.S. Treasury bill rate forgoes the opportunity to make a commercial loan at a higher rate of interest.

We refer to the difference between the costs imposed by regulation and the benefits resulting from regulation as the **net regulatory burden.** The concept of a net regulatory burden takes on greater significance in a world where financial innovation and improvements in telecommunications and computing have made financial transactions more footloose. Transactions that were traditionally conducted in one market may readily be transferred elsewhere. As we will see, regulatory costs have had a significant impact on both the menu and location of financial transactions.

Governments remain concerned about the prospects of losing markets to other locations. See Box 1.2 for a story that discusses the possibility for trading in U.S. government securities to migrate to other countries. And see Box 1.3 for a story that illustrates steps proposed by Germany to retain its place as a European and international financial center.

Box 1.2

"London, Tokyo Said Crucial to Market in U.S. Treasurys"

The London and Tokyo markets for U.S. Treasury securities could handle shifts in trading from the United States if cost differences favored the offshore markets, U.S. Federal Reserve economists said.

"The potential for such shifts could have important implications for the development of regulatory and oversight policies aimed at the government securities market in the U.S.," said Fed economists Brian Madigan and Jeff Stehm in a newly published paper.

The economists said various sources suggest that the volume in the global market for U.S. Treasury securities may range from $400 billion to $550 billion per day, including financing activities involving repurchase and reverse repurchase agreements with which market participants finance their positions. More than 95% of this activity takes place in the United States, they said, while 4% goes on in London and Tokyo. Dealings in London are about three times greater than in Tokyo, the two men said.

But the economists said that the figures for Tokyo and London may not accurately reflect the importance of these centers in allocating securities among final investors and in performing such functions as allowing for the adjustment of final exposures and pricing during critical periods when the U.S. markets are closed.

By creating liquidity around the clock, the London and Tokyo market "deepen the markets and thus strengthen the role of U.S. Treasury securities in serving as an interest-rate benchmark, an outlet for investable funds, and a risk-adjustment mechanism for financial markets worldwide," the economists said.

The Fed economists' comments came in "An Overview of the Secondary Market for U.S. Treasury Securities in London and Tokyo," a new paper in the Fed's finance and discussion series. Such writings are circulated for discussion and don't represent Fed policy.

Noting that "convenience appears to be by far the most important reason for investors to choose to trade U.S. Treasuries in London or Tokyo," the authors said that "the development of a substantial local organizational infrastructure also suggests that they could easily accommodate a shift of trading volume from New York should cost differences shift in their favor."

"As offshore repurchase markets and settlement alternatives for U.S. Treasuries develop, such accommodation becomes even easier," the economists said. "These factors should be taken into account in the development of policies toward the government securities market in the U.S."

Challenges in the Study of International Financial Markets and the Practice of International Financial Management

One of the primary challenges facing the student of international financial markets today is that while the importance of international finance has increased over the last 25 years, the study of international financial markets and the practice of international financial management have become far more demanding.

The Importance of Foreign Exchange outside the United States

The foreign exchange rate is usually considered "the most important price" for the economy. The intuition behind this remark is that most economies are small relative to the world, when measured in terms of gross domestic product (GDP). As small economies, most countries depend heavily on trade in goods and services. And most imports and exports of primary commodities like petroleum, copper, and lumber, or agricultural products are priced in US$—a foreign currency to all countries of the world except one. With oil at $20 per barrel, a change in the $/¥ exchange rate seems a nonevent to most

Box 1.3

"Germany Will Issue Short-Term Bills, Sign of Pressure from Euro-Currency"

By Matt Marshall
Staff Reporter of The Wall Street Journal

The German government will begin issuing short-term Treasury bills, the latest sign that the move toward a European single currency is forcing Germany to soften some of its conservative fiscal traditions.

Yesterday, the Bundesbank, Germany's central bank, announced it had endorsed Bonn's desire to begin issuing 10 billion marks ($6.52 billion) worth of "Bu-bills" on a quarterly basis with a six-month maturity. The first issue will be in July.

In a statement, the Bundesbank said the move was taken to "further enhance the standing of the federal government as a benchmark issuer and to strengthen the competitiveness of the German financial center, with a view also to European economic and monetary union."

For more than 40 years, Bonn has been forced to rely on longer-term securities to finance its debt, mainly bills with maturities of 5 to 10 years. That is because the Bundesbank feared that a shift to short-term bills would endanger Germany's culture of long-term, and therefore stable, financing.

But in recent years, that restriction had become increasingly costly. By not borrowing at less-expensive, short-term interest rates, Bonn lost an average 200 million marks of savings a year over the past 20 years, said Juergen Stark, the finance ministry deputy minister who announced the decision. In addition, Frankfurt was fast losing its reputation as a modern financial capital because it couldn't offer what in most countries is considered a basic financial instrument.

Saving money and boosting Frankfurt's financial reputation have both taken on added significance in view of the approaching 1999 deadline for European monetary union.

Most notably, Germany is struggling to rein in record public debt levels to under 60% of gross domestic product, the ceiling set by the Maastricht Treaty for participation in monetary union. On Wednesday, Bonn admitted for the first time that it would not likely meet that criterion, and a stagnant economy is only making Germany's financial situation worse.

Further, Germany's strength as a financial center has been challenged by other European nations, which issue their own Treasury bills, and which are all now jockeying to become benchmark issuers after the switch over to the Euro currency in 1999.

Analysts added that the Bundesbank's move will help the Euro compete as an international currency reserve, since short-term government-backed securities will be crucial if it is to compete with dollar-based securities.

Americans, but it has a direct consequence for all Japanese producers and consumers of oil products.

On the financial side, foreign investors have long been attracted to U.S. short-term financial instruments for the depth and liquidity of these markets. And non-U.S. investors have exhibited a greater propensity to hold foreign assets in their portfolios, both for higher expected rates of return and the advantages of diversification. The calculation of returns on these foreign investments depends a great deal on changes in the foreign exchange rate.

Foreign central banks have long followed exchange rates closely, not only because of a currency's impact on the domestic economy, but because foreign central banks were committed to use their international reserves (comprised mostly of US$) to support a pegged rate. An overvalued exchange rate could cost a central bank dearly through the loss of valuable US$ reserves that had been earned through foreign trade or borrowed from another central bank or international agency.

The Importance of Foreign Exchange in the United States

By comparison, the foreign exchange rate was probably *not* the most important price for a typical U.S. consumer, investor, or firm for most of the 20th century. Even though the United States has prided itself on being a free-trading nation, American reliance on international trade has been low relative to that of other countries. In 1950, for example, U.S. merchandise imports and exports *combined* were only 6.8 percent of U.S. GDP. The United States was by far the largest economy in the world in 1950—its GDP valued at $1.6 trillion (in 1992 dollars) was nearly 60 percent of world GDP.

In financial markets, U.S. individuals held few foreign portfolio investments. Controlling interests in foreign operations (direct foreign investments) were a minor part of the total operations of most U.S. firms. When U.S. firms borrowed capital, the debt was typically denominated in US$ and issued in U.S. markets.

At the national level, the United States' central bank, the Federal Reserve, held gold and foreign currency to support the value of the US$. However, because the Fed printed US$ which other central banks were obliged to hold, the Fed did not feel the pinch in the same way as other central bankers when official U.S. debts accumulated against a fixed stock of gold.

The collapse of the Bretton Woods system of pegged exchange rates in 1973 set the stage for a change in how Americans would view the foreign exchange rate and international financial markets.[3] Exchange rate volatility increased dramatically in the early years of the float, whether measured in nominal or real terms. Consequently, U.S. firms started to see substantial shifts in international competitiveness (in goods markets) and similarly these exchange rate shocks affected firms with debt or earnings streams denominated in foreign currency.

One imperfect indication of the impact of exchange rate variability on firms is reflected in corporate income and balance sheet figures as mandated by U.S. generally accepted accounting principles (GAAP). In Table 1.1, we show the largest foreign exchange accounting gains and losses realized by U.S. firms during three years: 1978, a weak US$ year; 1984, a strong US$ year; and 1998, a recent year.

The figures show that the impact of foreign exchange swings on accounting income has been substantial for some companies.[4] What these accounting numbers represent in *economic* terms is open to dispute, but the size of these numbers is too large for managers, accountants, or financial analysts to simply ignore.

In Table 1.2, we report the largest unrealized foreign exchange gains and losses by U.S. firms for 1984, 1993, and 1998. These figures represent the accumulation of unrealized foreign exchange gains and losses up to the reporting date.[5] Again, the interpretation of these figures is open to dispute, but the figures are too large to set aside without close examination. Taken together, Tables 1.1 and 1.2 suggest that exchange rate volatility in the post–Bretton Woods period might have had an impact on the performance of firms.

By 1998, U.S. GDP had advanced more than 3.5 times in *absolute* terms, reaching $7.5 trillion (in 1992 dollars). Even so, U.S. GDP declined in *relative* terms, to only 28.4

---

[3]There are many summaries of the development of the international monetary period and the major events surrounding the rise and fall of the Bretton Woods system. A particularly readable account is in Aliber (1987). For a highly detailed and documented account, see Dam (1982).

[4]Other, less well-known and smaller companies report a smaller absolute impact but are similar in relationship to operating income.

[5]These unrealized profits could represent, among other things, foreign currency denominated assets and liabilities that have not matured but have gained or lost US$ value at present exchange rates.

TABLE 1.1   Largest Realized Foreign Exchange Accounting Gains/Losses for U.S. Firms: Selected Years

Largest Realized Gains			Largest Realized Losses		
Company	*Amount ($ Millions)*	*Percent of Operating Income*	*Company*	*Amount ($ Millions)*	*Percent of Operating Income*
1998					
Chase Manhattan Corp.	$963	15.4%	General Motors	$−323	−1.5%
Bank of America Corp.	531	4.3	Seagate Technology	−252	−55.9
American International Group	339	4.0	UAL Corp.	−84	−3.7
State Street Corp.	289	41.5	ICN Pharmaceuticals	−81	−39.8
Republic New York Corp.	141	26.8	Texaco	−74	−1.9
Bank Boston Corp.	127	9.6	Mobil Corp.	−53	−1.1
Ford Motor Co.	97	0.3	Chevron Corp.	−47	−1.2
1984					
Exxon	109	0.8	General Motors	−115	−1.2
Ford Motor	75	1.3	Minnesota Mining and Manufacturing	−62	−3.7
Texaco	55	1.0	Atlantic Richfield	−61	−1.5
Pepsico	54	5.6	Goodyear Tire	−46	−4.3
Amoco	53	0.1	Gillette	−35	−8.1
1978					
IBM	113	1.5	Exxon	−316	−3.2
General Motors	63	0.7	Navistar	−107	−16.4
GTE	32	1.2	Texaco	−105	−3.8
General Electric	12	0.5	Varity Corp.	−91	−46.9
Air Products	10	0.4	Chevron	−87	−3.9

Note: Realized Gains/Losses represent the foreign exchange adjustment to income. Operating Income is before depreciation.

Source: Standard & Poor's, Compustat.

percent of world GDP in 1998.[6] Thus, the United States became a relatively smaller country in the world economy and substantially more reliant on open trading relations with the rest of the world. By 1998, U.S. merchandise exports and imports together approached 20 percent of U.S. GDP, or nearly three times the percentage in 1950.

On the financial side, U.S. investors have gradually diversified their portfolios into foreign securities (both stocks and bonds), the value of which depends directly on foreign exchange rates. U.S. firms have diversified their borrowing activities into other market locations and into non-US$ denominations—and their ability to raise funds and the costs of those funds depends on the exchange rate. There is some evidence that financial analysts paid too little attention to corporate foreign exchange gains and losses.[7] But empirical evidence also suggests that the stock price of certain U.S. firms (those with substantial foreign currency earnings or foreign competition) is sensitive to changes in the exchange rate.[8]

---

[6]According to the World Bank, the relative size of the U.S. economy appears even smaller (only 23 percent of world GDP) when national GDPs are combined using purchasing power parity exchange rates. See *World Development Indicators 2000,* World Bank (Washington, DC: World Bank, April 2000), pp. 10–13.

[7]See Bartov and Bodner (1994).

[8]See Allayannis (1996).

TABLE 1.2 Largest Unrealized Foreign Exchange Accounting Gains/Losses for U.S. Firms: Selected Years

	Largest Unrealized Gains			Largest Unrealized Losses		
Company	*Amount ($ Millions)*	*Percent of Operating Income*		*Company*	*Amount ($ Millions)*	*Percent of Operating Income*
1998						
IBM Corp.	$860	6.3%		Coca-Cola	$−1,320	−24.4%
Browning-Ferris	82	7.5		General Motors Corp.	−1,157	−5.4
Caterpillar Inc.	65	1.8		Phillip Morris	−1,081	−7.1
Loews Corp.	60	2.2		Mobil Corp.	−1,058	−21.4
Bausch & Lomb	41	10.0		Ford Motor Co.	−1,017	−3.1
				Goodyear Tire	−878	−56.3
				Gillette Co.	−826	−30.6
1993						
IBM	1,658	27.2		Philip Morris	−711	−7.2
Caterpillar	170	11.7		Mobil	−526	−8.1
Molex	102	48.9		General Motors	−494	−2.9
AMP	68	8.7		Goodyear Tire	−422	−29.5
LSI Logic	60	39.9		Coca-Cola	−420	−12.1
Honeywell	53	6.9		Gillette	−415	−32.5
Tektronix	51	37.2		Colgate-Palmolive	−373	−33.5
Woolworth	39	5.0		Exxon	−370	−3.1
Safeway	39	4.7		Unisys	−361	−33.8
Disney	37	1.4		Johnson & Johnson	−338	−11.5
1984						
BCE	53	2.1		IBM	−2,948	−20.4
IPL Energy	16	8.3		Mobil	−2,037	−30.7
Bow Valley Energy	11	4.1		Exxon	−1,818	−13.1
Abitibi Price	10	0.6		Ford Motor	−1,365	−23.8
Caterpillar	8	2.2		General Motors	−790	−8.2
Inter-City Products	4	3.6		Xerox	−537	−34.5
DeTomaso Ind.	1.4	16.6		Minnesota Mining and Manufacturing	−490	−29.0
Nike	0.8	0.7		Goodyear Tire	−466	−43.5
Reading & Bates	0.5	0.6		Union Carbide	−419	−31.7
Laidlaw	0.3	0.4		Johnson & Johnson	−366	−37.7

Note: Unrealized gains/losses represent the cumulative translation adjustment to retained earnings. Operating income is before depreciation.
Source: Standard & Poor's, Compustat.

The U.S. government (on behalf of all national taxpayers) now has its own reason for self-interest in the path of foreign exchange rates. At the end of 1999, the U.S. government had $3.3 trillion of its $5.8 trillion public debt in the form of marketable securities. Almost $1.3 trillion of that debt (or 40 percent of marketable securities) is held by foreigners. In contrast, five years earlier foreigners held only $641 billion in U.S. government securities, or about 20 percent of the total at that time. Thus, the United States depends heavily on foreign investors to purchase U.S. government debt, keep bond prices high, and keep the interest rate on government debt low. Foreign investors are less inclined to buy government debt at prevailing prices if there is an expectation that the exchange rate of the US$ will decline.

The Study of International Financial Markets: More Demanding

The study of international financial markets has become more demanding over the 25 years since the collapse of the Bretton Woods system. The historical data series are longer, encompassing more episodes, and there is greater volatility to explain. At the same time, innovation has brought us more financial products, each one in need of a pricing model and each one adding to the list of possible price correlations to analyze. Process innovation has given us more procedures, markets, and regulations to follow. And the creativity and research by financial economists have given us more realistic theoretical models and relevant empirical evidence to interpret.

The Practice of International Financial Management: More Demanding

The practice of international financial management has also become more demanding over the last 25 years. In part, this simply follows from the wider array of products and markets, and the need to understand the theoretical underpinnings and empirical behavior of prices in those markets. New techniques for forecasting, measuring performance, and managing risks also create a more demanding atmosphere for financial managers. Finally, greater price volatility in financial markets raises the opportunity cost of a wrong decision or an unexpected exchange rate change.

A Road Map for the Remainder of the Book

Summary of Major Topics

The next chapter rounds out Part I with an overview of international monetary systems and recent developments in international financial markets. We review the experience with the gold standard, the Bretton Woods system of pegged exchange rates, the post–Bretton Woods floating-rate standard, and the fledgling European Monetary Union. Then, to gain familiarity with some of the key market variables, we examine charts and descriptive statistics on exchange rate and interest rate behavior.

Part II focuses on the foreign exchange market. In Chapter 3, we first describe the structure of the market, the basic contracts and conventions, and how the main actors in the market are organized. Parity conditions and arbitrage play an important role for us. We develop the purchasing power parity theory in Chapter 4 and the interest rate parity theories (both *covered* and *uncovered* interest parity) in Chapter 5. We present empirical evidence on the parity conditions and discuss how situations of both parity and disparity have an impact on policy decisions.

Chapters 6, 7, and 8 highlight several key themes regarding foreign exchange: the macroeconomic determinants of spot rates, the pricing efficiency of foreign exchange markets, and techniques for forecasting rates. Under each heading, we lay out a theoretical framework and describe the behavior of prices or markets in accordance with theory. We then review the empirical evidence and draw conclusions regarding which theories or policies can be supported. Recent research suggests that there may be significant inefficiencies in foreign exchange markets at short horizons. We examine this evidence and its implications for forecasting.

In Part III, we examine the market for short-term bank deposits and loans (the Eurocurrency market in Chapter 9) and the market for longer-term fixed-income securities (the Eurobond market in Chapter 10) that collectively are known as the offshore financial markets. The offshore markets are another truly international market because they operate across national borders. Pricing in the offshore markets depends very much on cost savings because the markets operate in direct competition with onshore markets that are usually well entrenched. As we will see, offshore markets have prospered in their low operating cost and low regulatory cost environment. Their prosperity has policy implications for both the private and public sectors.

Part IV (Chapters 11, 12, and 13) is concerned with derivative securities. We examine the markets for futures, options, and swaps for both currencies and interest rates. The value of these securities is *derived* from an underlying asset (for example, a currency price), so it will be natural to express the value of a futures, option, or swap as a function of the underlying asset. When we measure the value of the derivative security as a function of the current *price* of the underlying asset, we define this as **marking to market.** In this way, owners of a portfolio of derivative securities can monitor the value of their portfolio, and they can express the value of the portfolio *conditional on* the value of the underlying assets.

Key issues in Chapter 11 (on futures) are the difference between futures contracts and forward contracts, and the information content in the term structure of forward rates. In Chapter 12, we develop the now conventional **Black-Scholes option pricing model** as applied to foreign currencies. The model has important insights for the management of risk in option positions. However, the jumpiness of currency prices may make this model inappropriate for pricing currency options. In Chapter 13, we rely on the marking-to-market approach to measure the riskiness of swap contracts if a default forces one counterparty to replace the contract at market prices.

International assets portfolios comprising bonds and equities are the topic of Part V. In these chapters, we are concerned with the calculation of risk and return in these international portfolios. In Chapter 14, we focus on the impact that currency hedging plays on the risk-return profile. In Chapter 15, we examine the natural diversification associated with an international equity portfolio.

Issues pertaining to the measurement and management of risk in international financial positions are addressed in Part VI (Chapter 16). We review both accounting and economic concepts of exposure as they face the corporate treasurer. And we demonstrate why both financial and operational hedging strategies may be needed for the firm to hedge the range of exposures that it faces in an international setting. We illustrate the use of regression analysis and scenario analysis to estimate a firm's exposure to exchange risk. We also describe the value-at-risk approach for measuring the exposure of pure financial positions, and provide an example.

Finally, in Part VII, we consider how regulators may give direction to international financial markets that appear so footloose and innovative when left to private hands. We focus on two issues in Chapter 17: (1) whether national financial market regulators should behave in a coordinated or competitive approach, and (2) whether foreign exchange market intervention can be effective in containing exchange rate behavior.

Typical Chapter Outline

In those chapters dealing with markets or instruments, a typical chapter begins with a description of the market and its principal institutional features. We then review or develop a theoretical framework for the pricing or price behavior of the instrument. Empirical evidence is presented to see whether predictions of the model are borne out.

Nearly every chapter concludes with a section on policy implications for private individuals or firms and implications for public policymakers. In these sections, we attempt to show the linkage between prices and policies that represents the main theme of this book.

Questions

1. Which financial markets and instruments available to players in the international financial markets today were not available in the 1950s or 1960s?

2. Why were the new financial markets and instruments you listed in response to question 1 developed, and why have they grown in importance and popularity?

3. What evidence supports the notion that the volatility of prices in financial markets has increased since the Bretton Woods system collapsed in 1973? Explain in general terms why volatility in financial markets has increased since 1973.

4. Is it more correct to say "The fall of Bretton Woods in 1973 allowed financial prices to become more volatile," or "An increase in volatility brought on the demise of Bretton Woods"? Discuss.

5. While concern about price variability remains important, market participants have become more concerned recently with counterparty risk, liquidity risk, delivery risk, and systemic risk. Why have these risks have become a source of greater concern?

6. Why would knowledge about the determinants of prices, the nature of price changes, the nature of price relationships among financial markets, and pricing efficiency be important for setting the policies of individuals or corporations?

7. Why would knowledge about the determinants of prices, the nature of price changes, the nature of price relationships among financial markets, and pricing efficiency be important for setting national and international financial policies?

8. Why might international financial markets be very important to a small country such as Portugal or Korea?

9. "Over the last 50 years, international financial markets have become more important to the United States." True or false? Explain.

References

Aliber, Robert Z. *The International Money Game,* 5th ed. New York: Basic Books, 1987.

Allayannis, George. "Exchange Rates, Hedging and the Value of the Firm." Ph.D. dissertation, Stern School of Business, New York University, 1996.

Bartov, Eli, and Gordon M. Bodnar. "Firm Valuation, Earnings Expectations, and the Exchange-Rate Exposure Effect." *Journal of Finance* 49, no. 5 (Dec. 1994), pp. 1755–85.

Dam, Kenneth W. *The Rules of the Game.* Chicago: University of Chicago Press, 1982.

2 AN OVERVIEW OF INTERNATIONAL MONETARY SYSTEMS AND RECENT DEVELOPMENTS IN INTERNATIONAL FINANCIAL MARKETS

"The way in which an international monetary system actually works may differ enormously from the written or intended rules in the treaty on which it is apparently based."

Ronald I. McKinnon (1993)

Learning Objectives

After reading this chapter, students should

1. Understand the main features of international monetary systems that have been in use over the 20th century.

2. Appreciate the risks associated with a change in the system or a system that does not operate as the formal rules might suggest.

3. Realize the extent of exchange rate movements since 1970 and observe examples of how volatile rates have been under pegged rate systems, floating rate systems, and the European Monetary System.

4. Realize the extent of interest rate movements since 1990, and observe examples of how volatile interest rates (and interest rate differentials) have been for several countries.

5. Be aware of the distinction between nominal magnitudes and real magnitudes for both exchange rates and interest rates.

6. Understand that price volatility has been a feature of international financial markets for many years, *a.* leading private investors to desire better understanding of the determinants of prices, better ways to forecast prices, and better tools for hedging price risks, and *b.* leading public policymakers to become more concerned about the risks of international financial markets and whether systems with lower exchange rate volatility are feasible.

23

For more than a century, financial markets have witnessed an evolution in international monetary arrangements from the classical gold standard of the 19th century, to the pegged exchange rate system known as Bretton Woods adopted in 1944, to the floating exchange rate system that began in the early 1970s. The possibility of change in international monetary arrangements—from pegged to floating rates, or vice versa—and the prospect that any system may not operate according to the stated "rules of the game" represent two of the major risks facing agents in international financial markets. Much of the drama in international finance is focused on the selection of an exchange rate system for a nation (or a set of nations) and on the uncertainty of how that system will operate in practice.

While the gold standard lacked a formal treaty or agreement, major industrial countries (and many smaller ones) elected to follow a set of monetary practices that allowed the gold standard to function effectively until the beginning of World War I in 1914. After two world wars and the worldwide Great Depression, the transition to pegged rates in 1944 was planned specifically to promote international monetary stability, trade, and growth. The Bretton Woods system gave a central role to gold, but it soon became apparent that the United States and the U.S. dollar were the real anchoring points of the system.

In contrast, the movement to a floating-rate system was not the free choice of policymakers. Rather, floating was the only system compatible with the separate macroeconomic choices of nations and the intense scrutiny of financial markets. The tendency for countries to place domestic economic priorities ahead of external economic commitments and the increase in international capital mobility meant that exchange rates needed to become more flexible to equilibrate international capital movements. But after a decade of floating, policymakers sought relief from increased exchange rate volatility either by intervention to keep exchange rates within **target zones,** or by the formation of regional currency blocs such as the **European Monetary System (EMS).** As we will see, these efforts have met with mixed success, but policymakers remain committed to influencing exchange rate behavior.

The objective of this chapter is to describe in broad terms the major operating principles—the "rules of the game"—of alternative international monetary agreements. We review the rules for the classical gold standard, the Bretton Woods system for pegged exchange rates, and the floating rate, U.S. dollar exchange rate system. We also review how these systems operated in practice, suggesting that the Bretton Woods system evolved into a U.S. dollar standard and that the system of freely floating exchange rates has been overlaid from time to time by central bank intervention.

While the classical gold standard is no longer a realistic option for major industrial countries, in the last ten years several smaller countries have introduced **currency boards** that share some characteristics with a commodity money system. We will comment on the development and operational aspects of a currency board.

The **European Union (EU),** formerly the **European Community (EC)** and before that the European Economic Community (popularly known as the Common Market), has been engaged in a financial experiment for over three decades. Initially, the objective was to limit the variability of European exchange rates against each other. This evolved into a system to limit European exchange rate variability against a common synthetic unit, the **European Currency Unit (ECU).** In the 1990s, European financial planning evolved still further by proposing to replace all national currencies with a common European currency (the euro) and a pan-European monetary policy directed by a new European central bank. We will review the rules of the game for monetary arrangements within the EMS and examine how well the EMS performed in practice.

We will also describe the impact of moving to the euro and a single European central bank, both for Europe and for the international monetary system.

The second section of this chapter presents a series of graphs that reflect various aspects of exchange rate and international interest rate behavior over recent years. We examine these graphs to gain greater familiarity with the behavior of key prices, pricing volatility, and pricing relationships in international financial markets. Reviewing the historical experience of international financial markets in this way is intended to convey a sense of the risks and opportunities facing treasurers, investors, and public policymakers—and also to convey a sense of the challenges facing researchers and analysts in these markets.

We conclude the chapter with a discussion of policy issues pertaining to private enterprises and public policymakers that are affected by the choice of international monetary arrangements.

International Monetary Arrangements in Theory and Practice

Neither a world central bank nor a world currency for international transactions exists. Thus, it has been necessary for trading nations to develop systems whereby national monies can be used to conduct international transactions such as the import and export of goods and services.[1] In this section, we review the principal **international monetary systems** that nations have adopted over the past century. Each system carries with it a set of rules—sometimes explicit in the form of laws or regulations, and sometimes implicit in the form of conventions or customs—which in international finance are commonly referred to as the **rules of the game.**

While the expression *rules of the game* is in common usage, the student will not easily find a definitive list of the most important rules to describe the operation of an international financial system. There are two reasons for this. First, since some of the rules are only conventions, they cannot be relied on as accurate descriptions for how a system will operate at any time. Second, even though some of the rules are written in the form of international treaties or regulations, national practices may depart from these rules.

Despite our inability to enumerate a definitive set of rules of the game, the general preference for having an international financial system based on rules (rather than on discretion) should be emphasized. In an integrated international economy, national economic policies hold the potential for harmful externalities (spillover effects). A well-functioning international financial system may be beneficial for securing the gains from international trade, but it also may be a conduit for the transfer of macroeconomic shocks from one nation to another.[2] The international financial system is like a factor of production that can promote the gains from trade and the economic integration of regions, but it can also impose costs if some nations use the international financial system to export their problems to other countries. An international financial system based on rules has evolved to balance these trade-offs. Still, economic policymakers often use discretion (and exempt themselves from the rules or modify the rules) when fundamentals change or a crisis situation is at hand.

---

[1]Transactions in goods and services (including interest payments for financial services) are referred to as *current account transactions*. Longer-term borrowing and lending transactions, whether by private residents or national governments, are classified as *capital account transactions*.

[2]The standard shocks include the transmission of inflation, growth, unemployment, and investment. See Krugman and Obstfeld (2000) or Pugel and Lindert (2000).

In one paper, Ronald McKinnon (1993) describes the operation of the principal international financial systems of the last century.[3] McKinnon organizes his review into seven separate episodes, each with their own set of rules:

1. The International Gold Standard, 1879–1913
2. The Spirit of the Bretton Woods Agreement, 1945
3. The Fixed-Rate Dollar Standard, 1950–1970
4. The Floating-Rate Dollar Standard, 1973–1984
5. The Plaza-Louvre Intervention Accords and the Floating-Rate Dollar Standard, 1985–1999
6. The Spirit of the European Monetary System, 1979
7. The European Monetary System as a "Greater DM" Area, 1979–1998

McKinnon emphasizes that the selection of rules to describe each system is his best assessment, but it remains controversial. We will draw on McKinnon's taxonomy to discuss the broad rules of the game for each system and the operation of each system in practice.[4] We take the liberty of extending the designation of the Plaza-Louvre Intervention Accords period through 1999 and the European Monetary System period through 1998. In addition, we propose an eighth system for the EMU beginning in 1999.

The International Gold Standard, 1879–1913

By 1879, virtually all the major industrial countries and most smaller nations had adopted the gold standard. Surprising as it may seem, no treaty marks the beginning of the international gold standard. Countries unilaterally elected to follow the rules of the gold standard system, which lasted until the outbreak of World War I in 1914 when European governments ceased to allow their currencies to be convertible into either gold or other currencies, causing the collapse of the gold standard.[5]

The centerpiece of the gold standard was the adoption of a "mint parity" (see Box 2.1, Rule I). For example, the United States adopted the gold standard in 1879 and defined the US$ as 23.22 fine grains of gold. With 480 fine grains per troy ounce, it took US$20.67 to equal one ounce of gold. Other countries linked their currencies to gold in a similar way, which then determined exchange rates.

Using this system, for example, the mint parity exchange rates were 4.856 US$/£, 5.183 FFr/US$, and 4.198 DM/US$ during the gold standard period. Because residents could move gold internationally and freely convert between gold and national currencies (See Box 2.1, Rules I and II), international arbitrage kept exchange rates within very narrow bands of the parity rate (within about 1 percent for rates quoted against the US$ and within 0.5 percent for rates within Europe). Convertibility made it prudent for central bankers to link the creation of national money to its gold backing (see Box 2.1, Rule III).

The operation of the **price-specie flow mechanism** under the gold standard reveals the basic intuition about exchange rates, international reserves, and capital flows under

---

[3]The period from 1914 to 1945 reflects the global turmoil of two world wars and the Great Depression, and no uniform system can be ascribed to this period. See also McKinnon (1996).

[4]For another account of the development of the international monetary system over the last century that focuses on the factors underlying a transition from one regime to the next, see Eichengreen (1996).

[5]The United States formally remained on the gold standard until 1933. Other countries attempted to return to the gold standard after World War I.

Box 2.1

Rules of the Game: The International Gold Standard, 1879–1913

I. Fix an official gold price or "mint parity" and allow free convertibility between domestic money and gold at that price.

II. Impose no restrictions on the import or export of gold by private citizens, or on the use of gold for international transactions.

III. Issue national currency and coins only with gold backing, and link the growth in national bank deposits to the availability of national gold reserves.

IV. In the event of a short-run liquidity crisis associated with gold outflows, the central bank should lend freely to domestic banks at higher interest rates (Bagehot's Rule).

V. If Rule I is ever temporarily suspended, restore convertibility at the original mint parity as soon as practical.

VI. As a result of these practices, the worldwide price level will be endogenously determined based on the overall world demand and supply of gold.

Source: Adapted from Ronald I. McKinnon, "The Rules of the Game: International Money in Historical Perspective," *Journal of Economic Literature* 31 (Mar. 1993), p. 4.

---

other systems. Suppose that country A runs a balance of trade surplus (exports exceed imports). Country A exports goods and imports gold from country B. The gold supply in country A expands, while it contracts in country B. Because of Rule III (Box 2.1), international reserves and the money supply expand in country A while they contract in country B. Goods prices in country A tend to rise while those in country B tend to fall, which acts to dampen the trade imbalance and stop the flow of gold between countries. The process illustrates an *automatic adjustment* to a trade imbalance, as long as countries submit to Rules I, II, and III (Box 2.1).

Under the gold standard, an *active* commitment to return to the original mint parity after any temporary suspension of convertibility (Box 2.1, Rule V) shows that national economic policies were at times managed to justify a particular mint parity rate. This long-term commitment made capital extremely mobile on the basis of a small interest differential if countries were to experience a substantial trade deficit and needed short-term financing. On the other hand, countries were *passive* with regard to money creation. The money supply reflected the amount of gold discoveries, and the world price level was determined endogenously based on money supply and money demand (Box 2.1, Rule VI). In this sense, all countries were treated *symmetrically*, even though countries differed in terms of economic power.

The international gold standard resulted in stable exchange rates. With stable exchange rates and a common monetary policy, prices of tradable commodities were equalized across countries to much the same degree as they were equalized within countries. Purchasing power parity, as measured by wholesale price indexes, also tended to hold. And real rates of interest similarly tended toward equality across a broad range of countries "to a degree not seen before or since."[6]

On the other hand, maintenance of the gold standard essentially made the workings of the internal economy subservient to balance in the external economy. Empirical evidence shows that domestic economies were not as stable or prosperous as some nostalgically remember. Figure 2.1 shows that while average inflation was low during the

---

[6]See McKinnon (1993, p. 11) and references therein. We define *purchasing power parity* in Chapter 4.

FIGURE 2.1   Wholesale Price Indexes in the United States and the United
Kingdom during the Gold Standard, 1870–1914

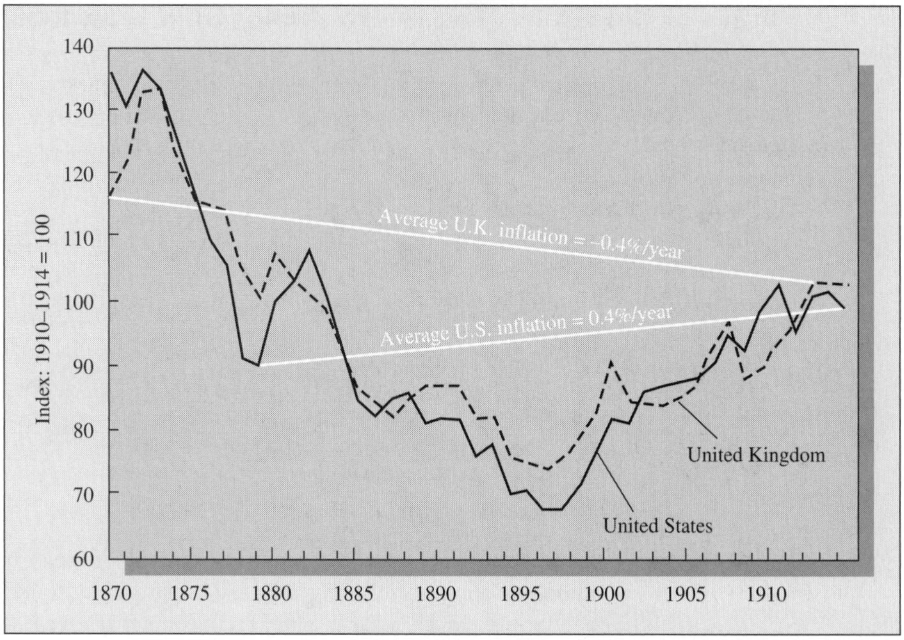

Note: Gold standard period begins 1870 in the United Kingdom and 1879 in the United States.
Source: Warren and Pearson, *Gold and Prices* (New York: John Wiley, 1935).

period of the international gold standard, inflation variability was quite high. A study by Richard Cooper (1984) showed that while *average* inflation during the gold standard was less than in the post–World War II period, *variability* in U.S. inflation was greater during the gold standard. Moreover, income growth was lower and average unemployment higher during the gold standard.

The end of the gold standard was precipitated by the start of World War I. But policymakers had already begun to put the management of the domestic economy ahead of an international commitment to stable exchange rates. The U.S. Federal Reserve System was established in 1913, to supervise banking and also "to furnish an elastic currency," unlike gold, which was added to the system largely by chance discoveries.

The Spirit of the Bretton Woods Agreement, 1945

The **Bretton Woods Agreement** is named after the resort in New Hampshire where it was adopted along with the Articles of Agreement for the **International Monetary Fund (IMF).** In essence, the Bretton Woods Agreement sought a set of rules that would remove countries from the tyranny of the gold standard and permit greater autonomy for national monetary policies.

The negotiators recognized the historical shortcomings of other systems and the trade-offs they would face in trying to balance "stable yet adjustable" exchange rates. For example, the British return to the gold standard from 1925 to 1931 was widely credited for the contraction of the British economy over this period, which in turn aggravated the Great Depression of the 1930s. So a return to gold was resisted. European experiments with floating exchange rates in the 1920s were seen as utter failures and no

---

Box 2.2

Rules of the Game: The Spirit of the Bretton Woods Agreement in 1945

I. Fix an official par value for domestic currency in terms of gold or a currency tied to gold as a numeraire.

II. In the short run, keep the exchange rate pegged within 1 percent of its par value, but in the long run leave open the option to adjust the par value unilaterally if the IMF concurs.

III. Permit free convertibility of currencies for current account transactions, but use capital controls to limit currency speculation.

IV. Offset short-run balance of payments imbalances by use of official reserves and IMF credits, and sterilize the impact of exchange market interventions on the domestic money supply.

V. Permit national macroeconomic autonomy; each member pursues its own price level and employment objectives.

Source: Adapted from Ronald I. McKinnon, "The Rules of the Game: International Money in Historical Perspective," *Journal of Economic Literature* 31 (Mar. 1993), p. 13.

---

foundation upon which to build a post–World War II recovery.[7] Exchange rates needed some flexibility so that national governments could tend to their own macroeconomic policymaking. But exchange rate flexibility needed to be controlled to prevent a recurrence of competitive devaluations as in the 1930s.[8]

The spirit of the Bretton Woods Agreement is summarized in Box 2.2. Official currency values would be set (or "pegged") either in terms of gold or another numeraire currency (Box 2.2, Rule I). Currency values were allowed to fluctuate within a narrow 1 percent band in the short run (Box 2.2, Rule II), but countries retained the option to change the official parity in response to a "fundamental disequilibrium" as long as the IMF concurred. Countries were permitted to pursue their own macroeconomic agenda (Box 2.2, Rule V), which was logically consistent with exchange rate pegging only if exchange controls on capital transaction were imposed (Box 2.2, Rule III).

Temporary payments imbalances of a seasonal or cyclical nature would be covered through a buffer stock of international reserves which could be supplemented through short-term borrowing at the IMF. Figure 2.2 illustrates the role of international reserves in a pegged exchange rate system. *DD* and *SS* represent the demand and supply curves, respectively, for £. The initial intersection at *a* is at a price of $2.80/£, the central parity rate for £ in the 1960s.

To analyze the role of international reserves, assume that the demand for £ falls to *D'D'* following a rise in British prices that makes British goods less attractive to Americans. With the demand for £ at *D'D'*, there is an excess supply of £ equal to *fg* at the lower intervention level $2.78/£, 0.75 percent below the central rate. Since the diagram represents *flows* per unit of time, the Bank of England must buy up *fg* pounds *each period* (at a cost of $2.78/£ × *fg* £) in order to keep the exchange rate from falling to price *e*. Notice that the Bank of England uses *US$ reserves* to buy up the excess supply of pounds.[9] Once reserves are depleted and no more can be borrowed, the central bank has no choice but to devalue (that is, lower the price of) its currency.

---

[7]See Chapter 17 for more on the behavior of floating rates during the 1920s.

[8]Such devaluations intended to boost domestic growth through cheaper exports and were known as "beggar-thy-neighbor" policies.

[9]Analogously, if the supply of pounds increases to *S'S'*, there is an excess supply of £ equal to *ij* at the lower intervention level $2.78/£, which the Bank of England must buy up to keep the exchange rate from falling to price *h*.

FIGURE 2.2   The Role of International Reserves in Exchange
Rate Determination

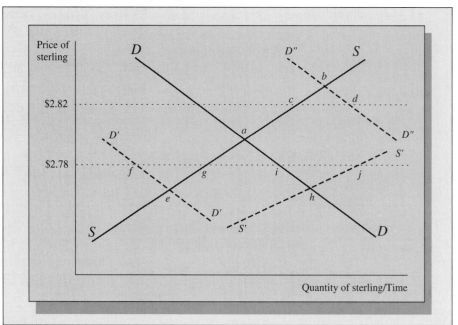

On the other hand, suppose that the demand for £ increases to $D''D''$ following a rise
in U.S. prices that makes British goods more attractive to Americans. Now there is an
excess demand for £ at the upper intervention level $2.82/£, 0.75 percent above the cen-
tral rate. The Bank of England must supply *cd* pounds per period (and accumulate
$2.82/£ $\times$ *cd* £) to keep the pound from appreciating (that is, rising in price above
$2.82). Notice that the excess demand for pounds need not force an appreciation of the
pound, as long as the Bank of England is willing to accumulate US$ reserves.[10]

The Fixed-Rate Dollar Standard, 1950–1970

Even though the Bretton Woods system was designed to permit each country to set its
currency value in terms of gold and create symmetry across all countries, in practice the
system evolved into a fixed-rate dollar standard. Except for the United States, the industrial countries set their official par values in terms of the U.S. dollar (Box 2.3, Rule
I) and endeavored to keep exchange rate changes to a minimum. In the 20 years from
1950 to 1970, the major industrial countries had only a handful of modest exchange rate
changes. Japan kept its exchange rate virtually unchanged at 360 ¥/US$ for 22 years.
Thus, countries other than the United States largely abandoned their monetary autonomy to support a fixed exchange rate and a common price level for tradable goods.

---

[10]If the Bank of England were to increase the British money supply based on its greater stock of US$
reserves, this would tend to increase British prices and reduce the demand for the pound, much like the
price-specie flow mechanism under the gold standard.

Box 2.3

Rules of the Game: The Fixed-Rate Dollar Standard, 1950–1970

Industrial Countries other than the United States

I. Fix an official par value for domestic currency in terms of the U.S. dollar, and keep the exchange rate within 1 percent of this par value indefinitely.

II. Permit free convertibility of currencies for current account transactions; use capital controls to insulate domestic financial markets, but begin liberalization.

III. Use the U.S. dollar as the intervention currency and keep official reserves in U.S. Treasury bonds.

IV. Elevate the importance of maintaining the fixed exchange rate; make domestic monetary policy subordinate to this target as well as to the price level of traded goods in the United States.

V. Limit current account imbalances by adjusting national fiscal policy (government expenditures minus tax revenues) to offset imbalances between private savings and investment.

United States

VI. Remain passive in the foreign exchange market; practice free trade without a balance of payments or exchange rate target.

VII. Keep U.S. capital markets open for borrowing and investing by private residents and foreign sovereigns.

VIII. Maintain an international creditor position in dollar-denominated assets, and limit fiscal deficits.

IX. Pursue an independent monetary policy that establishes a stable price level for tradable goods.

Source: Adapted from Ronald I. McKinnon, "The Rules of the Game: International Money in Historical Perspective" *Journal of Economic Literature* 31 (Mar. 1993), p. 16.

The United States found itself in a very different situation, both liberated and constrained by the so-called **redundancy problem.** In brief, the redundancy problem arises in a world with N countries because the policies of $N-1$ of those countries are sufficient to determine the policies of the Nth country. The Nth country must remain passive; it cannot act independently. To illustrate, in a two-country world (the United States and Germany) there is only one exchange rate. If Germany elects to fix the deutsche mark (DM) at 4.0 DM/US$, the United States must accept 0.25 $/DM as the central rate. In a three-country world, there are only two independent exchange rates, and so on.

Once $N-1$ signatory countries had set par values in terms of the US$, the United States had little choice but to remain passive in the foreign exchange market (Box 2.3, Rule VI). This was the liberating side. The United States alone could exercise monetary independence to provide a stable price level for tradable goods (Box 2.3, Rule IX), but then there was the constraining side of the fixed-rate dollar standard. The United States had to provide a stable world price level and a monetary policy that met the needs of the other $N-1$ countries. Otherwise tensions were bound to develop if the internal macroeconomic objectives of all N countries were not met. This was clearly a tall order to sustain over a 20-year period.

The system worked well in the 1950s. Europe and Japan found it convenient to rely on the United States to supply a stable price environment and for access to the dominant U.S. capital markets. In Europe, the Marshall Plan established the European Payments Union, which used the US$ as a unit of account and means of settlement. In Japan, the Dodge Plan supported a similar dollar-based price stabilization program. In the 1960s, Europe and Japan were hesitant to consider any exchange rate changes because large capital movements could be launched in anticipation of these changes.

FIGURE 2.3   The Triffin Dilemma

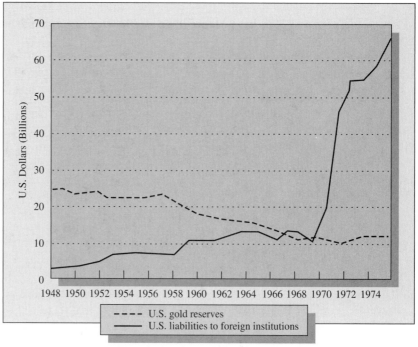

Source: *International Financial Statistics.*

From the U.S. perspective, some felt that the buildup of dollar exchange reserves in the 1950s was benign. As long as the United States provided a stable world price level, and the foreign buildup of reserves was demand-driven and based on a preference for high-quality, interest-bearing dollar assets rather than non-interest-bearing gold, one could argue that the international trading system was the beneficiary.

By the 1960s, the accumulation of U.S. liabilities abroad continued, leading to the famous **Triffin dilemma.** In 1960, Robert Triffin pointed out that based on the U.S. commitment to convert currency into gold at $35 per ounce, the stock of U.S. liabilities held by foreigners would exceed the U.S. gold reserves within a few years (see Figure 2.3). Even though U.S. monetary policy remained credible through the mid-1960s, the Triffin dilemma threatened to excite a speculative run on the U.S. gold stock.

Note that the $35 per ounce price of gold is *not* listed as a rule in Box 2.3. McKinnon (1993) argues that the U.S. commitment was "pro forma" only as a means of defining the value of the U.S. dollar in accordance with the articles of the IMF. Devaluation of the dollar was legally possible within the Bretton Woods Agreement. But the unwritten rules of the fixed-rate dollar standard kept U.S. policymakers uncertain. Concern over continued gold losses led to new restrictions on U.S. capital outflows (contrary to Box 2.3, Rule VII), and formal steps to make conversion of dollars into gold more costly.[11] Other stopgap measures were taken in the late 1960s; a two-tier market for gold

---

[11]These capital restrictions—the Interest Rate Equalization Tax (1963), the Voluntary Foreign Credit Restraint Program (1968), and the Office of Foreign Direct Investment (1970)—helped foster the growth of offshore capital markets. See Chapters 9 and 10.

was introduced to let the private market price of gold adjust upward while maintaining the $35 per ounce official price, and the **special drawing right (SDR)** was introduced as a "paper gold" substitute to increase the supply of nondollar international reserves.

These steps did not address the fundamental economic causes of tension in the fixed-rate dollar standard. During the height of the Vietnam War in the late 1960s, U.S. monetary policy turned expansionary, and U.S. inflation accelerated to 3.5 percent based on producer prices and 4.5 percent based on consumer prices.[12] The United States had dropped its commitment to Rule IX (Box 2.3) and the provision of a stable price anchor. In response, other countries (Germany, in particular) felt compelled to violate Rule IV (Box 2.3) and run tighter monetary policies to offset American excesses. Over time, U.S. inflation caused a loss of price competitiveness for U.S. exports. The U.S. trade balance and current account balance deteriorated sharply in 1968 and 1969. Capital markets sensed a need for change, and "hot money" flows added to the accumulation of dollar reserves offshore. The stage was set for a dramatic change.

On August 15, 1971, President Richard Nixon announced a devaluation of the dollar, changing its official parity rate to $42 for one ounce of gold. At the same time, Nixon officially "closed the gold window" by renouncing any commitment to exchange foreign dollar reserves for gold at even the official price (confirming what had been true in practice for several years). Exchange rates floated for the next few months as central banks allowed markets to search for equilibrium levels.

In December 1971, a meeting at the Smithsonian Institution resulted in a new set of exchange rate parities and a return to pegging. But this new par value agreement met with limited success. The Canadian dollar continued to float, as it had since June 1970. The British allowed sterling to float in June 1972. In March 1973, the Smithsonian Agreement was abandoned and all currencies of the major industrial countries were allowed to float against each other.

Meetings held during 1972 were unable to resolve the basic conflicts of a pegged exchange rate system in a world with free capital movements where policymakers are charged with the management of their national economies. First, policymakers wanted stable exchange rates in the short run with the freedom to run autonomous macroeconomic policies that would require exchange rate changes in the long run. Clearly, this was incompatible with high capital mobility. Speculators would surely anticipate discrete changes in a pegged-rate system. And policymakers were clearly unwilling to impose heavy-handed capital controls.

Second, policymakers were unable to overcome the redundancy problem. With N countries, there can only be $N - 1$ independent official targets for exchange rates and other macroeconomic variables. No matter how big or important countries are, they cannot *all* operate independently as if the others did not exist. If they do so, markets will find the inconsistencies and exploit them for profit. That, in essence, was at the heart of the downfall of the Bretton Woods system. Without an agreement on who would set the common monetary policy and how it would be set, a floating exchange rate system provided the only alternative.

The Floating-Rate Dollar Standard, 1973–1984

The floating-rate system that developed after the fall of Bretton Woods was not devoid of rules. The U.S. dollar remained the centerpiece of international financial markets. For

---

[12]By comparison, U.S. inflation had averaged about 1 percent per year from 1951 to 1967.

private and official purposes, the U.S. dollar fulfilled the primary functions of money—*medium of exchange, store of value, unit of account*—better than any alternative. In private transactions, nearly all exchange rates continued to be quoted in terms of the US$, which dominated the volume of trading in the foreign exchange market. Primary commodities continued to be priced in terms of the US$. And roughly 75 percent of claims (assets and liabilities) in offshore markets were denominated in the US$. In official transactions, roughly 75 percent of official reserves were held in US$ assets. To assess the external value of domestic currency, officials would typically refer to an exchange rate in US$. And when intervention was called for, it was generally conducted in US$.

While the system was called *floating,* it was far from a freely floating, laissez-faire system. Policymakers were unwilling to let "private market forces" be the sole determinant of exchange rates. This is not surprising. Given the importance of exchange rates to an economy, Richard Cooper (1984, p. 16) reminds us that

> It is inconceivable that a government held responsible for managing its economy could keep its hands off [the exchange rate]. And, sure enough, they have not left it alone.

The IMF also recognized that each country saw its exchange rate as an important policy variable and that the exchange rate policy of one country could have significant negative spillover effects on other countries. Therefore, in 1974 the IMF enacted a set of guidelines designed to limit the potential for conflicts regarding exchange rate policies.[13] The guidelines (still in effect) specified that member nations of the IMF:

1. Have an obligation to intervene to prevent "disorderly conditions" in the foreign exchange market.
2. Should avoid manipulating exchange rates to prevent balance of payments adjustment or gain an unfair competitive advantage in trade.
3. Should take into account the interests and policies of other members when setting their own intervention policies.

While these guidelines are not binding, they show that the IMF sanctions intervention as a method to promote orderly conditions in the foreign exchange market. In the name of maintaining "orderly market conditions" the IMF allows a broad range of intervention techniques—from simple smoothing operations intended to limit short-run volatility in exchange rates, up to exchange rate targeting operations designed to peg the value of a currency at a specific level or range. Indeed, many countries continued to peg their currencies to the US$ or the currency of a major trading partner after 1973.

Under the floating rate dollar standard, the task of smoothing short-run exchange rate movements fell primarily on industrial countries other than the United States (Box 2.4, Rule I). The United States remained more passive (Box 2.4, Rule VI), adopting a laissez-faire (or benign neglect) policy toward exchange rates. Currencies remained convertible for current account transactions (Box 2.4, Rule II). Access to U.S. capital markets was not restricted—the capital controls of the late 1960s were abolished in 1974—and other countries moved to eliminate the remaining restriction on capital account transactions (Box 2.4, Rules II and VII). Countries set their long-run monetary and macroeconomic policies largely independent of the United States (Box 2.4, Rule V), while the United States also set its policies without reference to the foreign exchange value of the US$ or to monetary policies elsewhere.

---

[13]The guidelines are specified in International Monetary Fund Guidelines (1974) and the Amendments to the Articles of Agreements (1978).

Box 2.4

Rules of the Game: The Floating-Rate Dollar Standard, 1973–1984

Industrial Countries other than the United States

I. Smooth short-term variability in the dollar exchange rate, but do not commit to an official par value or to long-term exchange rate stability.

II. Permit free convertibility of currencies for current account transactions, while endeavoring to eliminate all remaining restrictions on capital account transactions.

III. Use the U.S. dollar as the intervention currency (except for transactions to stabilize European exchange rates) and keep official reserves primarily in U.S. Treasury bonds.

IV. Modify domestic monetary policy to support major exchange rate interventions, reducing the money supply when the national currency is weak against the dollar and expanding the money supply when the national currency is strong.

V. Set long-run national monetary and price-level targets independently of the United States; let the exchange rate adjust over the long run to offset these differences.

The United States

VI. Remain passive in the foreign exchange market; practice free trade without a balance of payments or exchange rate target. No need for sizable official foreign exchange reserves.

VII. Keep U.S. capital markets open for borrowing and investing by private residents and foreign sovereigns.

VIII. Pursue a monetary policy independent of the exchange rate or policies in other countries, thereby *not* striving for a common, stable price level (or anchor) for tradable goods.

Source: Adapted from Ronald I. McKinnon, "The Rules of the Game: International Money in Historical Perspective," *Journal of Economic Literature* 31 (Mar. 1993), p. 29.

Essentially, the foreign exchange rate was left to play the role of a residual variable that did a great deal of the adjusting to offset the macroeconomic policy differences across countries. With little coordination of these policies, one would expect exchange rate volatility to increase sharply. It did, as we will detail later in this chapter.

The Plaza-Louvre Intervention Accords and the Floating-Rate Dollar Standard, 1985–1996

The United States had held a fairly passive stance toward US$ exchange rates during the first 10 years of the float.[14] In 1981, the introduction of an expansive U.S. fiscal policy (supported by President Ronald Reagan) combined with tight monetary control (guided by Federal Reserve chairman Paul Volcker) started the U.S. dollar on a prolonged appreciation. By early 1985, the U.S. dollar had appreciated nearly 50 percent (relative to 1980) in real terms against an average of the world's other major currencies (see Figure 2.9 on page 56).[15] As the U.S. dollar rose higher, some economists characterized its price behavior as a "speculative bubble" (meaning a movement greater than, and progressively greater than, justified by macroeconomic fundamentals) and predicted that the foreign exchange value of the dollar was not sustainable.[16]

---

[14]The U.S. intervention of November 1, 1978, is an exception we will review in Chapter 3.

[15]Real appreciation of currency *a* relative to *b* is appreciation of *a* by more than the excess of country *b*'s inflation rate relative to country *a*. See Chapter 4 for further discussion.

[16]For example, see Krugman (1985) and Frankel (1985).

Box 2.5

Rules of the Game: The Plaza-Louvre Intervention Accords and the Floating-Rate Dollar Standard, 1985–1996

Germany, Japan, and the United States (G-3)

I. Set broad target zones for the $/DM and $/¥ exchange rates. Do not announce the agreed-upon central rates, and allow for flexible zonal boundaries.

II. Allow the implicit central rates to adjust when economic fundamentals among the G-3 countries change substantially.

III. Central banks intervene collectively but infrequently to reverse short-run exchange rate trends that threaten a zonal boundary. Signal the collective intent by announcing rather than hiding intervention.

IV. G-3 countries hold reserves in each other's currencies; for the United States, this means building up reserves in deutsche marks, yen, and possibly other convertible currencies.

V. Sterilize the immediate impact of exchange market interventions by not adjusting short-term interest rates.

VI. Each G-3 country aims its monetary policy toward stable prices (measured by domestic consumer or wholesale prices or the GNP deflator), which indirectly anchors the world price level and reduces the drift in exchange rate target zones.

Other Industrial Countries

VII. Support or do not oppose interventions by the G-3 to keep the dollar within its target zone limits.

Source: Adapted from Ronald I. McKinnon, "The Rules of the Game: International Money in Historical Perspective," *Journal of Economic Literature* 31 (Mar. 1993), p. 32.

The strong dollar caused U.S. export firms to lose international competitiveness, and the U.S. trade balance deteriorated. Americans enjoyed the cheaper imports that accompany a strong currency, but import-competing firms naturally sought protection in the form of trade barriers. European policymakers leaned toward tighter monetary policies to halt the slide of their currencies, but the downside of tighter money was an adverse effect on domestic economic performance.

The entire episode convinced policymakers that (1) exchange rates were too important to be left to market forces, so intervention was deemed appropriate to smooth disorderly markets and halt market excesses, and (2) exchange rates were too important to be the residual from uncoordinated economic policies, so better policy coordination was required to establish a set of economic fundamentals that in turn would produce a smoother path of the exchange rate. As a result, since 1985 a new set of rules has evolved, emphasizing the role of exchange market intervention and macroeconomic policy coordination (see Box 2.5).

The first part of the policy sea change, the easy part, was foreign exchange intervention. Although the appreciation of the U.S. dollar peaked in early March 1985, the dollar did not initially fall by much and the U.S. Congress continued to favor import restrictions. On September 22, 1985, officials from the Group of Five (G-5) countries—Britain, France, West Germany, Japan, and the United States—met at the Plaza Hotel in New York City. The G-5 officials issued a communiqué announcing that they would intervene jointly to foster a dollar depreciation. The dollar fell sharply on this news and continued to decline through 1986.

The Plaza communiqué represented a sharp break with earlier policies. Exchange market intervention was often characterized by "leaning-against-the-wind" behavior to reverse a market trend. The Plaza meeting had the central banks leaning with the wind of the recently weak dollar. Further, exchange market interventions were often kept secret and were often the doings of a single central bank. The Plaza meeting resulted in a **coordinated intervention** among several central banks and an open announcement of intervention activity (Box 2.5, Rule III). The Plaza meeting provided a clear signal to markets that the major industrial countries were willing to intervene in a coordinated effort to influence exchange rates.

The dollar's fall continued into 1987, so much so that some European officials began to fear for the competitiveness of their own export industries. Policymakers from the G-5 countries plus Canada made another attempt at exchange rate cooperation in a meeting held at the Louvre in Paris on February 22, 1987. At the Louvre meeting, policymakers agreed "to foster stability of exchange rates around [their] current levels."[17] This was not an unusual statement as part of a press release from a meeting of international finance ministers, but the Louvre accord was more than an empty statement in praise of stability. The substance of the Louvre meeting was a set of target zones, or exchange rate ranges, that the central bankers agreed to defend using active foreign exchange intervention (Box 2.5, Rule I). The exact target zones were never published, but observers believed that the Louvre accord specified bands of ±5.0 percent around a central value of 1.8250 DM/$ and 153.50 ¥/$, the exchange rates of the Friday before the Louvre meeting.[18]

Critics of the Louvre Accord argued that the target zone strategy could have no real force, and the decision to keep the zonal boundaries secret was simply a device to prevent any evaluation of the policy's success. Indeed, policymakers have had to adjust the central rate of the "implied" target zones (consistent with Box 2.5, Rule II) and be flexible about the precise location of the target zone boundary (Box 2.5, Rule I). Intervention under the Louvre Accord seems to be more successful when accompanied by macroeconomic policy changes, and less successful when domestic monetary policy is preserved through **sterilized intervention.**[19]

The harder part of stabilizing exchange rates is achieving the macroeconomic fundamentals that themselves would produce stable exchange rates while allowing countries to achieve their internal macroeconomic goals along with free international capital flows. The Louvre Accord began a process toward greater and, it was hoped, better policy coordination (Box 2.5, Rule VI). Progress in this coordination process is essential to fundamentally affect the stability of exchange rates in the longer run.

The Spirit of the European Monetary System, 1979

At the same time that the international community was struggling to establish a viable set of international monetary arrangements, European nations pursued their own efforts to limit exchange rate fluctuations against each other and to establish coordinated macroeconomic policies across Europe.

In March 1971 with the Bretton Woods system still intact, the European Council (the body uniting Heads of State of the EU member countries) adopted the Werner plan,

---

[17]From the text of the G-6 communiqué, reproduced in Funabashi (1988, p. 280).

[18]Quoted in Funabashi (1988, p. 183).

[19]Sterilized intervention in the foreign exchange market leaves the domestic monetary base unaffected. See Chapters 6 and 17 for further discussion.

which was designed to move the Common Market countries (as the EU was then known) toward economic and monetary union. Under the Werner plan, the countries pledged to stabilize intra-European currency movements to a greater degree than European currencies were allowed to fluctuate against the US$. A time series chart of exchange rate movements thus traced out a "snake in the tunnel" with intra-European currency changes small (the snake) relative to the larger European currency changes against the US$ (the tunnel). After the breakdown of Bretton Woods and the Smithsonian Agreement, European countries met again in April 1972 and set the snake's band at ±2.25 percent and the tunnel's band at ±4.50 percent. In March 1973, the European Council voted to abolish the tunnel and let European currencies float against the US$ while preserving the snake.

The 1973–1978 period witnessed many currency realignments as well as entrances to and exits from the snake agreements.[20] In December 1978, the European Council voted to establish a European Monetary System (EMS) as of March 1979. The EMS was built upon three building blocks: The European Currency Unit (ECU), the **Exchange Rate Mechanism (ERM),** and the **European Monetary Cooperation Fund (EMCF).** Together these components linked together European exchange rates and monetary policies until the chaotic events of 1992 and 1993 (discussed later in this chapter) put the future of the EMS in jeopardy. The European Union overcame these episodes of turmoil and worked toward even closer financial cooperation through the formation of the **European Economic and Monetary Union (EMU)** in 1999. First, we describe the basic building blocks of the EMS.

The European Currency Unit.   The European Currency Unit (ECU) is a basket currency, defined as a fixed amount of the national currencies of the European Union member states. The basket was first defined in 1979, redefined in 1984 to include the Greek drachma, and revised once again in 1989 when the Spanish peseta and Portuguese escudo were added. The Maastricht Treaty (1992) barred further revisions to the ECU. In Table 2.1, we see that an ECU is a basket with 0.6242 DM, 1.332 French francs, 0.08784 British pounds, and so forth through the 12 component currencies. Because we cannot add together German marks, French francs, and British pounds, a column in Table 2.1 lists the $/foreign currency spot rate, which allows us to compute the US$ equivalent of each of the ECU's components.

Based on the spot rates for November 6, 1995, the value of the ECU was $1.3046. The table shows that Germany had the largest weight in the ECU (about one-third) followed by France (about one-fifth), the United Kingdom, and the Netherlands (about one-tenth each). Because the ECU was a fixed basket, the weight of each currency changed slightly as its US$ exchange rate changed.[21]

Prior to 1999, the ECU had a strange existence. No physical ECU coins or notes ever circulated. Private residents could use the ECU as a unit of account for bank accounts, and companies could use the ECU as a convenience for invoicing products. Central banks also used the ECU through the European Monetary Cooperation Fund, described below. On January 1, 1999 the **euro** (E) replaced the ECU on a one-for-one basis. From then on, all existing contracts (such as bank accounts, and government bonds) expressed in ECU were settled in euro.

---

[20]See van Ypersele and Koeune (1985, pp. 38–45) for a detailed analysis of the events of this period.

[21]We could also compute a forward rate for the ECU using $/foreign currency forward rates. There were similarly ECU futures contracts, ECU options, ECU interest rates, and ECU bonds. See Levich (1987) for an introduction to these instruments.

TABLE 2.1 Definition of the ECU and Recent Values

Country	Currency	Basket Amount at Sept. 21, 1989	Exchange Rate on Nov. 3, 1995 ($/foreign currency)	US$ Equivalent	Weighting (% of total)
Germany	DM	0.6242	0.701754	$0.4380	33.58%
France	FFr	1.332	0.203355	0.2709	20.76
United Kingdom	Pound	0.08784	1.5774	0.1386	10.62
Netherlands	Guilder	0.2198	0.62637	0.1377	10.55
Belgium	BFr	3.301	0.034153	0.1127	8.64
Italy	Lira	151.8	0.000626	0.0950	7.28
Spain	Peseta	6.885	0.008145	0.0561	4.30
Denmark	Krone	0.1976	0.181176	0.0358	2.74
Portugal	Escudo	1.393	0.00669	0.0093	0.71
Ireland	Irish Pound	0.00855	0.620347	0.0053	0.41
Luxembourg	LFr	0.13	0.034153	0.0044	0.34
Greece	Drachma	0.1976	0.00426	0.0008	0.06
Total				$1.3046	100.00%

Source: *ECU Handbook,* ECU Banking Association, 1992; spot exchange rates as quoted in *The Wall Street Journal,* Nov. 6, 1995; other entries are author's calculations.

The Exchange Rate Mechanism. The Exchange Rate Mechanism (ERM) was the centerpiece of the plan to limit exchange rate fluctuations across Europe. Each country that participated in the ERM agreed to limit the fluctuations of its currency around a central rate defined in terms of the ECU (Box 2.6, Rule I). In most cases, countries agreed to 2.25 percent bands on either side of their central rate (Box 2.6, Rule II). Italy was allowed a ±6.0 percent band, as were late arrivals to the ERM such as Spain (June 1989), the United Kingdom (October 1990), and Portugal (April 1992).[22]

The ERM set two conditions to assist with stabilization of exchange rates. First, intervention was mandatory if the exchange rate hit the limit of its allowed fluctuations, either ±2.25 percent or ±6.0 percent. Second, there was a "presumption of action" if the exchange rate passed its "divergence threshold," a distance roughly 75 percent of the maximum permitted fluctuation (Box 2.6, Rule III).[23]

Even though countries had pledged to work toward convergence of their macroeconomic policies (Box 2.6, Rule V), realignments were at times necessary. Twelve realignments occurred between 1979 and 1992, with the consent of other EU countries (Box 2.6, Rule IV). Each realignment corresponded to a discrete jump in the central rate from one level to another. We will review several realignments in the next section.

The European Monetary Cooperation Fund. The final leg of the EMS was the European Monetary Cooperation Fund (EMCF). The EMCF issued "official ECUs" to

---

[22]The United Kingdom joined the ERM earlier, but dropped out. Greece was never a part of the ERM. Italy's fluctuation band was reduced to 2.25 percent in January 1990.

[23]The divergence limit for the *i*th currency is computed as $D_i = 0.75 \times B \times (1 - W_i)$, where B is the intervention limit (either 2.25 percent or 6.0 percent) and W_i is the weight of the currency calculated at the central parity values. *The Financial Times* reported the divergence limits daily.

Box 2.6

Rules of the Game: The Spirit of the European Monetary System, 1979

All Member Countries

I. Fix a par value for each exchange rate in terms of the European Currency Unit, a basket weighted according to country size.

II. Keep exchange rates stable in the short run by limiting movements in bilateral rates to 2.25 percent on either side of the central rate.

III. When an exchange rate threatens to breech a bilateral limit, the strong currency central bank must lend freely to the weak-currency central bank to support the exchange rate.

IV. Adjust the par value in the intermediate term only if necessary to realign national price levels, and only with the collective agreement of other EMS countries.

V. Work toward a convergence of national macroeconomic policies that would lead to stable long-run par values for exchange rates.

VI. Maintain free currency convertibility for current account transactions.

VII. Hold foreign exchange reserves primarily in ECUs with the European Fund for Monetary Cooperation (EFMC), and reduce U.S. dollar reserves.

VIII. Repay central bank debts quickly from exchange reserves or by borrowing from the EFMC within strict long-term credit limits.

IX. No single country's money serves as a reserve currency nor does its national monetary policy serve (asymmetrically) as the nominal price anchor for the group.

Source: Adapted from Ronald I. McKinnon, "The Rules of the Game: International Money in Historical Perspective," *Journal of Economic Literature* 31 (Mar. 1993), p. 36.

European central banks through a series of revolving swaps. The central banks were obliged to exchange 20 percent of their gold and US$ reserves in exchange for official ECUs. Once created, EC central banks could mobilize their ECU reserves to intervene in support of the currencies (Box 2.6, Rule VII and VIII).

The European Monetary System as a "Greater DM" Area, 1979–1998

As proposed, the EMS appears to enshrine the symmetry of the EU member nations in a cooperative process. However, the EMS may represent another example of Ronald McKinnon's (1993) dictum that what you see isn't necessarily what you get in an international monetary agreement. In practice, the DM was the centerpiece of the ERM, and German monetary policy formed the anchor for the EMS price level (Box 2.7, Rule XV).[24] Thus, the operation of the EMS was subject to more strains than might have been foreseen, as the strongest country with the least inflation called the policy tune, rather than some equally weighted average of all the policy prescriptions of the member countries.

Most of the strains in the EMS over this period arose not so much from the EMS itself, but from the desire by some European leaders to achieve still closer economic and social union. In 1989, a European Council committee headed by European Commission President Jacques Delors presented a plan to establish a European Economic and

---

[24]McKinnon (1993, p. 36) observes that this outcome closely parallels the symmetry of Bretton Woods and the role played in practice by the United States in the fixed-rate dollar standard.

Box 2.7

Rules of the Game: The European Monetary System as a "Greater DM" Area, 1979–1992

All Member Countries

  I. through V. as in the "Spirit of the Treaty" (see Box 2.6)

  VI. Avoid using the credit facilities of the EFMC.

Member Countries except Germany

  VII. Intervene inside the formal bilateral parity bands to stabilize currency values vis-à-vis the deutsche mark (DM). Intervene in DM rather than in U.S. dollars.

  VIII. Keep exchange reserves in DM instruments as well as in U.S. Treasury bonds.

  IX. Adjust national monetary growth and short-term interest rates to support exchange market interventions.

  X. Subordinate national monetary policy so that long-term price inflation converges to or remains the same as that in Germany.

  XI. Continue to liberalize capital controls.

Germany

  XII. Remain passive in the foreign exchange market with respect to other EMS countries.

  XIII. Keep German capital markets open for borrowing and investing by foreign residents and sovereigns.

  XIV. Sterilize the effects of official intervention on the German monetary policy.

  XV. Set German monetary policy independently to serve as an anchor for the EMS price level.

Source: Adapted from Ronald I. McKinnon, "The Rules of the Game: International Money in Historical Perspective," *Journal of Economic Literature* 31 (Mar. 1993), p. 37.

Monetary Union (EMU). Under the EMU, a single European central bank would set monetary policy for a single European money, thereby abolishing national monies and an independent role for national central banks.

The Delors plan recommended a three-stage process to phase in EMU: (1) Bring all 12 member EC countries into the ERM while bringing tighter convergence of monetary policies to secure the ERM; (2) narrow the permissible bands of the ERM and permit a new European central bank to exercise more control of national monetary policies; (3) replace national monies with a common currency, placing responsibility for European monetary policy within a European central bank that reflects the interest of all EC countries.

The original timetable for the Delors plan called for a transition to stage 2 by January 1, 1994, and implementation of stage 3 by January 1, 1999. Doubts and debate about the economic feasibility and advisability of EMU persisted throughout the 1990s. Markets reacted continuously to economic and political news, wrestling with uncertainty as to what policies would be chosen to deliver EMU, which countries would join EMU, what final exchange rates would link the old European "legacy currencies," and when the EMU would start.

The EMS Crisis of 1992–1993. The Delors plan called for a transfer of national sovereign powers (that is responsibility for monetary policy and national monies) to a new EC institution. In December 1991, the EC drafted the **Maastricht Treaty,** a 250-page document that spelled out the steps needed to affect this transfer of policymaking authority. The Maastricht Treaty required approval by *all* 12 EC countries, either by a national referendum or parliamentary vote.

Many parts of the treaty were contentious, as one might expect with the transfer of precious sovereign economic powers to an untried and distant EC institution. The treaty went further than monetary unification, calling for centralization of foreign policies and defense policies as well as certain social policies. Still, backers of the treaty argued that there would be significant benefits for Europe associated with a single European money, and that a European monetary authority could represent the needs of all EC countries rather than be driven largely by Germany's Bundesbank.

In June 1992, Danish voters narrowly rejected the Maastricht Treaty. Because the treaty required the unanimous approval of all EC countries, the Danish vote put the future of EMU and the Delors timetable into question. The French vote was scheduled for September 20, and opinion polls showed sharp divisions.

Currency speculators sensed that the treaty was in trouble. If the EC stayed with its ERM rather than moving ahead to a single money, further exchange-rate realignments might be required (or desired). In September, speculative attacks hit the pound and the lira, as well as Sweden's krona and Finland's markka, two nonmembers of the EMS that had pegged their currencies to the ECU. The Bundesbank and other central banks intervened in accordance with ERM operating principles, but the reserve flows were too great to sustain. On September 17, Italy devalued the lira and then removed it from the ERM. Great Britain dropped out of the ERM, allowing the pound to depreciate after its finance minister had pledged not to.

Currency tensions persisted throughout 1993. The Portuguese escudo was devalued, the Spanish peseta was devalued twice, and the Swedish and Norwegian currencies were allowed to float. In the summer of 1993, speculative attacks continued on the French franc and other currencies. Central banks intervened heavily, but the French resisted a devaluation. To avoid a formal devaluation of the franc, new ± 15 percent bands were adopted for all ERM currencies (except for the guilder/DM). This change in the rules of the ERM game effectively abolished the old system, although many countries continued to keep their exchange rates within old ERM bands.

The Path to European Monetary Union.   Despite these seismic shocks, voting on the Maastricht Treaty continued. By November 1992, it was adopted and the European Union (EU) was born. However, many countries had negotiated the right to opt out of certain key provisions, including the EU's common monetary and defense institutions.

Planning for EMU continued. According to the Delors plan, countries had to meet various economic targets before joining the EMU. These **convergence criteria** included: (1) limit annual budget deficits to 3 percent of GDP, (2) limit total public debt to 60 percent of GDP, (3) establish consumer price inflation within 1.5 percent of the inflation of the three lowest EU countries, (4) establish long-term government bond yields to within two percentage points of the three lowest-inflation countries, and (5) maintain exchange rates within the traditional ERM band without devaluation for a period of two years. These criteria were very demanding. As of February 1997, only Luxembourg satisfied them. Undaunted, EU policymakers pressed on. Designs for new physical coins and notes were unveiled. Private firms and banks were compelled to follow suit, redesigning their accounting systems and financial software to accommodate the new euro.

The Spirit of the European Economic and Monetary Union, 1999

In May 1998, the European Council met to make two critical decisions: (1) which countries would participate in the launch of EMU, set for January 1, 1999, and (2) who

---

Box 2.8

Rules of the Game: The Spirit of the EMU, 1999

The "In Countries" (EU Countries Taking Part in EMU)

I. Offer admission to only those EU countries that meet the five convergence criteria—on budget deficits, total public debt, inflation, long-term interest rates, and ERM membership without devaluations for two years.

II. Fix a final conversion rate for exchanging old "legacy currencies" for the new surviving currency, the euro.

III. Establish a new European central bank that is independent from national governments and community institutions. The European Central Bank (ECB) has sole responsibility for monetary policy among EMU countries. The primary objective of the ECB is price stability across EMU countries.

IV. National central banks no longer have any monetary policy authority, but continue in existence to form (along with the ECB) a European System of Central Banks (ESCB) intended for regulation and monitoring EMU financial institutions.

V. National governments retain independence over other economic policies such as taxation and government expenditures, but within a set of commonly agreed rules (the Stability and Growth Pact).

VI. The euro replaces the DM as the principal currency of Europe. The euro acquires a greater role as an international reserve currency.

VII. The ECB allows the euro to float against the US$ and ¥.

The "Out Countries" (EU Countries *Not Initially* Taking Part in EMU)

VIII. "Out countries" retain their national currencies. However, these countries are encouraged to take part in a new Exchange Rate Mechanism whereby their currencies are permitted to fluctuate with a band 15 percent either side of a central rate against the euro. Participation in the new ERM-2 is voluntary.

IX. "Out countries" are encouraged to orient their policies toward stability and convergence with the euro area, to limit foreign exchange pressures versus the euro and to promote their eventual membership in EMU.

---

would be elected as president of the European Central Bank. Many observers had predicted a "narrow" EMU with only three or six countries going in at the start because of the stringent requirements on fiscal budget deficits and national debt levels. However, the European Council selected 11 countries—virtually all EU countries, except those that desired to opt out of the starting group (Denmark, Sweden, and the United Kingdom) and Greece, which wanted to join but clearly had not met the convergence requirements. Those countries that stayed out of the EMU were encouraged to take part in an ERM-2 that would allow for their eventual membership in ERM (Box 2.8, Rule VIII), and also encouraged to follow macroeconomic policies that would not put unnecessary pressure on their currencies versus the euro (Box 2.8, Rule IX).

Without question, the EU countries had made substantial progress toward meeting the Maastricht convergence requirements. However, the large initial EMU was made possible by a relaxed interpretation of the Maastricht criteria and a dose of "creative accounting" (straining Rule I in Box 2.8). For example, even though the debt-to-GDP ratios of Belgium and Italy exceeded 100 percent and, along with the Netherlands, Spain, and Germany, exceeded the 60 percent limit set by Maastricht, the European Council determined that *approaching* the 60 percent ceiling at a satisfactory pace was sufficient to qualify. To deal with excessive fiscal budget deficits, France and Italy resorted to one-time tricks (a payment from France Telecom and a repayable euro tax in Italy). Even

Germany redefined certain hospital debts as regional rather than national to improve the country's financial picture. The European Council did not challenge this accounting "magic."

According to EU rules, the European Central Bank (ECB) president was to be elected for an eight-year term. The first president would commence his or her duties on July 1 and guide the ECB in its preparations for the launch of EMU. However, the selection process at the May 1998 meeting was marred by disagreement and, some felt, compromise of the Maastricht principles (Box 2.8, Rule III). In November 1997, France nominated its own central bank governor, Jean-Claude Trichet, for the post. The front-runner had always been Willem Duisenberg, who had headed the Dutch central bank for many years and had led the European Monetary Institute, the predecessor of the ECB, since its inception. The lengthy debate among national finance ministers and heads of state ended with a compromise: Duisenberg would head the ECB for about half of the stipulated eight-year term, and then he would take "voluntary" retirement, to be replaced by Trichet. Most economists saw this as a bad signal, suggesting that the ECB might not be an independent policymaking body, or that politicians could force Duisenberg to step down if ECB policies were unpopular. In a December 1998 interview just prior to the launch of EMU, Duisenberg acknowledged the turmoil surrounding his appointment but reiterated that the primary goal of the ECB was price stability (Box 2.8, Rule III) and that he alone would decide on his length of term in office, which "might be eight years."[25]

The May 1998 meeting was also used to set irrevocable bilateral exchange rates among the 11 EMU countries (Box 2.8, Rule I). The European Council acted in May 1998 to preclude private speculation about last-minute exchange rate changes in the countdown to EMU. The Irish punt central rate change in March 1998, which we discuss in more detail later in this chapter, made clear that countries might indeed desire such changes prior to EMU. Because the ECU included amounts of pound sterling, Danish krone, and Greek drachma, the European Council could not set the final irrevocable conversion rates of national currencies against the euro until the end of December 1998.

For the last half of 1998, the ECB concentrated much of its efforts on finalizing the TARGET system for payments within the EMU, setting up supervisory and regulatory guidelines for banks, and getting ready for the changeover of computing and accounting systems to handle the euro (Box 2.8, Rule IV).[26] On December 22, 1998, the ECB helped coordinate a joint reduction in the key central bank interest rates to 3 percent (with the exception of Italy, which reduced its discount rate to 3.5 percent). This policy announcement halted speculation about what the ECB might do once it took full control under EMU.

On January 1, 1999, the final and "irrevocable" conversion rates of the 11 legacy currencies versus the euro were announced as shown in Table 2.2. The transition went smoothly in terms of execution of transactions in the foreign exchange market and the operation of the EMU payments and settlement system. Financial markets in the EMU countries redenominated all traded financial securities and instruments from their national currencies into euros. A new market for bonds denominated in euros is thriving. And the trend toward transnational mergers and acquisitions across firms within the EMU is growing. The last step on the path to monetary union is the introduction of

---

[25]Dagmar Aalund and Greg Steinmetz, "Duisenberg Doesn't Rule Out Full-Term Stay as ECB Chief," *Wall Street Journal,* December 18, 1998.

[26]TARGET (Trans-European Automated Real-Time Gross Settlement Express Transfer) is the payment system designed for processing cross-border transactions in euros across Europe.

TABLE 2.2   **Irrevocable Conversion Rates Set on January 1, 1999**
The Value of the Euro in Terms of the 11 Legacy Currencies of the
EMU Countries

Country	Units Equal to One Euro (E)	
Austria	13.7603	schillings
Belgium	40.3399	francs
Finland	5.94573	markkaa
France	6.55957	francs
Germany	1.95583	marks
Ireland	0.787564	punt
Italy	1,936.27	lire
Luxembourg	40.3399	francs
Netherlands	2.20371	guilders
Portugal	200.482	escudos
Spain	166.386	pesetas

physical euro notes and coins and the withdrawal of legacy currency notes and coins. This process is scheduled to begin on January 1, 2002, and to be completed no later than July 1, 2002.[27]

While the EMU is a functioning reality, concerns remain. We will discuss some of these concerns later in this chapter and in other sections of this book.

Recent Behavior of Prices in International Financial Markets

Let us now survey some recent series of prices in selected international financial markets. Our objective is to gain familiarity with some of the markets we will be studying in this book and to gauge the extent of price movements in recent years. We begin with exchange rates and then move on to international interest rates.

Exchange Rate Developments

Nominal Exchange Rates against the US$, 1970–1999.   Spot exchange rates for the period 1970–1999 are displayed in Figure 2.4. The data are monthly, bilateral exchange rates, calculated as an index of the spot rate in period t (expressed in US$ per foreign unit) relative to the spot rate in March 1973, or:

$$S_{\text{index},j,t} = 100 \times S_{j,t}/S_{j,\text{March}1973}$$

for j = Canada, Germany, Italy, Japan, Switzerland, and the United Kingdom. Values of S_{index} greater than 100 correspond to a nominal US$ depreciation (a foreign currency appreciation), and values less than 100 signify a nominal US$ appreciation (a foreign currency depreciation) relative to the base period, March 1973. (See Box 2.9 for a primer on foreign exchange market math and terminology.)

---

[27]For a preview of the new euro notes and coins, see the ECB website at <www.ecb.int>.

FIGURE 2.4   **Spot Exchange Rates versus US$**
January 1970–December 1999

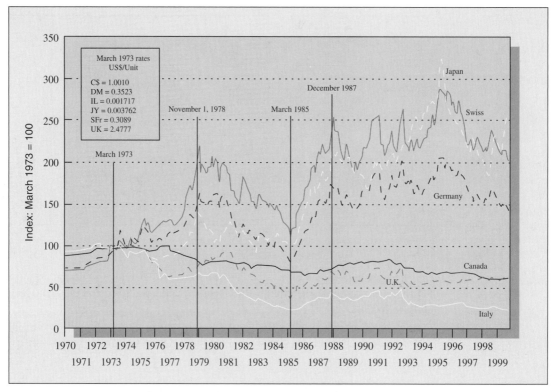

Source: *International Financial Statistics.*

One reason to explore these graphs is to sort through the "forests and the trees"—meaning the larger patterns and the smaller details—of exchange rate movements. In Figure 2.4, note the scale required to include these six countries on one graph—from a low of 28.1 for Italy in February 1985 to a high of 319.5 for Japan in May 1995. Thus, the Italian lira at its low depreciated to only 28 percent of its nominal value compared with its value at the start of the floating-rate period, while the Japanese yen at its high appreciated by 219 percent of its nominal value in March 1973. This is a wide variation in pricing. But because these are nominal exchange rates and bilateral rates against a single currency (the US$), substantial price movements may be expected.

At the start of the floating-rate period in March 1973, we observe that the DM and the Swiss franc (SFr) both rose by approximately 20–25 percent against the US$, then fell back to their March 1973 levels, then rose by about 20 percent, then fell, and then rose again by about 20–25 percent—all within the span of only two years. These sharp exchange rate movements made economists wonder whether it was rational for exchange rates to move so rapidly when placed against a background of limited macroeconomic developments.

These volatile episodes led economists to develop so-called *asset approaches* to exchange rate valuation. Under an asset approach, it is theorized that the current spot rate moves quickly to reflect future, and as yet unobserved, changes in macroeconomic fundamentals. Around this time, the expression *overshooting* was coined to characterize short-term exchange rate changes that exceeded the required change for long-run equilibrium. We will examine asset approaches and overshooting in Chapter 6.

Box 2.9

A Primer on Foreign Exchange Market Math and Terminology

Suppose the exchange rate for the pengo (a Hungarian silver coin used until 1946) versus the US$ changes from $0.25/pengo to $0.125/pengo. How should we describe this movement?

We could describe the change as an *appreciation* of the US$, because fewer US$ are needed to purchase a pengo. Or we could describe the change as a *depreciation* of the pengo because more pengos are required to purchase a US$ after the change (8 pengos/US$) than before the change (4 pengos/US$). An appreciation of one currency will always correspond to a depreciation of the other currency.

How should we measure the magnitude of the exchange rate change? The most widely used convention, and the convention we follow in this book, associates a move from $S_1 = \$0.25/\text{pengo}$ to $S_2 = \$0.125/\text{pengo}$ as a 50 percent appreciation of the US$ because $S_2 = S_1(1 - a)$ where a is the percentage rate of appreciation in the US$.

Note that the exchange rate change could also be described as a move from $E_1 = 4$ pengo/US$ to $E_2 = 8$ pengo/US$. Our convention defines this change as a 100 percent depreciation of the pengo, because $E_2 = E_1(1 + d)$ where d is the percentage rate of depreciation in the pengo.

In this example, we see that the percentage rate of depreciation in one currency is not the negative of the percentage rate of appreciation in the second currency.*

Consider one more example. Suppose that the pengo depreciates from 4 pengo/US$ (or $0.25/pengo) to 16 pengo/US$ (or $0.0625/pengo). This 300 percent depreciation of the pengo has the same meaning as a 75 percent appreciation of the US$.

The reader can see that this convention permits the depreciation of a currency to reach any positive value approaching infinity. But the percentage appreciation of a currency can be no more than 100 percent. These examples also illustrate that when we read that the "exchange rate has changed" by x percent, it is essential to know whether the statement refers to an appreciation or a depreciation and whether it refers to the pengo or the US$.

---

*Appendixes 4.1 and 5.1 introduce logarithmic returns that treat appreciations and depreciations symmetrically. Using log returns, the rate of appreciation will equal the negative of the rate of depreciation.

After two years of relative exchange rate stability, inflation in the United States picked up in early 1977. The US$ resumed its depreciation against the SFr, DM, and ¥ as seen by the spikes for these three currencies on November 1, 1978. Notice that by the same date the US$ had actually appreciated against the C$, £, and lira in Figure 2.4.

November 1, 1978, was a key date for the US$. The United States announced a major package of policy changes designed to halt inflation and stop the slide in the US$. Two of these changes—a hike in the Federal Reserve discount rate from 8 percent to 9 percent, and a new get-tough policy against inflation—were in the traditional policy arsenal. But the third leg of the policy package was a commitment by the United States to intervene in the foreign exchange market directly and purchase US$. The funds for these US$ purchases were to come from "Carter bonds"—direct obligations of the U.S. Treasury denominated in Swiss francs, deutsche marks, and yen, and sold to foreign residents—representing a brand-new way for the United States to show support for the US$.[28]

The depreciation of the US$ halted in November 1978. By late 1980 (coinciding with the election of Ronald Reagan), the US$ began a steady appreciation against most currencies that would last until February 1985. The experience of the $/£ rate was a bit different through this period as the £ appreciated from $1.59 in October 1976 to $2.43 in October 1980. North Sea oil discoveries came to fruition in this period, giving the United Kingdom a substantial current account surplus and some hedging demand for the pound as a "petrocurrency."

---

[28]Details of the Carter bond initiative are given in Chapter 3.

Having completed its long appreciation in early 1985, the US$ began another substantial depreciation which culminated in December 1987, taking the US$ to lows against the SFr, DM, and ¥ that exceeded the values hit in November 1978. This phase included the G-5 meeting at the Plaza Hotel in September 1985. As discussed earlier, at the Plaza meeting central bankers announced their desire to see the US$ depreciate further, which it did. After the G-6 meeting at the Louvre in February 1987, the slide in the US$ halted temporarily as intervention kept rates within undeclared target zones. However, after the October 1987 stock market crash, the US$ continued to depreciate for the rest of the year.

Since December 1987, we can see that spot SFr and DM rates have moved within fairly wide bands, of 20–25 percent from top to bottom. But the yen's movements have been less contained, as the yen reached new highs against the US$ in May 1995.

Our description of the patterns of the US$ rate over the post–Bretton Woods era suggests several major periods: the weak dollar from early 1976 to November 1978, the strong dollar from late 1980 to February 1985, and the weak dollar from March 1985 to December 1987 (see Figure 2.4). While there was substantial day-to-day variation, Figure 2.4 suggests that exchange rates appeared to have had a prominent "drift" factor over these three periods.

In recognition of this apparent pattern, some economists refer to a "long swings" hypothesis, where the exchange rate appears to have a nonzero drift factor for a long time, as if it were stuck moving primarily in one direction. But then something happens—perhaps something that can be measured such as a change in economic policy or a change in the makers of economic policy (a "regime shift"), or perhaps something that cannot be directly measured (a change in "sentiment")—causing the exchange rate to reverse course and run in the opposite direction for an extended period. Intuitively, this characterization is contrary to a "random walk" description of rates. In Chapter 7 and 8, we discuss the random walk versus long-swings hypothesis for foreign exchange rates. We also present evidence on whether trends can be identified in exchange rate series and used to earn profits in foreign exchange trading.

Nominal Exchange Rates in the ERM: The FFr/DM and Guilder/DM Rates.   The European Exchange Rate Mechanism (ERM) began in March 1979. The ERM established a set of central rates, and participating countries agreed to keep their exchange rates within a ±2.25 percent band, or ±6.0 percent in the case of Italy (and Spain, Portugal, and the United Kingdom when they joined the ERM). These bands were widened to ±15.0 percent after the ERM crisis in August 1993.

The ERM was intended to help foster a zone of "monetary stability." If successful, efforts to coordinate longer-run monetary and fiscal policies would result in monetary **convergence,** a narrowing of the range of inflation rates and nominal interest rates across ERM countries. Convergence of these key economic variables represented a necessary (and possibly sufficient) condition for stability in the ERM. Convergence of inflation rates across EU member countries and convergence of long-term interest rates generally improved since 1979. However, without complete convergence of inflation rates across ERM countries, price level differences accumulate over time, which increases the need for exchange rate realignments.

Whether the ERM helped to usher in a period of exchange rate stability across the EU was a subject of dispute. In the first 13 years of the ERM, 13 changes, or **realignments,** in the central rates were carried out (see Table 2.3). The length of time between realignments varied from as little as 67 days (separating the first and second realignments in 1979) to as long as 1,092 days (separating the 11 and 12 realignments in 1987

TABLE 2.3 Exchange Rate Realignments within the European Monetary System, 1979–1992
Percentage Change in Central Parity Rate[a]

Date	Deutsche Mark	Dutch Guilder	French Franc	Belgian-Lux. Franc	Italian Lira	Danish Krone	Irish Pound	Spanish Peseta[b]	Portuguese Escudo[c]	Days since Last Realignment[d]
24 September 79	+2.0					−3.0				195
30 November 79						−5.0				67
23 March 81					−6.0					479
5 October 81	+5.5	+5.5	−3.0		−3.0					196
22 February 82				−8.5		−3.0				140
14 June 82	+4.25	+4.25	−5.75		−2.75					112
22 March 83	+5.5	+3.5	−2.5	+1.5	−2.5	+2.5	−3.5			281
22 July 85	+2.0	+2.0	+2.0	+2.0	−6.0	+2.0	+2.0			853
7 April 86	+3.0	+3.0	−3.0	+1.0		+1.0				259
4 August 86							−8.0			119
12 January 87	+3.0	+3.0		+2.0						161
8 January 90					−3.7[e]					1092
14 September 92	+3.5	+3.5	+3.5	+3.5	−3.5	+3.5	+3.5	+3.5	+3.5	980

Notes:

a. Unshaded cells indicate the date of a realignment in the guilder/DM and FFr/DM central rates. See text for discussion and Figures 2.5a and 2.5b.

b. The Spanish peseta entered the ERM in June 1989 with a 6.0 percent band.

c. The Portuguese escudo entered the ERM in April 1992 with a 6.0 percent band.

d. All calendar days including weekends. For first realignment, we report number of days since EMS adoption on March 13, 1979.

e. The Italian lira adopted the 2.25 percent narrow band on this date.

Sources: European Economic Commission documents and *Financial Times*, various issues.

and 1990). Each realignment involved an appreciation of the DM against at least one other European currency. Most realignments led to an appreciation of the Dutch guilder, and most led to a depreciation of the Italian lira against the deutsche mark.

To illustrate the impact of realignments, Figure 2.5a shows the behavior of the FFr/DM rate over the 1975–1994 period and the six realignments affecting this bilateral rate. A band of 2.25 percent on either side of the central rate is also drawn.[29] Notice that in the first realignment, we observe a change in the central rate and a change in the upper and lower band values, but that the exchange rate movement itself is continuous, without a jump. In the second, third, fourth, and fifth realignments, the exchange rate jumps from one level to the next. And the new upper and lower intervention bands do not overlap with the old. In the sixth realignment, notice that the new lower band is less than the old upper band with only a small jump in the exchange rate.

Looking at Figure 2.5a, it is reasonable to ask whether the ERM acted to reduce exchange rate volatility and improve predictability for the FFr/DM rate. It is a difficult question to answer because we do not know what Figure 2.5a would have looked like without the ERM. It is clear, however, that the ERM did not prevent the FFr/DM rate from changing by a large amount (cumulatively) over the period, and that the ERM left market participants with the risk of a large jump in rates beyond the announced band

---

[29]The dates for the six realignments are shaded in Table 2.3. Notice that a realignment of the FFr/DM rate occurs on any date that the DM and FFr central rate does not change by the same percentage amount vis-à-vis the ECU.

FIGURE 2.5A   **FFr/DM: Spot Rates in the ERM**
January 1975–December 1994

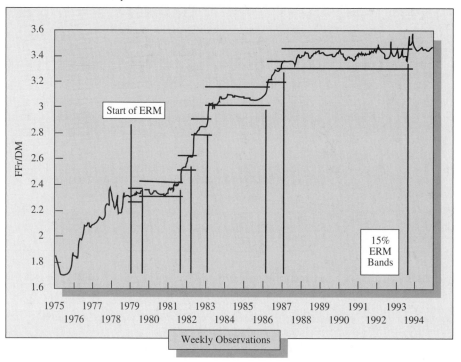

Source: Harris Bank database.

limits. These exchange rate jumps represent an important element of risk in exchange rate behavior.[30]

Now consider Figure 2.5b, which shows the guilder/DM rate over the 1975–1994 period (as well as a ±2.25 percent band) and the two realignments affecting this bilateral rate. The overall graph of the guilder/DM may look similar to the FFr/DM, but there are important differences. First, the guilder realigned against the DM on only two occasions. The exchange rate jump was small in both cases, and the new intervention bands overlap the old. Second, it appears that the guilder/DM rate operated well within its bands after the second realignment; the Dutch central bank even adopted a ±1 percent fluctuation band.

Finally, check the scale of Figures 2.5a and 2.5b. From the start of the ERM until December 1994, the FFr/DM rate changed from 2.3095 to 3.4428, representing a 49.1 percent depreciation of the FFr against the DM. Over the same period, the guilder/DM rate changed from 1.081 to 1.120, or a 3.6 percent depreciation of the guilder against the DM. Clearly, the guilder had more nearly stabilized its value against the DM.

Nominal Exchange Rates for Asian Currencies against the US$, 1990–1999.   Spot exchange rates for five Asian currencies for the period 1990–1999 are displayed in

---

[30]In Chapter 8, we describe a model for predicting realignments in rates that are banded within a target zone. Because currency option prices depend positively on volatility, a high option price may signal the market's belief that a target zone is no longer credible, raising the prospects for realignment.

FIGURE 2.5B   **Guilder/DM: Spot Rates in the ERM**
January 1975–December 1994

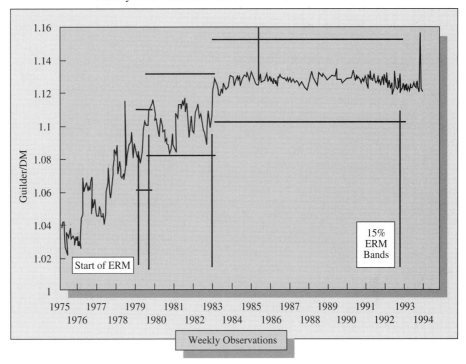

Source: Harris Bank database.

Figure 2.6. The monthly data are calculated as an index of the spot rate in period t. They are expressed in US$ per foreign unit relative to the spot rate in January 1990, or

$$S_{\text{index},jt} = 100 \times S_{j,t}/S_{j,\text{January}1990}$$

for j = Indonesia, Korea, Malaysia, Philippines, and Thailand. Again, values of $S_{\text{index},jt}$ greater than 100 correspond to a nominal US$ depreciation (a foreign currency appreciation), and values less than 100 signify a nominal US$ appreciation (a foreign currency depreciation).

Figure 2.6 shows the relative stability of these Asian currencies prior to July 1997. For example, the Thai baht was pegged to a basket of currencies (although heavily weighted to the US$) and traded in a narrow range from 25 to 26 baht/US$ until 1997. The Malaysian ringgit was also quite stable and actually appreciated from about 2.7 ringgit/US$ in 1990 to 2.5 ringgit/US$ in the spring of 1997. Indonesia's currency, the rupiah, followed a gliding peg; it depreciated steadily (but predictably) by about 4 percent per year, from 1,800 rupiah/US$ in 1990 to about 2,450 rupiah/US$ in the spring of 1997. From 1990 to 1994, the path of the Korean won was somewhat similar to the rupiah, showing a gradual but steady depreciation. The won actually strengthened versus the US$ into 1995 and 1996. The Philippine peso showed the most volatility prior to 1995, but then it, too, stabilized at around 26 pesos/US$ until the spring of 1997.

The break came in July 1997, when the Bank of Thailand was forced to allow the baht to float, and the baht lost more than half its value, depreciating from about 26 baht/US$ to 55 baht/US$ in January 1998. Soon after the Bank of Thailand's move,

FIGURE 2.6 Nominal Exchange Rates: Selected Asian Currencies versus the US$

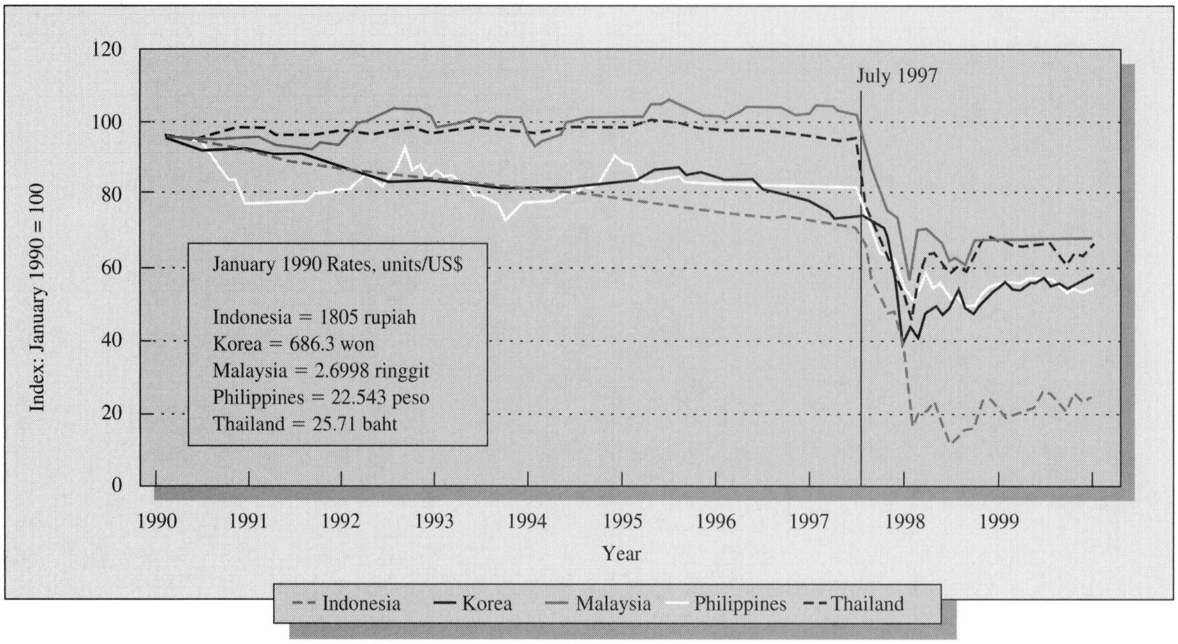

120
100
80
60
40
20
0
Index: January 1990 = 100
July 1997
January 1990 Rates, units/US$
Indonesia = 1805 rupiah
Korea = 686.3 won
Malaysia = 2.6998 ringgit
Philippines = 22.543 peso
Thailand = 25.71 baht
1990 1991 1992 1993 1994 1995 1996 1997 1998 1999
Year
Indonesia
Korea
Malaysia
Philippines
Thailand

Source: *International Financial Statistics.*

other Asian currencies started to depreciate, but the big drops in the rupiah and the won did not occur till late 1997 or early 1998. In June 1998, the rupiah rate reached 15,000/US$, a loss of 88 percent of its value relative to January 1990. Throughout 1999, these Asian currencies appeared to stabilize, but at far lower nominal values and after a period of extreme turbulence.

Volatility in Spot Exchange Rates. In Figure 2.7 we display the average absolute monthly percentage change for several bilateral exchange rates against the US$. In the early 1960s under Bretton Woods, month-to-month exchange rate changes were small, averaging only 0.1–0.2 percent in absolute value.

Toward the end of the 1960s, signs of stress on the pegged-rate system began to mount with increasing frequency. The United Kingdom devalued sterling by 14 percent on November 1967, the DM floated during October 1969 and was then revalued by 9 percent, and the Canadian dollar began floating in June 1970. Earlier, we reviewed the US dollar devaluation on August 15, 1971, the brief period of floating that followed, and the official realignments at the Smithsonian meeting on December 18, 1971. The United Kingdom permitted sterling to float in June 1972, and generalized floating began in January 1973 for the Swiss franc, in February 1973 for the Japanese yen and Italian lira, and in March 1973 for most other currencies.

In Figure 2.7, we see that these developments led to an increase in exchange rate volatility over the November 1967–February 1973 period to about 0.5 percent per month. From March 1973 onward under floating rates, we see that volatility increased further. The absolute month-to-month change for the deutsche mark, pound, and yen averaged about 2.0 percent per month in the first five years of floating, then increased

FIGURE 2.7   **Exchange Rate Volatility**
Average Absolute Month-to-Month Changes

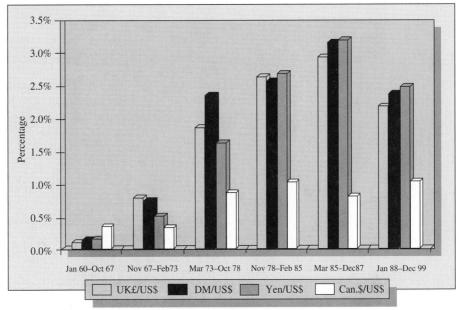

Source: *International Financial Statistics.*

to about 2.5 percent per month in the period through 1985, and finally climbed to about 3.0 per month in the period ending in December 1987. Since then, month-to-month changes for these currencies have tapered off to about 2.5 percent. The absolute month-to-month change for the Canadian dollar has been roughly 1.0 percent throughout the post–Bretton Woods period.

Another way to measure volatility utilizes the standard deviation (or σ) of percentage exchange rate changes. **Historical volatility** represents the standard deviation of previous exchange-rate changes. By construction, historical volatility represents past, realized exchange rate changes. **Implied volatility** represents the value of standard deviation implied by the market price of a currency option.[31] Implied volatility is a more forward-looking concept; it responds to how option traders believe currency volatility will unfold over the life of the option.

In Figure 2.8, we show graphs of the historical and implied volatility for the Yen/US$ and UK£/US$ exchange rates. These graphs support several conclusions about volatility. First, a general observation is that volatility varies from currency to currency. Second, historical volatility (represented in Figure 2.8 by the standard deviation of exchange rate changes over the previous 30 days) and implied volatility for a given currency are generally different, and sometimes by a substantial amount. This observation raises the question of how the two measures are related, and which measure (historical or implied) is a better indicator of future volatility.

Third, it appears that "volatility is volatile," whether measured using historical data or using implied measures from option prices. For the Yen/US$, for example, volatility

---

[31]We review option pricing models in Chapter 12.

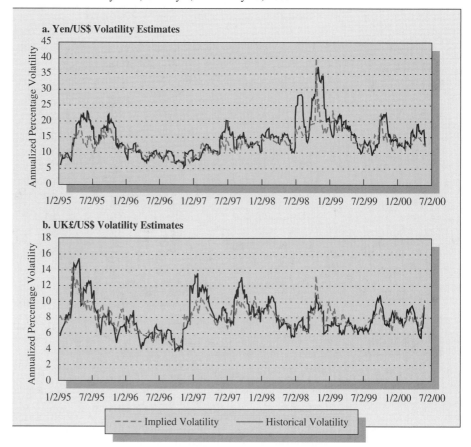

FIGURE 2.8 Historical and Implied Exchange Rate Volatility
Daily Data, January 2, 1995–May 15, 2000

Note: Historical volatility is based on percentage exchange rate changes over previous 30 trading days. Implied volatility is from the one-month currency option.

Source: Deutsche Bank, Datastream, and author's calculations.

has ranged between 5 percent and more than 35 percent on an annual basis.[32] This finding has several important implications.

While economists recognize that market conditions, including volatility, are prone to change, most economic models of exchange rates simplify matters and assume that σ does not vary over time. Figure 2.8 suggests that taking σ as a constant is a strong simplifying assumption. Allowing σ to vary raises other interesting questions, such as how should we model or describe the time-varying nature of σ_t—can we predict σ_t or does it move randomly? And how can we estimate σ_t—should we use a large amount of past data or only the most recent data?

In Chapter 12, we show that volatility is an important determinant of option prices. This fact and the evidence in Figure 2.8 imply that option prices (which are a proxy for the cost of hedging services) are likely to vary over time. Specifically, options are more

---

[32]To annualize volatility, we compute $t^{0.5}\,\sigma$, where σ is the standard deviation per period and t is the number of periods in a year. For example, if σ is measured from monthly data, $t = 12$.

costly in periods with high volatility. This will be another important consideration in the evaluation of alternative investing and borrowing strategies. It is possible that (ex ante) profitable investing or borrowing strategies occur at times when volatility is high, thus reducing the overall return–risk ratio.

In Part IV, on derivative securities, we discuss the impact of price changes on the value of a trading position. Greater volatility implies greater exposure, or value-at-risk (VAR), in a trading position. Financial risk managers require volatility estimates to measure the exposure (VAR) of a trading position. And regulators, as we discuss in Chapter 17, may rely on volatility to determine the capital requirements for banks with a given portfolio and VAR position. Thus, accurate and timely estimates of volatility now play a key role in the risk management and trading of international financial instruments.[33]

Real Effective Exchange Rates for Developed Countries.   We now examine several real effective exchange rates (REERs) over the floating exchange rate period. A **real exchange rate** is constructed by taking the nominal exchange rate (of two currencies) and deflating it by a relative price ratio (of two countries). Typically, analysts use a consumer price index (CPI) or producer price index (PPI) in the construction of the real exchange rate, but other prices such as unit labor costs are also used. By taking a weighted average of several exchange rates against the currency of interest, the analyst computes an **effective exchange rate.** Various weighting schemes are popular, usually assigning more weight on the basis of greater merchandise trade shares or larger national output. The use of different price indexes and different weights will result in some variation across different REER indexes. The figures are then normalized by setting the REER equal to 100 in a base period.[34]

In Figure 2.9, we present several REERs for the United States, Japan, and Canada. Perhaps the first point to notice about these graphs is that the range of values for the US$ REER varies between 90 and 138. This is a smaller range than we saw in Figure 2.4 for the various nominal exchange rates against the US$. Because exchange rate changes, in part, reflect inflation differences, we should expect that real exchange rates fluctuate less than nominal rates. In addition, by taking a weighted average across many currencies, appreciations against some currencies and depreciations against others tend to cancel out.

Still, Figure 2.9 shows a large amount of variability for a real rate considering that it reflects the relative competitiveness of one country, *on average and against all trading partners*. Consider the REER for the US$, which was close to 90 in mid-1980, and by February 1985 reached 138. Thus, by early 1985 U.S. goods were 53 percent more expensive than in 1980 when viewed in inflation-adjusted terms by the average foreigner. This is a tremendous relative price change that held a considerable *negative* impact for both export-oriented U.S. firms as well as import-oriented foreign firms and consumers. The mirror image of this relative price change was a substantial *positive* impact for both import-oriented U.S. firms and U.S. consumers as well as export-oriented foreign firms.

---

[33]We do not review it here, but the correlation of returns also influences the riskiness of a financial portfolio. By definition, Correlation of returns (£,¥) = Covariance (£,¥)/[σ(£) × σ (¥)]. We expect that time patterns in volatility, σ(£) and σ(¥), may induce time patterns in Correlation (£,¥). Campa and Chang (1995) show how option prices can be used to infer the time pattern in correlation.

[34]The base period may also represent an equilibrium period for purposes of purchasing power parity calculations. See the discussion in Chapter 4.

FIGURE 2.9   Real Effective Exchange Rates
Monthly Data, January 1979–December 1999

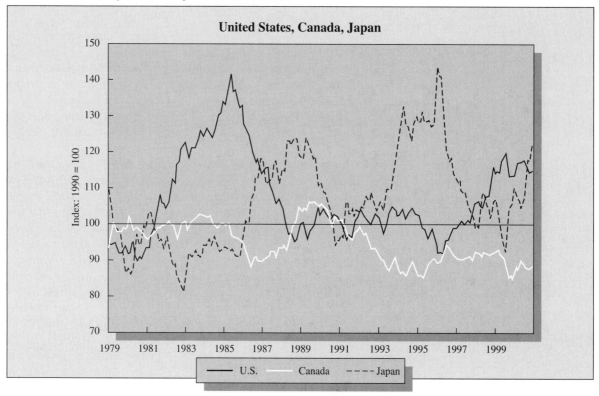

Source: J. P. Morgan.

The sharp rise in the REER for the US$ was immediately followed by an equally sharp and swift real depreciation, taking the US$ index back below 100 in spring 1988. Since 1988, variability in the US$ REER declined. But between April 1995 and June 1999, the US$ REER appreciated steadily from 92.8 to 116—a 25 percent increase.

The REER for the yen experienced wider swings from a low of 82.7 in October 1982 to 140 in April 1995. The relative undervaluation of the yen in the first half of the 1980s helped Japanese firms gain competitiveness in U.S. markets. Since 1990, the real effective value of the yen has climbed substantially, reducing the competitiveness of Japanese firms in export markets, and lowering the cost of imported products for Japanese firms and consumers. This pattern in the yen REER implies that Japanese firms had to generate productivity gains to retain Japan as an export base; otherwise, profit margins of Japanese export firms would fall. Since April 1995, the yen REER depreciated sharply until reaching 93 in August 1998, and then rebounded back to 120 at the end of 1999.

As we will discuss in Chapter 16, variation in real exchange rates contributes to the real operating exposure of firms and potentially to changes in firm values. Figure 2.9 shows that a necessary condition for real operating exposure—variable real exchange rates—has been a prominent feature of the last 25 years.

Real Effective Exchange Rates for Asian Currencies, 1990–1999.   Figure 2.10 shows real effective exchange rates for five Asian countries for the period 1990–1999. These are

FIGURE 2.10   Real Effective Exchange Rates—Selected Asian Countries
Monthly Data, January 1990–December 1999

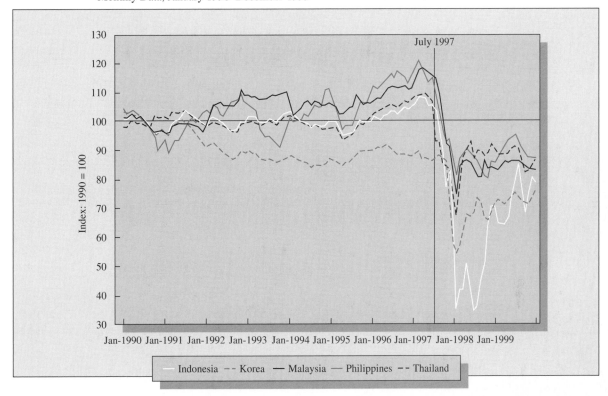

Source: J. P. Morgan.

the same five countries for which we presented nominal exchange rates in Figure 2.6. The comparison is interesting when we recall that nominal exchange rates were quite stable for Thailand and Malaysia, but the real exchange rates for these countries reveal some volatility as local goods prices did not move in synchronization with U.S. goods prices. By comparison, Indonesia's nominal exchange rate was gliding down at about 4 percent per year, but its real exchange rate showed only minor movements away from 100 until 1997. After July 1997, we see the substantial real depreciation that hit these countries, helping make their goods far cheaper in comparison to foreign goods. Note that by the end of 1999, much of this real depreciation had been reversed, indicating that the combination of nominal currency appreciation and local inflation pushed real exchange rates for these countries back toward their benchmark parity levels.

Interest Rate Developments

Short-Term Nominal Interest Rate Levels.   Eurocurrency interest rates are determined substantially by market forces and therefore represent a convenient way to compare interest rates on various currencies. In Figure 2.11, we show the behavior of the three-month Eurocurrency deposit rate for several currencies over the January 1, 1988–March 31, 2000, period.

FIGURE 2.11   Three-Month Eurocurrency Interest Rates: Recent Trends,
January 1, 1988–March 31, 2000

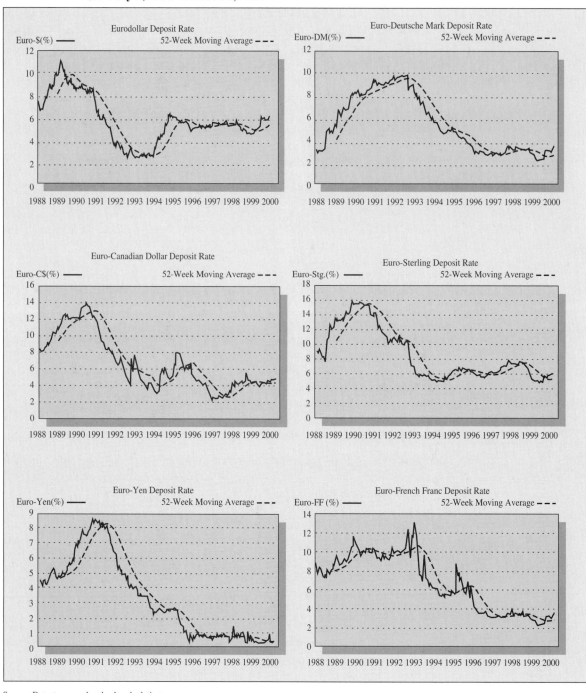

Source: Datastream and author's calculations.

First, consider the rates on Eurodollar deposits over this period. Notice that Eurodollar interest rates ranged from a high of more than 10 percent in early 1989 to a low of 3 percent in 1993. The downward path was fairly uninterrupted until the increase in early 1994. In comparison, the graph for Euro-DM interest rates shows an almost mirror-image pattern as Euro-DM rates rose from about 3.25 percent in early 1988 to over 10 percent in 1992. The increases in 1989 were linked to the announcement of unification of East and West Germany into a single German republic, and the expectation that inflation and the demand for investment funds would accelerate. A 700-basis-point (bp) decline in U.S. interest rates coupled with a 700 bp increase in German interest rates gives an indication of the strong forces acting on exchange rates over this period.[35]

The graph of Euro–Canadian dollar rates looks broadly similar to the Eurodollar graph, except that the peak in Euro-Canadian rates occurred in mid-1990, about one year after the U.S. peak. The Euro-yen shows a somewhat similar pattern, with the peak rate occurring later, in late 1990. Short-term Euro-yen rates fell sharply in 1995 and since then have hovered near zero, reflecting the Bank of Japan's efforts to stimulate growth using interest rate policy. These graphs illustrate the cyclical nature of interest rates and the "rolling" nature of interest rate peaks and troughs across various markets.

The Euro-sterling graph shows a different and interesting pattern. Euro-sterling rates hit 15 percent in the first half of 1990. In October 1990, the British government brought the pound into the ERM. The policy change linking £ and DM triggered a sudden drop in short-term £ interest rates. Euro-sterling rates continued to decline through 1991 until leveling off at about 10 percent, or roughly equal to Euro-DM rates. With the DM/£ exchange rate pinned down within the ERM (except for 6 percent bands), interest rates on Euro-DM and Euro-sterling should be similar or the sustainability of the exchange rate comes into question. By late 1992, the continuing British recession demanded attention and the British withdrew the pound from the ERM. Euro-sterling rates fell abruptly from 10 percent to 6 percent over the following six months. Since 1993, British interest rates have been freed from a link with the DM or the euro and have tracked within a narrower 5–8 percent range.

Nominal Interest Rate Differentials. The varying patterns of short-term interest rates suggest that interest rate differentials have probably displayed some severe swings. As we discuss in Chapter 5, the interest rate differential measures the incentive for borrowers or investors to adjust the currency composition of their portfolios. Under *covered interest parity,* the interest differential equals the forward exchange premium. Under *uncovered interest parity,* the interest differential equals the expected future exchange rate change.

Several interest differentials are displayed in Figure 2.12. Short-term interest differentials using the three-month Eurocurrency rates are on the left-hand side of the figure and long-term interest differentials using the 10-year government bond yields are on the right. As expected, we observe the sharp change in the Eurodollar − Euro-DM interest differential, from a 400-bp advantage favoring the US$ in 1989 to a 600-bp advantage favoring the DM in 1992. The Eurodollar − Euro-yen differential echoes the pattern for the DM, with nearly an 800-bp swing from early 1989 to 1991. Notice that in each case, the differential has reversed its path since 1992 and moved by several hundred basis points. Note that since 1995, both interest differentials have stabilized with a roughly 300-basis-point difference favoring the US$ over the DM, and a 500-basis-point margin favoring the US$ over the yen.

---

[35]A basis point is one one-hundredth of a percentage point, or 0.01 percent.

FIGURE 2.12 Interest Rate Differentials versus the US$: Recent Trends, January 1, 1988–March 31, 2000

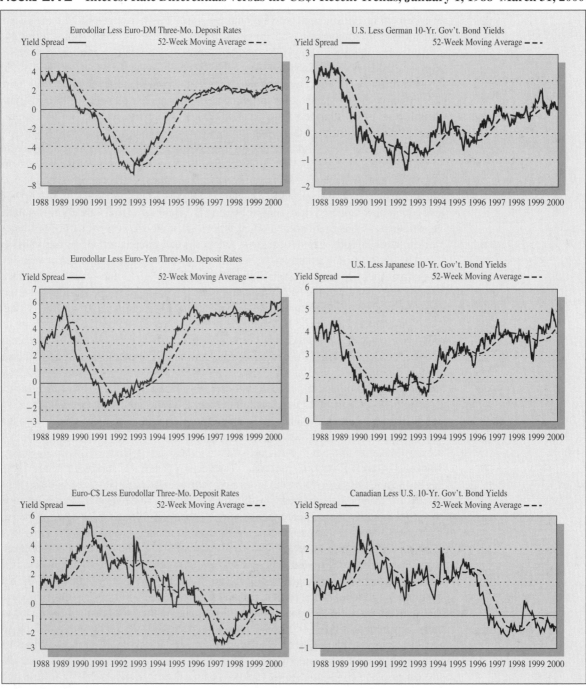

Source: Datastream and author's calculations.

The differentials for long-term interest rates show a similar overall pattern. But notice that the movement in terms of basis points is smaller. This reflects the longer maturity of these instruments and the greater impact on price that results from a given interest rate change for a long-term security.

The interest differentials reported in Figure 2.13 help explain the developments within the ERM over its turbulent years. The graph of the Euro-sterling − Euro-DM differential shows a 700-basis-point spread prior to the entry of sterling into the ERM. With entry in October 1990, the Euro-sterling rate fell sharply, but still left a 450-bp spread. Even though the Bank of England made a commitment to maintain the central value of the £ against the DM, the interest differential declined only gradually until reaching zero in the summer of 1992. Further declines in the Euro-sterling rate occurred only *after* the £ exited the ERM in September 1992. Sterling and DM interest rates are not linked within EMU, and since 1993, Euro-sterling rates have risen by roughly 400 basis points against the Euro-DM.

Notice that in the case of long-term interest rates, the October 1990 ERM entry coincided with a decline in long-term £ rates as well. But the convergence of long-term £ and DM interest rates was incomplete. When £ left the ERM, long-term £ rates were still 150 bp greater than long-term DM rates. Only recently in January 2000 did long-term sterling and DM interest rates reach equality.

The French franc–DM interest differentials are also shown in Figure 2.13. For the short-term Eurocurrency rate differentials, there was a gradual decline toward a zero differential, which was reached in early 1991. Recall from Figure 2.5a that the last change in the FFr/DM central rate occurred in January 1987. It required roughly *four years* for the Euro-FFr and Euro-DM rates to reach parity. We should inject that the onus was not only on the French, since we saw that Euro-DM interest rates were rising dramatically over this period. In Figure 2.13, we also note the sharp increases in short-term FFr rates during the summers of 1992 and 1993 when the narrow ERM bands were abandoned in favor of 15 percent bands. And the FFr-DM interest differential jumped again in the spring on 1995 and 1996 when renewed tension about the future of EMU erupted. Only in 1997 did FFr and DM interest rates reach a rough convergence, which became absolute for short-term rates in January 1999. Long-term FFr rates remained slightly higher than DM rates in 1999, even though both securities are actually denominated in euros. We will discuss this issue further in Chapter 14.

We conclude our review of interest differentials between several currencies and the DM on a favorable note with the case of the Dutch guilder. In Figure 2.13, we see that the Euro-guilder/Euro-DM differential had been small, oscillating within a 50-bp band through the 1990s. In fact Euro-guilder rates at times actually fell below Euro-DM rates. The interest rate differential on long-term bonds was also quite small, oscillating around zero from 1992 to 2000.

The graphs of interest differentials versus the DM serve to demonstrate the tempered response that market participants take to announcements of currency stabilization plans. A central bank's public commitment to a central rate does not *immediately* establish credibility to the extent that the market will post a zero interest differential vis-à-vis the pegging partner. It may require years of favorable experience before market participants are convinced that a central bank will not renege on its commitment to a central rate. Market participants know from experience that given a choice between an external commitment (to an exchange rate) and an internal commitment (to growth or full employment) that the internal commitment comes first and the external exchange rate target can be jettisoned.

FIGURE 2.13   **Interest Rate Differentials versus the DM: Recent Trends, January 1, 1988–March 31, 2000**

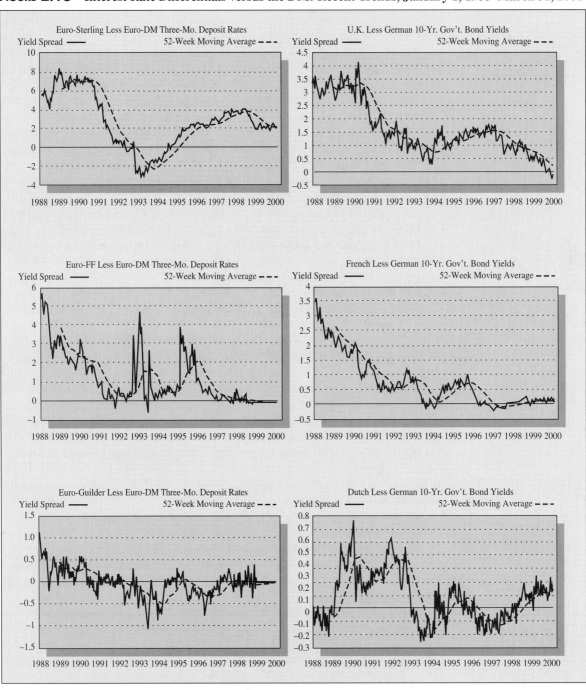

Source: Datastream and author's calculations.

FIGURE **2.14** U.S. Real Interest Rates
T-Bill Returns–CPI, Annual Data

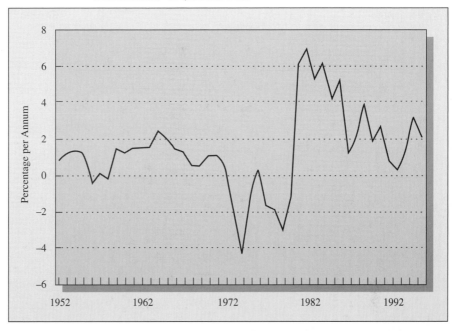

Source: *Stocks, Bonds, Bills and Inflation: 1997 Yearbook*, (Chicago: Ibbotson Associates, 1997); and author's calculations.

Real Interest Rates. Like other real magnitudes, the **real interest rate** reflects a nominal rate adjusted for inflation. The *expected* real interest rate equals the nominal interest rate minus the *expected* inflation rate, while the *realized* real interest rate equals the nominal interest rate minus the *realized* inflation rate. Since inflation may be approximated by a variety of inflation measures, the real interest rate is not a uniquely defined concept.

A graph of real interest rates for short-term US$ investments is displayed in Figure 2.14. During most of the post–World War II period, U.S. real interest rates hovered in the 1.0–2.0 percent range. After the first oil price shock in the early 1970s, inflation surged, making real interest rates negative. Toward the end of the 1970s in an attempt to wring inflation from the economy, nominal interest rates rose, taking real interest rates with them. Real US$ interest rates stayed high through most of the 1980s, before returning to the 1.0–2.0 percent range common in the 1950s and 1960s.

The real interest differential has also shown dramatic up-and-down behavior since the end of the Bretton Woods system. In Figure 2.15, we report one example, comparing the US$ against a portfolio of U.K., German, Japanese, and French interest rates. This interest differential varies from 3.0 percent in 1976 to −4.0 percent in 1979, back to 3.0 percent in 1982, and then turning negative in the late 1980s and early 1990s. The graph also suggests a positive correlation between the real interest differential and the foreign exchange value of the US$. Although far from being a perfect correlation, the relationship between the two series was strong from 1980 to 1984. The interest differential peaked in 1984, leading the peak in the US$ exchange rate.

Figure 2.16 shows the US$ − DM real interest rate differential from 1993 to April 2000. Over this period, the real interest differential ranged from +1.00 percent (in 1994

FIGURE 2.15   The Dollar and Real Interest Rate Differentials

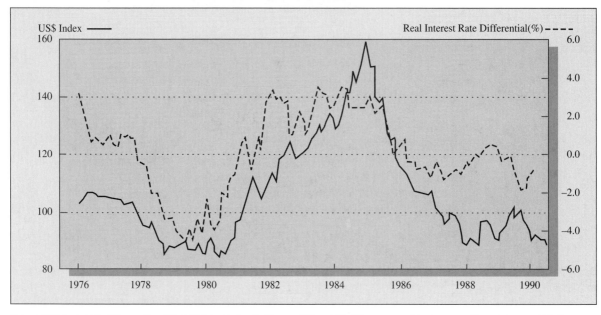

Notes: US$ Index is Federal Reserve Board Trade Weighted index; Real interest differential is U.S. rate less weighted average of Japan, Germany, United Kingdom and France.

Source: Merrill Lynch, *Currency and Bond Market Trends*, July 19, 1990.

FIGURE 2.16   DM/US$ Exchange Rate and U.S./German Real Interest-Rate Differentials (1993–1999)
10-Year Bond Yields Less Core CPI

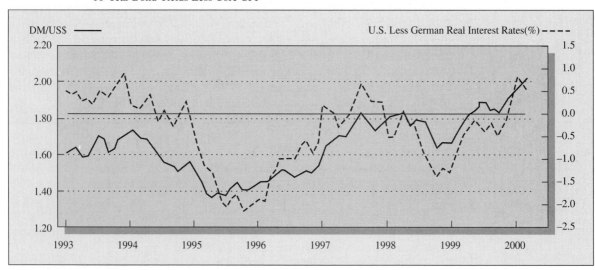

Source: Deutsche Bank, *Global FX Outlook and Strategy,* May 5, 2000, p. 19.

and 2000) to -2.00 percent (in 1995). Again the correspondence between the exchange rate and the real interest differential is pronounced.

Summary of Recent Developments

The graphs in this chapter offer an introduction to the variability found in prices in international financial markets over the past 20 years. Our focus on the markets in major industrial countries has been sufficient to illustrate tremendous variation in prices and experiences. The recent experience in Asian financial markets shows even more clearly the abrupt and substantial price changes that are possible when a country moves involuntarily from a regime of essentially pegged to floating exchange rates.

In this book, we will attempt to highlight those empirical regularities in the data that summarize the determinants of financial market prices and the relationships among those prices. The reader can appreciate that many idiosyncratic events ("the trees") helped to shape the specific graphs reviewed here. Nevertheless, we will try to uncover the general relationships ("the forest") that these graphs represent.

Policy Matters—Private Enterprises

The Conduct of Business under Pegged and Floating Exchange Rates

In this chapter, we have outlined the rules underlying the gold standard, pegged exchange rates, and floating exchange rates. And we have summarized some of the empirical findings about the behavior of market prices under these alternative systems.

In today's international business environment, firms face numerous exchange rate regimes. The demise of the Bretton Woods system brought a floating or flexible exchange rate regime to most major currencies. While the desire for exchange rate stability and predictability remains, many countries have found it difficult to deliver. In 1991, only 56 of the 156-member countries of the International Monetary Fund (IMF) declared themselves as following managed or independently floating exchange rate policies. The other 100 nations were pegged to a single currency or a composite indicator, or limited exchange rate flexibility by some other means. By 1998, with the IMF's membership having increased to 182 nations, these figures were nearly reversed, with 100 IMF member nations relying on managed or independently floating exchange rate policies. A minority of 82 countries imposed a currency peg or attempted to limit exchange rate flexibility.

In this section, we examine how the government's choice of an international monetary system affects the decisions that firms face.

Greater Exchange Rate Variability under Floating

Earlier in this chapter, we showed that the variability of exchange rates increased when the industrial countries abandoned the Bretton Woods systems for the floating-rate system. A study by Michael Mussa (1986) documents that this pattern has been true over the last 50 years in virtually every industrial country that has moved from a fixed-rate to a floating-rate regime. Similarly, countries that have moved away from floating rates and into pegged systems have seen a decline in exchange rate variability.

Since prices of many commodities and manufactured products tend to move sluggishly, the move to floating rates has increased variability in both real and nominal exchange rates.

Costs of Exchange Rate Variability

The nominal exchange rate is used to translate the value of nominal cash flows (such as sales revenues, interest payments, and royalties) and the value of nominal assets and liabilities (such as government bonds and bank debt). The real exchange rate measures the overvaluation or undervaluation of a currency, and thus indicates the change in international competitiveness for firms buying and selling real goods and for firms investing in real productive assets. Increasing volatility of nominal and real exchange rates raises important policy concerns for private individuals and enterprises.

Financial Decisions and Hedging.   Investors gain from holding assets in appreciating currencies while borrowers gain from holding liabilities in depreciating currencies. The increase in nominal exchange rate variability raises the importance of the choice of currency of denomination for cash flows and financial assets. An individual or firm with the ability to forecast exchange rates better than the market may feel that the possible reward for bearing this exchange rate exposure justifies the risks.

On the other hand, exchange rate variability may be a formidable deterrent for risk-averse individuals. Exchange rate variability thus increases the demand for financial instruments (such as futures, forwards, options, and swaps) that can be used to hedge or offset these currency risks. The tremendous growth in the markets for these instruments over the last 25 years can be attributed in large part to the increase in exchange rate and interest rate variability and the demand for hedging services.

Operating Decisions and Hedging.   Changes in real exchange rates affect the business success of firms, their operations, and ultimately their market value. Real exchange rate changes affect the competitiveness of an individual firm. But real exchange rate changes also affect the financial health of suppliers and customers. Other things being equal, the value of a firm increases as a real exchange rate change strengthens customers and suppliers, and weakens competitors.

Real exchange rate changes thrust critical business decisions onto the firm. For example, as the value of the yen appreciated from 200 ¥/$ to 150 ¥/$ to 100 ¥/$, the *yen revenue* associated with a $20,000 U.S. auto sale has declined. As the yen appreciated, Japanese automakers faced key decisions: When and by how much to raise the US$ price of autos? Should the Japanese change the characteristics of autos sold in the United States to make US$ price increases more acceptable? Should they abandon Japan as an export base for automobiles and move production elsewhere?

The increase in the variability of real exchange rates under a floating-rate regime raises the importance of these operating decisions for the firm.

Policy Matters—Public Policymakers

Earlier in this chapter, we examined the broad choices facing policymakers with respect to a gold standard, fixed exchange rates, and floating exchange rates. In this section, we review several current policy issues that affect exchange rate systems and the behavior of international financial markets.

Exchange Rate Policies in Emerging Markets

Currency Boards as an Exchange Rate System.   A **currency board** is a system aimed at establishing a fixed exchange rate between domestic currency and an external currency. Its operating principles are akin to the classical gold standard, and place severe restrictions on domestic monetary policies. Currency boards were fairly common in colonial nations where the local and colonial currencies were closely linked. Recently, several nations have introduced a currency board as their exchange rate regime. Their success has raised the visibility of this exchange rate regime.

A currency board fixes its exchange rate by making a commitment to exchange—on demand and without limit—domestic currency for foreign currency at a prespecified rate. To fulfill this commitment, the currency board will issue domestic money only when it has sufficient foreign currency reserves to meet its commitment. Thus, a currency board operates similarly to the classical gold standard (Box 2.1, Rule I) in that residents are free to convert domestic currency into foreign currency (and vice versa) at the official parity rate.[36]

A currency board linking the Hong Kong dollar to the US$ has operated since 1983. More recently, currency boards have been established in Argentina (1991) and Lithuania (1994) backed by the US$ and in Estonia (1992) linked to the DM. If the currency board follows its commitment exactly, domestic monetary growth will be constrained and the rate of domestic inflation should closely follow the inflation rate in the country whose currency serves as backing for the currency board.

Figure 2.17 shows the recent inflation experience for four countries with currency boards and the United States. Notice that the inflation rate in Hong Kong closely tracks the U.S. rate, but at a rate 5–7 percent per year higher. The explanation may be that certain nontraded goods (such as real estate) are in inelastic supply and their prices may rise more quickly in a developing economy. In late 1998 with the Asian financial crisis, inflation in Hong Kong dipped below the rate in the United States and actually turned negative throughout 1999.

The inflation record for Argentina is more unusual. Argentina experienced hyperinflation, with inflation running at several thousand percent per year as late as 1990. With the introduction of the currency board, Argentina's inflation fell sharply through 1993 and 1994. By 1995, inflation in Argentina was roughly identical to that in the United States, and actually fell below the U.S. rate for the remainder of the decade.

The record for Estonia is equally impressive. Estonia gained its independence from the Soviet Union in 1991 and it established its currency board in June 1992.[37] Estonia's inflation, which was running at several hundred percent per year in 1991 and 1992, has slowly been winding down, reaching the 20 percent range in 1995, and falling below a 10 percent annual inflation rate in 1998. The experience in Lithuania is very similar. Inflation in Lithuania was more than 500 percent per year in 1993, and by 1998 inflation had fallen to an annual rate of under 5 percent.

The recent success of currency boards raises an interesting question: Why can currency boards successfully contain domestic monetary growth while other commitments to monetary austerity have failed? The currency board gains credibility by its commitment to forgo the devaluation option. Sometimes this is backed with a "national law" in support of the currency board and its fixed rate. Not surprisingly, the initial view of a

---

[36]See Williamson (1995) for more on currency boards.

[37]Estonia's currency board was funded by the return of gold deposits it had made in the Bank of England prior to World War II. See Bennett (1995).

FIGURE 2.17   Consumer Price Inflation in Currency Board Countries and the
United States, 1990–1999
Percentage Inflation at Annual Rate

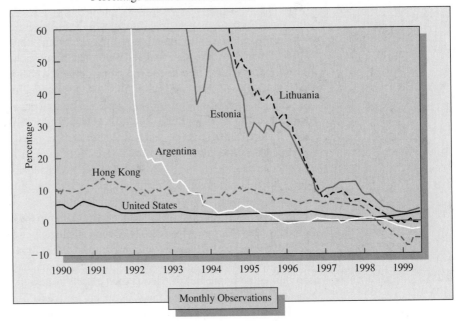

Source: *International Financial Statistics,* various issues.

currency board by market participants is usually skeptical; credibility in the marketplace must be earned through years of adherence to a commitment. In a politically unstable country, the currency board could be abolished along with the current government. And even a stable country may regret fixing against a very strong (or weak) currency.[38]

In Chapter 5, we review the uncovered interest parity rule which predicts that when the exchange rate of two countries is permanently fixed, the interest rates on these currencies should be similar. In the case of Hong Kong, Argentina, and Estonia, local currency interest rates have converged to a small differential vis-à-vis foreign currency interest rates (the US$ for Hong Kong and Argentina, and the DM for Estonia). Still, local interest rates are subject to jumps when credibility is threatened, such as the jump in Hong Kong interest rates during the Asian financial crisis in 1997, or the jump in rates in Argentina and Estonia after the Russian financial crisis in 1998.

Beyond Currency Boards to Full Dollarization

Given the success of currency boards in stabilizing exchange rates and lowering inflation, the reader might wonder why policymakers could be less than fully satisfied with a currency board and what policy could offer improved results. While a currency board ties the hands of local monetary authorities and removes practically any scope for an independent monetary policy, the nation still retains its own money. Thus, the country retains the option to abandon the currency board and devalue, an option that might look

---

[38]In January 1997, reports circulated that Lithuania would abandon its currency board in response to the 25 percent real appreciation of the US$.

attractive to exercise if other neighboring countries have devalued (and gained competitiveness) or if the currency board is under speculative attack. The country "pays" for its option by being forced to pay higher interest on loans in domestic currency—because lenders fear that they could be repaid in devalued units.

Since the start of its currency board in 1991, interest rates on Argentine pesos have exceeded the interest rate on US$ even though the Argentine government has committed to keep the peso/US$ exchange rate at 1:1. The differential has been 50–200 basis points which is nonnegligible. Moreover, interest rates in Argentina increased sharply in 1995 after the Mexican peso crisis (the "Tequila effect"), and again in 1998 after the Russian ruble crisis. On both occasions, real growth in Argentina slowed considerably. The 1995 tequila effect alone may have cost Argentina 14 percent of GDP.[39] To Argentine President Carlos Menem, this demonstrated the cost of the currency board when investors doubt the credibility of a government's commitment to maintain the exchange rate.

In January 1999, President Menem proposed "dollarizing" the Argentine economy, meaning to adopt the U.S. dollar as Argentina's sole currency. In some respects, this would not be a huge transition for Argentina. U.S. dollars circulate interchangeably for pesos in Argentina and roughly 60 percent of private sector deposits are in US$. Argentina could enact a dollarization policy on its own, simply by buying up all outstanding pesos in circulation (about $14.6 billion in 1999) using its reserves of US$ (about $18.3 billion).

What would be the ramifications of dollarization for Argentina? First, Argentina would lose the ability to pursue an independent monetary policy. But this has been true since the start of the currency board in 1991. Second, Argentina would lose the ability to act as a lender of last resort to domestic banks by issuing currency to financial institutions in distress. This also is not a change from the situation under a currency board. However, the Argentine government is free to use its excess US$ reserves to assist banks in distress, or alter reserve requirements on deposits in domestic banks.

Dollarization would impose one major cost on Argentina—the central bank would lose the seigniorage from printing domestic pesos. Simply put, the central bank holds US$ denominated assets that earn interest, and it issues noninterest-bearing peso coins and notes that circulate. The difference between the interest on its assets and its liabilities represents seigniorage. By some estimates, this loss could be about $14 billion, or 4 percent of Argentine GDP, but it could run higher.[40]

Would there be a net gain to Argentina from full dollarization? That depends on how frequent and how costly "Tequila effect" shocks to GDP are relative to the cost of lost seigniorage. As Argentina was hit twice in 10 years with a substantial downturn in GDP, one can understand the attraction of dollarization.[41]

Risks of Pegging—The Asian Currency and Russian Ruble Crises. The decade of the 1990s has clearly shown how pegged exchange rate regimes can be vulnerable to sudden and substantial exchange rate changes. However, the experience of Argentina, Hong Kong, and other currency board countries demonstrates that exchange rates can be stable, if the central bank commits to a "dull and boring" style of monetary policy— namely, a dependent policy that simply emulates the policy of the pegging partner.

---

[39]See François R. Velde and Marcelo Veracierto, "Dollarization in Argentina," *Chicago Fed Letter,* Federal Reserve Bank of Chicago, No. 142, June 1999.

[40]*Ibid.*

[41]For further discussion of dollarization in Argentina, see Velde and Veracierto, *ibid.,* and the IMF Economic Forum, "Dollarization: Fad or Future for Latin America," June 24, 1999 available at their web site, <www.imf.org>.

Keeping exchange rates pegged and stable is not a technological problem. The problem is that the technology is too constraining on local monetary authorities.

Many factors related to bank lending policies, transparency of corporate reporting, among other factors played a role in the Asian financial crisis.[42] But one factor that certainly led to the crisis is a violation of the "unholy trinity"—meaning the desire of countries to have (1) pegged exchange rates, (2) free capital mobility, and (3) scope for monetary policy independence. The Bretton Woods period showed time and again that countries can have two of these three policies, but they cannot sustain all three. A country (say, Argentina) can adopt pegged exchange rates (1) and permit free capital movements (2), but then it loses the ability to have an independent monetary policy. A country (say, United Kingdom) can seek its own monetary policy while permitting free capital movement, but then it loses the ability to have a pegged exchange rate. Or a country (say, Chile) can seek an independent monetary policy while under pegged exchange rates, but then it must impose barriers to capital mobility to segment its financial markets from its pegging partner.

The Russian ruble crisis came at the culmination of a six-year struggle by the former Soviet Union to develop a market economy and integrate Russia's fledgling financial markets into the global system.[43] In January 1998, the Russian ruble was pegged to the US$ with a 15 percent fluctuation band. Throughout 1997 and into 1998, the Russian economy faced a litany of problems—among them, falling commodity prices, soaring fiscal deficits, and real exchange rate appreciation—all of which combined to cast doubt on Russia's debt servicing capabilities. Over this period, the ruble was repeatedly attacked by speculators, and the central bank raised interest rates to 150 percent even though domestic inflation hovered below 10 percent. Russia was offered an IMF aid package of almost $23 billion, but speculation against the ruble and reserve losses continued. The Russian parliament resisted revenue-raising measures, and almost half of government tax receipts were going toward debt servicing. On top of this, equity prices tumbled and spreads on Russian eurobonds, offered to the market in 1996 at U.S. Treasury plus 345 basis points traded at spreads of 2,000 basis points.

In August 1998, the Russian government made a radical shift in policy, allowing the ruble to float, declaring a 90-day moratorium on repayment of corporate and bank debt owed to foreigners, and imposing extensive restrictions on foreign exchange transactions. The ruble plummeted in value, from about 6.25 ruble/US$ in July to over 20 ruble/US$ by year-end as shown in Figure 2.18. The real exchange rate for the ruble switched from substantially overvalued to undervalued within two months.

The events in Russia had only a limited and short-lived impact on Eastern Europe. But the need to raise capital and reduce exposure to risk led investors to liquidate both high-quality U.S. government securities and lower-credit-rated Brazilian Brady bonds during the fourth quarter of 1998. These dealings eventually pushed Long-Term Capital Management, the high-profile hedge fund, to the brink of bankruptcy in October 1998, and soon thereafter, the decision to float the Brazilian real in January 1999.

Concerns About EMU

The European Economic and Monetary Union (EMU) became a reality on January 1, 1999, after nearly forty years of hoping and about 20 years of serious planning. Most

---

[42]We discuss possible leading indicators of the Asian financial crisis in Chapter 8.

[43]This summary draws on the detailed discussion in the *69th Annual Report,* Bank for International Settlements, Basle, Switzerland, June 7, 1999, pp. 50–54.

FIGURE 2.18 **Russian Ruble Exchange Rates versus US$**

Nominal Rate (Ruble per US$, left scale); Real Effective Exchange Rate (right scale)

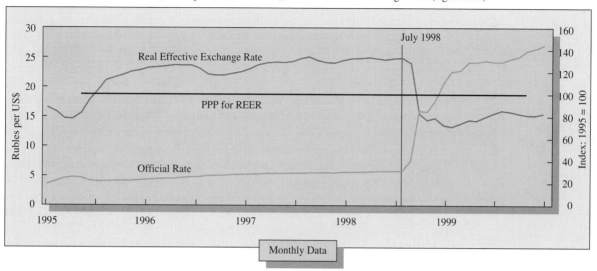

Source: *International Financial Statistics,* CD-ROM.

economists, and especially American economists, were long skeptical about EMU. The titles of their articles signaled their skepticism. Maurice Obstfeld chose "Europe's Gamble" for a 1997 article, and *The Economist* picked "An Awfully Big Adventure" for the theme of their 1998 survey on EMU.[44] Their skepticism was grounded in part in the belief that the European Union is not an ideal candidate for a currency union.

The theory of optimum currency areas (pioneered by Robert Mundell) asserts that three factors are critical for a successful currency union. First, factors of production (namely, capital and labor) should be mobile within the union. Second, the cyclical behavior of economic activity (expansions and contractions) should be highly correlated across member countries. And third, the union will benefit by an ability to make fiscal transfers from expanding regions to temporarily depressed regions in the event that points one and two are not met. Various studies conclude that the EU comes up short on all of these criteria. While financial capital has the potential for greater mobility, labor is notoriously immobile across Europe. Language, culture, and portability of social benefits are important barriers to labor moving across borders. The business cycles of EMU nations has historically been weakly correlated, although in part this may have been the result of different monetary policies as well as differences in the flexibility and exposure of the underlying real economies. And third, EMU is an *economic* union and not a *political* union. The tax revenues of the central EU government are tiny and fiscal transfers among EMU countries are accordingly small.

In contrast, many European economists and political leaders have focused on the known advantages and dynamic gains likely under EMU. In their calculus, the costs of sacrificing monetary sovereignty are small, while the benefits—of lower-transaction costs, lower-exchange rate risk, greater depth of financial markets across Europe, and

[44]Maurice Obstfeld, "Europe's Gamble," *Brookings Papers on Economic Activity,* No. 2, 1997; "An Awfully Big Adventure," *The Economist,* April 11, 1998.

greater capital mobility—are perpetual. The single currency, the euro, is likely to stimulate competition across the EU throughout private sector firms and among social welfare systems. Perhaps more important than its economic aspects, European leaders recognize that EMU is a political initiative to redress the balance of power vis-à-vis the U.S. dollar and give Europe a share of America's seigniorage rights.

While the EMU is now a reality, its presence raises many concerns about its viability and impact on international financial markets. We discuss several specific concerns.

The Problem of Asymmetric Shocks—An Irish Example.   Under EMU, a single currency replaces the national currencies of 11 nations.[45] Thus each nation loses the option of following a separate independent monetary policy and altering its exchange rate to reach its internal and external policy objectives. This reduction in policy choices can be important when countries are experiencing faster or slower economic growth than is sustainable long term. Typically, the problem is one of slower than desired growth, which can be addressed by either expansionary monetary policy or currency depreciation. But the opposite case, faster than desired growth, can be dampened by either contractionary monetary policy or currency appreciation.

From 1994 to 1998, thanks to various policy initiatives and special circumstances, annual real growth in Ireland averaged nearly 8.5 percent. Despite this growth, unit labor costs were declining and inflation was under control. Between 1995 and 1997, the Irish punt appreciated by almost 14 percent against the DM, but it then depreciated back toward its central rate as EMU became more certain. Given that Irish punt interest rates exceeded DM rates by roughly 200 basis points, further convergence in rates (that is, Irish rates falling) risked further stimulating the Irish economy. As a result, on March 19, 1998, Ireland requested a 3 percent revaluation of the punt's central rate.

The Irish revaluation sent two worrisome signals. First, that the single monetary policy under EMU could be constraining, so Ireland found it helpful to make a small adjustment while it had the option. Indeed, the Irish move raised the risk that other countries would follow suit and demand their own last-minute exchange rate changes before irrevocable conversion rates were set. Second, if exchange rate policy could be useful for a small, open economy the size of Ireland, it could arguably be even more important for France, Germany, Italy, and Spain, which have substantial trade-to-GDP ratios and less scope for adjusting quickly to unexpected real shocks.[46] The lack of national exchange rate policy under EMU could be a source of tension if national growth rates are not sufficiently correlated.

The Euro as an International Challenger to the U.S. Dollar.   As the currency of 11 nations, nearly 300 million people, and an annual GDP approaching $7 trillion, the euro could naturally aspire to a preeminent position in international financial markets and possibly challenge the dominant role played by the U.S. dollar over the last 50 years. As we will see in later chapters, once the volume of foreign exchange trading and securities outstanding in the 11 legacy European currencies is combined, the new EMU-wide and euro totals are substantial; in some cases, they rival those in the United States and the global US$ markets. Their size could give Euro-denominated security markets depth and liquidity that compares well with US$ markets. The concern (at least from the U.S. perspective) is that international investors might shift out of US$ securities into euro securities, thus damaging liquidity in the US$ market segments. U.S. officials have said

---

[45]Greece becomes the twelfth EMU nation on January 1, 2001.

[46]See Obstfeld (1998) for a more detailed analysis of Irish economic policies prior to EMU.

publicly that they welcome the euro, and see the threat to the US$ as minor, because any shift in the composition of asset portfolios will occur gradually.[47] The euro could, in fact, harbor a positive external for the United States. If the ECB is successful in delivering credible monetary policy with the resulting low and predictable inflation, the euro could gain popularity, leading the U.S. Fed to compete harder by increasing its own credibility.

The Euro and International Financial Markets.   The euro changes some basic aspects of international financial management for both European and non–European participants. For example, prior to 1999, a French investor that held shares of Italian and German firms considered these "foreign" investments, subject to additional currency risk but possibly offering a diversification benefit.[48] Now these shares are more "domestic" because they are denominated in the same currency and operating in the EMU that shares a common monetary policy. There may still be some diversification benefits, because the economic performance of France, Germany, and Italy need not be perfectly correlated even under EMU. To garner international diversification benefits, the French investor will have to look outside the EMU.

For the US$-based investor, various types of financial bets were popular in the run-up to EMU. "Convergence plays" were based on the assumption that interest rates in two potential EMU members would converge (so own the high-interest-rate currency and short the low-interest-rate currency). "Divergence plays" were based on the opposite assumption.[49] Now with EMU, all cross-currency plays among the 11 legacy currencies are gone.

For US$ based investors, introduction of the euro implies that the universe of investable currencies has shrunk by ten. If the United Kingdom joins EMU, another major currency and security market will come under the EMU umbrella. To obtain diversification benefits, the global currency or fixed income investor must turn to other countries, such as Australia, New Zealand, or the smaller emerging markets.

---

[47]See Michael R. Sesit, "New York Fed's McDonough Says U.S. Doesn't Look Upon the Euro as a Threat," *The Wall Street Journal,* November 19, 1997.

[48]We discuss international equity portfolios in detail in Chapter 15.

[49]We discuss these strategies in the context of uncovered interest parity in Chapter 5.

Summary

In this chapter, we first reviewed alternative methods of international monetary arrangements, including the classical gold standard, the Bretton Woods pegged exchange rate system, the floating-rate system, and the European Monetary System. Each system corresponded with certain "rules of the game," some of which were written and others unwritten. The gold standard operated most faithfully in accordance with its rules, but it was abandoned because nations wanted more control over their economic performance. In practice, the other systems tended to operate differently than their classic designs. The American economy and the US$ were at the center of Bretton Woods rather than gold; floating rates reverted to a form of managed floating and target zones; and Germany and the DM came to dominate the EMS, which for a time placed the future of the EMS in doubt.

We examined a set of graphs of international financial market prices to demonstrate the behavior of prices over the recent past. These graphs illustrated the extent of price variability in exchange rates and interest rates during the floating-rate period. In the last few years, financial crises in Asia, Russia, and Latin America have shown how rapidly exchange rate variability can erupt, leading to real sector effects on both the local economy and distant countries.

Exchange rate variability raises crucial strategic and managerial issues for firms and individuals. Exchange rate variability implies that firms may win big (or lose big) if they make the right (or wrong) choice regarding currency. This naturally raises the demand for products that will hedge some of the risks of exchange rate changes.

Governments have also been searching for ways to make their exchange rate and monetary policies more credible in order to reduce the risks of exchange rate changes and to improve their economic performance. The currency board seems to offer a way for some countries to gain credibility when other methods have failed. Argentina has proposed going a step further to full dollarization. The EMU is a new system that supplies a common currency to 11 nations that still hold sovereignty over their fiscal and political affairs. How EMU will perform in practice and how it will evolve can only be known with time.

Questions

1. What is meant by the expression "the rules of the game," as applied to an international financial system? Why are rules desirable for an international financial system?

2. In what ways are the policies of countries constrained when they participate in a pegged exchange rate system?

3. In what ways are the policies of countries constrained when they participate in a floating exchange rate system?

4. The period of the international gold standard allowed countries to achieve the twin objectives of strong growth and stable prices. True or false? Discuss.

5. On what basis was Robert Triffin able to predict a collapse of the Bretton Woods system as early as 1960? Why did the Bretton Woods system survive until 1973?

6. On what basis could it be argued that the United States defaulted on a major international commitment prior to the collapse of Bretton Woods?

7. What reasons support the argument that the European Monetary System was achieving its objectives prior to 1992?

8. Define the term *long swings* as it pertains to the US$ exchange rate during the floating-rate period. How would the existence of long swings affect financial managers?

9. Summarize the high and low measures of exchange-rate volatility shown for the DM in Figure 2.8. Does volatility appear to be constant or variable over time?

10. Real effective exchange rates appear to be less volatile than nominal exchange rates. Explain why.

11. Summarize the high and low measures for nominal interest rates shown for a single currency in Figure 2.11. In general, why do interest rates vary over time rather than take on a constant value?

12. Define the concept of "real interest rate." Discuss several ways to measure a real interest rate.

13. In general terms, discuss how the conduct of business is affected by whether pegged or floating exchange rates govern the international financial system.

14. In 1992, both the United Kingdom and Italy dropped out of the European Exchange Rate Mechanism. After the announcement, British interest rates fell and Italian interest rates rose. Explain why.

15. The Netherlands appears willing to pursue a European Monetary Union while Britain appears unwilling. List reasons that explain these apparent differences.

16. Today's interest rate on three-month US$ deposits is about 6.0 percent, while the three-month interest rate on Argentine pesos is about 7.5 percent. Discuss how this could happen even though Argentina has adopted a currency board.

17. What are the costs and benefits facing Argentina if the Argentines decide to abandon their currency board and adopt "full dollarization" in its place?

Exercises

1. Let the current Mexican peso (MP) rate be 4 MP/US$. Suppose the MP depreciates to 5 MP/$.
   a. Calculate the percentage depreciation of the MP.
   b. Express the foreign exchange rates in US$ terms and calculate the percentage appreciation of the US$.
   c. Does the MP depreciation in (a) equal the US$ appreciation in (b) multiplied by negative one? Why or why not?

2. Let the current MP exchange rate be 4 MP/US$.
   a. A forecaster predicts a 150 percent MP depreciation. What value of the exchange rate is the forecaster predicting?
   b. Another forecaster predicts a 60 percent US$ appreciation. What value of the exchange rate is this forecaster predicting?
   c. Do the two forecasters in (a) and (b) agree or disagree with each other? Explain.

3. Again, let the current MP/US$ rate be 4 MP/US$. Suppose the MP depreciates to 5 MP/$.
   a. Calculate the percentage depreciation of the MP using logarithmic returns (continuous compounding). [*Hint:* See Box 2.9 and Appendix 4.1]
   b. Calculate the percentage appreciation of the US$ using logarithmic returns (continuous compounding).
   c. Does the MP depreciation in (a) equal the US$ appreciation in (b) multiplied by negative one? Why or why not?

4. Let the current spot rate be 2.00 DM/US$.
   a. Forecaster A believes that in the next period, the DM rate will jump to 1.60 DM/US$ or 2.40 DM/US$ with equal probability. Calculate A's expected exchange rate.
   b. Forecaster B tracks the US$/DM exchange rate. His forecasts for the next period are 0.625 US$/DM and 0.416667 US$/DM with equal probability. Calculate B's expected exchange rate.
   c. Do A's and B's forecasts of exchange rates agree or disagree? Explain.

References

Bennett, Adam G. G. "Currency Boards: Issues and Experiences." *Finance and Development*, Sept. 1995, pp. 39–42.

Campa, José M., and P. H. Kevin Chang. "The Forecasting Ability of Correlations Implied in Foreign Exchange Options." New York University working paper, Nov. 1995.

Cooper, Richard N. "Recent History of World Monetary Problems." In *The Future of the International Monetary System*, T. Agmon, R. Hawkins, and R. Levich, eds. Lexington, MA: D. C. Heath, 1984.

Eichengreen, Barry. *Globalizing Capital: A History of the International Monetary System.* Princeton, NJ: Princeton University Press, 1996.

Frankel, Jeffrey A. "The Dazzling Dollar." *Brookings Papers on Economic Activity*, no. 1 (1985), pp. 199–218.

Funabashi, Yoichi. *Managing the Dollar: From the Plaza to the Louvre.* Washington, DC: Institute for International Economics, 1988.

International Monetary Fund, "Guidelines for the Management of Floating Exchange Rates," *IMF Annual Report,* Washington DC (1974), pp. 112–16.

International Monetary Fund, *Second Amendment, Articles of Agreement of the International Monetary Fund,* Washington, DC, 1976.

Krugman, Paul R. "Is the Strong Dollar Sustainable?" In *The U.S. Dollar—Recent Developments, Outlook, and Policy Options.* Federal Reserve Bank of Kansas City, 1985.

Krugman, Paul R., and Maurice Obstfeld. *International Economics: Theory and Policy,* 5th ed. Reading, MA: Addison-Wesley, 2000.

Levich, Richard M., ed. *The ECU Market* (London: Euromoney Publications), 1987.

McKinnon, Ronald I. "The Rules of the Game: International Money in Historical Perspective." *Journal of Economic Literature* 31 (Mar. 1993), pp. 1–44.

————. *The Rules of the Game: International Money and Exchange Rates.* Cambridge: MIT Press, 1996.

Mussa, Michael. "Nominal Exchange Rate Regimes and the Behavior of Real Exchange Rates: Evidence and Implications." *Carnegie-Rochester Conference Series on Public Policy* 25 (Amsterdam: North-Holland, 1986), pp. 117–213.

Obstfeld, Maurice. "EMU: Ready or Not?" *Princeton Essays in International Finance,* No. 209, July 1998.

Pugel, Thomas A., and Peter Lindert. *International Economics,* 11th ed. Burr Ridge, IL: Irwin/McGraw-Hill.

Williamson, John. *What Role for Currency Boards?* Washington, DC: Institute for International Economics, 1995.

Ypersele, Jacques van, and Jean-Claude Koeune. *The European Monetary System.* Cambridge, Eng.: Woodhead-Faulkner, 1985.

II FOREIGN EXCHANGE MARKETS

3 Market Structure and Institutions 78
4 International Parity Conditions: Purchasing Power Parity 111
5 International Parity Conditions: Interest Rate Parity and the Fisher Parities 142
6 Spot Exchange Rate Determination 183
7 Foreign Exchange Market Efficiency 227
8 Exchange Rate Forecasting 260

3 MARKET STRUCTURE AND INSTITUTIONS

"Although the rudimentary methods still survive, . . . the modern Foreign Exchange market is a highly developed and sophisticated institution . . . it now comes as near to the theoretical ideal of a perfect market as any market in existence."
Paul Einzig (1970)

Learning Objectives

After reading this chapter, students should

1. Understand how the foreign exchange market is organized and how trades take place in the interbank and the retail segments of the market.

2. Understand the institutional features of foreign exchange market products (such as spot, forward, and forex swap contracts) and the distinction between speculation and arbitrage.

3. Be familiar with the size and scope of the foreign exchange market and worldwide trading activity.

4. Understand the relationship among four prices: spot rates (S), forward rates (F), and money-market interest rates at home and in the foreign country (i_H and i_F) and be able to predict any single price on the basis of information about the other three.

5. Be able to explain how to construct a synthetic forward contract, or home or foreign interest-bearing asset or liability by using other financial instruments.

6. Realize the types of risks that foreign exchange traders face and how these risks can be controlled.

Markets for the exchange of national currencies have existed for centuries. For most of the 20th century, the foreign exchange market behaved as a mature industry. The list of market participants was static, comprised of commercial banks in the United States and universal banks elsewhere. The product list also was static, comprising only spot contracts and forward contracts with fixed, short-term maturities. Competition from exchange-traded products was nonexistent. And the structure of the market—that is, the relationship between dealing banks, brokers, and commercial customers, the technology of trading and the systems for clearing and settlement of positions—was well defined and static.

Over the last 25 years, financial innovation and competitive pressures have forced massive changes on the structure and institutions of the foreign exchange market. The list of foreign exchange market products has grown considerably. Banks now offer longer-term forward contracts with maturities up to five years (and longer for major currencies). Currency options (traded over the counter among banks and sold to commercial customers) are the fastest-growing segment of the market. Other products such as range forwards and participating forwards that combine characteristics of options and forwards also have been introduced. New centralized markets for exchange-traded currency and interest rate futures and options have developed in countries around the world. In many cases, these exchange-traded contracts offer deep and liquid markets, and stiff competition to traditional bank products.

New competitors have entered the market. Investment banking firms in the United States and securities firms worldwide now support trading activities in foreign exchange and interest rate products. Many corporate customers now have well-developed financial subsidiaries that seek a more direct role in the market. New ways of foreign exchange clearing and settlement are being developed that will dramatically reduce the extent of payments risk among banks. New communications technology that links market participants and automates transactions may herald the end of traditional foreign exchange "voice" brokers. And new Web-based trading systems now in development may threaten the dominant role of bank dealers by offering greater power and transparency to large corporate and institutional customers.

In this chapter, we review the institutional and structural arrangements within the foreign exchange market, beginning with an examination of the importance of the foreign exchange market as measured by the volume of trading activity and the profitability of currency trading. We then discuss the basic foreign exchange market products and demonstrate how they can be transformed into innovative new forms. Next, we review the foreign exchange market setting, including the structure of the market, the role of brokers, and competitive threats to the market. A discussion of policy matters and how they affect private enterprises and public policymakers concludes the chapter.

Importance of Foreign Exchange Market Trading

Origins of the Market

The foreign exchange market establishes the price of each (domestic) currency in terms of other (foreign) currencies. Normally, we associate each currency with a country and assume that only domestic currency is acceptable for domestic transactions. This convention establishes a necessary although insufficient condition for a foreign exchange market.

Consider international transactions between the United States and Germany. The United States imports Mercedes-Benz automobiles from Germany and exports Boeing aircraft. If German residents would accept and hold U.S. dollars (US$) in exchange for Mercedes automobiles, and if U.S. residents would accept and hold euros (€) in exchange for Boeing aircraft, there would be no need for a foreign exchange market. The problem of course is that neither the US$ (in Germany) nor the € (in the United States) is particularly efficient as a *medium of exchange*. As a consequence, Mercedes is likely to prefer payment in € while Boeing is likely to prefer payment in US$. If the seller of the good determines the currency of invoicing, the foreign buyer of the product is forced to enter the foreign exchange market to trade its domestic currency for an acceptable means of payment. Unless the German buyer (who wants to exchange € for US$) meets an American buyer (who wants to exchange US$ for €), the German buyer must convince a satisfied holder of US$ (probably a U.S. resident) to hold € instead.

The common solution to the international trade transaction between Germany and the United States is the **foreign exchange trader** or **dealer**—an agent who stands ready to buy and sell currencies out of inventory and who plans to earn a fair return for the costs and risks he or she incurs. The foreign exchange trader is an intermediary who smooths the transactions between German buyers of Boeing aircraft and American buyers of Mercedes automobiles, each of whom arrive at the market at irregular and unpredictable times.

In addition to the foreign exchange trader, other domestic residents may desire to hold assets denominated in foreign currencies. First, in countries that have experienced high and variable inflation (such as Argentina, Russia, Vietnam), domestic currency may be a poor *store of value*. As a result, residents of these countries often desire foreign currency denominated assets to protect their real wealth. Second, foreign currency balances may offset certain financial risks. Foreign currency denominated assets may serve as a direct hedge for the exchange risk associated with anticipated foreign currency liabilities. And even if no foreign purchases are planned, foreign assets (such as equities or bonds) may reduce the overall variability of returns (denominated in domestic currency) in an investment portfolio. Third, borrowers and investors may find that certain characteristics of a financial claim (such as its maturity or its tax status) can only be found in a foreign market, which may necessitate a transaction in foreign currency. Finally, domestic residents may simply view foreign currency assets as undervalued, and they may demand foreign exchange for pure speculative purposes to earn higher returns.

Thus, while domestic currency is usually the medium of exchange for domestic transactions, domestic residents may desire foreign currency as an asset or store of value.

Volume of Foreign Exchange Trading

Measuring the size of the foreign exchange market is difficult. No national or international agency is charged to regulate or monitor foreign exchange market practices, and no agency reports fundamental market data on trading volume. In April 1998, central banks and monetary authorities in 43 countries conducted surveys of their national markets to measure foreign exchange market activity. The results of this fifth triennial survey were compiled and reported by the Bank for International Settlements (BIS, 1999).

As a starting point, Table 3.1 reports the daily volume of foreign exchange trading by market location. The United Kingdom (meaning the London market) held the largest market share in 1998 with $637 billion per day in trading volume or 32.1 percent of the world market. The United States was second, with $351 billion, followed by Japan, with $149 billion. The data from previous BIS surveys show that the same countries held the top three positions for the past decade, but that growth in the United Kingdom, the United States, and Singapore was far greater than in Japan and other locations.

The first estimate of total daily worldwide foreign exchange trading volume in 1998 is $1.982 trillion. Each country adjusted its own data for "double counting" by counting a trade between two national institutions only once. To adjust for cross-border transactions, such as a trade between a U.S. bank and a U.K. bank, the BIS subtracts $540 billion per day from the previous total. To adjust for gaps in the survey coverage, the BIS adds another $58 billion per day. Thus the final estimate is $1.5 trillion per day or nearly *$400 trillion per year*. This estimate covers the "traditional" market segments

TABLE 3.1 Dimensions of the Foreign Exchange Market
Daily Volume of Trading by Location (in Billions of US$)

Country	April 1989 Turnover (% Share)	April 1992 Turnover (% Share)	April 1995 Turnover (% Share)	April 1998 Turnover (% Share)
United Kingdom	184 (25.6%)	290 (27.0%)	464 (29.5%)	637 (32%)
United States	115 (16.0)	167 (15.5)	244 (15.5)	351 (18)
Japan	111 (15.5)	120 (11.2)	161 (10.2)	149 (8)
Singapore	55 (7.7)	74 (6.9)	105 (6.7)	139 (7)
Germany	— (na)	55 (5.1)	76 (4.8)	94 (5)
Switzerland	56 (7.8)	66 (6.1)	86 (5.5)	82 (4)
Hong Kong	49 (6.8)	60 (5.6)	90 (5.7)	79 (4)
France	23 (3.2)	33 (3.1)	58 (3.7)	72 (4)
Australia	29 (4.0)	29 (2.7)	40 (2.5)	47 (2)
Others	96 (13.4)	182 (16.9)	248 (15.8)	332 (16)
Total	718 (100)	1,076 (100)	1,572 (100)	1,982 (100)
Adjustments				
Less cross-border double counting	−184	−291	−435	−540
"Net-net" turnover	534	785	1,137	1,442
Plus estimated gaps in reporting	56	35	53	58
Equals estimated global turnover in "traditional" market segments	590	820	1,190	1,500
Plus futures and options	30	60	72	129
Grand total	620	880	1,262	1,634

Notes:

• Country figures are net of local interdealer double counting.

• Survey data for 1989 drawn from 21 countries. Survey data for 1992 and 1995 drawn from 26 countries. Survey data for 1998 drawn from 43 countries. Different coverage may affect comparisons.

• Futures and options include OTC and exchange-traded contracts.

Source: Bank for International Settlements, *Central Bank Survey of Foreign Exchange and Derivatives Market Activity,* May 1996 (Table F-2 and Table 2-A) and May 1999 report (Table B-2).

of spot, forward, and swap contracts. Trading in currency futures and options adds another $129 billion per day to the estimate of trading volume in 1998.

Foreign exchange trading volume is clearly huge. In comparison, only $58.8 billion in securities was traded on the busiest trading day in the history of the New York Stock Exchange, April 19, 1999.[1] The annual volume of foreign exchange trading is 35 times larger than annual world trade (roughly $11 trillion, counting both world imports and exports in 1998) and even 10 to 12 times larger than world GDP (about $35 trillion in 1998).

Foreign Exchange Trading Profits

Another measure of the importance of foreign exchange trading is the profits associated with trading earned by major banks. Data for a sample of large banks that deal in foreign exchange are reported in Table 3.2. The data show the variability of trading income across banks and the dramatic growth in income over the last 20 years.

---

[1]*New York Stock Exchange Factbook* (1999).

TABLE 3.2   Foreign Exchange Trading Income of Selected Banks
In Millions of US$

Company	1977	1987	1997	1998	1999
Bank of New York	NA	NA	109	126	137
Chase Manhattan	55	385	790	936	807
Citicorp	68	453	1,486	1,628	1,569
Credit Suisse First Boston	NA	NA	699	97	897
Deutsche Bank	NA	NA	1,040	636	807
Mellon Financial Corp	6	8	118	165	173
Morgan (J. P.) & Co.	40	251	493	781	777
Republic National Bank	5	39	98	120	141
State Street Bank	2	21	159	177	209

Notes:
• Figures for Chase, Citicorp, and Mellon are revenues.
• Figures for Mellon and J. P. Morgan include other securities.
• Figures for Chase in 1977 and 1987 include Chemical Bank.
• Figures for Mellon and State Street for 1977 are for years 1980 and 1978, respectively.
• Figures for Deutsche Bank and Credit Suisse converted to US$ at average yearly exchange rate.
NA = Not available.
Source: Company annual reports.

For the banks in Table 3.2, Citicorp appears to have the largest profits from foreign exchange trading, followed by Credit Suisse, Deutsche Bank, and Chase Manhattan. Comparing 1999 with 1987, foreign exchange trading income at Chase Manhattan is up by only a factor of 2, while at J. P. Morgan it is up by a factor of 3, and up by factors of 10 at State Street Bank and more than 20 at Mellon. Some of this growth reflects the financial mergers of the 1990s (for example, Chase Bank merging with Chemical Bank and Citigroup buying up Salomon Smith Barney), and some reflects the increase in foreign exchange trading volume.

The performance of individual banks often shows striking year-to-year variability. For example, trading profits at J. P. Morgan hit $106 million in 1981 and fell to less than $30 million in 1984, a year of great strength in the U.S. dollar.[2] The following year, the dollar plunged and Morgan's trading profits jumped by a factor of nearly six. Bankers Trust (now part of Deutsche Bank) also experienced a rough cyclical pattern between 1981 and 1986. In 1987, foreign exchange trading profits soared by a factor of nine, only to plunge by 70 percent in the following year. In more recent times, as Table 3.2 shows, Credit Suisse earned almost $700 million in foreign exchange trading income in 1997, and almost $900 million in 1999. But its foreign exchange profits collapsed to under $100 million in 1998, the year the company incurred huge losses on failed Russian ruble contracts.

It would be very useful to understand the economic circumstances leading to these patterns in foreign exchange trading profits. Some rise in profits over time should be attributable to the increase in international trade and overall foreign exchange trading volume. Exchange rate variability may cause some changes in the product mix; when uncertainty increases, customers should prefer more hedging products (longer-term

---

[2]See the first edition of this text, Levich (1998, p. 70), for data covering the 1976–1991 period for 15 U.S. banks.

forwards and options) that have wider bid/ask spreads or larger fees. Certainly the cross-sectional variability of the results will be related to the differing amounts of capital committed to trading at the various banks. However, without knowledge of the capital amount, we cannot compute a ratio of return on capital. Competition also should figure as a negative factor, with larger numbers of competitors associated with smaller profits.

An intriguing feature of the data in Table 3.2 is that all of the reported profit figures are positive. It is often argued that foreign exchange trading is a **zero-sum game,** meaning that the sum of speculative trading profits across all participants is zero. If the zero-sum game description is correct, how can foreign exchange trading be profitable to all banks simultaneously?

Explaining the Profitability of Foreign Exchange Trading

One explanation for the results in Table 3.2 is that the data refer to a one-year interval. If we were to check quarterly, monthly, or daily data, negative trading profits would surely appear. Over the span of one year, however, the data suggest that longer-run profits exceed short-term losses.

A second factor is that through the sale and purchase of foreign exchange, banks are providing a service, for which they earn a reasonable return reflected in the spread charged to corporate customers. Only banks' *speculative* trading profits ought to conform to the predictions of a zero-sum game.

Albéric Braas and Charles Bralver (1990) argue that speculative position-taking by dealers in the interbank market is not a "reliable" source of profits, and that trading rooms make all or substantially all of their profits from a steady turnover in the interbank market and with retail customers. This view is anathema to traders. But consider the following rough calculation. If trading volume is $1.5 trillion per day or $390 trillion per year, and if customer trading accounts for only 10 percent of all transactions (the actual figure is higher, as we will see later in this chapter) and earns only 0.0002 (2 basis points), then all dealing banks together would earn $7.8 billion per year in spread income.

A final explanation for the persistence of commercial bank foreign exchange trading profits emphasizes the role of central banks. Intervention by central banks to reduce the volatility or misalignment in floating rates, or to support the central rates of the European Monetary System, has been a feature of markets for many years. While none of the major central banks explicitly seek profits as a goal of their intervention, several studies reviewed in Chapter 17 suggest that central banks have at times incurred substantial losses.[3]

The data in Figure 3.1 show the foreign exchange gains and losses for the U.S. Treasury and the Federal Reserve. Realized profits from foreign currency sales are typically small numbers, sometimes literally zero because many quarters contain no foreign currency sales. Two marked exceptions were 1987 and 1990, when U.S. authorities realized $3 billion and $1.5 billion, respectively, in profits. Recalling Figure 2.4, these were years of relative strength in the DM and yen.

However, "valuation profits," which represent unrealized gains and losses on outstanding positions of the U.S. Treasury and Federal Reserve, have shown far wider swings. Losses were typical for the years through 1984. An exception to this pattern of losses occurred in the early 1980s, when a U.S. intervention strategy, known as the **Carter bonds,** turned a sizable profit. (See Box 3.1)

---

[3]See especially Taylor (1982).

FIGURE 3.1   **Annual Profits and Losses on Official U.S. Intervention**
Realized Profits and Unrealized Profits on Outstanding Positions

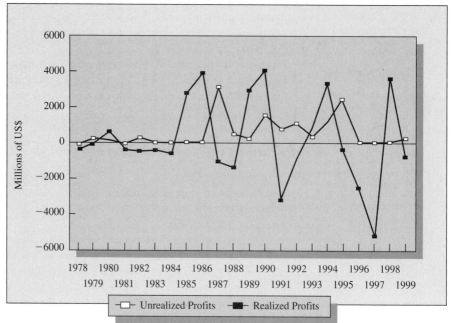

Note: Figures are net and represent the sum of Federal Reserve operations and U.S. Treasury operations in the Exchange Stabilization Fund and the General Account.

Source: Federal Reserve Bank of New York, *Quarterly Review,* various issues and the "Quarterly Report of Treasury and Federal Reserve Foreign Exchange Operations," *Federal Reserve Bulletin,* various issues.

Despite the profits on Carter bonds, overall valuation profits were systematically large and negative for the United States from 1971 until 1984. A study by Dean Taylor (1982) found that during the 1970s, the United States and other major central banks recorded substantial losses from foreign exchange intervention, totaling as much as $16.6 billion. In the context of a zero-sum game, it is possible that central banks played a large part in systematically transferring foreign exchange profits into the private sector, especially prior to 1984.

After the US$ peaked in early 1985, U.S. valuation profits soared throughout 1985 and 1986, along with the values of foreign currency holdings. Valuation profits reversed course in 1987 and 1988, and then turned positive again and headed higher in 1989 and 1990. Cumulative, outstanding unrealized profits for the U.S. Treasury and Federal Reserve hit a peak of $8.7 billion in January 1991.[4] These unrealized profits eroded, and turned into losses of about $350 million in June 1998. As of December 31, 1999, the U.S. Treasury and Federal Reserve had foreign currency holdings of about $32 billion; each 1 percent swing in exchange rates would amount to a $320 million swing in unrealized profits on this portfolio.

---

[4]Leahy (1995) argues that U.S. monetary authorities have earned positive profits since the beginning of floating rates in 1973. The profit calculations are sensitive to the initial foreign exchange position and the terminal date for calculating profits. For further discussion, see Edison (1993).

Box 3.1

How to Succeed at Intervention by Really Signaling

In 1978, the US$ was steadily losing value against most European currencies and the yen. Efforts to "talk up" the dollar had been unsuccessful. To reverse the dollar slide and signal to the market that serious monetary controls and inflation fighting policies were in place, the United States adopted an unusual strategy. On November 1, 1978, the Federal Reserve boosted the discount rate by one full percentage point, reiterated its policy of strict money supply growth, and announced a major intervention in the foreign exchange market. Specifically, the Treasury announced a plan to sell up to $10 billion in official obligations denominated in DM, SFr (Swiss francs), and ¥. The funds raised would be used, as needed, to support the US$ in the foreign exchange market.

These securities, dubbed "Carter bonds" after then President Jimmy Carter, were the first *public* borrowing by the United States in a foreign currency. In October 1961, the U.S. Treasury began issuing securities denominated in foreign currencies, but these were nonmarketable and offered only to foreign central banks.* Other countries had often issued sovereign debt in foreign currencies— Swedish debt in DM, Italian debt in ECU, and Mexican debt in US$ are only three of hundreds of examples. But the United States had never taken this course.

In December 1978, the U.S. Treasury issued (through the Bundesbank) $1.6 billion worth of DM-denominated notes. The three-year tranche carried a 5.95 percent interest rate and the four-year maturity was issued at 6.20 percent. Comparable securities denominated in US$ would

have cost the U.S. Treasury about 9.30 percent. In December 1978, the $/DM rate was about $0.55/DM. But when the Treasury repaid its DM debts in late 1981 and 1982, it paid only $0.40 to $0.45/DM as the US$ had strengthened considerably.

In January 1979, the U.S. Treasury issued (through the Swiss National Bank) $1.2 billion worth of SFr-denominated notes. The two-and-one-half-year tranche was sold to yield 2.35 percent and a four-year maturity was issued at 2.65 percent. Comparable securities denominated in US$ would have cost the U.S. Treasury about 9.50 percent. At the time of issue, the $/SFr rate was about $0.60/SFr. But when the Treasury repaid its SFr debts in July 1981 and January 1983, it paid only $0.45 to $0.50/SFr.

Both the DM and SFr transactions were clear moneymakers for the U.S. Treasury. The Treasury was speculating in the foreign exchange market in order to send a strong signal. But one could argue that the Treasury was doing so partly on the basis of "inside information" because it knew what macroeconomic policies had been set and believed (more than market participants) that these policies would be executed leading to a stronger US$. The strategy is similar to that of a corporation that repurchases its own equity shares in the marketplace on the grounds that the shares are undervalued by investors.

---

*Federal Reserve Bank of Chicago, *International Letter,* No. 385 and No. 387, Dec. 22, 1978, and Jan. 19, 1979.

As we pointed out in Chapters 1 and 2, central banks from many emerging markets lost substantial amounts in the 1990s by using US$ reserves to buy up domestic currency, which then depreciated by large amounts. Moreover, several European central banks incurred substantial losses as the European Monetary System broke down in 1992. These losses were transferred directly to private currency speculators (see Chapter 17).

Foreign Exchange Market Products and Activities

Spot and Forward Contracts

The most well-known products of the foreign exchange market are the spot contract and the forward contract. A **spot contract** represents a binding commitment for an exchange

TABLE 3.3 Dimensions of the Foreign Exchange Market

Daily Volume of Trading by Contract Type (in Billions of US$)

Contract Type	April 1989 Turnover (% Share)	April 1992 Turnover (% Share)	April 1995 Turnover (% Share)	April 1998 Turnover[b] (% Share)
Total	718[a] (100%)	1,076[a] (100%)	1,572 (100%)	1,441 (100%)
Spot	427 (69.5)	541 (50.7)	680 (43.3)	577 (40.0)
Outright forward	22 (3.6)	70 (6.6)	115 (7.3)	130 (9.0)
Foreign exchange swaps	165 (26.9)	457 (42.8)	777 (49.4)	734 (51.0)
Maturity				
$t \leq 7$ days	NA	294 (64.3)	552 (71)	529 (72)
7 days $< t \leq 1$ year	NA	158 (34.5)	218 (28)	192 (26)
$t > 1$ year	NA	5.5 (1.2)	8 (1)	10 (1)

Notes:

a. Sum of components do not add to total, as in original survey.

b. 1998 data are net of local and cross-border double-counting.

Source: Bank for International Settlements, *Central Bank Survey of Foreign Exchange and Derivatives Market Activity,* May 1996 (Tables 2-A, 2-B, 2-C, and 2-D); Bank for International Settlements, *Central Bank Survey of Foreign Exchange Activity,* March 1993 (Table 5-A), and Bank for International Settlements, *Central Bank Survey of Foreign Exchange and Derivatives Market Activity,* May 1999 (Table E-1).

of funds, with normal settlement and delivery of bank balances following in two business days, or one day in the case of North American currencies.

A **forward contract** is an agreement made today for an obligatory exchange of funds at some specified time in the future. The most common maturities for forward contracts are 1, 2, 3, 6, and 12 months. The settlement date for an *n*-month forward contract is determined by first determining the spot settlement date, and then picking the same day of the month *n* months forward.[5] The buyer (or seller) of a forward contract may settle his or her position by taking (or making) delivery of foreign exchange, or making a cash settlement based on the difference between the original forward rate and the present spot rate. Nonstandard maturities (such as 37 days or 81 days) are available, but transaction costs make them more expensive. No cash changes hands when a forward contract is arranged or at any time until the settlement date. Corporate customers gain access to the forward market on the basis of their credit standing; typically, there are no margin or collateral requirements.[6]

Data on the volume of trading by contract type are shown in Table 3.3. In 1989, and very likely in most earlier years, spot contracts accounted for the vast majority of foreign exchange trading. But the pace of spot trading slowed, measuring only 40 percent of all foreign exchange trading in 1998.

Forward contracts, labeled as "outright forwards" in Table 3.3, make up a small but growing fraction of foreign exchange trading volume, accounting for 9 percent of daily volume in 1998. Forward contracts typically involve a bank and a corporate counterparty and are used by corporations to manage their exposures to foreign exchange risk.

---

[5]One exception to this rule is that settlement cannot move forward into the next month. A one-month contract on January 27, 1992 (a Monday), should settle on February 29 (a Saturday). Since February 29 is not a business day and the next business day would be in March, settlement occurs on Friday, February 28.

[6]These terms are different than those of futures contracts, described in Chapter 11.

Foreign Exchange Swaps

The final category of contract, foreign exchange swaps, is less well-known but nevertheless represents a vital element in the market. A **foreign exchange swap** is the simultaneous sale of a currency for spot delivery and purchase of that currency for forward delivery.[7] Because each foreign exchange transaction involves two currencies and two "legs"—a sale of € is a purchase of dollars and a sale of dollars is a purchase of €—a foreign exchange swap can also be described as a simultaneous borrowing of one currency and lending of another currency. A dealer who owns spot € and then enters into a foreign exchange swap—selling € spot and buying it back for forward delivery—is managing the maturity structure of his or her currency position. We will describe the mechanics and use of foreign exchange swaps in greater detail later in this chapter.

Foreign exchange swaps have always been a major part of foreign exchange trading, especially among commercial bank dealers. In Table 3.3, we see that foreign exchange swaps have grown from 26.9 percent of all trading in 1989 to 51.0 percent in 1998. Foreign exchange swaps are typically short-term contracts with 72 percent having a maturity of less than one week, and the remainder having maturities of less than one year.

Types of Trading Activities: Speculation and Arbitrage

Trading activities link together the various segments of the foreign exchange market. In general, trading enhances the operational efficiency of the market and contributes to consistent pricing across market segments.

Speculation.   **Speculative transactions** expose the individual, trader, or corporation to price risk from foreign exchange rate changes. However, speculation entails more than simply the assumption of a risky position. An individual may hold a portfolio of risky securities that are selected naively to match his or her risk preferences. This may not indicate any desire to trade the portfolio actively, exploiting inside information, superior trading, or timing skills. **Speculation** under our definition implies financial transactions undertaken when an individual's expectations differ from the market's expectation.[8]

Arbitrage.   In contrast, **arbitrage** is the simultaneous, or nearly simultaneous, purchase of securities in one market for sale in another market with the expectation of a risk-free profit.

Spatial Arbitrage.   **Spatial arbitrage** suggests arbitrage between segments of the foreign exchange market that are physically separated. For example, purchasing € in Frankfurt at a rate of 0.66 £/€ and selling € in London at a rate of 0.67 £/€ illustrates a profitable spatial arbitrage. Arbitrage between the interbank forward market and a foreign exchange futures market (see Chapter 11) is another example of spatial arbitrage.

Because not all currency traders are housed in a centralized location, it is unlikely that they will quote exactly the same prices at the same instant. These price differences across traders are known as **price dispersion.** In a geographically dispersed market like foreign exchange, some price dispersion is inevitable, reflecting the cost of searching for

---

[7]This is *not* a capital market swap of the sort discussed in Chapter 13.
[8]See Kohlhagen (1979).

favorable prices and the uncertainty that expected arbitrage profits may disappear before all transactions can be completed.

Triangular Arbitrage.   Ignoring transaction costs, the prices for any three currencies (for example, U.S. dollars, British pounds, and Canadian dollars) must be consistent with the following relationship:

$$\frac{\text{US\$}}{£} = \frac{\text{US\$}}{\text{C\$}} \times \frac{\text{C\$}}{£} \tag{3.1}$$

Equation (3.1), known as **triangular parity,** applies to spot rates as well as to all forward rates. For example, if the U.S. dollar price of Canadian dollars is $0.70/C$ and the Canadian dollar price of £ is C$2.30/£, then the U.S. dollar price of £ must be $1.61/£.

If equation (3.1) did not hold, then profit opportunities would be available based on **triangular arbitrage.** For example, when:

$$S(\text{US\$}/£) > S(\text{US\$}/\text{C\$}) \times S(\text{C\$}/£) \tag{3.2}$$

triangular arbitrage profits may be captured by using US$ to buy C$ and then £, and then selling those £ for US$.

When transaction costs are present, each exchange rate has both a bid and an ask price. The arbitrageur buys at the dealer's ask price and sells at the dealer's bid price. In our example, arbitrage profits are present when

$$S(\text{US\$}/£,\text{bid}) > S(\text{US\$}/\text{C\$},\text{ask}) \times S(\text{C\$}/£,\text{ask}) \tag{3.3}$$

In our triangular arbitrage example, the C$/£ rate is called a **cross-rate,** a term used to describe exchange rates between non-US$ currencies. In a practical sense, the market for the direct exchange of C$ and £ does not exist. The C$/£ rate is calculated from the **direct rates** for $/C$ and $/£ quoted in these actively traded markets. A trader with C$ who wants to hold £ will actually engage in two transactions: (1) an exchange of C$ for US$, and (2) an exchange of US$ for £. That these two transactions are preferred to a direct exchange between C$ and £ suggests that the transaction costs must be lower. The time required to complete two transactions may also be shorter than the time required to arrange a direct trade of C$ for £, suggesting that the *liquidity risk* is smaller by trading through the US$.

The incentives for trading through the US$ would be more striking, for example, were we to consider, say, Mexican importers (with pesos) and Swedish exporters (expecting krona). Both parties would find it easier to trade their domestic currencies against the US$ in order to obtain a third currency. These examples illustrate the role of the US$ as a **vehicle currency** expediting the flow of transactions between smaller countries whose currencies have more limited circulation. The examples also suggest that the volume of US$ transactions in the foreign exchange market may be much larger than the U.S. share of world trade or the share of trade denominated in US$.

The data in Table 3.4 show that the US$ comprised 87 percent of the volume of transactions in the foreign exchange market in 1998, down from a 90 percent share in the 1989 survey and still higher percentages in earlier years. A 100 percent share would mean that the US$ was involved in every foreign exchange market transaction. The data imply that 13 percent of the transaction volume in 1998 did not involve the US$. Direct exchanges between the DM/¥, £/¥, DM/£, and the DM against other European Union currencies constitute the bulk of this 13 percent of the market representing "true" cross-rates.

Table 3.4 also shows that 52 percent of the transactions in 1998 involved either the DM, French franc, or another EMU currency. Will this market share rise or fall as a

TABLE 3.4 Dimensions of the Foreign Exchange Market

Daily Volume of Trading by Currency of Denomination (in Billions of US$)

Currency	April 1989 Turnover (% Share)	April 1992 Turnover (% Share)	April 1995 Turnover (% Share)	April 1998 Turnover (% Share)
U.S. dollar	90%	82%	83%	87%
Deutsche mark	27	40	37	30
Japanese yen	27	23	24	21
Pound sterling	15	14	10	11
Swiss franc	10	9	7	7
French franc	2	4	8	5
Canadian dollar	1	3	3	4
Australian dollar	2	2	3	3
ECU and other EMS	4	12	15	17
Other	19	11	10	15
Total	200	200	200	200

Note: Percentage shares sum to 200% because two currencies are involved in each transaction.

Source: Bank for International Settlements, *Central Bank Survey of Foreign Exchange and Derivatives Market Activity,* May 1996 (Table F-3); and Bank for International Settlements, *Central Bank Survey of Foreign Exchange and Derivatives Market Activity,* May 1999 (Table E-1).

result of the EMU? With the introduction of the euro in 1999, all of the cross-rate trades between the DM and other European legacy currencies ceased, which points to a decrease in market share. However, the share of transactions conducted in euros will rise if the euro acts as a vehicle currency in some foreign exchange transactions. Consider an exchange between Canadian dollars and British pounds. This transaction could be intermediated through the US$, as in equation (3.1a):

$$\frac{C\$}{£} = \frac{C\$}{US\$} \times \frac{US\$}{£} \tag{3.1a}$$

or through the euro, as in equation (3.1b):

$$\frac{C\$}{£} = \frac{C\$}{€} \times \frac{€}{£} \tag{3.1b}$$

Whether the US$ or the € plays the role of vehicle currency in this transaction depends on the depth and liquidity of the various markets. Even though C$/€ and €/£ markets have developed, both the C$/US$ and US$/£ markets have existed for many years. The US$ markets are well developed, with narrow spreads, which suggests that the US$ will continue as the vehicle currency in this transaction. But certainly the euro may play the vehicle currency role in some transactions, or grow into that role over time.

Covered Interest Arbitrage. Last, **covered interest arbitrage** describes capital flows that seek risk-free profits based on differences between the forward exchange premium and the relative rate of interest in domestic and foreign currency. Covered arbitrage transactions ensure the consistent pricing of spot rates, forward rates, and interest rates on securities that are alike in all respects except currency of denomination. Covered arbitrage transactions are profitable when the **interest rate parity** relationship is violated, as we examine in Chapter 5.

FIGURE 3.2   The Relationship between Spot and Forward Exchange Rates

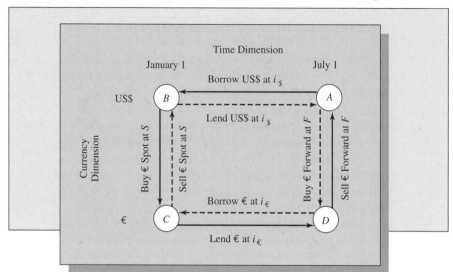

Note: A forward purchase of € (equivalent to a forward sale of US$) is shown by the arrow *AD*. This outright forward contract can be replicated by borrowing US$ (arrow *AB*), buying € in the spot market (arrow *BC*), and lending the € (arrow *CD*). The maturity of the forward contracts is identical to the maturity of the borrowing and lending contracts. A forward sale of the € can be described by reversing the direction of the arrows.

The Relationship between Spot and Forward Contracts

We now consider the relationship between spot and forward exchange rates, and the importance of this relationship for foreign exchange market products. Define the spot rate at time t (S_t) as the number of dollars per foreign currency ($/FC), and the forward rate at time t for delivery in n periods ($F_{t,n}$) also in $/FC. In Figure 3.2, we show the time dimension across two columns and the currency dimension across two rows.

Consider the case in which a manager wishes to own € on July 1, represented as point D in Figure 3.2. The manager has two alternative strategies to reach his goal. The first strategy has the manager calling a bank to arrange a forward purchase of €. We can represent this transaction by line segment AD, and a price of $F_{t,6}$ representing today's forward rate for delivery in six months. Alternatively, the manager could borrow US$ for six months (line segment AB and interest rate $i_{\$,6}$), use the borrowed US$ to purchase € at the spot exchange rate (line segment BC and price S_t), and then lend these € for six months (line segment CD and interest rate $i_{€,6}$). As the three contracts result in the same ultimate cash flows, we can refer to them as a **replicating portfolio.**[9] Using the replicating portfolio, the price of one € for delivery on July 1 has three components: $1/(1 + i_{€,6}/2)$, representing the present value of one €, S, the US$ cost of each €, and $(1 + i_{\$,6}/2)$ representing the cost of each borrowed US$. In the absence of transaction costs, taxes, or default, the price of the two alternatives must be identical:

$$F_{t,6} = S_t \frac{(1 + i_{\$,6}/2)}{(1 + i_{€,6}/2)} \tag{3.4}$$

---

[9]A forward sale of € for July 1 (line segment DA) could be replicated by reversing the three transactions: Borrow €, sell € in the spot market, and invest $.

Equation (3.4) shows that in the absence of transaction costs, taxes, or other barriers, a forward contract is equivalent to a spot contract, combined with borrowing and lending in two currencies. A forward contract is a type of **derivative security,** because the forward price is derived from the spot price and the borrowing and lending rates.

Earlier in this chapter, we defined the simultaneous borrowing and lending of bank deposits (line segments *AB* and *CD*) as a foreign exchange swap. In Table 3.3, we saw that swaps, particularly those with a maturity of one year or less, accounted for 51 percent of foreign exchange trading volume in 1998 while outright forwards accounted for only 9.0 percent of trading volume. These data suggest that most forward positions in the foreign exchange market are built using spot contracts and swaps.

Another implication of equation (3.4) is that forward contracts are *redundant;* that is, if forward contracts were suddenly outlawed, private agents could adjust by using spot contracts in addition to borrowing and lending of deposits. The existence of outright forward contracts can be explained by the reduction of transaction costs or increase in speed that they permit. This is a fundamental rather than a trivial result. In many cases, we will be able to show that a new financial product can be replicated by some combination of more elementary contracts. This finding has immediate applications: pricing a product, arbitraging a new product against other contracts, and laying off the risks in a new product.

The formulation of equation (3.4), in particular, isolating the forward rate on the left-hand side of the equation, is arbitrary. We could just as well have written:

$$(1 + i_{\$,6}/2) = F_{t,6}\frac{(1 + i_{\text{€},6}/2)}{S_t} \tag{3.5}$$

or

$$(1 + i_{\text{€},6}/2) = S_t\frac{(1 + i_{\$,6}/2)}{F_{t,6}} \tag{3.6}$$

Each variation represents an application that we will examine.

Synthetic Forwards.   Equation (3.4) indicates that if a forward contract did not exist, it might be replicated by using a spot contract combined with borrowing and lending. Forward contracts may be difficult to obtain for "exotic" currencies. But equation (3.4) offers an explanation: When controls are present on domestic borrowing and lending, it will be difficult for dealers to build forward contracts or to lay off the risks of their position. On the other hand, equation (3.4) suggests that as domestic money markets are liberalized, forward markets for currency should appear in the marketplace as "innovative" products.[10]

Another application of equation 3.4 is the creation of forward contracts with longer maturities than usual—say, 3, 4, 5, or perhaps 10 years. By combining a spot contract with fixed-rate, *n*-period borrowing and lending in the two currencies, an *n*-period forward exchange contract can be constructed. For example, assume that the spot rate is $1.05/€, and five-year interest rates in US$ and € are 6.0 percent and 4.5 percent, respectively. Ignoring transaction costs, a five-year forward exchange rate could be created at a price:[11]

---

[10]Examples of this are the development of Korean won and Greek drachma forward markets in the 1980s. See Frankel and MacArthur (1988) for a list of countries with forward currency markets.

[11]We assume zero-coupon interest rates to avoid dealing with intervening coupons in the securities. Intervening payments will be considered in the discussion of currency swaps in Chapter 13. See Antl (1983) for alternative approaches for computing the cost of long-term forwards.

$$F_{t,5 \text{ years}} = S_t \left[\frac{(1 + i_{\$,5 \text{ years}})}{(1 + i_{\euro,5 \text{ years}})} \right]^5 \tag{3.7}$$

$$F_{t,5 \text{ years}} = \$1.05 \left[\frac{(1 + .06)}{(1 + .045)} \right]^5 = \$1.1276$$

In the early 1980s, trading in longer-term forward contracts began to appear. An example of a page of quotations of long-term forward contracts is presented in Box 3.2.

Box 3.2

Example of Reuters Screen Page: Citibank Long-Dated Forward Rates, February 22, 1985

0949 CITIBANK N.Y. LONG DATED F.X. 212 207-3142 TX 66184 CILD

	1 YEAR	*2 YEAR*	*3 YEAR*	*4 YEAR*	*5 YEAR*	*10 YEAR*
STG	215/200	200/125	−100/+100	−50/+300	−50/+350	−20/+10
SF	1300/1250	2900/2600	4600/4100	5950/5550	7150/6550	
DM	1250/1230	2700/2500	4200/3900	5300/4900	6400/5900	102/90
JY	1040/1010	2250/2050	3300/3000	4400/4000	5400/5000	101/89
FFR	1225/1375	1800/2400	2200/3500	2600/4600	3000/5000	
HFL	1120/1090	2400/2200	3600/3200	4700/4200	5800/5200	
BFC	66/76	20/110	−20/−130	−60/+150	−220/+170	
BFF	49/59	10/80	−50/+90	−100/+110	−170/+110	
CAN	210/240	225/275	225/300	225/300	225/300	150/450

FEB 22 FRIDAY MORNING   INDICATIONS ONLY   S2-K2-2 REUTER MONITOR   1216

The entries on the sample Reuters page (above) are "swap points." To determine the outright forward rates, the swap points are added to the spot rates (bid and ask) if the swap points are in a rising sequence, the swap points are subtracted from the spot rates (bid and ask) if the swap points are in a falling sequence. For example:

DM:	*1 Year*	*5 Year*
Spot rates (DM/$)	3.3400/3.3420	3.3400/3.3420
Swap points	.1250/0.1230	.6400/0.5900
Outright forward rate	3.2150/3.2190	2.7000/2.7520
Bid/Ask spread	~ 0.12%	~ 1.93%
% Forward premium ≡ (F-S)/S	~ 3.68%	~ 18.38% (3.43%/year)

FFR:	*1 Year*	*5 Year*
Spot rates (FFR/$)	10.4000/10.4020	10.4000/10.4020
Swap points	.1225/ 0.1375	.3000/ 0.5000
Outright forward rate	10.5225/10.5395	10.7000/10.9020
Bid/Ask spread	~ 0.16%	~ 1.89%
% Forward premium ≡ (F-S)/S	~ 1.26%	~ 3.86% (0.76%/year)

FIGURE 3.3   **Long-Term Foreign Exchange Contracts and Counterparty Risk**

Five-Year Contracts Entered Into on 12/31/00, Maturing on 12/31/05

Customer A		Countibank		Customer B	
A/R on 12/31/05	A/P on 12/31/05	A/R on 12/31/05	A/P on 12/31/05	A/R on 12/31/05	A/P on 12/31/05
€ 89,500,000	$102,000,000	$102,000,000	€ 89,500,000	$100,000,000	€ 89,500,000
from Countibank	to Countibank	from Customer A	to Customer A	from Countibank	to Countibank
		A/R on 12/31/05	A/P on 12/31/05		
		€ 89,500,000	$100,000,000		
		from Customer B	to Customer B		

Note: Countibank sells € at $1.1397 (or $102,000,000/€89,500,000); Countibank buys € at $1.1173 (or $100,000,000/€89,500,000).

Pricing Long-Term Forward Contracts.   While equation (3.7) suggests an exact pricing formula for long-term forwards, other factors may influence actual long-term forward rates. John Hilley, Carl Beidleman, and James Greenleaf (1981) found that bid-ask spreads of actual (or outright) forward contracts exceeded the bid-ask spreads of synthetic forwards constructed using spot rates and long-term borrowing and lending. The authors offered several explanations for their results. First, as long-term forward markets were thin and illiquid, traders faced risks that they attempted to pass along to customers in the way of high spreads. Second, long-term contracts exposed the bank to considerably greater credit risks. A bank with a "square book"—that is, no net position by virtue of equal and offsetting contracts—is still exposed to **counterparty risk,** meaning the risk of default on the terms and conditions of a contract.

Consider a hypothetical example in which Countibank sells a five-year forward € contract to customer A and purchases a five-year forward € contract from customer B. In Figure 3.3, these forward contracts are shown as accounts receivable (A/R) and accounts payable (A/P). If there is no default, Countibank earns the spread between bid and ask prices on the five-year contracts. In our example, the profit is $2 million earned at the end of year 5. If customer A defaults at the end of year 2, the impact on Countibank depends on whether they retain the "right-of-offset." With the right-of-offset, customer A's failure to pay $ to Countibank relieves Countibank of the obligation to pay € to customer A. In this case, Countibank must replace its contract with A at current market prices. Countibank will incur a loss (or gain) equal to the percentage difference between the original five-year forward rate and the three-year forward rate used to replace it.[12] However, if Countibank does not have the right-of-offset, then customer A's inability to pay Countibank in full does not relieve Countibank of its obligation to pay A in full. In this case, Countibank may incur a 100 percent loss on its contract if it pays out € 89.5 million, yet as an unsecured creditor of A, it receives nothing in return.

Another reason may explain the reluctance of Countibank to quote more narrow spreads on five-year forward contracts, *and* the acceptance of these spreads by customers A and B. Even though Countibank has a square book, BIS capital adequacy

---

[12]It seems unlikely that customer A would default on a contract that produced profits for itself and losses for Countibank.

guidelines (see Chapters 16 and 17) require a capital commitment from Countibank to support its exposure to counterparty risk. The magnitude of that capital commitment, which may change over time as the risk changes, will determine whether or not the $2 million profit is a competitive return.[13] Thus, Countibank might set a *higher* price than implied by equation 3.7 in order to cover these costs.

Customer B might be willing to pay a higher price for the outright forward offered by Countibank. B's alternative is to create its own five-year forward by borrowing € for five years, swapping the proceeds into US$ and investing them for five years. Fresh borrowing reduces B's borrowing capacity, making it unavailable for other projects that may have a higher rate of return. If B has scarce borrowing capacity, the forward contract from Countibank may leave B free to borrow for other purposes.[14]

Synthetic Dollar Securities.   Equation (3.5) suggests that a dollar-denominated security could be constructed by combining a foreign currency denominated security with a forward contract of similar maturity and a spot contract. The synthetic security could be either an asset or a liability. Borrowing US$ (line segment *AB* in Figure 3.2) is equivalent to borrowing € (line segment *DC*) combined with a forward € purchase (line segment *AD*) and a spot € sale (line segment *CB*). A US$ asset would reverse the above transactions.

For example, suppose that U.S. and Canadian three-month Treasury bills earn 5.68 percent and 10.00 percent per year, respectively, and spot and forward currency rates are $0.8679/$C and $0.8598/$C, respectively. The combination of a Canadian Treasury bill with spot and forward currency contracts (a combination which as an asset we will call a currency-hedged position in Chapter 15) produces a synthetic US$ yield of:

$$(1 + i_{\$,3}/4) = \frac{F_{t,3}\,(1 + i_{\$C,3}/4)}{S_t}$$

$$= \frac{0.8598 \times (1 + .10/4)}{0.8679}$$

$$= 1.0154$$

$$\Rightarrow i_{\$,3} \quad = 0.0616, \text{ or } 6.16\% \text{ per annum}$$

In this example, the synthetic security offers a 0.48 percent yield advantage over the U.S. Treasury bill. Purchase of the synthetic security could involve additional transaction costs and exposure to default risk on the forward contract. The synthetic also could entail a loss of liquidity relative to a U.S. Treasury bill. However, liquidity might not be a prime consideration in this transaction when, for example, undertaken by a US$-based money market mutual fund seeking yield enhancement.

The above process could be put into reverse, creating a synthetic dollar loan from a foreign currency liability coupled with spot and forward currency contracts, a combination that will be labeled a "swap-driven" loan in Chapter 13. The strategy behind a swap-driven loan is to search for low borrowing costs in foreign currency which, when covered against exchange risk, produce costs below direct dollar-based funding.

Synthetic € Securities.   From the above examples, the replication of a € security follows easily. Borrowing € (line segment *DC* in Figure 3.2) is equivalent to borrowing

---

[13]A bank might attempt to impose a front-end fee to offset some of these costs, depending on market conditions.

[14]Most likely, A also has a foreign exchange line at Countibank, which we assume is underutilized.

US$ (line segment *AB*) combined with a forward € sale (line segment *DA*) and a spot € purchase (line segment *CB*). A € asset reverses the above transactions. Other non-US$ securities could be replicated using spot and forward contracts in these currencies.

For example, consider the case of a German manager who requires DM funds on a short-term basis. However, until the early 1990s, no DM commercial paper market existed comparable to the US$ commercial paper market. The manager could create synthetic DM commercial paper by borrowing US$ commercial paper (assume at 6.0 percent), selling the proceeds in the spot market for DM (assume at $0.5712), and buying enough US$ forward (assume at $0.5664) to cover the repayment of the outstanding commercial paper plus interest. The synthetic DM cost of these transactions would be:[15]

$$(1 + i_{DM,3}/4) = \frac{S_t(1 + i_{\$,3}/4)}{F_{t,3}}$$

$$= \frac{0.5712 \times (1 + .06/4)}{0.5664}$$

$$= 1.0236$$

$$\Rightarrow i_{DM,3} = 0.0944, \text{ or } 9.44\% \text{ per annum}$$

The manager would compare this cost of funding with other short-term alternatives, perhaps in the Eurocurrency market.

In the same fashion, a portfolio manager might want a Swiss Treasury bill as an asset, but none exist. A U.S. Treasury bill combined with spot and forward currency contracts would produce an asset free of default risk (except for the forward contract) and effectively denominated in Swiss francs.

The Foreign Exchange Market Setting

Comparing the Foreign Exchange Market with Other Markets

The foreign exchange market is an excellent example of a dispersed, broker-dealer market. Trading takes place 24 hours per day between banks located around the world. Bank traders act as **market makers;** they have financial capital committed to trading, they take positions, and they are exposed to the risks of price changes. In comparison, other major financial markets are centralized in a single physical place, such as the New York Stock Exchange (NYSE) using a specialist in an auction market format, and the Chicago Mercantile Exchange (CME) using an open-outcry system among many pit traders.

The physical differences among these markets correspond to important economic differences. In centralized markets, learning the price of a security is relatively easy; it is printed on the consolidated tape of all transactions on the NYSE, or posted above the floor of the CME. The record of these transactions is transmitted electronically worldwide. By funneling all orders to a single place, the system hopes to achieve efficient order execution as well as a kind of market democracy—anonymous orders that

---

[15]The calculation is approximate because it does not take into account delivery and settlement conventions in the commercial paper and foreign exchange markets.

are executed at the best available prices.[16] The NYSE and the CME are relatively transparent markets; the term *transparent* refers to the ease with which participants can see actual market prices and learn about other important market details—such as trading volume, insider transactions, block trading, and open interest—that are commonly reported in regulated public markets.

In a geographically dispersed market, it is relatively difficult to learn the best available price of foreign exchange. There are nearly 1,200 trading banks in the world and perhaps as many as 10,000 traders. At 10:00 A.M. in New York, more than 900 banks in North America and Europe may be open for business.[17] How can a trader be confident that he or she is locating the best prices amid this sea of counterparties? Electronic screens are used to display foreign exchange quotations for each of these banks, but the prices are usually "for indications only," meaning that actual transactions may or may not be possible at these prices. In this dispersed market setting, the role of **brokers**—agents who canvass the market for buyers and sellers, thereby reducing the economic costs of search—is very important. Because search costs are present, some price dispersion is possible.[18]

As trades are concluded, no consolidated record of all prices or transactions is kept. The foreign exchange market is said to lack transparency, because it is relatively difficult for *all* market participants to see actual market prices and learn about other potentially important aspects of trading in the market. Historically, this lack of transparency has given an advantage to larger market makers. New technology that increases transparency may threaten this advantage, as we describe in more detail later in this chapter.

In addition to being a centralized market, the CME and other futures exchanges are often noted for the *standardized* features of the contracts that are traded.[19] Futures contracts are often standardized according to the size of the contract, maturity date, delivery features, and so on. In addition, futures contracts are standardized with respect to price (there is one price per contract at any moment) and, by implication, the contract is also standardized with respect to its counterparty risk. Because all buyers or sellers of a futures contract have the exchange's **clearinghouse** as their counterparty, this risk is standardized.[20]

In contrast, the foreign exchange market is known for its ability to *customize* the features of a transaction. A buyer can enter into spot contracts for any size and forward contracts for any maturity date. However, because of market dispersion, foreign exchange market transactions that occur simultaneously may be booked at different prices; they will also have different counterparties and different counterparty risks. When bank failure is a concern, knowing the identity of the counterparties and their credit rating gains importance. Because the credit quality of all market makers may not be identical, the quality of their quotes also may not be identical. These factors also contribute to price dispersion.[21]

---

[16]Fragmentation of the NYSE, as a result of off-exchange, upstairs trading, or trading in a 144a market (see Chapter 10) could threaten efficient order execution. The same would apply to pit traders who have the flexibility to trade for their own accounts in advance of executing orders as agents for their customers.

[17]*Global Dealers Directory,* Republic National Bank of New York (1994).

[18]See Garbade and Silber (1976) on price dispersion in the U.S. government securities market.

[19]The markets also differ with respect to regulation. The foreign exchange market (aside from the capital adequacy rules we will discuss in Chapter 17) is largely a self-regulating market. There are no rules regarding information disclosure and no official trading halts when rumors are circulating.

[20]If there were more than one counterparty with differing risks, there would be more than one price at any moment. See Chapter 11 for more details on the clearinghouse.

[21]Market makers who are willing to trade in larger amounts and at prices close to their posted prices offer higher "quality" quotes. Precision in the administrative and back-office aspects of trading are also a part of "quality."

FIGURE 3.4   Structure of the Foreign Exchange Market

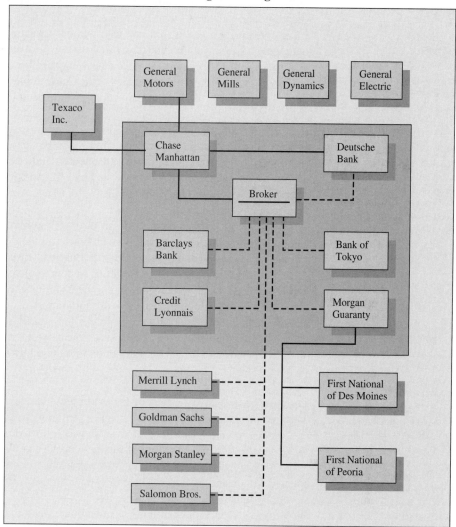

Note: A foreign exchange dealer at Chase Manhattan may execute transactions (indicated by solid lines) by direct dealing with another bank (say, Deutsche Bank) or using a broker. The broker collects quotations from other dealing banks and other financial institutions (indicated by broken lines). The traditional interbank market is in darker shading at the center of the diagram. Other participants are in the retail sector for at least some or all of their transactions. Smaller regional banks (lower right) and corporate customers (at top) execute foreign transactions through major banks and do not have direct access to foreign exchange brokers.

Tracking Foreign Exchange Transactions

A diagram representing the traditional structure of the foreign exchange market appears in Figure 3.4. We will use this diagram to visualize the two main segments of the market—the interbank market and the retail market—and their interrelationships.

The Interbank Market—Classic Connections.   Until 1992, a dealer at one bank (say, Chase Manhattan) had two ways to execute a purchase of spot currency. One way, known as "direct dealing," involves a direct telephone contact with a dealer at another bank. In Figure 3.4, this is indicated by a solid line connecting Chase Manhattan and Deutsche Bank. The second approach has the Chase trader telephone a foreign exchange (voice) broker, indicated by a solid line connecting Chase and the brokerage firm. The broker conveys two prices, bid and ask, without revealing the names of either bank counterparty. By convention, the Chase dealer may "take either price"; that is, buy at the ask price or sell at the bid price, or the dealer may decline to trade.

Direct dealing has its advantages. The Chase trader will save the commission charged by a broker. He or she may acquire some useful information from the other dealer about market developments or learn something about the other dealer's position from the way the dealer "shades" his price. If the Chase trader uses a broker, the broker's commission must be paid. But the trader may be offered a superior price if the broker has performed a thorough search of the market, indicated by the dotted lines linking the broker with other bank traders.[22] If the broker's quotation is accepted, the broker reveals the name of the counterparty to the Chase trader, so that the electronic transfer of deposits can be carried out.

In the 1980s, a refinement to direct dealing was introduced into the market. So-called automatic dealing systems permit direct communication of transaction prices, transaction quantities, and other market information between traders around the world. In the Reuters Dealing 2000-1 system, up to four "conversations" can be held at the same time on the same screen, permitting the trader to select the best transaction available among a small group of dealers (still short of polling *all* active dealers worldwide). Traditional telephone-based direct dealing is necessarily sequential, which introduces the risk that favorable prices will be lost as time passes. Automatic dealing systems also function to enter each accepted transaction into the trader's book and the bank's bookkeeping system.

The Interbank Market—Recent Innovations.   The foreign exchange brokerage industry received a jolt in 1992 with the introduction by Reuters of its automated brokerage system, *Reuters Dealing 2000-2*. This was followed in 1993 by two competitors: *MINEX,* backed by a consortium of Japanese banks and Dow Jones Telerate, and *Electronic Broking Service,* underwritten by Quotron and a consortium of U.S. and European banks.[23] Minex and EBS have since merged to form the EBS Partnership. The Reuters system permits dealers to enter their live prices into the system for broadcast. Prices appear on a screen as anonymous live quotations. Once a price is hit, the system checks for mutual credit availability between the two counterparties and completes the transaction with ticket writing and confirmations.

While these automated trading systems have only recently begun operation, they have already captured a substantial share of the traditional voice brokerage market. Data for spot trading in the United States show that the share of transactions handled through brokers rose from 34 percent in 1992 to 41 percent in 1998. In 1992, there were no electronic brokers with automated order-matching systems. But by 1998, these had captured $46 billion in daily volume, or 75 percent of the brokered transactions. The role of brokers in the overall U.S. foreign exchange market has grown smaller, around 23.6 percent in 1998, compared to nearly 50 percent in 1980. In London, the proportion of all foreign exchange transactions handled by brokers fell to 27 percent in 1998, from 35 percent in 1995. But as in the United States, electronic brokers are gaining a larger market share,

---

[22]The broker conveys the highest bid price available and the lowest ask price, a combination known as the "inside spread."

[23]See James Blitz, "Foreign Exchange Dealers Enter the 21st Century," *Financial Times,* Sept. 13 (1993).

about 41 percent of all brokered transactions, in the London market.[24] The EBS Partnership claims to be the leading electronic foreign exchange broker, in use at 800 banks and with a daily spot volume of $90 billion, or about 16 percent of the overall market.[25]

Another innovation affecting the foreign exchange market is the development of private systems for clearing and settlement. Until the early 1990s, the hundreds of thousands of transactions that occur daily were settled on a bilateral basis, with bilateral netting agreements in some cases.[26] With 1,000 trading banks there are nearly 500,000 pairs of banks, and each could have a trading relationship in one or more currencies. These paired arrangements expose the system to substantial liquidity and credit risks, and raise the transaction costs of clearing and settlement.

A multilateral netting system with banks clearing against a central clearinghouse substantially reduces transaction costs and liquidity risks. And if the agreements with the clearinghouse are structured to legally take the place of the original contracts between the trading banks, then the credit risk across the entire system is also reduced.[27] The leading multilateral netting firm is FXNET, owned by a consortium of 14 of the world's largest banks with most of the world's largest FX dealers on its client list.[28] Analysis by FXNET shows that its multilateral netting system can reduce daily settlement risks by more than 50 percent and gross payments by as much as 84 percent.

Corporate Foreign Exchange Trading—The Classic Relationship.   A corporate customer (say, General Motors) conducts its foreign exchange transactions through a commercial bank. The customer can often view the screens of various bank trading rooms and then decide to call a bank (or banks) to request a "live" quotation. Large customers that trade frequently might use an automated trading system (such as Reuters Dealing 2000-1) instead of the telephone to obtain quotations and execute transactions. The corporate customer would very likely contact the bank's corporate FX trader rather than the bank's interbank trader. The corporate trader would be aware of such factors as the customer's trading limit, trading style, and price sensitivity. The corporate trader asks whether the customer wishes to buy or sell and in what amount and then offers a quotation. This is a one-way quotation, instead of the two-way quotations that are the practice for transactions among interbank dealers. The corporate trader's price will reflect the interbank rate "plus X" if the customer is buying (or "minus X" if the customer is selling) where "X" is a markup ranging from zero on up.

Many corporations (such as General Motors or General Electric) have financial subsidiaries (General Motors Acceptance Corporation and General Electric Credit Corporation) which undertake a variety of sophisticated capital market transactions. Frequently, the credit ratings of these firms and financial subsidiaries exceed that of banks dealing in the foreign exchange market. The question has risen whether some of these corporations might gain more direct access to the foreign exchange market than through the traditional bank/customer relationship just described. This issue is discussed in Box 3.3.

---

[24]Based on press releases from the Federal Reserve Bank of New York and the Bank of England, September 29, 1998.

[25]From the EBS Partnership website at <www.ebsp.com>.

[26]Bilateral netting means that if Bank A owes £11 million to Bank B, and Bank B owes £10 million to Bank A, then only one transaction—a payment of £1 million from Bank A to Bank B—is executed, rather than the original two.

[27]See Cody (1990) for a thorough discussion of alternative netting arrangements.

[28]See <www.fxnet.com> for additional information about the company and its products.

Box 3.3

Why Can't Everyone Have Direct Access to the Interbank Foreign Exchange Market?

In 1981, Texaco negotiated a 50-50 joint venture with Charles Fulton Holdings Ltd., a London broker, to form Ful-Tex Euro Services Inc. The intention was to provide brokerage services in Eurocurrency deposits, certificates of deposit, and foreign exchange.* The motivation for the joint venture followed from the dispersed nature of the market. Even if Texaco had been offered the most favorable foreign exchange quotations (interbank + 0 percent), it might still be losing because of price dispersion in the market. By placing itself (through Ful-Tex) as a broker close to the center of market activity, Texaco might obtain valuable information about the timing of transactions. Texaco's strategic move opened the possibility of bringing other nonbank financial companies and industrial companies into the brokerage network.

At about the same time, the U.S. Justice Department filed suit against foreign exchange brokers in the United States, alleging that they had conspired to fix brokerage commissions on foreign exchange transactions. The suit was settled in January 1981 with a consent decree barring the establishment of set commission rates or enforcing compliance with them.†

These events of the early 1980s raise the question of how access to the brokerage network is determined. Could money-center banks restrict the use of brokerage services to themselves? In the early 1980s, Transamerica Inc., a San Francisco-based financial conglomerate, proposed a computer-based foreign exchange trading system (TAFEX). A central computer would match orders across all parties having access to the system. Small regional banks and multinational firms with heavy foreign exchange activity were anxious to enroll, but the important money-center banks were not keen to participate and the Transamerica proposal failed.

Access to the brokerage system defines pricing in the foreign exchange market: Those with access to brokers are in the interbank (or wholesale) market, those without access are in the corporate (or retail) market. Access to the brokerage system is based on two factors: credit quality and trading style. The practice of brokers announcing quotes anonymously is only efficient if the counterparty (when revealed) is an acceptable credit risk and reciprocal trading partner. Credit quality does not necessarily mean an AAA rating as banks with far lower credit ratings have been important foreign exchange market makers.‡ Trading style means that the counterparty must be a market maker; that is, someone willing to post two-way (bid and ask) prices, deal in normal quantities, and take both long and short positions.

With these "rules of engagement," some multinational firms might not be suitable counterparties for access to brokers, but some securities firms could qualify. Within the last decade, certain securities firms (see the lower part of Figure 3.4) have gained access to brokers for spot transactions. In most cases, these firms are still treated as retail customers for forward exchange transactions. Smaller regional banks (see lower right of Figure 3.4) are still outside the interbank market and treated as retail customers for foreign exchange transactions.

---

*See "Challenging a Bank Monopoly," *Business Week,* Nov. 16, 1981, p. 175.

†The suit named both the Forex Association of North America and the Foreign Exchange Brokers Association. See "Currency-Fee Fixing Alleged," *New York Times,* Jan. 22, 1980, p. D3; "U.S. Reaches Accord with Two Associations of Currency Traders," *The Wall Street Journal,* Jan. 7, 1981, p. 18.

‡Citibank, rated only BBB in 1991, has consistently ranked number one for service and popularity in polls conducted by *Euromoney*. Citibank has also held the largest market share of any bank in the foreign exchange market, about 9 percent in 1995. See "A Close Chase," *Euromoney,* May 1996, p. 60.

Corporate Foreign Exchange Trading—Recent Innovations.   The Internet and e-commerce are effecting many industries, and corporate foreign exchange trading may be in line for a dramatic changeover. Various companies are now developing business plans that bring a Web-based auction environment to corporate foreign exchange.

In April 2000, Currenex launched the first multibank Internet foreign exchange trading system.[29] The Currenex system works on an auction principle whereby corporate

---

[29]See the corporate website at <www.currenex.com> for further details.

users request quotations from participating banks. For example, suppose that Master-card International wishes to buy $10 million worth of Japanese yen in the spot market. Mastercard enters this request for bids into the system. All banks that participate in the Currenex system and with which Mastercard has a relation have a short period to enter a bid (about 20 seconds for major currencies, and longer for minor and exotic curren-cies). Once the bids have been received, Mastercard has five seconds to choose an ac-ceptable bank or decline completely. Mastercard can select any bid it wishes. In this yen transaction, for example, Mastercard could pass up the lowest price and favor another bank if it felt that other factors (back-office quality or credit issues) were important. Im-portantly, while Mastercard sees all of the quotes along with the name of each bank, the banks are not aware of the bids submitted by the other banks.

Currenex charges both banks and corporate customers a fee for using the service. The Currenex system and others like it improve the transparency for corporate cus-tomers and should lower the spreads charged to corporations as banks compete for busi-ness.[30] The system also simplifies the back-office, bookkeeping elements of currency trading. Banks may need to participate in new Internet-based trading systems in order to retain corporate customers. But falling spreads on corporate transactions will have an adverse effect on bank foreign exchange trading profits.

Counterparties and Concentration in the Foreign Exchange Market

Another dimension of foreign exchange trading is the distribution of trading by coun-terparty. Data from the 1998 BIS survey presented in Table 3.5 show that 82 percent of all spot trading is either interbank or between banks and financial institutions including investment banks and securities firms. Only 18 percent of spot trading is between banks and corporate customers. In earlier surveys, this figure was closer to only 10 percent. Given the huge volume of foreign exchange trading, it makes sense that only a small fraction of trading is connected with real customer economic activity.[31] The dispersed nature of the market helps to explain why there is so much trading among financial in-stitutions. Dealers trade with one another to acquire and lay off risks, and to discover transaction prices. As customer trading is only a small fraction of total foreign exchange trading, this underlies the great liquidity of the market for customer transactions.

Table 3.5 also shows that more than one-half of all foreign exchange deals represent cross-border transactions. In earlier surveys, this figure was as high as 67 percent. This confirms the international nature of the market and the concern about counterparty risks and clearing and settlement arrangements.

Finally, in Table 3.6 we show the estimated market shares of the top foreign ex-change dealers as of May 2000 as determined by *Euromoney* magazine.[32] Among the top 20 dealers, we find five institutions (Warburg Dillon Read, Goldman Sachs, Merrill

---

[30]See the website <www.CFOweb.com> for another example of a business-to-business currency auction style product. CFOweb.com is reported to have 2,300 customers signed up and four major banks, but the system is not open for live trading as of spring 2000. See "National/Global Forex Trading Sites May Erode Bank Revenues," *The American Banker,* May 5, 2000. Another entry in the electronic FX trading competition is FXall, operated by FX Alliance L.L.C., a joint venture combining 13 major banks and financial institutions including Bank of America, Credit Suisse, Goldman Sachs and J. P. Morgan. FXall may begin operating by year-end 2000. See the website <www.fxall.com> for further details.

[31]In comparison, more than 30 percent of outright forwards involve a corporate counterparty.

[32]See Philip Moore, "Deutsche Bank's Great Victory," *Euromoney,* May 2000.

TABLE 3.5 Dimensions of the Foreign Exchange Market, April 1998

Daily Volume of Trading by Contract Type, Counterparty, and Location of Counterparty

	Billions of US$				Percentage Share			
	Spot	Outright Forward	Foreign Exchange Swaps	Total Turnover	Spot	Outright Forward	Foreign Exchange Swaps	Total Turnover
Total	577.4	129.7	733.9	1413.9				
With dealers	347.7	49.1	511.7	881.5	60.2%	37.9%	69.7%	62.3%
Local	153.4	22.1	192.9	373.3				
Cross-border	194.3	27.0	318.8	513.1				
With other financial institutions	120.7	34.4	124.1	279.2	20.9	26.6	16.9	19.7
Local	58.2	23.1	48.9	130.2				
Cross-border	62.5	11.3	75.2	149.0				
With nonfinancial customers	109.0	46.2	98.1	253.2	18.9	35.6	13.4	17.9
Local	73.4	34.6	62.3	170.3				
Cross-border	35.6	11.5	35.8	83.0				
All local transactions	285.0	84.7	304.0	673.8	49.4	65.3	41.4	47.7
All cross-border transactions	292.3	49.9	429.9	745.1	50.6	38.5	58.6	52.7

Note: Turnover is measured net of local and cross-border interdealer double counting.

Source: Bank for International Settlements. *Central Bank Survey of Foreign Exchange and Derivatives Market Activity,* May 1999 (Table E-1).

TABLE 3.6 Concentration in the Foreign Exchange Market

Market Share of Top 20 Dealers, May 2000

Rank	Dealer	Estimated Market Share (%)	Cumulative Share (%)
1	Deutsche Bank	12.53%	12.53%
2	Chase Manhattan Bank	8.26	20.80
3	Citigroup	8.07	28.87
4	Warburg Dillon Read	5.02	33.88
5	HSBC	4.55	38.43
6	Goldman Sachs	4.38	42.82
7	J. P. Morgan	3.94	46.76
8	Merrill Lynch	3.27	50.02
9	Credit Suisse First Boston	2.89	52.91
10	Morgan Stanley Dean Witter	2.87	55.78
11	NatWest Global Financial Markets	2.71	58.50
12	Barclays Capital	2.07	60.57
13	Royal Bank of Canada	1.96	62.53
14	State Street Bank & Trust	1.95	64.48
15	Bank of America	1.86	66.34
16	ABN Amro	1.72	68.06
17	Bank of New York	1.24	69.30
18	Lehman Brothers	1.22	70.52
19	Credit Agricole Indosuez	1.02	71.54
20	Brown Brothers Harriman	0.74	72.28

Source: *Euromoney,* "Deutsche Bank's Great Victory," May 2000, p. 52.

TABLE 3.7   Trading Statistics for an Actual Spot DM Interbank Dealer

	Direct Transactions	*Brokered Transactions*	*Total Transactions*
Number of transactions	190	77	267
Value of transactions	$0.8 billion	$0.4 billion	$1.2 billion
Median transaction size	$3.0 million	$4.0 million	NA
Median spread size	DM 0.0003	NA	NA

Note: The above figures are daily averages for a single trader in the spot DM interbank market for the period Monday, Aug. 3, 1992–Friday, Aug. 7, 1992.
Source: Richard K. Lyons, "Tests of Microstructural Hypotheses in the Foreign Exchange Market," *Journal of Financial Economics* 39 (1995), pp. 321–51.

Lynch, Morgan Stanley Dean Witter, and Lehman Brothers) that are prominent investment banks and securities houses. This confirms that noncommercial banks have gained leading positions in the market. The survey found that Deutsche Bank was the largest foreign exchange dealer on a global basis across all currencies, with an estimated market share of 12.5 percent. In earlier years Citibank had achieved the number one ranking, with a market share of 8–10 percent. Note that the top 10 and top 20 firms collectively held market shares of 55.8 percent and 72.3 percent, respectively. By comparison, in its 1998 survey, *Euromoney* reported that the top 10 and top 20 firms had captured only 40 percent and 58 percent of the market. This trend toward increased concentration of business among fewer dealers was confirmed by the 1998 BIS foreign exchange survey, which did not, however, provide any details about the shares of individual banks.

Policy Matters—Private Enterprises

A Close-Up View on Foreign Exchange Trading

Stories of foreign exchange trading written by people close to the market emphasize the drama and sometimes frenzied pace of trading.[33] These accounts convey a good overall impression, but are usually lacking in details.

A study by Richard Lyons (1995) examines the behavior of an interbank spot DM trader in detail based on all transactions over a five-day period, August 2–7, 1992.[34] All of the trader's direct dealing transactions were executed on the Reuters 2000-1 communications system, so a complete record of each transaction—time, size, and price—was available. In addition, Lyons compiled the dealer's brokered transactions. The descriptive statistics in Table 3.7 show that the trader completed an average of 267 transactions per day, or about one transaction every 67 seconds.[35] The trader was involved in many more communications that did not result in a completed transaction. On an average day, this trader executed $1.2 billion in total transactions. Most trades were executed via

---

[33]See, for example, Coombs (1976), especially Chapter 6 on the market reaction to President Kennedy's assassination, and Krieger (1992) for a more recent account of foreign exchange trading.

[34]Studies that analyze the behavior of foreign exchange dealers and prices on a moment-to-moment basis form a new area of study called market microstructure analysis. See Bollerslev and Domowitz (1993) and Lyons (1997) for related articles.

[35]An average trading day for this dealer was 8:30 A.M. to 1:30 P.M.

FIGURE 3.5A   Net Trading Positions, August 3–August 7, 1992
(In US$ Millions)

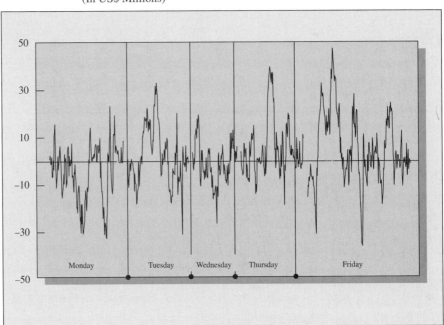

direct trading, but the median transaction size was larger in brokered trading. The median spread between bid and ask prices (whether quoted by this dealer or quoted to him by other dealers) was a scant DM 0.0003—3 "pips" to a dealer, or less than 0.02 percent of the spot rate.

Figures 3.5a and 3.5b show other dimensions of this trader's hectic pace. His position, long or short, trade by trade, and day by day, is displayed in Figure 3.5a. We see clearly how frequently the trader's position changes from long to short and vice versa during the day. We also observe that his daytime positions appear limited at about $40 million long or short. Notice also that his position returns close to zero at the end of each day, to safeguard against sharp overnight exchange rate changes such as those illustrated in Figure 3.5b.

Another study by Jian Yao (1997) analyzed the behavior of a spot DM trader at a major U.S. commercial bank over a 25-day period in late 1995. Yao observed immense efforts on the dealer's part to manage his inventory positions so that any undesired position was eliminated quickly (within five to six minutes) by actively initiating outgoing trades at other dealers' quotes. While inventory positions varied throughout the day, invariably the end-of-day position returned close to zero. While some conventional views allege that dealers actively speculate and earn their profits through speculation, Yao found that only a small percentage of the dealer's trades were his own initiated speculative transactions, and that the majority of his profits were earned through trades with the bank's retail customers rather than in interbank dealing or speculation.

Finally, a study by Roger Huang and Ronald Masulis (1999) examined the behavior of the bid-ask spread throughout the 24-hour day as dealers from around the world enter and leave the market. Huang and Masulis observed that the spread tends to be larger at the start of the trading day (as dealers develop a feel for the day) and at the end the trading day (as dealers rush to square their trading books). Spreads tend to narrow

---

FIGURE 3.5B   Transaction Prices: DM/US$ on August 3–August 7, 1992

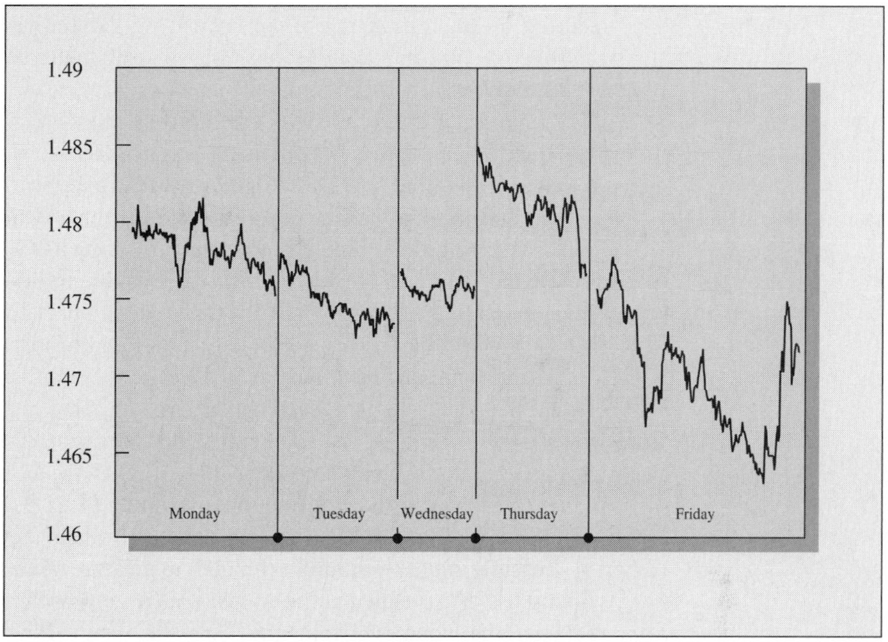

Note: The transactions are arranged in chronological sequence. The five panels represent trading on Monday–Friday. Notice that Friday and Monday appear to have the heaviest volume of trading.

Source: Richard Lyons, "Tests of Microstructural Hypotheses in the Foreign Exchange Market," *Journal of Financial Economics* 39 (1995), pp. 321–51.

when more dealers are offering quotes into the market, and when spot rate volatility is low. Spreads tend to widen at special times, in particular Mondays at the market opening, Fridays at the market closing, the last day of the month, and when there are regional holidays—again related to fewer dealers offering quotes at these times or eager to square their dealing books.

Controls over Foreign Exchange Trading

Managers have always been concerned about the risks of foreign exchange trading and various control measures are used to contain these risks.[36] **Exchange rate risk,** associated with unexpected exchange rate changes, can be addressed by placing limits on the size of open currency positions. These might include limits on an individual trader's position, overnight position limits that are more severe than daytime limits, and limits on the overall position of the trading room. **Interest rate risk** is associated with unexpected changes in forward exchange rates, because the term structure of forward premiums matches the ratio of the term structure of interest rates in the two currencies. Interest rate risks in trading can be contained by placing limits on the absolute size of a forward position, by restricting the permissible maturities, and by limiting the "gap," the difference in maturities of assets and liabilities for a single currency.

    Credit risk is another major trading risk associated with default on a contract. One example of credit risk, **rate risk,** applies to the case of default on an outstanding

---

[36]See Riehl and Rodriguez (1983) for a complete discussion of risk management of trading room and treasury operations.

contract, as we discussed earlier in connection with long-term forward contracts. The magnitude of rate risk depends on whether the bank retains the right-of-offset, the maturity of the contracts, and the underlying variability of prices. Rate risks can be controlled by limiting customer positions, placing maturity limits on each customer, and having a diversified portfolio of customers.

Another example of credit risk is **delivery risk,** which is associated with default on a contract in the process of settlement across time zones.[37] For example, assume that American bank A has sold DM 1.6 million to German firm G in exchange for $1 million for spot delivery on Tuesday, August 6, 1996. Bank A may deliver DM to firm G in Frankfurt during the morning before New York opens. Since US$ funds are officially cleared and settled in New York, firm G is unable to effect delivery of its $1 million obligation until 9:00 A.M. New York time, which normally is 3:00 P.M. in Frankfurt. If firm G declares bankruptcy before 3:00 P.M. Frankfurt time, bank A may suffer a total loss because the DM have already been paid out, and bank A stands as an unsecured creditor in a bankruptcy proceeding, hoping to receive all or part of its $1 million. One way to control delivery risk is to spread delivery time dates. For example, a customer with a $10 million foreign exchange limit, might have a limit of $2 million on any day. In this case, a default would lead to a maximum of $2 million subject to delivery risk, with the remaining $8 million subject to rate risk where the right-of-offset might apply.[38]

Recently, more analytical techniques to measure these risks have come into use. We will discuss the so-called **value-at-risk (VAR)** approach in Chapters 16 and 17. As important as these quantitative methods may be, they will be effective in controlling risks only when reporting systems are also in place and actively monitored by management.

Valuing Foreign Exchange Trading Profits

Perhaps because of the uncertainties in trading, many investors have been unwilling to place a high value on that portion of a bank's profits that are derived from trading. Thus, a bank that reports a rise in profits associated with an increase in trading profits may not see much of a stock price reaction. As one analyst commented, "If one sees dealing operations generating an increasingly high proportion of [a bank's] profits, this will lead to perceived poor quality of earnings, because the trading profits are so volatile."[39] In contrast, investors may view a bank's fee income from custodial services or acting as the depositary bank in an American Depositary Receipt program as nearly risk free, and award a higher stock price-to-earnings ratio.

Policy Matters—Public Policymakers

The design of clearing and settlement systems for foreign exchange, domestic bank deposits, and traded securities is receiving greater attention from public policymakers.[40] A

---

[37]Delivery risk is now sometimes referred to as *Herstatt risk,* commemorating the bankruptcy of the Herstatt Bank in West Germany in June 1974.

[38]The Federal Reserve has ruled that for certain short-term foreign exchange contracts, the right of offset is permitted.

[39]See "Giant HSBC Faces Nagging Questions over Stock and Bond Operations," *The Wall Street Journal,* Aug. 15, 1994, p. A7D.

[40]For example, see the remarks of Federal Reserve Chairman, Alan Greenspan (1990), former New York Federal Reserve Bank President, Gerald Corrigan (1989), and the Group of Thirty (1989). For further discussion, see Scarlata (1992).

study by Sawaichiro Kamata (1990) analyzes delivery risk in the foreign exchange market. As the United States is the nearest country to the east of the International Date Line and the Tokyo–New York time gap is the largest, and the US$/¥ currency market the most active, the dollar and the United States bear by far the largest burden of delivery risk. The netting systems discussed earlier would reduce but not eliminate the aggregate delivery risk in the system. A permanent solution to the problem of delivery risk would require the development of a "delivery versus payment" system in which there is a simultaneous exchange of the two legs of any transaction. An alternative private market solution to delivery risk is the so-called Continuous Linked Settlement (CLS) Bank. The CLS Bank acts as an escrow agent: it receives one leg of the transaction (say, ¥ headed for Tokyo), and does not release the funds until the second leg (say, US$ headed for New York) arrives at the CLS. The CLS Bank, owned by a consortium of major international banks, was expected to begin operation late in 2000.[41]

A recent report from the Bank for International Settlements (1996) suggests that foreign exchange settlement risk may be more than an intraday phenomenon as our earlier illustration portrayed. Because a bank may issue an irrevocable computer instruction before the settlement date, and because the bank may not know with certainty whether it has received the currency which it bought, the BIS report suggests that settlement exposures could last several days. The BIS report recognizes the significant potential benefits of multicurrency and multilateral netting arrangements being developed by private sector firms, and urges banks and central banks to work in cooperation to reduce exposure to settlement risk.

Finally, our analysis of synthetic instruments showed that it is relatively easy to overcome prohibitions and quantitative restrictions on many securities. Reliance on such restrictions as policy instruments should be less effective as a result.

---

[41]See Clive Davidson, "Settlement Solutions," *Risk,* November 1998, pp. 61–65, and Ottho Heldring, "Settle Down to Settling Up," *Risk,* October 1998, pp. 46–49.

Summary

The discussion in this chapter has highlighted the current structure and institutions in the foreign exchange market and the changes and competitive pressures affecting the market.

The basic foreign exchange products are spot contracts and interbank swap contracts. With these building blocks, traders can create forward contracts or offset the risks of outright forward positions. The process is extremely flexible, so that synthetic versions of spot, forward, and interest rate contracts can be constructed easily. Arbitrage of many varieties (spatial, triangular, and covered interest) plays an essential role in linking the prices of spot contracts and forward contracts.

The foreign exchange market processes more than $1.5 trillion of transactions each day. It is the largest financial market in the world and appears to generate considerable profits for commercial trading banks. Non-

bank financial firms, including investment banks, securities firms, and financial subsidiaries of industrial corporations, have increased their utilization of the foreign exchange and international money markets. Not surprisingly, the level of expertise among these nonbanks has increased, raising the incentives for them to have more direct and transparent access to the foreign exchange market. Direct access could include access to the traditional (i.e., voice/telephone) brokerage network (comparable to bank dealers), access to automated brokerage networks, access to Web-based auction systems, or access to clearing and settlement systems. Access to a trading system would very likely be determined on the basis of objective criteria, which raises the importance of counterparty credit risk assessment.

Foreign exchange trading is fast paced and involves numerous risks—price, interest rate, counterparty, liquidity, and so forth. Because of the fast pace and large turnover, dealers must manage their inventory positions continuously to keep them within acceptable limits, and typically near zero at day's end. Netting systems and continuous linked settlement systems are recent innovations designed to lower delivery risks to individual banks, as well as the systemic risk in global foreign exchange trading.

Questions

1. Explain how the nature of a currency as a domestic medium of exchange creates the need for foreign exchange markets. Provide an example.

2. Sometimes a currency, like the US$, can be used to conduct international transactions without the need for a foreign exchange market. For example, in 1995 the US$ could be used for transactions in Panama and Russia. Explain why these transactions occur without a foreign exchange market.

3. Explain why commercial banks appear to make consistent profits in trading foreign exchange. How can you reconcile these data on profitability with the idea that foreign exchange trading is a zero-sum game?

4. Explain the difference between a spot foreign exchange contract and a forward foreign exchange contract.

5. Contrast speculative trading with arbitrage trading.

6. What is the difference between spatial arbitrage and covered-interest arbitrage?

7. How would you explain the price dispersion across traders in the foreign exchange market?

8. What is the difference between a cross-rate and a direct rate in the foreign exchange market? How is a cross-rate derived from direct rates?

9. The US$ is used overwhelmingly as a vehicle currency in foreign exchange trading among non-US currencies. Why? What are the advantages of using the US$ instead of available cross-rates?

10. What is the relationship linking the spot rate, the forward rate, and interest rates in the domestic and foreign currencies?

11. Why is a forward foreign exchange contract called a redundant financial product?

12. How do you create a synthetic forward contract? What are the advantages to a firm of using a forward instead of a synthetic forward?

13. What difficulties might you encounter when creating a synthetic forward for "exotic" currencies?

14. Define *counterparty risk* in the foreign exchange market.

15. Define the *right-of-offset* in the foreign exchange market. What is its significance for a foreign exchange trader at a large bank?

16. Many countries have restrictions on the securities sold by corporations. For example, Germany did not allow a commercial paper market to develop until 1991. How could a German firm create a synthetic commercial paper program using other financial instruments?

17. What are the main structural differences between the foreign exchange market and a major stock market such as the New York Stock Exchange?

18. Contrast the clearing and settlement system in the foreign exchange market with that of centralized exchanges such as the Chicago Mercantile Exchange or the Chicago Board of Trade.

19. What are the main risks faced by players in the foreign exchange market?

Exercises

Cross Rates

1. Suppose the Canadian dollar is currently traded at 1.40 C$/$. The deutsche mark is traded at 1.39 DM/$. Ignoring transaction costs:

   a. Determine the C$/DM exchange rate consistent with these direct quotations.

  b. Suppose the C$/DM cross-rate in the market was at 1.05 C$/DM. Is there any arbitrage opportunity?

  c. How would you take advantage of any arbitrage situation?

  d. What is your profit?

2. Suppose the Mexican peso is currently traded at 7 MP/$. The yen is traded at 90 ¥/$.

  a. Determine the MP/¥ cross-rate.

  b. Suppose the MP/¥ cross-rate in the market was at 0.1 MP/¥. Is there any arbitrage opportunity?

  c. How would you take advantage of any arbitrage situation?

  d. What is your profit?

3. Suppose the French franc is currently traded in a French bank at 3.55 FFr/DM. The DM is traded in a German bank at 1.39 DM/$.

  a. Determine the FFr/$ direct rate that you expect to see.

  b. Suppose the FFr/$ was at 5.00 FFr/$. Is there any arbitrage opportunity?

  c. How would you take advantage of any arbitrage situation?

  d. What is your profit?

4. Suppose the Japanese yen is currently traded at 90 ¥/$. The Canadian dollar is traded at $1.40 C/$.

  a. Determine the ¥/C$ cross-rate.

  b. Suppose the ¥/C$ was at 60 ¥/C$. Is there any arbitrage opportunity?

  c. How would you take advantage of any arbitrage situation?

  d. What is your profit?

5. Suppose the FFr/DM cross-rate is currently at 3.55 FFr/DM, while the DM trades at 1.40 DM/$.

  a. What is the FFr/$ direct rate?

  b. Suppose the FFr suddenly depreciates to FFr 3.65 against the DM, the DM/$ rate stays constant, and the FFr/$ direct rate depreciates to 5.05 FFr/$. What would you do to take advantage of the arbitrage opportunity?

Covered Interest Arbitrage

6. Suppose the spot rate is $ 0.60/DM, $i_{\$,6}$ is 6.5 percent per annum and $i_{DM,6}$ is 9 percent per annum.

  a. What is your estimate of today's six-month forward $/DM rate?

  b. Suppose the six-month forward is quoted at $0.60/DM. What would you do to take advantage of the arbitrage opportunity? Where would you borrow and lend?

7. Suppose the spot rate is 100 ¥/$, $i_{\$,6}$ is 6.5 percent per annum and $i_{Yen,6}$ is 2.5 percent per annum.

  a. What is your estimate of today's six-month forward rate?

  b. Suppose the forward is currently quoted at 95 ¥/$. What would you do to take advantage of the arbitrage opportunity? Where would you borrow and lend?

8. Suppose the spot rate is 90 ¥/$, the three-month forward rate 88 ¥/$, and the three-month yen interest rate 2.5 percent.

  a. What is the implied three-month US$ interest rate?

  b. Suppose the actual three-month US$ interest rate is 10 percent. What would you do to profit from the arbitrage opportunity?

9. Suppose the current spot rate is $1.60/£, the one-year forward rate $1.50/£, and the British one-year interest rate 12 percent.

  a. What is the implied US$ one-year rate?

  b. Suppose the actual one-year US$ interest rate is 6 percent. What would you do to profit from the arbitrage opportunity?

Synthetic Securities

10. Suppose a German firm wishes to issue commercial in DM, but it is unable to do so in the German market.

  a. What can the firm do to replicate commercial paper (CP) securities without using German securities? Describe the transactions.

  b. Assume that the spot rate is $0.60/DM. The three-month forward rate is $0.58/DM. The three-month US$ CP rate is 8 percent. At what rate can the German firm expect to issue synthetic DM three-month CP?

11. Suppose a Canadian bond portfolio manager wishes to enhance his yield on Canadian short-term bills. Current one-year Canadian T-bills yield 13 percent. The current spot rate is 1.40 C$/$. The one-year forward rate is 1.50 C$/$. The U.S. one-year T-bill rate is 6 percent.

  a. What yield could the portfolio manager obtain by creating synthetic Canadian T-bills?

  b. What incentive is there in terms of yield enhancement to build a synthetic C$ security?

References

Antl, Boris. "Long-Term Forward Contracts." In *Swap Financing Techniques,* ed. B. Antl. London: Euromoney Publications, 1983.

Bank for International Settlements. *Central Bank Survey of Foreign Exchange and Derivatives Market Activity 1995.* Basle, Switzerland, May 1996.

———. *Central Bank Survey of Foreign Exchange Market Activity in April 1992.* Basle, Switzerland, Mar. 1993.

———. *Settlement Risk in Foreign Exchange Transactions.* Basle, Switzerland, Mar. 1996.

Bollerslev, Tim, and Ian Domowitz. "Trading Patterns and Prices in the Interbank Foreign Exchange Market." *Journal of Finance* 48, no. 4 (Sept. 1993), pp. 1421–43.

Braas, Albéric, and Charles N. Bralver. "An Analysis of Trading Profits: How Most Trading Rooms Really Make Money." *Journal of Applied Corporate Finance* 2, no. 4 (Winter 1990), pp. 85–90.

Cody, Brian J. "Reducing the Costs and Risks of Trading Foreign Exchange." *Business Review.* Federal Reserve Bank of Philadelphia (Nov./Dec. 1990), pp. 13–23.

Coombs, Charles A. *The Arena of International Finance.* New York: John Wiley, 1976.

Corrigan, E. Gerald. "Legislative Priorities." Federal Reserve Bank of New York, *Quarterly Review* 14, no. 1 (Summer 1989), pp. 1–16.

Edison, Hali J. *The Effectiveness of Central-Bank Intervention: A Survey of the Literature After 1982.* Princeton Special Papers in International Economics, no. 18, July 1993.

Einzig, Paul. *The History of Foreign Exchange.* 2nd ed. London: St. Martin's Press, 1970.

Frankel, Jeffrey A., and Alan T. MacArthur. "Political vs. Currency Premia in International Real Interest Differentials." *European Economic Review* 32, no. 5 (June 1988), pp. 1083–1121.

Garbade, Kenneth D., and William L. Silber. "Price Dispersion in the Government Securities Market." *Journal of Political Economy* 84 (1976), pp. 721–40.

Global Dealers Directory. New York: Republic National Bank of New York, 1994.

Greenspan, Alan. "Clearing and Settlement: Past and Future." Remarks before the American Bankers Association, Orlando, FL, October 22, 1990.

Group of Thirty. *Clearance and Settlement Systems in the World's Securities Markets.* New York: Group of Thirty, Mar. 1989.

Hilley, John L., Carl R. Beidleman, and James A. Greenleaf. "Why There Is No Long Forward Market in Foreign Exchange." *Euromoney* (Jan. 1981), pp. 95–103.

Huang, Roger D., and Ronald W. Masulis. "FX Spreads and Dealer Competition Across the 24-Hour Trading Day." *Review of Financial Studies* 12, no. 1 (Spring 1999), pp. 61–93.

Kamata, Sawaichiro. "Measuring Herstatt Risk." *Bank of Japan Monetary and Economic Studies* 8, no. 2 (Sept. 1990), pp. 59–74.

Kohlhagen, Steven W. "The Identification of Destabilizing Foreign Exchange Speculation." *Journal of International Economics* 9, no. 3 (Aug. 1979), pp. 321–40.

Krieger, Andrew J. *The Money Bazaar: Inside the Trillion Dollar World of Currency Trading.* New York: Times Books, 1992.

Leahy, Michael P. "The Profitability of U.S. Intervention in the Foreign Exchange Market." *Journal of International Money and Finance* 14, no. 6 (Dec. 1995), pp. 823–44.

Levich, Richard M. *International Financial Markets* (Burr Ridge, IL: Irwin/McGraw-Hill, 1998).

Lyons, Richard K. "A Simultaneous Trade Model of the Foreign Exchange Hot Potato." *Journal of International Economics* (May 1997), pp. 275–98.

———. "Tests of Microstructural Hypotheses in the Foreign Exchange Market." *Journal of Financial Economics* 39 (1995), pp. 321–51.

New York Stock Exchange Factbook. New York: New York Stock Exchange, 1999.

Riehl, Heinz, and Rita M. Rodriguez. *Foreign Exchange and Money Markets.* New York: McGraw-Hill, 1983.

Scarlata, Jodi G. "Institutional Developments in the Globalization of Securities and Futures Markets." Federal Reserve Bank of St. Louis, *Review* 74, no. 1 (Jan./Feb. 1992), pp. 17–30.

Taylor, Dean. "Official Intervention in the Foreign Exchange Market, or, Bet Against the Central Bank." *Journal of Political Economy* 90, no. 2 (Apr. 1982), pp. 356–68.

Yao, Jian. "Essays on Market Making in the Interbank Foreign Exchange Market." Unpublished Ph.D. dissertation, New York University, August 1997.

4 INTERNATIONAL PARITY CONDITIONS: PURCHASING POWER PARITY

"Under the skin of any international economist lies a deep-seated belief in some variant of the PPP theory of the exchange rate."
Dornbusch and Krugman (1976)

Learning Objectives

After reading this chapter, students should

1. Know how parity conditions can be used to understand the interrelationships among exchange rates, interest rates, and other variables in a perfect capital market.

2. Be able to describe the usefulness of purchasing power parity (PPP) and calculate PPP exchange rates.

3. Understand the connection between real exchange rates and PPP.

4. Be familiar with various empirical techniques for testing PPP, and with the strength of the evidence regarding PPP as a short-run and long-run relationship.

5. Be able to give examples of how private individuals and public policymakers would use their knowledge of PPP for strategic and policy decisions.

In the study of economics, one encounters many so-called parity or equilibrium conditions that link prices or price movements in seemingly distinct markets. The study of international financial markets is well represented by several important and useful parity conditions.

In Chapters 4 and 5, we review these parity conditions from several different perspectives. First, we develop the parity conditions themselves from basic principles, pointing out the key assumptions upon which each parity condition depends. As we will see, the international parity conditions are most easily developed in the context of the **perfect capital market (PCM)** assumptions (that is, no transaction costs, no taxes, and complete certainty) common to many analyses in financial theory.[1] Second, we explore the impact of relaxing the key assumptions underlying each parity condition to examine

---

[1]Fama and Miller (1972, pp. 1–143) develop the perfect capital market assumptions and their implications for financial models.

whether the parity condition is likely to hold when the assumptions are made more realistic. Third, we review the empirical evidence on each parity condition. One objective of this discussion is to analyze the appropriateness of different empirical techniques in the analysis of parity conditions. As we will see, certain empirical methods that are popular for the analysis of economic data (such as linear regression) are often inappropriate for the analysis of financial parity conditions. We suggest other, more direct, tests to determine the validity and implications of our parity relationships.

In this chapter, we begin with an overview of the importance of the parity conditions in the study *and* practice of international finance. We present a summary of the principal parity conditions. The focus of Chapter 4 is a detailed analysis of purchasing power parity (PPP). We develop the theory of purchasing power parity and then review the empirical evidence. In the final two sections of the chapter, we consider the role of PPP in policy decisions for both private enterprises and public policymakers. The remaining parity conditions are covered in Chapter 5.

The Usefulness of Parity Conditions in International Financial Markets

Parity conditions play a key role in our understanding of international financial markets and in a decision maker's strategic posture toward the markets. The parity conditions can usefully be thought of as international financial "benchmarks" or "break-even values"—defining points where the decision maker in private enterprise is indifferent between the two strategies summarized by the two halves of the parity relation. As we will see from the standpoint of a private enterprise, the decision to borrow in one currency or another, to locate a plant in one country or another, to measure exposure to currency risks using one formula or another, and other financial decisions, may boil down to a judgment about the validity of one or more parity conditions.[2] And from the standpoint of a public policymaker, a judgment regarding whether the nation's currency is "fairly" valued versus "overvalued" or "undervalued," an opinion regarding whether the nation's capital markets are functioning efficiently or inefficiently, and a conclusion regarding the ability of monetary and fiscal policies to produce the desired macroeconomic results—each of these may rest on our view about one or more of the parity conditions.

As a result, the decision maker will find it useful to have information about the validity of the parity conditions. For example, if the empirical evidence reveals sizable and prolonged departures from PPP, the decision maker will conclude that the selection of a manufacturing location could leave the firm exposed to substantial exchange rate risk. But if the data support PPP, then the location choice could be based on present prices and principles of comparative advantage, as if the choice were between two locations within the same country.[3]

The parity conditions are important in international finance because when they hold, they imply "points of indifference" between two alternative financial choices. When the parity conditions are invalid, they indicate market forces favoring one financial alternative over another. Empirical evidence on the international parity conditions

---

[2]This statement applies to the narrow economic determinants of borrowing and investment strategies, and not to cultural or psychological factors that may also play a role.

[3]We ignore for now the importance of political risk that could have a significant influence over location choices.

is important, because there will be an implication for the decision maker *when the parity conditions hold and when they do not hold.*

This may be a surprising conclusion to someone who has thought, "Well, if PPP or another parity relationship is false, I should not use them in my analysis." As we shall argue, contrary to the previous quotation, the parity conditions become *most* intriguing when they are false. Because the parity conditions rely heavily on arbitrage, a violation of parity often implies that a direct or indirect profit opportunity (or cost advantage) is available to the decision maker. It is when the data reveal departures from parity that the decision maker should be *most* interested in knowing precisely the direction and duration of departures from parity. At these times, the decision maker in private enterprise faces the greatest opportunities but not necessarily the greatest risks.

An Overview of International Parity Conditions in a Perfect Capital Market

Our analysis of international parity conditions begins by assuming a perfect capital market (PCM) setting, not because we believe this is an accurate picture of the world, but because it eases the analysis and provides a useful benchmark for comparison with other, more realistic assumptions.[4] The standard PCM assumptions are (1) no transaction costs, (2) no taxes, and (3) complete certainty.[5] With these strong assumptions, it should be intuitively clear that profit-maximizing agents will act to eliminate all arbitrage opportunities—between goods in one country and goods in another, between spot and forward exchange, and between real and financial assets, along with all other arbitrage opportunities. It is correct to use the word *arbitrage* because in the PCM, complete certainty implies no risks. Thus, different financial opportunities can be evaluated as if their costs were known and certain.

In Figure 4.1, the four principal parity conditions—purchasing power parity, interest rate parity, Fisher parities, and the forward rate unbiased theory—are summarized in words and algebraic symbols, and the economic driving forces underpinning them are noted. To give a preview of these conditions, purchasing power parity is based on the arbitrage of goods sold in two different countries and priced in two different currencies. Interest rate parity relies on the arbitrage between spot and forward exchange rates and short-term money market instruments. The Fisher parities concern the pricing of money market instruments—and the arbitrage between nominal assets and real assets, or the arbitrage between nominal assets denominated in two different currencies. And the forward rate unbiased theory relates the two basic ways that one can purchase currency for delivery at a future time $t + n$—either with a forward contract purchased on day t for delivery on day $t + n$, or a spot contract for delivery on day $t + n$.

As we will see, even though there are four parity conditions, only three of these are independent, because the fourth parity condition can be derived from the other three. And there is a "hidden" assumption—perhaps better thought of as a fifth parity condition—that real interest rates in the two economies are equal. This additional assumption is discussed when we review the Fisher parities in Chapter 5.

---

[4]The perfect capital market we describe is distinct from the "efficient capital market" discussed in Chapter 7. A PCM will of course be efficient, but capital markets not satisfying the PCM assumptions could also be efficient if equilibrium pricing obtains and no unusual profit opportunities are available.

[5]With no transaction costs, all participants have equal and costless access to information. Therefore, they share homogeneous expectations about future outcomes. All buyers and sellers of securities are "small" and cannot individually influence prices; all participants are price takers. See Fama and Miller (1972), pp. 20–22.

FIGURE 4.1   Parity Relationships in International Finance

Based on the Perfect Capital Market Assumptions: No Transaction Costs, No Taxes, Complete Certainty

Theory	*In Words*	*In Symbols*	*Driving Forces*
Purchasing Power Parity			
Absolute version	The price of a market basket of U.S. goods equals the price of a market basket of foreign goods when multiplied by the exchange rate	$P_{US} = P_{UK} \times \text{Spot}$	Arbitrage in goods
Relative version	The percentage change in the exchange rate equals the percentage change in U.S. goods prices less the percentage change in foreign goods prices	$\Delta\text{Spot} = \Delta P_{US} - \Delta P_{UK}$	Arbitrage in goods
Interest Rate Parity			
	The forward exchange rate premium equals (approximately) the U.S. interest rate minus the foreign interest rate	$(F - S)/S = i_\$ - i_\pounds$	Arbitrage between the spot and forward exchange rates, and money market interest rates
Fisher Parities			
Fisher Effect (Fisher Closed)	For a single economy, the nominal interest rate equals the real interest rate plus the expected rate of inflation	$i_\$ = r_\$ + E(\Delta\tilde{P}_{US})$	Desire to insulate the real interest against expected inflation. Arbitrage between real and nominal assets.
International Fisher Effect (Fisher Open)	For two economies, the U.S. interest rate minus the foreign interest rate equals the expected percentage change in the exchange rate	$i_\$ - i_\pounds = E(\Delta\tilde{S}\text{pot})$	Arbitrage in bonds denominated in two currencies
Forward Rate Unbiased			
	Today's forward premium (for delivery in n days) equals the expected percentage change in the spot rate (over the next n days)	$(F_t - S_t)/S_t = (E(\tilde{S}_{t+n}) - S_t)/S_t$	Market players monitor the difference between today's forward rate (for delivery in n days) and their expectation of the future spot rate (n days from today)

Note: Explanation of symbols:

Delta (Δ) in front of a variable means "percentage rate of change."

Tilde ($\sim$) indicates a random variable whose precise value is determined in the future.

All exchange rates S (spot) and F (forward) are in $/£ terms. We arbitrarily pick the United States, the United Kingdom, US$ and £ to illustrate these parity conditions.

Purchasing Power Parity in a Perfect Capital Market

The Law of One Price

Our first parity condition, purchasing power parity (PPP), is built on the notion of arbitrage across goods markets and the Law of One Price.[6] The **Law of One Price** is the

---

[6]The theory of purchasing power parity is associated with Gustav Cassel (1922), who advanced it as a technique for setting exchange rates after the disruptions to financial markets during World War I. The essential elements of PPP have been traced back to David Hume and David Ricardo. For more on the origins of PPP, see McKinnon (1979, Chapter 6).

principle that in a PCM setting, homogeneous goods will sell for the same price in two markets, taking into account the exchange rate. So, the Law of One Price predicts that if the price of wheat is $4.50/bushel in the United States and the $/£ exchange rate ($S$) is $1.50/£, then the price of wheat in the United Kingdom should be £3.00/bushel. In symbols, we have:

$$P_{US, \text{ wheat}} = S_{\$/£} \times P_{UK, \text{ wheat}} \qquad (4.1)$$

In theory, the Law of One Price applies equally to any homogeneous product whether a good or a service. The law is enforced by arbitrage across markets (we called this spatial arbitrage in Chapter 3), buying where the product is cheap and selling where the product is dear. This enforcement mechanism is especially effective under our PCM assumption where the transportation costs necessary for product arbitrage are zero, and uncertainties (such as whether the products really are homogeneous and whether quoted prices will still be valid once we have crossed the ocean to take advantage of a price difference) are assumed away. In the real world, these factors (and many others) would matter, and we will discuss this possibility later.

Absolute Purchasing Power Parity

Purchasing power parity builds on the Law of One Price by analyzing the behavior of the exchange rate and aggregate price indexes in two countries. Suppose we consider a U.S. price index (P_{US}) and a U.K. price index (P_{UK}), each defined as a weighted average (with weights W_i of the prices of the same set of N goods, or:

$$P_{US} = \sum_{i=1}^{N} W_{US, i} P_{US, i} \qquad\qquad P_{UK} = \sum_{i=1}^{N} W_{UK, i} P_{UK, i}$$

As defined, P_{US} and P_{UK} represent the weighted average price *level* for goods in the U.S. and U.K. market baskets respectively.

Absolute purchasing power parity predicts that these two price measures will be equal after adjusting for the exchange rate. In symbols, we write this as:

$$P_{US} = S_{\$/£} \times P_{UK} \qquad (4.2)$$

Even under the PCM assumptions, we can see that the absolute version of PPP contains a flaw (really an additional implicit assumption) that may make it unsuitable for drawing economic inferences. As we have defined our price indexes, absolute PPP will require that the consumption baskets (really the consumption weights on individual goods) are identical across the two countries. When this assumption fails, absolute PPP will fail, even though there are no arbitrage opportunities in the goods market. Examples illustrating how differing consumption weights and relative price changes affect absolute PPP are shown in Box 4.1.

Another shortcoming of absolute PPP is that countries usually report price indexes rather than the absolute level of prices in local currency terms. Thus, we are most likely to see data on price indexes reported as 112.7 or 125.9, with a reference noting that the index took on the value 100 at a particular time. With price indexes as a unit-free magnitude, absolute PPP cannot be used.

Relative Purchasing Power Parity

Relative purchasing power parity offers a way to deal with many of the shortcomings that plague absolute PPP. Suppose that absolute PPP is violated so that equation (4.2)

Box 4.1

Absolute PPP Comparisons with Alternative Market Baskets and Alternative Inflation Scenarios

Consider the examples outlined in the tables for Box 4.1. Suppose the consumption basket in both the United States and the United Kingdom consists of only two goods: oil and butter. In the United States, take consumption of 25 barrels of oil (at $18.00/barrel) and 200 pounds of butter (at $1.50/pound) as establishing a base case for comparison. U.S. consumption is split 60–40 percent between oil and butter, and the average price level is $11.40. Now, assume that U.K. consumption of oil and butter is 3 barrels and 64 pounds, respectively.* Assume further that the exchange rate is $1.50/£, thus removing any arbitrage profit opportunities in either oil or butter. As a result, consumption weights in the United Kingdom for oil and butter are 36 percent and 64 percent. The average price level in the United Kingdom is thus £4.96. The ratio P_{US}/P_{UK} = $11.40/£4.96 = $2.30/£ and bears no resemblance to the actual spot exchange rate of $1.50/£.

Now consider case 2 for the United Kingdom, where the consumption weights on oil and butter match those for the United States. The new P_{UK} is £7.60 and the ratio P_{US}/P_{UK} = $11.40/£7.60 = $1.50/£—an exact match for the spot exchange rate. Case 2 demonstrates that if consumption patterns were identical in the United States and the United Kingdom, the ratio of basket prices would match the spot exchange rate.

Now suppose we let the United Kingdom be subject to an inflationary shock of 20 percent that affects all goods equally (neutral inflation). In U.K. case 3, we see that this sends the U.K. price of oil and butter up to £14.40 and £1.20, respectively. To maintain the Law of One Price, this inflation is associated with a 20 percent depreciation of the pound, to $1.25/£.† If we assume that consumption is unaffected by this neutral inflation (which is most likely the

case over the long run), the U.K. price level rises to £9.12. The new ratio P_{US}/P_{UK} = $11.40/£9.12 = $1.25/£—again an exact match for the spot exchange rate.

As a final example, consider a change in relative prices between oil and butter. Specifically, let the price of oil in the United States rise by 25 percent to $22.50/barrel while letting butter remain at $1.50/pound. If we go back to our initial exchange rate of $1.50/£, the 25 percent *relative* price change between oil and butter also is felt in the United Kingdom. In this example, let the consumption of oil fall by 20 percent in *both* countries and consumption of butter fall by 10 percent in *both* countries. Now examine U.S. case 2 and U.K. case 4. We see that the consumption weights have changed for oil and butter, but they remain identical *across* countries. The new ratio P_{US}/P_{UK} = $14.625/£9.75 = $1.50/£—which again matches the spot exchange rate exactly.

The bottom line of all these examples is that for absolute PPP to hold, the consumption weights for all goods must be identical across countries. If this assumption fails, then even when the Law of One Price holds, statisticians will measure deviations from absolute PPP. However, in this situation, deviations from absolute PPP will *not* imply arbitrage opportunities in the goods markets.

---

*Note that this example takes the United Kingdom as a smaller country with consumption only 20 percent as much as in the United States.

†The original exchange rate was $1.50/£ or £0.6667/$. A 20 percent pound depreciation implies that 20 percent more pounds will be needed to buy foreign currency. We compute 1.20 × £0.6667/$ = £0.80/$ or $1.25/£.

---

holds at time $t + 1$ only if another parameter, call it K, is introduced into the equation, so that:

$$P_{US,\, t+1} = K \times S_{\$/£,\, t+1} \times P_{UK,\, t+1} \qquad (4.3a)$$

If absolute PPP were to fail by the same proportion at an earlier time t, we could describe this by:

$$P_{US,\, t} = K \times S_{\$/£,\, t} \times P_{UK,\, t} \qquad (4.3b)$$

Absolute PPP Comparisons with Alternative Market Baskets and Alternative Inflation Scenarios

United States: Base Case 1

Commodity	Quantity	Price/Unit (Dollars)	Percent Weight	$P_i \times W_i$
Oil	25 bbl.	$ 18.00	60%	$10.80
Butter	200 lbs.	1.50	40	0.60
Basket		750.00	100	11.40

United Kingdom: Case 1, Weights Unequal to U.S. Weights

Commodity	Quantity	Price/Unit (Pounds)	Percent Weight	$P_i \times W_i$
Oil	3 bbl.	£ 12.00	36%	£4.32
Butter	64 lbs.	1.00	64	0.64
Basket		100.00	100	4.96

United Kingdom: Case 2, Weights Equal to U.S. Weights

Commodity	Quantity	Price/Unit (Pounds)	Percent Weight	$P_i \times W_i$
Oil	5 bbl.	£ 12.00	60%	£7.20
Butter	40 lbs.	1.00	40	0.40
Basket		100.00	100	7.60

U.K.: Case 3, Weights Equal to U.S. and Neutral Inflation

Commodity	Quantity	Price/Unit (Pounds)	Percent Weight	$P_i \times W_i$
Oil	5 bbl.	£ 14.40	60%	£8.64
Butter	40 lbs.	1.20	40	0.48
Basket		120.00	100	9.12

United States: Case 2, Nonneutral Inflation

Commodity	Quantity	Price/Unit (Dollars)	Percent Weight	$P_i \times W_i$
Oil	20 bbl.	$22.50	62.5%	$14.0625
Butter	180 lbs.	1.50	37.5	0.5625
Basket		720.00	100.0	14.6250

U.K.: Case 4, Weights Equal to U.S. and Nonneutral Inflation

Commodity	Quantity	Price/Unit (Pounds)	Percent Weight	$P_i \times W_i$
Oil	4 bbl.	£15.00	62.5%	£9.3750
Butter	36 lbs.	1.00	37.5	0.3750
Basket		96.00	100.0	9.7500

Taking the ratio of the U.S. price level at time $t + 1$ relative to its level at time t that is, the ratio of equation (4.3a) to (4.3b), we have:

$$(1 + p_{US}) = (1 + s) \times (1 + p_{UK}) = 1 + s + p_{UK} + s \times p_{UK} \qquad (4.4)$$

where each lowercase letter (p and s) represents the percentage change in the variable with an uppercase letter. Rearranging terms, we have:

$$p_{US} = s + p_{UK} + s \times p_{UK} \qquad (4.5)$$

So, if the U.K. prices rose by 20 percent (say from 100 to 120), and the US$ depreciated by 10 percent (say from $1.50 to $1.65), then it would be necessary for U.S. prices to rise by 32 percent (from 100 to 132) to maintain relative PPP. For small percentage changes in prices and exchange rates, or when continuous rates of change are used, the final cross-product term ($s \times p_{UK}$) can be ignored.[7] In this case, we can write the classic statement of **relative PPP:**

$$\boxed{s = p_{US} - p_{UK}} \tag{4.6}$$

$$\boxed{\begin{array}{ccc} \% \text{ exchange rate} = & \% \text{ change in} - & \% \text{ change in} \\ \text{change} & \text{U.S. prices} & \text{U.K. prices} \end{array}}$$

Equation (4.6) describes relative PPP using percentage changes in exchange rates. But often we are really interested in the *level* of the exchange rate that satisfies PPP. By definition, the **PPP spot rate** is the spot rate that reestablishes PPP relative to some base period.[8] Consequently, the PPP spot rate is the exchange rate that would just offset the relative inflation between a pair of countries since the base period. Taking the ratio of equations (4.3a) and (4.3b) and rearranging terms gives us the answer:

$$\frac{S_{\$/£,\, t+1}}{S_{\$/£,\, t}} = \frac{P_{US,\, t+1} / P_{UK,\, t+1}}{P_{US,\, t} / P_{UK,\, t}}$$

So

$$S_{PPP,\, t+1} = S_{\$/£,\, t} \frac{P_{US,\, t+1} / P_{UK,\, t+1}}{P_{US,\, t} / P_{UK,\, t}} \tag{4.7a}$$

or,

$$S_{PPP,\, t} + 1 = S_{\$/£,\, t} \frac{P_{US,\, t+1} / P_{US,\, t}}{P_{UK,\, t+1} / P_{UK,\, t}} \tag{4.7b}$$

Consider the following numerical example. Assume that the nominal exchange rate in the base period was $1.50 and that prices of U.S. goods had risen by 8 percent and prices of U.K. goods had risen by 4 percent. Using equation (4.7b), the PPP spot rate is $1.50/£ × 1.08/1.04 = $1.5577/£. A nominal exchange rate of $1.5577/£ would reestablish PPP in comparison to the base period. When the nominal exchange rate equals its PPP value, both the real exchange rate (defined shortly) and international price competitiveness (between U.S. and U.K. goods) are unchanged relative to the base period. Nominal exchange rates greater than $1.5577/£ represent £ "overvaluation" ($ undervaluation), and nominal exchange rates less than $1.5577/ £ represent $ "overvaluation" (£ undervaluation).

At this point, it is important to stress that the purchasing power parity conditions—equations (4.6), (4.7a), or (4.7b)—do not imply anything about causal linkages between prices and exchanges rates or vice versa. Both prices *and* exchange rates are (endogenous

---

[7]See Appendix 4.1 for a brief review of continuous or logarithmic rates of return.

[8]Ideally, a base period is one where the exchange rate takes a value that allows both countries to achieve their domestic and international policy objectives (i.e. internal and external balance). In practice, the choice of a base period is subjective. Some researchers select a period immediately after a major exchange rate change. Others take an average over several years to represent the base-period values. Still others, such as Williamson (1985), use formal models to estimate the base-period PPP exchange rate.

variables) jointly determined by other variables in the economy. Thus, for example, a change in a nation's money supply policy, tax (fiscal) policy, or commercial (tariff) policy may affect *both* domestic prices and the exchange rate. Because the impact of these changes may be felt at different times, one may get the impression that "prices cause the exchange rate" or that "the exchange rate causes prices." No general conclusion like this can be made; any conclusion regarding causality will depend chiefly on the situation at hand.[9]

Purchasing power parity should not be thought of as a causal relationship. Rather, it is an equilibrium condition that must be satisfied when the economy is at its long-term (steady-state) equilibrium. Even though there may be no simple causal links between exchange rates and prices, knowledge of the PPP condition can be a powerful tool if there is a tendency for PPP to hold.

The Real Exchange Rate and Purchasing Power Parity

The **real exchange rate** is another useful concept in international finance, and its measurement is closely connected with the purchasing power parity condition. We commonly encounter real magnitudes in macroeconomics. Nominal income (Y), nominal wages (W), and nominal interest rates (i) have their *real* counterparts. Real magnitudes are constructed from nominal magnitudes by adjusting for the appropriate price levels (P) or inflation rates. It is useful to think of the term *real* as a shorthand way of saying "real goods and services." In other words, a real magnitude attempts to filter out the effects of inflation to isolate the impact on quantities of goods and services.

Real Income: A Digression and Review.   A simple, noninternational example will illustrate the major points. Suppose that nominal income (Y) is \$55,000/year. Real income ($Y_{Real} = Y/P$) could be measured as:

$$\text{Real income} = \frac{\$55,000/\text{year}}{\$250/\text{market basket}} = 220 \text{ market baskets/year}$$

This clearly shows that real income is measured in terms of real goods and services.

Usually, however, real income is expressed as an index relative to a base year because the price level itself is usually expressed as an index rather than in \$/market basket. In our example, if real income in 2000 is 220 market baskets/year, then define this as 100. In 2001, if nominal income rises by 10 percent to \$60,500, and the price of a market basket rises by 8 percent to \$270, then real income is now 60,500/270 = 224.07 market baskets/year. To express real income in 2001 as an index, compute:

$$\text{Index (2001)} = \text{Real income (2001)/Real income (2000)}$$

$$= 224.07/220$$

$$= 1.0185$$

The calculation implies that real income has risen by 1.85 percent.

---

[9]For example, a country with a pegged exchange rate may expand its money supply and experience inflation at a higher rate than its pegging partner. When the country devalues its currency, it may appear that "prices cause exchange rates." On the other hand, a country may devalue its currency in order to improve its export competitiveness and its balance of trade. The devaluation raises the prices of imported goods and puts pressure on the country to permit higher domestic wages and prices. When this occurs, it may appear that "exchange rates cause prices." Both examples show that other factors, domestic monetary and fiscal policies, were behind the changes in the exchange rate and local prices.

Work through the previous example with the rate of inflation in the market basket as 10 percent instead of 8 percent. With nominal income and the inflation rate *both* rising by 10 percent, there is no change in real income. This is a general and important result. *When all nominal magnitudes rise by the same percentage amount, we expect that there will be no change in any real magnitude.*[10]

Real Exchange Rates: An Illustration.   Now let's apply what we have just developed to the case of exchange rates. A nominal exchange rate (such as $S = \$1.50/\pounds$) measures the rate of exchange between the currencies of two sovereigns. Currency traders quote nominal exchange rates, which are essential for expressing cash flows denominated in one currency in terms of another currency. The real exchange rate is calculated by correcting the nominal exchange rate for the price levels in the two countries. Consider a case in which absolute purchasing power parity holds:

$$\$1.50/\pounds = \frac{(\$1,500 \text{ Price/U.S. good})}{(\pounds 1,000 \text{ Price/British good})} \qquad (4.8a)$$

Dividing the left-hand side of above by the right-hand side yields:

$$\frac{\$1.50/\pounds}{\dfrac{\$1,500 / \text{U.S. good}}{\pounds 1,000/\text{British good}}} = 1 \text{ U.S. good} / \text{British good} \qquad (4.8b)$$

In other words, when PPP holds, identical U.S. goods and British goods exchange for each other on a one-for-one basis. The **units of the real exchange rate** are therefore:

$$\frac{\text{U.S. goods}}{\text{British goods}} \quad \text{or} \quad \frac{\text{British goods}}{\text{U.S. goods}}$$

The real exchange rate measures the international price competitiveness (and changes in competitiveness) of domestic versus foreign products after adjusting for the exchange rate change and inflation. Examining equation (4.8a), it should be clear that when the exchange rate changes by the same percentage as the relative price of U.S.-to-British goods, then the real exchange rate is unchanged. To put this another way, *in periods when PPP holds, the real exchange rate is constant.*

Like most real magnitudes, the real exchange rate is usually expressed as an index relative to a base year. We can define an **index of the real exchange rate** as:

$$\text{Spot (Real, } t) = \frac{\text{Spot (Nominal, } t)}{\text{Spot } (PPP,\, t)} \qquad (4.9)$$

For example, if today's spot exchange rate is $\$1.80/\pounds$ and the PPP spot rate is $\$1.50/\pounds$, the real exchange rate index is 1.20 or 120. At this rate, the £ is "overvalued" on a PPP basis. £1 exchanges for $1.80, rather than $1.50 as it should under PPP; or 1.0 British good can be exchanged for 1.2 U.S. goods. With an overvalued £, sellers of British

---

[10]This result is sometimes referred to as the *neutrality of money,* or the *homogeneity postulate.* As a long-run proposition, it is useful to assume that nominal magnitudes are homogeneous of degree one (i.e., changing on a one-for-one basis with the money supply). In the short run, prices of individual goods may change at different speeds, resulting in relative price changes and relative price risk. A companion long-run proposition is that real magnitudes are homogeneous of degree zero (i.e., changing on a zero-for-one basis with the money supply). However, we will see in Chapter 6 that in the short run a pure monetary shock may lead to a real exchange rate change and real exchange rate risk.

goods have "lost competitiveness" on international markets—for every $1.80 worth of international money, a buyer could purchase either 1.0 British good or 1.2 U.S. goods. It would be equivalent in this case to say that the US$ is "undervalued," pointing out that it should take only $1.50 to purchase one £ but that the actual cost is $1.80. And with the undervalued US$, sellers of American goods have "gained competitiveness" on international markets because for a given amount of funds a buyer can purchase goods in the ratio of 1.2 U.S. goods to only 1.0 British good. On the other hand, if today's spot exchange rate were $1.35/£, the real exchange rate index is 0.90, or 90. At this exchange rate, we would say that the £ is undervalued on a PPP basis or, equivalently, that the US$ is overvalued.

Relaxing the Perfect Capital Market Assumptions

While starting out with the assumptions of a perfect capital market is useful for exploring the interrelationships of prices and exchange rates, the PCM leaves some doubt about how PPP might survive in the real world of transaction costs, taxes, and uncertainty. The basic impact, however, can be easily grasped because PPP (along with the other parity conditions) relies on the process of arbitrage to enforce parity.

Transaction Costs

To begin, consider how the purchasing power parity condition would be affected by the presence of transaction costs. We consider two types of transaction costs: *transport costs* and *menu costs*.

When transport costs are present, arbitrage will not take place to take advantage of a deviation from parity unless the absolute magnitude of the deviation is greater than the transport costs involved in undertaking the arbitrage. This constraint has the effect of creating a "neutral band" within which no arbitrage transactions will occur. Deviations from parity that are smaller than transport costs will persist, because it is not profitable for arbitrageurs to eliminate them.

Transport costs are positively related to the weight, bulk, and value of goods, and the distance between shipping points. If distance were the only factor, then one would expect that price differences between New York and Toronto (550 miles apart) would tend to be smaller than price differences between New York and Los Angeles (3,000 miles apart). Charles Engel and John Rogers (1996) show that, holding distance and product categories constant, deviations from PPP are wider and more variable between U.S. and Canadian cities than between cities in the same country. The authors conclude that "the border matters" as an additional contributing factor to deviations from PPP. In a related finding, John Helliwell (1998) shows that a Canadian province is 12 times more likely to trade merchandise and 40 times more likely to trade services with another Canadian province than with an American state of similar size and distance. Thus, the border matters even between countries that share a common language and a long history of open borders.

Menu costs are another potential factor behind deviations from PPP. Prices of commodities like oil, copper, and coffee are set in markets and change continuously in response to market forces. But prices of other goods such as automobiles, magazines, and restaurant meals are *administered prices* determined by managers. Because there are costs associated with changing prices, such as potential for lost sales, costs of notifying distributors, and costs of reprinting price lists (or restaurant menus), managers are reluctant to change prices unless the benefits of a price change exceed menu costs. Thus, goods prices are likely to be "sticky" and slow to change, while exchange rates, like other financial prices, move rapidly. Menu costs permit larger deviations from PPP. However, the likelihood of goods arbitrage or administered price changes puts a limit on the size of PPP deviations.[11]

Transaction costs lead to a neutral band around the PPP line, within which it is not profitable to execute arbitrage transactions. However, it seems reasonable to assume that there is no reason for the presence of transaction costs to favor either positive or negative deviations from PPP. Therefore, we conclude that transaction costs give rise to deviations from PPP, but not necessarily to deviations that are biased in either direction. So, even when transaction costs are present, we can continue to think of PPP as a useful benchmark when adjusted by an appropriate measure of the neutral band.

Taxes

In the case of purchasing power parity, taxes have an effect similar to transaction costs. For example, to take advantage of deviations from PPP, arbitrageurs would incur tariffs or duties on the goods they are arbitraging. These tariffs reduce the effective amount of funds available for arbitrage by an amount $(1 - \tau)$ where τ is the percentage tariff rate. A tax of this type will simply widen the neutral band within which no profitable arbitrage opportunities are available.

Uncertainty

When certainty is assumed, the calculation of the incentives to buy U.S. or foreign goods is straightforward, because all parameters needed to make the calculation are known. When uncertainty enters, our calculation is subject to errors and risks.

Suppose that a deviation between wheat prices in Chicago and London appears, so that $P_{UK,wheat} \times S_{\$/£} < P_{US,wheat}$. The arbitrageur intends to buy wheat in London and transport it to Chicago for sale. However, arbitrageurs may be uncertain whether they can conduct transactions at the posted prices. The arbitrageur who expects to sell in the Chicago spot market faces the risk of a price change during shipment. And if the arbitrageur hedges this risk by selling the wheat forward for delivery in seven days in the Chicago market, he or she faces the risk that the shipping time may be more or less than seven days.

These examples suggest that the goods arbitrage that underlies PPP may be hindered by uncertainty. Risk-averse arbitrageurs will seek a greater profit to compensate for these risks, thus leading to a wider neutral band around PPP exchange rates.

Note that the relaxation of each assumption—transaction costs, taxes, and uncertainty—results in a wider band around the PPP line before arbitrage becomes profitable. None of these examples, however, suggested a bias in the average size of PPP deviations. Scenarios that could lead to a bias in PPP deviations are discussed later in this chapter.

---

[11]Sercu (1989) models foreign exchange as an option that gives the owner the right to buy foreign goods. As deviations from PPP increase, the option becomes in the money, which raises the likelihood of exercise and caps the deviations from PPP. See also Sercu, Uppal, and Van Hulle (1995).

Empirical Evidence on Prices and Exchange Rates

The raw material for a test of relative PPP is usually one time series of exchange rates and two series of price indexes from the corresponding countries. Still, practical questions are left unanswered. Economists have long debated whether the PPP doctrine applies to the short run or to the long run and whether the relevant inflation rate is on a narrow class of goods (such as traded goods) or a broader class of goods (such as the consumer price index).[12] While PPP is built on commodity arbitrage and the Law of One Price, it is generally agreed that the doctrine of PPP pertains to fairly broad aggregates of goods. Empirically, while there are instances in which PPP is valid on a short-run basis—such as in hyperinflationary economies or where "dollarization" has taken place (to be explained later)—it is generally agreed that PPP describes a long-run phenomenon owing to the fast speed of adjustment in exchange rates relative to the slow rate of change in goods prices.

Empirical Methods, or How to Test a Parity Condition

As described in Figure 4.1, all of the parity conditions involve an expression whereby some left-hand-side (LHS) terms are equated to some right-hand-side (RHS) terms. As a result, the techniques for testing the empirical validity of the parity conditions could share a common approach. Any parity condition could be viewed as a 45° line passing through the origin with the LHS and RHS variables plotted on the vertical and horizontal axes. Thus, parity conditions could be tested by running the simple linear regression:

$$LHS_t = \alpha + \beta \, RHS_t + \epsilon_t$$

where

α = an intercept term,
β = a constant slope coefficient
ϵ_t = a classical error term.[13]

Parity, it could be argued, holds when the data cannot reject a (joint) null hypothesis such that $\alpha = 0$, $\beta = 1$, and the error terms have classical properties.

While regression tests of parity conditions are commonly observed in the literature, we will argue that the regression method of testing is useful only in a few special cases. In many cases, the results of a regression test can be completely misleading. In the context of financial arbitrage conditions, more simple and direct measures will be proposed to test whether a parity condition is valid and whether a parity condition is a useful construct for economic and financial decision making.

Evidence on the Law of One Price

Evidence on the Law of One Price for individual commodities is a logical starting point. Peter Isard (1977) investigated the movements of the dollar prices of German goods relative to their American equivalents, concluding that in reality the Law of One Price is "flagrantly and systematically violated by empirical data . . . Moreover, these relative

---

[12]For surveys of the literature on purchasing power parity, see Officer (1976), Katseli-Papaefstratiou (1979), McKinnon (1979, Chapter 6), Froot and Rogoff (1995), and Rogoff (1996).

[13]Classical error terms are drawn from the normal distribution with mean $\mu = 0$ and standard deviation $\sigma = \sigma_o$. The serial correlation of error terms $\epsilon_t \, \epsilon_{t \pm k}$ is zero for any value $k \neq 0$.

price effects seem to persist for at least several years and cannot be shrugged off as transitory" (p. 942). However, Crouhy-Veyrac et al. (1982) examined categories of goods at a more disaggregated level and found evidence more favorable to the Law of One Price.

As simple as the Law of One Price may seem, researchers face numerous problems in testing it. Seemingly "homogeneous" goods may differ in a number of important respects that undermine tests of the Law of One Price. For example, quality differences across goods are often important. This could include different grades of products (such as in oil or agricultural products) or the ability of a manufacturer to supply products on time and with few defects. Products might be sold in conjunction with various services such as product guarantees, after-sales services (such as installation or repair), or with favorable credit or financing terms included. Merchants also might offer discounts or rebates making transaction prices lower than printed "list" prices.

One of the most visible tests of the Law of One Price is the Big Mac Index published annually in *The Economist* magazine. This "Hamburger Standard" shows the average price of a Big Mac sandwich in various countries around the world.[14] The results of the 2000 survey are graphed in Figure 4.2. The average price of a Big Mac in the United States was $2.51, but internationally, one could pay as little as $1.19 (in Malaysia) or as much as $3.58 (in Israel). Note also that in 23 countries Big Macs are cheaper than in the United States, and in only 8 countries more expensive. This could be taken as an indication that the US$ was relatively overvalued in April 2000.

In a PCM world where sandwiches can be transported for free without getting cold, Figure 4.2 suggests that consumers could engage in profitable international Big Mac arbitrage. In the real world, we suspect that McDonald's is exploiting the barriers to arbitrage as a means to *price discrimination,* charging higher prices where income is high and fast food adds value, and charging lower prices where income is low and substitutes for the Big Mac are plentiful. We will return to the Big Mac Index later in this chapter when we discuss corporate policies in light of the evidence on PPP.

With the rise of e-commerce, investigating the Law of One Price becomes easier and violations more puzzling. A recent *Wall Street Journal* article highlighted the case of a popular book that sold for $16.20 at Amazon.com (United States), for $13.52 at Amazon.co.uk (Britain) and for $27.00 at Amazon.de (Germany).[15] The explanation for these pricing differentials is in part that historic agreements exist among book resellers in Germany to adhere to a uniform (and usually high) fixed price. So far, Amazon.de has respected the fixed-price agreement. But e-commerce is likely to hasten the end of such practices and reduce discrepancies from the Law of One Price, at least for tradable goods.

Relative PPP: Evidence on Recent Quarterly Data

A set of quarterly data for the $/DM exchange rate and U.S. and German consumer prices over the 1973–1999 period is displayed in Appendix A at the end of the book. The first three columns report the spot exchange rate, the German consumer price index, and the U.S. consumer price index (CPI). The remaining columns show the PPP spot rate, the real exchange rate, and the percentage deviation from PPP. These series are

---

[14]There is only one McDonald's restaurant in Africa, so to measure the relative purchasing power of various African currencies, a South African merchant bank (Investec) has proposed its own index based on a 375 ml bottle of clear lager beer. Like the Big Mac, beer has local inputs, but beer is also tradable. See "Through a Glass, Drunkenly," *The Economist,* May 8, 1999.

[15]See Neal A. Boudette, "In Europe, Surfing a Web of Red Tape," *The Wall Street Journal,* October 29, 1999. Price differences across Europe for bigger-ticket items like automobiles and cameras were far larger.

FIGURE 4.2

Big Mac Prices in US$ Relative to U.S. Price
U.S. Price Is $2.51/Big Mac

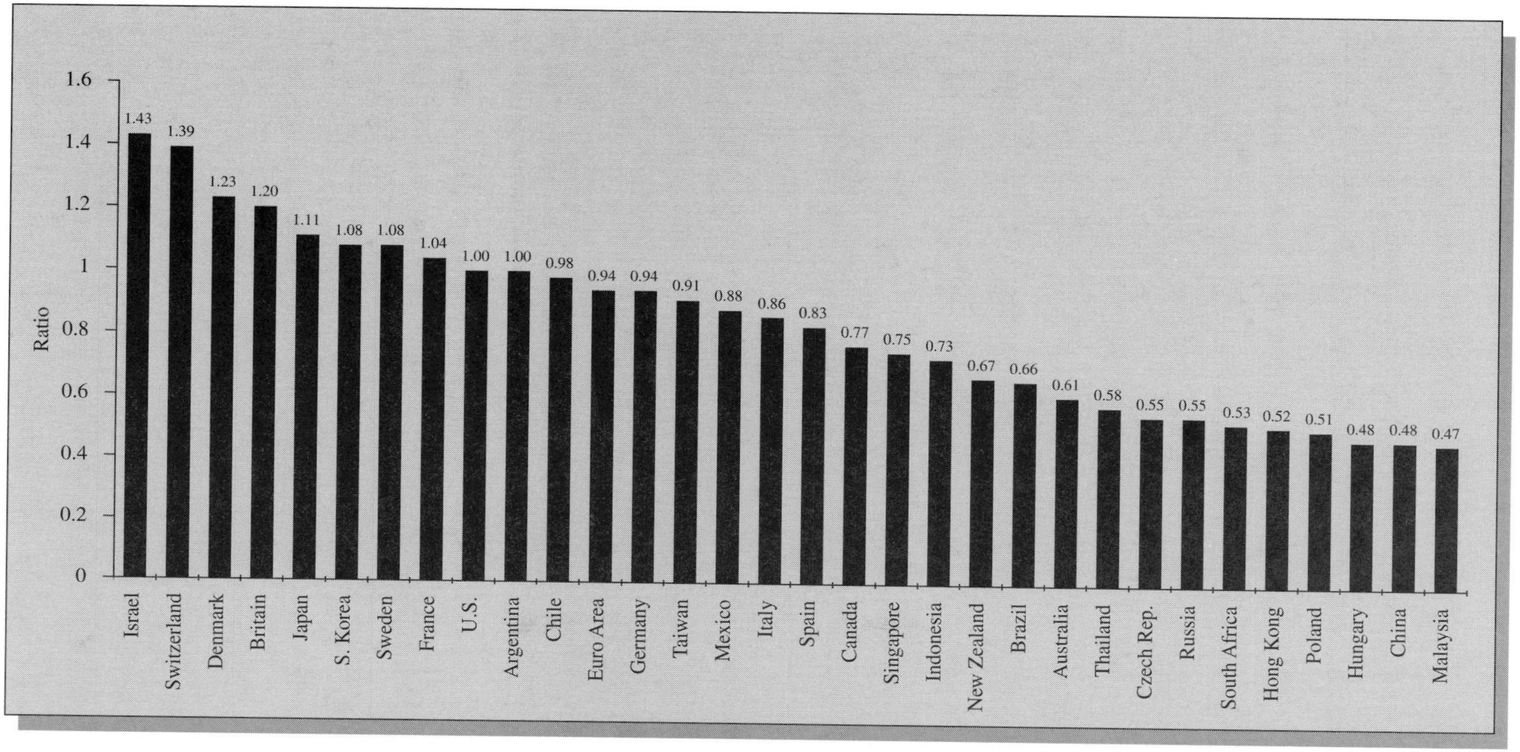

Country	Ratio
Israel	1.43
Switzerland	1.39
Denmark	1.23
Britain	1.20
Japan	1.11
S. Korea	1.08
Sweden	1.08
France	1.04
U.S.	1.00
Argentina	1.00
Chile	0.98
Euro Area	0.94
Germany	0.94
Taiwan	0.91
Mexico	0.88
Italy	0.86
Spain	0.83
Canada	0.77
Singapore	0.75
Indonesia	0.73
New Zealand	0.67
Brazil	0.66
Australia	0.61
Thailand	0.58
Czech Rep.	0.55
Russia	0.55
South Africa	0.53
Hong Kong	0.52
Poland	0.51
Hungary	0.48
China	0.48
Malaysia	0.47

Source: *The Economist*, April 29, 2000.

FIGURE 4.3   **Quarterly Deviations from Relative PPP**
CPI: Germany and the United States, 1973–1999

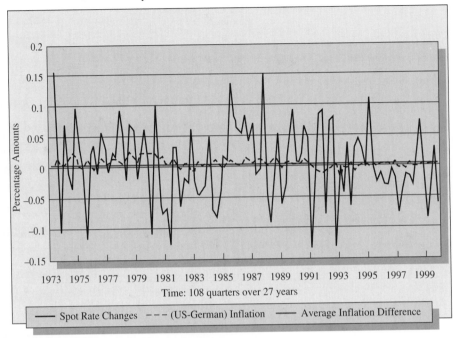

Note: Estimating the regression model $s_t = \alpha + \beta (p_s - p_{DM})_t$ we find:

$\alpha = 0.003$	$\beta = 0.15$	$R^2 = 0.003$	$N = 107$
(0.007)	(0.83)	D-W = 1.83	

with standard errors in parentheses, showing that the $\alpha = 0$ and $\beta = 0$ hypothesis is plausible. So, both the regression estimates and a visual inspection of Figure 4.3 support the conclusion that PPP is a poor explanation of exchange rate changes on a period-by-period basis.

Source: *International Financial Statistics,* and author's calculations.

calculated using the raw data and the formulas developed earlier in this chapter. Notice that we have taken the first period as a base period and defined the real exchange rate as 1.0 in that period.

Consider the period 1973.1–1980.4, during which the $/DM rate rose by nearly 50 percent in nominal terms, from $0.3523/DM to $0.5105/DM. However, the index of U.S. prices rose by nearly 100 percent (from 32.88 to 65.45) and the German prices rose by almost 50 percent (from 54.62 to 78.34). Over this interval of time, we can see that the exchange rate change was nearly matched by the difference between U.S. and German inflation rates. With these exchange rate and price changes, there should have been little change in the real exchange rate. Our calculation shows a real exchange rate of 1.0441, or a small real appreciation of the DM (meaning a DM overvaluation by 4.41 percent on a PPP basis).

To examine the relative PPP condition using a regression test, we would compare the exchange rate change to the contemporaneous inflation differential, using the equation:

$$s_t = \alpha + \beta (p_\$ - p_{DM})_t + \epsilon_t \qquad (4.10)$$

This regression test is a very "demanding" test of PPP in the sense that the exchange rate change is compared to the inflation differential period by period, which is quarter by quarter in this data set. Figure 4.3 graphs spot rate changes and inflation rate differences

FIGURE 4.4   **PPP: Germany and the United States, 1973–1999**
Wholesale and Consumer Price Indexes

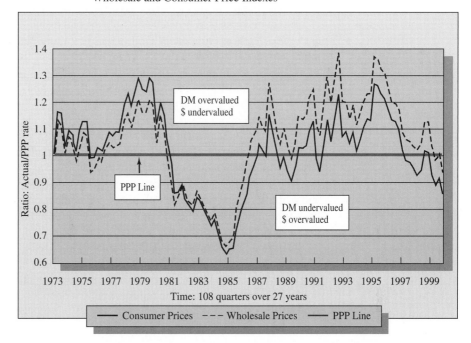

Note: The PPP line represents the nominal exchange rate that would restore PPP using 1973.1 as the base period. The other two lines plot the real exchange rate, defined by the ratio of the nominal exchange rate to its PPP value. The tendency of the exchange rate to revert back to its PPP value is evidence in favor of PPP as a long-run relationship. See Appendix A at the back of the book for details of the calculation.

Source: *International Financial Statistics,* and author's calculations.

(based on the data in Appendix A). Changes in the spot exchange rate form a turbulent series compared to the inflation differential that generally hovers around 0–2 percent per quarter. In Figure 4.3, it appears that there is little relationship between the two series. With a formal regression test, we find coefficients with standard errors in parentheses:

$$\alpha = 0.003 \qquad \beta = 0.15 \qquad R^2 = 0.003 \qquad N = 107$$
$$(0.007) \qquad\qquad (0.83) \qquad\quad D\text{-}W = 1.83$$

showing that $\alpha = 0$ and $\beta = 0$ hypothesis is plausible. Thus, both the regression esti-mates and a visual inspection of Figure 4.3 support the conclusion that PPP is a poor ex-planation of exchange-rate changes on a period-by-period basis. Based on these data, we can infer that quarterly exchange rate changes are driven by factors other than the con-temporaneous inflation differential.

    Figure 4.4 presents the same data on prices and exchange rates in an alternative way, using a graph of the real exchange rate based on equation (4.9). Both the CPI and WPI are used and there is a high correlation between the two real exchange rate series. The series begin at parity and move on the basis of *cumulative* exchange rate changes and inflation since the base period. Figure 4.4 suggests that the real exchange rate may stray from 1.0 (the value consistent with PPP) by a large amount—as much as 28 per-cent real DM appreciation (based on consumer prices) in 1979.3, and 38 percent real US$ appreciation in 1984.4. Clearly 1979 would have been a difficult year to be a

German exporter (and Volkswagen made its decision to invest in the United States at about this time) and 1984 would have been a tough year to be a U.S. exporter (and Caterpillar Tractor made its foreign investment decisions about this time).

But there appears to be a tendency for the real rate to return to PPP, in the sense that each series tends to cross the PPP line every few years. In these examples, counting the initial period, the two series cross the PPP line 14 and 12 times, respectively, in 27 years, an average of about once every 2–3 years. The longest waiting time was six years (between 1980.4 and 1987.1) for the CPI and fully 10 years (between 1989.2 and 1999.2) for the WPI. The shortest was a matter of only one or two quarters.

The tendency for a series to wander away from its average value and then return at later points in time is called **mean reversion.** The visual impression left by Figure 4.4 is that currencies go through periods of undervaluation and overvaluation that can be large, but there is a tendency for PPP to reassert itself as time passes. This would imply that PPP holds in the sense that deviations from parity can be both positive and negative, and that after some period of time there is a tendency for the exchange rate to revert back toward its PPP level. In Chapter 8, we will discuss how this property can be used in forecasting.

Corporate investment and capital budgeting decisions rely on cash flow calculations that are greatly simplified when PPP is assumed.[16] How competitive conditions will evolve over the life of a project and the rate at which foreign currency cash flows will be converted into domestic funds are better understood by analyzing the **deviations from PPP:**

$$d_t = s_t - (p_\$ - p_{DM})_t$$

rather than by the results of a regression like (4.10). This suggests that an analysis of PPP should focus on the *magnitude* of PPP deviations and the *length of time* that they persist. These measures reveal the size and duration of competitive shocks, and whether on average foreign currency cash flows will be converted at PPP rates.

In the case of the \$/DM rate from 1973 to 1999, the average deviation from parity in any quarter using the CPI was a mere 0.02 percent and not significantly different from zero. The average length of time required for the exchange rate to cross the PPP line (based on the CPI) was a little less than two years. However, using the WPI, the average deviation from parity in any quarter was 4.10 percent, an amount significantly greater than zero. With PPP calculated using the WPI, we found that the index was greater than 1.0 for most of the period from mid-1986 onward, with only one dip below 1.0 in 1989 and another in 1999. Taken together, these findings suggest that PPP held on average over the period using the CPI, but not using the WPI. With large temporary deviations possible using either index, there can be substantial competitive risks present for businesses producing in one country and selling goods in another.[17]

Relative PPP: Evidence from Hyperinflationary Economies

Other empirical evidence on PPP is worth highlighting. In a regression test (like equation 4.10) using data from Germany, which experienced hyperinflation during the

---

[16]See Lessard (1979) for a discussion on this issue.

[17]As an exercise, use data for Japan or another country and repeat the same calculations. What do you conclude? Next, try the same calculations for neighboring countries—the United States and Canada or Germany and the Netherlands. What do you conclude? Finally, try the same calculations for the United States, and one highly inflationary economy: Israel, Brazil, or Mexico. What do you conclude?

1920s, and three foreign countries, Jacob Frenkel (1980) concluded that in most cases the German exchange rate moved on a one-for-one basis with respect to the inflation differential. During a hyperinflation period, exchange rate changes may be dominated by contemporaneous developments in domestic inflation. In this case, even the demanding regression-style test tends to support PPP.

In the limit, businesses and consumers in a hyperinflationary economy may attempt to abandon their domestic currency, substituting a more stable unit of account, such as the US$, in its place. A wide-scale replacement of domestic currency by the US$ for purposes of quoting prices (unit of account), making transactions (medium of exchange), and holding wealth (store of value) has been termed **dollarization.**[18] In the 1980s and 1990s, reports of dollarization were common for some Latin American countries experiencing high inflation and in some newly capitalistic countries such as Vietnam and the former Soviet Union republics.

Dollarization works as follows. Suppose a television set in Mexico City is priced at 1,200 pesos, reflecting a $400 TV price and 3 peso/$. If the peso devalues to 6 peso/$, the price of the TV set would be changed immediately to 2,400 pesos. In effect, the TV set has been "priced" in US$. The exchange rate change has been immediately "passed through" into the local currency price. For these goods, PPP holds immediately since merchants *use* PPP to calculate their local prices. If all goods and services, including labor rates, in the local economy were priced in this manner (and indexed to the exchange rate), dollarization would lead to a PPP pattern of exchange rates and prices.

Relative PPP: Evidence from Long-Run Data

Most recently, empirical tests of PPP have used longer time series of prices and exchange rates to see if the use of more data enables researchers to reach more definitive conclusions regarding PPP. As our visual inspection of Figure 4.4 suggests, if there is a tendency for the real exchange rate to return to its PPP value, then it can be argued that PPP holds in the long run. This tendency for a time series to revert back to its mean is characteristic of a *stationary time series*. A **random walk** is an example of a *nonstationary time series* because it holds no tendency to return to its starting value (or any other value). Some researchers have not rejected the possibility that real exchange rates (as well as nominal exchange rates) evolve as a random walk without any mean reverting properties.[19]

To investigate this possibility, Niso Abuaf and Philippe Jorion (1990) examined 80 years of $/£ and $/FFr exchange rates. The time series graphs of these two exchange rates (see Figure 4.5) show clearly that the nominal exchange rate has no tendency to return to any particular level over the entire sample period.[20] The real exchange rate, however, demonstrates a clear tendency to revert back to its central value. Abuaf and Jorion computed that the rate of reversion toward the mean is such that a 50 percent overvaluation relative to PPP would take three to five years to be cut in half, and that the real exchange rate requires about three years on average to cross the PPP line. It is important to stress that while Abuaf and Jorion analyze 80 years of data, this does not imply that it takes 80 years for PPP to hold! Rather, it takes a large amount of data to have the real

---

[18]In Chapter 2, we referred to the case where the US$ is used in all transactions and completely replaces the local currency as *full dollarization.*

[19]See Meese and Rogoff (1988) or Mark (1990).

[20]In more technical terms, the nominal exchange rate is a nonstationary series.

FIGURE 4.5   Real and Nominal Exchange Rates over a Long-Run Period

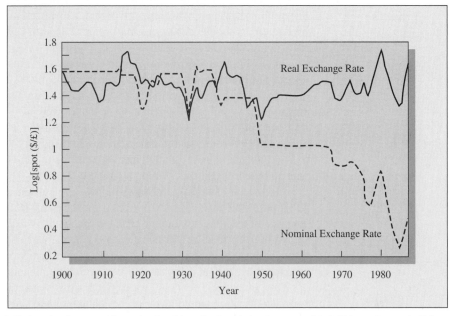

Dollar/pound exchange rate. Time-series plot of the real and nominal exchange rate of the British pound versus the U.S. dollar ($/£), based on annual averages. The real exchange rate is obtained by deflating the nominal exchange rate by the ratio of wholesale price indexes. The vertical scale is measured as the logarithm of the exchange rate. The real exchange rate is translated so that the 1900 value is equal to that of the nominal exchange rate.

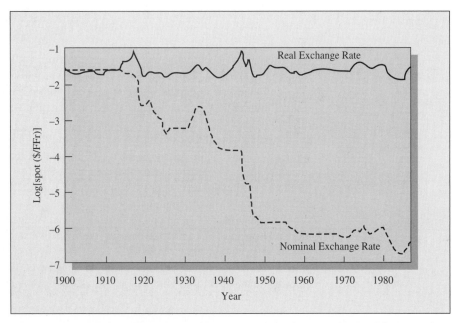

Dollar/French franc exchange rate. Time-series plot of the real and nominal exchange rate of the French franc versus the U.S. dollar ($/FFr), based on annual averages.

Source: Niso Abuaf and Philippe Jorion, "Purchasing Power Parity in the Long-Run," *Journal of Finance* 45, no. 1, Mar. 1990, pp. 171–72.

exchange rate go through enough cycles to be able to measure the average length of one cycle with reasonable precision.

Maurice Obstfeld (1995) looks at exchange rate changes and inflation over a 20-year period (1973–1993) in the modern float. A regression such as equation (4.10) is estimated, using data for 22 Organization for Economic Cooperation and Development (OECD) countries. Obstfeld reports regression estimates with standard errors in parentheses as:

$$\alpha = -0.066 \qquad \beta = 1.011 \qquad R^2 = 0.97$$
$$(0.193) \qquad\qquad (0.038) \qquad\qquad N = 22$$

These results show convincingly that over the modern period, the long-run variation in exchange rate changes across countries is largely dependent on differences in rates of inflation.

Empirical Tests of PPP: Is the Real Exchange Rate Constant?

Perhaps the most difficult problem in testing the empirical validity of PPP is that the real exchange rate itself need not be constant. Real variables (such as real income or the real exchange rate) may change *permanently* if there is a corresponding permanent real disturbance. The real exchange rate could change on a permanent basis if a real shock affected one country but not its trading partners.

One real shock in particular has attracted considerable interest. Suppose a country experiences real productivity gains in its traded-goods sector. Wages will rise in this sector but not prices, because prices are held in check by international competition. However, because the country draws its labor from a single domestic pool, wages in the nontraded, or service, sector also rise, leading to a rise in non-traded-goods prices and the overall consumer price index. If this hypothesis—known as the **Balassa-Samuelson hypothesis**—holds, then countries that have experienced high productivity gains, higher real income growth and higher real incomes should have appreciating real exchange rates (when other factors are held constant).

The classic test case for the Balassa-Samuelson hypothesis has been Japan, where fast economic growth went hand in hand with a sustained appreciation in Japan's real exchange rate against the US$. Over the 1960–1997 period, Japanese industrial production grew more than 2 percent per year faster than in the United States. The difference in growth was even more pronounced in the 1960s and 1970s. As Figure 4.6 shows, the yen steadily appreciated in real terms over the 1960s and 1970s, with greater appreciation evident using the CPI as we expected, and with no tendency to revert back toward a mean value. Notably, from 1978 to 1998, U.S. and Japanese industrial production have grown at almost identical rates. And over this period the real yen/dollar rate has shown some tendency to revert toward its 1978 level.

Assuming that the long-run real exchange rate is constant is of course a convenience, one that might plausibly be based on the assumption that while real shocks occur, they may affect all countries more or less equally, leaving the long-run real exchange rate unchanged. Still, for countries that experience country-specific real shocks a change in the long-run real exchange rate remains a possibility.[21]

---

[21]See Edison (1987) for an analysis of 90 years of $/£ exchange rates. PPP generally holds, but there is a shift in the level of the equilibrium real exchange rate over the period.

FIGURE 4.6   Real Yen/$ Exchange Rate

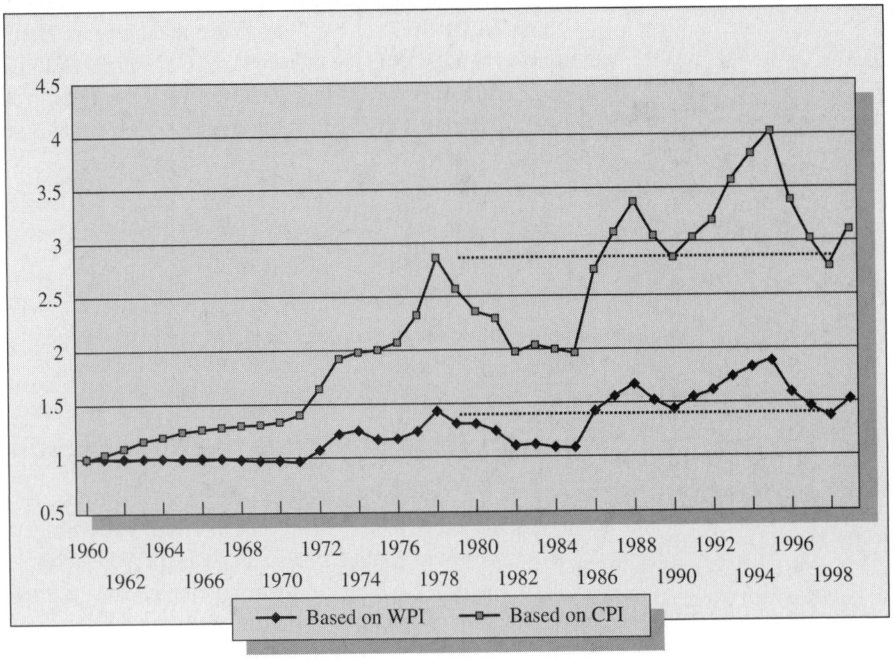

Source: *International Financial Statistics,* and author's calculations.

Empirical Tests of PPP: The Final Word

Empirical tests confirm that PPP is a poor description of exchange rate behavior in the short run, where exchange rates are quite volatile and domestic prices are somewhat sticky. But in longer-run analysis, it appears that PPP offers a reasonably good guide. In his review of the literature, Kenneth Rogoff (1996) suggests that for a broad sample of countries, the half-life of deviations from PPP may be around three to five years, meaning that deviations from PPP dampen out at a rate of about 15 percent per year. More recent analysis by Mark Taylor and David Peel (2000) suggests that the speed of return to PPP may increase when the deviation is larger. These findings of mean reversion are good news, and in Chapter 8 we will discuss how this property can be used in forecasting. However, large potential deviations from PPP spell competitive risks that firms must prepare to manage.

Policy Matters—Private Enterprises

The Role of Parity Conditions for Management Decisions

An important theme of this book is that parity conditions play an important role in the formation of strategies toward international financial markets formulated by people in private enterprise; that is, individuals acting on their own behalf and decision makers acting on behalf of firms. In this section, we develop this theme further, showing how the parity conditions impact many investment and financial management decisions facing individuals and firms.

Earlier in this chapter, we referred to the parity conditions as *benchmarks* or *break-even points*. When parities hold, a source of risk and a source of opportunity disappear; therefore, a decision point is removed. In particular, when PPP holds, a firm can make its selection of a production location on the basis of comparative advantage (according to traditional trade theory) without concern that a nominal exchange rate change will alter its competitiveness. When PPP holds, exchange rate changes do not affect the real costs of goods produced or the real revenues from goods sold, and so this channel of exchange risk is removed.

As we will be able to show at the end of Chapter 5, if all of the parity conditions were valid *at each and every moment in time* there would be no important financial managerial decisions to make since all choices would be fairly priced vis-à-vis the alternatives. The empirical evidence will show that while many of the parity conditions may hold "in most cases" or "on average," at many times the parity conditions are violated. As a result, managers are not relieved from having to make critical financial decisions.

We will distinguish two categories of financial decisions: **profit maximizing** and **risk managing.** If managers can identify those deviations from parity that are small and growing larger, or those that are already large and likely to persist, then active, profit-maximizing decisions will follow. Other things being equal, managers prefer to locate production in countries with undervalued currencies that benefit competitiveness, and managers prefer to earn revenues in markets with overvalued currencies. These profit-maximizing decisions assume that managers can move quickly enough to capture a parity deviation and that the risks involved are not excessive.

On the other hand, managers may believe that the parity conditions hold "on average," but they are not able to detect whether a deviation from parity is likely to be transitory or persistent. However, knowing that deviations from parity occur—and they have both uncertain size and duration—managers may adopt strategies that reduce their exposure to the risks of deviations from parity. For example, spreading production locations across countries is one way (albeit costly) to deal with the risk of PPP deviations.

Thus, understanding the magnitude and duration of deviations from the parity conditions will form the foundation for many of the decisions that international financial managers are asked to make.

Purchasing Power Parity and Managerial Decisions

The purchasing power parity condition rests heavily on the Law of One Price, a "law" that empirical observation shows (Isard 1977, p. 942) is "flagrantly and systematically violated."[22] In the case of commodities such as oil, grain, and metals, this result might be rationalized by a number of arguments—the heterogeneity of varieties for a commodity seemingly as homogenous as oil, coffee, or copper; the cost of transoceanic shipment; and the uncertainty of price changes while on route. Still, in a number of instances international price differentials in some commodities have been both large and persistent. Presumably, buyers of these commodities (such as, international steel, food, and electrical firms) stand to make substantial gains by locating the low-cost source of their inputs worldwide.[23]

---

[22]More recently, Cooper (1993) has commented that "anyone who does serious comparative shopping knows that the Law of One Price does not, in fact, obtain."

[23]Cooper (1993) cites the substantial price differential in copper between the United States and the London Metal Exchange that persisted for nearly two decades.

Box 4.2

Gray Markets and the Law of One Price

The strong US$ of the mid-1980s led to the development of so-called gray markets, whereby individuals would legally import goods from a foreign market (e.g., Germany at existing DM prices for goods) and then sell the imports at low prices (based on the strong $) in competition with U.S. distributors of the same products. In some cases, conversion costs were incurred—so a gray-market Mercedes would need to be refitted from European "specs" to American "specs" in order to pass emissions and safety requirements. But in other cases, such as Sony portable "boom boxes" or Nikon cameras, no conversion was necessary. Gray-market sellers could compete with—and usually undercut—traditional merchants who sold the imports at United States "list" prices.

While these gray-market activities were not illegal, some companies actively tried to derail them. Duracell, the Connecticut-based battery company, went so far as to ask U.S. Customs and then the U.S. courts to block the importation of Duracell batteries (made in Belgian factories 100 percent owned by Duracell) on the grounds of trademark infringement.* The activity of independent wholesalers buying up Duracell batteries in Europe and selling them throughout the United States was probably disruptive to Duracell's U.S. operations, but it was not illegal. On the other hand, some foreign companies used the strong dollar to find novel ways to promote the sales of their products in

the United States. In late 1984, Harrod's (the upscale London department store) rented space in the ballroom of New York's Waldorf-Astoria Hotel in order to bring its merchandise closer to U.S. buyers who thought that $1.05/£ was an opportunity too good to miss. With the strength of the Japanese yen, which broke below 100 ¥/$ in June 1994 and traded below 85 ¥/$ for several months in 1995, U.S. department stores should have found it worthwhile to set up displays in Tokyo hotels. To economize on Tokyo rents, U.S. merchants could probably use cable television or a home shopping network to reach Tokyo shoppers. Or follow the strategy of L. L. Bean, the mail-order merchandiser of outdoor clothing, by sending catalogs with US$ prices to Japanese home shoppers.

---

*Duracell argued that its branded product involved an implicit set of services, such as controlled shipping conditions and product freshness, that could not be guaranteed with gray market imports. Duracell lost its case. See Cooper (1993). In a very similar case, L'anza (a California maker of hair care products) was selling its products to overseas distributors at discounts of 35 to 40 percent, only to find the products being shipped back to the United States by third parties. L'anza claimed copyright infringement, but the U.S. Supreme Court ruled that the firm could not stop these gray-market transactions. See "Supreme Court Decision Limits Ability to Block 'Gray Market,'" *The Wall Street Journal,* March 9, 1998.

Purchasing Power Parity and Product Pricing Decisions

More interesting perhaps are the international price differentials across "branded goods," more interesting because these prices are set by brand managers or marketing managers rather than by market forces. As we will discuss in Chapter 16, customers prefer to face stable prices in their own local currency, and firms like to oblige their customers. This is true for every country in which a multinational firm operates. When exchange rates fluctuate, a multinational firm must decide whether to let its prices fluctuate in its home market, its foreign markets, or both. But at times it seems as if firms have tried to keep their prices *fixed* in *both* home and foreign markets (in terms of local currency) and then to erect barriers that separate the markets. *Price discrimination* of this sort is profitable for the firm, as long as it keeps "gray-market" arbitrageurs (described in Box 4.2) from exploiting these international price differences.

The Big Mac Index (see Figure 4.2) shows the extent to which international price discrimination is possible for a particular product. While the pricing decision for a product is complex, we can list some of the major factors that contribute to international

FIGURE 4.7   Factors Leading to Deviations from Big Mac Parity and Product X Parity

	Big Macs	*Product X*
Production Location	More than 18,000 restaurants in 91 countries	
Production Costs		
Materials	Wheat and beef produced locally, traded internationally	
Labor	Local labor, nontraded	
Overhead	Real estate, nontraded	
Product Characteristics		
Tradable/nontradable	Nontradable good	
Durable/nondurable	Nondurable good	
Differentiated	Differentiated product	
Warranties/service	Produced by firm with reputation for quality and consistency	
Price elasticity	May be price inelastic	
Close substitutes	Close substitutes in some locations	
Market leader	Leader in many locations	
Industry Characteristics		
Local competitors	Many fast-food merchants	
Foreign competitors	Foreigners must use direct investment to compete	
Profit margins	Higher on prepared/processed food	
Cyclical/noncyclical	Noncyclical	
Market Characteristics		
Level of income	Dining out rises with income	
Tariff or trade barriers	Few entry barriers to restaurants	
Distance between markets	Markets often close together	

Note: Pick your own candidate for a "Product X." A 12-ounce can of Coca-Cola, an "AAA" Duracell battery, or a Hilton Hotel room are examples. In the right-hand column, evaluate each product, market, and industry characteristic for your "Product X." What impact will these characteristics have on the pricing of your product from country to country? Overall, do you think that your product will exhibit larger or smaller deviations from the Law of One Price than we saw in Figure 4.2 for the Big Mac?

price variation, in Figure 4.7.[24] The Big Mac is a nontradable and nondurable product; it is a differentiated product with an implied warranty associated with the reputation of the McDonald's Corporation. All of these factors permit McDonald's to set the profit-maximizing price in a country, ignoring the prospect of Big Mac arbitrage. On the other hand, Big Macs are produced locally in 91 countries, always with local labor and on local land, and usually with locally produced materials. Thus, production costs vary with location. Income levels vary greatly across markets, from China (with a GNP of $500–$1,000 per capita) to Switzerland (with a GNP of nearly $35,000 per capita). And the availability of close substitutes are a factor, with "fast-food" street-corner vendors plentiful and popular in many parts of Asia. All of these factors come together to influence the local pricing decisions for the Big Mac—and how local prices respond when the local exchange rate changes against the US$.

---

[24]See Pugel and Lindert (2000) for a detailed discussion of international price discrimination.

How would the international pricing of other products compare with the pattern for the Big Mac? As a classroom exercise, consider another product (such as, a 12-ounce can of Coca-Cola, an "AAA" Duracell battery, a Hilton Hotel room) and discuss how you would set prices for the product in various parts of the world. It may be helpful to use the data on Big Macs in Figure 4.2 as a reference point.

To illustrate the exercise, we turn the tables on the British publication *The Economist* and investigate *their* international pricing based on the newsstand prices listed on the cover of each issue. The April 9, 1994, issue of *The Economist* listed newsstand prices in 28 countries, 12 of which were included in the Big Mac Index.

The results for all 12 countries are plotted in Figure 4.8. The U.S. newsstand price of *The Economist* was $3.50, and US$ equivalent prices ranged from $2.77 in Britain to $8.17 in Japan. We examine *The Economist* prices in US$ to permit a comparison with Big Mac pricing.[25] We can see that pricing for *The Economist* in China and Hong Kong is considerably steeper than Big Mac pricing there. Perhaps *The Economist* is appealing to a more narrow, higher-income market segment than McDonald's is aiming for or perhaps there are fewer close substitutes for *The Economist* magazine. We see that pricing in Russia is at parity with the United States. Interestingly, the cover quotes the Russian price as *US$3.50*, reflecting dollarization in the Russian economy. Prices of *The Economist* in most European countries seem to be roughly in line with Big Mac prices.

Atish Ghosh and Holger Wolf (1994) investigated whether newsstand prices of *The Economist* over an 18-year period were adjusted strategically to pass through the impact of exchange rate changes, or whether prices were changed infrequently in a lumpy manner consistent with menu costs. The authors reported that the data were consistent with the view that the publisher attempts to stabilize local currency prices and that price changes are infrequent owing to menu costs. The authors also argued that this non-strategic behavior may be mistaken for strategic local price changes in response to exchange rate changes. This strategic behavior, called **exchange rate pass-through,** is a common way for firms to manage the risk of foreign currency operating cash flows. We will discuss this in more detail in Chapter 16.

Policy Matters—Public Policymakers

The international parity conditions developed in this chapter (and in Chapter 5) play an important role in the variety of public policy discussions. At a point in time, each parity condition gives a snapshot view of one segment of the international financial markets. At a point in time, we learn whether a currency is overvalued or undervalued relative to a particular PPP standard and we observe a rough estimate of the market's expectations regarding future exchange rate changes (from the Fisher parities developed in Chapter 5). Over a longer time frame, the validity of the parity conditions provides information on the functioning of international financial markets, such as how much risk is present in the volatility of real exchange rates and whether financial markets efficiently reflect information about future exchange rate changes.

Purchasing power parity is an important construct for policymakers, even though PPP is not a model of short-run or even long-run exchange rate determination. Deviations from PPP, by definition, measure changes in a country's international competitiveness. At times, national policymakers have welcomed a real depreciation of their currency as a

---

[25]*The Economist* is printed in various locations around the world with input from journalists stationed in Great Britain and elsewhere. A comparison of international prices with British prices may be more suitable.

FIGURE 4.8 **Big Mac Prices and The Economist Prices in US\$ Relative to U.S. Price**

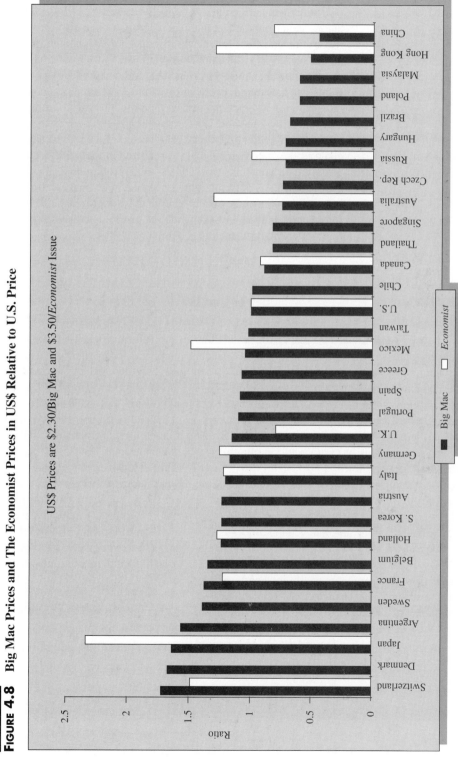

US\$ Prices are \$2.30/Big Mac and \$3.50/*Economist* Issue

Source: *The Economist*, April 9, 1994, and author's calculations.

means of spurring economic recovery through export-led growth. In other cases, national policymakers have embraced real appreciation, perhaps as a symbol of national strength, but more tangibly as a means to raise domestic living standards through cheaper imports.

Still, there are limitations on the usefulness of PPP in policy decisions. These limitations stem from the fact that real macroeconomic disturbances call for a change in the real exchange rate. Earlier, we introduced the Balassa-Samuelson hypothesis, which predicts larger PPP deviations for pairs of countries with different income levels.

Consider a country experiencing rapid real productivity increases. The country also is likely to have rapid income growth and real currency appreciation. The real exchange rate change will be permanent as the productivity differential is sustained relative to other countries. Or consider a country that liberalizes its capital markets to permit greater foreign investments that had been constrained in earlier years. This real change could lead to a permanent real depreciation of the home currency as local investors rebalance their portfolios to include a larger proportion of foreign investments.

Thus, PPP is a useful guide for public policymakers. It reveals whether a currency is overvalued or undervalued relative to a simple standard. But PPP is not a substitute for a complete model of exchange rate determination to understand whether exchange rates reflect all fundamental economic variables.

Summary

In this chapter, we introduced the main parity conditions that one encounters in the study of international finance: purchasing power parity, interest rate parity, the Fisher parities, and the unbiased forward rate condition. These parity conditions are a useful way to compare alternative international market opportunities. The parity conditions are important whether they hold empirically or not, because violations of parity could imply direct or indirect profit opportunities.

Our focus in this chapter has been on purchasing power parity (PPP). While PPP is built upon the Law of One Price, we stressed the relative version of PPP, which may be valid even if the absolute version of PPP is violated. Two constructs—PPP and the real exchange rate—are closely linked. When relative PPP holds, the real exchange rate and competitiveness are unaffected by nominal exchange rate changes. Relaxing the perfect capital market assumptions may lead to deviations from PPP, but these deviations should be limited in magnitude, falling within a neutral band on either side of the parity line. Relaxing the perfect capital market assumptions should not lead to a bias in measured PPP deviations.

The empirical evidence on PPP is sensitive to the empirical techniques applied. Regression tests of PPP are very demanding and tend to reject PPP when we look at short time intervals (quarters) and short sample periods. If we look at longer time intervals, regression tests tend to support PPP. Another way to check PPP is to measure the tendency for mean reversion in the real exchange rate. Empirical evidence supports this tendency. However, real exchange rates, like any other real variable, may change when there are real shocks to the economy. So, we cannot consider a reversion to an initial PPP value as a certainty, even in the long run.

The PPP paradigm plays a role in pricing decisions for private enterprises. If product markets are well arbitraged, then there are limits to how far prices of goods may diverge across countries. However, anecdotal evidence suggests that there is considerable scope for charging different prices in different markets, especially for "branded products" and in markets where incomes and the availability of product substitutes differ.

APPENDIX 4.1
PPP, CONTINUOUS COMPOUNDING, AND LOGARITHMIC RETURNS

In this chapter, several parity conditions were developed that involved the percentage rate of change in one variable. The percentage rate of change can be computed simply as:

$$\Delta X_{t+1} = (X_{t+1} - X_t)/X_t \qquad \text{(A4.1)}$$

But in many situations, it will be easier and more accurate to measure the percentage rate of change in continuous, or logarithmic terms as:

$$x_{t+1} = ln(X_{t+1}/X_t) = ln\,(X_{t+1}) - ln\,(X_t) \qquad \text{(A4.2)}$$

where *ln* represents the natural logarithm.

Consider this example. If the variable *X* rises from $X_t = 100$ to $X_{t+1} = 110$, the percentage change is 10 percent. This figure represents "simple interest" or "simple compounding" as if the 10 units of growth were paid once at the end of the single period. The logarithmic return in this case would be:

$$x_{t+1} = ln(110/100) = ln\,(1.10) = 9.5310 \text{ percent} \qquad \text{(A4.3)}$$

The logarithmic return assumes that the growth in *X* occurs continuously—a small amount every instant—and is compounded continuously. The logarithmic return is just another way to express the growth of *X* from 100 to 110 over some period of time. Note that $100 \times e^{0.09531} = 110$.

Why bother to use a logarithmic rate of return instead of a simple rate of return? In our discussion of purchasing power parity, equation (4.5) included a cross-product term ($s \times p_{UK}$) that was essential to make the equation hold true. Suppose we go back to our original expressions (4.3a and 4.3b), take their ratio, and then take logs:

$$ln\frac{P_{US,\,t+1}}{P_{US,\,t}} = ln\frac{K \times S_{\$/£,\,t+1} \times P_{UK,\,t+1}}{K \times S_{\$/£,\,t} \times P_{UK,\,t}}$$

or

$$ln(P_{US,t+1}) - ln(P_{US,t}) =$$
$$ln(S_{\$/£,t+1}) - ln(S_{\$/£,t}) + ln(P_{UK,t+1}) - ln(P_{UK,t})$$

or

$$p_{US} = s + p_{UK}$$

where the lowercase letters now represent the **continuous rate of return** of the uppercase variable, and for convenience we omit the $t+1$ subscript. Notice that the cross-product term has been eliminated by using logarithms and the continuous rate of return. One reason for using the continuous return is to simplify the analysis of a regression equation by eliminating one term.

Note also that many of the economic variables used in international finance, such as goods prices, stock prices, and exchange rates, are often expressed as indexes. Without loss of generality, we can define the initial value of any index as unity. Because the logarithm of unity is zero, measuring the logarithmic return in equation (A4.2) becomes:

$$x_{t+1} = ln(X_{t+1}/X_t) = ln\,(X_{t+1}) - ln\,(1.0) = ln\,(X_{t+1}) \qquad \text{(A4.4)}$$

Adopting this convention (taking the initial value of a series as unity) allows us to assert that the logarithm of a variable, $x = ln(X)$, represents the continuous rate of change in the variable.

Questions

1. Define the necessary conditions for a perfect capital market. Why do these assumptions make the analysis of international parity conditions easier?

2. Define and contrast absolute and relative purchasing power parity. Provide an example of each.

3. When does a change in nominal level of prices in two countries *not* imply any change in real exchange rates?

4. Define the real spot exchange rate between two currencies. What are the "units" of the real exchange rate?

5. "When purchasing power parity holds, the real exchange rate is constant." Discuss.

6. Describe several alternative methods for testing purchasing power parity. What is the most appropriate method?

7. What empirical evidence tends to show that PPP holds in the long term?

8. "When PPP holds, managers can choose their production location solely on the basis of comparative advantage." Is this statement true or false? Why?

9. Empirical evidence shows frequent deviations from purchasing power parity. Do these deviations always represent profit opportunities for business managers?

10. Empirical evidence shows frequent deviations from purchasing power parity. What kind of threats and opportunities does this open up for financial managers?

Exercises

1. Suppose a Big Mac at a McDonald's in New York costs $2.50 and FFr 15 in Paris.
   a. What spot exchange rate establishes the Law of One Price for these two commodities?
   b. If the current spot exchange rate is FFr 5/$, what is the real exchange rate? What are the units of the calculation?
   c. According to your calculation, is the dollar overvalued or undervalued? How about the French franc?

2. A bottle of champagne costs FFr 150 in a Paris wine store. The same bottle of champagne costs DM 45 in a Frankfurt wine store.
   a. What spot exchange rate establishes the Law of One Price for these two commodities?
   b. If the current spot exchange rate is 3.55 FFr/DM, what is the real exchange rate? What are the units of the calculation?
   c. According to your calculation, is the DM overvalued or undervalued?

3. Data on price indexes and exchange rates in 1973 and 1993 for 22 OECD countries are available at the author's website*. Estimate a regression of the form:

$$Y_i = a + bX_i$$

   where Y is the exchange rate change over the 20-year period and X is the total inflation over 20-year period for $i = 1, \ldots 22$ countries. Do your results come close to the results computed by Obstfeld (1995) and reported in this chapter?

4. Suppose the expected annual inflation rate in the United Kingdom is 4.5 percent and that in the United States 3 percent. According to PPP, will the dollar appreciate or depreciate? By what percentage?

5. Suppose the current spot rate is $1.55/£ on the first of January. By year-end, the U.S. CPI is expected to climb from 144 to 150 and the U.K. CPI from 120 to 130. According to PPP, what is the expected spot rate on December 31?

6. Consider the following data for the United States and Surlandia for the years 1975–1980.

	1975	1976	1977	1978	1979	1980
Pengo/$	8.5	17.4	28.0	34.0	39.0	39.0
Surlandia CPI	100	312	599	838	1118	1511
U.S. CPI	161.2	170.5	181.5	195.4	217.4	246.8

   a. According to the purchasing power parity theory, by how much is the pengo overvalued or undervalued at the end of 1980?
   b. On what basis could someone refute your calculation?

7. In the above table of numbers for Surlandia and the United States, the nominal bilateral exchange rate at the end of 1980 was reported as 39.0 pengos/$. What was the real bilateral exchange rate?

8. Try your hand at testing the Law of One Price by checking the purchase price of a book at Amazon.com from their sites in the United States (*www.amazon.com*), Germany (*www.amazon.de*), and Britain (*www.amazon.co.uk*). Try several different books—perhaps *Galileo's Daughter*, by Dava Sobel (the book we presented data on in this chapter), or use another book. How similar are the three prices? Would it be cheaper to buy from one of the foreign sites than a domestic site after taking transactions costs into account?

---

*See the author's website at
<www.stern.nyu.edu\~rlevich\book1\datafile.htm>.

References

Abuaf, Niso, and Philippe Jorion. "Purchasing Power Parity in the Long Run." *Journal of Finance* 45, no. 1 (Mar. 1990), pp. 157–74.

Cassel, Gustav. *Money and Foreign Exchange After 1914.* London: Constable, 1922.

Cooper, Richard N. "An Overview of (Older) Exchange Rate Theory." In *Japan and International Financial Markets: Analytical and Empirical Perspectives,* Ryuzo Sato, Richard M. Levich, and Rama Ramachandran, eds. Cambridge: Cambridge University Press, 1993.

Crouhy-Veyrac, L.; M. Crouhy; and J. Melitz. "More About the Law of One Price." *European Economic Review* 18 (1982), pp. 325–44.

Dornbusch, Rudiger, and Paul R. Krugman. "Flexible Exchange Rates in the Short Run." *Brookings Papers on Economic Activity,* no. 3 (1976), pp. 537–84.

Edison, Hali J. "Purchasing Power Parity in the Long Run: A Test of the Dollar/Pound Exchange Rate (1890–1978)." *Journal of Money Credit and Banking,* Aug. 1987, pp. 376–87.

Engel, Charles, and John H. Rogers. "How Wide Is the Border?" *American Economic Review* 86, no. 5 (December 1996), pp. 1112–25.

Fama, Eugene F., and Merton H. Miller. *The Theory of Finance.* New York: Holt, Rinehart and Winston, 1972.

Frenkel, Jacob A. "Exchange Rates, Prices and Money: Lessons from the 1920s." *American Economic Review* 70 (1980), pp. 235–42.

Froot, Kenneth A., and Kenneth Rogoff. "Perspectives on PPP and Long-Run Real Exchange Rates." In *Handbook of International Economics,* vol. 3, G. Grossman and K. Rogoff, eds. Amsterdam: North-Holland, 1995.

Ghosh, Atish R., and Holger Wolf. "Pricing in International Markets: Lessons from *The Economist*." NBER Working Paper No. 4806, July 1994.

Helliwell, John. *How Much Do National Borders Matter?* (Washington, DC: Brookings Institution), 1998.

Isard, Peter. "How Far Can We Push the Law of One Price?" *American Economic Review* 67, no. 6 (Dec. 1977), pp. 942–48.

Katseli-Papaefstratiou, Louka T. "The Reemergence of the Purchasing Power Parity Doctrine in the 1970s."

Princeton Special Papers in International Economics, no. 13, 1979.

Lessard, Donald R. "Evaluating Foreign Projects: An Adjusted Present Value Approach." In *International Financial Management: Theory and Application.* D. Lessard, ed. Boston: Warren, Gorham, and Lamont, 1979.

Mark, Nelson. "Real Exchange Rates in the Long-Run: An Empirical Investigation." *Journal of International Economics* 28 (1990), pp. 115–36.

McKinnon, Ronald I. *Money in International Exchange.* Cambridge: Cambridge University Press, 1979.

Meese, Richard, and Kenneth Rogoff. "Was It Real? The Exchange Rate Interest Differential Relation over the Modern Floating Exchange Rate Period." *Journal of Finance* 43 (1988), pp. 933–48.

Obstfeld, Maurice. "International Currency Experience: New Lessons and Lessons Relearned." *Brookings Papers on Economic Activity,* no. 1 (1995), pp. 119–220.

Officer, Lawrence H. "The Purchasing Power Parity Theory of Exchange Rates: A Review Article." *IMF Staff Papers,* 23 (Mar. 1976).

Pugel, Thomas A., and Peter Lindert. *International Economics,* 11th ed. Burr Ridge, IL: Irwin/McGraw-Hill, 2000.

Rogoff, Kenneth. "The Purchasing Power Parity Puzzle," *Journal of Economic Literature* 34 (June 1996), pp. 647–68.

Sercu, Piet. "Foreign Exchange as an Option on Traded Goods." Working Paper, Louvain, Belgium, Apr. 1989.

Sercu, Piet; Raman Uppal; and Cynthia Van Hulle. "The Exchange Rate in the Presence of Transaction Costs: Implications for Tests of Purchasing Power Parity." *Journal of Finance* 50, no. 4 (Sept. 1995), pp. 1309–19.

Taylor, Mark P., and David A. Peel. "Nonlinear Adjustment, Long-Run Equilibrium and Exchange Rate Fundamentals." *Journal of International* Money *and Finance* 19, no. 1 (February 2000), pp. 33–53.

Williamson, John. *The Exchange Rate System.* Policy Analyses in International Economics, no. 5, rev. ed. Washington: Institute for International Economics, June 1985.

5 INTERNATIONAL PARITY CONDITIONS: INTEREST RATE PARITY AND THE FISHER PARITIES

"From 1884 [the Indian rupee] fell much more rapidly than before, and the difference in the two rates of interest rose accordingly . . . Since the two bonds were issued by the same government, possess the same degree of security, are quoted side by side in the same market and are in fact similar in all important respects except in the standard in which they are expressed, the results afford substantial proof that the fall of [the Indian rupee] was discounted in advance."

Irving Fisher (1896)

Learning Objectives

After reading this chapter, students should

1. Understand the interest rate parity (IRP) relationship, which expresses the relationship between today's spot exchange rate, forward exchange rate, and home and foreign interest rates.

2. Be familiar with various empirical techniques for testing IRP, and the strength of the evidence regarding interest rate parity in various markets.

3. Know how to undertake risk-free arbitrage transactions to take advantage of deviations from interest rate parity.

4. Understand the International Fisher Effect (uncovered interest parity, UIP) that expresses the relationship between today's spot exchange rate, today's home and foreign interest rate, and the expected future spot exchange rate.

5. Be familiar with various empirical techniques for testing uncovered interest parity, and the strength of the evidence regarding UIP.

6. Be able to give examples of how private individuals and public policymakers would use their knowledge of UIP for strategic and policy decisions.

In this chapter, we continue our discussion of the parity conditions that form the foundation for a study of international financial markets. Our focus now shifts to parity conditions that link the spot and forward exchange markets with the international money and bond markets.

Our analysis moves along lines similar to those in Chapter 4. We first develop the parity conditions in a theoretical setting, starting with the perfect capital market (PCM) assumptions that we used earlier. We then analyze the impact of relaxing the PCM assumptions. Unlike Chapter 4, we now find that by relaxing our assumptions on taxes and complete certainty, persistent deviations from the basic parity pricing rules may result. Once again, we follow the theoretical discussion with a review of the empirical evidence on each parity condition. And once again, we show that some popular analytic techniques (such as linear regression) are often inappropriate to test the validity of a financial parity condition. We propose other, more direct, statistical tests.

This chapter begins with a reprise of the main international parity conditions. Our next stop is the interest rate parity condition, where we develop the theory and review the empirical evidence. The interest rate parity condition offers us an easy opportunity to relax the PCM assumptions and show the effect of introducing taxes into our financial calculations. As we will see, taxes may dramatically alter the conventional interest rate parity condition. We then present the Fisher parities, named for Irving Fisher, who formally derived these relationships in the late 19th century. As the reader now expects, we first develop the Fisherian theories and then examine the empirical evidence. We then introduce the forward rate unbiased condition as the final parity relationship. When uncertainty is introduced, deviations from the Fisher parities and the forward rate unbiased condition will emerge. We discuss how these deviations could be the result either of a market inefficiency or an additional risk premium term in each parity condition. We close the chapter with a discussion of the impact that these financial parity conditions have on decisions by private and public policymakers.

The Usefulness of the Parity Conditions in International Financial Markets: A Reprise

The reader may wish to refer again to Figure 4.1, where all of the parity conditions are summarized. We discussed purchasing power parity in Chapter 4, which leaves us three parity conditions to review that involve the price relationships among foreign exchange market, international money, and bond market products. Compared to PPP, which involved arbitrage in goods, it should be clear that violations in the remaining parity conditions may present more immediate profit opportunities because the cost of entering into financial transactions is typically less than in goods markets. However, financial markets are often subject to controls or restrictions and taxes that limit the ability of market participants to complete an arbitrage transaction. When controls or taxes are present that create a deviation from a parity condition, the magnitude of the deviation reveals how advantageous (read *profitable*) it would be for an agent to "overcome" the control or tax.

As with PPP, financial market transactions often involve risk. We outlined several risk categories in Chapter 3 as they applied to foreign exchange trading. Some of these risks, such as price risk, credit risk, and country risk, may apply to the parity conditions we consider in this chapter if the agent is unable to hedge or otherwise eliminate them. Risk and uncertainty may result in persistent violations of the Fisher parities and the forward rate unbiased condition.

As we illustrated in Chapter 4, the violation of a parity condition is not a signal to ignore the parity condition. If a parity condition is validated by the data, then both borrowers and investors will be indifferent between the two alternatives described on either side of the parity expression. If a parity financial condition is violated, a direct opportunity for profit (or cost savings) may be present.

However, we must be careful to understand the source of a violation of a simple parity condition derived from PCM assumptions. If the parity condition is violated because taxes are present, agents (whether borrowers or investors) must compare their own effective tax rate to that in the market to see whether the parity violation presents an opportunity in their case. Similarly, if the parity condition is violated because of uncertainty, agents must compare their risk aversion to that in the market. Agents who are less risk averse than the overall market will find that the violation of parity presents a profit opportunity. And agents who are more risk averse than the overall market will find that the violation of parity presents a hedging opportunity.

Interest Rate Parity: The Relationship between Interest Rates, Spot Rates, and Forward Rates

Interest rate parity (IRP) establishes the linkages across spot and forward currency markets simultaneously with domestic and foreign security markets.[1] IRP draws on the principle that, in equilibrium, two investments exposed to the same risks must have the same returns. IRP is maintained by arbitrage. We will initially propose **covered interest arbitrage,** a form of "round-trip arbitrage," as the activity that enforces IRP. Later, we will see that another style of arbitrage, which we label **one-way arbitrage,** is a more powerful factor in limiting the size of IRP deviations and a useful financial policy for managers.

Interest Rate Parity in a Perfect Capital Market

Imagine that an investor can place \$1 in a US\$ security that earns an interest rate $i_\$$ for one period and pays its interest once at the end of the period. The ending wealth from this US\$ investment would be:

$$\$1 \times (1 + i_\$)$$

Alternatively, the investor could take this \$1, convert it into UK£ at the current spot rate (S_t), take the entire amount and invest it in a UK£ security that earns interest at $i_£$ for one period, and at the same time sell the proceeds of the investment (principal and interest) at the current one-period forward rate, $F_{t,1}$. By selling the UK£ proceeds in the forward market, we say that the investor is **covering** his or her exposure to UK£ exchange rate changes.[2] The ending wealth from this UK£ investment would be:

$$\$1 \times \frac{1.0}{S_t} \times (1 + i_£) \times F_{t,1}$$

The pair of securities should be identical in all respects—that is, maturity, credit risk, liquidity risk—except for currency of denomination.[3] When these conditions are met, the two investments should produce identical ending wealth, or:

$$\$1 \times \frac{1.0}{S_t} \times (1 + i_£) \times F_{t,1} = \$1 (1 + i_\$)$$

---

[1]John Maynard Keynes (1923) made an early formulation of the interest rate parity theory. But the relationship was well known to earlier market participants. See Frenkel and Levich (1979) for references to Ricardo, Cournot, Walras, and Goschen, all written in the 19th century.

[2]In this example, our investor is a US\$-based investor, so US\$-denominated investments are risk free in nominal terms. Our US\$-based investor could be American, but he or she also could be Swiss, Mexican, or from any other country.

[3]The US\$ security need not be issued by an American party, nor the UK£ security by a British party.

Rearranging terms, we have:

$$\frac{F_{t,1}}{S_t} = \frac{1 + i_{\$}}{1 + i_{\pounds}}$$

And subtracting 1.0 from each side of the equality results in:

$$\boxed{\frac{F_{t,1} - S_t}{S_t} = \frac{i_{\$} - i_{\pounds}}{1 + i_{\pounds}}} \tag{5.1}$$

$$\boxed{\begin{array}{c} \% \text{ forward} \\ \text{premium} \end{array} = \begin{array}{c} \% \text{ interest} \\ \text{differential} \end{array}}$$

Equation (5.1) represents the *exact* formulation of the interest rate parity condition. The $(1 + i_{\pounds})$ term in the denominator of the interest differential is sometimes omitted on the grounds that the interest rate for one period—such as 1/12 of the per annum (p.a.) rate for monthly data, or 1/4 of the p.a. rate for quarterly data—is usually very small. But omitting this term results in an approximation, and inaccurate answers.[4] The term $(F - S)/S$ is called the **forward premium.** When $F > S$, the UK£ is more expensive in the forward market, so the term *forward premium* seems natural. When $F < S$, the UK£ is cheaper in the forward market. Thus, the term **forward discount** is often used when $(F - S)/S < 0$.[5]

Examples of Interest Rate Parity Prices.   Consider the following hypothetical numerical examples.

Example A.   Suppose that the rates for US$ and UK£ securities and exchange rates are:

$$i_{\$, \text{ 3-month}} = 5.96\% \text{ p.a.} \qquad\qquad S_t = \$1.5000/\pounds$$

$$i_{\pounds, \text{ 3-month}} = 8.00\% \text{ p.a.} \qquad\qquad F_{t, \text{ 3-month}} = \$1.4925/\pounds$$

An investor placing $100 in the three-month US$ security has an ending wealth of $100 $\times (1 + 0.0596/4) = \$101.49$. An investor placing $100 in the three-month UK£ security and covering the exchange risk has an ending wealth of $100 $\times (1 + 0.08/4) \times$ 1.4925/1.50 = $101.49. Therefore, the two investments produce identical results. Note that all interest rates were transformed to their *per period* values because this corresponds to the interest that an investor would earn over the three-month investment period. Note also that the forward discount on UK£ $[(F - S)/S = -0.50\%]$ is exactly equal to the interest differential between the US$ and UK£:

$$\frac{(i_{\$} - i_{\pounds})}{(1 + i_{\pounds})} = \frac{(0.0596/4 - 0.08/4)}{(1 + 0.08/4)} = -0.005$$

With £ at a forward *discount*, U.K. interest rates are higher than U.S. interest rates to preserve IRP.

---

[4]This denominator term disappears when we use continuous or logarithmic rates of return. See Appendix 5.1.

[5]Note that the terminology is symmetric. If the UK£ is at a forward premium, the US$ will be at a forward discount. And if the UK£ is at a forward discount, the US$ will be at a forward premium.

Example B.   Suppose that the rates for US$ and € securities and exchange rates are:

$$i_{\$, \, 6 \, month} = 6.10\% \text{ p.a.} \qquad S_t = \$1.0550/€$$

$$i_{€, \, 6\text{-month}} = 3.56\% \text{ p.a.} \qquad F_{t, \, 6\text{-month}} = \$1.0682/€$$

An investor placing $100 in the six-month US$ security has an ending wealth of:

$$\$100 \times (1 + 0.0610/2) = \$103.052$$

An investor placing $100 in the six-month € security and covering his or her exchange risk has an ending wealth of:

$$\$100 \times (1 + 0.0356/2) \times 1.0682/1.0550 = \$103.052$$

Therefore, the two investments produce identical results. Again, all interest rates were transformed to their *per period* values because this corresponds to the interest that an investor would earn over the six-month investment period. Note also that the forward premium on €: [$(F - S)/S = 1.25\%$] is exactly equal to the interest differential between the US$ and €:

$$\frac{(i_\$ - i_€)}{(1 + i_€)} = \frac{(0.0610/2 - 0.0356/2)}{(1 + 0.0356/2)} = 0.0125$$

With € at a forward *premium*, euro interest rates are lower than US$ interest rates to preserve IRP.

Equation (5.1) and Figure 5.1 provide an easy way to determine whether IRP holds or not with any set of numbers. In Figure 5.1, we plot the forward premium or discount against the interest rate differential. The 45° line represents the combination of all points where the forward premium is equal to the interest differential—the **interest rate parity line.** Our examples A and B result in points *A* and *B*, both of which plot on the interest rate parity line.

Examples of Covered Interest Arbitrage to Exploit Deviations from Interest Rate Parity.   Imagine, in example A, that the forward rate had been $F' = \$1.52/£$ instead of $1.4925/£. With the higher forward rate, investors now favor UK£ investments over US$ investments. This results in point *A'* on Figure 5.1. The location of point *A'* implies an incentive for risk-free covered arbitrage flows out of US$ and into UK£. For an investor who held US$ securities initially, the necessary transactions are as follows:

Transactions for a Covered Arbitrage Outflow	*Marginal Impact on Market Prices*
1. Sell US$ security at 5.96%	$i_\$$ rises, ↑
2. Buy £ spot at $1.50	S_t rises, ↑
3. Buy UK£ security at 8.00%	$i_£$ falls, ↓
4. Sell £ forward at $1.52	F_t falls, ↓

These four transactions describe covered interest arbitrage.[6] The profit from making these transactions is $0.0187 per $1.00, which is approximately the percentage deviation from interest rate parity, defined as:

---

[6]We also could call it round-trip arbitrage (see Figure 3.2). In round-trip arbitrage, a person can begin with $1, conduct four transactions, and wind up with more than $1.

FIGURE 5.1   The Interest Rate Parity Line
Equilibrium and Disequilibrium Points

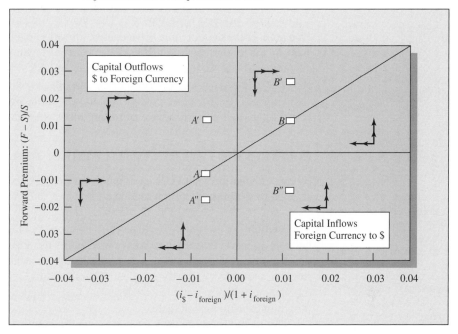

Note: Points A and B are on the interest rate parity line. Points off the parity line generate economic incentives for capital to flow out of investments in one currency and into another currency. The arrows indicate the marginal impact of arbitrage transactions on prices of F, S, $i_\$$, and i_{foreign}.

$$d_t = \frac{F_{t,1} - S_t}{S_t} - \frac{i_\$ - i_£}{1 + i_£} \tag{5.2}$$

Notice in Figure 5.1 that the marginal impact of each of these transactions has the effect of pushing the configuration of rates back toward IRP and the absence of covered interest arbitrage profits.

Now imagine another modification to example A, a forward rate $F'' = \$1.48/£$ instead of $\$1.4925/£$. With the lower forward rate, investors favor US\$ investments over UK£ investments. This results in point A'' on Figure 5.1. The location of point A'' implies an incentive for risk-free covered arbitrage flows out of UK£ and into US\$. For an investor who held UK£ securities initially, the necessary transactions are as follows:

Transactions for a Covered Arbitrage Inflow	Marginal Impact on Market Prices
1. Sell UK£ security at 8.00%	$i_£$ rises, ↑
2. Sell £ spot at \$1.50	S_t falls, ↓
3. Buy US\$ security at 5.96%	$i_\$$ falls, ↓
4. Buy £ forward at \$1.48	F_t rises, ↑

The profit from making these covered interest arbitrage transactions is \$0.0085 per \$1.00, which is approximately the percentage deviation from interest rate parity. Once again, we see from Figure 5.1 that each of these transactions has the effect of pushing the configuration of rates back toward IRP and the absence of covered interest arbitrage profits.

Summary of Interest Rate Parity.   The interest rate parity line represents the break-even point or the dividing line between investments in the domestic security and investments in the foreign security that have been covered against exchange risk. At points to the north and west of the line, capital flows from US$ to foreign currency should take place. At points to the south and east of the line, incentives favor capital flows from foreign currency to US$.[7] At points on the interest parity line, the *covered return* on invested funds and the *covered cost* of raising funds are identical across currencies.

Relaxing the Perfect Capital Market Assumptions

By relaxing the stringent PCM assumptions, we can examine how interest rate parity is affected by the presence of transaction costs, taxes, and uncertainty.

Transaction Costs.   Interest rate parity is enforced by arbitrage transactions. It follows intuitively that arbitrage will not take place unless the absolute magnitude of the deviation from parity exceeds the cost of undertaking the arbitrage transactions. This constraint has the effect of creating a "neutral band" within which covered interest arbitrage transactions will not occur. Deviations from IRP will persist because it is not profitable for arbitrageurs to exploit them.

The neutral band can be described by two limiting values on the forward premium, an upper limit (P_U) and a lower limit (P_L). These price limits for covered interest arbitrage are developed in Appendix 5.2.

The impact of a 1 percent neutral band on covered interest arbitrage opportunities is illustrated in Figure 5.2. Notice that point A'' (with forward premium -1.33 percent and interest differential -0.50 percent) is now bound within the neutral band. Point A'' should now be considered an *equilibrium point* because no covered interest arbitrage profits are available at A'' after transaction costs are taken into account. As a result, no arbitrage forces act on point A''. Point A'' would remain until other economic forces affected either the forward premium or interest rates. The other points in Figure 5.2 (A', B', and B'') are outside the neutral band. These should be considered *disequilibrium points* that represent arbitrage profit opportunities.

While transaction costs act as a barrier to the execution of arbitrage transactions, there is no reason for the presence of transaction costs to favor either positive or negative deviations from parity *for points inside the neutral band*. Therefore, we conclude that transactions costs give rise to deviations from IRP, but not necessarily to deviations that are biased in either direction. When transaction costs are present, all points within the neutral band are equilibrium points, not simply those points on the original parity line.

Taxes.   In financial markets, some taxes (such as stamp taxes and transfer taxes) are applied to the activity of transacting. As we argued in Chapter 4, these kinds of taxes can be modeled as transaction costs. These taxes would widen the neutral band around the original parity line.

---

[7]We might have labeled these flows as between the United States and foreign countries or vice versa. But as we will see in our discussion of offshore currency markets (Chapter 9), US$ and foreign currency deposits and loans could be booked in many different countries.

FIGURE 5.2 **The Interest Rate Parity Line**
Transaction Costs and the Neutral Band

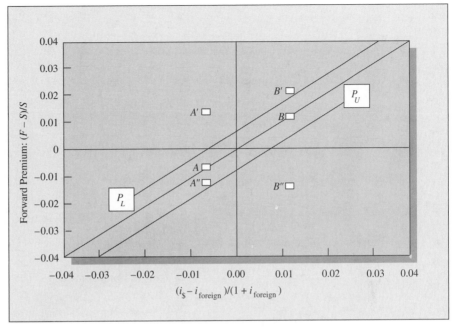

Note: Points *A*, *A″*, and *B* are inside the neutral band and considered equilibrium points with no arbitrage profit possibility. For points *A′*, *B′*, and *B″*, the profit opportunity is greater than the cost of executing arbitrage transactions.

Taxes on income and capital gains may have a different impact than tariffs on goods or transfer taxes. Our interest rate parity condition balanced *pretax* returns from two alternative investments. Clearly arbitrageurs are more interested in the balance between *after-tax* returns. But if taxes are levied by a single tax authority, and the tax rates applied to the two investments are identical, leaving $(1 - \tau)$ of each investment alternative, then taxes do not alter an arbitrageur's decision to choose one investment or another. The original parity condition remains a valid rule for selecting an investment on an after-tax basis as well as a pretax basis.

Now consider a case where both ordinary income and capital gains are taxed, but they are taxed at different rates—τ_y and τ_k, respectively.[8] In the United States, firms whose primary source of income is not related to foreign exchange and financial market activities may claim capital gains tax status for gains and losses on forward foreign exchange contracts. Interest paid and interest earned, however, qualifies for treatment as ordinary income for tax purposes. On an after-tax basis, therefore, equation (5.1) should be modified as follows:

$$\frac{F_{t,1} - S_t}{S_t} \times (1 - \tau_k) = \frac{i_\$ - i_£}{1 + i_£} \times (1 - \tau_y) \tag{5.3a}$$

or

---

[8]This analysis was developed in Levi (1977).

FIGURE 5.3   Interest Rate Parity Lines
Pretax (*PT*) and After-Tax (*AT*) Lines

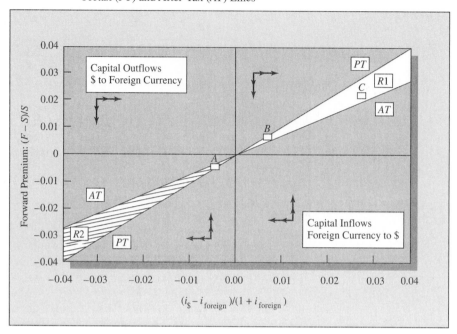

$$\frac{F_{t,1} - S_t}{S_t} = \frac{i_\$ - i_\£}{1 + i_\£} \times \frac{1 - \tau_y}{1 - \tau_k} \qquad (5.3b)$$

In equation (5.3b), we see that if the tax rates on capital gains and ordinary income are identical, then the IRP equation *with* taxes becomes identical to the IRP equation *without* taxes shown in equation (5.1). However, tax rates on capital gains frequently are lower than tax rates on ordinary income.

To explore this possibility, examine the case where $\tau_y = 50$ percent and $\tau_k = 25$ percent. In this case, the ratio $(1 - \tau_y)/(1 - \tau_k) = 0.50/0.75 = 0.67$. In other words, the *after-tax* interest rate parity line (*AT*) has a slope of 0.67 compared with the *pretax* interest rate parity line (*PT*) that has a slope of unity. These parity lines are plotted in Figure 5.3.

This case presents our first example of how the relaxation of a PCM assumption leads to a fundamentally different result. In Figure 5.3, points *A* and *B* (and other points along *PT*) are equilibrium, no-arbitrage points on a pretax basis, but they appear to lead to profits on an after-tax basis. The intuition for this result is clear: Because the tax system allows arbitrageurs to retain more of their gains obtained in forward contracts, a 2.0 percent forward premium offers the same after-tax gains as a 3.0 percent interest differential.

Which is the "correct" IRP line: Line *PT* in equation (5.1) or line *AT* in equation (5.3b)? Unfortunately, the situation is slightly more complicated. We described the "tax system" as if there were only one tax system and all investors were subject to it, but every country has its own tax system with its own rules. For example, the United States has usually required that financial assets be held for a period of time (the rules have varied between 6 and 18 months) in order to qualify for capital gains tax treatment. In this case, U.S. arbitrageurs would face parity line *PT* for short-term securities, and parity line *AT* for long-term securities. However, other countries (such as Canada) have not had a mandatory holding period to qualify for capital gains tax treatment; therefore, arbitrageurs from these countries face parity line *AT* for securities of any maturity.

For short-term securities, therefore, it would be possible for one group of arbitrageurs (say, Americans) to face parity line *PT*, while another group of arbitrageurs (say, Canadians) face parity line *AT*. Arbitrageurs subject to different tax rules will not find themselves looking at the same break-even values when considering an arbitrage possibility. Consider a point like *C* in region *R*1, the wedge in the northeast quadrant of Figure 5.3. In this region, Americans (who face equal tax rates on capital gains and ordinary income, and parity line *PT*) would want to arbitrage out of foreign currency and into US$. But at the same point, Canadians (who face unequal tax rates on capital gains and ordinary income, and parity line *AT*) would want to arbitrage out of US$ and into foreign currency. And *both* Americans and Canadians would be correct to do so on an *after-tax* basis.

The final resting place of point *C* is ambiguous. If Americans are the dominant force in the market, *C* will be pushed closer to line *PT*, giving pure, after-tax profit opportunities to any Canadian who can conduct the arbitrage.[9] If non-Americans are dominant, then *C* will be pushed closer to line *AT*, resulting in pure, after-tax profit opportunities to any American who can conduct the arbitrage. It is also clear that *R*1 is a region where the capital flows are ambiguous; indeed, they are two-way flows, from US$ to foreign currency and vice versa. And a similar pattern would be detected in region *R*2.

To conclude, our discussion of taxes suggests that differential capital gains and ordinary income tax rates could play an important role in systematically tilting the 45° slope of the traditional IRP line. Whether this will have an observable impact on actual data is difficult to say; this depends on the exact tax rates, the number of people who are subject to those rates, and transaction costs which may dominate the role of taxes. It is also possible that the marginal transactions in these capital markets are executed by international investors who operate offshore at low, or perhaps zero, marginal tax rates. Were this the case, the traditional IRP line (see Figure 5.1) would continue to represent the market's equilibrium, and investors who faced differential tax rates on ordinary income and capital gains would see this as a profit opportunity.

Uncertainty. All prices in covered interest arbitrage (S, F, $i_\$$, and $i_£$) are observed before conducting the transaction, but still there are elements of risk. For example, the arbitrageur may be uncertain whether he or she can conduct transactions at the posted prices. Placing orders takes time, and market prices may change. In addition, the foreign currency denominated investment may reflect risks not present with the domestic currency asset. The foreign currency investment includes a forward contract issued by a bank, which is subject to default risk. The foreign currency investment may be traded in

---

[9]Most models presume that the supply of arbitrage funds is virtually unlimited and that an infinite amount of capital would come forward to capture a risk-free profit. In the real world, partaking in arbitrage requires capital and the return on capital committed to arbitrage must be at least as great as capital committed to other activities. Therefore, unlimited capital may not be available to take advantage of risk-free arbitrage profits.

another marketplace that exposes the arbitrageur to an additional country risk, or a risk of exchange controls.[10] All of these risks serve to inhibit the process of arbitrage and widen the neutral band around the traditional parity line.

Empirical Evidence on Interest Rate Parity

A test of the interest rate parity condition—equation (5.1)—requires data on the forward and spot exchange rates and interest rates on foreign currency and domestic currency denominated securities. As noted earlier, the securities should have the same maturity as the forward contract and be *comparable in all respects*—credit risk, liquidity risk, and so on. Until the 1960s, tests of IRP used short-term government securities. These securities were risk free to local investors, but foreign investors faced an additional risk—that the foreign government could impose exchange controls. Since covered interest arbitrage involves two securities, any potential arbitrageur faces additional risks with the foreign security investment. Early studies found deviations from IRP which were attributed to transaction costs, differential market liquidity, differential investment risks, and a failure of the supply of arbitrage funds to respond with perfect elasticity in response to an arbitrage incentive.[11]

With the introduction of the Eurocurrency markets in the 1960s, it became possible to examine two securities (such as Eurocurrency deposits) that were alike in all respects, *including* their exposure to country risks, and differed only in terms of their currency of denomination.[12] For example, a one-month Euro-$ deposit issued by a bank in Zurich and a one-month Euro-£ deposit issued by the *same* bank in Zurich would be one such pair of securities. Eurodeposits satisfied the comparability criterion more so than government securities.

Having selected the data, we now must decide how to analyze it. Even though the IRP line (Figure 5.1) is a 45° line passing through the origin, a test of whether $\alpha = 0$ and $\beta = 1$ in the following simple linear regression would not be appropriate:

$$\frac{(F_{t,1} - S_t)}{S_t} = \alpha + \beta \frac{(i_{\$,\,t} - i_{£,\,t})}{(1 + i_{£,\,t})} + \epsilon_t$$

Given the role played by transaction costs (see Figure 5.2), it is clear that observations could cluster inside the neutral band in any number of ways. Clustering tightly along the 45° line is not necessary for the elimination of covered interest arbitrage profit opportunities. And clustering loosely about the 45° line (but outside of the neutral band) would leave many covered arbitrage opportunities available.

Similarly, measuring the average deviation from IRP would not be informative.[13] The reason again is simple. Suppose we observed one deviation of +3.0 percent and another deviation of −3.0 percent. Together, the average deviation is zero, but if transaction costs were only 0.50 percent, then two substantial profit opportunities were passed over by the market.

The essence of an arbitrage condition in a financial market is that *each and every observation is a potential arbitrage opportunity*. The IRP condition is valid if a high

---

[10]Country risk and exchange-control risk can be standardized by considering only securities that are issued within the same regulatory regime, such as the Euromarket. See Chapter 9.

[11]For a review of these early papers, see Officer and Willett (1970) and Frenkel and Levich (1975).

[12]See Chapter 9 for a full discussion of the Eurocurrency market.

[13]As an exercise, explain why measuring the average deviation made sense in the context of PPP, but not in the context of IRP.

percentage of observations fall within the boundary conditions created by transaction costs. Thus, a meaningful test of the IRP condition relies on the percentage of sample observations within a band consistent with the cost of executing arbitrage transactions. If the percentage of observations inside the neutral band is high and the percentage of points outside the band is small (and their occurrence unpredictable), then IRP holds in the sense that there are few opportunities for profitable covered interest arbitrage transactions.

Empirical Evidence on the Neutral Band.   Robert Aliber (1973) examined two histograms of deviations from IRP, one using Treasury securities and another using Eurocurrency deposits. He concluded that the distribution of deviations from IRP was much more tightly clustered around zero with Eurocurrency deposits, so that IRP applied to the Eurocurrency market. Jacob Frenkel and Richard Levich (1975) made direct estimates of the separate elements of transaction costs and measured the number of observations contained within a neutral band generated by these costs. They concluded that IRP held in the Eurocurrency markets because a large percentage of observations were captured within the neutral band. Points outside the band were few and far between, making simple trading rules unprofitable.[14] Using government securities, a smaller percentage of observations were bound within the neutral band. Still, outliers could be accounted for by assuming reasonable size elasticities in the supply of arbitrage funds.

More recent studies concluded that Frenkel and Levich (1975) overstated the size of the neutral band relevant for IRP, either because the number of transactions was smaller or the estimates of transaction costs themselves were smaller.[15] For example, Alan Deardorff (1979) showed that "one-way" arbitrage (described at the end of this chapter) could substantially reduce the size of the neutral band. Still, the general result—that IRP holds in the short-term Eurocurrency market after accounting for transaction costs—remains intact.

Recent Data and Interest Rate Parity Calculations.   A sample of recent data for assessing the IRP condition is presented in Appendix B at the end of the book. Data on three-month Eurodeposits for US$, UK£, and DM, and three-month forward premiums are included.

A graph of deviations from IRP—calculated from equation (5.2)—using the data in Appendix B is presented in Figure 5.4. The graph shows that the deviations from IRP using Eurodeposits are typically small; only a few observations are greater than 10 basis points in absolute value. Deviations based on arbitrage between U.S. and foreign Treasury bills (not shown) are substantially larger, often 50–100 bp or more. These results show that the interest rate parity condition is extremely robust in the Eurocurrency market.

Interest Parity with Longer-Term Securities.   An early analysis by John Hilley, Carl Beidleman, and James Greenleaf (1981) showed that there could be substantial deviations from IRP using forward contracts with three, four, and five years to maturity. The authors argued that bank traders were reluctant to carry the extra trading risks and

---

[14]One such trading rule would be: if a deviation from parity exists in period t, carry out arbitrage transactions in period $t + 1$. This rule acknowledges that there may be a time lag between receiving information and executing an arbitrage transaction.

[15]See also McCormick (1979), Bahmani-Oskooee and Das (1985), and Clinton (1988).

FIGURE 5.4   **Deviations from Interest Rate Parity Using Three-Month Eurorates**
January 3, 1997–December 31, 1998

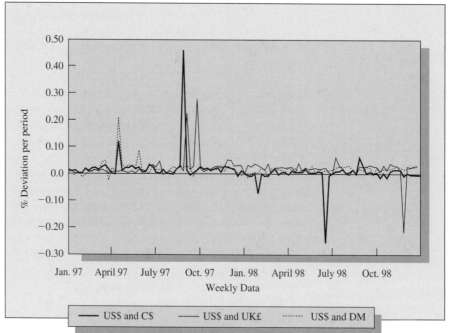

Source: Bank of Montreal/Harris Bank, *Weekly Review,* and author's calculations.

capital costs associated with long-dated forward contracts. Still, some customers were attracted to long-dated forwards, perhaps because they faced still higher costs in creating their own synthetic long-term forward positions.

More recently, Helen Popper (1993) analyzed long-term covered interest parity using five-year and seven-year securities and the interest differential implied by currency swaps of matching maturities.[16] For her sample of major countries in the mid-1980s, Popper found that deviations from long-term covered interest parity are only slightly higher (about 10 bp) than deviations from short-term covered interest parity.

In a related study, however, Donna Fletcher and Larry Taylor (1994) examined 5-, 7-, and 10-year securities for deviations from long-term covered interest parity. They reported that in every test market, there are significant deviations from parity that represent profit opportunities even after adjusting for transaction costs. Deviations from parity open a window of opportunity for firms and may partly explain the rapid growth in long-term currency swaps.

Interest Parity and Capital Controls.   On the issue of IRP and government securities, Michael Dooley and Peter Isard (1980) attempted to measure the risk factor inherent in arbitrage between national securities. The difficulty in making such an estimate is that capital controls *in place* (such as interest rate restrictions or deposit limitations on foreigners) are not "risky" because they are known to investors. Known controls represent costs; unknown future controls represent risks. Dooley and Isard estimated that during

---

[16]Currency swaps are discussed in detail in Chapter 13.

the 1970–1973 period of controls in Germany the interest differential between government securities and Euro-DM deposits that could be attributed to political risks may have been as high as 1–2 percent per annum.[17] When the capital control program ended in 1974, the raw interest differential between onshore and offshore DM securities returned to its previous small magnitude.[18]

The Fisher Parities

In a financial market, prices tend to reflect information. The Fisher parities describe how information regarding expected inflation and expected exchange rates are captured in current interest rates. From previous course work or personal experience, most people are familiar with one Fisher parity relationship—sometimes called the **Fisher Effect**—which relates the nominal interest rate to the expected rate of inflation in a single country.[19] Fisher also posited that the interest rate differential across pairs of currencies embodies information, but this time information about the likely exchange rate change between these units of account. We will call this relationship the **International Fisher Effect**, although some authors use the term **uncovered interest parity**.[20]

The Fisher Effect

The link between the nominal interest rate (i) and inflation (p) in a single economy is so often invoked that the measure of the real interest rate ($r = i - p$) might be understood as merely a definition. But the Fisher Effect really represents another example of arbitrage, this time between real assets and nominal (or financial) assets within a single economy. If for the moment we assume that inflation is zero, individuals balance their choice between the purchase of goods today versus investment (and purchase of goods in the future) so that $1 spent today yields the same utility as $1 invested at ($1 + r$) and spent in the future.

Imagine an individual in our PCM setting who holds $1 in cash and faces an expected (and therefore known) rate of inflation, $E(\tilde{p})$. He can use his cash to purchase a commodity such as gold or paper clips.[21] At the end of one period, his commodity

---

[17]German controls at this time acted to restrict the inflow of capital *into* Germany by nonresidents. These accounts were subject to the so-called Bardepot requirements that placed a progressively larger percentage of the account into a non-interest-bearing reserve. Consequently, nonresidents were willing to accept far lower interest rates on Euro-DM deposits, because these were not subject to German controls and nonresidents received interest on the entire amount of the deposit. The interest differential between onshore and offshore DM reached 10 percent per annum in 1973. Switzerland had similar disincentives for nonresident Swiss franc accounts at this time.

[18]Otani and Tiwari (1981) investigated interest rate parity on Japanese yen (¥) securities in London and Tokyo, finding that substantial deviation from IRP existed in the 1970s for those who could borrow at the lower Euro-¥ rate in London and invest at the higher Gensaki rate in Tokyo. Capital controls precluded most investors from doing this arbitrage. In May 1979, Gensaki assets became available to nonresidents and interest rates between Gensaki assets and Euro-¥ deposits converged. Arbitrage had established IRP between Euro-¥ and Euro-$ assets throughout the 1970s. See also Ito (1986, 1988).

[19]The Fisher parities honor Irving Fisher (1867–1947), regarded by many as the greatest American economist.

[20]The terminology of *uncovered interest rate parity* is slightly awkward because *uncovered* implies a risky situation while interest rate parity refers to risk-free arbitrage.

[21]When there is neutral inflation, all commodities increase in price at the same rate, so all commodities serve equally well as an inflation hedge. In practice, commodities with a high value-to-weight ratio may be preferred, but storage and insurance costs must be considered.

holdings can be liquidated for $1[1 + E(\tilde{p})]$. To reestablish indifference between this commodity purchase and an interest-bearing security, the security would need an end-of-period value of $1(1 + r)[1 + E(\tilde{p})]$. However, the return on the security will normally be quoted in nominal terms to yield $1(1 + i)$, from which it follows that:

$$(1 + i) = (1 + r)[1 + E(\tilde{p})]$$

or

$$i = r + E(\tilde{p}) + r E(\tilde{p})$$

In countries where the rate of inflation is high, the final cross-product term can be important. But in most developed countries where inflation and the real interest rate are low, the Fisher Effect is usually approximated as:

$$\boxed{i = r + E(\tilde{p})} \qquad (5.4)$$

$$\boxed{\frac{\%\ \text{nominal}}{\text{interest rate}} = \frac{\%\ \text{real}}{\text{interest rate}} + \frac{\%\ \text{expected}}{\text{interest rate}}}$$

To execute the arbitrage implied by the Fisher Effect, individuals would move out of financial assets into commodities when inflation is high but not fully reflected in nominal returns. Similarly, when inflation is receding, individuals would prefer financial assets to lock in higher returns that would no longer be available through storing commodities.[22] When the Fisher Effect holds, nominal assets (meaning financial assets) fully reflect expected inflation and preserve the real rate of return.

The International Fisher Effect

In addition to performing a balancing act within a single economy, Fisher also realized that interest rates across countries must be set with an eye toward expected exchange rate changes. In our PCM setting, the derivation of the International Fisher Effect is another straightforward application of arbitrage. Assume again that an investor can place $1 in a US$ security that earns an interest rate $i_\$$ for one period, and pays its interest once at the end of the period. The ending wealth from this US$ investment is:

$$\$1 \times (1 + i_\$)$$

Alternatively, the investor could take the $1, convert it into UK£ at the current spot rate (S_t), and then invest the entire proceeds in a UK£ security that earns interest at $i_£$ for one period. Given the investor's expected future spot rate, $E(\tilde{S}_{t+1})$, the ending wealth from this UK£ investment is:

$$\$1 \times \frac{1.0}{S_t} \times (1 + i_£) \times E(\tilde{S}_{t+1})$$

Under our PCM assumptions, the two investments share the same maturity, risk, and final currency of denomination, and therefore should produce identical ending wealth, or:

---

[22]The mechanism may be more applicable to countries with poorly developed capital markets where commodities and real estate are preferred stores of value against inflation.

$$\$1 \, (1 + i_\$) = \$1 \times \frac{1.0}{S_t} \times (1 + i_£) \times E(\widetilde{S}_{t+1})$$

Rearranging terms, we have:

$$\frac{E(\widetilde{S}_{t+1})}{S_t} = \frac{1 + i_\$}{1 + i_£}$$

Subtracting 1.0 from each side of the equality results in:

$$\boxed{\frac{E(\widetilde{S}_{t+1}) - S_t}{S_t} \quad \frac{i_\$ - i_£}{1 + i_£}} \tag{5.5}$$

$$\boxed{\begin{array}{cc} \% \text{ expected exchange} = & \% \text{ interest} \\ \text{rate change} & \text{differential} \end{array}}$$

Once again, it is common to see the right-hand side of equation (5.5) simply approximated by $i_\$ - i_£$ when $i_£$ is small.

The International Fisher Effect in equation (5.5) looks much like the interest rate parity condition shown in equation (5.1), but there is an important difference. Under interest rate parity, all four variables (F_t, S_t, $i_\$$, and $i_£$) can be observed at the time of arbitrage *even in the real world.* In the case of the International Fisher Effect, only three variables (S_t, $i_\$$, and $i_£$) can be observed at the time of investment. The fourth variable, $E(\widetilde{S}_{t+1})$, is an expectation that is not realized until the conclusion of the investment. So, in the real world the foreign investment proposed in the International Fisher Effect contains **exchange risk.** Even in the real world, the exchange risk of the foreign investment in interest rate parity has been extinguished using a forward contract. Some numerical examples of the International Fisher Effect are developed in Box 5.1.

The International Fisher Effect and Exchange Rate Predictions. Equation (5.5) represents one equation with one unknown, namely, the expected future spot rate. Therefore, we could use equation (5.5) to compute the market's **implied future spot rate,** conditional on today's spot rate and the pair of interest rates. The equation is:

$$E(\widetilde{S}_{t+1}) = \frac{1 + i_\$}{1 + i_£} \times S_t \tag{5.6}$$

To take a numerical example, suppose that the current spot rate is $1.50/£ and that $i_\$ =$ 6 percent and $i_£ = 8$ percent. Then the market's implied future spot rate is $1.4722/£. A future spot rate of $1.4722/£ will balance the return on a US$ investment and the expected return on an uncovered UK£ investment.

The securities used in equation (5.6) should be identical in all respects—maturity, credit risk, liquidity risk—except for currency of denomination. The International Fisher Effect predicts that when US$ interest rates are higher than foreign interest rates, the market expects the US$ to *depreciate*, $E(\widetilde{S}_{t+1}) > S_t$. The logic underpinning this result is that investors must be paid a higher interest rate to compensate them for a unit of account that is expected to depreciate in value. In the same spirit, the International Fisher Effect predicts that when US$ interest rates are lower than foreign interest rates, the market expects the US$ to *appreciate*, $E(\widetilde{S}_{t+1}) < S_t$. The economic logic is similar: Investors willingly accept a lower interest rate when they hold a unit of account that is

Box 5.1

Deviations from Uncovered Interest Parity, or How Exchange Rate Changes Can Substantially Raise (or Lower) the Cost (or Return) on Your Funds

Ex ante, the International Fisher Effect predicts that the cost of borrowing (or the return on investment) will be identical no matter which currency the borrower (or investor) selects. Ex post, *deviations* from the International Fisher Effect reveal where it was better to borrow or invest on an uncovered basis.

Consider the following way to borrow $1 million and pay very high interest. In the first quarter of 1973, prior to the collapse of Bretton Woods, spot UK£ was $2.3519, so borrowing £425,188.15 was equivalent to borrowing $1 million. The cost of borrowing pounds for three months was 9.00 percent per annum. On March 30, 1973, the UK£ had appreciated to $2.4755. Thus, it required $1,076,235.70 to pay off the UK£ loan with interest. This implied a cost of 7.62 percent per quarter, or 30.48 percent per annum. The details of the transaction are shown below. Borrowing on an uncovered basis in this instance resulted in extremely high-cost funds indeed.

Example: First Quarter of 1973

Borrow £425,188.15 on January 5, 1973
    (at 2.3519 $/£, this is $1,000,000)
Pay interest of 2.25% per quarter (9.00% per annum)
Pay back £434,754.88 on March 30, 1973
    (at 2.4755 $/£, this is $1,076,235.70)
Cost of US$ funds = 1,076,235.70/1,000,000
                  = 7.62% per quarter
                  = 30.48% per annum

Now consider another case of borrowing $1 million that resulted in a very low interest cost. In the fourth quarter of 1973, spot DM was $0.4142, so borrowing DM 2,414,292.61 was equivalent to borrowing $1 million. The cost of borrowing DM for three months was 6.125 percent p.a. By the end of 1973, the DM had depreciated to $0.3702. So, it required only $907,457.00 to pay off the DM loan with interest. This implied a cost of −9.25 percent per quarter, or −37.00 percent per annum. The details of the transaction are shown below. Borrowing on an uncovered basis in this instance resulted in very low-cost funds.

Example: Fourth Quarter of 1973

Borrow DM 2,414,292.61 on September 28, 1973
    (at 0.4142 $/DM, this is $1,000,000)
Pay interest of 1.53% per quarter (6.125% per annum)
Pay back DM 2,451,261.47 on December 28, 1973
    (at 0.3702 $/DM, this is $907,457.00)
Cost of US$ funds = 907,457.00/1,000,000
                  = − 9.25% per quarter
                  = −37.00% per annum

Of course, one could turn these examples around and present them as ways to *earn* extremely high or low returns on uncovered foreign currency investments.

expected to appreciate in value. When the International Fisher Effect holds, the ending wealth from holding $1 in any security is identical regardless of the currency selected.[23]

The intuition behind these predictions becomes clearer if one associates changes in nominal interest rates with changes in expected inflation. For example, capital may not be attracted by high interest rates when they are largely a compensation for high expected inflation and currency depreciation. Similarly, countries with traditionally low interest rates, such as Switzerland, have not found it difficult to attract capital because their currencies have been strong in nominal terms, offsetting the effect of low interest rates.

---

[23]Irving Fisher's (1896) own example was that of two bonds issued by the government of India—both traded on the London market, with similar liquidity, maturities, and credit risks. But one bond paid its coupons in gold and the other in silver. The prices and interest rates on the two bonds adjusted in advance of changes in the gold/silver price in a way consistent with the International Fisher Effect.

Equation (5.6) can be rewritten to generate seemingly different exchange rate predictions.

$$S_t = \frac{1 + i_£}{1 + i_\$} \times E(\widetilde{S}_{t+1}) \tag{5.7}$$

which is approximately equal to

$$S_t = \frac{E(\widetilde{S}_{t+1})}{1 + (i_\$ - i_£)} \tag{5.7a}$$

Equation (5.7a) shows that the current spot exchange rate S_t is equal to the discounted present value of the future expected spot rate $E(\widetilde{S}_{t+1})$ where the interest differential $(i_\$ - i_£)$ is the discount factor. Equation (5.7a) embodies the so-called **asset approach to exchange rates.** It predicts that a currency's value, like the value of any other financial asset is equal to the present value of what people expect the asset to be worth in the future.[24]

To take a numerical example, suppose that the market expects the future spot rate will be \$1.60/£ and that $i_\$ = 6$ percent and $i_£ = 8$ percent. Then the current spot rate will be set at \$1.6302/£. This current spot rate acts to balance the return on a US\$ investment and the expected return on an uncovered UK£ investment.

Equation (5.7) predicts that with the expected future spot rate given and foreign interest rates given (that is, conditioning on these two variables), an increase in US\$ interest rates should coincide with an appreciation of the US\$.[25] An increase in $i_\$$ that leaves $E(\widetilde{S}_{t+1})$ unchanged more likely reflects a change in the real interest rate. This generates a capital inflow into US\$ and an appreciation of the US\$.

It is important to stress why these two versions of uncovered interest parity lead to such radically different predictions. In equation (5.6), the reader can think of S_t and $i_£$ as fixed, so a rise in dollar interest rates can only be a compensation for future dollar depreciation, meaning that $E(\widetilde{S}_{t+1})$ rises. However, in equation (5.7) the reader should think of $E(\widetilde{S}_{t+1})$ and $i_£$ as fixed, so a rise in dollar interest rates makes the dollar more attractive without fear of future depreciation, and so S_t falls. Both equations are meaningful, but they are based on different working assumptions.

The International Fisher Effect and Real Interest Rate Parity.   An alternative derivation of the International Fisher Effect helps to reveal an important implicit assumption underlying the basic international parity conditions. This derivation is based on the Fisher Effect and purchasing power parity. Suppose that the Fisher Effect is valid in the United States. Therefore, we have:

$$i_\$ = r_\$ + E(\widetilde{p}_\$) \tag{5.8}$$

If the Fisher Effect were also at work in a second country, the United Kingdom, for example, then we could write:

$$i_£ = r_£ + E(\widetilde{p}_£) \tag{5.9}$$

Subtracting expression (5.9) from expression (5.8) produces:

$$i_\$ - i_£ = r_\$ - r_£ + E(\widetilde{p}_\$) - E(\widetilde{p}_£) \tag{5.10}$$

---

[24]Note that this simple formula ignores any premium for foreign exchange risk, country risk, or loss of liquidity that could be associated with a foreign currency investment.

[25]This is the representation of uncovered interest parity presented in Krugman and Obstfeld (1994), pp. 352–57.

This says that the nominal interest differential is equal to the real interest differential plus the expected inflation differential. If we assume that real interest rates are equal across the two countries, $r_\$ - r_£ = 0$, then our expression simplifies to:

$$i_\$ - i_£ = E(\tilde{p}_\$) - E(\tilde{p}_£) \tag{5.11}$$

By assuming further that PPP holds using expected inflation rates, we have:

$$i_\$ - i_£ = E(\tilde{s}_{\$/£}) \tag{5.12}$$

which is the International Fisher Effect of equation (5.5).

This derivation is useful because it reveals that the International Fisher Effect implicitly assumes that real interest rates are equal across countries. As we will see, this assumption may often be violated, providing a reason behind deviations from the International Fisher Effect.

Relaxing the Perfect Capital Market Assumptions

Transaction Costs and Taxes.   As the reader will suspect, introducing transaction costs into the Fisher parities has much the same effect as with other parity conditions. Transaction costs create a barrier that results in a neutral band around the parity line. Taxes such as stamp duties and transfer fees are analogous to transaction costs. But differential taxes on income and capital gains hold the prospect for tilting the traditional parity line, as we saw in Figure 5.3. Both borrowers and investors will assess the International Fisher Effect on an after-tax basis rather than a pretax basis.

Uncertainty.   Allowing for conditions of uncertainty makes an enormous difference in the International Fisher Effect. The uncovered interest parity condition involves a comparison between the ending wealth on a domestic currency investment [$\$1(1 + i_\$)$] and an uncovered foreign investment [$\$1 \times (1 + i_£) \times E(\tilde{S}_{t+1})/S_t$]. The ending value of the foreign investment depends on the expected, and uncertain, future spot rate, $E(\tilde{S}_{t+1})$, while the domestic investment does not.

The critical question is: Do investors require an **exchange-risk** (or **currency-risk**) **premium** to hold the foreign investment? It could be that investors judge that exchange risk is a *diversifiable* risk and therefore they do not require a payment for holding it. It could also be the case that even if exchange risk cannot be diversified, a group of investors are *risk neutral;* that is, they are indifferent between two investments with different risks as long as they have identical expected returns. A pool of risk-neutral investors would preserve the International Fisher Effect even if the exchange risks could not be diversified away.

If neither of these conditions are met, then uncertainty will lead to an exchange-risk (or currency-risk) premium and systematic deviations from the International Fisher Effect. These deviations, however, would not represent unusual profit opportunities or market pricing errors. Ex ante deviations from the International Fisher Effect would reflect the fair pricing of an additional risk. At the moment, there is some dispute about the existence, magnitude, and possible causes of an exchange-risk premium. We take up this topic again in Chapter 7 as it pertains to tests of foreign exchange market efficiency.

Empirical Evidence on the International Fisher Effect

Testing the International Fisher Effect requires data on expected exchange rates and interest rates on a pair of securities denominated in domestic and foreign currencies. Obtaining data on *expected* exchange rates is difficult because expectations are usually not observed directly in the marketplace. Enterprises (e.g., banks, securities companies, and forecasting firms) and individuals produce forecasts of the future spot exchange rate, but these forecasts need not represent widely held views that we could confidently label as "the market's expected exchange rate."[26]

Alternatively, we could assume that the market's expectations are rational and unbiased. If so, the actual future spot rate is equal to the expected future spot rate augmented by an error term with the classical properties, or:

$$S_{t+1} = E(\tilde{S}_{t+1}) + \epsilon_{t+1}$$

With this assumption of *rational expectations,* we can rewrite the International Fisher Effect as:

$$\frac{(S_{t+1} - S_t)}{S_t} = \frac{(i_\$ - i_£)}{(1 + i_£)} + \epsilon_{t+1} \tag{5.13}$$

Confronted with another parity condition, we might again propose a test of whether $\alpha = 0$ and $\beta = 1$ in the simple linear regression:

$$\frac{(S_{t+1} - S_t)}{S_t} = \alpha + \beta \frac{(i_\$ - i_£)}{(1 + i_£)} + \epsilon_{t+1} \tag{5.14}$$

This test would reveal whether the interest differential provides a good forecast of the future spot rate change. But it would not provide us with useful information regarding the performance of domestic versus foreign currency investments (on an uncovered basis), which is the basic arbitrage opportunity underlying the International Fisher Effect.

Data for a test of the International Fisher Effect using US$ and DM rates for the period 1973–1998 are presented in Appendix C at the end of the book. Notice that we have selected data at time intervals that match the maturity of the interest rates. This results in a time series of observations that are independent and nonoverlapping. In other words, the three-month interest rates set on January 1 are compared with the exchange rate change over the January 1–April 1 period, and then the next interest rates selected are on April 1.[27]

Figure 5.5 presents a graph of the interest differential on Euro-$ and Euro-DM deposits at quarter t and the spot exchange rate change ($/DM) one quarter in the future. The graph shows that exchange rate changes form a volatile series that switches between sizable positive and negative values. In comparison, the interest differential is a relatively smooth and calm series that takes on positive values over most of the sample period. Figure 5.5 suggests little relationship between the current interest differential and the future realized exchange rate change. In a formal regression test of equation (5.12), we find coefficients with standard errors in parentheses:

$\alpha = 0.007$	$\beta = -0.070$	$R^2 = 0.001$	$N = 108$
(0.008)	(0.827)	$D\text{-}W = 1.75$	

These results clearly reject the $\alpha = 0$ and $\beta = 1$ hypothesis.

---

[26]Individual exchange rate forecasts are still important to analyze. See Chapters 7 and 8 and the discussion of market efficiency and forecasting. See also Frankel and Froot (1987) and Takagi (1991) on the rationality of exchange rate expectations.

[27]Monthly, weekly, or daily data on three-month interest rates could have been used, but then the deviations from the International Fisher Effect would exhibit positive serial correlation even if the International Fisher Effect were valid. The International Fisher Effect error of January 1 (ϵ_1) would be highly correlated with the error of January 2 (ϵ_2), and the error of January 3 (ϵ_3), and so on, because the magnitude of the January 1 error is not learned until April 1.

FIGURE 5.5   **Deviations from the International Fisher Effect**

$/DM: Spot Rate Change and Three-Month Eurorate Differential

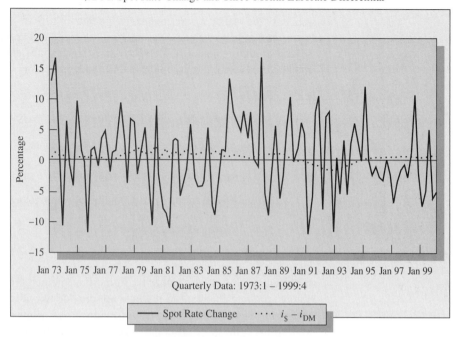

Quarterly Data: 1973:1 – 1999:4

Source: Bank of Montreal/Harris Bank, *Weekly Review,* and author's calculations.

Suppose instead that we assess the International Fisher Effect by measuring the deviation between the exchange rate change and the interest differential

$$d_{t+1} = \frac{(S_{t+1} - S_t)}{S_t} - \frac{(i_\$ - i_£)}{(1 + i_£)} \tag{5.15}$$

In Figure 5.5, we observe both positive and negative deviations—periods when the interest differential overestimates and underestimated the future exchange rate change. The average deviation across the 27-year sample period is 0.14 percent per quarter (0.56 percent per annum) and is not significantly different from zero. The same general result—a small average deviation from the International Fisher Effect that is not significantly different from zero—is found using the US$ paired with other foreign currencies.[28] Therefore, it can be argued that even though the International Fisher Effect condition performs poorly in any individual period, over extended periods of time it appears that the interest differential tends to provide an offset to the realized exchange rate change. Currencies with high interest rates tend to *depreciate* and currencies with low interest rates tend to *appreciate* along the lines predicted by the International Fisher Effect.

Figure 5.6 makes the same point by tracking a $100 investment in three-month Eurodeposits first in US$ and then in DM uncovered against exchange risk. If the International Fisher Effect held, the two investments would produce the same terminal wealth. After 1973, the two terminal wealth lines cross 12 times in 27 years, which suggests a long-run tendency for the interest differential to offset exchange rate changes.

---

[28]The test was repeated for the other eight currencies in the Harris Bank database—C$, UK£, Belgian, French, and Swiss francs, lira, guilder, and ¥—all with similar results.

FIGURE 5.6 **Cumulative Wealth: US$ and DM Investments**
Three-Month Eurorates, Uncovered

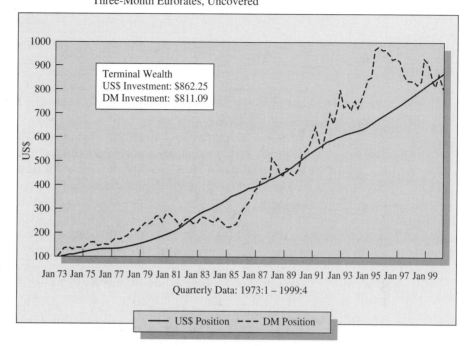

Note: For the US$ position, terminal wealth is the value of $100 invested at the three-month Eurodollar rate and rolled over every quarter at the prevailing interest rate. For the DM position, terminal wealth is the value of $100 converted to DM at the spot rate, invested at the three-month Euro-DM rate, and converted back to US$ at the end-of-quarter spot rate. This amount is then rolled over every quarter at the prevailing spot rates and DM interest rate.

Source: Bank of Montreal/Harris Bank, *Weekly Review,* and author's calculations.

However, even if the International Fisher Effect were to hold in the long run, it would not imply that borrowers and investors can be *totally* passive or indifferent about the selection of the currency of denomination of their liabilities or their assets. One reason for this is that the series of deviations (d_t) might have a time pattern that could be exploited, even though the *average* deviation tended to be small. If a discernible time pattern is present, borrowers and investors could shift back and forth between currencies to earn extra profits. A second reason to look beyond the simple average of deviations from the International Fisher Effect is that even though a US$ and foreign currency security have the same *average* return, they might entail different risks. Clearly, agents would prefer to use the currency that left them exposed to fewer risks. We take up both of these issues in the policy discussion at the end of this chapter.

The Forward Rate Unbiased Condition

Given the PCM assumptions, it follows from interest rate parity in equation (5.1) and the International Fisher Effect in equation (5.5) that the expected percentage change in the exchange rate will equal the forward exchange premium:

$$\boxed{\frac{E(\widetilde{S}_{t+1}) - S_t}{S_t} = \frac{F_{t,1} - S_t}{S_t}} \tag{5.16}$$

$$\boxed{\begin{array}{cc} \% \text{ expected exchange} = & \% \text{ forward} \\ \text{rate change} & \text{premium} \end{array}}$$

If the average deviation between today's forward rate $(F_{t,1})$ and the *actual* future spot exchange rate (S_{t+1}) is small and near zero, we say that the forward rate is an **unbiased predictor** of the future spot rate.

The forward rate unbiased condition is monitored by speculators, who in the PCM setting trade in forward contracts only at prices equal to the expected future spot rate. When we relax the PCM assumptions, it is clear that the forward rate unbiased condition depends on two further assumptions:

(I) **Market Efficiency:** $\qquad\qquad\qquad\qquad E(\widetilde{S}_{t+1}) = S_{t+1}$

Speculators are able to form unbiased expectations of future spot rates; and

(II) **Forward Rate Pricing:** $\qquad\qquad\qquad F_{t,1} = E(\widetilde{S}_{t+1})$

Speculators choose to trade forward contracts at prices equal to their expectations of future spot rates.

If either of these assumptions fail, the forward rate will be a **biased predictor** of the future spot rate.

Interpreting a Forward Rate Bias

If assumption I is violated, a forward rate bias signifies market inefficiency. In this case, exploiting the pattern of forward rate bias offers a pure profit opportunity based on the market's inability to form rational or unbiased forecasts of the future spot rate. However, a forward bias could result from a failure of assumption II, the "pricing rule" used by the market for setting forward prices. Specifically, forward prices could reflect a risk premium (RP) such that $F_{t,1} = E(\widetilde{S}_{t+1}) + RP_t$. In this case, exploiting the pattern of forward rate bias could lead to speculative profits, but these profits would reflect the risk incurred. Thus, a forward rate bias *does not necessarily imply* a foreign exchange market inefficiency.

Empirical Evidence on the Forward Rate Unbiased Condition

A test of the forward rate unbiased condition requires a series of forward rates and expected future spot rates. As discussed, measurements on the market's expected future spot rate are difficult to obtain. So again we start by assuming rational or unbiased expectations whereby the actual future spot rate is equal to the expected future spot rate augmented by an error term. With this assumption, we can rewrite the forward rate unbiased condition as:

$$\frac{(S_{t+1} - S_t)}{S_t} = \frac{(F_{t,1} - S_t)}{S_t} + \epsilon_{t+1} \tag{5.17}$$

Tests Using the Level of Spot and Forward Exchange Rates

By inspecting equation (5.17), we see that the left and right sides of the equation will be identical (except for the error term) when S_{t+1} equals $F_{t,1}$. Graphs of the forward rate and the realized future spot rate for the one-month and three-month \$/DM rates are presented in Figure 5.7. As we did previously, the sequence of observations is again constructed to be nonoverlapping at one-month intervals in the one-month forward contract

FIGURE 5.7A   **One-Month Forward and Future Spot Rates**
$/DM Rates: January 1979–December 1998

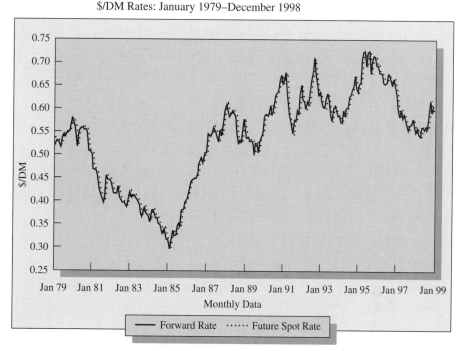

Source: Bank of Montreal/Harris Bank database and author's calculations.

FIGURE 5.7B   **Three-Month Forward and Future Spot Rates**
$/DM Rates: January 1979–December 1998

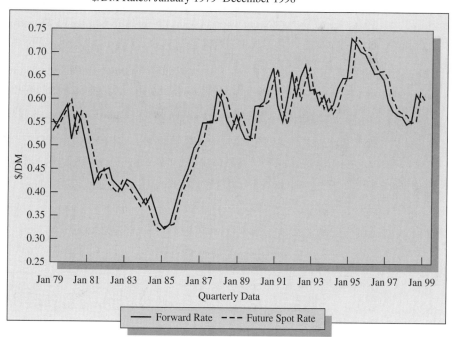

Source: Bank of Montreal/Harris Bank database and author's calculations.

TABLE 5.1   Regression Tests of Forward Rate Unbiased Condition
January 1979–December 1998; Three-Month Forward Rates

	Levels			Percentage Changes		
	$S_{t+n} = \alpha + \beta F_{t,n} + e_t$			$ln\,(S_{t+n}/S_t) = \alpha + \beta\, ln\,(F_{t,n}/S_t) + e_t$		
Country	α	β	R^2	α	β	R^2
Belgium	0.002	0.933	0.89	−0.216	−0.025	0.00
	(0.001)	(0.036)		(0.721)	(1.119)	
Canada	−0.004	1.005	0.91	−0.532	−0.788	0.02
	(0.028)	(0.035)		(0.289)	(0.597)	
France	0.014	0.917	0.90	−0.144	0.506	0.00
	(0.006)	(0.035)		(0.758)	(0.814)	
Germany	0.018	0.963	0.90	0.394	−0.540	0.01
	(0.021)	(0.037)		(0.806)	(0.823)	
Italy	0.000	0.949	0.94	0.994	1.497	0.05
	(0.000)	(0.028)		(1.094)	(0.714)	
Japan	0.000	0.969	0.95	3.491	−3.212	0.12
	(0.000)	(0.026)		(1.111)	(0.984)	
Netherlands	0.018	0.960	0.89	0.463	−0.969	0.01
	(0.018)	(0.037)		(0.778)	(0.892)	
Switzerland	0.030	0.948	0.88	1.132	−1.024	0.02
	(0.027)	(0.041)		(1.018)	(0.770)	
United Kingdom	0.140	0.918	0.86	−1.180	−1.935	0.06
	(0.070)	(0.041)		(0.727)	(0.893)	

Notes: (1) Sample size, $N = 80$ nonoverlapping observations

           (2) Standard errors in parentheses

Source: Bank of Montreal/Harris Bank database and author's calculations.

and at quarterly intervals in the three-month forward contract. Thus, each successive observation is an independent observation—a fresh "time at bat" for the forward rate to predict the future spot rate.

Each graph reveals that the forward rate and the future spot rate track along a very similar path. Therefore, we expect that a regression of the *level* of the future spot rate against the *level* of the present forward rate, such as:

$$S_{t+1} = \alpha + \beta\, F_{t,1} + \epsilon_{t+1} \tag{5.18}$$

would produce coefficients α and β near 0 and 1, respectively, and a high R^2 for the regression. In Table 5.1, we see that the data correspond well to the $\alpha = 0$ and $\beta = 1$ hypothesis.

Inspection of Figure 5.7 reveals another interesting pattern. It appears as if the forward rate tracks "below" the future spot rate when the spot rate is rising, and "above" the future spot rate when the spot rate is falling. As a result, the forward rate misses all of the "turning points" in the spot rate series.

Tests Using Forward Premiums and Exchange Rate Changes

Our perception of the forward rate as a predictor changes when we examine *percentage changes* in exchange rates rather than the *levels*. In percentage change form, the forward rate unbiased condition of equation (5.15) requires us to compare the present *forward premium* with the expected future *exchange rate change*.

Figure 5.8 shows a graph of the present forward premium and the actual future exchange rate change for the $/DM rate at one-month and three-month maturities. The graphs show that actual exchange rate changes form a volatile series while the forward premium is a relatively smooth and calm series. Testing the joint hypothesis $\alpha = 0$ and $\beta = 1$ in a regression such as:

$$\frac{(S_{t+1} - S_t)}{S_t} = \alpha + \beta \frac{(F_{t,1} - S_t)}{S_t} + \epsilon_{t+1} \qquad (5.19)$$

tests whether the current forward rate premium is an unbiased predictor of the future exchange rate change. In Table 5.1, we see that the $\alpha = 0$ and $\beta = 1$ hypothesis is rejected for the DM and every other currency in the sample; the data indicate that β is negative and significant for several currencies. Thus, the analysis of exchange rate changes suggests that the forward premiums are a poor predictor of the future exchange rate change, and oftentimes a biased predictor. As we will see in Chapters 7 and 8, this empirical finding may offer good news through the hope it offers forecasters to beat the forward rate at forecasting exchange rate changes.

On the other hand, we can look at the forward rate bias in a more simplistic way by examining the sequence of forecasting errors, the ϵ_{t+1} in equation (5.17). Figure 5.8 shows that the deutsche mark was at a (positive) forward premium over nearly the entire decade of the 1980s even though the $/DM rate both appreciated and depreciated over the period. Examination of subperiods sometimes suggests that a forward rate bias is present in the market. For example, in the first half of the 1980s, it is clear that the forward rate underestimated the strength of the US$. The statistics in Table 5.2 establish that a statistically significant *negative* bias was indeed present in the market for many currencies during this period. However, it is also clear that the forward rate underestimated the weakness of the US$ in the latter half of the 1980s. The statistics support a significant *positive* bias in the market for many currencies during the late 1980s. Over the entire decade, these two biases cancel out, and it could be claimed that the forward rate was actually unbiased over the longer sample period.[29]

Policy Matters—Private Enterprises

As we have argued, the parity conditions play an important role in the formation of strategies toward international financial markets. We have referred to the parity conditions as benchmarks or break-even points.

When interest rate parity (IRP) holds, the covered cost of funds is identical across all currencies and the covered return on funds is identical across all currencies; there are neither bargains nor bad deals on a covered basis. And when IRP holds, covering an exchange risk using a forward contract bears the same cost as covering the risk using borrowing and lending with money market instruments.

When the International Fisher Effect holds, the expected cost of borrowed funds is identical across currencies and the expected return on invested funds is identical across

---

[29]The results in Table 5.2 show that the forward premium is near the center of the distribution of actual exchange rate changes and is unbiased in this *unconditional* sense. However, *conditional* on the size of the forward premium, the results in Table 5.1 show that the forward premium itself is not the best available forecast.

FIGURE 5.8A Forward Premium and Spot Rate Change
$/DM One-Month Forward Rates: January 1979–December 1998

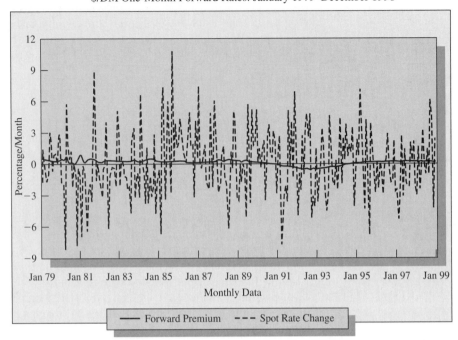

Source: Bank of Montreal/Harris Bank database and author's calculations.

FIGURE 5.8B Forward Premium and Spot Rate Change
$/DM Three-Month Forward Rates: January 1979–December 1998

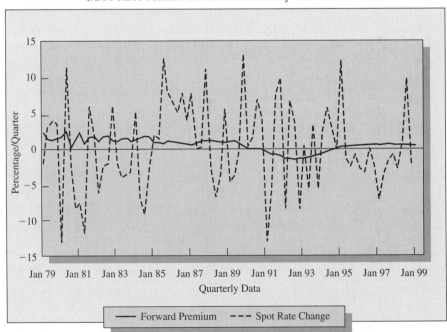

Source: Bank of Montreal/Harris Bank database and author's calculations.

TABLE 5.2 Deviations from Forward Rate Unbiased Condition
Percentage Forecast Errors of Three-Month Forward Premia

Currency	Period 1 Jan. 1980–Feb. 1985	Period 2 Mar. 1985–Dec. 1988	Combined Period Jan. 1980–Dec. 1988
Belgium	−3.829	3.087	−1.062
	(−2.514)[a]	(2.029)[b]	(−0.864)
Canada	−0.690	1.170	0.054
	(−1.401)	(1.878)[b]	(0.131)
France	−3.624	3.055	−0.953
	(−2.560)[a]	(2.096)[b]	(−0.821)
Germany	−4.302	2.615	−1.535
	(−3.025)[a]	(1.677)	(−1.287)
Italy	−2.577	3.395	−0.188
	(−2.031)[a]	(2.395)[a]	(−0.177)
Japan	−1.846	3.614	0.338
	(−1.201)	(2.294)[a]	(0.283)
Netherlands	−4.316	2.852	−1.448
	(−3.056)[a]	(1.821)[b]	(−1.206)
Switzerland	−4.545	2.459	−1.743
	(−2.811)[a]	(1.349)	(−1.308)
United Kingdom	−3.162	2.718	−0.810
	(−2.388)[a]	(1.977)[b]	(−0.755)

Notes: *T*-values in parentheses.
[a] Significant at the 5% level.
[b] Significant at the 10% level.
Source: Richard M. Levich, "Is the Foreign Exchange Market Efficient?" *Oxford Review of Economic Policy* 5, no. 3 (1989), pp. 40–60.

currencies on an uncovered basis. Some currencies may have high nominal interest rates and others may have low nominal interest rates, but when the expected exchange rate change is taken into account, all currencies bear the same expected nominal interest rate when expressed in the same numeraire. As a result, monetary assets retain their value despite exchange rate changes because, when the International Fisher Effect holds, the interest rate provides an offset.

When the forward rate unbiased condition holds, the expected cash flows associated with hedging or not hedging a currency exposure are identical. When the forward rate equals the expected future spot rate, those who hedge (and convert their foreign currency assets and liabilities to domestic currency at the forward rate), and those who do not hedge (and convert their foreign currency positions at the expected future spot rate) have the same expected domestic currency results.

If all of the parity conditions were valid *at each and every moment in time,* then all financial choices would be fairly priced compared with the alternatives. But the empirical evidence shows that while many of the parity conditions may hold in most cases or on average, at times the parity conditions are violated. As a result, managers may have an opportunity to make profit-maximizing decisions by exploiting deviations from the parity conditions. Or if managers assess a risk of large deviations from the parity conditions, then strategies to avoid or hedge these risks may be called for. We examine some of these situations in the context of the three parity conditions.

FIGURE 5.9   Example of One-Way Arbitrage in Foreign Exchange and
Security Markets

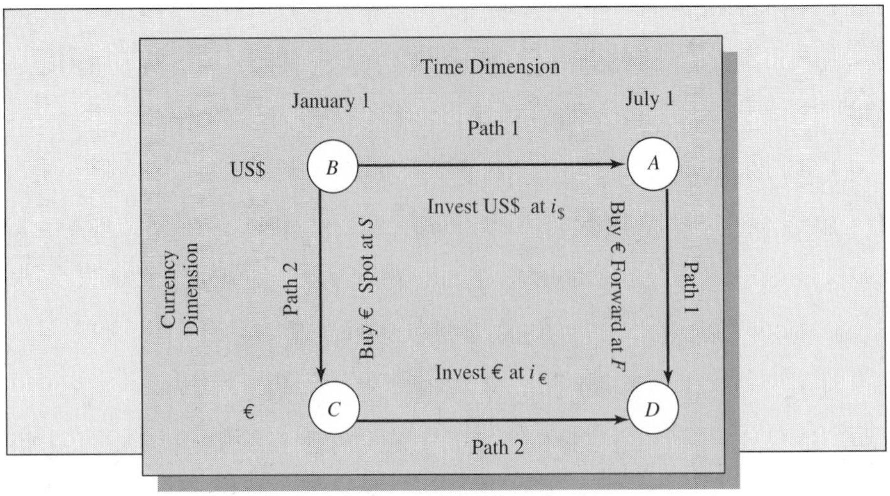

Note: A manager who holds US$ can obtain € in the future by following two alternative paths.
            By taking the low-cost path, the manager is engaging in one-way arbitrage.

Path 1:   Invest US$ for six months, buy € forward on January 1 for July 1 delivery

            Cost $= F_{\text{Jan 1, July 1}}/(1 + i_{\$, \text{6 months}})$

Path 2:   Buy € spot on January 1, invest € for six months

            Cost $= S_{\text{Jan 1}}/(1 + i_{€, \text{6 months}})$

Application 1: Interest Rate Parity and One-Way Arbitrage

The interest rate parity condition was developed based on covered interest arbitrage between domestic and foreign currency denominated securities. When IRP is violated, we
showed (see Figure 5.1) that round-trip arbitrage results in risk-free arbitrage profits.
Closer examination of the basic transactions reveal that one-way arbitrage imposes a
tighter constraint on the size of IRP deviations. An example of one-way arbitrage is suggested by Figure 5.9.

Suppose that an investor holds US$ cash and wishes to make a € payment in six
months. The investor has two alternatives to choose between:

Path 1:   Buy € at the six-month forward rate $(F_{t,1})$ for delivery on July 1, and
           hold US$ assets for six months (earning $i_\$$) until then.

Path 2:   Buy € at the spot rate (S_t) for immediate delivery, and hold € assets for
           six months (earning $i_€$) until July 1.

In the absence of transaction costs, the two alternatives will be identical. But when
transaction costs are present, an investor may favor one alternative over another, even
though no round-trip arbitrage profits are possible. One-way arbitrage then is simply
picking the lowest-priced alternative (when buying) or the highest-priced alternative
(when selling) for a transaction between any two corners of the box in Figure 5.9.[30] As
long as there is an ongoing flow of international transactions (for example, people who

---

[30]There are 12 possible one-way arbitrage transactions between the corners of the box in Figure 5.9. As
an exercise, can you list them?

Box 5.2

An Example of One-Way Arbitrage Profits When There Are No Round-Trip Arbitrage Profits

Suppose that you are given the following prices as true transaction prices:

Spot €:	$1.0430–$1.0440
1-month Forward €:	$1.0448–$1.0458
1-month Euro €:	3.0625–3.1875% p.a.
1-month Euro $:	5.4375–5.5625% p.a.

First, check if you could earn arbitrage profits by round-trip arbitrage in the counterclockwise direction; that is, borrowing $ for 30 days, buying € spot, investing € for 30 days, and selling € forward.* Note that borrowing $ and buying € spot represent costs, while investing € and selling € forward are returns. Thus the calculation is:

$$\frac{(1 + 0.055625/12) \times 1.0442}{(1 + 0.030625/12) \times 1.0448} = 1.0015$$

So borrowing $1 winds up costing us more than $1. Therefore, there is no profit opportunity here.

Now check if you could earn arbitrage profits by round-trip arbitrage in the clockwise direction; that is, borrowing €, selling € spot, investing $, and buying € forward. Note that borrowing € and buying € forward represent costs, while investing $ and selling € spot are returns. Thus the calculation is:

$$\frac{(1 + 0.031875/12) \times 1.0458}{(1 + 0.054375/12) \times 1.0432} = 1.0006$$

*Note that we use the ask price when buying a currency or borrowing and the bid price when selling a currency or investing.

So borrowing € 1 winds up costing us more than € 1. Therefore, there is no profit opportunity here either. The calculations show that transactions costs preclude the possibility of profitable round-trip arbitrage.

Now suppose that the firm has a payment of € 1 million due in 30 days and you want to lock in a price today. Suppose that the manager has access to the same quotes as above. What is the best way for the manager to transact?

The manager could travel along path 1 (as in Figure 5.9), first investing his US$ for 30 days and then selling US$ for € at the forward rate. The cost of path 1 is:

$$\frac{1.0458 \text{ } \$/€}{1 + 0.0543175/12} = 1.0411 \text{ } \$/€$$

The manager could travel along path 2 (as in Figure 5.9), first selling US$ for € at the spot rate and then investing his € for 30 days. The cost of path 2 is:

$$\frac{1.0442 \text{ } \$/€}{1 + 0.030625/12} = 1.0415 \text{ } \$/€$$

Path 2 is preferred because it entails a lower cost.

Note that even though no covered arbitrage profits exist, the manager is not indifferent between the two alternatives in this transaction. By taking advantage of the lower cost in path 2, the manager will bring the two price paths into closer alignment. The search for one-way arbitrage profits makes it unlikely that round-trip arbitrage profits are available.

---

have US$ today but want € in six months, or people who will receive € in six months but want US$ today), the search for one-way arbitrage opportunities will severely limit the possibility of round-trip, covered interest arbitrage profits. See Box 5.2 for a numerical example illustrating the possibility of one-way arbitrage when round-trip arbitrage profits are absent.

In a study based on intraday prices, S. Ghon Rhee and Rosita Chang (1992) found that the occurrence of a round-trip arbitrage profit opportunity is exceedingly rare—most often no sample points and occasionally 2–3 percent of a sample. On the other hand, profit opportunities in one-way arbitrage seemed to occur frequently, ranging from 20 to 90 percent of the sample observations. Thus, even though data strongly support the IRP condition, managers may find that volatile prices create many opportunities for one-way arbitrage.

Application 2: Credit Risk and Forward Contracts— To Buy or to Make?

Another decision related to interest rate parity is whether to use an outright forward contract for hedging (represented by line segment *AD* in Figure 3.2) or a synthetic forward contract (namely, borrowing and lending in the two currencies in conjunction with a spot contract, represented by line segments *AB*, *BC*, and *CD* in Figure 3.2) constructed by the manager.[31] When IRP holds, the two choices are, of course, identical.

Suppose now that firms reflect different credit risks, which for convenience we summarize in declining credit quality as a letter rating such as *AAA*, *AA*, *A*, *BBB*, *BB*, and so forth. In constructing a money-market hedge—at cost $S_t(1 + i_\$)/(1 + i_\epsilon)$ when buying € forward, and at cost $(1 + i_\epsilon)/[(1 + i_\$)S_t]$ when selling € forward—credit rating is likely to play a role in the determination of the two interest rates, with lower-rated firms paying higher interest rates on the borrowing leg.[32] But when we examine a table of exchange rates in the newspaper or on a Reuters screen, there is no mention of foreign exchange dealers differentiating their quotes on the basis of credit rating. What implications follow when $F_{t,1}$ is set apparently without reference to credit quality, while the synthetic forward contract is so clearly dependent on credit quality?

Glenn Boyle (1992) showed that these conditions lead firms with lower credit rating and firms with lower borrowing capacity to prefer to hedge using a bank forward contract rather than a money-market hedge. Such lower-rated firms save to the extent that credit risk is priced in bank loans but not in forward contracts. And firms with low borrowing capacity prefer to use the bank's credit capacity (with a forward) rather than their own (building a synthetic forward) with a money-market hedge. Why should banking practices exclude credit risk from forward contract pricing? Although banking practices are not uniform, a corporate foreign exchange line at a bank is not "committed" like a regular lending facility. So, the foreign exchange line can be revoked at any time. The bank may deal with credit risk by offering the lower-rated firm a smaller foreign exchange line and shorter forward contract maturities. These techniques may suffice and be less cumbersome compared with constructing a separate risk-adjusted forward exchange rate for each firm.[33]

Application 3: Interest Rate Parity and the Country Risk Premium

Yet another implication of IRP for financial managers is the use of deviations from IRP based on government securities as a measure of political risk differences between countries. To evaluate risky cash flows from foreign countries, managers will need to use a risk-adjusted discount rate. IRP provides a market-determined measure of this discount rate.

---

[31]The synthetic forward is sometimes called a **money-market hedge** in this context.

[32]The notation omits reference to bid and ask prices. Hedgers pay the higher (asked) price for contracts they buy and receive a lower (bid) price for contracts they sell.

At present, a AAA firm might pay 0.0625–0.125 percent per annum for a one-year lending commitment, while a BBB firm would pay in the 0.25–0.50 percent range. Longer commitments are available at higher costs and higher-rated firms could opt to have longer commitments than weaker-rated firms. If the firm draws on its lending facility, the BBB firm pays a higher markup (over prime or LIBOR) than the AAA firm.

[33]The same issue will arise when offering swap quotes to clients of differing credit quality.

Application 4: Are Deviations from the International Fisher Effect Predictable?

Even if deviations from the International Fisher Effect were zero on average, a nonrandom pattern of deviations could represent an attractive profit opportunity. Robert Cumby and Maurice Obstfeld (1981) examined a series of 312 International Fisher Effect deviations for six currencies against the US$ over the July 1974–June 1980 period. They used seven-day Eurocurrency interest rates and seven-day exchange rate changes and tested to see whether the deviations from the International Fisher Effect were random. In five of the six currencies, the authors reported significant departures from random behavior; in other words, the deviations were correlated over time so that past deviations could be used to predict future deviations. Cumby and Obstfeld did not compute the profits available from exploiting the pattern of International Fisher Effect deviations in a trading rule, but later studies did (see Chapters 7 and 8).[34]

Application 5: Are Deviations from the International Fisher Effect Excessive?

Under a system of pegged exchange rates, any interest rate differential represents a departure from the International Fisher Effect *as long as the exchange rate peg is expected to hold*. Trying to profit from this sort of Fisher deviation is indeed currency speculation. Naturally, the game can be played in two directions: (1) invest in the high-interest-rate currency when you expect the peg to hold, and (2) borrow the high-interest-rate currency when you expect the peg to change by more than the interest differential.

Strategy 1: Investing in the High-Interest-Rate Currency.   A recent application of this principle was the surge of U.S. investment into Mexican government securities. During 1992, peso-denominated, short-term securities had yields of 7–16 percentage points greater than US$ government securities. With the foreign exchange value of the peso depreciating gradually, at about 5 percent per year, the realized International Fisher Effect deviations were substantial, enough to draw large sums of U.S. investment into Mexico. For example, in late 1992 the Fidelity Short-Term World Income Fund, a $631 million fund managed by Fidelity Investments of Boston, held almost 17 percent of its assets in peso-denominated securities.[35] This strategy failed in late 1994, when the peso suffered a maxi-devaluation and took back more than the excess interest paid on peso securities.

A slightly more complex application of the same principle involved currencies within the European Exchange Rate Mechanism (ERM). As we described in Chapter 2, currencies within the ERM were pegged to one another, but within bands of 2.25 percent for most currencies and 6.0 percent for the British pound and Italian lira. Suppose, as was the case in early 1991, that three-month Euro-£ interest rates were 14 percent while comparable Euro-DM interest rates were 9 percent. By borrowing Euro-DM and investing in Euro-£, the speculator would earn 5 percent per annum. As long as the DM/£ rate did not depreciate by more than 5 percent per annum, the strategy would add incremental profits to a short-term investment portfolio.[36] These strategies worked

---

[34]See also Cumby and Obstfeld (1984) for updates and extensions of this test.

[35]See the fund's annual report of October 31, 1992. The *New York Times* (Apr. 22, 1993) reported that Fidelity was probably the largest single owner of Mexican Treasury securities. See Uchitelle (1993).

[36]Notice that these profits would be *incremental* profits. A U.S. fund manager with $1 million in U.S. Treasury bills could use these assets to collateralize a futures contract position or a bank position on the Euro-DM/Euro-£ bet. The fund manager would continue to receive risk-free interest from the U.S. Treasuries.

reasonably well through the early 1990s, as the ERM held up and interest rate differentials persisted.

Strategy 2: Borrowing the High-Interest-Rate Currency.   In September 1992, the ERM came under stress and fears mounted that several currencies would have to devalue or exit the ERM. Anticipating this, speculators had an opportunity to invoke an alternative strategy—borrowing the high-interest-rate currency while owning the low-interest-rate currency and betting *against* the preservation of the ERM. In early September 1992, three-month Euro-£ rates were only 0.50 percent higher than Euro-DM rates. Euro-lira rates, however, were some 6.00 percent higher than Euro-DM rates. Still, paying this interest differential for a few weeks was a modest cost relative to the exchange rate changes that occurred—a 14 percent depreciation of the pound (from 2.78 DM/£ to 2.40 DM/£) and a 13 percent depreciation of the lira (762 lira/DM to 863 lira/DM).[37]

Application 6: International Fisher Effect and Diversification Possibilities

As we have seen, deviations from the International Fisher Effect across major currencies during the floating-rate period have been both positive and negative, averaging near zero. We know that *active speculators* may make extraordinary gains by moving into those currencies where the exchange rate gain outweighs the interest rate cost, or where the interest rate gain outweighs the exchange rate loss. But can *passive investors* use the principle of portfolio diversification and capture diversification gains by holding a diversified portfolio of international currencies on an unhedged basis?

The answer is suggested by Figure 5.10. The annual return from investing in US$ averaged 8.85 percent with a standard deviation of 3.6 percent over the 21-year period. Holding C$ on an uncovered basis was slightly less attractive, but more than twice as risky. Investing in the other major currencies resulted in higher average US$ returns (from 60 basis points in Germany to more than 200 basis points in Japan), but because of the substantial variability, the returns were not significantly higher than the US$ return.[38] The message of Figure 5.10 is that even with a tendency for the International Fisher Effect to hold on average, the low-cost, low-risk way to borrow (or invest) US$ on a passive basis is to work directly through US$ instruments (or synthetic US$ instruments, that is, covered foreign currency instruments). Considering short-term, money-market instruments, there are no meaningful diversification gains from using foreign currencies on an uncovered basis. Diversification gains will appear, however, when we look at portfolios of long-term international bonds (Chapter 14) and portfolios of international equities (Chapter 15).

---

[37]It was reported (Jaffe and Machan, *Forbes*, Nov. 9, 1992, pp. 40–42) that George Soros, the well-known international financier, made about $1.5 billion in one month on an ERM speculation of this sort. His percentage profit was probably in the 10–14 percent range, but was made larger through the use of leverage. Had the pound and the lira not dropped out of the ERM, Soros would have lost an amount proportional to the interest differential.

[38]To see this, examine Figure 5.6 again and note that the cumulative wealth lines cross nine times in 21 years. This suggests a tendency for uncovered interest parity to hold between US$ and DM investments after two to three years, on average.

FIGURE 5.10 U.S. Dollar Return and Risk on Uncovered Investing in Different Currencies, 1973–1993

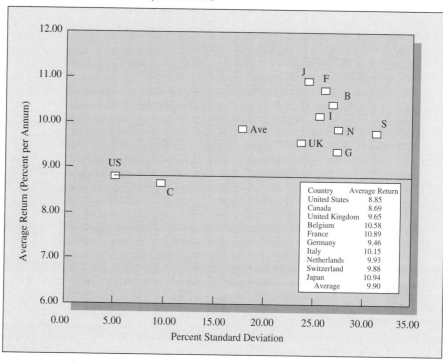

Country	Average Return
United States	8.85
Canada	8.69
United Kingdom	9.65
Belgium	10.58
France	10.89
Germany	9.46
Italy	10.15
Netherlands	9.93
Switzerland	9.88
Japan	10.94
Average	9.90

Note: US$ return on investing is computed as the return on investing in foreign currencies on an uncovered basis, using three-month Eurocurrency deposits. Average and standard deviation is computed over 84 quarterly observations. "Ave" represents the average result from an evenly weighted portfolio of all nine foreign currencies.

Application 7: International Fisher Effect, Long-Term Bonds, and Exchange Rate Predictions

The International Fisher Effect in expression (5.6) provided a link between the current spot exchange rate, interest rates, and the implied future spot exchange rate.

$$E(\tilde{S}_{t+1}) = \frac{1 + i_\$}{1 + i_£} \times S_t \qquad (5.6)$$

The interest rates in expression (5.6) apply to a one-period investment. We can extend our interpretation of the International Fisher Effect to the case of long-term bonds. The future spot exchange rate that equilibrates the value of *n*-period investments in US$ or UK£ bonds is:

$$E(\tilde{S}_{t+n}) = \frac{(1 + i_{\$,n})^n}{(1 + i_{£,n})^n} \times S_t \qquad (5.20)$$

Consider the following example, where the current spot rate is $1.50/£ and the 10-year US$ and UK£ interest rates are 6.0 percent and 8.0 percent per annum, respectively. With these values, the implied future spot exchange rate that satisfies the International Fisher Effect is $1.2443/£. The path of the $/£ exchange rate over the 10-year period is graphed in Figure 5.11. The steady depreciation of UK£ at roughly 2 percent per year traces out the Fisher path. Note that this path, *and only this path*, makes the value of the

FIGURE 5.11   **International Fisher Effect over 10 Years**
Initial Spot \$1.50/£, $i_\$ = 6\%$, $i_£ = 8\%$

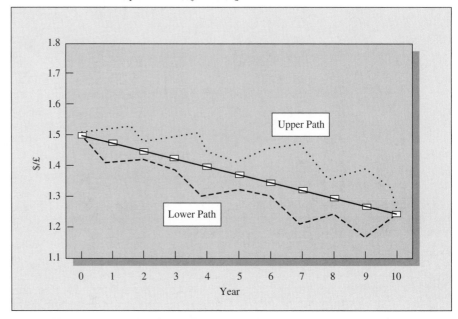

Note: The equilibrium path of the exchange rate according to the International Fisher Effect is $E(S_{t+n}) = S_t[(1 + i_\$)/(1 + i_£)]^n$. This path is the solid line. The other paths (shown with dotted and dashed lines) are hypothetical, but are constrained to have the same starting and ending values, and the same average rate of change over the 10-year period.

two investments equal at all times over the 10 years. If the exchange rate had followed the upper path from \$1.50 to \$1.2443, then US\$-based investors would have preferred the UK£ bond (and US\$-based borrowers would have preferred the US\$ bond). Had the exchange rate followed the lower path from \$1.50 to \$1.2443, then US\$-based investors would have preferred the US\$ bond (and US\$-based borrowers would have preferred the UK£ bond).[39]

Figure 5.11 suggests that our shorthand expression for the International Fisher Effect in expression (5.5) reflects an important assumption—namely, the predicted annual exchange rate change is constant over the life of the investment. Only then will (risk-neutral) investors be indifferent between the two bonds. If the expected path of the exchange rate does not follow this constant path, then borrowers and investors must use the net present value rule to decide between the two bonds.[40]

Policy Matters—Public Policymakers

The international parity conditions developed in this chapter also play a role in public policy discussions.

---

[39]Note that these predictions are reversed for UK£-based investors and borrowers. Can you explain why?

[40]Note that these results are valid if the bond is a zero-coupon bond or a coupon-paying bond. Can you explain why?

The Fisher parities can provide information regarding how closely national financial markets are linked to one another, and what price, if any, a nation is paying for perceived political and economic risks. From our discussion of the International Fisher Effect, we can express the real interest differential as:

$$r - r^* = [i - E(\tilde{p})] - [i^* - E(\tilde{p}^*)]$$

where r, i, and $E(\tilde{p})$ are the real interest rate, nominal interest rate, and expected inflation, respectively, and the asterisk represents a foreign variable. Jeffrey Frankel and Alan MacArthur (1988) showed how the real interest differential can be rewritten as the sum of three terms:

$$r - r^* = (i - i^* - fd) + [fd - E(\tilde{s})] + [E(\tilde{s}) - E(\tilde{p}) + E(\tilde{p}^*)] \qquad (5.21)$$

where *fd* is the forward discount $(F - S)/S$, and $E(\tilde{s})$ is the expected exchange rate change. The first term is the covered interest differential. When i and i^* are taken as the local interest rates in the two countries (instead of the Eurorates), this differential measures the "political risk premium" or "country risk premium." Frankel and MacArthur argued that this differential is an appropriate measure of *capital mobility* across the two markets. The second term in equation (5.21) is the deviation from the forward rate unbiased condition and measures the exchange-risk premium, or the currency-risk premium. The final term in expression (5.21) measures the expected real depreciation of the currency.

In their analysis of 24 countries over the September 1982–March 1987 period, Frankel and MacArthur showed that for most of the large industrialized countries and several other countries known to have few capital controls (such as Hong Kong and Singapore), the deviations from covered-interest parity were small over the entire period or declining through the period, suggesting high capital mobility. But even in the remaining countries, the political-risk premium was generally not as large as the currency-risk premium.

The interest rate differential may be a useful indicator of policy credibility for countries following pegged exchange rate policies. Uncovered interest parity implies that the nominal interest differential $(i - i^*)$ should be zero for a pair of countries with pegged exchange rates. We have seen numerous instances in the past (such as European Union countries or the United States and Mexico in the early 1990s) where an interest rate differential was the harbinger of a future exchange rate change. A positive interest differential could be related to a difference in real interest rates $(r - r^*)$ where the higher real rate reflects a high investment demand for funds. But the positive interest differential could reflect a country risk premium, or higher expected inflation, $E(p) - E(p^*)$, and some probability that domestic policymakers will be forced to devalue their currency. A positive interest differential may provide an early-warning device about the perceived credibility of a fixed exchange rate policy.

Summary

In this chapter, we concluded our discussion of the international parity conditions. We focused on those parity conditions that relate prices in the foreign exchange market with interest rates in domestic and foreign securities markets.

Interest rate parity (IRP) is the purest form of arbitrage in international financial markets. The interest rate parity line establishes the break-even line where the return on a foreign currency investment *covered against exchange risk* is identical with the return on a domestic currency investment. The interest rate parity line also determines the break-even line where the cost of a foreign currency loan *covered against exchange risk* is identical with the cost of a domestic currency loan. Deviations from interest rate parity represent attractive profit opportunities for both investors and borrowers. Empirical evidence generally supports IRP, especially for short-term maturities and interest rates set in the Euromarkets. However, other evidence suggests that deviations from parity may appear in the very short run or for long-term maturities. These deviations offer opportunities for investment managers to raise their returns and for corporate treasurers to lower their cost of funds *without increasing their exposure to currency risks.*

The International Fisher Effect establishes the break-even line between investments in domestic securities and investments in foreign securities where the exposure to currency risk is not covered. When international investors are risk neutral toward currency risk, the International Fisher Effect provides an estimate of the market's expectation of the future spot exchange rate. The International Fisher Effect predicts that high-interest-rate currencies tend to depreciate while low-interest-rate currencies tend to appreciate. The predictions of the International Fisher Effect and purchasing power parity are consistent if we assume that currencies with high interest rates go hand-in-hand with high inflation rates. Periods where the interest rate differential does not match the anticipated exchange rate change represent potential profit opportunities for investors and borrowers. But these are *risky opportunities* because the investor or borrower is exposed to currency risks.

The forward rate unbiased condition is a logical consequence of IRP and the International Fisher Effect. The empirical evidence suggests that over long periods, the forward rate appears to be unbiased in the sense that periods of positive and negative bias offset each other. During shorter time intervals, on the other hand, it appears that the forward premiums are a poor predictor of the future exchange rate change. In this sense, the data hold the promise that models may be able to outperform the naive forward premium as a predictor of the future exchange rate change.

APPENDIX 5.1
INTEREST RATE PARITY, THE FISHER PARITIES, CONTINUOUS COMPOUNDING, AND LOGARITHMIC RETURNS

The continuous rate of return can be used in connection with interest rate parity and the International Fisher Effect. In IRP (equation 5.1), we balanced the return on a US$ investment with the covered return on a UK£ investment. If we assume that the interest rates on the two securities are in continuous terms, the arbitrage condition becomes:

$$\$1 \, e^{i_\$} = \$1 \, \frac{1}{S(\$/£)} \, e^{i_\$} \, F(\$/£)$$

or

$$\frac{F(\$/£)}{S(\$/£)} = e^{i_\$ - i_£}$$

Taking logarithms, we have:

$$\ln\left(\frac{F}{S}\right) = i_\$ - i_£$$

Notice that the $[1 + i_£]$ term in the denominator of our original IRP condition—equation (5.1)—has now vanished. The same follows easily for the International Fisher Effect condition, which can be written with continuous rates of return as:

$$\ln[E(\widetilde{S}_{t+1})/S_t] = i_\$ - i_£$$

The $[1 + i_£]$ term in equation (5.5) is thereby eliminated in the denominator.

Using continuous returns rather than simple returns is especially helpful when analyzing a time series of prices or returns. Suppose that over N periods, a security appreciates from price P_0 to price P_N. The total price change $(P_N - P_0)$ can be decomposed into a sequence of prices changes $(P_N - P_{N-1})$ $+ (P_{N-1} - P_{N-2}) + \ldots + (P_2 - P_1) + (P_1 - P_0)$. The **logarithmic returns** over these N periods: $ln(P_N/P_{N-1})$, $ln(P_{N-1}/P_{N-2}), \ldots ln(P_2/P_1), ln(P_1/P_0)$, when added together yield the total return $ln(P_N/P_0)$. The simple mean and standard deviation of logarithmic returns result in unbiased estimates of average return and volatility. These statistics can be computed easily within a common spreadsheet program or standard statistical software.

A sequence of **simple returns,** in comparison, would require the computation of the geometric mean of the series to have an unbiased estimate of the mean. For example, suppose a security price starts with $P_0 = 100$, then $P_1 = 50$, then $P_2 = 100$. The return sequence is -50 percent, $+100$ percent. A simple average of these two numbers $(+25$ percent) overestimates the average return. Suppose instead that the price series is $P_0 = 100$, then $P_1 = 200$, then $P_2 = 100$. The return sequence is $+100$ percent, -50 percent. Again, a simple average of these two numbers $(+25$ percent) overestimates the average return. Clearly, a portfolio manager would welcome being rewarded on the basis of the simple average of simple rates of return.

As an exercise, compute logarithmic returns in these examples to convince yourself that this approach removes the bias. Compute the geometric mean of the returns to show that this approach is also able to remove the bias. The use of continuous, or logarithmic, returns is by far the easier technique to remove any bias from the estimate of the mean, especially for long time series of data.

APPENDIX 5.2
TRANSACTION COSTS AND THE NEUTRAL BAND SURROUNDING THE TRADITIONAL INTEREST RATE PARITY LINE

To develop the idea of a neutral band, consider the process of covered interest arbitrage when transaction costs are present.[41] Let the parameters t, t^*, t_S, and t_F represent the *fixed* percentage costs of transacting in the domestic securities market, foreign securities market, spot foreign exchange market, and forward foreign exchange market, respectively. For an arbitrageur who begins with domestic securities and considers a covered outflow from domestic to foreign securities (as set forth in the chapter), the trade-off between remaining in domestic securities (with return i) versus undertaking a costly outflow into foreign securities (with return i^*) is given by:

$$(1 + i) = (1 - t)(1 - t^*)(1 - t_S)(1 - t_F)(1 + i^*)\frac{F}{S}$$

where the right-hand-side term reflects the fact that four transaction costs would have to be paid to undertake the covered outflow.[42] To simplify the notation, let the total transaction costs be represented by $\Omega = (1 - t)(1 - t^*)(1 - t_S)(1 - t_F)$. It

follows that the lower limit on the forward premium (P_L) needed to make an outflow profitable would be:

$$\frac{F - S}{S} = \frac{(1 + i) - (1 + i^*)\,\Omega}{(1 + i^*)\,\Omega} \equiv P_L \qquad (A5.1)$$

In a similar fashion, the trade-off between remaining in foreign securities or undertaking a costly inflow to domestic securities (as set forth in the chapter), would be balanced when the following relationship holds:

$$(1 + i^*) = \frac{(1 - t)(1 - t^*)(1 - t_S)(1 - t_F)(1 + i)\,S}{F}$$

Thus, it follows that the upper limit (P_U) on the forward premium needed to make an inflow profitable would be:

$$\frac{F - S}{S} = \frac{(1 + i)\Omega - (1 + i^*)}{(1 + i^*)} \equiv P_U \qquad (A5.2)$$

Together, the conditions in equations (A5.1) and (A5.2) imply that, in equilibrium, and to preclude covered interest arbitrage opportunities, the forward premium (P) must be within the band given by:

$$P_U \le P \le P_L$$

Within this neutral band, profit opportunities are outweighed by transaction costs.

---

[41]The exposition is adapted from Frenkel and Levich (1975).

[42]As an exercise, compute the size of the neutral band for an investor who begins with $ *cash* rather than $ securities. You should find that the size of the band is smaller. Explain why.

Questions

1. Describe how covered interest arbitrage acts to enforce interest rate parity. Describe the impact of each transaction on interest rates and exchange rates. Provide one example using data from today's newspaper.
2. Define the Fisher Effect and the International Fisher Effect (uncovered interest parity). How are these effects similar and how are they different?
3. Describe the forward rate unbiased condition.
4. If the forward rate unbiased condition is true, then the forward rate should not vary from the future spot rate by more than 1 percent. Is this statement true or false? Explain.
5. Discuss the impact of transaction costs on the interest rate parity condition.
6. Discuss the impact of taxes on the interest rate parity condition.
7. We can measure the deviations from interest rate parity on an ex ante basis, but we can only measure the deviations from the Fisher International Effect on an ex post basis. Is this statement true or false? Discuss.

8. Describe several alternative methods for testing the interest rate parity condition. What is the most appropriate method?
9. What empirical evidence tends to show that the interest rate parity condition holds in the long term?
10. If the forward unbiased condition holds, financial managers should regularly hedge their foreign exchange exposure. Is this statement true or false? Why?
11. When interest rate parity holds, it does not matter which currency you choose for borrowing or lending purposes. Is this statement true or false? Why?
12. Empirical evidence shows that there are sometimes deviations from interest rate parity and the International Fisher Effect. What kind of threats and opportunities does this open up for financial managers?
13. In the case of a pegged exchange system, when would an interest rate differential appear between government securities of the two countries?

Exercises

Interest Rate Parity

1. Suppose the U.S. and U.K. three-month interest rates are, respectively, 6 percent and 8 percent per annum and that the spot rate is $1.55/£.
   a. Calculate the forward premium (or discount) on the £ expressed on a per annum basis.
   b. What value of the three-month forward rate establishes interest rate parity?
2. Suppose the spot rate is $0.20/FFr. The U.S. one-year rate is 6 percent. The forward rate is $0.1923/FFr.
   a. What is the current one-year French interest rate that will satisfy the interest rate parity?
   b. Suppose the one-year French interest rate is instead 12 percent. What kind of arbitrage would you perform to take advantage of this opportunity?
   c. Suppose the U.S. tax rate on capital gains and the tax rate on interest earned and paid are 15

percent and 40 percent, respectively. What is the new forward rate (F') that would satisfy IRP on an after-tax basis?
   d. Suppose all the variables took the values from part a. Would there be any arbitrage opportunity on an after-tax basis?
3. Assume that the Citibank trading room is dealing on the following quotations:
   Spot sterling = $1.5000
   Euro-sterling interest rate (6 months) = 11 percent p.a.
   Euro-$ interest rate (6 months) = 6 percent p.a.

   Also assume that Barclays Bank is quoting forward sterling (6 months) at $1.4550.
   a. Describe the transactions you would make to earn risk-free covered interest arbitrage profits.
   b. How much profit would you expect to make?

Fisher International Effect

4. The following data were taken from the July 28, 1994, issue of Merrill Lynch's *Currency and Bond Market Trends*.

	Japan	Britain	United States
Spot exchange rates:	98.75 ¥/$	$1.53/£	
5-year bonds	3.73%	7.94%	6.88%
10-year bonds	4.34	8.24	7.24
20-year bonds	4.70	8.26	7.40

Compute the break-even exchange rate for investors, weighing the choice between $-bonds and yen-bonds, and between $-bonds and pound-sterling bonds for each of the three maturities. (*Note*: Assume that interest is paid twice yearly.)

5. In 1986, the Seagram Company of Canada issued Swiss franc bonds (SFr 250,000,000) due September 30, 2085, with a 6 percent coupon. Assume that a similar bond denominated in US$ would have required a 9 percent coupon and that the spot rate on the issue day was $0.50/SFr.
   a. Compute the break-even exchange rate for the redemption of the Seagram bond at maturity.
   b. Discuss why Seagram may have issued this bond rather than a US$-denominated bond.

6. Suppose that the interest rates in question 5 reflect a 0.5 percent per annum currency-risk premium for bond investors to willingly hold US$-denominated bonds.
   a. Compute the expected exchange rate on the maturity date of the bond.
   b. How does the currency-risk premium affect the choice by Seagram to issue a US$- or SFr-denominated bond?

References

Aliber, Robert Z. "The Interest Rate Parity Theory: A Reinterpretation." *Journal of Political Economy* 81, no. 6 (Dec. 1973), pp. 1451–59.

Bahmani-Oskooee, Mohsen, and Satya P. Das. "Transaction Costs and the Interest Rate Parity Theorem." *Journal of Political Economy* 93, no. 4 (Aug. 1985), pp. 793–99.

Boyle, Glenn W. "Cash Position, Credit Risk and Hedging." *Journal of International Financial Management and Accounting* 4, no. 1 (Spring 1992), pp. 1–12.

Clinton, Kevin. "Transaction Costs and Covered Interest Arbitrage: Theory and Evidence." *Journal of Political Economy* 96, no. 2 (Apr. 1988), pp. 358–70.

Cumby, Robert E., and Maurice Obstfeld. "International Interest Rate and Price Level Linkages under Flexible Exchange Rates: A Review of Recent Evidence." In *Exchange Rate Theory and Practice*, ed. John Bilson and Richard Marston. Chicago: University of Chicago Press, 1984.

————. "A Note on Exchange-Rate Expectations and Nominal Interest Differentials: A Test of the Fisher Hypothesis." *Journal of Finance* 36, no. 3 (June 1981), pp. 697–703.

Deardorff, Alan V. "One-Way Arbitrage and Its Implications for the Foreign Exchange Markets." *Journal of Political Economy* 87, no. 2 (Apr. 1979), pp. 351–64.

Dooley, Michael P., and Peter Isard. "Capital Controls, Political Risk, and Deviations from Interest Rate Parity." *Journal of Political Economy* 88, no. 2 (April 1980), pp. 370–84.

Fisher, Irving. "Appreciation and Interest." *Publication of the American Economic Association* 11, no. 4 (Aug. 1896), pp. 331–442.

Fletcher, Donna J., and Larry W. Taylor. "A Non-Parametric Analysis of Covered Interest Parity in Long-Date Capital Markets." *Journal of International Money and Finance* 13, no. 4 (Aug. 1994), pp. 459–75

Frankel, Jeffrey A., and Kenneth A. Froot. "Using Survey Data to Test Standard Propositions Regarding Exchange Rate Expectations." *American Economic Review* 77, no. 1 (Mar. 1987), pp. 133–53.

Frankel, Jeffrey A., and Alan T. MacArthur. "Political vs. Currency Premia in International Real Interest Differentials." *European Economic Review* 32, no. 5 (June 1988), pp. 1083–1121.

Frenkel, Jacob A., and Richard M. Levich. "Covered Interest Arbitrage: Unexploited Profits?" *Journal of Political Economy* 83, no. 2 (Apr. 1975), pp. 325–38.

————. "Transaction Costs and the Efficiency of International Capital Markets: Tranquil versus Turbulent

Periods." In *Inflation, Unemployment and Monetary Control,* ed. K. Brunner and M. Neumann. Supplement to *Kredit und Kapital,* vol. 5. Berlin, 1979.

Hilley, John L.; Carl R. Beidleman; and James A. Greenleaf. "Why There Is No Long Forward Market in Foreign Exchange." *Euromoney,* Jan. 1981, pp. 95–103.

Ito, Takatoshi. "Capital Controls and Covered Interest Parity," *Economic Studies Quarterly* 37, no. 3 (Sept. 1986), pp. 223–41.

————. "Use of (Time Domain) Vector Autoregressions to Test Uncovered Interest Rate Parity." *Review of Economics and Statistics,* no. 2 (May 1988), pp. 296–305.

Jaffe, Thomas, and Dyan Machan. "How the Market Overwhelmed the Central Banks." *Forbes,* Nov. 9, 1992, pp. 40–42.

Keynes, John Maynard. *A Tract on Monetary Reform.* London: Macmillan, 1923.

Krugman, Paul R., and Maurice Obstfeld. *International Economics: Theory and Policy,* 3rd ed. New York: HarperCollins, 1994.

Levi, Maurice D. "Taxation and 'Abnormal' International Capital Flows." *Journal of Political Economy* 85, no. 3 (June 1977), pp. 635–46.

McCormick, Frank. "Covered Interest Arbitrage: Unexploited Profits?: Comment." *Journal of Political Economy* 87, no. 2 (Apr. 1979), pp. 411–17.

Officer, Lawrence H., and Thomas D. Willett. "The Covered-Arbitrage Schedule: A Critical Survey of Recent Developments." *Journal of Money, Credit and Banking* 2 (1970), pp. 247–57.

Otani, Ichiro, and Siddhart Tiwari. "Capital Controls and Interest Rate Parity: The Japanese Experience 1978–1981." *IMF Staff Papers* 28, no. 4 (Dec. 1981), pp. 793–815.

Popper, Helen. "Long-Term Covered Interest Parity: Evidence from Currency Swaps." *Journal of International Money and Finance* 12, no. 4 (Aug. 1993), pp. 439–48.

Rhee, S. Ghon, and Rosita P. Chang. "Intra-Day Arbitrage Opportunities in Foreign Exchange and Eurocurrency Markets." *Journal of Finance* 47, no. 1 (Mar. 1992), pp. 363–79.

Takagi, Shinji. "Exchange Rate Expectations: A Survey of Survey Studies." *IMF Staff Papers* 38, no. 1 (Mar. 1991), pp. 156–83.

Uchitelle, Louis. "High Mexican Interest Rates Are Luring Wall Street Cash," *New York Times*, Apr. 22, 1993, p. A1.

6 SPOT EXCHANGE RATE DETERMINATION

"The approximate random-walk behavior of nominal and real exchange rates is a major source of embarrassment for efforts to model the economic determinants of exchange-rate behavior; virtually all structural models of exchange rate behavior are empirically outperformed by a simple random-walk model . . . This conclusion might suggest that nothing can confidently be said about the economic determinants of exchange rate behavior. I shall argue, however, that such a nihilistic conclusion is unwarranted."

Michael Mussa (1990)

Learning Objectives

After reading this chapter, students should

1. Understand that the spot exchange rate, like other financial assets, reflects what investors believe will happen to key variables now and in the future.

2. Know the impact that changes in (*a*) the nation's money supply, (*b*) real income, (*c*) short-term interest rates, and (*d*) inflation rates are likely to have on the spot exchange rate in the context of the monetary approach to exchange rates.

3. Be able to define *exchange rate overshooting* and understand its causes and implications.

4. Know the impact that changes in (*a*) the nation's bond supply, and (*b*) current account are likely to have on the spot exchange rate in the context of the portfolio balance approach to exchange rates.

5. Be familiar with the empirical evidence linking macroeconomic variables to the spot exchange rate, and how "news" about macroeconomic variables can quickly affect the spot exchange rate.

Exchange rates are the quintessential international financial variable, a factor in virtually every international financial market decision. For most countries, the exchange rate is the single most important price in the economy. Economists have studied exchange rates intensely for the last 25 years. Yet, to many economists, exchange rate models built around a set of structural macroeconomic variables seem to have little power to explain the patterns of short-term exchange rate behavior.

Financial economists at banks, securities firms, and elsewhere also have been hard at work analyzing the variables that might impact foreign exchange rates. With daily trading over US$1.5 trillion, market participants approach their craft in a serious and methodical way. In no way is this structured and analytical approach better exemplified than in the foreign exchange market's pursuit of "news" regarding macroeconomic, financial, and political events. Perhaps these efforts of financial economists merely represent the required "due diligence"—if there is even a small chance that macroeconomic analysis has a payout, then a major institution must make a good-faith effort. But the depth to which market economists follow macroeconomic developments suggests that an understanding of the macroeconomic news is critical for understanding (and perhaps predicting) exchange rate behavior.

The above paragraphs may imply a conflict between academic and financial market economists when it comes to modeling exchange rate behavior, but this is not really the case. The view that exchange rates follow a simple random walk and evolve without regard to macroeconomic fundamentals is an extreme characterization, and we believe a false one. Michael Mussa (1990, in the lead quote) writes that the random-walk behavior of exchange rates is only "approximate." As we will explore in this chapter (and Chapters 7 and 8), the presence of non-random-walk behavior offers market economists an opportunity to add value. Second, while the link between exchange rates and macroeconomic variables may be difficult to uncover, there is evidence that such a link exists in the short run and to a greater extent in the long run.

Financial market economists are trained to be skeptical. The principal result from models of exchange rate determination is that the exchange rate is a forward-looking variable that should be priced in the same way as other financial assets. Just as the price of an equity share reflects (in theory) the net present value of all of the cash flows that accrue to its owner, the current price of foreign exchange can be shown to equal (in theory) the net present value of all the fundamental variables that affect the exchange rate. This immediately suggests why the exchange rate would be difficult to model and even more difficult to forecast. The current exchange rate already reflects the expected values of future macroeconomic variables.

In this chapter, we use several news items about macroeconomic events to show the forward-looking nature of the foreign exchange market and the difficulties we face in modeling exchange rates. We survey some of the stylized models of exchange rate determination developed over the last 25 years. We outline the broad predictions of these models, and then we analyze the empirical evidence to determine whether these models offer a satisfactory explanation for exchange rate behavior. We conclude with a discussion of policy choices that affect private enterprises and public policymakers in connection with exchange rate models.

News and Foreign Exchange Rates: An Introduction

Financial markets are preoccupied with news. To illustrate this point, consider Figure 6.1, which presents a sample "trader's calendar." For each trading day, a notation appears listing the macroeconomic data to be announced. In addition, a trader's calendar also may show the value of a consensus forecast for the news release, or the forecast for the news announcement as prepared by the firm's research staff. A calendar of expected macroeconomic announcements is a regular part of many financial newspapers, such as the *Financial Times* and *The Wall Street Journal,* that attempt to prepare their readers for upcoming announcements and the possible market response.[1]

---

[1]In their proprietary research reports, many financial company research teams include a calendar of macroeconomic announcements and their own forecasts. The Bank of Montreal puts its calendar of economic events online at <www.bmo.com/economic/econ.htm>.

FIGURE 6.1   Announcements of Macroeconomic Data during the Week of June 12, 2000

Date	United States	Eurozone	Japan	United Kingdom	Others
Monday, June 12		**Italy: Industrial Production** (April) 0.3% (−0.1%)	**Bank of Japan Monetary Policy Meeting**	**Producer Price Index** Outputs (May) 0.5% (0.2%)	**Switzerland: Producer Price Index** (May) 2.8% (2.9%)
Tuesday, June 13	**Retail Sales** (May) −0.2% (0.1%)	**Germany: Current Account** (April) €5.9 bn (€4.0 bn)	**Industrial Production** (April) −0.4% (NA)	**Retail Price Index** (May) 1.0% (0.3%)	**Sweden: Unemployment Rate** (May) 4.7% (4.4%)
		Spain: Consumer Price Index (May) 0.4% (0.1%)	**Manufacturing Shipments** (April) −0.3% (NA)	**EU Harmonized Consumer Price Index** (May) 0.6% (0.6%)	
Wednesday, June 14	**Consumer Price Index** (May) 0.0% (0.2%)	**Germany: Consumer Price Index** (May) Flat (Flat)	**Bank of Japan Monthly Survey released**	**Unemployment** (May) −28,800 (−10,000)	**Canada: Auto Sales** (April) 6.5% (2.0%)
		France: Current Account (March) €3.2 bn (€2.3 bn)	**Bank of Japan Governor Hayami speech**		**Australia: Real GDP** (1st Q 2000) 1.0% (0.3%)
Thursday, June 15	**Jobless Claims** (Week to June 3) 309,000 (285,000)	**Germany: Retail Sales** (April −4.9% (2.0%)		**Retail Sales** (May) −0.3% (0.6%)	**Sweden: Real GDP** (1st Q 2000) 0.8% (NA)
	Industrial Production (May) 0.9% (−0.2%)	**Portugal: Consumer Price Index** (May) 1.1% (0.5%)			**Canada: Manufacturing Shipments** (April) 3.8% (0.5%)
Friday, June 16	**Housing Starts** (May) 1.66 mn (1.63 mn)	**France: Trade Balance** (April) €1.15 bn (€1.1 bn)			**Canada: Consumer Price Index** (May) −0.4% (0.2%)

Notes: First figure is previous actual value; figure in parentheses is market forecast of announcement; mn = million; bn = billion; NA = not available.

Sources: *Financial Times,* June 12, 2000; "International Economic Briefing," Bank of America, June 12, 2000; "FX Pulse," Morgan Stanley Dean Witter, June 1, 2000.

Even though news seems to figure prominently in the daily activities of foreign exchange market participants, it can be very confusing to read through the (ex post) journalistic explanations of day-to-day exchange rate movements. The confusion comes from the market's different response on two different days to what appears to be the same news item.

For example, in a period of floating exchange rates we might have read that following an increase in the U.S. money supply, the US$ *fell* because the news generated inflationary expectations. But on another occasion, we might have read that following a similar increase in the U.S. money supply, the US$ *rose* because the news generated expectations that the Federal Reserve would tighten money growth and raise interest rates. Along the same lines, we might have read that following an upsurge in the U.S. fiscal budget deficit, the US$ *fell* because the news generated expectations that the Fed would monetize the deficit; but on another occasion, we might have read that the US$ *rose* because the news generated expectations that further government borrowing and higher interest rates would result.[2]

---

[2]These examples are adapted from Frenkel (1985).

This kind of market behavior may seem irrational. In response to what *seems* to be the same news story, the US$ sometimes rises in value and sometimes falls. One might suppose that rationality would dictate an unambiguous link between a news announcement and an exchange rate reaction.

Two reasons explain why we do not find a simple, unambiguous link between a news announcement and an exchange rate reaction. First, the foreign exchange market, like other financial markets, is a *forward-looking* market. Once a news item has occurred, traders are concerned whether the news represents a *permanent* change or only a *transitory* phenomenon. And they are also concerned with whether other macroeconomic shocks are made more (or less) likely following today's news. In each newspaper analysis of the market, note that the phrase "generated expectations" appeared. The news item itself is important, but so is the scenario of future policy and market responses that follow from the news.

Second, while two news announcements may seem similar, on closer examination we may conclude that they are not. For example, an increase in the current account deficit between the United States and Japan may have resulted from an increase in U.S. imports from Japan or a decrease in Japanese imports from the United States. An increase in the interest differential between the United States and Germany may have come about because of an increase in U.S. interest rates or a decrease in German interest rates. Or an increase in U.S. GNP may have been driven by any of its many components. In each case, the market might rationally respond in a different way to what *appears* to be the same piece of news because some underlying aspects of the stories were in fact different.

The reader may feel that this description is a recipe that means anything can happen and be justified in the foreign exchange market. Readers with this feeling have detected one of the troubling aspects of financial markets—there is a story or scenario that rationalizes any market price or market reaction.[3] However, this is not quite the right interpretation. The purpose of this chapter is to show that every analysis and every forecast of an exchange rate is conditional on (1) some assumptions about certain key variables both today and in the future, and (2) a model that links together these variables. We feel that this is a valuable lesson, because it helps the reader appreciate the critical role of assumptions and models when trying to understand the connection between macroeconomic variables and the exchange rate.

Exchange Rates and News Stories: Three Illustrations

To illustrate the idea of confusing exchange market responses to macroeconomic and political news, consider the three "stories" reported in Box 6.1. Imagine that these stories appeared on the Reuters news service. By their nature, stories appear one at a time, so that while one news item is being reported, all other facts about the economy are presumed to be unchanged. The news service puts us in a *ceteris paribus* (all other things being equal) setting common to macroeconomic analysis.

Story 1: An Increase in the U.S. Money Supply.   Consider the first news item announced at time t_1—that the U.S. money supply grew by $3 billion in the most recent week. For many years, the Federal Reserve has announced the weekly U.S. money supply figures at 4:00 P.M. every Thursday. Assume that the consensus market forecast on money

---

[3]For example, on December 31, 1999, equity shares of Amazon.com were valued at $30 billion based on a belief that Amazon.com will one day be a very profitable company. So far, however, Amazon.com has not had a single profitable quarter, let alone a string of profits that would justify its stock price to many investors.

Box 6.1

The Reaction of the Spot Exchange Rate to News Announcements on Macroeconomic and Political Events

Imagine that you are the chief euro trader for a large bank. The Reuters screen on your desk prints out the following messages:

1. The Federal Reserve announces that the money supply grew by $3 billion in the most recent week.
2. Rates for three-month U.S. Treasury bills jump from 3.50 percent to 3.60 percent during the morning trading. Other rates along the term structure respond accordingly.
3. The General Accounting Office (GAO) announces that the U.S. fiscal budget deficit for the year ending next June 30 is expected to reach $250 billion.

In each of the above cases, describe how you think the US$/€ rate will respond to the news item. In each case, devise a scenario under which:

a. The euro would rise in value in response to the news item.

b. The euro would fall in value in response to the same news item.

See the text for a description of some sample scenarios following these news items.

---

supply growth was $2 billion, so that realized money growth exceeded the predicted growth—a "positive surprise." Why might the US$ weaken in response to this news? One simple answer is that the market feels that the higher money supply will be maintained. With national output constant, a larger money supply leads to a higher price level. If both prices and exchange rates are perfectly flexible, then the US$ will weaken immediately. These events are diagrammed in Figure 6.2, with the paths of the money supply, price level, and exchange rate indicated by path *a* for this scenario. The interest rate does not change since the price level is constant after the monetary shock under this scenario.

Could the US$ strengthen in response to the *same* news item? Suppose that market participants believe that the Federal Reserve has "discipline" and that it will drain reserves from the banking sector in the coming weeks to make up for its past excessive money supply creation. In this case, the market projects an unusually low growth in the money supply. As tighter money is projected, interest rates are projected to rise, and thus interest rates rise immediately in anticipation. Higher US$ interest rates attract capital, and the US$ rises. These events are diagrammed in Figure 6.2, with the paths of the money supply, price level, and exchange rate indicated by path *b* for this scenario.

Paths *a* and *b* are only two extreme choices: *a*, where the money supply shock is taken to be a one-time and permanent shock to the *level* of the money supply; and *b*, where the money supply shock is taken to be transitory and offset in one period. Clearly, any number of other scenarios could be possible.[4] A natural question to ask is: Which is the correct response of the exchange rate to the news—path *a* or path *b*? The answer, unfortunately, is that both responses are correct, but to different scenarios derived from the same news announcement.

Story 2: An Increase in U.S. Interest Rates.   Consider the second news item, that U.S. interest rates at all maturities along the term structure of interest rates have risen by 0.10

---

[4]In Figure 6.2, path *c* describes a permanent change in the rate of growth of the money supply. In this scenario, inflation turns positive after t_1, the interest rate jumps, and the US$ steadily depreciates.

FIGURE 6.2   **The Reaction of the US$ to a Money Supply Announcement: Alternative Scenarios**

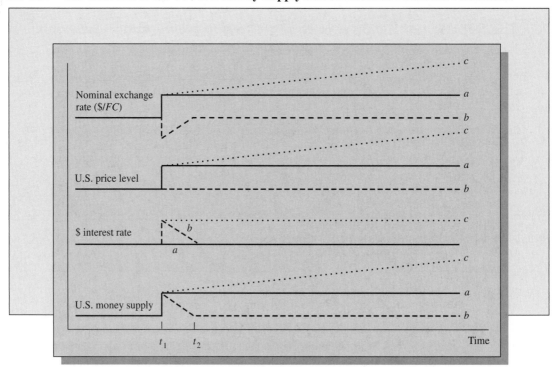

Note: In response to an increase in the domestic money supply at time t_1, interest rates, the price level, and the US$/FC exchange rate may follow various paths (indicated by a, b, and c) depending on the expected path of the money supply at time t_2 and beyond.

percent or 10 basis points (bp). Assume that the market consensus was for no change in interest rates, so the entire 10-bp increase comes as an unexpected surprise. Could the US$ be *weaker* as a result of this news? It could be that US$ interest rates have risen because of concern about rising U.S. inflation (the Fisher Effect). Following purchasing power parity, a weaker US$ would be expected—call this path d (not graphed in Figure 6.2). Might the US$ *strengthen* in response to the same news item? If market participants were attracted by the higher yields now available on US$ securities, capital flows to the United States would contribute to a stronger US$—call this path e (also not graphed).

Again, we can ask the question: Which is the correct response of the exchange rate to an increase in the level of interest rates—a weaker currency or a stronger currency? The answer again is that both responses may be correct. The weaker US$ (path d) assumes that the rise in U.S. interest rates is stemming from inflationary concerns, and therefore a rise in the *nominal* interest rate, but not necessarily the real interest rate. The stronger US$ (path e) assumes that inflation is under control, so the higher interest rate corresponds to an increase in the *real* interest rate. And a higher real interest rate draws in foreign capital and raises the foreign exchange value of domestic currency. Because nominal U.S. interest rates respond to both real and inflationary factors, the exchange rate response must be ambiguous.[5]

---

[5]The general problem is that the Fisher Effect equation for the nominal interest rate gives us one equation with two unknown variables (the real interest rate and the expected rate of inflation). A domestic bond trader could refer to the foreign exchange market for confirmation of whether real or inflationary forces are behind an interest rate change.

FIGURE 6.3 The Trade-Weighted Dollar versus the U.S.–Foreign Interest Differential: 1976–78 and 1979–80

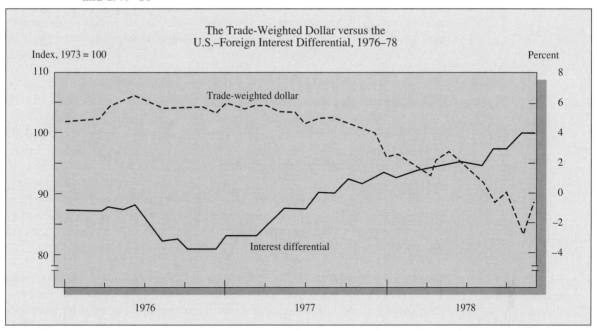

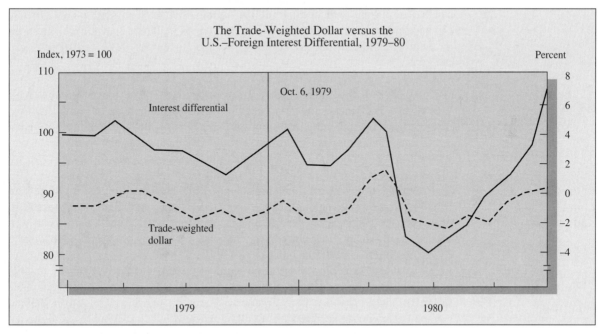

Source: Federal Reserve Bank of Chicago, *International Letter,* no. 441, Feb. 13, 1981.

Figure 6.3 provides a vivid illustration that the interest rate–exchange rate correlation can be either positive or negative. From 1976 to 1978, the differential between U.S. and foreign interest rates rose from −4 percentage points to +4 percentage points.

Despite this sharp increase in U.S. interest rates, the trade-weighted value of the dollar depreciated by almost 20 percent, from 105.0 in mid-1976 to 85.0 by November 1978. This is certainly an example of negative correlation between interest rates and exchange rates as in path *d*. In the following two years, the correlation between exchange rates and interest rates turned significantly positive. Clearly, higher U.S. interest rates were stimulating US$ currency purchases during the latter period while the reverse was evident during the earlier period.

We can see both patterns in Figure 6.3, but what factors lay behind this change in behavior? Two important policy events took place during these periods. First, the official intervention of November 1, 1978 (see Chapters 2 and 3) was intended to convince the market that U.S. policymakers were serious about controlling inflation and arresting the downward slide in the US$. Second, on October 6, 1979, the U.S. Federal Reserve announced a change in its operating procedures. The Fed's new policy emphasized containing the growth rate of monetary aggregates within announced limits, allowing interest rates to take on greater volatility. Together, these policy changes led markets to believe that U.S. inflation would be kept under control, so that changes in nominal interest rates would be tantamount to changes in real interest rates, thus causing interest rates and exchange rates to move more in concert.

Story 3: An Increase in the U.S. Current Account Deficit.   The final news item concerns an announcement that the U.S. current account deficit will reach an annual rate of $250 billion. Assume that the GAO's announcement is credible and that previously the market's consensus estimate for the current account was a smaller deficit of, say, $200 billion. This is news of a larger than expected current account deficit. It is useful to recall that the current account can be defined as the difference between a nation's exports (X) and imports (M) of goods and services, plus all unilateral transfers (U) from domestic to foreign residents, or:

$$CA = X - M + U \tag{6.1}$$

Using other accounting identities, we can also show that the current account reflects a nation's rate of savings and that this can be divided into two pieces: net public savings measured as government tax collections (T) minus government expenditures (G), and net private savings measured as private savings (S^P) minus private investment (I), or:

$$CA = (T - G) + (S^P - I) \tag{6.2}$$

Could the US$ *weaken* following news of a higher-than-expected current account deficit? Referring to equation (6.1), the larger current account deficit could be the result of an unexpected shortfall in exports or an increase in imports. If these movements were viewed as permanent, traders could conclude that a weaker US$ would be required to encourage exports and reduce imports.

A weaker US$ could follow based on other channels of analysis. From equation (6.2) we see that a larger current account deficit could be financed by either larger public sector borrowing ($T - G < 0$) or larger private sector borrowing ($S^P - I < 0$). Suppose that the larger current account deficit will be financed by a larger public sector deficit, $T - G < 0$, also commonly known as the *fiscal budget deficit.* Let B denote the *supply* of U.S. government bonds and SF the US$ value of the *supply* of foreign government bonds, determined by multiplying the stock of foreign bonds (F) by the spot exchange rate (S). If the larger U.S. fiscal budget deficit is financed by issuing government bonds, then the ratio B/SF increases. If the relative supply of U.S. government bonds exceeds the (given) relative demand for U.S. government bonds, $(B/SF)_{\text{supply}} > (\overline{B/SF})_{\text{demand}}$, it follows that prices must change to restore equilibrium. One route is for domestic bond prices to fall to reflect their excess supply $(B\downarrow)$. But another route is for the US$ to weaken $(S\uparrow)$ until $(B/SF)_{supply} = (\overline{B/SF})_{demand}$.

Could the US$ *strengthen* in response to news of a higher-than-expected current account deficit? Suppose as in equation (6.2) that the higher current account deficit has its source in greater private sector investments. We might associate these larger investments with greater real rates of return. If so, foreign capital will flow willingly to finance these investments. In doing so, the US$ will strengthen. Suppose instead that the higher current account deficit has its source in greater public sector expenditures $(G\uparrow)$ and a larger supply of U.S. government bonds $(B\uparrow)$. Other things being equal, this expansionary fiscal policy should raise interest rates on U.S. government bonds. If foreign investors judge that this higher level of government borrowing and expenditure is sustainable, then the higher interest rate will attract foreign capital and the US$ will strengthen. **Sustainability** is a key issue here. When foreign investors are confident that U.S. government bonds will be paid off with future tax revenues instead of fresh money creation, the value of the US$ may remain steady or move higher following an increase in the fiscal budget deficit.[6]

Once again, we can ask the question: Which is the correct response of the exchange rate to a larger than expected current account deficit—a weaker currency or a stronger currency? The reader can now anticipate that either response may be correct. If traders take the larger current account deficit as a sign that U.S. goods are too expensive relative to foreign goods, then the US$ will weaken. Or if traders believe that the deficit will be financed by larger government bond offerings (B) but that foreign appetite for these bonds is nearly saturated, then a weaker US$ $(S\uparrow)$ will be required to equilibrate the supply and demand for U.S. and foreign bonds. However, if the current account deficit is associated with greater private investment opportunities, or higher government interest rates and sustainable fiscal balance, then the US$ will strengthen as foreign capital flows toward these opportunities.

The empirical evidence displayed in Table 6.1 shows that during the 1974–1984 period, the foreign exchange value of the US$ was correlated significantly with the budget deficits in the United States and in foreign countries. The first regression equation shows that the link between a larger budget deficit and a stronger currency was established empirically in the 1974–1981 period. This relationship persisted over the 11 quarters through 1984:3, explaining 97 percent of the variation in rates over this decade.[7]

News and Foreign Exchange Rates: A Summary

Examining the response of exchange rates to these three hypothetical news stories leaves us with both good news and bad news. The good news is that exchange rate behavior could be rational after all, even though exchange rates have been shown to move in opposite directions in response to what appears to be the same news item. Our analysis shows that news items that appear to be the same may differ in some critical respect, and that this causes the exchange rate to respond differently following what might seem to be similar economic events. The bad news of course is that exchange rate modeling—not to mention exchange rate prediction—can be extremely complex. Still, a number of key principles stand out as summarized in Box 6.2.

---

[6]For more on the issue of sustainability and the path of the foreign exchange rate, see Krugman (1985).
[7]The model is extended and used to forecast in Chapter 8.

TABLE 6.1   Real Exchange Rates and the Fiscal Budget Deficit

Period	a_0	a_1	a_2	a_3	R^2	Rho
1974–1981:4	4.59	3.4	−4.3	2.96	0.88	0.59
	(85.4)	(3.7)	(−3.1)	(2.1)		
1974–1984:3	4.61	3.46	−4.48	3.22	0.97	0.62
	(191.4)	(4.5)	(−7.6)	(3.1)		

Regression estimates for the equation

$$REX = a_0 + a_1 (R^* - R) + a_2 B + a_3 B^*$$

where

       REX is the real, trade-weighted US$ exchange rate

       R is the real interest rate

       B is the budget deficit as a percentage of GNP

and variables with (without) an asterisk represent trade-weighted foreign (U.S.) values, respectively.

Data are quarterly; *t*-statistics are in parentheses.

Source: Michael Hutchison and Adrian Throop, "U.S. Budget Deficits and the Real Value of the Dollar." Reprinted from the Federal Reserve Bank of San Francisco *Economic Review,* no. 4, 1985. The opinions expressed in this article do not necessarily reflect the views of the management of the Federal Reserve Bank of San Francisco, or of the Board of Governors of the Federal Reserve System.

Exchange rates deviate from their expected path only in response to unanticipated events.[8] If nothing significant is announced during the day, no significant exchange rate movements should be expected. Point 1 is simply the principle of market efficiency, which we discuss further in Chapter 7. From point 2, it is clear that a single variable explanation of the exchange rate cannot be supported. A variety of monetary and real variables affect the demand for a currency or for financial assets denominated in that currency. And because the exchange rate is a relative price, changes in these variables in either the home country or the foreign country can affect the exchange rate. And point 3 reminds us that the character of the economic news and the context in which it occurs help formulate the scenario that traders extrapolate from a particular news story. It is this scenario for the future that determines how the exchange rate reacts to news.

If it were possible to describe how the exchange rate would respond to each news report, then we would have an economic model of exchange rate determination. In the remainder of this chapter, we will examine a number of alternative models of exchange rate determination that merit consideration.

Flow versus Stock Models of the Exchange Rate

A model of exchange rate determination requires the specification of demand and supply curves, the intersection of which determines a price.

---

[8]We say "deviations about the expected path," because the foreign exchange rate could change with an expected drift or pattern. For example, if countries A and B have inflation rates of 5 percent and 10 percent, respectively, we would expect that B's currency would depreciate at 5 percent per year to preserve PPP. A change of this amount would not therefore be unexpected.

Box 6.2

Foreign Exchange Rate Behavior: Major Concepts

1. Only unanticipated events cause exchange rates to deviate from their expected path of movement.
2. Factors that increase the demand for a currency tend to raise the price of that currency. The demand for a nation's money as a currency or as an investment choice depends on a small group of factors, including:

   - National income
   - Real interest rates
   - Inflation rate
   - Changes in national wealth (through the current account)
   - The preferred currency mix for holding financial wealth
   - Financial risk factors
   - Political risk factors

   When a change in one of these variables occurs—either in the home country or in the foreign country, since it is relative values that determine the exchange rate—we should be able to predict the direction of change in the exchange rate that will follow.
3. The "character" and the "context" of the economic news item will greatly influence the "nature" of the exchange rate response that follows. By "character," we mean whether the news item represents:

   - An unanticipated or anticipated disturbance.
   - A permanent or transitory disturbance.

   - A shock affecting the level of a variable or its rate of change.
   - A real or nominal (monetary) disturbance.
   - A shock affecting a single industry sector or an economywide shock.
   - A shock to beliefs that were weakly held (and therefore easily changed) or strongly held.

   By "context," we mean a variety of factors including (but not limited to):

   - Whether the monetary authorities are perceived to have discipline relative to their targets.
   - Whether foreign demand for home country currency and securities is satiated or growing.
   - Whether prices in the economy are free to adjust quickly (rather than sticky).
   - Whether the shock resulted from a change in exports (rather than imports), a change in public savings (rather than private savings), and so forth.

   By the "nature" of the exchange rate response, we mean:

   - Whether the exchange rate jumps immediately to its next long-term equilibrium and stays there at rest.
   - Whether the exchange rate overshoots its next long-run equilibrium and continues to adjust following its initial jump.

An Overview of the Flow Approach

Until the early 1970s, most attempts to model the demand and supply for foreign exchange concentrated on the *flows* of currency passing through the foreign exchange market. Foreign exchange was thought to be in demand or supply largely as a *medium of exchange* for executing international trade transactions. Bretton Woods had left various capital controls in place. Consequently, foreign exchange was not extensively used as a *store of value;* investment portfolios were more concentrated in domestic assets. The demand for foreign exchange was thus derived from the consumers' ultimate demand for a *flow* of foreign goods and services.

In a two-country setting, the flow demand for British pounds (UK£) represents American demand for British goods and services. The supply of UK£ represents the demand for American goods by British residents.[9] The intersection of the two schedules determines the US\$/UK£ exchange rate (see Figure 2.2, Chapter 2). In a flow specification, exchange rate changes result from shifts in the flow demand or flow supply of goods and services. An increase in the demand for British goods and services, *ceteris paribus,* tends to increase the \$/£ exchange rate, while an increase in the demand for U.S. goods and services tends to lower the \$/£ exchange rate.

As we saw in Chapter 2, the flow concept could be especially useful under a pegged exchange rate system because the gap between supply and demand measures the rate at which a central bank is depleting (or adding to) its stock of international reserves. Balance of payments data showing the flow of international transactions could provide useful information. The sustainability of the pegged rate could be assessed by comparing the central bank's stock of international reserves to their rate of depletion.

Regardless of whether a pegged-rate regime is in place, the flow approach suggests a sluggish pattern of exchange rate behavior. The demand and supply for foreign exchange are derived from consumer demands for goods and services and the principles of *comparative advantage* that determine where these goods are produced. For example, if British consumers buy wheat that comes from the United States, and American consumers buy cheese that comes from Britain, we assert that both consumption preferences and production possibilities are slow to change. Hence, the demand and supply curves in a flow specification would be slow to change, producing a sluggish bias toward exchange rate movements.

An Overview of the Stock Approach

The stock approach focuses on the total quantity of currency outstanding at a moment in time. Currency is treated as an asset—one that is infinitely durable, which can be transferred but not destroyed. At a moment in time, the stock of currency is in fixed supply. At the equilibrium currency price, the stock of currency is willingly held. Figure 6.4 provides an example of the stock approach for the static case where the supply of currency is fixed. Holding demand constant, an increase in the supply of £ to S' (through money creation or issuing sterling bonds) leads to a fall in the price of £ to point *b*. Holding supply constant, an increase in the demand for £ to D' (because of changes in investor wealth or increased expected returns or lower risk on £ assets) leads to a rise in the price of sterling to point *c*. In general, the supply of sterling may grow at some variable rate, and demand (which is also subject to change) may or may not keep pace. The dynamic interplay between demand and supply determines the current price of sterling.

The stock approach is also referred to as the **asset approach.** This term evokes another aspect of the stock approach, namely that the current exchange rate is set to equilibrate the (risk-adjusted) expected rate of return on assets denominated in different currencies. Thus, in the asset approach the current spot exchange rate is set equal to the present discounted value of the expected future spot exchange rate. We developed this idea in Chapter 5 as the Fisher International Effect (uncovered interest parity) and repeat equation (5.7) below for convenience.

$$S_t = \frac{1 + i_{\pounds}}{1 + i_{\$}} \times E(\widetilde{S}_{t+1}) \tag{5.7}$$

---

[9]The demand and supply schedules are examples of *reciprocal* demand and supply curves; that is, the demand for US\$ is identical to the supply of UK£, and the supply of US\$ is identical to the demand for UK£.

FIGURE 6.4 Determination of Exchange Rates: A Stock Approach

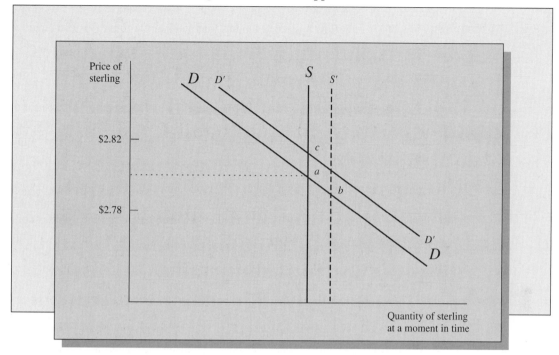

Equation (5.7) tells us that once $E(\widetilde{S}_{t+1})$, $(1 + i_\$)$, and $(1 + i_\pounds)$ are known, the current spot rate must take on a unique value, in order to equalize expected returns on US\$ and UK£ investments. In Chapter 5, we also saw that equation (5.7) is approximately equal to

$$S_t = \frac{E(\widetilde{S}_{t+1})}{1 + (i_\$ - i_\pounds)} \tag{5.7a}$$

which again shows that the current spot rate can be thought of as the discounted present value of the expected future spot rate, where the interest differential $(i_\$ - i_\pounds)$ is the discount factor. It is worthwhile repeating that the discount factor in this simple formula ignores any premium for foreign exchange risk, country risk, or loss of liquidity that could be associated with a foreign currency investment.

The asset approach gained favor among economists in the late 1960s and early 1970s, in part because financial market transactions became more important as capital flow restrictions and currency convertibility rules were removed. More likely, the popularity of the asset approach stemmed from its links to other popular theories of financial asset pricing and market efficiency.

The asset approach to exchange rates is inherently forward-looking. If an event occurs that affects domestic or foreign returns, or the expected future spot rate, the asset approach predicts that the spot rate will respond immediately to this news. As a result, the asset approach predicts that the current spot rate should reflect—in the sense of a net present value—everything that is known or expected to happen in the macroeconomic environment. This notion of **market efficiency** predicts quick movements in the exchange rate to reflect new information.

Combining Flow and Stock Concepts of the Exchange Rate

Obviously, foreign exchange is used as both a medium of exchange and a store of value, so aspects of both flow and stock models may have a role to play in exchange rate determination. An overall equilibrium in the foreign exchange market requires a balance in both flow *and* stock aspects of the market. The impact of integrating the flow and stock models is presented in Appendix 6.1. At this point, we summarize the main conclusions of that analysis.

First, stock concepts (as in the asset approach) are of primary importance for the determination of exchange rates in the short run. Since asset portfolios can be rebalanced quickly and at low cost, these actions will influence exchange rate behavior (and vice versa) over the short run.

Second, flow imbalances can be maintained over the short run as long as surplus countries are willing to accumulate assets and deficit countries are willing to run down assets or accumulate foreign debts. Eventually, however, flow imbalances cannot be left unchecked. Because no surplus country wants to accumulate foreign assets indefinitely (the risks of counterparty default are high along with the cost of forgone consumption), and no deficit country wants to accumulate liabilities to foreigners indefinitely (the marginal cost of debt is rising, and debt service payments lower present consumption). The flow side becomes an anchor for the exchange rate in the long run.

Third, elements of the flow model and the stock model are related. A country that runs a current account surplus accumulates wealth, and may use this wealth to bid for international assets in a different mixture than the deficit country that relinquished its wealth. Thus, transfers of wealth through the current account may tilt the demand for currencies in the foreign exchange market.

With these general points in mind, let us turn to specific models of exchange rate determination.

Asset Models of the Spot Exchange Rate[10]

A useful way to begin is with Figure 6.5, which illustrates the two main categories of asset models, the monetary and portfolio-balance models, and several variants of each model. All asset models of exchange rate determination assume a high degree of capital mobility between assets denominated in different currencies. In these models, **perfect capital mobility** is implied by the interest rate parity condition, for which there is strong empirical support. Models based on the asset approach begin by specifying a menu of assets. The interrelationship between the demand and the supply of those assets determines the price of foreign exchange.

The **monetary approach** is distinguished in part by the menu of assets under consideration. In the monetary approach, the menu is short and simple—the only assets are domestic and foreign money, M and M^*. As we will see, the monetary approach also can be characterized by the assumption that domestic and foreign currency denominated bonds display **perfect substitutability.** If investors are indifferent between holding foreign and domestic bonds when they receive an interest differential on the bonds equal to the expected exchange rate change—what we defined as the International Fisher Effect—then the two bonds are **perfect substitutes.**

---

[10]See Levich (1985), MacDonald and Taylor (1992), and Taylor (1995) for surveys.

FIGURE 6.5 A Family Tree of Exchange Rate Models

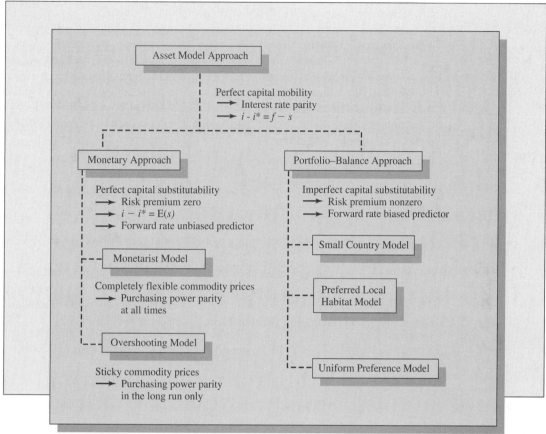

Note: The asset approach to exchange rates has two primary branches: the monetary approach, which focuses primarily on the demand and supply for money, and the portfolio-balance approach, which emphasizes the demand and supply of money and bonds. Each theory has several variations that introduce other assumptions about conditions in goods markets and financial markets.

Source: Adapted from Jeffrey A. Frankel, "Monetary and Portfolio Balance Models of Exchange Rate Determination," in *Economic Interdependence and Flexible Exchange Rates,* eds. Jagdeep S. Bhandari and Bluford H. Putnam (Cambridge, MA: MIT Press, 1983).

In the **portfolio-balance approach,** the menu of assets is expanded to include domestic and foreign bonds (B and F) as well as domestic and foreign monies. The portfolio-balance approach can also be characterized by the assumption that domestic and foreign currency denominated bonds do not display perfect substitutability. When investors require a risk premium in addition to the expected percentage exchange rate change to establish indifference between holding foreign and domestic bonds, the two bonds are **imperfect substitutes.**

The Monetary Approach

The monetary approach to exchange rate determination is a direct outgrowth of purchasing power parity and the quantity theory of money. While PPP concludes that the exchange rate is the relative price of goods in two countries, monetary theory suggests that the spot exchange rate (S) is the relative price of two monies. In this context, it follows that exchange rate behavior reflects the evolution of the relative supplies and demands for two monies. Within the monetary approach, there are two models, the flexible-price model and the sticky-price (overshooting) model.

Flexible-Price Models.   The flexible-price model assumes that domestic good prices are fully flexible. That is, if the domestic money supply increases by x percent, then domestic goods prices rise immediately by x percent, and domestic currency depreciates immediately by x percent. The flexible price monetarist model implies that purchasing power parity holds continuously and that the real exchange rate never changes. To begin, note that the price level (P) in each country can be related to the ratio of money supply (M) to money demand (L) as:

$$P = \frac{M}{L(Y,i)} \qquad \text{for the home country}$$

and

$$P* = \frac{M*}{L(Y*,i*)} \qquad \text{for the foreign country}$$

The demand for money is hypothesized to be positively related to real income (Y), which represents the transactions demand for money, and negatively related to the interest rate (i), which represents the opportunity cost of holding money balances. Now, recall the purchasing power parity condition from equation (4.2):

$$S_{\text{home/foreign}} = \frac{P}{P*}$$

By substituting, we have:

$$S_{\text{home/foreign}} = \frac{P}{P*} = \frac{M/L(Y,i)}{M*/L(Y*,i*)}$$

A common specification of the money demand function is:

$$L(Y,i) = K\, Y^{\eta}\, e^{-\epsilon i}$$

where K is a constant (representing the inverse of the velocity of money), η is the income elasticity of the demand for money, and ϵ is the interest rate semielasticity of the demand for money. Making these substitutions, we get:[11]

$$S = \frac{P}{P*} = \frac{MK*\, Y*^{\eta}\, e^{\epsilon i}}{M*\, KY^{\eta}\, e^{\epsilon i*}} \tag{6.3}$$

Finally, taking natural logarithms of the above, we have:

$$\ln S_t = (m - m*)_t + \eta(y* - y)_t + (k* - k)_t + \epsilon(i - i*)_t \tag{6.4}$$

where lowercase letters (m, k, y) represent the natural logarithm of uppercase letters (M, K, Y), and t is a time subscript.

Equations (6.3) and (6.4) give us the "predictions" of the **flexible-price monetary model.** From equation (6.3), we can see that if the domestic money supply (M) increases, domestic currency will depreciate proportionately. For example, if the domestic money supply doubles, the foreign exchange value of domestic currency is cut in

---

[11]For simplicity only, we assume identical elasticities in both countries, so that $\epsilon = \epsilon*$ and $\eta = \eta*$.

TABLE 6.2 Implied Regression Coefficients in Various Exchange Rate Equations

Spot rate a function of: *Coefficient defined as:*	$(m - m^*)$ a_1	$(y - y^*)$ a_2	$(i - i^*)$ a_3	$(\pi - \pi^*)$ a_4	$(b - f)$ a_5
Traditional flow model		+	−		
Modern asset models					
Monetary Approach					
Flexible-price model (6.4)	+	−	+	+	
Overshooting model (6.5)	+	−	−		
Real interest differential (6.6)	+	−	−	+	
Portfolio-Balance Approach			−		+

Note: Spot rate expressed as *ln(S)* in domestic currency/foreign currency terms:

    $(m - m^*)$ = log of domestic relative to foreign money supplies

    $(y - y^*)$ = log of domestic relative to foreign real income

    $(i - i^*)$ = interest rate differential, domestic minus foreign

    $(\pi - \pi^*)$ = inflation rate differential, domestic minus foreign

    $(b - f)$ = log of domestic relative to foreign bond supplies

half—much like the impact on the price of equity shares when there is a 100 percent stock dividend.

Equation (6.3) also predicts that domestic currency will appreciate in response to a rise in domestic real income (Y) or a fall in domestic interest rates (i), because both changes would increase the demand for domestic money. Notably, both of these predictions are contrary to those that come from traditional theories based on trade or capital flows. The monetarist result can be explained with the following logic. While it is true that a rise in U.S. real income will lead to a greater demand for imports and an increased demand for foreign currency, this is only a partial equilibrium result that neglects capital flows that also respond to an increase in U.S. income. Monetary theory argues that in general equilibrium, the net effect of higher U.S. income should be a US$ appreciation because the increase in the demand for money and the corresponding improvement in the capital account exceeds the decline in the trade balance.

Similarly, as discussed in Chapter 5, the positive relationship between interest rates and currency value focuses on real interest rates. Monetary theory, however, emphasizes the change in nominal interest rates associated with monetary shocks and inflation. As we will see, the monetary approach may be modified to include a real interest rate term as well as an inflation term.

We can rewrite equation (6.4) in a linear form that will be suitable for empirical tests using linear regression, such as:

$$\ln S_t = a_0 + a_1(m - m^*)_t + a_2(y^* - y)_t + a_3(i - i^*)_t + u_t$$

where u is an error term. The signs of the regression coefficients (a_1, a_2, and a_3) are discussed below and summarized in Table 6.2.

Equation (6.4) is in "rate of change" form because the logarithm of a variable approximates its percentage change.[12] Thus, equation (6.4) predicts that the rate of change

---

[12]Recall that the continuous rate of change in a variable over the time interval [0,t] is ln (X_t/X_0). Without loss of generality, we can define the base value as $X_0 = 1$, in which case the continuous rate of change in the variable is simply ln (X_t). See Appendix 4.1 for a review of continuous compounding.

in the spot rate depends on the rate of change in the foreign and domestic money supplies, on the rate of change in foreign and domestic real incomes, on the *levels* of foreign and domestic interest rates, and on the rate of change in other factors that are lumped into the terms k and k^*. Note that the coefficient of $(m - m^*)$ is 1, predicting that a change in the growth of domestic money by x percentage points will lead to an increase in the *rate* of depreciation of domestic currency by x percentage points.

Like all asset models, the monetary approach is a forward-looking model. This may be unclear because equations (6.3) and (6.4) specify the level and the rate of change in the exchange rate at time t as functions of other variables, also valued at time t. The explanation is that the interest differential term $(i - i^*)$ is itself equal to the expected rate of change in the exchange rate, $\ln [E(\tilde{S}_{t+1})/S_t]$. Thus the exchange rate (or its rate of change) at time t depends on the expected exchange rate (or its rate of change) at time $t + 1$. This "trick" can be repeated again and again—the exchange rate at $t + 1$ depends on the exchange rate at $t + 2$, and the exchange rate at $t + 2$ depends on the exchange rate at $t + 3$, and so on. By implication, the spot exchange rate depends on the expected path of the exchange rate through all future points in time, much the same as the price of a share of stock depends on all future cash flows accruing to the shareholder.[13]

The model summarized in equations (6.3) and (6.4) assumes that the prices of goods are fully flexible and that PPP holds at all times using a broad price index. These are extreme assumptions given that the validity of PPP has been questioned. One natural modification is to assume that PPP holds, but only for *traded* goods. The presence of nontraded goods and services (labor services, in particular) may pose a significant barrier to the continuous validity of PPP. Since the importance of services in the economy tends to rise with income, taking account of relative price changes between traded and nontraded goods may be particularly important when applying the monetary approach to countries with substantial income differences.[14]

The monetary approach can easily accommodate a modification that allows the relative prices of traded and nontraded goods to vary.[15] The monetary approach can also accommodate a setting in which goods prices are not fully flexible.

Sticky-Price (Overshooting) Monetary Models.   The assumption that domestic goods prices are fully flexible is a powerful simplification. It implies that purchasing power parity holds continuously and that the real exchange rate never changes. Such stability in the real exchange rate is not consistent with the observed history of real exchange rates among major currencies. However, the basic monetary model can be refined to produce real exchange rate variability and increased variability in the nominal exchange rate—two results that more closely match the behavior of floating exchange rates over the last 25 years.

The **sticky-price monetary model** was introduced by Rudiger Dornbusch (1976) to highlight the impact of assuming that the speed of adjustment of goods prices is slow relative to the speed of adjustment of asset prices. When a central bank announces its money supply figures, it is well accepted that traders in financial markets respond quickly, adjusting the prices of various securities and their portfolio positions until a new equilibrium is reached. At the same time, it is also well accepted that store managers at Wal-Mart, McDonald's, and elsewhere essentially ignore these money supply

---

[13]We show this more rigorously in Appendix 6.2.

[14]Balassa (1964) is credited with this insight.

[15]See Appendix 6.3 for details.

FIGURE 6.6   Time-Series Pattern of Variables in the Sticky-Price (Overshooting) Monetary Model

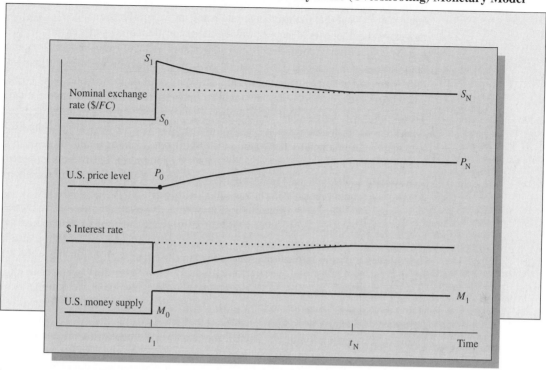

Note: In response to a one-time, permanent, unanticipated jump in the domestic money supply, the U.S. interest rate falls, and the US$ depreciates. Over time, the excess money supply leads to U.S. price inflation, and U.S. interest rates rise as the liquidity effect dissipates and the US$ gradually appreciates. In the long run, U.S. interest rates return to their original level and the US$ has depreciated in nominal terms, but the real exchange rate is unaffected.

announcements. Their prices remain virtually the same after the central bank speaks, and change only gradually in response to general inflationary pressures.

When goods prices are sticky, Dornbusch showed that it is necessary for asset prices to move by more than in the flexible price case, in order for markets to reach a temporary equilibrium. Dornbusch also showed that the gradual adjustment of goods prices following a monetary shock imparts a **dynamic adjustment path** to the exchange rate, so that while the real exchange rate changes in the short run (as there are PPP deviations), it reverts to its original level in the long run.

The Dornbusch model is built on three assumptions: perfect capital mobility (meaning the interest rate parity condition), slow price adjustment, and perfect certainty. The final assumption should be stressed. The results that follow from this model are not an indication that traders are unclear about what shocks are hitting the market or how to respond to them. Indeed, given the assumptions in the model, the exchange rate path that is derived is the *only* equilibrium path—the *only* time sequence of exchange rates that accurately reflects the nature of the shock and removes all unusual profit opportunities in financial markets.

The basic mechanics of the model can be understood with the aid of Figure 6.6, which traces out the path of the key variables over time in response to an unanticipated, permanent increase in the money supply of the domestic country. This money shock will eventually lead to inflation and currency depreciation (as we expect with a monetary model); but we are interested in the dynamic adjustment path to this result. Prior to this monetary shock, we assume that interest rates in the domestic and foreign countries are equal ($i = i*$) and that the exchange rate is resting in equilibrium at its PPP rate, S_0. The monetary shock occurs at time t_1, raising the domestic money supply from M_0 to M_1.

Note that in the goods market, the domestic price level is unchanged at P_0 immediately following this shock. However, there is plenty of action in the asset markets. The domestic interest rate falls owing to an excess supply of money (the *liquidity effect*), and capital flows out of the country, attracted by the higher foreign interest rate. Traders now face a dilemma: How can they willingly hold domestic currency that will depreciate over the long term *and* also pays a low interest rate? The answer is that if the exchange rate were to depreciate by too much in the short run (from S_0 to S_1), then the currency would be set to appreciate (from S_1 to S_N) over the long term. The currency appreciation could exactly offset the low interest rate on domestic currency, leaving traders as well off as if they held foreign currency assets (the interest rate parity condition).

Over time, the excess supply of money works its way into the goods market, domestic prices rise gradually, interest rates rise gradually, and the exchange rate appreciates gradually. In the long run, the economy is once again in equilibrium at a higher price level (P_N) and higher (depreciated) exchange rate (S_N), but at the same real exchange rate as before the shock.

This relationship, where the immediate, short-run change in the nominal exchange rate exceeds the long-run change in the nominal exchange rate, is defined as **overshooting**.[16] Because goods prices are sticky in the short run, the real exchange rate also follows an overshooting path. Thus, a monetary disturbance which in the long run has only *nominal effects* (changing the price level and the nominal exchange rate) has *real effects* in the short run by changing the real exchange rate and the competitiveness of firms in international trade.

Within the Dornbusch model, the magnitude of exchange rate overshooting depends on a variety of technical factors.[17] The path of the exchange rate is given by the following equation:

$$s_t = (m - m*)_t + \eta\, (y* - y)_t + (1/\theta)\, (i - i*)_t \qquad (6.5)$$

where θ is the rate at which the exchange rate adjusts toward its long-run equilibrium and the other variables are as in our earlier monetarist equation (6.4). Note that in the overshooting model of equation (6.5), the expected coefficient of *(i − i*)* is negative (see Table 6.2).

The Dornbusch overshooting model has been modified and extended by several authors. Jeffrey Frankel (1979) argued that the pure monetarist model was deficient because the nominal interest rate (*i*) reflects both inflation and the real interest rate. Frankel's modification resulted in another exchange rate equation:

$$s_t = (m - m*)_t + \eta\, (y* - y)_t + (1/\theta)\, (r - r*)_t + \epsilon(\pi - \pi*)_t \qquad (6.6)$$

where r and $r*$ are the domestic and foreign real interest rates and π and $\pi*$ are the domestic and foreign inflation rates. By replacing ($i - i*$) with terms in r and π, equation (6.6) associates higher real interest rates with currency appreciation and higher inflation with currency depreciation. In other words, we expect the coefficient of ($r - r*$) to be negative and the coefficient of ($\pi - \pi*$) to be positive (see Table 6.2).

---

[16]For other possible definitions of overshooting, see Levich (1981).

[17]These include the interest elasticity of the demand for money and the rate of adjustment in domestic goods prices.

The Portfolio-Balance Approach

Like other asset models of the exchange rate, the portfolio-balance approach focuses on the excess demand for financial assets relative to their supply. The portfolio-balance model has two financial assets (money and bonds) and two countries (home and foreign). We assume that home country agents are free to allocate their wealth (W) among three holdings: domestic money (M), domestic bonds (B), and foreign bonds (F, valued at SF). The accounting identity $W \equiv M + B + SF$ defines home country wealth. In portfolio-balance models, the exchange rate establishes an equilibrium (a balance) in investor portfolios comprised of domestic money and domestic and foreign bonds.

The bonds we have in mind are government bonds, so their supply is closely connected to the country's fiscal budget deficit. The greater the deficit, the larger the supply of bonds.

The demand for bonds depends on two factors: First, the domestic demand for domestic bonds should be positively related to the domestic interest rate, i; and, second, domestic demand for foreign bonds should be positively related to the foreign interest rate augmented by the expected exchange rate change, $i^* + E(s)$. Thus, the balance between domestic bonds and foreign bonds (B/SF) in a portfolio should be positively related to $\phi = i - i^* - E(s)$. This quantity (ϕ) is the expected excess return on domestic currency bonds over foreign currency bonds. A rise in the domestic interest rate, a fall in the foreign interest rate, or a decrease in the expected rate of domestic currency depreciation will lead investors to reallocate their portfolios out of foreign bonds and into domestic bonds.

Unlike the monetary approach, the portfolio-balance approach allows imperfect substitutability between domestic and foreign currency bonds, with $\phi \neq 0$. In principle, two assets could be imperfect substitutes for a variety of reasons: liquidity, tax treatment, default risk, political risk, and exchange risk. In these stylized models of exchange rate determination, the role of exchange risk is emphasized. The parameter ϕ defines the **exchange-risk premium**.[18]

The second element in the demand for bonds is wealth itself. As W increases, individuals hold more of each asset (M, B, and F) in their portfolios. How individuals spread their wealth across M, B, and F has an important impact on the exchange rate.

The most simple assumption about investors' asset preferences is that they are similar across countries. This similarity, labeled the **uniform preference model** in Figure 6.5, would make sense if both domestic and foreign investors consumed the same basket of goods and therefore found it sensible to hold identical investment portfolios. Under the uniform preference model, if wealth grows faster in the home or foreign country, there is no exchange rate impact because investors from both countries bid for assets in the same proportions.

An alternative assumption is that residents of both the home and foreign countries prefer to hold a larger fraction of their wealth in local bonds.[19] In Figure 6.5, this is labeled the **preferred local habitat model.** To be more precise, the preferred local habitat model assumes that $B_H/W_H > F_H/W_H$ and $F_F/W_F > B_F/W_F$ where the subscripts H and F indicate home and foreign residents. To make this case more concrete, suppose that the two countries are the United States and Japan. Assume that individuals in the United

---

[18]This formulation assumes that the bonds are one-period maturity and default free. There are no expected capital gains or losses on the bonds. The term *currency-risk premium* is also used.

[19]A third version, the small country model, assumes that residents of the small country hold both home and foreign bonds while residents of the large country hold only their own domestic bond.

TABLE 6.3   The Portfolio-Balance Approach: Effects of Macroeconomic Shocks
on the Exchange Rate

Model		Variable	Impact on S from Increase in Variable ($\partial S/\partial X_i$)
Portfolio balance:			
All versions	B	Supply of home country bonds	+ Home currency depreciates
	F	Supply of foreign country bonds	− Home currency appreciates
	i	Domestic interest rate	− Home currency appreciates
	i*	Foreign interest rate	+ Home currency depreciates
	E(s)	Expected rate of home currency depreciation	+ Home currency depreciates
Portfolio balance:			
Preferred local habitat version	W	Home country wealth	− Home currency appreciates
	CA	Home country current account surplus	− Home currency appreciates

States hold bond portfolios that are 90 percent in US$ and 10 percent in ¥, while individuals in Japan hold bond portfolios that are 30 percent in US$ and 70 percent in ¥.[20] If wealth expands at a faster pace in Japan than in the United States, under our limited assumptions, portfolio demands would tend to tilt toward the ¥.

International trade provides an important channel for the transfer of financial wealth. A country's current account (a flow item in the balance of payments) measures a country's change in its international investment position. For example, a home country with a current account deficit, where imports of goods and services exceed exports, pays for its excess current consumption and investment by lowering its stock of foreign assets ($F_H\downarrow$) or issuing new bonds that are held by the foreign country ($B_F\uparrow$).

Consider a specific example that uses our earlier assumptions about U.S. and Japanese portfolio preferences. If the United States runs a $1 billion current account deficit, then $1 billion of wealth moves from U.S. hands (where it is invested 90 percent in US$ and 10 percent in ¥) to Japanese hands (where it is invested 30 percent in US$ and 70 percent in ¥). The transfer of wealth would tend to shift demand toward the Japanese yen and ¥ assets and away from US$ assets. The portfolio-balance model, with demand given by preferred local habitat, predicts a correlation between current account surpluses (deficits) and strong (weak) currencies.

The effects of various macroeconomic shocks on the exchange rate as predicted by the portfolio-balance approach are summarized in Table 6.3. Note carefully that these relationships are derived on the assumption that all other aspects of the economy are unchanged. Thus, an increase in the domestic bond supply (B) leads to a depreciation of the home currency, under the assumption that the domestic interest rate (i) is fixed and all the adjustment takes place in S. Note also that the relationship between interest rates

---

[20]These bond allocations may reflect that domestic investors tend to consume domestic goods and use domestic assets as a hedge. Having a preferred allocation between domestic and foreign bonds implies that the bonds are imperfect substitutes.

and exchange rates in the portfolio-balance approach agrees with the overshooting model and real interest differential versions of the monetary approach (see Table 6.2).

Empirical Evidence on Exchange Rate Models

An assessment of the empirical evidence is important for understanding the validity and usefulness of models of exchange rate determination. Our review of empirical evidence is divided into three sections: (1) **in-sample results** designed to measure how well actual exchange rates conform to the predictions and specifications of an estimated model; (2) **postsample results** designed to measure how accurately a model can forecast exchange rates once the model's coefficients have been estimated; and (3) tests focusing on the **role of news** designed to measure the relationship between unanticipated exchange rate movements and unanticipated macroeconomic events.

The initial analysis of the monetary approach produced generally favorable results. But by the late 1970s, the results became at best mixed and often inconsistent with the theoretical predictions of the monetary approach. Confidence in the monetary approach in particular (and the asset approach in general) was further shaken when postsample studies showed that the popular models had little if any prediction power. This failure may have been related to the turbulent structural changes that occurred in the late 1970s. More recent postsample studies have offered more encouraging results, especially when the postsample forecast horizon is long, allowing greater time for fundamental economic variables to take hold.

Studies emphasizing the role of news have been consistently encouraging to the asset approach. News items pertaining to variables that macroeconomists would include in a model of exchange rate determination consistently explain a large percentage of short-run exchange rate behavior. Both the speed of the market's reaction and the directional response of the exchange rate reinforce the notion that rational economic principles consistent with the asset approach play an important role in driving exchange rate behavior. In this sense, the asset approach is a useful guide to interpreting the relationship between macroeconomic variables and the foreign exchange market.

In-Sample Results

In-sample analysis of an exchange rate model is structured to test whether the relationship between an economic variable and the exchange rate (meaning the regression coefficient) is as predicted by the model, and whether the variables taken as a group (the model) explain a significant proportion of exchange rate variability in the sample. Usually the analysis focuses on a time series of observations for a single exchange rate.[21] The model is supported when the regression coefficients are significant and with the correct sign, and the proportion of exchange rate variability explained (measured by R^2) is significant.

Estimating the coefficients of a regression equation—such as shown in equations (6.4), (6.5), or (6.8)—is somewhat trickier than it might seem. The "independent" variables, or the right-hand-side variables, are not truly independent in these equations. The money supply, as a policy variable, could be dependent on income growth; income

---

[21]One departure from that pattern is a study by Bilson (1982) that examines how well monetary variables explain the variability of exchange rates *across* countries. Bilson reports that the fitted exchange rates compare favorably to actual exchange rates.

TABLE 6.4   Empirical Evidence: The Monetary Approach in the 1920s

Dependent Variable: ln S_t	Constant	m	m^*	y	y^*	π	R^2	D.W.	ρ
Mark/Pound Feb. 1921– Aug. 1923	−6.030 (1.696)	.970 (.092)				3.886 (1.131)	.99	2.56	.89
Franc/Pound Feb. 1921– May 1925	.001 (.010)	.999 (.099)	−.972 (.099)	.188 (.281)	.926 (.520)	3.914 (.970)	.92	1.86	1.00
Franc/Dollar Feb. 1921– May 1925	.006 (.011)	.995 (.099)	−.995 (.100)	.225 (.327)	−.369 (.370)	3.971 (.974)	.86	1.81	1.00

Note: Monthly data, standard errors in parentheses.

> m = ln ("domestic" money), mark or franc
>
> m^* = ln ("foreign" money), pound or dollar
>
> y = ln ("domestic" production), German or French
>
> y^* = ln ("foreign" production), British or American
>
> π = forward exchange premium: $(F - S)/S$
>
> D.W. = Durbin-Watson statistic

Estimation note: The mark/pound exchange rate equation was estimated using two-stage least squares following Fair's method with lagged values of the dependent and independent variables, a constant, time, and time squared as instruments, ρ is the final value of the autocorrelation coefficient; an iterative Cochrane-Orcutt transformation was employed. R^2 was computed as $1 - \text{var}(\hat{u}_t)/\text{var}(\ln S_t)$. The franc/pound and the franc/dollar exchange rate equations were estimated in first difference form using the Theil-Goldberger mixed-estimation procedure with stochastic restrictions.

Source: Jacob A. Frenkel, "Exchange Rates, Prices and Money: Lessons from the 1920s," *American Economic Review* 70 (1980).

growth may depend on interest rates, and so forth. As a result, ordinary least squares (OLS) regression techniques which presume the independence of all right-hand-side variables are usually not appropriate. A variety of more advanced econometric techniques have been applied in some of the studies we review.[22]

One series of exchange rate data that show tremendous variability—and therefore provide something substantial for a model to explain—are German exchange rates during the 1920s. During the 16 months of hyperinflation in Germany (August 1922–November 1923), the German price level exploded by a factor of 1.02×10^{10} and the exchange rate paralleled this behavior. Jacob Frenkel (1976) estimated a flexible price monetarist model for the mark/pound exchange rate over this period and found results fully consistent with the monetary approach (see Table 6.4). The coefficient of the domestic money supply is not significantly different from 1.0, and the coefficient of the interest differential is positive and significant. The equation explains 99 percent of the exchange rate variability over the sample period. In some ways these results should be expected, because monetary shocks dominated this period and purchasing power parity was maintained throughout. Nevertheless, it is reassuring to find that the monetary approach provides a good fit to the data when its fundamental assumptions are met.

---

[22]For example, most major exchange rates (for example, $/£, $/¥, $/DM) include the US$. Therefore, the equation for each exchange rate includes U.S. macroeconomic variables, and estimation errors for each currency are positively correlated. Estimation efficiency can be increased by pooling the exchange rates into one larger system. See Baillie and McMahon (1989) for further discussion.

FIGURE 6.7   The Monetary Approach in the 1920s

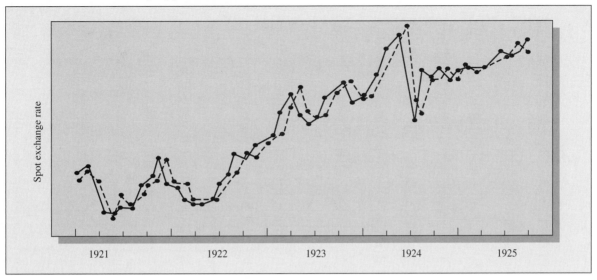

Note: Plot of the French franc/British pound exchange rate. The solid line is the actual spot exchange rate and the broken line is the fitted rate. The fitted regression is ln (FFr/UK£) = 0.001 + 0.999m − 0.972m* + 0.188y + 0.926y* + 3.914π where these variables represent the log of the money supply, production in France and the United Kingdom, respectively, and forward exchange premium. See Table 6.4 for more information.

Source: Jacob Frenkel and Kenneth Clements, "Exchange Rates in the 1920s: A Monetary Approach," in *Development in an Inflationary World,* ed. J. Flanders and A. Razin (New York: Academic Press, 1981). Copyright Academic Press, reprinted with permission.

The other results in Table 6.4 describe the franc/pound and franc/dollar exchange rates, all of which operated under flexible exchange rates at this time but, unlike Germany, were not experiencing hyperinflationary conditions. The empirical results again show a close correspondence to the predictions of the monetary approach—that is, coefficients of M and M* approximately +1.0 and −1.0, respectively, and a positive and significant coefficient on the interest differential. The income coefficients in these equations are not significant.[23]

The graph of the actual and fitted exchange rates in Figure 6.7 for the franc/pound shows how well the model tracks the actual exchange rate, and why the model achieves a high R^2. On the other hand, the graph also shows how time series models commonly miss "turning points" in the data, and are therefore not likely to be useful for profitable exchange rate forecasting.

The return of flexible exchange rates in the 1970s offered another laboratory for testing the monetary model. John Bilson (1978) selected the DM/£ exchange rate for the period April 1970–May 1977. His estimates of the regression parameters (see Table 6.5) are broadly consistent with the flexible-price monetary approach.[24] The coefficients on

---

[23]The results of these two equations are somewhat misleading because they were estimated using a procedure (mixed estimation) that augments the sample information using prior information about the coefficients. Since the sample information was not conclusive enough by itself, the results should be interpreted to mean that the data are *consistent* with the monetary approach, but they could be consistent with other models as well.

[24]Bilson used mixed estimation—mixing sample information and prior information—to obtain these results. A conservative conclusion is that the DM/£ data for this period are *consistent* with the monetary approach, but they could also be consistent with other models.

TABLE 6.5   Empirical Evidence: The Monetary Approach in the 1970s

$$S_t = \alpha_0 + \alpha_1 m_t + \alpha_2 m^*_t + \alpha_3 (i - i^*) + \alpha_4 y_t + \alpha_5 y^*_t + \alpha_6 t$$

Variable	Coefficient	T-value
Constant	−1.3280	
m	1.0026	6.259
m^*	−0.9846	6.258
$(i - i^*)$	1.3853	2.792
y	−0.9009	3.341
y^*	1.0183	3.623
t	−0.0049	3.247

Standard Error of Regression:	0.0276
R-squared:	0.9807
Durbin-Watson	1.9707

Note: Dependent variable is monthly DM/£ exchange rate for the period April 1970–May 1977. All independent variables in log form except interest rates (i and i^*) and time trend (t). Estimated using Theil-Goldberger mixed-estimation technique.
Source: John F. O. Bilson, "The Monetary Approach to the Exchange Rate: Some Empirical Evidence," *IFM Staff Papers* 25 (Mar. 1978), pp. 48–75.

domestic and foreign money supplies are nearly +1 and −1, respectively, as predicted by the model. The interest differential and income terms are also significant and correctly signed. An additional term that is not part of the simple monetary model—"time," denoting a time trend—also is significant. Since Bilson's analysis is performed on monthly data, the time coefficient implies a 0.49 percent per month (about 6.04 percent per year when compounded) exogenous appreciation of the DM/£ rate. This suggests that other forces were in place, perhaps of a portfolio-balance nature, causing traders to shift out of £ and into DM over this period.

Estimates of the real interest differential model—equation (6.6)—applied to the monthly DM/$ rates in the 1970s were reported by Frankel (1979) and are reproduced in Table 6.6. The results strongly support the model. The coefficient of the money supply differential is significantly positive and insignificantly different from 1.0. The coefficient of the income term is significant, bears the correct sign, and has a reasonable magnitude. Likewise, the coefficients of the real interest differential and the inflation differential have the predicted signs and plausible values. Together these coefficients support the notion of exchange rate overshooting in response to unanticipated monetary shocks.

A graph of the actual and fitted values of the equation (in Figure 6.8) reveals that the model explains a large proportion of exchange rate variability, and that it also follows the broad swings in the market: the deutsche mark's appreciation in 1974, its depreciation in 1975, and its appreciation from 1976 to 1977. Unfortunately, the regression begins to fall off-track in early 1978. The DM appreciates in January and February of 1978, and continues to appreciate until the central bank intervention on November 1, 1978. Meanwhile, German monetary growth in 1978 exceeded U.S. monetary growth, helping to push the fitted DM/$ value up, indicating a DM depreciation.

This development signals both bad news and good news for the monetary approach. The bad news is that this particular specification of a monetary model of the exchange rate was breaking down. The fitted values for the DM/$ rate were diverging in magnitude and direction from the actual values. Structural changes in the conduct of U.S.

TABLE 6.6 **Empirical Evidence: The Real Interest Differential Approach in the 1970s**
(July 1974–February 1978)

Technique	Constant	m − m*	y − y*	r − r*	π − π*	R^2	D.W.	ρ	Number of Observations
OLS	1.33	.87	−.72	−1.55	28.65	.80	.76		44
	(.10)	(.17)	(.22)	(1.94)	(2.70)				
Fair	1.39	.97	−.52	−5.40	29.40			.46	41
	(.12)	(.21)	(.22)	(2.04)	(3.33)				

Note: Monthly data July 1974–February 1978. Standard errors in parentheses.
  Dependent variable = ln (DM/$) spot rate.

  $m − m* = ln$ (German M_1/U.S.M_1)

  $y − y* = ln$ (German production/U.S. production)

  $r − r* =$ Short-term German–U.S. interest differential

  $π − π* =$ Expected German inflation differential, proxied by long-term government bond differential

  D.W. = Durbin-Watson statistic

  ρ = Autocorrelation coefficient

Estimation note: OLS = Ordinary least squares

  Fair = Instrumental variables are industrial WPI inflation differential and lagged values of the following: exchange rate, relative industrial production, short-term interest differential, and expected inflation differential. The method of including among the instruments lagged values of all endogenous and included exogenous variables, to ensure consistency while correcting for first-order correlation, is attributed to Ray Fair.

Source: Jeffrey A. Frankel, "On the Mark: A Theory of Floating Exchange Rates Based on Real Interest Differentials," *American Economic Review* 69 (1979), pp. 610–22.

FIGURE 6.8 **Empirical Evidence: The Real Interest Differential Approach and the DM/$ Rate**
(July 1974–February 1978)

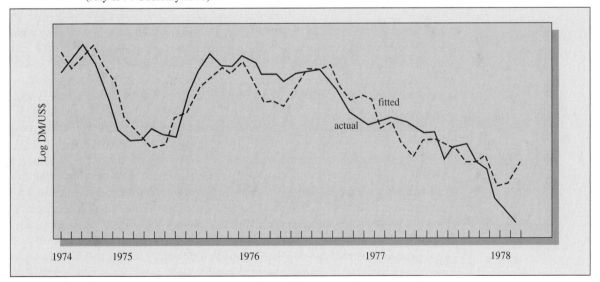

Note: The actual exchange rate is the log of the DM/US$ rate and the fitted line is the estimate from the OLS regression in Table 6.6. The fitted regression is log (DM/US$) = 0.87 (m − m*) − 0.72 (y − y*) − 1.55 (r − r*) + 28.65 (π − π*) where these variables represent the log of the money supply (M_1), production, short-term interest rates, and expected inflation in the United States and Germany, respectively. See Table 6.6 for more information.

Source: Jeffrey A. Frankel, "On the Mark: A Theory of Floating Exchange Rates Based on Real Interest Differentials," *American Economic Review* 69 (1979), pp. 610–22.

monetary policy, the conduct of central bank exchange market intervention, the impact of financial innovation on money demand, and changing international portfolio preferences may have played some part in making the structural relationships of the early 1970s no longer valid at the start of the 1980s.

The good news, often overlooked, is that the model in Figure 6.8 provided a six-month leading indicator that the US$ was undervalued on the basis of the monetary approach. The objective of the stylized models reviewed in this chapter is *not* to obtain leading indicators for the sake of forecasting. But the reversion of the DM/$ rate toward values suggested by a monetary model supports the model as a useful benchmark, even though its tracking on a quarter-by-quarter basis is unsatisfactory. We will discuss this further in Chapter 8, on forecasting.

At the start of the 1980s, monetary models became more suspect owing to structural changes in the conduct of monetary policy which made it less appropriate to treat the entire flexible exchange rate period as a single uniform period. Coupled with the advent of the Reagan fiscal expansion, attention shifted to the role played by fiscal deficits and their impact on the real interest differential. Results presented earlier (Table 6.1) show the substantial role played by these two variables over the floating-rate period in general, and the first half of the 1980s in particular. Few studies of the portfolio-balance approach were ever reported, and those that did generally produced results unfavorable to the model.[25] However, a number of studies used portfolio-balance variables (such as the accumulated current account balance over the last *n* periods) to augment a model of exchange rate determination.

The apparent failure of simple asset models to explain exchange rate movements in 1978–1980 in addition to a new study of postsample forecasting performance led researchers to focus less attention on developing models of exchange rate determination. We now turn to see why the postsample studies may have had this effect.

Postsample Results

Another technique to measure the validity and usefulness of a model of exchange rate determination is to estimate the model using data from one time period (the in-sample period) and then to measure its forecasting properties in a subsequent period (the postsample period). A postsample analysis is sometimes seen as a "horse race" among models—to judge which model performs best and at a minimum to see whether any model consistently outperforms a naive benchmark (such as the random walk with no drift forecast).

The first study of exchange rates in the modern flexible rate era to employ the postsample methodology was conducted by Richard Meese and Kenneth Rogoff (1983a). This influential study compared the postsample forecasting accuracy of several macroeconomic and pure forecasting models. The macroeconomic models relied on at most five variables: the money supply, real income, short-term interest rates, expected long-run inflation, and the cumulative trade balance. The pure forecasting models included both univariate autoregressive models, multivariate (or vector) autoregressive models, a simple random walk without drift, and the forward exchange rate. The competing models were estimated with monthly data beginning in March 1973. The first forecast period was November 1976. Then the data for December 1976 were added, models were rees-

---

[25]See Branson, Halttunen, and Masson (1977, 1979) for an example of a portfolio-balance study. Frankel (1983) reports results for several variants of the portfolio-balance model, but none produce estimates consistent with the model.

TABLE 6.7   **Empirical Evidence: Postsample Results**
(Root Mean Square Forecast Errors)

Exchange Rate	Horizon	Pure Forecast Models				Macroeconomic Models		
		Random Walk	*Forward Rate*	*Univariate Autoregression*	*Vector Autoregression*	*Frenkel-Bilson*	*Dornbusch-Frankel*	*Hooper-Morton*
$/DM	1 month	3.72	3.20	3.51	5.40	3.17*	3.65	3.50
	6 months	8.71*	9.03	12.40	11.83	9.64	12.03	9.95
	12 months	12.98	12.60*	22.53	15.06	16.12	18.87	15.69
$/¥	1 month	3.68*	3.72	4.46	7.76	4.11	4.40	4.20
	6 months	11.58*	11.93	22.04	18.90	13.38	13.94	11.94
	12 months	18.31*	18.95	52.18	22.98	18.55	20.41	19.20
$/£	1 month	2.56*	2.67	2.79	5.56	2.82	2.90	3.03
	6 months	6.45*	7.23	7.27	12.97	8.90	8.88	9.08
	12 months	9.96*	11.62	13.35	21.28	14.62	13.66	14.57
Trade-weighted dollar	1 month	1.99*	N.A.	2.72	4.10	2.40	2.50	2.74
	6 months	6.09*	N.A.	6.82	8.91	7.07	6.49	7.11
	12 months	8.65*	14.24	11.14	10.96	11.40	9.80	10.35

*Lowest RMSE forecast.

Notes: Root mean square errors are approximately in percentage terms.

The three structural models are estimated using Fair's instrumental variable technique to correct for first-order serial correlation.

Frenkel-Bilson: Flexible-price monetary model

Dornbusch-Frankel: Sticky-price monetary model

Hooper-Morton: Monetary model with cumulative current account balance terms

All models use seasonally unadjusted data. Competing models were estimated with monthly data beginning March 1973. The first forecast period is November 1976. Then the data for December 1976 were added, models reestimated, and new forecasts generated. The sample period ends on June 1981. Thus, forecasts were constructed on 55 consecutive months.

Source: Reprinted from Richard Meese and Kenneth Rogoff, "Empirical Exchange Rate Models of the Seventies: Do They Fit Out of Sample?" *Journal of International Economics* (1983), pp. 3–24, with kind permission of Elsevier Science—NL, Amsterdam

timated, and new forecasts were generated. Forecasts of 1, 3, 6, and 12 months to match the forward rate maturity were constructed on 55 consecutive months until June 1981 using this recursive procedure. Forecasting accuracy was measured using the root mean squared error (RMSE) criterion.[26]

The Meese and Rogoff results (see Table 6.7) show that a macroeconomic model achieved the lowest RMSE (3.17 percent) in the 1-month $/DM forecast horizon, and the forward rate achieved the lowest RMSE (12.60 percent) in the 12-month $/DM forecast horizon. In the other 10 cases, the random walk with no drift model $[E(\widetilde{S}_{t+1}) = S_t]$ produced the lowest RMSE. In summarizing their results, Meese and Rogoff (1983a, p. 3) observed:

> We find that a random-walk model performs as well as any estimated model at the 1- to 12-month horizons ... The structural models perform poorly despite the fact that we base their forecasts on actual realized values of future explanatory variables.

These results were naturally very disappointing to those who had spent a great deal of time and effort trying to model exchange rates. Others took these results as a challenge to understand what factors were behind the poor postsample performance of these

---

[26]The *root mean squared error (RMSE)* is a common measure of postsample forecasting accuracy. RMSE is calculated by taking each forecast error (u_i), squaring it (u_i^2), adding up all of these terms ($\Sigma_i u_i^2$), dividing by the number of forecasts (n) to compute the mean, and then taking the square root.

structural macroeconomic models. Could the results be attributed to chance (sampling error), model misspecification, parameter (coefficient) instability, instability in the money demand function, or an inappropriate empirical proxy for money?[27]

Upon reflection, however, it does not seem so surprising or so damaging that Meese and Rogoff obtained the results they did. The postsample periods, November 1976–June 1981, contain the substantial U.S. intervention announced on November 1, 1978, and the changeover in U.S. monetary targeting procedures announced in October 1979. The evidence we reviewed in the last section showed that the macroeconomic models used for comparison by Meese and Rogoff began to break down (on an *in-sample* basis) in this 1978–1979 period. Considering the turbulent nature of those years, it may not seem so surprising that structural economic models, with parameters estimated from historic data, offered poor short-run forecasts compared to a naive random-walk forecast.

Later papers by James Boughton (1984) and V. S. Somanath (1986) found that in the 1982–1983 period (shortly after the years studied by Meese and Rogoff) various structural model specifications could outperform the random walk in postsample tests. Michael Hutchison and Adrian Throop (1985, p. 39) found that in a 1982–1984 post-sample period, a model based on the real interest differential alone produced RMSE for the trade-weighted US$ of 18.1 percent—worse than the RMSE of 14.7 percent for the random-walk model. However, when Hutchison and Throop applied their complete model with fiscal budget balances augmenting the real interest differential, the post-sample RMSE fell to only 5.4 percent, far lower than for the random-walk model. These results support the view that the original Meese and Rogoff results may have been particular to the time period selected and its unusual structural instability.

In a follow-up study, Meese and Rogoff (1983b) reported that in forecasting beyond one year, their structural models tend to outperform the random-walk model, again in terms of RMSE. Still more compelling evidence is reported by Nelson Mark (1995), who found that at long horizons, economic models often predicted a large, and statistically significant portion of actual exchange rate changes. For example, at the four-year horizon, Mark found that the overshooting model explains more than 80 percent of $/DM exchange rate changes, a result that far exceeds the performance of the random walk, with or without drift.

Overall, these results suggest that macroeconomic models of exchange rates, estimated using historic data, may be useful for forecasting exchange rates—more so when the structural characteristics underlying the model are stable and when the forecasting horizon is long, permitting economic fundamentals to take hold. But even during turbulent periods when models cannot be estimated with precision and their forecasts do not outperform a random walk, we need not draw the conclusion that exchange rates are moving randomly and "irrationally" with respect to economic fundamentals. Economic news might still be an important determinant of exchange rates within the context of a rational economic model. This is the topic we examine next.

The Role of News

Another strand of empirical research relating spot exchange rates to fundamentals is referred to as the "role of news." In some respects, these studies are similar to so-called

---

[27]In a follow-up paper, Meese and Rogoff (1983b) ruled out parameter sampling error as the reason for poor out-of-sample performance. Instead, they suggest that model misspecification resulting from instability in the underlying money demand function and insufficient attention to risk factors and shifting real exchange rates may underlie their earlier results.

FIGURE 6.9   Anticipated and Unanticipated Depreciation of the Dollar, February 1973–January 1980

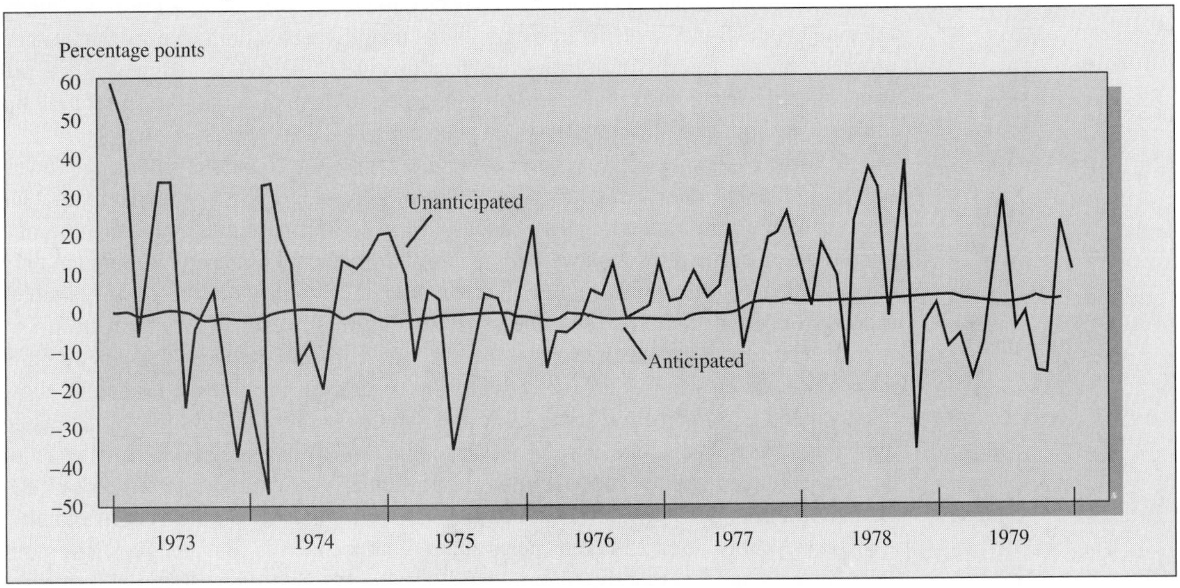

Note: The data are monthly, expressed at annual percentage rates. The unanticipated depreciation of the dollar is the difference between actual depreciation of the dollar and anticipated depreciation. The exchange rate is the nominal effective exchange rate. Anticipated depreciation is measured by the short-term interest differential between the United States and a trade-weighted average of the interest rates of five foreign countries. The weights equal those used in calculating the exchange rate. See Dornbusch (1980, pp. 162) for detailed explanations of anticipated values and data sources.

Source: Rudiger Dornbusch, "Exchange Rate Economics: Where Do We Stand?" *Brookings Papers on Economic Activity,* no. 1 (1980), pp. 145–85.

event studies of financial markets that examine how share prices respond to unanticipated events believed to affect a firm's market value. In the case of foreign exchange, it can be shown (see Appendix 6.2) that the present spot rate reflects a discounted, weighted sum of the expected values of all *future* exogenous fundamental variables. One implication of this insight is that the exchange rate departs from its equilibrium path only in response to unanticipated events, that is, unanticipated changes in fundamentals, or "news."

To test for the role of news, we must be able to classify prices and events into their anticipated and unanticipated components. For the spot exchange rate, let S define the actual spot rate at time t, and S^A represent the spot rate that had been anticipated for time t by the market. The difference, $S - S^A$, defines S^U, the unanticipated component of the exchange rate at time t. We cannot observe S^A directly, so an assumption must be made. Usually for horizons of one month or more, S^A is defined by the forward rate; for horizons of one week or less, S^A is defined by the present spot rate. We can use similar notation—X, X^A, X^U—to define the actual, anticipated, and unanticipated components of an economic variable. Also in these cases, X^A is not directly observed; it is usually taken from surveys of market participants or economic forecasters. X^U defines the difference $X - X^A$.

The objective of news studies is threefold: (1) to determine what kind of news the market is reacting to, (2) to measure the directional response of the market to this news, and (3) to estimate the proportion of exchange rate variability that is explained by macroeconomic news. To illustrate this empirical approach, refer to Figure 6.9, which shows a time series graph of the anticipated and unanticipated US$ exchange rate in nominal terms calculated on a trade-weighted basis. The line showing the anticipated component is measured by the interest differential. It shows little variability over the entire seven-year period. The unanticipated portion shows substantial variability, as month-to-month exchange rate changes have a large random element. A priori, we might imagine that it would be difficult to explain the unanticipated component because, in an efficient market, traders learn from their past mistakes (the past unanticipated component), thus rendering the sequence of pricing errors random or serially uncorrelated. Intuitively, it should be difficult to explain such a series using regression analysis.

In Table 6.8 (panel A), we reproduce several regression equations reported by Dornbusch (1980). The dependent variable is S^U as in Figure 6.9. The independent variables are a set of X^U, or news about macroeconomic variables: the current account, income, and interest rates. The estimates show that the current account and interest rates are the only two significant variables. Together, unanticipated developments in these two variables account for 61 percent of the variance in unanticipated US$ exchange rate changes.

Dornbusch conducted similar tests for the $/DM and $/¥ exchange rates on monthly data over the same sample period. These results, displayed in Table 6.8 (panel B), show that as much as 60 percent (for the DM) and 80 percent (for the ¥) of the variability in unanticipated exchange rate changes are accounted for by news regarding a small set of economic fundamentals. These results are particularly remarkable. Even though exchange rate changes may appear to be random (unconditionally), the bulk of monthly changes appear to be explained by news about macroeconomic fundamentals. These results strongly suggest that the foreign exchange market pays close attention to macroeconomic fundamentals, and that the volatility in the market closely parallels the unpredictability of the underlying fundamentals.

Empirical evidence on the role of news is also available at extremely short horizons. Several studies have analyzed the reaction of exchange rates to macroeconomic news over a one-day or less horizon. In these cases, the anticipated exchange rate change (S^A) is taken to be zero, implying that the entire realized exchange rate change is unanticipated. The anticipated announcement of macroeconomic fundamentals (X^A) is taken from survey data.

Craig Hakkio and Douglas Pearce (1985) examined the reaction of spot exchange rates to weekly U.S. money supply announcements and monthly inflation, industrial production, and unemployment announcements from September 1977 to March 1984. The authors reported that the spot exchange rate responds quickly (by 4:30 P.M. following a 4:00 P.M. announcement) and significantly to unanticipated money supply changes in the post-October 1979 period. A positive money surprise leads to an appreciation of the dollar, consistent with the view that the Federal Reserve would quickly move to offset the positive money surprise.[28] The authors found that exchange rates did not react to other macroeconomic news during this period.

Michael Klein, Bruce Mizrach, and Robert Murphy (1991) studied the reaction of the exchange rate to monthly U.S. trade balance announcements over the 1980–1988 period. They divided their sample period into two parts—before and after the Plaza Agreement of September 1985. The data confirmed that after the Plaza meeting, the dollar tended to depreciate significantly on days when a surprise increase in the U.S. trade deficit was reported. These unanticipated announcements explain roughly 40 percent of the variation in the $/DM and $/¥ exchange rates on these announcement days.

Ethan Harris and Natasha Zabka (1995) analyzed the impact of monthly news about U.S. employment. The authors found that in the 24-hour window surrounding the announcement, news of greater than anticipated employment tends to appreciate the US$

---

[28]Tandon and Urich (1987) report similar results.

TABLE 6.8   Equations Explaining Unanticipated Depreciation in the Dollar

Panel A Unanticipated Depreciation of the Nominal Effective Exchange Rate of the Dollar

		Independent Variables: News About				Summary Statistics			
Equation	Constant	U.S. Current Account	U.S. GNP	Foreign GNP	U.S. Interest Rates	R²	D.W.	SEE	ρ
A-1	3.5 (1.88)	−0.49 (−2.62)	1.86 (1.35	−1.86	—	0.41	2.13	6.2	—
A-2	2.7 (1.69)	−0.31 (−1.82)	0.47 (0.33)	−0.78 (0.57)	13.33 (1.99)	0.63	2.03	5.5	−0.24
A-3	3.1 (2.47)	−0.27 (−2.19)	—	—	13.79 (2.53)	0.61	2.13	5.1	−0.28

Panel B Unanticipated Depreciation of the Dollar-Yen and Dollar-Mark Exchange Rates

		Independent Variables: News About					Summary Statistics			
Country and Equation	Constant	U.S. Current Account	U.S. GNP	Foreign GNP	U.S. Interest Rates	Interest Differential	R²	D.W.	SEE	ρ
Japan										
B-1	−3.81 (−0.45)	1.35 (4.21)	−2.63 (−4.03)	2.27 (1.13)	—	—	0.73	2.11	8.7	0.75
B-2	0.60 (0.27)	1.40 (5.70)	−1.71 (−2.12)	1.71	13.0 (2.03)	—	0.82	2.09	8.0	—
B-3	−0.29 (−0.08)	1.39 (4.43)	−2.45 (−2.81)	2.45	—	−2.14 (−0.73)	0.71	1.85	8.1	0.32
Germany										
B-4	2.29 (1.22)	1.38 (1.93)	0.53 (−0.76)	—	26.1 (3.51)	—	0.62	2.22	7.6	−0.40
B-5	1.37 (0.42)	1.01 (1.50)	—	—	13.0 (1.36)	—	0.32	2.09	10.2	—

Note: Monthly data, mid-1973 to mid-1979; *t*-statistics in parentheses.

Unanticipated depreciation ≡ Actual depreciation − anticipated depreciation, where Anticipated depreciation = short-term interest differential between U.S. and foreign countries. Effective exchange rate and foreign GNP in panel A defined on a trade-weighted basis using weights: Canada = 0.2405; France = 0.1640; Germany = 0.2340; Japan = 0.2160; United Kingdom = 0.1440. News about independent variables ≡ Actual value − Anticipated value. See Dornbusch (1980, pp. 162) for detailed explanations of anticipated values and data sources.

D.W. = Durbin-Watson statistic

SEE = Standard error of regression estimate

ρ = Auto correlation coefficient

Source: Rudiger Dornbusch, "Exchange Rate Economics: Where Do We Stand?" *Brookings Papers on Economic Activity*, no. 1 (1980), pp. 145–85.

relative to other major currencies.[29] The authors found that employment growth tends to raise short-term interest rates (suggesting a fear of Fed tightening), which leads to a rise in the US$. The effect is significant and explains about 10–15 percent of the variation in exchange rates on the announcement days. The announcement effect became more significant during 1991–1995 compared with an earlier period.

---

[29]Results for the Canadian dollar are not significant.

Taken as a group, these results strongly suggest that the foreign exchange market pays close attention to macroeconomic fundamentals of the sort that economists believe are driving exchange rates. The reaction to news is often extremely fast and typically in the direction consistent with our models.[30]

Policy Matters—Private Enterprises

For business managers, portfolio managers, and individual investors, the foreign exchange rate is a key variable in all aspects of international financial decision making. All of these parties are "consumers" of exchange rate forecasts. All need to have some measure of exchange rates over the time period of their decision horizons. Some of these parties may also be "producers" of currency forecasts. An issue facing some managers is whether the evidence suggests that economic fundamentals are an important determinant of exchange rates. Could managers attempt to use fundamentals to forecast better than the random walk?

The models of exchange rate determination reviewed in this chapter highlight both strengths and limitations of the structural economic approach. The asset models offer us a stylized representation of how economic fundamentals come together to determine an exchange rate. The models are rich in the sense that a wide variety of economic shocks can be considered. The forward-looking nature of the models provides an underpinning that helps us better understand exchange rate volatility.

The empirical evidence shows that the models are indeed helpful to understand wide cross-sectional differences in exchange rates—why there are roughly 1,200 Korean won per US$ but only 0.6 UK£ per US$. Similarly, the empirical evidence shows that exchange rates often conform to the predictions of an economic model during periods of hyperinflation and during more normal periods as long as there are no abrupt changes in monetary and fiscal policy behavior. However, at critical times, such as the U.S. monetary policy shift in October 1979, a model may break down, making its predictions misguided.

Despite these risks, the evidence suggests that economic fundamentals are more likely to assert themselves in setting currency values as the horizon increases. As PPP holds better in the long run, so do models such as the monetary approach, which relies heavily on PPP.

Yet even in the very short run (a few hours or one day), the evidence supports an important role for economic fundamentals. Exchange rates may be volatile in the short run because the economic environment is noisy and unpredictable. Currency traders move rates quickly in response to news about current (and future) fundamentals. The market may appear irrational because it sometimes follows the money supply announcements, and at other times it follows the trade balance, the CPI, or the employment report. But this style of rotation could itself be rational if policymakers are themselves temporarily focusing on one indicator or if volatility in that indicator is unusually large.

Thus, contrary to the notion that exchange rates are driven by arbitrary trends or random elements, much of the evidence we have reviewed suggests that exchange rates

---

[30]A study by Almeida, Goodhart, and Payne (1998) examines the response of the DM/US$ rate to macroeconomic news at five-minute intervals. Another study, by Bosner-Neal, Roley, and Sellon (1998), investigates the response of US$ exchange rates to changes in the U.S. Federal funds target rate. Both studies find a significant relationship between these news events and unanticipated exchange rate changes.

move to a great extent in response to or anticipation of economic fundamentals. However, the anticipatory nature of financial markets and the high speed of adjustment in asset markets (relative to goods markets) may result in exchange rates that are highly volatile and largely unpredictable. News about fundamentals is, by definition, the unpredictable component. Thus, even if exchange rates are driven entirely by fundamentals, business managers may still face a risky environment.

Policy Matters—Public Policymakers

Some of the issues raised in the last section are understandably of interest to public policymakers. If the level and volatility of the exchange rate create competitive problems for local businesses, this is a public policy concern. Today, nearly all countries are "small" and openness to international transactions is generally high and growing. The price of foreign exchange and its volatility are therefore important agenda items for public policymakers in most countries.

We will consider three general areas for public policy concerns regarding exchange rates: (1) Is the *level* of the exchange rate set as a fair reflection of economic fundamentals? (2) Is exchange rate *variability* excessive? (3) How would prospective policy changes affect the level and variability of exchange rates?

Any answer to questions 1 and 2 must begin with the selection of a suitable benchmark. Concepts such as "fair valuation" and "excessive volatility" compel us to ask, "Relative to what standard?" Our discussion in this chapter has relied on the notion that the price of foreign exchange is largely determined by asset market considerations. This has been a useful paradigm for organizing the theory of exchange rate determination and for uncovering many empirical regularities between exchange rates and economic variables.

On the other hand, we understated somewhat the complexity of a complete asset model of exchange rate determination. In the real world, the supply of money and government bonds is stochastic. Demand and supply for assets are interdependent: Private demand depends on the discipline of the official supply process and the likelihood of intervention; official supply, including intervention, depends on the strength of private demand.

To make things still more complicated for policymakers, an asset market benchmark relies heavily on expectations that are not observable and are difficult to approximate empirically. Therefore, price changes do not depend on the realization of a change in fundamentals; the *expectation* of a future disturbance, or a change in market confidence or sentiment, is sufficient to move exchange rates immediately.

For example, if speculators push up the price of orange juice futures several weeks prior to a crop-damaging freeze in Florida, we would be unlikely to conclude that speculators cause weather. Rather, the speculators took expectations into account for pricing. If these expectations about the weather are unrealized, it seems unfair to conclude that speculators, setting prices ex ante, behaved irrationally unless these expectations are repeatedly unrealized.

Policymakers are concerned about irrational or excessive speculative behavior. Swings in nominal and real exchange rates have been so substantial over the past 20 years that an explanation based on **speculative bubbles** has been entertained. To model a speculative bubble, we assume that the exchange rate can be decomposed into a **fundamentals term** and a **bubble term**: $S_t = \overline{S} + B_t$. Thus, the observed exchange rate can deviate from its fundamentals value by the amount of the bubble. To qualify as a true speculative bubble, however, the bubble must grow over time, so that $\hat{B}_{t+1} = B_t(1 + \lambda)$ with $\lambda > 0$. Thus, speculators buy spot exchange at price S_t knowing that it is overvalued relative to fundamentals, because they expect a gain as the speculative bubble grows in the next period, pushing the expected spot rate to $\hat{S}_{t+1} = \overline{S} + (1 + \lambda)\hat{B}_t$. As the process goes on, the spot exchange rate becomes more and more overvalued relative to fundamentals—until the bubble bursts.

Many tests of excessive exchange rate volatility and of speculative bubbles have been conducted. Some of these have rejected the "no-bubbles" hypotheses and favored the "excess volatility" hypothesis.[31] It is difficult to interpret these studies for several reasons. The most obvious problem inherent in these tests is the need to select a benchmark ($\overline{S}$) representing the fundamentals value. As our discussion has shown, many models might be put forward as benchmarks, most of which could rely heavily on unobserved future variables. Tests of excess volatility and no bubbles are really testing two hypotheses: one concerning the benchmark model and another concerning excess volatility. If a study finds excess volatility, it could be simply because the benchmark model is incorrect. The small sample sizes also make it difficult to reach a firm conclusion. If a currency is overvalued for several years at an expanding rate, one can expect to support a bubbles interpretation. But as Frankel (1985) points out, if the overvaluation is small and lasts only a few months or quarters, it is very difficult to detect and distinguish from normally high price volatility. In other words, we may be able to rule out prolonged episodes of bubble-like behavior, but not be able to rule out a repeating series of shorter and smaller bubbles.

As we have seen, there are a number of explanations for exchange rate volatility without appealing to speculative bubbles. Volatility in real variables (such as oil price shocks, oil discoveries, German unification); volatility in policy variables (such as monetary policy discipline, fiscal discipline); failed attempts at policy coordination (such as Europe's Exchange Rate Mechanism in the fall of 1992); and price stickiness in commodity markets will naturally enhance exchange rate volatility.

Public policymakers also rely on models to gauge how exchange rates will react to policy changes, or to examine how policies might be changed to obtain a desired exchange rate result. A clear message from the asset approach to exchange rates is that (1) markets respond quickly to news and (2) policy surprises will induce volatility (overshooting). A further reason for policies to be predictable, and surprises few, is that nominal shocks (which wash out in the long run) have real effects in the short run. These short-run real exchange rate effects in turn may stimulate demand for trade protection, unemployment assistance, and other costly programs.

A broader issue worthy of consideration is that models of exchange rate determination can be looked upon as studies in *positive economics,* asking whether the level and volatility of exchange rates are consistent with a credible model. Public policymakers are often, and rightfully, concerned with issues of *normative economics,* asking whether the level and volatility of exchange rates are consistent with values that allow countries to reach their domestic and international economic policy objectives—often cryptically referred to as internal and external balance. A conflict develops when exchange rates are a fair reflection of economic fundamentals (and the uncertainties therein), but the exchange rates prove inconsistent with other policy objectives. To resolve the conflict, policymakers could attempt either to change economic fundamentals or to alter policy

---

[31]See MacDonald and Taylor (1992), pp. 11–16. Bartolini and Bodnar (1996) reject the excess volatility interpretation.

objectives. An alternative dilemma appears when the foreign exchange markets are judged to be inefficient and a poor reflection of economic fundamentals. If actual exchange rates stray far from their fundamentals values, then the argument for central bank intervention is enhanced. Market inefficiencies provide a ready justification for exchange market intervention to correct a private market failure. We take up the topic of foreign exchange market efficiency in the next chapter.

Summary

In this chapter, we have examined the economic determinants of spot exchange rates. In the last 25 years, economists have adopted the asset approach to exchange rates as the main paradigm for explaining exchange rate movements. The asset approach defines an equilibrium as a set of prices where all assets are willingly held. In the monetary approach, the exchange rate establishes the relative price of two monies, while in the portfolio-balance approach, the exchange rate equilibrates the relative risk and return of domestic and foreign assets. The asset approach is forward looking and emphasizes the role of expectations. Unfortunately, expectations cannot be observed directly, which complicates empirical testing and interpretation of market behavior.

Empirical evidence suggests that during some periods—the 1920s hyperinflation, the early 1970s, and over the longer run—exchange rate behavior is significantly related to fundamentals. Also, in the very short run exchange rate changes often closely follow news about fundamental economic events. Thus, while exchange rate movements may *approximate* a random walk (recall the lead quote to this chapter from Michael Mussa), the evidence shows a significant link between exchange rates and many of the macroeconomic variables used to model exchange rates. This is basically good news for private agents seeking to understand the main determinants of exchange rates, and for public policymakers who hope that exchange rates reflect macroeconomic fundamentals.

Still, economic models of exchange rates have often been unreliable and unsuitable for forecasting. This could be the result of underlying economic instability that makes regression estimation difficult, or it could be the result of misspecified economic models of the exchange rate.

APPENDIX 6.1
THE IMPLICATIONS OF FLOW AND STOCK EQUILIBRIUM ON THE FOREIGN EXCHANGE RATE

An overall equilibrium in the foreign exchange market would balance both flow and stock dimensions of the market. To examine the impact of integrating the flow and stock models, consider Figure 6A.1 on p. 220. Stock demand and supply schedules are shown in the northeast quadrant, and flow demand and supply schedules (with positive numbers emanating from the origin) are shown in the northwest quadrant.[32] Take the initial condition as an equilibrium in both the stock market (at point *A*) and in the flow market (at point *a*), each showing an exchange rate of $0.50/DM. This represents a long-run,

steady-state equilibrium that, absent any shocks, would not be disturbed.

Now consider a shock to the stock demand schedule. Suppose that for some reason (perhaps because of healthy prospects relating to the formation of the European Community or a reduction in the cost of trading in the German market) investors seek to increase permanently their holdings of DM-denominated assets. We represent this in Figure 6A.2 on p. 221 by an outward shift in the stock demand schedule to *D'D'* intersecting the stock supply schedule at *b* or $0.52/DM. The appreciation of DM occurs immediately to "clear" the stock market. On the flow side, the stronger DM has resulted in an excess flow supply of DM in the amount *bc*. The flow demand for German goods has fallen with the appreciating DM, while the flow supply for U.S. goods has risen along with

---

[32]The supply curve in Figure 6A.1 on p. 220 represents the supply of German government bonds offered to non-German investors, which is a positive function of the exchange rate.

FIGURE 6A.1   Determination of Exchange Rates: A Simultaneous Stock and Flow Approach

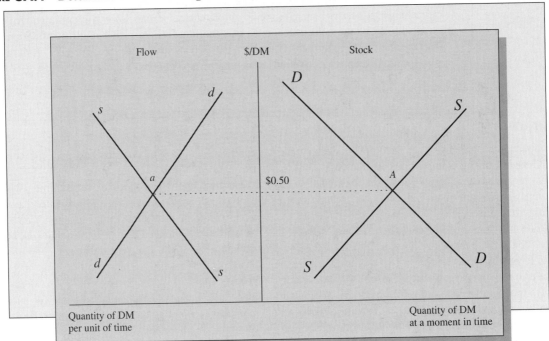

the depreciating dollar. With the weaker dollar, the United States runs a current account surplus equal to the amount *bc* per period. The current account surplus implies that the United States is accumulating foreign assets, so over time the stock supply schedule shifts outward, eventually reaching *S'S'*.

A stylized version of the time path of the exchange rate following this permanent stock demand shock is shown in Figure 6A.3 on p. 221. The jump in the exchange rate occurs immediately to clear the stock market. Since the United States cannot run a current account surplus indefinitely—nor Germany a current account deficit indefinitely—the exchange rate changes gradually to bring about a long-run equilibrium in both the stock and flow dimensions.

Now consider a shock to the flow demand schedule. Suppose that for some reason (perhaps because U.S. consumers believe that German goods have better quality, style, after-sales service, and so forth) consumers seek to increase permanently their purchase of German goods and services. We represent this in Figure 6A.4 on p. 222 by an outward shift in the flow demand schedule to *d'd'* intersecting the flow supply schedule at *c* or $0.52/DM. The appreciation of the DM does not occur immediately because in this stylized model the exchange rate is determined in the stock market, which is unaffected. With the exchange rate at $0.50/DM, there is excess flow demand for DM in the amount *ba*. With the increase in demand for German goods, the United States runs a current

account deficit equal to the amount *ba* per period. The current account deficit implies that the United States is reducing its stock of foreign assets, so over time the stock supply schedule shifts inward, eventually reaching *S'S'*.

Figure 6A.5 on p. 222 contains a stylized version of the time path of the exchange rate following this permanent flow demand shock. The exchange rate changes gradually to clear the flow market, while the stock market is cleared at all times. Again the logic is that the current account imbalance cannot persist indefinitely, so that the exchange rate must eventually bring about a long-run equilibrium in both stock and flow dimensions.[33]

Figures 6A.4 and 6A.5 illustrate one important stylized finding in models of exchange rate determination. The stock side is of primary importance for the determination of exchange rates in the short run. Because asset portfolios can be rebalanced quickly and at low cost, these actions will influence exchange rate behavior (and vice versa) over the short run. Flow imbalances can be maintained over the short run as

---

[33]Strictly speaking, the requirement of a current balance assumes no growth in the economy. A growing economy can support a larger current account deficit for a longer period, based on the prospect of higher income to service and retire foreign debts incurred. In this section, we abstract from these growth issues. See Howard (1989) for further discussion.

FIGURE 6A.2 Stock and Flow Reactions to Permanent Increase in the Stock Demand for German Assets

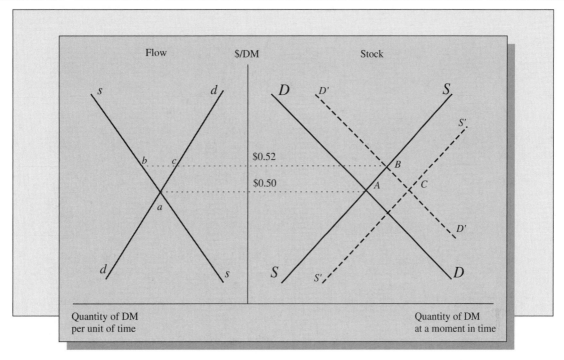

FIGURE 6A.3 Exchange Rate Response to Permanent Increase in the Stock Demand for German Assets

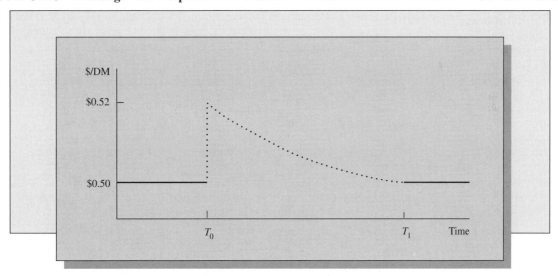

long as surplus countries are willing to accumulate assets and deficit countries are willing to run down assets or accumulate foreign debts. Eventually, however, flow imbalances cannot be left unchecked. Because no surplus country wants to accumulate foreign assets indefinitely (the risks of default are high,

along with the cost of forgone consumption), and no deficit country wants to accumulate liabilities to foreigners indefinitely (the marginal cost of debt is rising and will eventually cut into present consumption). The flow side becomes an anchor for the exchange rate in the long run.

FIGURE 6A.4   Stock and Flow Reactions to Permanent Increase in the Flow Demand for German Goods

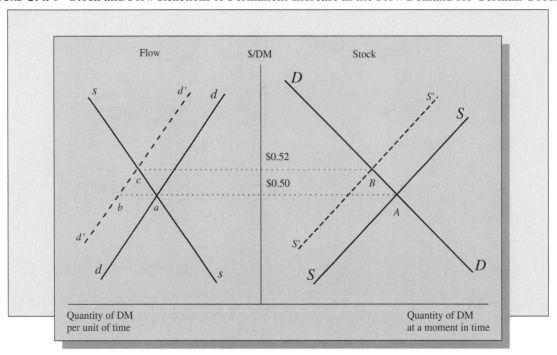

FIGURE 6A.5   Exchange Rate Response to Permanent Increase in the Flow Demand for German Goods

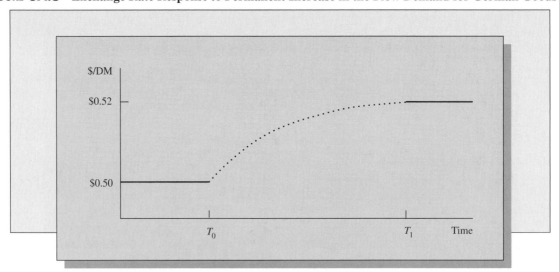

APPENDIX 6.2
DEMONSTRATION THAT THE PRESENT EXCHANGE RATE REFLECTS ALL FUTURE EXOGENOUS MACROECONOMIC VALUES

In both the monetary approach and the portfolio balance approach to exchange rate determination, the exchange rate (or its logarithm) was shown to depend on (1) a set of macroeconomic variables and (2) the expected exchange rate change. In the pure monetarist model, the equation is:

$$s_t = (m - m^*)_t + \eta\,(y^* - y)_t + (k^* - k)_t + \qquad (6.1a)$$
$$\epsilon(E[\Delta s_{t+1}])_t$$

where we have substituted $E(\Delta s_{t+1})$ for $i - i^*$ in equation (6.4). In the portfolio balance model, a standard equation is:

$$e_t = -\alpha - \beta\,(i - i^*)_t - \beta\,(E[\Delta s_{t+1}]) + b_t - f_t \qquad (6.2a)$$

where b_t and f_t represent the logarithm of the supply of domestic bonds and foreign bonds, respectively. For convenience, let z represent the vector of fundamental economic factors driving the exchange rate. Then any asset model of the exchange rate can be written as:

$$s_t = z_t + \epsilon[E(s_{t+1}) - s_t] \qquad (I)$$

Rearranging terms, equation (I) becomes:

$$(1 + \epsilon)\,s_t = z_t + \epsilon\,E(s_{t+1})$$

or

$$s_t = \frac{1}{(1 + \epsilon)}\,z_t + \frac{\epsilon}{(1 + \epsilon)}\,E(s_{t+1}) \qquad (II)$$

Equation (II) shows that the present spot rate is a function of present macroeconomic fundamentals (z_t), and the expected future spot rate in period $t + 1$. But what then is the expected future spot rate of period $t + 1$? Applying equation (II), we see that:

$$s_{t+1} = \frac{1}{(1 + \epsilon)}\,z_{t+1} + \frac{\epsilon}{(1 + \epsilon)}\,E(s_{t+2})$$

So the expected value of s_{t+1} is then:

$$E(s_{t+1}) = \frac{1}{(1 + \epsilon)}\,E(z_{t+1}) + \frac{\epsilon}{(1 + \epsilon)}\,E(s_{t+2}) \qquad (6.3a)$$

Substituting equation (6.3a) into (II) yields:

$$s_t = \frac{1}{(1 + \epsilon)}\,z_t + \frac{\epsilon}{(1 + \epsilon)^2}\,E(z_{t+1}) + \frac{\epsilon^2}{(1 + \epsilon)^2}\,E(s_{t+2}) \qquad (IIa)$$

Equation (IIa) shows that the present spot rate is a function of present macroeconomic fundamentals (z_t), the expected value of future fundamentals [$E(z_{t+1})$], and the expected future spot rate in period $t + 2$. But what then is the expected future spot rate of period $t + 2$? Applying equation (II) once again, we have:

$$s_{t+2} = \frac{1}{(1 + \epsilon)}\,z_{t+2} + \frac{\epsilon}{(1 + \epsilon)}\,E(s_{t+3})$$

So the expected value of s_{t+2} is then:

$$E(s_{t+2}) = \frac{1}{(1 + \epsilon)}\,E(z_{t+2}) + \frac{\epsilon}{(1 + \epsilon)}\,E(s_{t+3}) \qquad (6.4a)$$

Substituting equation (6.4a) into (IIa) yields:

$$s_t = \frac{1}{(1 + \epsilon)}\,z_t + \frac{\epsilon}{(1 + \epsilon)^2}\,E(z_{t+1}) + \frac{\epsilon^2}{(1 + \epsilon)^3}\,E(z_{t+2}) +$$
$$\frac{\epsilon^3}{(1 + \epsilon)^3}\,E(s_{t+3}) \qquad (IIb)$$

Equation (IIb) shows that the present spot rate is a function of present macroeconomic fundamentals (z_t), the expected value of future fundamentals [$E(z_{t+1})$], the expected value of future fundamentals [Ez_{t+2}], and the expected future spot rate in period $t + 3$. This substitution can be continued indefinitely, until obtaining:

$$s_t = \frac{1}{(1 + \epsilon)}\,\Sigma_i\,[\epsilon/(1 + \epsilon)]^i\,E(z_{t+i}) \qquad (III)$$

Equation (III) posits that the present exchange rate is equal to a discounted sum of the expected value of all future fundamental variables (the z's) from now into the indefinite future. The formulation is general and applies in any asset framework whether the fundamentals are monetary or portfolio balance in nature. Equation (III) predicts that the exchange rate will depart from its equilibrium path only in response to unanticipated events (meaning "news") because the exchange rate already reflects the expectation of all fundamental variables from the present into the indefinite future.

APPENDIX 6.3
THE MONETARY MODEL OF EXCHANGE RATE DETERMINATION WITH TRADED AND NONTRADED GOODS

To account for traded and nontraded goods, assume that the aggregate price level is calculated by taking a geometric average of the prices of traded goods (P_T) and nontraded goods (P_N), so that:

$$P = P_N^\alpha P_T^{1-\alpha}, \qquad P^* = P_T^{*\alpha^*} P_T^{*1-\alpha^*}$$

where α and α^* are the domestic and foreign expenditure shares on nontraded goods. When PPP applies to traded goods only, we have:

$$S = \frac{P_T}{P^*_T} = \frac{(P_T/P_N)^\alpha}{(P_T^*/P_N^*)^{\alpha^*}} \times \frac{P}{P^*}$$

By substituting the expression for P/P^* in equation (6.3), we obtain:

$$S = \frac{(P_T/P_N)^\alpha}{(P_T^*/P_N^*)^{\alpha^*}} \frac{M}{M^*} \frac{Y^{*\eta}}{Y^\eta} \frac{K^*}{K} e^{\epsilon(i - i^*)}$$

And taking logarithms, we obtain the linear expression:

$$s_t = \alpha \ln (P_T/P_N) - \alpha^* \ln (P_T^*/P_N^*) + (m - m^*)_t + \eta (y^* - y)_t + (k^* - k)_t + \epsilon(i - i^*)_t$$

Note that this expression is identical to equation (6.4), with two additional terms added for changes in the traded/nontraded goods price ratios in the domestic and foreign countries.

Questions

1. How would you explain the seemingly contradictory reaction of the foreign exchange market, sometimes rising and sometimes falling, in response to similar news announcements?

2. The foreign exchange market reacts only on unanticipated news. Is this statement true or false? Explain.

3. The asset models of foreign exchange pricing see foreign exchange primarily as a medium of exchange for executing international trade transactions. Is this statement true or false? Explain.

4. Describe how an increase in the foreign demand for U.S. goods and services would impact supply and demand curves in the flow and stock models of exchange rate determination.

5. Describe how an increase in the stock demand for U.S. assets impacts demand and supply curves in the flow and stock models of exchange rate determination.

6. Explain how a shift in the supply and demand for US$ affects the exchange rate in the flow model of exchange rate determination.

7. Discuss the similarities and differences between the monetary approach and the portfolio-balance approach to the determination of exchange rates.

8. Describe and contrast the monetarist and the overshooting models of exchange rate determination.

9. Can the monetarist model predict changes in the real exchange rate?

10. According to the monetarist model, a rise in the domestic interest rate will result in a fall in the domestic currency. Is this statement true or false? Explain.

11. According to the monetarist model, a rise in domestic real income will create added demand for domestic money, thus provoking a rise in the price of domestic currency. Is this statement true or false? Explain.

12. What is the difference between in-sample and postsample testing of foreign exchange models?

13. The experience of the 1970s and 1980s shows that exchange rates can be highly volatile. Does this experience suggest that economic factors are unrelated to exchange rate behavior?

14. Define the term *speculative bubble*. Explain how a speculative bubble could develop in the foreign exchange market.

15. How would you devise a governmental policy of communication to the markets to avoid extreme volatility in the foreign exchange market?

References

Almeida, Alvaro; Charles Goodhart; and Richard Payne. "The Effects of Macroeconomic News on High Frequency Exchange Rate Behavior." *Journal of Financial and Quantitative Analysis* 33, no. 3 (Sept. 1998) pp. 383–408.

Baillie, Richard, and Patrick McMahon. *The Foreign Exchange Market: Theory and Econometric Evidence.* Cambridge: Cambridge University Press, 1989.

Balassa, Bela. "The Purchasing-Power Parity Doctrine: A Reappraisal." *Journal of Political Economy* 72 (1964), pp. 584–96.

Bartolini, Leonardo, and Gordon M. Bodnar. "Are Exchange Rates Excessively Volatile? And What Does 'Excessive Volatility' Mean, Anyway?" *IMF Staff Papers* 43, no. 1 (Mar. 1996), pp. 72–96.

Bilson, John F. O. "The Monetary Approach to the Exchange Rate: Some Evidence." *IFM Staff Papers* 25 *(Mar. 1978), pp. 48–75.*

————. "Comment on Willett and Sweeney," in *The International Monetary System: A Time of Turbulence,* ed. J. Dreyer, G. Haberler, and T. Willett. Washington, DC: American Enterprise Institute, 1982.

Bosner-Neal, Catherine; V. Vance Roley; and Gordon H. Sellon, Jr. "Monetary Policy Actions, Intervention, and Exchange Rates: A Reexamination of the Empirical Relationships Using Federal Funds Rate Target Data." *Journal of Business,* Apr. 1998, pp. 147–77.

Boughton, James M. "Exchange Rate Movements and Adjustment in Financial Markets: Quarterly Estimates for Major Currencies." *IMF Staff Papers* 31 (Sept. 1984), pp. 445–68.

Branson, William H.; Hannu Halttunen; and Paul Masson. "Exchange Rates in the Short Run: The Dollar-Deutschemark Rate." *European Economic Review* 10, no. 3 (1977), pp. 303–24.

————. "Exchange Rates in the Short-Run: Some Further Results," *European Economic Review* 12, no. 4 (1979), pp. 395–402.

Dornbusch, Rudiger. "Exchange Rate Economics: Where Do We Stand?" *Brookings Papers on Economic Activity,* no. 1 (1980), pp. 145–85.

————. "Expectations and Exchange Rate Dynamics." *Journal of Political Economy* 84, no. 6 (Dec. 1976), pp. 1161–76.

Frankel, Jeffrey A. "The Dazzling Dollar." *Brookings Papers on Economic Activity,* no. 1 (1985), pp. 199–218.

————. "Monetary and Portfolio Balance Models of Exchange Rate Determination." In *Economic Interdependence and Flexible Exchange Rates,* ed. Jagdeep S. Bhandari and Bluford H. Putnam. Cambridge: MIT Press, 1983.

————. "On the Mark: A Theory of Floating Exchange Rates Based on Real Interest Differentials." *American Economic Review* 69 (1979), pp. 610–22.

Frenkel, Jacob A. "Exchange Rates, Prices and Money: Lessons From the 1920s." *American Economic Review* 70 (1980), pp. 235–42.

————. "A Monetary Approach to the Exchange Rate: Doctrinal Aspects and Empirical Evidence." *Scandinavian Journal of Economics* 78, no. 2 (May 1976), pp. 200–24.

————. "Commentary on 'Causes of Appreciation and Volatility of the Dollar.'" *The U.S. Dollar—Recent Developments, Outlook, and Policy Options,* Federal Reserve Bank of Kansas City, 1985.

Hakkio, Craig, and Douglas Pearce. "The Reaction of Exchange Rates to Economic News." *Economic Inquiry,* Oct. 1985, pp. 621–36.

Harris, Ethan S., and Natasha M. Zabka. "The Employment Report and the Dollar." Federal Reserve Bank of New York, *Current Issues in Economics and Finance* 1, no. 8 (Nov. 1995).

Howard, David. "Implications of the U.S. Current Account Deficit." *Journal of Economic Perspectives* 3, no. 4 (Fall 1989), pp. 153–65.

Hutchison, Michael, and Adrian Throop. "U.S. Budget Deficits and the Real Value of the Dollar." *Economic Review*, Federal Reserve Bank of San Francisco, 1985, pp. 26–43.

Klein, Michael; Bruce Mizrach; and Robert G. Murphy. "Managing the Dollar: Has the Plaza Agreement Mattered?" *Journal of Money Credit and Banking* 23, no. 4 (Nov. 1991), pp. 742–51.

Krugman, Paul. "Is the Strong Dollar Sustainable?" *The U.S. Dollar—Recent Developments, Outlook, and Policy Options*, Federal Reserve Bank of Kansas City, 1985, pp. 103–32.

Levich, Richard M. "An Examination of Overshooting Behavior in the Foreign Exchange Market." *Group of Thirty Occasional Studies*, no. 3. New York: Group of Thirty, 1981.

————. "Empirical Studies of Exchange Rates: Price Behavior, Rate Determination and Market Efficiency." In *Handbook of International Economics,* ed. Ronald Jones and Peter Kenen. Amsterdam: North-Holland, 1985.

MacDonald, Ronald, and Mark P. Taylor. "Exchange Rate Economics: A Survey." *IMF Staff Papers* 39, no. 1 (Mar. 1992), pp. 1–57.

Mark, Nelson C. "Exchange Rates and Fundamentals: Evidence on Long-Horizon Predictability and Overshooting." *American Economic Review* 85, no. 1 (Mar. 1995), pp. 201–18.

Meese, Richard, and Kenneth Rogoff. "Empirical Exchange Rate Models of the Seventies: Do They Fit Out of Sample?" *Journal of International Economics* 14 (1983a), pp. 3–24.

————. "The Out-of-Sample Failure of Empirical Exchange Rate Models: Sampling Error or Model Misspecification?" In *Exchange Rates and International Macroeconomics,* ed. J. Frenkel. Chicago: University of Chicago Press, 1983b, pp. 67–112.

Mussa, Michael. "Exchange Rates in Theory and Reality." *Princeton Essays in International Finance*, no. 179, Dec. 1990.

Somanath, V. S. "Efficient Exchange Rate Forecasts: Lagged Models Better than the Random Walk." *Journal of International Money and Finance* 5 (1986), pp. 195–220.

Tandon, Kishore, and Thomas Urich. "International Market Response to Announcements of U.S. Macroeconomic Data." *Journal of International Money and Finance,* Mar. 1987, pp. 71–84.

Taylor, Mark. "The Economics of Exchange Rates." *Journal of Economic Literature* 33, no. 1 (Mar. 1995), pp. 13–47.

7 FOREIGN EXCHANGE MARKET EFFICIENCY

"There just aren't so many secrets any more. The farmers in Vietnam are walking around with mobile phones. They know the market price as soon as I do."

A Rotterdam spice trader, reported in *The Economist,* Dec. 19, 1998, p. 55.

Learning Objectives

After reading this chapter, students should

1. Know the definition of foreign exchange market efficiency and why market efficiency studies are often difficult to interpret.
2. Be familiar with several technical trading models that have been used to investigate the efficiency of the spot foreign exchange market.
3. Have an understanding of the empirical evidence on spot market efficiency.
4. Be familiar with several techniques that have been used to investigate the efficiency of the forward foreign exchange market.
5. Have an understanding of the empirical evidence on forward market efficiency.
6. Understand that foreign exchange speculation is always risky so that evidence of trading profits in the past does not mean that these profits were excessive relative to the risk incurred or that they will continue into the future.

In this chapter, we introduce the principles of market efficiency and review the empirical evidence on efficiency as they apply to the foreign exchange market. The notion of market efficiency and the efficient market hypothesis entered the vocabulary of finance in the 1960s.[1] Most empirical tests at that time were conducted on stock market prices, but some initial tests of foreign exchange market efficiency were carried out using as the experimental laboratory the flexible exchange rates of Canada from the 1950s and of several European countries from the 1920s.[2] Empirical work on the efficiency of foreign

---

[1]See Fama (1970) for a review of this early literature and studies from the 1950s and 1960s. The sequel, Fama (1991), extends this review with the major themes of the 1970s and 1980s.

[2]Poole (1966, 1967) analyzes Canadian exchange rates in the 1950s. For an analysis of exchange rate behavior in the 1920s, see Giddy and Dufey (1975) and Poole (1967).

exchange markets accelerated after the introduction of floating exchange rates in the early 1970s, and there is now a substantial body of evidence.[3]

The concept of market efficiency plays an important role in the study of financial markets. Implicitly or explicitly, an assumption about market efficiency enters into any theoretical or practical analysis of financial markets.

In a market economy, prices play a critical role—namely, they are assumed to assemble and process available information, and thus convey useful signals. When the market does this efficiently, prices function as "sufficient statistics" that lead agents to the same decisions as if they had access to the original raw information. The exchange rate models we developed in Chapter 6 rely on the assumption that asset prices are set in efficient markets. Our preference for models like those in Chapter 6 is based on the premise that agents (in efficient markets) act to keep exchange rates at or near their equilibrium levels.

As a practical matter, market efficiency is an important benchmark that has a strong bearing on policies in the private sector pertaining to risk management and forecasting, and policies in the public sector pertaining to central bank intervention. If empirical evidence shows that foreign exchange markets are not efficient, then unusual (meaning risk-adjusted) profit opportunities are being missed and private agents could formulate strategies to capture them. When foreign exchange markets are not efficient, exchange rate forecasts that outperform the forecasts implicit in present market prices can be formulated. A failure to find market efficiency is probably the most tantalizing possibility that private agents hope to encounter. Public policymakers, on the other hand, would interpret a lack of foreign exchange market efficiency as a "market failure." A failure of markets to set prices at their equilibrium values implies that costs are being incurred somewhere by someone; for example, in the form of reduced output, greater unemployment, or higher goods prices. If these failures are serious and costly enough, policies to restore market efficiency, such as jawboning foreign exchange traders or calling for central bank intervention, could be contemplated.

On the other hand, if empirical evidence shows that markets are efficient, then private enterprises can take market prices as the best possible reflection of available information. Outforecasting the market will be difficult, as will be earning unusual profits from open, speculative positions. If markets are efficient, then public policymakers cannot blame "the market" for a ¥ that is "too high," a £ that is "too low," or a $ that is "too volatile." In an efficient market, prices accurately capture the available information, so markets are simply the messengers conveying the news of underlying and anticipated conditions in macroeconomic variables, the stickiness of domestic prices, or other factors that determine the pattern of foreign exchange rates.

Our interpretation of efficiency thus draws a distinction between *market efficiency* and *optimality*. Market efficiency concerns the narrow question of whether private agents set prices that fully reflect available information. An efficient financial market is efficient informationally—a market that removes all unusual profit opportunities. Market efficiency is a less demanding test than the broader question of whether market prices are optimal in any sense—whether exchange rates are consistent with an efficient allocation of productive resources, targets for internal–external balance, or other public policy objectives. If markets are efficient, public policymakers may still be unhappy with the level or course of exchange rates. But in this case, policies must deal with the

---

[3]Surveys of the literature have been prepared by Levich (1979, 1985) and Hodrick (1987). See also Baillie and McMahon (1989), especially Chapters 2 and 4.

root causes of exchange rates themselves rather than with exchange rates per se, which are more a symptom of these underlying causes.

The remainder of this chapter continues with a discussion of the theory of market efficiency, in which we define the characteristics of an efficient market. We highlight the distinction between the efficient market hypothesis and the random-walk model of asset prices, which is sometimes incorrectly identified as a requirement for market efficiency. In the following sections, we survey a number of studies of efficiency in foreign exchange markets.[4] Empirical tests concerning risk-free arbitrage between markets have generally concluded that once transaction costs and other factors are considered, foreign exchange markets are efficient in that few unexploited profit opportunities remain.

Empirical tests that focus on risky profit opportunities in spot and forward speculation reveal many departures from what we will call the **simple efficiency model,** which assumes a world of risk-neutral investors. These results do not allow us to reject categorically the efficient market hypothesis, because risk-neutral pricing may not be a suitable assumption for the foreign exchange market. Investors instead may demand a currency risk premium that varies over time. Nevertheless, these empirical results carry important implications for private enterprises and public policymakers. One implication that we examine is the possibility of earning speculative profits by using technical trading models. A second implication is the possibility to outforecast the forward rate by building a composite forecast that combines additional information with the forward rate. The broader implications of the empirical evidence on market efficiency for private enterprises and public policymakers are examined in the final two sections of this chapter.

Theory of Market Efficiency

A capital market is said to be efficient if prices in the market fully reflect available information. When this condition is satisfied, market participants cannot earn economic profits (that is, unusual or risk-adjusted profits) on the basis of available information. This classic definition, which was developed formally by Eugene Fama (1970), applies to the foreign exchange market as well as to other asset markets.

As stated, the definition is too general to be tested empirically. We need to give some substance to the terms *fully reflect* and *available information.* In this section, we discuss the terms *fully reflect* and *available information* so that we can conduct tests of foreign exchange market efficiency and interpret their results.

Defining the Equilibrium Benchmark

The term *fully reflect* implies the existence of an equilibrium model (or benchmark), which might be stated either in terms of equilibrium prices or equilibrium expected returns. In an efficient market, we expect to have actual prices conform to their equilibrium values, and actual returns conform to their equilibrium expected values.

These conditions can be made more precise. If we define $\tilde{r}_{j,t+1}$ as the actual one-period rate of return on asset j in the period ending at time $t + 1$, and $E(\tilde{r}_{j,t+1} | I_t)$ as the expected value of that return conditional on available information (I) at time t, then the **excess market return** (Z) can be written:

---

[4]Efficiency in the currency futures market, currency option market, and Eurocurrency and Eurobond markets is discussed later in the context of those particular markets.

FIGURE 7.1   **Efficient Market Behavior with a Constant Equilibrium Expected Return**

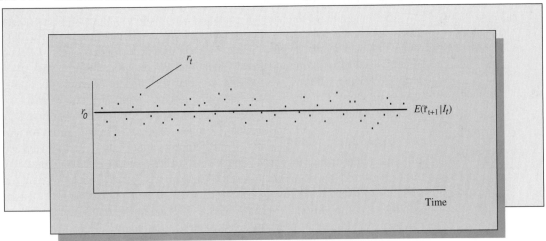

Note: In an efficient market, the actual returns, r_t, oscillate randomly about the equilibrium return, $E(\tilde{r}_{t+1}|I_t)$. Because the equilibrium return is assumed constant, actual returns appear to move randomly about a constant.

$$Z_{j,t+1} = r_{j,t+1} - E(\tilde{r}_{j,t+1}|I_t) \tag{7.1}$$

An **efficient market** has two defining characteristics: First, the expected excess market return, $E(Z_{j,t+1}|I_t)$, should equal zero; and second, $Z_{j,t}$ is uncorrelated with $Z_{j,t \pm k}$ for any value of k. These two properties together imply that the sequence $\{Z_t\}$ is a **fair game** with respect to I_t. In other words, the market is efficient if, on average, errors in the formulation of expectations about prices or returns are zero, and these errors follow no pattern that might be exploited to produce profits.

At times, it may be more convenient to think about efficiency in terms of the level of prices rather than rates of return. The link between today's price (P_t) and the expected future price $E(P_{t+1}|I_t)$ is given by:

$$E(P_{t+1}|I_t) = [1 + E(\tilde{r}_{t+1}|I_t)] P_t \tag{7.2}$$

where $E(\tilde{r}_{t+1}|I_t)$ is the expected equilibrium yield on spot market speculation. Again, market efficiency requires that the sequence of expected errors (X) follows a fair-game process.

$$X_{t+1} = P_{t+1} - E(\tilde{P}_{t+1}|I_t) \tag{7.3}$$

Pictures of Efficient Markets

When Equilibrium Expected Returns are Constant.   To help visualize the requirements of a fair-game process, Figure 7.1 illustrates the case of efficient market behavior when the expected equilibrium return is constant (r_o). The actual rate of return series $\{r_t\}$ oscillates randomly about the expected return series $[E(\tilde{r}_{t+1}|I_t) = r_o]$ so that the expectational errors $\{Z_t = r_t - r_o\}$ conform to the requirements of a fair game.

Now consider the asset prices that could have generated the returns in Figure 7.1. When prices evolve as a **random walk,** then tomorrow's price (P_{t+1}) is equal to today's price (P_t) augmented by an error term (u_{t+1}). We can write this as:

$$P_{t+1} = P_t \times e^{(r_0 + u_{t+1})}$$

Taking the natural logarithm, we have:

$$\ln(P_{t+1}) - \ln(P_t) = r_0 + u_{t+1} \qquad (7.4)$$

If $r_0 = 0$, then we say that prices follow a random walk without drift.[5] If $r_0 \neq 0$, then we say that prices follow a random walk with drift.[6]

Recall our the discussion of the International Fisher Effect—equation (5.5) that modeled the future spot exchange rate (S_{t+1}) as the current spot rate (S_t) adjusted by the return differential on the two currencies. Again, if we augment the International Fisher Effect with an error term (u), we have:

$$S_{t+1} = S_t \times e^{[(i_\$ - i_£) + u_{t+1}]}$$

Taking the natural logarithm, we have:

$$\ln(S_{t+1}) - \ln(S_t) = (i_\$ - i_£) + u_{t+1} \qquad (7.5)$$

The above expression portrays the spot exchange rate as following a random walk with drift equal to the interest differential. The reader can refer back to Figure 5.11 to observe an example of a constant drift path in the \$/£ exchange rate with $i_\$ = 6$ percent and $i_£ = 8$ percent.

See Box 7.1 for an example of how to create your own random-walk series of exchange rates and a diagram like Figure 7.1.

When Equilibrium Expected Returns Wander Substantially.   Now consider a case where the equilibrium expected return wanders substantially over time as in Figure 7.2. Efficient market behavior continues to require that actual returns oscillate randomly about expected returns to meet the criterion of a fair game. However, in this case it is clear that the underlying asset prices did not evolve as a random walk with zero drift, or a random walk with constant drift, or a random walk with any other obvious pattern of deterministic drift.

Could the equilibrium required rate of return on a security wander substantially as in Figure 7.2? The existence of a *business cycle* where the expected rate of return on capital changes over time is an example that corresponds to Figure 7.2. The business cycle could result from any set factors, but as long as the business cycle is not a deterministic phenomenon, asset prices need not follow a random walk with a constant or deterministic trend.

Could the equilibrium level of the spot exchange rate wander substantially? In Chapter 6, we examined several models that could produce such a pattern. The monetary model of the exchange rate with perfect flexibility in domestic goods prices is one example. In the context of this model, when the fundamental determinants of exchange rates are serially correlated, then equilibrium exchange rates will also be serially correlated.[7]

In the sticky-price version of the monetary model, we saw (in Figure 6.6) that in response to an unanticipated increase in the domestic money supply, the exchange rate depreciates immediately by an amount greater than what is required in the long run, and

---

[5]Strictly speaking, the random walk also requires that the distribution of the error term (u) is independent and distributed identically over time.

[6]This is sometimes called *constant drift* or *linear drift*.

[7]Be sure you see that no profit opportunities are available in this case. Even though the money supply is changing in a correlated pattern, interest rates change to offset any profitable exchange rate change.

Box 7.1

Exchange Rate Levels and Changes Generated Using the Random-Walk (No-Drift) Model

In this experiment, we generated 200 random numbers (u_t, $t = 1, \ldots 200$), using the random number generator in Excel and placed the numbers in Column A of a spreadsheet. This can be done by clicking on the "TOOLS" menu and then "DATA ANALYSIS" and then "Random Number Generation." We selected the normal distribution with mean 0 (to demonstrate the "no-drift" case) and standard deviation 1, and used the number 3,388 (an arbitrary choice) as the "random seed" requested by Excel.

Our Excel column B started with an initial exchange rate (S_1) of 50. Each successive exchange rate is the previous rate augmented by the random number: $S_t = S_{t-1} + u_t$. In column C, we measured the percentage change in the rate from one observation to the next.

The graph of the level of exchange rates appears in Figure A below. It may look as if there are patterns in the series, but there are none because every successive change is the result of a random number. The graph of percentage changes appears in Figure B below. The time series plot shows little correlation from one observation to the next. The changes are distributed approximately normally as we would expect since the random numbers were generated from a normal distribution. The mean change is not significantly different from zero (representing the no-drift assumption). The standard deviation of the changes in Figure B is about 2.1 percent, which represents the standard deviation of the random numbers (1) divided by the mean of the spot rate series in Figure A (about 45.5).

To see what happens in the case of a linear (or constant) drift, repeat this exercise, but pick random numbers with a mean of 0.1, 0.2, or −0.15 instead of zero.

FIGURE A
Exchange Rate Levels

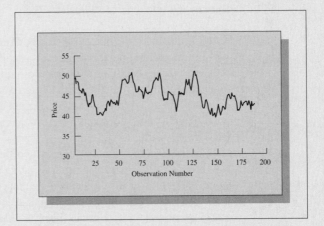

FIGURE B
Exchange Rate Percentage Changes

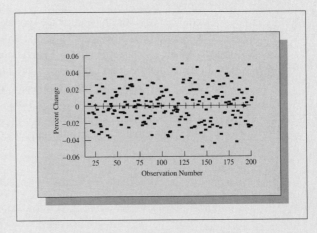

FIGURE 7.2   Efficient Market Behavior When the Equilibrium Expected Rate of Return
Wanders Substantially

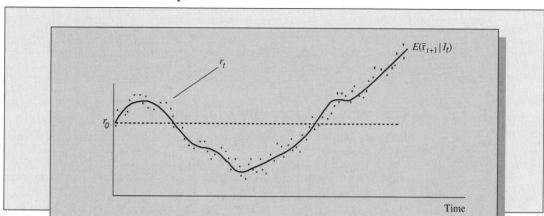

Note: In an efficient market, the actual returns, r_t, oscillate randomly about the equilibrium return, $E(\tilde{r}_{t+1}|I_t)$. Because the equilibrium return is allowed to wander, actual returns appear to move in a serially correlated pattern relative to the dashed line.

then appreciates asymptotically back to its long-run equilibrium value. During the adjustment period, exchange rate changes are serially correlated and efficient market behavior would require that actual exchange rates oscillate randomly about the benchmark. Again, because the interest differential along the adjustment path always equals the percentage exchange rate change, there are no profit opportunities even though the adjustment path exhibits a trend.

Interpreting Efficient Market Studies

Now let us turn to the problem of interpreting efficient market tests. In Figure 7.1, the series $\{r_t\}$ appears to be priced efficiently against the benchmark $E(\tilde{r}_{t+1}|I_t) = r_0$, but it would be priced inefficiently versus any other choice. Similarly, in Figure 7.2, the series $\{r_t\}$ appears to be priced efficiently against the benchmark $E(\tilde{r}_{t+1}|I_t)$, but it is priced inefficiently against the benchmark $E(\tilde{r}_{t+1}|I_t) = r_0$. This illustrates that all tests of market efficiency are tests of a *joint hypothesis*—(1) the hypothesis that defines market equilibrium prices or market equilibrium returns as some function of the available information set, and (2) the hypothesis that market participants have actually set prices or returns to conform to their expected values. For empirical studies that reject market efficiency, it is impossible to determine whether an incorrect specification of the market's equilibrium benchmark is responsible for the rejection or whether market participants were indeed inefficient information processors. For studies that cannot reject market efficiency, it could be argued that the wrong equilibrium price or return process was assumed as the benchmark. And that relative to another standard, the market is really inefficient and unusual profit opportunities are available.[8]

---

[8]A specification that takes the current spot exchange rate as the equilibrium (having equilibrated market supply and market demand for foreign exchange) would assume away all need for efficient market tests. By this benchmark, the market is perpetually efficient.

The theory of exchange rate determination developed in Chapter 6 found that various exchange rate levels and paths of adjustment could be proposed as equilibrium paths. It need not be the case that the equilibrium exchange rate takes on a constant value, or that it follows a simple linear trend, or some other deterministic pattern. The theoretical criterion of efficiency is for exchange rates to deviate randomly and with mean zero from their *equilibrium* value, which we have argued could itself wander substantially and in a serially correlated fashion.

Defining the Available Information Set

It is common to distinguish three types of market efficiency depending on the information set, I_t. These are:

- *Weak form,* in which the current price reflects all information in the historic series of prices.
- *Semistrong form,* in which the current price reflects all publicly available information.
- *Strong form,* in which the current price reflects virtually all available information, including proprietary and insider information.

The terminology was introduced by Fama (1970), who in the sequel (1991) to his original review of the efficient market literature proposed the following taxonomy:

- *Tests of return predictability,* indicating studies that examine whether returns can be predicted by historic prices or historic information on fundamental variables.
- *Event studies,* referring to studies that examine how prices respond to public announcements.
- *Tests for private information,* indicating studies that examine whether specific investors have information not in market prices.

Fama (1991) argues that the new terminology is more descriptive of the empirical work and consistent with current usage. The importance of specifying the information set (I_t) remains intact.

Weak Form Tests and Tests of Predictive Ability.   Given our discussion of equilibrium or benchmark models, it is apparent that weak form tests of market efficiency (or tests of predictive ability) must be formulated and interpreted with caution. Specifically, a test of whether the exchange rate follows a random walk or some other time series process *cannot* be offered as a test of efficiency when divorced from a model of the equilibrium exchange rate.

Analysis of the statistical properties of exchange rates, however, may be useful for descriptive purposes. For example, measuring deviations from PPP (Chapter 4) is useful for assessing changes in competitiveness across countries. Measuring historical exchange rate volatility may be useful for the pricing of currency options (Chapter 12). And measuring the magnitude and variation in forward rate forecasting errors, $F_{t,n} - S_{t+n}$ may be useful for assessing the risks of maintaining open foreign exchange positions (Chapter 11). However, without a benchmark, these data—while useful to know and helpful for decision making—cannot be taken as indicators of foreign exchange market efficiency.

Semistrong Form Tests and Event Studies.   Similarly, semistrong form tests that draw on publicly available information (such as forward exchange rates and interest rates) will be heavily dependent on the model of equilibrium. Monetary models of the exchange rate assume that financial assets denominated in different currencies are perfect substitutes. With this assumption, we showed in Chapter 6 that the interest differential between domestic and foreign assets should equal the anticipated exchange rate change, and the forward premium is an unbiased forecaster of the future exchange rate change. However, within the class of portfolio-balance models, financial assets denominated in different currencies are imperfect substitutes. According to this benchmark, the forward premium is a biased forecaster of the anticipated exchange rate change as a result of an exchange-risk premium. Clearly, we must agree on the exchange rate model before we can interpret semistrong form tests of market efficiency.

Empirical tests of the role of news are event studies that illustrate similar joint-hypothesis testing problems. In response to news about the money supply, interest rates, the fiscal budget deficit, and so on, we showed in Chapter 6 that a currency might logically appreciate or depreciate depending on the scenario for the future, which is typically unknown at the time of the news release.

Strong Form Tests and Private Information.   Strong form tests of market efficiency examine whether market prices fully reflect information available only to market insiders. This information set could include knowledge of intervention in the market by central bankers that is often kept secret, knowledge of customer orders that is available to interbank market makers, and proprietary models of exchange rate forecasting that have not been published or made available to a wide audience.

Official intervention, whereby central banks buy and sell their own currency, has its counterpart in the private market, whereby corporations may issue new shares or buy back existing shares on a strategic basis. At times, central banks have behaved opportunistically—intervening in the foreign exchange market and altering fundamental policies that are known to affect exchange rates—and earned profits from their activities.[9] At other times, central banks have behaved defensively—intervening to protect a fixed rate—and suffered huge losses.[10] If intervention is used to signal a target range of acceptable exchange rates and the commitment of the central bank to fundamental policies consistent with these rates, the market may not be strong-form efficient if this information is kept secret.[11] As the central bank is the consummate insider, we could expect that foreknowledge of intervention transactions could be a valuable piece of information to have.[12]

Others with proprietary information—bank traders or professional foreign exchange forecasters or analysts—may have in some way paid for their special knowledge or position. It should be made explicit that we are not referring to illegally obtained insider information. The speculator who owns a seat on a currency futures exchange or the developer of a complex econometric model of exchange rates may have access to

---

[9]The Carter Bonds discussed in Chapter 3 are an example.

[10]The losses incurred by the Bank of England prior to the withdrawal of £ from the ERM in 1992 and the losses incurred by the Bank of Thailand prior to floating the baht in 1997 are recent examples.

[11]See Mussa (1981) for the view that central banks intervene to signal policy commitments. Lewis (1995) finds evidence that foreign exchange intervention can be a useful signal for future monetary policy.

[12]See Dominguez and Frankel (1990) on the impact of intervention on exchange rate expectations.

information that is not generally available. In this case, equilibrium in the information market requires that one earn a fair return on investments in proprietary information.

Extensions of Efficient Market Theory

The basic model of market efficiency as proposed by Fama (1970) contains some stringent assumptions that are at odds with the real world. In particular, our basic model assumes that there are no transaction costs, so all information is freely available to all agents. Furthermore, all agents are assumed to have homogeneous expectations, and so they evaluate their common information set in an identical manner. While the assumption of a frictionless world with identical representative agents would be sufficient to produce an efficient market, neither of these assumptions is necessary to sustain the efficient market hypothesis.[13] Large transaction costs may reduce the volume of transactions in a market. However, when transactions occur they could fully reflect available information. It is also true that not all investors evaluate information in a similar fashion. However, unless one group can consistently use available information to make better judgments about price than the market, this is not a case against market efficiency.

Further research on these issues—costly information and investor heterogeneity—has provided some new insights into the efficient market hypothesis. If market prices were a full reflection of all available information, there would be no incentive for agents to collect and pay for information. On the other hand, if all agents behaved this way and no one collected information, market prices could get far out of line and there would be great incentives to collect information. The conundrum is that as private individuals pay for information and act on it, market prices move to reflect this information, and market prices are observed freely by other agents. The situation describes a free-rider problem that limits the incentives for agents to collect information. When information is costly, markets cannot be efficient with prices representing the full reflection of *all* available information.

A solution to this case was offered by Sanford Grossman and Joseph Stiglitz (1980), who assume that there is a market for information which is similar to other competitive markets. A marginal-cost versus marginal-benefit rule applies: Agents make investments in information up to the point that the marginal return on their investment equals the marginal cost. Agents who elect to invest in information expect compensation in terms of a higher level of profits. As long as the information industry itself is competitive, with free entry and free exit, there will be no excess returns from the collection of information. However, if the information industry is not fully competitive, then information takes on an insider character and excess returns from the collection of information are possible.

The case of investor heterogeneity has been examined by Stephen Figlewski (1978), who assumes that investors may differ with respect to their information sets, their methods of forming expectations, their risk preferences, and their endowments of wealth. In this framework, the willingness of investors to bet on different speculative outcomes will vary. The key point in Figlewski's analysis is that observed market prices reflect the weighted average of actual "dollar votes" that make up the market's demand schedule. Those agents with limited wealth, high risk aversion, or weakly held expectations are underrepresented in the market, and those with higher wealth, low risk aversion, and strongly held views tend to be overrepresented. Thus, it is possible for agents

---

[13]See Fama (1970, p. 387).

with superior information or analytical skills to be underrepresented in the market and for agents with inferior information or analytical skills to be overrepresented. In the short run, therefore, prices do not fully reflect *all* available information, only the information of market participants as weighted by their actual positions.

Over time, however, market participants who have superior information will tend to amass wealth by virtue of their profitable speculation, and markets will tend to become more efficient as they become more dominated by wealth in the hands of these superior players. However, the process is not monotonic because even poorly informed participants occasionally win and receive back a transfer of wealth from those players we label superior. In this framework, market efficiency is not an either/or proposition. Markets are neither entirely inefficient nor entirely efficient. Instead, they are somewhere in the middle—tending toward greater efficiency, but not necessarily in a smooth, uninterrupted fashion.

Empirical Evidence on Exchange Market Efficiency[14]

Rather than test directly whether prices or returns in the foreign exchange market conform to their equilibrium-expected values, empirical studies have preferred to test for the availability of unusual or risk-adjusted profit opportunities. In the case of certainty or risk-free investments, we expect that arbitrage will quickly eliminate any profit opportunities. In arbitrage, the equilibrium-expected return is zero. Looking at the case of uncertainty or risky investments, some positive level of profit is consistent with an equilibrium return on nondiversifiable risks. In these cases, it is necessary to have an appropriate benchmark to gauge whether unusual or excessive profits are present.

Market Efficiency with Certainty and Risk-Free Investment

In this section, we review arbitrage only within the spot and forward foreign exchange market. The role of arbitrage for the efficiency of futures, options, offshore currency and bond markets, and swap markets will be discussed in later chapters.

Tests for efficiency of arbitrage pricing relationships usually entail similar methodology—namely, examination of a market price in relation to an arbitrage boundary condition (often based on the transaction costs of undertaking the arbitrage). Points that lay anywhere inside the boundary generate no arbitrage profits and are therefore efficient; all other points imply the existence of profit opportunities and market inefficiencies. Using the arbitrage criteria, a market is deemed efficient when a large percentage of observations fall within the boundaries, when the outliers are only a small measure away from the boundaries, and when those outliers are scattered widely over time. In an efficient market, arbitrage opportunities should be both small and rarely observed.

The most basic arbitrage in the foreign exchange market is spatial arbitrage, which reduces the dispersion of price quotations across individual market makers. Some price dispersion is consistent with market efficiency since there is a cost of searching for spatial arbitrage profits and some price risk associated with exploiting them. In addition, however, price dispersion that reflects quotations of different "quality" (such as quotations from a bank with a low credit rating or questionable back-office practices) will

---

[14]Surveys of the literature have been prepared by Levich (1985) and Hodrick (1987).

persist. These issues have not been explored rigorously on data from the foreign exchange market.

The major testing ground for market efficiency in the case of certainty has been the analysis of covered interest arbitrage. As we learned in Chapter 5, when the interest rate parity relationship does not hold, it may be possible to undertake covered interest arbitrage transactions to earn risk-free profits.

Various explanations—transaction costs, noncomparable risk in securities, exchange controls, political risk, and taxes—have been proposed to account for deviations from interest rate parity. Research suggests that all of these factors may play a role, and that the covered interest arbitrage profit opportunities are more apparent than real. That is, after one adjusts for these additional factors, most profit opportunities are either nonexistent or not risk free.

In Chapter 5, we reviewed studies by Robert Aliber (1973) and Frenkel and Levich (1975, 1977, 1981), which confirm that deviations from interest rate parity in the Eurocurrency markets are small and that a high percentage of deviations are smaller than transaction costs. Therefore, the linkages between the foreign exchange and short-term Eurocurrency markets are efficient in that few opportunities for risk-free arbitrage exist.

When we relax some of the key assumptions of interest rate parity, the empirical results become more ambiguous. For example, if domestic securities (such as Treasury bills or commercial paper) are selected, Frenkel and Levich (1975, 1977) reported that a much larger fraction of observations are outside of the arbitrage boundary condition. These apparent departures from market efficiency have been analyzed further using several techniques. Frenkel and Levich concluded that finite price elasticities, still large enough to be consistent with a competitive market, would be sufficient to push prices in the currency and security markets against the arbitrageur, thus canceling these apparent profit opportunities.

Jeffrey Frankel and Alan MacArthur (1988) extended the analysis of covered interest rate differentials to a wider group of countries—24 countries including smaller industrialized countries and 7 lesser developed countries—over the 1982–1987 sample period. The authors concluded that deviations from interest rate parity fall within a fairly narrow range for most major industrial countries as well as Hong Kong and Singapore.

The empirical results are somewhat ambiguous in the case of arbitrage between longer-term forward contracts and longer-term securities. John Hilley, Carl R. Beidleman, and James A. Greenleaf (1981) reported that rates quoted by banks for three- to five-year forward contracts were inconsistent with interest rate parity. The authors, however, suggested that the opportunity for banks to earn a small arbitrage profit may not compensate them for the costs of keeping capital tied up for three to five years, for the adverse impact on balance sheet ratios, and for the credit risks of the transaction. These costs have gained prominence now that banks face explicit capital requirements for transactions that once may have been considered as off-balance-sheet. If undertaking arbitrage uses capital, banks will engage in arbitrage only if it produces a competitive rate of return.

Similarly, other studies reviewed in Chapter 5 (Popper, 1993, and Fletcher and Taylor, 1994) reported larger deviations from interest rate parity for longer-term maturities. This apparent inefficiency may reflect the early development of this market and thinness in executing covered, risk-free arbitrage transactions.

Market Efficiency with Uncertainty and Risky Investment

Introducing uncertainty adds complexity as well as realism to tests of foreign exchange market efficiency. When the future spot rate is a random variable, the investor who holds a net (asset or liability) position in foreign currency is exposed to foreign exchange risk. As we noted earlier, prices of spot and forward exchange in an efficient market should be set so that unusual profits from risky investment opportunities are quickly eliminated. Because a test of market efficiency tests a joint hypothesis, the specification of the expected equilibrium return for bearing exchange risk is critical. However, there is no general agreement on the appropriate model for the equilibrium pricing of foreign exchange risk. So, tests of efficiency under uncertainty will not lead to definitive results.

There are basically two techniques for bearing exchange risk: spot speculation and forward speculation. In spot speculation, the investor borrows domestic currency at interest rate i, buys foreign exchange in the spot market at rate S_t, and invests in a foreign currency denominated security at interest rate i^*. A forward speculator can establish a similar long position simply by buying foreign exchange in the forward market at rate F_t. In either case, the profit depends on the expected future spot rate $[E(S_{t+1}|I_t)]$, which is uncertain. When interest parity holds, $F_t = S_t(1 + i)/(1 + i^*)$ and spot and forward speculation are equivalent investments that produce the same expected profits. Institutional factors and transaction costs will lead investors to pick the spot or forward market as the preferred venue for speculation.

Spot Market Efficiency: Design of the Tests.   The primary technique for testing spot market efficiency has been to compute the profitability of various mechanical, or technical, trading strategies. Most of these studies are examples of weak form tests (or tests of return predictability) that use only the past series of exchange rates to generate buy and sell trading signals. We will examine only two technical trading rules: the filter rule and the moving average crossover rule. Many other variations on these rules and other completely different trading systems are of course possible and in use. We chose these two because they are representative of rules tested in the literature and used in practice.

A **filter rule** is defined by a single parameter (f), the filter size. An f percent filter rule identifies trends and generates buy and sell signals according to the following design: Buy a currency whenever it rises f percent above its most recent trough; sell the currency and take a short position whenever the currency falls f percent below its most recent peak. Typically, f is chosen to be a small number (1 percent, 2 percent, 3 percent, etc.).[15]

Figure 7.3 illustrates the operation of a 1 percent filter rule on a hypothetical series of \$/€ exchange rates. At the start of the process (t_1), the speculator has no foreign exchange positions. But he or she does have capital that earns interest at the risk-free rate and allows the speculator to enter into the transactions that follow. At time t_2, the € is assumed to have risen by 1 percent. The filter rule signals an upward trend in the €, and so the trading strategy calls for a spot € purchase. By virtue of monitoring US\$/€ rates, the trading signal also calls for a spot sale of the US\$. Our speculator borrows an amount of US\$ and uses it to purchase € spot, which is invested in an interest-bearing account. Our speculator's position (long € and short US\$) is described by the T-account corresponding to time t_2. The cost of taking on this position is the interest differential ($i_{t2,\$} - i_{t2,€}$). The cost of holding this position for m days is $C = \Sigma_{t2}^{t2+m}[(i_{t,\$} - i_{t,€})]$. The expected return on the currency position is $\tilde{R} = \ln[E(\tilde{S}_{t2+m})/S_{t2}]$, which should be positive as $E(\tilde{S}_{t2+m}) > S_{t2}$. The expected profit ($\tilde{\pi}$) from using the filter rule strategy at time t_2 is then $E(\tilde{\pi}_{t2}) = \tilde{R} - C$.

By time t_3, the € has hit its peak. But the filter rule does not signal a change until time t_4. At time t_4, a sell signal causes the speculator to sell the original € position (using

---

[15]A filter rule could be a two-parameter rule with an x percent filter applied for upward movements and a y percent filter for downward movements.

FIGURE 7.3 **Mechanics of a Filter Rule in the Foreign Exchange Market**

Time series graph of $/€ exchange rate

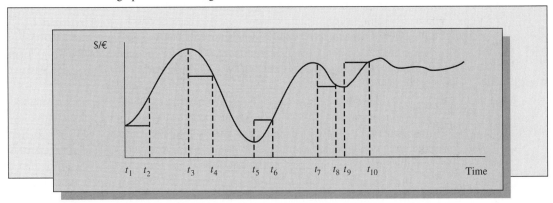

Speculative trading position over time

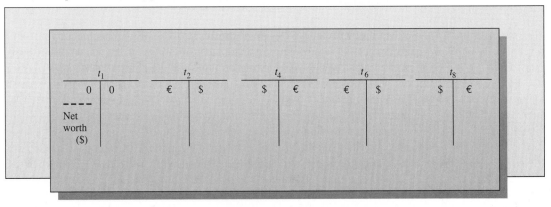

Note: An f percent filter rule generates buy signals when the currency rises f percent above an interim trough (at points t_2, t_6, and t_{10}), and sell signals when the currency falls f percent below an interim peak (at points t_4 and t_8). Initially (at t_1), the speculator has a net worth that allows him to execute transactions, but he holds no foreign exchange positions. After a buy signal, the speculator takes a long position in € by borrowing US$ and buying € in the spot market. After a sell signal, the speculator sells his € holdings and takes a short position in € by borrowing € and buying US$ in the spot market. These transactions and positions are described in the T-accounts at the bottom of this figure.

the proceeds to repay the US$ loan) and short the € (at S_{t4}) in anticipation of a further fall in its price. The speculator's new position (long US$ and short €) is shown by the T-account corresponding to time t_4. The cost of taking on this position is the interest differential ($i_{t4,€} - i_{t4,\$}$). The cost of holding this position for n days is $C = \Sigma_{t4}^{t4\,+\,n} [(i_{t,€} - i_{t,\$})]$. The expected return on the currency position is $\tilde{R} = \ln \{S_{t4}/[E(\tilde{S}_{t4\,+\,n})]\}$. This return is positive as $S_{t4} > E(\tilde{S}_{t4\,+\,n})$, the expected price at which the speculator will cover the short position. The expected profit ($\tilde{\pi}$) on the filter rule strategy is again $\tilde{R} - C$.

As time continues, Figure 7.3 shows how the speculative positions change in response to exchange rate changes. Time t_8 illustrates a "whipsaw," or a false signal. At t_8, the € has fallen by 1 percent and the speculator establishes a short € position. In this case, however, the € turns up, and at time t_{10} the speculator covers the short position and buys € in anticipation of a further rise. Selling at t_8 and buying back at t_{10} results in a loss on the exchange rate change. A closer look at the mechanics of the filter rule along with numerical calculations are shown in Box 7.2.

Box 7.2

Tracking Positions and Profits in a Technical Trading Rule: A Numerical Example

In this box, we show the operation of a technical trading rule in more detail, based on the example in Figure 7.3 and a 1 percent filter rule. The figures are entered in a table that appears below.

At time t_1, assume that the spot rate is \$0.95/€ and the speculator has no position in the market. At time t_2 (call it day 10), the spot rate is up by 1 percent to \$0.9595/€. The speculator borrows \$1,000, converts this into € at the spot rate, and invests €1,042.21. At time t_3, 20 days later, the spot rate reaches \$0.9975. The US\$ liability position is \$1,003.33, reflecting 20 days of interest at 6.5 percent. The € asset position is €1,044.24, reflecting 20 days of interest at 3.5 percent. The net gain in US\$ terms is \$38.29, reflecting the appreciation of the € in the spot market.

At time t_4 (call it day 40), the € has fallen by 1 percent from its peak. The technical rule issues a sell signal and the speculator sells his € (which has continued to accrue interest for 10 days), pays off his US\$ liability, and realizes a gain of \$26.92. These transactions are summarized in the row labeled $t_{4,P1}$ where P1 indicates "Part 1 of the transaction." Now the speculator shorts € (in the amount €1,012.63) and converts this in the spot market to take

a long position of \$1,000. This transaction is summarized in the row labeled $t_{4,P2}$ where P2 indicates "Part 2 of the transaction."

As time goes on, the € depreciates to \$0.94/€ at time t_5. The speculator has a net gain from the short position, even after adjusting for 30 days of interest owed on the € borrowing and interest earned on the US\$ asset. When the € appreciates by 1 percent above its trough to \$0.9494 at time $t_{6,P1}$, the speculator closes out his position for a gain of \$42.36. The speculator then borrows \$1,000, converts this into € at the spot rate (\$0.9494), and invests the proceeds in €, expecting the € to appreciate by more than the interest differential between US\$ and €.

At time t_8, the filter rule issues another signal to short € and the speculator shorts € at \$0.9603. By time t_9, the € has depreciated somewhat to \$0.9560, but then it appreciates by 1 percent to \$0.9656. The speculator covers his short position at time $t_{10,P1}$ and realizes a small loss (\$4.30). The rule signals another long € position at time $t_{10,P2}$.

Overall, the profits from the four transactions entered into at times t_2, t_4, t_6 and t_8 are \$72.76, or slightly more than 7.0 percent of the speculator's average \$1,000 position.

Positions, Profits and Losses Day-by-Day Using a Technical Trading Model

Time*	Day	Spot	i_S	$i_€$	Value of $ Position	Value of € Position	Net $ Gain/Loss†
t_1	1	0.9500	6.0%	3.0%	0.00	0	0
t_2	10	0.9595	6.0	3.5	−$1,000.00	€1,042.21	0
t_3	30	0.9975	6.5	3.0	−1,003.33	1,044.24	38.29
$t_{4,P1}$	40	0.9875	6.5	3.0	−1,005.14	1,045.11	**26.92**
$t_{4,P2}$	40	0.9875	6.5	3.0	1,000.00	−1,012.63	0
t_5	70	0.9400	6.0	3.5	1,005.42	−1,015.16	51.16
$t_{6,P1}$	80	0.9494	6.0	3.5	1,007.09	−1,016.15	**42.36**
$t_{6,P2}$	80	0.9494	6.0	3.5	−1,000.00	1,053.30	0
t_7	120	0.9700	6.5	3.0	−1,006.67	1,057.39	19.00
$t_{8,P1}$	130	0.9603	6.5	3.0	−1,008.48	1,058.27	**7.78**
$t_{8,P2}$	130	0.9603	6.5	3.0	1,000.00	−1,041.34	0
t_9	135	0.9560	6.0	3.5	1,000.90	−1,041.78	4.97
$t_{10,P1}$	145	0.9656	6.0	3.5	1,002.57	−1,042.79	**−4.30**
$t_{10,P2}$	145	0.9656	6.0	3.5	−1,000.00	1,035.67	0

Cumulative sum of profits (losses) on transactions 72.76

*Times refer to Figure 7.3.

†A bold entry indicates where a position is closed out and profit (or loss) is realized.

It is important to note that the speculator's profit (π) represents the *incremental return* from accepting a foreign exchange risk. Recall that the speculator has pledged, either implicitly or explicitly, a certain amount of capital (net worth) that allows him or her access to the borrowing and lending capabilities of the foreign exchange market. The speculator's capital is assumed to earn interest at a competitive market rate (R_F). Thus, the total return from committing this capital to a trading strategy is $R_F + \pi$.

Note also that the strategy outlined in Figure 7.3 could be applied to the currency futures markets. In this case, the graph would represent the \$/€ price of a € currency futures contract. A long € position implies *buying* the € futures, and a short € position implies *selling* the € futures. It would not be necessary to take into account the interest cost of any short position or interest earned on any long position because the futures price itself already reflects these interest rates through the interest rate parity condition. Once again, any gain or loss on these futures contracts represents an incremental return from accepting foreign exchange risk. In order to trade in futures contracts, our speculator is required to place U.S. Treasury bills in a margin account. The speculator continues to earn the risk-free rate of interest on this margin, so the total return from committing capital to this trading strategy is again $R_F + \pi$.

Specifying a **moving average crossover rule** requires two parameters: the length (S, in trading days) of the shorter moving average (MA_S) and the length (L, in trading days) of the longer moving average (MA_L). An S/L moving average rule is defined as follows: "If $MA_S > MA_L$, buy the foreign currency. If $MA_S < MA_L$, sell the foreign currency. If $MA_S = MA_L$, take no position." Possible values of S/L are 1/5 (representing today's price relative to the last week), 5/20 (representing this week's price relative to the last month), 1/200 (representing today's price relative to the last 200 trading days), and so on. The intuition of a moving average crossover rule is again to identify trending behavior in exchange rates. When $MA_S > MA_L$, the currency's value in the recent past exceeds its value in the more distant past, which in moving average models signals that an upward trend is developing.

Figure 7.4 illustrates the operation of a 1/200 moving average crossover rule using actual daily prices for the DM/\$ rate over a period extending from 1986 to 1992. As in our previous example, we assume that the speculator has no initial foreign exchange positions but has capital that permits entry into the transactions that follow. The first signal appears at time t_1 when the spot rate (MA_S) exceeds the 200-day moving average (MA_L), thus triggering a buy signal. Since this exchange rate is quoted as DM/\$, our speculator borrows an amount of DM and uses it to purchase US\$, placing the funds in an interest-bearing account. The position is closed out at time t_2 when the spot rate (MA_S) falls below the 200-day moving average (MA_L), thus setting off a sell signal. Our speculator sells his US\$ position and shorts the US\$, using the proceeds to go long the DM. Note that (ignoring interest rates) the position taken at time t_1 was not profitable since the speculator bought US\$ at a higher price than he later sold them.

Following the passage of time in Figure 7.4, the reader can see (again ignoring interest rates) that the short US\$ position taken at time t_2 resulted in a positive currency return when closed out at time t_3. The long US\$ position taken at time t_3 posted a negative currency return when closed out at time t_4. But shorting the US\$ at time t_4 resulted in a sizable currency return when the position was covered by buying US\$ at a lower price at time t_5. The reader can see that the other transactions triggered by this moving average rule basically had the speculator buying US\$ at low prices and selling US\$ for DM at high prices, especially the longer swings over periods t_6, t_7, t_8, t_9, and t_{10}. Note that the signals from a moving average rule could entail frequent trading, such as in the

FIGURE 7.4   **Illustration of 1/200 Moving Average Crossover Rule**
DM Spot (Daily): July 10, 1986–July 23, 1992

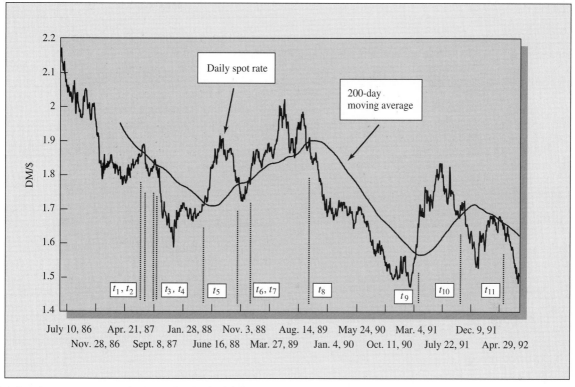

Note: A *moving average crossover rule* generates buy signals when the short-term moving average rises above the long-term moving average (at points like t_1, t_3, and t_5), and sell signals when the short-term moving average drops below the long-term moving average (at points like t_2, t_4, and t_6).

neighborhood of time t_{11} when the long-term moving average crosses the spot exchange rate at several points.

Profits from speculation using a moving average crossover rule are computed in an identical manner to the filter rule—namely, cumulative currency returns (R) minus cumulative interest costs (C). Profits are again interpreted as the incremental return over the rate of interest earned on the speculator's collateral capital. The moving average crossover rule could be applied to currency futures as well as interbank spot exchange rates.

Spot Market Efficiency: Empirical Evidence.   The application of any technical trading system, including the two we have just described, entails two steps: (1) identifying trends in exchange rates and (2) establishing market positions to profit from the continuation of that trend. The null hypothesis of market efficiency is that the cost of taking on the foreign exchange position should exactly offset the anticipated exchange rate change resulting in no net expected profit. If the trends have been identified based on a sequence of publicly observed prices, then no profits ought to be earned by using the technical strategy. The alternative hypothesis of course is that the trading strategy produces profits (and perhaps unusual, risk-adjusted profits).

TABLE 7.1   Filter Rules: Annual Percentage Profits and Losses Adjusted for Interest Rate Differentials

Country	Sample Period	Filter Size						
		0.01	0.03	0.05	0.10	0.15	0.20	0.25
Belgium	Mar 73–Sept 75	10.17	13.49	14.35	3.55	−7.42	−7.97	−12.05
	Sept 75–Nov 81	5.58	2.54	3.04	3.07	3.19	0.64	−0.91
	Sept 75–Nov 81							
	First half	4.11	−2.83	5.52	5.36	3.55	1.85	0.71
	Sept 75–Nov 81							
	Second half	8.78	5.88	2.28	3.63	8.98	0.01	−3.53
Canada	Mar 73–Sept 75	−0.72	−0.93	−2.57	0	—	—	—
	Sept 75–Nov 81	4.95	1.62	1.33	3.71	3.08	2.26	−1.34
	First half	2.93	0.20	−0.79	0	—	—	—
	Second half	8.02	3.37	4.20	4.06	2.64	0.76	0
France	Mar 73–Sept 75	17.31	12.15	21.85	10.03	−1.51	−0.90	−6.02
	Sept 75–Nov 81	5.93	5.53	2.11	−0.89	−2.49	−0.12	−2.43
	First half	−0.64	−1.16	−2.99	−2.23	−6.46	0	—
	Second half	12.13	11.30	5.11	0.44	3.22	0.008	−2.57
Germany	Mar 73–Sept 75	5.71	6.42	11.65	−6.10	−8.30	−16.54	−26.17
	Sept 75–Nov 81	5.77	5.36	5.79	3.62	3.08	0.22	−1.42
	First half	4.98	−0.08	5.14	6.11	4.76	3.72	2.43
	Second half	10.74	9.82	6.91	3.43	6.91	−1.23	−3.66
Italy	Mar 73–Sept 75	6.51	5.57	−1.66	0.29	−1.69	−3.55	0
	Sept 75–Nov 81	3.72	4.08	5.86	−0.09	7.76	12.90	12.72
	First half	7.14	6.08	4.19	−8.35	14.36	13.54	12.55
	Second half	4.81	5.65	10.52	5.43	6.91	3.14	0.80
Japan	Mar 73–Sept 75	3.89	5.29	2.56	−2.95	1.00	0	—
	Sept 75–Nov 81	13.08	7.62	7.28	10.83	5.46	0.64	−1.07
	First half	15.45	9.17	15.48	14.27	11.89	10.34	8.74
	Second half	17.28	9.41	5.31	14.64	6.34	−1.20	−2.68
Netherlands	Mar 73–Sept 75	17.06	13.20	2.91	.54	10.85	−18.89	−4.42
	Sept 75–Nov 81	9.85	4.37	3.03	3.57	3.77	0.48	−2.07
	First half	4.24	1.82	2.32	4.80	4.00	2.44	1.29
	Second half	16.05	6.38	2.83	3.71	7.51	−1.07	−4.66
Switzerland	Mar 73–Sept 75	10.44	−0.11	8.00	2.26	−6.78	−16.13	13.04
	Sept 75–Nov 81	7.54	10.27	3.3	5.62	4.79	3.34	1.12
	First half	11.09	11.87	1.97	6.07	9.95	10.65	9.30
	Second half	8.19	13.13	7.55	8.18	5.58	7.38	−8.80
United Kingdom	Mar 73–Sept 75	8.88	10.32	3.06	−1.06	3.50	0.82	0
	Sept 75–Nov 81	11.46	7.57	4.32	4.77	3.09	0.44	−2.66
	First half	11.12	11.11	7.68	5.01	−0.22	−3.11	−6.69
	Second half	12.58	3.93	0.12	3.19	3.35	−0.49	−4.98

Source: Michael Dooley and Jeffrey Shafer, "Analysis of Short-Run Exchange Rate Behavior: March 1973 to November 1981," in *Floating Exchange Rates and the State of World Trade and Payments,* ed. D. Bigman and T. Taya (Cambridge, MA: Ballinger, 1984).

The first empirical studies to report on the profitability of using filter rules in the foreign exchange market were prepared by Michael Dooley and Jeffrey Shafer (1976, 1983). A sample of their results based on daily spot rates for nine currencies over the 1973–1981 period is shown in Table 7.1. Dooley and Shafer's calculations are adjusted to reflect the interest expense and interest income of long and short positions. Transaction costs are incorporated by using bid and ask foreign exchange quotations. Remember that the figure reported is the *incremental* return for bearing open foreign exchange positions, implying that the speculator would earn the stated return *plus* a return on his or her initial capital stake.[16]

The results indicate that small filters ($f = 1$, 3, or 5 percent) would have been profitable for all currencies over the entire sample period. For larger filters ($f = 10$, 15, 20, and 25 percent) the results were more variable, but still these rules were profitable in more than one-half of the subperiods. However, even with the small filters there appears to be some element of riskiness in these trading rules because each filter would have generated losses in at least one currency during at least one subperiod. Even so, for three currencies (yen, guilder, and pound sterling) every small filter was profitable in every subperiod. The authors did not report any measures of statistical or economic significance of these profits. But basing the study on more than 8.5 years of daily data (more than 2,200 observations per currency) suggests that profitability of small filter rules has been a persistent phenomenon in the floating-rate period. When Dooley and Shafer applied filter rules to hypothetical randomly generated prices, they found that filter rules typically produce trading loses. This result is not surprising since random numbers do not contain any meaningful patterns. But this only heightens the puzzle about why there is some pattern of serial dependence in exchange rates that can be observed by speculators but that is not apparently used in money markets to produce interest rates that offset short-term exchange rate changes.

A study by Richard Sweeney (1986) used a similar filter rule technique on daily exchange rates for 10 currencies over the April 1973–December 1980 sample period and reached similar conclusions.[17] Filters of 0.5, 1, 2, 3, 4, 5, and 10 percent led to trading profits in more than 80 percent of the cases. The results for the smaller filters (0.5, 1, and 2 percent) were again superior. Sweeney divided his sample into a 2.5-year estimation period followed by a 5-year postsample period. Filter rules that were profitable in the first period tended to be profitable in the second. Under the assumption of constant exchange rate volatility, Sweeney calculated that in about one-third of the cases, the profits from filter trading were statistically significant. Again, the results were more pronounced for the smaller filters.

Stephan Schulmeister (1987, 1988) conducted an in-depth analysis of the \$/DM rate over the April 1973–October 1986 period. In addition to the filter and moving average models, he also tested a momentum model (based on the rate of change in past exchange rate) and a combination model involving both moving average and momentum models. Some of the empirical results are summarized in Table 7.2.

Schulmeister's results suggest that most of these technical models would have resulted in profitable trading strategies even after adjusting for interest expense and transaction costs. The filter rules did not stand out, however. Over the entire 13.5-year period, the 2 percent filter achieved average returns of 8.2 percent, which is statistically greater than zero. The results for the 1 percent and 3 percent filters are positive but not significant. A check of the nine subperiods (each 1.5 years long) shows several periods of losses with the filter rule. In contrast, the moving average rules are profitable in each of the nine subperiods analyzed. Over the entire sample, the moving average rules

---

[16]Note also that the returns are on unlevered positions. The use of leverage and margin increases the return and risk of these positions proportionately. See the returns as calculated in Box 7.2.

[17]Sweeney imposes a restriction on short foreign currency positions. From an initial position in US\$, a buy signal triggers a move into foreign currency while a sell signal results in a move back into US\$. Profits from this trading rule are evaluated vis-à-vis the benchmark of buying and holding the foreign currency. The same methodology was used by Cornell and Dietrich (1978) in an analysis of five currencies over the March 1973–September 1975 period.

TABLE 7.2   **Annual Percentage Rates of Return from Following Trading Rules for the DM/$ Exchange Rate, April 2, 1973–October 1, 1986**

Sample Period	Filter			Moving Average Crossover			Momentum	
	1.0%	2.0%	3.0%	MAS: 3 MAL: 10	5 10	4 16	K: 8	10
Apr 73–Oct 74	16.5%	19.9%	25.3%	24.1%	35.3%	32.5%	31.1%	29.1%
	(1.29/39)	(1.36/13)	(1.46/5)	(1.56/34)	(2.25/27)	(1.91/16)	(1.95/57)	(1.67/45)
Oct 74–Apr 76	9.8	8.7	−13.9	14.3	12.6	17.0	14.3	13.0
	(1.46/19)	(1.11/5)	(−9.75/2)	(1.92/30)	(1.62/24)	(2.06/20)	(1.83/48)	(1.78/38)
Apr 76–Oct 77	2.9	6.3	−6.9[a]	4.1	4.1	6.0	2.8	5.5
	(0.43/5)	(0.65/1)		(0.98/44)	(1.01/40)	(1.53/26)	(0.71/66)	(1.32/58)
Oct 77–Apr 79	−0.3	−4.6	−8.0	8.2	13.7	7.9	1.2	11.3
	(−0.03/34)	(−0.61/11)	(−0.87/5)	(1.12/33)	(1.88/30)	(1.05/25)	(0.14/67)	(1.52/53)
Apr 79–Oct 80	4.4	4.5	5.6	16.6	16.9	14.5	12.6	13.7
	(0.52/22)	(0.47/5)	(1.36/3)	(2.38/34)	(2.48/26)	(2.37/22)	(1.85/46)	(1.96/40)
Oct 80–Apr 82	13.6	20.4	−14.7	11.0	8.1	10.5	1.5	5.4
	(1.09/56)	(1.47/17)	(−1.11/14)	(0.87/33)	(0.74/28)	(0.93/28)	(0.15/40)	(0.53/48)
Apr 82–Oct 83	−4.5	2.3	−1.5	10.2	9.9	6.6	12.2	16.1
	(−0.59/44)	(0.31/11)	(−0.25/3)	(1.34/37)	(1.30/35)	(0.85/21)	(1.50/45)	(1.79/35)
Oct 83–Apr 85	−1.8	−7.8	7.8	28.2	30.0	20.9	32.1	27.3
	(−0.17/53)	(−0.58/19)	(0.68/4)	(2.48/30)	(2.41/28)	(1.85/18)	(2.76/40)	(2.64/34)
Apr 85–Oct 86	9.7	23.5	21.3	12.2	5.8	13.7	12.2	18.4
	(0.84/58)	(1.23/15)	(1.16/8)	(1.01/46)	(0.50/41)	(1.19/20)	(1.02/59)	(1.57/42)
Apr 73–Oct 86	5.6%	8.2%	1.6%	14.3%	15.1%	14.4%	13.3%	15.5%
	(1.76/332)	(2.14/97)	(0.39/44)	(4.39/321)	(4.56/280)	(4.40/196)	(4.03/468)	(4.69/393)

Notes: The t-statistic in parentheses with the number of the degrees of freedom test the mean of the single rates of return against a hypothesized value of zero.
[a]No t-statistic could be calculated (only one observation).
Source: Stephan Schulmeister, "An Essay on Exchange Rate Dynamics," working paper, Austrian Institute of Economic Research, 1987.

resulted in annual profits of 14–15 percent, which is statistically greater than zero. The additional rules based on exchange rate momentum and the "combination rule" (which takes positions only if both signals are in agreement) performed much the same as the moving average rules. Schulmeister suggests that one reason behind the profitability of trading rules is that exchange rate changes and speculative profits appear to be distributed nonnormally. There are too many small exchange rate changes relative to a normal distribution, but also too many large exchange rate swings (also relative to the normal). The implication from the latter is that once an exchange rate move has started, it is likely to proceed more or less uninterrupted, which allows market technicians time to identify a profitable investment opportunity.

Richard Levich and Lee Thomas (1993) added more weight to the evidence on the profitability of filter rules and moving average crossover rules. They used the largest sample of any study—3,800 daily observations over the period from January 1976 to December 1990—and based their analysis on currency futures prices, thus removing the need for a concurrent sample of daily interest rates. The results are summarized in Table 7.3.

Once again, filter rules and moving average crossover rules appear to produce profitable trading signals. The profits are lower for the Canadian dollar (C$), which has lower volatility than the other currencies in the sample. The profits for the moving average rules are generally higher than those for the filter rules. Notice that the small filter rules and the shortest run moving average rules entail considerable trading activity.

TABLE 7.3   Profitability of Filter Rules and Moving Average Rules, Percent per Annum
Sample Period, January 1976–December 1990

| Currency Sample Size | Filter Size (in %) | | | | | | Average Profit | Moving Average: Short-term (days)/ Long-term (days) | | | Average Profit |
	0.5	1.0	2.0	3.0	4.0	5.0		1/5	5/20	1/200	
DM (N = 3786)											
Actual profit	1.9	8.9	5.6	7.7	7.8	7.9	6.6	5.6	11.1	7.6	8.1
No. of trades	833	411	193	99	62	41		950	212	79	
Rank in 10,000	7652	9998	9808	9975	9981	9991		9786	10,000	9990	
UK£ (N = 3786)											
Actual profit	10.0	6.6	6.2	7.8	6.7	4.9	7.0	8.1	8.8	9.4	8.8
No. of trades	793	432	192	108	69	53		935	192	42	
Rank in 10,000	9994	9852	9850	9961	9907	9609		9975	9987	9993	
C$ (N = 3785)											
Actual profit	2.9	3.5	1.4	0.7	1.5	1.0	1.8	3.1	2.6	2.1	2.6
No. of trades	309	119	51	28	15	11		957	190	91	
Rank in 10,000	9969	9989	9089	7845	9317	8672		9977	9917	9804	
¥ (N = 3533)											
Actual profit	6.7	7.8	8.0	7.3	10.2	8.5	8.1	7.8	10.5	8.7	9.0
No. of trades	777	412	170	98	60	44		866	190	87	
Rank in 10,000	9883	9965	9973	9945	9997	9987		9957	10,000	9994	
SFr (N = 3786)											
Actual profit	7.2	6.5	3.4	7.1	9.8	5.8	6.6	7.5	4.4	8.7	6.9
No. of trades	907	541	253	127	78	64		975	213	71	
Rank in 10,000	9873	9808	9680	9872	9991	9702		9912	9235	9987	

Source: Reprinted from Richard M. Levich and Lee R. Thomas, "The Significance of Technical Trading-Rule Profits in the Foreign Exchange Markets: A Bootstrap Approach," *Journal of International Money and Finance* 12, no. 5 (Oct. 1993), pp. 451–74, with kind permission of Elsevier Science Ltd, Kidlington, UK.

Over the 15-year sample period, 930 total transactions amount to 62 transactions per year. Levich and Thomas estimate that the transaction costs associated with this level of trading activity would amount to between 1.62 percent and 2.60 percent per annum, which would eliminate most of the profits in the DM and C$ 0.5 percent filter rule and in the C$ 1/5 moving average rule. In all other cases, transaction costs would not make a significant dent in trading profits.

Levich and Thomas (1993) introduce a novel way to measure the statistical significance of technical trading results. To gauge whether their profit figures are unusual or not, Levich and Thomas generate random series of exchange rates, each series constructed by shuffling the actual series of exchange rate changes and thus preserving the actual distribution of the exchange rate series. Each technical rule is then applied to each random series and the profit measured. This procedure is repeated 10,000 times to generate an empirical distribution of profits. The profits of the original series can then be compared with the profits from the randomly generated series. Under the null hypothesis, if there is no information or signals in the original sequence of data, the profits obtained from trading in the original series should not be significantly different from the profits available in the shuffled series. As Table 7.3 shows, the profits in the original series typically rank highly in the empirical distribution of 10,000 series. These results give strong support to the notion that significant patterns occur in the original exchange rate series.

Forward Market Efficiency: Design of the Tests.   Tests of forward market efficiency generally focus on the relationship between the *current n*-period forward rate, $F_{t,n}$, the *expected* future spot rate, $E(S_{t+n}|I_t)$, and the *actual* future spot rate, S_{t+n}. By definition, the forward exchange market is efficient when forward prices fully reflect available information. The term *fully reflect* is particularly troublesome in the forward market. Some economic models cast the equilibrium value of the forward rate as simply the expected value of the future spot rate. For our purposes, this will be called the **simple efficiency hypothesis.** The simple efficiency hypothesis reflects the following two hypotheses:

(I) Rational expectations:	$E(S_{t+n}|I_t) = S_{t+n}$
(II) Forward rate pricing:	$F_{t,n} = E(S_{t+n}|I_t)$

$$(7.6)$$

The assumptions in (7.6) could also be labeled the **no currency-risk premium hypothesis.** In Chapter 5, they were referred to as the *forward rate unbiased* condition.

Other economic models, however, conclude that the equilibrium forward rate reflects a currency risk premium. We will call this the **general efficiency hypothesis.** The general efficiency hypothesis reflects the following two hypotheses:

(I) Rational expectations:	$E(S_{t+n}|I_t) = S_{t+n}$
(II) Forward rate pricing:	$F_{t,n} = E(S_{t+n}|I_t) + RP_{t,n}$

$$(7.7)$$

where $RP_{t,n}$ represents the currency risk premium at time t for maturity n. In the case of general efficiency, $F_{t,n}$ becomes a biased predictor of S_{t+n}.

The assumptions for both simple efficiency and general efficiency again highlight that a test of market efficiency relies on a joint hypothesis. Market efficiency always requires that market participants are able to form rational, forward-looking expectations. But forward rate pricing may or may not include a risk premium. As a result, the relationship between the current forward rate ($F_{t,n}$) and the future spot rate (S_{t+n}) is ambiguous, *even in an efficient market.*

Most tests of forward market efficiency employ regression methodology to examine the relationship between the future spot rate (or the future spot rate change) and the past forward rate (or the past forward rate premium). For example, in a regression of the form:

$$S_{t+n} = a + b\,F_{t,n} + c\,X_t + e_t \qquad (7.8)$$

we test whether $a = 0$, $b = 1$ and the coefficient of any other variable, X_t, is $c = 0$ under the null hypothesis of simple efficiency.[18] The residuals, e_t, should be free of serial correlation. If $b \neq 1$ or $c \neq 0$ or if there is serial correlation in the residuals, we reject the simple efficiency hypothesis. When we reject simple efficiency, it may be possible to use equation (7.8) to form forecasts that outperform the forward rate.[19]

We can recast equation (7.8) in rate-of-change form, asking whether the forward exchange *premium* embodies useful information regarding the future spot exchange *change*. A regression equation suitable for this question is:

$$\ln (S_{t+n}/S_t) = a + b\,\ln (F_{t,n}/S_t) + c\,\ln (X_t) + e_t \qquad (7.9)$$

---

[18]To test general efficiency, the equation $S_{t+n} = a + b\,(F_{t,n} - RP_{t,n}) + c\,X_t + e_t$ could be estimated using a suitable proxy for *RP*.

[19]Improved forecasting performance will depend on the stability of the regression parameters and the structure of residuals in the postsample forecasting period.

Again, simple efficiency requires that $a = 0$, $b = 1$ and $c = 0$. Were this not the case, it becomes possible to use equation (7.9) to form forecasts that outperform the forward premium.[20]

It is difficult to link regression results to conclusions about market efficiency because of the ambiguity regarding a currency risk premium. Graham Elliott and Takatoshi Ito (1995) have argued recently that regression methodology has further limitations because there is no simple relation between regression results and profit opportunities in forward markets. For example, suppose that the forward rate is unbiased ($S_{t + n} - F_{t,n} = 0$) as a result of taking on $+1$ values in some months and -1 values in others. If sophisticated speculators can correctly identify the sign of the forward error period by period, potentially they can earn a profit in every period. In this case, an unbiased forward rate *understates* potential forward market profits.

On the other hand, suppose that the forward rate is biased ($S_{t + n} - F_{t,n} \neq 0$). Linking a forward rate bias to profit opportunities presumes that speculators can identify the direction of bias in advance. This may be difficult given the random behavior of exchange rates. In this case, a biased forward rate *overstates* potential forward market profits.

Thus, more direct tests of forward market efficiency examine whether unusual profit opportunities exist in the forward market, or whether it is possible to outperform the forward rate as a forecaster of the future spot rate. However, the usual efficient market caveats apply: When a currency risk premium exists, the profits earned through forward speculation may only reflect a fair premium for the additional risk incurred. Thus, beating the forecasting performance of the forward rate need not be an indication of market inefficiency.

Forward Market Efficiency: Empirical Evidence.   A good place to begin the analysis of forward market efficiency is to take a second look at Figures 5.7 and 5.8 and Table 5.1. In Figure 5.7, we saw that forward rates and future spot exchange rates move in tandem. The regression estimates in Table 5.1 showed that the coefficient of the forward rate is very close to $+1.0$, its expected value under the null hypothesis of simple efficiency. The R^2 of these regressions is very high, confirming that the bulk of the variability in the future spot rate is explained by the lagged forward rate.

In Figure 5.8, we saw that the correspondence between the forward *premium* and future spot exchange rate *changes* is very weak. The regression estimates in Table 5.2 reveal that the coefficient of the forward rate is most often far from $+1.0$; in six of the nine cases, b is negative and in four cases significantly less than zero. These results make a strong rejection of the forward premium as an unbiased predictor of the future exchange rate change.

Kenneth Froot and Richard Thaler (1990, p. 182) reviewed many of these same regression tests, and concluded that the estimated b coefficient—in equation (7.9)—is "reliably less than one" and "frequently . . . less than zero." Because simple efficiency rests upon two hypotheses, there are two explanations for the empirical rejection of the $b = 1$ hypothesis. First, $b < 1$ could be explained by a time-varying currency-risk premium such that higher US$ interest rates imply greater risk when investing in US$ assets. Alternatively, if we maintain that currency risk is diversifiable or that investors are risk neutral, $b < 1$ could be evidence of expectational errors and against rational expectations.

Froot and Thaler reviewed both explanations. Various techniques have been developed to identify a currency-risk premium. Some of these rely on statistical measures of

---

[20]See footnote 19. The same caveat applies here.

risk. Others measure currency risk as a *systematic risk* parameter in a capital asset pricing model. Still others take currency forecasts as a measure of expectations, $E(S_{t+n}|I_t)$, and identify the risk premium as the forward rate minus the forecast.[21] None of these techniques successfully demonstrates a relationship between a currency-risk premium and the forward rate bias.

Expectational errors are the other chief explanation behind the forward rate bias. Expectational errors arise naturally in a world of uncertainty. But market efficiency posits that markets learn so errors do not persist. In the changeover to floating exchange rates and other regime shifts, it is natural to expect a slow learning process as market agents need time to understand new policies and become convinced that they are permanently in place. Karen Lewis (1989) showed that even when slow learning is incorporated into investor's expectations of the U.S. money supply process, roughly half of the forward rate bias observed in the 1980–1985 US$ appreciation is still unaccounted for.

Many empirical studies have investigated whether other variables [X in the context of equations (7.8) and (7.9)] can be used to significantly augment the forecasting performance of the forward exchange rate. As a group, these studies cast more doubt on whether the forward rate can be considered an unbiased predictor, or the best available predictor of the future spot rate. We will briefly review some of the variables used in these studies.

1. *Historic forecast errors.* In an efficient market, historic forward rate forecast errors should not be useful for explaining current forward rate forecast errors. Lars Hansen and Robert Hodrick (1980) studied this issue, using weekly data on the three-month forward rate for seven major currencies in the 1973–1979 period. They found that in three currencies, historic forward rate forecast errors were significant for explaining the current forward rate forecast error. The strongest evidence was in the case of the deutsche mark, where historic forecast errors explained 13.5 percent of the variance in observed forward rate forecasting errors. This may seem like a small number relative to the total variability in forward rate forecasting errors. But 13.5 percent is a large number relative to zero and, as we will see in Chapter 8, large enough to be used by a speculator to earn substantial trading profits.

2. *Multiple forward rates.* Equations (7.8) and (7.9) implicitly assume that the future spot exchange rate is related to its own forward exchange rate. In an efficient market, forecast errors should not be related to forward premiums of other currencies, since the information content in these prices should be reflected directly through the forward rate of the currency in question. Robert Hodrick and Sanjay Srivastava (1984) examined the relationship between forward rate forecasting errors for a single currency and forward premium for a family of five currencies (the French franc, deutsche mark, Japanese yen, British pound, and Swiss franc) using monthly data for the February 1976–September 1982 period. The authors found that for three currencies (the yen, pound, and Swiss franc) a significant relationship exists between future forward rate forecast errors and the presently observed forward premium for the family of five currencies. This technique explains between 16 percent and 22 percent of the variance in forward rate forecast errors.

3. *"Large" and "small" contemporaneous forward premiums.* Under simple efficiency, the forward premium forecasting error should be unrelated to any observable

---

[21]Domowitz and Hakkio (1985) present a statistical analysis of currency risk and the forward discount. Frankel (1982) estimates currency risk in a capital asset pricing model (CAPM) setting. Frankel and Froot (1987) use survey data to estimate the currency risk premium.

variable. John Bilson (1981) examined nine major currencies over the July 1974–January 1980 period to see if forecast errors are related to contemporaneous forward premiums. He used all currencies together in a pooled time series–cross-section analysis, which raises the sample size and increases the precision of the estimated regression coefficients. The first results (with standard errors in parentheses) were:

$$\text{Percent forecast error} = \ln (S_{t+1}/S_t) - \ln (F_t/S_t) = 3.123 - 0.852 \ln (F_t/S_t)$$
$$(1.18) \quad (0.18)$$

The R^2 of this equation is only 2.9 percent, but it firmly rejects the hypothesis that the forward premium is an unbiased predictor of the future spot exchange rate change.

Concerned that these results may be driven by outlying observations, Bilson divided the forward premiums into two groups: those greater than 10 percent in absolute value (FP_{Large}) and those less than 10 percent in absolute value (FP_{Small}). The final estimated equation is:

$$\text{Percent forecast error} = -0.741 \, FP_{Small} - 1.280 \, FP_{Large}$$
$$(0.15) \quad\quad\quad (0.12)$$

which shows that the bias in the forward premium appears to be even *greater* when the forward premium takes on extreme values.

The real challenge, however, is whether this forecasting equation can generate trading profits in a postsample period. To conduct this test, Bilson used his regression estimates to produce a forecast of the future spot exchange rate. The difference between the forward rate and the estimated future spot rate provides an estimate of the expected profit for each currency. A portfolio of forward contracts is designed to profit from the exchange rate forecasts.[22] In the 51-week postsample period, Bilson's speculative portfolio earned a return that is significantly greater than zero and substantially the same as what the model predicted.

4. *A contemporaneous professional forecast.* Another selection of X_t in equation (7.8) is a set of two variables: the current spot rate and a current forecast from a professional forecasting service. This regression of the future spot rate against the current spot rate, the forward rate, and a professional forecast resembles a *composite forecast* (discussed in more detail in Chapter 8). It offers a standard test for unbiasedness in the forward rate, and it also illustrates a useful approach for measuring the value of a forecast from a professional forecasting service. The regression format is well suited for measuring the marginal value of an additional forecasting variable; if the variable picks up a significant coefficient, it improves the fit of the equation (at least on an in-sample basis).

Bilson (1983) presented an analysis along these lines using currency forecasts from Predex, a New York–based professional forecasting service. The regression was estimated using techniques similar to those in Bilson (1981). Data for several currencies, several forward rate maturities, and many time periods were pooled into a single regression to increase the sample size and the precision of the regression estimates.

The results of the regression, shown in Table 7.4, suggest that the coefficients of the forward rate do not equal unity, so the forward rate does not optimally reflect all of the information necessary to predict the forward rate. The same could be said of the coefficient of the Predex forecast, which is small numerically but statistically different from zero in four of five currencies. Bilson's (1983) analysis illustrates a worthwhile technique for measuring the marginal value of a forecast sold by a professional service. It

---

[22]The portfolio weights come from the estimated covariance of profits in each currency.

TABLE 7.4   Regression Weights in a Composite Exchange Rate Forecast

Currency	Spot	Predex	Forward
Canadian dollar	0.41	0.05	0.54
	(5.52)	(3.20)	
French franc	1.07	0.03	−0.10
	(8.99)	(2.14)	
German mark	1.13	0.05	−0.18
	(11.29)	(2.91)	
Japanese yen	0.83	0.02	0.15
	(10.51)	(0.96)	
British pound	0.65	−0.02	0.37
	(8.19)	(1.93)	

Note: The figures in parentheses are *t*-statistics. Coefficients have been constrained to sum to unity.

Source: John F. O. Bilson, "The Evaluation and Use of Foreign Exchange Rate Forecasting Services," reprinted from Richard J. Herring, ed., *Managing Foreign Exchange Risk* (New York: Cambridge University Press, 1983), with the permission of Cambridge University Press.

also shows that (on an in-sample basis) the forward rate can be beaten when augmented by a combination of public information (the spot rate) and private information (the professional forecast).

5. *The contemporaneous PPP spot rate.* Another study by Bilson (1984) is similar in spirit to the study just described. The spot exchange rate, forward rate, and purchasing power parity rate are selected as the variables to explain the future spot rate. The model is estimated over the 1973–1982 period using regression techniques that pool observations across currencies. The coefficient of the PPP variable is shown to be small but statistically significant, making a useful contribution to the information contained in the spot and forward exchange rates. The results show that the inclusion of the PPP spot rate increases the explanatory power of the equation, and raises the potential profits for speculators who incorporate the PPP spot rate into their exchange rate forecast.

Policy Matters—Private Enterprises

The implications of efficient market studies for business are potentially far-reaching. When markets are believed to be efficient, business executives have few incentives to invest in information for the purpose of forecasting exchange rates. Such information is already reflected in market prices. Unusual profit opportunities from foreign exchange speculation are not present in an efficient market. On the other hand, business practices that reduce transaction costs can be pursued without fear of incurring opportunity costs. In particular, hedging foreign currency obligations by covering them at the current forward rate would not incur any opportunity costs for the firm. If the forward rate is equal to the expected future spot rate, firms that hedge will not sacrifice any expected value in their cash flows, but they will reduce the volatility in these flows. Consequently, efficiency will encourage hedging behavior. Put another way, there is little incentive for firms to maintain open foreign exchange positions if there is no expected profit associated with bearing this risk.

When markets are perceived to be inefficient, managerial policies toward foreign exchange management will be considerably different. When markets are inefficient, risk taking in foreign exchange will, on average, offer higher returns per unit of risk than in other markets. Firms will be better off then by actively managing their foreign exchange risks, and selectively taking positions based on available foreign exchange forecasts.

The evidence in this chapter shows many reasons to be skeptical about the unbridled efficiency of the foreign exchange market. A variety of techniques—simple trend-following rules in the spot market and in the futures market, and straightforward multiple regression models in the forward markets—show that speculative profit opportunities have been available and models that outperform the forward rate forecast can be constructed. While no study has shown that these profits are *unusually high* on a *risk-adjusted* basis, many studies have shown persistent profits over fairly long periods of time. Firms that have some tolerance for bearing risks could well consider using the methods described in this chapter for either speculative or selective hedging purposes.[23]

In drawing a conclusion about market efficiency and the possibility of superior forecasting rules and profit opportunities, corporate managers and private investors need to keep several warnings in mind. First, spirited data analysis can very likely uncover significant trends in spot exchange rates, or a model with some power to predict future spot rates. While "data snooping" or "data mining" can often find (ex post) trading rules that would have worked, it is only a violation of market efficiency, strictly speaking, if these rules can be applied successfully ex ante. Rules that have worked in the past are often used in the future, thereby affecting market prices and rendering the rule obsolescent. Thus conclusions regarding market efficiency are on more solid ground when based on a long period of analysis that includes a postsample analysis.

Second, it is important but often difficult to account for risk in market-efficiency tests. While several profitable trading and/or forecasting opportunities in spot and forward markets were noted, none of these was risk free. Moreover, the standard deviation of speculative returns or exchange rate changes, may not be sufficient to describe the riskiness of these apparent market inefficiencies. Many studies have shown that exchange rate changes are distributed nonnormally, with too many observations in the extreme tails of the distribution compared to the normal. This property—so-called fat-tailed distributions—means that extreme exchange rate changes are more likely than one would expect given the volatility based on a normal distribution. Fat-tailed distributions increase the risks for speculators.[24]

In some cases, government intervention in the currency market may contribute to this statistical finding. For example, the Exchange Rate Mechanism (reviewed in Chapter 2) called on participating European governments to keep their currencies within a 2.25 percent band around a central rate. Intervention within the band helped to keep most exchange rate changes fairly small. But on those occasions when the central bank abandoned its central rate, unusually large changes would result. The usual measure of volatility (standard deviation, σ) does not adequately describe the risk in this case.

The same tendency for the statistical measure σ to understate risk happens for currencies that are "pegged but adjustable." In this case, there is usually a very large chance that the peg will hold, so most daily price changes will be small. But there is a finite probability that the peg will break, resulting in a large exchange rate movement. The distribution of exchange rate changes in this case is highly nonnormal. Indeed, the

---

[23]This view is becoming more widespread. For example, Froot and Thaler (1990, p. 190) conclude: "Taken as a whole, the evidence suggests that explanations which allow for the possibility of [foreign exchange] market inefficiencies should be seriously investigated."

[24]Some studies (Hsieh, 1988) have shown that volatility in the foreign exchange market varies according to the day of the week, with Mondays and Fridays the most volatile days.

distribution may appear bimodal, with a large probability of a small change in rates and small probability of a large discrete exchange rate change.

This phenomenon is often referred to as a **peso problem,** a term that refers to the substantial change in the Mexican peso exchange rate in 1976 after the rate had been pegged to the US$ for the previous 23 years. But the term *peso problem* is applied to any situation where there can be a discrete jump in prices or shift in policy regimes. Risk in the case of a peso problem is poorly described by the usual σ measure, since there is a finite probability of a discrete jump in prices.

Issues pertaining to the measurement of risk cloud the interpretation of efficient market studies, because inefficiency implies high returns relative to the risk incurred.

Policy Matters—Public Policymakers

Public policymakers also take an interest in the efficiency of foreign exchange markets. If markets are efficient, then the level of exchange rates and their volatility is, on average, a fair reflection of underlying economic fundamentals. If policymakers feel that exchange rates are "misaligned" or "excessively volatile," the cause of these concerns would likely be traced to shocks to certain key economic variables (such as the money supply, real income, inflation), the inherent uncertainty about the future path of these variables, and the ability of the economy to adjust to shocks as they occur—as in the sticky-price, overshooting model of the exchange rate. In other words, in an efficient market, the level and volatility of exchange rates are due to fundamental factors rather than a misreading of these factors by private foreign exchange market participants.

If policymakers conclude that the foreign exchange market is inefficient, the policy prescription to remedy the situation is not clear because the causes of inefficiency are themselves unclear. One plausible explanation for market inefficiency is excessive and destabilizing private speculation. According to this view, short-term exchange rate movements are determined by traders who use chartist techniques instead of relying on macroeconomic fundamentals. As a result, trending behavior and bandwagons may develop in exchange rates. Excessive speculation of this sort could be portrayed as short run and mainly affecting the volatility of rates rather than their level. But these short-run dynamics now associated with "noise traders" could develop into longer swings where the exchange rate deviates substantially from its fundamental value.

Another explanation of market inefficiency is that there is too little stabilizing speculation. In this view, profit opportunities in the foreign exchange market are the result of slow and predictable price changes. These should attract speculators. But profit opportunities persist because even though trading volume in the interbank foreign exchange market is huge, some evidence suggests that there is relatively little risk taking in the market, especially over medium- and longer-term horizons.

Consider the behavior of two major players in the foreign exchange market: bank traders and corporations. Bank traders may hold their position for only a few minutes or a few hours, typically closing out these positions overnight.[25] Corporations may hold large foreign exchange positions for longer periods, but they do not usually manage these positions continuously for pure profits. Suppose a corporation has a €1 million payable due in one year. If the manager anticipates a strong € (in particular, stronger

---

[25]See Lyons (1995) and the discussion in Chapter 3.

than today's forward rate), he may choose to buy €1 million forward. Once the manager hedges, the firm's policies may not allow him to buy more € if he is extremely confident of a stronger €, or to sell € forward, even if the manager's forecast now points to a weak €. Thus a large group of informed market participants with substantial currency positions may be unable to make stabilizing speculative transactions when market prices stray away from fundamentals.

A final important theme is that public policy itself—central bank intervention in the foreign exchange market—may be a fundamental cause of foreign exchange market inefficiency. In Chapter 3, we reported evidence that central banks have sometimes lost huge amounts through intervention in the foreign exchange market. This was true of many central banks in the 1970s and of European central banks in the latter years of operation of the Exchange Rate Mechanism. A study by Kathryn Dominguez and Jeffrey Frankel (1993) examined the relationship between central bank intervention and exchange rate volatility. Their analysis shows mixed results. Prior to the 1985 Plaza Hotel meeting, U.S. and German central bank intervention could be associated with higher volatility in US$ exchange rates. But since then, it appears that intervention has had an opposite effect of reducing measured exchange rate volatility.

William Silber (1994) took a close look at the efficiency of futures markets and attempted to show the role of government. Silber selected 12 futures contracts for which there is a long history of daily price data. He applied moving average crossover rules to each series to measure the profitability of technical trading strategies. To select the parameters of the moving average crossover rule, Silber searched over a grid of values where the short-term moving average parameter ranges from 1 to 15 days and the long-term moving average parameter ranges from 16 to 200 days (in increments of 2 days). Having measured the profitability in year t for each rule over this 16×92 ($= 1,472$) grid, Silber took the "best rule" and applied it in the *next* period. Thus, Silber's results in Table 7.5 represent a true out-of-sample analysis.

The evidence suggests that in currencies and short-term interest rates, where governments maintain a significant involvement, there is a tendency for technical trend-following rules to result in profits. Crude oil is another case where political factors also strongly influence market prices. However, the markets for precious metals (silver and gold) and equities (the S&P 500) show no tendency to permit profits from the use of naive technical trading rules.

Silber's tests are intriguing for two reasons. First, the results are true postsample findings; a speculator could have obtained these results with available information. Moreover, these results suggest a link between public policies toward exchange rates and opportunities open to private speculators. The process of government intervention in foreign exchange markets may be an important feature that distinguishes currency markets from other financial markets.

Along somewhat the same lines, Blake LeBaron (1999) investigated the profitability of technical trading models from 1979–1992 for the DM and ¥.[26] LeBaron reported that if the days when the Federal Reserve actively intervenes are removed from the sample, there is a dramatic decline in the level and significance of technical trading profits. A cautious interpretation is advised because, as LeBaron concluded, "It is not clear that the Federal Reserve *causes* inefficiencies in the foreign exchange market, or just happens to be around when they occur."

---

[26]See Neely (1998) for a related study that reaches similar conclusions.

TABLE 7.5   Moving Average Trading Rules in Currency Futures and Other Futures Markets

	(1)	(2)	(3)	(4)	(5)	(6)	(7)	(8)	(9)
	Number of Years	Average Annual Returns	Standard Deviation of Returns	Sharpe Ratio [(2)/(3)]	Average Trades per Year	Average Annual Returns after Transaction Costs	T-Statistic on Column 6 Returns	Average Annual Returns: Buy and Rollover	Sharpe Ratio [(6)/(3)]
German mark	12	0.0980	0.1176	0.8333	17.08	0.0937	2.72	−0.0197	0.797
3-month Eurodollar	8	0.0034	0.0038	0.8947	16.75	0.00298	2.53	0.0036	0.785
Swiss franc	12	0.10103	0.1311	0.7727	12.25	0.0982	2.67	−0.0268	0.749
Japanese yen	12	0.0742	0.1112	0.6673	17.08	0.0699	2.17	0.020	0.629
British pound	12	0.0580	0.1198	0.4841	16.58	0.0539	1.55	0.0047	0.4495
Canadian dollar	12	0.0253	0.0429	0.5897	25.50	0.0189	1.52	0.0148	0.441
Crude oil	7	0.199	0.4151	0.479	31.71	0.1673	1.07	0.117	0.403
3-month sterling	8	0.0024	0.0054	0.4444	28.63	0.00168	0.88	−0.0046	0.312
U.S. T-bonds	12	0.0450	0.1406	0.3201	24.42	0.0377	0.93	0.0371	0.267
Silver	11	−0.003	0.3159	−0.009	30.18	−0.0271	−0.28	−0.2224	−0.086
Gold	12	−0.0270	0.2337	−0.1155	18.92	−0.0364	−0.54	−0.121	−0.15
S&P 500	8	−0.1120	0.2195	−0.5103	15.88	−0.1152	−1.48	0.0672	−0.524

Note: All tests are on futures contracts. Calculations based on daily data. Moving average crossover rules, $MA(i,j)$, are analyzed over all combinations $i = 1, 2, \ldots$ 15; $j = 16, 18, 20, \ldots, 200$. Best rule in year t is applied in year $t + 1$. Analysis of best rule is updated annually.

Source: William L. Silber, "Technical Trading: When It Works and When It Doesn't," *Journal of Derivatives* (Spring 1994). Reprinted with permission from *The Journal of Derivatives Quarterly*, a publication of Institutional Investor, Inc., 488 Madison Avenue, New York, NY 10022.

Summary

In this chapter, we reviewed the theory and empirical evidence on market efficiency, as applied to the foreign exchange market. As a theoretical matter, market efficiency represents a joint hypothesis: one hypothesis about the equilibrium prices or returns in a market, and a second hypothesis about the ability of markets to set actual prices or returns in conformity with the equilibrium. Market efficiency requires that expectational errors follow a fair-game process. When markets are efficient, no excess profit opportunities are consistently available to market participants.

The empirical evidence in the case of certainty is clear-cut and supportive of market efficiency. Once transaction costs and other factors are taken into account, most risk-free arbitrage profit opportunities in foreign exchange are quickly eliminated. However, empirical tests of market efficiency under uncertainty are difficult to interpret. Many studies have reported techniques for profitable trading or superior forecasting in both spot and forward markets. These studies are compelling because the results have been persistent over the floating-rate period. However, all reported profit opportunities involve risk, so the risk-return ratio from (apparent) foreign exchange market inefficiencies must be compared with the risk-return trade-off in other markets.

Questions

1. Describe three forms of market efficiency. Give an example of each one in the context of the foreign exchange market.

2. Describe the joint hypothesis that underlies all tests for market efficiency.

3. Define filter rules and moving average crossover rules for trading in the foreign exchange market. Under what circumstances would these methods be profitable for a currency trader?

4. How would you determine whether the profits earned by a currency trader were excessive and thus indicative of market inefficiency?

5. How does a currency-risk premium affect the notion of efficiency in the foreign exchange market?

6. If the foreign exchange market is efficient, a corporation does not need to hedge at all. Is this statement true or false? Explain.

7. When the market is inefficient, a corporation should actively manage its currency positions to capture extraordinary returns. Is this statement true or false? Explain.

8. How could government intervention in the currency market impact foreign exchange market efficiency?

9. What is the "peso problem"? How does the presence of a peso problem affect our ability to test for efficiency in the foreign exchange market?

Exercises

1. This exercise is based on the simulation of exchange rates in Box 7.1.

   a. Using Excel or other statistical software, replicate the graph in Figure A. Recall that the data were generated using a starting exchange rate $S_0 = 50$, and subsequent exchange rates determined by $S_t = S_{t-1} + u_t$, where u_t are random numbers drawn from a normal distribution with mean of 0, a standard deviation of 1, and a "random seed" of 3,388.

   b. Pick another random seed value, generate another set of u_t, and plot the new values for S_t and the percentage change in S_t. Do you observe any patterns in your new graphs? Would you feel confident building a technical trading rule on the basis of these patterns?

   c. Now, select another set of u_t but now with a mean of 0.2 and a random seed of 3,388. Plot these new values of S_t and the percentage change in S_t. Do you observe any patterns in your new graphs? Would you feel confident building a technical trading rule on the basis of these patterns?

2. *Examine the daily closing price data on the DM/$ rate in file E07.XLS that was used to construct Figure 7.4. Suppose you were using a 1 percent filter rule to trade the DM and US$.

   a. On what day would the 1 percent filter rule have issued its *first* signal? Was this a buy or a sell signal? At what price did the trade occur?

   b. On what day would the 1 percent filter rule have issued its *second* signal? Was this a buy or a sell signal? At what price did the second trade occur?

   c. Calculate the profit from the first trade. Assume that transaction costs are 0.02 percent and that interest rates were constant over the period with $i_{DM} = 3.0$ percent and $i_{\$} = 5.5$ percent.

   d. Repeat questions a, b, and c assuming a 2 percent filter rule.

3. *Examine the daily closing price data on the DM/$ rate in file E07.XLS that was used to construct Figure 7.4. Suppose you were using a 1/200 moving average rule to trade the DM and US$.

   a. On what day would the 1/200 moving average rule have issued its *first* signal? Was this a buy or a sell signal? At what price did the trade occur?

   b. On what day would the 1/200 moving average rule have issued its *second* signal? Was this a buy or a sell signal? At what price did the second trade occur?

   c. Calculate the profit from the first trade. Assume that transaction costs are 0.02 percent and that interest rates were constant over the period with $i_{DM} = 3.0$ percent and $i_{\$} = 5.5$ percent.

4. Suppose that a technical trading rule leads to profits of 10 percent per annum (after transaction costs and interest expense) over a five-year period. The trader can commit an initial stake of $100,000.

   a. Calculate the expected wealth of the trader after five years if he puts his *entire* stake, including interim gains and losses, at risk in each trade.

_____

*Data from this exercise are provided on the author's website at <www.stern.nyu.edu/~rlevich/book1/datafile.htm>.

b. Now suppose that the trader uses his $100,000 as a 10 percent margin in order to take an initial position of $1 million. Calculate the expected ending wealth of this trader after five years if he puts his *entire* stake, including interim gains and losses, at risk in each trade.

c. Discuss the risks associated with the trading style in question *b* that are not present with the trading style in question *a*.

d. What assumptions underlie the calculation in question *b*?

5. Under the simple efficiency hypothesis, the relationship between the future spot rate (S_{t+n}), the current three-month forward rate ($F_{t,3}$), and other information (X_t) should be given by equation (7.8)

$$S_{t+3} = a + b F_{t,3} + c X_t + e_t$$

with $a = 0$, $b = 1$, and $c = 0$. Assume that you analyze a set of data for the $/£ exchange rate, and you can estimate quite precisely that $a = 0$, $b = 0.85$, and $c = 0.15$ when X_t is the PPP rate for the $/£.

a. Does the above information help confirm or reject the simple efficiency hypothesis?

b. Suppose that the current spot rate (S_t) is $1.50/£, the three-month forward rate is $1.46/£ and the PPP exchange rate is $1.54/£. What is your forecast of the $/£ spot rate three months from now?

c. Based on your forecast, would you speculate by taking a long or short position in the pound? Would you prefer to take your speculative position in the spot market or in the forward market?

References

Aliber, Robert Z. "The Interest Rate Parity Theory: A Reinterpretation." *Journal of Political Economy,* Dec. 1973, pp. 1451–59.

Baillie, Richard, and Patrick McMahon. *The Foreign Exchange Market: Theory and Econometric Evidence.* Cambridge: Cambridge University Press, 1989.

Bilson, John F. O. "The Evaluation and Use of Foreign Exchange Rate Forecasting Services." In *Managing Foreign Exchange Risk,* ed. R. Herring. Cambridge: Cambridge University Press, 1983.

———. "The 'Speculative Efficiency' Hypothesis." *Journal of Business* 54, no. 3 (July 1981), pp. 435–51.

———. "Purchasing Power Parity as a Trading Strategy." *Journal of Finance*, July 1984, pp. 715–25.

Cornell, W. Bradford, and J. Kimball Dietrich. "The Efficiency of the Market for Foreign Exchange under Floating Exchange Rates." *Review of Economics and Statistics* 60, no. 1 (Feb. 1978), pp. 111–20.

Dominguez, Kathryn, and Jeffrey Frankel. "Does Foreign Exchange Intervention Matter? Disentangling the Portfolio and Expectations Effects of the Mark." NBER Working Paper No. 3299, Mar. 1990.

———. *Does Foreign Exchange Intervention Work?* Washington, DC: Institute for International Economics, 1993.

Domowitz, Ian, and Craig Hakkio. "Conditional Variance and the Risk Premium in the Foreign Exchange Market." *Journal of International Economics* 19 (1985), pp. 47–66.

Dooley, Michael P., and Jeffrey Shafer. "Analysis of Short-Run Exchange Rate Behavior: March 1973–September 1975." International Finance Discussion Papers, No. 76. Washington, DC: Federal Reserve System, 1976.

———. "Analysis of Short-Run Exchange Rate Behavior: March 1973–November 1981." In *Exchange Rate and Trade Instability,* ed. D. Bigman and T. Taya. Cambridge, MA: Ballinger, 1983.

Elliott, Graham, and Takatoshi Ito. "Heterogeneous Expectation and Tests of Efficiency in the Yen/Dollar Forward Foreign Exchange Rate Market." NBER Working Paper No. 5376, Dec. 1995.

Fama, Eugene F. "Efficient Capital Markets: A Review of Theory and Empirical Work." *Journal of Finance* 25 (1970), pp. 383–417.

———. "Efficient Capital Markets: II." *Journal of Finance* 46, no. 5 (Dec. 1991), pp. 1575–1617.

Figlewski, Stephen. "Market Efficiency in a Market with Heterogeneous Expectations." *Journal of Political Economy* 86, no. 4 (Aug. 1978), pp. 581–97.

Fletcher, Donna J., and Larry W. Taylor. "A Non-Parametric Analysis of Covered Interest Parity in Long-Date Capital Markets." *Journal of International Money and Finance* 13, no. 4 (Aug. 1994), pp. 459–75.

Frankel, Jeffrey A. "In Search of the Exchange Risk Premium: A Six Currency Test Assuming Mean Variance Optimization." *Journal of International Money and Finance* 1, no. 3 (Dec. 1982), pp. 255–74.

Frankel, Jeffrey A., and Kenneth A. Froot. "Using Survey Data to Test Standard Propositions Regarding Exchange

Rate Expectations." *American Economic Review* 77, no. 1 (Mar. 1987), pp. 133–53.

Frankel, Jeffrey A., and Alan T. MacArthur. "Political vs. Currency Premia in International Real Interest Differentials." *European Economic Review* 32, no. 5 (June 1988), pp. 1083–1121.

Frenkel, Jacob A., and Richard M. Levich. "Covered Interest Arbitrage: Unexploited Profits?" *Journal of Political Economy* 83, no. 2 (Apr. 1975), pp. 325–38.

———. "Covered Interest Arbitrage in the 1970s." *Economic Letters* 8, no. 3 (1981), pp. 267–74.

———. "Transaction Costs and Interest Arbitrage: Tranquil versus Turbulent Periods." *Journal of Political Economy* 85, no. 6 (Dec. 1977), pp. 1209–26.

Froot, Kenneth A., and Richard H. Thaler. "Anomalies: Foreign Exchange." *Journal of Economic Perspectives* 4, no. 3 (Summer 1990), pp. 179–92.

Giddy, Ian H., and Gunter Dufey. "The Random Behavior of Flexible Exchange Rates." *Journal of International Business Studies* 6, no. 1 (1975), pp. 1–32.

Grossman, Sanford J., and Joseph E. Stiglitz. "On the Impossibility of Informationally Efficient Markets." *American Economic Review* 70 (1980), pp. 393–408.

Hansen, Lars P., and Robert J. Hodrick. "Forward Exchange Rates as Optimal Predictors of Future Spot Exchange Rates: An Econometric Analysis." *Journal of Political Economy* 88 (Aug. 1980), pp. 829–53.

Hilley, John L.; Carl R. Beidleman; and James A. Greenleaf. "Why There Is No Long Forward Market in Foreign Exchange." *Euromoney* (Jan. 1981), pp. 95–103.

Hodrick, Robert J. *The Empirical Evidence of the Efficiency of Forward and Futures Foreign Exchange Markets.* Chur, Switzerland: Harwood Academic Publishers, 1987.

Hodrick, Robert J., and Sanjay Srivastava. "An Investigation of Risk and Return in Forward Foreign Exchange." *Journal of International Money and Finance* 3, no. 1 (Mar. 1984), pp. 5–29.

Hsieh, David A. "The Statistical Properties of Daily Foreign Exchange Rates: 1974–1983." *Journal of International Economics* 24 (1988), pp. 129–45.

LeBaron, Blake. "Technical Trading Rule Profitability and Foreign Exchange Intervention." *Journal of International Economics* 49 (Oct. 1999), pp. 125–43.

Levich, Richard M. "The Efficiency of Markets for Foreign Exchange: A Review and Extension." In *International Financial Management: Theory and Application,* ed. Donald Lessard. Boston: Warren, Gorham and Lamont, 1979.

———. "Empirical Studies of Exchange Rates: Price Behavior, Rate Determination and Market Efficiency." In *Handbook of International Economics,* ed. R. Jones and P. Kenen. Amsterdam: North-Holland, 1985.

Levich, Richard M., and Lee R. Thomas. "The Significance of Technical Trading-Rule Profits in the Foreign Exchange Market: A Bootstrap Approach." *Journal of International Money and Finance* 12, no. 5 (Oct. 1993), pp. 451–74.

Lewis, Karen K. "Are Foreign Exchange Intervention and Monetary Policy Related, and Does It Really Matter?" *Journal of Business* 68, no. 2 (Apr. 1995), pp. 185–214.

———. "Can Learning Affect Exchange Rate Behavior?: The Case of the Dollar in the Early 1980s." *Journal of Monetary Economics* 23 (Mar. 1989), pp. 79–100.

Lyons, Richard K. "Tests of Microstructural Hypotheses in the Foreign Exchange Market." *Journal of Financial Economics* 39 (1995), pp. 321–51.

Mussa, Michael. "The Role of Official Intervention." Group of Thirty Occasional Papers, no. 6 (New York: Group of Thirty), 1981.

Neely, Christopher, J. "Technical Analysis and the Profitability of U.S. Foreign Exchange Intervention." *Review,* Federal Reserve Bank of St. Louis, July/Aug. 1998, pp. 3–17.

Poole, William. "The Canadian Experiment with Flexible Exchange Rates." Unpublished Ph.D. dissertation, University of Chicago, 1966.

———. "Speculative Prices as Random Walks: An Analysis of Ten Time Series of Flexible Exchange Rates." *Southern Economic Journal* 33 (1967), pp. 468–78.

Popper, Helen. "Long-Term Covered Interest Parity: Evidence from Currency Swaps." *Journal of International Money and Finance* 12, no. 4 (Aug. 1993), pp. 439–48.

Schulmeister, Stephan. "Currency Speculation and Dollar Fluctuations." *Quarterly Review*. Banca Nazionale del Lavoro, no. 167 (Dec. 1988), pp. 343–65.

———. "An Essay on Exchange Rate Dynamics." Discussion Paper IIM/LMP 87-8. Wissenschaftszentrum Berlin fur Sozialforschung. Berlin, 1987.

Silber, William L. "Technical Trading: When It Works and When It Doesn't." *Journal of Derivatives* 1, no. 3 (Spring 1994), pp. 39–44.

Sweeney, Richard. "Beating the Foreign Exchange Market." *Journal of Finance,* Mar. 1986, pp. 163–82.

8 EXCHANGE RATE FORECASTING

"My father was in the import-export business and he used to ask me to predict exchange rates. It's an experience that did not bring us much closer."

University economist speaking at conference on international finance

Learning Objectives

After reading this chapter, students should

1. Understand how to use a simple framework to organize the process of forecasting foreign exchange rates.

2. Be familiar with findings from various studies that suggest how different techniques may be beneficial for forecasting exchange rates in certain circumstances.

3. Know the difference between accurate and useful forecasts, and why useful forecasts may be a better technique for evaluating forecaster performance.

4. Know how to evaluate the track record of a forecaster using accuracy measures and the percentage correct approach.

5. Be able to use several specific techniques for forecasting exchange rates at the short-, medium-, and long-run horizons.

Exchange rate forecasts play a fundamental role in nearly all aspects of international financial management. This is obviously the case for financial transactions. To evaluate foreign borrowing or investment opportunities, forecasts of future spot exchange rates are necessary to convert expected foreign currency cash flows into their expected domestic currency value. And short-term hedging or cash management decisions often rely on a forecast of expected exchange rate movements. Exchange rate forecasts also enter into the firm's operating and strategic decisions, such as where in the world to source inputs and sell final products. And for long-term strategic decisions, such as whether to build or acquire productive resources in a particular country, the firm needs forecasts of exchange rates to measure the competitiveness of alternative location choices.

While numerous business and financial decisions depend on exchange rate forecasts, there is considerable skepticism about the possibility of accurate or useful forecasts. Sometimes this pessimistic view has been fostered by the alleged poor performance of popular models of exchange rate determination. If economists are not able to describe the fundamental determinants of exchange rates, the argument goes, clearly economic models will not be very helpful for forecasting. Another argument against successful forecasting is based on foreign exchange market efficiency. If markets are efficient, and prices fully reflect all available information, including structural economic information, then *unanticipated* exchange rate movements are only the results of unanticipated events—and by definition, these cannot be forecast.

Recently, several well-known economists have summarized this pessimistic view regarding our ability to explain exchange rate movements after the fact, or to forecast exchange rate changes before the fact. Richard Meese, whose study (with Kenneth Rogoff) highlighted the forecasting superiority of the random-walk model versus structural models, has argued:

> Economists do not yet understand the determinants of short- to medium-run movements in exchange rates. Neither models of exchange rates based on macroeconomic fundamentals nor the forecasts of market participants as embodied in the forward rate or survey data can explain exchange rate movements better than a naive alternative such as a random-walk model. Worse yet, exchange rate changes are hard to explain after the fact, even with the knowledge of actual fundamental variables. It remains an enigma why the current exchange rate regime has engendered a time series database where macroeconomic variables and exchange rates appear to be independent of one another.[1]

Along the same lines, but not quite so pessimistic, Jeffrey Frankel and Kenneth Froot have written that:

> It is now widely accepted that standard observable macroeconomic variables are not capable of explaining, much less predicting ex ante, the *majority* of short-term changes in the exchange rate.[2]

In this chapter, we propose a more optimistic view toward exchange rate forecasting than that suggested by the above comments. Some of the foundation for this optimism was laid in Chapter 6, where during certain periods we saw a significant association between exchange rate movements and traditional macroeconomic fundamentals. We also showed evidence that some structural models appeared capable of outperforming the random walk in out-of-sample tests, and that short-run exchange rate changes were not dissociated with economics events. Rather, foreign exchange changes appeared closely connected with "news" about key fundamental economic variables. In Chapter 7, we saw that certain technical models appeared able to generate buy and sell signals in the spot market, which led to substantial speculative profit. And other econometric tests showed that available information could improve the ability of the forward rate to track the future spot rate.[3]

Despite these rays of hope, the reader would be wise to maintain a healthy skepticism on the topic of exchange rate forecasting. While forecasting economic variables may be possible, forecasting them for profit should not. Market prices (of spot and forward exchange) should already reflect the information in our forecasts. All of the exchange rate models we have discussed and all of the econometric techniques we will propose are well known and in the public domain. If these models and forecasting techniques are in widespread use, it is reasonable to presume that there are no unusual profits to be made by using what is already known.

---

[1]Meese (1990), p. 132.

[2]Frankel and Froot (1990), p. 181, emphasis added.

[3]Note, however, that these two strands of reasoning are at odds with each other. Chapter 6 says that forecasting is possible because economic models work and fundamentals matter, while Chapter 7 suggests that forecasting is possible because markets are not efficient. We will address this seeming contradiction.

We begin this chapter by developing its central theme—that more insights about exchange rate forecasting are possible if we clearly define the market setting, meaning the exchange rate system, the forecasting horizon, and the units of the forecast. Narrowing the problem in this way, we argue, may make it possible to identify a forecasting approach that shows promise based on an empirical track record. We show several real-life examples of how this classification system (exchange rate system, horizon, and unit of forecast) combined with the economic foundations developed in Chapters 6 and 7 can be applied to exchange rate forecasting.

Further, we will show that the forecasting performance of any model (say, purchasing power parity) is usually measured in a much too demanding fashion—usually how accurately the individual model performs for forecasting a single currency—that at the same time does not shed light on the value of the forecast in guiding hedging or investment decisions. We will propose an alternative measure of forecaster performance—usefulness rather than accuracy—and demonstrate that this measure is more appropriate and meaningful for a broad class of financial decisions. Along the same lines, we will argue that the *economic value* of an exchange rate forecast is its *marginal value* when added to the other information at hand. Thus, analyzing forecasts one by one may seriously overstate or understate their value in financial decision making.

We then present some specific examples of forecasting methods. In particular, we reexamine the evidence for trends versus random walks in short-run exchange rate movements, and we review the evidence for forecasting exchange rates in the longer run. We also introduce the composite forecasting technique and show how it has been applied to exchange rate forecasting. We conclude the chapter by reviewing various policy issues and problems facing consumers and producers of exchange rate forecasts. In this chapter, we omit our usual discussion of policy issues facing public policymakers.

Resolving Controversies in Exchange Rate Forecasting

The Forecasting Approach and the Market Setting

The demands of managers for exchange rate forecasts are extremely varied.[4] Forecasts are required for currencies that float against the US\$, that are pegged within stated intervention bands, and that are traded within hybrid or mixed systems. Forecasts are required by traders for very short-run horizons, by treasury managers for the short- to medium-run horizons, and by corporate planners for long-run horizons. And when an investor holds a nominal asset (for example, a Mexican bond that pays the owner 1 million pesos in five years), he or she needs a forecast of the *nominal* US\$/peso exchange rate to value the asset. While an investor who owns 1 million square feet of factory space in Mexico City would prefer a forecast of the *real* US\$/peso exchange rate in order to value this asset.

With this wide range of objectives, it seems unlikely that a single forecasting approach would be advisable or lead to similar results in these varied settings. We propose that much of the confusion regarding whether successful exchange rate forecasting is possible (and how to go about it) can be resolved by adopting the framework presented in Figure 8.1. We will focus on three key factors: the exchange rate system, the forecasting horizon, and the units of the foreign exchange rate.

---

[4]In this chapter, we focus on forecasts of the exchange rate and exchange rate changes. Forecasts of exchange rate volatility (σ) are discussed in Chapter 12.

FIGURE 8.1   A Framework for Forecasting Exchange Rates

Factor	*Examples*
1. Exchange Rate System*	
Pegged	Bretton Woods period
Floating	Post–Bretton Woods period for many major countries
Hybrid systems	Bloc pegging [such as the European Monetary System], managed floating, target zones
2. Forecast Horizon	
Very short term	1, 2, 3 minutes, hours, days
Short term	1, 2, 3 weeks, months
Medium term	1, 2, 3 quarters
Long term	1, 2, 3 years, decades
3. Foreign Exchange Units	
Nominal	Home currency/Foreign currency
Real	Adjusted for relative inflation, deviations from PPP

*A list of all members of the IMF and their present exchange rate systems is reported every month in *International Financial Statistics.* As of December 31, 1998, 65 countries were classified on pegged rates, 46 countries as independently floating, 54 countries as managed floating, and 17 countries in bloc pegging or other arrangements.

Exchange Rate System.   The **exchange rate system** has an important effect on how we approach the exchange rate forecasting question. Under a **pegged exchange rate** regime, an exchange rate between two countries is allowed to vary within narrow bands. The pegged regime is maintained ultimately by central bank intervention at the upper and lower intervention points (recall Figure 2.2). Central bank intervention is supported by international reserves, which each country holds in finite supply. As long as the inflationary experience of the countries is similar, the pegged rate may be sustained. A prolonged period of inflation differences precedes a change in the international competitiveness of our countries, leading to a current account deficit and a loss of reserves in the higher inflation country. This situation is not sustainable in the long run.

Under a pegged-rate system, once an exchange rate becomes misaligned, the likely *direction of change* in the exchange rate is fairly easy to predict: depreciation in countries that have experienced losses in international reserves, excess inflation and current account deficits, and appreciation where there has been relatively low inflation and current account surpluses.[5] It also may be possible to infer the likely *magnitude of change* in the exchange rate needed to restore equilibrium. The deviation from purchasing power parity offers one natural estimate of the likely exchange rate change.[6] More complex estimates based on the change needed to restore external balance also may be computed.[7]

---

[5]Eichengreen, Rose, and Wyplosz (1995) establish these empirical regularities, and others, in a study of 81 devaluations and 20 revaluations in 20 OECD countries, 1959–1993.

[6]The PPP equilibrium rate can be computed in many ways: using different base years, base periods, and price indexes. So there is no *unique* PPP rate. For a sense of the variation in PPP rates and methodologies, see the recent estimates from several financial institutions, such as the UBS *PPP Chart Book,* Deutsche Bank's *FX Weekly,* and J. P. Morgan's *World Financial Markets.* The Deutsche Bank publication is available at the author's website <www.stern.nyu.edu/~rlevichbook1/links.htm>, and data on J. P. Morgan currency indexes are on the company's website <www.jpmorgan.com>.

[7]See Williamson (1985) for measures of the "Fundamental Equilibrium Exchange Rate." A recent monograph by Hinkle and Montiel (1999) extends this style of analysis to developing countries.

FIGURE 8.2   Actual and PPP Spot Rates: Mexico
Quarterly Data, 1957–1979

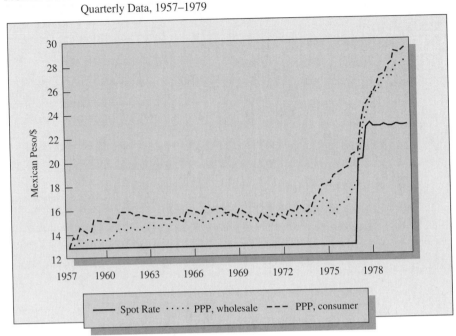

Note: Calculation uses 1957:1 as a base period.

Source: Author's calculations; data from *International Financial Statistics*.

While economic models may assist with the direction and magnitude of a likely exchange rate change (under pegged rates), these models offer little guidance about the *timing of change* since the decision to adjust the peg is typically a *political* decision. As such, the political party in power may resist a depreciation of the peg, feeling that a devaluation would confirm that its past policies were excessively inflationary and that a devaluation might ignite new rounds of wage and price inflation.

The experience of Mexico in the 1950s and 1960s broadly conforms to this description. As shown in Figure 8.2, the Mexican peso (MP) was pegged to the US$ at 12.5 MP/US$ from the early 1950s until mid-1976. Mexican inflation exceeded U.S. inflation throughout the 1950s and 1960s, leading to a PPP rate of roughly 15 MP/US$ (arbitrarily using the first quarter of 1957 as a base period). But this deviation from PPP was sustained for more than 15 years. In 1973, Mexican inflation accelerated, and the PPP rate rose to 19 MP/US$ using wholesale prices, and 21 MP/US$ using consumer prices. On September 1, 1976, the Mexican peso was devalued to 20 MP/US$. This change was clearly in the direction suggested by PPP and also remarkably close to the magnitude predicted by PPP. Purchasing power parity theory, however, offered little guidance on the timing of the exchange rate change.

Economists have attempted to model the political and economic events that might presage an exchange rate change. John Bilson (1979) examined a monetary model of the exchange rate and an international liquidity variable (measured as the stock of international reserves relative to the monetary base) as indicators of discrete exchange rate changes. He found that the monetary model frequently offers a good proxy for the magnitude of devaluation and that the international liquidity ratio provides a leading indicator of the actual devaluation date. Examples of this approach for three devaluations of Latin American currencies are shown in Figure 8.3. In each case, when the international liquidity indicator falls substantially relative to its historical norm, the actual exchange rate depreciates thereafter within one to two years. The technique is not foolproof, but as Bilson (1979, p. 79) concludes, "the two indicators . . . appear to offer exchange rate forecasters a great deal of useful information."[8]

Under a **floating exchange rate system,** the exchange rate is free to adjust quickly in response to changing relative macroeconomic conditions. A floating exchange rate reflects the speculative dynamics of the market—with prices moving by large amounts in response to unanticipated changes in economic fundamentals, and short-run price movements overshooting their required long-term adjustment. Forecasting in a floating exchange rate environment is easier when the market is efficient in processing available information, but forecasting for profit can be more difficult for the same reason.

Forecasting under various **hybrid exchange rate systems**—such as the European Monetary System (bloc pegging), managed floating, or a target zone system—could reflect elements of both the pegged and floating process. Under the Exchange Rate Mechanism (ERM) of the European Monetary System, exchange rates are guided primarily by market forces within the upper and lower intervention points. At the extremities of the band, the question of sustainability of the central rate versus realignment becomes critical. At the extremities of the band, the "one-way bet" described for pegged rates becomes operative. PPP will likely give a reasonable approximation of where the next central rate realignment is headed. But the timing of the realignment is uncertain, guided again by economic considerations (such as the stock of international reserves and the willingness to incur intervention losses) and political considerations (such as the strength of the country's commitment to the ERM).

The DM/Italian lira rate illustrates this situation well. Figure 8.4 shows that in 1988 the lira became increasingly overvalued against the DM within the ERM. This overvaluation continued and even widened during 1990 and 1991. In September 1992, the lira broke loose from its ERM ties with the DM and was permitted to depreciate, roughly restoring its PPP value.

While the timing of an ERM realignment is uncertain, several techniques may be useful. The standard approach considers the interest differential as an implicit exchange rate forecast.[9] The interest differential implies a forward rate. When this forward is outside the ERM band, some probability of realignment is present.[10] However, the implied forward rate measure tends to be a late signal of actual realignment.

An alternative approach proposed by José Campa and Kevin Chang (1996) uses option prices on European cross-rates (like the FFr/DM and DM/£) to measure the "intensity" of exchange rate realignments, where intensity is the product of the probability and magnitude of a realignment. One step in their argument is that the upper limit of the

---

[8]More recently, Klein and Marion (1997) and Kaminsky, Lizondo, and Reinhart (1998) have investigated leading economic and political indicators of exchange rate changes. Berg and Pattillo (1999) evaluate several models for predicting currency crises and find that their predictive power is limited. Research on "speculative attacks" and balance of payments crises (Krugman, 1979, and Flood and Garber, 1983) also addresses the timing of major exchange rate changes.

[9]See Svensson (1992, 1993) for a survey of the literature on target zones and the credibility of commitments to the ERM, and Rose and Svennson (1994) for an update.

[10]For example, on February 18, 1983, the FFr/DM spot rate was 2.8363, less than the upper limit of 2.8977 (See Figure 2.5a). However, with the three-month Euro-FFr and Euro-DM interest rates at 23.75 percent and 5.625 percent, to preserve interest rate parity, the forward FFr/DM rate traded at 2.9629, greater than the upper limit. The FFr devalued several weeks later on March 18 (See Table 2.3).

FIGURE 8.3 Leading Indicators for Exchange Rate Changes in Mexico, Peru, and Ecuador

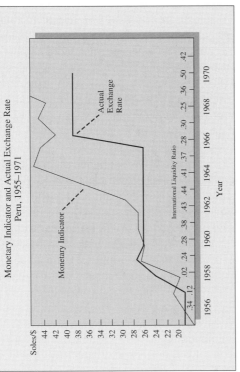

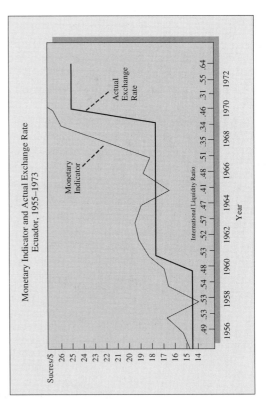

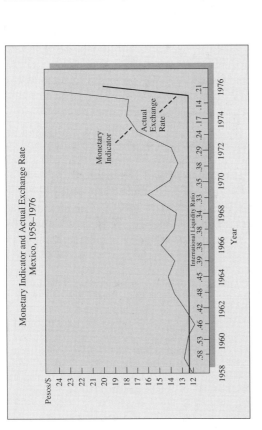

Note: *Monetary Indicator* is the prediction of the equilibrium exchange rate based on the monetary model. *International Liquidity Ratio* is international reserves as a percentage of high-powered money.

Source: Bilson (1979)

FIGURE 8.4   **Actual and PPP Spot Rate—DM/Italian Lira**

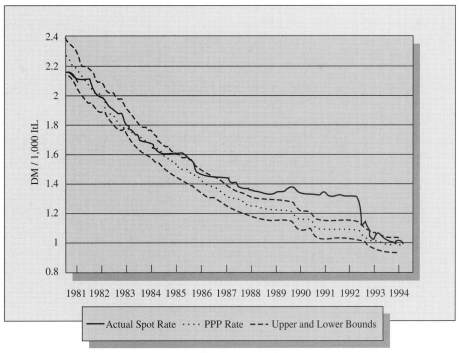

Note: The three lines moving together in the graph represent the estimated PPP rate and its upper and lower bound. During the late 1980s and early 1990s, the lira became progressively overvalued against the DM on a PPP basis, until the lira was devalued in September 1992.

Source: Swiss Bank Corporation, *PPP Chart Book,* Aug. 1994.

ERM band places an upper limit on the price of an option—if the upper band is credible.[11] Campa and Chang show that option prices provide a far earlier signal of ERM realignment than the simple interest differential. For more on the use of option prices for currency forecasting, see Box 12.2 in the chapter on options.

The recent experience of the Mexican peso illustrates the difficulty of forecasting a managed float. In the early 1990s, the MP was permitted to depreciate along a glide path of about 5 percent per year. In Figure 8.5, we see that at the end of 1993 the MP traded at 3.1 MP/$ and was overvalued by conventional PPP measures (3.5 MP/$ using the CPI and 4.1 MP/$ using the PPI, taking the first quarter of 1985 as a base period).[12] The overvaluation persisted until late 1994, supported largely by a favorable domestic investment climate and strong foreign capital inflows.

Mexico's international reserves surged during this period, from about $5 billion in 1990 to nearly $30 billion in early 1994 (see Figure 8.6). Capital inflows continued to support the peso into January 1994 despite an armed uprising in Chiapas. After presidential candidate Colosio was assassinated in March, Mexico's reserves fell by more

---

[11]For example, consider a three-month call option on the DM written in 1992 with a strike price of 3.35 FFr/DM. The upper limit of the FFr/DM rate was then 3.4293 FFr/DM. The present value of the call cannot exceed the present value of the largest payout (0.793 FFr) if the upper limit of 3.4293 FFr/DM is fully credible. A higher option price would imply some probability of ERM collapse.

[12]By some methods the extent of overvaluation is even greater. See Swiss Bank Corporation, *PPP Chart Book* (1994), p. 23.

FIGURE 8.5   **Actual and PPP Spot Rates: Mexico**
Quarterly Data, 1985:1–1995:4

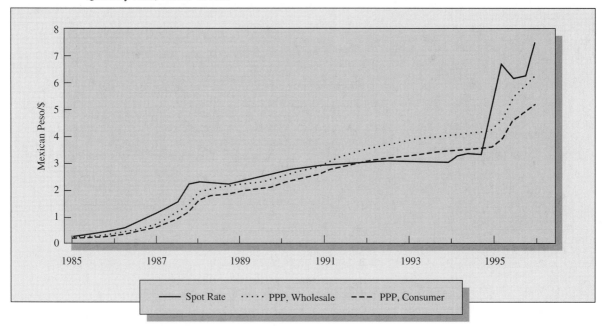

Note: Calculation takes 1985:1 as a base period.

Source: Author's calculations; data from *International Financial Statistics.*

than $10 billion. Capital inflows dried up, but the government resisted devaluation, reportedly from a "not-on-my-watch" mentality. Mexico continued to lose reserves in October and November (see Figure 8.6). When new president Ernesto Zadillo took office on December 1, he saw there was little choice but to devalue the peso and let it float freely.[13]

The peso collapsed, depreciating by 100 percent from about 3.40 MP/$ before the crisis to 6.82 MP/$ in March 1995. The peso became undervalued on a PPP basis, but a period of undervaluation is common after a devaluation.[14] Local prices and the PPP rate rose at a faster rate in 1995. By year-end, the peso hit 7.50 MP/$.

Forecast Horizon.   Another important element in selecting a forecasting approach is the *forecast horizon*. It seems reasonable to assume that some techniques would be more suitable for very short-run forecasts while others are more effective at longer-run horizons. For example, many macroeconomic fundamentals (such as inflation, national income, and the trade balance) are reported on a monthly or quarterly basis and sometimes after a long time lag, which makes it difficult to forecast *daily* exchange rates using fundamentals. On the other hand, using a random-walk model to forecast exchange rates 5

---

[13]An important forecasting issue is whether investors learned the value of reserves in a timely manner. See "Peso Surprise," *The Wall Street Journal,* July 6, 1995, for an account of the Mexican crisis.

[14]See Eichengreen, Rose, and Wyplosz (1995) for an analysis of the behavior of various macroeconomic variables before and after changes in pegged exchange rates.

FIGURE 8.6   Mexico's International Reserves

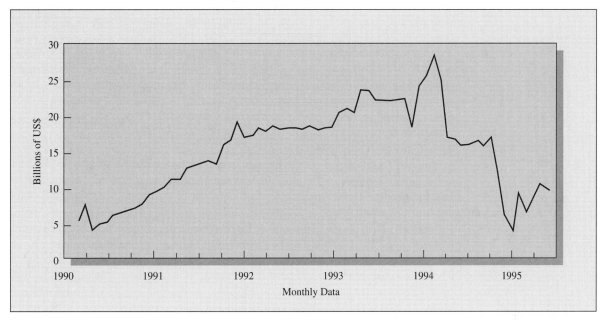

Source: *International Financial Statistics.*

or 10 years in the future seems to place virtually no weight on economic fundamentals, which could have a dramatic effect on rates over such a long period.

Market participants seem to recognize that constraining themselves to a single model for exchange rate forecasting needlessly imposes a high cost. In a survey of several hundred London foreign exchange market participants, Mark Taylor and Helen Allen (1992) reported that 90 percent of respondents place greater reliance on technical models for their very short-run (intraday to one-week) forecasts. As the forecast horizon lengthens, more respondents turn to fundamentals to guide their exchange rate expectations. At the one-year (or longer) horizon, roughly 85 percent of the respondents rely primarily on economic fundamentals.

Some of the empirical evidence that we have already reviewed supports this assignment of technical models to short-run forecasts and fundamental models to longer-run forecasts. In Chapter 7, we saw that various technical models appeared to successfully predict the trend behavior of daily spot exchange rates. These studies showed the effectiveness of filter rules, moving average crossover rules, and other technical indicators for many currencies over most of the floating exchange rate period. A study by Chuck Kwok and Linda Van de Gucht (1991) applied the filter rule technique to DM/$ exchange rates sampled at 30-minute intervals over the February 1, 1985–August 15, 1989, period. The results show strong evidence that small filter rules applied to high-frequency, intradaily exchange rates result in statistically significant trading profits throughout the period. With these results, the preference for using technical models to forecast short-run directional changes in exchange rates is easily understood.

We also demonstrated in Chapter 6 that a large proportion of unanticipated exchange rate changes is associated with "news" about macroeconomic fundamentals—such as the money supply, national income, the trade balance, and the current account.

It follows that firms might invest resources in an attempt to forecast these fundamentals more accurately than the consensus forecast, with the expectation of earning a payoff through short-run speculation in the foreign exchange market around the dates of macroeconomic news announcements.[15]

At the other end of the horizon spectrum, we indicated that certain fundamental factors may have a tendency to exert themselves clearly in the longer run. For example, while deviations from purchasing power parity may be large and persistent, they have a tendency to dampen out over time. Thus, while PPP is a poor stand-alone predictor of the exchange rate on a period-by-period basis, it may offer useful supplemental information about the drift of the exchange rate over time. We will see an empirical demonstration of this in the next section.

In the middle range of horizons, forecasting exchange rates may become more difficult. These horizons may be too short for fundamental factors to take effect, and too long for technical factors to offer useful signals. This is unfortunate because it is in these horizons that many financial hedging decisions are planned. Still, in the next section we will refer to several types of **composite forecasts** that suggest that more creative and efficient use of available information may produce significant forecasting gains.

Foreign Exchange Units.   Finally, it is necessary for forecasters to clarify the *units of the exchange rate* they wish to forecast, thus making a distinction between real and nominal exchange rates. In the short run with price levels relatively constant, changes in the nominal exchange rate and the real exchange rate are virtually the same. But in the longer run, the nominal and real exchange rates may take substantially different courses. Investors who hold nominal assets, such as Eurocurrency deposits or foreign government bonds, need to forecast the nominal exchange rate in order to estimate the domestic currency value of their foreign assets.

We have expressed some optimism about forecasting the nominal exchange rate in the very short run, but as the forecasting horizon lengthens, forecasting the nominal exchange rate becomes more subject to error. In part, this reflects the statistical phenomenon that the forecast error of any series, even a **stationary series,** increases with the forecasting horizon.[16] More details on the forecasting properties of stationary series versus the random walk, a **nonstationary series,** are reviewed in Box 8.1.

The greater problem is that as time passes, a central bank may permanently increase its nominal money supply (relative to output), thus raising its nominal price level and causing the nominal exchange rate to climb to a new level. As we saw in Figure 4.5, the nominal exchange rate has no affinity for a mean value. Since the nominal money supply can be expanded without limits, the nominal exchange rate is not anchored at any fixed value. Thus, holders of long-term nominal assets are at risk that these assets could be greatly depreciated over time.

In comparison, the real exchange rate may be difficult to predict in the short run. Deviations from PPP of 10 percent, 20 percent, 30 percent, and more may be observed

---

[15]A real-life illustration of this approach is described in Jeffrey L. Hiday, "How Do You Make $3.5 Million or So in Two Minutes?" *The Wall Street Journal,* February 10, 1997. Traders at Goldman Sachs reportedly purchased positions totaling $500 million in interest rate futures contracts at 8:28 A.M., two minutes before a scheduled announcement of U.S. employment figures. The announcement surprised the market—but not these traders, who closed out their positions moments later and pocketed their profits. Hiday's article cautions that these large bets do not always pay off, but the style of short-run speculation based on fundamental news announcements is well established.

[16]A stationary series is one generated by drawings from the same, unchanging probability distribution. The mean of a stationary series is the same whether we sample the first 100 observations, the last 100, or any other subsample.

in any year. However, over the long run the tendency for PPP to hold means that periods of over- and undervaluation should cancel out, so that the real exchange rate will be stationary, reverting back to its mean (equilibrium) level. A long-run forecast of the real exchange rate can be made with relative confidence, especially under the assumption that real shocks in the two economies will be similar.[17] (Again, see Box 8.1 for details.)

Holders of real, productive assets need to know the real exchange rate in order to value the expected cash flows generated by their real assets. Suppose an investor owns real productive assets in Mexico and generates income by selling a product at price P_t^* (in MP) which is valued at P_t^*/S_t in US\$. If the real exchange rate is constant, any MP depreciation ($S\uparrow$) will be matched by local inflation ($P*\uparrow$), thus preserving the US\$ value of Mexican sales. Holders of real, productive assets should be more concerned about the real exchange rate than the nominal exchange in order to value their assets. The predictability of the long-term real exchange rate is an important assumption often invoked to value foreign investment projects. In a world where nominal shocks dominate and real shocks are somewhat evenly distributed across countries over time, we may expect that it would be easier to forecast the real exchange rate in the long run than to forecast the nominal exchange rate.

Forecast Performance Evaluation: Accurate versus Useful Forecasts

Another source of controversy surrounding the value of exchange rate forecasts is the method of measuring performance. The traditional econometric approach begins with the forecast error made at time t, defined as:

$$e_t = \frac{(\hat{S}_{t,j} - S_{t+j})}{S_{t+j}}$$

where $\hat{S}_{t,j}$ is the j-period ahead forecast made at time t and S_{t+j} is the actual spot rate at time $t + j$. Intuitively, it seems natural to prefer forecasts that produce smaller errors. Thus, criteria such as the following are often adopted as measures of performance:

Mean Error:	ME	$= (\Sigma_i\, e_i)/n$
Mean Absolute Error:	MAE	$= (\Sigma_i\, |e_i|)/n$
Mean Squared Error:	MSE	$= (\Sigma_i\, e_i^2)/n$
Root Mean Squared Error:	RMSE	$= \sqrt{\text{MSE}}$

It is possible to produce a small mean error as a result of large negative and positive individual errors. Therefore, in practice, the MAE and RMSE are more commonly used to estimate the average error size.[18]

But all of these traditional measures could be seriously misleading when the forecast is used for financial hedging or speculative purposes. Consider the forecasts

---

[17]If real shocks are dissimilar, there may be a permanent change in the real exchange rate. For countries at similar stages of development (e.g., the United States and Canada), it may be plausible to assume that real shocks are similar. But they need not be; one country could experience war, climate changes, mineral discoveries, and so on, which the other country does not. For countries at different stages of development (e.g., the United States and Mexico), it is more plausible to assume that some real productivity shocks will effect the two countries differently over long periods.

[18]In theory, the MAE is appropriate when the cost of a forecast error varies linearly with the magnitude of the error. The RMSE is appropriate when the cost of a forecast error is a quadratic function of the magnitude of the error.

Box 8.1

The Difference between Forecasting a Random Walk and an "Almost Random" Walk

Students often encounter the term *random walk* in discussions of efficiency and forecasting in financial markets. A random walk is a very special kind of series; a series that is "almost" a random walk behaves very differently. The following equation describes an exchange rate where each current value (S_t) depends on an earlier value (S_{t-1}) plus a random error term (u_t).

$$S_t = \phi S_{t-1} + u_t \qquad (8A.1)$$

When the parameter $\phi = 1$, the spot rate evolves as a random walk without drift. In the random-walk case, today's exchange rate (S_t) is the same as yesterday's exchange rate (S_{t-1}) except for the random-error term. Expressed somewhat differently, the exchange rate change ($S_t - S_{t-1}$) is simply a random error term (u_t).

Forecasting an exchange rate like that shown in equation (8A.1) is not so difficult. Always begin by writing down the definition of the rate for the date in which we are interested. Suppose we want to predict the exchange rate one step ahead. This is defined as:

$$S_{t+1} = \phi S_t + u_{t+1} \qquad (8A.2)$$

Suppose we want to predict the exchange rate two steps ahead. This is defined as:

$$S_{t+2} = \phi S_{t+1} + u_{t+2}$$

By using the definition of S_{t+1} given in equation (8A.2), we can rewrite the above equation as:

$$S_{t+2} = \phi (\phi S_t + u_{t+1}) + u_{t+2}$$

or

$$S_{t+2} = \phi^2 S_t + u_{t+1} + u_{t+2} \qquad (8A.3)$$

The three-step-ahead exchange rate is defined as:

$$S_{t+3} = \phi S_{t+2} + u_{t+3}$$

By using the definition of S_{t+2} given in equation (8A.3), we can rewrite the above equation as:

$$S_{t+3} = \phi (\phi^2 S_t + \phi u_{t+1} + u_{t+2}) + u_{t+3}$$

or

$$S_{t+3} = \phi^3 S_t + \phi^2 u_{t+1} + \phi u_{t+2} + u_{t+3} \quad (8A.4)$$

So in general, the *n*-step-ahead definition of the exchange rate is:

$$S_{t+n} = \phi^n S_t + \phi^{n-1} u_{t+1} \qquad (8A.5)$$
$$+ \phi^{n-2} u_{t+2} + \ldots \phi u_{t+n-1} + u_{t+n}$$

Figure A
Making *n*-Step-Ahead Forecasts
With First-Order Autoregressive, $\phi = x$

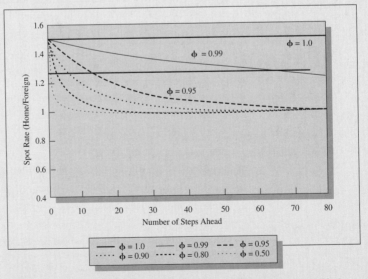

Note: If the exchange rate follows a random walk ($\phi = 1.0$), the forecast for any period in the future will be identical to the current spot rate (1.5 in the above chart). But if $\phi < 1.0$, the exchange rate will revert back to its mean value (1.0 in the above chart). The spot rate $S = 1.25$ shows where one-half of the gap between 1.5 and 1.0 has been reversed.

Now let's forecast! To forecast S_{t+n}, we take the expectation, $E(S_{t+n})$, which is the expectation of the right-hand-side of equation (8A.5). But note that the expectation of every error term is zero, $E(u_i) = 0$. So, our forecast of any future spot rate is:

$$E(S_{t+n}) = \phi^n S_t \qquad (8A.6)$$

For the random walk, $\phi = 1$. So, the forecast of the spot rate for *any* future date is simply today's spot rate. In Figure A, the current spot rate is shown as 1.5 units. The forecast for any future date is simply the horizontal line at 1.5.

But suppose that the exchange rate is not quite a random walk. Suppose that ϕ is 0.99, or 0.95, or 0.90 rather than unity. Now the term ϕ^n is less than 1 and greater than zero, and ϕ^n decreases as n increases. Thus, the exchange rate in the future will decay back toward its mean value. In Figure A, we have taken $S = 1$ as the mean value of the spot rate. If the exchange rate is hit with a shock ($u_t \neq 0$) and moves away from its mean, with $\phi < 1$ the rate has a tendency to return back to its mean. When $\phi < 1$, the exchange rate can be called a stationary or mean-reverting series. In our example, starting from a 50 percent overvaluation (relative to the mean), it takes about 6, 13, or 65 periods for the rate to make up half of its overvaluation (to a value of 1.25) when $\phi = 0.90, 0.95$, and 0.99, respectively.

How much confidence do we have in these forecasts? Going back to the definition of S_{t+n} in equation (8A.5), the variance of the forecast is the variance of the right-hand-side terms. The variance calculation is simplified because each random error term has the same variance. So, we have:

$$\sigma^2(S_{t+n}) = \sigma^2(u)\,(1 + \phi + \phi^2 + \phi^3 + \ldots \phi^n)$$

For the random walk, $\phi = 1$. Thus, the variance of the forecast for *any* future date increases along with the length of the forecast, *and it grows without bounds!* In Figure B, we show how the forecast variance grows in a linear fashion for the case $\phi = 1.0$ and $\sigma^2(u) = 1.0$.

But suppose that ϕ is 0.99, or 0.95, or 0.90 rather than unity. Now the terms ϕ^i are less than 1 and approach zero as n increases. Now the forecast variance grows as the horizon increases, but reaches a limit as $n \to \infty$.*

Overall, if an exchange rate follows a random walk without drift (1) any forecast of the future is the same as today's rate, no matter how far ahead we forecast, and (2) the exchange rate has no tendency to return toward its (prior) mean value. The random walk is an example of a *nonstationary* series. However, if ϕ is only slightly less than unity, the series will have a tendency to return back toward its mean level, and the forecast variance is finite. These cases with $\phi < 1$ are examples of *stationary* series. The small difference in ϕ creates a big difference in how we think about the exchange rate process.

---

*The limit of the geometric summation is $\sigma^2(u)/(1 - \phi^2)$.

FIGURE B
Variance of *n*-Step-Ahead Forecasts
With First-Order
Autoregressive, $\phi = x$

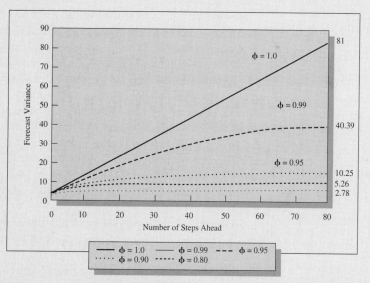

Note: When $\phi = 1.0$, the exchange rate follows a random walk and the variance of the forecast errors grow without bounds. When $\phi < 1$, the variance is bounded. When $n = 80$, the variance is 40.39, 10.25, 5.26, and 2.78 for $\phi = 0.99, 0.95, 0.90$, and 0.80, respectively. These calculations assume that $\sigma^2(u) = 1.0$.

FIGURE 8.7   **Illustrating a Pitfall in Forecast Error Analysis**
Two Forecasts of the US$/£ Exchange Rate

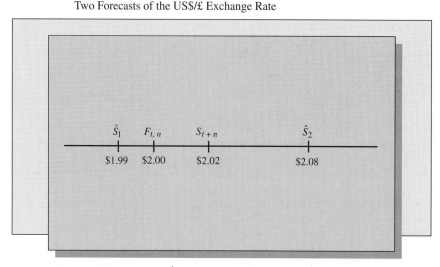

Note: One forecast of the US$/£ exchange rate, $\hat{S}_1$ = $1.99, predicts a depreciation of £ relative to the forward rate. Another forecast, $\hat{S}_2$ = $2.08, predicts an appreciation of £ relative to the forward rate. Given the actual future spot rate of $2.02, forecast $\hat{S}_2$ is on the right side of the market, even though forecast $\hat{S}_1$ was more accurate.

represented in Figure 8.7. The present forward rate is $2.00/£, and two alternative forecasts are $\hat{S}_1$ = $1.99/£ and $\hat{S}_2$ = $2.08/£. When the future spot rate is realized, let its value be $2.02/£. So, the error associated with $\hat{S}_1$ is −$0.03 and the error associated with $\hat{S}_2$ is +$0.06. If these individual forecasts are representative of a series of forecasts, conventional analysis would show that forecast 1 is superior to forecast 2 because forecast 1 is more accurate.

However, a closer look at these forecasts reveals that forecast 1 in effect advised speculators to short £ in the forward market, and advised US$-based investors to hedge their long £ positions in advance of a predicted depreciation of £. In Figure 8.7, we can see that this hedging and speculative advice was incorrect because £ actually appreciated relative to the forward rate. Forecast 2 was not very accurate, but it led to correct and profitable advice: US$-based speculators would have profited by establishing long forward £ positions and US$-based investors should not have hedged their existing long £ positions.

Our example shows that it is important to distinguish between accurate forecasts and useful forecasts. **Accurate forecasts** have small forecasting errors gauged by traditional statistical measures such as the MAE or RMSE. **Useful forecasts** are those on the "right side of the market" and lead to profitable speculative positions and correct hedging decisions.

Some market participants need both accurate and useful forecasts. For example, a portfolio manager following forecast $\hat{S}_2$ might have taken large £ positions in anticipation of a 4 percent return on the currency (based on the $2.08 forecast relative to the $2.00 forward rate). If so, he may have been very disappointed to earn only 1 percent on the currency position (based on the $2.02 actual spot rate relative to the $2.00 forward rate).

But other market participants are primarily interested in useful forecasts. For example, consider the treasurer of a U.S. multinational firm that holds a £1 million account receivable. Following forecast $\hat{S}_2$, the treasurer decides not to hedge this receivable since the forecast calls for a stronger £. In our example, this turns out to be the correct hedging decision. Assuming that our treasurer does not have the authority to increase his £ position, his decision not to hedge the £ receivable is correct and he does not incur any incremental loss from the lack of forecasting accuracy.

To measure how often a forecaster's advice has been on the "right side of the market," we must have a measure of "the market." In the absence of a currency risk premium, "right side of the market" implies "right side of the forward rate." Thus, useful forecasts are those that lead to correct hedging decisions. By this measure, forecasts are either "correct" or "incorrect" leading to a simple binomial test for the presence of forecasting expertise or market timing ability.[19] To begin this test, consider the 2×2 matrix below:

		Actual Exchange Rate Change	
		$S_{t+j} > F_{t,j}$	$S_{t+j} < F_{t,j}$
Predicted Exchange Rate Change	$\hat{S}_{t,j} > F_{t,j}$	Correct	Incorrect
	$\hat{S}_{t,j} < F_{t,j}$	Incorrect	Correct

A forecaster's performance in terms of usefulness can be summarized by the percentage of correct forecasts. We define the percentage of correct forecasts as:

$$p = \frac{r}{n}$$

where

r = number of correct forecasts

n = total number of forecasts

A test for forecasting expertise, or market timing, is simply:

$$H_0: p = 0.5 \text{ (no timing or expertise)}$$

$$H_1: p > 0.5 \text{ (positive timing or expertise)}$$

According to the binomial distribution, the expected value of p is r/n, and the standard deviation of p is $\sqrt{p(1-p)/n}$. An example of this method is presented in Box 8.2.

Assessing the Economic Value of Currency Forecasts

A related source of confusion surrounding forecast performance evaluation is the connection between statistical significance and economic significance. As we just examined,

---

[19]When a risk premium ($RP_{t,j}$) is present, the comparison should be drawn to the market's expected future spot rate ($F_{t,j} - RP_{t,j}$) rather than simply the forward rate. If the probability of correct forecasts in up and down markets is allowed to differ, then the simple binomial test must be modified. See Henriksson and Merton (1981) for the theoretical development and Cumby and Modest (1987) for an application to foreign exchange forecasting.

Box 8.2

Evaluating a Forecasting Track Record Using the Percentage Correct Method

Consider a forecaster who makes 100 forecasts as summarized in the table below. The overall track record is 60 correct forecasts out of 100 total forecasts, so $p = r/n = 0.60$. Under the null hypothesis of no expertise, the forecaster would expect a track record of $p^* = 0.50$.

The statistical test we propose is much the same as the analysis of coin-tossing experiments where the problem is to calculate the probability of tossing 60 heads in 100 attempts with a fair coin. In our case, we want to determine whether the realized track record represents real forecasting expertise or simply a run of good luck. In coin-tossing experiments, p is generated from a binomial distribution. If the sample size is large, we can use the normal distribution as a close approximation.

Our estimate of p is 0.60. Under the null hypothesis, $\sigma(p) = [p^* \times (1 - p^*)/n]^{0.5} = (0.5 \times 0.5/100)^{0.5} = 0.05$. Using the normal approximation, the test statistic:

$$Z = \frac{(p - p^*)}{\sigma(p)}$$

allows us to test the null hypothesis. In this case:

$$Z = \frac{(0.6 - 0.5)}{0.05} = 2.0$$

Thus, the realized track record in this example is two standard deviations greater than 0.50. By consulting a normal distribution table, we find that a Z-score of 2.0 corresponds with a probability of about 2.3 percent. The right-tail probability area (labeled p_1) shown in the figure represents the probability that the observed (or a superior) track record could have occurred by pure chance. In this case, because p_1 is only 2.3 percent, we would most likely reject the "good luck" explanation, and conclude that the track record shows genuine forecasting expertise.

As with any statistical method, there is a chance that we will reach a false conclusion. Consider another forecaster who genuinely possesses expertise and an average track record of 60 percent. Nevertheless, there is a probability (p_2) that in any sample of 100 forecasts, his or her number of correct forecasts will be below 50.

	Forecast ($/£)	Forward Rate	Actual Future Spot Rate	Correct	Not Correct
1	1.52	1.50	1.51	Yes	
2	1.47	1.50	1.51		No
3	1.49	1.48	1.53	Yes	
. . .	. . .	. . .	. . .	. . .	. . .
99	1.63	1.60	1.58		No
100	1.65	1.60	1.62	Yes	
Total				60	40

the link between accurate forecasts and economic value is ambiguous. An accurate forecast on the wrong side of the forward rate has no economic value. On the other hand, an inaccurate forecast could be extremely valuable if it frequently puts the investor on the right side of the market. In a study of 42 Japanese currency forecasters, Graham Elliott and Takatoshi Ito (1999) showed that these forecasters are less accurate than the random-walk forecast. Nevertheless, the forecasts of 32 of the 42 forecasters are useful for generating profits at the one-month horizon.

Gordon Leitch and J. Ernest Tanner (1991) concluded that conventional tests based on accuracy and R^2 in regression analysis may be misleading if investors adopt forecasts on the basis of usefulness or profitability criteria.[20] For example, a regression model that explains only 5–10 percent of exchange rate changes might seem of little value. As we

---

[20]See also Elliott and Ito (1999) for examples using foreign exchange forecasts.

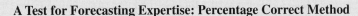

A Test for Forecasting Expertise: Percentage Correct Method

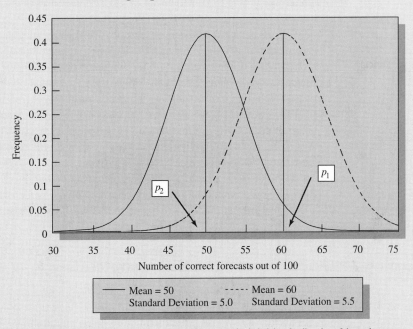

Mean = 50	Mean = 60
Standard Deviation = 5.0	Standard Deviation = 5.5

Note: In a sample of 100 forecasts, a forecaster with no expertise in judging the direction of the exchange rate has some probability (p_1) of turning in a superior track record of 60 or better out of 100. And a superior forecaster who averages 60 out of 100 correct forecasts has a probability (p_2) of a track record that is worse than 50 percent.

will show in the next section, a model with a small but statistically significant explanatory power may result in highly profitable currency trading strategies. A possible explanation for this is that a marginal change in a forecasting equation may substantially alter the *direction* of the forecast, and thus have a significant effect on profitability even though it stems from a negligible change in forecasting accuracy.

But even the link between useful forecasts and economic value is ambiguous. A statistically significant track record of 55–60 percent correct forecasts may be insufficient to produce profitable results. This would occur if the profits on the correct forecasts did not exceed the losses on the incorrect forecasts. On the other hand, a small excess of correct predictions (or even *no* excess of correct predictions) can lead to considerable profit.

One explanation for this outcome is that the forecaster may be better at forecasting large changes. For example, suppose that every incorrect forecast produces a loss of

−0.1 percent while every correct forecast produces a gain of 0.6 percent. If correct and incorrect forecasts are equal in number, the forecasts generate an average profit of 0.25 percent per forecast. A similar illustration can be found in the context of a technical trading model. A technical trading model is likely to reverse one incorrect decision quickly, resulting in a small loss, while allowing one correct decision to run on into a lengthy profitable string. But even in a hedging context, a 60 percent track record of correct forecasts gives the firm three correct decisions for every two that are incorrect—a result that could put the firm well ahead of a strategy of simply guessing or following a naive hedging rule.

Finally, in most analyses of currency forecasting models, the model's performance is measured in isolation: for a single currency, a single horizon, and as the sole explanatory measure of the currency's future value. While the business success of professional forecasters (who charge for their forecasts) may depend on their track record measured in isolation, users of a forecast should be more interested in the forecast's *marginal* value, measured by its marginal impact on accuracy, usefulness, and speculative or hedging performance. This notion suggests that a forecast could be either accurate or useful, but if it is highly correlated with other available forecasts, the forecast does not have much marginal value. On the other hand, a forecast could be neither particularly accurate nor useful, but if it is *not* highly correlated with other available forecasts, the forecast could have a large impact on a composite forecast produced by aggregating available information. We will examine this method of forecasting in the next section.

Forecasting Methods: Some Specific Examples

In this section we summarize several methods of forecasting exchange rates that appear to have enjoyed some success. We will discuss why these methods appear to have been successful and what factors distinguish these models from those often considered by economists.

Short-Run Forecasts: Trends versus Random Walk

As we have discussed, many economists have concluded that short-run exchange rate movements are nearly random, so that a random-walk (with zero drift) forecast is the best short-term forecast that one can formulate. At the same time, we have highlighted technical, trend-following models that appear to earn profits from exploiting patterns in spot rates. These results stand in contradiction. How can exchange rates appear random to some researchers yet display patterns to other researchers?

Papers by John Bilson (1990, 1993) help to resolve this issue. Bilson argues that most studies of exchange rate behavior have used *linear regression* models similar to:

$$\text{Future trend} = \beta_0 + \beta_1 (\text{Past trend}) + e \tag{8.1}$$

to examine whether current exchange rate movements can be used to forecast the future. When equation (8.1) is estimated, the regression coefficient (β_1) is typically insignificantly different from zero. The results for the major currencies in Table 8.1 show that the β_1 coefficient (with the exception of the ¥ at one week) is not significant, and that the R^2 of these regressions is generally less than 1 percent. Hence, these results support a random-walk view—the future trend appears unrelated to the past trend.

The problem with this methodology, Bilson points out, is that linear regression analysis assumes a linear (proportionate) relationship. For example, if the past trend

TABLE 8.1   Linear Regressions of Future Trend versus Past Trend in Spot Exchange Rates

$$\ln(\text{Spot}_t/\text{Spot}_{t-1}) = \beta_0 + \beta_1 \ln(\text{Spot}_{t-1}/\text{Spot}_{t-2}) + \epsilon_t$$

Currency	Interval[a,b]	N	β_1 (t-ratio)	R^2	F (probability)	D.W.	Normality[c]	Heteroscedasticity[d]
Canadian dollar	1 week	938	0.0474 (1.45)	0.002	2.11 (.147)	2.00	.000	.065
	1 month	216	−0.0680 (1.00)	0.005	0.99 (.321)	2.00	.000	.811
	1 quarter	72	0.1030 (0.86)	0.011	0.75 (.391)	1.99	.529	.225
German mark	1 week	938	0.0378 (1.16)	0.001	1.34 (.248)	2.00	.000	.000
	1 month	216	−0.0073 (0.10)	0.000	0.01 (.915)	2.00	.008	.839
	1 quarter	72	0.0918 (0.76)	0.008	0.57 (.345)	1.90	.538	.735
Japanese yen	1 week	938	0.0729 (2.23)[e]	0.005	4.99 (.026)	2.01	.000	.006
	1 month	216	0.0633 (0.93)	0.004	0.86 (.354)	2.00	.115	.077
	1 quarter	72	0.1364 (1.15)	0.018	1.31 (.256)	1.97	.328	.472
Swiss franc	1 week	938	0.0139 (0.42)	0.000	0.18 (.671)	2.00	.000	.005
	1 month	216	0.0421 (0.62)	0.002	0.38 (.536)	2.01	.003	.292
	1 quarter	72	0.0364 (0.30)	0.001	0.09 (.765)	1.90	.922	.882
British pound	1 week	938	0.0310 (0.95)	0.001	0.90 (.342)	2.00	.000	.022
	1 month	216	0.1077 (1.59)	0.012	2.51 (.114)	2.01	.003	.147
	1 quarter	72	0.1984 (1.61)	0.036	2.59 (.112)	1.84	.683	.724

Notes:

a. Sample periods are January 3, 1975–December 31, 1992, for weekly data; 1975:1–1992:12 for monthly data; and 1975:1–1992:4 for quarterly data.

b. Regressions are estimated using OLS in MICROFIT version 3.0 software. Sample observations are nonoverlapping.

c. Normality test is based on skewness and kurtosis of residuals. Statistic reports probability that residuals are normally distributed.

d. Heteroscedasticity test is based on a regression of squared residuals on squared fitted values. Statistic reports probability that residuals are homoscedastic.

e. T-ratio for β_1 in Japanese yen, 1-week interval is 1.89, using White's heteroscedastic-consistent estimate of the standard error. The p-value on β_1 is 0.059 with this adjustment.

Source: Author's calculations. Weekly data are from *Harris Bank Weekly Review*; monthly data are end-of-month values and quarterly data are end-of-quarter values from *International Financial Statistics*.

FIGURE 8.8   Past Trends and Future Returns for Three Currencies

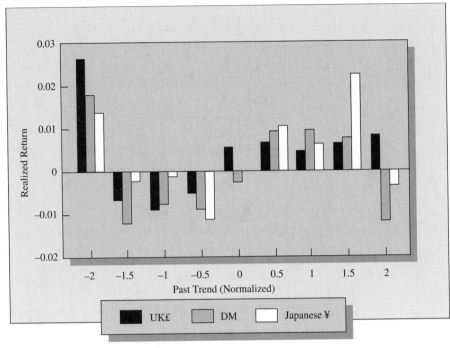

Note: Data are monthly over the period April 1975–April 1991. Past trend is measured by the change in the spot rate over a three-month period normalized by dividing by standard deviation (about 6 percent). Future return is measured by the one-month return on a long forward contract position.

Source: John F. O. Bilson, " 'Technical' Currency Trading," in *The Currency-Hedging Debate,* ed. Lee R. Thomas (London: IFR Publishing, 1990).

movement in the exchange rate is +10 percent, equation (8.1) predicts a larger movement in the future than if the past trend movement in the exchange rate had been only +5 percent. Most technical models would make far weaker quantitative predictions: If the exchange rate has gone up (down) in the past, it is likely to go up (down) in the future. Technical models do not impose a linear relationship such as that given in equation (8.1).

To better reflect the aims of technical analysis, Bilson graphs the relationship between the past spot rate trend and the future realized speculative return for the DM, £, and ¥ over the period from April 1975 to April 1991. Data on the spot rate trend (on the *X*-axis) are grouped into nine intervals, expressed in terms of σ, the volatility of the exchange rate trend.[21] As Figure 8.8 shows, the data clearly reject a linear relationship between past and future trends. Instead, in the interval (−1.5σ, +1.5σ) current upward (downward) trends seem to be followed by further upward (downward) movements. Thus, technical trend following might be successful in these regions, even though the relationship is not proportional.

However, for larger movements (1.75σ and greater), Figure 8.8 suggests that a reversal of direction is more likely than a continuation. These extreme data points run contrary to a linear relationship between past and future exchange rate changes. But they seem more consistent with a technical explanation that markets may become "overbought" or

---

[21]In these data, σ is about 6 percent.

TABLE 8.2 Regression Coefficients to Explain Future Currency Trend Using Dummy Variables Representing Past Currency Trend

Dummy Variable	Past Trend ($\Delta S_t/\sigma$)	Coefficient	T-Statistic
D_1	$\Delta S_t/\sigma < -1.75$	1.16	1.62
D_2	$-1.75 < \Delta S_t/\sigma < -1.25$	-0.31	0.64
D_3	$-1.25 < \Delta S_t/\sigma < -0.75$	-0.69	1.80
D_4	$-0.75 < \Delta S_t/\sigma < -0.25$	-0.80	2.50
D_5	$-0.25 < \Delta S_t/\sigma < +0.25$	-0.14	0.42
D_6	$+0.25 < \Delta S_t/\sigma < +0.75$	0.97	3.08
D_7	$+0.75 < \Delta S_t/\sigma < +1.25$	0.81	2.19
D_8	$+1.25 < \Delta S_t/\sigma < +1.75$	0.95	2.07
D_9	$+1.75 < \Delta S_t/\sigma$	-0.26	0.52

Notes: Sample period is April 1975–April 1991, using monthly data. The past trend variable is the percentage change in the spot rate normalized by its standard deviation. The regression is estimated after pooling the data for DM, £, and ¥.

When these dummy variables are combined to form the following "trend" variables:

Trend 1	$\Delta S_t > 0$		$D = +1$
	$\Delta S_t = 0$		$D = 0$
	$\Delta S_t > 0$		$D = -0$
Trend 2		$\Delta S_t/\sigma > +0.25$	$D = +1$
		$-0.25 \leq \Delta S_t/\sigma \leq +0.25$	$D = 0$
		$\Delta S_t/\sigma < -0.25$	$D = -1$
Trend 3		$0.25 \leq \Delta S_t/\sigma \leq +1.75$	$D = +1$
		$-0.25 \leq \Delta S_t/\sigma \leq +0.25$	$D = 0$
		$-1.75 \leq \Delta S_t/\sigma \leq -0.25$	$D = -1$

each "trend" variable is positively and significantly related to the future exchange rate return.

Bilson concludes: "The results demonstrate that there has been a predictable pattern of serial correlation in exchange rates which has not been captured by linear regression models."

Source: John F. O. Bilson, "Value, Yield, and Trend: A Composite Forecasting Approach to Foreign Exchange Trading," in *Strategic Currency Investing,* ed. A. Gitlin. Chicago: Probus, 1993.

"oversold" and that a trend reversal—perhaps stemming from a fundamental policy change or simply a change in sentiment—is more likely than a continuation.

The data in Figure 8.8 can be transformed into a dummy variable regression of the form:

$$\text{Future return}_t = \beta_0 + \beta_1 D_{1,t-1} + \beta_2 D_{2,t-1} + \ldots + \beta_9 D_{9,t-1} + e_t \quad (8.2)$$

where each dummy variable (D_i) takes the value +1 if the past price trend falls within a specified interval (see Table 8.2 for intervals), and zero otherwise. Equation (8.2) tests whether the "pattern" we observe in Figure 8.8 is significant or not. The results in Table 8.2 show that four of the dummy variables are significant and two others are marginally significant. When *trend* is defined in this nonlinear fashion, Bilson shows that future return is significantly related to past trend.[22]

Thus, the failure of traditional econometric models to find a connection between past trends and future trends may be the result of flawed methodology. The underlying relationships may be nonlinear. If so, linear regression will be unable to uncover them.

---

[22]Bilson shows that current trend could be defined in other ways, as in the notes to Table 8.2. Current trend so defined explains (in terms of R^2) 3–8 percent of the future trend, but still the relationship generates substantial trading profits.

Long-Run Forecasts: Reversion to the Mean?

The likelihood that long-term foreign exchange rate forecasting will be successful is enhanced when an economic model such as purchasing power parity or current account balance acts as an anchor to rein in unexpected short-term exchange rate changes. The notion of an anchor represents a long-term equilibrium value of the exchange rate that will always exert a force on the exchange rate. Without such an anchor, the exchange rate becomes a nonstationary series that may wander to any conceivable level.

In some early studies, economists could not reject the hypothesis that the real exchange rate follows a random walk, given by:

$$S_{real, t+1} = \phi \, S_{real, t} + e_{t+1}$$

with $\phi = 1$. This finding disturbed many economists. Because the real exchange rate measures the competitiveness between countries, it seems questionable that this variable could wander in an unconstrained fashion. The real exchange rate, most economists contend, ought to be determined by real factors and not allowed to take on any arbitrary value as in a random walk.

One statistical approach that helps restore a sense of anchoring is *cointegration* testing. To explain, imagine that one series follows a random walk. As a nonstationary series, it cannot be explained in terms of its own history. Imagine a second series that is also nonstationary and cannot be explained in terms of its own history. If series 1 and series 2 are related (by a cointegrating relationship), then the movement of the two series *relative to each other* is constrained. In our context, the real exchange rate may be nonstationary, but if it is related to a second series (such as relative inflation differentials), then the movement of the real rate is in this sense "connected" to fundamentals.[23]

Another approach is to question the reliability of the estimate of ϕ. If $\phi = 1$, the real exchange rate follows a random walk, a nonstationary series. But if $\phi = 0.999$, the series is stationary and will show an affinity to return to its mean value if temporarily disturbed. (See Box 8.1 for review.) Thus, the value of ϕ is critical and precision estimation matters greatly. Niso Abuaf and Philippe Jorion (1990) develop this argument carefully. For long time series of the \$/£ and \$/FFr, the authors show that ϕ is less than 1, so that the real exchange rate series is stationary and mean reverting (see Figure 4.5). And for the recent floating rate period, Abuaf and Jorion report that ϕ is closer to 0.98–0.99. For monthly data, this implies that "a 50 percent overappreciation of a currency with respect to PPP would take three to five years to be cut in half."[24]

Further tests for mean reversion were conducted by Philippe Jorion and Richard Sweeney (1996) on real exchange rates for 10 major countries. Over the 1973–1983 period, Jorion and Sweeney also find that the ϕ coefficient is close to 1.0, but significantly less than 1.0. Making use of this information improves forecasting accuracy (relative to the random-walk model) in 10 years of out-of-sample forecasts (1983–1993). Another test of mean reversion, by James Lothian and Mark Taylor (1996), examines nearly 200 years of data on dollar-sterling and French franc–sterling real exchange rates. Lothian and Taylor conclude that a significant tendency toward mean reversion ($\phi < 1.0$) was evident as early as 1973. Again, these authors conclude that taking mean reversion into account had a significant beneficial effect on forecasting accuracy, especially at horizons of three to five years.

---

[23]See Coughlin and Koedijk (1990) for further discussion of the cointegration approach and exchange rates.

[24]Abuaf and Jorion (1990), p. 173.

Finally, a study by Nelson Mark (1995) provides strong evidence that the long-run path of the exchange rate can be accurately gauged from knowledge of the current level of the rate relative to its equilibrium value in a monetary model. The adjustment path corresponds broadly to the overshooting path described in Figure 6.6—the movement toward the equilibrium should be greater the further into the future we forecast. Indeed, Mark's results conform to this hypothesis. Mark found that on an in-sample basis, his model explains (in terms of R^2) between 50 and 75 percent of the variation in the DM, SFr, and ¥ rates at the three- and four-year horizons.[25] Figure 8.9 shows how the correspondence between the actual exchange rate (indicated by open circles) and the fitted exchange rate (indicated by solid circles) improves as the forecast horizon lengthens to three and four years. Even in out-of-sample forecasts, Mark's model significantly outperforms the naive random walk, reducing the MSE by 20 percent, to 59 percent.

Overall, these results suggest that, at the long-run horizon, there is considerable reason to be optimistic that one can construct a forecast of the real exchange rate that is superior to the random walk. This optimism relies on an assumption of stationary real rates, which implies a reversion to the mean real rate, or a reversion to the equilibrium exchange rate implied by macroeconomic fundamentals.

Composite Forecasts: Theory and Examples

Economic theories usually begin with an internally consistent set of assumptions to develop a stylized model of exchange rate determination. The hope is, of course, that the stylized model captures every facet of exchange rate determination so that the model is both internally consistent and complete. Forecasting models, on the other hand, tend to take a more pragmatic approach. Rather than be doctrinaire, a forecasting model may simply draw on what works from available theoretical models.

Composite forecasting illustrates this principle. A composite forecast brings together the information in alternative forecasting models in an attempt to outperform any of the individual forecasts. In practice, the technique may be successful if individual forecasts reflect complementary elements of information.

Consider a manager with access to several alternative exchange rate forecasts. Assuming that historic data are available on these forecasts, we can compute the mean (μ) and standard deviation (σ) for each series of forecast errors and graph them as in Figure 8.10. The graph shows forecaster 5 with the smallest average error, forecaster 4 with the lowest standard deviation of forecast errors, and so forth. Which forecaster should the manager select?

The manager need not be restricted to the use of a single forecast. In principle, the manager could draw on all of the information in the available pool of forecasts. A variety of alternative weighting systems is possible. The manager could take the arithmetic average of all forecasts, assigning a weight of $w = 1/n$ to each of the n available forecasts. Alternatively, greater weight could be assigned to forecasts that have been more accurate. One such scheme assigns a set of weights:

$$w_i = \frac{(1/\sigma_i)}{(\Sigma_i \, 1/\sigma_i)} \qquad i = 1, \ldots n \qquad (8.3)$$

producing weights that are inversely proportional to each forecast's standard deviation.

---

[25]The results are less striking for the Canadian dollar.

FIGURE 8.9   Evidence on Long-Horizon Predictability in the DM/$ Rate

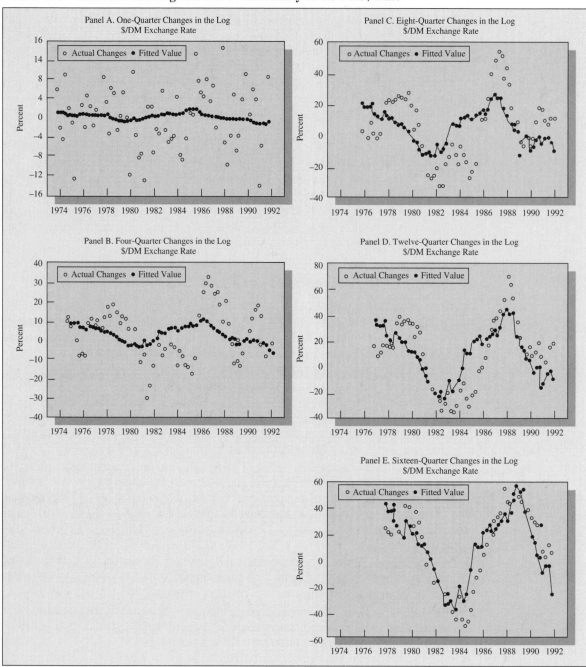

Source: Nelson C. Mark, "Exchange Rates and Fundamentals: Evidence on Long-Horizon Predictability and Overshooting," *American Economic Review* 85, no. 1 (Mar. 1995), p. 211.

Figure 8.10 suggests that a set of weights (w_i) could be chosen to minimize (or maximize) the average forecast error, conditional on the standard deviation. This approach (similar to a portfolio allocation) generates a locus $S^C S^C$, which represents all the

FIGURE 8.10   **Illustrating the Potential Gains from Composite Forecasting over Individual Forecasts**

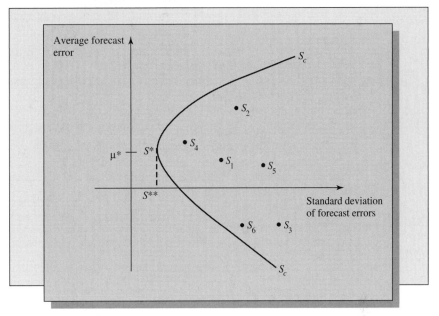

Note:

$S_1, S_2, \ldots S_3$ represent individual forecasters;

$S_c S_c$ is the locus of composite forecasts formed by various weighted combinations of individual forecasts;

S^* is the composite forecast with the smallest standard deviation; and

$S^{**} = S^* - \mu^*$ is the forecast with an average error of zero (unbiased) with the smallest standard deviation.

Source: Richard M. Levich, "Composite Forecasts," in *The Management of Foreign Exchange Risk,* 2nd ed., ed. Boris Antl and Richard Ensor (London: Euromoney Publications, 1983), p. 100.

possible forecasts that could be formed with alternative weighting schemes. The weighting scheme that produces S^* appears desirable as it corresponds to the minimum standard deviation forecast. But on an in-sample basis, an alternative forecast can be constructed, $S^{**} = S^* - \mu^*$, that is both unbiased (average error of zero) and has the minimum standard deviation.

Linear regression is a simple method to determine the weights in a composite forecast. With n forecasts ($\hat{S}_i, i = 1, \ldots n$), the weight ($w_i$) on each forecaster can be estimated from the following equation:

$$\hat{S}_{C,t} = w_1 \hat{S}_{1,t} + w_2 \hat{S}_{2,t} + \ldots + w_n \hat{S}_{n,t} \tag{8.4}$$

Each regression coefficient is interpreted as the *marginal value* of information from the ith forecast, conditional on the information in the other $n - 1$ forecasts. Thus, an individual forecast might be fairly accurate, but of little value if it replicates the information in other available forecasts. Alternatively, an individual forecast could be biased or inaccurate, but capture some information that is missing in the other forecasts.

One drawback of the composite approach is that the weights must be estimated from in-sample data. If the accuracy or the correlation structure of the individual forecasts should change, then the composite forecast need not be superior when applied to out-of-sample data. Still, a simple average that assigns a fixed weight ($1/n$) and draws

TABLE 8.3   Composite Currency Forecasts: Postsample Results

Currency	Percentage Correct One-Month	Percentage Correct Three-Month
Canadian dollar	70.0*	76.7*
Pound sterling	66.7*	43.4
Belgian franc	73.3*	83.3*
French franc	73.3*	80.0*
German mark	80.6*	90.3*
Italian lira	77.4*	71.0*
Dutch guilder	86.7*	83.3*
Swiss franc	70.0*	60.0*
Japanese yen	51.6	32.3
Average	72.2*	68.9*

*Significant at the 5% level.

Notes: Each composite forecast is based on up to 11 advisory service forecasts and the forward rate. Individual forecasts made during a two-week interval are combined with the forward rate quoted on Friday at the end of an interval. Forecasts are weighted inversely proportional to their in-sample forecast error standard deviation. The sample periods are as follows:

One-month horizon: "In-sample" is 115 two-week intervals from January 11, 1974–June 9, 1978. "Postsample" is 33 two-week intervals from July 21, 1978–September 28, 1979.

Three-month horizon: "In-sample" is 110 two-week intervals from January 11, 1974–March 31, 1978. "Postsample" is 33 two-week intervals from July 21, 1978–September 28, 1979.

Source: Richard Levich, "Composite Forecasts," in *The Management of Foreign Exchange Risk,* 2nd ed., ed. Boris Antl and Richard Ensor (London: Euromoney Publications 1983).

on no in-sample characteristics (μ, σ, or correlation structure) may produce a superior and more steady forecasting record.

In Chapter 7, we saw several examples of the composite forecasting approach. Individual forecasting candidates, such as the current spot rate, the current forward rate, lagged forward rates, a current professional forecast, and the current PPP rate, were used in various combinations. All of the cases we reviewed showed that the combination of forecasters into a single composite improved forecasting performance relative to the forward rate alone.

An additional case was reported by Levich (1983), who combined the forecasts of as many as 11 advisory services and the forward rate using weights as in equation (8.3) and adjusting for in-sample bias. The results in Table 8.3 show that in a postsample period, the composite forecast produced a highly significant record of correct forecasts.[26]

Another practical illustration of composite forecasting is provided by companies that collect forecasts from many economic and financial forecasters and publish so-called consensus forecasts. Foreign Exchange Consensus Forecasts, a London company, surveys more than 250 forecasters monthly and publishes a consensus forecast reflecting the mean value of available forecasts.[27] Periodically, the company also asks forecasters to assess the probability that exchange rates will fall within certain prespecified ranges. Survey information of this sort helps to gauge the chances (as assessed by these forecasters) that an exchange rate might differ from its mean or expected value.[28] In

---

[26]See Goodman (1982) for an analysis of the record of percentage correct forecasts using pairs of technical trading models.

[27]Further information is at the company's website <www.consensuseconomics.com>.

[28]This survey technique is described in "A Consensus FX View with a Twist," *International Treasurer,* August 5, 1996.

some case, these results are particularly interesting when they reveal a huge spike of probability for a zero or small change in the rate, and a small lump of probability for larger changes.

Policy Issues and Special Forecasting Problems

Selecting or implementing a currency forecasting program raises a number of challenging policy issues. It will be useful to divide these into two broad categories: problems facing "consumers" of forecasts and problems facing "producers" of forecasts.

Consumers of Exchange Rate Forecasts

Perhaps the first problem facing the consumer is which forecasting method to follow or which foreign exchange advisory service forecasts to purchase. Our earlier discussion suggested that, before this question can be asked, consumers must decide on their forecasting horizon. Different forecasting techniques will often be more successful for different horizons. Then consumers must assess their loss function. Will the forecasts be used primarily for hedging decisions, asset and liability portfolio management, or longer-run strategic planning? Once this is decided, consumers can determine whether to measure forecasting performance using accuracy, usefulness, or some combination of the two. And, after the performance criteria have been established, consumers can consider whether any forecasting approach adds value relative to naive decision rules, and whether marginal gains obtained from using more than one forecaster outweigh the cost of additional forecasters.

For example, take the case of a corporate treasurer who is required to make hedging decisions on foreign currency receivables with a maturity of under one month. At that horizon, the treasurer might consider forecasts from a technical trading model. Suppose also that the treasurer operates under a policy directive that permits hedging from 0 to 100 percent of his or her cash inflows but rules out the ability to increase a long position in foreign currency or take a short position. In this situation, the treasurer's decisions on how to manage his or her receivables will depend heavily on the direction of change in the exchange rate (relative to the forward) and not on the magnitude of the error.[29] The treasurer should judge the technical model on the percentage correct method discussed in Box 8.2. And if the treasurer had been using another forecasting model previously, he or she should measure the value of the new forecast based on the marginal or incremental gain expected by using the new forecast in place of, or in addition to, the old forecast.

Or consider a corporate strategic planner who must evaluate foreign investment projects where revenues will not begin for 5 years and will last for as long as 25 years. In this case, the planner definitely should consider a long-term forecasting model, perhaps based on a structural model or PPP. Because the planner must decide between projects in various countries based on the magnitude of returns, forecast accuracy is important. The marginal value of the forecast is again related to how the planner's decisions change relative to his decisions made without benefit of the new forecast.

---

[29]If the treasurer's only choices were "hedge 100 percent" or "hedge 0 percent," then the direction of the forecast would be the sole determinant of the treasurer's decision.

After a forecast method is adopted, consumers face the problem of how to integrate currency forecasts into their business decisions. We have not stressed the role that forecast uncertainty might play for consumers. For example, suppose our forecasts predict that £ will appreciate by $+0.2$ percent and ¥ will depreciate by -0.2 percent against the US$. Are these really different forecasts, or should both be considered as forecasts of no change? If these are considered as precise forecasts with little estimation error, managers will be encouraged to take extreme speculative positions. In this case, a manager will go long £ and short ¥ in amounts conditioned only by his or her capital stock and risk preferences. This position is extremely risky if the exchange rate forecasts are uncertain. In general, portfolio allocations and hedging decisions depend on the accuracy of exchange rate forecasting and many services present forecasts without standard errors.

Producers of Exchange Rate Forecasts[30]

Like consumers, producers of forecasts must first settle on the desired forecasting horizon before selecting a forecasting approach. Technical models have shown greater success in forecasting short-term horizons. Economic fundamentals appear to have greater reliability over longer horizons.

Producers of forecasts face the problem of operating in a competitive industry. To be successful, it is not enough for a forecaster to forecast well by some arbitrary standard; it is necessary to forecast better than the market as a whole. However, even if a forecaster succeeds in doing this, he or she faces the "speculative efficiency" problem—namely, that market prices will come to incorporate his or her forecasts, rendering them without any further value. To continue adding value, a forecaster must have access to a superior model, superior data, or superior assumptions about the future course of exogenous variables than other forecasters in the industry.

Forecasters also face numerous econometric problems. One worth commenting on is the decision to revise a forecasting model as time passes. It is common to assume that econometric modeling improves as sample observations accumulate. This may be true, but as the market learns more, the ability of the model to produce valuable forecasts will decline. It also is argued that the performance of an econometric model may actually *decline* as the sample period *expands*. This would be expected if the new sample observations are drawn from a different period that reflects a different economic policy regime.

Special Problems in Exchange Rate Forecasting

For producers of exchange rate forecasts, econometric modeling assumes a certain degree of stability or stationarity in the system. Producers rely on stability and stationary conditions in order to select their in-sample period for estimation and to increase their

---

[30]While most exchange rate forecasts are proprietary and their producers charge a fee for obtaining them, a few forecasts are available online at no cost. For example, see the "Global Economic Forum" posted by Morgan Stanley at <www.msdw.com/gef/index.html>, and the "Weekly International Economic Briefing" posted by the Bank of America at <http://corp.bankofamerica.com/research/e_international_perspective. html>.

estimation precision. Consumers of exchange rate forecasts also rely on stability and stationarity. In order to select among forecasters or forecasting methods, they need to know whether past performance is any indication of future forecasting ability.

In the international financial environment, the biggest risks arise when structural breaks interrupt the stability and stationarity of an exchange rate series. The classic examples are the structural breaks associated with changes in the central rate of a pegged-rate system, realignments of exchange rates within a hybrid system like the ERM, or changes in government intervention policy within a target zone system. But other events, such as the change in U.S. monetary policy targeting in 1979 and the unification of East and West Germany in 1992, had a significant impact on forecasting in foreign exchange markets while these events were unfolding. Structural changes of this sort pose the greatest risk, both because exchange rate changes are likely to be more extreme and because the historical database may no longer be appropriate as the basis for future forecasts.

The difficulty of forecasting financial variables is well known. In the summer of 1988, the Japanese yen exchange rate was approximately 125 ¥/$. Economists using a PPP benchmark, presumably as a long-run guide, felt that the yen should drift toward 188 ¥/$. Market efficiency and the random-walk view supported a continuation of the then-current 125 ¥/$ rate. With the Japanese running a substantial current account surplus with the United States, other economists argued that a further 20 percent devaluation of the US$ to 100 ¥/$ was needed to reestablish current account balance.[31]

Some observers regarded this as an inconsistency—that the PPP equilibrium should point "north" of 125 ¥/$ while the current account equilibrium should be "south" of 125 ¥/$. For some it confirmed how little economics can foretell about exchange rates. For us, however, this situation points out the risks of forecasting in an environment that is susceptible to a structural change.

Since 1988, the Japanese bilateral trade surplus with the United States declined from $50 billion and then increased, reaching new highs in 1994. Over the same period, the yen initially weakened, reaching 158 ¥/$ in April 1990, but it fell below 100 ¥/$ in 1994. The current account has been a highly significant explanatory variable for the ¥/$ rate, as the forecasting equation in Figure 8.11 shows. And forecasters who got the current account right proved to get the direction and general level of the exchange rate right. If a sudden structural change in the spending patterns of Japanese (and U.S.) consumers were to occur, perhaps brought about by major structural changes in the access of Japanese consumers to international consumer goods markets, it is possible that the Japanese current account surplus would decline. And as it did, the yen would depreciate toward its PPP level. In this scenario, the PPP and current account equilibria would result in consistent exchange rate forecasts.

The wide array of ¥/$ exchange rate forecasts may signal that some economists were counting on a major structural change while others were not. With well-trained and well-informed economists presenting forecasts ranging from 100 to 188 ¥/$, it is no wonder that there is opportunity for exchange rate forecasters who perform only slightly better than average.

---

[31]See "Oh, Dear, Where Should the Dollar Be?" *Business Week*, July 7, 1988, pp. 117–19.

FIGURE 8.11   The Japanese–U.S. Trade Balance and the Yen/Dollar Exchange Rate

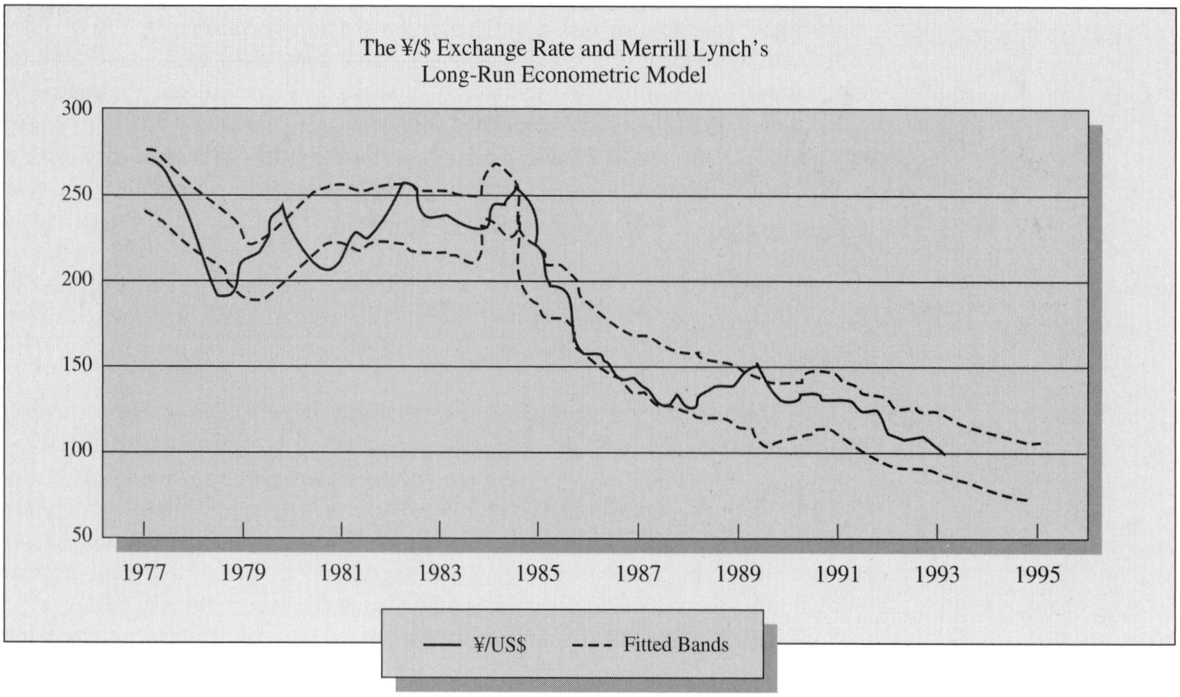

The ¥/$ Exchange Rate and Merrill Lynch's
Long-Run Econometric Model

— ¥/US$ - - - Fitted Bands

Note: The fitted equation is:

$$¥/US\$_t = 226.50 + 3.822\ (r_t^{US} - r_t^J) + 3.01\ (C_t^{US} - C_t^J) + 27.93\ (db_t)$$
$$(85.3)\quad\ (4.32)\qquad\qquad\quad (22.2)\qquad\qquad (2.72)$$

with *t*-values in parentheses, $R^2 = 0.89$, and Durbin-Watson = 0.51.

The variables in the equations are: *r*, the long-term government bond yield; *C*, the cumulative current account balance as a percentage of GNP; and *db*, a dummy variable for the speculative bubble period in late 1984.

Source: Merrill Lynch, *Currency and Bond Market Review,* Sept. 15, 1994.

Summary

Forecasts of exchange rates raise some of the more puzzling aspects of foreign exchange. Many economic studies conclude that exchange rates evolve as a random walk, and that many forecasts are no more accurate than the random-walk or forward-rate models. At the same time, many professional economists believe that exchange rates evolve with detectable trends, and the prevalence of currency forecasters suggests that some financial managers find value in their forecasts.

In this chapter, we have argued that economic modeling can make a contribution to currency forecasting once three key factors are specified: the exchange rate system, the forecast horizon, and the units of the foreign exchange rate. With these factors well specified, we argued that it was possible to formulate a sensible, and possibly successful, approach to currency forecasting. We also highlighted the difference between accurate and useful forecasts. While economists typically judge a model on the basis of accuracy, professional economists may take a more pragmatic stance and judge a forecast by its ability to achieve correct hedging decisions or speculative profits. We reviewed several cases in which accurate forecasts might not be profitable, and vice versa.

Second, we reviewed several specific examples of exchange rate forecasting. We argued that the failure to reject the random-walk model of exchange rates may stem from reliance on linear regression testing. In comparison, technical trend-following rules rely on a nonlinear relationship. We also reviewed evidence that the long-run forecasting ability of certain structural exchange rate models far exceeded the basic random-walk model of the exchange rate. And we reviewed the composite forecasting approach as a practical way to combine the information in alternative currency models.

Both consumers and producers of exchange rate forecasts face special problems because of the competitive and dynamic nature of currency markets. Knowing how the forecast will be used and knowing whether the forecast should be evaluated on the basis of accuracy, usefulness, or both are key elements for consumers to understand. For producers of forecasts, success depends in part on whether past economic relationships will persist in the future. Structural changes in the international economy represent one of the biggest challenges to forecasters.

Questions

1. Explain the difference between an accurate forecast and a useful forecast. Who needs an accurate forecast?

2. Describe and provide examples of different exchange rate systems that countries use. How do they affect the timing of exchange rate changes? How would a forecaster approach the different systems in making exchange rate forecasts?

3. How does the forecasting horizon affect the choice of a forecasting model?

4. Short-term exchange rate forecasting requires a strong emphasis on economic fundamentals. Is this statement true or false? Explain.

5. Purchasing power parity measures are a powerful tool for short-term forecasting. Is this statement true or false? Explain.

6. What is the difference between real exchange rate forecasting and nominal exchange rate forecasting? Which one is the most useful to financial planners? To foreign currency traders?

7. Explain the limitations of the regression method in forecasting future exchange rates using current and past exchange rates.

8. What is a mean-reverting series? Why is the concept of mean reversion helpful for making long-term exchange rate forecasts?

9. What is composite forecasting? Under what conditions would a composite forecast outperform individual forecasts?

10. What are the main problems facing forecasters who use econometric models to forecast exchange rates?

Exercises

1. Assume that your company exports to Japan and earns yen revenues. Thus, forecasts of the ¥/$ rate are important. Suppose two forecasters issue their predictions for the ¥/$ exchange rate. The current spot rate is 90 ¥/$. Forecaster A predicts a rate of 98 next month and forecaster B predicts a rate of 88. The forward rate is at 89, reflecting the interest rate differential between the two currencies. One month later, the spot rate reaches 92 ¥/$.

   a. Which of the forecasters, A or B or the forward rate, made the most accurate forecast?

   b. Which forecast is the most useful?

2. You are the treasurer of a large multinational company. Suppose that you receive every month exchange rate forecasts for the ¥/$ exchange rate from five different forecasting institutions: A, B, C, D, and E. From your past experience, the best forecaster has been firm C, followed by A, D, B, and E.

   The historic RMSE (standard deviation of forecasting errors) for the five forecasters and the current predictions are shown in the following table:

Forecaster	RMSE	Yen Forecast
A	7	80
B	15	82
C	5	85
D	10	81
E	20	88

a. Calculate the composite forecast that results from weighting these five forecasts evenly.

b. Calculate a composite forecast that assigns greater weight to forecasts with greater accuracy.

c. Discuss the advantages and disadvantages of using the forecast in exercise (*b*) versus (*a*).

3. Suppose you are evaluating two forecasters based on the following information:

Forecaster A made 30 "correct" forecasts of a total of 50 during the last year. Forecaster B made 114 "correct" forecasts of a total of 200 during the last year.

a. What is the probability that forecaster A's track record of correct forecasts was due simply to chance? (*Note:* You may use the normal approximation to the binomial distribution.)

b. What is the probability that forecaster B's track record of correct forecasts was due simply to chance? (*Note:* You may use the normal approximation to the binomial distribution.)

c. Discuss whether you would prefer to use the forecasts prepared by A or B.

4. As a multinational firm with sales in Japan, you require forecasts of the ¥/$ exchange rate. You have been using a professional forecasting firm, Crystal Ball Associates, and now want to measure the performance of their predictions. The following is a table showing the Crystal Ball forecasts, the actual end-of-period rates, and the one-period-ahead forward rates all in ¥/$.

a. Calculate the performance of the Crystal Ball forecasts and the forward rate using the MSE and RMSE methods to measure their accuracy.

b. Calculate the performance of the Crystal Ball forecasts and the forward rate using the percentage-correct method to measure their usefulness.

c. Has Crystal Ball Associates demonstrated unusual forecasting expertise according to the percentage-correct method?

d. Compare your results using the two methods. What do you conclude?

Period	*1*	*2*	*3*	*4*	*5*	*6*	*7*	*8*	*9*	*10*	*11*	*12*
Crystal Ball Associates forecast (end of period)	100	106	102	108	115	109	103	95	93	90	91	85
Actual spot rate (end of period)	101	110	108	105	110	110	98	90	91	85	88	84
1-period-forward rate	98	105	100	102	108	112	105	98	90	89	90	86

References

Abuaf, Niso, and Philippe Jorion. "Purchasing Power Parity in the Long Run." *Journal of Finance* 45, no. 1 (Mar. 1990), pp. 157–74.

Berg, Andrew, and Catherine Pattillo. "Are Currency Crises Predictable? A Test," *IMF Staff Papers* 46, no. 2 (June 1999), pp. 107–38.

Bilson, John F. O. "Leading Indicators of Currency Devaluation." *Columbia Journal of World Business* 14, no. 4 (Winter 1979), pp. 62–76.

———. " 'Technical' Currency Trading." In *The Currency-Hedging Debate,* ed. Lee R. Thomas. London: IFR Publishing, 1990.

———. "Value, Yield, and Trend: A Composite Forecasting Approach to Foreign Exchange Trading." In *Strategic Currency Investing,* ed. A. Gitlin. Chicago: Probus, 1993.

Campa, José Manuel, and P. H. Kevin Chang. "Arbitrage-Based Tests of Target-Zone Credibility: Evidence from ERM Cross-Rate Options." *American Economic Review* 86, no. 4 (Sept. 1996), pp. 726–40.

Coughlin, Cletus C., and Kees Koedijk. "What Do We Know about the Long-Run Real Exchange Rate?" *Review,* Federal Reserve Bank of St. Louis, 72, no. 1 (Jan. 1990), pp. 36–48.

Cumby, Robert, and David Modest. "Testing for Market Timing Ability: A Framework for Forecast Evaluation." *Journal of Financial Economics* (Sept. 1987), pp. 169–89.

Eichengreen, Barry; Andrew K. Rose; and Charles Wyplosz. "Exchange Market Mayhem: The Antecedents and Aftermath of Speculative Attacks." *Economic Policy,* no. 21 (Oct. 1995), pp. 249–312.

Elliott, Graham, and Takatoshi Ito. "Heterogeneous Expectation and Tests of Efficiency in the Yen/Dollar Forward Foreign Exchange Rate Market." *Journal of Monetary Economics* 43, no. 2 (Apr. 1999), pp. 435–56.

Flood, Robert P., and Peter M. Garber. "A Model of Stochastic Process Switching." *Econometrica* 51 (1983), pp. 537–51.

Frankel, Jeffrey A., and Kenneth A. Froot. "Chartists, Fundamentalists, and Trading in the Foreign Exchange Market." *American Economic Review* 80, no. 2 (May 1990), pp. 181–85.

Goodman, Stephen. "Two Technical Analysts Are Even Better Than One." *Euromoney* (Aug. 1982), pp. 85–96.

Henriksson, Roy, and Robert Merton. "On Market Timing and Investment Performance, II: Statistical Procedures for Evaluating Forecasting Skills." *Journal of Business* 54, no. 4 (Oct. 1981), pp. 513–34.

Hinkle, Lawrence E., and Peter J. Montiel. *Exchange Rate Misalignment Concepts and Measurement for Developing Countries.* Washington, DC: World Bank, 1999.

Jorion, Philippe, and Richard J. Sweeney. "Mean Reversion in Real Exchange Rates: Evidence and Implications for Forecasting. *Journal of International Money and Finance* 15, no. 4 (July/Aug. 1996), pp. 535–50.

Kaminsky, Graciela; Saul Lizondo; and Carmen M. Reinhart. "Leading Indicators of Currency Crises," *IMF Staff Papers* 45, no. 1 (March 1998), pp. 1–48.

Klein, Michael, and Nancy Marion. "Explaining the Duration of Exchange-Rate Pegs." *Journal of Development Economics* 54, no. 2 (Dec. 1997), pp. 387–404.

Krugman, Paul. "A Theory of Balance of Payments Crises." *Journal of Money, Credit and Banking* 11, no. 3 (1979), pp. 311–25.

Kwok, Chuck C. Y., and Linda Van de Gucht. "An Empirical Examination of Foreign Exchange Market Efficiency: Applying the Filter Rule Strategy to Intra-Daily DM/$ Exchange Rates." *Journal of International Financial Management and Accounting* 3, no. 3 (Autumn 1991), pp. 201–18.

Leitch, Gordon, and J. Ernest Tanner. "Economic Forecast Evaluation: Profits versus the Conventional Error Measures." *American Economic Review* 81, no. 3 (June 1991), pp. 580–90.

Levich, Richard M. "Composite Forecasts." In *The Management of Foreign Exchange Risk*, 2nd ed., ed. Boris Antl and Richard Ensor. London: Euromoney Publications, 1983.

Lothian, James R., and Mark P. Taylor. "Real Exchange Rate Behavior: The Recent Float from the Perspective of the Past Two Centuries." *Journal of Political Economy* 104, no. 3 (June 1996), pp. 488–509.

Mark, Nelson C. "Exchange Rates and Fundamentals: Evidence on Long-Horizon Predictability and Overshooting." *American Economic Review* 85, no. 1 (Mar. 1995), pp. 201–18.

Meese, Richard. "Currency Fluctuations in the Post-Bretton Woods Era." *Journal of Economic Perspectives* 4, no. 1 (Winter 1990), pp. 117–34.

Rose, Andrew K., and Lars E. O. Svensson. "European Exchange Rate Credibility Before the Fall." *European Economic Review* 38, no. 6 (June 1994), pp. 1185–1216.

Svensson, Lars E. O. "An Interpretation of the Recent Research on Exchange Rate Target Zones." *Journal of Economic Perspectives*, Fall 1992, pp. 119–44.

———. "Assessing Target Zone Credibility: Mean Reversion and Devaluation Expectations in the ERM, 1979–1992." *European Economic Review*, May 1993, pp. 763–802.

Taylor, Mark, and Helen Allen. "The Use of Technical Analysis in the Foreign Exchange Market." *Journal of International Money and Finance*, June 1992, pp. 304–14.

Williamson, John. *The Exchange Rate System.* Policy Analyses in International Economics, no. 5, rev. ed. Washington: Institute for International Economics, June 1985.

III OFFSHORE FINANCIAL MARKETS

9 The Eurocurrency Market 296
10 The Eurobond Market 333

9   THE EUROCURRENCY MARKET

"International deposits are intrinsically vulnerable to more than one source of sovereign risk because they transcend national borders. A typical Eurodollar deposit—for example, a dollar-denominated deposit liability of the London branch of a German bank—is potentially vulnerable to adverse actions taken by the government in the jurisdiction where the bank resides, where the head office is chartered, or . . . where payments denominated in dollars are ultimately cleared and settled."

Richard J. Herring (1991)

Learning Objectives

After reading this chapter, students should

1. Understand the factors that led to the development of the offshore Eurocurrency markets and how the market was able to compete with traditional onshore banking markets.

2. Know the factors that determine the relationship between bank deposit rates and bank lending rates in the onshore and offshore markets.

3. Be aware of the types of risks faced by depositors in offshore markets.

4. Be aware of the types of risks faced by borrowers in offshore markets.

5. Recognize the difficulties of regulating the offshore markets, and appreciate some of the actions taken by public policymakers to regulate the activities of the offshore market.

6. Realize how the offshore market concept increased international competition and spawned an offshore market in the United States and in other countries.

In this chapter, we describe the pricing and policy issues that pertain to the Eurocurrency market. The Eurocurrency market owes its existence to differences in national financial regulation combined with declining barriers to international capital movements. The Eurocurrency market and its offspring—the Eurobond, Eurocommercial paper, and Euroequity markets—comprise some of the most important financial innovations of the last 40 years. These innovations are examples of **unbundling,** in this case, separating the exchange risk of one currency (the U.S. dollar, for example) from its indigenous regulatory environment and combining it with the regulatory climate and political risk of another financial center (such as London). The Eurocurrency market and the Eurobond

Box 9.1

Did You Request the Eurorate or the Euro Eurorate?

Until 1999, when a boss asked for information on current Eurorates, the dutiful employee would return with a table of short-term interest rates. The word *Eurorates* meant Eurocurrency interest rates, which meant interest rates on Euro-$, Euro-£, Euro-DM, Euro-¥, and so on. But beginning in January 1999, when asked for information about euro rates (as opposed to Eurorates), the clever employee might return with a set of exchange rates for the euro (€) against other currencies such as the $, £, or ¥. But what if we wanted the *interest rate* on the euro, in either the onshore or the offshore market? What would we request to be sure we got a table of interest rates and not exchange rates?

First, we should review which countries have adopted the euro as official legal tender. As of 2001, those countries are the European Monetary Union 12 (Austria, Belgium, Finland, France, Germany, Greece, Ireland, Italy, Luxembourg, Netherlands, Portugal, Spain), sometimes referred to as the euro zone, euro area, or euroland. A deposit denominated in euros in any of these countries would be an *onshore euro deposit*. While a deposit denominated in euros in any other place—such as New York, London, Singapore, or Zurich—would be an *offshore euro deposit*.

Next, what will we call the interest rates on deposits or loans denominated in euros? The market has adopted two naming conventions for short-term interest rates on the euro.* The euro overnight index average (EONIA) is an onshore index of overnight euro interest rates from across the euro zone as compiled by the European Banking Federation. Its offshore counterpart, using overnight interest rates in London, is dubbed EURONIA. These interest rates are important for banks in the euro zone that need to borrow euros to meet regulatory requirements, or for banks that have excess euros to lend. As of June 2000, average daily volume in EONIA transactions was about €43 billion, compared to about €15 billion in daily EURONIA transactions.†

For other short-term lending, the euro interbank offered rate (EURIBOR) exists for lending within the euro zone. The offshore counterpart has been dubbed Euro LIBOR, meaning the London interbank offered rate for offshore lending denominated in euros. We discuss the nature of LIBOR rates later in this chapter. The London International Financial Futures Exchange (LIFFE) maintains an active market in three-month EURIBOR and Euro LIBOR contracts. We introduce these futures contracts later in this chapter, and go into more detail regarding their pricing and use in Chapter 11.

---

*See "Practical Issues Arising from the Euro," June 1999, published periodically by the Bank of England and available at its website <www.bankofengland.co.uk>.
†Ibid., June 2000, p. 18.

---

market (discussed in Chapter 10), virtually nonexistent until the late 1950s, have grown to become major centers of activity and in many instances the preferred markets for raising or investing funds.

To be precise, the **Eurocurrency market** is the market for deposits placed under a regulatory regime different from that applied to deposits used to execute domestic transactions. In most cases, this definition corresponds to US$ deposits outside the United States, UK£ deposits outside the United Kingdom, and so forth—simply the market for deposits denominated in a currency different from the indigenous currency of the financial center. However, several countries have set up special regulations to permit "Eurocurrency deposits" on domestic turf. For example, in the United States, dollar deposits at so-called **international banking facilities (IBFs)** are subject to a lower regulatory burden than ordinary dollar deposits in U.S. banks. IBF deposits are tantamount to Eurodeposits, but they are available only to nonresidents, and IBF accounts may not be used to conduct transactions within the United States.

Since the Eurocurrency market has expanded to financial centers outside Europe (such as the Bahamas, Singapore, Bahrain), the term *offshore* is more appropriate to describe its location. And we use the term *onshore* to mean the traditional, domestic

FIGURE 9.1   Sectors of the International Money Markets

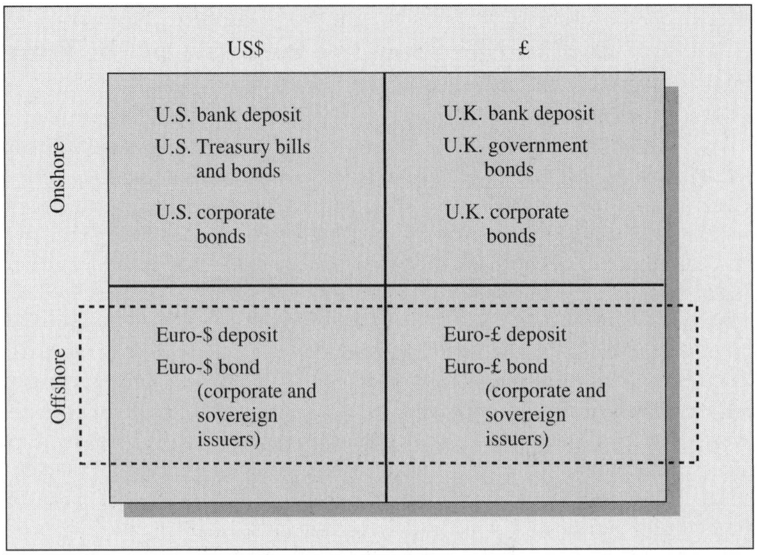

	US$	£
Onshore	U.S. bank deposit U.S. Treasury bills and bonds U.S. corporate bonds	U.K. bank deposit U.K. government bonds U.K. corporate bonds
Offshore	Euro-$ deposit Euro-$ bond (corporate and sovereign issuers)	Euro-£ deposit Euro-£ bond (corporate and sovereign issuers)

Note: The offshore market is like a parallel market that offers bank instruments and securities that compete with similar financial products in the traditional, onshore market.

marketplace. But the key distinction between offshore and onshore markets is the regulatory environment, not location. Because the prefix *Euro* is now also the name of a currency, the naming of offshore deposits denominated in euros requires special care, as discussed in Box 9.1

Figure 9.1 shows a stylized interpretation of international financial markets. The columns represent two currencies, the currency dimension of the market. The rows represent the onshore and offshore markets, the geographic, political, and regulatory dimension of the market.

Clearly, investors (borrowers) can choose between assets (liabilities) denominated in US$ and £. Markets for US$ securities compete with markets for £ securities. In Chapter 3, we showed how forward exchange contracts could be used to transform a £ (or US$) security in one market to a similar synthetic US$ (or £) security. Thus, synthetic dollar-denominated securities compete with conventional dollar-denominated securities, and synthetic £-denominated securities compete with conventional £-denominated securities.

However, a second dimension of competition exists in international financial markets. Securities in the onshore market bear certain regulatory costs and political risks. If these costs or risks become large, agents have an incentive to cross into the offshore markets and devise new securities and institutional structures. Thus, financial products (beginning with deposits and loans but including more complex financial instruments) produced in the offshore markets compete with products from the traditional onshore market base. As Figure 9.1 suggests, all types of agents—banks, corporate borrowers, and sovereign issuers—have made use of the offshore market.

The offshore market portrayed in Figure 9.1 is in effect a **parallel market** in competition with the onshore market. We expect to find competition among private agents in onshore and offshore markets. However, public policymakers have not been idle observers of this market. We will also describe the competitive give-and-take among regulatory bodies, which seeks to influence the location of these financial market transactions.

This chapter begins with a historical overview, which highlights the effect of regulation on the development of the Eurocurrency markets. We describe the process of deposit creation and statistics on the growth of the market. Then we analyze the pricing of Eurocurrency deposits and loans, followed by an analysis of market share and pricing across competing offshore centers. As in other chapters, we conclude with a discussion of policy matters and how they affect private enterprises and public policymakers.

Historical Overview

The Origins of Supply and Demand for Offshore Banking

The Eurocurrency market was not planned as a new stock exchange or a futures and options exchange might be planned today. Rather, the market evolved through a combination of forces that presented an opportunity for innovation. The practice of banks accepting deposits in a currency other than the native currency of the realm was not new—at least not in Europe, where it had been a normal part of banking for hundreds of years. After World War II, Canadian, Swiss, and U.K. banks commonly accepted U.S. dollar deposits, which they placed in U.S. money-market instruments through their New York correspondent banks. The innovation came in the mid-1950s when rather than simply return their U.S. dollars to the U.S. money market, these banks elected to lend these funds within Europe to finance foreign trade or other economic projects.

Any market can be characterized by its supply and demand components, which is a useful way to think about the origins of the Eurocurrency market.

In a sense, a supply of funds to the Eurodollar market was always present. International commodities such as oil, agricultural products, and precious metals were often priced in terms of U.S. dollars. So Europeans held balances in U.S. dollars to execute transactions, to act as a hedge against foreign exchange changes, and to serve as a store of value. The supply of U.S. dollars was also enriched by Russians and other Eastern European depositors who at the time were reluctant to hold their U.S. dollars (needed for international trade transactions) in accounts in the United States. Most likely these depositors remembered that Russian-owned dollar balances had been impounded by the Alien Property Custodian during World War II.[1] Rather than risk confiscation, the Russians deposited their dollars in London and Paris with affiliates of state-owned Russian banks.[2] Still another boost to the market came in 1958 with a general relaxation of exchange controls throughout Europe and a return to external convertibility for the British pound. Private individuals could now hold their U.S. dollars earned through international trade rather than being required to sell them to the central bank.

In a sense, too, the demand for funds in the Eurodollar market was always latent. Borrowers will always line up to borrow cheaper funds because, after all, there is no risk to them in doing so. But demand for Eurodollars multiplied after the sterling crisis of 1957, when the Bank of England restricted the use of sterling for financing foreign trade

---

[1]Friedman (1969), p. 7.

[2]The Paris bank, Banque Commerciale pour l'Europe du Nord, carried the cable address "EUROBANK," which later became synonymous with the general activity of accepting deposits offshore. See Kvasnicka (1969). The United States froze Iranian deposits in 1979, Libyan deposits in 1988, and Iraqi deposits in 1991, suggesting that the Russians were right to be concerned.

and external loans. British merchant banks responded with a pragmatic solution: Use the U.S. dollar, which was not regulated by the Bank of England to conduct these transactions from accounts based in London. Once the advantage of this approach was evident, European banks began to actively solicit U.S. dollar deposits.

Onshore Banking Regulations Boost the Offshore Market

Banking regulations in the United States helped to serve up a fresh, continuing supply of funds to the Eurodollar market. Under **Regulation Q,** the Federal Reserve established ceilings on the interest rate that banks could pay on deposits of various sizes and maturities. No interest was allowed on demand deposits, and from January 1957 until November 1964, a ceiling of 1 percent interest was applied to time deposits of less than 90 days. Given these restrictions, depositors were willing, if not eager, to search for higher returns offshore.

At about the same time, other U.S. regulations helped to bolster the demand for Eurodollar loans. Responding to the undesired buildup of dollars overseas (dollars that the United States was obliged to convert into gold at $35 per ounce), the United States adopted the **interest equalization tax (IET)** in 1963. The IET amounted to an excise tax on U.S. purchases of new or outstanding foreign securities. By raising the price of long-term borrowing, the United States encouraged foreigners to go elsewhere for borrowed funds. The Eurodollar market provided one outlet, the Eurobond market another.

Finding that the IET was ineffective in stopping the capital outflow, other U.S. regulations were imposed. The so-called **Foreign Credit Restraint Program** (voluntary in 1965 and mandatory in 1968) set specific limits on the volume of bank lending that U.S. banks could conduct with foreigners.[3] Foreign subsidiaries of U.S. multinational firms were included in the "foreign" classification.

Thus, a large group of borrowers was given strong incentives to investigate the Eurocurrency markets. None of these measures were effective in achieving their stated objective of reducing the U.S. capital outflow—perhaps because so many loopholes existed (for example, U.S. capital flows to Canada were exempted) or because larger macroeconomic constraints had to apply.[4]

European governments also experimented with capital controls during this period, which similarly helped to promote the nondollar segments of the Eurocurrency market. In the early 1970s, the Bundesbank required foreigners with onshore DM accounts to place a fraction of their funds in non-interest-bearing accounts. At roughly the same time, the Swiss National Bank imposed heavy interest rate penalties on nonresidents with onshore Swiss franc accounts. Both Germany and Switzerland were trying to limit nonresident demand for their currencies. Rather than face these controls and risks of future controls, agents deposited DM and Swiss francs offshore. The German capital controls expired in 1974, and the Swiss interest rate penalties were abolished in December 1979.[5]

The Offshore Markets Endure

It is noteworthy that even though the initial stimulus for the Eurocurrency markets is long gone, as are the U.S. regulations that offered a warm and nurturing environment,

---

[3]For details of these programs, see Clendenning (1970), pp. 202–4.

[4]If the United States runs a current account surplus, as it did in the 1960s, it must also run a capital account deficit, buying bonds from foreigners to finance the purchase of U.S. goods and services.

[5]For an analysis of the impact of German capital controls on the differential between onshore and offshore interest rates, see Dooley and Isard (1980). The Swiss control program is described in various issues of the "International Letter," Federal Reserve Bank of Chicago, over the 1974–1979 period.

the Eurocurrency markets are still with us—and larger and healthier than ever.[6] This is noteworthy because it illustrates a *hysteresis* effect—the idea that certain economic decisions are difficult to reverse, even when the initial conditions behind those decisions have disappeared.[7] Writing in 1970, E. Wayne Clendenning (1970, p. 24) argued:

> The major factors favoring the development of the Eurodollar market were the rigidities in the U.S. banking system ... and ... the fact that European banks were able and willing to operate on relatively narrow interest margins. This situation ... enabled the market to provide benefits to all three major groups involved—the owners of the U.S. dollar deposits, the European banks operating as intermediaries, and the final borrowers.

Once the genie of lower-cost, less-regulated banking was out of the bottle, it was impossible to get people back to the usual ways of doing business, even though many of the rules and regulations that initially fostered the Eurodollar market had been abolished.

Clendenning (1970, p. 22) and Paul Einzig (1970) linked the success of the Eurocurrency market with the decision to lend offshore and to create a market with both depositors and borrowers. Today, we describe the innovation that permits the Eurocurrency market to sustain its existence as "unbundling"—taking the exchange risk of one currency and combining it with the regulatory climate and political risk of another financial center. As long as the regulatory burden that exists in the offshore market is lower than it is onshore, offshore banks possibly can reduce their costs, passing on more favorable rates to both depositors and borrowers, and keeping a profit for themselves. We will incorporate these ideas in the discussion that follows on market growth and pricing.

Growth of the Eurocurrency Market

In this section, we review data on the overall size and growth of the Eurocurrency market as well as its composition by currency and region.

The process of Eurocurrency deposit creation is outlined in Box 9.2. By tradition, this process is described as if the Euromarket were a closed banking system whereby funds are deposited, lent, redeposited, and re-lent. Since the statutory reserve requirement on Eurocurrency deposits is zero, the initial concern was that the Eurodeposit creation process could go on indefinitely.[8]

This concern was not well founded, primarily because the Euromarket is but one segment of an international banking market. The deposit creation process associated with fractional reserve banking may be stopped abruptly if funds borrowed in the Euromarket are spent, invested, or deposited back in the United States in the "onshore" banking system.[9] Moreover, the vast majority of deposits in the Eurocurrency market are term deposits instead of demand deposits. This rules out early withdrawals that might lead to a run of withdrawals on Eurobanks. In practice, Eurobanks tend to follow a conservative strategy of accepting short-term deposits with interest rates determined by

---

[6]The IET and the Foreign Credit Restraint Program were eliminated in January 1974. Regulation Q was gradually phased out, starting in March 1980 and completed in March 1986.

[7]For example, workers hired during an expansion may not be fired during a recession when the cost of firing is high. And firms may be slow to rehire workers during an expansion who were fired during a recession. Or home insulation installed when oil is $40/barrel may not be removed when oil reaches $20/barrel.

[8]Even though the statutory reserve requirement on Eurocurrency deposits is zero, banks may keep a small amount of prudential reserves.

[9]*Leakage* of funds from the offshore to the onshore market may occur to offset the original leakage of funds from the onshore to offshore market.

Box 9.2

Creating Eurodollars

In this box, we illustrate the mechanics of Eurodollar deposit creation and the overall growth of the Eurodollar market. For ease of exposition, we assume a 19th-century paper-check technology instead of today's electronic funds transfers.

To begin, assume that Adam Smith (an American) holds a $100 deposit with a New York bank, shown in Round 1 as Smith's asset and a liability of the New York bank, marked (1) below, Smith decides to open an account in London. He does so by writing a check on his New York bank, carrying it to London, and depositing it (2). The London bank accepts the check, opens an account for Smith (3), and sends the check for collection to its New York correspondent, which deducts $100 from Smith's account and credits that amount to the London bank's *nostro* (meaning "own") account (4).

Eurodollar Creation: Round 1

Adam Smith		NY Bank		London Bank	
(1) NY bank $100		A. Smith $100 (1)		(3) NY bank $100	A. Smith $100 (3)
------		------			
(2) NY bank −$100		A. Smith −$100 (4)			
(2) London bank $100		London bank $100 (4)			

After Smith's transaction, there are 100 Eurodollars measured by the liabilities of the London bank. Note also that U.S. dollars are cleared and settled in New York, an institutional feature that underlies the problem of delivery risk as discussed in Chapter 3.

The London bank may wish to increase its earnings on the $100 above the interest paid on its *nostro* account, and it can do so by making a loan. Suppose that in Round 2 David Hume (a Swiss) comes to the London bank for a $100 loan, shown in Round 2 as the London bank's asset and a liability for Hume (5). The London bank issues a check to Hume, which he takes to a Zurich bank for deposit (6). The Zurich bank accepts the check and sends it to New York for collection (7). The New York bank debits the London bank's *nostro* account and credits the Zurich bank's *nostro* account (8).

----

market conditions, and matching them against loans with interest rates indexed to a market rate that is reset periodically.

The data in Figure 9.2 report the overall growth of Eurocurrency deposits. The market has grown from essentially zero in 1960 to roughly $9.5 trillion on a gross basis and $5.5 trillion on a net basis (netting out all interbank deposits) in 1999—*larger* than the U.S. money supply as measured by M2. The market's annual rate of growth exceeded 20 percent for many years, but it tapered off to only 5 percent over the 1990s.

Once exclusively dollar denominated, the Eurocurrency market stabilized during the 1970s with a dollar share of roughly 75–80 percent. Recently, however, the dollar's share has fallen below 50 percent. Simply as a matter of accounting, the dollar's share of the Eurocurrency market rises and falls as the dollar appreciates and depreciates against other currencies. The overall composition of the Eurocurrency market in 1999 is shown in Figure 9.3. After the US$, offshore euros (€) and the so-called EMU legacy currencies (the deutsche mark, French franc, Italian lire, and others) make up 28 percent

After Hume's transaction, there are 200 Eurodollars—the $100 liability of the London bank to Smith and the $100 liability of the Zurich bank to Hume. The liabilities of the New York bank remain at $100. The process of lending and redepositing could continue until Euromarket deposits reached:

$$D = R/r$$

where

R = initial injection of funds into the Euromarket
r = fraction of reserves held against deposits
$1/r$ = deposit-reserve multiplier

If $r = 0$, then in theory, deposit creation within the Euromarket could go on indefinitely, creating a huge inverted pyramid of deposits backed by only $100 of base reserves in the New York bank. This certainly presents the image of a market at risk if Messrs. Smith, Hume, and their friends were to arrive at their respective banks at the same time to withdraw their funds. This risk is highly unlikely since nearly all Eurodeposits are term deposits (which can be withdrawn only at maturity) rather than demand deposits (which can be withdrawn at any time on short notice).

Eurodollar Creation: Round 2

London Bank		*Zurich Bank*		*David Hume*	
(6) NY bank −$100		(7) NY bank $100	D. Hume $100 (7)	(6) Zurich bank $100	London bank (5) $100
(5) D. Hume $100					

N.Y. Bank	
	London bank (8) −$100
	Zurich bank (8) $100

of the market. The Japanese yen, U.K. pound, and Swiss franc each have small shares. And other currencies—Euro-Australian dollars, Euro-New Zealand dollars, Euro-Canadian dollars, and so on—make up the final 5 percent slice. These market shares were quite stable over the 1990s.

The wide geographic spread of the offshore banking market is illustrated in Figure 9.4. Overall, Europe has been the dominant region (62.8 percent in 1999), and the United Kingdom (19.9 percent in 1999) the dominant country. Within Europe, Germany was the number two location in 1999, with a 9.2 percent share, surpassing France for the first time in 25 years. Japan's market share stood at almost 15 percent in 1990 after a period of capital market liberalization, but its share fell to only 5.7 percent in 1999.[10] The United States has roughly maintained its market share (11.6 percent in 1999). The

---

[10]See Watson et al. (1986) for a discussion of capital market liberalization in Japan.

FIGURE 9.2   **Dimensions of the International Banking Market**
Total of Offshore Deposits and Share Denominated in US$

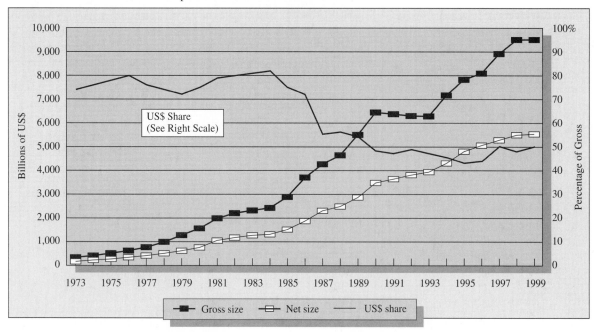

Note: Break in data sources as described below; US$ share based on liabilities in industrial reporting countries only.

Sources: For 1973–1986, Morgan Guaranty Trust Co., *World Financial Markets,* various issues; for years 1987–1999, Bank for International Settlements, *International Banking and Financial Market Developments,* various issues.

FIGURE 9.3   **Percentage of Euromarket Deposits by Currency in 1999**
Total Euromarket Deposits: $9.5 Trillion

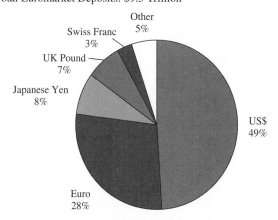

Note: Shares based on liabilities in reporting countries only.

Source: Bank for International Settlements, *International Banking and Financial Market Developments,* June 2000.

establishment in 1981 of international banking facilities (IBFs), which permit offshore transactions for non-U.S. residents, helped the United States to attract deposits from the Caribbean and elsewhere. The remaining cross-border deposits (18.8 percent in 1999) are spread over a number of other countries, but predominantly the Cayman Islands (6.8

FIGURE 9.4   **Euromarket Deposits by Location**
Percentage Shares, Total in US$ Billion

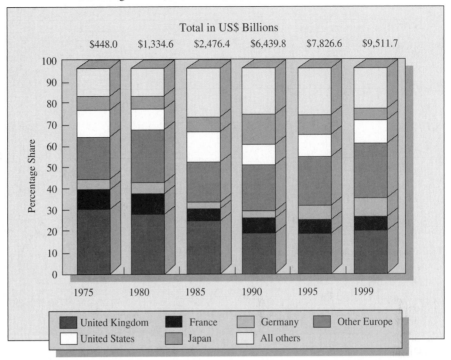

Source: Bank for International Settlements, *International Banking and Financial Market Developments,* various issues.

percent share), Singapore (4.44 percent share) Hong Kong (3.9 percent share), and the Bahamas (2.5 percent share).[11]

Pricing of Eurocurrency Deposits and Loans

To approach the question of how Eurocurrency interest rates are determined, we propose conducting the analysis using a *loanable funds* framework. It is convenient to imagine a world with *n* currencies and *n* countries or financial centers.

Pricing in the Case of One Currency and Two Financial Centers

To begin, consider the case of one currency (the U.S. dollar) and two financial centers (New York and London). Suppose that in the onshore market, the demand (*D*) for funds depends on the required rate of return on available projects, while the supply (*S*) of funds depends on individuals' rates of time preference. The curves take on the expected slopes, as illustrated in Figure 9.5. In the absence of transaction costs, equilibrium is at point *A*.

---

[11]Some of the increase in the "all others" category around 1985 (and the decline in Europe as a location) may be spurious, because the Bank for International Settlements increased its reporting coverage.

Figure 9.5   **Determination of Onshore and Offshore Interest Rates**

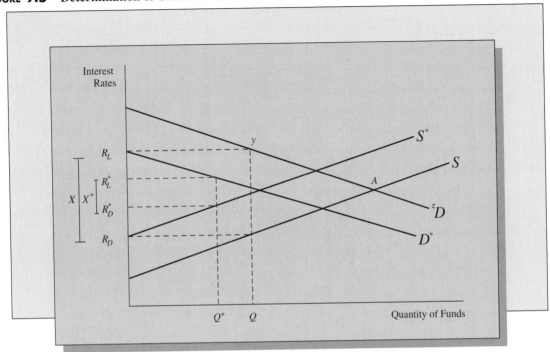

Note: Determination of onshore and offshore interest rates: one currency, one offshore financial center, no capital controls.

Source: Adapted from Richard Levich, "The Euromarkets After 1992," in *European Banking in the 1990s,* ed. J. Dermine (London: Basil Blackwell, 1990), pp. 373–99.

However, banks incur costs in collecting deposits and in servicing loans. The major categories of costs are (1) non-interest-bearing reserves at the Federal Reserve, (2) FDIC insurance, (3) credit review, (4) asset-liability risk management, (5) taxes, and (6) administrative overhead. More details on these costs are presented in Box 9.3. If these costs are summarized by amount X, then the onshore market will reach an equilibrium with deposit rate R_D, lending rate R_L, and market size Q, as shown in Figure 9.5.

Where can a Eurodollar market fit into this picture? Assume that a new market in U.S. dollar-denominated funds opens in London. Americans will supply dollars to the offshore market only if they are compensated for bearing the extra costs and risks associated with London. Since Americans can earn R_D with minimum inconvenience and no political risks in the onshore market, the supply curve to the offshore market (S^*) will begin at R_D.[12] Similarly, in the absence of capital controls, no borrower would travel to London to pay a higher price for funds. Therefore, the demand curve for offshore funds (D^*) must begin at R_L, reflecting the unfunded projects along segment yz of the onshore demand curve D.

The offshore dollar market exists only if it is able to collect deposits and service loans at a profit. We can see that if this cost remains as X, the Eurodollar market will not exist. However, if the cost of collecting deposits and servicing loans in the offshore mar-

---

[12]We are assuming the nonexistence of Russians, Iranians, Iraqis, or others who view the United States as risky and who would deposit funds offshore at rates *below R_D.*

Box 9.3

Costs of Collecting Deposits and Servicing Loans

The table below outlines the major categories of costs associated with collecting bank deposits and servicing bank loans. We will examine these costs in more detail.

The impact of non-interest-bearing reserves is influenced by both the level of interest rates and the reserve requirements. Suppose member banks of the Federal Reserve System are required to hold 8 percent of their deposits as non-interest-bearing reserves (r).* With only $92 available to lend (at interest rate R_L), for every $100 earning interest (at interest rate R_D), when R_D = 10 percent, R_L must exceed R_D by 0.87 percent simply to cover the interest on bank deposits.†

Onshore Market (United States)	Offshore Market
1. Zero interest on mandatory reserves	1. Market interest on voluntary reserves
2. FDIC insurance	2. No deposit insurance
3. Credit review/loan collection	3. Known, higher-quality credits
4. Asset–liability risk management	4. Floating-rate interest plus maturity matching
• Default risk	5. Tax havens or other incentives
• Interest rate risk	6. Large volume, shell operation, low overhead
• Pre-payment risk	
5. Taxes	
6. Administrative overhead	

Since 1970, the level of US$ interest rates has varied substantially, with the Federal Funds rate reaching 17 percent in 1981. Since 1960, the Federal Reserve has set reserve requirements on various categories of deposits ranging between 3 percent on time deposits in rural banks to 17 percent on demand deposits in urban banks. These figures vividly illustrate how non-interest-bearing reserves could induce a substantial wedge between onshore deposit and lending rates. In comparison, when Eurobanks hold reserves, these may be invested in safe and liquid instruments (e.g., U.S. Treasury bills) that earn a market interest rate.

Another cost assessed on banks is FDIC deposit insurance that until 1989 was fixed at $1/12$ of 1 percent of all deposits. These premiums have been raised since 1990 and are now related to the risk characteristics of the bank.

Other costs of collecting deposits and servicing loans are more difficult to quantify. Onshore banks usually hold a mixed portfolio of assets (short-term consumer loans, long-term residential mortgages, various corporate loans) funded by deposits of varying maturities. The loan portfolio gives the bank an exposure to default risk. In addition, the bank bears an interest rate risk as the time profile (duration) of its loan portfolio and its deposit portfolio are not perfectly matched. These kinds of risks must be monitored and included in the bank's operating costs.

In comparison, deposits in the offshore market are typically accepted for a fixed term, say 1, 3, 6, or 12 months, and at a fixed rate of interest for the term. Offshore loans may be made for a longer term, but the interest rate is reset every three months (to the prevailing three-month LIBOR rate) or every six months (to the prevailing six-month LIBOR rate). This practice reduces the Eurobank's exposure to interest rate risks, because the interest rates charged to borrowers are more closely linked to interest rates paid to depositors.

Last, offshore banks tend to operate in locations that offer tax advantages and may require lower staffing and overhead costs than onshore operations. Taken together, all of these factors suggest that the cost of collecting deposits and servicing loans will be substantially less offshore than onshore.

---

*Reserve requirements are outlined in Federal Reserve Regulation D. Reserve requirements on deposits from offshore branches are treated in Regulation M.
†Interest paid on deposits [$R_D X$] is set equal to interest earned on amounts available to lend [$X(1 - r) R_L$]. Solving, we have $R_L = R_D / (1 - r)$.

ket (X^*) is less than in the onshore market, we can determine the offshore deposit rate R_D^*, lending rate R_L^*, and market size Q^*.[13] Because Eurobanks (1) earn interest on their voluntary level of reserves, (2) do not pay FDIC-like insurance, (3) deal primarily with known, high-quality credits, (4) use floating interest rate arrangements and maturity matching to minimize interest rate risks, (5) often operate in tax havens or under other special tax incentives, and (6) operate a wholesale business with lower overheads than onshore operations, we fully expect to find $X^* << X$.

With $X^* << X$, Figure 9.5 shows the normal relationship between onshore and offshore interest rates, that is:

$$R_L > R_L^* > R_D^* > R_D \tag{9.1}$$

In more familiar terms, this inequality states that for US\$, the New York lending rate ("prime") exceeds the **London interbank offered rate (LIBOR),** which exceeds the **London interbank bid rate (LIBID),** which in turn exceeds the marginal cost of funds (either a certificate of deposit rate or the Federal Funds rate) of a New York bank. In recent times, the LIBOR-LIBID spread (for US\$) has varied from about 0.125 to 0.25 percent while the spread between the prime rate and the Federal Funds rate has varied from about 2 to 3 percent.

A sample of onshore and offshore deposit and borrowing rates for several countries on June 20, 2000, is reported in Table 9.1. For every country, we see that the prime commercial bank lending rate exceeds LIBOR for that currency, and the LIBID exceeds a typical onshore deposit rate. Thus, the data correspond with the broad prediction of equation (9.1).[14]

It is important to note that Eurocurrency rates are quoted for various maturities. The standard maturities are 1, 3, 6, and 12 months, but rates are also quoted for overnight and seven-day funds as well as maturities longer than one year. See Table 9.2 for a sample of rates for various currencies and maturities.

Can Offshore and Onshore Markets Coexist?

The offshore market exists by driving a wedge into the onshore financial market; it provides a similar financial service at a lower cost. An important question, however, is: How can the onshore and offshore markets coexist? If the offshore market provides a similar service at a lower cost, what prevents all onshore transactions from migrating to the offshore market?

In our stylized model, offshore depositors bear the additional risk of exchange controls or taxes, plus inconvenience with deposits outside their home country. The interest differential between a Eurodollar deposit in London and a certificate of deposit in a New York bank ($R_D^* - R_D$) measures the extra compensation paid to depositors to offset these factors. Figure 9.6 shows this differential for the US\$. In the early 1980s, R_D^* often exceeded R_D by 50–100 basis points (bp). Recently, the differential has dropped to under 25 bp.

For borrowers, size and credit quality may act as barriers that restrict some firms from access to the offshore market. The interest differential between the New York prime rate and LIBOR ($R_L - R_L^*$) measures the cost of failing to gain access to offshore

---

[13]Note how this approach to determining the size of the banking market differs from the fractional reserve multiplier approach used in Box 9.2.

[14]For reasons we will discuss shortly, the prime lending rate may not adequately capture the true cost of borrowing onshore in every country.

TABLE 9.1 **Deposit Rates and Borrowing Rates: Onshore and Offshore**
Percentage per Annum as of June 20, 2000

	Prime Lending Rate (R_L)	Offshore Borrowing Rate: LIBOR (R_L^*)	Offshore Deposit Rate: LIBID (R_D^*)	Onshore Deposit Rate (R_D)
Canada	7.50	5.9063	5.8125	3.70
Euro area	NA	4.5313	4.4375	3.04
Japan	1.375	0.1875	0.0938	0.03
Switzerland	4.75	3.4375	3.3125	3.29
United Kingdom	7.00	6.1875	6.0313	6.00
United States	9.50	6.8125	6.6875	5.99

Note: LIBID and LIBOR rates are in London, except for £ where offshore rates refer to a continental Europe location. LIBID, LIBOR, and deposit rates are for three-month maturities. Prime lending rates may not be comparable, because lending practices may vary across countries. A single representative prime lending rate is not available for the 11 euro area countries. See the European Central Bank website <www.ecb.int/stats/nrir> for information about the range of interest rates.

Sources: LIBOR and LIBID are from *Financial Times,* June 21, 2000. Prime lending rates are from *The Economist,* June 17, 2000. Onshore deposit rates are from Datastream (Canada and United States), European Central Bank *Monthly Bulletin* (euro area), *The Economist* (Japan), UBS (Switzerland), and Nat West (United Kingdom).

TABLE 9.2 **A Sample of Recent Eurocurrency Rates**
June 20, 2000

	One Month	Three Months	Six Months	One Year
U.S. dollar	$6\frac{23}{32}$–$6\frac{5}{8}$	$6\frac{11}{16}$–$6\frac{13}{16}$	$6\frac{31}{32}$–$6\frac{7}{8}$	$7\frac{1}{16}$–$7\frac{3}{16}$
Euro (€)	$4\frac{7}{16}$–$4\frac{11}{32}$	$4\frac{7}{16}$–$4\frac{17}{32}$	$4\frac{5}{8}$–$4\frac{19}{32}$	$4\frac{27}{32}$–$4\frac{31}{32}$
Japanese yen	$\frac{1}{16}$–$\frac{5}{32}$	$\frac{3}{32}$–$\frac{3}{16}$	$\frac{3}{16}$–$\frac{5}{16}$	$\frac{3}{8}$–$\frac{9}{32}$
U.K. pound	$5\frac{15}{16}$–$6\frac{1}{16}$	$6\frac{1}{2}$–$6\frac{5}{16}$	$6\frac{5}{16}$–$6\frac{5}{8}$	$6\frac{1}{2}$–$6\frac{11}{32}$
Swiss franc	$3\frac{3}{16}$–$3\frac{5}{16}$	$3\frac{5}{16}$–$3\frac{7}{16}$	$3\frac{1}{2}$–$3\frac{5}{8}$	$3\frac{13}{16}$–$3\frac{29}{32}$
Canadian dollar	$5\frac{1}{4}$–$5\frac{27}{32}$	$5\frac{13}{16}$–$5\frac{29}{32}$	$5\frac{7}{8}$–6	$6\frac{3}{32}$–$6\frac{5}{16}$
Singapore dollar	$2\frac{23}{32}$–$2\frac{31}{32}$	$2\frac{21}{32}$–$2\frac{13}{16}$	$2\frac{3}{4}$–$2\frac{27}{32}$	3–$3\frac{1}{4}$

Note: Rates applicable to interbank deposits of $1 million minimum (or equivalent).
Source: *Financial Times,* June 21, 2000.

lending terms. Figure 9.7 shows this differential for the US$. Contrary to our model, in the early 1970s LIBOR often exceeded prime. This suggests that prime did not capture the entire cost of borrowing onshore, as banks often required compensating balances (earning less than market interest rates) of borrowers.

Throughout the 1980s and until recently, the prime-LIBOR spread has risen to nearly 3 percent. But this overstates the burden on large- and medium-sized borrowers in the onshore market because competition has forced many onshore banks to lend at rates below prime.[15] The Federal Reserve Board conducts a survey to gauge the lending terms

---

[15]Even small borrowers have gained access to the Eurocurrency loan market through adjustable-rate home mortgages that are indexed against LIBOR and sold as pass-through certificates to offshore investors. See Kenneth R. Harney, "A New Hybrid Loan Designed to Draw Foreign Investors," *Philadelphia Inquirer* (Oct. 22, 1989), p. K-1.

FIGURE **9.6**   **Deposit Rates for US$**
Onshore (CD Rate) and Offshore (LIBID)

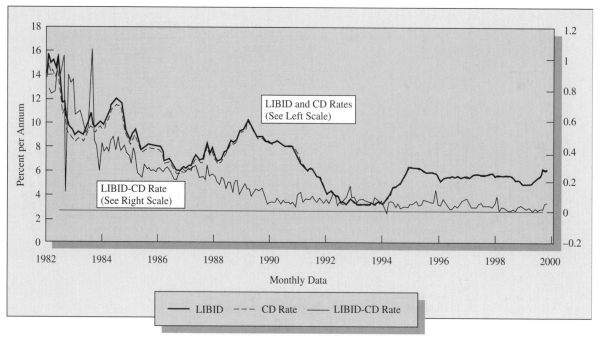

Sources: LIBID is the three-month deposit rate on Eurodollars in London, OECD *Financial Statistics Monthly* (disk series INT.E.A1) supplemented with
International Financial Statistics, series 60D; CD rate is the monthly average of secondary market prices, *International Financial Statistics,* series 60LC.

at U.S. commercial banks.[16] These data show that since 1985, between 60 percent and 80
percent of (the value of) short-term loans (under one year) have been made at below-
prime terms. A growing percentage, exceeding 50 percent in 1995, of (the value of) long-
term loans has also been made at below-prime terms. In the mid-1980s, below-prime
short-term loans tended to be priced about one percentage point under prime. But by
1995, the pricing advantage was slightly more than two percentage points under prime.

The Impact of Capital Controls and Taxes

When capital controls are present, the relationship between onshore and offshore interest rates given in inequality (9.1) may be affected.[17] For example, when there are controls on the movement of funds into the onshore market, such as we described for
Germany and Switzerland in the early 1970s, we find $R_D^* < R_D$. Depositors accepted
lower rates offshore because the onshore rates as quoted did not account for the cost of
the controls in place and the prospective controls. Indeed, for several weeks in 1973,
Euro–Swiss franc and Euro–DM deposit rates were *negative*. Depositors accepted these
"lower" offshore rates because after factoring in the cost of onshore controls they were
at least as favorable as the effective rates available to nonresidents in onshore Swiss

---

[16]See "Terms of Lending at Commercial Banks," Table 4.23, in selected issues of the *Federal Reserve
Bulletin.*

[17]For an analytical treatment of this case, see Levich and Hawkins (1981), p. 398.

FIGURE 9.7   **Borrowing Rates for US$**
Onshore (Prime) and Offshore (LIBOR)

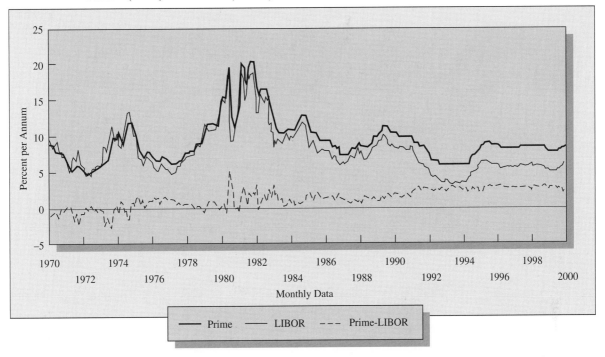

Source: LIBOR is the three-month Eurodollar rate. Both the prime rate and LIBOR are monthly averages of daily rates from *International Financial Statistics,* series 60P and 60LDD.

franc and DM accounts. Euro-Swiss franc deposit rates were again negative for four weeks at the end of 1978 when controls applied to nonresident Swiss franc accounts were near their peak.

Similarly, when the onshore market is experiencing a "capital crunch"—a period when interest rate ceilings or central bank lending guidelines lead to a shortage of funds—borrowers may venture offshore prepared to pay $R_L^* > R_L$. Again, the reasoning is that R_L (as quoted) is not a true market clearing price for funds. At these times, borrowers willingly pay a "higher" interest rate offshore.[18]

The German controls on onshore deposits were removed in 1973, and the Swiss controls were abolished in 1979. Controls affecting lending are sporadic, not the norm, in the major industrial countries. Therefore, in the analysis that follows, we will assume that no onshore capital controls are in place, so that onshore and offshore interest rates satisfy expression (9.1).

Market Share and Pricing in Competing Offshore Centers

Now consider the case of one currency (the U.S. dollar) and several offshore centers (London, Frankfurt, Singapore, and Beijing). In Figure 9.8, we continue to assume that the demand for dollars offshore is described by D^*, which reflects the underlying set of

---

[18] R_L^* may exceed R_L temporarily at the end of the tax year when firms need funding to complete merger and acquisition deals.

FIGURE 9.8   Determination of Offshore Interest Rates and Market Shares

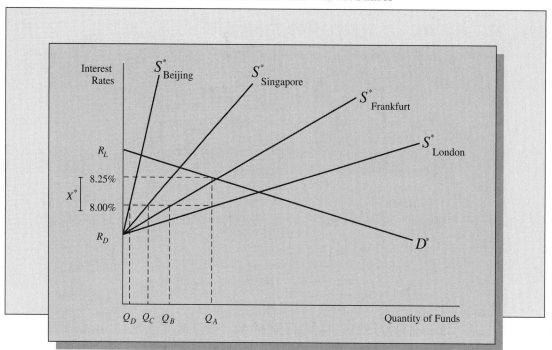

Note: Determination of onshore and offshore interest rates: one currency, four offshore financial centers, no capital controls.

Source: Adapted from Richard Levich, "The Euromarkets After 1992," in *European Banking in the 1990s*, ed. J. Dermine (London: Basil Blackwell, 1990), pp. 373–99.

projects. The supply of funds to each offshore center depends on depositors' assessments of the costs of using the center—associated with known taxes and capital controls as well as the inconvenience of time-zone differences—and the risks (of future taxes and capital controls). In principle, each center might have its own cost for collecting deposits and servicing loans. For simplicity, assume that these costs are identical across centers and equal to 0.25 percent. In Figure 9.8, this selection of X^* results in a London deposit rate of 8.00 percent and lending rate of 8.25 percent and a London market size of Q_A.

If a Frankfurt offshore center is to develop, it must offer loans at 8.25 percent to compete with the price charged in London. As a result, Frankfurt can pay no more than 8 percent on deposits, and it must be satisfied with a market size of Q_B. A similar story applies to Singapore with a resulting market size of Q_C and Beijing, with a market size of Q_D. In our example, once the most efficient and least risky financial center has set the price of loans, other centers must follow suit, leaving quantity as the only other variable to adjust.[19]

In reality, if Germany or Singapore were saddled with higher operating costs, it might be able to set a higher R_L^* and still attract borrowers. But its loan portfolios would have higher credit risks than London. Figure 9.8 also suggests that countries which depositors view as more risky will need more favorable regulations to lower their costs and reduce their lending rates.

---

[19]An offshore center might adjust its deposit rates higher than 8.00 percent in our example, but this might signal that it was a less convenient or more risky center.

FIGURE 9.9   **The Structure of International Financial Markets: Many Currencies, Many Markets**
Currency of Denomination × Country of Issue

	United States	United Kingdom	Germany	Switzerland	Singapore	Brazil
US$	**NY US$** NY IBF US$	London US$	Frankfurt US$	Zurich US$	Singapore US$	
UK£	NY IBF £	**London £**	Frankfurt £	Zurich £	Singapore £	
€	NY IBF €	London €	**Frankfurt €**	Zurich €	Singapore €	
SFr	NY IBF SFr	London SFr	Frankfurt SFr	**Zurich SFr**	Singapore SFr	
S$		London S$		Zurich S$	**Singapore S$**	
Real						**Rio Real**

The General Case with Many Currencies and Many Financial Centers

Figure 9.9 illustrates the general case of *n* currencies and *n* financial centers. Regulatory costs and political risks vary as we move from column to column. Exchange risks vary as we move from row to row. The contents of each cell correspond to a set of interest rates representing deposits, loans, and other securities available in that marketplace. The cells along the northwest-southeast diagonal of Figure 9.9 represent the onshore market, and the remaining cells represent the offshore market.

Arbitrage and Interest Rate Parity: Once Again.   We have analyzed the interest rate differential between an onshore market (New York dollars) and offshore market (London dollars) using a loanable funds approach. We argued next that arbitrage and regulatory competition should keep the offshore interest rates for a single currency nearly equal. With pricing nearly equal, the market share of an offshore financial center depends on both the costs of using the center and the perceived risks of capital controls and new taxes. Finally, the interest rate differential between offshore instruments should conform to the interest rate parity condition, which was derived in Chapter 5 as equation (5.1). So, for example, the interest differential between Zurich dollars and Zurich sterling in Figure 9.9 should equal the forward exchange premium between U.S. dollars and U.K. pounds, or:

$$\frac{F_{t,1} - S_t}{S_t} = \frac{i_{\$,\text{Zurich}} - i_{£,\text{Zurich}}}{(1 + i_{£,\text{Zurich}})}$$

Figure 9.9 helps to underscore why tests of interest rate parity may fail when the arbitrage is between traditional, onshore securities. In arbitrage between U.S. Treasury bills and U.K. treasury bills (examples of New York US$ and London £ securities, respectively), two dimensions of risk are changed: exchange risk and political risk. The forward exchange contract hedges only the exchange risk portion of the interest differential, not the political risk portion.

Policy Matters—Private Enterprises

Concerns of Depositors

In our model of Eurocurrency rates (Figure 9.5), we assumed that depositors associate greater risks with offshore deposits than onshore deposits. These risks include the risk of exchange controls, blocked funds, or other events that could affect the timely return of the deposits or the amount returned.

The Riskiness of Offshore Deposits.   Specifying the precise nature of these risks is difficult because the circumstances of every **cross-border deposit** transaction are difficult to characterize. For example, a typical cross-border deposit might involve a *US$* deposit by a *Philippine* citizen in the *London* branch of a *Japanese* parent bank. Potentially, any of four governments could intercede to create a risk for this depositor. If a dispute arises between the depositor and the bank in a cross-border transaction, it is difficult to know in advance which country will claim jurisdiction and which legal precedents apply.

A further complication concerns whether the offshore bank is organized as a separate subsidiary or a branch of the parent bank. As a separate legal entity, a subsidiary could be expropriated or become insolvent, leaving the depositor without recourse to the parent. The liabilities of a branch, in contrast, are ultimately the responsibility of the parent bank.

The simple distinction between assets and liabilities in banking frequently offers a useful guide for sorting out the complex legal issues that arise in a cross-border banking dispute. The bank's assets include its cash in the vault and its loan portfolio. If the bank is the victim of a robbery or failed loans, the bank's obligation to meet its liability to depositors goes on. On the other hand, a bank deposit is the liability of the bank and the asset of a depositor. If the depositor becomes subject to a confiscation of funds or an exchange control regulation, the bank is not normally obligated to undo the government's restrictive policy toward the depositor. Some examples may help to clarify these points.

Examples of Risk in Cross-Border Deposit Transactions.[20]   Many disputes during the 20th century between depositors and banks—including exchange controls and blocked funds—have stemmed from war and revolution aimed at the confiscation of bank assets or depositors' accounts.

Cases Favorable to the Bank.   Those cases that have been judged favorable to the bank seem to rely on the legality of the confiscation of depositor assets. For example, *Arab Bank* v. *Barclays Bank* (1954) pertains to the case of Arab Bank (Jerusalem) and its deposit at the Jerusalem branch of Barclays Bank (London). On May 15, 1948, British rule over Palestine ended and war broke out between Palestinian Arabs and the State of Israel. In July, Arab Bank moved its head office from Jerusalem to Amman, Jordan. In December, Israel passed emergency regulations to confiscate the property of absentees. At the request of the new custodian for absentee property, Barclays Bank transferred the balance of Arab Bank's account to the custodian. Arab Bank argued that, as a consequence of the war, its deposit at Barclays (Jerusalem) had been "destroyed" and replaced

---

[20]These examples and many others are described in detail in Herring and Kübler (1995). We include the date of the most recent court decision pertaining to the case.

by a new right against the head office of Barclays in London. The British House of Lords disagreed, finding that the site of the deposit remained in Israel and that Barclays had acted properly in paying out the deposit to the new custodian for absentees.

Similarly, after the Castro revolution in 1959, the government of Cuba passed Law No. 78, which established the Ministry of Recovery of Misappropriated Property. Using this law, Cuban branches of the Chase Manhattan Bank (New York) were instructed to transfer the balances of various accounts held by former government officials and their families to the Ministry of Recovery. In *Perez* v. *Chase Manhattan Bank* (1984), the courts concluded that the confiscation was proper under the act-of-state doctrine. Cuba was the site of the deposit as well as the depositor; Chase Manhattan Bank had discharged its responsibility by payment to the Cuban government.

In *Braka* v. *Bancomer* (1985), U.S. depositors held US$ certificates of deposit (CDs) with Bancomer at its head office in Mexico City. During the balance of payments crisis of 1985, the Mexican Ministry of Treasury ordered Bancomer to redeem these deposits with pesos calculated at the official exchange rate instead of the free-market exchange rate.[21] Even though some CD purchases and interest payments were directed through Bancomer's New York office, the court held that the site of these deposits was in Mexico City. The act-of-state doctrine implied that the deposits were rightfully subject to Mexico's exchange control regulations.

Cases Favorable to the Depositor.   Those cases that have been judged favorable to the depositor have relied on various principles that make the home office ultimately liable for many of the transactions entered into by its branches around the world.

Sokoloff v. *National City Bank of New York* (1928)—the predecessor of Citibank—describes the case of Boris Sokoloff, a Russian citizen, who in June 1917 made a US$ deposit in New York with an equivalent amount in rubles credited to the Petrograd (St. Petersburg) branch. Sokoloff made some withdrawals from the account and in November 1917 attempted to transfer all of the remaining balances. For reasons that are unclear, but possibly including civil disorder, the transfer was not made, and in August 1918 the new Soviet government closed the Petrograd branch. The court ruled in favor of Sokoloff. The court cited the communication failures between the bank and the depositor. But the court also noted that the United States had not recognized the Soviet government, and so the act-of-state principles did not apply.

In *Garcia* v. *Chase Manhattan Bank* (1984), the depositor held peso-denominated CDs issued by a Cuban branch of the Chase Manhattan Bank. Garcia's deposit balances had been transferred to the Castro government, as in the *Perez* v. *Chase Manhattan Bank* case discussed earlier. In this case, however, Chase officials had made assurances to Garcia that the CDs were guaranteed by the New York office and could be repaid by presenting the CDs at any Chase office worldwide. The court concluded that Chase's obligation to Garcia was not extinguished by virtue of the fact that Chase had paid out funds to a third party (the Cuban government).[22] The court compared the nationalization of deposits in Cuba to an armed robbery of the Cuban branches, which would still leave the bank liable for its obligations to depositors.

In *Vishipco* v. *Chase Manhattan Bank* (1981), the depositor had held a Vietnamese piastre account at the Saigon branch of Chase Manhattan Bank. With the fall of Saigon to Communist forces looming, Chase officials closed the Saigon branch on April 24,

---

[21]Deposits that left the United States as dollars and returned as pesos were labeled "burro-dollars."

[22]In *Perez* v. *Chase Manhattan Bank,* a similar guarantee from a Chase employee was alleged. But the court ruled for Chase in that case.

Box 9.4

Risk in Cross-Border Transactions: The Wells Fargo–Citibank Case*

In June 1983, Wells Fargo Asia Limited (WFAL), a Singapore-chartered, wholly owned subsidiary of Wells Fargo Bank, made two six-month deposits of $1 million each with Citibank's Manila branch. On October 15, 1983, the Philippine government imposed exchange controls requiring prior approval by the central bank for repayments of principal on foreign obligations to foreign banks. Citibank did not repay the deposits when they matured in December 1983 and Wells Fargo took legal action in February 1984.

Under the principle of *corporate responsibility,* one could argue that the parent retained responsibility for deposits at the Philippine branch. Clearly Citibank had the ability (that is, the financial capacity) to repay the deposits; as an operational matter, payment would have been effected electronically through facilities in New York (recall Box 9.2). However, the *separate entity* principle recognizes that the WFAL deposits were booked in the Philippines and thus subject to the sovereign risk of the Philippines. For Citibank (Manila or New York) to have repaid the deposits at maturity without government approval would have flouted the spirit and possibly the letter of the Philippine law.

Throughout the lengthy legal battle, the case seemed to revolve around several points: (1) Was the matter a question for Philippine or New York law? (2) Would the deposits be repaid through New York or Manila? (3) Could

Citibank draw on its Philippine or worldwide assets to repay the WFAL deposits? (4) If Citibank repaid the deposits from New York using its worldwide assets, would this contravene the Philippine exchange control law?

In an unusual twist to the case—as part of an appeal to the U.S. Supreme Court in 1989—the Department of State, the U.S. Treasury, the Board of Governors of the Federal Reserve System, the Federal Deposit Insurance Corporation, the Office of the Comptroller of the Currency, *and* the Solicitor General filed a friend-of-the-court brief supporting Citibank. In part, this brief claimed that allowing the deposit to be cleared and settled through New York would give WFAL "something it did not bargain for and had no right to receive—dollar-denominated deposits that are exempt from federal reserve requirements and insurance assessments but *legally payable in the United States.*"[†]

Despite this impressive support for Citibank, the U.S. circuit court finally ruled in favor of Wells Fargo on June 26, 1991. In deciding this case, the court focused on the distinction between the physical location of "repayment" (where the liability will be discharged, New York in the case of Eurodollars) and the location of the assets (that is, the assets of Citibank Manila or the assets of Citibank worldwide) that may be used for "collection" to satisfy the liability. WFAL could have stipulated that collection on its Manila deposits be made at Citibank (New York), in effect

---

1975, without notifying depositors. In finding for Vishipco, the court ruled that by operating as a branch in Vietnam, Chase accepted the risk that it would be liable elsewhere. The court also concluded that the act-of-state principle did not apply; the new Vietnamese government had seized the assets and physical facilities of Chase, not the property of the depositors.[23]

The most recent legal case involving Eurocurrency deposits is the *Wells Fargo Asia Limited* v. *Citibank* (1991) case, which we review in Box. 9.4.

Finally, the United States has itself been the source of political risk in several high-profile international incidents. The United States sought to freeze Iranian deposits during the embassy hostage seizure (November 1979), to freeze Libyan deposits after alleged terrorist incidents (1988), and to freeze the deposits of Panama's president Manuel Noriega (1990) in connection with a drug-trafficking charge.

The original freeze order in the Iranian case pertained to both dollar and nondollar deposits in U.S. banks and foreign branches of U.S. banks. The freeze on nondollar deposits in foreign branches was quickly rescinded out of fear of repercussions from for-

---

[23]However, other Vietnamese cases against Banque Nationale de Paris tried in French courts ruled in favor of the bank. See Herring and Kübler (1995), fn. 56.

demanding a parental guarantee on repayment of the deposits. If this had been done, presumably the rate of interest on Citibank (Manila) deposits would have been identical to the interest on similar deposits placed with Citibank (New York). In fact, the rate of interest paid by Citibank (Manila) was higher than the rate available at Citibank (New York), as our analytical model predicts. However, the court ruled that under New York law, unless there were an agreement to the contrary, a creditor may collect a debt at any place that the parties have agreed it is repayable. Because there was no agreement forbidding the collection in New York, and repayment of dollar deposits through New York is a normal business practice, the court sided with WFAL.

Moreover, the court found that Citibank had not satisfied its good faith obligation to seek the Philippine government's approval to repay the WFAL deposits. WFAL had recovered $934,000 of its $2 million deposit in 1985 after Citibank petitioned the Philippine central bank for permission to use its worldwide assets for this purpose. In 1987, a U.S. district court allowed Wells Fargo to recover the remainder of its deposit in New York. At that time, the court concluded that because the Citibank branch in Manila was not a separate legal entity, Philippine law would not be violated by a repayment from Citibank's worldwide assets.

In our theoretical analysis (in Figure 9.5), the higher rate of interest paid on Eurodeposits represents compensation for the greater sovereign risk to which these deposits are exposed compared with onshore deposits.[‡] If depositors desire protection against these sovereign risks, it seems reasonable that the cost of this guarantee would be equal to the offshore-onshore deposit rate differential. The situation is analogous to a U.S. bank loan to a foreign subsidiary of a U.S. industrial firm. If the parent is required to guarantee the loan against the risk of exchange controls that might block repayment by the foreign subsidiary, then the interest rate on the loan should be lower, reflecting the reduction in sovereign risk and the credit risk of the parent.

The *WFAL* v. *Citibank* case may have important implications for the practice of deposit taking in offshore markets. As the court upheld WFAL, offshore banks may respond by having depositors expressly acknowledge that offshore deposits are subject to particular sovereign risks. Without this, offshore depositors in a branch of a U.S. bank would seem to be exempt from certain exchange control risks, although they remain exposed to the risk that their assets could be confiscated through an act of state.

---

[*]See Herring and Kübler (1995, pp. 965–7) for a summary of the legal arguments in the case.

[†]Ibid., p. 966, italics in original.

[‡]If the offshore bank were established as a subsidiary instead of a branch, differential credit risk (between the offshore subsidiary and the parent) could affect the deposit rate differential. As a practical matter, it seems unlikely that a parent would allow an offshore subsidiary to fail unless the parent itself also declared bankruptcy.

---

eign governments. The prospects for freezing dollar deposits worldwide rested on the premise that all dollar accounts are cleared through New York and that the government could block access of all banks to these clearing facilities.[24] Some funds were released to offset U.S. claims against Iran. In January 1981, the hostages were released and Iranian deposits were unblocked.

In the Libyan case, a Libyan government bank held deposits with Bankers Trust and Manufacturers Hanover Trust. Both banks required Libya to hold a US$ balance in the New York office, but excess amounts were transferred daily to the London offices. The courts held that British law applied to the London deposits. The London Eurodollar deposits were to be paid even if it meant payment in physical US$ rather than using the customary electronic transfer system. Eventually, the U.S. Treasury permitted electronic payment, although payment could have been made in UK£.

Earning Offshore Deposit Rates with Minimal Risk.   The primary concern of many depositors is simply to gain access to the offshore market and to find a location that is

---

[24]CHIPS, the Clearing House Interbank Payment System, is a privately owned electronic funds transfer system that handles more than 90 percent of the world's dollar transactions. See Timberlake (1992).

as free as possible from political risks. Access to offshore quotations is usually restricted to large players with deposits in excess of $1 million. Comparable rates may be available in somewhat smaller amounts for wealthy individuals who partake of special banking services for high-net-worth clients. Small investors participate in the offshore deposit market indirectly through money-market mutual funds.

Selecting a safe offshore market for deposits also deserves some attention since the alternatives run the gamut from small island economies (such as Grand Cayman Island and the Netherlands Antilles), through countries in various stages of development (like Hong Kong, Mexico, and the Philippines), to advanced financial centers (including London, Frankfurt, Singapore, and Zurich). Let us focus primarily on the first two categories. An offshore banking center situated on an island economy may appear risky and vulnerable. The operation may appear to be only a shell, with minimal office space and employees, which may add to the appearance of vulnerability. In comparison, an offshore bank's presence in the larger countries may be more substantial. More physical facilities and employees may suggest a more stable operation. But this need not be the case.

To understand why, consider a (geographically) small offshore banking center. Virtually all of its loans will be to entities who reside elsewhere, outside of the offshore center. Were this offshore center subjected to government controls or threats of expropriation, the parent bank could still recover its loans. The parent could simply instruct the borrowers to make their repayments to another offshore branch. Thus, the ability of the initial offshore branch to service its deposits would be unaffected.

Now consider the loan portfolio of a larger offshore banking center, such as the Philippines. The loan portfolio of many Philippine branches could contain a substantial number of *domestic* Philippine loans. Thus, threats to control or expropriate bank assets could have credibility because there are valuable assets at the offshore bank that could be seized. In this respect, small banking centers may harbor fewer risks than those that reside in larger or more developed countries.

Concerns of Borrowers

Borrowing Onshore Versus Offshore.   Borrowers are heavily attracted by low-cost funding. Risk that a bank will not roll over a maturing loan, the advantage of diversifying one's sources of funding, and concerns over how a bank would treat a borrower in default are all additional considerations that lead a borrower to favor one bank lender over another. But price is the primary factor. Our model suggested that, other things being equal, borrowers will find lower-cost funds in the offshore market. Can this really be the case, especially when banks operate in both the onshore and offshore markets and borrowers can readily see into both settings?

Our model concluded that the onshore lending rate (R_L) is typically greater than the offshore lending rate (R_L^*). In the 1960s before the rise of the Eurodollar market, the agreed-upon definition of the *prime* lending rate was "the interest rate banks charge their best business customers."[25] Once banks began to write loans indexed to LIBOR, the standard definition of *prime* was no longer valid. Large and creditworthy companies could receive loans indexed to LIBOR at a substantial savings relative to a loan indexed to prime.

But the interest differential illustrated in Figure 9.7 gives only a vague indication of the true differences in the costs of borrowing in the two markets. The reason is that the

---

[25]Ritter and Silber (1970), p. 67.

reference rate (prime or LIBOR) is only one element in the overall cost of bank funding. First, banks historically have required borrowers to post some form of collateral, often in the form of compensating balances, to secure a loan. Compensating balances held at less than the market rate of interest act to raise the cost of bank funding. This practice has diminished for larger, high-rated firms that have access to the commercial paper market.[26] Second, prime and LIBOR are only an index or reference rate. The interest rate on a bank loan is usually quoted as the index plus x, where x is 0.0 percent, 0.25 percent, 0.50 percent, 1.0 percent, or more. Alternatively, the interest could be quoted as $(1 + y)$ times the index. Usually, y is a positive number. But when the index is prime, we noted earlier that a top-rated borrower could be quoted an interest rate that equates to an amount less than prime. Third, a borrower may be required to pay a lump-sum, up-front fee for the privilege of borrowing or for the benefit of having a bank commitment to lending for a given period of time. When all of these factors are taken together, the all-in cost of funds in the onshore and offshore market may be more similar than suggested by Figure 9.7.

How then would a firm choose to borrow in the onshore or offshore banking market? One factor is that prime is an **administered rate,** set within a bank and adjusted from time to time as short-term interest rates change. But the adjustment is usually made with a lag. Banks may be reasonably slow to lower prime as rates are falling, and somewhat slow to raise them when rates rise. LIBOR, on the other hand, is a **market-determined rate** that changes daily in response to market conditions. For a longer-term loan that requires several interest rate resets, if the costs initially appear similar across LIBOR and prime loans, a firm might prefer the LIBOR loan if rates were predicted to fall and the prime loan if rates were predicted to rise. Alternatively, the decision could be made as part of a hedging plan with a preference for LIBOR or prime liabilities to offset the firm's assets that have payoffs linked to LIBOR or prime.

Eurocurrency Loans and Interest Rate Risk.   The second major issue facing borrowers in offshore financial markets is how to deal with the *interest rate risk* that is associated with Eurocurrency loans. Suppose in June 2000 a firm obtains a $1 million loan for two years priced at LIBOR plus 0.5 percent. Assume further that the loan specifies that three-month LIBOR will govern the pricing. Once the interest rate on the loan has been set initially (for one quarter) it will be reset on the seven following quarterly anniversary dates until the loan matures. This process illustrates a **floating-rate loan.** Since LIBOR changes over time, this part of the pricing is risky. We assume that the add-on term (0.5 percent in this case) is fixed and therefore not risky.[27]

Borrowing on floating-rate terms may be desirable if the firm expects that short-term interest rates will fall over the two-year period. The borrowing terms also may be useful for establishing a hedge if the firm has assets with payoffs positively linked to LIBOR. If neither of the above conditions is the case, a two-year floating-rate loan exposes the firm to the risk that LIBOR will rise over the term of the loan.

Borrowers may choose to hedge this risk using **Eurodollar interest rate futures contracts.** At this time, we will describe only the basic hedging mechanism. A complete discussion of futures contracts and hedging appears in Chapter 11. A family of Eurodollar

---

[26]Commercial paper (CP) is an unsecured, uncollateralized, short-term obligation of the firm issued directly to private investors. CP is a liquid claim; thus, investors willingly accept a lower return. This has made CP a preferred mechanism for short-term loans rather than bank borrowing.

[27]A bank could retain the option to raise (or lower) the add-on term if there is a material decline (or improvement) in the firm's credit quality.

TABLE 9.3   Prices of Eurodollar Interest Rate Futures
June 20, 2000

						Yield		
				Eurodollar (CME)—$1 million; pts of 100%				
	Open	*High*	*Low*	*Settle*	*Chg.*	*Settle*	*Chg.*	*Open Interest*
July	93.17	93.17	93.16	93.16	−.01	6.84	+.01	41,818
Aug	93.11	93.11	93.10	93.10	−.01	6.90	+.01	10,368
Sept	93.07	93.07	93.04	93.05	−.02	6.95	+.02	625,571
Dec	92.88	92.88	92.85	92.86	−.04	7.14	+.04	506,608
Mr01	92.87	92.89	92.85	92.86	−.05	7.14	+.05	369,350
June	92.86	92.88	92.83	92.84	−.05	7.16	+.05	247,216
Sept	92.87	92.88	92.84	92.85	−.05	7.15	+.05	215,972
Dec	92.83	92.86	92.81	92.82	−.05	7.18	+.05	156,626
Mr02	92.89	92.92	92.87	92.88	−.04	7.12	+.04	133,746
June	92.89	92.92	92.88	92.89	−.04	7.11	+.04	93,409
Sept	92.89	92.93	92.87	92.89	−.04	7.11	+.04	106,461
Dec	92.85	92.89	92.84	92.85	−.04	7.15	+.04	75,648
Mr03	92.90	92.94	92.90	92.91	−.04	7.09	+.04	78,748
June	92.90	92.93	92.88	92.90	−.05	7.10	+.05	53,407
Sept	92.89	92.92	92.87	92.88	−.05	7.12	+.05	48,142
Dec	92.83	92.85	92.81	92.82	−.05	7.18	+.05	37,529
Mr04	92.87	92.90	92.85	92.86	−.06	7.14	+.06	36,134
June	92.85	92.87	92.83	92.83	−.06	7.17	+.06	33,191
Sept	92.83	92.85	92.80	92.81	−.06	7.19	+.06	28,792
Dec	92.75	92.76	92.72	92.73	−.06	7.27	+.06	27,104
Mr05	92.76	92.79	92.75	92.76	−.06	7.24	+.06	20,238
June	92.73	92.76	92.72	92.73	−.06	7.27	+.06	13,135
Sept	...	...	...	92.70	−.06	7.30	+.06	10,738
Dec	...	...	...	92.63	−.05	7.37	+.05	7,774
Mr.06	...	...	...	92.67	−.05	7.33	+.05	8,086
June	92.66	92.66	92.63	92.64	−.05	7.36	+.05	7,352
Sept	...	...	...	92.61	−.05	7.39	+.05	6,672
Dec	...	...	...	92.54	−.05	7.46	+.05	6,660
Mr07	...	...	...	92.58	−.05	7.42	+.05	5,137
June	...	...	...	92.55	−.04	7.45	+.04	3,813
Sept	...	...	...	92.53	−.04	7.47	+.04	3,363
Dec	...	...	...	92.46	−.04	7.54	+.04	4,816
Mr08	...	...	...	92.49	−.04	7.51	+.04	3,957
June	...	...	...	92.47	−.03	7.53	+.03	4,169
Sept	92.48	92.49	92.44	92.44	−.03	7.56	+.03	3,952
Dec	...	...	...	92.38	−.03	7.62	+.03	2,976
Mr09	...	...	...	92.41	−.03	7.59	+.03	2,315
June	92.42	92.42	92.37	92.38	−.02	7.62	+.02	2,364
Sept	...	...	...	92.36	−.02	7.64	+.02	2,167
Dec	...	...	...	92.29	−.02	7.71	+.02	1,623
Mr10	92.32	92.36	92.32	92.32	−.02	7.68	+.02	1,090

Estimated volume 318,792; volume Monday 282,778; open interest 3,384,489, − 49,689.

Source: Adapted from *The Wall Street Journal,* June 21, 2000.

interest rate futures contracts is actively traded on the Chicago Mercantile Exchange. The underlying asset reflected in these contracts is a three-month Eurodollar deposit. A sample of prices for June 20, 2000, is shown in Table 9.3. As the table reveals, contracts mature on a regular basis—March, June, September, and December of every year—for a range of dates as far as 10 years into the future.

If the two-year Eurodollar loan described above was to have its seven interest rate resets in September, and December of 2000, March, June, September and December of 2001, and March 2002, the risk of rising Eurodollar interest rates could be hedged by selling a strip of seven Eurodollar interest rate futures contracts, meaning one contract for each of the seven periods.[28] Because interest rates and futures prices move inversely (by convention), a rise in LIBOR will lead to a fall in futures prices. Thus, a short futures position will earn a profit to offset an increased interest rate cost.

Eurodollar interest futures contracts may be particularly useful for hedging short-term interest rate risks or risks for individual anniversary dates. If the firm has a longer-term loan, say three, five, or seven years, indexed to LIBOR, it may be more efficient to enter into an *interest rate swap* for hedging all of the uncertain future interest payments. An interest rate swap is an over-the-counter bank product that amounts to a collection (or strip) of interest rate futures contracts. As such, there may be some savings from scale economies associated with an interest rate swap compared with a strip of interest rate futures. Swaps are discussed in detail in Chapter 13.

Policy Matters—Public Policymakers

From time to time since its inception, the Eurocurrency market has raised significant concerns for policymakers. These concerns have not been shared equally by all nations. For some offshore financial centers—Luxembourg, Bermuda, small Caribbean nations, Middle Eastern nations, and Singapore—the rise of the Eurocurrency market has meant an important boost to employment and economic activity. For other nations—particularly the United States but also other major industrial countries—the rise of the Eurocurrency market was perceived as a threat to their ability to control macroeconomic conditions within their borders, and perhaps even as a threat to the fundamental safety and soundness of the financial system. With the passage of time, most of these fears about the Eurocurrency market have been put to rest, either through new policy agreements or a better understanding of how the Euromarkets operate.

As we suggested initially with Figure 9.1, the Eurocurrency markets are now acknowledged as fully competitive with the traditional onshore banking system. Rather than attempt to stamp out the Euromarkets, policymakers have opted to factor in the Euromarkets when setting domestic monetary and financial policies. And in some cases, policymakers have elected to adapt their local regulations and compete head-on with the Euromarkets.

Offshore Markets and Macroeconomic Stability

In its early years, the Eurocurrency market was often portrayed in terms that would frighten all but the most die-hard believer in free markets. The Eurocurrency market, it was alleged, enjoyed its high rate of growth because of a high deposit multiplier permitted by the absence of reserve requirements. This vast offshore credit expansion led to a loss in the effectiveness of national monetary control, the argument continued, and produced an inflationary bias in the industrial countries. The Eurocurrency market, in truth, lacked formal supervision and a lender of last resort. Allegedly, this left the market open to a run on deposits that could fold back on the onshore financial systems. At

---

[28]For the time being, we assume that the maturity dates of the futures contract and the interest rate reset dates are identical. If they are not, another element of uncertainty exists.

times, the stability and impact of the Eurocurrency markets seemed to genuinely concern financial policymakers.[29]

One might initially wonder how the Eurocurrency markets could escape the attention of European regulators. One answer is that in the United Kingdom, the Bank of England is primarily concerned with controlling the pound sterling money supply and sterling inflation, regulating the activities of British banks, and serving as the country's lender of last resort. While the Bank of England might have attempted to control Eurodollar borrowing and lending activities, it viewed these activities as outside its sphere of responsibility or influence. Had the Bank of England acted alone to supervise the Eurocurrency market, the activities would very likely have migrated to another, more hospitable regulatory climate. British banks had traditionally accepted deposits in many currencies, so the development of the Eurocurrency market was not out of keeping with the activities of an international financial center such as London. Finally, the Eurocurrency market helped the British financial system out of a nasty bind in the 1950s: how to enhance the international role of British banks while controlling their use of sterling in external markets. Instead of a heavy, repressive hand, the Bank of England adopted what Paul Einzig (1970, p. 17) called a policy of "benevolent neutrality" toward the Euromarkets.

Could the Offshore Markets Expand Indefinitely?

One factor that made the Eurocurrency market stand out was the absence of any reserve requirement on deposits and the potential for a limitless (and therefore dangerous) expansion of offshore deposits. But precise estimates of this deposit multiplier were hard to come by. Andrew Crockett (1976, p. 382), citing an internal working paper of the International Monetary Fund, reported that early estimates of the multiplier ranged from 0.50 to nearly 100. The problem in implementing multiplier analysis, Crockett argued, is that this framework is not applicable in an unregulated market driven by pure demand and supply forces. The reason that the combination of a $100 initial deposit and a 20 percent reserve requirement can be counted on to generate $500 in total bank deposits (in a closed banking system) is that the reserve requirement imposes a cost that exceeds the prudential reserves that banks would hold in an unregulated market. As a result, banks are likely to be fully "loaned up" so that the reserve requirement imposes a binding constraint on their ability to write loans. Without a reserve requirement, banks would continue to conduct business as any financial intermediary—writing loans as long as their marginal return exceeds their marginal costs.

Crockett (1976, p. 383) concluded that the size of the Eurocurrency market is determined "not by specific portfolio constraints put on banks but rather by the supply and demand for loanable funds" as we have presented in this chapter. Even though the market has no required reserves, the interaction of supply and demand for funds means that "the specter of uncontrolled credit expansion, made possible by an infinite [deposit] multiplier, is illusory" (Crockett, p. 384).

Approaches to Regulating Offshore Markets

While ruling out an infinite multiplier is comforting, it leaves unclear exactly how policymakers might attempt to control the Euromarkets. Another important insight for our understanding of the Eurocurrency market is that all banks that are significant

---

[29]See Ritter and Silber (1970, p. 179) and their discussion of Euromarkets and the national "Worry Meter."

producers of offshore deposits are also major producers of onshore deposits. No bank is important in the offshore market if it does not have a strong domestic base. As a consequence, the operations of offshore banks are well integrated with their onshore banking activities. The integration of offshore and onshore banking activities holds the key for how Eurocurrency markets can be "regulated" and kept from derailing national monetary policies.[30]

As our figures in this chapter have shown, under conditions of reasonable capital mobility, Eurocurrency interest rates are closely linked to those in domestic money markets of the same currency because Eurocurrency deposits are reasonably close substitutes for deposits in the domestic banking system. A decrease in the domestic money supply, for example, should lead to both higher domestic interest rates and higher Eurocurrency interest rates. In principle, the domestic monetary authority could retain adequate control over the rate of domestic monetary expansion if it takes the Euromarkets into account when formulating its targets. This is certainly easier said than done, but it nevertheless leaves the possibility for national monetary control alive. The central bank always loses some control when more financial activity takes place outside of central bank member banks. Still, monetary control is possible as long as there is a predictable link between the two sectors.

One word of warning is needed here, however. If Eurocurrency deposits and domestic banking deposits are deemed to be perfect substitutes, then domestic monetary authorities will not be able to exercise control through reserve requirements and other mechanisms that act as a tax on domestic banking. Any attempt to raise the burden of taxation on domestic banking activities would simply be offset by expansion in the Eurocurrency market.

The integration of the offshore and onshore banking systems suggests a far greater stability for the overall system. In effect, international banks pool their activities and hold reserves for the integrated worldwide system. Finding a high ratio of deposits to reserves in the London branch of a U.S. bank is no more a sign of instability than finding a high ratio of deposits to reserves in the suburban branch of the same bank. The presumption in both cases is that if funds were required at either branch, they would be forthcoming from the parent—the deposit multiplier in any slice of the bank is not meaningful.

Stability in the Eurocurrency markets is also enhanced through other mechanisms. We pointed out earlier that Eurobanks tend to follow a hedging strategy. Interbank Eurocurrency deposits and loans tend to be traded through a brokerage network similar to foreign exchange.[31] As most deposits are accepted for a fixed term and loan rates are reset periodically to LIBOR, exposure to interest rate risks can be kept to a minimum. Moreover, Eurobanks bear the market test through the scrutiny of depositors. Operating in an unregulated market is not a license for imprudent bank lending. Banks with more risky loan portfolios will see their deposit rates rise relative to other more conservatively managed banks (see Box 9.5).

The Basle Concordat.   A milestone for the Eurocurrency markets was reached in the early 1970s when discussions on how to monitor and regulate key aspects of the offshore markets finally reached fruition. One possible approach was to regulate on a

---

[30]The integration thesis is developed in Aliber (1980).

[31]Ellis (1981) claims that after receiving a large deposit from a nonbank, a Eurobank will usually immediately lend it out in the interbank market for as little as $1/32$ of 1 percent. With margins this low, it is not unusual for a deposit to be lent and re-lent several times before finding a nonbank borrower.

Box 9.5

Japanese Banking Woes: The Daiwa Banking Scandal and the Japan Premium

The major money center banks channel huge sums between depositors and borrowers. Accordingly, markets closely monitor the creditworthiness of banks. Many well-known American banks (such as Bank of America, Chase Manhattan, Citibank, Continental Illinois and others) saw their credit rating deteriorate in the 1980s following losses in real estate loans, developing-country sovereign debt, oil sector loans, and so forth. Each of these institutions paid a premium for borrowing relative to more highly rated banks.

In the summer of 1995, concern over credit quality shifted to Japanese banks. Prices of real estate and stocks had skyrocketed in Japan throughout the 1980s. When the economic bubble in Japan burst (the Nikkei stock index fell from nearly 40,000 in January 1990 to 15,000 in the third quarter of 1992), analysts thought that Japanese banks must have incurred huge losses on their real estate portfolios. Analysts could only make educated guesses about loan losses since it was not until 1993 that Japanese banks were required to disclose a small portion of their nonperforming assets. The Ministry of Finance reckoned that bad loans at Japanese banks totaled about ¥40 trillion (roughly $400 billion), but some independent analysts estimated twice this amount.*

Against this background, a small "Japan premium" developed in the offshore market, forcing Japanese banks to pay a fraction of a percent higher than other banks.

In September 1995, Daiwa Bank announced that more than $1 billion had been lost through unauthorized bond dealing in the bank's New York office. The difficulties were compounded by the accumulation of these trading losses over many years and the apparent failure of Daiwa's managers to notify Federal Reserve Bank officials in the United States until eight weeks after they learned of the fraud. Market analysts who thought the Japanese banks

held risky loan portfolios now feared that bank managers might be unaware of the true state of their own operations.

With the revelations from Daiwa unfolding, the **Japan premium** (the extra cost of LIBOR funding for Japanese banks) rose to 0.3 percent for some banks (such as the Bank of Tokyo) to 0.6 percent for other banks, and in some cases even higher.[†] The Japan premium diminished in 1996, but then resurfaced in early 1997 as falling Tokyo equity prices raised concerns about the ability of Japanese banks to meet their capital adequacy requirements. In November 1997, the Japan premium spiked to over 0.75 percent, coinciding with the failure of Yamaichi Securities, once Japan's fourth largest securities firm. Another spike to over 0.50 percent hit in November 1998, about the time that Long Term Credit Bank, another major Japanese financial institution, was nationalized.

The Japan premium clearly had a detrimental impact on Japanese banks. Either the banks absorbed the increased funding cost, which reduced profits, or they tried to pass the extra costs on to borrowers, which may have caused borrowers to patronize other banks. Either way, there was a clear market incentive for acting prudently in the international financial markets.

A recent research paper by Joe Peek and Eric Rosengren (1999) analyzes the Japan premium in detail. These authors find that the premium declined when either banks or the Japanese government took definitive actions (such as injecting funds into the banking system), but that mere announcements of plans or intentions had no significant impact.

---

*Gerard Baker, "Hidden Behind a Screen of Stability," *Financial Times*, Oct. 24, 1995, p. 17.
[†]*The Financial Times* ("Japan Bank Chief Tries to Calm Loan Fears," Oct. 25, 1995) quotes a Reuters report that the premium had reached one full percentage point.

---

territorial basis. Under this approach, the country in which a deposit was issued would impose reserve requirements on both domestic banks and branches and subsidiaries of foreign banks. Since offshore banking is footloose, the territorial approach would be effective only if agreement was reached among *all* countries, small and large, that might potentially harbor Eurobanks.

Eurocurrency banks could instead be regulated on a domiciliary approach requiring the country in which the headquarters of the bank is domiciled to impose consistent regulations across all offshore branches and subsidiaries. The latter approach would "only" require agreement across major industrial countries where the parents of all major Eurobanks reside. To escape the domiciliary approach, a large bank could move its headquarters to a regulation-free ministate. But this might not be a wise strategy, given (among other things) the value that depositors place on lender-of-last-resort facilities.

The approach taken by the Bank for International Settlements (BIS) to regulate the Eurocurrency markets was along the lines of the domiciliary approach.[32] In the Basle Concordat (1974), the United States and 30 other countries agreed to assume lender-of-last-resort responsibility for their offshore banks. In 1980, the BIS announced an agreement among central banks requiring commercial banks headquartered within their territories to consolidate their worldwide accounts. This agreement enabled bank examiners to regulate offshore and onshore operations on a consistent basis.

Competing for Markets: U.S. Policy Initiatives

Once the fear of unstable and uncontrollable Euromarkets had dwindled, U.S. policymakers (among others) turned their attention to the problem of *attracting* offshore banking activities within their regulatory borders.[33] By the end of the 1970s, the gross size of the Eurocurrency market exceeded $1 trillion. While U.S. banks were active in the Euromarkets, no offshore banking activities were located within U.S. borders. To attract offshore banking to the United States, regulations needed to be changed.

The Rise of International Banking Facilities.   In December 1981, the Federal Reserve Board amended its regulations to allow the creation of **international banking facilities (IBFs).** An IBF is essentially a "separate set of books" established within an existing U.S. banking institution: a U.S. chartered depositary institution, a U.S. branch or agency of a foreign bank, or a U.S. office of an Edge Act corporation would qualify. An IBF is exempt from deposit reserve requirements, interest rate ceilings, and federal deposit insurance. In effect, the IBF legislation creates an offshore banking environment located physically within the United States. These changes in federal regulation were necessary, but in some cases not sufficient, to make IBFs fully competitive with true offshore banking operations. State taxation of banking profits and activities was the culprit. Several states (New York and California among others) granted special tax status to IBFs to enable their establishment within state borders.[34]

To prohibit all U.S. banking activity from migrating to IBFs, important restrictions are placed on their operations. First and foremost, IBFs may not deal with U.S. residents, other than their parent institution and other IBFs. And those allowed transactions that involve nonresidents must relate to the customer's business activities *outside* the United States. This regulation is intended to prevent IBFs from competing directly with domestic credit sources for finance intended for domestic economic activity. Other restrictions (1) limit the maturity of IBF deposits—two days or greater initial maturity to keep IBF deposits from offering a close substitute for checking accounts; (2) restrict the size of IBF deposits—they must be greater than $100,000 to promote a wholesale market; and (3) disallow the issuance of negotiable instruments that could be traded in a secondary market and compete with domestic money market instruments.[35]

---

[32]For a thorough discussion of these events, see Dam (1982), pp. 320–28.

[33]The notion that financial market regulators actually "compete" for markets has been developed by Kane (1987). See Levich (1990), pp. 404–8, for an extension to the Euromarkets.

[34]In Florida, IBFs are exempt from all local taxes. See Chrystal (1984), p. 6.

[35]Interbank transactions with other IBFs are exempt from the maturity and size restrictions.

FIGURE 9.10 U.S. International Banking Facilities

Liabilities at Year-End, US$ Billions

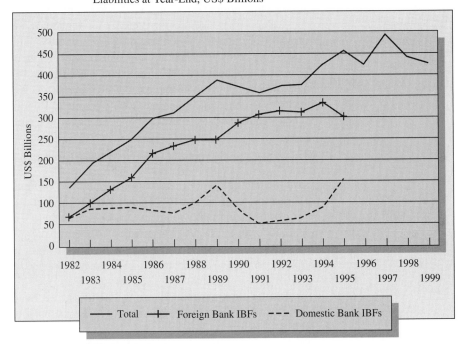

Sources: The years 1982–1986 are from Moffett and Stonehill (1989), who quote Federal Reserve sources; year totals for 1987–1999 are from Bank for International Settlements, "International Banking and Financial Market Developments," Table 2A, various issues; foreign component from Federal Reserve Bulletin, Table 4.30, various issues; domestic component computed by subtraction.

Following these regulatory changes, IBFs grew rapidly, reaching $300 billion in liabilities at the end of 1986 and rising gradually to $450 billion in 1995 (see Figure 9.10). Almost one-half of IBF offices are located in New York (followed by California, Florida, and Illinois in number of offices) and the larger share of IBF activity originates with foreign bank IBFs.[36]

In the push to establish IBFs and alter state and local tax laws, many claims and predictions were made. Initially some people thought that a U.S. offshore market might pose a severe competitive threat to London as the preeminent offshore financial center.[37] While competition or the threat of competition is always a concern, London has survived the rise of IBFs. In part, this reflects some important advantages that London retains. First, London's offshore market is not encumbered by the restrictions placed on IBF deposits and loans. London, because of its historic commitment to open financial markets, may be viewed as a superior location of activity. And finally, London's time zone remains an important advantage. Unless New York bankers are willing to extend

[36]Following the U.S. regulatory change, other nations have moved to permit offshore banking centers. Notably, the Japanese Offshore Market (JOM) began operations in December 1986, reaching $192 billion in assets by the end of 1987. The JOM is designed to compete with Hong Kong and Singapore for the dominant position as an Asian-Pacific financial center. Other countries, including Canada, have announced plans to develop international banking centers. See Moffett and Stonehill (1989).

[37]For example, Stanislas Yassukovich, "Could the Euromarkets Leave London?" *Euromoney,* Oct. 1981, pp. 249–53.

their trading hours into the European business day, IBFs are not able to compete effectively for this business.[38]

Coupled with the prediction of London's demise was the view that U.S. IBFs would rise in importance and generate a growing volume of business that their parent institutions would not have gained otherwise. Contradicting this prediction, the initial growth of IBF deposits appears to coincide with a decline in deposits at other offshore centers in the Caribbean and other U.S. time-zone centers. In fact, Michael Moffett and Arthur Stonehill (1989) reported that major banks have retained their offshore branch operations to deal with U.S. domestic residents, even though they run active IBF operations. Further, Moffett and Stonehill's survey suggested that the U.S. time zone has not proved to be a significant advantage for IBFs and that on balance IBFs have not resulted in a significant expansion of the parents' customer base.

Growth in deposits held at IBFs stalled in the 1990s (see again Figure 9.10). In 1999, IBF deposits totaled $424 billion, or slightly less than in 1995.

Beyond IBFs: Foreign Currency Deposits in the United States.   The factors that continue to differentiate IBF deposits from those in true offshore markets are the restriction on access by domestic residents and the restriction against nonresidents using IBF accounts to conduct domestic business activity. The situation raises the question of why limitations have been placed on domestic residents' access to foreign currency deposits placed in U.S. banks. In international financial centers such as London, no restrictions exist on the issuance or use of deposit accounts in the world's many currencies. U.S. policies in this area date to 1973. After the collapse of the Bretton Woods system, U.S. bankers sensed that the demand for accounts in units other than the US$ was likely to increase—and U.S. banks wanted to participate in that market. Responding to the president of the Bank of America, the chairman of the Federal Reserve Board of Governors wrote:

> The greater scope for movements out of dollars into foreign-currency assets could at times pose an increased threat to the international stability of the dollar. At the present time, therefore, the Board of Governors does not believe that the Bank of America should undertake to provide foreign-currency deposit facilities in the United States.[39]

Recall that the United States was still under a capital restraint program that limited loans to foreign entities. Subsequent requests from U.S. banks received similar replies noting that it would not be in the "public interest" for member banks to issue foreign currency time deposits at U.S. offices. Attempts by some banks to issue US$ accounts indexed to a foreign currency were disallowed on the grounds that these constituted securities, which at the time could not be issued by commercial banks. In the mid-1980s, mutual funds filled a gap in the retail market by organizing money-market mutual funds denominated in foreign currencies, usually the DM, £, and ¥. These open-end funds held foreign currency denominated certificates of deposit offshore and issued shares to domestic investors.

Finally, on December 23, 1988, the Federal Reserve ruled that U.S. banks could offer foreign currency denominated accounts starting January 1, 1990. This ruling raises

---

[38]U.S. banks could hold a possible time zone advantage; namely, access to the last central bank to close ahead of the international date line. IBFs could be favored for US$ transactions that require "good funds" at the last possible moment on any day.

[39]Correspondence from Arthur F. Burns to A. W. Claussen, Oct. 23, 1973, in *Currency and Bond Market Trends,* Merrill Lynch, Feb. 17, 1989, p. 3.

many questions involving reserve requirements, deposit insurance, and some elements of political risk. Advertising and promotion of these new accounts is rare. It is not clear whether costly regulations make it prohibitive to offer this product within the U.S. market, or whether few marketing efforts have been made to promote it. This may reflect another hysteresis effect, whereby the old way of guiding nondollar accounts of residents to foreign markets is continued even though new regulations would permit them to be placed within the United States.

Offshore Markets: European Policy Concerns

The European Union (EU) has attempted to create a single market in both goods and services. To create a level playing field in financial services, the EU has sought to harmonize rules on withholding taxes and disclosure of interest paid to depositors and shareholders. One EU country, Luxembourg, stands out because it imposes no withholding tax on investment income and resolutely refuses to supply information about depositors to other tax authorities. These are long-standing policies for Luxembourg, a prominent center for both Eurocurrency and Eurobond markets.

Events took an important turn in 1989 when Germany imposed a 10 percent withholding tax on investment income, and then raised this tax to 30 percent in January 1993. The net flow of capital from Germany to Luxembourg between 1991 and 1994 hit an estimated DM 120 billion.[40] This raised at least two problems for Germany: (1) the lost tax revenue, and (2) the difficulty in monitoring the effective German money supply.

In response, Luxembourg officials agreed to modify their tax and reporting policies, but only after all industrial countries have shut down their tax loopholes (in particular, Britain's Channel Islands and the Dutch-affiliated Netherlands Antilles). Without broad-based harmonization of tax and disclosure policies, Luxembourg officials are right to claim that an EU-wide policy would very likely drive the offshore market on to Switzerland, Singapore, or elsewhere. An EU policy to require harmonization of withholding taxes and disclosure would clearly be detrimental to Luxembourg, which generates 20 percent of its GDP from financial services. But there could also be a wider impact on the cost of capital for EU firms.[41]

The situation is especially disturbing for Germany because German banks constitute the largest segment in Luxembourg. Germany could respond by removing the secrecy provisions of German banks, but this would be extremely unpopular. In its place, the German authorities have mounted a campaign to identify banks and individual bankers involved in tax evasion schemes with Luxembourg.[42] The campaign bore some fruit when raids by tax inspectors contributed to the early retirement of the chairman of Dresdner Bank and other bank officials were convicted of abetting tax evasion. In June 1998, a well-publicized raid by 300 tax inspectors at the headquarters of Deutsche Bank put more bank officials and customers under investigation.[43]

---

[40]Peter Gumbel, "Luxembourg Sops Up Neighbor's Capital," *The Wall Street Journal,* Nov. 16, 1994, p. A22.

[41]A study for the Luxembourg Bankers Association calculated that establishing an EU withholding tax on interest policy could increase the cost of capital in the EU by 0.3 percent. See Philip Eade, "Facing Up to Harder Times," *Euromoney,* May 1996, pp. 132–34.

[42]See "German Tax Probe Widens," *The Wall Street Journal,* Jan. 5, 1996, p. A6; "A Tax Haven Is Living on Borrowed Time," *The Wall Street Journal,* Aug. 23, 1996, p. A6.

[43]See "Tax Raids: Sleepless in Frankfurt, Again," *The Economist,* June 20, 1998.

Negotiations took a more positive turn in June 2000 when EU members agreed to scrap their bank secrecy laws and provide information on nonresidents' savings accounts.[44] But the agreement is far from a final deal. EU members have until December 2000 to draw up the details of which tax data to exchange, and until December 2002 to persuade third countries (the United States, Switzerland, and others) to introduce their own information exchange regimes. The details of the information swap will be critical. For example, Luxembourg has argued that investment funds pay dividends rather than interest and therefore should be exempt from tax withholding.[45] Luxembourg should have an ally in the United Kingdom, which also supported an exemption for Eurobonds, our topic for Chapter 10. Eurobonds have historically paid interest on a gross basis without withholding taxes.

----

[44]See "EU Agrees Big Changes to Bank Secrecy Laws in War on Tax Evasion," and "Europe's Tax Data Swap," *Financial Times,* June 21, 2000.

[45]See "Bid to Break Deadlock over Withholding Tax," *Financial Times,* October 29, 1999.

Summary

In this chapter, we examined the principles underlying the formation of the Eurocurrency market. The offshore market can be likened to a parallel market that offers similar services to the onshore market, but in a different regulatory climate. These regulatory differences permit offshore markets to offer higher deposit rates and lower lending rates than in the traditional onshore market. Arbitrage tends to keep offshore rates similar for any individual currency across market centers. Offshore rates in different currencies generally reflect the interest rate parity condition.

Barriers are needed to keep the onshore and offshore markets separate and permit a coexistence of both markets. Offshore depositors face additional risks of exchange controls and blocked funds. The legal status of cross-border deposits is complicated. Offshore deposi-tors are exposed to risk when an act-of-state occurs, but very often the parent bank bears the ultimate responsibility for branch deposits. Offshore borrowers do not face these risks, but their access to the market may be limited by size and credit quality.

Regulation, or the absence of it, has been an important issue throughout the existence of the Eurocurrency market. The Basle Concordat helped to clarify regulatory responsibility for the Euromarket. Regulators generally have responded to the Euromarket by liberalizing their onshore markets and, in some cases, establishing competing markets such as the International Banking Facilities in the United States. The Eurocurrency market is now a mature marketplace that is well integrated with domestic banking and financial markets.

Questions

1. What are the main factors that contributed to the creation and development of Eurocurrency markets?

2. What is the difference between onshore markets and offshore markets?

3. The United States could have an offshore market for US$ in the United States. Is this statement true or false? Explain.

4. Describe the multiplier effect in the case of the creation of Eurodollars. Use a basic example.

5. What are international banking facilities (IBFs) and why were they created? Discuss why the IBFs did not impact London's market share of the Eurocurrency market.

6. Describe the relationship between the onshore deposit rate, the offshore deposit rate, the onshore lending rate, and the offshore lending rate. Look in today's newspaper (*The Wall Street Journal* or *Financial Times*) and see if this relationship holds for US$ rates. What about € or UK£ rates?

7. What kind of risk does a depositor incur when maintaining an offshore account? What kind of risk does a borrower incur when maintaining an offshore loan?

8. From the standpoint of a depositor, what factors differentiate the appeal of two offshore banking centers?

9. What did the *Wells Fargo Asia Limited* vs. *Citibank* case demonstrate as far as legal issues of Eurocurrency markets are concerned?

10. How would a firm choose between onshore and offshore borrowing? What kind of interest rate expectations would favor onshore borrowing as opposed to offshore borrowing?

11. How could firms and financial institutions use the Eurocurrency markets to hedge their interest rate risk exposure?

12. Are the Eurocurrency markets a threat to the stability of the world financial system? Give both sides of the argument.

13. Discuss the control mechanisms available to national financial market regulators to limit the possible negative impact of the Eurocurrency markets. What are the limitations facing national financial market regulators?

14. Define the term *Japan premium* as it is used in the Eurocurrency market. What factors have contributed to the Japan premium?

Exercises

1. Suppose the Eurodollar deposit rate in London is 6.5 percent and the dollar deposit rate in New York is 6.0 percent.
   a. What factors could explain the interest rate differential between the two locations?
   b. Suppose the British Treasury imposes a 0.1 percent tax on deposits taken in London. What impact will this have on funds deposited in London?
   c. Suppose that all offshore centers are subject to the same 0.1 percent tax on deposits? What impact will this have on offshore markets?
   d. Returning to the original proposition, suppose the Fed increases short-term rates in the United States by 0.5 percent. What impact would you expect in the offshore rates?

2. Atlantic Richfield, a big U.S. oil and gas company, has a large amount of debt indexed to short-term Eurodollar rates. A $100 million facility at Deutsche Bank is due in six months in mid-December 2000. Atlantic Richfield pays LIBOR +0.25 percent and the treasurer expects to roll over the $100 million for another three months. The treasurer is expecting interest rates to go up during the next six months.
   a. Use Table 9.3 to illustrate how Atlantic Richfield could hedge its interest rate exposure using futures traded on the Chicago Mercantile Exchange (CME). Show all the steps, now and in December. (*Hint:* For convenience, assume that CME maturity dates coincide with the firm's rollover dates.)

   b. Suppose in December that LIBOR is 6.50 percent. Will the firm have a gain or a loss from its hedge? How large is the gain or loss in dollar terms? How much interest (in dollars) will the firm pay to Deutsche Bank for the three-month period commencing in December?
   c. What if LIBOR is 7.50 percent in mid-December? Will the firm have a gain or a loss from its hedge? How large is the gain or loss in dollar terms? How much interest (in dollars) will the firm pay to Deutsche Bank for the three-month period commencing in December?

3. General Motors finances itself, among other channels, by using one-year, floating-rate notes whose rates are recalculated every three months at LIBOR + ⅛. A new $250 million issue with a one-year maturity is planned for mid-September 2001.
   a. Describe how GM could hedge its interest payments for the year. (*Hint:* For convenience, assume that CME maturity dates coincide with the firm's rollover dates.)
   b. Using Table 9.3, what is the yearly rate that GM can secure if it hedges?
   c. Calculate GM's total costs for the $250 million issue, assuming that it hedges.

4. The ABC firm is considering borrowing $50 million for one year, either at a fixed rate of 6.50 percent in the U.S. domestic market or at a floating rate indexed to three-month LIBOR + ¼ in the Eurocurrency market. Currently, three-month

LIBOR is 5.25 percent and it is expected to remain constant for the year.

a. How much would ABC save if it uses the Euromarkets and these expectations are met? (*Hint:* For convenience, assume that CME maturity dates coincide with the firm's rollover dates.)

b. What are the risks in using a Euromarket loan?

c. Calculate the eventual saving for ABC if LIBOR increases by .50 percent every three months.

5. Suppose that three-month Eurodollars are quoted in the interbank markets at 6.0 percent to 6.125 percent by London banks, and 6.25 percent to 6.375 percent by Singapore banks.

a. Explain how you could attempt to make arbitrage profits in the above case.

b. How large is the profit from arbitraging $1 million in this case?

c. What risks and/or costs do you face in attempting the arbitrage?

6. Consider Watanabe Bank in Japan. It has a portfolio of $10 billion in loans to AA-rated companies. The loans are priced at US$ LIBOR + 25 bp. The bank also has a portfolio of $5 billion in loans to BBB-rated companies. These loans are priced at US$ LIBOR + 50 bp.

a. Suppose that the Watanabe Bank is subject to a Japan premium in the Euromarket equal to 10 bp. Calculate the impact on the bank's revenues as a result of the Japan premium.

b. Now suppose the Japan premium rises to 30 bp. Again, calculate the impact on the bank's revenues as a result of the Japan premium.

c. Suppose that the Japan premium is predicted to remain at 30 bp for some time. What changes would you recommend for the bank's lending strategy? What other changes could you propose to improve the bank's profitability?

References

Aliber, Robert Z. "The Integration of the Offshore and Domestic Banking System." *Journal of Monetary Economics* 6 (1980), pp. 509–26.

Chrystal, K. Alec. "International Banking Facilities." *Monthly Review,* Federal Reserve Bank of St. Louis, Apr. 1984, pp. 5–11.

Clendenning, E. Wayne. *The Euro-Dollar Market.* Oxford: Oxford University Press, 1970.

Crockett, Andrew D. "The Euro-Currency Market: An Attempt to Clarify Some Basic Issues." *IMF Staff Papers* 23, no. 2 (July 1976), pp. 375–86.

Dam, Kenneth W. *The Rules of the Game.* Chicago: University of Chicago Press, 1982.

Dooley, Michael P., and Peter Isard. "Capital Controls, Political Risk, and Deviations from Interest Rate Parity." *Journal of Political Economy,* 1980, pp. 370–84.

Einzig, Paul. *The Euro-Dollar System,* 4th ed. London: St. Martin's Press, 1970.

Ellis, John G. "Eurobanks and the Interbank Market." *Bank of England Quarterly Bulletin,* Sept. 1981, pp. 351–64.

Friedman, Milton. "The Euro-Dollar Market: Some First Principles." *Morgan Guaranty Survey,* Oct. 1969, pp. 4–14.

Herring, Richard J. "Comment on Savona: Who Bears the Risk of Controls on Eurodeposits, Some Recent Developments." In *Protectionism and International Banking,* ed. Gerhard Fels and George Sutija. London: Macmillan, 1991, pp. 62–77.

Herring, Richard, and Friedrich Kübler. "The Allocation of Risk in Cross-Border Deposit Transactions." *Northwestern University Law Review* 89, no. 3 (Spring 1995), pp. 942–1028.

Kane, Edward J. "Competitive Financial Reregulation: An International Perspective." In *Threats to International Financial Stability,* ed. R. Portes and A. Swoboda. London: Cambridge University Press, 1987.

Kvasnicka, Joseph G. "Eurodollars—An Important Source of Funds for American Banks." *Business Condition,* Federal Reserve Bank of Chicago, June 1969.

Levich, Richard M. "The Euromarkets After 1992." In *European Banking in the 1990s,* ed. J. Dermine. Oxford: Basil Blackwell, 1990.

Levich, Richard M., and Robert G. Hawkins. "Foreign Investment." Chapter 18 in *Financial Markets and Institutions,* 2nd ed., ed. Murray Polakof and Thomas Durkin. Boston: Houghton Mifflin, 1981.

Moffett, Michael H., and Arthur Stonehill. "International Banking Facilities Revisited." *Journal of International Financial Management and Accounting* 1, no. 1 (Spring 1989), pp. 88–103.

Peek, Joe, and Eric S. Rosengren. "Determinants of the Japan Premium: Actions Speak Louder than Words," NBER Working Paper No. 7251, July 1999.

Ritter, Lawrence S., and William L. Silber. *Money.* New York: Basic Books, 1970.

Timberlake, Richard H. "Clearinghouse Associations." In *The New Palgrave Dictionary of Money and Finance,* ed. P. Newman, M. Millgate, and J. Eatwell. London: Macmillan, 1992.

Watson, Maxwell; Donald Mathieson; Russell Kincaid; and Eliot Kalter. *International Capital Markets.* Occasional Paper No. 43. Washington, DC: International Monetary Fund, Feb. 1986.

10 THE EUROBOND MARKET

"Indeed, it is paradoxical that a law which was intentionally prejudicial to the interests of foreign borrowers, had the effect of creating the largest international capital market the world has known."

Frederick G. Fisher, III (1988)

Learning Objectives

After reading this chapter, students should

1. Understand the factors that led to the development of the offshore Eurobond market and its sustained growth even after key U.S. capital controls were eliminated in 1974.

2. Be familiar with the regulatory and institutional characteristics of the Eurobond market that enable it to compete with traditional onshore bond markets.

3. Be aware of the typical yields on Eurodollar bonds in comparison to the yields on US$ denominated bonds in the onshore market.

4. Understand how various companies and the U.S. Treasury have used the Eurobond market to gain a funding advantage.

5. Appreciate how the Rule 144a market developed in the United States in response to the Eurobond market.

The Eurobond market is the market for long-term debt instruments issued and traded in the offshore market. Like the Eurocurrency market, the necessary condition for the development of a Eurobond market is differences in national regulation. Increasing capital mobility and greater ease in telecommunications have provided the sufficient conditions, allowing the Eurobond market to flourish. From a base of zero in the late 1950s, the Eurobond market has grown to an annual volume of new issues that often nears or surpasses the annual volume of new U.S. corporate bond issues. Through regulatory differences as well as innovations in market processes and product offerings, the Eurobond market has carved out an important niche in the international capital market, providing benefits to investors and borrowers—and on occasion profits to the parties who intermediate the transactions. Similar to the Eurocurrency market, the Eurobond market is in effect a **parallel market,** but one that has *not* put its chief rivals—the onshore markets for domestic and foreign bonds—out of business.

To be precise, a **Eurobond** was once defined as a debt instrument (1) underwritten by an international syndicate, and (2) offered for sale simultaneously in a number of countries.[1] As a consequence of (2), a Eurobond is usually denominated in a currency (or unit of account) that is foreign to a large number of buyers. With the introduction of the **bought deal,** in which a single underwriter commits to an entire issue in advance, the first criterion may be lost as a distinctive element of a Eurobond issue.

In contrast, a **domestic bond** is an obligation of a domestic issuer that is underwritten by a syndicate of domestic investment banks, denominated in domestic currency, and offered for sale in the domestic market. A **foreign bond** is similar to a domestic bond except that the issuer of the foreign bond is a foreign entity, which may be beyond the legal reach of investors in the event of default. For this reason, some domestic institutional investors may follow charters that restrict or prohibit purchasing foreign bonds. The definition of a "domestic" or "foreign" bond that we adopt comes from the nationality of the *issuer* in relation to the *marketplace*.[2] The term *foreign* may lead to some confusion in this context. A US$ bond issued in the United States by General Motors and a ¥ bond issued in Japan by Toyota are both domestic bonds from the standpoint of the regulations that govern their initial offering and secondary market trading. From the *investor perspective,* Americans (Japanese) would view the Toyota (General Motors) bond as foreign in the sense that the investment is denominated in a foreign currency and traded in a foreign marketplace. Foreign currency denominated bonds play an important role in international portfolio diversification, as we will discuss in Chapter 14.

Particular segments of the foreign bond market (as defined from the issuer perspective) sometimes take on colorful names. For example, US$ obligations of non-U.S. firms that are underwritten and issued in the U.S. market are called **Yankee bonds.** Japanese yen obligations of non-Japanese firms that are underwritten and issued in the Japanese market are called **Samurai bonds.** And British pound sterling obligations of non-U.K. firms that are underwritten and issued in the U.K. market are called **Bulldog bonds.** These names and others have proliferated along with the development of international financial markets. (See Box 10.1 for a distinction between Eurobonds and euro-denominated bonds.)

In the next section we present a historical overview of the Eurobond market and link it with data on the growth of issuing activity. Next, we review the regulatory and institutional characteristics of the Eurobond market and contrast them with those in traditional onshore bond markets. Then, we describe the process of issuing a Eurobond and suggest how the market has responded to the pressures that arise from operating in a largely unregulated environment. We then offer empirical evidence on the pricing of Eurobonds, making use of several case studies. The final two sections review the policy issues that confront both private enterprises and public policymakers when domestic, foreign, and Eurobond markets are all active simultaneously but with different elements of regulation.

[1]Levich (1985, p. 258). Some organizations (the BIS and the OECD, for example) refer to "external bonds" or "international bonds" rather than Eurobonds, perhaps to suggest that the scope of the market extends beyond Europe. In this book, we will classify the Eurobond and foreign markets as two elements of the international bond market.

[2]A global bond offering combines elements of both domestic and foreign bonds. We discuss global bonds later in this chapter. Brady bonds and other emerging market bonds are discussed in Chapter 14.

Box 10.1

Eurobonds Are Not the Same as Bonds Denominated in Euros

Prior to 1999, if a German firm issued a bond denominated in Italian lire to Italians, we would have called this a foreign bond. Or if a German firm issued a bond denominated in DM to Italian, French, and Spanish investors, we could have called this a Eurobond. With the advent of European Economic and Monetary Union (EMU), the euro is the common domestic currency of all 12 euro-zone countries. Now, if a German firm issues a bond denominated in euros to Italian, French, and Spanish investors, or if an Italian government agency issues a bond denominated in euros to Austrian and Dutch investors, these are classified as domestic bonds. Collectively, all of these domestic bonds are known as euro-zone, euro-area, or euroland bonds. They are

not Eurobonds in the sense commonly used in international finance—meaning bonds issued in the offshore market.

So let's test ourselves. If a German firm were to issue a bond denominated in euros to Swiss, British, and Danish investors, this would be a Eurobond because the euro is not the domestic currency of any of these three countries. As it happens, it is a euro-denominated Eurobond. But if U.S., Swiss, or British firms offer euro-denominated bonds for sale in Frankfurt, Paris, and Milan, these would be foreign bonds. In these cases the euro is the local currency of Frankfurt, Paris, and Milan, but the issuers are from outside the EMU.

Historical Overview and Dimensions of the Eurobond Market

There is disagreement surrounding the exact starting point for the Eurobond market. Citing World Bank records, M. S. Mendelsohn claims that Petrofina, SA, the Belgian petroleum company, deserves the honor for its $5 million issue in 1957.[3] Frederick Fisher cites SACOR, the Portuguese petroleum company, for its 1961 bond issue denominated in European Units of Account (EUA).[4] Over the 1957–1962 period, more than $500 million was raised through 22 Eurobond issues. At about this time the Eurocurrency market—the offshore market for short-term loans and deposits—was taking shape. Given the large share of international transactions denominated in US$, it was reasonable to predict that Europeans and other offshore residents would soon demand longer-term offshore assets denominated in US$, as well as European currencies. Although natural forces were in place, the development of the Eurobond market was about to receive an important, policy-induced stimulus.

A First Stimulus to the Eurobond Market: The IET

Driven out of concern for a deteriorating U.S. balance of payments, President John F. Kennedy proposed the enactment of the **interest equalization tax (IET)** on July 18, 1963. As we explained in Chapter 9, the IET operated like an excise tax on purchases of new or outstanding foreign stocks and bonds issued or trading in the United States. The rate of tax varied with maturity, ranging from 2.75 percent for bonds with three years remaining to maturity and extending to 15 percent for equities or for bonds with more than 28½ years remaining to maturity. It was estimated that the tax raised the effective cost of foreign borrowing in the United States by about 1 percent, thus bringing the cost of U.S. funds into rough alignment, or equalization, with foreign rates.

---

[3]Mendelsohn (1980), p. 137.
[4]Fisher (1988), p. 11.

The design of the IET played a larger role than expected. While a 1 percent increment in cost may seem modest, the full amount of the interest equalization tax was due at the time the foreign security was purchased. This was a powerful disincentive that effectively closed down the Yankee bond market, and it was a powerful inducement for foreign borrowers to migrate offshore and set up a US$-denominated bond market in London and Luxembourg.

The IET was proposed as a temporary measure to reduce U.S. capital outflows and take pressure off the U.S. balance of payments. However, the IET was renewed several times—expanded to cover short-term bank lending to foreigners, and extended so that the president could vary the tax rate allowing an effective annual increment to borrowing costs of 0 to 1.5 percent

A Second Round of Stimulus to the Eurobond Market

As the IET proved ineffective in resolving the U.S. balance of payments dilemma, still further policy measures were taken. In February 1965, President Lyndon Johnson imposed a Voluntary Foreign Credit Restraint (VFCR) program that set voluntary limits on the direct foreign investments made by U.S. corporations. Firms making a "positive" contribution to the U.S. balance of payments (such as through increased exports or increased dividend repatriation) were allowed some additional rights to make foreign investments. By January 1968, however, the VFCR limits on foreign investment were made mandatory, administered through a newly created Office of Foreign Direct Investment (OFDI). The VFCR and OFDI programs effectively forced U.S. multinationals offshore to meet the financing needs for their foreign projects.

In Table 10.1, we see that the (gross) volume of Eurobond issues reached $5.9 billion in 1972, substantially greater than the volume of foreign bonds that until 1960 had been the sole component of the international bond market. The growth of the Eurobond market during this period was aided substantially by the cushion of U.S. regulation. With direct competition from the Yankee bond market (located in New York) effectively removed, Euromarket participants were able to develop professional relationships among themselves and client relationships with issuers, as well as issuing techniques, clearing and settlement arrangements, and products well suited to the new market.

The Eurobond Market Endures

Both the IET and OFDI programs were extended several times until January 1974, when both were scrapped. In Table 10.1, we see that Eurobond market volume collapsed in 1974 to one-third of its 1972 level. The US$ segment fell further to only one-quarter of its 1972 level. The foreign bond market, however, showed steady growth over the early 1970s. Sensing the market's possible demise, the April 1973 cover of *Euromoney* magazine depicted the Eurobond market as a picked-over skeleton lying lifeless in the desert. With U.S. controls abolished, wasn't it likely that foreign borrowing activity would return to its traditional home in New York?

Any prediction of the demise of the Eurobond market would have been wildly premature. During the remainder of the 1970s, both the foreign bond market and the Eurobond market grew at a similar pace, each sharing roughly 50 percent of international bond issues. But during the 1980s, the Eurobond market surged. Since 1985, roughly 80 percent of all international bond issues have been floated in the Euromarket, surpassing 85 percent in 1994 (see Figure 10.1). New issue volume in the Eurobond market has

TABLE 10.1   **Eurobonds, Foreign Bonds, and U.S. Corporate Bonds:
Volume of New Issues**
Millions of U.S. Dollars

Year	Eurobonds Total	Eurobonds Euro-$ Bonds	Foreign Bonds	Total International Bond Issues	U.S. Corporate Bond Issues[a]
1970	$ 2,908	$ 1,775	$ 1,595	$ 4,503	$ 25,384
1971	3,491	2,221	2,644	6,135	24,775
1972	5,936	3,908	3,412	9,348	19,434
1973	3,931	2,447	3,646	7,577	13,649
1974	1,955	996	4,723	6,678	25,903
1975	8,130	3,738	11,346	19,476	32,583
1976	14,036	9,276	18,190	32,226	26,453
1977	17,222	11,627	16,205	33,427	24,072
1978	13,590	7,290	20,154	33,744	19,815
1979	18,256	12,565	22,264	40,520	25,814
1980	23,724	16,427	17,950	41,674	41,587
1981	31,427	26,830	21,369	52,796	37,653
1982	51,499	43,959	26,397	77,896	44,278
1983	48,196	38,428	27,828	76,024	47,369
1984	78,937	63,593	27,953	106,890	73,357
1985	130,766	96,822	31,229	161,994	119,559
1986	180,944	118,096	39,359	220,303	231,936
1987	127,040	58,070	40,252	167,292	209,279
1988	166,428	74,539	48,274	214,702	202,215
1989	212,800	117,500	42,900	255,700	179,694
1990	180,100	70,000	49,800	229,900	188,778
1991	258,100	81,600	50,600	308,700	286,930
1992	276,100	103,200	57,600	333,700	378,058
1993	394,600	147,700	86,400	481,000	486,879
1994	368,400	149,400	60,200	428,600	365,050
1995	371,300	144,400	96,000	467,300	408,806
1996	589,800	268,700	119,000	708,800	567,671
1997	735,100	361,700	96,500	831,600	708,188
1998	768,488	396,313	100,883[b]	869,371	923,771
1999	1,051,425	505,412	289,915	1,341,340	818,694
Compound Growth	20.31%	19.49%	17.94%	19.64%	12.33%

[a]Public, domestic offerings by U.S. corporations only.

[b]Author's estimate.

Sources: Morgan Guaranty Trust, *World Financial Markets,* various issues; OECD, *Financial Market Trends,* various issues; *Federal Reserve Bulletin,* various issues; International Securities Market Association, *Annual Reports.*

exceeded the volume of U.S. corporate (public) bond issues in 9 of the last 18 years (see Table 10.1) and surpassed *$1 trillion* in new issues in 1999.

The Eurobond market has grown in other dimensions as well. In the 1970s, the US$-denominated segment comprised nearly two-thirds of the market. Between 1990 and 1995, the market share of the US$ fell to between 30 and 40 percent with the DM, £, and ¥ taking about 10 percent each, and the remainder spread across the C$, FFr and other currencies (see Figure 10.2). The ECU garnered more than 12.5 percent of the Eurobond market in 1991, before the ERM collapse. This trend away from the US$

FIGURE 10.1   **Eurobonds and Foreign Bonds**
Percentage of Total International Bonds

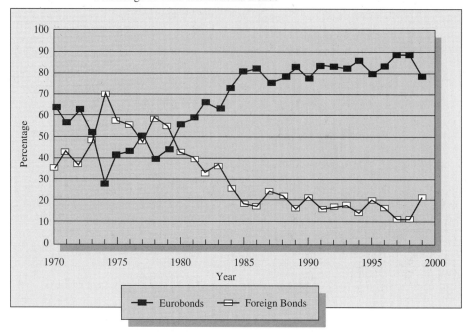

Source: OECD, *Financial Market Trends,* various issues, and International Securities Market Association, *Annual Reports.*

FIGURE 10.2   **Eurobond Issues by Currency, 1970–1995**
Market Shares Total 100%

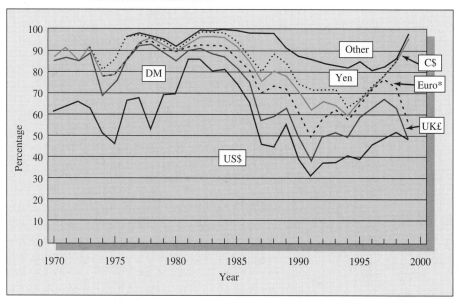

*Prior to 1998, bonds denominated in ECU.

Source: OECD, *Financial Market Trends,* various issues, and International Securities Market Association, *Annual Reports.*

FIGURE 10.3   Secondary Market Trading in Eurobonds
Annual Turnover in Euroclear and Cedel Combined

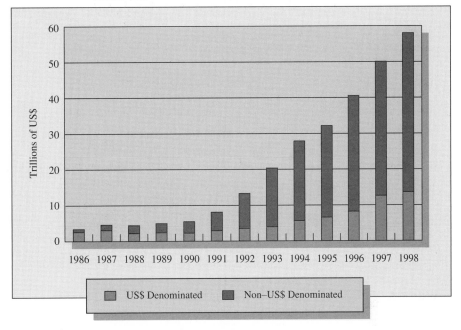

Source: Datastream.

illustrated the innovative style of the market. Increasingly, Eurobonds were issued in currencies *other* than the US$, and then combined with a currency swap to achieve lower cost funds in US$, DM, or another traditional unit of account. This technique seeks to exploit pricing opportunities in the non-US$ segments of the Eurobond market.

After 1995, the US$ share of the Eurobond market expanded, exceeding 50 percent in 1998. The Euro returned as an important currency in the Eurobond market in 1998 with a 12 percent share in 1998. With the start of EMU in 1999, the Euro's share expanded to 39 percent as the DM, FFr, Italian lire and other legacy currencies fell out of use. Overall, almost 95 percent of all Eurobonds issued in 1999 were denominated in either US$, Euro or UK£.

At the same time, the market has grown in terms of the maturities that can be issued. The most common maturity for a Eurobond is now in the range of 5 to 7 years, but issues extending to 10 and 20 years and more are also regularly observed. The average issue size also has grown, surpassing $100 million in 1986, with some issues in excess of $1 billion. Larger issue size is associated with greater liquidity. Finally, secondary market trading in Eurobonds accelerated in the 1980s, reaching more than $6 trillion annually in 1990 and approaching $60 trillion in 1998 (see Figure 10.3). The growth in liquidity has been aided by Euroclear and Cedel, the major privately owned electronic clearing and settlement systems for Eurobonds.

Clearly, the Eurobond market did not expire once American regulations such as the IET and OFDI were abolished in 1974. The Eurobond market must have retained a number of advantages that, once learned, were hard to give up. We now describe some of the most important regulatory and institutional characteristics of the Eurobond market that have helped to secure its place as a thriving parallel market.

TABLE 10.2   Comparative Characteristics of Bond Issues in the International Bond Market

	U.S. Market: Domestic and Foreign Bonds	Non-U.S. Market: Domestic and Foreign Bonds	Eurobond Market
Regulatory bodies	Securities and Exchange Commission	Official agency approval	Minimum regulatory control
Disclosure requirements	More detailed • High initial expense • High ongoing expense • Onerous to non-U.S. firms	Variable	Determined by market practices
Issuing costs	0.75–1.00%	Variable to 4.0%	2.0–2.5%
Rating requirements	Yes	Usually not	No, but commonly done
Exchange listing	Usually not listed	Listing is usual	Listing is usual
Queuing	No queue	Queuing is common	No queue
Currency of denomination restrictions	United States does not restrict the use of US$	Part of queuing • Many foreign countries (Germany, Switzerland) have in past or now restrict use of currency	No restrictions on use of US$ or C$
Speed of issuance	Relatively slow until Rule 415 on "shelf registration"	Variable	Usually fast—"bought deal" leads to fast issuance
Borrower/Issuer incentives	(+) Large market, great depth (−) Disclosure is costly to foreigners, speed	(+) Local visibility, diversification of funding sources (−) Markets may be small, queuing may prevail	(+) Lower annual interest expense, speed of placement (−) Cannot sell issue in U.S. until seasoned
Lender/Investor incentives	(+) Great depth and liquidity, appeal of standardized information (−) Reporting to tax authorities, withholding tax prior to 1984	(+) Diversified currency portfolio (−) Reporting to tax authorities and withholding taxes may apply	(+) Diversified currency portfolio, bearer bonds, no withholding tax on interest payments (−) Less liquidity and information disclosures

Source: Based on Richard M. Levich, "A View from the International Capital Markets," p. 261. Reprinted with permission from *Deregulating Wall Street,* edited by Ingo Walter (New York: John Wiley, 1985). Copyright © 1985 by John Wiley & Sons, Inc.

Regulatory and Institutional Characteristics of the Market

Some of the major regulatory and institutional characteristics of the international bond market are displayed in Table 10.2. Features of the onshore markets in the United States and elsewhere are summarized in columns 1 and 2, while the characteristics of the offshore or Eurobond market are shown in column 3. Highlighting the role played by regulation, Table 10.2 begins with the regulatory body that oversees each marketplace.

Regulatory Bodies and Disclosure Practices

In the United States, a public bond offering must conform to the rules laid down by the Securities and Exchange Commission (SEC). Bonds offered in other countries also have similar official agencies that guide the process of a public bond offering. A primary objective of the SEC is investor protection. To that end, all bond issues offered for sale to the public must be accompanied by a prospectus which provides detailed disclosures on the nature of the security under offer, the financial condition of the firm issuing the bond, and other pertinent information about the risks facing the firm and the industry that might affect the buyer of the security. Preparation of the prospectus for a proposed offering is an expensive and time-consuming matter. Not only is the initial expense high, but also the issuer has the ongoing expense of preparing quarterly financial reports to keep public bondholders apprised of the firm's financial condition.

An SEC filing for a public bond offering is even more onerous for non-U.S. firms. U.S. financial markets are open to non-U.S. firms, but only on the basis of *national treatment;* that is, all those who aspire to a public securities offering in the United States must provide financial information prepared according to U.S. generally accepted accounting principles (GAAP). These rules differ in many respects from the accounting rules used outside of the United States.[5] For example, non-U.S. companies often prepare only semiannual financial statements. Moreover, many of the items required by U.S. GAAP, such as segmental disclosures of sales and profits by major product lines and geographic regions, are not required in some non-U.S. GAAP. Disclosure of these items would entail costly preparation expense. Moreover, it can be argued that disclosure of certain financial information could be costly from a strategic standpoint, as the firm may wish to restrict certain bodies—labor unions, competitors, government regulators—from access to particular information. Thus, some non-U.S. firms (more so than non-U.S. governments) have been reluctant to use the U.S. capital markets.

A public bond issue in countries other than the United States (see column 2) also requires the approval of an official agency, sometimes housed within the treasury or finance ministries or within a separate SEC-like body. While non-U.S. agencies also require the preparation and release of financial information, these same agencies generally practice *reciprocity;* that is, the financial statements of the firm's home country are accepted "as prepared" (or with only small changes) to qualify for a public bond offering. For example, Switzerland, which until 1991 was the most active foreign bond market, does not require non-Swiss issuers coming to the Swiss market to produce Swiss GAAP financial statements.

Issuing practices in the Eurobond market, in comparison, are far less rigid. The essential difference between domestic or foreign bonds issued onshore and Eurobonds is that Eurobonds are not public offerings. Eurobonds are treated by most countries as private placements that are offered by the underwriter to a professional investment adviser, who buys the bond for an institutional account or a retail customer. Therefore, only a minimal level of regulation impacts a Eurobond either when it is issued or in the secondary market. Disclosure requirements are determined by market practices. This implies that little documentation may be required for a well-known issuer (such as Exxon, Nissan Motors, or Nestlé) regarded as having high credit quality. This market-determined behavior toward disclosure has allowed the speed of Eurobond offerings to accelerate, especially since the late 1970s. Less-than-prime borrowers also participate in the Eurobond market following practices that have evolved in the market for the presentation of information in an offering circular or prospectus.

Issuing Costs, Ratings, and Exchange Listings

Other practices, such as normal issuing costs and the decision to obtain bond ratings and exchange listings, also vary across the markets. Posted issuing costs in the Eurobond

---

[5]For more on national differences in accounting principles and their impact, see Choi and Levich (1990) and Choi and Mueller (1992).

market are higher than in the U.S. market. However, "give-backs" have been common in the Eurobond market, so the actual issuing cost paid by issuers is probably less than the quoted figures. What matters to the firm, of course, is its all-in cost of funds, which as we will see has often been less than the alternative cost in the onshore market.

While bonds issued publicly in the U.S. market are always rated, ratings of firms or the particular issue are not required in the Eurobond market. Some evidence suggests that ratings do improve the terms at which an issuer can raise funds, so it has become increasingly common to obtain ratings for Eurobonds.[6]

Exchange listing for bonds is uncommon in the United States. Only a few hundred bonds are listed on the New York Stock Exchange and the American Stock Exchange out of nearly 10,000 corporate and sovereign issues trading in public hands. In contrast, exchange listing for Eurobonds, usually in Luxembourg or London, is the rule rather than the exception. Exchange listing helps to increase the marketability of Eurobonds because some institutions are allowed to purchase only securities listed on an exchange. However, most actual trading of Eurobonds occurs in an over-the-counter setting. The exchange listing serves primarily as a mechanism for reporting an end-of-day price quotation.

Queuing, Currency of Denomination, and Speed of Offering

Other factors that play an important role in an issuer's preference for a marketplace are queuing, currency of denomination, and speed of issue. The practice of **queuing** may not be familiar to readers in the United States, because the timing of access to the U.S. capital market is not under government control. By comparison, the timing of issues in non-U.S. (onshore) markets is (or has been) generally controlled by the local regulatory body. Queuing of new issues is an important tool of macroeconomic policy outside the United States because most foreign capital markets are far smaller than those in the United States, and the markets could be disrupted by large issues or bunching of issues. Thus, queuing is a policy instrument intended to reduce "congestion" in the market and promote better pricing for those at the head of the queue.

Furthermore, **credit rationing** is a more common policy instrument in some countries. The regulatory body may allocate places in the queue according to national or regional priorities. Queuing clearly limits free access to the capital market and may thus limit the amount of funds available to a borrower and raise the price charged on those funds.

Along the same lines, the United States does not restrict the use of the US$ as a unit of account in transactions at home or around the world. The rationale for doing so may be based on economic reasoning—the damage inflicted on the United States by unauthorized use of the US$ as a unit of account is low and the monitoring costs are high; or based on philosophical principles—issuers are simply free to choose the US$ as their unit of account. Whatever the case, no restrictions have been imposed on the use of the US$ and the C$.

In comparison, many foreign countries in the past have restricted or still restrict the use of their currency as a unit of account. The rationale is again that foreign countries have smaller capital markets and view control of their unit of account as part of national monetary policy. Until 1989, bond issues denominated in DM had to be cleared with the

---

[6]Standard & Poor's and Moody's rate Eurobonds as well as onshore bond issues. See Fisher (1988), p. 129.

Bundesbank, Germany's central bank, to obtain authorization for issue.[7] Similarly, it has been only since 1984 that guidelines governing the issuance of Euro-¥ bonds by residents and foreign companies were eased. And as well, only since 1984 that non-Japanese financial institutions were permitted to lead manage Euro-¥ issues.[8] Clearly, underwriters possessed the financial technology needed to issue Euro-DM and Euro-¥ bonds prior to these rule changes. But both of these restrictions were binding because the cost (to a large underwriter) of violating a central bank directive would not have been worth the profit on the bond issue. To the present day, there are no Eurobonds denominated in Swiss francs, in deference to the Swiss National Bank policy to control the use of the Swiss franc as a unit of account.

Queuing, currency of denomination restrictions, and other factors come together to determine the speed with which a bond can be issued. While there is no queue in the U.S. market and no restriction on the use of the US$, filing an SEC registration document might require four weeks or more for approval *after* it has been prepared and submitted. Fisher (1988, pp. 118–19) estimates that 60 days may elapse between the initial meeting with underwriters to discuss terms and conditions and the actual offering date of securities. The process of **shelf registration** (SEC Rule 415) adopted in 1982 has sped up the process. Under a shelf registration, the issuer files a prospectus with the SEC that covers all anticipated new borrowings within a 12-month period. Once approved, the issuer may go to the capital market on very short notice (typically one week) after a short "prospectus supplement" has been filed which provides the exact terms for the new issue and information on any new material changes to the borrower's financial condition. The process in a non-U.S. bond market involves a variable amount of time, including the waiting time for the government to approve the prospectus and any waiting time in the queue.

The issuing process in the Eurobond market, however, may be remarkably fast. From the time of an initial organization meeting with the firm to discuss basic terms and conditions of the offering, Fisher (1988, pp. 81–82) estimates that only 19 days may elapse until the offering day and another 19 days (38 days in total) until the closing and delivery of funds to the issuer. A bought deal, in which the underwriter commits to specific terms if the issuer will accept them within a set period of time, speeds the Eurobond issuance process still faster. Speed is valuable because it allows issuers to capture windows of opportunity to issue bonds at particularly favorable terms and conditions.

Summing Up: The Pros and Cons of Onshore and Offshore Markets

All of these factors taken together leave borrowers (issuers) and lenders (investors) with various incentives for using a marketplace, as summarized in the final two rows of Table 10.2. From the issuer's perspective, the U.S. market is large and deep, so it easily accommodates most large issues and longer-maturity issues. However, the U.S. market places a high weight on ratings, and the information disclosure required for a U.S. public offering may be costly to non-U.S. issuers. The Eurobond market definitely offers greater speed of placement to an issuer. Initial underwriting expenses are higher, but the ongoing interest expense, as we will see, is often lower. Sales of a new Eurobond are

---

[7]*Financial Market Trends,* May 1990, p. 38.
[8]See Watson et al. (1986), p. 23.

initially limited to offshore investors because a Eurobond is not a registered security and cannot be sold to U.S. investors until a seasoning period has passed.[9] This may have been a consideration for issuers in the 1970s, when the Eurobond market was smaller than the U.S. bond market.

From an investor perspective, the size and depth of the U.S. market also offers an attraction. Some investors may value the extent of information disclosure which the U.S. market epitomizes. However, U.S. securities are typically in registered form so that ownership may be tracked. And until 1984, foreign owners of U.S. securities were subject to a 30 percent withholding tax on interest payments. By comparison, bonds in the Eurobond market are issued in bearer form and there are no withholding taxes on interest payments. Retail investors who desire anonymity (either for its own sake or for tax evasion) have been attracted to the Eurobond market. Institutional investors, who are audited and pay taxes, value the Eurobond market as a way to earn additional returns through currency appreciation while simultaneously reducing risk through currency diversification. Institutional investors may also feel that their exposure to credit risk is reduced by access to a worldwide pool of issuers. And many institutional investors may find the absence of withholding taxes a convenience, especially if they are tax-exempt in their home countries. In comparison with the U.S. bond market, the Eurobond market may be less liquid and offer less information disclosure about the issuers. But these features will matter less to retail investors who buy bonds to hold rather than to trade, and who put more weight on name (of issuer) recognition rather than accounting information and credit rating.

In summary, issuers have been attracted to the Eurobond market by its speed of issue and competitive pricing. Investors have been drawn to the Eurobond market through the availability of bearer bonds and the lack of withholding taxes. These features have given the Eurobond market an edge over onshore markets and enabled it to expand even after U.S. capital controls were abolished in 1974. Issuing practices in the Eurobond market have needed to keep pace with this growth in a highly competitive environment, as we describe in the next section.

Issuing Practices and Competitive Conditions in the Eurobond Market

It is worthwhile to examine Eurobond underwriting practices for two reasons. First, as a largely unregulated market with free entry, free exit, and few restrictions on related financial activities, capital requirements, and the like, this market has survived and prospered without the regulatory safety net that is so common in most onshore securities markets. Such an examination is important to understand how the market operates and to judge whether new regulations or market practices should be considered. Second, as the United States was the last remaining industrial nation that separated commercial banking (associated with deposit taking and bank lending) from investment banking (meaning securities underwriting), the Eurobond market may be a useful laboratory to consider how financial markets in the United States might fare now that these activity restrictions have been relaxed. The U.S. practice of separating commercial banking

---

[9]The seasoning period was 90 days until 1990, when Regulation S was changed to impose a 30-day waiting period. The rationale for a seasoning period may be that after a period of time the market efficiently establishes prices, thus protecting investors from the purchase of bonds that are mispriced on issue or during the underwriters' support period.

from investment banking was ushered in by the Glass-Steagall Act, passed in 1933.[10] The law remained in place for 66 years, until abolished by the November 1999 financial services bill.[11] Despite Glass-Steagall, some U.S. commercial banks were permitted to underwrite corporate securities on a small scale.[12] However, it is interesting to note that for more than 40 years, the Eurobond market offered a way for U.S. commercial banks to circumvent Glass-Steagall prohibitions and to underwrite all manner of corporate securities through their offshore affiliates.

A Brief Sketch of Eurobond Underwriting

A Eurobond offering brings together the bond issuer and the bond investor. The supply side (the issuer) and the demand side (the investor) are brought together by intermediaries that fulfill some or all of the following services: lead management, underwriting, and bond sales. In the case of a bought deal, all of these services are provided by a single intermediary. In a bought deal, the lead manager approaches the issuer with a proposal to raise funds under specific terms: issue size, currency, maturity, coupon payments, and other features that may enhance the volume or price of the issue. Once the manager commits to raise funds on specific terms, the manager assumes the underwriting risks of the issue.

Underwriting risk reflects the possibility that the sale price of the bonds may not match the price promised to the issuer. In other words, if the manager commits to raise $100 million in a seven-year bond issue with 8 percent annual coupons, he or she must provide this amount even if investors are willing to pay only $98 million for the bonds. A sudden rise in interest rates, a decline in the issuer's credit quality, or a shift in investor preferences away from US$-denominated investments are but three examples of underwriting risks.

When lead management, underwriting, and sales are conducted within a single firm, a Eurobond issue can proceed very quickly in a few days or less. The investment bank or securities firm that undertakes a bought deal must have considerable expertise in the markets. The initial design and pricing of the bond requires knowledge of both the market conditions and the issuer's credit quality and market standing. The manager must have sufficient financial capital to withstand the underwriting risks. And the manager must have links with investors providing the ability to place the bonds quickly, before market conditions change.

Traditionally, the lead management, underwriting, and sales functions of a Eurobond offering were divided among several parties. A diagram of a typical Eurobond offering is shown in Figure 10.4. The "management group" organizes most of the activities related to the initial bond offering. The group meets with the issuer to design the

---

[10]The Glass-Steagall Act was passed in the wake of the Great Depression, amidst allegations that commercial banks had engaged in questionable securities activities and that these contributed both to the stock market crash of 1929 and the wave of bank failures that followed thereafter. Research by White (1986) and Benston (1990) shows that many of these allegations were unfounded, and indeed the failure rate of banks with securities affiliates was lower than for other banks. Further analysis of the historical origins of the Glass-Steagall Act is in Walter (1985).

[11]See Barth, Brumbaugh, and Wilcox (2000) for a discussion of the Gramm-Leach-Bliley Act of November 1999 and its potential impact on "broad banking" in the United States.

[12]In the 1990s, the Federal Reserve allowed banks to generate 10 percent of their revenues from so-called ineligible activities, such as underwriting corporate debt and equity securities. The Federal Reserve proposed raising this limit to 25 percent of bank revenues. See Jeffrey Taylor and Stephen E. Frank, "Federal Reserve Set to Ease Rules on Banks' Expansion," *The Wall Street Journal,* Aug. 1, 1996.

FIGURE 10.4   Structure of a Eurobond Syndication

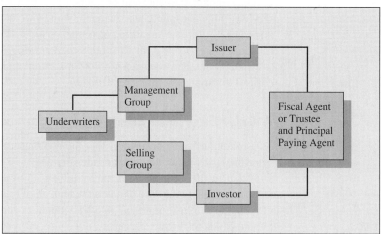

details of the bond issue—issue size, currency, maturity, coupon, and so forth—and assembles other firms (labeled "underwriters") to share in the underwriting risks of the issue. Finally, the management group organizes a "selling group" of firms that place the bonds with the ultimate investors in the issue. In practice, a single firm may play more than one role. For example, the lead management firm typically bears some of the underwriting risk and often participates in the selling group.

For our purposes, the important element of Figure 10.4 is that members of the selling group are distinct from the underwriters of the bond issue. In other words, members of the selling group in a Eurobond syndicate do not bear *true* underwriting risks, as in a U.S. bond syndicate. To understand this point, it is useful to review the formation of a Eurobond syndicate. The lead manager invites other firms to participate in the selling group. Historically, the invitation would come by telex in the form of an offering circular describing the characteristics of the bond in broad terms. Because of the need to move quickly, no formal agreement is signed between the parties; thus, the lead manager has no legally binding way to transfer underwriting risk to the selling group.[13]

Tensions and Incentives within a Eurobond Syndicate

In the early days of the Eurobond market, both selling agents and lead managers were comfortable with this arrangement. Selling agents from small banks and securities firms were happy to avoid taking on any underwriting risks in return for the prospective fees and prestige associated with a Eurobond deal. Lead managers at larger firms, on the other hand, felt that they had the market power to enforce discipline on the syndicate. With so many firms seeking to participate in the selling group, the lead manager could form syndicates with large selling groups. Lead managers were confident that the bond

---

[13]Fisher (1988, p. 92) discusses this topic in greater detail. Lead managers have other techniques—variable payment of selling fees, invitations to future Eurobond issues—to enforce discipline within the selling group. Sellers wish to protect their own reputations and have a natural incentive to sell bonds whether or not there is a binding commitment.

issue would be fully subscribed and that the selling group would meet their (nonbinding) selling commitments out of fear of being dropped from future syndicates.

This imbalance of power between lead managers and the selling group put stresses on the market. Lead managers have incentives to propose sweeter deals for issuers in order to enhance their volume of business. Better terms for issuers meant higher bond prices and lower yields. Lead managers felt that they could form syndicates to sell "overpriced" bonds because of eagerness on the part of smaller firms to join the syndicate. However, if the bonds received a poor reception in the market, bonds left unsold were marked down in price, thus cutting into the profits of the selling group and of any investors who purchased the bonds at par. Financial journalists characterized this situation in the Eurobond primary market as "excessive competition"—too many selling firms with too little power relative to lead managers and the inability to refuse participation in badly priced bond deals, leading to an oversupply of bonds at posted terms. Note that excessive competition is not bad for issuers in the market, but it could be harmful to lead managers and investors (see Box 10.2).

It is important to note another characteristic of the Eurobond primary market at this point. During the 1960s and 1970s, Eurobonds were *not* sold in the primary market on a **fixed-price reoffering** basis.[14] Thus, an informed institutional investor might assess a particular new issue and bid only 98 percent of par, believing that the issue had been overpriced. At the same time, a less-well-informed retail customer might find that his or her portfolio manager paid 100 percent of par for the same bond. This **variable-price reoffering** system points out a second problem facing the Eurobond market: "stuffing" of retail accounts with badly priced bonds. As the portfolio managers were often employed by the same financial institutions as the selling group, portfolio managers faced a possible *conflict of interest*—to assist their colleagues in the selling group by selling as many bonds as possible at full price, or to maximize the performance of their retail clients' investment portfolios.[15]

The Gray Market

In the 1970s, market participants developed a method to deal with the problem of excessive competition. To protect themselves from accepting bonds that could not be sold at par or were likely to decline in value in the aftermarket, firms could sell their allotment of bonds forward for delivery on a when-issued basis. Once a bond issue was announced, a selling firm might decide to sell the bond immediately (for forward delivery) at 98 percent or 99 percent of par.[16] This strategy would hedge the selling firm against further price declines but still allow the firm to participate in the syndicate, to appear in the tombstone announcing the deal, and to stay in good standing with the lead manager for the next deal. And if the price discount was less than the selling commission, the selling firm could even make a small profit. This practice of trading in Eurobonds on a

---

[14]A fixed-price reoffering system (the practice in the U.S. corporate bond market) requires that all bonds are sold on issue day at a fixed price to all buyers whether they are large institutions or small investors. Selecting this single fixed price is critical because the underwriters bear the risk of unsold bonds.

[15]Concern over conflicts of interest was a common argument for Glass-Steagall policies that limited securities underwriting activities within commercial banks. Most common conflicts—such as using the proceeds of an offering to pay off bank debt, selling securities into bank-managed trust accounts, and so on—would violate existing U.S. banking or securities laws. For more on conflicts, see Walter (1985), chapters 8 and 9.

[16]If the seller's fees were 1 percent, then selling at 99 percent of par would reflect a break-even, no-profit, selling price.

Box 10.2

"Excessive Competition" in the Eurobond Market

The Eurobond market is unregulated and competition in the market is intense. Occasionally, some participants complain that competition is "excessive." It is important to understand (1) that this "problem" affects the *business* of Eurobond underwriting, but it is beneficial for the issuers, and (2) that the Eurobond market has grown and developed despite, or because of, intense competition.

In the early days of the Eurobond market, underwriting fees ranged from 2.0 percent to 2.5 percent, depending on maturity. A bond sold at par ($100) might net the issuer only $97.50, the balance divided among the lead manager and members of the selling group. These fees were considerably higher than in the U.S. corporate bond market, but comparable to or slightly less than continental European markets.*

To gain market share, underwriters could propose larger deals to issuers at lower interest rates. Having underwriters compete in this way clearly benefits the issuer. If the bond issue sells out on stated terms, all parties are happy. However, if the offering sells poorly, the underwriter is left with unsold bonds that are held in inventory (hoping for a price rise) or marked down in price and sold immediately, cutting into underwriting profits.

The Eurobond market has often experienced this tendency. For example, in 1985 a *New York Times* article reported that "in their eagerness to win the business of these companies, international commercial and investment banks have been so aggressive in setting low yields that the bankers have been left with billions of dollars in unsold bonds."[†]

Who gains and who loses as a result of excessive competition? Access to low-cost funds clearly benefits the issuer. Investors must be on guard to discern deals that are priced too high relative to comparable bonds in other markets. The market itself could be harmed if losses force underwriters to drop out of the market, leaving the surviving underwriters free to raise underwriting fees. But entry into the Eurobond business is unrestricted, so Eurobond underwriters cannot charge monopolistic prices. Securing business relationships with large issuers is so important that Eurobond underwriters have kept fees low and appear to operate at little or no profit.

In 1994, a *Wall Street Journal* headline declared "Eurobond Market No Longer Affords Investment Banks Big Profit Margins" and went on to describe ever-increasing competition in the market.[‡] By 1994, the nominal measure of underwriting fees was about 1.4 percent. But because of discounting to clear out unsold offerings, the actual profit margin was estimated at 0.50 percent by some, and as little as 0.25 percent by others—hardly enough to cover administrative costs.[§] As a result, many banks do not see Eurobond underwriting as a profitable activity on its own but as a way to attract other forms of business to the bank.

---

when-issued basis, called the **gray market** or premarket, began with prices circulated over telephone lines. A few years later, gray market prices were published in newsletters and circulated across market participants. By the early 1980s, gray market prices were posted on trading screens. See Box 10.3 for an illustration of gray market prices.

Lead managers initially criticized the gray market as a factor undermining syndicate discipline and promoting instability in the primary market. Some lead managers attempted to censure firms that participated in the gray market by tracking bonds that were allocated to the firm but wound up being dumped in the gray market. But since Eurobonds are either in bearer (physical) form or traded electronically using Euroclear or Cedel on a "fungible" basis—meaning that a bond number is selected at random to transfer from a seller to a buyer—it was not possible for lead managers to effectively monitor gray market transactions, especially if they occurred through third-party intermediaries.

Ultimately, the gray market provided a means for the selling group to refuse to participate in badly priced deals. Prices in the gray market provided useful information that lead managers and issuers could not easily ignore. Offering terms or issue sizes could be

*Levich (1985), p. 269.
†Fred R. Bleakley, "The Eurodollar Bond 'Mess'," *The New York Times,* Feb. 14, 1985.
‡Glenn Whitney, "Eurobond Market No Longer Affords Investment Banks Big Profit Margins," *The Wall Street Journal,* Oct. 31, 1994, p. A9D.

§The 0.50 percent estimate is from *ibid.* The 0.25 percent figure is from Richard Lapper, Martin Brice, and Graham Bowley, "Warburg Exit Highlights Pressure on Margins" *Financial Times,* Jan. 16, 1995, p. 20.

Source: Reprinted with permission of the artist, Roger Beale.

adjusted in response to gray market prices, thus reducing the tendency toward over-priced bonds and an oversupply of bonds in the aftermarket.

The gray market also provided a means for the retail investor to monitor the performance of his or her portfolio manager. Traditionally, Eurobonds were offered using a variable-price reoffering system. As a result, institutional buyers with better information and more clout could buy bonds at prices *below* par while retail investors were sold bonds at par. This form of price discrimination against retail buyers is commonly called stuffing. Retail investors could now monitor gray market prices to detect stuffing and move their accounts if no other remedy were available.[17]

[17]Alternative issuing procedures, such as the fixed-price reoffering system, prevent retail investors from being stuffed. In a fixed-price reoffering deal, the lead manager and members of the selling group agree to sell the issue at a common price to all investors on issue day, which implies no discounting to large institutional buyers. Underwriting fees are far smaller (in the neighborhood of 0.25–0.375 percent) in a fixed-price reoffering issue, but if the issue is priced correctly, members of the selling group will not find themselves cutting prices and giving up fees in order to move their bonds out of inventory.

Box 10.3

Examples of Gray Market Prices in the Eurobond Market

Gray market prices have been circulated among market participants for many years. The table below shows two bonds, one issued in 1983 and the other in 1993.

The first bond, from Weyerhauser Capital Corporation, NV, was issued through the Netherlands Antilles subsidiary of the U.S. timber and paper company. The issue amount of $60 million was typical for this time, and the bond was listed in Luxembourg. The bond was issued at par (100),

but it traded in the gray market at a discount of 1.25–1.50 percent below par. In the row marked "total commission," we see that the selling concession (the amount of fees allocated to a member of the selling group) was 1.25 percent. Thus, a Eurobond trader was willing to give up his or her entire selling concession, or a bit more, to make a sale in the gray market. This bond was apparently overpriced at par, but "fairly priced" at its gray market discount.

	Issuer and Date of Issue	
	Weyerhauser Capital Corp, NV (1983)	*Osaka Gas (1993)*
Amount	US$60 million	US$250 million
Maturity	7 years (due November 15, 1990)	5 years (due May 26, 1998)
Coupon	11.5%	5.75%
Issue price	100	101.489
Fixed reoffer price	N.A.	99.889
Listing	Luxembourg Stock Exchange	London Stock Exchange
Total commission	1.875%	1.875%
	Management and underwriting fees, 0.625%; selling concession, 1.25%	Management and underwriting fees, 0.275%; selling concession, 1.6%
Lead manager	Morgan Stanley International	Goldman Sachs International
Gray market price	Minus 1.5 to 1.25	100.25
Market commentary	"A fairly priced deal, say traders."	"The issue blew out in 15 minutes according to the lead manager."

Source: *AGEFI* issue 492, October 29, 1983, p. 1677. *International Financing Review*. issue 977, May 1, 1993, pp. 60–61.

The second bond was issued by Osaka Gas of Japan. Note the larger amount ($250 million), which was more typical of 1993, and the bond listing in London. Although the issue price of the bond was 101.489 (percent of par), it was slated for sale initially at 99.889 (percent of par) on a fixed reoffer price basis. Note that this 1.6 percent difference happened to be the selling concession, so again it appears that the selling group would not profit from a sale at this price.* However, the gray market price (called the

premarket price in 1993) was 100.25. Thus, these bonds were apparently in heavy demand, selling for 0.361 more in the gray market than the posted initial offering price. The market commentary about the Osaka Gas bond confirms this heavy demand.

---

*It is difficult to say for sure, since the lead manager could compensate a selling member from his or her own fees or in some other way.

Evidence of Competition among Eurobond Lead Managers

As the previous discussion suggests, the Eurobond market has been characterized by (1) competition to participate in the selling group and (2) competition to lead manage primary issues. Various statistics demonstrate the competitive nature of the primary market. In Table 10.3 we report the concentration ratios for Eurobond underwriting from

TABLE 10.3 Concentration Ratios in Eurobond Underwriting, 1978–1998

Year	Top 1	Top 5	Top 10	Top 15	Top 25
1978	23.0%	49.0%	61.0%	70.0%	82.0%
1979	11.0	34.0	49.4	60.0	76.0
1980	10.0	33.0	47.0	57.0	72.0
1981	13.0	37.0	52.0	63.0	76.0
1982	15.2	41.9	57.0	64.8	77.2
1983	16.7	40.2	54.4	64.5	78.3
1984	16.6	44.0	60.6	69.7	81.9
1985	14.1	37.3	55.7	65.9	81.5
1986	11.2	35.9	55.0	66.0	79.9
1987	13.6	37.5	55.6	67.2	79.7
1988	10.0	34.6	52.2	66.0	81.4
1989	15.0	42.8	60.3	71.3	83.7
1990	9.2	31.2	48.8	62.3	79.7
1991	8.5	32.5	52.5	67.2	83.3
1992	7.8	30.5	50.0	62.8	80.5
1993	6.7	26.5	45.8	59.1	78.4
1994	8.2	31.1	50.1	63.0	77.3
1995	6.6	27.8	47.3	60.8	76.8
1996	7.7	28.6	48.2	61.9	77.2
1997	NA	NA	NA	NA	NA
1998	10.0	39.5	67.3	80.2	90.5
1999	9.1	37.9	63.6	77.6	84.9[a]
Average	11.6%	35.9%	54.0%	65.7%	79.9%

[a]Top 20 firms only.

Note: Eurobonds include issues in all currencies. Percentages are calculated by allocating the full amount of the issue to sole lead manager and equal amounts to joint lead managers. Years 1994–1999 represent all international bonds rather than Eurobonds. See text for explanation.

Sources: Richard M. Levich, "A View from the International Capital Markets," p. 273, for years 1978–1982. Reprinted with permission from *Deregulating Wall Street,* edited by Ingo Walter (New York: John Wiley, 1985). Copyright © 1985 by John Wiley & Sons, Inc. Updated for years 1983–1993 and 1996–1999 from data in *Euromoney,* various issues. Updated for years 1994–1995 courtesy of Capital Data, London.

1978 to 1998. The concentration ratio measures the percentage of business captured by various layers of lead managers. The table shows that the top 5 lead managers tended to account for approximately 36 percent of all Eurobond primary issues, while the top 10 lead managers captured a 54 percent share. In comparison, the concentration ratios in the U.S. corporate underwriting business tend to be about 65 percent and 85 percent for the top 5 and top 10 firms, respectively. Thus, Eurobond underwriting has been spread more thinly across more participants than in the U.S. market, although in recent years concentration appears on the increase. This coincides with mergers and acquisitions among some of the largest international underwriters, for example Citibank and Salomon Smith Barney, Deutsche Bank and Bankers Trust, among many others.

In Table 10.4 we report the rankings (i.e., "league tables") for the top underwriters for six years during the 1978–1999 period. These data suggest that there has been considerable mobility of firms across these leader tables. Only 2 firms (Deutsche Bank and Credit Suisse First Boston) appear in the top 10 in all selected years. And 3 U.S. firms (Morgan Guaranty, Merrill Lynch, and Salomon Brothers) rank in the top 10 for four of the selected years. The other 16 Eurobond underwriters have rotated positions among

TABLE 10.4 Top Underwriting Firms in the Eurobond Market and Their Rankings, Selected Years

Rank	1978 Firm Name	1978 Market Share	1982 Firm Name	1982 Market Share	1986 Firm Name	1986 Market Share	1990 Firm Name	1990 Market Share	1993 Firm Name	1993 Market Share	1999 Firm Name	1999 Market Share
1	Deutsche Bank	23.3%	Credit Suisse	15.1%	Credit Suisse	11.2%	Nomura	9.2%	Goldman Sachs	6.7%	Merrill Lynch	9.1%
2	West Deutsche Landesbank	9.8	Deutsche Bank	10.4	Nomura	7.8	Credit Suisse	6.6	Deutsche Bank	6.2	Morgan Stanley Dean Witter	8.1
3	Credit Suisse	6.3	Morgan Stanley	7.9	Deutsche Bank	6.7	Deutsche Bank	6.3	Morgan Stanley	4.6	Salomon Smith Barney	7.6
4	Dresdner Bank	5.6	Morgan Guaranty	4.2	Morgan Guaranty	5.4	Daiwa Securities	4.7	Credit Suisse	4.5	Deutsche Bank	7.4
5	S. G. Warburg	3.6	Salomon Brothers	3.8	Daiwa Securities	4.8	Salomon Brothers	4.4	Merrill Lynch	4.5	Credit Suisse	5.7
6	Amro Bank	2.8	Merrill Lynch	3.6	Morgan Stanley	4.8	Morgan Guaranty	4.0	Lehman Brothers	4.3	Goldman Sachs	5.7
7	Commerzbank	2.6	Swiss Bank Corp.	3.6	Salomon Brothers	4.6	Nikko Securities	3.7	Nomura	4.3	Warburg Dillon Read	5.5
8	European Banking Co. Ltd.	2.4	S. G. Warburg	3.4	Banque Paribas	3.7	Merrill Lynch	3.6	Salomon Brothers	4.2	J. P. Morgan	5.2
9	Union Bank of Switzerland	2.3	Goldman Sachs	2.5	Merrill Lynch	3.3	Goldman Sachs	3.2	Banque Paribas	3.4	Lehman Brothers	5.1
10	Banque Nationale de Paris	2.1	Société Générale	2.1	Nikko Securities	2.8	Banque Paribas	3.2	Morgan Guaranty	3.0	ABN Amro	4.1

Sources: For years 1978 and 1982, Richard M. Levich, "A View from the International Capital Markets," p. 272. Reprinted with permission from *Deregulating Wall Street*, edited by Ingo Walter (New York: John Wiley, 1985). Copyright © 1985 by John Wiley & Sons, Inc.; for years 1986, 1990, 1993, and 1999, *Euromoney*, various issues.

TABLE 10.5 Number of Lead Managers for Agencies with Three or More Eurodollar Bond Issues

Number of Issues	Number of Lead Managers							
	1	*2*	*3*	*4*	*5*	*6–10*	*> 10*	*Total*
3	29	29	31	NA	NA	NA	NA	89
4	14	12	14	13	NA	NA	NA	53
5	1	3	6	5	5	NA	NA	20
6–10	6	0	6	4	5	16	NA	40
11–15	0	0	0	1	1	5	2	9
16–20	4	0	0	0	0	2	0	6
> 20	0	0	0	0	0	0	2	2
Total	54	47	57	23	11	23	4	219

Note: Figures reflect issues outstanding on April 29, 1994. Agencies include corporations, government bodies, and supranational agencies. Bond issues include straight bonds, zero-coupon bonds, and floating-rate notes.

Source: Author's calculation based on information in *Weekly Eurobond Guide,* April 29, 1994.

the top 10. In 1978, the strong DM helped promote DM bond issues at the expense of US$ issues. At the time, all DM bond issues were required (by Bundesbank directive) to be lead-managed by German banks. Not surprisingly, several German institutions moved near the top of the league tables. By 1982, a strong US$ had propelled US$ issues back into fashion and U.S. underwriters made a strong showing in the league tables, notably Morgan Guaranty, which had opened its London Eurobond office only in 1979 and by 1982 had moved into fourth place. And in the late 1980s, assisted by the relaxation of capital controls and a buoyant stock market, Japanese underwriters advanced to hold several top positions in the Eurobond rankings. Notably, no Japanese underwriters occupy a top 10 position in the 1999 ranking.

The data in Table 10.4 suggest that there is competition and mobility among Eurobond underwriters. However, our analysis suggests that certain external factors and regulations also assisted firms to rise or fall in the league tables. These external factors have had an important impact on competitive conditions in the Eurobond underwriting market.

Finally, the data in Table 10.5 show another aspect of competition in the Eurobond market. One important element of a competitive market is the willingness to switch suppliers. Table 10.5 reports the number of lead managers used to launch Eurobond issues for firms with three or more issues outstanding as of April 29, 1994.[18] The table shows that of the 89 firms with three Eurobond issues outstanding, 29 firms used two different lead managers to handle the issues and 31 firms employed three lead managers—a separate lead manager for each Eurobond issue. In a similar fashion, Table 10.5 shows that 53 firms had four bond issues outstanding at the time of the compilation, but only 14 firms used a single lead manager for all of their issues; 39 firms employed more than one lead manager. Overall, 75 percent of the 219 firms in the sample used more than one lead manager to handle their Eurobond business. This is clear evidence that issuers are prepared to switch lead managers when competitive conditions warrant.

---

[18]The data come from the April 29, 1994, issue of the *Weekly Eurobond Guide,* a directory of information about all Eurobonds traded as of that date. For a table based on October 28, 1983, data that showed a similar pattern, see Levich (1985), p. 274.

The explanation for this behavior, which contrasts with what we observe in U.S. underwriting, may relate to the information and disclosure requirements of the Eurobond market. As a Eurobond issue does not require detailed disclosures, an underwriter does not need access to privileged or up-to-the-minute information about an issuer to launch a deal. Public information may be sufficient to satisfy investor needs. Thus, managers may feel free to approach issuers for their Eurobond underwriting business even when there is no close or long-standing relationship between the two parties. This freedom to solicit business is probably most evident when the Eurobond issue is launched as a bought deal with fixed terms offered to the issuer. In this situation, managers are free to make full use of their product innovation skills and market timing with the prospect of winning new customers.

Another Innovation: Global Bonds

Similar to a Eurobond, a **global bond** issue is offered for sale in many countries simultaneously. Unlike a Eurobond, a global bond is a registered security, usually in the United States and sometimes in other countries as well. Global bonds are held in common depositories (such as Cedel, Euroclear, or Depository Trust Company in the United States) that enhance secondary market trading in local markets and between investors in different regions. The global bond strategy is designed for issuers with substantial funding needs who can benefit by reaching the widest possible investor audience. The size of issue, combined with widespread distribution, and secondary market trading opportunities offers a liquid investment that investors find attractive. Thus, even though the global bond offering strategy incurs additional floatation costs, the issuer may enjoy a lower all-in cost of funds.[19]

The World Bank undertook the first global bond in 1989 with a $1.5 billion issue. Since then, the global bond structure has been used by other international organizations, public enterprises, and government (sovereign) borrowers. Global bond offerings totaled $15.4 billion in 1991 (5.0 percent of all international bonds) rising to $44.2 billion in 1994 (10.3 percent of all international bonds) and to $101.5 billion in 1997 (12.2 percent of all international bonds).[20]

The largest global bond offering in the short history of this instrument was launched in late June 2000. Deutsche Telekom raised $14.5 billion in a multicurrency global bond offering, with tranches in US$, euros, sterling, and yen.[21] The size of the deal reflects the huge appetite for capital among major telecommunication firms.

Electronic Bond Offering Format.   The World Bank's $3 billion global bond issued on January 19, 2000, shows an innovation within an innovation.[22] Dubbed an *electronic bond,* or *E-bond,* this five-year issue was sold and distributed entirely over the Internet. Keeping with tradition, the bond was offered through underwriters, but all information dissemination and order entry was handled through the Internet. Moreover, retail investors with two large firms (Charles Schwab and Fidelity) were eligible to submit their

---

[19]For an introduction to the market, see "The Rise of Global Bonds," *Financial Market Trends,* no. 58 (June 1994), pp. 55–61.

[20]*Financial Market Trends,* no. 61 (June 1995), pp. 101–3, and no. 68 (Feb. 1998), p. 61.

[21]See "Telekom Bond Issue Could Hit $15 Billion Record," *Financial Times,* June 27, 2000, p. 17, and "Deutsche Telekom Charms U.S. Investors with Generous Returns on Bond Offering," *Financial Times,* June 30, 2000.

[22]See <www.worldbank.org/debtsecurities> for more information about the World Bank's E-bond.

orders as well through the same channels as large institutional buyers. The E-bond format has the potential to offer advantages to the issuers and investor. First, it allows the World Bank to monitor the order flow in real time to gauge demand for the issue. Second, it allows all investors to purchase bonds in the primary market at identical transaction fees. This maximizes the potential demand for the issue. The smallest order ($1,000) was from a retail investor, while the largest order ($250 million) was from an institutional money manager. The World Bank chose an underwritten issue to ensure a commitment to active secondary market making. But, in principle, the electronic bond could have been offered directly to investors without the added expense of underwriting fees.

Pricing Eurobonds

As a parallel or offshore market, the Eurobond market must offer prices and terms that are advantageous to both issuers and investors to attract them from the traditional onshore markets. In the Eurocurrency market (Chapter 9), we saw that the wide spread between deposit and lending rates gave Eurobanks an opening to compete—offering higher rates to depositors and lower rates to borrowers, and still earning a spread for their intermediation. The same principle could apply in the Eurobond market.

Suppose that underwriting fees in the U.S. domestic corporate bond market were 2 percent and our firm issues an 8 percent coupon bond with a seven-year maturity. After issuing the bond at par ($1,000), our firm receives only $980 after underwriting fees. The cost of funds to the firm on a current-yield basis is 8.16 percent (= 80/980). The cost over the seven-year period is 8.39 percent, acknowledging that the firm must repay $1,000 per bond at the end of year 7.[23] The investor earns a current yield and yield-to-maturity of 8 percent The effective lending and borrowing spread (for this coupon and maturity bond) is thus 8.00–8.39 percent.

Suppose now that underwriting fees were only 1 percent in an offshore market and our firm issues a seven-year bond with a higher 8.05 percent coupon bond in order to attract an onshore investor. If this bond is issued at par ($1,000), the firm receives $990 after underwriting fees. This makes the cost of funds to the firm on a current basis 8.13 percent (= 80.5/990). The all-in cost over the seven-year period is 8.24 percent. Thus, the effective lending and borrowing spread is 8.05–8.24 percent, more narrow than when underwriting fees were 2 percent.

Market Segmentation and the Pricing of Eurobonds

While lower underwriting fees, in theory, would open up a marketplace for investors to earn higher returns and issuers to bear lower costs, this is *not* the secret underpinning the success of the Eurobond market. Indeed, the figures customarily presented show that underwriting fees in the Eurobond market are *higher* than those in the U.S. corporate bond market.[24] These same data suggest that Eurobond underwriting fees are sometimes lower than in other non-U.S. domestic markets.

How can both issuers and investors benefit from an offshore market that typically charges higher underwriting fees than in the onshore market? From the issuer's side, the

---

[23]This is an internal rate of return or yield-to-maturity calculation.

[24]For estimates of the gross spreads in onshore and offshore bond markets, see Levich (1985), p. 269.

answer is that underwriting fees are a one-time cost and only part of the total cost. There may be certain cost savings because the Eurobond market often allows firms to issue bonds more quickly and with lower disclosure costs.

More important are the ongoing savings that come from a lower annual interest cost in the Eurobond market than in the onshore market. The Eurobond market has appeared to function as a **segmented capital market,** where bond prices are determined primarily by Eurobond market participants who give less than full regard to how these bonds would be priced in the onshore market. By comparison, in an **integrated capital market,** a bond with specific terms and conditions would be priced identically by investors in the onshore market and in the Eurobond market. Arbitrage between the onshore and offshore bond markets leads the markets toward integration.

In the case of the Eurobond market, it is often suggested that the early years of the market were dominated by small retail investors who evaluated bond prices on different terms than the institutional investors who traded in the onshore markets.[25] The argument is that these retail investors were less concerned about cryptic issuer ratings and more swayed by name recognition. To the extent that these investors willingly paid higher prices for debt securities in the Eurobond market, issuers were offered a price incentive to issue Eurobonds instead of onshore bonds.

Eurobonds and Secrecy

This behavior, however, only raises the question: Why would investors sacrifice yield by buying Eurobonds when instead they could purchase essentially identical bonds onshore? The answer relies on the secrecy of the Eurobond market and its implication for taxes. While essentially all securities in the United States are **registered securities** (with the name of the owner registered on the books of the issuing company), Eurobonds are **bearer securities.** Possession of a bearer bond is evidence of ownership because the issuer does not maintain a list. A significant fraction of Eurobonds are held in physical form. The owner of a Eurobond literally clips a coupon and takes it to a bank for payment in order to receive the annual interest payment. The large majority of Eurobonds are deposited with Euroclear and Cedel, the two electronic clearing and settlement firms. Euroclear and Cedel associate each bond with a numbered account; only the portfolio manager can link an investor name to each numbered account. Thus, the identity of Eurobond investors is held secret.

At present, there are no laws in the major Eurobond markets that require issuers or portfolio managers to disclose the identity of investors, or to disclose interest payments made to investors. Furthermore, there are no withholding taxes applied to Eurobond coupon payments. In contrast, U.S. federal law requires that a payer of interest obtain the Social Security number or tax identification number from anyone to whom interest is paid. A payer who is unable to obtain this number is obligated to withhold an amount (now typically 20 percent) that is paid to the U.S. Treasury.

Since the Eurobond market shields the identity of the investor and no withholding taxes are applied to coupon payments, the burden of reporting interest income from Eurobonds rests with the investor. If the investor fails to report Eurobond interest income, an 8 percent Eurobond yield would be equivalent to a 10 percent onshore yield if the tax rate is 20 percent, or to a 16 percent onshore yield if the tax rate is 50 percent. Thus, when tax evasion is a factor, retail investors would be content with a much smaller

---

[25]See Smith and Walter (1990), chap. 8.

TABLE 10.6   Pricing of U.S. Treasury Securities and a Sample of Six Eurodollar Bonds

Issuer	Description	First Call	Issue Size (in millions of dollars)	Security Guaranty	Rating	Percent Yield to Maturity
U.S. Treasury	13.75% notes due 8/15/87	None	NA	NA	NA	11.22%
GMAC Overseas Finance	12.00% notes due 10/1/87	None	100	PG	AA	11.00
Coca-Cola International Finance	11.75% notes due 6/1/88	None	100	PG	AA	11.11
Union Bank of Switzerland	10.75% notes due 11/15/87	None	200	PG	AAA	10.15
Deutsche Bank Finance	11.625% notes due 10/29/87	None	100	PG	AAA	11.14
Prudential Overseas	12.75% notes due 10/15/87	None	150	NP	AAA	11.27
Xerox Financial	13.25% notes due 8/15/87	None	100	NP	AA	11.39

Note: PG = Parental guarantee; NP = Negative pledge, meaning that the borrower pledges not to offer improved security arrangements to other investors on bonds of similar status to this bond, without offering the equivalent security to the investors in this issue.

Source: Eurobond data are from *Weekly Eurobond Guide*, Oct. 28, 1983; U.S. Treasury yield as reported in the *Wall Street Journal*, Oct. 31, 1983.

Eurobond yield compared with onshore yields that are subject to registration and/or disclosure and taxation.[26]

While the initial development of the Eurobond market relied on the retail investor, the increased volume of new issues since the mid-1980s could only be supported by a surge in institutional investors. It is reasonable to assume that institutional investors are honest taxpayers, so that their investments in Eurobonds are not driven by tax evasion. Some institutional investors who hold tax-free status (such as pension funds and university endowments) may find that Eurobonds are a more convenient vehicle for cross-border or cross-currency investing. The Eurobond market offers a greater variety of high-quality issuers, ease of clearing and settlement, and larger issues with good liquidity. Thus, unlike many onshore bond markets that are small or saddled with restrictions, the Eurobond market is attractive to institutional investors.

Eurodollar Bond Prices: Some Examples

The ongoing factor contributing to the differential pricing of Eurobonds over onshore bonds appears to be market segmentation—a different assessment of prices and risks between participants in the Eurobond market and those in onshore markets. To illustrate this point, consider the bonds listed in Table 10.6 as of October 28, 1983. The U.S. Treasury notes carried a yield to maturity of 11.22 percent. Many investors, particularly

---

[26]Note that tax *avoidance,* that is, structuring your investments so that they are subject to favorable tax treatment, is legal. Tax *evasion* is not legal.

FIGURE 10.5   Onshore U.S. Corporate Bonds, Eurodollar Bonds, and U.S. Government Bonds, 1984–2000
Yields and Yield Differentials

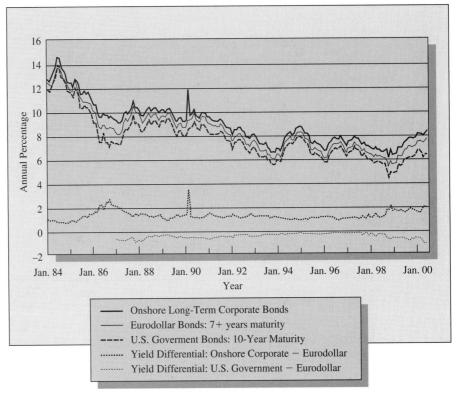

Source: Datastream.

Americans, view the U.S. Treasury as the most creditworthy issuer of US$ bonds and the U.S. Treasury market as the most liquid in the world.

In comparison, none of the six Eurodollar bonds in Table 10.6 held a higher credit rating, a shorter maturity, or more favorable call features. Yet four of the Eurodollar bonds carried a lower yield than the U.S. Treasury note. Clearly, the investors in the U.S. dollar segment of the Eurobond market were willing to give up yield in comparison to an onshore U.S. Treasury note.

The magnitude of the yield differential between offshore and onshore bonds has varied over time, and there also are differences across firms. Throughout 1983 and 1984, some well-known firms were able to obtain funding in the Eurobond market at yields below the rate on a U.S. Treasury bond of comparable maturity. These favorable funding opportunities coincided with a period of substantial US$ appreciation in the foreign exchange market. If Eurodollar bonds are bought primarily by non-U.S. investors whose base currency is not the US$, these investors may be more willing to sacrifice yield when they expect foreign exchange gains from a strong US$.[27]

A general picture of the yields on onshore corporate bonds, Eurodollar bonds, and U.S. government bonds (all with longer-term maturities) appears in Figure 10.5. These

---

[27]Again, this hypothesis assumes that the markets are segmented so that non-U.S. investors prefer to buy US$ bonds in the Euromarket instead of the U.S. market.

three indexes of bond yields tend to move together over time. The onshore yields always exceed the Eurodollar yield (by 25 to 150 basis points), and the Eurodollar yields usually exceed the U.S. government yield (also by 25 to 150 basis points). In some periods, Eurodollar bonds were in such heavy demand that many yields fell *below* U.S. government yields.

Onshore–Offshore Arbitrage Opportunities

As we have seen, during some periods (such as 1984–1985), certain U.S. firms were able to issue Eurodollar bonds not only at prices below onshore rates but also at prices below U.S. Treasury rates. This yield relationship raises the prospect of arbitrage—for firms to issue debt in the Eurodollar market and close their position by purchasing U.S. Treasury securities with the same maturities. We discuss this strategy for firms in the next section.

But the yield relationship also raises the question of whether the *U.S. Treasury itself* might reduce its funding costs by going to the Eurobond market. In fact, the U.S. Treasury initiated a Eurobond strategy in October 1984 just as the yield differential favoring Eurodollar bond issuers was becoming more attractive.

The first U.S. Treasury Eurobond—the so-called **specially targeted Treasury notes**—was issued on October 24, 1984. It was a $1 billion issue carrying a coupon of 11.375 percent maturing on September 30, 1988. On the same date, the U.S. Treasury issued a regular Treasury note with the same coupon and maturity in the onshore market. Thus, the two Treasury securities were alike in all respects, except that the specially targeted Eurobond was in bearer form and available for sale only to foreign investors, while the onshore issue was available in registered form only and for sale to both American and foreign investors.[28] The result of the auction was that the specially targeted issue Eurobond was sold for 32 basis points *less* than the regular onshore issue.

If we accept the claim that the two securities were alike in all respects with the exception of the bearer versus registered feature, then the 0.32 percent difference measures the value that Eurobond investors placed on the secrecy associated with bearer bonds. Eurobond investors might also have bid up the value of the specially targeted Treasury issues because of the "scarcity value" of the U.S. Treasury as an alternative AAA-rated issuer. Investors with a AAA-rated portfolio would prefer to hold securities from many issuers to diversify their exposure to credit risk. If there are few AAA issuers, a new AAA issuer with its first Eurobond might expect to receive a very warm welcome from the market. Still, offshore investors could have purchased as much U.S. Treasury debt as they desired in registered form in the onshore U.S. market. So the 0.32 percent differential can be attributed to the value of secrecy rather than to scarcity.

Eurodollar Bond Prices: A General Model

Arbitrage should link the prices of Eurodollar bonds with the prices of similar bonds in the onshore market.[29] Prices of Eurodollar bonds depend on a range of factors that reflect

---

[28]It might be argued that the regular onshore issue had somewhat better liquidity as it benefited from the highly developed market that trades in U.S. government securities. This would enhance the price paid for the onshore security.

[29]The author assumes that the reader is familiar with those factors that influence the rate of interest on government securities with different terms to maturity (the *term structure of interest rates*) in the onshore market, as well as the impact of different default characteristics on bond prices (the *risk structure of interest rates*). See Van Horne (1998) for review.

TABLE 10.7   **Empirical Results on U.S. Public Utility Offerings in the Eurodollar Bond Market**

Dependent Variable	Regression Coefficient b_E Location of Sale Eurobond Market	T-value	Adjusted R^2
Issuer's interest cost	−0.520	4.34	0.587
Investor's reoffering yield	−0.831	7.24	0.614
Underwriting spread	+1.290	31.69	0.846

Note: Based on sample of 229 bond issues, including 38 Eurodollar issues and 191 domestic issues.

Issuer's interest cost is calculated as internal rate of return for the issuer's net proceeds, interest and principal repayments less the yield-to-maturity basis of an equivalent maturity U.S. Treasury issue. *Investor's reoffering yield* is computed as an investor's yield-to-maturity for the issue less the yield-to-maturity of an equivalent maturity U.S. Treasury issue. *Underwriter's spread* is a percentage of bond value.

Each dependent variable was regressed against 11 independent variables and a constant term. The adjusted R^2 refers to the overall regression. We report the regression coefficient only for the one location-of-sale variable.

Source: David S. Kidwell, M. Wayne Marr, and G. Rodney Thompson, "Eurodollar Bonds: Alternative Financing for U.S. Companies," *Financial Management* (Winter 1985), pp. 18–27.

the characteristics of the issue, the issuer, and current market conditions. Controlling for these factors, we would like to measure the marginal impact of changing the location of the bond issue from the onshore market to the Euromarket. A paper by David Kidwell, Wayne Marr, and Rodney Thompson (1985) attempted to answer this question by estimating a regression of issuer cost (Y_1), reoffering yield (Y_2), and underwriting spread (Y_3) against a set of control variables (X_i) and a dummy variable for the location of sale (EURO). Thus the authors use a regression equation like:

$$Y_i = b_0 + b_1X_1 + b_2X_2 + \ldots + b_nX_n + b_E \text{ EURO}$$

and estimate the coefficients using a sample of 229 bonds issued by U.S. public utilities over the 1979–83 period. The regression coefficient b_E measures the marginal impact on yield for a bond issued in the Eurobond market (EURO = 1). The sample contained 38 Eurodollar bonds and 191 bonds issued in the U.S. corporate bond market. The analysis controls for various X_i variables: issuer rating, issue size, call features, current U.S. Treasury interest rates, recent volatility in U.S. Treasury interest rates, and other factors. The authors' results are summarized in Table 10.7.

For this sample of bonds, issuers in the Eurobond market saved 0.52 percent per annum, compared with the estimated cost of a similar issue in the onshore U.S. corporate bond market. Investors were willing to buy the Eurodollar bonds, sacrificing 0.83 percent per annum in yield relative to a similar onshore US$ bond. Both estimates are significantly different from zero. The underwriting spread for the Eurodollar bonds was greater by 1.29 percent, but not large enough to nullify the issuer's overall cost savings.

In further analysis, Kidwell et al. (1985) show that the foreign exchange value of the US$ is another significant variable for Eurodollar bond pricing. When the dollar is expected to appreciate, the authors show that investors are more willing to purchase Eurodollar bonds at still lower yields. And while the underwriting spread is larger in the Eurodollar market than onshore, the evidence shows that the spread was declining with time through the sample period.

Policy Matters—Private Enterprises

Private participants in the Eurobond market have spotted numerous advantages in the market that have helped it develop into its present status. From the investor's standpoint, we have documented that the retail investor has often sacrificed yield, apparently in exchange for a bearer instrument with no withholding taxes and no disclosures made to the tax authorities.

For the institutional investor, the Eurobond market offers a wide array of corporate and sovereign issuers and currencies (US\$, €, £, ¥, and others) with which to form well-diversified portfolios.[30] The large size of some issues, particularly global bonds, and electronic trading and settlement makes some Eurobonds well suited for institutional investors. In addition, institutional investors may feel that they can wield more power in the Eurobond market, where variable-price reoffering issuance methods are still practiced, as opposed to the fixed-price reoffering system of the onshore U.S. corporate bond market.

The Eurobond market has also been a venue for financial innovation. Institutional investors may find Eurobonds with unusual features that allow them to tailor a portfolio or take on uncommon bets. Bonds with equity or currency warrants attached, with interest payments linked to various economic events, with prices linked to equity or commodity indexes, with rights to convert the bond into equity, and so forth are fairly common in the Eurobond market. Bonds with these special features may have extremely risky or skewed payoff profiles, but they are structured—really "disguised"—as bonds and therefore can be sold to fixed-income investors.

The other main participants in the Eurobond market are corporate and sovereign issuers. There is compelling evidence that issuers have made prudent use of the Eurobond market, often raising funds at significantly lower cost than alternative onshore sources. For issuers, the principal policy issue is how to make the most effective use of this alternative marketplace. We will discuss two policies here. The first policy pertains to arbitrage between the Eurobond market and onshore markets. The second policy concerns funding strategies and opportunities for the issuer to exploit its excess borrowing capacity and scarcity.

Onshore–Offshore Arbitrage Once Again: Exxon Capital Corporation

When Eurobond interest rates are below rates in the onshore market, issuers have an incentive to borrow offshore. When Eurobond rates are lower than the yield on government securities, issuers have an incentive to engage in arbitrage by issuing securities offshore and covering their liability with a purchase of risk-free government securities whose cash inflows match the cash outflows of the Eurobond. If the matching is perfect and the government securities can be pledged to pay off the Eurobond liability, the transaction qualifies as a pure arbitrage, which should enhance the value (and therefore the future borrowing capacity) of the issuer.

While many instances of this type of arbitrage have likely occurred, one conducted by Exxon Capital Corporation (ECC), a wholly owned subsidiary of Exxon Corporation,

---

[30]The possibilities for currency diversification in bond portfolios are reviewed in Chapter 14.

Figure 10.6   Exxon Capital Corporation, Zero-Coupon Notes of 2004

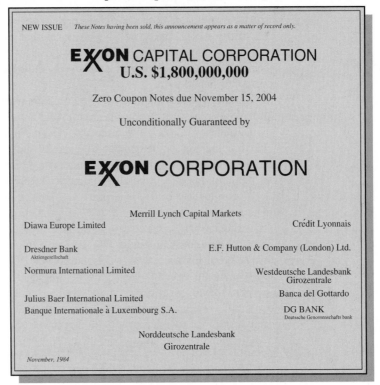

Source: Exxon Capital Corporation.

has been well documented by John Finnerty (1985).[31] On October 19, 1984, ECC issued $1.8 billion principal amount of zero-coupon notes due November 15, 2004, as shown in the tombstone in Figure 10.6. The issuing cost for ECC in the Eurobond market was 11.65 percent, compounded annually, giving ECC net proceeds of $198.6 million from the issue.[32] To effect the arbitrage, ECC would purchase zero-coupon U.S. Treasury bonds that also were due on November 15, 2004. In the week prior to ECC's issue, the yield on zero coupon U.S. Treasuries for this maturity ranged between 11.75 percent and 11.90 percent, compounded semiannually. Thus, ECC could have purchased $1.8 billion of U.S. Treasuries in the range of $178.4 million to $183.5 million.[33] Thus, ECC realized a profit of $15–20 million, depending on the interest rate it was able to secure on the U.S. Treasuries.

How was Exxon Capital Corporation able to accomplish this? In theory, a perfect capital market would have granted *anyone* the opportunity to borrow in the Euromarket at very favorable terms, assuming that he or she had pledged U.S. Treasury securities (AAA-rated collateral). In practice, however, Eurobond investors might doubt whether

---

[31]A more recent example involves the Euro-yen market in the spring of 2000. Bonds due in 2002 issued by the World Bank and by the Kingdom of Spain were trading at lower yields than comparable onshore Japanese government issues.

[32]Calculated as $1,800,000,000/(1.1165)^{20} = \$198,654,294$.

[33]Calculated as $1,800,000,000/(1 + .1175/2)^{40} = \$183,457,542$ and $1,800,000,000/(1 + .119/2)^{40} = \$178,333,964$.

the U.S. Treasuries had been deposited in an irrevocable trust for the benefit of the investors. ECC also had the accumulated financial market expertise to carry out the transaction quickly and at low cost. In theory, ECC could have conducted the deal even without any available borrowing capacity, again because the U.S. Treasury securities would be sufficient collateral for the issuance of the Eurobonds. In practice, ECC chose not to link the U.S. Treasuries (as if they were collateral) to the Eurobonds. Instead, the ECC zero-coupon notes were unconditionally guaranteed by Exxon Corporation. In all probability, Exxon's name-recognition value and parental guarantee resulted in a lower issue cost for ECC. Thus, excess or unused borrowing capacity is an important element in executing arbitrage transactions in the Eurobond market.

The ECC zero-coupon issue also depended on investors to buy the issue on favorable terms. As bearer securities, the ECC issue grants anonymity to the investor, and the zero-coupon feature eliminates the reinvestment risk of periodic coupon payments. Moreover, at this time Japanese investors could classify the increase in the note's value as a capital gain, which is nontaxable. In addition, Japanese investors were prohibited from buying a "defaced security," such as a stripped U.S. Treasury security created by an investment house. These and other factors came together to leave the Eurobond market as the only marketplace capable of satisfying the demand (particularly the Japanese demand) for low credit risk, US$ denominated, bearer, zero-coupon bonds. Thus, firms such as Exxon and other well-capitalized firms have been able to exploit arbitrage opportunities.

Using the Eurobond Market to Enhance the Value of the Firm

A second, more general policy issue is how the Eurobond market fits into a firm's overall funding strategy. Empirical evidence suggests that the Eurobond market may hold opportunities for the issuer to exploit its excess borrowing capacity and scarcity value. The lower interest rate available to some firms in the Eurobond market gives one measure of this value. Yong Cheol Kim and René Stulz (1988) measured the impact of Eurobond offerings on the value of the issuing firm's equity shares. Using a sample of 183 Eurobonds issued over the period 1975–1985, Kim and Stulz showed that in the two-day period surrounding the announcement of a Eurobond offering, equity shares exhibited significant positive abnormal returns, averaging 0.46 percent. This equity share price reaction was greatest during the January 1979–June 1984 subperiod when the interest differential between U.S. corporate bonds and Eurodollar bonds was at its greatest. Kim and Stulz argued that only firms with an ability to offer low default risk bonds benefited from this interest rate relationship. The incentive for Eurodollar bond financing persisted for some time, because debt offerings require time to launch and there is a limit to the amount of debt that a firm can issue and still retain its reputation and scarcity value among offshore investors.

A good illustration of how a firm's issuing advantage in the Eurobond markets changes over time is provided by the U.S. Treasury. Earlier, we highlighted the specially targeted U.S. Treasury note issued on October 24, 1984. The U.S. Treasury issued $1 billion of these notes at 0.32 percent less than the cost of a comparable regular U.S. Treasury note. Trying to extend the cost savings, the U.S. Treasury followed up with three additional $1 billion specially targeted bond issues in December 1984 (due February 15, 1990); June 1985 (due August 15, 1990); and February 1986 (due February 15, 1996). These bonds were issued at savings of 0.07 percent, 0.19 percent, and 0.05 percent, respectively, as shown in Figure 10.7. By May 1986, the yield on the fourth specially targeted U.S. Treasury was identical with the regular onshore issue of the same

FIGURE 10.7   Yield Spread: Specially Targeted U.S. Treasury Note Minus
Regular U.S. Treasury Note

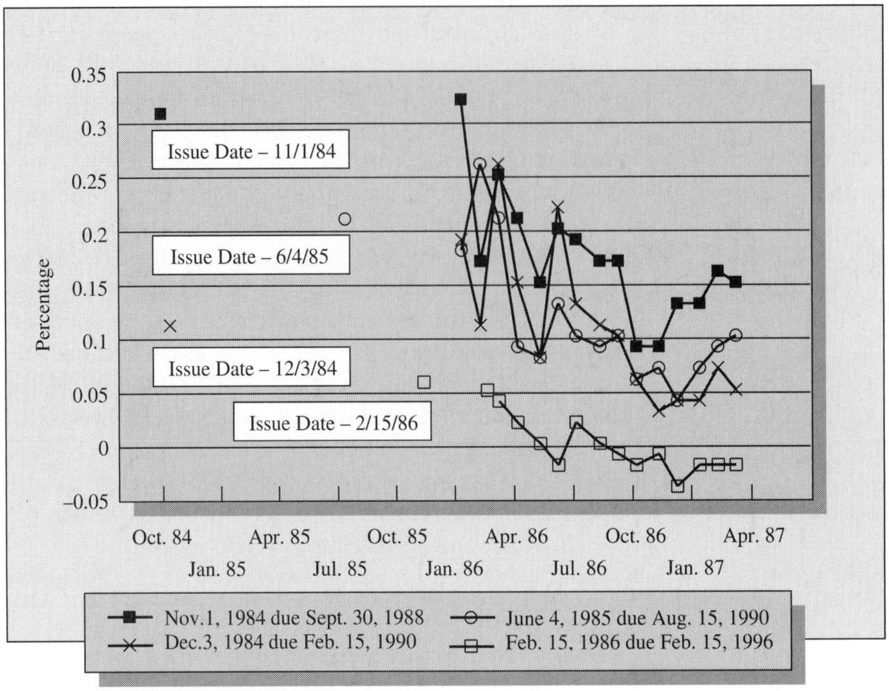

Note: Legend lists issue date and maturity date of each bond.

Source: Data are from Bloomberg pages, various dates, included in Kristina Borsy, "Foreign-Targeted Treasury Issues,"
unpublished MBA thesis, New York University, May 1988.

maturity. And later that year, the yield on the fourth specially targeted U.S. Treasury exceeded the yield on the comparable regular U.S. Treasury bond. By mid-1986 and after $4 billion of issues, the apparent cost incentive for the U.S. Treasury to issue bonds in the Eurobond market had vanished.

While the U.S. Treasury exhausted its scarcity value, private firms continued to use the Eurobond market to capture special windows of opportunity when their scarcity value in the market was high. See Box 10.4 for several recent examples.

Policy Matters—Public Policymakers

The Eurobond market has not attracted as much concern among policymakers as the Eurocurrency market. In the early 1970s, the Eurobond market was a fairly small component of the international bond market. And the abolition of U.S. capital controls in 1974 was expected to halt its development. It was only in 1982 that the total volume of Eurobond issues (across all currencies) first exceeded the volume of U.S. corporate bond issues. The US$ segment of the Eurobond market has never outpaced the U.S. corporate bond market (in terms of new issue volume) although it nearly did so in 1982. Still, by 1985 the annual volume of Eurobond issues was running in excess of $100 billion, often exceeding the volume in the U.S. corporate bond market. The Eurobond market was too large to be ignored by U.S. financial regulators or by European policymakers. We will discuss each of them in turn.

Box 10.4

Recent Cases of Scarcity Value in the Eurobond Market

Usually an issuer requires a strong credit rating, high name recognition, or both along with infrequent visits to the capital market to earn a scarcity value, and issue bonds at a premium relative to other firms. For example, in August 1995 Merck & Company, the U.S. pharmaceutical firm, issued a $500 million, 10-year bond. Merck is rated AAA, and analysts felt that the rarity of a Merck offering made the bond particularly attractive to institutional investors in Asia and Switzerland. The bond was offered at a yield equal to the U.S. Treasury rate plus 31 basis points.[a]

Another rare offering came from the Coca-Cola Company in October 1995. Coca-Cola, rated AA, had not issued a Eurodollar bond for 10 years. The company offered a $250 million five-year bond priced to yield only 18 basis points over the equivalent U.S. Treasury rate. About 90 percent of the issue was placed with Swiss retail investors "for whom the issue's rarity value proved to be an attraction," it was reported.[b]

Harvard University, rated AAA, spotted an opportunity in the short-term end of the Eurodollar market. In January 1996, Harvard issued its second Eurobond, a three-year issue at a rate of 5.307 percent, only 5.7 basis points above the comparable U.S. Treasury bond.[c]

Kellogg's, the U.S. cereal maker, suffered a credit downgrade from AAA to AA, but still the company was able to issue $500 million of seven-year bonds at only 20 basis points over the U.S. Treasury rate. "Kellogg is such a household name, people aren't really bothered by the downgrade," it was reported.[d] Moreover, this was Kellogg's only Eurodollar bond, a sign of true scarcity.

In February 1997, Siemens, the German electronic and engineering company, made a 10-year, $1.5 billion offering, the firm's first in 25 years.[e] The issue had three tranches (DM, Dutch guilders, and French francs), each with a 5.5 percent coupon. Siemens effectively exploited rising sentiment toward the single currency by pledging to redenominate each tranche into euros as each currency enters the European Monetary Union. This would enhance the liquidity of the overall issue in later years. The bond was oversubscribed by three to four times and sold at narrow spreads relative to each benchmark.

But scarcity isn't always everything. In November 1996, the Russian government sold $1 billion of Eurobonds—its first international bond offering since the Russian Revolution in 1917. The five-year bonds were rated BB− and sold at 345 basis points above the U.S. Treasury rate.[f] Less than two years later, the Russian government defaulted on these bonds, leaving investors with only a small fraction of their initial investment.

All of these examples illustrate that good credit quality and name recognition can enable a firm to gain access to low-cost funds in the Euromarket. Expertise to tailor the maturity, amount, coupon, and other features of the bond, and to sell it into the appropriate retail or institutional market, are essential aspects of a successful offering. Scarcity, or infrequent offerings, are another element that contribute to lower borrowing costs.

Students may follow the pricing of new issues in the Eurobond market by reading the "International Bonds" column in the *Financial Times* or the "New Securities Issues" column in *The Wall Street Journal*. Both newspapers report the yield spread on newly issued bonds relative to the appropriate government benchmark rate.

---

[a]Conner Middelmann, "Merck Capitalises on Rarity Value with $500m Deal," *Financial Times,* Aug. 3, 1995.
[b]Richard Lapper and Connor Middelmann, "Coca-Cola Deal Taps Strong Swiss Retail Demand," *Financial Times,* Oct. 25, 1995, p. 34.
[c]*International Herald Tribune,* Frankfurt edition, Jan. 5, 1996, p. 12.
[d]Conner Middelmann, "Kellogg Well Received Despite Downgrading," *Financial Times,* Jan. 16, 1997.
[e]Conner Middelmann and Edward Luce, "Siemens Uses EMU Angle," *Financial Times,* Feb. 12, 1997.
[f]"Russia's $1 bn Eurobond Popular," *Financial Times,* Nov. 21, 1996.

The U.S. Competitive Response

We have discussed two U.S. policy changes that could be viewed as responses to the competitive challenge from the Eurobond market. First is the "shelf registration" procedure introduced in 1982 with Rule 415. The Eurobond market always offered a shorter launch time for issuing a security. Around 1982, the bought deal shortened the time requirement in the Eurobond market still further. Rule 415 could be interpreted as a response by U.S. regulators to compete with the more favorable offering conditions available in offshore markets. By lowering the amount of paperwork and time required for a capital issue, Rule 415 lowered the issuing costs of public offerings in the U.S. corporate bond market.

A second important rule change occurred in July 1984. Foreigners purchasing bonds issued in the United States after that date were exempt from withholding tax on interest payments. Ostensibly, the rule change was an attempt to increase the attractiveness of U.S. federal debt to foreigners, and thus shift the demand curve outward, raise the price, and lower the interest cost of U.S. Treasury debt. But by dropping the withholding tax on interest paid to foreigners, the U.S. corporate bond market became more comparable to the Eurobond market from the standpoint of foreign investors. Also in connection with these new regulations, U.S. corporations were permitted to issue Eurobonds in bearer form without going through a foreign-based, separately capitalized financing affiliate as had been the law previously. The catch was that these bearer securities could be sold *only* to foreigners. This rule change made it less costly for U.S. firms to enter the Eurobond market by avoiding the cost of setting up a separate offshore financial affiliate. Indeed, the evidence shows that more and smaller U.S. corporate issuers entered the Eurobond market after this rule change.[34]

The Rule 144a Market.   The **Rule 144a market** represents the most important competitive response by the United States to the Eurobond market. Introduced in April 1990, the Rule 144a market essentially takes the private placement market within the United States and enhances it by adding the right to transfer the 144a security to another "qualified institutional buyer." All types of securities—equity, debt, rights, warrants—may be issued in the Rule 144a market. A private placement market existed in the United States prior to April 1990.[35] In this market, a corporation or individual sells a security to one or more institutional buyers. Because the security is not offered publicly, the SEC rules regarding disclosure and investor protection do not apply. However, the buyer's ability to transfer the security is severely curtailed, as dividing and transferring the security could quickly transform it into a public offering. The innovation of the 144a market is to permit transfer of the security to another qualified institutional buyer without obtaining prior approval from the SEC.

Thus, the Rule 144a market is similar in many respects to the Eurobond market. In the Rule 144a market, issuers are free to provide whatever accounting information and disclosures they choose. There is no requirement for U.S. GAAP statements and no lengthy SEC approval process for an offering prospectus. Rule 144a securities are sold to "professional investors" like those in the Eurobond market. And like the Eurobond market, investors retain the right to sell their investment, although in the Rule 144a market the sale must be to another qualified institutional buyer.

An example of a Rule 144a tombstone is shown in Figure 10.8. Note the wording at the top of the tombstone which states that the securities have *not* been registered under the Securities Act of 1933. Note also the wording that the securities are for sale *only* to qualified institutional buyers. When Rule 144a was formulated, a **qualified institutional buyer** was defined as any registered investment adviser with more than $100 million under management.

---

[34]See Thomas, Saudagaran, and Shroff (1994).
[35]See Carey et al. (1993) for an extended discussion of the U.S. private placement market.

FIGURE 10.8   Atlas Copco AB, Rule 144A American Depositary Shares

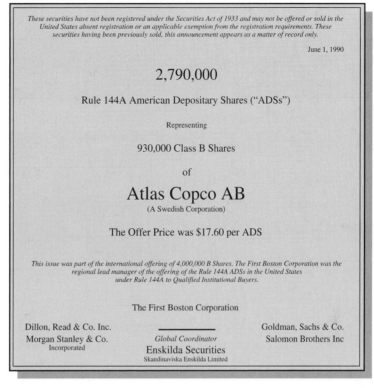

These securities have not been registered under the Securities Act of 1933 and may not be offered or sold in the United States absent registration or an applicable exemption from the registration requirements. These securities having been previously sold, this announcement appears as a matter of record only.

June 1, 1990

2,790,000

Rule 144A American Depositary Shares ("ADSs")

Representing

930,000 Class B Shares

of

Atlas Copco AB
(A Swedish Corporation)

The Offer Price was $17.60 per ADS

This issue was part of the international offering of 4,000,000 B Shares. The First Boston Corporation was the regional lead manager of the offering of the Rule 144A ADSs in the United States under Rule 144A to Qualified Institutional Buyers.

The First Boston Corporation

| Dillon, Read & Co. Inc. | | Goldman, Sachs & Co. |
| Morgan Stanley & Co. Incorporated | *Global Coordinator* Enskilda Securities Skandinaviska Enskilda Limited | Salomon Brothers Inc |

Source: Atlas Copco AB.

The Rule 144a market has been very successful. In Figure 10.9 we see that the volume of Rule 144a securities grew at a rapid pace, reaching $91 billion in 1993 before falling back in 1994 and 1995 and then climbing to over $300 billion in 1998 and 1999. Debt securities make up close to 90 percent of the Rule 144a market. Somewhat surprising, perhaps, is that nearly three-fourths of all Rule 144a issues have been made by American issuers. The explanation for this is that American issuers also find it costly to comply with SEC rules for a public offering.[36] American issuers also enjoy the speed of the Rule 144a market, which now allows the use of Internet road shows rather than in-person investor conferences. In addition, some investments may be too complex to explain easily and therefore are unsuitable for a retail investment clientele through a U.S. public offering. These investments may be better suited for a professional or institutional clientele.

Anecdotal evidence also suggests that the Rule 144a market has resulted in lower issuing costs than for private placements. Investors are willing to pay more for a 144a bond than for a private placement, because the 144a bond has liquidity and can be sold to another qualified buyer. On the other hand, investors have been willing to pay less for a 144a bond than for a similar registered bond. This 144a premium was about 10 basis points in 1995 but has declined as more investors have been drawn to the 144a market.[37]

---

[36]See Carey et al. (1993) for further discussion of the Rule 144a market.

[37]See Patrick McGeehan, "Money Raised in Private Placement of Issues Doubles as Companies Take Advantage of SEC's Rule 144a," *The Wall Street Journal*, Jan. 2, 1998, p. R38.

FIGURE 10.9   The Rule 144a Market

Gross Proceeds from New Issues—Debt and Equity Issues

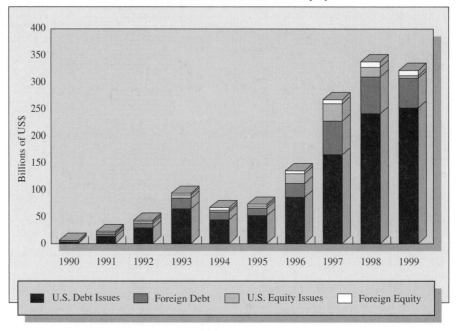

Note: Rule 144a market began in April 1990. Figures for 1990 represent April 1990–December 1990.
Source: Securities Data Company.

European Union and the Eurobond Market

In 1985, the European Commission drafted a plan to move the member nations of the European Community (EC) to a single unified market by 1992.[38] Dubbed "Europe 1992," the plan called for unified banking and financial markets as well as markets for goods and services. As an initial element of the plan, European policymakers agreed to abolish all capital controls among participants in the European Monetary System (EMS) by July 1, 1990, a deadline that was met.

The bulk of the Europe 1992 plan pertaining to financial services addressed the removal of internal barriers affecting financial markets within the EC. The broad goals of the plan were:

1. A minimal amount of regulation shared by all EC countries.

2. Complete freedom to offer financial services throughout the EC based on mutual recognition of national laws, regulations, and practices.

3. Home country control over all activities supervised by firms headquartered in the home country.

The first point signifies a common core of regulation to be shared by all EC countries. This common core is intended to safeguard certain fundamental public goods dealing with the safety and solvency of the financial system, as well as setting minimum standards for investor, depositor, and consumer protection. The second goal, of mutual

---

[38]Commission of the European Communities (1985).

recognition, leaves scope for accommodating differences in regulation across countries. Rather than to straitjacket regulation across the EC, this feature allows for competition among regulatory bodies and dynamic adjustment. The third goal, of home country control, reflects a domiciliary approach along the lines of the Basle Concordat discussed in Chapter 9. Home country control both preserves national sovereignty in these areas and exploits existing regulatory and supervisory bodies without the need for a new supranational agency for the European Community.

Taken together, these principles circumvent the need to homogenize a long list of financial regulations and practices, thus speeding up the ultimate goal of unifying the internal financial markets. Furthermore, by exploiting competition among regulatory authorities, the EC will ultimately achieve a market-determined level of regulation that is more responsive to market conditions than one designed ex ante by a supranational body and then revised subject to long and variable lags.

The Europe 1992 plan laid down a workable foundation. However, a great many details were left unspecified. The resolution of these issues bears heavily on the Euromarkets.[39] The specification of these common core regulations is still evolving within the present European Union (EU). The primary areas that bear on the Eurobond market are the harmonization of tax rates on interest payments; dividends, capital gains, and withholding practices; and the harmonization of disclosure and reporting of interest and dividends to tax authorities (meaning rules on secrecy).

First consider the rules for *residents* of each EU country. Most EU countries withhold tax on interest payments to residents. Two countries that do not, Denmark and the Netherlands, report interest payments to the tax authorities. Luxembourg stands out as the only country with neither withholding tax nor reporting to authorities of interest paid to residents. However, *nonresidents* of Denmark, Luxembourg, and the Netherlands have neither a withholding tax nor the reporting to authorities of interest paid. No withholding tax and no reporting to authorities is also the practice for dividends paid to both residents and nonresidents of Ireland and the United Kingdom.

How taxation and disclosure to tax authorities are treated within the common core of EU regulation is of critical importance to the Eurobond market. If, for example, EU countries agree on a unified withholding tax rate, or if EU countries agree to inform tax authorities of all interest and dividends payments, the tax evasion element of the Eurobond market could vanish. If the rules require withholding taxation and/or disclosure only for residents, then the definition of *resident* will be important. Will *resident* be defined broadly to mean resident of the EU, or narrowly to mean resident of a single country?

The resolution of these issues is important because the Eurobond market is to some extent a footloose industry. EU policymakers want to harmonize their financial policies to create a level playing field free from competitive distortions. Creating a level playing field across Europe is only half the problem that policymakers face. The taxation and disclosure policies must be commensurate with those in other world financial centers. Otherwise, there is the possibility that the Eurobond market will migrate—to Switzerland, the U.S. Rule 144a market, or elsewhere. As the Europeans have been the beneficiaries of excess U.S. financial market regulation, they can hardly question that this migration will occur. The only question can be: How sensitive will the migration be in response to a given difference in regulatory burdens? Now that institutional investors play a greater role in the Eurobond market, the sensitivity of the market to tax regulations may be less than it was in the early years of the market.

---

[39]For further discussion, see Levich (1993) and the collection of studies in Dermine (1993).

Summary

The Eurobond market operates in a largely unregulated and, consequently, a highly competitive environment. Over the years, market participants have developed their own practices for designing, issuing, pricing, and trading Eurobonds. In the formative years, onshore regulations (such as the IET and VFCR) and onshore practices (such as queuing and credit rationing) provided an active stimulus to the Eurobond market. But even after these regulations and practices were dropped or softened, the Eurobond market survived and expanded because of its flexibility and innovative style.

Issuers have often raised funds at lower cost with Eurobonds than in onshore markets. This suggests a form of market segmentation where Eurobond investors are willing to pay higher prices than onshore investors for the same security. Knowing this, issuers may target the Eurobond market to take advantage of a window of opportunity or even to arbitrage between the offshore and onshore markets.

Public policymakers have responded to the growth of the Eurobond market by modifying onshore market regulations. In the United States, the Rule 144a market emulates some key features of the Eurobond market. And regulatory changes, contemplated in the European Union, that affect the disclosure of information about interest payments could seriously affect the Eurobond market.

Questions

1. What are the most distinctive features of a Eurobond compared with a traditional onshore bond?

2. What is a samurai bond? What is a bulldog bond?

3. Describe how U.S. regulations in the 1960s and 1970s played a role in the development of the Eurobond market.

4. What is the difference between public offerings and private placements? How does the distinction play a role in the Eurobond market?

5. Give a brief explanation of Rule 144a. Compare and contrast the Rule 144a market with the Eurobond market.

6. Discuss the factors an issuer must consider before deciding between a Eurobond issue or a domestic bond issue.

7. What is underwriting risk? Who bears the underwriting risk in the case of a bought deal?

8. How could the variable-price reoffering method of Eurobond underwriting lead to stuffing the accounts of retail investors?

9. What role has the gray market played in the Eurobond market?

10. Is competition greater in the Eurobond market or in the U.S. domestic bond market? Explain.

11. Would you say that the Eurobond market and the domestic U.S. bond market are integrated? Why? Provide an example.

12. Suppose that firm ABC has issued seven-year straight US$ bonds in both the Eurobond market and the U.S. domestic market. Would you expect the yield-to-maturity on the two bonds to be identical?

13. How did the EU approach the issue of regulation of international financial markets across the area? What impact might the EU approach have on the Eurobond market?

14. What role have taxes played in the development of the Eurobond market?

Exercises

1. Suppose IBM is issuing $100 million of seven-year Eurobonds priced at U.S. Treasury minus 25 basis points. There is great demand for the issue, and you are willing to bid 102 for 10 percent of the issue.

   a. If you actually get your bid executed, how much will you pay for the bond?

   b. A year later, the IBM Eurobonds are traded on the Luxembourg Stock Exchange at 105. What is the value of your investment? What is your capital gain (loss)?

c. You decide to sell the bond at the above price to pursue other opportunities. What amount of withholding taxes are you required to pay?

2. Suppose Credit Suisse First Boston (CSFB) is the sole lead manager in a $100 million bought deal for the World Bank. CSFB decides to price the seven-year issue at par to yield 8 percent.

a. What will CSFB's position be if the Fed decides to increase short-term interest rates by 50 basis points during the offering period?

b. Instead of the Fed move described in a above, suppose that international trade talks break down, leading to a depreciation of the dollar on currency markets. What will CSFB's position be in this case?

c. Calculate the gain or loss for CSFB if the seven-year Eurobond rate rises to 8.25 percent on the offering day. (*Note:* Eurobonds pay interest only once each year.)

d. Suppose CSFB collects 2 percent in fees for lead managing the issue. Again, calculate the overall gain or loss for CSFB if the seven-year Eurobond rate rises to 8.25 percent on the offering day.

e. (Optional) How could CSFB hedge the risks described in a and b?

3. Suppose Mobil Oil Company is able to issue $500 million worth (face value) of 10-year, zero-coupon Eurobonds at a yield of 8 percent.

a. How much capital would Mobil raise with this issue? (Assume that there are no underwriting fees.)

b. At the same time, suppose that 10-year, stripped zero-coupon U.S. Treasury bonds were traded at a yield of 8.25 percent. Describe how Mobil could arbitrage between the U.S. market and the Eurobond market. Calculate Mobil's profit from this arbitrage transaction.

c. When does Mobil earn the profit you calculated in b?

4. Suppose two similar seven-year maturity bonds are issued at par, one in the U.S. domestic market and the second in the Eurodollar bond market. Underwriting fees are 2.5 percent in the U.S. market and 1 percent in the Eurobond market.

a. If the U.S. domestic bond has an initial yield of 10 percent, what is the effective spread between lending and borrowing rates in this market?

b. If the Eurodollar bond has an initial yield of 10.5 percent, what is the effective spread between lending and borrowing rates in this market?

c. Suppose that the U.S. bond is subject to a withholding tax of 20 percent on the interest paid. What yield would an investor accept on the Eurobond issue to make him or her indifferent between the two issues?

References

Barth, James R.; Dan Brumbaugh, Jr.; and James A. Wilcox. "The Repeal of Glass-Steagall and the Advent of Broad Banking." *Journal of Economic Perspectives* 14, no. 2 (Spring 2000), pp. 191–204.

Benston, George J. *The Separation of Commercial and Investment Banking: The Glass-Steagall Act Revisited and Reconsidered.* New York: Oxford University Press, 1990.

Carey, Mark; Stephen Prowse; John Rea; and Gregory Udell. "The Economics of Private Placements: A New Look." *Financial Markets Institutions and Instruments* 2, no. 3 (Aug. 1993), pp. 1–67.

Choi, Frederick D. S., and Richard M. Levich. *The Capital Market Effects of International Accounting Diversity.* Homewood, IL: Dow Jones–Irwin, 1990.

Choi, Frederick D. S., and Gerhard G. Mueller. *International Accounting,* 2nd ed. Englewood Cliffs, NJ: Prentice Hall, 1992.

Commission on the European Communities. *Completing the Internal Market: White Paper to the European Council.* Brussels, June 1985.

Dermine, Jean. *European Banking in the 1990s,* 2nd ed. London: Basil-Blackwell, 1993.

Financial Market Trends. Paris: Organization for Economic Cooperation and Development, various issues.

Finnerty, John D. "Zero Coupon Bond Arbitrage: An Illustration of the Regulatory Dialectic at Work." *Financial Management,* Winter 1985, pp. 13–17.

Fisher, Frederick G. *Eurobonds.* London: Euromoney Publications, 1988.

Kidwell, David S.; M. Wayne Marr; and G. Rodney Thompson. "Eurodollar Bonds: Alternative Financing for U.S. Companies." *Financial Management* (Winter 1985), pp. 18–27.

Kim, Yong Cheol, and René M. Stulz. "The Eurobond Market and Corporate Financial Policy: A Test of the Clientele Hypothesis." *Journal of Financial Economics* 22 (Dec. 1988), pp. 189–205.

Levich, Richard M. "The Euromarkets after 1992." In *European Banking in the 1990s,* 2nd ed., ed. J. Dermine. London: Basil Blackwell, 1993.

———. "A View from the International Capital Markets." In *Deregulating Wall Street,* ed. I. Walter. New York: John Wiley, 1985.

Mendelsohn, M. S. *Money on the Move.* New York: McGraw-Hill, 1980.

Smith, Roy C., and Ingo Walter. *Global Financial Services.* New York: Harper and Row, 1990.

Thomas, Jacob K.; Shahrokh Saudagaran; and Peter Shroff. "U.S. Corporate Borrowing in the Eurodollar Market." Working Paper, Columbia University, 1994.

Van Horne, James C. *Financial Market Rates and Flows,* 5th ed., Englewood Cliffs, NJ: Prentice Hall, 1998.

Walter, Ingo, ed. *Deregulating Wall Street.* New York: John Wiley, 1985.

Watson, Maxwell; Donald Mathieson; Russell Kincaid; and Eliot Kalter. *International Capital Markets.* Occasional Paper No. 43. Washington, DC: International Monetary Fund, Feb. 1986.

Weekly Eurobond Guide. London: Association of International Bond Dealers, weekly issues.

White, Eugene N. "Before the Glass-Steagall Act: An Analysis of the Investment Banking Activities of National Banks." *Explorations in Economic History* 23 (1986), pp. 33–55.

IV   DERIVATIVE SECURITY MARKETS: FUTURES, OPTIONS, AND SWAPS

11   Currency and Interest Rate Futures   374
12   Currency and Interest Rate Options   418
13   Currency and Interest Rate Swaps   475

11 CURRENCY AND INTEREST RATE FUTURES

"My nomination for the most significant financial innovation of the last twenty years is: financial futures—the futures exchange style trading of financial instruments."

Merton Miller (1986)

Learning Objectives

After reading this chapter, students should

1. Understand the distinctions between futures contracts and forward contracts.
2. Know the institutional arrangements for trading futures contracts, including the notions of cash settlement and marking to market.
3. Be able to graph the payoffs of a futures contract as a function of the price of the underlying asset, and graph similar payoff profiles or combinations of futures contracts.
4. Be able to show how futures contracts can be used to hedge an open, risky position.
5. Be aware that futures prices may contain a risk premium and, if so, that the futures price will not equal the market's expectation of the future spot price of the underlying asset.
6. Know that futures markets are a business and that exchanges initiate new contracts when there is sufficient demand from hedgers or speculators, but regulators are often concerned that futures markets may exacerbate market volatility.

A **forward contract** is an agreement struck today that binds two counterparties to an exchange at a later date. We introduced **currency forward contracts** in Chapter 3 as a method for buying or selling a given amount of foreign currency at specified dates in the future—often one, three, or six months ahead, but possibly one, three, or five years ahead. Forward contracts exist for other financial transactions—forward contracts for equity shares (common in Europe) and forward contracts for government securities (common in many markets)—as well as for goods and services—forward contracts for college tuition or for an artist's services. In each case, the forward contract establishes an *obligation* for two counterparties to make an exchange at a specified future date.

The possibility of default poses a potentially serious problem for counterparties in a forward contract. Suppose I agree to buy oil forward at $30 per barrel for delivery on

June 30, 2003, and when this date arrives, oil can be purchased in the spot market for $25 per barrel. In this situation, the *buyer* has a strong incentive to default and save the $5 per barrel cost of fulfilling the forward commitment. Similarly, someone who sold yen forward on August 28, 1998, for delivery in one year at 136.71¥/$ incurred an opportunity loss of 0.001643$/¥ based on the actual spot rate on August 27, 1999, of 111.63¥/$. In this situation, the *seller* has a strong incentive to default and deliver his or her yen to the spot market for the higher price.

How can counterparties separated by great distances and lacking complete information about one another overcome this inherent risk? One method is to make forward contracts only with people of high character, reputation, and credit quality, so that the likelihood of a default is minimized. This is roughly the method adopted by banks dealing in forward contracts.

Another method, associated with **futures contracts,** calls for both counterparties to post a "good-faith bond" that is held in escrow by a reputable and disinterested third party. In case of default, the bond is available to compensate the nondefaulting counterparty. Futures exchanges use a modification of this approach, requiring each counterparty to post a bond in the form of a *margin requirement,* but in an amount that varies from day to day as the futures contract loses or gains value. The procedure of adjusting the posted bond, known as **marking to market,** is one of the important features of a futures contract, and a characteristic that distinguishes a futures contract from a forward contract.

It is common to associate futures contracts with physical commodities such as agricultural commodities (like corn and wheat), primary commodities (like lumber or copper), or precious metals (like silver and gold). Indeed, prior to 1972, futures contracts were associated exclusively with these physical commodities. But with the rise of exchange rate volatility (see Figure 2.7) and interest rate volatility (see Figure 2.11), the demand for financial hedging instruments multiplied.

Because banks offered a well-developed market in spot and forward currency contracts, the need for currency futures contracts in 1972 might have been questioned. The story goes, however, that in 1971 Chicago banks refused to enter a forward contract with Professor Milton Friedman, a future Nobel laureate in economics at the University of Chicago. Professor Friedman wanted to sell the UK£ forward and profit from its expected devaluation. The commercial banks declined his business, probably not out of fear of default but because the contract size was small relative to their normal transactions. Professor Friedman encouraged local futures market officials to consider currency futures as a promising business to supplement commodity futures trading.[1]

After the devaluation of the pound sterling in November 1967, a rash of international financial crises ensued: two-tier gold pricing in 1968, DM revaluation in 1969, floating the Canadian dollar in 1970, temporary DM and Dutch guilder floating in 1971, followed by the de facto float of most major currencies from August 15, 1971, until the Smithsonian agreement on December 1971. All of this set the stage for the International Monetary Market (IMM) of the Chicago Mercantile Exchange (CME) to introduce trading in foreign currency futures in May 1972. Once the UK£ was allowed to float in June 1972 followed by generalized floating of other currencies in early 1973, the prospects for currency futures as a business was given an immediate boost.

With currency futures "up and running," futures exchange officials realized that futures contracts could be structured around the prices of other financial instruments and

---

[1]See Rodriguez and Carter (1979), p. 154, or Miller (1986), p. 464.

intangibles (such as price indexes) and not only physical or tangible commodities as in the past. And with interest rate volatility increasing, there was ready demand for contracts from both hedgers and speculators. Trading in interest rate futures (on GNMA contracts) began in October 1975 on the Chicago Board of Trade (CBOT). These were followed by Treasury bill futures contracts in 1976, Treasury bond futures contracts in 1977, and Eurodollar interest rate futures contracts in 1981.

Since futures contracts and organized futures markets have been around for centuries (the CBOT began trading futures in 1865, but trading in other countries began far earlier), it may seem odd to associate the present-day term *derivative* with a futures contract. But as we showed in Chapter 3, the cash payoffs of forward currency contracts are *derived from* other, basic financial instruments.[2] In this sense, forward contracts and futures contracts are redundant because their cash payoffs can be replicated using other financial instruments.

This raises two natural questions: Why does a redundant security exist? And what benefits can come from a redundant security? Of the many reasons postulated about why forward and futures contracts exist, the most basic reason is reduced transaction costs. The existence of the derivative security results in faster and lower cost execution of transactions relative to other means of contracting. The various "design features" of futures contracts, as we will see in this chapter, promote a liquid and efficient order flow between anonymous counterparties, while they effectively manage the issue of counterparty default.

The benefits of financial futures contracts are clear to market economists who view the huge increases in trading volume as a confirmation that access to the market improves welfare. Futures contracts offer a means for risk management and risk spreading that potentially improves welfare for everyone even though it creates no tangible output.[3] Some economists, market regulators, and the general public are not convinced. The lower transaction costs of a futures exchange clearly encourage trading. But this may be bad, it is argued, for individuals who unwittingly extend their risky positions and for the entire economy if futures market volatility spills over into other markets.

Economists presume that volatile weather conditions generate a demand for corn and wheat futures, but that futures trading does not affect the weather. The stock market crash of October 1987 caused many people to rethink the relationship between derivative markets and the underlying cash markets, and to ask whether new public policy safeguards are required.

In the remainder of this chapter, we review the basic institutional features of currency and interest rate futures, and highlight the distinctions between futures and forward contracts. An important characteristic of futures is their symmetric payoff profile, which comes from the *obligation* of a counterparty to pay off in both good and bad outcomes. We then compare the pricing of futures contracts and forward contracts and examine the factors that lead to price differences. We also review the term structure of forward rates in both currency and interest rates and examine whether longer-term forward contracts contain a risk premium. Among the policy issues that affect private individuals, we explore the decision to use futures or forwards when both contracts are

---

[2]In Chapter 3 we showed that the forward rate is determined by interest rate parity based on the spot rate, the domestic interest rate, and the foreign interest rate. Futures pricing relies on the same formula—referred to as the cost-of-carry model—where we interpret i_{FC} as the cost of storing the underlying futures commodity.

[3]The cash flows in futures contracts are a zero-sum game. There is some loss of human and physical resources associated with running the exchange.

available. We conclude the chapter with a discussion of public policy issues, including a return to the question of whether futures markets promote volatility and whether policies to impede trading in futures are warranted.

Distinctions between Futures and Forwards: Institutions and Terminology

While both forward and futures contracts entail a binding contract executed today for settlement at a future specified date, there are important differences between the two transactions.

Dispersed versus Centralized Trading

Forward contracts, whether for currencies or interest rates, are usually traded by commercial banks, investment banks, or securities firms. As we discussed in Chapter 3, the interbank market is geographically dispersed and open 24 hours a day. Market makers use direct dealing to trade with one another over telephone lines or computer networks, or they rely on brokers to arrange transactions.

In contrast, futures contracts trade on *centralized exchanges.* Until recently, this meant physical centralization. All futures contracts traded in a specified area, known as a *pit,* and trading took place only during specified trading hours. Pit traders use a system called *open outcry* to communicate and execute trades with one another. In 1992, the Chicago Mercantile Exchange launched GLOBEX, a computer-based system to allow after-hours trading of its listed futures contracts. Since then, some exchanges (like the French MATIF and German-Swiss EUREX) have centralized the exchange by using electronic computer systems exclusively. Other futures exchanges (such as Singapore and the CME) operate an open outcry system for some contracts and an electronic system for others.

A centralized exchange has advantages with respect to **price discovery,** which refers to the ability of market participants to observe or "discover" the current market price. In a centralized market, traders observe all transaction prices as posted by the exchange. We say that the futures market exhibits transparency. In the futures market, anonymous orders enjoy the democracy of the marketplace. By comparison, price discovery may be compromised in a geographically dispersed market. In the interbank forward foreign exchange market, there is no centralized record of prices. At times, some dealers may have difficulty gauging the market price when some price quotations represent true transactions and others are for "indications only." So the interbank market lacks transparency.

Customized versus Standardized Transactions

Transactions in the interbank forward market are *customized* and flexible to meet customer preferences. While certain maturities (such as 1, 3, 6, and 12 months) are popular for currency forwards, a counterparty can request a quotation for *any* forward maturity and for *any* contract size.

By comparison, transactions in the futures markets are highly standardized. The exchange designs the contracts and sets their specifications in order to obtain regulatory permission to begin trading. Each futures contract specifies a contract size or quantity of the underlying asset. Contract expiration dates are also standardized—often maturing in

March, June, September, and December as well as the two months nearest to the present date. In addition, the exchange will standardize delivery terms for futures contracts, daily price-limit movements, minimum price fluctuations, and the trading days and hours.

Standardization may be anathema in the fashion industry, but in the futures market it is an effective means to promote trading and liquidity. Since all futures contracts for a given asset and maturity (such as "March 2001 yen") are identical, in the same sense as all common equity shares of IBM are identical, futures can be traded continuously, much as if they were equity shares.

To see why futures contracts are relatively more liquid than forwards, assume that today (June 15) I purchase a six-month yen forward contract from Bank XYZ for delivery on December 15. Suppose that after 10 weeks (on September 1), the yen has appreciated and I want to secure my profit. To begin, my contract now has a maturity of about 15 weeks (or 105 days). This is a nonstandard maturity. I could try to sell my contract to another party, but there is no active market for 15-week forward contracts with Bank XYZ as a counterparty. I could go back to Bank XYZ and ask them to buy it back. But Bank XYZ probably would decline for similar reasons—the original forward contract has been rolled into their overall book, and it would be a nuisance to attempt to reverse the transaction. The solution (from Bank XYZ or another bank) would be to initiate a second forward contract on September 1, whereby I sell yen forward for delivery on December 15. This would be an expensive alternative because 15-week forward contracts are not actively quoted in the market.[4]

Alternatively, suppose that on June 15 I purchase a yen *futures* contract expiring on December 15. If I decide to sell my December yen contract after any period of time—10 minutes, 10 days, or 10 weeks—I will find that the December yen futures contract is still trading on the futures exchange. Selling the contract closes my position and secures my gain or loss on the contract.

As we discuss in the next section, futures contracts are standardized in another important facet: counterparty risk.

Variable Counterparty Risks versus the Clearinghouse

Forward market transactions link banks with other banks (the interbank market) or banks with customers (the retail market). As we discussed in Chapter 3, each counterparty to a transaction assumes the credit risk and the risk of default of the other counterparty. That is why bank credit officers make a detailed appraisal of the credit and risk quality of any potential counterparty before trading particulars are discussed. As the geographically dispersed market for forwards leads to some price variability, it also leads to some variability in counterparty risk. Banks compensate by lowering the credit limits or the maturity limits of more risky counterparties.

Every futures contract traded on an organized exchange, by comparison, has the **clearinghouse** as *one* of the two counterparties. The clearinghouse may be a separately chartered corporation or a division of the futures exchange.[5] In either case, the clearing-

---

[4]The 15-week contract might involve a three-month forward (from September 1 to December 1) and 14 one-day rollovers until final maturity on December 15.

[5]For example, the clearinghouse for the CBOT is the Board of Trade Clearing Corporation. See <www.botcc.com> for further information. The clearinghouse for the New York Futures Exchange is the Intermarket Clearing Corporation, which is a wholly owned subsidiary of the Options Clearing Corporation (OCC). The OCC acts as the clearing organization for all exchange-traded option contracts in the United States. See the OCC website at <www.optionsclearing.com> for further information.

house is the legal entity on one side of *every* futures contract, and it stands ready to meet the obligations of the futures contract vis-à-vis every customer of the exchange. Thus, a broker-transmitted buy order for yen futures from Aunt Millie in Ohio may be matched in the futures pit against a sell order for yen futures from Mega Corporation of Liverpool. But each customer's legal contract is with the clearinghouse. The clearinghouse therefore standardizes the counterparty risk of all futures contracts, and facilitates trade between buyers and sellers who remain anonymous to one another.

This organization structure may offer an advantage, especially when bank credit quality is in doubt. The failure of the Herstatt Bank in Germany, the Franklin National Bank in the United States, and the British merchant bank Baring Brothers (among others) illustrates the reality of bank counterparty risk. Some counterparties may prefer the creditworthiness of a clearinghouse, which is backed by substantial capital reserves. In the United States, a clearinghouse of a major exchange has never defaulted on an obligation. The importance of the clearinghouse in the Baring Brothers debacle is discussed in Box 11.1.

Cash Settlement and Delivery versus the Marking-to-Market Convention

Another distinction between forwards and futures concerns the obligations of a buyer or seller between the point of entering into the contract and the point of closing out and settling or selling the contract. An illustration will help to convey the main points.

Tracking a Forward Contract. Suppose that on June 15 I wish to purchase €1 million for forward delivery on September 15 at a price of $1.10/€. To execute this contract as a retail customer of a large commercial bank, I would first need to have an established line of credit with the bank. This relationship is essential since the bank normally would not require specific credit or capital commitments to execute an individual contract. Suppose that this background due diligence is complete. I execute my forward purchase on June 15, but *no funds change hands at this time*. I am now "long forward €" for delivery on September 15. For the next three months, the value of the € gyrates, but still no money changes hands.

On September 15, the forward contract matures and it is time to settle up and/or take delivery. There are two possibilities. First, I may take delivery of the €1 million on September 15. In that case, I pay the bank $1,100,000 in exchange for €1 million delivered to my account. Second, I may not take delivery of the € and instead settle up with the bank for the gain or loss on the forward contract. If € is valued in the spot market on September 15 at $1.12, then the bank pays me $20,000. If € is valued in the spot market on September 15 at only $1.07, then I pay the bank $30,000.

The essential feature of a forward contract is that *no cash flows take place until the final maturity of the contract.*

Tracking a Futures Contract. Now suppose that on June 15, I purchase September € futures contracts traded on the CME and, for convenience, assume that the price is the same at $1.10/€.[6] To establish a €1 million "long futures" position, I will need to purchase eight contracts because each CME contract represents €125,000. To enter into this transaction, I must have an authorized futures trading account with a securities or

---

[6]We will soon examine whether it is reasonable for the prices of forwards and futures to be identical.

Box 11.1

Rogue Trading Sinks Baring Brothers—But Not the Futures Market

In 1995, speculative trading by a 28-year-old trader contributed to bringing down Baring Brothers and Company bank, a 233-year-old institution that was, among other distinctions, banker to the Queen of England. The British trader, Nicholas Leeson, had been hired from Bankers Trust in 1992 to build a global fixed-income derivatives operation in Singapore. He may have enjoyed some early successes, but in 1994 Leeson started to trade in the Nikkei 225 index of Tokyo securities. Ostensibly, Leeson was taking a low-risk arbitrage strategy—buying the Nikkei 225 index and shorting a similar index of the Osaka exchange traded on the Singapore International Monetary Exchange (SIMEX), or vice versa, to take advantage of small price differences. In reality, Leeson was accumulating a large speculative position in the Nikkei 225 index futures. After the Kobe earthquake on January 16, the Nikkei index fell, from almost 20,000 on January 1 to only 18,000 after the earthquake. Leeson's position lost value, but he apparently bought still more Nikkei futures in an attempt to recoup his losses.

By the end of February, the Nikkei sank below 17,000. Many of Leeson's losing trades were "hidden" in Account 88888. The exhibit (at right) shows a daily activity statement for this account as reported by the *Financial Times*. The account had a deficit of more than ¥59 billion, or about $610 million. These losses may have been hidden

from Leeson's supervisors in London, but in no way were they hidden from the market. As the value of Leeson's Nikkei futures contracts sank, he needed to post additional margin. Indeed, as *The Wall Street Journal* reported, "The flow of margin money is the sign investigators point to when they suggest that Baring's managers in London knew what Mr. Leeson was doing. Often when a company has to come up with fresh margin money, it has to go to a bank. At least 15 Japanese banks had lent a total of $715 million to Barings, much of it to cover margin calls on Japanese futures."*

While rogue trading and lax internal controls sank Baring Brothers, the futures markets survived. Thanks to the clearinghouse and the marking-to-market convention money flowed from Baring Brothers to the clearinghouse and on to other counterparties on a regular basis. When Baring Brothers finally defaulted, all losses (except for the last day's trading) had already been paid over to the clearinghouse.

Still, puzzles remain. At the peak of their dealings, Barings controlled 27,000 contracts on the SIMEX alone, representing a $2.4 billion open interest. The SIMEX permits speculators to hold no more than 1,000 contracts. Some-

---

*"Barings PLC Officials May Have Been Aware of Trader's Position," *The Wall Street Journal,* Mar. 6, 1995, p. 1.

---

brokerage firm. The broker requires that I post (in advance of any trades) a good-faith deposit (known as *margin*) either in the form of cash, a bank letter of credit, or short-term U.S. Treasury securities.[7] The **initial margin** is the amount of margin that must be on hand when the initial buy or sell order for the futures contract is placed. The initial margin varies from contract to contract and from time to time. But for the sake of illustration, let us assume that the initial margin in this case is 4 percent, which corresponds to $44,000.

Now suppose that on June 16, the September € future falls in value and ends the day trading at $1.095. Taking $1.095 as the **settlement price** (the price used for settling up the value of the margin account), my broker calculates that I would incur a $5,000 loss if the futures contract were sold at this price. Thus, the remaining value of my margin account has been reduced to $39,000. Now suppose that on June 17 the September € futures falls further to $1.089. The value of my eight futures contracts is now $1,089,000. Thus, the remaining value of my margin account has been reduced to

---

[7]If I choose to use U.S. Treasuries, I continue to accrue the interest earnings.

how, the Singapore and Japanese regulators failed to spot this abuse.[†]

On March 6, 1995, ING Group, the Dutch banking giant, agreed to buy Baring Brothers and assume "substantially all" of its liabilities for the nominal sum of £1. Nick Leeson was released from a Singapore jail in July 1999 after serving 3½ years of a 6½-year sentence for fraud. He owes £100 million to his creditors, who allow him to retain 35 percent of his speaking fees plus a monthly allowance of £3,000 from his frozen assets.

[†]None of the questionable futures trades by Barings took place on the CME. The CME limits speculators to holding 5,000 Nikkei contracts. See "Exchanges Boost Nikkei 225 Futures Margins," *The Wall Street Journal*, Mar. 1, 1995.

Baring Futures (Singapore) Pte Ltd
20 Raffles Place, 24th Floor, Ocean Towers, Singapore 0104
Tel: 5395571/5395572

Client	: Baring Futures (Singapore) Ltd	Account No: 88888
Address	: c/o Singapore Office	
	20 Raffles Place	Date: 24/02/95
	24th Floor, Ocean Towers	Page: 26
	Singapore 0104	Daily Activity Statement
Attention	: Nick Leeson	

DAILY STATEMENT OF UNREALISED PROFIT AND LOSS

. . . .

7. Equity Balance	0.00	−59,239,120,000.00 (¥)
8. Collateral Securities Held	. . . .	. . . .

Source: *Financial Times*, Friday, Mar. 3, 1995, p. 1.

$33,000. We will define this value, equal to 75 percent of the initial margin, as the **maintenance margin.**

If my margin account falls below the maintenance margin value, my broker will issue a **margin call** and demand that I restore my margin account to the level of the *initial margin* before the end of the day.[8] If not, the broker may elect to sell my futures contract and return any remaining proceeds of the margin account to me.

Assume that the September € futures falls to a settlement price of $1.080/€. My margin account has been reduced to only $24,000—below the maintenance margin level. The broker will issue a margin call for $20,000 (the so-called **variation margin**) to restore an initial margin of $44,000.

Now consider the happier case (for me) where the € appreciates in value to $1.11/€. In this case, the broker would credit my margin account for $10,000—equal to the $0.01 gain on €1 million—bringing the total to $54,000. These excess margin funds could be withdrawn and put to some other use. Although as the reader might suspect, with high

----

[8]In some cases, as long as 24 hours may be granted to fulfill a margin call.

FIGURE 11.1   **March 1985 DM Futures**
Prices and Margin Account

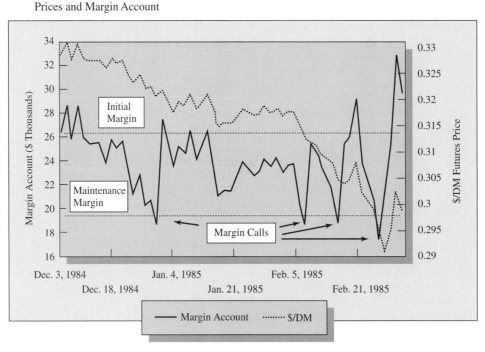

Note: The initial margin is $26,176 or 8 percent of the initial contract value. As the value of the DM falls (right scale), the value of the margin account falls. There is a margin call on December 28 and the trader adds $7,700 to the account to restore the initial margin. There are three additional margin calls in February. The overall loss on the transaction is $28,600 = $29,576 (ending value of margin account) − $26,176 (initial value of margin account) − $32,000 (margin calls). This loss can also be calculated as the change in the futures price ($0.3272 − $0.2986) × 1,000,000 = $28,600.

levels of exchange rate volatility, I might elect to simply keep my excess margin funds close at hand.

The process of updating a margin account on a daily basis to reflect the market value of the underlying position is known as marking to market. To some economists, *marking to market is the defining feature of a futures market.* Unlike a forward contract, a futures contract may "spin off" cash flows in and out of the margin account on a daily basis.

Tracking Two Real-Life Futures Contracts.   In Figure 11.1 we show the actual prices of the March 1985 DM futures contract over the three-month period from December 3, 1984, to February 28, 1985, and the margin account for a trader with a long DM1 million position. We assume (hypothetically) that the initial margin is 8 percent and the maintenance margin is 6 percent. The initial contract price is $0.3272/DM, so the initial margin is $26,176 (8 percent of $327,200). In the first three trading days, the DM appreciates, so the margin account grows. But as the DM falls, the margin account declines until December 27, when the margin account drops below the maintenance margin level of $19,632 (6 percent of $327,200). The trader adds new funds to his margin account on December 28, but the slide in the DM continues, leading to three additional margin calls in February 1985.

FIGURE 11.2   September 1985 DM Futures
Prices and Margin Account

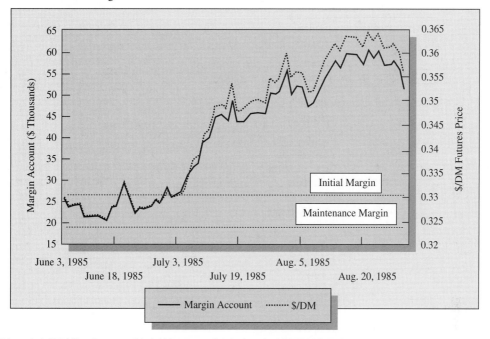

Note: The initial margin is $26,448, or 8 percent of the initial contract value. As the value of the DM rises (right scale), the value of the margin account increases. The margin account always stays above the required maintenance margin, so no additional margin calls are required. The overall gain on the transaction is $25,000 = $51,448 (ending value of margin account) − $26,448 (beginning value of margin account). This gain can also be calculated as the change in the futures price ($0.3556 − $0.3306) × 1,000,000 = $25,000.

At the end of the period, the DM futures price is $0.2986/DM. Thus, the long futures position has produced a loss of $0.0286/DM, or a $28,600 loss. In terms of the margin account, its ending value is $29,576, reflecting an initial value of $26,176 plus $32,000 in margin calls—or an overall loss of $28,600.

We show a similar experiment for a happier speculator in Figure 11.2 by tracking the September 1985 DM futures over the period June 3, 1985–August 30, 1985, and the margin account for a trader with a *long* DM1 million position. Keeping the same initial margin and maintenance margin requirements (8 percent and 6 percent), the initial contract price of $0.3306/DM leads to an initial margin of $26,448 (8 percent of $330,600). The September DM futures depreciate for the first 10 days, so the margin account declines but never pierces the maintenance margin level. The September DM strengthens to $0.3556/DM on August 30, resulting in a gain of $25,000 to the speculator. There are no margin calls in this example, and the trader could elect to withdraw surplus funds from his margin account as the DM strengthens.

Marking to Market and Initial Margins.   Small initial margins in a futures market are possible since the trader is required to replenish his or her margin account on a daily basis following adverse price movements. Relying on the marking-to-market convention, the clearinghouse can contract with diverse counterparties around the world because each margin account of these counterparties is replenished on a daily basis as necessary, or closed out in the event of a failed margin call.

TABLE 11.1   Top Futures Contracts Worldwide, 1999

Rank	Contract	Size	Exchange	Volume (millions)
1	Euro-BUND	€100,000	EUREX	121.3
2	Eurodollar	$1,000,000	CME	93.4
3	U.S. T-Bond	$100,000	CBOT	90.0
4	Euro-BOBL	€100,000	EUREX	45.5
5	Crude oil	Barrels 1,000	NYMEX	37.8
6	3-mo Euribor	€1,000,000	LIFFE	35.7
7	10-yr T-note	$100,000	CBOT	34.0
8	3-mo sterling	£500,000	LIFFE	27.2
9	S&P 500	$250 × Index	CME	27.0
10	German BUND*	DM 250,000	LIFFE	22.8
11	Interest rate	R$50,000	BM & F	22.2
12	Aluminum	Tons 25	LME	22.2
13	French CAC 40	€ × Index	MONEP	21.0
14	Natural gas	10,000MM BTU	NYMEX	19.2
15	Euro-SCHATZ	€100,000	EUREX	17.7
16	KOSPI 200	Won 500,000 × Index	KSE	17.2
17	5-yr T-note	$100,000	CBOT	17.0
18	Copper	Tons 25	LME	16.8
19	Gold	Kg 1	TOCOM	16.0
20	Corn	Bushels 5,000	CBOT	15.7
21	3-mo Euro-¥	¥100,000,000	TIFFE	14.6
22	Platinum	Grams 500	TOCOM	13.3
23	German DAX	€25 × Index	EUREX	12.9
24	Soybeans	Bushels 5,000	CBOT	12.5
25	Brent crude oil	Barrels 1,000	IPE	12.2

*Contract discontinued during 1999.

Notes: Currency symbols: R$—Brazilian reals.
Futures exchanges: BM&F—Bolsa de Mercadorias & Futuros (Brazil); CBOT—Chicago Board of Trade; CME—Chicago Mercantile Exchange; EUREX—exchange named for merger of former German DTB and Swiss SOFEX exchanges; IPE—International Petroleum Exchange (London); KSE—Korea Stock Exchange; LIFFE—London International Financial Futures and Options Exchange; LME—London Metal Exchange; MONEP—Monetary Exchange of Paris; NYMEX—New York Mercantile Exchange; TOCOM—Tokyo Commodity Exchange; TIFFE—Tokyo International Financial Futures Exchange.

Source: *Futures Industry Institute Factbook,* at <www.fiiweb.org/factbook> and various futures exchange websites.

Description of Futures Contracts

The focus in this chapter is on currency and interest rate futures. Futures markets on these financial instruments were developed in the mid-1970s. Since their introduction, the markets have expanded dramatically—in terms of numbers of futures exchanges, numbers of different contracts, and trading volume. In 1999, currency futures contracts were traded on at least 12 different exchanges worldwide in 8 countries and interest rate futures contracts were traded on 29 different exchanges worldwide in 24 countries.[9] Still more trading takes place in equity futures and stock index futures in addition to futures on agricultural commodities, metals, energy products, and others.

---

[9]See the *Futures and Options Factbook* prepared by the Futures Industry Institute for a listing of futures and options contracts and markets. The *Factbook* is available at <www.fiiweb.org/factbook>.

TABLE 11.2   **Daily Volume of Trading in Interest Rate Derivatives**
April 1998 (US$ Billions)

	OTC/Interbank	*Exchange-Listed*
Forward rate agreements	$ 96.5	NA
Futures	NA	$1,192.5
Options	45.9	193.1
Swaps	201.1	NA
Other derivatives	0.0	NA
Total	$343.6	$1,365.6

Note: OTC data are from Table E-37. Exchange-listed data are from Table 20A and reflect the average of 1998Q1. Survey data are "net-gross" estimates, meaning that transactions between banks in a single country have been netted out, but transactions between banks across countries have *not* been netted out. The data reflect a BIS survey of banks, and results are not directly comparable with volume data from futures and option exchange organizations.

Source: Bank for International Settlements, *Central Bank Survey of Foreign Exchange and Derivatives Market Activity, 1998,* May 1999, and *International Banking and Financial Market Developments,* Aug. 1998.

In Table 11.1 we report the top futures contracts in 1999 ranked according to their trading volume. Of the 25 contracts listed, 9 are for metals or commodities, 4 are for stock indexes, and the remaining 12 are interest rate futures. The top contract in terms of volume is the Euro-BUND futures contract traded on the EUREX, the European exchange that reflects the merger between the former German DTB and Swiss SOFEX exchanges. The Euro-BUND contract is an interest rate futures contract related to long-term German government interest rates. Assuming 260 trading days in 1999, the Euro-BUND futures traded an average of €46.6 billion per day. The Eurodollar futures contract traded on the CME was the second most actively traded futures contract in 1999, with 93.4 million contracts over the year. However, because each Eurodollar future represents a notional value of $1 million, the average daily volume for this contract is over $359 billion per day, or roughly seven times greater than the Euro-BUND.[10] By comparison, the US$/Brazilian real futures was the currency futures contract with the highest volume in 1999 trading 11.4 million contracts over the year, or roughly $2.2 billion per day in notional value.

We reported in Chapter 3 that the vast majority of foreign exchange transactions are conducted in the interbank market, and not using exchange-listed contracts. The situation is reversed for interest rate futures products. The 1998 Bank for International Settlements survey reports that the trading volume of exchange-listed interest rate futures contracts is nearly $1.2 trillion per day, more than 10 times as great as the interest rate forward contracts that are traded over the counter among banks.[11] Likewise, trading in interest rate options is far more active on organized exchanges than in the over-the-counter market. As Table 11.2 shows, the estimated daily volume of trading in interest rate derivatives is of the same order of magnitude as the volume of foreign exchange trading summarized in Table 3.1.

---

[10]The average US$/€ exchange rate during 1999 was about $1.06/€.

[11]We define an interest rate forward contract, also called a forward rate agreement, later in this chapter.

TABLE 11.3   Specifications for Selected Currency Futures Contracts

Market[a]	Currency[b]	Contract Size	Minimum Price Change	Value of One Tick
CME	€	€ 125,000	$ 0.0001	US$ 12.50
	¥	¥ 12,500,000	$ 0.000001	US$ 12.50
	C$	C$ 100,000	$ 0.0001	US$ 10.00
	£	£ 62,500	$ 0.0002	US$ 12.50
NYBOT	US$ Index[c]	$1,000 × index	0.01 index points	US$ 10.00
	€/£ cross	€ 100,000	€ 0.0001	£ 10.00
	€/¥ cross	€ 100,000	€ 0.01	¥ 1,000
TIFFE	US$	US$50,000	¥0.05	¥2,500

[a]CME—Chicago Mercantile Exchange; NYBOT—New York Board of Trade; TIFFE—Tokyo International Financial Futures Exchange.

[b]Currency futures generally have maturity months of March, June, September, and December. The expiration date for U.S.-traded futures is the second business day preceding the third Wednesday of the contract month (except for Canadian dollars, which expire on the business day immediately preceding the third Wednesday of the contract month). The settlement date for U.S.-traded futures is the third Wednesday of the contract month.

[c]The US$ index is a trade-weighted average of the US$ against 10 major currencies, as computed by the Federal Reserve.

Source: *Futures Industry Institute Factbook* at <www.fiiweb.org/factbook>.

Contract Specifications

We now outline some of the important specifications for a small sample of currency and interest rate futures contracts.[12]

Currency Futures.   Of the top six most actively traded currency futures contracts in the world, five are on the CME. The most active currency futures contract in 1998 was the US$ futures traded on the Bolsa in São Paulo, Brazil. The Japanese yen contract on the CME was the second most active currency futures, trading 5.9 million contracts in 1998. The contract size for several CME currency futures is reported in Table 11.3. These are futures contracts *on* foreign currency, so the contract is a set number of foreign currency units. The minimum price change allowed for each contract (also known as **one tick**) is listed along with the value of one tick, which is simply the contract size multiplied by the minimum price change.

In Table 11.4 we show a table of currency futures prices as reported in *The Wall Street Journal*. The newspaper reports the opening, high, low, and settlement prices for each contract. The settlement price is the basis on which mark-to-market margin requirements are computed and usually represents the closing price for the day. Below each panel of numbers, the newspaper reports the daily trading volume.

In the far right column is a notation for the **open interest** in each contract. Open interest represents the number of futures contracts outstanding for which delivery is obligated. When a contract begins initial trading, there are zero contracts outstanding and no open interest. The first transaction obligates a seller to deliver to a buyer and creates *one unit* of open interest. Before expiration, a seller who closes his or her position by

---

[12]Very detailed and up-to-date information about currency and interest rate futures contract specifications is readily available through the exchanges' websites; for example, <www.cme.com>, <www.cbot.com>, <www.liffe.com>, and <www.matif.com>.

TABLE 11.4   Recent Prices of Selected Currency Futures: June 20, 2000

```
                        CURRENCY
                                         Lifetime      Open
           Open  High   Low Settle Change High  Low Interest
   JAPAN YEN (CME)-12.5 million yen; $ per yen (.00)
Sept .9612 .9663 .9592 .9642 + .0026 1.0272 .9300 34,902
Dec  .9794 .9820 .9786 .9805 + .0026 1.0434 .9225    623
   Est vol 9,444; vol Mon 19,964; open int 75,827, −5,263.
   DEUTSCHEMARK (CME)-125,000 marks; $ per mark
Sept .4935 .5200 .4915 .4925 − .0007 .5250 .4596    631
   Est vol 4; vol Mon 76; open int 1,181, −9.
   CANADIAN DOLLAR (CME)-100,000 dlrs.; $ per Can $
June .6818 .6818 .6797 .6798 − .0027 .7005 .6547 17,871
Sept .6835 .6838 .6809 .6812 − .0028 .7017 .6623 51,126
Dec  .6850 .6850 .6825 .6827 − .0029 .7025 .6640  4,886
Mr01 .6849 .6849 .6849 .6843 − .0029 .7040 .6672    586
June  ....  ....  .... .6859 − .0029 .6990 .6695    165
   Est vol 4,985; vol Mon 11,091; open int 74,648, +1,054.
   BRITISH POUND (CME)-62,500 pds.; $ per pound
Sept 1.5148 1.5228 1.5072 1.5214 + .0056 1.6780 1.4700 25,896
Dec  1.5252 1.5280 1.5120 1.5246 + .0056 1.6500 1.4730    255
   Est vol 6,695; vol Mon 4,382; open int 52,425, −133.
   SWISS FRANC (CME)-125,000 francs; $ per franc
Sept .6195 .6224 .6171 .6212 + .0015 .7063 .5783 34,655
   Est vol 6,140; vol Mon 10,681; open int 54,430, +520.
   AUSTRALIAN DOLLAR (CME)-100,000 dlrs.; $ per A.$
Sept .6036 .6070 .6014 .6053 + .0021 .6699 .5672 14,963
Dec  .6060 .6060 .6050 .6063 + .0021 .6704 .5740    171
Mr01  ....  ....  .... .6073 + .0021 .6390 .5700    377
   Est vol 503; vol Mon 3,343; open int 23,987, −1,762.
   MEXICAN PESO (CME)-500,000 new Mex. peso, $ per MP
Sept .09860 .09890 .09820 .09843 − 00025 .10470 .08500 10,567
Dec  .09580 .09600 .09575 .09583 − 00025 .10290 .09200  1,359
Mr01   ....   ....   .... .09340 − 00025 .10005 .09120    496
   Est vol 2,697; vol Mon 2,176; open int 23,832, +23.
   EURO FX (CME)-Euro 125,000; $ per Euro
Sept .9642 .9672 .9583 .9633 − .0013 1.1136 .8991 52,683
Dec  .9648 .9690 .9648 .9686 − .0013 1.0572 .9046    572
   Est vol 9,156; vol Mon 14,597; open int 73,739, −2,448.
```

Source: *The Wall Street Journal,* June 21, 2000.

buying a contract from someone who previously owned a contract acts to reduce open interest by one unit. At maturity, open interest is once again zero.

Open interest is a measure of how much risk taking and positioning there is in a contract. Note in Table 11.4 how large open interest is in the near-term currency futures contracts and how this tails off sharply. The daily change in open interest is reported at the bottom of each panel.

Currency futures contracts are of course traded in other markets. NYBOT trades a contract on the US$ Index, which represents a trade-weighted basket of currencies from 10 U.S. trading partners. The US$ Index may be useful for taking a general position against the US$ or against a portfolio of foreign currencies. NYBOT and several other exchanges have also introduced **cross-rate futures** such as the €/£ and €/¥ rates.[13] As we noted in Chapter 3, the percentage of currency trading that involves the US$ has declined in recent years, so the demand for hedges in these non-US$ currencies may be growing.

Finally, we should remember that *outside the United States, the US$ is a foreign currency* upon which traders may wish to hedge or speculate. Thus, many countries

---

[13]All European cross-rate contracts (DM/FFr, DM/Lira, and others) among the euro-zone currencies disappeared on January 1, 1999, with the introduction of the euro as the single currency for all EMU countries.

TABLE 11.5   Specifications for Selected Interest Rate Futures Contracts

Market[a]	Underlying Asset: Interest Rate Futures on	Contract Size	Minimum Price Change	Value of One Point
CME	3-month Euro $	$1,000,000	$0.05	$25.00
LIFFE	3-month Euro SFr	SFr 1,000,000	SFr 0.01	SFr 25.00
TIFFE	3-month Euro ¥	¥100,000,000	¥0.05	¥2,500
LIFFE	3-month London £	£500,000	£0.01	£12.50
LIFFE	3-month EURIBOR	€ 1,000,000	€ 0.005	€ 25.00
SFE	90-day bank bills	A$1,000,000	A$0.01	A$25.00
CBOT	U.S. Treasury bonds	$100,000	$1/32	$31.25
LIFFE	U.K. government bond (long gilt)	£50,000	£1/0.01	£10.00
EUREX	Euro-BUND (8½–10½-yr German bonds)	€ 100,000	€ 0.01	€ 10.00
EUREX	Euro-BOBL (3½–5-yr German bonds)	€ 100,000	€ 0.01	€ 10.00

[a]CME—Chicago Mercantile Exchange; LIFFE—London International Financial Futures Exchange; SFE—Sydney Futures Exchange; CBOT—Chicago Board of Trade.

Source: *Futures Industry Institute Factbook,* and various exchange publications.

have a US$ futures contract that is priced in terms of their own domestic currency. For example, a US$ contract traded in ¥ (in Tokyo) is reported in Table 11.3.

Interest Rate Futures.   Trading in interest rate futures is spread across several major futures in exchanges in Chicago, London, Frankfurt, Tokyo, and elsewhere. A few specifications for a small group of interest rate futures is presented in Table 11.5. In the top half of the table, we list several short-term interest rate futures beginning with Eurocurrency interest rates for the US$, SFr, and ¥, followed by several domestic short-term interest rates including London sterling, euro-zone euros, and Sydney Australian dollars.[14] For these futures contracts, the underlying asset is the three-month interbank offered rate for the respective interest rates, with the exception of the Aussie dollar contract, where the underlying asset is a 90-day interest rate on bank-accepted bills of exchange. Whether the underlying instrument is a deposit rate or borrowing rate, these interest rate futures can be used to hedge both risky borrowing and investment situations.

As shown in Table 11.5, contract sizes vary. In each case, however, the contract size represents the notional amount of principal on which to compute interest payments or receipts. And in many cases, the minimum price change is one basis point, though the very actively traded contracts such as the Euro-$, EURIBOR, and Euro-¥ have instituted a minimum price change of half a basis point. The value of one point in the futures price equals the contract size multiplied by one basis point, which is then divided by four to reflect the three-month tenure of the underlying instrument.

In Table 11.6 we show a table of interest rate futures prices as reported in *The Wall Street Journal.* As with currency futures, the newspaper reports the opening, high, low, and settlement prices for each contract. For the Eurodollar futures contract, the table

---

[14]Recall our discussion in Chapter 9, Box 9.1. EURIBOR is an onshore rate based on a survey of banks located in the euro zone. LIFFE also trades a Euro LIBOR contract where the underlying interest rate is a three-month Euro sampled from banks located offshore, mainly in London.

TABLE 11.6 Recent Prices of Selected Interest Rate Futures: June 20, 2000

INTEREST RATE

TREASURY BONDS (CBT)-$100,000; pts. 32nds of 100%

	Open	High	Low	Settle	Change	Lifetime High	Lifetime Low	Open Interest
June	97-16	98-05	97-09	97-12	– 5	99-28	88-22	11,277
Sept	97-15	98-04	97-07	97-10	– 5	99-24	88-19	376,451
Dec	97-17	98-01	97-09	97-09	– 5	99-09	88-31	3,834
Mr01	....	....	....	97-09	– 4	98-06	88-06	313

Est vol 200,000; vol Mon 96,488; open int 391,886, –2,855.

TREASURY BONDS (MCE)-$50,000; pts. 32nds of 100%

	Open	High	Low	Settle	Change	Lifetime High	Lifetime Low	Open Interest
June	97-11	97-31	97-11	97-16	– 3	99-28	88-25	44
Sept	97-12	98-04	97-07	97-12	– 4	99-18	92-23	5,141

Est vol 3,300; vol Mon 2,974; open int 5,187, –201.

TREASURY NOTES (CBT)-$100,000; pts. 32nds of 100%

	Open	High	Low	Settle	Change	Lifetime High	Lifetime Low	Open Interest
June	98-18	98-285	98-17	98-195	– 4.0	99-30	93-11	22,432
Sept	98-165	98-215	98-085	98-12	– 4.0	99-20	94-22	560,294

Est vol 140,000; vol Mon 88,052; open int 582,947, +7,917.

10 YR AGENCY NOTES (CBT)-$100,000; pts. 32nds of 100%

	Open	High	Low	Settle	Change	Lifetime High	Lifetime Low	Open Interest
June	....	....	....	92-17	– 9.0	93-045	88-08	6,048
Sept	92-26	92-26	92-15	92-165	– 8.5	93-045	88-045	34,575

Est vol 7,500; vol Mon 10,528; open int 40,623, +83.

5 YR TREAS NOTES (CBT)-$100,000; pts. 32nds of 100%

	Open	High	Low	Settle	Change	Lifetime High	Lifetime Low	Open Interest
June	98-285	98-31	98-265	98-27	– 3.5	00-005	96-10	10,332
Sept	98-29	98-305	98-24	98-255	– 3.5	99-24	96-14	367,783

Est vol 51,000; vol Mon 40,837; open int 378,115, –10,967.

2 YR TREAS NOTES (CBT)-$200,000; pts. 32nds of 100%

	Open	High	Low	Settle	Change	Lifetime High	Lifetime Low	Open Interest
June	99-07	99-08	99-06	99-06	– 2.5	99-225	98-06	2,359
Sept	99-047	99-047	99-025	99-03	– 2.5	99-07	98-025	50,016

Est vol 2,300; vol Mon 859; open int 52,375, –76.

30-DAY FEDERAL FUNDS (CBT)-$5 million; pts. of 100%

	Open	High	Low	Settle	Change	Lifetime High	Lifetime Low	Open Interest
June	93.485	93.490	93.485	93.485	....	94.130	93.465	8,706
July	93.45	93.45	93.44	93.44	– .01	94.06	93.18	26,576
Aug	93.40	93.41	93.40	93.41	....	93.73	93.12	9,482
Sept	93.29	93.30	93.29	93.29	– .01	93.64	92.98	7,115
Oct	93.24	93.24	93.22	93.23	– .02	93.52	92.93	289

Est vol 3,100; vol Mon 3,703; open int 52,330, +982.

MUNI BOND INDEX (CBT)-$1,000; times Bond Buyer MBI

	Open	High	Low	Settle	Change	Lifetime High	Lifetime Low	Open Interest
June	96-24	96-29	96-16	96-17	+ 4	96-29	89-08	7,675
Sept	95-15	96-06	95-10	95-13	– 2	96-06	90-03	18,102

Est vol 2,400; vol Mon 1,710; open int 26,177, +31.
Index: Close 96-15; Yield 5.99.

TREASURY BILLS (CME)-$1 mil.; pts. of 100%

	Open	High	Low	Settle	Chg	Discount Settle	Discount Chg	Open Interest
Sept	93.93	93.99	93.93	93.94	– .02	6.06	+ .02	532

Est vol 38; vol Mon 7; open int 787, –2.

LIBOR-1 MO. (CME)-$3,000,000; points of 100%

	Open	High	Low	Settle	Chg	Settle	Chg	Open Interest
July	93.33	93.33	93.32	93.32	– .01	6.68	+ .01	20,222
Aug	93.23	93.24	93.22	93.22	– .02	6.78	+ .02	9,714
Sept	93.17	93.17	93.17	93.17	– .01	6.83	+ .01	2,342
Oct	....	....	....	93.12	– .02	6.88	+ .02	1,417
Nov	....	....	....	93.04	– .03	6.96	+ .03	855
Dec	....	....	....	92.80	– .04	7.20	+ .04	160

Est vol 2,923; vol Mon 4,151; open int 42,057, +1,799.

EURODOLLAR (CME)-$1 million; pts of 100%

	Open	High	Low	Settle	Chg	Yield Settle	Yield Chg	Open Interest
July	93.17	93.17	93.16	93.16	– .01	6.84	+ .01	41,818
Aug	93.11	93.11	93.10	93.10	– .01	6.90	+ .01	10,368
Sept	93.07	93.07	93.04	93.05	– .02	6.95	+ .02	625,571
Oct	92.92	92.92	92.90	92.90	– .02	7.10	+ .02	1,378
Dec	92.88	92.88	92.85	92.86	– .04	7.14	+ .04	506,608
Mr01	92.87	92.89	92.85	92.86	– .05	7.14	+ .05	369,350
June	92.86	92.88	92.83	92.84	– .05	7.16	+ .05	247,216
Sept	92.87	92.88	92.84	92.85	– .05	7.15	+ .05	215,972
Dec	92.83	92.86	92.81	92.82	– .05	7.18	+ .05	156,626
Mr02	92.89	92.92	92.87	92.88	– .04	7.12	+ .04	133,746
June	92.89	92.92	92.88	92.89	– .04	7.11	+ .04	93,409
Sept	92.89	92.93	92.87	92.89	– .04	7.11	+ .04	106,461
Dec	92.85	92.89	92.84	92.85	– .04	7.15	+ .04	75,648
Mr03	92.90	92.94	92.90	92.91	– .04	7.09	+ .04	78,748
June	92.90	92.93	92.88	92.90	– .05	7.10	+ .05	53,407
Sept	92.89	92.92	92.87	92.88	– .05	7.12	+ .05	48,142
Dec	92.83	92.85	92.81	92.82	– .05	7.18	+ .05	37,529
Mr04	92.87	92.90	92.85	92.86	– .06	7.14	+ .06	36,134
June	92.85	92.87	92.83	92.83	– .06	7.17	+ .06	33,191
Sept	92.83	92.85	92.80	92.81	– .06	7.19	+ .06	28,792
Dec	92.75	92.76	92.72	92.73	– .06	7.27	+ .06	27,104
Mr05	92.76	92.79	92.75	92.76	– .06	7.24	+ .06	20,238
June	92.73	92.76	92.72	92.73	– .06	7.27	+ .06	13,135
Sept	....	....	....	92.70	– .06	7.30	+ .06	10,738
Dec	....	....	....	92.63	– .05	7.37	+ .05	7,774
Mr06	....	....	....	92.67	– .05	7.33	+ .05	8,086
June	92.66	92.66	92.63	92.64	– .05	7.36	+ .05	7,352
Sept	....	....	....	92.61	– .05	7.39	+ .05	6,672
Dec	....	....	....	92.54	– .05	7.46	+ .05	6,660
Mr07	....	....	....	92.58	– .05	7.42	+ .05	5,137
June	....	....	....	92.55	– .04	7.45	+ .04	3,813
Sept	....	....	....	92.53	– .04	7.47	+ .04	3,363
Dec	....	....	....	92.46	– .04	7.54	+ .04	4,816
Mr08	....	....	....	92.49	– .04	7.51	+ .04	3,957
June	....	....	....	92.47	– .03	7.53	+ .03	4,169
Sept	92.48	92.49	92.44	92.44	– .03	7.56	+ .03	3,952
Dec	....	....	....	92.38	– .03	7.62	+ .03	2,976
Mr09	....	....	....	92.41	– .03	7.59	+ .03	2,315
June	92.42	92.42	92.37	92.38	– .02	7.62	+ .02	2,364
Sept	....	....	....	92.36	– .02	7.64	+ .02	2,167
Dec	....	....	....	92.29	– .02	7.71	+ .02	1,623
Mr10	92.32	92.36	92.32	92.32	– .02	7.68	+ .02	1,090

Est vol 318,792; vol Mon 282,778; open int 3,384,489, –49,689.

SHORT STERLING (LIFFE)-£500,000; pts of 100%

	Open	High	Low	Settle	Change	Lifetime High	Lifetime Low	Open Interest
June	93.80	93.81	93.79	93.80	– .01	95.17	92.47	160,364
July	93.75	93.75	93.75	93.75	– .01	93.77	93.55	1,569
Aug	....	....	....	93.72	– .01	93.63	93.61	300
Sept	93.69	93.70	93.67	93.68	– .02	95.13	92.80	195,731
Dec	93.59	93.59	93.55	93.56	– .03	98.80	92.61	184,367
Mr01	93.51	93.51	93.47	93.49	– .03	95.08	92.55	103,114
June	93.46	93.46	93.41	93.43	– .03	95.08	92.49	66,923
Sept	93.42	93.43	93.38	93.40	– .03	95.09	92.41	62,694
Dec	93.39	93.41	93.36	93.38	– .04	95.07	92.31	44,948
Mr02	93.42	93.42	93.38	93.39	– .03	95.13	92.34	36,198
June	93.37	93.37	93.37	93.37	– .04	95.10	92.39	10,910
Sept	93.39	93.39	93.39	93.38	– .03	95.11	92.38	11,680
Dec	....	....	....	93.39	– .03	95.11	92.45	6,044
Mr03	93.43	93.43	93.43	93.44	– .03	94.69	92.49	4,662
June	....	....	....	93.50	– .03	93.88	92.77	1,020
Sept	93.53	93.54	93.53	93.54	– .03	93.59	92.90	630
Dec	....	....	....	93.61	– .03	93.67	92.92	1,068
Mr04	....	....	....	93.68	– .03	93.70	93.01	1,030
June	....	....	....	93.69	– .03	93.72	93.04	326

Est vol 75,328; vol Mon 59,715; open int 893,583, –7,807.

LONG GILT (LIFFE) (Decimal)-£50,000; pts of 100%

	Open	High	Low	Settle	Change	Lifetime High	Lifetime Low	Open Interest
June	114.53	114.68	114.40	114.44	– .38	115.41	109.97	7,988
Sept	114.46	114.46	114.00	114.13	– .38	115.09	110.82	65,209

Est vol 19,772; vol Mon 9,598; open int 73,197, –1,618.

3 MONTH EURIBOR (LIFFE) Euro 1,000,000; pts of 100%

	Open	High	Low	Settle	Change	Lifetime High	Lifetime Low	Open Interest
July	95.44	95.46	95.43	95.44	....	95.49	95.32	10,021
Sept	95.26	95.28	95.23	95.26	– .01	97.16	95.02	343,912
Dec	94.97	94.98	94.92	94.95	– .04	97.00	93.36	230,505
Mr01	94.93	94.94	94.88	94.90	– .05	96.96	94.62	162,573
June	94.86	94.86	94.80	94.83	– .04	96.85	94.52	109,117
Sept	94.80	94.81	94.75	94.77	– .04	96.75	94.44	98,354
Dec	94.71	94.71	94.65	94.67	– .04	96.58	92.57	58,583
Mr02	94.74	94.74	94.69	94.70	– .04	96.48	94.33	47,970
June	94.70	94.70	94.65	94.67	– .04	96.37	94.29	27,903
Sept	94.65	94.67	94.62	94.63	– .04	96.25	94.24	18,623
Dec	94.56	94.57	94.53	94.55	– .04	96.06	94.06	13,619
Mr03	94.55	94.58	94.55	94.56	– .04	96.01	94.05	8,751
June	94.52	94.54	94.52	94.53	– .04	95.45	93.99	4,633
Sept	94.48	94.51	94.48	94.49	– .04	95.15	93.91	4,118
Dec	....	....	....	94.40	– .04	95.07	93.80	2,304
Mr04	94.43	94.43	94.43	94.41	– .04	94.50	93.83	1,977
June	....	....	....	94.37	– .04	94.43	93.79	541
Sept	....	....	....	94.31	– .04	94.40	93.73	638

Est vol 257,550; vol Mon 171,326; open int 1,144,177, +4,502.

3-MONTH EUROSWISS (LIFFE)
SFr 1,000,000; pts of 100%

	Open	High	Low	Settle	Change	Lifetime High	Lifetime Low	Open Interest
Sept	96.26	96.27	96.22	96.25	– .01	98.36	96.05	57,219
Dec	95.87	95.89	95.85	95.87	– .02	98.12	95.72	36,292
Mr01	95.89	95.89	95.87	95.89	– .01	98.04	95.70	16,789
June	95.80	95.83	95.80	95.82	– .02	97.47	95.65	5,324
Sept	95.76	95.76	95.76	95.76	– .03	96.76	95.59	5,357
Dec	95.66	95.66	95.66	95.66	– .03	96.46	95.45	7,710
Mr02	95.71	95.71	95.71	95.71	– .03	96.14	95.50	732

Est vol 9,557; vol Mon 14,121; open int 129,423, +1,711.

CANADIAN BANKERS ACCEPTANCE (ME)-C$1,000,000

	Open	High	Low	Settle	Change	Lifetime High	Lifetime Low	Open Interest
July	94.06	94.07	94.06	94.05	– 0.02	94.07	93.83	1,063
Sept	93.96	93.97	93.93	93.93	– 0.05	95.24	93.48	73,061
Dec	93.84	93.84	93.81	93.81	– 0.05	95.13	93.34	43,204
Mr01	93.79	93.79	93.76	93.76	– 0.05	95.10	93.16	23,789
June	93.76	93.77	93.75	93.75	– 0.04	95.07	93.07	11,640
Sept	93.75	93.75	93.73	93.73	– 0.04	93.87	93.06	6,565
Dec	93.75	93.75	93.73	93.73	– 0.04	94.74	92.97	2,132
Mr02	....	....	....	93.73	– 0.04	94.73	93.25	2,742
June	....	....	....	93.73	– 0.04	93.42	92.95	1,725
Sept	....	....	....	93.73	– 0.04	93.39	93.11	615
Dec	....	....	....	93.71	– 0.04	93.06	93.06	200

Est vol 14,866; vol Mon 11,376; open int 166,811, –5,777.

10 YR. CANADIAN GOVT. BONDS (ME)-C$100,000

	Open	High	Low	Settle	Change	Lifetime High	Lifetime Low	Open Interest
June	....	....	....	100.42	– 0.33	102.00	96.90	7,103
Sept	101.03	101.03	100.77	100.79	– 0.33	101.70	97.85	44,645

Est vol 9,634; vol Mon 1,767; open int 51,748, –34.

EUROYEN (SIMEX)-Yen 100,000,000 pts. of 100%

	Open	High	Low	Settle	Change	Lifetime High	Lifetime Low	Open Interest
Sept	99.69	99.72	99.69	99.70	....	99.80	97.94	76,544
Dec	99.56	99.59	99.56	99.57	....	99.67	97.90	84,286
Mr01	99.47	99.51	99.46	99.48	+ 0.01	99.59	98.08	82,061
June	99.37	99.41	99.36	99.39	+ 0.01	99.47	98.17	65,013
Sept	99.24	99.30	99.24	99.26	+ 0.01	99.33	98.01	60,039
Dec	99.13	99.14	99.13	99.13	+ 0.02	99.18	97.84	21,687
Mr02	....	....	....	99.02	+ 0.02	99.06	98.17	12,441
June	....	....	....	98.91	+ 0.03	98.91	98.11	1,780
Sept	....	....	....	98.75	+ 0.02	98.75	98.35	745
Dec	....	....	....	98.60	+ 0.02	98.61	98.28	335
Mr03	....	....	....	98.49	+ 0.02	98.51	....	200

Est vol 28,411; vol Mon 50,309; open int 405,131, –79,551.

5 YR. GERMAN EURO-GOVT. BOND
(EURO-BOBL) (EUREX)-Euro 100,000; pts. of 100%

	Open	High	Low	Settle	Change	Lifetime High	Lifetime Low	Open Interest
Sept	103.82	103.82	103.67	103.70	– 0.12	141.43	101.74	280,246
Dec	....	....	....	103.50	– 0.17	103.55	102.25	1,030

vol Tue 231,825; open int 281,276, +12,237.

10 YR. GERMAN EURO-GOVT. BOND
(EURO-BUND) (EUREX)-Euro 100,000; pts. of 100%

	Open	High	Low	Settle	Change	Lifetime High	Lifetime Low	Open Interest
Sept	106.10	106.25	105.92	106.12	– 0.01	106.56	101.18	544,382
Dec	105.81	105.81	105.69	105.75	– 0.01	105.86	102.66	6,975
Mr01	....	....	....	105.62	– 0.01	....	....	3,102

vol Tue 558,000; open int 554,459, +15,407.

2 YR. GERMAN EURO-GOVT. BOND
(EURO-SCHATZ) (EUREX)-Euro 100,000; pts. of 100%

	Open	High	Low	Settle	Change	Lifetime High	Lifetime Low	Open Interest
Sept	101.81	101.81	101.71	101.72	– 0.09	102.55	101.03	275,689
Dec	....	....	....	101.50	+ 0.04	101.74	101.50	1,208

vol Tue 174,217; open int 276,897, +13,951.

Source: *The Wall Street Journal,* June 21, 2000.

also shows the *yield* based on the settlement price, which by definition is simply (100 − futures price) in the case of short-term interest rate futures.

This convention establishes an inverse relationship between the futures price and the underlying interest rate. For example, in Table 11.6, the price of the December 2000 Eurodollar futures is 92.36, corresponding to a 7.14 percent per annum interest rate. A higher price such as 93.86 corresponds to a lower interest rate (6.14 percent), while a lower price such as 91.86 corresponds to a higher interest rate (8.14 percent).

Notice also in the case of Eurodollar futures that the family of interest rate futures (each one with a three-month Eurodollar deposit as the underlying asset) extends into the future for 10 years. The structure of these prices has a distinct pattern—from 93.16 (6.84 percent) for the nearest maturity contract (July 2000) to 92.32 (7.68 percent) for the March 2010 contract. Like the term structure of interest rates, two broad forces may underlie the term structure of Eurodollar interest rate futures prices: (1) speculative expectations that short-term Eurodollar interest rates are likely to rise, and (2) risk premiums such that interest rates are somewhat higher than their expected values (and prices are somewhat lower than their expected values). The column for open interest shows that there was a very active market in Eurodollar futures two years ahead and even four or more years ahead. Lower trading volume at more distant horizons may also have an impact on market prices.

The bottom half of Table 11.5 shows several futures contracts for long-term interest rates on U.S. and foreign government securities. The quotation convention differs for long-term interest rate futures, as the minimum price change for U.S. government bonds is ¹⁄₃₂ of a point while the minimum price move for U.K. and German bonds is one basis point. The value of one point is simply the contract size times the minimum price change as a percentage per annum.

Long-term and short-term interest rate futures differ in another more important and complicated respect. With short-term interest rate futures, the underlying financial instrument is uniform and simply defined. With long-term interest rate futures, the underlying financial instrument may not be uniform because dozens of government bonds with different maturities and coupons are traded in the cash marketplace. The exchanges have designed their futures contracts to cope with this complication.

In brief, their solution is to set the interest rate futures price based on the yield of a hypothetical or **notional bond** with a given yield and maturity. For U.S. T-bond futures, the notional yield is 6 percent on a 15-year bond; for the U.K. long gilt (government) bond, the notional yield is 7 percent on a 8.75–13-year bond; and for the German Bund, the notional yield is 6 percent on a 8.5–10-year bond. These notional yields are arbitrary choices, but intended to be representative of yields in each market.[15] Each exchange then computes a **conversion factor** for each government bond that may be delivered to satisfy the obligation of the seller if the seller is asked to deliver the underlying bond. The conversion factor implies that a seller could deliver *fewer* units of a more valuable bond (one with a higher coupon and/or shorter maturity than the notional), but would have to deliver *more* units of a less valuable bond (one with a lower coupon and/or longer maturity than the notional). Since the seller will generally elect to deliver the **cheapest-to-deliver** acceptable bond, the cheapest-to-deliver bond will generally determine the price of the interest rate futures contract.

---

[15]The notional interest rate for the U.S. bond had been 8 percent until March 2000, and the notional interest rate for the U.K. long gilt had been 9 percent until December 1998. These changes were made in recognition of a lower interest rate environment than in earlier years.

FIGURE 11.3   **Payoff Profiles for Currency Forwards**
Long at \$1.10/€ and Short at \$1.08/€

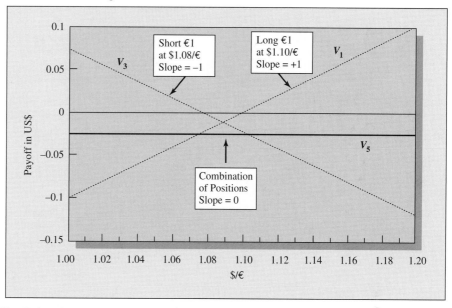

Note: V_1 shows the value of a long forward position in € established at \$1.10/€. V_3 shows the value of a short forward position in € established at \$1.08/€. V_5 shows the value of a combination of both short and long positions. The slope of V_5 is zero, showing that this position is not exposed to exchange rate changes.

Payoff Profiles for Futures and Forward Contracts

To better understand the risks and rewards of using futures and forward contracts, it is useful to trace the **payoff profiles** for these contracts. A payoff profile is a graph of the value of a contract (or the profit and loss on a contract) plotted against the price of the underlying financial instrument.

Currency Contracts.   For the sake of illustration, consider someone with a *long forward* € contract entered into at a price $F_{t,n} = \$1.10/€$. At maturity, the value of the contract is:

$$V_1 = N\,(S_{t+n} - F_{t,n})$$
$$= €1\,(S_{t+n} - \$1.10/€)$$

where N is the notional principal of the contracts in € (in this case $N = 1$) and S_{t+n} is the spot rate on the maturity date of the forward contract. Note that the *units* of V_1 are US\$. Since $F_{t,n}$ is a constant, the value of the forward contract at maturity varies one for one with the future spot rate.

A graph of this relationship is shown in Figure 11.3. Notice that the slope $(\partial V_1/\partial S_{t+n})$ of the value line is one. So, if $S_{t+n} = \$1.12/€$, then $V_1 = \$0.02$; and if $S_{t+n} = \$1.07/€$, then $V_1 = -\$0.03$.

Suppose that we hold a long position for €750,000 instead of only €1. The value of this position is:

FIGURE 11.4   **Payoff Profiles for Currency Forwards**
Long €750,000 and Short €500,000

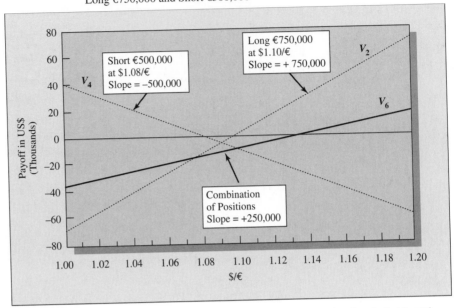

Note: V_2 shows the value of a long forward position in € established at $1.10/€. V_4 shows the value of a short forward position in € established at $1.08/€. V_6 shows the value of a combination of both short and long positions. The slope of V_6 is 250,000, showing that this position is exposed to exchange rate changes.

$$V_2 = €750,000\ (S_{t+n} - F_{t,n})$$

$$= €750,000\ (S_{t+n} - \$1.10/€)$$

A graph of this relationship is shown in Figure 11.4. The graph appears identical to the previous graph, but notice that the slope $(\partial V_2/\partial S_{t+n})$ of the value line is $+750,000$, reflecting the larger long € position.

Now consider a *short forward* € contract entered into at a price of $F_{t,n} = \$1.08/€$. At maturity, the value of this contract is:

$$V_3 = N\ (S_{t+n} - F_{t,n})$$

$$= -€1\ (S_{t+n} - \$1.08/€)$$

where N is the notional principal value of € forward contracts sold or shorted (in this case $N = 1$).

As we see from the graph of this relationship in Figure 11.3, the value at maturity of this short position varies inversely with the future spot rate. So, if $S_{t+n} = \$1.11/€$, $V_3 = -\$0.03$, and if $S_{t+n} = \$1.04/€$, $V_3 = \$0.04$. Again, note that the values of V_3 are expressed in US$. The slope $(\partial V_3/\partial S_{t+n})$ of the value line is -1.

Suppose that we held a short position for €500,000 instead of only €1. The value of this position at maturity is:

$$V_4 = -€500,000\ (S_{t+n} - F_{t,n})$$

$$= -€500,000\ (S_{t+n} - \$1.08/€)$$

A graph of this relationship also is shown in Figure 11.4. The graph of V_4 appears slightly different than V_3, but note that we still observe the linear relationship between the value of the forward position and the underlying spot rate. The slope $(\partial V_4/\partial S_{t+n})$ of the value line is $-500,000$, reflecting the magnitude of this short € position.

Combinations of Currency Contracts.   Now consider the results of combining positions 1 and 3 in the same portfolio. The combination of buying €1 forward at $1.10/€ and selling €1 forward at $1.08/€ results in a value:

$$V_5 = V_1 + V_3 = -\$0.02$$

In Figure 11.3, we can think of the combination of the long € and short € positions as the "vertical summation" of the two payoff profiles, V_1 and V_3.

Note that V_5 is flat or invariant with respect to the future spot rate, $\partial V_5/\partial S_{t+n} = 0$. Any single position, or portfolio of positions, whose value does not vary as a function of the spot exchange rate will be deemed *hedged against exchange risk* or *not exposed to exchange risk*.[16]

Now consider the results of combining positions 2 and 4 into one portfolio. The combination of buying €750,000 forward at $1.10/€ and selling €500,000 forward at $1.08/€ results in a value:

$$V_6 = V_2 + V_4$$
$$= €750,000\,(S_{t+n} - \$1.10/€) - €500,000\,(S_{t+n} - \$1.08/€)$$
$$= €250,000\,S_{t+n} - \$285,000$$

Notice that the exposure of this portfolio is long €250,000 as measured by the slope $(\partial V_6/\partial S_{t+n})$ of the value line. In Figure 11.4, we see that the combination $V_6 = V_2 + V_4$ is exposed to foreign exchange risk since the value of V_6 varies along with the exchange rate.

Interest Rate Contracts.   The mechanics and payoff profiles for interest rate futures and forward contracts are in many ways similar to those for currency futures and forward contracts. In a generic interest rate futures contract, the value of the contract at maturity is proportional to the interest differential between the futures price and the interest rate at maturity:

$$V = N\,(S_{i,t+n} - F_{i,t,n})$$

where N is the factor of proportionality, representing the notional principal value of long (or short) futures contracts, $F_{i,t,n}$ is the futures rate on interest rate i at time t that matures n periods later, and $S_{i,t+n}$ is the (spot) interest rate on the maturity date of the futures contracts. In the following analysis, we consider short-term interest rates where the futures price (F) and the spot price (S) are defined as 100 minus the appropriate interest rate.

Consider someone with a long position in the March 2010 Eurodollar futures contract, entered into at a price $F_{i,t,n} = 92.32$, which is the settlement price reported for June 20, 2000, in Table 11.6. At maturity, the value of this contract is:

---

[16]Strictly speaking, the value of this position is not exposed to exchange risk at horizon $t + n$ since this is the maturity of the spot and forward contracts. There could be exposure at other horizons. See the formal definition of exposure in Chapter 16.

FIGURE 11.5   **Payoff Profiles of Interest Rate Future**
Long at 92.32 and Short at 92.32

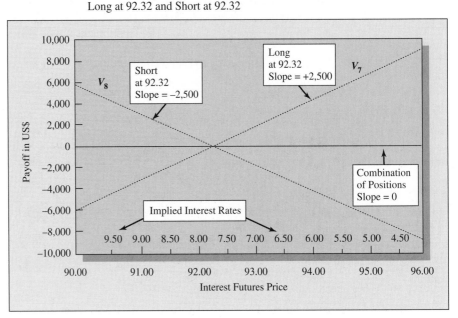

Note: V_7 shows the value of a long Eurodollar interest rate futures established at 92.32. The slope of line V_7 is $2,500 per 100 basis points. V_8 shows the value of a short Eurodollar interest rate futures established at 92.32. The slope of line V_8 is $-\$2,500$ per 100 basis points. V_9 shows the value of a combination of both short and long positions. The slope of V_9 is zero, showing that this position is not exposed to interest rate changes.

$$V_7 = N\,(S_{\text{Euro-\$},t+n} - F_{i,t,n}) \times 0.01/4$$

$$= \$1,000,000\,(S_{\text{Euro-\$},t+n} - 92.32) \times 0.01/4$$

$$= \$2,500\,(S_{\text{Euro-\$},t+n} - 92.32)$$

where N is the notional size of one Eurodollar futures contract on the CME, and $S_{\text{Euro-\$},t+n}$ is the spot, three-month Eurodollar rate on the maturity date of the contract.[17] Multiplying by 0.01/4 converts the spot and futures prices into percentage points for a three-month period, so the value of one *basis point* is $25 for this contract. Note that the *units* of V_7 are US$.

A graph of this relationship is shown in Figure 11.5. Notice that the slope $(\partial V_7/\partial S_{\text{Euro-\$},t+n})$ of the value line is $2,500, indicating that each full percentage point is worth $2,500. So, if $S_{\text{Euro-\$},t+n} = 93.32$ (a 6.68 percent interest rate), then $V_7 = \$2,500$; and if $S_{\text{Euro-\$},t+n} = 91.32$ (an 8.68 percent interest rate), then $V_7 = -\$2,500$. In other words, if interest rates fall, futures prices rise and a long position makes a profit. If interest rate rise, then futures prices fall and a long position makes a loss.

Everything we have just said about long positions applies in the opposite way for a short interest rate futures position. The value of a short interest rate futures position in the March 2010 Eurodollar futures contract, entered into at the same settlement price ($F_{i,t,n} = 92.32$ on June 20, 2000) is:

---

[17]On the CME, the final settlement price for the Eurodollar futures contract is the 11:00 A.M. (London time) cash market offered rate (LIBOR) for three-month Eurodollar time deposits as determined by the British Bankers Association (BBA). For more details of the BBA methodology, see <www.bba.org.uk>.

$$V_8 = -N\,(S_{\text{Euro-\$},t+n} - F_{\text{Euro-\$},t,n}) \times 0.01/4$$

$$= \$1,000,000\,(92.32 - S_{\text{Euro-\$},t+n}) \times 0.01/4$$

$$= \$2,500\,(92.32 - S_{\text{Euro-\$},t+n})$$

A graph of this relationship also is shown in Figure 11.5. The slope $(\partial V_8/\partial S_{\text{Euro-\$},t+n})$ of the value line is $-\$2,500$. So, if $S_{\text{Euro-\$},t+n} = 91.32$ (an 8.68 percent interest rate), then $V_8 = \$2,500$; and if $S_{\text{Euro-\$},t+n} = 93.32$ (a 6.68 percent interest rate), then $V_8 = -\$2,500$. In other words, if interest rates rise, futures prices fall and a short position makes a profit. If interest rates fall, futures prices rise and a short position makes a loss.

The combination of these two short and long positions also is shown in Figure 11.5. Not surprisingly, the short and long positions offset each other and produce zero payoff independent of the future interest spot interest rate.

While the examples have expressed the value of the interest rate futures in terms of US\$, it may be more practical to use basis points as a measure of value. Value in a long position (V_L) is proportional to $(S_{i,t+n} - F_{i,t,n})$, since the contract is purchased at $F_{i,t,n}$ and liquidated at $S_{i,t+n}$, while value in a short position (V_S) is proportional to $(F_{i,t,n} - S_{i,t+n})$ since the contract is sold at $F_{i,t,n}$ and bought back at $S_{i,t+n}$. We use this convention in Box 11.2 to illustrate the use of interest rate futures to hedge the risks of future investment and borrowing at uncertain interest rates.

Futures Pricing and Forward Pricing

Our payoff profile graphs show the value of a forward or futures contract *at maturity*. This value is well defined because both forward and futures prices converge to the spot rate at maturity. In other words, a forward currency contract with delivery in two days is identical to a spot currency contract, which by convention also grants delivery in two days.

The more difficult problem to address is the fair price of a forward or futures contract *prior to maturity*. Most economists agree that, in theory, forward and futures prices reflect several factors: expectations of rates in the future, risk premiums reflecting uncertainty about expectations, pricing errors as a result of a failure to form rational expectations about the future, and pricing errors that result from unexpected events. As we discussed in the chapter on market efficiency, it is important to understand the relationship between forward rates and future spot rates in order to gauge whether forward rates are a useful guide to future spot rates and whether risk taking in forward markets is rewarded, on average.

Forward Pricing and the Cost-of-Carry Model

Forward Currency Rates.   The most common method for determining the price of a forward contract is the so-called **cost-of-carry model,** which relates the forward price of the underlying asset or commodity to its spot (or current) price, plus the cost of storage. In foreign exchange, the physical costs of storage are essentially zero. What matters is the financial cost of interest forgone on the currency we borrow, offset by the interest earned on the currency we hold in storage. As we established in Chapters 3 and 5, interest rate parity predicts that the forward exchange rate (in US\$/FC) at time t for delivery n periods from now will be set so that:

$$F_{t,n} = S_t\,\frac{(1 + i_{\$,t})}{(1 + i_{FC,t})}$$

Box 11.2

Hedging the Interest Rate Risk in Planned Investment and Planned Borrowing

A treasurer who plans to invest excess cash balances at a future date $(t + n)$ faces risk, because the interest rate (i_{t+n}) on this planned investment is uncertain. The treasurer's interest earnings are $N(100 - S_{i,t+n})$ where N is the investment amount and $S_{i,t+n}$ is 100 minus the appropriate short-term interest rate. In Figure A, the line marked with the symbol □ shows the uncertain interest earnings assuming $N = 1$. A long interest rate futures position results in profits equal to $N(S_{i,t+n} - F_{i,t,n})$. The value of the long interest rate futures is also shown in Figure A marked with the symbol ■ for a futures position taken at 92.5 and $N = 1$.

The combined value (V_{10}) of these two positions is:

$$V_{10} = \text{Interest earnings} + \text{Gain/loss on Long futures}$$
$$= (100 - S_{i,t+n}) + (S_{i,t+n} - F_{i,t,n})$$
$$= 100 - F_{i,t,n}$$

Thus, a long futures position is a complete hedge for a planned investment. In the example, a futures price of 92.50 leads to a stable 7.50 percent return on a planned investment, labeled V_{10} in Figure A.

FIGURE A   **Hedging the Interest Rate Risk of a Planned Investment Using a Long Interest Rate Futures Contract at 92.5**

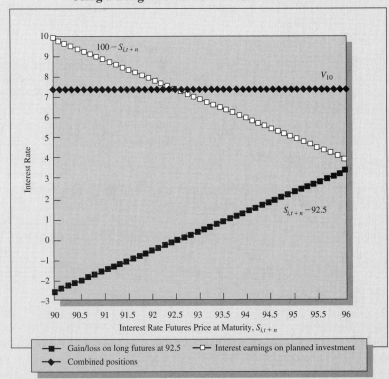

Note: The combination of a long interest rate futures at 92.5 and a planned investment leads to an investment whose value does not depend on the future spot interest rate.

The analysis is much the same for a treasurer who plans to borrow at a future date. The interest cost is uncertain, but it will be equal to $N(100 - S_{i,t+n})$ where N is the borrowing amount and $S_{i,t+n}$ is 100 minus the appropriate short-term interest rate. In Figure B, the line marked with the symbol □ shows the uncertain interest cost assuming $N = 1$. A short interest rate futures position results in profits equal to $N(F_{i,t,n} - S_{i,t+n})$. The value of the short interest rate futures is also shown in Figure B marked with the symbol ■ for a futures position taken at 94.5 and $N = 1$. The combined value (V_{11}) of these two positions is:

$$V_{11} = \text{Borrowing costs} - \text{Gain/Loss on short futures}$$

$$= (100 - S_{i,t+n}) - (F_{i,t,n} - S_{i,t+n}) = 100 - F_{i,t,n}$$

Thus, a short futures position is a complete hedge for a planned borrowing. In the example, a futures price of 94.50 leads to a stable 5.50 percent return on a planned borrowing, labeled V_{11} in Figure B.

In these two examples, we implicitly assume that the treasurer selects an appropriate interest rate futures contract. Thus, if the planned investment is in three-month Treasury bills, the investor uses the Treasury bill futures contract. If the planned borrowing is at the Eurodollar interest rate, the treasurer uses the Eurodollar interest rate futures contract.

FIGURE B   **Hedging the Interest Rate Risk of a Planned Borrowing Using a Short Interest Rate Futures Contract at 94.5**

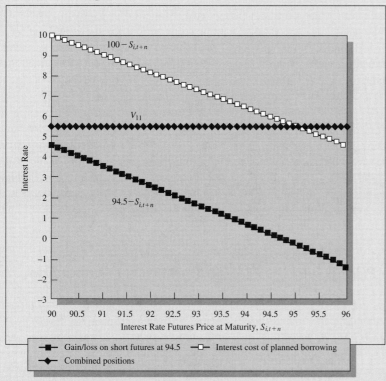

Note: The combination of a short interest rate futures at 94.5 and a planned borrowing leads to a borrowing cost that does not depend on the future spot interest rate.

where S_t is the spot exchange rate (in US$/FC) and the two interest rates have the same maturity as the forward contract.

Interest rate parity helps us to understand how the forward exchange rate is determined. However, it is an incomplete answer because the right-hand-side variables are endogenously determined and in turn are dependent on other economic variables.

Forward Interest Rates.   Similar to a forward exchange rate, a **forward interest rate** is an interest rate quoted today that applies to a financial transaction (either borrowing or lending) at some date in the future. A **forward rate agreement (FRA)** is the more common name for a forward interest rate.

A parity framework can also be developed to establish prices of FRAs. This parity framework is based on the **pure expectations model** of the term structure of interest rates. Consider a simple example. Define $i(0,1)$ as the one-period interest rate for a transaction that begins today ($t = 0$) and define $i(0,2)$ as the two-period interest rate, again for a transaction that begins today. Both $i(0,1)$ and $i(0,2)$ are interest rates for the same currency. Now, consider two investments:

$$V_A = [1 + i(0,2)]^2$$

equal to the ending value of a two-period investment begun today; and

$$V_B = [1 + i(0,1)] \times [1 + i(1,1)]$$

equal to the ending value on a sequence of two one-period investments, where $i(1,1)$ represents the one-period interest rate beginning one period from now (an example of a forward interest rate). Even though $i(1,1)$, is uncertain and cannot be observed directly today, an investor could lock in $i(1,1)$ by investing for two periods at $i(0,2)$ and borrowing for one period at $i(0,1)$. The implied value of the forward interest rate is:

$$i(1,1) = \frac{[1 + i(0,2)]^2}{[1 + i(0,1)] - 1}$$

The above illustration can be generalized. Based on the **term structure of interest rates,** which we will take as the collection of today's interest rates for various maturities: $i(0,1)$, $i(0,2)$, ... $i(0,n)$, it is possible to estimate all the implied one-period interest rates starting at any date in the future. And using the same parity approach, it is also possible to estimate all the implied forward rates for two periods, three periods, and so forth starting at any date in the future.[18]

Futures Pricing and the Marking-to-Market Convention

A Sketch of the Theory.   While both futures and forward contracts allow someone to enter into a binding agreement for an exchange at some later date, we have noted that these contracts have different institutional features. A forward contract, by convention, requires no commitment of capital and no cash flows until the maturity date. Only at maturity is there an exchange of funds for either delivery or cash settlement of the gains (or losses) on the contract.

---

[18]For example, $i(4,6)$, which is the implied two-period interest rate beginning four periods from now, can be estimated as the solution to $[1 + i(0,6)]^6 = [1 + i(0,4)]^4 \times [1 + i(4,6)]^2$.

A futures contract traded on an organized exchange requires an initial margin requirement from the buyer (or seller) plus a commitment to supply additional margin if the contract falls in value (or accumulate additional margin if the contract rises in value). If speculators expected the futures contract to accumulate cash over its life, then futures prices would *exceed* forward prices. Speculators would rather get their winnings sooner than later. But if speculators expected the futures contract to require margin calls over its life, then futures prices would be *lower* than forward prices. Since theory allows for both possibilities, we cannot draw a conclusion.

Two additional factors affect the appeal of futures versus forwards. Since it is not known a priori whether the futures contract will make or lose value, we can conclude that the marking-to-market feature of futures contracts imposes a cash-flow risk that is not present with forward contracts. As a theoretical matter, this risk should *decrease* the attractiveness of futures relative to forwards. On the other hand, futures contracts are traded on exchanges that enhance their liquidity relative to forward contracts. Since investors and speculators place a positive value on liquidity, this factor may *increase* the attractiveness of futures relative to forwards.

Overall, then, the theoretical relationship between futures and forward prices is ambiguous.[19]

The Empirical Evidence.   Several authors have investigated whether there is any pricing differential between futures and forward contracts on the same underlying financial asset. An early study by Bradford Cornell and Mark Reinganum (1981) examined the difference between futures and forward prices for foreign exchange. Their results show that the average difference between futures and forward prices is not significantly different from zero. A more recent study by Carolyn Chang and Jack Chang (1990) updates these results and aligns the delivery dates more carefully for futures and forward contracts. The empirical results are not affected. The authors conclude that futures and forward prices for foreign exchange are not statistically different from each other.

For our purposes, then, we will regard the pricing of futures and forward contracts as similar and we will consider that the research findings on currencies are applicable in other markets. Nevertheless, it is important to remember that futures and forwards have different institutional features that may attract different groups of market participants.

The Term Structure of Forward Rates

The discussion of forward prices should make it clear that the **term structure of forward rates**—that is, the set of today's forward prices for maturities 1, 2, . . . *N* periods into the future—is closely related to the term structure of interest rates.

The Term Structure of Forward Currency Rates.   In the case of foreign currencies, we have used the interest parity relationship to show the link between forward rates for maturity *n* periods and a pair of interest rates for the same maturity:

$$F(0,n) = S \frac{[1 + i_{\$}[(0,n)]}{[1 + i_{FC}(0,n)]} \tag{11.1}$$

---

[19]If forward prices and interest rates are uncorrelated, futures and forward prices are identical. See Cox, Ingersoll, and Ross (1981). Nonzero correlation and institutional differences may cause some agents to prefer forwards over futures, as we discuss later.

FIGURE 11.6   Term Structure of US$ and FC Interest Rates
Three Scenarios: Rising, Flat, Falling

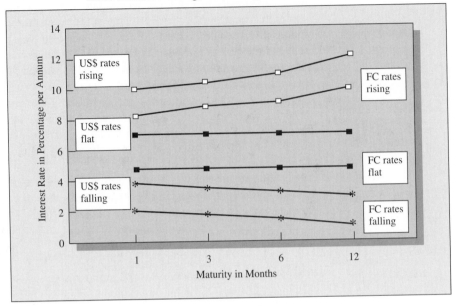

where $F(0,n)$ is the forward rate at time 0 for maturity n periods, S is the spot rate in $/FC, and $i_\$(0,n)$ and $i_{FC}(0,n)$ are interest rates at time 0 for maturity n periods.[20] Thus, the forward rates for 1, 3, 6, and 12 months would reflect the relative yields on the US$ and FC for 1, 3, 6, and 12 months, respectively.

Equation (11.1) shows that the *relative yields,* not the absolute yields, determine the term structure of forward exchange rates. In Figure 11.6, we show several term structures of interest rates for the US$ and an FC. In the top pair (marked by □), interest rates start at $i_\$ = 10$ percent and $i_{FC} = 8$ percent for the one-month maturity and gradually rise with the term structure. In the middle pair (marked by ■), interest rates start at $i_\$ = 7$ percent and $i_{FC} = 5$ percent for the one-month maturity and remain flat across the term structure. In the final pair (marked by *), interest rates start at $i_\$ = 4$ percent and $i_{FC} = 2$ percent for the one-month maturity and gradually fall with the term structure.

In Figure 11.7 we show the pattern of forward rates implied by these term structures when the spot exchange rate is $0.50/FC. Each scenario results in a similar pattern of forward rates as shown in Figure 11.7 because the interest differential is approximately 2 percent a year at each term to maturity. Therefore, the forward premium is approximately 2 percent a year at each maturity. The rising forward rate reflects the compounding of this differential over longer periods.

The Term Structure of Forward Interest Rates.   In an earlier section, we showed that forward interest rates could be extracted from the term structure of interest rates using the parity principle. Thus, the one-period interest rate beginning in period 1 could be calculated by solving:

---

[20]Strictly speaking, the interest rates should be *zero-coupon interest rates* since the forward contract does not entail any intermediate cash flows.

FIGURE 11.7   Term Structure of $/FC Forward Rates under All Three Scenarios

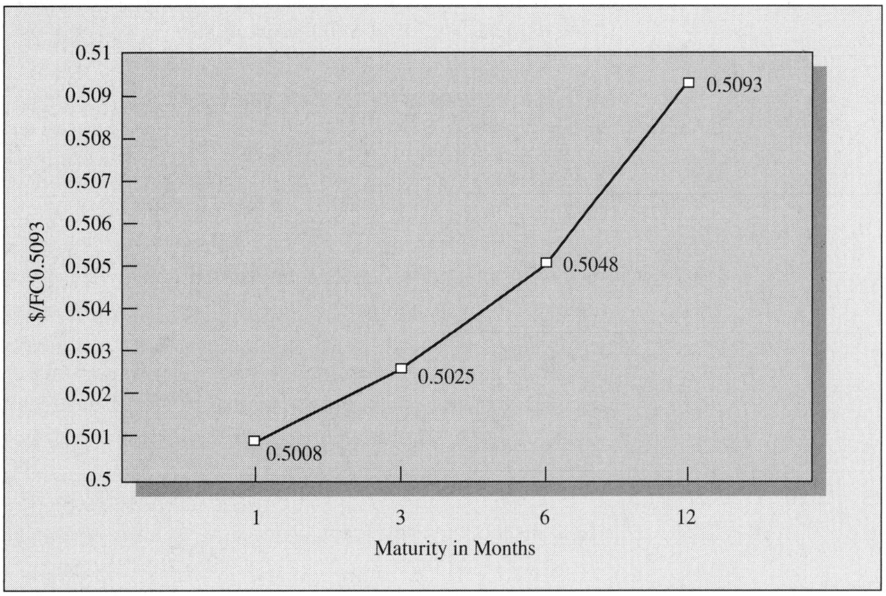

Note: Following from interest rate parity, the forward rate is $S \times (1 + i_\$)/(1 + i_F)$. The term structure of forward rates therefore is closely related to the relative term structure of US$ and foreign currency interest rates.

$$[1 + i(1,1)] = \frac{[1 + i(0,2)]^2}{[1 + i(0,1)]} \tag{11.2}$$

The one-period interest rate beginning in period 2 could be calculated by solving:

$$[1 + i(2,1)] = \frac{[1 + i(0,3)]^3}{[1 + i(0,2)]^2} \tag{11.3}$$

The one-period interest rate beginning in period 19 could be calculated by solving:

$$[1 + i(19,1)] = \frac{[1 + i(0,20)]^{20}}{[1 + i(0,19)]^{19}} \tag{11.4}$$

and so on. In this section, we comment on the pattern of these future short-term rates, which we define as the **term structure of implied forward interest rates.**

It is beyond the scope of this book to develop formally, but a few points can be made intuitively. In those segments of the term structure where interest rates are rising, the term structure of forward interest rates is also rising. Thus, a rising term structure is often interpreted (under the pure expectations hypothesis) as a signal of rising short-term interest rates in the future. In those segments of the term structure where interest rates are declining (sometimes called an inverted term structure of interest rates), the term structure of forward rates is declining. And a declining term structure is often interpreted (under the pure expectations hypothesis) as a signal of declining short-term interest rates in the future.

Equations such as (11.2), (11.3), and (11.4) tell us that there is a link between the pricing of forward interest rate contracts and the term structure of interest rates. In Table 11.6, we saw that the term structure of three-month Eurodollar futures contracts exhibited a clear and sharply rising pattern. This pattern was consistent with a rising term structure of interest rates. Because the term structure of forward rates may include a risk premium, the prices in Table 11.6 may or may not signal a forecast of rising short-term interest rates. We discuss this issue now.

A Risk Premium in Forwards?

A natural question to ask is whether forward rates are a pure reflection of future expectations or whether other factors play a role. As we pointed out earlier, this is also a useful question to ask. If the forward rate embodies expectations, it is an inexpensive source of forecasts, and if the forward does not reflect expectations, the forward market may offer a lucrative venue for speculation. However, before we can draw conclusions about the forward market, we need to consider whether the forward rate includes a risk premium.

To begin, let us examine the sources of forecasting error contained in the forward rate. The forward rate at time t for maturity n periods from now can be related to the future spot rate S_{t+n} plus an error term e_{t+n}, as in equation (11.5).

$$F_{t,n} = S_{t+n} + e_{t+n} \qquad (11.5)$$

Next, inspect the error term:

$$e_{t+n} = F_{t,n} - S_{t+n}$$

By simply adding and subtracting the market's expected future spot rate $[E(S_{t+n})]$ and the "true" or unbiased expected future spot rate $[E^*(S_{t+n})]$, we can rewrite the error term as follows:

$$
\begin{aligned}
e_{t+n} = \;&[F_{t,n} - E(S_{t+n})] && \text{<risk premium>} && (11.6)\\
&+ [E(S_{t+n}) - E^*(S_{t+n})] && \text{<forecast bias>}\\
&+ [E^*(S_{t+n}) - S_{t+n}] && \text{<rational error>}
\end{aligned}
$$

Equation (11.6) shows that the forward rate forecast error has three components: a **risk premium,** defined as the difference between the forward rate and the market's expected future spot rate; a **forecast bias,** defined as the difference between the market's forecast and the fully informed, unbiased expectation; and a **rational error** that reflects pricing errors associated with unexpected events.

We introduced the notion of a currency risk premium in Chapter 7 in our discussion of market efficiency. A number of theories have been put forward to justify a risk premium in the forward market. We will review several of these models.

The Currency Risk Premium and the Quality of Money Balances.   An intuitive way to begin thinking about the risk premium on forward currency contracts relies on the relationship between the forward rate, spot rate, and yields that we developed in Chapter 3 and we repeat below:

$$F(0,n) = S\,\frac{[1 + i_\${(0,n)}]}{[1 + i_{FC}(0,n)]} \qquad (11.1)$$

The **Fisher Effect** (introduced in Chapter 5) posits that each nominal interest rate, $i_\$$ and i_{FC}, reflects a real interest rate (r) and an expected rate of inflation $[E(p)]$. Models of the term structure of interest rates extend the Fisher Effect, positing that longer-term interest rates may reflect liquidity risk premiums $[\sigma(lp)]$ or inflation risk premiums

[$\sigma(p)$]. By substitution of these factors into equation (11.1), we can see that the forward currency premium reflects not only the relative levels of real interest rates and inflation, but also the respective premiums for liquidity risk premiums and inflation variability, so that:

$$\frac{F(0,n)}{S} = \frac{1 + r_\$(0,n) + E_\$(p,n) + \sigma_\$(lp,n) + \sigma_\$(p,n)}{1 + r_{FC}(0,n) + E_{FC}(p,n) + \sigma_{FC}(lp,n) + \sigma_{FC}(p,n)} \tag{11.7}$$

By inspection of equation (11.7), we can see that in the case where real interest rates and expected inflation are identical in the two countries, and the two risk premium factors are zero, then the forward rate is identical with the current spot rate. This is sensible because, without a real interest differential or an inflation differential, there is no reason (in the context of this model) for the exchange rate to change.

Now assume that the volatility factors are positive *and* not equal across countries. Specifically, assume that $\sigma_\$(lp) > \sigma_{FC}(lp)$ or $\sigma_\$(p) > \sigma_{FC}(p)$. With this assumption, the US\$ will sell at a forward discount—that is, $F(0,n) > S$—even though there is no expected depreciation in the exchange rate. The intuition behind this result is that investors would prefer to hold assets in a unit of account with fewer inflationary shocks and with a smaller liquidity risk premium. Investors prefer the currency that offers a higher quality of monetary services and lower volatility of returns, even when the exchange rate is not expected to change over the investment horizon.[21]

The Currency Risk Premium and Portfolio Theory.   An alternative explanation for a currency risk premium stems from portfolio theory applied to the open economy. In a two-country world, assume that investors from country A are net creditors (holding claims against country B) and residents of country B are net debtors. As net creditors, the investors from country A generate earnings in currency B. Assuming that investors from country A are risk averse, they will demand hedging services to sell their currency B earnings forward in exchange for currency A. This generates a net demand for currency A in the forward market that cannot be satisfied without disturbing the portfolio balance of other investors. As a result, the forward rate for currency A includes a positive risk premium (that is, its forward price exceeds the expected future spot rate) paid for by investors from country A who demand hedging services.

Empirical Evidence on the Currency Risk Premium.   In equation (11.6) we showed that the forward rate forecast error is comprised of three pieces: a risk premium, a forecast bias, and a rational error of expectations. Assuming (as we should) that the rational error is zero, we cannot use the forward rate forecast error to estimate the risk premium unless we also have an estimate of the forecast bias.

Research to measure and validate a currency risk premium has taken two directions. First, if we assume that currency forecasts are unbiased, then $F_{t,n} - S_{t+n}$ is the risk premium. But to *validate* this conclusion, we need to show that $F_{t,n} - S_{t+n}$ varies along with other factors that in theory move the risk premium. Unfortunately, this line of research has been unable to show a significant and plausible relationship between the risk premium and fundamental factors.[22]

The second line of research relies on surveys of currency forecasters to generate the forecast bias. Then the risk premium is measured by subtracting the forecast bias from

---

[21]See Fama and Farber (1979).
[22]For a review of this evidence, see Lewis (1995), p. 1938.

Box 11.3

Using Futures Contracts for Transferring and Sharing Risks

Here's a riddle: Name something that in the aggregate does not exist yet helps people in an economy efficiently reach their objectives. The answer? It's futures contracts.

The classic case begins with a farmer in Kansas who has planted wheat in April and worries over what the price will be at harvest time in September. At the same time, there is a baker who expects to bake bread in September; while she owns the breadmaking equipment, she does not own any wheat. The farmer is "long wheat" for September delivery. And the baker is "short wheat," also for September delivery. Stylized balance sheets for the farmer and the baker could look like this:

Farmer April (without Futures)		Baker April (without Futures)	
Assets	*Liabilities*	*Assets*	*Liabilities*
Receipts for sale of 100 bushels of September wheat at unknown price			Payments for 100 bushels of September wheat at unknown price

Now suppose that the farmer sells a futures contract on September wheat, and the baker buys a futures contract on September wheat. The farmer agrees to deliver 100 bushels of wheat for, say, $15/bushel, and the baker agrees to accept the 100 bushels and make a payment of $15/bushel. Their new balance sheets look like this:

Farmer April (with Futures)		Baker April (with Futures)	
Assets	*Liabilities*	*Assets*	*Liabilities*
Account Receivable: $1,500	Must deliver 100 bushels of September wheat	Will receive 100 bushels of September wheat	Account Payable: $1,500

Notice that the farmer is short one futures contract and the baker is long one futures contract. So it would be correct to claim that in the aggregate, futures contracts do not exist, because there is no net supply of futures contracts. Every long position is matched by an equal and offsetting short position somewhere in the market. But the futures

---

the forward rate forecast error.[23] Using this method, Kenneth Froot and Jeffrey Frankel (1989) conclude that some of the forward rate forecast error may be the result of a risk premium. But they cannot reject the hypothesis that all of the forward rate error is due to poor survey forecasts and that none is the result of a time-varying currency risk premium.

Thus, the existence of a currency risk premium remains a matter of debate. Further research is in progress to test if other models of the risk premium or other empirical methods can identify a significant currency risk premium that varies along with the forward rate forecasting error.

Policy Matters—Private Enterprises

Our graphs of the payoff profiles associated with futures and forward contracts offer an indication about the role for these contracts in financial management. Futures and forwards can be used for two distinct purposes: (1) to take on additional risk and speculate on the price of the underlying financial claim, or (2) to lay off existing risks and hedge

---

[23]One possible problem with this method is that the surveys may not measure the market's true currency expectations.

contracts have eliminated the *price* uncertainty faced by both the farmer and the baker. This example illustrates the role that futures contracts play in risk sharing, or distributing the risks of price changes among market participants.

Note that other uncertainties and risks could remain. One is the farmer's risk of a crop failure. He is obligated to deliver 100 bushels of September wheat by either growing it or buying it from someone else if his crop fails. Another is the baker's risk that she may not need all 100 bushels of wheat in September, perhaps because tastes or recipes change. But the baker is obligated to take and pay for the wheat.

In our simple example, there is only one futures contract affecting the farmer and the baker. In practice, the farmer could have sold his wheat futures to a speculator (speculator A), who bought based on the belief that wheat prices would rise. And the baker could have purchased her wheat futures from Speculator B, who sold based on the belief that wheat prices would fall. This extension illustrates how futures contracts can assist in risk transfer, transferring risks from those who do not want to hold them (the farmer and the baker) to those who do (speculators A and B). Note again that in this example there are two futures contracts outstanding (so open interest is 2), but the aggregate supply of futures contracts is zero, because the number of long positions is equal to the number of short positions.

Our example uses wheat, but similar examples could be crafted in financial markets. The yen currency futures market links together individuals and firms, some with natural long yen positions (from exporting to Japan), others with natural sort yen positions (from importing from Japan), and speculators who want to take positions based on their beliefs about the $/¥ price. The interest rate futures market links together some individuals and firms who plan to borrow money (and worry about rising interest rates), some who plan to invest money (and worry about declining interest rates), and speculators who want to take positions based on their beliefs about the course of interest rates.

In our first example, from a managerial perspective, either the farmer or the baker could regret the decision to use futures. If the price of wheat goes to $20, the farmer will regret selling at $15, and he may fall behind other farmers who did not hedge and who therefore have more capital for next year's season. And similarly, if the price of wheat goes to only $12, the baker will regret buying forward at $15 and she may be unable to sell bread as cheaply as other bakers who did not hedge. The futures market hedges price risks, but it cannot deal with competitive risks when farmers or bakers do not all follow identical hedging strategies.

against price movements in the underlying financial claim. Transactions on a futures exchange could link together two speculators: an individual in Denver who buys € futures on the expectation the € will rise in value, and an individual in Minneapolis who sells € futures on the expectation that the € will fall. Transactions on a futures exchange could also link two hedgers together: a New York importer who wants to buy € to cover a future € liability to a Frankfurt firm, and a Boston exporter who wants to sell € to offset a future € receivable from a German customer.[24] And transactions could link one speculator with one hedger on either the buy or sell side.

As these sketches suggest, futures and forward markets allow for efficient **risk sharing** across individuals. Risk is traded—either acquired or laid off—using futures and forward markets, allowing individuals to achieve a more desirable allocation of risk. For more on risk transferring and risk sharing, see Box 11.3.

In this section, we consider two issues facing private enterprises (1) the decision to use futures versus forwards contracts, and (2) the decision to introduce a new futures contract for trading. Decisions about the use of forwards and futures for hedging and risk management are discussed in Chapter 16.

---

[24]Similar examples using interest rate futures or commodity futures are also valid.

Deciding on Futures versus Forwards

As the payoff profiles indicate, both futures and forward contracts lead to the same value at maturity. What distinguishes futures and forwards are the intermediate cash flows associated with marking to market, the various aspects of futures that are standardized, and the trading mechanism.

The decision to use futures or forwards depends on the purpose and scale of the transaction. We have highlighted two stylized purposes: hedging and speculation. Hedgers who buy or sell a contract to offset an underlying business transaction have little need for liquidity. Hedgers who match the maturity of their hedge contract to their underlying exposure do not intend to trade or liquidate their contract prior to maturity. The added liquidity of a futures contract is not valued by hedgers, and the marking-to-market feature would create undesired cash flow risk. Therefore, when prices are similar, hedgers will prefer interbank forward contracts, if they have the scale of activity and credit rating to gain access to the market.

If scale or credit rating precludes access to the interbank market, hedgers will migrate to the futures market. Since futures contracts have standard delivery dates, hedgers may be unable to construct a perfect hedge, which they could in the interbank market. The hedgers may elect a futures contract with an earlier delivery date or a delivery date just after the maturity of their underlying exposure.

For example, suppose that the € liability of our New York importer is due on September 25 and that the September currency futures contract matures on September 15. The importer could buy the September contract, leaving himself with 10 days of risk due to the mismatch of maturity dates. Or the importer could buy the December contract and then sell it prior to maturity on September 25. In this case, the importer incurs a *basis risk* because the price of the December contract may not be perfectly correlated with the spot currency price on September 25.

In contrast to a hedger, a speculator relies heavily on market **liquidity**—the ability to buy and sell quickly with transactions having little impact on market prices. As we reviewed, interbank forward contracts are relatively illiquid. A short-term speculator may prefer to trade in exchange-traded futures contracts as long as the smaller scale of the market is acceptable and the speculator is able to meet the explicit margin requirements of the market. Larger-scale speculators may prefer the interbank market. But they will more likely trade in spot contracts that are extremely liquid.

New Futures Contracts and Trading Arrangements

While futures exchanges are a heavily regulated business, they are still managed, like any privately owned company, to extend the use of their products and to increase the profitability of the exchange. To further their objectives, the exchange will design and introduce new futures contracts and new trading relationships.

Success and Failure of New Futures Contracts.   Although there has been a worldwide proliferation of trading in financial futures, success in the introduction of futures contracts is far from assured. Initial costs are high to design a contract, win regulatory approval, provide physical trading space and back-office support, and attract traders. In 1995 alone, 41 new futures contracts were introduced on exchanges around the world.[25]

---

[25]*Futures and Options World: Directory and Review 1996,* p. 9.

By some estimates, only 30 percent of new futures contracts reach a profitable trading volume.[26]

Those contracts that are successful help to illustrate how futures contracts provide a value-added service for financial managers. The likelihood of success for a new futures contract is greater when there is a large underlying cash market with high price variability that attracts both speculators and hedgers. Success is also more likely when price variability is uncorrelated with other futures contracts. If prices of a new futures contract were perfectly correlated with prices of an existing futures contract, then the new contract would not increase speculative or hedging opportunities. Thus, successful futures contracts fulfill a demand, much like ordinary consumer products, for speculative or hedging services that cannot be met by other products. In this sense, successful futures contracts help to "complete" the financial market.[27]

For currencies, it is clear that the $C, £, and ¥ are separate financial assets. Using £ futures to hedge ¥ exposure would be a poor cross-hedge since the correlation between price movements on these currencies is low. Thus, separate futures contracts for these currencies makes sense. In contrast, the Saudi Arabian riyal, the Liberian dollar and the Hong Kong dollar, are separate currencies, but there is no demand for a futures market in these currencies because they are pegged to the US$. Thus, there is little need to hedge US$ exchange risk in these currencies, and available currencies futures (in US$/£, US$/¥, US$/€, and so forth) can be used to hedge risks against these third currencies.[28]

The DM, French franc, and Belgian franc were also separate currencies, but from 1989 until 1998 they participated in the European Exchange Rate Mechanism (ERM) to limit exchange rate variability. Thus, US$ exchange rate risk against the French franc was highly correlated with US$ exchange rate changes against the DM and the Belgian franc. As long as the ERM stayed intact, there was little need to support separate futures contracts of the US$ against the individual ERM currencies. The DM contract was sufficient to hedge US$ risk against ERM currencies during periods of EMS stability. But during periods of EMS realignment (noted in Table 2.3) the DM contract was an imperfect and inefficient contract for hedging US$ exchange risk against other EMS currencies.

For interest rate futures, we observe a range of futures contracts specifying different maturities (from overnight rates to long-term bonds) and different instruments (from commercial paper, to bank lending rates, to government securities). It is clear that these underlying instruments are separate and distinct, but the high correlation of interest rates within a currency unit makes it harder to predict if any individual interest rate futures contract will succeed.

In addition, as we show in Appendix 11.1, some interest rate futures contracts in currency B can be replicated by interest rate futures contracts in currency A combined with currency futures contracts linking A and B. In particular, we show that a three-month Euro–foreign currency (FC) interest rate futures contract for the interval $(t_1, t_1 + 3$ months) can be replicated by a three-month Eurodollar interest rate futures plus long and short positions in the $/FC currency futures contracts at maturities t_1 and $t_1 + 3$ months. Thus, managers could have hedged Euro-£, Euro-¥, and Euro-lira

---

[26]Kolb (1991), p. 48.

[27]See Black (1986).

[28]The Hong Kong dollar is an example of how the 1997 political changeover from British to Chinese rule in Hong Kong stimulated some demand for hedging and speculative contracts. In December 1994, the unpegging of the Mexican peso also accelerated the demand for futures contracts, which the CME reintroduced after an absence of almost 20 years.

FIGURE 11.8 Top 10 Futures Exchanges in 1998 and 1999

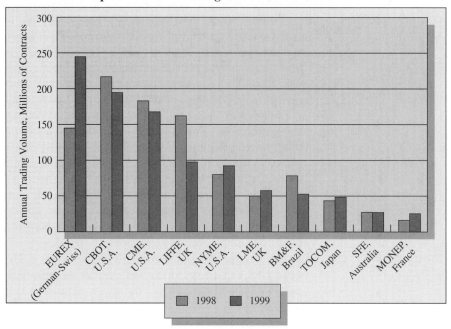

Source: Galen Burghardt, "Equities Saved the Year," *Futures Institute Magazine,* Feb. 2000.

interest rate risks using this synthetic approach long before actual Euro-FC contracts became available. These types of replicating strategies may limit the range of nondollar interest rate futures contracts that are needed to complete the market and sustain hedging and speculative activity.

The Internationalization of Futures Markets. The internationalization of futures markets reflects elements of both competition and cooperation. While U.S. futures exchanges have dominated trading volume and product innovation for many years, foreign markets have developed, spurred on by volatility in their own financial market prices. Clearly, foreign market participants possess the accumulated experience of operating in their local cash market instruments. So it is natural to find futures contracts on Brazil's BOVESPA index traded in Sao Paulo, and futures contracts on yen interest rates traded on the Tokyo Stock Exchange in Japan, and so forth. In 1993, the volume of futures contracts traded on non-U.S. exchanges surpassed U.S. exchange trading volume for the first time after years of U.S. domination. In 1999, U.S. futures exchanges accounted for only 38.2 percent of the 1.25 billion futures contracts traded that year.[29] The CBOT and CME, which had been the number one and two exchanges in the world in 1998, were overtaken by EUREX. Figure 11.8 shows the top 10 futures exchanges in the world ranked on the basis of trading volume. The list includes exchanges from five continents.

Another layer of competition covers European exchanges and the quest for market share in new euro-linked products that have replaced the broad array of contracts linked with the 12 European legacy currencies. LIFFE, which had been the number one

---

[29]Galen Burghardt, "Equities Saved the Year," *Futures Institute Magazine,* Feb. 2000.

exchange in Europe for many years, was overtaken in 1999 by EUREX, which appeared to be the winner in the early rounds of this competition. A key to this success was the Euro-BUND contract, which LIFFE dominated when it offered the German (DM) Bund contract. But in 1997, EUREX introduced its own Bund contract with electronic trading, rather than the open outcry system used at LIFFE. Within months, EUREX had taken virtually all of the Bund futures trading volume. In 1999, more than 121 million Euro-BUND futures contracts were traded on EUREX versus none at LIFFE. In addition, EUREX introduced very successful contracts for short- and medium-term German securities. LIFFE retains prominence in the Euribor contract.

In some cases, however, competition has given way to cooperation. Foreign futures markets have at times attempted to compete directly with U.S. futures markets over contracts on the same underlying asset. Thus, we have seen a Eurodollar futures contract traded on the CME, LIFFE, SGX-DT (Singapore Exchange Derivatives Trading Limited, formerly known as SIMEX), and other exchanges. Initially some exchanges tried to compete on the basis of product differentiation; that is, redesigning the contract with different sizes, expiration dates, or delivery specifications to attract trading volume. These product modifications did little to attract trading.

At some point, it became apparent that foreign markets had their own competitive advantage that could not be duplicated by U.S. futures markets, namely, their *time zone advantage*. With this insight, the strategy for foreign futures market was to offer a futures contract with *identical specifications* as the contract traded on the dominant futures market. Then market participants could trade in the dominant market during normal business hours, and, if desired, make offsetting transactions in the foreign (or *satellite*) futures market. Or, the ordering could be reversed—taking a position initially in the satellite market, and then making an offsetting transaction in the dominant, home market.

This strategy reached a new pinnacle in 1984 when the CME and SIMEX established their so-called **Mutual Offset System (MOS)** for the CME's Eurodollar futures contract. Under this agreement, SIMEX began trading Eurodollar futures contracts with exactly the same contract specifications as those on the CME. With the MOS, positions taken on one exchange could be transferred to the other for purposes of consolidating or offsetting a position. In March 1996, the CME and SIMEX extended their MOS agreement. This time the CME adopted the contract specifications of the successful SIMEX Euroyen contract.[30] LIFFE has negotiated a similar mutual offset system with TIFFE for its Euroyen contract that took effect in April 1996. And in November 1996, the CME entered into yet another agreement to permit trading in LIFFE and MATIF interest rate futures contracts on the CME. These alliances effectively extended the trading day to as much as 16 hours.[31]

Electronic trading is another means of extending the trading day around the world and creating a virtual 24-hour market. In 1987, the CME developed its GLOBEX system—an electronic order-entry and matching system for trading CME futures (and futures from other participating exchanges) during hours when the local open-outcry pits are closed. GLOBEX enjoyed some early success by bringing contracts from the CME, CBOT, and MATIF together in one electronic marketplace. However, the CBOT dropped out in 1994 and other major exchanges, such as LIFFE, have not allowed their

---

[30]The CME and SGX-DT contracts are absolutely identical. The closing settlement price for the Eurodollar contract is determined by the CME. The closing settlement price for the Euroyen contract is determined by the SGX-DT, which happens to use the settlement price as determined by TIFFE.

[31]See "LIFFE Paves Way for Euroyen Futures," *Financial Times,* January 21–22, 1995, and information at CME and LIFFE websites <www.cme.com> and <www.liffe.com>.

contracts to trade on GLOBEX. In January 1997, MATIF announced that it would drop out of GLOBEX in May 1998 when its contract expired. Today, the system has evolved into the "GLOBEX Alliance," linking five exchanges (the CME, SGX-DT, Brazil's MB&F, Paris Bourse, and the Montreal Exchange) in a system that permits cross-exchange trading privileges to members, and cross-margining of positions.[32]

Policy Matters—Public Policymakers

Futures exchanges affect the public directly because they offer firms and individuals an opportunity to transact in futures contracts, and indirectly as there may be side effects from market transactions. It is no surprise that futures markets are heavily regulated. We will consider two issues that are prominent in the public policy debate: whether futures markets affect the volatility of cash market prices and whether, in the public interest, it makes sense to slow down the pace of futures market trading.

Futures Prices and Cash Market Volatility

The possible link between futures markets and cash market volatility has been a topic of concern for many years. One image of a futures market portrays screaming traders consumed in wild speculation in the trading pit. Another image captures conservative farmers who want to sell their wheat forward for a safe return and conservative bakers who want to buy their wheat forward and also obtain certainty. The fear of promoting futures markets is that the wild, speculative side could exacerbate price movements and have an impact on the *real economy* of wheat growers and wheat consumers, as well as those far removed from this market.

Sorting out this issue is difficult, in part because causality is in question. It is doubtful whether econometric analysis can ever determine whether factors are causally linked because a third, unobserved factor may be involved. We observe fire trucks at the scene of many fires. We observe that hospitals are home to many unhealthy people. We cannot conclude that the former causes the latter. The presence of volatility in many prices when these commodities or financial instruments trade on a futures exchange does not imply that futures markets are the cause of this price volatility. As we argued earlier, the sequence is usually the reverse—only those contracts that have naturally volatile cash market prices will engender successful futures markets. However, once the futures market is in place, is its effect on cash market price volatility positive, negative, or neutral?

Most studies of the issue adopt an "events study" methodology, measuring the volatility of cash market prices before and after the introduction of a futures market. The classic study by Holbrook Working (1960) examined the market for onions, which had a futures market during the period 1942–1958. Working showed that greater hedging activity on the futures market was associated with smaller price variability in cash onion prices over the season. A related study by Roger Gray (1963) showed that the ban on onion futures trading (following the 1958 Onion Futures Act, U.S. Public Law 85-839) led to a period of increased volatility in onion prices like that common before active futures trading. Numerous studies of other markets and other sample periods using

---

[32]See <www.globexalliance.com> for further information.

alternative statistical techniques have tended to support the price stabilizing effect of futures markets, although not in all cases.[33]

The issue of futures market activity and cash market volatility became less clear and more of a public issue after the stock market crash of Monday, October 19, 1987. After the precipitous 22.6 percent drop in the Dow Jones Industrial Average in one day, policymakers asked more forcefully whether trading in financial futures and options may have exacerbated the day's trading, even if the existence of futures markets was not the direct cause of the crash.

As we have noted, one of the attractions of futures markets is their greater liquidity relative to certain interbank market transactions. Thus, it is natural to expect, especially during fast-moving markets, that traders will prefer to transact in the futures market instead of the underlying cash markets.

This was allegedly the case during the 1987 crash. With prices of stock index futures falling, program traders attempted to arbitrage by buying the low-priced futures and selling the higher-priced cash shares (index arbitrage). When sales of the underlying cash shares became difficult to execute—because of clogged phone lines, delays in price reporting, and order imbalances—traders accelerated their sales on the futures market. A presidential commission to investigate the crash recommended, among other things, the establishment of "circuit breakers" so that a large daily price swing would trigger a temporary halt to program trading or trading in general.[34]

This kind of "crisis intervention" has not been recommended for either the currency or interest rate futures market. Nevertheless, the persistent expansion of futures trading continues to concern policymakers.

Transaction Costs and Transaction Taxes

Part of the attraction of a futures market is the low cost and speed of transacting. Futures markets attract traders. If these traders are the right type—namely, *stabilizing speculators*—then futures trading ought to reduce price volatility as speculators endeavor to keep market prices close to their fair, equilibrium value.[35] It has been recognized for some time that futures markets could also attract *destabilizing speculators*, but most economists have presumed that their effect would be short-lived as destabilizing speculators would tend to lose money and exit the market.

Some economists now question this view. They posit that "noise traders" may operate in futures markets (as well as other financial markets). A **noise trader** is someone who buys on the basis of a positive price shock and sells on the basis of a negative price shock, even when these price shocks are based on random noise rather than a true change in underlying fundamentals. According to this view, noise traders may temporarily destabilize the market and initiate a trend in one direction, which is profitable for them to follow. Thus, the impact of noise traders is a permanent increase in the volatility of financial prices, which is not associated with any underlying source of true, economic uncertainty.

If noise trading is an important feature of financial markets, then steps to increase the cost of trading ("to throw sand into the gears" of the market, in James Tobin's

---

[33]Figlewski (1981) concludes that trading in GNMA futures contracts coincided with an increase in GNMA rate volatility. Although this was the first financial futures contract introduced, it proved to be unsuccessful and trading was stopped. See Johnston and McConnell (1989).

[34]See the NYSE website at <www.nyse.com/press> for the current of size of various circuit breakers.

[35]Recall the discussion of equilibrium pricing in Chapter 7 on market efficiency.

phrase) may benefit national welfare. It has been argued that a tax on trading activity would "curb instability introduced by speculation, reduce the diversion of resources into the financial sector of the economy, and lengthen the horizons of corporate managers."[36]

Market economists have been highly skeptical of this argument. A central issue is whether a transaction tax assessed in one country can be collected, or whether trading will simply migrate to another more hospitable location. We have some experience on this point. In Chapter 10, we saw that international bond issues were quick to migrate to London and Luxembourg after the introduction of the interest equalization tax (IET) in 1963. The IET generated almost no tax revenue and did not stem the outflow of capital.

Along the same lines, Steven Umlauf (1993) reported that the Swedish experience with transaction taxes had much the same effect. Large blocks of transactions migrated to London. The evidence suggests that volatility actually *increased* (rather than decreased) with the higher transaction taxes, but the increase was not significant.[37]

Overall, there is strong evidence that traders will shift their trading location or shift into untaxed securities, so that taxation revenue will be overstated unless these behavioral changes are taken into account. There is less direct evidence that transaction taxes will have any impact on price volatility. The accumulated evidence on futures markets and price volatility suggests that any policy that reduces the role of futures markets may actually increase volatility in cash market prices.

---

[36]See Summers and Summers (1989).
[37]For further evidence, see Campbell and Froot (1994).

Summary

Futures markets on currencies and interest rates have developed over the last 25 years. Like futures on agricultural commodities and precious metals, currency and interest rate futures are standardized contracts that permit trade among hedgers and speculators around the world in a centralized marketplace. Trading among anonymous counterparties in futures is made possible by (1) the clearinghouse, which provides a standardized, high-quality counterparty to each transaction; and (2) the marking-to-market convention that minimizes the need for credit checks, relying instead on a system of margin requirements.

While futures and forward contracts are similar, institutional differences make them different. As an empirical matter, there appears to be little difference in the prices of futures and forwards. We argued that futures markets may attract smaller investors who desire liquidity, and forward markets may be preferred by larger agents (hedgers especially) who do not value liquidity.

Futures contracts are traded for various maturities ranging to 10 years or more for some instruments. The term structure of interest rates is an important tool for understanding the basic structure of futures prices. Expectations play a role in the pricing of futures contracts, but in theory risk premiums may also contribute to pricing. The empirical evidence for a currency risk premium is inconclusive.

The growth of trading in financial futures has coincided with an increase in volatility in financial prices. As a practical matter, the demand for a new futures contract depends on the presence of volatility in the underlying asset and the absence of another futures contract capable of hedging the price risk. However, once a liquid futures contract exists, the possibility of spillovers from the futures market to the underlying cash market is possible. Empirical evidence often suggests that futures markets help reduce volatility in underlying cash markets. Still, policies such as transaction taxes have been adopted in some countries and are under consideration in others as a way to reduce financial market price volatility associated with financial futures.

APPENDIX 11.1
SYNTHETIC INTEREST RATE FUTURES[38]

In this appendix, we will show that a synthetic nondollar interest rate futures contract can be constructed using available futures contracts, specifically by using Eurodollar interest rate futures in conjunction with currency futures contracts. This technique permits us to construct interest rate futures contracts denominated in Euro-¥, Euro-DM, Euro-£, and any other Euro-denomination that has an active currency futures market. This approach, another example of a **replicating portfolio approach,** is general and could be applied to construct synthetic Eurocurrency interest rate futures of any maturity. However, to simplify the exposition, we assume that the maturity of the nondollar borrowing period matches the maturity of the Eurodollar interest rate futures contract.

The General Setting

The setting is as follows. Assume that today (time t_0) a treasurer plans to borrow foreign currency (FC) at time t_1 to be repaid at time t_2. At time t_0, the FC interest rate at t_1 is uncertain. It is this risk that the treasurer wants to hedge.

In Figure 11A.1 we show a familiar looking diagram (recall Figure 3.2) depicting time along the horizontal dimension and currency along the vertical dimension. Spot and forward

[38]This appendix draws heavily on Koh and Levich (1994).

exchange rates measure the cost of shifting between dollars and foreign currency, while interest rates measure the cost of shifting cash flows across time. From the interest rate parity condition, we know that the rate for a forward transaction on t_1 is given by:

$$\frac{F_{t_1}}{S_{t_0}} = \frac{1 + i_{\$t_0,t_1}}{1 + i_{FC,t_0,t_1}} \tag{11A.1}$$

and the rate for a forward transaction on t_2 is given by:

$$\frac{F_{t_2}}{S_{t_0}} = \frac{1 + i_{\$t_0,t_2}}{1 + i_{FC,t_0,t_2}} \tag{11A.2}$$

where

$$S_{t_0} = \text{spot exchange rate in US\$/FC at time } t_0$$
$$F_{t_1} = \text{forward exchange rate at } t_0 \text{ for delivery at time } t_1$$
$$F_{t_2} = \text{forward exchange rate at } t_0 \text{ for delivery at time } t_2$$
$$i_{\$,t_0,t_1} = \text{US\$ interest rate for the period } t_0 \text{ to } t_1$$
$$i_{\$,t_0,t_2} = \text{US\$ interest rate for the period } t_0 \text{ to } t_2$$
$$i_{FC,t_0,t_1} = \text{FC interest rate for the period } t_0 \text{ to } t_1$$
$$i_{FC,t_0,t_2} = \text{FC interest rate for the period } t_0 \text{ to } t_2$$

Note that equation (11A.2) can be rewritten using implied forward interest rates—defined in equations (11.2), (11.3), and (11.4) in the main chapter—to give the result:

$$\frac{F_{t_2}}{S_{t_0}} = \frac{(1 + i_{\$,t_0,t_1})(1 + i_{\$,t_1,t_2})}{(1 + i_{FC,t_0,t_1})(1 + i_{FC,t_1,t_2})} \tag{11A.3}$$

FIGURE 11A.1 **Synthetic Eurocurrency Interest Rate Pricing**

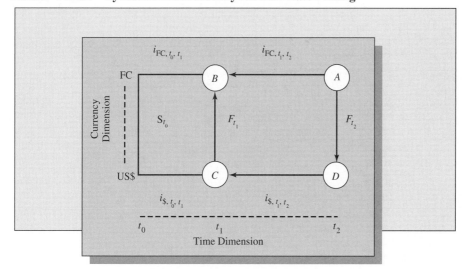

where

$i_{\$,t_1,t_2}$ = implied forward US$ interest rate at time t_0 for the period t_1 to t_2

i_{FC,t_1,t_2} = implied forward FC interest rate at time t_0 for the period t_1 to t_2

Equating S_{t_0} obtained in equations (11A.1) and (11A.3) gives the following relationship:

$$1 + i_{FC,t_1,t_2} = \frac{F_{t_1}}{F_{t_2}}(1 + i_{\$,t_1,t_2}) \qquad (11A.4)$$

Notice that equation (11A.4) is analogous to the traditional interest rate parity formula in equation (11A.1) except that the near-term cash flows pertain to a future time (t_1) rather than to the present time (t_0).

Equation (11A.4) predicts that the implied forward interest rate on FC is uniquely related to the implied forward interest rate on US$ and the term structure of forward exchange rates. The sale of an FC interest rate futures contract (line segment *AB* in Figure 11A.1) is replicated by combining the sales of a currency futures contract for date t_2 (segment *AD*) with the sale of a US$ interest rate futures contract (segment *DC*) and the purchase of a currency futures contract for date t_1 (segment *CB*).

A Specific Example

Consider the case of a treasurer who plans to borrow £1 million in the Eurocurrency market for three months beginning March 15, 1998. Assume that today (December 15, 1997) the treasurer could hedge the cost of borrowing with a forward rate agreement (FRA) obtained from a bank. Alternatively, the treasurer could implement the synthetic approach by (1) sell-ing the March 1998 Eurodollar futures (segment *DC*) and cov-ering the exchange risk by buying the near-term March 1998 currency futures (segment *CB*) and selling the far-term June 1998 currency futures (segment *AD*). These flows are illus-trated in Figure 11A.2.

We can assess the theoretical Euro-£ borrowing rate im-plied by these futures transactions by using equation (11A.4) and Figure 11A.2. Assume that the observed market prices are:

$$AD = 1.555 \ \$/\pounds$$

$$DC = [1 + 0.06\,(90/360)] = 1.015$$

$$CB = 1.567 \ \$/\pounds$$

So $[1 + i_\pounds\,(90/360)] = 1.015 \times (1.567/1.555) = 1.022833$. Therefore, our estimate of $i_\pounds$ is 9.13 percent, which represents the effective £ borrowing rate over the March 15–June 15, 1998, interval, using the synthetic approach.

A Final Note

The method for replicating a foreign currency interest rate fu-tures contract is very general. We could use it to create interest rate futures in the £, DM, and ¥, as well as the lira, won, or peso. Any currency with a currency futures contract can be combined with the Eurodollar futures to create an FC interest rate futures. Thus, the Eurodollar interest rate futures may be another **vehicle contract.** Traders who want to hedge lira, won, or peso interest rate risk may prefer to use the Eurodol-lar interest rate futures (in conjunction with currency futures contracts), rather than to rely on thinly traded interest rate fu-tures and forward rate agreements in the FC where borrowing and lending take place.

FIGURE 11A.2   **Example of Synthetic Euro-£ Hedge**

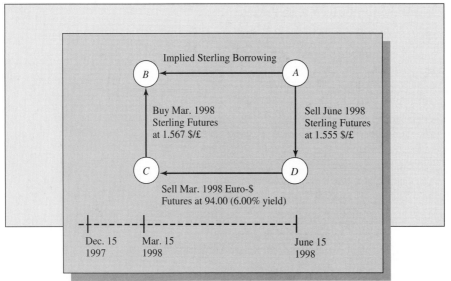

Questions

1. What does it mean to mark an investment to market?

2. A futures contract is a redundant instrument; that is, it can be replicated using other, simpler, financial instruments. What benefits come from the existence of futures contracts?

3. What are the four characteristics cited in the chapter that differentiate a futures contract from a forward contract?

4. What services does the clearinghouse in the futures markets deliver to its clients?

5. What is the difference between a maintenance margin and a variation margin?

6. What is a notional bond? What does it mean when a trader delivers the cheapest-to-deliver bond at maturity? What determines the conversion factor?

7. State the arbitrage condition that links the interest rate futures contract and the current borrowing/lending condition in the market.

8. Define what it means to be hedged against foreign exchange risk.

9. Suppose you believe that the euro will rise sharply against the dollar over the next three months (i.e., the future spot rate will be higher than that predicted by the covered interest parity). What position on the futures market would you take to benefit from your speculation?

10. Suppose at the end of the year you have a capital gain on a T-bond. You would like to lock in your profits now but would rather wait for the year to end to delay the capital gain tax until next year. How would you use the futures markets to achieve your objective? What are the risks of your strategy?

11. Suppose your firm will receive dividends in one month. You want to invest these funds in short-term instruments at today's interest rate, which you find particularly attractive. How would you lock in your future interest income using interest rate futures?

12. What are the factors that might imply a different valuation for futures and forwards for the same maturity?

13. How does the shape of the spot yield curve influence the theoretical price of interest rate futures?

14. Describe the cost-of-carry model of pricing for a futures contract. What determines a currency futures price? What would explain the difference in price between the theoretical futures price and the actual futures price?

15. Suppose that spot SFr trades at $0.66/SFr and three-month futures contracts on DM trade at $0.69/SFr. Is the SFr three-month interest rate higher or lower than the US$ equivalent?

16. Describe how a forward interest rate can be derived. Find a numerical example in today's newspaper.

17. What risks associated with a futures position are not present in a forward position? What risks associated with a forward position are not present in a futures position?

18. What are the main features a speculator would look for in deciding between a futures market and a forward market? A hedger?

19. How could the existence of a futures market possibly increase the volatility of prices in the underlying cash market? Could it have the opposite effect and decrease volatility in cash market prices?

20. Describe the meaning of *noise trading*. How could noise trading affect the volatility of market prices?

Exercises

Arbitrage in the Currency Futures Market

1. Consider the following:

   Spot rate: $0.65/SFr

   Swiss one-year interest rate: 9 percent

   U.S. one-year interest rate: 5 percent

   a. Calculate the theoretical price of a one-year futures contract.

   b. What would you do if the futures price was quoted at $0.65/SFr in the marketplace? Where would you borrow? Lend? Calculate the gain on a $100 million arbitrage transaction.

   c. What would you do if the future price was quoted at $0.60/SFr in the marketplace? Where would you borrow? Lend? Calculate the gain on a $100 million arbitrage transaction.

2. Consider the following prices:

   Spot rate: ¥100/$

   U.S. one-year interest rate: 5 percent

   Futures price: ¥97.62/$

   a. What value of the one-year Japanese interest rate will remove arbitrage incentives conditional on the spot rate, futures price, and U.S. interest rate?

   b. If the yen interest rate is higher than the one found above, what would you do to take advantage of arbitrage opportunities?

   c. If the yen interest rate is lower than the one found above, what would you do to take advantage of arbitrage opportunities?

Arbitrage in the Interest Rate Futures Markets

3. Suppose the interest rate futures contract for delivery in three months is currently selling at 110. The deliverable bond for that particular contract is a 25-year bond, currently traded at 100 with a coupon rate of 10 percent. The current three-month rate is 7 percent.

   a. Is there any arbitrage opportunity? If the answer is yes, what would you do and what would be your potential gain from an arbitrage transaction?

   b. What is the theoretical price of the futures contract?

   c. Suppose the price was 95 instead of 110. What would you do to take advantage of arbitrage opportunities?

Spread Risk in the Eurocurrency Market

4. The portfolio manager of the WXYZ pension fund wants to protect herself against a decline in future interest rates. The fund's planned short-term investments are placed in three-month Eurodollar deposits at the LIBID rate. The current LIBID-LIBOR spread in the interbank market is 7.375–7.500 percent, and the current price of a CME futures contract (which settles on the basis of three-month Eurodollar LIBOR) is 92.50, reflecting a 7.500 percent interest rate.

   a. How could the WXYZ fund use the futures market to hedge itself? What is the minimum interest that the firm locks in?

   b. Suppose that at maturity, Eurodollar rates have fallen to 6.375–6.500 percent in the interbank market. Evaluate the hedge. What deposit rate has the fund secured?

   c. Suppose that at maturity, Eurodollar rates have increased to 8.375–8.625 percent in the interbank market. Assume that the LIBID-LIBOR spread has widened because of greater interest rate and macroeconomic uncertainty. Now evaluate the hedge. What deposit rate has the fund secured?

Forward Interest Rates

5. Check today's newspaper and locate values for today's three-month, six-month, one-year, and two-year interest rates on government securities.

   a. Calculate the market's implied value of the three-month interest rate beginning three months from now.

   b. Calculate the market's implied value of the one-year interest rate beginning one year from now.

References

Black, Deborah G. "Success and Failure of Futures Contracts: Theory and Empirical Evidence." *Monograph Series in Finance and Economics,* no. 1986-1. New York: New York University Salomon Brothers Center for the Study of Financial Institutions, 1986.

Campbell, John Y., and Kenneth A. Froot. "International Experience with Securities Transaction Taxes." In *The Internationalization of Equity Markets,* ed. J. Frankel. Chicago: University of Chicago Press, 1994.

Chang, Carolyn W., and Jack S. K. Chang. "Forward and Futures Prices: Evidence from the Foreign Exchange Markets." *Journal of Finance* 45, no. 4 (Sept. 1990), pp. 1333–36.

Cornell, Bradford, and Mark R. Reinganum. "Forward and Futures Prices: Evidence from the Foreign Exchange Markets." *Journal of Finance* 36, no. 5 (Dec. 1981), pp. 1035–45.

Cox, John C.; Jonathan E. Ingersoll, Jr.; and Stephen A. Ross. "The Relation between Forward Prices and Futures Prices." *Journal of Financial Economics* 9, no. 4 (1981), pp. 321–46.

Fama, Eugene F., and Andre Farber. "Money, Bonds and Foreign Exchange." *American Economic Review* 69 (Sept. 1979), pp. 639–49.

Figlewski, Stephen. "Futures Trading and Volatility in the GNMA Market." *Journal of Finance* 36, no. 2 (May 1981), pp. 445–56.

Froot, Kenneth A., and Jeffrey A. Frankel. "Forward Discount Bias: Is It an Exchange Risk Premium?" *Quarterly Journal of Economics* 104 (Feb. 1989), pp. 139–61.

Gray, Roger W. "Onions Revisited." *Journal of Farm Economics* 45, no. 2 (May 1963), pp. 273–76.

Johnston, Elizabeth T., and John J. McConnell. "Requiem for a Market: An Analysis of the Rise and Fall of a Financial Futures Contract." *Review of Financial Studies* 2, no. 1 (1989), pp. 1–23.

Koh, Annie, and Richard M. Levich. "Synthetic Eurocurrency Interest Rates Futures Contracts: Theory and Evidence." In *Japan and International Financial Markets: Analytical and Empirical Perspectives,* ed. Ryuzo Sato, Richard M. Levich, and Rama Ramachandran. Cambridge: Cambridge University Press, 1994.

Kolb, Robert W. *Understanding Futures Markets.* Miami, FL: Kolb Publishing, 1991.

Lewis, Karen K. "Puzzles in International Financial Markets." In *Handbook of International Economics.* vol. 3; ed. G. Grossman and K. Rogoff. Amsterdam: North-Holland, 1995.

Miller, Merton H. "Financial Innovation: The Last Twenty Years and the Next." *Journal of Financial and Quantitative Analysis* 21, no. 4 (Dec. 1986), pp. 459–71.

Rodriguez, Rita M., and E. Eugene Carter. *International Financial Management,* 2nd ed. Englewood Cliffs, NJ: Prentice Hall, 1979.

Summers, Lawrence H., and Victoria P. Summers. "When Financial Markets Work Too Well: A Cautious Case for a Securities Transactions Tax." *Journal of Financial Services Research* 3 (1989), pp. 261–86.

Umlauf, Steven R. "Transaction Taxes and Stock Market Behavior: The Swedish Experience." *Journal of Financial Economics* 33 (Apr. 1993), pp. 227–40.

Working, Holbrook. "Price Effects of Futures Trading." *Food Research Institute Studies,* vol. 1 (1960).

12 CURRENCY AND INTEREST RATE OPTIONS

"Setting a currency option price is fairly simple. You just plug six variables into a computer model and out pops a price—assuming you have the correct model."

A statement once heard at a now defunct option trading desk

Learning Objectives

After reading this chapter, students should

1. Be familiar with the basic terminology of option contracts and the institutional arrangements for trading options.

2. Understand the determinants of put and call option prices *at* maturity.

3. Understand the determinants of put and call option prices *prior to* maturity.

4. Understand the relationship among put prices, call prices, and forward rates, and how to apply the put-call-forward parity formula.

5. Realize that a simple option can be replicated by borrowing (or lending cash) and holding a fractional position in the underlying asset—and that this replicating portfolio concept can be used to (*a*) construct an option, (*b*) price an option, and (*c*) hedge an option position.

6. Understand the concept of implied volatility and its relation to historic volatility.

7. Be familiar with the notion of delta hedging as a way to manage the risk in an option portfolio.

8. Know that models for pricing currency options are very useful but that actual option prices may deviate from the predictions of popular models.

Option contracts on foreign exchange and interest rates are among the most recent financial innovations. Options on currencies and debt instruments were traded over the counter among banks in the late 1970s. Exchange-traded options on currencies began trading on the Philadelphia Stock Exchange (PHLX) in 1982, and interest rate options began trading on the Chicago Mercantile Exchange (CME) in 1985. Since their introduction, the markets for exchange-traded currency and interest rate options have expanded in many directions—more option exchange markets around the world, more currencies and debt instruments on which options are traded, option contracts with longer maturities, more styles of option contracts, and greater volume of trading activity.

Options on foreign currencies and interest rates bear many similarities to options on equities, which began trading on the Chicago Board Options Exchange in 1972 and had been traded on a customized, over-the-counter basis since the 1920s. Much of the terminology is the same, as are the basic pictures of an option's value at and prior to maturity. However, several aspects of currency and interest rate options are special. These special attributes help to shed light on the pricing and behavior of exchange rates and global interest rates as well as other financial options. Currency and interest rate options provide another marketplace where investor sentiment about the future behavior of prices is expressed. This is a potentially important feature as option prices may allow us to learn more about the determinants of currency and interest rate behavior.

As we will see, the essential characteristic of an option contract is its *asymmetric* payoff profile; that is, if the price of an underlying asset moves in one direction ("up" for a call and "down" for a put), the price of an option on that asset will generally rise. However, if the price of the underlying asset moves in the opposite direction, option prices will generally fall, but the option price cannot fall below zero. Thus, the owner of an option can participate in upside gains, but losses are limited to the amount of the initial option purchase price. By comparison, recall that a futures contract displays a *symmetric* payoff profile so that both upside gains and downside losses are virtually unlimited.

This chapter is about option contracts, and we will see that there are many varieties of them. In addition, many financial products are now available that embody optionlike features. Some of these products, such as **rights** or **warrants,** are really options under another name. Other products—such as an interest rate **cap,** which puts a ceiling or upper limit on a price that can be paid; a **floor,** which puts a lower limit on a price that can be paid; or a **collar,** which combines a cap and a floor—are simply more conventional or descriptive names for optionlike features that an investor or borrower might wish to have for hedging or speculative purposes. Other products may contain **embedded options** that add or subtract from the value of an otherwise conventional asset. A *callable bond* often bears a lower price (higher return) than a *noncallable bond* because the issuer retains the right to retire the bond if interest rates fall beyond some point. A **dual-currency bond** often bears a higher price (lower return) than a typical single-currency bond because the owner has purchased the right to have the bond repaid in the second currency if the second currency strengthens.[1]

Some business arrangements might be referred to as **implicit options,** because the optionlike feature is not mentioned explicitly. For example, a seller's price list grants a customer the right to buy items on the list at specified prices for a specified period of time. A seller whose price list is marked "Prices valid until December 31" has given customers an option, while a seller whose price list is marked "Prices subject to change without notice" has not. An issuer of a bond or taker of a mortgage holds the right to default. This may not be stated in the financial contract. But borrowers may avail themselves of the bankruptcy laws in order to obtain a better resolution of debts, rather than exhausting all of their present resources and forgoing the chance for future revenues in an effort to meet all of the terms of their original contract.

An option contract is another example of a **redundant security,** that is, a financial instrument whose cash payoffs may be replicated by a set of basic transactions in more traditional financial claims.[2] Demonstrating that a common option contract is equivalent

---

[1]A dual-currency bond is similar to a convertible bond that converts into equity shares if the performance of the underlying shares is strong.

[2]Recall the discussion in Chapter 3. We argued that forward contracts were redundant because their cash flows could be perfectly replicated using spot contracts plus borrowing and lending.

to a **replicating portfolio** of other financial claims is a neat theoretical device, but one that also has powerful practical applications. First, the replicating portfolio provides a technique for pricing an option contract. In a perfect capital market, an option contract would attain the same price as the set of contracts that can replicate it. Second, the replicating portfolio provides a technique for hedging the risk in an option contract. A long (or short) position in an option can be hedged by selling (or buying) a **synthetic option** built from the set of transactions making up the replicating portfolio.

An option contract is yet another example of a derivative security. In other words, the value of an option is "derived from" the value and the anticipated behavior of an underlying asset. As in any derivative market, contracts have **zero-net supply;** for every buyer of a contract, there must be a seller. The profit (or loss) that the buyer of a call earns, is exactly equal to the loss (or profit) that the seller of the call earns. Like the futures market, the options market as a whole is a **zero-sum game** before we take transaction costs into account. Despite being redundant and in zero-net supply, options add value by allowing private agents to hedge against or to hold particular risks, and to do so at lower transaction costs. Public policymakers must consider whether option trading leads to any negative externalities, such as greater currency volatility or wider bid/ask spreads.

In the remainder of this chapter, we first describe the basic terminology and nomenclature used in the market and the institutions that organize trading in option contracts. We introduce graphs that portray the value of option contracts at maturity and the payoff profiles to buyers and sellers of options. We review prices of options as posted in the newspaper in order to understand market mechanics and the relationship between options with differing characteristics prior to maturity. We then discuss formal mathematical models for pricing options on spot currency and options on interest rate and currency futures contracts. As we will see, these models are derived from a strict set of assumptions about currency and interest rate behavior. Empirical evidence on pricing efficiency in the currency options market is presented that shows, in part, that a popular currency option pricing model underprices deep out-of-the-money options, especially when a currency is expected to move sharply. As in other chapters, we conclude by reviewing various policy issues that affect private market participants and public policymakers. In particular, we discuss the shortcomings of formal models as a guide to option pricing and the impact of option trading on currency price volatility.

First Principles: Terminology and Institutions

Before delving into any of the substantive issues involving option contracts, it is important to lay out the essential terminology and institutional practices. With options, there appears to be a great deal of terminology, which in part reflects the profusion of option contracts and markets that have developed over the short life of the market.

Types of Contracts

To begin, the standard definition of a conventional option is:

> The right, but not the obligation, to buy (or to sell) a fixed quantity of an underlying financial asset or commodity at a given price on (or before) a specified date.

From this definition, we can see the need to provide a few more details. On the one hand:

> A **call option** bestows on the owner the right, but not the obligation, to buy the underlying financial asset or commodity.

On the other hand:

> A **put option** conveys to the owner the right, but not the obligation, to sell the underlying financial asset or commodity.

The option definition also specifies when the option can be exercised. Again, there are two generic types, a European option and an American option:

> A **European option** can be exercised once only at the maturity date.

> An **American option** can be exercised at any time on or before the maturity date of the option.

Thus, we can have a European call and an American call as well as a European put and an American put.

The basic definition also refers to an underlying financial asset or commodity. With currency options, there are two choices. An **option on spot** takes spot foreign exchange as the underlying asset. If such an option is exercised, spot foreign exchange is transferred. Alternatively, there are also **options on futures.** If such an option is exercised, positions in the underlying currency futures contract are created: a long position (at the strike price) for the holder of a call or seller of a put, and a short position (at the strike price) for the holder of a put or seller of a call.[3] With interest rate options, the underlying contract is typically an interest rate futures. The interest rate futures could be on a three-month Eurodollar deposit, a long-term Treasury bond, or any of a myriad of other interest-bearing instruments. Again, when an interest rate futures option is exercised, appropriate long or short positions in the underlying futures contracts are established.

Only a bit more terminology is needed to get us started. The given price specified in the contract is called the **strike price** or the **exercise price.** The maturity date specified in the option is sometimes called the **expiration date.** The price paid for the option is usually called the **option premium.**

A complete description on an American call option on spot € might read:

> Example 1:   The right to buy € 1 million for $1.10 per € from today until expiration on December 15, 2001.

while a description of a European put option on Swiss franc futures would read:

> Example 2:   The right to sell SFr 10 million March 2002 futures for $0.65 per SFr on (and only on) March 15, 2002.

Notice that both of the above hypothetical options on foreign currency used the US$ as the second currency or numeraire currency. From these examples, you should be able to convince yourself that:

> In Example 1:   A "call on €" is identical to a "put on US$."
> In Example 2:   A "put on SFr" is identical to a "call on US$."

In other words, someone who holds the right to "buy €" appears similar to someone who has the right to "sell US$" when the strike price is given in US$/€. In the same fashion, someone who holds the right to "sell SFr" appears similar to someone who has the right to "buy US$" when the strike price is given in US$/SFr. This equivalence will be very

---

[3]To clarify this, recall that the owner of a futures call has the right to buy a futures, so the seller of a futures call must deliver a long position if the call is exercised (i.e., the seller takes a short position). The owner of a put has the right to sell a futures, so the seller of a futures put must deliver a short position (i.e., the seller takes a long position). Because futures contracts have zero-net supply, the underlying positions must be "created" before they can be delivered.

FIGURE 12.1   Top 10 Options Exchanges in 1998 and 1999

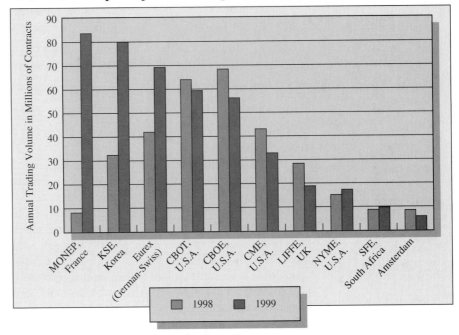

Sources: Galen Burghardt, "Equities Saved the Year," *Futures Institute Magazine,* Feb. 2000; and author calculations.

useful when the reader uses computer software for determining the prices of currency options.

With the rise of significant trading volume in **cross-exchange rates**—notably the £/¥, DM/¥, DM/£, and DM against other European currency rates—options written in currency pairs that do not involve the US$ have been introduced. These **cross-rate options** gained further popularity after 1991 as exchange rate volatility among European currencies increased.[4] Of course, cross-rate options for the DM against other European currencies vanished in 1999 with the introduction of the euro and EMU. Cross-rate options on the €/¥, €/£, and other pairs began trading in 1999. Cross-rate options possess the same characteristics as conventional US$-denominated currency options; only the numeraire of the underlying asset is different.

Location and Scale of Trading

In 1999, options were traded on at least 47 different exchanges around the world. Only 8 exchanges listed currency options, and 22 exchanges listed interest rate options.[5] Organized exchanges represent a small part of the global market for options on currencies, but they are the dominant venue for interest rate options. Figure 12.1 shows the top 10 option exchanges in 1999 (ranked by number of contracts traded) and their trading volume in 1998. In 1998, three U.S. exchanges (the Chicago Board of Trade, the Chicago Mercantile Exchange, and the Chicago Board Options Exchange) occupied the

---

[4]For more on this issue, see Campa and Chang (1996) and Malz (1996).
[5]*Futures Industry Institute Factbook,* at <www.fiiweb.org/factbook>.

TABLE 12.1   Top Option Contracts Worldwide, 1999

	Rank[a]	Contract	Exchange	Volume (millions)
Top 10 contracts	1	KOSPI 200	KSE	79.9
	2	French CAC 40	MONEP	75.6
	3	US T-bond	CBOT	34.7
	4	German DAX	EUREX	32.6
	5	S&P 100	CME	25.6
	6	Euro-BUND	EUREX	24.9
	7	Eurodollar	CME	24.9
	8	S&P 500	CME	23.3
	9	10-yr T-note	CBOT	9.7
	10	South Africa All Share Index	SAFEX	8.5
Next 5 interest rate contracts	13	3-mo sterling	LIFFE	6.5
	18	3-mo EURIBOR	LIFFE	4.8
	27	5-yr T-note	CBOT	2.5
	30	German BUND[b]	LIFFE	1.8
	31	Euro-BOBL	EUREX	1.8
Top 5 currency contracts	42	US$/¥	CME	1.1
	50	Flexible currency options	BM&F	0.8
	58	US$/R$	BM&F	0.7
	64	Customized currency options	PHLX	0.5
	92	US$/£	CME	0.2

[a]Rank among all traded option contracts, excluding individual equities.
[b]Contract discontinued during 1999.

Notes: Currency symbols: R$—Brazilian reals.
  Futures exchanges: BM&F—Bolsa de Mercadorias & Futuros (Brazil); CBOT—Chicago Board of Trade; CME—Chicago Mercantile Exchange; EUREX—exchange named for merger of former German DTB and Swiss SOFEX exchanges; KSE—Korea Stock Exchange; LIFFE—London International Financial Futures and Options Exchange; MONEP—Monetary Exchange of Paris; PHLX—Philadelphia Stock Exchange; SAFEX—South Africa Futures Exchange.

Sources: *Futures Industry Institute Factbook,* at <www.fiiweb.org/factbook>; and various futures exchange websites.

top three positions. In 1999, these U.S. exchanges were overtaken by three non-U.S. competitors—MONEP (Paris), Korea Stock Exchange, and EUREX (German-Swiss). The volume on MONEP and KSE is dominated by highly successful stock index option contracts. EUREX has grown thanks to several new interest rate contracts on the Euro that effectively replace the interest rate contracts on many of the 12 legacy interest rates.

Table 12.1 lists the most heavily traded option contracts in 1999. There are 4 interest rate options (the U.S. T-bond, Euro-BUND, Eurodollar, and 10-year U.S. T-note) on the top 10. Other interest rate futures options such as the three-month sterling contract and the Euro-BOBL rank further down the list. The US$/¥ futures option on the CME is the most active currency option, but its trading volume is light compared to the most active interest rate options.

Currency Options.   Currency options are traded over-the-counter by banks and on organized futures and options exchanges. Surveys conducted by the Bank for International Settlements (BIS, 1996, 1999) show that the volume of currency option trading among banks reached $87.1 billion per day in April 1998, more than double the $41 billion per day traded in April 1995. In comparison, currency option trading on organized

FIGURE 12.2   Volume of Currency Options Traded on Organized Exchanges

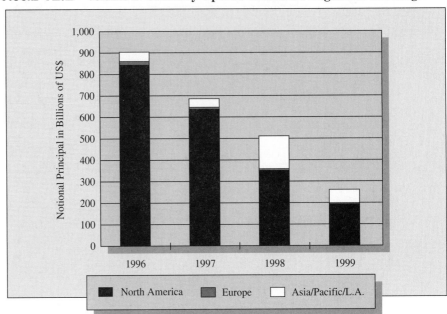

Source: Bank for International Settlements, *International Banking and Financial Market Developments,* various issues.

exchanges was only $1.8 billion per day in the first quarter of 1998, down from about $3.75 billion per day in 1995.

The recent decline in annual turnover on currency option exchanges is shown in Figure 12.2. Indeed, turnover was even greater earlier in the 1990s. The great majority of currency option turnover is on North American exchanges, specifically the CME and PHLX exchanges.

Another vehicle for trading in currency options is through the use of listed rights or warrants issues. These rights or warrants are issued by private companies, sold to individual investors, and often listed for trading on a stock exchange. A tombstone for a foreign exchange warrant issued by Citicorp is shown in Figure 12.3. These warrants are custom products that are launched when underwriters sense that market demand for a product with special features is high. The warrant illustrated in Figure 12.3 was for an option with a five-year maturity, which lets us examine how the market prices options for this unusually long horizon.

Interest Rate Options.   Like currency options, interest rate options are traded over the counter by banks and on organized futures and options exchanges. BIS surveys (BIS, 1996, 1999) show that the OTC trading in interest rate options has grown from $28.0 billion per day in April 1995 to $45.9 billion per day in April 1999. Trading on organized exchanges, however, accounts for more than 80 percent of the turnover, rising from $128.4 billion per day in 1995 to $193.1 billion per day in 1998. The recent growth of trading on organized exchanges is shown Figure 12.4. The majority of interest rate option turnover is on North American exchanges; European exchanges, however, account for 25 to 30 percent of the market. Referring back to Table 12.1, we see that options on the U.S. T-bond and the Euro-BUND are the most actively traded interest rate

FIGURE 12.3   Example of a Foreign Exchange Warrant Issued by Citicorp
on June 26, 1987

Source: Citicorp.

contracts. However, these contracts reflect only $100,000 and €100,000, respectively, of
the underlying asset. The Eurodollar futures option reflects an underlying position of
$1 million, which makes it the most active interest rate contract in value terms.

Contract Specifications

The organized exchanges have standard contract specifications and market conventions,
while contract attributes are often customized in the over-the-counter market. Reviewing the practices on the organized exchanges is a useful means of understanding the various features of an option contract that must be specified in order to determine an
option's price and its trading behavior.

Currency Options.   Some essential characteristics of currency option contracts on the
CME and PHLX are summarized in Table 12.2. A contract on the CME represents twice
as many currency units as a PHLX contract. Designing contract sizes in this fashion
makes them more attractive to market participants by facilitating arbitrage between the

FIGURE 12.4   Volume of Interest Rate Options Traded on Organized Exchanges

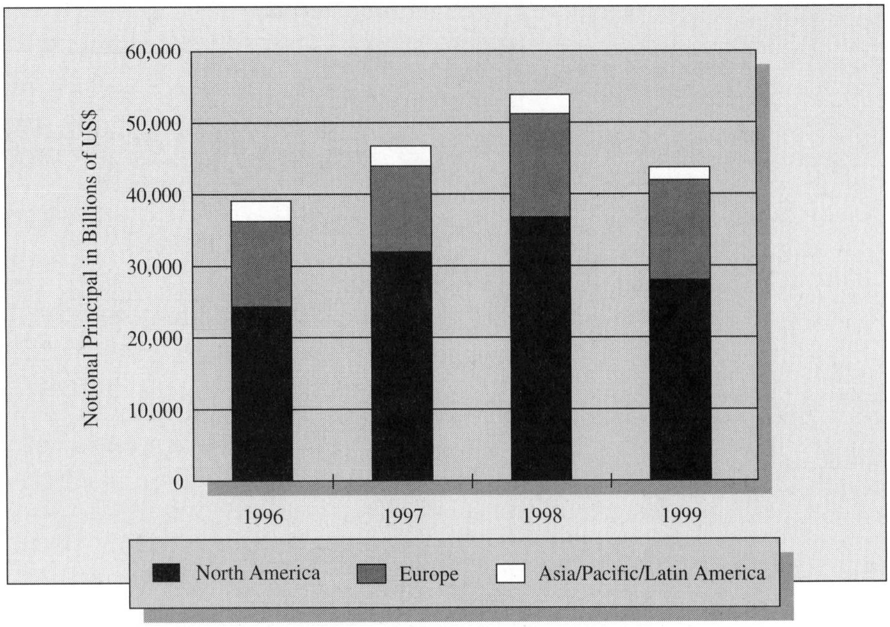

Source: Bank for International Settlements, *International Banking and Financial Market Developments,* various issues.

TABLE 12.2   Contract Specifications for Selected Currency Option Contracts

Market	Currency	Underlying Asset	Contract Size	Strike Price Interval	Minimum Price Change	Value of One Point
CME	€	€ futures	€ 125,000	$0.01	$0.01	$12.50
	¥	¥ futures	¥ 12,500,000	$0.0001	$0.0001	$12.50
	C$	C$ futures	C$ 100,000	$0.005	$0.01	$10.00
	£	£ futures	£ 62,500	$0.02	$0.02	$ 6.25
PHLX	€	€ spot	€ 62,500	$0.02	$0.01	$ 6.25
	¥	¥ spot	¥ 6,250,000	$0.05	$0.0001	$ 6.25
	C$	C$ spot	C$ 50,000	$0.005	$0.01	$ 5.00
	£	£ spot	£ 31,250	$0.01	$0.01	$ 3.125

Notes:

1. All CME options are American options. PHLX trades both American and European options.

2. All CME options have maturity dates of March, June, September, and December plus the two additional near-term months. The expiration date of these options is the Saturday before the third Wednesday of the month, so the preceding Friday is the last trading day. Settlement day is the third Wednesday of the month.

3. Conventional PHLX options have the same maturity dates and expiration dates as CME options. In addition, PHLX trades "end-of-month" currency options that expire on the last Friday of the three nearest months, and "long-term" currency options that expire in June and December with maturities up to 24 months from the date of issue.

4. Currency options are *not* subject to daily price limit movements.

5. The permitted strike price interval may vary depending on option maturity.

Source: Chicago Mercantile Exchange (1987) and Philadelphia Stock Exchange (1994) and updates from these exchanges' websites at <www.cme.com> and <www.phlx.com>.

two markets. In addition, contract sizes have been set so that an even multiple of contracts results in 1 million units of the underlying currency—32 contracts in the case of PHLX £ contracts, 16 contracts for PHLX € contracts, 8 contracts for CME € contracts, and so forth.

The strike price interval is set so that as the currency price changes over time, new option contracts are opened up to begin trading.[6] The value associated with the minimum price movement is determined by multiplying the contract size by the minimum price movement.

All options contracts traded on the CME or the PHLX are in fact issued by the Options Clearing Corporation (OCC), and bear their guarantee of performance.[7] The owner of an option does not need to perform an individualized credit analysis of each counterparty in an option transaction that takes place on these organized exchanges. The counterparty in every case is the OCC. If owners of a call option choose to exercise their option, the exchange clearinghouse will randomly select option sellers (writers) who will provide a position in the underlying asset; that is, they will provide spot currency in the case of a PHLX option, or they will take a short futures position (assigned at the strike price) for a CME option on futures. The OCC is obligated to meet this contractual commitment to option holders if any private counterparties default.

To gain familiarity with these contract specifications, we present tables with actual option prices from Tuesday, June 20, 2000, as reported in the newspaper.[8] Prices on PHLX options on spot currency are shown in Table 12.3a.

Consider the August 2000 €/$ call option with a strike price of $0.96. The closing, or settlement, price of the option was reported as 1.89 cents or $0.0189 *per unit,* which in this case means *per* €. Since the contract size is €62,500, the buyer of this call option would expect to pay 62,500 × $0.0189 = $1,181.25 plus commission charges. The September 2000 €/$ put option with a strike price of $0.94 would have an analogous interpretation. The reported settlement price of this option was 1.26 cents or $0.0126 per unit. The buyer of this put option would expect to pay 62,500 × $0.0126 = $787.50, plus commission charges.

Table 12.3b reports prices on CME options on currency futures.[9] The structure of the table is somewhat similar to the PHLX table giving the contract size and strike price reported for each currency. For the Japanese yen, we see that the price of a September 2000 ¥/$ call option with a strike price of 9600 (meaning $0.0096 per yen) is 2.41 cents, or $0.0241 per 100 yen. The cost of purchasing this option would be 12,500,000 × $0.0241 ÷ 100 = $3,012.50, plus commissions. The August 2000 ¥/$ put option with a strike price of 9800 (meaning $0.0098 per yen) is 2.61 cents, or $0.0261 per 100 yen. The cost of purchasing this option would be 12,500,000 × $0.0261 ÷ 100 = $3,262.50, plus commissions.

Note that both Tables 12.3a and 12.3b report the daily trading volume and open interest over all strike prices for each currency option.

---

[6]When a new contract month is listed initially, the rules of the CME require that nine strike prices be established for both puts and calls. The central strike price is the one nearest to the underlying futures price, with four strike prices higher and four lower. "Using Currency Futures and Options," Chicago Mercantile Exchange (1987), p. 21.

[7]The OCC holds an AAA credit rating from Standard & Poor's. See *Creditweek,* Standard & Poor's Corporation, Feb. 1, 1993 or the OCC website at <www.optionsclearing.com>.

[8]Only the nearest-term option prices are reported in the newspaper, and not all strike prices are reported. Recall that longer-term options are available, but these also tend to be more thinly traded.

[9]Again, only the near-term option prices are reported, and only some strike prices.

TABLE 12.3A   Recent Prices of PHLX Spot Currency Options: June 20, 2000

■ **PHILADELPHIA SE £/$ OPTIONS** £31,250 (cents per pound)

Strike Price	CALLS Jul	CALLS Aug	CALLS Sep	PUTS Jul	PUTS Aug	PUTS Sep
1.500	2.24	2.87	3.39	0.87	1.50	2.04
1.510	1.62	2.32	2.95	1.33	1.94	2.49
1.520	1.17	1.83	2.38	1.86	2.45	2.99

Previous day's vol., Calls 6 Puts 82 Prev. day's open int., Calls 1.814Puts 922

■ **PHILADELPHIA SE EURO/$ OPTIONS** €62,500 (cents per €)

Strike Price	CALLS Jul	CALLS Aug	CALLS Sep	PUTS Jul	PUTS Aug	PUTS Sep
0.940	2.44	3.04	3.62	0.46	0.86	1.26
0.960	1.23	1.89	2.49	1.19	1.67	2.07
0.980	0.53	1.15	1.62	2.38	2.78	3.19

Previous day's vol., Calls 265Puts 28. Prev. day's open int., Calls 4.111Puts 888

Source: *Financial Times,* June 21, 2000.

Interest Rate Options.   As a group, interest rate options are far more diverse than currency options. As we noted earlier, interest rate options are traded in more countries and on more exchanges than currency options. Added to this, each market tends to offer a variety of interest rate options—short-term (three-month) instruments, medium-term instruments (2–5 years to maturity), and long-term securities (10 years and more). Some interest rate options pertain to private sector instruments (such as Eurocurrency deposits, bankers acceptances, and mortgage securities) while many others take government notes or bonds as the underlying security. Because of this diversity, we will provide only a brief description of selected interest rate option contracts. We will focus on Eurocurrency interest rate options and government bond interest rate options because these are most likely to be germane for international investors and financial managers.

A sample of contract specifications for selected interest rate options is presented in Table 12.4. The underlying asset for each option is an interest rate futures contract traded on the same exchange as the option. The upper part of the table shows short-term interest rate options, four that take the interest rate on various three-month Eurocurrency deposits as the underlying asset and one that takes a three-month domestic interest rate as the underlying asset. For these particular financial instruments, interest rates are quoted as "add-on" rates. As we saw in Chapter 11, the market has adopted the convention that:

$$\frac{\text{Eurocurrency interest rate}}{\text{futures price}} = 100.00 - \text{Eurocurrency interest rate}$$

So, a strike price of 95.25 implies an interest rate of 4.75 percent. At the CME, strike prices are set every 0.50 percent for interest rates above 9.00 percent, and every 0.25 percent for interest rates below 9.00 percent. Eurocurrency interest rates are quoted to the nearest basis point (or 1/100 of 1 percent). The value of one basis point for each of these short-term options is determined by a general formula: contract size $\times$ 0.0001 $\times$ number of months/12. For the Eurodollar option contract, this results in $1,000,000 $\times$ 0.0001 $\times$ 3/12 = $25.

A sample of actual option prices from June 20, 2000, is shown in Table 12.5. The panel labeled EURODOLLAR (CME) reports the closing settlement prices for the op-

TABLE 12.3B   Recent Prices of CME Options on Currency Futures:
June 20, 2000

CURRENCY

JAPANESE YEN (CME)
12,500,000 yen; cents per 100 yen

Strike	Calls-Settle			Puts-Settle		
Price	Jly	Aug	Sep	Jly	Aug	Sep
9550	1.49	....	2.67	0.57	....	1.76
9600	1.20	1.86	2.41	2.41	1.44	2.00
9650	0.95	1.61	....	....	....	....
9700	0.75	1.39	1.96	1.96	....	2.53
9750	0.59	....	....	....	....	....
9800	0.46	1.04	1.58	1.58	2.61	3.14

Est vol 1,424 Mn 372 calls 150 puts
Op int Mon 22,761 calls 22,558 puts

EURO FX (CME)
125,000 euro; cents per euro

Strike	Calls-Settle			Puts-Settle		
Price	Jly	Aug	Sep	Jly	Aug	Sep
940	25.30	....	35.30	2.10	....	12.30
950	17.80	....	29.10	4.50	7.50	16.00
960	11.30	....	23.30	8.00	10.80	20.00
970	6.90	13.50	18.90	13.60	....	25.50
980	4.20	9.90	15.00	20.80	....	31.50

Est vol 287 calls 482 puts
Op int 9,927 calls 3,663 puts

CANADIAN DOLLAR (CME)
100,000 Can.$, cents per Can.$

Strike	Calls-Settle			Puts-Settle		
Price	Jly	Aug	Sep	Jly	Aug	Sep
6700	1.17	....	1.38	0.05	0.16	0.27
6750	0.74	....	1.03	0.12	0.28	0.42
6800	0.39	....	0.73	0.27	....	0.61
6850	....	....	0.50	....	0.73	0.87
6900	0.08	0.21	0.33	....	....	1.20
6950	0.06	....	0.21	....	....	....

Est vol 69 Mn 79 calls 38 puts
Op int Mon 1,775 calls 1,990 puts

BRITISH POUND (CME)
62,500 pounds; cents per pound

Strike	Calls-Settle			Puts-Settle		
Price	Jly	Aug	Sep	Jly	Aug	Sep
1500	2.54	....	3.80	0.40	....	1.68
1510	1.82	2.54	3.18	0.68	1.40	2.06
1520	1.24	1.98	2.66	1.10	....	2.52
1530	0.80	1.54	....	1.66	....	....
1540	0.50	1.20	1.82	2.36	....	3.66
1550	0.30	0.90	1.48	....	3.04	....

Est vol 249 Mn 228 calls 76 puts
Op int Mon 8,090 calls 6,499 puts

SWISS FRANC (CME)
125,000 francs; cents per franc

Strike	Calls-Settle			Puts-Settle		
Price	Jly	Aug	Sep	Jly	Aug	Sep
6100	1.36	....	2.00	0.24	....	0.90
6150	1.01	....	....	0.39	....	....
6200	0.73	....	1.46	0.60	....	1.34
6250	0.50	....	1.25	....	....	....
6300	0.34	0.72	1.05	....	....	....
6350	0.22	....	0.88	....	....	....

Est vol 80 Mn 48 calls 38 puts
Op int Mon 4,324 calls 1,370 puts

Source: *The Wall Street Journal,* June 21, 2000, and the Chicago Mercantile Exchange website at <www.cme.com>.

tion on a three-month Eurodollar futures contract. The left-hand column lists the various strike prices, from 9275 (representing 7.25 percent) to 9400 (representing 6.00 percent).[10] The remainder of the table shows the prices of calls and puts maturing in July, August, and September 2000. Consider the August call option with a strike price of 9300. The closing or settlement price of the option was reported as 0.125, or 12.5 basis

---

[10]Again, only the near-term option prices are reported, and only some strike prices.

TABLE 12.4 Contract Specifications for Selected Interest Rate Futures Option Contracts

Contract	Market	Underlying Asset: Interest Rate Futures on	Contract Size	Minimum Price Change	Value of One Point
Euro-$	CME	3-month Euro $	$1,000,000	$0.01	$25.00
Euribor	LIFFE	3-month Euribor	€1,000,000	€0.01	€25.00
Euro-SFr	LIFFE	3-month Euro SFr	SFr 1,000,000	SFr 0.01	SFr 25.00
Euro-¥	TIFFE	3-month Euro ¥	¥100,000,000	¥0.01	¥2,500
Short sterling	LIFFE	3-month London £	£500,000	£0.01	£12.50
US T-bond	CBOT	US Treasury bonds	$100,000	$1/64	$15.625
Long gilt	LIFFE	UK govt. bond	£100,000	£0.01	£10.00
Euro-BUND	EUREX	German govt. bond, 8.5–10.5 yrs.	€100,000	€0.01	€10.00
Euro-BOBL	EUREX	German govt. bond, 3.5–5.0 yrs.	€100,000	€0.01	€10.00

Notes:

1. All options are American style.

2. Expiration dates are March, June, September, and December in all cases with lead months.

Source: *Futures Industry Institute Factbook.*

points. Since each basis point for this contract is worth $25, the buyer of this call option would expect to pay $12.5 \times \$25 = \$312.50$, plus commission charges.

Looking back at Table 12.4 we see several options where the underlying asset is a futures on a long-term interest rate. Each interest-rate future is a contract on a **notional government bond**—a hypothetical bond with a defined coupon yield. These futures contracts have been designed such that the **notional yield** is 6 percent for the U.S. bond, 7 percent for the U.K. bond, and 6 percent for the German bond. This system, as we discussed in Chapter 11, allows the owner of a futures contract to deliver any one of several government bonds within a designated set of acceptable bonds, each one bearing a conversion factor.

For U.S. bonds, the pricing convention uses quotes in 32nds (of 1 percent) for futures but quotes in 64ths (of 1 percent) for options. So the value of one point for U.S. T-bond options is given by the formula $\$100,000 \times 0.01 \times 1/64 = \$15.625$. For U.K. government bonds (known in the market as *gilts*), and German government bonds (known in the market as *bunds*), the pricing convention uses quotes to the nearest basis point. So the value of one point for U.K. and German bonds is simply the contract size $\times 0.0001$.

Actual option prices from June 20, 2000, for U.S. T-bonds and German Eurobunds are shown in Table 12.5. The panels labeled T-BONDS (CBT) and 10 YR. GERMAN EURO GOV'T BD (EUROBUND) (EUREX) report the closing settlement prices for these two options on futures contracts. The left-hand column lists various strike prices, from 95 to 100 for the U.S. T-bond and from 105.00 to 107.50 for the German Eurobund. Recall from Chapter 11 that the T-bond futures contract is for a notional 6 percent bond with at least 15 years remaining until maturity, while the German Eurobund futures contract is for a notional 6 percent bond with 8.5–10.5 years remaining until maturity. Thus, strike prices greater than 100 imply a higher yield than the notional bond, while strike prices greater than 100 imply a lower yield than the notional bond.

The other columns in the table show the prices of calls and puts for several maturities. Consider the September call option on U.S. T-bond futures with a strike price of 98. The closing or settlement price of the option was reported as 1-10, or $1^{10}\!/_{64}$ *percentage*

TABLE 12.5 Recent Prices of Selected Interest Rate Futures Options: June 20, 2000

Short-Term Interest Rates   *Long-Term Interest Rates*

■ SHORT STERLING OPTIONS (LIFFE) £500,000 100-rate

Strike Price	CALLS			PUTS		
	Jun	Sep	Dec	Jun	Sep	Dec
93750	0.050	0.065	0.105	0	0.135	0.295
93875	0	0.030		0.075	0.225	
94000	0	0.010	0.040	0.200	0.330	0.480
94125	0	0.005		0.325	0.450	
94250	0	0	0.015	0.450	0.570	0.705
94375	0	0		0.575	0.695	

Est. vol. total, Calls 1635 Puts 5884. Previous day's open int., Calls 401660 Puts 358859

EURODOLLAR (CME)
$ million; pts. of 100%

Strike Price	Calls-Settle			Puts-Settle		
	Jly	Aug	Sep	Jly	Aug	Sep
9275	0.305	0.315	0.320	0.005	0.015	0.025
9300	0.100	0.125	0.145	0.050	0.075	0.095
9325	0.010	0.020	0.035	0.210	0.220	0.235
9350	....	0.007	0.010	....	....	0.455
9375	....	....	0.005	....	....	0.700
9400	....	....	0.002	....	....	0.950

Est vol 67,149;
Mn vol 40,805 calls 24,941 puts
Op int Mon 936,322 calls 849,761 puts

T-BONDS (CBT)
$100,000; points and 64ths of 100%

Strike Price	Calls-Settle			Puts-Settle		
	Jly	Aug	Sep	Jly	Aug	Sep
95	2-21	2-39	....	0-01	0-20	....
96	1-22	1-54	2-14	0-02	0-35	0-59
97	0-33	1-14	....	0-13	0-58	....
98	0-07	0-47	1-10	0-51	1-27	1-53
99	0-01	0-27	....	1-45	2-06	....
100	0-01	0-14	0-32	2-44	....	3-10

Est vol 55,000;
Mn vol 19,000 calls 12,283 puts
Op int Mon 222,012 calls 273,028 puts

T-NOTES (CBT)
$100,000; points and 64ths of 100%

Strike Price	Calls-Settle			Puts-Settle		
	Jly	Aug	Sep	Jly	Aug	Sep
96	2-24	2-30	2-40	0-01	0-07	0-17
97	1-25	....	1-53	0-01	0-15	0-30
98	0-30	0-58	1-12	0-06	0-34	0-52
99	0-03	0-28	0-45	0-43	1-04	1-21
100	0-01	0-11	0-24	....	....	1-63
101	....	0-04	0-12	....	....	2-51

Est vol 40,000 Mn 15,835 calls 5,181 puts
Op int Mon 249,967 calls 206,777 puts

5 YR TREAS NOTES (CBT)
$100,000; points and 64ths of 100%

Strike Price	Calls-Settle			Puts-Settle		
	Jly	Aug	Sep	Jly	Aug	Sep
9800	0-52	....	1-07	0-01	0-12	0-21
9850	0-23	0-40	0-50	0-04	0-21	0-31
9900	0-04	....	0-34	0-17	0-36	0-47
9950	0-01	0-12	0-22	....	....	1-03
10000	0-01	....	0-13	....	..	1-26
10050	....	....	0-08	....	..	....

Est vol 4,600 Mn 1,789 calls 3,364 puts
Op int Mon 77,554 calls 105,127 puts

10 YR. GERMAN EURO GOV'T BD
(EUROBUND) (EUREX)
100,000;pts. In 100%

Strike Price	Calls-Settle			Puts-Settle		
	Jly	Aug	Sep	Jly	Aug	Sep
10500	1.12	1.39	1.61	0.01	0.27	0.49
10550	0.66	1.02	1.28	0.04	0.40	0.66
10600	0.29	0.73	0.98	0.17	0.61	0.86
10650	0.08	0.49	0.73	0.46	0.87	1.11
10700	0.01	0.32	0.53	0.89	1.20	1.41
10750	0.01	0.19	0.37	1.38	1.57	1.75

Vol Tu 74,785 calls 55,003 puts
Op int Mon 620,467 calls 528,289 puts

Sources: *Financial Times,* June 21, 2000, for short sterling option prices; *The Wall Street Journal,* June 21, 2000, for all other prices.

points. Since each $\frac{1}{64}$ point for this contract is worth $15.625, the buyer of this call option would expect to pay 74 × $15.625 = $1,156.25, plus commission charges. The price of the August put option on German Eurobund futures with a strike price of 107.50 closed at 1.57, or 157 basis points. The buyer of this put option would expect to pay 157 × €10.00 = €1,570.00, plus commission charges.

Option Pricing: An Introduction

The distinctive characteristic of an option contract is its asymmetric payoff profile. We will examine this property first with currency options and then with interest rate options.

Spot Currency Options: Prices at Maturity

Consider the following hypothetical call and put options on the British pound. Each option has a strike price (K) of $1.50/£ and an option premium of about $0.10.[11] If we designate C and P as the values of the call and put prices, then at maturity:

$$C = \text{Max } [0, S - K] \tag{12.1a}$$

and

$$P = \text{Max } [0, K - S] \tag{12.1b}$$

where S is the spot price of the pound at the maturity of the option.[12] It is clear from equations (12.1a) and (12.1b) that the value of an option at maturity can never be negative.

A graph of the profit profile for this hypothetical call option on the British pound is shown in Figure 12.5a. For spot prices less than or equal to $1.50, the expiration value of the call is zero. The buyer of the hypothetical call suffers a loss equal to the $0.10 premium he or she originally paid for the option. At spot prices greater than $1.50, the expiration value of the option is positive (equal to $S - $1.50), which reduces the call buyer's losses. The break-even exchange rate is $1.60, and at exchange rates greater than $1.60, the call buyer earns a profit. The seller of our hypothetical call has a "mirror image" profit profile. The seller keeps the option premium when the spot rate is less than or equal to $1.50, because the call is not exercised. At spot rates greater than $1.50, the seller's profits are reduced because he or she must deliver pounds at $1.50 even though they could be sold for more in the market.

A graph of the profit profile for our hypothetical put option is shown in Figure 12.5b. For spot prices greater than or equal to $1.50, the expiration value of the put is zero. The buyer of the hypothetical put suffers a loss equal to the option's $0.10 original purchase price. At spot prices less than $1.50, the expiration value of the put is positive (equal to $1.50 - S) which reduces the put buyer's losses. The break-even exchange rate is $1.40; at exchange rates less than $1.40, the put buyer earns a profit. The seller of this hypothetical put has a mirror-image profit profile. The seller earns the option premium when the spot rate is greater than or equal to $1.50, because the put is not exercised. At spot rates less than $1.50, the seller incurs losses because he or she must purchase pounds at $1.50 even though pounds could be bought for less in the market.

Note that the combination of buying a call and selling a call (see Figure 12.5a) produces a horizontal profit line at zero (without taking transaction costs or commissions into account). Similarly, the combination of buying a put and selling a put (in Figure 12.5b) also produces a horizontal profit line at zero. This is a trivial result, but shows again that we can add together (vertically) the profits from two option positions similar to how we treated futures positions.

Note also that the buyer of either a put or call faces limited liability in that his or her loss is capped at the initial option premium paid. The seller of a call faces unlimited liability as the underlying asset could appreciate without limit. The seller of a put faces a

---

[11]The price is determined by the Garman-Kohlhagen model with US$ and UK£ interest rates at 5.0 percent, time to maturity of 360 days, and volatility of 17.65 percent.

[12]Notice that the value of these *conventional options* (as we will label them) at maturity depends only on S at maturity and K, and *not* on the path by which S was established. In contrast, some options allow the owner to buy (sell) at the average price over a period, or at the highest (lowest) price over a period. These *exotic* or *path-dependent* options are discussed in Appendix 12.3.

FIGURE 12.5A   Buyer and Seller of a Spot Currency Call on £ with Strike at $1.50/£

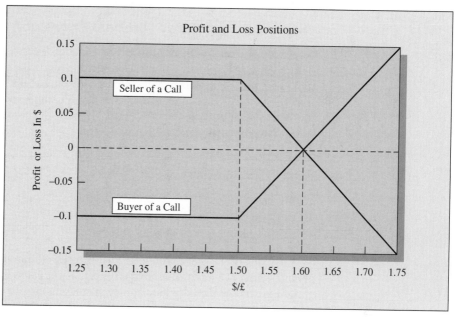

FIGURE 12.5B   Buyer and Seller of a Spot Currency Put on £ with Strike at $1.50/£

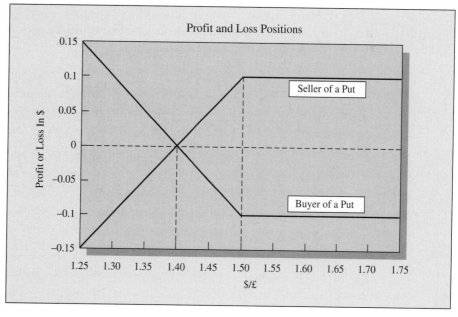

large liability, which is limited by the fact that the price of the underlying cannot fall below zero.[13]

Interest Rate Futures Options: Prices at Maturity

The profit profiles for interest rate option contracts are broadly similar to what we have just outlined for currency options. Consider the following hypothetical call and put options on a Eurodollar interest rate futures contract. Let the strike price (K) for each option be 9600 (corresponding to a 4.00 percent Eurodollar interest rate) and assume that the option premium is 0.25.[14] If we use C^f and P^f to represent the values of call and put prices (and the superscript f indicates a futures option), then at maturity:

$$C^f = \text{Max}\,[0, F - K] \qquad (12.2a)$$

and

$$P^f = \text{Max}\,[0, K - F] \qquad (12.2b)$$

where F is the price of the underlying Eurodollar futures contract on the maturity of the option.

A graph of the profit profile for the hypothetical Eurodollar call option is shown in Figure 12.6a. The interpretation of this graph is similar to that for Figure 12.5a once we take into account the inverse relationship between interest rates and futures prices. For futures prices less than or equal to 96.00 (corresponding to interest rates greater than or equal to 4.00 percent), the expiration value of the call is zero. The buyer of the hypothetical call suffers a loss equal to the original premium paid for the option (in this case 25 basis points $\times$ \$25/bp = \$625). If the Eurodollar futures price at maturity exceeds 96.00, the expiration value of the option is positive (equal to $F - 96.00$ basis points), which reduces the call buyer's losses. The break-even Eurodollar futures rate is 96.25, corresponding to an interest rate of 3.75 percent. If interest rates fall below 3.75 percent, the call buyer earns a profit. The seller of our hypothetical call has a mirror-image profit profile.

A graph of the profit profile for the hypothetical Eurodollar put option is shown in Figure 12.6b. The interpretation of this graph is also similar to that for Figure 12.5b once we take into account the inverse relationship between interest rates and futures prices. For futures prices greater than or equal to 96.00 (corresponding to interest rates less than or equal to 4.00 percent), the expiration value of the put is zero. The buyer of the hypothetical put incurs a loss equal to the original premium paid for the option (in this case 25 basis points $\times$ \$25/bp = \$625). If the Eurodollar futures price at maturity is less than 96.00, the expiration value of the put is positive (equal to $96.00 - F$ basis points) which reduces the put buyer's losses. The break-even Eurodollar futures rate is 95.75, corresponding to an interest rate of 4.25 percent. If interest rates rise above 4.25 percent, the put buyer earns a profit. The seller of our hypothetical put has a mirror image profit profile.

---

[13]If the £ price fell to zero, the seller of the put would lose \$1.50 per pound. The seller cannot lose more than this amount.

[14]The price is determined by Black's model—equation (12.10a)—with $F = K = 96.00$, $r_d = 4$ percent, $t = 1$, and $\sigma = 0.68$ percent.

FIGURE 12.6A   Euro-$ Interest Rate Call with Strike at 96.00

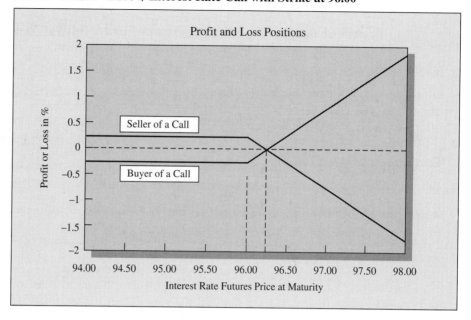

FIGURE 12.6B   Euro-$ Interest Rate Put with Strike at 96.00

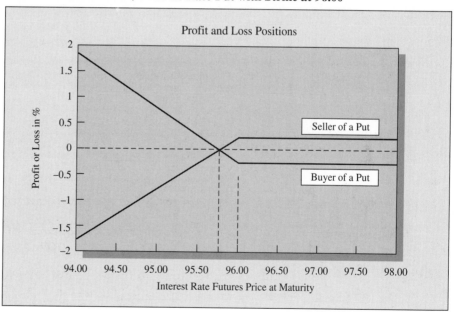

Based on Figures 12.5 and 12.6, we can design various applications for put and call options. These are discussed in Box 12.1.

Box 12.1

Practical Applications of Currency and Interest Rate Options

Options can be applied to reach many investment and financing objectives. In this box, we describe how options can be used for speculation—about the direction of prices and about their volatility—and for hedging against the risk of price changes or volatility changes.

Options and Speculation

As a *speculative investment,* buyers of calls (see Figures 12.5a and 12.6a) are generally "bullish" about the underlying asset. Their speculation is profitable if the underlying asset rises to a level greater than the strike price plus the option premium. This interpretation is also valid for interest rate futures, keeping in mind that a rising interest rate futures price corresponds to a falling interest rate environment. Speculative sellers of calls must have essentially opposite expectations.

In a corresponding way, speculative buyers of puts (see Figures 12.5b and 12.6b) are generally "bearish" about the underlying asset. Their speculation is profitable if the underlying asset falls to a level less than the strike price

minus the option premium. Speculative buyers of interest rate puts hold a bet that interest rates will rise by more than the strike price plus the option premium. And speculative sellers of puts have essentially opposite expectations.

A speculator could also have a view about volatility. For example, prior to the introduction of a new currency stabilization program, a speculator might expect to see a decline in volatility. By simultaneously selling a call and a put with the same strike price, the speculator generates a payoff profile known as a *short straddle* as in Figure A.* We assume that the option premium is $0.05 and the strike price is $1.50/£. The short straddle strategy generates a profit as long as currency rates stabilize *within* the range ($1.40 − $1.60).

On the other hand, suppose that a speculator expects an increase in volatility, either because a stabilization program is about to collapse or a pending election may result in fiscal laxity or fiscal stringency. Simultaneously buying a call

---

*If the put and call are sold at different strike prices, the strategy is called a *strangle.*

FIGURE A   **A Short Straddle in the $/£**
Profit and Loss Positions

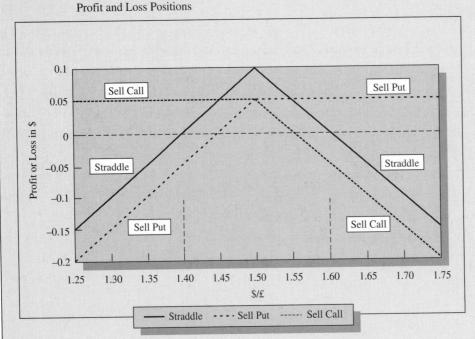

and a put with the same strike price is called a *long straddle* and generates a payoff profile as shown in Figure B. Again, we assume that the option premium is $0.05 and the strike price is $1.50/£. This strategy generates a profit as long as currency volatility increases, pushing rates *outside* the range ($1.40 − $1.60).

Options and Hedging

Options contracts also fulfill a *hedging function*. Those who hold or expect to hold an obligation to deliver pounds in the future may wish to protect themselves against an unexpected rise in the price of £ by purchasing a call option. As shown in Figure C, if £ appreciates above $1.50, hedgers will exercise their option. Buying a call in this example establishes a cap on the amount that hedgers pay for the £. In this case, the cap is $1.50/£, not counting the $0.05/£ cost of the call option itself. Notice the asymmetric nature of the hedge (labeled "Combined Position" in Figure C). If £ depreciates below $1.50 hedgers let their call expire without value, but they enjoy a gain from their underlying short £ position.

Similarly, those who hold or expect to hold an obligation to receive pounds in the future may wish to protect themselves against an unexpected fall in the price of £ by purchasing a put option. As shown in Figure D, if £ depreciates below $1.50, hedgers will exercise their option. Buying a put in this example establishes a floor on the amount that the hedgers receive for £. In this case, the floor is $1.50/£, not counting the $0.05/£ cost of the put option itself. Again, notice the asymmetric nature of the hedge (labeled "Combined Position" in Figure D). If £ appreciates above $1.50 hedgers let their put expire without value, but they enjoy a gain from their underlying long £ position.

A hedging motive also can drive the purchase or sale of interest rate futures. A portfolio manager who expects to invest funds for a three-month period at the Eurodollar interest rate is concerned about an unexpected fall in interest rates. Buying an interest rate call that gains value as interest rates fall would act as a hedge for the expectant investor. This strategy establishes an interest rate floor, similar to our example. On the other hand, a corporate treasurer who expects to borrow funds for a three-month period at the Eurodollar interest rate is concerned about an unexpected rise in interest rates. Buying an interest rate put that gains value as interest rates rise would act as a hedge for the expectant borrower. This strategy establishes an interest rate cap.

FIGURE B   A Long Straddle in the $/£
Profit and Loss Positions

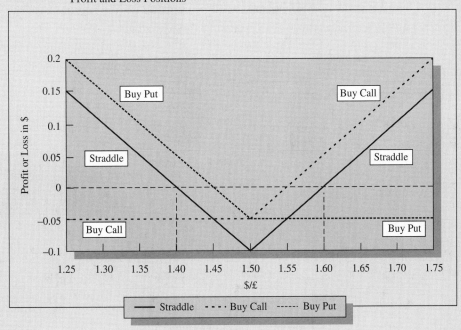

Box 12.1 (continued)

Practical Applications of Currency and Interest Rate Options (continued)

Another basic strategy combines a cap and a floor to establish a *collar*. Consider a firm that has a long £ position presently valued at $1.50/£. The firm can hedge against £ depreciation by buying a put (with a strike at $1.40), but this requires a cash outlay (say $0.06). The firm can earn some income (say $0.04) by selling a call (with a strike at $1.60), which caps its participation in any £ appreciation.

The collar establishes upper and lower limits on the value of the £ position as shown in Figure E. Collars of various sizes can be constructed by varying the strike prices on the put and call options. Collars for short £ positions also can be constructed, as can collars on interest rates, using the same techniques with interest rate options.

FIGURE C   Using a Call to Hedge a Short Pound
Profit and Loss Positions

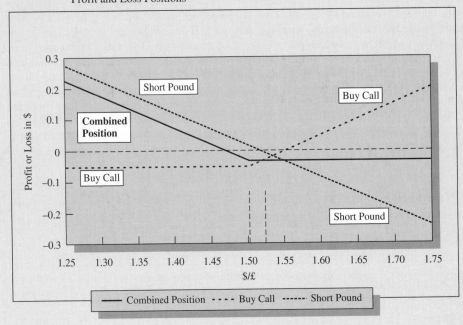

FIGURE D   **Using a Put to Hedge a Long Pound**
Profit and Loss Positions

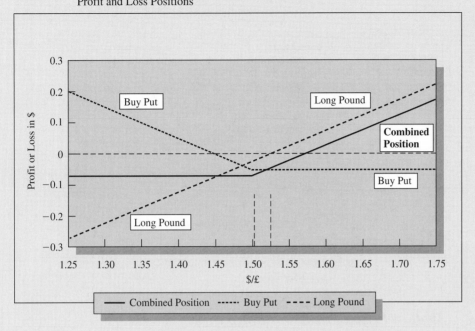

FIGURE E   **Combining a Floor and Cap: A Collar**
Profit and Loss Positions at Maturity

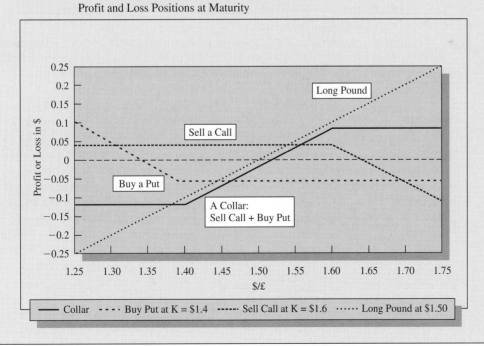

FIGURE 12.7   Call Options on Spot Yen

Seven Strike Prices at Three Maturities

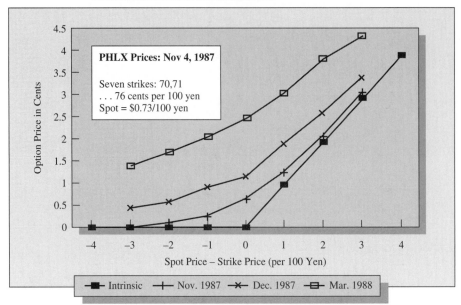

Option Prices Prior to Maturity

At maturity, the value of an interest rate or currency option is known with certainty. On the expiration date, the option price is governed by equations (12.1) and (12.2).[15] Prior to maturity, while the option is still "alive," market forces play a role in determining a fair price for the option. We can learn about some patterns of option prices prior to maturity by examining actual market prices.

In general, we can say that the option price is composed of two pieces: its **intrinsic value** as given by equations (12.1) and (12.2), and its **time value,** which represents the present value of the expected payouts from the option, given that the option is exercised. Both the intrinsic value and the time value are always non-negative amounts.

In Figure 12.7 we graph the value of many of the yen calls trading on the PHLX on November 4, 1987. Notice that the spot price minus the strike price is placed on the horizontal axis rather than simply the underlying spot (or asset) price. Drawing the graph this way allows us to examine the pattern of option prices for a given maturity while varying the amount by which the options are in or out of the money. On this trading day, the spot yen closed at $0.73/¥100, or about 137 ¥/$. The PHLX was trading yen calls with strike prices of $0.70, $0.71, . . . and $0.76 per ¥100. Calls with a strike price of $0.73 are plotted at 0.0 on the *X*-axis and designated as "at the money." Calls with a strike price of $0.72 and below are plotted with positive values and designated as "in the money" as they have positive intrinsic value. While calls with a strike price of $0.74 and above are plotted with negative values on the *X*-axis and designated as "out of the money" because they have zero intrinsic value.

---

[15]The owner of the option will have to exercise his or her option or sell it to obtain the option's terminal value, depending on the rules of the option market. After maturity, the value of any option is zero since the rights explicit in the option have expired.

FIGURE 12.8   **Put Options on Short Sterling Interest Rate Futures**
Prices on Tuesday, June 20, 2000

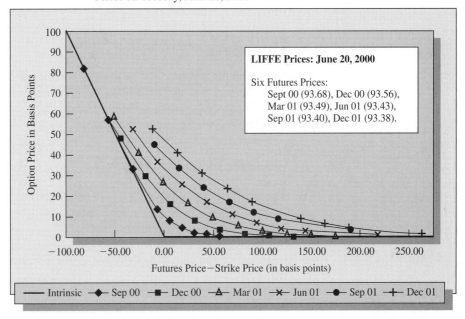

Source: LIFFE, *Daily Information Bulletin,* June 20, 2000.

The graphs in Figure 12.7 have some interesting features. First, we can see that options with more time to maturity have a higher value. Second, we observe that as options become deeper in the money or deeper out of the money, their value appears to asymptotically approach the intrinsic value. This is especially noticeable for the November and December options. Finally, the curvature of each graph shows some distinctive patterns. For the shortest-term November option, the curvature is fairly abrupt because the graph hugs the intrinsic value. For the longest-term March option, the curvature is more gentle. In every case, however, the slope of the graph for deep out-of-the-money call options approaches zero. And the slope of each graph for deep in-the-money call options approaches one. This slope, usually called *delta* (representing $\Delta_C = \partial C / \partial S$), reflects the rate of change of the call price with respect to the underlying spot asset price. We can see that Δ_C is bounded between 0 and 1 ($0 \leq \Delta_C \leq 1$).

In Figure 12.8, we graph the values of various put options on the three-month short sterling interest rate futures contract.[16] These data were reported in Table 12.5 and have been supplemented by three longer maturities for June, September, and December 2001. Normally, the option price would be plotted on the vertical axis against the futures price on the horizontal axis. In Figure 12.8, the *X*-axis is scaled by the strike price (X = Futures price − Strike price) in order to illustrate the general pattern of futures option pricing.

As we can see, Figure 12.8 shows many similarities to Figure 12.7. Like options on spot currency, options on futures with more time to maturity have a higher value. Second, as options on futures become deeper in or out of the money, their value appears to asymptotically approach the intrinsic value. Finally, the curvature of each graph has its own distinctive pattern. The slope of each graph reflects the rate of change in the put

---

[16]The underlying asset in each case is a three-month sterling interest rate futures contract. The different months represent different delivery dates for this contract.

price with respect to the underlying futures price, $\Delta_p = \partial P/\partial F$. We can see that the put delta is negative and bounded between -1 and 0 $(-1 \le \Delta_p \le 0)$.

Option Pricing: Formal Models

To learn more about the pricing of currency or interest rate options, it is necessary to examine prices in the context of a particular set of assumptions. We will begin by describing models for pricing options on spot currency. We then briefly review models for pricing options on currency futures and interest rate futures.

Pricing Spot Currency Options

The Discrete Time Binomial Model.   The **binomial model** offers a useful way to explore both the factors that determine option prices and the way in which option contracts can be replicated by common financial market transactions. Imagine a two-period case where the current spot exchange rate is $S_1 = \$1.40/£$.[17] In the second period, the exchange rate may move up (taking the value S_{2u}) or it may move down (taking the value S_{2d}). The question we wish to answer is, How much would someone pay today for a call option (C_1) granting the right to buy £1 at an exercise price (K) equal to S_1?

To answer the question, we need to add a few more assumptions about market conditions and the (stochastic) behavior of the spot exchange rate. Assume that interest rates are 9 percent in the domestic currency (US\$) and 12 percent in the foreign currency (£). Finally, assume that the exchange rate change depends on two factors: (1) the interest rate differential as in the International Fisher Effect, and (2) a random jump term depending on the volatility of exchange rates. Thus, if the spot rate goes up, it does so by a multiplicative factor u, where $u = \exp[(r_d - r_f) + \sigma]$, and if the spot rate goes down, it does so by a multiplicative factor d, where $d = \exp[(r_d - r_f) - \sigma]$.[18] With volatility set at 10 percent, the values of u and d are 1.0725 and 0.8781, respectively.

To summarize, the path of the spot rate is shown in Figure 12.9. The spot rate begins at \$1.40/£ and either rises to \$1.5015 $(= u\, S_1)$ or falls to \$1.2293 $(= d\, S_1)$. The value of the call option with $K = \$1.40/£$ will be \$0.1015 if the spot rate rises, or \$0 if instead the spot rate falls.

How much should an investor pay for a contract that pays off either \$0.1015 or \$0 depending on the path of the exchange rate? The answer can be found by showing that the exact same payoff pattern can be replicated using common financial transactions such as borrowing and lending.

Table 12.6a shows the cash flows from a particular combination of borrowing and lending in an environment where the spot £ rate can be strong (S_{2u}) or weak (S_{2d}). First, borrowing \$0.41903 in period 1 leads to a cash inflow that must be repaid with interest in period 2 whether spot £ rises or falls. Second, with spot £ valued at \$1.40, buying £0.330785 $(= \Delta_C)$ in period 1 leads to a cash outflow of \$0.46310.[19] With accrued in-

---

[17]This example is adapted from Bodurtha and Courtadon (1987).

[18]In general, $u = \exp[(r_d - r_f)t/n + \sigma\sqrt{t/n}]$ and $d = \exp[(r_d - r_f)t/n - \sigma\sqrt{t/n}]$ where t is the maturity of the option in years, n is the number of periods or number of price jumps, and r_d and r_f are the domestic and foreign interest rates on a continuous per annum basis. Both t and n are set equal to 1 in this example. The expression $y = \exp(x)$ is the same as $y = e^x$.

[19]Calculated as \$0.41903 $\times$ exp (0.09) = \$0.46310.

FIGURE 12.9   Binomial Currency Option Example

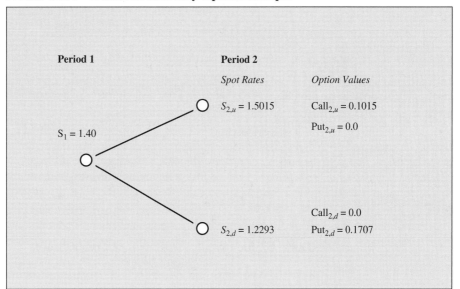

terest at 12 percent, the value of this sterling holding in period 2 is \$0.56000 if sterling rises, but only \$0.45849 if sterling falls. As we can see, the combination of borrowing dollars and purchasing sterling in the proportions chosen leads to cash flows in period 2 that exactly match those of the call option. By the laws of financial arbitrage, if the call option leads to the same payoff stream as the set of common transactions, then the call option must have the same initial price—in this case, \$0.04407/£.

The combination of borrowing dollars and investing in roughly one-third of a pound is called a **replicating portfolio** for a call option on one pound sterling. The same technique can be used to show that a put option on the pound can also be replicated using common financial transactions.

Figure 12.9 shows the value of a put on £1 with an exercise price of \$1.40/£, using the same assumptions as we had in our earlier example. The put is worthless if the price of spot £ rises to S_{2u} or worth \$0.1707 if the £ falls to S_{2d}.

In Table 12.6b we show a set of cash flows for another particular combination of borrowing and lending transactions. The first component is lending \$0.86047 in period 1. At the prevailing 9 percent interest rate on US\$, this will return \$0.94151 in the second period whether the spot rate rises or falls.[20] The second component is borrowing £0.556129 ($= \Delta_p$), which equates with \$0.77858 in period 1 when the spot rate is \$1.40. Given the 12 percent interest rate on £, we must pay back £0.627033 in period 2, which equates to \$0.94151 if £ rises but only \$0.77084 if £ falls. As we see in Table 12.6b, the combination of lending dollars and borrowing sterling in the proportions chosen leads to cash flows in period 2 that exactly match those of the put option. By the laws of financial arbitrage, since the put option leads to the same payoffs as the combination of borrowing and lending transactions, then the put option must have the same initial price—in this case, \$0.08188/£.

---

[20]As before, calculated as \$0.86047 $\times$ exp (0.09) = \$0.94151.

TABLE 12.6A   **Replicating Portfolio for a Call on £**
A Numerical Example of the Binomial Model

| | Cash Flows | Cash Flows in Period 2 | |
Transaction	Period 1	if $S_1 \uparrow S_{2u}$	if $S_1 \downarrow S_{2d}$
Dollar borrowing (B)	+$0.41903	−$0.45849	−$0.45849
Spot £ purchase ($\Delta_C S_1$)	−$0.46310	+$0.56000	+$0.45849
Sum of above ($B + \Delta_C S_1$)	−$0.04407	+$0.10151	$0.0
Call option purchase	(C_1)	+$0.10151	$0.0

Note: The values of B, L, Δ_C, and Δ_P are determined using the formulas in Appendix 12.1, assuming r_d = 9 percent, r_f = 12 percent, σ = 10 percent, t = 1, n = 1, and S_1 = $1.40/£, as discussed in the text.

TABLE 12.6B   **Replicating Portfolio for a Put on £**
A Numerical Example of the Binomial Model

| | Cash Flows | Cash Flows in Period 2 | |
Transaction	Period 1	if $S_1 \uparrow S_{2u}$	if $S_1 \downarrow S_{2d}$
Dollar Lending (L)	−$0.86047	+$0.94151	+$0.94151
Spot £ borrowing ($\Delta_p S_1$)	+$0.77858	−$0.94151	−$0.77084
Sum of above ($L + \Delta_p S_1$)	−$0.08188	$0.0	+$0.17067
Put option purchase	(P_1)	$0.0	+0.17067

Note: The values of B, L, Δ_C, and Δ_P are determined using the formulas in Appendix 12.1, assuming r_d = 9 percent, r_f = 12 percent, σ = 10 percent, t = 1, n = 1, and S_1 = $1.40/£, as discussed in the text.

The reader may wonder how we are able to determine the value of borrowing (B) or lending (L) in local currency and the position in the underlying asset (ΔS_1) to construct the replicating portfolio. Actually, B, L, and ΔS_1 can be determined uniquely once the initial spot rate (S_1), the strike price (K), the jump factor or volatility (σ), the two interest rates (r_d and r_f), and the time to maturity (t = 1 in this case) are given. The formulas are shown in Appendix 12.1.

For our purposes, the important point so far is that the currency option can be replicated using appropriate combinations of ordinary borrowing and lending transactions. The replicating portfolio concept is the same idea that we used in Chapter 3 to show that forward contracts could be mimicked using combinations of other commonly available contracts. The same principles we applied in Chapter 3 apply here as well. The replicating portfolio notion is critical both for determining the price of a put or call option and for devising a strategy to hedge the risks of options. We have just seen how the replicating portfolio concept allows us to determine the price of a put or call option. It also follows that a trader who has sold a put (or call) could buy a *synthetic* put (or call) using the replicating portfolio approach in order to hedge his or her position. We will discuss the notion of hedging option positions in more detail later in this chapter.

FIGURE 12.10   Binomial Currency Option Example: Multiple Periods
to Expiration

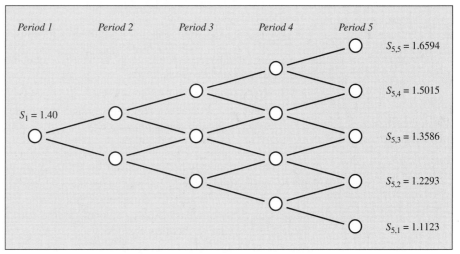

Extending the Discrete Time Binomial Model.   The two-period binomial model represents a very simple setting, but it can be extended to a multiperiod setting. Figure 12.10 illustrates a binomial model extended to cover four one-quarter time periods. The figure shows a "tree diagram" that is characteristic of this approach. At each node (indicated as a circle in Figure 12.10) the exchange rate may take a discrete jump up (governed by the process $S_{t+1} = S_t u$) or a jump down (governed by the process $S_{t+1} = S_t d$). Keeping the interest rates and volatility as in our previous example, we calculate the multiplicative factors $u = 1.043416$ ($u = \exp[(r_d - r_f)/4 + \sigma\sqrt{1/4}]$) and $d = 0.944122$ ($d = \exp[(r_d - r_f)/4 - \sigma\sqrt{1/4}]$). The ending value of the exchange rate after four quarters of evolution is reported on the right-hand side of Figure 12.10. The value of a put or call option at each node (that is, each discrete point in time) could be computed using the same replicating portfolio approach as we described for the two-period binomial case.[21] The binomial approach may seem somewhat arcane and laborious, but it is the workhorse model for pricing American options, especially when there is an incentive to exercise the option early, meaning before expiration.

The Continuous Time Lognormal Approach.   While it is a useful way to conceptualize the problem of option pricing, the multiperiod binomial model does not adequately depict the evolution of a currency price that changes from moment to moment and the need to set option prices that also change on a moment-by-moment basis. So imagine that we take the multiperiod binomial model depicted in Figure 12.10 and divide the time period into n periods of length dt. As $n \to \infty$, $dt \to 0$. And imagine that the movement in the spot rate in each period becomes infinitesimally small, with either positive or negative sign. We could then attempt to solve the multiperiod, binomial pricing problem for the case where n is very large, dt becomes very small, and the spot exchange rate

---

[21]For further discussion of the binomial method applied to currencies, see Bodurtha and Courtadon (1987), pp. 10–15.

movement is small and random. Under certain restrictive assumptions, the solution to this mathematical problem yields a single equation for pricing European style put and call options. The model also provides option values for American options when early exercise is deemed unlikely.[22]

The essential assumptions of the continuous time lognormal approach are:

1. The underlying currency price evolves continuously with mean rate of change μ and standard deviation σ.[23]
2. Both domestic and foreign interest rates are constant at r_d and r_f, respectively.
3. There are no taxes or other barriers such as transaction costs, margin requirements, or limits to short sales.

With these assumptions, it is possible to imagine a scenario in which a trader, after buying a call, continuously hedges himself by selling $\Delta_{C(S,t)}$ units of foreign currency as S and t change. From Table 12.6a, we can see that this position is riskless, so it should cost the risk-free rate of interest.[24] Similarly, a trader who buys a put could continuously hedge himself by purchasing $\Delta_{P(S,t)}$ units of foreign currency as S and t change. From Table 12.6b, we know that this position also is riskless, so it should also earn the risk-free rate of return.[25] These scenarios imply a partial differential equation that can be solved subject to the constraint that the ending value of the option is its intrinsic value. The solution to this differential equation yields the equations for valuation of European options on spot currency given below:[26]

$$\text{Call price: } C(S,t) = S \exp(-r_f t)N(x + \sigma\sqrt{t}) - K\exp(-r_d t)\,N(x) \quad (12.3a)$$

$$\text{Call delta: } \partial C/\partial S = \Delta_{C(S,t)} = \exp(-r_f t)N(x + \sigma t) > 0$$

$$\text{Put price: } P(S,t) = S\exp(-r_f t)[N(x + \sigma\sqrt{t}) - 1] - K\exp(-r_d t)[N(x) - 1] \quad (12.3b)$$

$$\text{Put delta: } \partial P/\partial S = \Delta_{P(S,t)} = \exp(-r_f t)[N(x + \sigma\sqrt{t}) - 1] < 0$$

where

N ($\bullet$) is the cumulative normal distribution
$x = [\ln(S/K) + (r_d - r_f - \sigma^2/2)t]/\sigma\sqrt{t}$

Inspection of equations (12.3a) and (12.3b) reveals that both put and call prices depend on only six parameters: S, K, r_d, r_f, t, and σ. Conditional on the other parameters remaining constant, the marginal effect of a change in each parameter is shown in Table 12.7. The marginal impact of S and K on put and call prices is consistent with what was suggested by the data in Table 12.3 and Figure 12.7. Within the context of the continu-

---

[22]For a comparison between the binomial and continuous lognormal option pricing models, see Bodurtha and Courtadon (1987), pp. 18–20.

[23]This assumption implies that the exchange rate evolves as a diffusion process of the form $dS/S = \mu\,dt + \sigma\,dz$. The instantaneous drift in the currency is μ and dt is an instant of time. The instantaneous standard deviation is σ and z is a standard normal variate that is independent and identically distributed over time.

[24]In Table 12.6a, we showed that buying a call is equivalent to the transactions $B + \Delta_C S_t$. Hedging by selling Δ_C units of foreign currency valued at S_t, gives the trader an overall position of $B + \Delta_C S_t - \Delta_C S_t = B$, which represents a riskless loan.

[25]In Table 12.6b, we showed that buying a put is equivalent to the transactions $L + \Delta_P S_t$. Hedging by buying Δ_P units of foreign currency valued at S_t, gives the trader an overall position of $L + \Delta_P S_t - \Delta_P S_t = L$, which represents a riskless asset.

[26]The continuous time lognormal approach to European option pricing was first developed by Black and Scholes (1973). Garman and Kohlhagen (1983) extended the Black-Scholes model to currencies.

TABLE 12.7   Marginal Effect of a Parameter Change on Option Prices

Variable	Price Effect on Call Option	Price Effect on Put Option
Spot price ↑ ($S\!\uparrow$)	Call price ↑	Put price ↓
Exercise price ↑ ($K\!\uparrow$)	Call price ↓	Put price ↑
Domestic interest rate ↑ ($r_d\!\uparrow$)	Call price ↑	Put price ↓
Foreign interest rate ↑ ($r_f\!\uparrow$)	Call price ↓	Put price ↑
Spot rate volatility ↑ ($\sigma\!\uparrow$)	Call price ↑	Put price ↑
Time to maturity ↑ ($t\!\uparrow$)	Ambiguous effect, depends on r_d, r_f, and σ	Ambiguous effect, depends on r_d, r_f, and σ

Note: Partial price effects pertain to the continuous time lognormal approach for options on spot currency.

ous time lognormal approach, the effect of r_d and r_f on put and call prices is consistent with our development of the replicating portfolio notion in Tables 12.6a and 12.6b. In the case of a call on £, a rise in r_d lowers the amount of US$ one could borrow in period 1 (keeping the cash flows in period 2 as before). As the call is a leveraged contract that replicates the effect of borrowed domestic currency, its equilibrium price rises with a rise in domestic interest rates. In the case of a call on £, r_d could be thought of as a "cost of funds" and r_f as a "yield on the position." With this in mind, we can see that a currency option is analogous to an option on a dividend-paying stock. In this case, £ represents the underlying asset and r_f represents its dividend rate, which is assumed to be paid continuously throughout the option's life. Similar logic can be applied for changes in r_d and r_f for the case of puts.

Our discussion of the replicating portfolio also implied that an increase in σ would increase both put and call prices. An increase in σ raises the multiplicative factor u and the potential payout of a call if the spot rate jumps higher, without lowering its payout if the spot rate falls (since the payout is bounded at zero). Analogously, an increase in σ lowers the multiplicative factor d and raises the potential payout of a put if the spot rate falls, without lowering its payout if the spot rate increases (again, the payout of the put is bounded at zero).

Only the marginal impact of time, which is listed as ambiguous in Table 12.7, appears to be at odds with the market data presented earlier in Figure 12.7. Inspection of equations (12.3a) and (12.3b) shows that time interacts with (that is, multiplies) both interest rate terms and the volatility parameter. Increasing time has a positive effect on an option's value because it allows more opportunities for volatility to work its way and propel the option into the money. But since an option also represents an implicit financing cost, greater time implies a greater cost of replicating the option. If volatility is fairly small relative to the interest differential, it will make sense for the owner of an option to exercise it early (if this is permitted, as in American options), and save the sure cost of the interest differential rather than to wait for the unlikely event of a large favorable spot rate move. We will further discuss early exercise later in this chapter.

Equations (12.3a) and (12.3b) can be calculated once values for all six parameters are determined. Figure 12.11a shows a graph of call option values plotted against S conditional on $K = 100$, $r_d = 4.0$ percent, $r_f = 6.0$ percent, $\sigma = 15$ percent and $t = 1$, 60, 90, and 365 days to maturity. Note that the curvature of the pricing graph becomes greater as the option gets closer to maturity. The slope of the price graph ($\Delta_{C(S,t)}$) still ranges between 0 and 1, but the transition between 0 and 1 occurs much more quickly

FIGURE 12.11A   **Call Option Prices and Maturity**
$r_d = 4\%, r_f = 6\%$, Volatility = 15%, $K = 100$

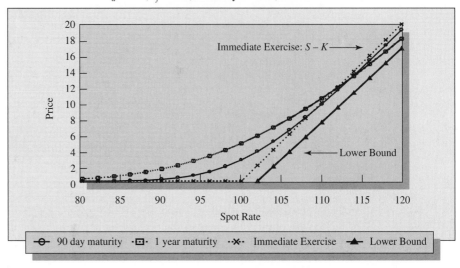

FIGURE 12.11B   **Call Option Deltas and Maturity**
$r_d = 4\%, r_f = 6\%$, Volatility = 15%

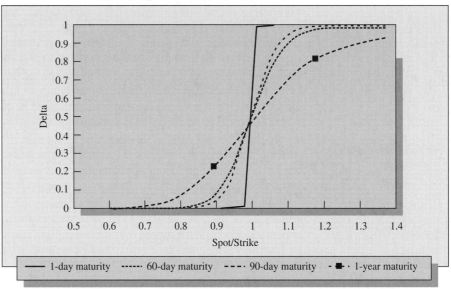

for options closer to expiration. A graph of $\Delta_{C(S,t)}$ in Figure 12.11b explicitly shows its sensitivity to changes in S and t. For an option with one day to maturity, a small change in the spot price in the vicinity of the strike price will shift delta from its lower limit of 0 to its upper limit of 1. But with one year to maturity, the same spot rate change has a much smaller impact on delta.

Our emphasis here on this relationship stems from the importance of delta for managing trading risks in option positions. In the context of the continuous time lognormal approach, delta represents the probability that an option will expire in the money. Delta also represents the **hedge ratio,** meaning the amount of the underlying asset that when combined with an option would result in a risk-free (or **delta neutral**) trading position. If we stick with the assumption that the underlying asset evolves continuously over time, then traders could reduce their risks (in theory to zero) if they could rebalance (or **delta-hedge**) their position *continuously* as the spot rate changes. Figure 12.11b provides an indication of how much rebalancing might be needed as spot prices and time change.

Arbitrage Boundary Conditions and Pricing.   In the analysis so far, we have shown that options can be replicated by simple transactions in common financial instruments. It follows that the prices of options are constrained to lie within certain boundaries. If these **boundary conditions** are violated, arbitrage profit opportunities are available. In a well-functioning financial market, we would expect very few true arbitrage opportunities. Still these arbitrage boundary conditions are extremely useful for summarizing the price relationships among options and other financial instruments.[27]

To begin, we know that option prices are nonnegative, so that:

$$C \geq 0; P \geq 0; C^* \geq 0; P^* \geq 0$$

where C and P are call and put prices of European currency options and C^* and P^* are call and put prices of American currency options. Because owners of an option are not required to exercise it, they would never pay to get rid of the option. Therefore, zero is the absolute lower bound for an option's price.

We also know that the underlying currency price represents the absolute upper bound for the prices of European and American calls, so that:

$$C \leq S; C^* \leq S$$

If this condition were violated, it would pay arbitragers to buy the underlying currency and sell calls.

Along the same lines, the prices of European and American puts cannot exceed the strike price of the contract, or:

$$P \leq K; P^* \leq K$$

No one would pay more than $1.50/£ for the right to sell at $1.50/£. This contract would only break even if the £ were valued at zero and became worthless.

The above conditions do not place very tight bands on the prices of European or American puts or calls. Far tighter bands can be deduced once we recognize that puts and calls on currencies must conform to pricing relationships against each other as well as currency forward contracts. In Figure 12.12, we graph the payoff profile for buying a European call and selling a European put, both with the same exercise price (K) and the same maturity (T). The combination of the put and call positions gives the same payoff profile as a forward position established at the strike price. So, being long a call and short a put (at the same exercise price) must be equivalent to holding a long forward position. Analogously, being short a call and long a put (at the same exercise price) must be equivalent to holding a short forward position. This property allows us to determine a link between put and call prices as well as forward rates.

---

[27]For more details on arbitrage pricing relationships in options, see Gibson (1991) and Grabbe (1986).

FIGURE 12.12   **Buying a Call and Selling a Put Replicates Buying a Forward**
Profit and Loss Positions at Maturity

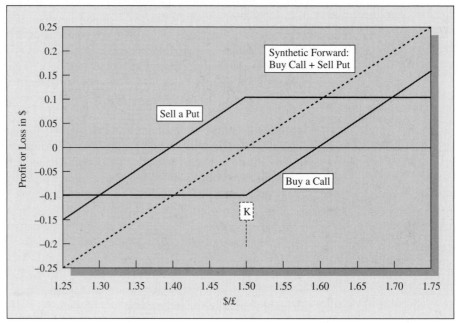

In Table 12.8, we see that buying a call and selling a put (labeled the option portfolio) entails an initial cash flow of $-C + P$. At maturity, either the call is in the money (and worth $S_T - K$) or the put is in the money (and also worth $S_T - K$). The option portfolio always returns $S_T - K$. As we have seen in Chapters 3 and 11, a long forward foreign exchange position can be replicated by borrowing the domestic currency and lending the foreign currency. Thus, in the initial period, we borrow the present value of the option strike price [$K \exp(-r_d T)$]. At maturity, we must repay an amount equal to the strike price ($-K$). To complete the forward position, we invest an amount of foreign currency equal to the present value of the currency spot rate [$S_1 \exp(-r_f T)$]. At maturity, this investment returns an amount of foreign currency now valued at S_T. Thus, the forward contract (in Table 12.8) always returns an amount $S_T - K$. By the law of financial arbitrage, it must be the case that for European options:

$$-C + P = +K \exp(-r_d T) - S_1 \exp(-r_f T) \qquad (12.4)$$

Equation (12.4) is often referred to as **put-call parity,** but it applies to European options only. If we divide each side of equation (12.4) by $\exp(-r_d T)$ and recall that based on interest rate parity the T-period forward rate $F_{1,T}$ equals $S_1 \exp(r_d T - r_f T)$, then the expression becomes:

$$C - P = \frac{(F_{1,T} - K)}{\exp(r_d T)} \qquad (12.5)$$

Equation (12.5) is often referred to as **put-call-forward parity.** Like other parity conditions, put-call-forward parity can be viewed as a pricing rule, a formula for creating synthetic securities, or the basis for an arbitrage trading strategy. Assuming that there are

TABLE 12.8   **Put-Call-Forward Parity for European Currency Options**

Portfolios	Cash Flows Period 1	Cash Flows in Period 2 if $S_2 \leq K$	Cash Flows in Period 2 if $S_2 > K$
Option Portfolio			
Buy call	$-C$	0	$S_2 - K$
Sell put	$+P$	$S_2 - K$	0
Sum of above	$-C + P$	$S_2 - K$	$S_2 - K$
Forward Contract			
Borrow domestic currency	$+Ke^{-rd}$	$-K$	$-K$
Invest foreign currency	$-S_1 e^{-rf}$	$+S_2$	$+S_2$
Sum of above	$+Ke^{-rd} - S_1 e^{-rt}$	$S_2 - K$	$S_2 - K$

Note: Since the cash flows in period 2 are the same for the option portfolio as for the forward contract, the price of these two portfolios must be the same in period 1. Thus, you have: $-C + P = +Ke^{-rdr} - S_1 e^{-rf}$

no transaction costs or taxes, equation (12.5) implies that for the same strike price (K) the call price is related to the put price by:

$$C = P + \frac{(F_{1,T} - K)}{\exp(r_d T)} \tag{12.6a}$$

and the put price is related to the call price by:

$$P = C - \frac{(F_{1,T} - K)}{\exp(r_d T)} \tag{12.6b}$$

Equation (12.6a) implies that buying a European call is equivalent to buying a put and buying a forward contract. Clearly, if the price of buying this synthetic call (C_{syn}) were not identical to the price of the true call (C), then arbitrage profit opportunities would be available. Similarly, equation (12.6b) implies that buying a put is equivalent to buying a call and selling a forward contract. If the price of the synthetic put (P_{syn}) were not identical to the price of the true put (P), arbitrage profit opportunities would be possible.

Put-call-forward parity in equation (12.5) has another interesting implication. For puts and calls written at a strike price equal to the currency forward rate, put-call-forward parity implies that the put price and call price should be identical, that is, $C = P$. If investors pay the same amount for a call (which rises in value as the future spot rate exceeds the strike price) as they would pay for a put (which rises in value as the future spot rate falls short of the strike price), intuition might dictate that the forward rate must lie at the center of distribution of expected future spot rates. A link between put-call-forward parity and market sentiment is discussed in Box 12.2.

Pricing Currency and Interest Rate Futures Options

The distinctive feature of a futures option is that the underlying asset is a commodity or financial futures contract. With this in mind, the basic pictures of the option's intrinsic value and its payoff profile at expiration are identical to those we have seen for spot currency options (Figures 12.5a, 12.5b, 12.7, 12.11a, and 12.11b) except that the futures price appears on the horizontal axis (see Figures 12.6a, 12.6b, and 12.8). The thought experiment of constructing a binomial tree, with a futures contract as the underlying asset, could also be performed. These experiments would show that a futures option can be replicated by continuously adjusting the delta position in the underlying asset, as we

Box 12.2

A Link between Put Prices, Call Prices, and Market Sentiment

From put-call-forward parity, we know that when $K = F$, we expect to find that $C = P$ for puts and calls on the same currency and with the same maturity. Since a call gains value when the underlying asset price rises and the put gains value when the underlying asset price falls, $C = P$ suggests that the forward rate should lie near the center of the distribution of expected future spot rates.

Suppose instead that we look at puts and calls that are somewhat out of the money. Later in this chapter, we show that out-of-the-money options tend to be overpriced by the market, especially when markets feel there is a likelihood of a price jump in a favorable direction. Examining whether the market pays more for an out-of-the-money call than for an out-of-the-money put may indicate whether market sentiment favors an upward or downward move in the underlying asset.

A **risk reversal** is measured by the difference in price between calls and puts whose strike prices are spaced symmetrically about the current spot rate. For example, we could take out-of-the-money calls with a delta of 0.25 and compare them with out-of-the-money puts with a delta of -0.25. When this risk reversal is positive, market participants are willing to pay more for the right to *buy* a currency at a given maximum strike than they are willing to pay for the right to *sell* a currency at a symmetric minimum strike price. A positive risk reversal, defined as the call price minus the put price suggests that greater probability is attached to a large appreciation (of the underlying currency). A negative risk reversal indicates that greater probability is attached to a currency depreciation.[*]

The figures in this box show risk-reversal prices for the US$/€ and the ¥/US$ from July 1998 to June 2000. The graphs show the difference in price between an out-of-the-money (25-delta) call and an out-of-the-money (25-delta) put. Throughout most of 1998, the positive risk reversal on the US$/€ indicated market sentiment toward appreciation of the euro versus the US$. The negative risk reversal on the ¥/US$ throughout much of June 1999 onward indicates market sentiment favoring a depreciation of the US$.

---

[*]For further discussion of risk reversal and the market's expectations regarding future currency movements, see Neil Cooper and James Talbot, "The Yen/Dollar Exchange Rate in 1998: Views from the Options Market," *Bank of England Quarterly Bulletin*, Feb. 1999, pp. 68–77.

Three-Month Risk Reversal Prices
US$ versus €

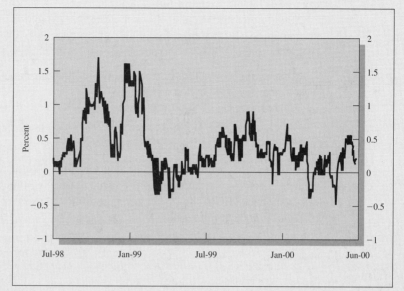

Three-Month Risk Reversal Prices
¥ versus US$

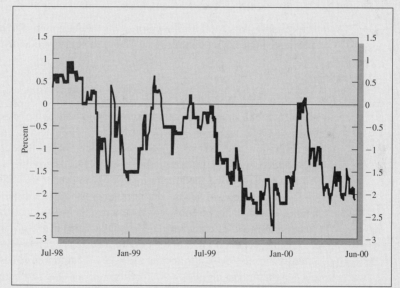

Note: The risk reversal is the price difference between a 25-delta call and a 25-delta put. For example, if the call is quoted at an 11 percent implied volatility and the put is quoted at a 9 percent implied volatility, then the risk reversal is quoted as 2.0 percent. Strike prices are in US$/€ for the euro options and in ¥/US$ for the yen options.

Source: Deutsche Bank, *Foreign Exchange Weekly,* June 23, 2000.

had with options on spot. The one difference, however, is that a futures position can be undertaken with no initial cash outlay.[28] Thus, there is no interest cost necessary to finance the delta position in a futures option.

Taking this into account, Fischer Black (1976) applied the continuous time lognormal approach for European options on commodity futures contracts. Assumptions analogous to those that we laid out earlier apply once again, namely:

1. The underlying *futures price* evolves continuously with mean rate of change μ and standard deviation σ.[29]

2. The domestic interest rate is constant at r_d.

3. There are no taxes or other barriers such as transaction costs, margin requirements, or limits to short sales.

As in our earlier discussion, these assumptions imply that a trader can continuously rebalance a position in futures options and the underlying future contract to earn the risk free rate. Black (1976) shows that the equilibrium valuation of the European futures call (C^f) and European futures put (P^f) is:

$$C^f(F,t) = F \exp(-r_d t)N(y) - K \exp(-r_d t)N(y - \sigma\sqrt{t}) \tag{12.7a}$$

$$P^f(F,t) = -F \exp(-r_d t)N(-y) + K \exp(-r_d t)N(-y + \sigma\sqrt{t}) \tag{12.7b}$$

where

$N(\bullet)$ is the cumulative normal distribution
$y = [\ln(F/K) + (\sigma^2/2)t]/\sigma\sqrt{t}$

The delta for these options now represents the rate of change in the option price with respect to the underlying futures price. This can be derived analytically, with the result that:

$$\Delta_C = \partial C^f/\partial F = \exp(-r_d t)N(y)$$

$$\Delta_P = \partial P^f/\partial F = -\exp(-r_d t)N(-y)$$

As before, call deltas are bounded between 0 and 1, while put deltas are bounded between -1 and 0.

Equations (12.7a) and (12.7b) are generic—that is, they apply to any commodity futures option, whether the commodity is lumber, oil, currency, or a short-term interest rate. All that matters is the specification of the evolution of the futures price (as a continuous diffusion process) and that the domestic interest rate is constant. With these assumptions, a riskless hedge can be constructed between the futures contract and the futures option, which in turn yields equations (12.7a) and (12.7b) as the pricing models.[30]

It may seem odd that in the case of a currency futures option, the foreign currency interest rate (r_f) does not appear explicitly in equations (12.7a) and (12.7b). While r_f plays a major part in linking the forward rate and the spot rate by means of interest rate

---

[28]There is a margin requirement in futures, but this acts as a good-faith bond. The individual still retains ownership of the margin assets and the interest that these assets earn.

[29]This assumption implies that the futures price evolves as a diffusion process of the form $dF/F = \mu \, dt + \sigma \, dz$. The instantaneous drift in the futures price is μ and dt is an instant of time. The instantaneous standard deviation is μ and z is a standard normal variate that is independent and identically distributed over time.

[30]The interest rate options traded on LIFFE are futures-style options, meaning that futures positions are marked to market daily, giving rise to positive or negative variation margin flows. In this case, the relevant interest rate is $r_d = 0$. Equations (12.7a) and (12.7b) can be simplified accordingly.

parity, it plays no part in the link between the price of currency futures and the price of an option on currency futures.

Prices of European futures options are also subject to similar boundary conditions as we saw for options on spot currency. It remains true that (1) the combination of a long call and short put position replicates the payoffs for a synthetic long futures position and (2) the combination of a short call and long put position replicates the payoffs for a synthetic short futures position (see Figure 12.12). As a result, *put-call-forward parity* [equation (12.5)] can be recast as **put-call-futures parity** with the equation:

$$C^f - P^f = \frac{(F_{1,T} - K)}{\exp(r_d T)} \tag{12.8}$$

where F now symbolizes a futures contract instead of a forward contract. As we have done many times with parity conditions, any term can be isolated on the left-hand side to demonstrate a pricing rule, a formula for creating synthetic securities, or the basis for an arbitrage trading strategy. Assuming that there are no transaction costs or taxes, equation (12.8) implies that for the same strike price (K) the call price is related to the put price by:

$$C^f = P^f + \frac{(F_{1,T} - K)}{\exp(r_d T)} \tag{12.9a}$$

The put price is related to the call price by:

$$P^f = C^f - \frac{(F_{1,T} - K)}{\exp(r_d T)} \tag{12.9b}$$

Equation (12.9a) implies that buying a European call is equivalent to buying a put and buying a futures contract. Similarly, equation (12.9b) implies that buying a put is equivalent to buying a call and selling a futures contract. If these are not satisfied, then arbitrage profit opportunities are available between synthetic futures options and true futures options.

Empirical Evidence on Option Prices

A large number of empirical studies have examined how well actual option prices conform to the predictions of theoretical models. In this section we will highlight only a few studies that focus on currency and interest rate options.

Arbitrage Boundary Conditions

A natural starting point is to test the efficiency of the market in eliminating arbitrage profit opportunities. These empirical tests measure only whether options are priced efficiently relative to other options and other financial instruments. They do not rely on the accuracy of option prices in an absolute sense. Boundary conditions were discussed earlier, leading up to several explicit parity conditions: put-call parity, put-call-forward parity, and put-call-futures parity. As we argued in Chapter 5, the preferred way to test a boundary or parity condition is to count the number of times the condition is violated after having made suitable adjustments for transactions costs and the time synchronization of the data.

James Bodurtha and Georges Courtadon (1986) present a rigorous analysis of arbitrage boundary conditions based on an initial sample of more than 50,000 spot currency option trades on the PHLX. The authors show that when data on last daily trades are used (such as are commonly reported in the newspapers), numerous boundary violations are discovered if transaction costs are ignored. However, once the data are restricted to those combinations within a 15-minute period and transaction costs are considered, boundary violations are shown to be extremely rare.

Other studies have examined arbitrage boundary conditions for currency futures options traded on the CME (Ogden and Tucker, 1987) and for U.S. Treasury bond futures options traded on the CBOT (Jordan and Seale, 1986). Both studies used very large data samples and found almost no violations of the key arbitrage boundary conditions.

Pricing Efficiency and Pricing Biases

The second type of empirical test is aimed at measuring the accuracy of a particular option pricing model. This is a more stringent and difficult test to accomplish because (1) we must obtain all of the inputs required by the particular option pricing model, and (2) any test of pricing accuracy is a joint test of both the validity of the model and the ability of investors to set market prices equal to model prices.

As we discussed earlier, the continuous time lognormal model—equations (12.3a) and (12.3b)—for pricing options on spot currency has six data inputs: S, K, r_d, r_f, T, and σ. To test the model, we need a set of prices on put and call options plus measurements on the six data inputs taken at the same time as the option prices. There is no difficulty measuring K and T since they are explicitly specified in the option contract. There should be little difficulty in measuring S, r_d, and r_f at times that coincide with the option prices. Eurocurrency interest rates are often used to represent the opportunity cost of funds for option market participants.

Only the volatility parameter (σ) cannot be observed directly, so it must be estimated. There are two basic techniques to estimate σ. First, we can compute a statistical estimate of σ based on *historical* data. However, this approach does not provide an unambiguous answer since we must select a sample period and a statistical estimator of volatility. Second, we can compute the so-called **implied volatility,** namely, the volatility figure that equates the "model price" from a particular option pricing equation with the "market price" as observed in the option market. But clearly, the current implied volatility cannot be used to test the accuracy of a pricing equation, since implied volatility is itself constructed to produce a perfect fit between the model price and the market price.

Bodurtha and Courtadon (1987) have prepared an extensive study on the accuracy of both European and American option pricing models based on the assumption of continuous time lognormal currency rates. For their estimate of volatility, they take a value for σ based on the previous day's implied volatility. Their empirical analysis is based on 15,000 randomly selected prices from a database of over 100,000 trades during the March 1983–March 1985 period on PHLX currency options.

The authors report numerous results for puts and calls; for in-the-money, at-the-money, and out-of-the-money options; for options with short, medium, and long maturities; and for currencies maintaining a positive and negative interest differential against the US$. Each classification could be important to specify how the European and American models perform under various conditions.

Across the entire 15,000-trade sample, Bodurtha and Courtadon conclude that the average pricing error for the European model is not significantly different from zero. However, "underpricing" (meaning model price less than market price) is significantly more common than "overpricing" (that is, model price greater than market price) for European options. The American model tends, on average, to significantly overprice currency options. The results for the entire sample seem to be dominated by the results for puts. The European model significantly overprices puts, and the American model overprices puts even more so. Both European and American models exhibit unbiased pricing for calls.

The pricing bias appears smallest (although still significant) for in-the-money options. Perhaps this makes intuitive sense because the bulk of the option price for this category is intrinsic value and little is time value. European models tend to significantly underprice in-the-money options, while American models tend to significantly overprice them. The largest pricing bias (significant and on the order of about 18 percent) appears in out-of-the-money options. European and American models produce similar prices for out-of-the money options since the value of early exercise is low for the currencies in this particular sample. Both European and American models significantly overprice out-of-the-money put options, and significantly (and substantially) underprice out-of-the-money call options.

Further research by Eduardo Borenzstein and Michael Dooley (1987) focused on the underpricing of out-of-the-money calls. Borenzstein and Dooley examine PHLX currency options for a similar period, February 1983–June 1985. Their results show that if we maintain the lognormal continuous time model with a single value of σ, a substantial pricing bias results which increases for options that are further out of the money. Figure 12.13 shows this result for the DM and ¥, where the notation σ^* represents the value of σ, which produces the best fit between model prices and market prices for all options in the sample, across all strike prices. The authors also show that this pricing bias has a significant time pattern as the bias is significantly larger with shorter intervals to maturity.

Borenzstein and Dooley then study the performance of an alternative option pricing model—a "pure jump" model which assumes that the exchange rate changes at some steady rate ($\mu\ dt$) but is then augmented by an additional term reflecting a constant probability of discrete jumps drawn from a Poisson distribution. If an exchange rate evolves in this fashion, out-of-the-money options should have higher values. As the authors explain:

> For an out-of-the-money option it is only the probability of an exchange rate reaching values higher than the exercise price that gives the option a positive price. Now consider the price of an option at a moment in time close to maturity; if the exchange rate follows a diffusion process, the chances of its rising above the exercise price may be very small, but if it is a jump process, all that might be required is that it takes one jump before maturity. It follows that investors would price the option correspondingly higher.[31]

Empirical evidence in Figure 12.14 shows that a pure jump model clearly outperforms the alternative continuous diffusion model and eliminates the pricing bias for out-of-the-money calls. Recall that the sample period includes the rapid appreciation of the US$ that culminated in March 1985. The results support the interpretation that the chance of a large, sudden appreciation of the DM or the ¥ accounted for the high prices of out-of-the-money call options during this period.

Policy Matters—Private Enterprises

Can Option Pricing and Trading Be Made an Exact Science?

The existence of explicit formulas for pricing options sometimes lends the impression that option trading is an exact science. Indeed this is *not* the case, as our review of empirical evidence suggested. The Black-Scholes (lognormal continuous time) model is

---

[31]Borensztein and Dooley (1987), p. 665.

FIGURE 12.13 **Exercise Price Bias in Call Options with the Continuous Time Lognormal Model**
September 1984–June 1985

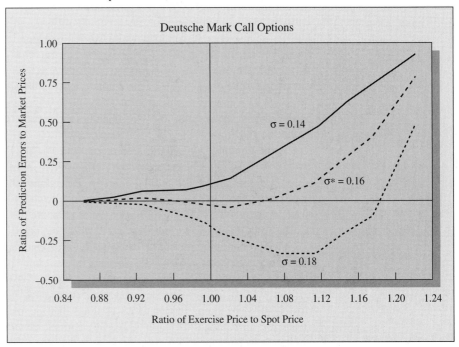

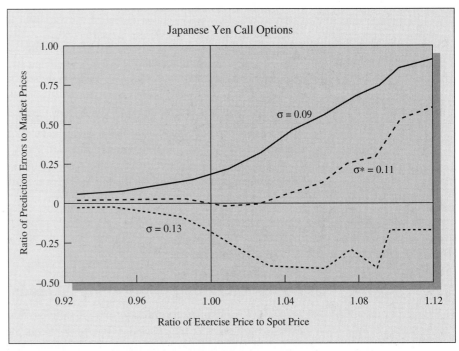

Note: The prediction error is the difference between the market price and the model price. Each curve is based on a model price with σ equal to the constant as noted. The curve labeled σ* produced the best fit between model and market prices.

Source: Eduardo R. Borensztein and Michael P. Dooley, "Options on Foreign Exchange and Exchange Rate Expectations," *IMF Staff Papers* 43, no. 4 (Dec. 1987), pp. 643–80.

FIGURE 12.14   Exercise Price Bias in Call Options with the Continuous Time
Lognormal Model and the "Pure Jump" Model
September 1984–June 1985

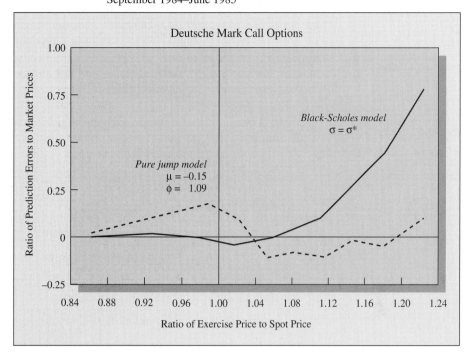

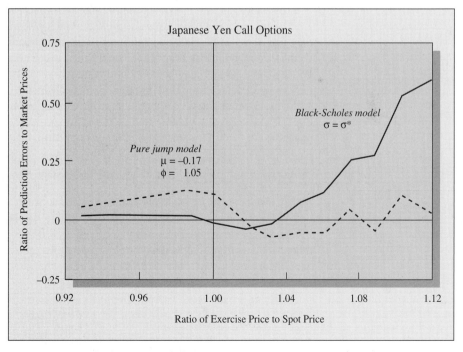

Note: The pure jump model assumes that the $/FC rate behaved as if there were a constant probability of a φ–1 percent
jump (depreciation) of the US$ exchange rate.

Source: Eduardo R. Borensztein and Michael P. Dooley, "Options on Foreign Exchange and Exchange Rate Expectations,"
IMF Staff Papers 43, no. 4 (Dec. 1987), pp. 643–80.

one possible model whose predictions may or may not conform closely with prices observed in the market. The importance of the Black-Scholes model, however, has been elevated by various market practices. For example, in the over-the-counter market, option prices are not quoted in dollars as they are on the PHLX or CME. Rather, prices are quoted in units of volatility. A bank trader might quote a price of 14.2 percent volatility for a six-month, at-the-money ¥ call option, or a price of 5.7 percent volatility for a three-month, at-the-money C$ put option.[32] Market convention then uses the Black-Scholes model to convert these volatilities into U.S. dollar prices.

Another market practice entails measuring the sensitivity of an option position to changes in market fundamentals. In particular, traders want to measure the sensitivity of their option positions to changes in each of the five parameters in the option pricing model, namely:

$$\partial C / \partial S = \text{Delta} \qquad\qquad (\Delta)$$

$$\partial C / \partial \sigma = \text{Kappa (or vega)} \qquad\qquad (\kappa)$$

$$\partial C / \partial t = \text{Theta (or time decay)} \qquad\qquad (\theta)$$

$$\partial C / \partial r_d = \text{Domestic interest rate partial} \qquad\qquad (\rho_d)$$

$$\partial C / \partial r_f = \text{Foreign interest rate partial} \qquad\qquad (\rho_f)$$

And since traders place such importance on delta as a risk measure, the sensitivity of delta to changes in the spot rate is also monitored.

$$\partial^2 C / \partial S^2 = \text{Gamma} \qquad\qquad (\gamma)$$

The Black-Scholes model has gained importance because each one of the above risk measures can be written down mathematically once we have a well-specified equation for *C* the call price.[33] We will discuss these risk measures in the next section.

A fundamental policy issue for private market participants is how much reliance they can place on formal models of option pricing (such as Black-Scholes) to guide them in pricing and risk management decisions. As the empirical evidence shows, the Black-Scholes model may lead to significant over- or underpricing of options, particularly those that have little time left until expiration and those that are out of the money. Although the usefulness of a model depends on its predictions rather than its assumptions, it may be worthwhile to review the assumptions of the Black-Scholes model to understand its possible shortcomings when applied to options on foreign exchange.

Is Volatility Constant or Does Volatility Vary?

First, consider volatility, which is assumed to be a constant parameter over the life of the option. In practice, measures of historical volatility display considerable variation. In Figure 12.15, we see that the estimate of volatility based on the prior 20 trading days (about one month) has ranged from below 5 percent to above 30 percent for the yen over

---

[32]To see the current values of implied volatilities for foreign currency options, see the Federal Reserve Bank of New York website at <www.ny.frb.org/pihome/statistics/vrate.shtml>. The Fed reports implied volatilities (both bid and offer prices) for horizons of one week, one month, and so on out as far as three years. Further information about implied volatility and how the Federal Reserve collects its data is available at <www.ny.frb.org/pihome/statistics/vbground.html>. Historic data on implied volatility can be downloaded at <ftp://ftp.ny.frb.org/forex/>.

[33]A comparable set of risk measures apply also for put prices.

FIGURE 12.15   Estimates of $/Yen Spot Rate Volatility Based on 20 and 260 Trading Days

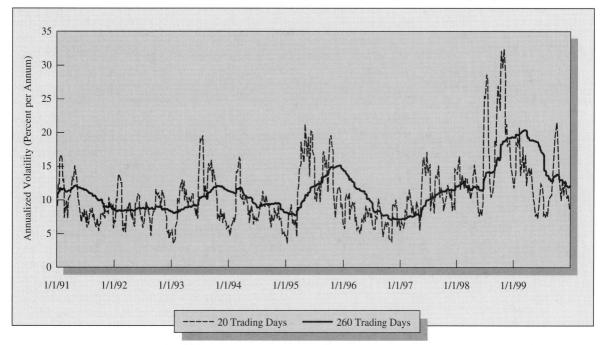

Source: Federal Reserve data and author's calculations

the years 1991–1999. One-month volatility is clearly not a constant across these 108 months.[34] The apparent lack of constancy raises the issue of whether the empirical time patterns in volatility can be modeled.[35] The estimate of volatility for the yen based on the prior 260 trading days (about one year) shows much less variation, but still ranges between 7 percent and 20 percent over the nine-year period. The two graphs in Figure 12.15 suggest that there may be some mean-reversion in volatility, whereby σ varies in the short run with a tendency to return back toward its longer-run value. If so, a trading strategy based on buying options when volatility is low and selling or writing options when volatility is high would be profitable. However, it should be clear that volatility is the *result* of macroeconomic fundamentals. There is no reason that σ should be constant although it may be convenient and not inappropriate to model it as constant over certain periods.

The currency option market itself seems to acknowledge the empirical finding that volatility is not a constant as assumed within the Black-Scholes framework. As we mentioned, option traders conventionally quote their "prices" to one another using σ. The fact that traders offer different quotes on σ for options with differing strikes and differing maturities immediately calls into question the assumption of constant volatility. In fact, the quotations for σ in the OTC market (and the implied σ from the PHLX) market

---

[34]Strictly speaking, the Black-Scholes model requires constant volatility only *within* the one month of a one-month option. The sequence from one month to the next need not be constant.

[35]Modeling σ(*t*) as a function of lagged values of σ, or lagged values of other variables, is a natural approach.

FIGURE 12.16   The Strike-Price Structure of Quoted OTC Volatility and
Implied PHLX Volatility: The "Smile Effect"

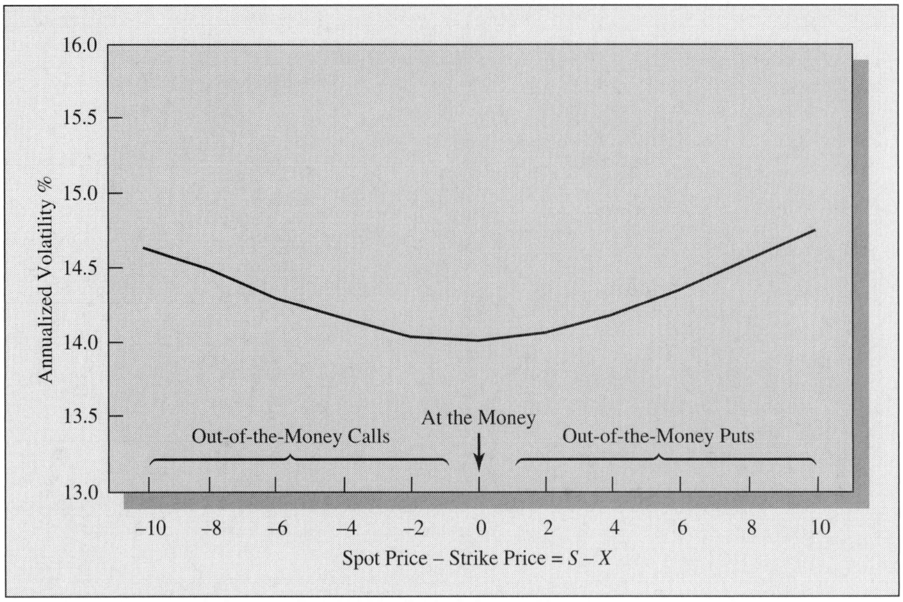

Note: When $S - X < 0$, we have out-of-the-money calls. When $S - X > 0$, we have out-of-the-money puts.

often have a distinctive pattern as shown in Figure 12.16. The quoted value of volatility often takes a minimum for at-the-money options, and then rises for out-of-the-money puts and calls. This empirical pattern has been dubbed the "smile effect."[36] The explanation for the smile effect may in part be institutional since out-of-the-money options tend to be thinly traded and subject to higher liquidity risk. But an alternative explanation—that currency prices evolve subject to discrete jumps rather than continuous change—is also plausible.

Estimating Volatility Using the Historical and Implied Approaches.   A related issue is how to estimate σ. Volatility can be estimated from historical data, but option pricing theory provides no guidance about how the estimate should be constructed. Should we use the last 20 trading days, the last 260, or more? Should we weight all observations equally or weight more recent observations more heavily? If we use daily data, should we construct an annualized volatility measure by multiplying by $\sqrt{260}$ (the number of trading days per year) or by $\sqrt{365}$ (the number of calendar days in the year)? Should we use the classical statistical estimator of volatility, $\sigma^2 = \Sigma (x_1 - \bar{x})^2/(n - 1)$, or an alternative estimator based on the daily range of prices?

Alternatively, we could let the market guide us in estimating σ by using the implied volatility approach. Recall that implied volatility is the volatility figure that equates the

---

[36]There may be a smile effect using only calls or only puts if the distribution of exchange rates is very fat-tailed. In this case, the market price will exceed the model price for deep out-of-the-money options. If instead the distribution is nonnormal and skewed left or skewed right, we may observe a half-smile (dubbed a "smirk") where only deep in- or deep out-of-the-money options are overvalued.

Box 12.3

What Does Implied Volatility Predict?

No matter how volatility is determined, if the currency option market is efficient, we should find that today's implied volatility provides an unbiased estimate of the future (realized) volatility over the life of the option. This is an implication of market efficiency.

The evidence in Philippe Jorion (1995) suggests that for an individual currency option, implied volatility is a significant variable for explaining future volatility. However, implied volatility is a fairly poor predictor of future volatility since it can explain only about 10–15 percent in terms of an R^2. Moreover, implied volatility appears to be a biased forecaster of the future. Jorion's results show that if implied volatility is high relative to its average, a forecast should be scaled back. And if implied volatility is low relative to its average, it should be grossed up. These findings suggest a lack of efficiency and a profitable trading rule strategy, but no empirical evidence on trading profits is available.

Shang-Jin Wei and Jeffrey Frankel (1991) also found that the implied volatility for one-month currency options is not significantly related to the realized volatility in the ensuing one-month period. As in any test of market efficiency, the results depend on having the correct equilibrium model of asset pricing. As we have seen, empirical

studies question the precision of the basic Black-Scholes model for pricing currency options. So, this may contribute to the lack of correlation between implied and realized volatility. However, Wei and Frankel found that the market tends to accurately foresee the *direction of change* in volatility; that is, option prices tend to increase (decrease) prior to periods when spot rate volatility increases (decreases). In this sense, the option market appears to behave efficiently.

José Campa and Kevin Chang (1995) examined a related aspect of implied volatility as a predictor—whether the implied volatility of a longer-maturity option contract contains information about the implied volatility of shorter-maturity option contracts. The question is much like that asked in research on the term structure of interest rates where, according to the expectations hypothesis, forecasts of future short-term interest rates are embedded in current long-term interest rates. Campa and Chang analyzed daily option prices on DM, ¥, £, and SFr options with maturities of 1, 2, 3, 6, and 12 months over the period from December 1, 1989, to August 31, 1992. The authors reported that the current spread between long-run and short-run volatility significantly predicts the direction of change in volatility of future short-run options.

"model price" from a particular option pricing equation with the "market price" as observed in the option market. To implement this approach, we need to select a "market price." But for any single currency there are many market prices reflecting (1) puts and calls, (2) different maturities, and (3) different strikes. If the Black-Scholes model were valid, each option would return the same volatility figure because volatility is assumed constant. In practice, however, we are likely to find a "smile effect" which implies that the price (that is, volatility) of a recently issued one-year at-the-money option cannot be used as an unbiased guide to the price of an already existing one-year out-of-the-money option. The possible use of implied volatility as a forecasting tool is discussed in Box 12.3.

Other Shortcomings of Option Pricing Models

The Black-Scholes model also assumes that domestic and foreign interest rates are constant over the option's life. This is a suspicious assumption on its face, but particularly so in the case of exchange rates, since exchange rate changes are often closely connected to interest rate movements. The assumption is even more suspicious in the case of options on interest rate futures. If interest rates were constant, there would be little need for a product to hedge interest rate risks.

Formal models such as Black-Scholes have also facilitated risk management by allowing option traders to calculate their exposure to changes in the list of parameters that determine option prices. The delta, gamma, kappa, and theta terms defined earlier measure the sensitivity of option prices to these parameters. But notice that delta (along with the other risk measures) is a *partial derivative* (for example, $\Delta_C = \partial C/\partial S$) computed under the assumption that all other factors are held constant, rather than a *total derivative* (for example, $\Delta_C = dC/dS$). Thus, each popular risk measure will understate exposures when shocks to the spot rate and volatility happen concurrently (and the risks compound) while they overstate exposures when shocks to the spot rate and volatility happen concurrently (and the risks offset). More important, the risk measures are themselves dependent on the validity of the model equation. And as we have seen, there is reason to be suspicious that any single equation model with fixed parameters can offer a good approximation to market prices in a world where policy shifts and exchange rate jumps are a somewhat common occurrence.

Policy Matters—Public Policymakers

Options Markets and Price Volatility in Underlying Markets

For public policymakers, the establishment and growth of currency and interest rate options markets raises a number of complex issues. As with any derivatives market, a generic question is whether the existence of the option market leads to negative spillover effects, such as an increase in the volatility of the underlying asset. This question can be asked for any asset that has an option or futures market. In the case of foreign exchange, there are some additional considerations to the argument.

In the first decade or so of the currency option market, writers of options could not hedge themselves by turning to an interbank market and buying an offsetting position. More likely, traders would "delta-hedge" their position as follows. After selling a £1 million call option with $\Delta_C = 0.50$, traders would buy a synthetic call by borrowing an amount of US\$ (*B*) and purchasing Δ_C units of £. Then if spot £ rises, Δ_C would rise, perhaps to 0.60. The traders would adjust their hedge by borrowing more US\$ and buying more spot £. The marginal impact of this spot £ purchase would be to *further* increase the spot price of £. The process is symmetric in the reverse direction. If spot sterling were to fall, and Δ_C also fell to 0.40, traders would reduce their US\$ borrowing and sell spot £, thus putting more downward pressure on spot £.

We can see that delta hedging is an example of a **dynamic hedging strategy** or a strategy that is continuously adjusted in response to market conditions. This strategy also tends to reinforce exchange rate movements: buying when the spot rate is going up and selling when the spot rate is headed down. Were this a complete description of the process, it would be possible to argue that the option market induces greater exchange rate volatility. However, several factors mitigate this conclusion.

First, delta hedging is performed on the trader's overall option portfolio and not on each individual option separately. Thus, a trader with the following book:

Short, £10,000,000 Call $\Delta_C = $ $0.50 \Rightarrow$ Delta hedge $=$ £5,000,000

Short, £20,000,000 Put $\Delta_P = -0.25 \Rightarrow$ Delta hedge $= -$£5,000,000

actually holds a delta neutral book because the delta positions for each option are additive and, in this case, offset each other. Thus, there need not be a great deal of delta hedging by traders, even if there is an active options market.

Second, the option market is a derivative market. Customers who demand option-like products could replicate them synthetically using continuous rebalancing of spot and forward currency positions. The option market only lowers the transaction cost of establishing positions that the trader could already create.

Finally, the option market remains small relative to the entire foreign exchange market. Even if delta hedging were a popular risk-management tool, it is not clear that it could have much impact on the behavior of currency rates.

Capital Requirements for Option Traders

A related public policy concern is the risk to which option traders are exposed and how capital requirements for these risks should be measured. If a valid option pricing model were available, meaningful risk measures could be calculated for any option position. As we have suggested, it may not be possible to write down a single equation model of option prices that fits well with market prices across a broad range of market conditions.[37] Still, having a model is only part of the story.

All of the risk measures we have described apply to "differentially small" shocks to one of the proximate determinants of the option price. If a large shock hits the spot rate, then a delta neutral option portfolio will experience a change in valuation. This is the meaning of "gamma risk," where the delta neutral hedge changes with the level of the spot rate. We illustrated this in Figure 12.11b, where delta changes gradually with longer-term options but very abruptly with short-term options.

These factors suggest that there are additional elements of risk in option trading than those that can be simply deduced from a stylized model of option pricing. Risks of larger price movements and their impact on the integrity of the option trading system are policy issues that we will reexamine in Chapter 17.

---

[37]More advanced theoretical option pricing models examine the pricing of options when (1) interest rates are stochastic, (2) volatility is stochastic, and (3) the underlying distribution of exchange rates is not lognormal, such as when the exchange rate is subject to jumps. See Hull and White (1991) and DeRosa (1992), pp. 188–95, for examples.

Summary

Options on currencies and interest rates have been actively traded since the late 1970s. Most currency options trade in the interbank market while most interest rate options are listed on exchanges. The defining feature of an option contract is its asymmetric payoff profile, offering limited loss (gain) and unlimited gain (loss). Used individually, options can put a floor on the lowest price or a cap on the highest price for a transaction in the underlying asset. Options can be used in combinations to achieve exposure to (or protection from) rising volatility or falling volatility, or to achieve a collar on transaction prices.

At maturity, the prices of options are known with certainty. Prior to maturity, option prices depend on a small set of factors: the asset's current price, the strike price, interest rate(s), time to maturity, and volatility. Using the binomial model, we showed that a call option can be replicated by borrowing money and holding some fraction (delta) in the underlying asset, and that a put option can be replicated by borrowing some fraction (delta) in the underlying asset and investing in the safe asset. This replicating approach showed how to price an option, and how to hedge an option position using a delta hedge.

The continuous time lognormal model is the most popular way of assessing the value of an option on a financial instrument. The Garman-Kohlhagen model can be applied to options on spot currency, and Black's model can be applied to options on futures, including interest rate futures. In these models, interest rates and volatility are assumed constant over the life of the option. Volatility is the only unobserved variable in an option pricing model. There is no unique method for estimating volatility. Most studies suggest that volatility varies over time. This raises doubts about the validity of conventional option-pricing models, and risks for people who use these models for pricing options or for hedging option positions.

Empirical evidence suggests that option markets are very efficient in the sense that few arbitrage boundary violations are observed. On the other hand, market prices of options are often substantially greater than the model prices of options, especially for deep out-of-the-money options. This result could mean that the continuous time lognormal model for option prices is correct and the option market is inefficient, or that the option market is really efficient, but that the assumptions of the continuous time lognormal model are false. Nonnormal (fat-tailed) exchange rate distributions, time-varying volatility, exchange rate jumps, and measurement error in estimating volatility are some of the possible explanations for the market's apparent overpricing of deep out-of-the-money options.

APPENDIX 12.1
DETERMINATION OF THE REPLICATING PORTFOLIO IN THE TWO-PERIOD BINOMIAL MODEL

A call option on £ can be replicated by an amount of dollar borrowing (B) and spot sterling purchase (Δ_C). Using Table 12.6a and algebraic symbols to represent the cash flows, we can solve for B and Δ_C as shown below. All of the magnitudes ($C_{2u}, C_{2d}, S_1, S_{2u}, S_{2d}, r_d, r_f, t$, and n) are known; only B and Δ_C are unknown.

Transaction	Cash Flows Period 1	Cash Flows in Period 2 if $S_1 \uparrow S_{2u}$	if $S_1 \downarrow S_{2d}$
Dollar borrowing	B	$-B \exp(r_d t/n)$	$-B \exp(r_d t/n)$
Spot £ purchase	$\Delta_C S_1$	$-\Delta_C S_{2u} \exp(r_f t/n)$	$-\Delta_C S_{2d} \exp(r_f t/n)$
Purchase call option on £	C_1	C_{2u}	C_{2d}

We solve for Δ_C and B, using methods for two equations and two unknowns.

Equation I. $C_{2u} = -B \exp(r_d t/n) - \Delta_C S_{2u} \exp(r_f t/n)$

Equation II. $C_{2d} = -B \exp(r_d t/n) - \Delta_C S_{2d} \exp(r_f t/n)$

The solution is:

$$\Delta_C = \frac{(C_{2d} - C_{2u})}{[S_1 (u - d) \exp(r_f t/n)]}$$

$$B = \frac{[u\, C_{2d} - d\, C_{2u}]}{[\exp(r_d t/n)\,(u - d)]}$$

We showed in the main text that $C_1 = B + \Delta_C S_1$. The only inputs needed to determine the current value of an option with expiration one period from now are (1) the distribution of the spot price at expiration, associated with the current spot rate and the expected rate of appreciation and depreciation, (2) the exercise price of the option, and (3) the prevailing interest rates.

In the same fashion, we can replicate a put option on £ by an amount of dollar lending (L) and spot sterling borrowing (Δ_P). Using Table 12.6b and algebraic symbols to represent the cash flows, we can solve for L and Δ_P. All of the magnitudes ($C_{2u}, C_{2d}, S_1, S_{2u}, S_{2d}, r_d, r_f, t$, and n) are known; only L and Δ_P are unknown.

Transaction	Cash Flows Period 1	Cash Flows in Period 2 if $S_1 \uparrow S_{2u}$	if $S_1 \downarrow S_{2d}$
Dollar lending	L	$-L \exp(r_d t/n)$	$-L \exp(r_d t/n)$
Spot £ borrowing	$\Delta_P S_1$	$-\Delta_P S_{2u} \exp(r_f t/n)$	$-\Delta_P S_{2d} \exp(r_f t/n)$
Purchase put option on £	P_1	P_{2u}	P_{2d}

We solve for Δ_P and L, using methods for two equations and two unknowns.

Equation I. $P_{2u} = -L \exp(r_d t/n) - \Delta_P S_{2u} \exp(r_f t/n)$

Equation II. $P_{2d} = -L \exp(r_d t/n) - \Delta_P S_{2d} \exp(r_f t/n)$

The solution is:

$$\Delta_P = \frac{(P_{2d} - P_{2u})}{[S_1 (u - d) \exp(r_f t/n)]}$$

$$L = \frac{[d\, P_{2u} - u\, P_{2d}]}{[\exp(r_d t/n)\,(u - d)]}$$

APPENDIX 12.2
BOUNDARY CONDITIONS, EARLY EXERCISE, AND OPTION PRICES

Equation (12.4) can be used to determine a more useful lower bound for a European option price. Since put and call prices are always nonnegative, it must be the case that:

$$C \geq S_0 \, exp(-r_f T) - K \exp(-r_d T) \qquad \text{(12A.1)}$$

$$P \geq K \exp(-r_d T) - S_0 \, exp(-r_f T) \qquad \text{(12A.2)}$$

If both domestic and foreign interest rates were zero in equation (12A.1), the lower bound for a European call is simply its intrinsic value, $S - K$. But if r_f is greater than r_d (so that the foreign currency trades at a forward discount), then the lower bound for a European option is less than its intrinsic value. The same reasoning applies to equation (12A.2) and European puts. If both domestic and foreign interest rates are zero, the lower bound for a European put is its intrinsic value, $K - S$. But if r_d is greater than r_f, then the lower bound for a European option is less than its intrinsic value.

Figure 12A.1 shows the usefulness of the lower bound given by equation (12A.1). The lower bound for a European call has a flatter slope and lies to the right of the $S - K$ locus because of the interest differential and the effect of discounting over time. As Figure 12.7 suggests, at some point the value of a European call intersects the $S - K$ locus, indicating that it would be preferable to exercise the option were this permitted. The point where $S - K$ exceeds the lower bound of equation (12A.1) is where:

$$S - K \geq S \exp(-r_f T) - K \exp(-r_d T)$$

or

$$S \, [1 - \exp(-r_f T)] \geq K \, [1 - \exp(-r_d T)] \quad \text{(12A.3)}$$

Along the same lines, the value of a European put intersects its intrinsic value locus ($K - S$) at some point, indicating that it would be preferable to exercise the option were this permitted. Again, this point occurs where $K - S$ exceeds the lower bound of equation (12A.2), so that:

$$K - S \geq K \exp(-r_d T) - S_0 \, \exp(-r_f T)$$

or

$$K \, [1 - \exp(-r_d T)] \geq S \, [1 - \exp(-r_f T)] \quad \text{(12A.4)}$$

Equations (12A.3) and (12A.4) are *necessary conditions* for the early exercise of an option. These conditions apply only to American options; European options cannot be exercised prior to expiration. However, equations (12A.3) and (12A.4) are *insufficient conditions* for early exercise. Sufficient conditions for early exercise are that the value of the American option is less than the option's intrinsic value, or:

$$C^* < S - K \qquad \text{for calls} \qquad \text{(12A.5)}$$

$$P^* < K - S \qquad \text{for puts} \qquad \text{(12A.6)}$$

From our discussion in this chapter, it should be clear that the value of an American currency option is always at least as great as the value of a similar European currency option. Intuitively, this is because an American option embodies the possibility for early exercise. Based on equations (12A.3) and (12A.4) and Figure 12.17, we can conclude that early exercise is an important consideration only when (1) the interest differential between foreign and domestic currencies is large, and (2) the option is very deep in the money.

We will not discuss the development of a model for American currency option pricing in detail.[38] The general approach usually relies on a multiperiod application of the binomial model. The value of the American option at maturity is (as it is for all options) the maximum of its exercise value or zero. At each node *prior* to maturity, the value of the option is determined as the maximum of its exercise value or its value from being kept alive for one more period. This procedure is repeated until the value of the option at the first node is determined. Application of the binomial approach requires analytical approximations, based on the number of nodes to consider, the magnitude of each spot rate change, and the number of exchange rate paths to evaluate. Computer programs have been developed to calculate values of American currency options using these approximations.

---

[38]For more details on American option pricing, see Bodurtha and Courtadon (1987) and DeRosa (1992), chapter 8.

FIGURE 12A.1   Currency Calls and Puts and Early Exercise

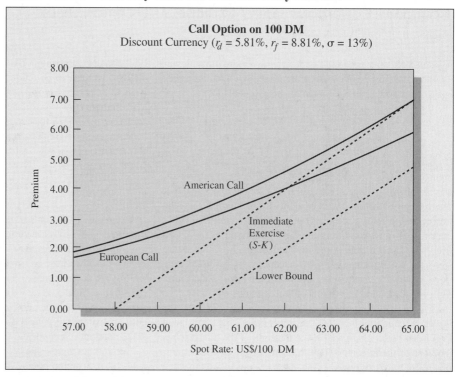

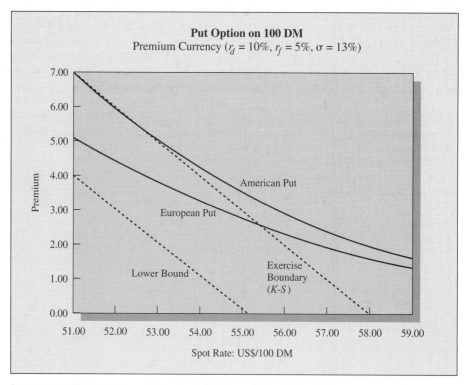

Source: David F. DeRosa, *Options on Foreign Exchange* (Chicago: Probus, 1992), p. 161.

APPENDIX 12.3
INTRODUCTION TO EXOTIC OPTIONS

A conventional option has a fixed-length maturity and results in a payoff that depends only on the price of the underlying asset (upon exercise or at maturity) in comparison to a fixed strike price. **Exotic options** include a wide variety of options with some unusual feature pertaining to the calculation of the underlying asset price, the calculation of the strike price, or the expiration conditions. An exotic option, like a conventional option, is a *contingent claim* that obtains value *contingent on* the occurrence of an event (or events). As long as the contingency can be well specified, agents can write an option contract and agree to payments if the contingency occurs.

All exotic options are traded in the over-the-counter market. Many exotic options are known as **path-dependent options,** since the payoff depends not simply on the terminal value of the underlying asset, but on its price history prior to exercise or expiration. We will briefly describe several of the more popular exotic options—**average rate options, barrier options, and basket options.**[39]

Average Rate Options

An average rate option (sometimes called an "Asian" option) may be attractive for several reasons. Because the payoff depends on an average rate instead of the rate on a single day, the contract is less susceptible to a sharp price swing on the expiration day. Some forecasters predict the average rate over a period (and not the end-of-period rate), making the average rate option the most direct way to apply an average rate forecast. Many firms use an average exchange rate to translate or convert foreign cash flows over a reporting period, again making the average rate option the most direct way to hedge these risks. Finally, an average rate option should always be less expensive than a conventional option. The reasoning is that the standard deviation of an average is always smaller than the standard deviation of an individual price in the series.

The payoff for an average rate option is defined by Max[0, $A - K$] for a call and Max[0, $K - A$] for a put, where A is the *average* spot rate and K is the strike price.[40] The word *average* is in italics because there are many ways to compute an average. For example, we could compute either arithmetic or geometric averages.

If we elect the arithmetic average, there is (as yet) no simple formula for pricing the option. If we use the geometric average, a mathematical formula is available.[41] For any set of numbers, the geometric average will be less than the arithmetic average. It follows that the price of a geometric average rate call option will be less than the price of an arithmetic average rate call option. And the price of a geometric average rate put option will be greater than the price of an arithmetic average rate put option.

The average we compute could be based on one observation per week, per day, per hour, and so forth. This sampling frequency is important since we know that the standard deviation of an average of 52 observations (one per week) is less than the standard deviation of an average of 12 observations (one per month). Consequently, the greater the sampling frequency, the lower the price of the average rate option.

Barrier Options

A **barrier option** is an exotic option where the expiration (or birth) of the option depends on the underlying asset crossing a specified price level, or barrier. A **knock-out option** is one that automatically expires when the underlying asset price crosses the preset barrier, while a **knock-in option** is one that automatically comes to life when the barrier is penetrated.

The most common types of knock-out options are the "down-and-out" call and the "up-and-in" put. Consider a down-and-out € call with a strike at $0.90 and an out-barrier of $0.88. As long as the spot € rate stays above $0.88, the down-and-out call functions as a conventional option. But if the $0.88 barrier is hit, the call expires worthless.

Clearly, the down-and-out call must be less valuable than a conventional call option, since the maturity of the down-and-out call is less than (and at most equal to) a conventional call. Thus, a bullish € speculator, confident that the € will appreciate above $0.90 (and never below $0.88) would be attracted by the down-and-out call. A corporate hedger also might buy the down-and-out call to lock in a $0.90 ceiling on a planned € purchase, but would willingly let the option expire if the € drops below $0.88. Implicitly, the corporate hedger must feel that € will stay near this lower level.

The "up-and-out" put functions in an analogous way. With a strike at $0.90 and a put-barrier at $0.92, the up-and-out put functions as a conventional put as long as the € stays below $0.92. If € appreciates to $0.92 or above, the up-and-out put expires.

---

[39]For a general description of other exotic options see Gastineau (1992). For a more detailed analysis, see DeRosa (1992), chapter 10.

[40]The *average strike option* is another style of average option. The payoffs depend on the terminal spot rate and a strike price computed from an average of intervening spot rates.

---

[41]See Ruttiens (1990).

Once again, the value of an up-and-out put is less than (and at most equal to) a conventional put. So, a bearish € speculator, confident that the € will depreciate below $0.90 (and never cross above $0.92) would be attracted by the up-and-out put. And a corporate hedger might buy the up-and-out put to lock in a $0.90 floor on a planned € sale, but would willingly let the option expire if the € appreciates above $0.92.

A knock-in option is one that comes into existence, and *remains* in existence, once the option-barrier is hit. Knock-in options could be attractive to speculators who feel that spot rate changes are serially correlated or that a big movement will follow once the barrier is penetrated. An up-and-in call or down-and-in put would fit this strategy.

A corporate hedger who plans to buy euros and fears a rise in the € above $0.92, might not want to pay the full price of a call with a $0.92 strike. Buying an up-and-in call option (with a strike at $0.90 and an in-barrier at $0.92) will cost less than a conventional option and possibly provide a better fit to his or her exchange rate scenario. Similarly, a corporate hedger who plans to sell euros and fears a fall in price below $0.88 might not want to pay the full price on a put with a $0.88 strike. Buying a down-and-in put (with a strike at $0.90 and an in-barrier at $0.88) will save money and still put a $0.88 floor under the € sale.

The reader can check that conventional European options, that live from writing until expiration, can be decomposed into two barrier options, such as:

$$C_{\text{conventional}} = C_{down\text{-and-out}} + C_{down\text{-and-in}}$$

$$P_{\text{conventional}} = P_{up\text{-and-out}} + P_{up\text{-and-in}}$$

From the above, it is clear that barrier options are always cheaper than conventional European options.

Basket Options

A **basket option** refers to an option on a basket of assets, such as currencies. The price of the option will be based on the volatility of the portfolio. The basket option should be cheaper than a collection of individual options when the assets in the basket are imperfectly correlated.

A straightforward application is for a U.S. importer with purchases in Canada (invoiced as C$) and the United Kingdom (invoiced in UK£). The importer could purchase at-the-money calls for C$ and UK£ separately to cover the amounts of each individual invoice. These options would be priced based on the volatility of each currency, $\sigma_{\text{C\$}}$ and $\sigma_{\text{UK£}}$. Alternatively, the importer could purchase an at-the-money call for a *portfolio* of C$ and UK£. The volatility of the portfolio, $\sigma_{\text{Portfolio}}$, will be less than either $\sigma_{\text{C\$}}$ or $\sigma_{\text{UK£}}$, resulting in a lower option price.

Questions

1. What is the difference between an American option and a European option? Which one should trade at a higher price?

2. A call option that gives you the right to buy the yen also gives you the right to sell the US$. Is this statement true or false? Explain.

3. What is the main reason behind the use of OTC options versus exchange-traded options? Why would a firm call a bank and enter an agreement using OTC options rather than use an exchange-traded option?

4. If the current exchange rate is $0.86/€, the strike price of a call option expiring in three months is $0.90/€ and the option premium is $0.05/€, what is the intrinsic value of the option? What is its time value?

5. Look in the newspaper for yesterday's prices of € call options on the PHLX. Graph the option prices in the format used in Figure 12.7.

6. Suppose a U.S.-based firm has a receivable position for € 10 million. In order to hedge its exchange rate exposure, would the firm use a call or a put on the €? Would the firm buy or sell the option?

7. What are the main differences between hedging interest rate exposure with options and hedging with futures contracts?

8. What is the difference between options on spot currency and options on currency futures?

9. Suppose an investor purchased an interest rate call option to buy a 10-year maturity 9 percent bond at the strike price of 100. The underlying bond is currently trading at a yield of 8 percent. Is this option in the money or out of the money?

10. If investors want to protect themselves against a rise in interest rates, should they buy or sell a *call* option on interest rate futures or a *put* option?

11. What is the delta of an option? The gamma? What are the fundamental assumptions that underlie the calculation of the delta?

12. How can option traders hedge their position using their knowledge of delta? In what circumstances do we call a portfolio delta neutral? Is a delta neutral portfolio at any risk of loss?

13. Some people have argued that the Black-Scholes model is not ideal for assessing the value of interest rate and currency options. Why is this?

14. Suppose you can buy on the PHLX a call option to buy yen at $0.01/¥ for maturity in two months. The premium is 1.26 cents per 100 yen. What would be the total cost of purchasing this call option?

15. Suppose the yen is trading at ¥100/$, the Japanese interest rate is 2.5 percent, and the U.S. interest rate is 6 percent. A European call option at a strike of 100 with a two-month maturity is currently trading at 1.93 cents per 100 yen and the put option at the same strike and the same maturity trades at 2.00 cents per 100 yen. Determine whether there is an arbitrage opportunity in the option market, using the put-call parity.

16. OTC options traders often quote option prices using volatility and deriving the actual price in dollars through options models like the continuous time lognormal model. If an option (call or put) is being quoted at 14 percent volatility by trader A and at 15 percent volatility by trader B, which trader—A or B—has the better price?

17. Some people have argued that the option market tends to increase the volatility of the underlying asset. If a trader is short call options on a currency, what effect would the trader's delta hedging strategy have on the underlying currency market?

18. If the market is efficient, what is the ideal measure of volatility that should be used when estimating the value of an option?

19. Explain several alternative methods for estimating the volatility for a three-month DM option. Discuss the pros and cons of using these different methods.

20. Explain the smile effect.

21. "Setting a currency option price is fairly simple. You just plug six variables into a computer model and out pops a price—assuming you have the correct model." Discuss.

Exercises

Option Strategies

Options can be used in an unlimited numbers of ways, with one option or a bundle of them. Bundling options (calls and/or puts) with different maturities and/or different strike prices help create many varieties of payoff patterns, which may fit an investor's objectives, either for speculation or hedging. Payoffs for a bundle of options are determined by adding the different positions acquired or sold. Profits and losses from positions in individual options are added to determine the overall profit and loss picture. The following exercises will cover some of the most widely used option strategies.

1. A *straddle* is the simultaneous buying or selling of both a call and a put with the same exercise price and the same maturity.

   a. Suppose that the yen is currently traded at ¥99.77/$. On the PHLX, the Call August 100 is traded at $0.0193 and the Put August 100 at $0.0183.

- What is the cost to an investor purchasing this straddle?
- When would the position start making money? Graph the payoff at maturity.
- What are the expectations of an investor who purchases this straddle?
- What are the risks?

   b. Suppose the German mark is currently traded at $0.63/DM. On the CME, the Call August 63 is traded at $0.0102/DM and the Put August 63 at $0.0093/DM.

- What is the cost for an investor purchasing a straddle? Shorting a straddle?
- When does an investor make money on a short straddle position? Graph the payoff at maturity.
- What are the risks in the position compared with a long straddle position?
- What are the investor's expectations if he or she is short a straddle?

2. A *spread* is a combination of two or more call options (or put options) on the same underlying asset with different strike prices or times to maturity. Some options are bought while others are sold, or written.

   a. Suppose the German mark is traded at $0.6319/DM. On the PHLX, the Call July 63 is traded at $0.0085 and the Call July 64 at $0.0043.
      - What is the cost for an investor purchasing a *bullish spread,* that is, buying the Call July 63 and selling the Call July 64?
      - When would the position start making money? What is the maximum payoff the investor can expect? Graph the payoff at maturity.
      - How would you exploit mispricing in the call option markets using spreads?

   A *bearish spread* is buying the Call July 64 and selling the Call July 63.

   b. What is the cost of the bearish spread strategy? What are the investor's expectations? Graph the payoff at maturity.

   c. Suppose the British pound is trading at $1.55/£. On the CME, the Put July 1.550 is trading at $0.0164/£ and the Put July 1.525 at $0.0054/£.
      - What is the cost for an investor purchasing the Put July 1.55 and selling the Put July 1.525?
      - When would the position start making money? What is the maximum payoff the investor can expect? Graph the payoff at maturity.
      - How would you exploit mispricing in the put option markets using spreads?

3. A *butterfly spread* is created by simultaneously selling one call with a low strike price and one call with a high strike price as well as buying two calls with a midlevel strike price. Suppose the following call options on Swiss francs are traded on the CME:

   Call August 74.50: $0.0135/SFr
   Call August 75.50: $0.0115/SFr
   Call August 76.50: $0.0075/SFr

   Consider a *butterfly spread* created by simultaneously selling one call with a 74.50 strike and one call with a 76.50 strike and buying two calls with a 75.50 strike.
   - What is the cost of the strategy?
   - When would the position start making money? What is the maximum payoff the investor can expect?
   - Graph the payoff at maturity. Compare the payoff pattern with that of a straddle.

Discrete Time Binomial Model

4. Suppose the yen is traded at ¥100/$ on January 1. The one-year Japanese yen interest rate is 2.5 percent. The one-year U.S. Treasury bill yields 5.5 percent. The volatility of the ¥/$ exchange rate is 17 percent. Suppose there is a call on the yen with exercise price ¥100/$ and maturity of one year.

   a. In a simple binomial model with only two scenarios (¥ up or down), what is the expected value of the ¥ at the end of the year according to both scenarios? (Use the simplified formula to calculate the multiplicative factors u and d.)

   b. What is the value of the call at maturity, considering the two scenarios?

   c. Using the formulas in Appendix 12.1, show how a combination of borrowing and lending can replicate the payoff of the call. What is the value of the call today?

   d. Suppose the volatility of the exchange rate increases to 25 percent. What would be the effect on the value of the call?

Put-Call-Forward Parity

5. Using put-call-forward parity, demonstrate that the price of a call with the strike price equal to the futures price is equal to the price of a put with the same strike price and the same maturity.

6. Suppose call options on the DM with a strike price of $0.63/DM and maturity of one month are traded at $0.01/DM. One-month futures on the DM are traded at $0.624/DM. One-month U.S. Treasury bills yield 5.5 percent. One-month German government securities yield 7.5 percent. The spot $/DM exchange rate is $0.625/DM.

   a. Using put-call-forward parity, determine the value of a put option on DM with a strike price of $0.63 and one month maturity.

   b. How would you take advantage of arbitrage opportunities if you find that the actual price of the put is below the theoretical price determined using the parity condition?

Hedging

7. The treasurer of XYZ company is expecting a dividend payment of DM 10 million from a German subsidiary in two months. Her expectations of the future DM spot rate are mixed: The DM could strengthen or stay flat over the next two months. The current spot exchange rate is $0.63/DM. The two-month futures rate is at $0.6279/DM. The two-month German interest rate is 7.5 percent. The two-month U.S. T-bill yields 5.5 percent. Puts on the DM with maturity of two months and strike price of $0.63 are traded on the CME at $0.0128/DM. Compare the following choices offered to the treasurer:

   • Sell a futures on the DM for delivery in two months for a total amount of DM 10 million.

   • Buy 80 DM put options on the CME with expiration in two months and strike price equal to the current spot rate.

   • Set up a forward contract with the firm's bank.

   a. What is the respective cost of each strategy?

   b. Which strategy would best fit the treasurer's mixed forecast for the future spot rate of the DM?

8. Refer to the previous question. Suppose the DM actually rose in value to $0.67/DM when the dividend payment is made.

   a. Which of the three strategies enables the treasurer to take advantage of the rise in the DM against the dollar?

   b. What is the final gain (loss) incurred in each case?

9. Suppose a trader at Citibank has the following positions on her book:

   Short £15 million call
   Short £30 million put

   The delta is 0.60 on the call and −0.30 on the put.

   a. Calculate the delta hedge for each position.

   b. What exposure does the trader have on her portfolio?

10. Refer to the previous question. Suppose that a change in the spot rate implies a change in the delta for the call from 0.60 to 0.65, and a change in the delta of the put from −0.30 to −0.25. What adjustments would the trader have to make to keep a delta neutral portfolio?

References

Bank for International Settlements. *Central Bank Survey of Foreign Exchange Market Activity 1995.* Basle, Switzerland: BIS, May 1996.

Bank for International Settlements. *Central Bank Survey of Foreign Exchange and Derivatives Market Activity 1998.* Basle, Switzerland, May 1999.

Black, Fischer. "The Pricing of Commodity Contracts." *Journal of Financial Economics* 3 (Jan.—Mar. 1976), pp. 167–79.

Black, Fischer, and Myron Scholes. "The Pricing of Options and Corporate Liabilities." *Journal of Political Economy* 81 (May–June 1973), pp. 637–59.

Bodurtha, James N., and Georges Courtadon. "Efficiency Tests of the Foreign Currency Options Market." *Journal of Finance* 41, no. 1 (Mar. 1986), pp. 151–62.

———. "The Pricing of Foreign Currency Options." *Monograph Series in Finance and Economics.* No. 1987-4/5, New York: New York University Salomon Brothers Center for the Study of Financial Institutions, 1987.

Borensztein, Eduardo R., and Michael P. Dooley. "Options on Foreign Exchange and Exchange Rate Expectations." *IMF Staff Papers* 43, no. 4 (Dec. 1987), pp. 643–80.

Campa, José M., and P. H. Kevin Chang. "Arbitrage-Based Tests of Target-Zone Credibility: Evidence from ERM Cross-Rate Options." *American Economic Review* 86, no. 4 (Sept. 1996), pp. 726–40.

———. "Testing the Expectations Hypothesis on the Term Structure of Volatilities in Foreign Exchange Options." *Journal of Finance* 50, no. 2 (June 1995), pp. 529–47.

Cooper, Neil, and James Talbot. "The Yen/Dollar Exchange Rate in 1998: Views from the Options Market." *Bank of England Quarterly Bulletin,* Feb. 1999, pp. 68–77.

DeRosa, David F. *Options on Foreign Exchange.* Chicago: Probus, 1992.

Garman, Mark B., and Steven W. Kohlhagen. "Foreign Currency Option Values." *Journal of International Money and Finance* 2, no. 3 (1983), pp. 231–37.

Gastineau, Gary L. *Dictionary of Financial Risk Management.* Chicago: Probus, 1992.

Gibson, Rajna. *Option Valuation: Analyzing and Pricing Standardized Option Contracts.* New York: McGraw-Hill, 1991.

Grabbe, J. Orlin. *International Financial Markets.* New York: Elsevier, 1986.

Hull, John, and Alan White. *Introduction to Futures and Options Markets.* Englewood Cliffs, NJ: Prentice Hall, 1991.

Jordan, J., and W. Seale. "Transactions Data Tests of Minimum Prices and Put-Call Parity for Treasury Bond Futures Options." *Advances in Futures and Options Research* 1 (1986), pp. 63–87.

Jorion, Philippe. "Predicting Volatility in the Foreign Exchange Market." *Journal of Finance* 50, no. 2 (June 1995), pp. 507–28.

Malz, Allan M. "Using Option Prices to Estimate Realignment Probabilities in the European Monetary System: The Case of Sterling-Mark." *Journal of International Money and Finance* 15, no. 5 (Oct. 1996), pp. 717–48.

Ogden, J., and A. Tucker. "The Relative Valuation of American Currency Spot and Futures Options: Theory and Empirical Tests." *Journal of Futures Markets* 7 (Dec. 1987), pp. 695–703.

Ruttiens, Alain. "Classical Replica." *Risk* 3 (Feb. 1990), pp. 33–36.

Wei, Shang-Jin, and Jeffrey A. Frankel. "Are Option-Implied Forecasts of Exchange Rate Volatility Excessively Variable?" NBER Working Paper No. 3910, Nov. 1991.

13 CURRENCY AND INTEREST RATE SWAPS

"Swaps are the glue that binds together the world's financial system."

The Economist, June 10, 2000, p. 81.

Learning Objectives

After reading this chapter, students should

1. Be familiar with the historical origins of the swap market, the size and growth of the market, and the notion of gross exposure.

2. Understand the cash flows that counterparties are obligated to make in interest rate and currency swaps.

3. Understand how swaps can be used to transform financing on fixed-rate terms into floating-rate terms (or vice versa), or financing in home currency terms into foreign currency terms (or vice versa).

4. Recognize that swaps are equivalent to a collection of forward contracts and commitments.

5. Understand the notion of a par swap and how, over time, swaps can become "in the money" or "out of the money."

6. Be aware of the price risks associated with swaps, how these risks can be measured using the "simulation approach," and how these risks can be managed more effectively.

The market for currency and interest rate swaps is the most recent addition to the international financial markets. From the first currency swap in August 1981 and the first interest rate swap in 1982, the market has grown to enormous proportions, with more than $45 *trillion* in "notional principal value" of outstanding swap contracts by year-end 1999.

The swaps we analyze in this chapter might be better termed *capital market swaps.* That would help to differentiate them from the foreign exchange swap transactions discussed in Chapter 3 which represented simply a simultaneous borrowing and lending of short-term bank deposits denominated in two different currencies with interest paid at maturity. In this chapter, a **swap** represents an agreement to exchange cash flows between two parties, usually referred to as **counterparties.** A **swap agreement** commits each counterparty to exchange an amount of funds (determined by a formula) at regular

475

intervals until the swap expires. In the case of a currency swap, there is an initial exchange of currency and a reverse exchange at maturity.

As we saw with futures and options, swaps are another example of a derivative security. In this case, a swap can be shown to be equivalent to a collection of forward contracts that call for an exchange of funds at specified times in the future. Like forward contracts, a swap can be used to speculate, to hedge an exposure, or to replicate another security in an effort to enhance investment returns or to lower borrowing costs.

Because a swap can be replicated using forward contracts, it is natural to ask why the swap market exists and why it has grown so popular. The answer has several pieces that we will examine in this chapter. Part of the answer is that a swap reduces transaction costs by allowing the counterparties to arrange in one transaction (the swap) what would take many transactions (using forward contracts) to replicate. In addition, the legal structure of a swap transaction may have advantages that reduce the risk to each counterparty in the event of a default by the other counterparty.

In the early years of the market, most swaps could be described as "plain vanilla." For example, the exchanges in the classic **fixed-floating interest rate swap** were based on the simple differential between a fixed US$ interest rate (say, today's five-year Treasury bond rate) and a floating US$ interest rate (say, the six-month Eurodollar rate measured every six months). Each counterparty would pay (or receive) the difference between the fixed and floating interest rate times the **notional value** of the agreement. Likewise, the classic **fixed-rate currency swap** committed the counterparties to an exchange of payments governed by the simple differential between, say, the interest rate on a seven-year US$ corporate bond and the interest rate on a seven-year SFr corporate bond.

In recent years, more exotic swap contracts have been developed. Rather than oblige one counterparty to pay an amount: $A_{\text{Vanilla}} = i_{\text{Fixed}} - i_{\text{Floating}}$, a swap could call for the payment of an amount $A_{\text{Exotic}} = \beta_0 + \beta_1 i_{\text{Fixed}} - \beta_2 i_{\text{Floating}}$ where β_0, β_1 and β_2 are parameters specified in the swap contract. Clearly, a swap can call for an exchange of funds governed by *any* formula that one can write. But the basic approach to swap valuation remains straightforward and intuitive. Once we specify the expected cash flows of the swap and their riskiness, a swap can be valued using a net present value approach.

However, calculating the price of these exotic swaps and the exposure borne by an uncovered counterparty is exceedingly difficult. In this chapter, we will focus primarily on the economic fundamentals and financial characteristics of basic interest rate and currency swap agreements.

In the sections that follow, we begin by describing the origins of the swap market and the role played by capital controls. The growth of the market and some description of the players is also discussed. We then develop the basic pictures that describe the cash flows of simple interest rate and currency swaps. We use these to examine the risks that are borne by the counterparties in a swap transaction. An important theme is how one should measure these risks. We outline a simulation approach for measuring market risk and show that the time pattern of behavior in the floating interest rate is a key determinant of risk for interest rate swaps. With the building blocks in place, we outline the determinants of swap prices. For interest rate swaps, the relationship between swap rates and interest rate futures contracts is examined.

The swap market has spawned numerous policy issues, especially as cases involving large losses incurred by corporations and financial portfolio managers have come to light. We review the major policy issues that affect private enterprises in their use of the swap market. And, in the final section, we consider those issues that are of primary concern to public policymakers in this new and fast-growing financial market.

FIGURE 13.1   The Origins of a Capital Market Swap

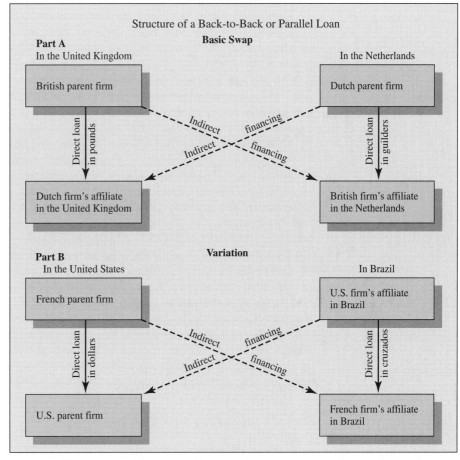

Source: D. K. Eiteman, A. I. Stonehill, and M. H. Moffett, *Multinational Business Finance,* 6th ed. (Exhibit 8.4 from p. 215), © 1992 by Addison Wesley Publishing Company Inc. Reprinted by Permission of Addison-Wesley Longman Publishing Company Inc.

Origins and Underpinnings of the Swap Market

The concept of counterparties agreeing to a long-term exchange of financial payments existed prior to the development of the swap market. Examining these precursors will help us to understand more about the modern swap contract.

The Role of Capital Controls

Part A of Figure 13.1 shows a British parent firm operating in the United Kingdom and a Dutch parent firm operating in the Netherlands. Suppose that the British parent wishes to make a loan to its affiliate in the Netherlands. This seems like a simple transaction. But suppose that this transaction is taxed. In the post–World War II period, Britain operated under a variety of capital controls. One control, known as the *investment dollar,* required a British investor to purchase foreign currency intended for overseas investment from a limited pool of funds. These funds were scarce and therefore traded at a premium.[1]

Rather than submit to the exchange control, the British firm could (legally) arrange for a Dutch parent firm in the Netherlands to lend to the British firm's Dutch affiliate, while at the same time arranging for a loan from the British parent to a British affiliate of the Dutch parent firm. This "double loan" arrangement was sometimes called a **back-to-back loan** or a **parallel loan.** Since the British parent would have paid a tax by taking the direct financing route, the parent (through its subsidiary) would willingly pay a slightly higher interest rate to the Dutch parent and charge a slightly lower interest rate to the Dutch firm's affiliate in order to effect this indirect financing of its own Dutch affiliate.

In much the same fashion, suppose a Brazilian affiliate of a U.S. parent firm had accumulated substantial profits beyond what it desired to reinvest locally or was allowed to repatriate home. The Brazilian affiliate could effectively transfer funds to its U.S. parent if it made a loan to a Brazilian affiliate of a French firm and the French parent simultaneously lent funds to the U.S. parent. Since the legal barrier to repatriation imposes a cost, the U.S. firm is willing to provide a financial incentive to the French firm to take part in the deal. Part B of Figure 13.1 illustrates these transactions.

While back-to-back and parallel loans were a useful device, they also presented certain drawbacks. First, identifying a counterparty was time-consuming and costly. Second, the initial capital market barrier was circumvented by two loans. These loans, while paired in the eyes of the counterparties, were legally separate and distinct loans. Therefore, default on one loan by one counterparty would not release the other counterparty from fulfilling its commitments under the second loan. Finally, as these transactions are indeed loans, they would appear on the counterparties' accounting statements or on balance sheet for accounting and regulatory purposes. Thus, there could be repercussions on the firm's unused borrowing capacity, credit rating, and so on.

Factors Favoring the Rise of Swaps

In the early 1980s, the currency swap evolved as a way to simplify and speed the exchange of currency cash flows between counterparties. Lowering transaction costs is a basic, but critical, ingredient in the introduction of a new financial product. In addition, the currency swap effectively linked the two cash flows. The counterparties to a swap compare the cash flows moving in each direction and pay only the net difference between them. Thus, if firm A is obliged to pay firm B $1 million and B is obliged to pay A €1 million, when the spot rate is $1.05/€ firm B simply delivers $50,000 to firm A.

The cash flows of a swap were linked; if firm A could not pay firm B, then firm B felt excused from having to pay firm A. Whether swaps always reflect this **right-of-offset** is a critical point that we will discuss in more detail. Finally, as a new financial product, the currency swap was not covered by any accounting disclosure or security registration requirements. A firm could treat a currency swap as an **off-balance-sheet item,** in this case representing a contingent responsibility to make (or receive) payments. If the swap was not disclosed, investors and regulators could not estimate the value or risk of these contingent claims.

While the desire to reduce the costs of overcoming barriers to the international movement of capital played a major role in the development of the currency swap market, other factors also have been important. Corporate name recognition, tax status, and

---

[1]For more on exchange control programs, see Rosenberg (1983), p. 13. For a discussion of the investment currency market, see *Bank of England Quarterly Bulletin* (1976).

FIGURE 13.2   **Interest Rate and Currency Swaps Outstanding at Year-End**
Notional Principal Value in Trillions of US$

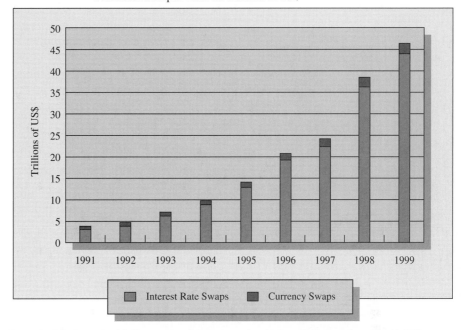

Source: Bank for International Settlements, *Quarterly Review,* various issues, and BIS press release, May 18, 2000.

innovative financial product design have given cost advantages to some firms, thus promoting the use of swaps. We will amplify the other reasons why swaps have gained such popularity later in this chapter.

Swaps Outstanding, the Volume of Transactions, and Gross Exposure

The swap market grew rapidly, from zero in 1980 to more than $45 trillion in outstanding swaps in December 1999 (see Figure 13.2). This figure represents the notional value of outstanding swaps, defined as the underlying amount on which swap payments are based. Although currency swaps were introduced first, interest rate swaps quickly raced ahead and now account for roughly 90 percent of outstanding swaps. About 40 percent of these swaps have a maturity of less than 2 years, and another 35 percent have maturities between 2 and 5 years; the remaining 25 percent of swaps outstanding have maturities greater than 5 years, with some exceeding 10 years.

Currency swaps naturally involve the US$ and other currencies, but interest rate swaps are conducted in many currencies as well. The US$–¥ pair represented the largest segment of the currency swap market in 1991, with 24.4 percent of the market (see Table 13.1). But more than half of all currency swaps written in 1991 did not involve the US$. The data for April 1995 show a substantial increase in currency swaps involving the US$–¥ and US$ versus other currencies. In the April 1998 BIS survey, the US$–¥ pair remained the most active segment of the currency swap market, with a 27.2 percent share. However, swaps between the US$ and the DM, French franc, or other EMU currencies accounted for 33.6 percent of the total market, suggesting that US$/€ currency swaps should comprise a large segment of the market.

TABLE 13.1   Composition of Swaps Written Annually by Currency
Notional Principal in Billions of U.S. Dollars

	1991		April 1995[a]		April 1998[a]	
	Amount	*Percentage*	*Amount*	*Percentage*	*Amount*	*Percentage*
Currency Swaps						
Yen-Dollar	$ 80	24.4%	$ 439	41.6%	$ 701	27.2%
Others-Dollar	60	18.3	416	39.4	1,542	60.0
Non-Dollar	188	57.3	200	19.0	332	13.8
Total	$ 328	100.0%	$ 1,055	100.0%	$ 2,575	100.0%
Interest Rate Swaps						
US$	$ 926	57.1%	$ 4,367	26.8%	$ 9,312	23.2%
DM	103	6.3	1,694	10.4	12,117	30.2
Yen	194	12.0	4,464	27.4	3,669	9.1
Others	399	24.6	5,793	35.5	15,088	37.5
Total	$1,622	100.0%	$16,318	100.0%	$40,186	100.0%

[a]Data for April 1995 and 1998 were reported on a daily basis and converted to annual figures by the author by multiplying by 260 trading days per year.

Sources: Data for 1991 are from *Derivatives: Practices and Principles,* Group of Thirty, Washington, DC, July 1993. Data for April 1995 are from *Central Bank Survey of Foreign Exchange and Derivatives Market Activity, 1995.* Bank for International Settlements, May 1996 Table D-8 and Table 10-A-1. Data for April 1998 are from the BIS survey of the same title, Tables E-20, E-21, and E-30.

More than half (57.1 percent) of all interest rate swaps written in 1991 involved US$-based rates. The remainder of the interest rate swap market was linked to interest rates in DM, ¥, and other currencies. The data for April 1995 and 1998 show that the volume of transactions in non-US$ interest rate swaps has grown considerably, to nearly 75 percent of this market segment. New interest rate swaps involving DM expanded nearly eightfold between 1995 and 1998 as the DM became a more certain proxy for the pending EMU. The volume of yen interest rate swaps actually declined in 1998.

The swap market has developed an infrastructure so that swap transactions occur among dealers in the interbank or over-the-counter market as well as with final customers. In Table 13.2, we see that much of the annual flow of swap activity is with final customers, but that this percentage has declined from nearly 70 percent in 1987 to only 47 percent in 1997. Financial institutions such as securities houses, investment companies, and insurance firms form the largest group of final customers. The market among dealers is expanding at a greater rate than the market among end-users of swaps.[2] Note, however, that the dealers' share of the swap market is still much lower than we observe in the foreign exchange market, where interbank transactions account for more than 80 percent of trading activity. The dealer market is heavily concentrated among the world's largest banks and financial institutions. In the United States, for example, Julapa

---

[2]In April 2000, a group of large swap dealers announced plans to form an electronic dealing network for online trading and negotiation of interest rate derivatives. The joint venture, called SwapsWire, was expected to begin live trading late in 2000 and then expand to permit broader trading among the interbank community and end users in 2001. See <www.swapswire.com> for further information.

TABLE 13.2   Composition by Counterparty of New Swaps Written Annually
Notional Principal in Billions of U.S. Dollars

| | | | Counterparty | | | | |
| | | | End-Users | | | | |
Year	Total	Dealers	Subtotal	Financial Institutions	Corporations	Governments	Others
1987	474	144 (30.4%)	330 (69.6%)	203	86	35	6
1988	692	222 (32.1%)	470 (67.9%)	282	127	52	9
1989	1,012	368 (36.4%)	644 (63.6%)	370	186	63	25
1990	1,477	546 (37.0%)	931 (63.0%)	472	286	98	75
1991	1,950	865 (44.4%)	1,085 (55.6%)	591	362	111	21
1992	3,124	1,402 (44.9%)	1,722 (55.1%)	933	548	191	50
1993	4,400	2,059 (46.8%)	2,341 (53.2%)	1,193	787	251	110
1994	6,620	3,280 (49.6%)	3,340 (50.4%)	1,740	1,286	233	81
1995	9,154	5,144 (56.2%)	4,010 (43.8%)	2,437	1,292	281	0
1996	14,437	7,424 (51.4%)	7,014 (48.6%)	4,986	1,697	330	0
1997	18,202	9,625 (52.9%)	8,577 (47.1%)	6,272	1,744	561	0

Source: Data for years 1987–1991 are from *Derivatives: Practices and Principles,* Group of Thirty, Washington, DC, July 1993. Data for years 1992–1997 are from Bank for International Settlements, *Quarterly Review* of *International Banking and Financial Market Developments,* Aug. 1998 and Aug. 1999. Data reflect both currency and interest rate swaps.

Rungkasiri (1989) reported that only 235 banks (of more than 14,000) participated in the swap market and 90 percent of the swap activity was conducted by only 17 banks.[3]

While the total notional principal value of swaps outstanding exceeds $45 trillion, this measure vastly overstates the amount of payments exchanged or the value of capital at risk. A more meaningful indicator of the economic significance of outstanding swaps is their **gross market value** which reflects the cost that one counterparty would pay to replace a swap at market prices in the event of default. Thus, gross market value represents the **gross exposure** associated with swap contracts. The Bank for International Settlements (BIS) estimated that gross market value in December 1999 was about $250 billion for currency swaps (or 10.2 percent of notional value) and about $1,150 billion for interest rate swaps (or 2.6 percent of notional value).[4]

Together, currency and interest rate swaps have a gross market value of $1,400 billion, or 3.0 percent of the outstanding notional value. Certainly $1,400 billion seems like a large number, but it is really small in comparison to the banks' exposures in traditional loan portfolios and their cross-border exposures to other banks. As we examine later in this chapter, the use of bilateral netting agreements and collateral arrangements significantly reduces the actual exposure of swap dealers below gross market value.

The Basic Cash Flows of a Swap Transaction

Perhaps the easiest way to describe the essential cash flows in a swap and to demonstrate the motivation underlying a swap transaction is to work through a hypothetical

---

[3]For further analysis of the determinants of commercial banks activities in the swap market, see Jagtiani (1996).

[4]Bank for International Settlements, *Quarterly Review,* June 2000, p. 81.

FIGURE 13.3   The Basic Cash Flows of a Currency Swap

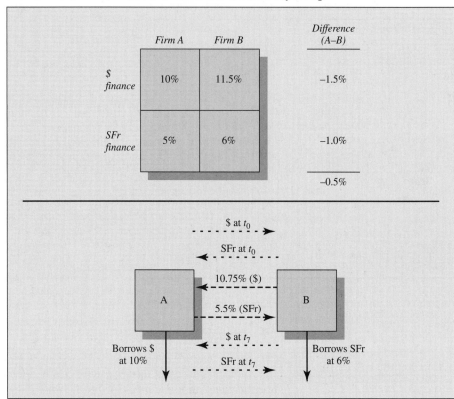

Notes: The amounts in the top panel show that firm A has a comparative advantage in borrowing US$ while firm B has a comparative advantage in borrowing SFr. If A desires SFr funds and B desires US$ funds, each can lower its borrowing costs by borrowing in the comparative advantage currency and swapping.

The cash flows and costs are summarized in the lower panel. A and B exchange US$ for SFr from the bond issues in period t_0. Firm A pays 10.0 percent + 5.5 percent and receives 10.75 percent, for a net cost of 4.75 percent. Firm B pays 6.0 percent + 10.75 percent and receives 5.5 percent, for a net cost of 11.25 percent. Each firm saves 0.25 percent over its alternative cost of funds. In period t_7, A and B reexchange US$ for SFr to retire their bond issues.

example. We begin with a description of a generic currency swap and then examine the cash flows in a generic interest rate swap.

Currency Swap

In Figure 13.3 we show two firms, A and B, each of which can issue a seven-year bond in either the US$ or SFr market. The annual interest costs for firm A are assumed to be 10 percent and 5 percent in the US$ and SFr market, respectively, and 11.5 percent and 6 percent for firm B. Firm A enjoys an *absolute advantage* in both credit markets. It is able to borrow at a lower interest cost than firm B in either market, most likely because firm A possesses a stronger credit rating.

But notice that firm A's credit advantage differs in the two markets. In the US$ market, firm A is awarded a 1.5 percent interest rate advantage relative to firm B, while in the SFr market, the interest differential between A and B is only 1.0 percent. Thus, firm A enjoys a *comparative advantage* in the US$ bond market and firm B has a comparative advantage in the SFr bond market. From the principles of trade theory, we know that it is possible for A and B to engage in mutually beneficial trade. Using reasoning from trade theory, both firm A and firm B can benefit by borrowing in their comparative advantage currencies and then swapping to obtain lower-cost financing in terms of the other currency.

To illustrate the transactions in a currency swap, we assume that in period t_0, firm A issues a seven-year bond for US$100 million at 10 percent and firm B issues a seven-year bond for SFr150 million at 6 percent. Assume that the spot exchange rate at t_0 is S_0 = SFr1.50/$, so that the principal amounts of these two loans are equal. Next, A lends its US$100 million to B, charging 10.75 percent per annum (fixed) while B lends its SFr150 million to A at a rate of 5.5 percent per annum (fixed). In years t_1 until t_7, firms A and B make interest payments to each other as stipulated in the swap agreement, *plus* paying interest on the original bonds they have issued. At time t_7, the swap contract matures. A and B make their final interest payments to each other, and reexchange the original principal amounts, which A and B use to retire their outstanding bonds.[5]

What is the result of this strategy? Firm A pays 5.5 percent (to B) on its SFr150 million loan. But firm A also pays 10.0 percent interest on its US$ bonds while receiving 10.75 percent interest on its US$100 million loan to B—or a net inflow of 0.75 percent. Thus, A pays (approximately) 4.75 percent net interest on its SFr loan.[6] This represents a 0.25 percent savings in relation to its own cost of borrowing SFr.

Firm B pays 10.75 percent (to A) on its US$100 million loan. But B also pays 6.0 percent interest on its SFr bonds and receives 5.5 percent interest on its SFr150 million loan to A—or a net outflow of 0.5 percent. Thus, B pays (approximately) 11.25 percent net interest on its US$ loan.[7] This represents a 0.25 percent savings in relation to its own cost of borrowing US$.

Together, A and B save 0.5 percent, an amount that could be determined in advance from the interest differentials assumed at the top of Figure 13.3. In a real transaction, if A and B are corporations or institutions, a bank or swap dealer would intermediate the transaction and charge a fee, thus reducing the aggregate interest savings available to A and B.

The Role of Market Segmentation and Saturation.   Two important questions require consideration: What is the source of these financing savings? And are they consistent with an efficient international financial market? The situation portrayed in Figure 13.3 reflects **capital market segmentation.** In other words, a case where two capital markets (the United States and Switzerland in our case) reach different evaluations about two firms and apply a different interest cost conditional on the risk of the firm. This is not an efficient outcome. If all factors are truly held similar, the price of risk (in this case, a unit of A's risk or B's risk) must be similar in **integrated markets.** A dissimilarity between the United States and Switzerland in the *relative pricing* of A and B bonds suggests either an arbitrage profit opportunity or that some factor has been omitted from the analysis.[8] These alternatives are explored in Box 13.1.

---

[5]Note that the spot rate at maturity, S_7, does not play a role. The reexchange of $100 million for SFr150 million (in effect, at S_0) eliminates any currency risk to retire the outstanding bonds.

[6]The calculation is approximate because 1 percent interest on US$ is not precisely the same as 1 percent interest on SFr.

[7]Again, the calculation is approximate because 1 percent interest on US$ is not precisely the same as 1 percent interest on SFr.

[8]An absolute pricing differential between firms A and B may be consistent with differential credit risks. And an absolute pricing differential between US$ and SFr bonds may be consistent with an expected change in the US$/SFr exchange rate.

Box 13.1

A Summary of the IBM/World Bank Currency Swap

The interest rates in the figure below summarize the borrowing costs of IBM and the World Bank in both the US$ (United States) and SFr (Swiss) bond markets in mid-1981. The World Bank had an absolute advantage in the US$ market, while IBM had an absolute advantage in the SFr bond market. The World Bank could issue seven-year US$ bonds in the U.S. market at rates roughly 40 basis points over U.S. Treasuries of the same maturity, while IBM could issue seven-year SFr bonds in the Swiss market at rates roughly equal to Swiss treasuries of the same maturity. Examining these borrowing costs, we see that the firms could save 25 bp by entering into a currency swap.

Although the exact details are confidential, the figures below summarize the cash flows in the swap. IBM and the World Bank issued Swiss franc and US$ bonds respectively and then exchanged the cash proceeds of these bond

issues. It was presumed that IBM agreed to pay the World Bank a fixed interest rate of 40 bp over the initial U.S. Treasury rate while the World Bank agreed to pay IBM a fixed interested rate of 10 bp over the initial Swiss Treasury rate.* The total cost for IBM was (Swiss Treasury + 0 bp) + (U.S. Treasury + 40 bp) − (Swiss Treasury + 10 bp) = U.S. Treasury + 30 bp; so IBM saved 15 bp. The total cost for the World Bank was (U.S. Treasury + 40 bp) + (Swiss Treasury + 10 bp) − (U.S. Treasury + 40 bp) = Swiss Treasury + 10 bp; so the World Bank saved 10 bp. At the termination of the swap in year 7, the firms reexchanged the original principal amounts and retired their outstanding bonds.

─────────

*See Bock (1983) for a more detailed discussion of the IBM–World Bank currency swap.

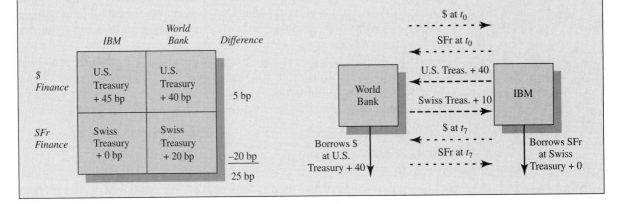

A review of the world's first currency swap between the World Bank and IBM will shed some light on this. The estimated costs for the World Bank and IBM to borrow in the US$ and SFr markets are shown in Box 13.1. In 1981, both IBM and the World Bank were rated AAA for credit risk. But in the real world, all AAA credits are not necessarily awarded the same interest cost of funds, even if the bond issues share similar characteristics. The reasoning is based, in part, on **saturation** and **scarcity value.** Other things being equal, investors seeking a portfolio of AAA bonds prefer to hold bonds from a broad set of issuers in order to diversify the idiosyncratic risks of any single issuer. An issuer who has not saturated the market may enjoy a scarcity value and be able to issue bonds at a lower rate. This effect is more likely among AAA-rated issuers, given their small universe.

FIGURE 13.4   The Basic Cash Flows of an Interest Rate Swap

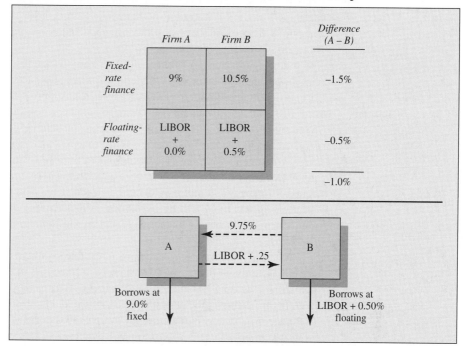

Notes: The figures in the top panel show that firm A has a comparative advantage in borrowing on fixed-rate terms while firm B has a comparative advantage in borrowing on floating-rate terms. If A desires floating-rate funds and B desires fixed-rate funds, each firm *appears* able to obtain lower borrowing costs by borrowing in its comparative advantage market sector and swapping. See the text and Box 13.2 for a discussion of why these cost savings may be illusory.

The cash flows and interest costs of the swap are summarized in the lower panel. Firm A pays 9.0 percent + LIBOR + 0.25 percent and receives 9.75 percent for a net cost of LIBOR − 0.50 percent. Firm B pays LIBOR + 0.50 percent + 9.75 percent and receives LIBOR + 0.25 percent for net cost of 10.00 percent. Each firm appears to save 0.50 percent over its alternative cost of funds. These interest rates are computed as a percentage of the notional principal value of the swap.

Note that there is no exchange of notional principal amounts in an interest rate swap.

Until 1981, the World Bank was a frequent issuer of bonds in the Swiss market in order to capture the low nominal interest rate in SFr.[9] With the demand for World Bank bonds saturated at prevailing rates, Swiss investors demanded a higher interest rate to hold additional World Bank bonds. IBM, on the other hand, viewed itself as a US$-based firm and borrowed exclusively in the US$ bond markets. Swiss investors were willing to pay a premium (reflecting a scarcity value) to bring IBM as a new AAA-issuer into their portfolios.

The bottom line of this transaction was that the World Bank saved about 10 basis points (SFr) and IBM saved about 15 basis points (US$) by virtue of the currency swap.

Interest Rate Swap

In Figure 13.4, we show two firms, A and B, that can issue a US$-denominated bond in either fixed-rate or floating-rate terms. The annual interest costs are assumed to be 9.0 percent and 10.5 percent, respectively, for A and B in the fixed-rate bond market. In

---

[9]The World Bank's strategy relied on the assumption that persistent deviations from uncovered interest rate parity would favor SFr borrowing.

addition, each firm can arrange floating-rate financing, perhaps through bank lending or a commercial paper (CP) program. In the floating-rate case, we assume that firm A pays six-month LIBOR plus 0 basis points, while firm B pays six-month LIBOR plus 50 basis points. This example assumes that interest is paid semiannually and the floating interest rate is reset every six months.[10]

Once again, it is apparent that firm A enjoys an absolute advantage in both the fixed- and floating-rate credit markets. Firm A is able to borrow on better terms than firm B in both markets, most likely because firm A represents a better overall credit risk.

But again, it appears that A's credit advantage differs across the two markets. In the fixed-rate market, A is granted a 1.5 percent lower interest cost while in the floating-rate market the interest rate advantage is only 0.50 percent. Thus, firm A enjoys a comparative advantage in the fixed-rate bond market, and firm B has a comparative advantage in the floating-rate bond market. Once again, we can reason that it may be possible for A and B to engage in mutually beneficial trade. The basic principle is as before—both A and B appear to benefit by borrowing in their comparative advantage markets and then swapping to obtain lower cost financing in their preferred method of long-term financing.

To explain the transactions in an interest rate swap, assume that in period t_0, firm A issues a seven-year bond for $100 million at a fixed rate of 9 percent and firm B obtains bank financing for $100 million at a floating rate equal to six-month LIBOR + 0.5 percent. In our example, the principal amounts are identical, so there is no need to actually exchange principal as in the currency swap example. However (and as if there were an exchange of principal), A agrees to pay LIBOR + 0.25 percent interest on $100 million to B, while B agrees to pay 9.75 percent interest on $100 million to A. In years t_1 until t_7, firms A and B make interest payments to each other as stipulated in the swap agreement, *plus* paying interest on the original bonds they have issued. At time t_7, the swap contract matures. A and B make their final interest payments to each other, A retires its outstanding bond issue, and B pays off its bank loan.

What is the result of this strategy? Firm A pays LIBOR + 0.25 percent (to B) and 9.0 percent on its fixed-rate bonds, while receiving 9.75 percent interest from B—or a net interest cost of LIBOR − 0.50 percent. Thus, A saves 0.50 percent in relation to its own cost of floating-rate funds.

Firm B pays 9.75 percent (to A) and LIBOR + 0.50 percent on its outstanding floating-rate bonds, while receiving LIBOR + 0.25 percent interest from A—or a net interest cost of 10.0 percent. Thus, B saves 0.50 percent in relation to its own cost of fixed-rate funds.

Together, A and B save 1 percent, an amount that could be determined in advance from the interest differentials assumed at the top of Figure 13.4. In a real transaction, if A and B are corporations or institutions, a bank or swap dealer would intermediate the transaction and charge a fee, thus reducing the aggregate interest savings available to A and B.

The Role of Segmentation and All-In Cost Differences.   Again, we are curious about the source of these apparent financing savings for users of interest rate swaps and

---

[10]Other floating-rate financing conventions are also possible. For example, a Eurobond that pays interest only once a year could float on the basis of one-year LIBOR. A bank loan that requires payment of interest on a quarterly basis could float on the basis of three-month LIBOR. Many other benchmarks for the payment of floating-rate interest (such as the prime lending rate or five-year government bond rate) are possible.

whether they are consistent with an efficiently operating capital market. In this case—two U.S. companies borrowing in the US$ market—it seems less likely that the capital market could be segmented as hypothesized in the currency market. But elements of segmentation could be involved. It may be that different groups of investors or different groups of analysts follow firms A and B. If so, then different pricing terms between fixed and floating interest are possible.

But it is important to see that floating-rate finance combined with a fixed-floating swap (**synthetic fixed-rate finance**) is not necessarily identical to actual fixed-rate financing. First, the all-in costs of the two techniques over the full seven-year period may differ. The fixed-rate bond will have higher underwriting and front-end fees that may total 1.0–1.5 percent of principal.[11] Floating-rate finance may be obtained through a commercial paper (CP) program or through a bank loan. In the CP program, the issuer pays a lower underwriting fee (perhaps 0.625 percent), but this fee is paid periodically (every six months) as the CP matures and is reissued (that is, "rolled over"). In a long-term bank loan priced in reference to LIBOR, the bank will charge an initial fee for setting up the loan, but there will be an ongoing facility fee charged periodically. Thus, the costs of floating-rate finance and fixed-rate finance are typically closer together than the raw periodic interest rates would suggest.

Second, the risks of the two techniques may differ as well. The fixed-rate financing alternative gives the firm funding at a known cost for the full maturity of the issue—7 to 10 years or longer. The synthetic alternative (floating-rate finance combined with a swap) leaves several elements of risk open. **Rollover risk** represents the chance that the firm may suffer a decline in its credit quality (below investment grade) and become unable to issue short-term paper in the commercial paper market. In the same fashion, if the firm borrowed against an uncommitted, six-month bank facility, the bank might refuse to renew the commitment if the firm's credit quality declines. The firm can buy insurance to guarantee its credit rating and protect itself against rollover risk. This may cost the firm about 0.75 percent per annum in fees, but save it about 0.25 percent in annual interest expense.

The synthetic alternative may also leave the firm exposed to a **basis risk** if its floating-rate financing is at the CP rate (or prime in the case of a U.S. bank loan) but it receives floating-rate interest based on LIBOR. There is a basis risk if the spread between the rate paid (CP or prime) and the rate received (LIBOR) is not constant. To guarantee this risk, an additional swap between CP and LIBOR is needed, which may cost about 0.15 percent.

Finally, the fixed-rate financing alternative may include a call provision that allows the issuer to repay the bonds early after three to four years. In the synthetic alternative, the firm could buy an option for the right to enter into an additional swap that would effectively offset the remaining transaction in the final years of the original swap.[12] The cost of this option could be 0.4 percent per annum.

Once all of these additional costs and risks have been taken into account, the actual benefits of fixed-rate financing versus an *equivalent* synthetic alternative are fairly small. Vipul Bansal et al. (1993) estimated that the net saving may be only 0.12 percent and growing smaller, as we detail in Box 13.2.

Thus, the underlying rationale for the interest rate swap is its role in facilitating interest rate risk management, rather than closing a (presumed) segmentation barrier and cost differential across the fixed- and floating-rate portions of the debt market. Speed

---

[11]These front-end fees include legal, accounting, and advertising expenses.

[12]The right to enter into a swap is called a *swaption*.

Box 13.2

Comparing Genuine Fixed-Rate and Synthetic Fixed-Rate Financing: A Detailed Example*

Suppose a firm with an A credit rating can issue a seven-year fixed-rate bond (callable after three years) with a 12.75 percent coupon payable semiannually. Suppose that the same firm can issue six-month commercial paper (CP) at 8.875 percent when LIBOR is 8.50 percent. By entering into a fixed-floating swap, paying 11.27 percent (a midpoint rate) in exchange for LIBOR, the firm creates synthetic fixed-rate financing. The apparent savings associated with the synthetic approach is computed as:

Apparent Savings

= Genuine fixed rate − Synthetic fixed rate

= 12.75% − [CP − (LIBOR + 11.27%)]

= 12.75% − [(LIBOR + 0.375%) − (LIBOR + 11.27%)]

= 1.105 percent

This simple, back-of-the-envelope calculation leaves out two major categories of costs—floatation costs and costs to offset additional risks in the synthetic approach—that differ between the two alternatives. We will examine these costs for a hypothetical $100 million debt issue. All costs in parentheses are hypothetical, but reasonable, guess values for actual costs.

Floatation Costs

Genuine Fixed-Rate.   To issue a seven-year bond, we must pay the underwriter's spread (1 percent) plus various front-end costs to cover accounting and legal expenses ($125,000). The firm must cover additional expenses ($45,000 every six months) to pay for the bond trustee,

registrar, and disbursement of coupons in addition to the semiannual coupon ($6,375,000). Thus, the "all-in" costs of the genuine fixed-rate approach are given in the table below. These cash flows imply a cost of 6.55 percent per six-month period, or 13.09 percent per annum on a semiannual bond basis.

Period	Year	Net Cash Flow
0	0	+$ 98,875,000
1	0.5	− 6,420,000
2	1.0	− 6,420,000
. . .	. . .	. . . .
13	6.5	− 6,420,000
14	7.0	− 106,420,000

Synthetic Fixed-Rate.   To follow this strategy, the firm must issue CP every six months and pay the CP dealer's fee (0.0625 percent or $62,500). The firm must cover the cost of disbursements and other administrative expenses ($38,000) every six months, plus additional accounting costs ($3,800) because of the synthetic structure. The swap dealer will charge a spread above the midpoint rate, so the cost of the swap will be closer to 11.33 percent. Every time the CP is rolled over, the firm will pay the swap dealer and the add-on above LIBOR (11.33 percent + 0.375 percent = 11.71 percent per annum, or $5,852,500 every six

_____
*The figures in this example are taken from Bansal et al. (1993).

may also be a factor because the synthetic alternative can be completed in a day, while issuing a fixed-rate bond could require more than a week (under Rule 415) or longer if a fresh offering prospectus is required.

Risks in Swaps

Our examples have demonstrated that a swap is a collection of exchanges between two counterparties. These exchanges are well defined; they occur on specified dates and according to specified terms. Since swaps can be used for two generic purposes—to lay months).[†] In the final period, the firm repays its CP with interest but does not incur a $62,500 charge since the CP is not rolled over. Thus, the all-in costs of the synthetic approach are:

Period	Year	Net Cash Flow
0	0	+$ 99,937,500
1	0.5	− 5,960,500
2	1.0	− 5,960,500
...	...	....
13	6.5	− 5,960,500
14	7.0	− 105,898,000

These cash flows imply a cost of 5.96 percent per six-month period, or 11.93 percent per annum on a semiannual bond basis.

A Preliminary Comparison.   Based on these floatation cost estimates, the synthetic fixed-rate structure now looks more attractive (13.09 percent − 11.93 percent = 1.16 percent) than before (1.105 percent).

Controlling for Additional Risk Factors

If the firm opts for the synthetic approach in an attempt to lower its funding costs, the firm exposes itself to several additional risks. Each of these risks can be insured against, but only for an additional cost as we outline below.

Roll-over Risk.   If the firm suffers a decline in its credit quality, the firm may be excluded from the CP market. This

[†]The current value of LIBOR is not in the calculation since the firm both pays and receives LIBOR.

is a serious risk, since lack of access to funds may jeopardize the firm's business project and its ability to earn income to meet its various obligations, including its outstanding swap. The firm can purchase a CP backup facility from its bank, and draw against these funds if necessary. The cost of this facility may be 0.45 percent.

Basis Risk.   The synthetic rate paid by the firm is CP − (LIBOR + 11.27 percent). If CP and LIBOR rise or fall in unison, there is no basis risk. The firm faces the risk that the CP rate rises and LIBOR falls. The firm can insure against this risk by purchasing a CP/LIBOR swap, for about 0.16 percent.

Equalizing the Call Provisions.   The genuine fixed-rate alternative may contain a call provision in year 3. The synthetic fixed-rate choice obliges the firm to swap payments over the full seven-year period. The firm can replicate the call provision by purchasing an option for the right to reverse the swap in year 3. The cost of this swaption may be about 0.40 percent.

A Final Comparison

The overall cost of controlling for the additional risks in the synthetic fixed-rate alternative is 0.45 + 0.16 + 0.40 = 1.01 percent. This brings the total cost of the synthetic fixed-rate approach to 11.93 percent + 1.01 percent percent = 12.94 percent, or only 0.15 percent below the cost of genuine fixed-rate funds. The costs in this example are hypothetical but realistic. In an actual case, the costs could be more or less, depending upon market conditions and the specific firm. The example illustrates the way to make a valid comparison between the genuine and synthetic fixed-rate alternatives. It also shows that the cost differences are far less than a simple comparison might suggest.

off risks (meaning to hedge) and to take on risks (that is, to speculate)—a counterparty should consider two categories of risks.

Swap Risks for the Hedger

Let's look first at the hedging motive behind swaps. Consider the currency swap involving IBM that we described in Box 13.1. For the purposes at hand, let's assume that IBM's revenues are primarily denominated in US$, so US$ financing represents the prudent financing alternative. In this case, IBM is primarily concerned about a default by its swap counterparty.

Default risk in the case of a swap raises many of the same issues discussed in Chapter 3 concerning default in forward contracts. Suppose that the World Bank defaults on its obligation to IBM in year 4 of its seven-year currency swap, and that IBM retains the right-of-offset. Default under these conditions implies that the mutual exchanges scheduled for years 5, 6, and 7 will not occur. To recover its hedged position, IBM needs to find a substitute counterparty to agree to a new three-year currency swap.

Once there is a default, IBM faces **market risk** because the three market prices that play a role in the swap—$i_\$$, i_{SFr}, and the SFr/$ spot rate—may have changed. By reviewing Box 13.1, the reader can see that IBM will be worse off if $i_\$$ increases and i_{SFr} falls in comparison to the values on the original swap date. The new three-year swap could require IBM to pay out higher US$ interest in order to obtain the SFr interest it needs to service its outstanding SFr bonds.

In addition, IBM faces the risk of a stronger SFr relative to the rate on the original swap date. Suppose that the original swap required IBM to exchange SFr150 million for $100 million to reflect the original 1.50 SFr/$ exchange rate. If the SFr has appreciated to 1.35 SFr/$, IBM will be forced to deliver $111,111,111 to obtain SFr150,000,000 in a new three-year swap.

To summarize, if IBM's motive in the swap is hedging, then risk depends on the probability of default by the counterparty. Once a default has occurred, IBM's risk depends on (1) how far market prices have moved since entering into the swap, and (2) how much time remains in the swap. If there is no default, then the paths of $i_\$$, i_{SFr}, and the spot rate (SFr/$) during the life of the swap are of little concern to IBM.[13] If there is no default, the swap allows IBM to obtain fixed US$ financing at known costs.

Swap Risks for the Speculator

Now suppose that the speculative motive lies behind the swap transaction. Consider a treasurer who believes that short-term interest rates will *rise* over the next three years. The treasurer enters into a swap to *receive* floating-rate (LIBOR) interest and *pay* fixed-rate interest. The purpose of the swap is to earn income for the treasurer if his or her interest rate forecast is correct. The cash flows of this swap are summarized in Figure 13.5. The floating-rate interest receipts in this example are taken from the CME Euro-$ interest rate futures contract prices in Table 11.6 for the 12 contracts spanning Sept 00 (rate 6.95 percent), Dec 00 (rate 7.14 percent), . . . through June 03 (rate 7.10 percent).[14]

Our example shows that the treasurer could have speculated on rising interest rates by taking a short position in a strip of Euro-$ interest rate futures for delivery dates at 3, 6, 9, . . . and 36 months into the future. This also suggests that a swap can be priced by replicating its cash flows using futures contracts, a point we will develop later.

---

[13]Under prior accounting rules, IBM would not have been required to disclose any particulars of this individual swap agreement. However, under new accounting rules known as FAS 133, that take effect for fiscal years beginning after June 15, 2000, IBM will be required to document that the swap represents a true hedge. If the swap is not linked to another underlying transaction and therefore not classified as a hedge, then IBM will be required to report the change in the swap's market value and include this figure in the calculation of current income.

[14]The reader may feel that there is very little variation in the Euro-$ interest rates and prospective floating rate receipts over the 12 quarters. This impression reflects the picture only on June 20, 2000. Using data for June 27, 1994, Euro-$ interest rates ranged from 5.22 percent (for the Sept 94 contract) to 7.46 percent (for the June 97 contract). See Appendix 13.1 for this example.

FIGURE 13.5   Anticipated Cash Flows of an Interest Rate Swap
On $1 Million notional value

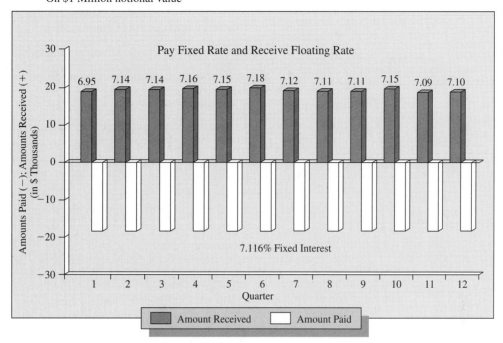

Notes: The above figure shows the anticipated cash flows for a hypothetical fixed-floating interest rate swap. The anticipated floating rate is taken from the Eurodollar futures contract traded on the CME and reported in Table 11.6. The floating-rate receipts are drawn as positive numbers, and are proportional to the interest rate for the three-month Eurodollar futures contract. The fixed-rate payments are drawn as negative numbers of a fixed size. The example shows a par swap where the present value of payments and receipts are equal.

Finally, assume that the treasurer's swap is a **par swap** where the present value of the expected cash payments and receipts are equal.[15] Initially, a par swap has no value and no cash changes hands between the treasurer and his or her swap counterparty.

To show that the swap exposes the treasurer to risk, assume that short-term interest rates fall below the levels anticipated in Figure 13.5. If rates fall, the treasurer receives smaller cash flows than anticipated originally. Thus, we can say that the swap has "negative value" or it is "out of the money."[16] The value of the swap is its mark-to-market value based on current expectations of the floating-rate interest receipts. Had interest rates risen rather than fallen, the swap would have "positive value" and be "in the money." Clearly, the notion of negative and positive value would be reversed in these examples if the treasurer had contracted to pay floating and receive fixed-rate interest. These cases are summarized in Table 13.3.

Our example shows that the treasurer, like any speculator, needs to keep track of the mark-to-market value of his or her swap in order to decide whether to continue the bet or close out the position. The treasurer (as speculator) is primarily concerned about market risk, which in an interest rate swap depends critically on the anticipated time

[15]In this example, a fixed rate of about 7.116 percent equalizes the net present value of expected inflows and outflows.

[16]Another way to see that the swap has negative value is by recalling that the swap is a collection of short positions in Euro-$ futures contracts. As interest rates fall, futures prices rise, creating a loss on the short futures position.

TABLE 13.3   **Profit and Loss from Entering into an Interest Rate Swap When Interest Rates Are Variable**

		Behavior of Floating Interest Rates	
		Interest Rates Rise Relative to Expectations	*Interest Rates Fall Relative to Expectations*
Speculative Position	*Pay Floating and Receive Fixed*	Speculative loss, swap has negative value, out-of-the-money swap	Speculative gain, swap has positive value, in-the-money swap
	Pay Fixed and Receive Floating	Speculative gain, swap has positive value, in-the-money swap	Speculative loss, swap has negative value, out-of-the-money swap

path of the underlying floating-rate interest and the maturity of the swap contract. The treasurer also is concerned about default risk by the counterparty, but this risk can be minimized by selecting a AAA-rated swap counterparty.

Two examples of the potential for speculative gain and loss in a fixed-floating interest rate swap are outlined in Box 13.3 on pages 494–5.

Measuring the Risks of Swaps

Our discussion has highlighted two elements of swap risk: default risk and market risk. In this section, we focus primarily on market risk, which plays a role for the speculator and the hedger (in the event of a default).[17]

A naive approach to measure the market risk of a swap is based on asking what happens to the value of a swap if underlying interest rates and exchange rates take on particular values at specified times during the swap. For example, in the interest rate swap in Figure 13.5 we could ask what the value of the swap will be if the floating rate (LIBOR) falls to 4 percent in quarter 2 and stays at 4 percent for the remainder of the swap. Or we could ask what the swap will be worth if the floating rate rises to 6 percent in quarter 2, rises to 7 percent in quarter 3, and then returns to 5.25 percent for the remainder of the swap. As the reader can see, a sizable number of interest rate scenarios might be evaluated in this way.

To make this "what if" approach practical, the analyst might consider several particular scenarios. The analyst could follow the value of the swap under the worst-case scenario, in which the floating rate falls to the lowest rates that can be envisioned. Similarly, the analyst could investigate the best-case scenario, the most likely case, or the case consistent with a particular interest rate forecast.

While it may be interesting to examine the value of the swap under a variety of special scenarios, each one suffers from having been selected in an ad hoc way. We would really like to measure the market risk of the swap in a manner consistent with the actual underlying volatility of interest rates. This objective requires us to specify a process that

---

[17]For a discussion of swap pricing with default risk, see Solnik (1990).

FIGURE 13.6 **Behavior of Short-Term Interest Rates and the Valuation of Fixed-Floating Swap**

Valuation Effects for Paying Fixed and Receiving Floating

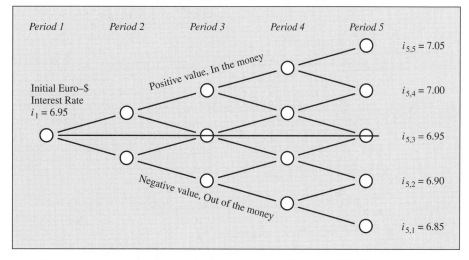

Notes: After the swap is agreed to in period 1, the floating interest rate may either rise or fall. We show this as a rise or fall in the interest rate by 0.05 percent in each period. The initial floating Eurodollar interest rate in Figure 13.6 is 6.95 percent. If this interest rate rises, the counterparty who receives floating rate interest will gain. The swap obtains a positive value, and is referrred to as in the money. If the floating interest rate falls, the counterparty who receives floating rate interest will lose. The swap obtains a negative value, and is referred to as out of the money.

governs the time series evolution of the market interest rate. If we can specify such a process, then it is possible to estimate the market risk throughout the life of a swap. These estimates are based on the **simulation approach.**

Using Simulation to Estimate the Risks of Swaps

Starting from its initial level, the market interest rate is subject to changes driven by unexpected events. These changes can be modeled as small upward or downward moves in the market interest rate. We illustrate this in Figure 13.6, taking the initial Euro-$ interest rate as 6.95 percent, the same initial interest rate we used in Figure 13.5. Period by period, the interest rate is subject to small upward and downward changes that will push this particular swap into or out of the money.

For descriptive purposes, it is reasonable to model the interest rate as a diffusion process, analogous to our assumption about exchange rates in Chapter 8.[18] In the short run, the interest rate is likely to remain near its original value, but in the longer run, there is an increasing likelihood that it will deviate. This potential for an interest rate change represents a risk that we illustrate in Figure 13.7a and label the **diffusion effect.** We see that this risk increases along with the maturity of the swap.[19]

---

[18]The diffusion process for interest rates (i_t) can be represented by an equation such as $i_t = i_{t-1} \exp(x)$ where x is normally distributed with mean zero and standard deviation σ.

[19]The risk is one-sided since if interest rates wander in the opposite direction, the swap will have positive value for the counterparty who has no incentive to default in this case.

Box 13.3

Interest Rate Volatility and the Potential for Gain and Loss in an Interest Rate Swap Contract

In Chapter 2, we presented several graphs to illustrate the volatility of interest rates in the 1980s and 1990s. Volatility exposes the speculator in swaps to potential gains and losses. To illustrate this, we show the impact of changes in the three-month Eurodollar interest rate for a hypothetical three-year fixed-floating interest rate swap.

In the first quarter of 1987, the three-month Eurodollar interest rate stood at 6.4375 percent while the yield on a

three-year U.S. Treasury bond was about 6.50 percent. To receive floating-rate funds, the speculator might have had to pay the fixed rate plus, say 0.625 percent or 7.125 percent. As it turned out, short-term interest rates rose substantially, all the way to 10.3125 percent in the second quarter of 1989. In this case, the speculator enjoyed a net positive inflow over the life of the swap, as shown in the figure below.

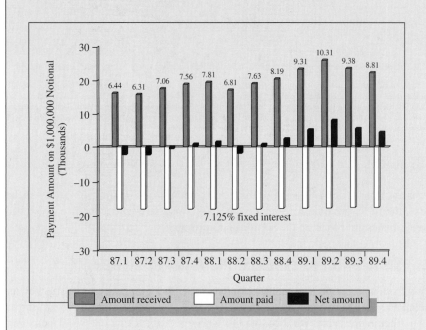

However, time plays another role in the risk of a swap that carries a negative effect. As time passes, the swap requires fewer exchanges between the counterparties. Thus, a large interest rate swing far into the future is not so damaging since fewer payments remain in the swap. In addition, the present value of these payments is lower simply because they are assumed to take place further into the future. This decline in risk with the passage of time is called the **amortization effect** and is also graphed in Figure 13.7a.

The overall risk of a swap reflects a combination of these two elements. The general shape of the overall risk is shown in Figure 13.7b. But the specific shape of the curve, in particular the shape of the diffusion effect, depends on a number of factors: the maturity of the swap, the volatility of interest rates, and the initial level of the interest rate.

Assuming a notional principal value of $1 million, the owner of this swap would have received net payments of more than $25,000 over the three-year period, or 2.5 percent of the notional principal value. This example shows why the speculator will demand adequate credit quality, or collateral, from a swap counterparty.

In contrast, at the start of 1990, the three-month Eurodollar interest rate was 8.375 percent while the yield on a three-year U.S. Treasury bond stood at 8.0 percent. A speculator might have had to swap Treasury plus, say 0.60 percent or 8.6 percent, in exchange for floating-rate receipts. As it turned out, short-term interest rates fell substantially, all the way down to 3.125 percent in the fourth quarter of 1992. In this case, the speculator incurred heavy cash flow losses, as shown in the figure below.

Assuming a notional principal value of $1 million, the owner of this swap would have paid out nearly $73,000 over the three-year period, or 7.3 percent of the notional principal value. This example also shows the market risk of swaps for the speculator, and demonstrates again why collateral may be required if a counterparty's credit quality is not adequate.

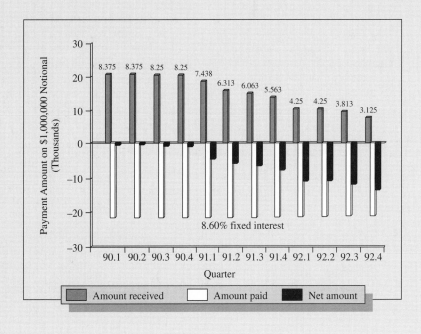

A study by Katerina Simons (1989) illustrates the simulation approach and shows how certain variables affect the amount at risk in an interest rate swap.[20] Simons assumes that the market interest rate (i_t) evolves so that:

$$i_t = i_{t-1} \exp(x) \tag{13.1}$$

where x is normally distributed with mean zero and standard deviation σ. Historical data for US$ Treasury securities from the January 1979–March 1987 period were used to calculate volatility measures (σ) ranging from 19.5 percent for 1-year interest rates to 14.2 percent for 10-year interest rates. The simulation approach uses random numbers to

---

[20]The approach could be applied to a currency swap as well.

FIGURE 13.7A   **The Amortization Effect and the Diffusion Effect in a Long-Term Interest Rate Swap**

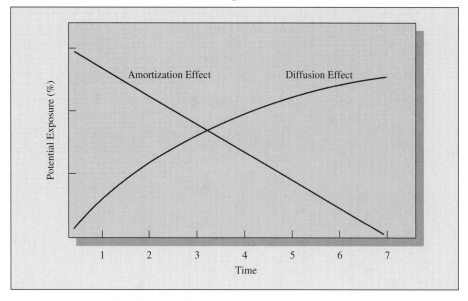

FIGURE 13.7B   **The Overall Risk in a Long-Term Interest Rate Swap**

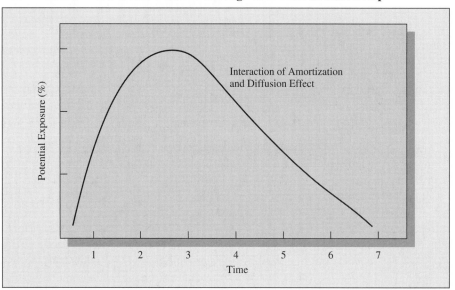

trace out how interest rates might evolve conditional on the process specified in equation (13.1). Simons uses 5,000 trials and can thus measure the **expected exposure** averaged across all 5,000 simulations. And she can also estimate the risk associated with unusual or atypical interest rate patterns.

The graphs in Figure 13.8a and 13.8b show the expected exposure as a percentage of notional principal value for a variety of conditions. Figure 13.8a clearly shows that

FIGURE 13.8A   Expected Credit Exposures on Interest Rate Swaps:
The Maturity Effect

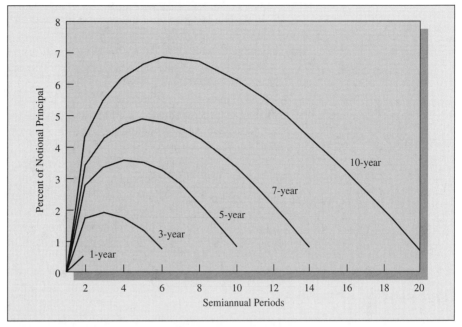

Source: Katerina Simons, "Measuring Credit Risk in Interest Rate Swaps," *New England Economics Review* (Nov./Dec. 1989), pp. 29–38.

FIGURE 13.8B   Expected Credit Exposures on 10-Year Interest Rate Swaps:
The Interest Rate Level Effect

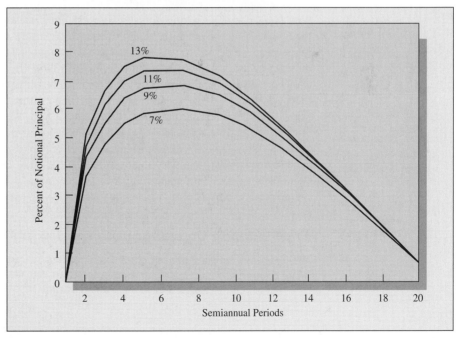

Source: Katerina Simons, "Measuring Credit Risk in Interest Rate Swaps," *New England Economics Review* (Nov./Dec. 1989), pp. 29–38.

the maximum potential exposure increases with longer-term swaps. Figure 13.8b shows the impact of the initial level of interest rates conditional on the maturity of the swap. Greater interest rate volatility (σ) would also increase the risk of swaps.

It is important to stress that the graphs show the *expected exposure*. Thus, about half of the simulations produced amounts at risk that were greater than (and also less than) the amount traced out by the graph. A more conservative approach to measuring the amount at risk might focus on the 90 percent or 95 percent confidence limits, which are substantially greater than the expected values.

As in any empirical exercise, it is important to mention some of the limitations of the analysis. First, the simulation method often assumes that interest rates evolve in a smooth process. Second, it commonly assumes that the evolutionary shocks to interest rates are normally distributed. These two points suggest that the simulations may understate actual exposure, since interest rates are sometimes nonnormally distributed and subject to jumps, much like other financial assets. Finally, the simulations are based on historical estimates of interest rate volatility that may not accurately reflect prospective volatility during the life of the swap.

Despite these limitations, the simulation approach offers many useful insights into the nature of exposure facing swap market participants.

The Pricing of Swaps

As a derivative instrument, the intuition underlying swap pricing is straightforward. A swap is a contract that we enter into today for a collection of exchanges that will take place in the future. The swap price, therefore, should be based on the net present value of the cash flows expected in these future exchanges.

In addition, numerous parity or arbitrage linkages among swap contracts aid in the determination of swap prices. Figure 13.9 illustrates that two currencies, X and Y, have both fixed-rate and floating-rate segments. Interest rate swaps, as we have described them, operate between the fixed and floating segments of a single currency.[21] The currency swap we described was between two fixed-rate bond issuers, or the "fixed-fixed currency swap" linking cells *A* and *C* in Figure 13.9.

We can see from Figure 13.9 that with an interest rate swap in currency X (line segment *AB*) and a fixed-fixed currency swap (line segment *AC*), we could construct a "cross-currency interest rate swap" (line segment *BC*). Similarly, the same fixed-fixed currency swap (line segment *AC*) could be combined with an interest rate swap in currency Y (line segment *CD*) to produce a separate "cross-currency interest rate swap" (line segment *AD*). Finally, a "floating-floating currency swap" (line segment *BD*) appears identical to a combination of three swaps (*BA* + *AC* + *CD*) or a single interest rate swap (*BA*) plus a cross-currency interest rate swap (*AD*).

Price Quoting Conventions in the Swap Market

While the concepts in Figure 13.9 are useful tools, swap dealers typically post prices for interest rate swaps and cross-currency interest rate swaps. With these basic elements,

---

[21]Figure 13.9 simplifies by suggesting that there is only one floating-rate segment. In reality, swaps between the fixed-rate Treasury bond and floating rates such as LIBOR, Treasury bills, commercial paper, Federal funds, and prime are also quoted.

FIGURE 13.9   Swaps and Linkages across International Capital Markets

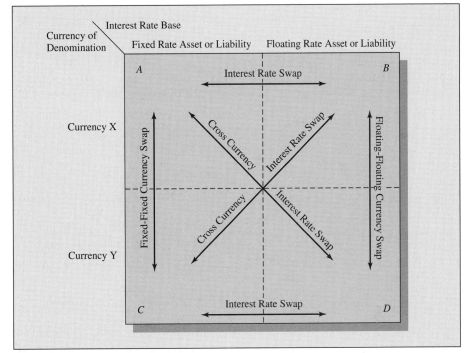

Examples of securities in different market segments:
   A Dollar-denominated straight Eurobond
   B Eurodollar floating-rate note (FRN)
   C Samurai bond
   D Euroyen floating-rate note (FRN)

market participants can construct the prices of fixed-fixed currency swaps and floating-floating currency swaps.

Table 13.4 presents a sample of swap quotations from a major dealer. Various interest rate swap quotations within the US$ segment are shown in panel A of Table 13.4. Various cross-currency interest rate swap quotations for the US$ against other currencies are shown in panel B of Table 13.4. A diagram illustrating how the quotations apply to the dealer and the counterparties is in panel C.

To demonstrate the use of Table 13.4 for constructing a fixed-fixed currency swap, consider the following example. Suppose a U.S. firm (A) issues a seven-year Euro-¥ straight bond with a coupon of 3.80 percent, and that a Japanese firm (B) issues a seven-year Euro-$ straight bond with a coupon of 7.40 percent.[22] Assume that A wishes to obtain fixed-rate US$ financing and that B wishes to obtain fixed-rate ¥ financing and that both are willing to trade at the quotes in Table 13.4 from the swap dealer at Merrill Lynch. The relevant prices to use will be the seven-year T-bond versus LIBOR quotes for US$ interest rate swaps in panel A, and the Japanese yen cross-currency swap in panel B.

---

[22]On the date of the example (August 7, 1996), seven-year Japanese government bonds traded at 2.72 percent and seven-year U.S. government bonds traded at 6.32 percent. The borrowing rates for firms A and B are hypothetical.

TABLE 13.4   **An Example of Price Quotations in the Swap Market**
Posted Rates as of August 7, 1996

Panel A: U.S. Dollar Interest Rate Swaps

	Treasury	Treasury vs. LIBOR		Treasury vs. T-Bills		Treasury vs. CP	
Maturity	*Yield*	*Bid*	*Offer*	*Bid*	*Offer*	*Bid*	*Offer*
2	5.94	18	20	−21	−16	12	16
3	6.12	19	21	−23	−18	13	17
4	6.20	24	26	−18	−13	18	22
5	6.28	27	29	−18	−13	20	24
7	6.32	33	35	−15	−10	26	30
10	6.53	35	37	NA	NA	NA	NA

Note: Quotes are in basis points over/under Treasury bond yields.

Panel B: Non-U.S. Dollar Interest Rate Swaps

	Japanese Yen		Pound Sterling		Deutsche Mark		Swiss Franc	
Maturity	*Bid*	*Offer*	*Bid*	*Offer*	*Bid*	*Offer*	*Bid*	*Offer*
2	1.49	1.53	6.507	6.557	4.035	4.085	2.990	3.090
3	1.97	2.01	6.939	6.989	4.615	4.665	3.370	3.470
4	2.37	2.41	7.185	7.235	5.130	5.180	3.670	3.770
5	2.69	2.73	7.375	7.425	5.520	5.570	3.910	4.010
7	3.10	3.14	7.670	7.720	6.090	6.140	4.260	4.360
10	3.385	3.425	7.960	8.010	6.500	6.550	4.610	4.710

Note: Quotes are on an actual/365 day semi-annual basis.

Panel C: Diagram of Price Quoting Conventions in the Swap Market
Swap Quotes

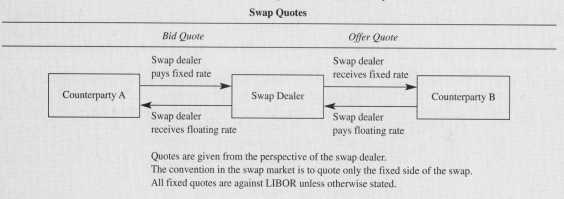

Quotes are given from the perspective of the swap dealer.
The convention in the swap market is to quote only the fixed side of the swap.
All fixed quotes are against LIBOR unless otherwise stated.

Source: Panels A and B are from Merrill Lynch Global Swap Desk, Aug. 7, 1996, private correspondence to the author. Panel C is from Merrill Lynch, *Currency and Bond Market Trends,* Mar. 16, 1989.

To convert its fixed-rate Euro-¥ bond into a fixed-rate US$ liability, firm A enters into two swaps with Merrill Lynch:

1. A cross-currency swap paying $-LIBOR and receiving 3.10 percent in ¥.

2. An interest rate swap paying 6.67 percent in $ (equal to the 6.32 percent T-bond rate + 0.35) and receiving $-LIBOR.

TABLE 13.5 **Construction of a Fixed-Fixed Currency Swap**
Data for August 7, 1996; see Table 13.4

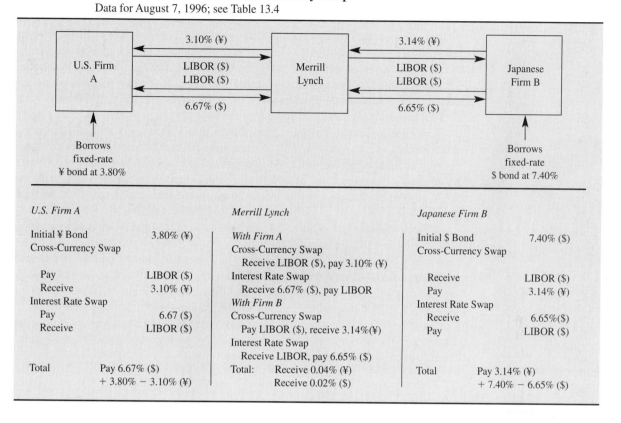

We can see that the two LIBOR portions cancel, leaving firm A with a fixed-rate US$ liability costing 7.37 percent.

Firm B also enters into two swaps with Merrill Lynch:

1. A cross-currency swap receiving $-LIBOR and paying 3.14 percent in ¥.
2. An interest rate swap receiving 6.65 percent in $ (equal to the 6.32 percent T-bond rate + 0.33) and paying $-LIBOR.

Again, we can see that the two LIBOR portions cancel, leaving firm B with a fixed-rate ¥ liability costing 3.89 percent.

As the intermediary in this transaction, Merrill Lynch earns 0.04 percent in ¥ and another 0.02 percent in US$ on a per annum basis over the seven-year life of the swap.[23] In addition, Merrill Lynch receives a fee for originating each swap. All of these transactions are summarized in Table 13.5.

The Fundamental Determinants of Swap Prices

The more fundamental question about swap pricing concerns how the numbers in Table 13.4 are determined and what economic relationship they bear to other financial prices.

---

[23]Spreads have narrowed considerably since 1988 when they were about 0.06 percent in both the $ and ¥ markets.

This is a more difficult question to answer in mathematical detail, so we will only sketch the essential elements.[24]

The fixed-floating interest rate swap is priced using arbitrage to equate the expected present value of the cash inflows and outflows. The expected values of the floating interest rate may be taken from the yield curve or from interest rate futures prices, if a futures contract is traded on the particular floating rate index. Given values for the floating interest rate, the fixed rate is selected as the *internal rate of return* that renders the expected present value of the floating rate cash flows equal to the expected present value of the fixed rate cash flows.

Consider an example using the three-month Euro-$ rates in Figure 13.5. These rates establish the expected present value of cash flows for the floating-rate leg of the swap. Using numerical search methods, we find that a fixed rate of 7.116 percent produces a nearly identical present value of cash flows.[25] If the three-year Treasury were trading at 6.436 percent, then the swap rate would be estimated as *3-year Treasury + 68 basis points*.

By convention, dealers quote only the fixed side of the market; it is understood that (in our example) the dealer will exchange the floating rate leg for Treasury plus 68 basis points. This method allows a dealer to issue a quote that can be valid for one hour or longer and afford some protection against interest rate risk. In practice, the dealer would of course include a spread ranging from as little as 2 basis points to 20 basis points or more depending on the marketplace and market conditions.[26] In our example, the dealer might quote *3-year Treasury + 66/70 basis points,* meaning that he or she would pay Treasury + 66 in exchange for receiving LIBOR, and receive Treasury + 70 in exchange for paying LIBOR.

Policy Matters—Private Enterprises

Applications of Swaps: Capturing Arbitrage Opportunities, Reducing Risks, Enhancing Sales

Our discussion of swaps focused primarily on their role in connection with borrowing. Indeed, this remains an important function of currency swaps. It is often presumed that international capital markets are at least partially segmented, meaning that investors from different markets are willing to pay different prices for the same securities. Market segmentation of this sort may present firms with an opportunity to exploit their comparative advantage in a foreign capital market and swap into their desired unit of account. A firm's own borrowing strategy may produce a temporary market saturation effect, leading to windows of opportunity in other financial markets. But swaps have found a far wider range of applications over their short history.

In the same way that interest rate and currency futures can be used to hedge or offset financial risks, interest rate and currency swaps have become a common device that replicate the function of bundles of interest rate and currency futures contracts. For example, a financial firm that has acquired floating-rate accounts receivable may hedge its exposure through an interest rate swap instead of using a strip of interest rate futures. Or

---

[24]The reader is referred to Marshall and Kapner (1993) and Beidleman (1991) for more details.

[25]Our calculation uses the same fixed rate to discount all cash flows. In practice, it is more appropriate to use the zero-coupon interest rate for the maturity of the cash flow. For details, see Appendix 13.1.

[26]See Table 13.4 or the table with end-of-chapter exercise 11 to review the spreads in the various markets.

a manufacturing firm with a steady inflow of foreign currency from a royalty or leasing agreement may find it more convenient to sell this multiperiod revenue stream forward with a currency swap, rather than to deal in a collection of currency forward contracts.

Swaps also offer a mechanism for the firm to transform its capital structure without incurring the expense of redeeming its existing debt and issuing new debt. For example, suppose our firm begins exporting to Japan. With a substantial quantity of ¥ receivables, the treasurer feels it would make sense to have long-term ¥ payables to offset the firm's currency exposure. Rather than undertake a new bond issue, the treasurer can instead commit to a long-term currency swap, delivering ¥ in exchange for US$. This strategy could be especially sensible if our firm has little chance for a successful ¥ bond issue. This situation also illustrates how a swap might enhance product sales. If product pricing in ¥ would strengthen our firm's exports to Japan, a currency swap could make it reasonable to adopt this pricing strategy and yet keep currency risks in check.

Swaps also can be used to circumvent capital controls on various financial market transactions. A currency swap can duplicate the cash flows of parallel loans, but with the advantage of lower costs and lower risks. In a situation where a bond issue in currency X must be approved by an official agency or lead-managed by a foreign firm, we may elect to issue bonds in US$ with our preferred lead manager and then swap into currency X.

Along the same lines, interest rate swaps might allow the firm to exploit windows of opportunity in a particular capital market segment. The swap can proceed quickly without the need for SEC registration and documentation as in a long-term bond issue. The firm can then hedge its position to obtain the desired exposure to fixed- or floating-rate terms.

Interest rate swaps, similar to currency swaps, may be used as a means to enhance sales or to develop new financial products. It may be advantageous to offer our customers financing on either fixed- or floating-rate terms at their preference. Whichever terms they pick, we can aggregate these positions and then use interest rate swaps to manage the firm's overall exposure to interest rate risk.

Pricing Interest Rate Swaps: The Source of Gains

The recent tendency of lower-rated firms to prefer floating-rate finance combined with a swap to obtain fixed-rate finance has raised questions about pricing and market segmentation. Our earlier discussion suggested that segmentation seems unlikely in a single currency's capital market, and that pricing differences between true fixed-rate finance and floating-rate finance combined with a swap may be exaggerated.

The strategy of floating-rate finance combined with a swap has an alternative interpretation based on asymmetric information. Sheridan Titman (1992) argued that all firms would prefer to borrow long-term to avoid interest rate risk. But in so doing, "good firms" with sound projects are pooled with "bad firms," so lenders (who are unable to distinguish between good and bad firms) raise the interest cost to all. When managers have better information about their firms than lenders, good firms that expect their credit quality to improve will opt for short-term financing and then hedge the interest rate risk with a swap. The strategy benefits the firm since it obtains lower-cost funds initially and in the future if higher credit quality is achieved. The lending bank is protected since it can monitor the firm closely and refuse, if necessary, to roll over its short-term loan. The additional risk of the interest rate swap is small relative to the principal risk of the loan.

Consistent with Titman's model, we observe that most firms that borrow short term and swap to obtain fixed-rate terms have only A or BBB credit rating while higher-rated firms generally issue fixed-rate debt and swap into floating-rate terms. In this context,

Titman shows that lower-rated firms, in effect, pay for the opportunity to swap, which amounts to a transfer to higher-rated firms (and intermediaries).[27]

Applications of Swaps: Magnifying Risk and Return

Many of the illustrations in this chapter have linked a swap with a bond issue, but these decisions are separable. A firm can issue a bond in one year and then decide to swap later, using the swap as a risk management tool. However, a firm could enter into a swap without a prior bond issue. This transaction is the same as a pure speculation on the direction of exchange rates or interest rates.

The swaps discussed in the chapter could be termed "plain vanilla" as the payoffs are governed by the simple differential between two specific interest rates. But more exotic swaps could be designed, with payoffs proportional to twice the interest differential or three times the interest differential, or the square or cube of the interest differential. In principle, these exotic contracts could reduce the firm's exposure to risk from its core business activities. But it is also true that exotic swaps are a way to enhance speculative return and risk, if these contracts are not tempered with other hedging transactions.

The Gibson Greetings & Procter and Gamble Cases.   Two recent cases have demonstrated how exotic swaps can put a corporate treasurer at substantial risk. Gibson Greetings (a Cincinnati-based company with $500 million in annual sales) lost $20 million in an interest rate swap whose payments were proportional to LIBOR squared.[28] Procter & Gamble (P&G) (also based in Cincinnati and with $30 billion in annual sales) lost $157 million on an exotic swap whose payments ("in most cases") were defined by the formula:[29]

$$17.0415 \times \text{(5-year Treasury rate)} - \left(\frac{\text{Price of 6.25 percent}}{\text{Treasury due 8/2023}} \right) - 0.75\%$$

The amount of interest that P&G would pay under this formula is shown in Table 13.6.

This arrangement would have reduced P&G's funding costs below the commercial paper rate if short-term interest rates fell. But if interest rates rose, P&G was subject to enormous borrowing costs on its $200 million notional value.

Both Gibson Greetings and P&G closed out their swap positions to cap their losses, and both firms filed suit against the swap dealer (Bankers Trust), alleging that the dealer failed to make sufficient disclosures of the risks involved in the transaction. Bankers Trust claimed that it had acted in good faith and that, in the case of P&G, it was dealing with a sophisticated investor with extensive experience in exotic derivatives.

Gibson Greetings settled its case in November 1994 after Bankers Trust agreed to accept only $6 million of the $20 million owed to it. In December 1994, Bankers Trust paid a $10 million fine to federal securities regulators to settle charges that the firm willingly supplied misleading information to Gibson Greetings.[30] P&G added a second

---

[27]Titman (1992, p. 1514) asserts that in a typical swap, the party that swaps floating for fixed pays about 70 basis points above the difference between LIBOR and the Treasury bond rate. So if the lower-rated firm could borrow short-term at LIBOR+2.0 percent, then the borrowing cost after the swap would be LIBOR+2.7 percent.

[28]J. Neu, "Gibson Greetings Goes for It," *International Treasurer,* Sept. 19, 1994.

[29]F. Norris, "Procter's Tale: Gambling in Ignorance," *New York Times,* Oct. 30, 1994, section 3, p. 1.

[30]S. Lippin and J. Taylor, "Bankers Trust Settles Charges on Derivatives," *The Wall Street Journal,* Dec. 23, 1994.

TABLE 13.6   Interest Cost (Premium over the CP Rate) in the Procter & Gamble/Bankers Trust Interest Rate Swap

		30-Year Interest Rate		
		6%	*7%*	*8%*
5-Year	*5%*	−0.75%	−0.75%	4.2%
Interest	*6*	−0.75	10.8	21.2
Rate	*7*	15.1	24.9	38.2

money-losing DM interest rate swap to its lawsuit, bringing its total claim against Bankers Trust to $200 million. P&G and Bankers Trust settled their dispute in May 1996, after Bankers Trust agreed to absorb at least $150 million of P&G's loss.[31] Around this time, it was reported that some banks had chosen to absorb losses on swap transactions, rather than risk bad publicity or litigation.[32]

These two examples demonstrate that the treasurer must use considerable skill in evaluating complex swap contracts. At a minimum, the treasurer should calculate the impact of various combinations of interest rates (as in Table 13.6) and exchange rates (when these are relevant for the swap) to determine which combinations pose the greatest potential loss. For example, in Table 13.6, the combination of a 7 percent 5-year rate and an 8 percent 30-year rate poses the greatest threat. Then the treasurer should assess the probability of this adverse event. So-called **stress-testing** that uses simulation to estimate the probability of extreme events has become another element of a treasurer's tool kit.

Even stress-testing may underestimate risks as it may assume a known distribution of underlying financial prices, and it may assume that the treasurer can terminate the swap at its fair market value at any time. The later assumption may be suspect in the case of an exotic swap that was custom designed by a swap dealer, and especially so when market prices are moving quickly in an adverse direction.

What drives a treasurer to seek out such exotic swaps is itself an interesting question. A recent survey found that 20 percent of U.S. firms view their treasurer's office as a profit center.[33] Perhaps some firms reason that the expertise embodied in the treasurer's office can be parlayed into extra returns. But the recent experience provides evidence on the risk of this strategy.

Formation of AAA-Rated Subsidiaries

A more humble issue facing swap market participants is the concern over counterparty default. To enhance their position in the market, many swap dealers have established subsidiaries apart from their parent organizations, and funded these subsidiaries with separate capital. Furthermore, in many cases these subsidiaries have arranged for insurance

---

[31]See L. Hays, "Bankers Trust Settles Dispute with P&G," *The Wall Street Journal,* May 10, 1996.

[32]See. A. Sikri, "Quietly, Bankers Eat Clients' Losses Tied to Derivatives," *The Wall Street Journal,* Apr. 29, 1996.

[33]The survey was conducted by *Treasury and Risk Management* magazine and cited in "Just What Firms Do With Derivatives Is Suddenly a Hot Issue," *The Wall Street Journal,* Apr. 14, 1994, p. A1.

from nonrelated insurance carriers to guarantee their ability to perform as a counterparty in swap transactions. The net result of this business strategy is a derivatives subsidiary that holds a AAA credit rating.[34] The subsidiary uses this rating to enhance its appeal as a swap counterparty, especially for longer-term swaps.[35]

The ability of the subsidiary to obtain private insurance for its overall activities suggests a fair amount of confidence in assessing the risks of swap trading. We now turn to this issue from the public policy standpoint.

Policy Matters—Public Policymakers

A Large-Scale Default Hits the Swap Market

Bank regulators became interested in the swap market in the late 1980s as the market expanded sharply and for the first time experienced the angst of a major default. The setting was the British sterling segment of the interest rate swap market. During the 1980s, more than 100 city council governments entered into swap agreements, most often agreeing to pay floating-rate interest while receiving fixed-rate interest. One council (the London community of Hammersmith and Fulham) was reported to have engaged in over 600 swaps with notional value over £6 billion (or $9.5 billion).[36]

But the floating Euro-£ rate rose from about 8.1 percent in May 1988 to 15.2 percent in December 1989, sending most interest rate swaps deeply out of the money and leaving local governments in a pool of red ink. To the rescue came British government auditors, who concluded that the local government financial officials did not have the authority to enter into the swap contracts in the first place. The auditors essentially decided that local officials were permitted to raise funds, collect taxes, make disbursements, and so on, but legally they were not permitted to enter into swap transactions on behalf of their communities.

A British court confirmed this interpretation and voided all swap contracts between banks and local governments. The House of Lords, the British equivalent of the U.S. Supreme Court, concurred, stating that "a local authority has no power to enter into a swap transaction."[37] With this decision, losses estimated at £500–£600 million were spread across 78 banks.

BIS Capital Requirements for Swap Transactions

With the myth of safety shattered, bank regulators banded together through the Basle Committee of the Bank for International Settlements (BIS) to develop a set of capital requirements for swap transactions. These regulations governing credit risk went into effect in 1988.

---

[34]See *Standard & Poor's Structured Finance* (Nov. 1993) for a review of the Banque Paribas subsidiary (known as Paribas Dérivés Garantis) and Goldman Sachs subsidiary (known as GS Financial Products US L.P.) and a discussion of their business plans and risks facing separate derivatives products companies.

[35]Empirical support for this proposition is in Jagtiani (1995).

[36]U.K. Court Rules Borough, Banks' Rate Swaps Illegal," *The Wall Street Journal,* Nov. 6, 1989.

[37]"Law Lords Give Their Reasons for Ruling All Council Swaps Illegal," *Financial Times,* Jan. 25, 1991, p. 18.

TABLE 13.7 The Original Exposure Method for BIS Capital Adequacy Requirements

	Conversion Factor for	
Maturity	*Interest Rate Swaps*	*Exchange Rate Swaps*
Less than one year	0.5%	2.0%
One to two years	1.0	5.0
For each additional year	1.0	3.0

Capital requirements then computed as:

$$\text{Notional value of swap} \times \text{Conversion factor} \times \text{Risk weight}$$

Examples:

1. One year, $100,000,000 $/DM currency swap, counterparty is an OECD bank

   $100,000,000 \times 0.05 \times 0.20 = \$1,000,000$

2. Seven year, $100,000,000 fixed-floating interest rate swap, counterparty is major industrial firm

   $100,000,000 \times 0.07 \times 0.50 = \$3,500,000$

Source: Basle Committee on Banking Supervision, *Treatment of Potential Exposure for Off-Balance-Sheet Items* (Basle, Switzerland: BIS, Apr. 1995).

The BIS regulations allow two methods for calculating capital requirements for swap transactions. The **original exposure** method is outlined in Table 13.7. Using this method, the capital requirement is the product of the notional value of the swap, a conversion factor (as displayed in Table 13.7), and a risk weight determined by the nature of the counterparty. Governments are assigned a risk weight of 0, banks from OECD countries a risk weight of 0.2, and major industrial firms a risk weight of 0.5. Some examples of the original exposure approach are calculated in Table 13.7.

The **credit exposure** method defines exposure as the sum of **current exposure** measured as the mark-to-market value of the swap, plus **potential exposure** determined by an add-on factor using the information in Table 13.8. The ultimate capital requirement equals the credit exposure multiplied by a risk weight appropriate for the swap counterparty. Some examples of the credit exposure approach are illustrated in Table 13.8.

As the reader can observe, the formulas under either method bear little relationship to the structure of swap risks represented in Figure 13.7. Some deficiencies are glaring. All currency swaps command the same capital requirements whether the swap is written against a fairly tranquil currency like the Canadian dollar or a more volatile currency. All interest rate swaps command the same capital requirements whether written against tranquil interest rates or during turbulent periods.

The virtue of the BIS requirements is their simplicity and ease of implementation at banks with either high or low expertise in risk management. Clearly, there is no attempt to fine-tune the capital requirements to the actual behavior of financial prices.

In 1995, the BIS proposed to allow banks to use their own in-house risk measurement systems for measuring their exposure to **market risk,** meaning the price risk, of their swap and derivative security positions. These techniques for measuring market risk, often referred to as **value-at-risk,** will be discussed in Chapters 16 and 17.

TABLE 13.8   The Credit Exposure Method for BIS Capital Adequacy Requirements

Credit exposure defined as "current exposure" (as determined by mark-to-market valuation) plus "potential exposure" (as determined by an add-on factor).

The add-on factors (applicable for swaps with positive, negative or zero mark-to-market value) are:

	Add-on Factor for	
Maturity	*Interest Rate Swaps*	*Exchange Rate Swaps*
Less than one year	0.0%	1.0%
One to five years	0.5	5.0
Five years or more	1.5	7.5

Capital requirements then computed as:

$$\text{Credit exposure} \times \text{Risk weight}$$

Examples:

1. Two year, $10,000,000 interest rate swap, counterparty is a major industrial firm; assume swap is "in the money" by $200,000.

   Current exposure = Max [200,000 ; 0] = $200,000

   Potential exposure = $10,000,000 × 0.005 = $50,000

   Capital requirement = (200,000 + 50,000) × 0.50 = $125,000

2. Two year, $10,000,000 interest rate swap, counterparty is a major industrial firm; assume swap is "out of the money" by $200,000.

   Current exposure = Max [–200,000 ; 0] = $0

   Potential exposure = $10,000,000 × 0.005 = $50,000

   Capital requirement = (0 + 50,000) × 0.50 = $25,000

Source: Basle Committee on Banking Supervision, *Treatment of Potential Exposure for Off-Balance-Sheet Items* (Basle, Switzerland: BIS, Apr. 1995).

In June 1999, the BIS proposed still further modifications to its capital adequacy rules. This new proposal would introduce the credit rating of the swap counterparty as another factor helping to determine the capital requirements.

Netting Agreements and the Risk Exposure of Swap Transactions

Although the rate of default on swap contracts has been extremely low, the rapid expansion of the market naturally raises concerns about credit risk.[38] As swap volume increases, a bank may enter into dozens, and perhaps hundreds of swaps (on various

---

[38]A survey conducted by the International Swap Dealers Association in 1992 estimated that the cumulative total of losses was only 0.0115 percent of the notional principal value of swaps. See *International Financing Review,* Aug. 1, 1992.

TABLE 13.9   An Illustration of a Master Swap Agreement

			Summary of Transactions with Counterparty A, as of Dec. 31, 2000			
Date of Swap	*Currency*	*Maturity (Years)*	*Notional Amount*	*Contract Description*	*Value*	*Replacement Cost*
Jan. 15, 2000	US$	3	10,000,000	Pay fix / receive LIBOR	$50,000	$ 50,000
Jan. 20, 2000	US$	5	5,000,000	Pay fix / receive CP	$20,000	$ 20,000
Mar. 1, 2000	€	5	20,000,000	Receive fix / pay LIBOR	$25,000	$ 25,000
Mar. 15, 2000	UK£	7	10,000,000	Receive fix / pay LIBOR	$15,000	$ 15,000
July 15, 2000	US$	3	10,000,000	Receive LIBOR / pay fix	−$60,000	0
July 20, 2000	US$	7	5,000,000	Receive CP / pay fix	−$30,000	0
Totals					$20,000	$110,000

Note: This table summarizes the current credit exposure of a bank with a single counterparty (A) as of Dec. 31, 2000 based on six swaps agreed to during 2000. If A could default on individual swaps, A would choose to default on swaps 1–4, but not 5 and 6. The bank would lose $110,000 in this case. But if A cannot selectively default (as in a master swap agreement), then the bank's exposure is only $20,000.

currencies, maturities, and interest rate bases) with a single counterparty. Swaps also tend to accumulate from the practice of entering into an additional swap to reverse a position, rather than simply closing out a swap prior to maturity.

Assume that our bank has six swaps outstanding with counterparty A as described in Table 13.9. The credit risk our bank faces is a default by firm A. But notice that our bank's relationship with A has an asymmetry. If A should enter bankruptcy and default on its counterparty commitment, A may demand payment on all swaps that have positive value to them, while A willingly cancels all swaps that have negative value. The common term for this behavior is *cherry-picking.*

A strategy developed by dealers to combat cherry-picking is the so-called **bilateral closeout netting agreement,** under which the counterparties agree that in the event of default, the financial obligation between the counterparties will be based on the *net value* of the transactions. A **master swap agreement,** now sometimes called a **global master swap agreement,** is a term describing transactions that are included under such a netting agreement.

In Table 13.9, four of the six swaps have positive value and two of the swaps have negative value. The first swap listed has a value of $50,000, which we recall indicates that at current prices the bank expects to receive $50,000 more (in present value) than it pays out under the swap. If counterparty A defaulted on this swap, the bank would need $50,000 to replace it. The next three swaps also have positive value. But the last two swaps in Table 13.9 have negative value. If counterparty A defaulted on swaps 5 and 6, the bank would be better off and would not replace them.

If our bank has a bilateral closeout netting agreement, the current exposure of the six swap transactions is $20,000. This represents the **net exposure** of the portfolio of swaps covered by the netting agreement. If there were no netting agreement, counterparty A would have an incentive to cherry-pick; A would like to default on contracts one through four, while collecting on contracts five and six. In this case, the bank's current exposure is $110,000, as shown in the final column of Table 13.9.

Our example shows that netting agreements have the potential to dramatically reduce current credit exposure. In addition, the adoption of netting agreements also would tend to reduce, on average, a counterparty's exposure to potential credit risk.[39]

Most banks use master swap agreements, in part to reduce the paperwork associated with swap transactions, but primarily to reduce the credit exposures with counterparties in the event of default. In July 1994, the Basle Committee on Banking Supervision approved a plan to allow the use of bilateral closeout netting agreements when calculating current credit exposures.[40] Banks with acceptable netting agreements may calculate their exposure as 40 percent of gross exposure plus 60 percent of net exposure. Thus, if net exposure were zero, the method leads to a 60 percent reduction in the exposure measure. This plan could greatly reduce the capital requirements for exposures to counterparty credit risks.

---

[39]See Hendricks (1994) for an analysis of this issue.

[40]Basle Committee on Banking Supervision, *The Treatment of the Credit Risk Associated with Certain Off-Balance-Sheet Items* (Basle, Switzerland: BIS, July 1994): Text available at <www.bis.org>.

Summary

The currency and interest rate swap market began in the early 1980s. By 1999, the notional principal value of swaps outstanding surpassed $45 trillion. This figure adequately shows the tremendous growth of the market. However, because swap counterparties exchange only the net amount of their obligations and because swap dealers use bilateral netting agreements, this notional aggregate vastly overstates the amount at risk in the swap market.

In many of our examples, we showed that swaps could reduce the net cost of borrowing. Swaps are also used to manage currency and interest rate risks at lower costs and more quickly than alternative means. Currency swaps developed as a response to market segmentation and other barriers, where capital markets in different countries assigned different relative costs to borrowers. We argued that market segmentation was most likely not responsible for the development of the interest rate swap market. Instead, we proposed an argument that relied on asymmetric information as the rationale for interest rate swaps.

A swap contract is a derivative security that represents a set of forward obligations between counterparties. Once these forward cash flow obligations are specified, we can use ordinary discounting methods to estimate the net present value of cash inflows and outflows under the swap. Comparing the present value of inflows and outflows leads us to label swaps as at the money, in the money, or out of the money. The net present value approach implies that swaps can be marked to market like other derivative securities, so that the value of swaps can be tracked over time.

The idea of tracking a swap's value over time leads to the simulation method for measuring the market risk of swaps. After a swap is written, the amortization effect results in a reduction in risk as the number of exchanges decreases over time. However, the diffusion effect produces a steady increase in risk as prices diverge and the swap goes into or out of the money. The risk in swaps is asymmetric because a counterparty will not default on a swap that is in the money from their perspective.

Now that major defaults have occurred in swaps, market regulators have proposed methods for measuring the risks of swaps and now require banks to hold capital in the event that swap counterparties default. The development of exotic swap contracts and gyrating prices have also caused treasurers to reexamine their systems for evaluating the costs and benefits of using swaps.

APPENDIX 13.1
VALUING THE CASH FLOWS IN AN INTEREST RATE SWAP

In column 2 of the table below, we show the interest rates on a strip of 12 Eurodollar interest rate futures contracts traded on the CME as of June 27, 1994.* These rates are assumed to represent the expected interest rate at the start of each three-month period. For a $1 million notional principal amount, the amount of floating rate interest received is (1 + Eurodollar rate/400) × $1 million as shown in column 4. A fixed rate of 6.709745% is shown in column 3 and the fixed-rate payments on a $1 million notional principal amount are listed in column 5. The amounts in columns 4 and 5 are plotted below, similar to our Figure 13.5. The net amount of cash payments (−) or receipts (+) are in column 6. A net present value (NPV) factor is entered in column 7, based on the interest on the fixed interest rate. This NPV factor could be modi-fied to reflect a different "zero-coupon" interest rate consistent with a single payment at maturities 0.25 years, 0.50 years, . . . and so on.

The sum of the items in column 8 is nearly zero (0.0015), indicating that the expected NPV for the buyer (or seller) of the swap is zero. Counterparties with good credit quality could enter into this swap without any funds changing hands initially, because the market value (mark-to-market value) of this swap is zero. As interest rates change, the value of the swap will become either positive or negative.

—————

*See Table 11.6 in Richard M. Levich, *International Financial Markets* (Burr Ridge, McGraw-Hill/Irwin, 1998), p. 365.

Valuing the Cash Flows in an Interest Rate Swap

(1) Date	(2) Variable 3-month Euro-$	(3) Fixed Rate 6.709745%	(4) Amount Received Floating	(5) Amount Paid Fixed	(6) Amount Net	(7) NPV Factor	(8) NPV of Net Amount
Sep. 94	5.22%	6.710%	13050.00	−16774.36	−3724.36	0.983896	−3664.38
Dec. 94	5.92	6.710	14800.00	−16774.36	−1974.36	0.96805	−1911.28
Mar. 95	6.19	6.710	15475.00	−16774.36	−1299.36	0.95246	−1237.59
Jun. 95	6.48	6.710	16200.00	−16774.36	−574.362	0.937122	−538.247
Sep. 95	6.71	6.710	16775.00	−16774.36	0.6375	0.92203	0.587794
Dec. 95	6.95	6.710	17375.00	−16774.36	600.6375	0.907181	544.8868
Mar. 96	7.00	6.710	17500.00	−16774.36	725.6375	0.892571	647.6831
Jun. 96	7.10	6.710	17750.00	−16774.36	975.6375	0.878197	856.8017
Sep. 96	7.19	6.710	17975.00	−16774.36	1200.638	0.864054	1037.415
Dec. 96	7.35	6.710	18375.00	−16774.36	1600.638	0.850139	1360.764
Mar. 97	7.36	6.710	18400.00	−16774.36	1625.638	0.836448	1359.761
Jun. 97	7.46	6.710	18650.00	−16774.36	1875.638	0.822977	1543.607
					Sum = 1032.65		Sum = 0.001508

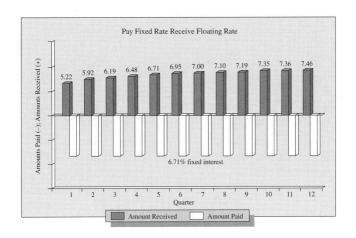

Questions

1. Describe the advantages of a swap agreement over a back-to-back loan.

2. How can a swap be used to circumvent capital controls on financial market transactions?

3. Describe a fixed-floating interest rate swap in terms of forward (futures) contracts. Explain the advantages of a swap agreement compared to forward contracts.

4. A fixed-rate payer in a fixed-floating interest rate swap can be viewed as short the bond market. Is this statement true or false? Explain.

5. A floating-rate payer in a fixed-floating interest rate swap can be viewed as short the bond market. Is this statement true or false? Explain.

6. What are the differences, in terms of required cash flows, between an interest rate swap and a currency swap? Describe both.

7. Explain how firms can take advantage of comparative and absolute advantages in different credit markets using currency swap agreements.

8. Describe a cross-currency interest rate swap in terms of interest rate swaps and currency swaps.

9. Explain the role of a swap dealer.

10. What is counterparty risk in a swap agreement? What is market risk in a swap agreement? What is the right-of-offset in a swap agreement?

11. Define *master swap agreement*. Why is a master swap agreement important for swap dealers?

12. Describe the simulation approach to measuring the risk of swaps. What is the main drawback of the method?

13. Describe the diffusion effect and the amortization effect in swaps.

14. What is the best way to price a swap?

15. What does it mean for a firm to mark its portfolio of swaps to market?

16. Define *in-the-money swap* and *out-of-the-money swap*.

17. Describe the swap contracts and the circumstances that led to the default by British municipal councils in the late 1980s.

18. How can a firm or a financial institution transform its capital structure by using swaps?

19. Suppose that a bank earns 10 percent semiannual on a five-year loan and that the bank finances itself with six-month LIBOR. How could a five-year swap agreement in which the bank pays a fixed rate and receives a floating rate be of benefit?

20. Who are the main players in the swap market? What is the rationale behind the creation of AAA-subsidiaries by large banks to handle swap transactions?

21. In 1994, Procter & Gamble lost $157 million in a swap transaction with Bankers Trust. On page 504, we showed the formula for the rate of interest for payments by P&G under the swap agreement. What was the rationale behind the deal for P&G? For Bankers Trust? Under what circumstances would P&G gain (lose) from the transaction?

Exercises

1. Suppose firm ABC can issue seven-year bonds in the United States in US$ at the fixed rate of 8 percent and in Switzerland in SFr at 13 percent. Suppose firm XYZ can issue seven-year bonds at the fixed rate of 10 percent in the United States in US$ and at 14 percent in Switzerland in SFr.
   a. Which firm has a comparative advantage in the Swiss capital market?
   b. How would you advise both firms so that they take advantage of each other's comparative advantage in the U.S. and Swiss capital markets?
   c. How much could be saved in borrowing costs by both firms?
   d. What factors could be responsible for the relative comparative advantages in international credit markets?

2. Suppose two parties enter a five-year interest rate swap to exchange one-year LIBOR plus 50 basis points (bp) for a fixed rate on $100 million notional principal.
   a. If LIBOR is predicted to be 10 percent in year 1, 9 percent in year 2, 9 percent in year 3, 8 percent in year 4, and 8.5 percent in year 5, what cash flows will be exchanged between the two parties? Assume a flat Eurodollar yield curve at 10 percent.
   b. What is the value of the swap?
   c. What fixed rate in the swap agreement will make the value of the swap equal to zero?

3. Estimate the current value of the following five-year swap agreement:
   • Pay fixed rate of 5 percent.
   • Receive fixed rate of 10 percent.
   Assume a flat yield curve at 7 percent.

4. Suppose the one-year LIBOR is forecast to fluctuate as follows:
   Year 1: 5.0%
   Year 2: 5.5%
   Year 3: 6.0%
   Year 4: 7.0%
   Year 5: 7.5%

   Determine the swap quote a dealer would post on fixed-floating five-year $100-million interest rate swap. Suppose the floating index is the one-year LIBOR, and the five-year Treasury rate is 6 percent.

5. Suppose the U.S. yield curve is flat at 7 percent and the Swiss yield curve is flat at 12 percent. The current US$/SFr exchange rate is 5.25 SFr/$.
   a. What will be the swap rate on an agreement to exchange every year $1 million for Swiss francs over the next five years?
   b. Suppose that the counterparty paying US$ defaults in year 3. The US$ has depreciated to 5 SFr/$. What is the net result for the SFr-paying counterparty? How much will the firm lose (gain) when it negotiates a new swap contract for the remaining two years?

6. The following is the seven-year swap agreement entered by the World Bank and IBM in 1981:
   • The World Bank borrowed at U.S. Treasury plus 40 bp, received U.S. Treasury plus 40 bp

from IBM, and paid Swiss Treasury plus 10 bp to IBM.
   • IBM borrowed at Swiss Treasury, received Swiss Treasury plus 10 bp from the World Bank, and paid the World Bank U.S. Treasury plus 40 bp.
   • The current SFr/US$ rate was 1.50 SFr/US$. The World Bank exchanged with IBM $100 million for SFr 150 million.
   a. How would you define this swap? What are the risks for both counterparties?
   b. What is the total costs and savings for each party?
   c. Suppose the World Bank defaults in year 2 of the agreement. U.S. interest rates went up from 9 percent to 12 percent and SFr interest rates fell from 5 percent to 4.5 percent. The exchange rate is now 1.35 SFr/$. Design a new swap agreement that would restore IBM's position. What is the magnitude of the loss incurred by IBM?

7. Suppose the seven-year Treasury yields 8 percent. What will be the bid and offer quote proposed by a dealer in the following fixed-floating seven-year swap:
   • Fixed-rate payer pays fixed rate of 8.5 percent and receives six-month LIBOR.
   • Floating-rate payer pays six-month LIBOR and receives fixed rate 8.25 percent.
   a. What is the bid-offer spread?

8. Suppose a bank has a portfolio of fixed rate seven-year mortgages. The total principal amount is $100 million and the interest rate is 10 percent. Interest is paid semiannually and principal is scheduled to be repaid at maturity. The bank finances its loan portfolio with six-month CDs at an interest rate equal to six-month LIBOR plus 25 basis points. The current interest rate on futures contracts is 9 percent.
   a. Describe the interest exposure of the bank, supposing no prepayment during the length of the loans. At what point does the bank begin to lose money on its borrowing/financing position?
   b. Suppose a seven-year fixed-floating interest rate swap is available with a notional amount of $100 million for the following terms:
   • Pay fixed 9 percent every six months.
   • Receive six-month LIBOR.

How can the bank use this swap to hedge its interest rate exposure?

c. Calculate the spread the bank would lock in if it chooses to enter the swap agreement?

d. Suppose in year 2 that 20 percent of the mortgages are prepaid. What is the position of the bank regarding its interest rate exposure? How can it adjust its swap position?

e. What risk does the bank face if it has to reverse part of its swap position? What is the market value of the loss (gain) incurred by the bank when it reverses part of the swap if the yield curve is flat at 10 percent?

9. Suppose a life insurance company issued $100 million of five-year guaranteed investment contracts that commit it to pay a fixed rate of 9 percent semiannually. Suppose the company is able to invest $100 million in a five-year semiannual floating-rate instrument yielding six-month LIBOR plus 100 bp.

a. Describe the interest exposure by the insurance company. At what point would the company

not be able to earn enough on the floating rate instrument to pay for its fixed obligations?

b. Suppose a five-year fixed-floating interest rate swap is available in the market with a notional amount of $100 million with the following terms:
  · Receive fixed 8.5 percent every six months.
  · Pay six-month LIBOR.
  How can the insurance company use this swap to hedge its interest rate exposure?

c. Calculate the spread the company would lock in if it chooses to enter the swap agreement?

10. Consider the following tables showing the swap transactions between the ABC Bank and XYZ, Inc. Suppose that XYZ files for bankruptcy and the firm defaults on its swap agreements with ABC Bank.

a. Calculate the potential loss of ABC Bank assuming that its swaps with XYZ are not in a master swap agreement.

b. Calculate the potential loss of ABC Bank, assuming that its swaps with XYZ are all part of a single master swap agreement.

Summary of Transactions with Counterparty XYZ as of Dec. 31, 2001

Date of Swap	Currency	Maturity (years)	Notional Amount	Contract Description	Value
Sept. 1, 2001	€	5	20,000,000	Receive fix / pay LIBOR	$25,000
Mar. 15, 2001	UK£	7	10,000,000	Receive fix / pay LIBOR	$15,000
June 6, 2001	US$	3	10,000,000	Receive LIBOR / pay fix	−$60,000
Aug. 31, 2001	US$	7	5,000,000	Receive CP / pay fix	−$30,000

11. Examine the following table of interest rate swap price quotations published in the *Financial Times* of June 20, 2000.

a. Make some general observations about the spreads in the table. Do these patterns seem logical?

b. Suppose firm A had issued a seven-year floating rate US$ bond at LIBOR + 0 and wanted to swap it into fixed-rate terms.

According to the information in the table, what fixed rate would firm A wind up paying after entering into the swap?

c. Suppose firm B had issued a five-year fixed rate £ bond and wanted to swap it into floating-rate terms. According to the information in the table, what fixed rate would firm B receive from its bank swap counterparty?

Interest Rate Swaps

Jun 20	Euro		£ Stlg		SwFr		US $		Yen	
	Bid	*Ask*	*Bid*	*Ask*	*Bid*	*Ask*	*Bid*	*Ask*	*Bid*	*Ask*
1 year	4.98	5.02	6.50	6.53	3.95	3.98	7.16	7.19	0.30	0.33
2 year	5.20	5.24	6.50	6.54	4.13	4.21	7.22	7.25	0.53	0.56
3 year	5.30	5.34	6.54	6.58	4.21	4.29	7.22	7.25	0.75	0.78
4 year	5.39	5.43	6.50	6.55	4.26	4.34	7.22	7.25	0.97	1.00
5 year	5.47	5.51	6.48	6.53	4.30	4.38	7.22	7.25	1.19	1.22
6 year	5.54	5.58	6.46	6.51	4.35	4.43	7.23	7.26	1.39	1.42
7 year	5.61	5.65	6.44	6.49	4.40	4.48	7.23	7.26	1.57	1.60
8 year	5.66	5.70	6.41	6.46	4.45	4.53	7.23	7.26	1.71	1.74
9 year	5.71	5.75	6.40	6.45	4.50	4.58	7.23	7.26	1.83	1.86
10 year	5.74	5.78	6.39	6.44	4.54	4.62	7.23	7.26	1.93	1.96
12 year	5.81	5.85	6.35	6.42	4.60	4.70	7.25	7.28	2.10	2.13
15 year	5.90	5.94	6.27	6.36	4.67	4.77	7.25	7.28	2.28	2.31
20 year	5.95	5.99	6.11	6.24	4.73	4.83	7.25	7.28	2.39	2.42
25 year	5.96	6.00	6.00	6.13	4.75	4.85	7.24	7.27	2.41	2.44
30 year	5.95	5.99	5.93	6.06	4.76	4.86	7.23	7.26	2.42	2.45

Bid and ask rates as of close of London business. US$ is quoted annual money actual/360 basis against 3 months LIBOR, £ and Yen quoted on a semi-annual actual/365 basis against 6 months LIBOR, Euro/Swiss Franc quoted on annual bond 30/360 basis against 6 month EURIBOR/LIBOR with the exception of the 1-year rate, which is quoted against 3-month EURIBOR/LIBOR.

Source: *Financial Times,* June 21, 2000. (Original source: Garban-Intercapital plc.)

References

Bansal, Vipul K.; James L. Bicksler; Andrew H. Chen; and John F. Marshall. "Gains from Synthetic Financings with Interest Rate Swaps: Fact or Fantasy?" *Journal of Applied Corporate Finance* 6, no. 3 (Fall 1993), pp. 91–94.

Beidelman, Carl R. *Cross-Currency Swaps.* Homewood, IL: Irwin, 1991.

Bock, David. "Exchanges of Borrowings." In *Swap Financing Techniques,* ed. B. Antl. London: Euromoney Publications, 1983.

Eiteman, David K.; Arthur I. Stonehill; and Michael H. Moffet. *Multinational Business Finance,* 6th ed. Reading, MA: Addison-Wesley, 1992.

Hendricks, Darryll. "Netting Agreements and the Credit Exposures of OTC Derivative Portfolios." *Quarterly Review,* Federal Reserve Bank of New York (Spring 1994), pp. 7–18.

"The Investment Currency Market." *Bank of England Quarterly Bulletin* 16, no. 3 (Sept. 1976), pp. 314–22.

Jagtiani, Julapa. "Characteristics of Banks That Are More Active in the Swap Market." *Journal of Financial Services Research* 10, no. 2 (June 1996), pp. 131–41.

Marshall, John F., and Kenneth R. Kapner. *The Swaps Market.* Miami, FL: Kolb Publishing, 1993.

Rosenberg, Michael R. "Foreign Exchange Controls: An International Comparison." In *International Finance Handbook,* ed. A. George and I. Giddy. New York: John Wiley, 1983.

Rungkasiri, Julapa. "Bank Participation in the Swap Market." Unpublished Ph.D. dissertation, New York University, 1989.

Simons, Katerina. "Measuring Credit Risk in Interest Rate Swaps." *New England Economics Review* (Nov./Dec. 1989), pp. 29–38.

Solnik, Bruno. "Swap Pricing and Default Risk: A Note." *Journal of International Financial Management and Accounting* 2, no. 1 (Spring 1990), pp. 79–91.

Titman, Sheridan. "Interest Rate Swaps and Corporate Financing Choices." *Journal of Finance* 47, no. 4 (Sept. 1992), pp. 1503–16.

V INTERNATIONAL ASSET PORTFOLIOS

14   Bond Portfolios   518

15   Equity Portfolios   554

14 BOND PORTFOLIOS

"It is better to have loaned and lost than never to have loaned at all."

Attributed to Leon Frazer, second president of the Bank for International Settlements (Kindleberger, 1984).

Learning Objectives

After reading this chapter, students should

1. Be familiar with the overall composition of the global bond market and the relative importance of various locations and currencies.

2. Know how to calculate the *unhedged* return (in US$) on a foreign currency bond.

3. Know how to calculate the *hedged* return (in US$) on a foreign currency bond.

4. Be aware of the benefits from holding a global portfolio of bonds (either hedged or unhedged) versus a portfolio of only US$ bonds.

5. Understand the notion of active versus passive hedging of currency risk in a global bond portfolio.

Unlike the markets we discussed in Parts II and III, bonds have been issued and traded in financial markets for centuries. International bond transactions have played a colorful and important role in the development of international economic and political relations. Creditor nations such as the Netherlands in the 17th century, Britain in the 18th century, and Germany and France prior to World War I had well-developed arrangements for direct loans and bonds, many of which were exchange listed and traded.

Foreign lending through debt issues often helped to finance a war, and an absence of funding sometimes helped to end one. Foreign lending financed national expansion (such as America's Louisiana Purchase from France) and national economic development (such as the building of canals and railroads). The experience of the United States, a young, developing nation in the mid-19th century, invites us to make comparisons with contemporary emerging markets:

> United States borrowing in Britain began in the 1830s at the level of the separate states; most of the Southern members among them later defaulted, if not shortly after 1837 [the collapse of the cotton boom], at least during the Civil War, with massive losses for British (and Continental) investors. The federal government had borrowed in the Netherlands in the 1790s, and in 1803 for the Louisiana Purchase. With the outbreak of war with Mexico, it began borrowing in European capital markets more generally. The capital inflow was to rise in the

1850s, and spread from London to Continental centers such as Frankfurt where the federal government, the states, and even such cities as Wheeling, Covington and Sacramento, to say nothing of New York, San Francisco and New Orleans, were to have their bonds listed 1854–6. The borrowing shifted from governments to railroads . . . The houses of Morgan, Seligmann and Drexel fanned out . . . over Europe to raise money for investment in the United States.[1]

Charles Kindleberger's (1984) discussion of international lending during these periods is remarkable in two ways. First, it documents the extensive use of direct loans and bond financing among nations in a period without any of the electronic or telecommunication equipment we now consider essential to a financial market. Second, and perhaps more astounding, is the recurrence in Kindleberger's accounts of words like *crisis, panic, bubble, mania,* and *war* throughout the three centuries before World War I. How prone markets and economies were to excesses, yet how resilient were the forces propelling capital across borders.

Since the start of the 20th century, international bond markets have been confronted by wars, depressions, recessions, and crises. Over the last two decades, however, these markets have enjoyed a fairly sustained relaxation of the policy-induced barriers to the international flow of capital. Fewer restrictions on foreign capital outflows and a lower incidence of withholding taxes on interest payments to foreigners are two examples of this trend. The popularity of deficit (fiscal) financing among governments also has contributed to the large supply of government bonds for investors to consider. Finally, the technological and institutional changes of the last decade have greatly facilitated the development of international bond markets.

Between 1981 and 1999, world bond markets expanded more than sevenfold, reaching $29.9 trillion in total bonds outstanding.[2] Of this worldwide total—which includes government bonds, domestic corporate bonds, foreign bonds, and Eurobonds— 41.1 percent were issued in (and then traded in secondary markets in) the United States. Japan and Germany are the second and third largest bond markets with 17.6 percent and 8.2 percent shares, respectively. Eurobonds that are issued and traded in the offshore market, rather than in a single geographic location, comprise 15.6 percent of all outstanding bonds. Seven other countries hold at least a 1 percent market share (see Figure 14.1a). Combining the 12 markets of the EMU countries, the Euroland bond market comprises about 22.4 percent of all bonds outstanding in 1999, making it the second largest bond market after the United States.

The composition of global bond markets by currency has a similar pattern with 48.9 percent of the worldwide total denominated in US$. The euro and yen rank second and third with 23.4 and 19.0 percent shares, respectively. Numerous other currencies account for small shares (see Figure 14.1b).

Thus, the majority of bonds outstanding at the end of 1999 were neither issued in the United States nor denominated in US$. Given the substantial size of the world bond market and the great advances in telecommunications, the reader might expect that U.S. investors would allocate a substantial fraction of their bond portfolios to bonds issued in foreign markets or denominated in foreign currencies. This prediction, however, is contradicted by the stylized facts of international investing. As Table 14.1 reports, foreign holdings account for only 3.3 percent of U.S. residents' overall bond portfolios. Residents

---

[1]Kindleberger (1984), p. 222.

[2]This figure excludes bond markets in emerging market countries in Asia, Latin America, and elsewhere that would add another $1.2 trillion to the value of outstanding bonds at year-end 1999.

FIGURE 14.1A   **Composition of Global Bond Markets by Market Location, 1999**

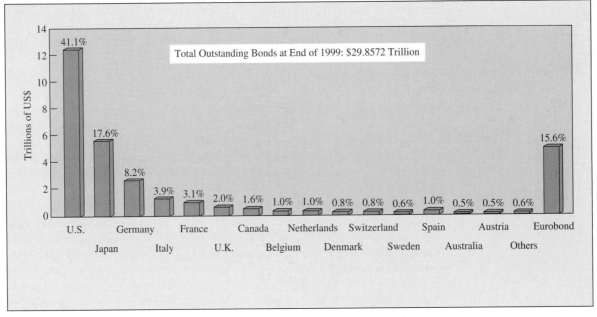

Note: The figure on the top of each bar represents the percentage relative to the total of all bonds outstanding, $29.8572 trillion.

Source: "Size and Structure of the World Bond Market: 2000," Merrill Lynch, April 2000.

FIGURE 14.1B   **Composition of Global Bond Markets by Currency, 1999**

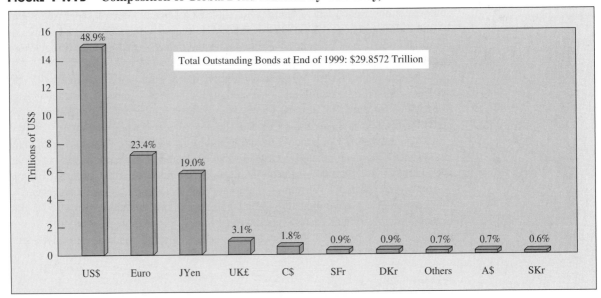

Note: The figure on the top of each bar represents the percentage relative to the total of all bonds outstanding, $29.8572 trillion.

Source: "Size and Structure of the World Bond Market: 2000," Merrill Lynch, April 2000.

TABLE 14.1   Holdings of Foreign Securities by Residence of Investor

Residence of Investor	*1970*	*1975*	*1980*	*1985*	*1990*	*1995*
Canada						
Overall portfolio	NA	4.0	3.6	4.5	4.2	NA
Stocks	NA	7.1	6.0	6.5	6.6	12.0
Bonds	1.7	1.2	0.8	2.4	2.2	3.0
Germany						
Overall portfolio	4.9	2.4	2.7	5.8	10.2	NA
Stocks	NA	NA	NA	NA	NA	18.0
Bonds	NA	NA	NA	NA	NA	6.0
Japan						
Overall portfolio	NA	1.3	2.0	6.9	10.7	NA
Stocks	NA	NA	NA	NA	NA	4.0
Bonds	NA	NA	NA	NA	NA	12.0
United Kingdom						
Overall portfolio	9.5	8.6	11.4	27.5	31.9	NA
Stocks	NA	NA	16.9	24.8	23.5	23.0
Bonds	NA	NA	6.4	32.3	61.4	38.0
United States						
Overall portfolio	NA	2.3	2.2	2.2	2.7	NA
Stocks	NA	1.4	1.5	2.0	3.3	9.9
Bonds	2.6	3.0	2.8	2.4	2.4	3.3

Source: Figures for 1970–1990 are from Tesar and Werner (1995) and figures for 1995 are from Linda Tesar, "Gains from Trade" class notes, University of Michigan, Winter 1999.

of Germany and the United Kingdom have tended to allocate a greater percentage of their bond portfolios toward foreign bond markets.[3] But even in these countries, the percentage allocation into foreign markets (and foreign currencies) is low relative to a naive allocation that assigns portfolio weights in proportion to market capitalization values.[4]

Another approach for calculating a desirable set of investment weights for each national market comes from portfolio theory, according to which allocations are selected to maximize the expected investment return per unit of risk. Because the correlation among national bond market returns is low, portfolio theory again predicts (as we will show) that investors would hold fairly broadly diversified international portfolios, especially investors from smaller countries where the national market is more obviously incompletely diversified. But the stylized facts of international investing again are inconsistent with the predictions of simple portfolio theory.

---

[3]Bond holdings for the United Kingdom may be inflated by the presence of the Eurobond market, where ultimate ownership is difficult to identify.

[4] Under EMU barriers to investment in other euro-zone countries will decline, which should increase the allocation of funds to these countries and reduce home country bias, as it is traditionally measured. Whether this should be called a true increase in foreign investment is debatable. This is because in some cases (for example, the insurance industry) EU regulations allow investors to treat government securities of any euro-zone country on a par with those issued by the investor's home country. In other case (for example, a French mutual fund aimed at retail investors) the fund manager may continue to classify securities issues by a German firm as foreign.

This tendency of private investors to "overweight" their portfolios with greater-than-expected allocations of domestic financial assets is termed **home country bias.** The presence of home country bias is a puzzle that has attracted a new wave of research interest.[5]

One standard explanation of why foreign investments are underweighted refers to higher barriers and costs to investment, such as transactions costs, taxes, time zone differences, language barriers, and so forth. While technological improvements have overcome many of the mechanical barriers to international investing, administrative costs are higher in comparison with domestic investing. The bid-ask spread on securities is inversely related to market size and trading volume. Smaller markets outside the United States typically have substantially greater transaction costs associated with trading.

Another explanation behind home country bias relies on the extra risks of foreign investing, in particular currency risk, and various political risks such as exchange controls or expropriation without full compensation. However, as portfolio theory predicts and new empirical studies confirm, the risk of an individual market is small in the context of an investor's overall portfolio.

In this chapter, we will describe the dimensions of the world's major bond markets. We then review the pattern of bond market returns, focusing primarily on average rates of returns and volatility in returns in both individual markets and portfolios. We focus on government bonds because these account for two-thirds of all bonds and the government sector is usually the largest and most liquid sector in each national market.

To investigate the pattern of bond market returns, we take the viewpoint of an investor. We begin by demonstrating how to calculate the return and risk on a foreign bond, both on an unhedged basis and on a currency-hedged basis. We then review the empirical evidence on return and risk for investments in foreign bonds. The beneficial effect of international diversification shows up clearly in our results measured either on an unhedged or currency-hedged basis. These results reinforce the home country bias puzzle.

Our results raise several policy issues for individual investors and investment managers. One issue is whether the performance gains from international bond portfolios are a figment of the sample period or a fundamental property of an international strategy. We argue that the performance gains in international bond portfolios are real, and represent a form of **central bank risk** diversification, which diversifies the investor's exposure to national interest rate risks. A second issue concerns the value of selective or active currency hedging rather than the passive rules of never hedging or always hedging. We show that selective currency management strategies offer a possible strategy for improving the risk-return opportunities open to international bond investors. The chapter concludes with a discussion of two public policy themes: the market for Brady Bonds and emerging market debt, and the future of European bond markets after EMU.

Dimensions of National Bond Markets

As Figure 14.2 shows, national bond markets have grown rapidly over the last decade. The total market size—measured as the market value of bonds outstanding—grew from under $4 trillion in 1981 to $29.9 trillion in 1999. This measure includes publicly issued government, corporate, and foreign bond markets in 20 developed countries as well as

---

[5]See Lewis (1995) for a review of literature on home country bias. This topic is discussed more fully in Chapter 15.

FIGURE 14.2   Global Bond Market and U.S. Bond Market Share
Value of Bonds Outstanding, 1981–1999

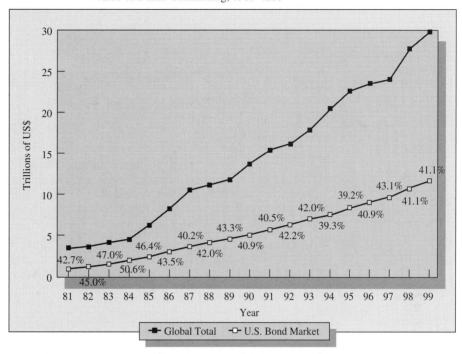

Note: The U.S. figure shows the value of U.S. government, corporate, and Yankee bonds and its percentage relative to the world total.

Source: "Size and Structure of the World Bond Market: 2000," Merrill Lynch, April 2000.

the Eurobond market.[6] The sustained growth of the world bond market reflects two broad trends: (1) the tendency of governments to run fiscal deficits and turn to bond financing, and (2) the rapid expansion of corporate borrowing. Growth has declined somewhat in the last few years, associated with smaller North American fiscal deficits and smaller deficits across Europe as preparation for EMU.

Bonds Outstanding by Market Location

Over the 1980s and 1990s, the United States was the largest bond market. In Figure 14.2, we see that the U.S. share has ranged between 50.6 percent of the world total in 1984 down to 39.2 percent in 1995. Japan and Germany ranked number two and three consistently until 1998. With the advent of EMU, the Euroland bond market comprises about 22.4 percent of all bonds outstanding in 1999, making it the second largest bond market after the United States. Seven other countries had at least a 1 percent share of the world market in 1999 (see Figure 14.1a). The Eurobond market, offshore and not attached with any individual country, accounted for 15.6 percent of all bonds outstanding in 1999.

---

[6]The 20 countries are the United States, Japan, Germany, Italy, France, Canada, United Kingdom, Netherlands, Belgium, Denmark, Sweden, Switzerland, Spain, Australia, Ireland, Iceland, Norway, Austria, Finland, and New Zealand. Publicly issued bonds include Rule 144a issues in the United States, but exclude private placements and official debts held by governments. Bond markets in emerging market countries would add another $1.2 trillion. Data are from Merrill Lynch (2000).

FIGURE 14.3   **Composition of Bond Markets by Sector, 1999**
Percentage Shares

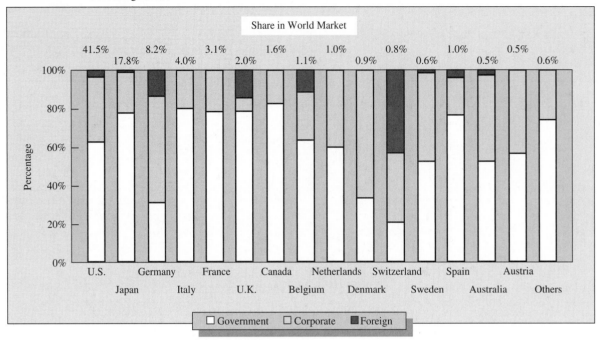

Note: The total of all bonds outstanding is $25.2125 trillion, excluding $4.6447 trillion of Eurobonds issued by various governments, public enterprises, banks, and international organizations.

The composition of global bond market by sector is government (54.3 percent), corporate (26.5 percent), foreign (3.7 percent), and Eurobond (15.6 percent). The composition of global bond market by issuer is government, including public enterprises and international organizations (59.4 percent), and corporate (40.6 percent).

Source: Author's calculations based on "Size and Structure of the World Bond Market: 2000," Merrill Lynch, April 2000, and *Annual Report,* Bank for International Settlements, June 2000.

Bonds Outstanding by Market Segment

Debt issued by governments or government agencies accounted for 59.4 percent of the world bond market in 1999.[7] In 16 of the 20 markets included in this sample, government debt accounted for more than half of the outstanding supply of bonds (see Figure 14.3). Germany, Denmark, Norway, and Switzerland were the exceptions.

The second largest market sector is corporate bonds, which represented 40.6 percent of the world market in 1999.[8] The corporate market exceeded the government sector in Germany, Denmark, Norway, and Switzerland.

The foreign bond market, discussed in Chapter 10, accounted for only 3.7 percent of the outstanding bonds in 1999. The United States has been the largest center for issuing foreign bonds. Yankee bonds outstanding in 1999 totaled $422 billion, or about 38 percent of all foreign bonds. The foreign bond sector in Germany has grown to roughly equal the Yankee bond market. In Switzerland, the foreign bond market *is* the largest sector, exceeding both the corporate and government sectors (see Figure 14.3).

---

[7]This figure falls to 54.3 percent if we exclude government issues in the Eurobond and foreign bond segments.

[8]This figure falls to 26.5 percent if we exclude corporate issues in the Eurobond and foreign bond segments.

Return and Risk in National Bond Markets

Before examining the evidence on the performance of various national and international bond markets, it will be useful to review the calculation of returns on a foreign bond—in foreign currency terms, in US$ terms, and on an unhedged and currency-hedged basis.[9] For the sake of convenience, we assume that our investor treats the US$ as his **base currency** (the numeraire currency used by the investor for measuring performance). In general, the return on a foreign bond, measured in US$ terms, will have three components:

1. Interest income earned or accrued.
2. The capital gain or loss on the bond, resulting from the inverse relationship between interest rates and bond prices.
3. The foreign exchange gain or loss, applied to the above two items.

For convenience, we assume that the bonds are government bonds and free of default risk or exchange controls.[10] In general, a change in the credit quality of the issuer would generate another source of gain or loss on the bond.[11] Finally, we assume that the bond has a long maturity (say 3, 5, or 10 years) which exceeds the time interval used for measuring returns.

Calculating Unhedged Returns in US$ Terms

In this section, we show the calculation of monthly returns for a US$-based investor. Let B_t represent the initial purchase price of the bond in foreign currency (FC) terms. And let S_t represent the spot exchange rate, in \$/FC terms, on the purchase date. The product, $B_t S_t$, is the US$ purchase price of the foreign bond. After one month, the value of the bond is $\widetilde{B}_{t+1}$, representing the initial bond price plus the price change over the month ($\widetilde{\Delta}_{t+1}$) plus accrued interest (C_{t+1}).[12] So the value of the bond after one month in US$ terms is the product $\widetilde{B}_{t+1}\widetilde{S}_{t+1}$, where:

$$\widetilde{B}_{t+1} \equiv B_t + \widetilde{\Delta}_{t+1} + C_{t+1}$$

Note the role played by interest rate risk: If interest rates rise, bond prices fall ($\widetilde{\Delta}_{t+1} < 0$); and if interest rates fall, bond prices rise ($\widetilde{\Delta}_{t+1} > 0$).

The continuous rate of return on the foreign bond *measured in US$* and *on an unhedged basis* is:[13]

$$\widetilde{R}_{\$,U} = \ln\left(\frac{\widetilde{B}_{t+1}\widetilde{S}_{t+1}}{B_t S_t}\right) = \ln\left(\frac{\widetilde{B}_{t+1}}{B_t}\right) + \ln\left(\frac{\widetilde{S}_{t+1}}{S_t}\right) = \widetilde{B}_{FC} + \widetilde{S}_{US\$,FC} \qquad (14.1)$$

---

[9]We use the term *foreign bond* from now on in this chapter simply to indicate a foreign currency denominated bond, rather than a segment of the market in which foreign firms make public offerings in local currency. See Chapter 10 for the proper distinction between domestic bonds, foreign bonds, and Eurobonds.

[10]Bonds issued by governments and private enterprises from emerging market economies carry substantial credit risks.

[11]The credit quality of a corporate issuer and the required yield on a corporate bond could change even when the general level of default-free interest rates is constant.

[12]The tilde (~) over a variable indicates a random variable whose realized value is uncertain. We assume that the coupon or interest payment (C_{t+1}) is virtually certain.

[13]Note that these are nominal returns, before factoring the rate of inflation. The appropriate inflation rate adjustment depends on what and where the investor consumes.

TABLE 14.2   Currency Market Return and Bond Market Return Combinations

		Currency Market Returns			
		Negative		*Positive*	
Bond Market Returns	*Negative*	FC interest rates ↑ Spot FX ↓	(A)	FC interest rates ↑ Spot FX ↑	(C)
	Positive	FC interest rates ↓ Spot FX ↓	(D)	FC interest rates ↓ Spot FX ↑	(B)

Equation (14.1) shows that the unhedged US$ return on the foreign bond has two pieces: (1) the return on the bond in foreign currency terms ($\tilde{B}_{FC}$); and (2) the return on the foreign currency used to buy the bond ($\tilde{S}_{US\$,FC}$). Again, notice that the return on the bond in foreign currency terms is uncertain because of the possible capital gain or loss on the bond. But the return measured in US$ has an additional source of uncertainty, namely, the foreign exchange gain or loss.

The variance of the returns in equation (14.1) reflects the variance of each term and the covariance between the returns on the foreign bond and the returns on spot foreign exchange, or:

$$\sigma^2(\tilde{R}_{\$,U}) = \sigma^2(\tilde{B}_{FC}) + \sigma^2(\tilde{S}_{US\$,FC}) + 2\,\text{Cov}\,(\tilde{B}_{FC}; \tilde{S}_{US\$,FC}) \qquad (14.2)$$

As a theoretical matter, the covariance term can be either positive or negative. Let us examine the covariance term more closely, using the possibilities described in Table 14.2.[14]

Cases A and B result in a positive covariance between currency and bond market returns. In cases A and B, the investor either makes a loss on *both* his currency and bond positions or profits on *both* his currency and bond positions. Cases A and B have a Fisherian foundation. In case A, a forecast of future inflation may raise interest rates (bond market losses) and depress the foreign exchange rate (currency market losses). A low inflation forecast would reverse the scenario, landing us in case B.

Cases C and D result in negative covariance between currency and bond market returns. Case C corresponds to a tight monetary policy that raises interest rates (bond market losses) but attracts foreign capital and appreciates the exchange rate (currency market gains). Case D suggests a low interest rate environment (bond market gains) that encourages an outflow of funds and a weaker currency market (currency market losses).

A portfolio manager needs to understand the mathematics in equation (14.2) because covariance could substantially increase (or decrease) the riskiness of an investment in a foreign bond. A portfolio manager also needs to understand the economics behind Table 14.2. If foreign interest rates are headed down, the manager may want to buy foreign bonds. But if lower interest rates imply a weaker currency (case D), the manager must weigh this possibility and consider a hedge to limit currency losses.

Overall, Table 14.2 shows that the covariance of bond returns and currency returns could be either positive or negative, and possibly changing over time. Covariance could also be a function of the time horizon—perhaps negative in the short run and positive in the long run. We will make use of Table 14.2 later in this chapter.

---

[14]This exposition draws on Putnam (1990).

We show the details of calculating unhedged returns using a numerical example in Box 14.1.

Calculating Currency-Hedged Returns in US$ Terms

Suppose our investor wishes to lower his exposure to currency risk. After buying the foreign bond at a price B_t, one possible strategy is to sell *all* future coupon payments forward in exchange for US$ as well as sell the final return of principal forward. This strategy is much like a currency swap that eliminates *all* currency risks and transforms this foreign bond into a US$ bond. The return on this **swapped bond** should be nearly identical to a US$ bond of the same maturity.

Suppose instead that our investor pursues a less extreme strategy toward currency risk.[15] Namely, he sells a one-month forward currency contract (priced at F_t) for an amount equal to next month's estimated value of the bond with accrued interest, $\tilde{B}_{t+1}$, where:

$$\tilde{B}_{t+1} \equiv B_t + \hat{\Delta}_{t+1} + C_{t+1}$$

If our investor guesses right, and $\tilde{B}_{t+1} = \hat{B}_{t+1}$, then he has made a perfect hedge. The US$ value of his foreign bond is $\hat{B}_{t+1}F_t$ and the continuous rate of return measured in US$ is:

$$\tilde{R}_{\$,H^*} = \ln \frac{\hat{B}_{t+1}F_t}{B_t S_t} = \ln \frac{\hat{B}_{t+1}}{B_t} + \ln \frac{\hat{F}_t}{S_t} = \hat{B}_{FC} + F_{US\$,FC} \qquad (14.3)$$

where the H^* subscript indicates a perfect hedge. The return $R_{\$,H^*}$ also has two pieces: the return on the bond in foreign currency terms ($\hat{B}_{FC}$) plus the one-month forward premium ($F_{US\$,FC}$). The variance of returns in equation (14.3) is:

$$\sigma^2(\tilde{R}_{\$,H^*}) = \sigma^2(\hat{B}_{FC}) + \sigma^2(F_{US\$,FC}) + 2\,\text{Cov}\,(\hat{B}_{FC}; F_{US\$,FC}) \qquad (14.4)$$

As an empirical matter, $\sigma^2(\tilde{R}_{\$,H^*})$ should be less than $\sigma^2(\tilde{R}_{\$,U})$ because the volatility of the forward premium is far smaller than the volatility of exchange rate changes (see Figures 5.8a and 5.8b).

In the more likely case, our investor cannot perfectly predict the future price of the foreign bond. We define the **prediction error** as the actual minus the expected bond price, or:

$$\tilde{\epsilon}_{t+1} \equiv \tilde{B}_{t+1} - \hat{B}_{t+1} = \tilde{\Delta}_{t+1} - \hat{\Delta}_{t+1}$$

The term $\tilde{\epsilon}_{t+1}$ and its volatility represent the interest rate risk in the foreign bond market. If $\tilde{\epsilon}_{t+1} > 0$, our hedge amount was too small and the unexpected (positive) excess value of the bond is valued at S_{t+1}. Conversely, if $\tilde{\epsilon}_{t+1} < 0$, our hedge amount was too large and we need to buy unexpected additional funds in the market at S_{t+1}. In general, once the value of the future exchange rate is known, we measure the continuous rate of return on the foreign bond *measured in US$* and *on a currency-hedged basis* as:

$$\tilde{R}_{\$,H} = \ln \left[\frac{\hat{B}_{t+1}F_t + \tilde{\epsilon}_{t+1}\tilde{S}_{t+1}}{B_t S_t} \right]$$

$$= \ln \left[\frac{\hat{B}_{t+1}F_t}{B_t S_t} \left(1 + \frac{\tilde{\epsilon}_{t+1}\tilde{S}_{t+1}}{\hat{B}_{t+1}F_t} \right) \right]$$

---

[15]There are many techniques for hedging foreign exchange risks. For now, we consider only the use of forward contracts.

Box 14.1

Calculation of Prices and Returns for a Five-Year Swiss Bond on an Unhedged Investment

In this box, we present a detailed example to show the calculation of returns from an investment in a foreign bond from the perspective of both domestic and foreign currency-based investors. We consider a five-year Swiss bond, priced at par with a 4.00 percent coupon paid annually. The initial spot exchange rate is $S_0 = \$0.65/\text{SFr}$, so the purchase of a SFr1 million bond requires an outlay of $650,000. These figures are recorded in the row labeled "Year 0" in the accompanying table.

At the end of year 1, assume that i_{SFr} falls to 3.75 percent, so the value of the bond rises.* Including the SFr40,000 coupon payment, the return for the first year is 4.80 percent in SFr terms. We also assume that spot SFr has weakened to $0.625 (case D in Table 14.2), perhaps because lower Swiss interest rates have encouraged capital flows to other countries. Thus, the US$ value of the Swiss bond is only $630,705.29 and the value of the coupon is only $25,000. In US$ terms, the first-year return, which reflects the coupon and exchange rate loss, is only 0.87 percent (see the row labeled "Year 1" in the table).

At the end of year 2, assume that i_{SFr} falls to 3.50 percent, so the value of the bond rises again. In SFr terms, the return including the capital gain on the bond is 4.35 percent, again exceeding the coupon rate. This time we assume that spot SFr strengthens to $0.635 (case B in Table

14.2), perhaps because lower interest rates have begun to stimulate the Swiss economy and foreign investor demand. In period 2, the US$ return is 5.94 percent. US$ returns are higher than SFr returns because of the foreign exchange gain over the period.

In year 3, we assume that i_{SFr} increases to 3.75 percent and that higher interest rate draws in capital and spot SFr appreciates to $0.66/SFr (case C in Table 14.2). The Swiss investor has a capital loss on the bond which eats into the SFr40,000 coupon payment. But the U.S. investor has a foreign exchange gain that more than compensates and, once again, US$ returns are higher than SFr returns.

In year 4, we assume that i_{SFr} increases again to 3.85 percent, but this change is accompanied by inflationary fears, and spot SFr depreciates to $0.655/SFr (case A in Table 14.2). Swiss investors have a small capital loss on the SFr bond that detracts from the SFr40,000 coupon payment. U.S. investors fare worse because they have a foreign exchange loss as well.

---

*The value of the bond is calculated as the net present value of the remaining SFr cash flows, discounted at the current SFr interest rate, which we assume applies to the remaining maturity of the bond.

$$= \ln\left(\frac{\hat{B}_{t+1}}{B_t}\right) + \ln\left(\frac{F_t}{S_t}\right) + \ln\left[(1 + \frac{\tilde{\epsilon}_{t+1}\tilde{S}_{t+1}}{\hat{B}_{t+1}F})\right]$$

$$= \hat{B}_{\text{FC}} + F_{\text{US\$,FC}} + \ln\left[(1 + \frac{\tilde{\epsilon}_{t+1}\tilde{S}_{t+1}}{\hat{B}_{t+1}F})\right] \tag{14.5}$$

Equation (14.5) shows the return on a **currency-hedged foreign bond.** This return has three pieces: the return from the predicted price change on the bond in foreign currency terms, the forward premium (or discount) on the foreign currency used to buy the bonds, and a residual term representing the unpredicted price change in the *foreign* bond that is valued at the future uncertain spot exchange rate. Notice that the US$ returns on the first two pieces are certain, because the predicted end-of-month value of the bond has been sold forward at a price F_t. The uncertainty in currency-hedged returns stems from the error in predicting future foreign bond prices ($\tilde{\epsilon}_{t+1}$) compounded by the uncertain future spot rate ($\tilde{S}_{t+1}$). We show the details of a numerical example in Box 14.2.

Under very general and plausible assumptions, the variance of hedged returns will be smaller (and very likely much smaller) than the variance of unhedged returns:

The bond is redeemed in year 5 and investors are paid SFr1,040,000 representing the return of principal and the last coupon payment, for a final period return of 3.78 percent. Assuming the final exchange rate is $0.6575, U.S. investors receive $683,800, which implies a 4.16 percent return over the price of the bond in year 4.

Over the five-year period, the average annual return is 3.90 percent in SFr terms, and 4.13% in US$ terms.[†] The US$ return is slightly higher because the SFr appreciated somewhat over the five-year period. The volatility of returns is 0.70 percent for SFr returns and 2.40 percent for US$ returns.[‡] Note that the returns for this bond are more volatile when measured in US$ terms, because of the additional foreign exchange risk. Note also that the volatility of annual SFr returns represents the role of interest rate risk. This is a risk-free, Swiss government security. The five-year return is known with certainty (in SFr terms), but the set of one-year returns has variability as a result of changing interest rates.

[†]The average SFr return is 3.9 percent instead of 4.0 percent (the coupon rate) because we have measured continuous returns.
[‡]Volatility is measured by the sample standard deviation, which is $(N/N-1)^{0.5}$ times the population standard deviation.

Year	SFr Bond Price (= B_t)	Swiss Interest Rate	Spot Rate US$/SFr	US$ Value of SFr Bond Price (= $B_t \times S_t$)	Cash Flow SFr	Cash Flow US$	Return SFr	Return US$
0	1,000,000.00	4.00%	0.6500	650,000.00	(1,000,000.00)	(650,000.00)		
1	1,009,128.46	3.75	0.6250	630,705.29	40,000.00	25,000.00	4.80%	0.87%
2	1,014,008.18	3.50	0.6350	643,895.20	40,000.00	25,400.00	4.35	5.94
3	1,004,825.31	3.75	0.6600	663,184.70	40,000.00	26,400.00	2.99	6.86
4	1,001,444.39	3.85	0.6550	655,946.70	40,000.00	26,200.00	3.58	2.82
5	1,000,000.00	NA	0.6575	657,500.00	1,040,000.00	683,800.00	3.78	4.16
						Average return	3.90%	4.13%
						Volatility of return	0.70%	2.40%

$$\sigma^2(\tilde{R}_{\$,H}) < \sigma^2(\tilde{R}_{\$,U})$$

In the special case where future foreign bond prices are perfectly predictable, the variance of hedged returns is zero:

$$\sigma^2(R_{\$,H}) = 0$$

when $\epsilon_{t+1} = 0$. The special case applies to short-term, one-period investments (such as those described in Chapter 3) where we showed that a foreign asset combined with a currency forward contract can produce a certain US$ return.

Empirical Evidence on Return and Risk in Global Bond Markets

To summarize the risk and return in global bond markets, it is convenient to rely on national bond market indexes. Several financial institutions compile these indexes. Salomon Brothers produces indexes for eight major bond markets, using all government bonds with maturities five years or greater. Returns weighted by market value are

---

Box 14.2

Calculation of Prices and Returns for a Five-Year Swiss Bond on a Currency-Hedged Investment

This box contains an example of the calculation of returns for a currency-hedged bond. We build on the assumptions set forth in Box 14.1. We consider a five-year Swiss bond, priced at par with a 4.00 percent coupon paid annually. We assume that the spot exchange rate and Swiss interest rates evolve in the same pattern as in Box 14.1. To make our calculations we need two additional assumptions. First, a series of one-period forward rates is included. The SFr is at roughly a 1 percent forward premium, and slightly larger when SFr interest rates fall. Second, for our estimate of the expected future bond price $(\hat{B}_{t+1})$ we take the previous value of the bond (B_t) plus the coupon payment. This assumption is equivalent to assuming a constant interest rate environment.

Consider the calculation for the first year. The initial value of the bond is SFr1,000,000. With SFr40,000 of interest expected, the investor hedges by selling SFr1,040,000 $(\hat{B}_{t+1})$ forward at a price of $0.6560/SFr (F_t). The proceeds from this transaction are $682,240. However, because SFr interest rates dropped, the bond price rose to SFr1,009,128. Therefore, the investor owns bonds and coupons valued at

SFr9,128 *more* than expected. This additional amount (ϵ_{t+1}) must be marked to market at the current spot rate ($0.625/SFr), which gives a US$ value of $5,705. The total rate of return over the first period is ln[(682,240 + 5,705)/650,000] = 5.67 percent. This is the currency-hedged return. The figures are in the row labeled "Year 1" in the table. The calculation for the second year is much the same.

Now consider the third period. At the start of period 2, SFr interest rates are low and the value of the bond is SFr1,014,008. Our investor hedges by selling SFr1,054,008 forward for one-period delivery. In period 3, however, interest rates rise and the value of the bond falls to SFr1,004,825. With the annual SFr40,000 coupon, our investor has sold SFr9,183 *more* SFr than he actually owns. To meet his forward contract obligation, the investor must buy an additional SFr9,183 in the spot market at $0.66/SFr or a total cost of $6,060.70. The overall return in period 3 is 4.38 percent. The calculation in the fourth year is much the same.

The fifth year is slightly different because it is the last year of the bond. Our hedging rule has called for the

---

computed on a monthly basis, including capital gains, coupon payments, and currency effects. J. P. Morgan also compiles a family of government bond market indexes for eight countries. Morgan's indexes focus on **investable issues** only—that is, bond issues that trade relatively frequently and in liquid markets, so that investors could reasonably attempt to replicate the performance implied by the Morgan indexes.[16] Using these indexes, we will look at returns on an unhedged basis, on a currency-hedged basis, and then examine an efficient frontier of investments formed by mixtures of domestic and international bonds.

Returns on Unhedged Bonds

In Table 14.3, we report the average annual return and risk *measured in US$ terms* for the eight bond markets covered by Salomon Brothers from January 1978 to September 1989. The statistics on risk and return for these markets are also graphed in Figure 14.4. The data show that average returns on U.S. bonds are near the middle of the group— higher than four countries and lower than three. However, the risk of non-U.S. bond

---

[16]For a more complete description of the J. P. Morgan Government Bond Index, see *World Financial Markets,* Nov. 22, 1989, or the J. P. Morgan website <www.jpmorgan.com>.

investor to sell forward the current value of the bond plus anticipated interest. In period 4, the value of the bond is SFr1,001,444, but the investor knows that the bond will be redeemed at par plus the final coupon. So, it is rational to hedge by selling forward only SFr1,040,000.

Over the five-year period, the average return from the currency-hedged program is 5.05 percent in US$ terms. This is higher than the 4.16 percent return on an unhedged

basis that we calculated in Box 14.1. The reason is that the SFr was at a forward premium over the entire period, and we tended to sell most of the bond proceeds at the forward rate. Note, however, the difference in volatility. By currency hedging, the volatility of returns has fallen to only 0.55 percent—far less than on an unhedged basis (2.40 percent) and even less than the volatility facing Swiss investors (0.70 percent).

Year	SFr Bond Price $(= B_t)$	Forecast of SFr Bond Price $(= \hat{B}_{t+1})$	Residual Amount (ϵ_{t+1})	Swiss Interest Rate	Spot Rate US$/SFr (S_t)	Forward Rate US$/SFr (F_t)	US$ Value of SFr Bond Price $(= B_t \times S_t)$	Cash Flow SFr	US$ Value of Hedge Cash Flow $(\hat{B}_{t+1} \times F_t)$	US$ Value of Residual Cash Flow $(\epsilon_{t+1} \times S_{t+1})$	Return SFr	Return US$
0	1,000,000.00			4.00%	0.6500	0.6560	650,000.00	(1,000,000.00)				
1	1,009,128.46	1,040,000.00	9128.46	3.75	0.6250	0.6325	630,705.29	40,000.00	682,240.00	5,705.29	4.80%	5.67%
2	1,014,008.18	1,049,128.46	4879.72	3.50	0.6350	0.6440	643,895.20	40,000.00	663,573.75	3,098.63	4.35	5.55
3	1,004,825.31	1,054,008.18	−9182.88	3.75	0.6600	0.6675	663,184.70	40,000.00	678,781.27	(6,060.70)	2.99	4.38
4	1,001,444.39	1,044,825.31	−3380.92	3.85	0.6550	0.6625	655,946.08	40,000.00	697,420.89	(2,214.50)	3.58	4.72
5	1,000,000.00	1,041,444.39	−1444.39	NA	0.6575	NA	657,500.00	1,040,000.00	689,956.91	(949.69)	3.78	4.92
									Average return		3.90%	5.05%
									Volatility of return		0.70%	0.55%

markets (measured by standard deviation of returns) was consistently higher than the risk of the U.S. bond market.

In Table 14.3, we also report two popular measures of investment performance: total return divided by risk, R_i/σ, and return in excess of the risk-free rate divided by risk, $(R_i - R_F)/\sigma$.[17] The total-return/risk ratio for the US$ bond portfolio is 0.92, exceeding that for any individual bond market. The excess-return/risk ratio for the US$ bond portfolio is 0.11, exceeding the ratio for all other bond markets except Britain and Japan. These statistics suggest that when measured in US$ terms, we expect the performance of the U.S. bond market to be superior to that of most individual bond markets.

An international investor is unlikely to specialize in the bonds from an individual country. Portfolio theory suggests that there are diversification gains whenever the returns on individual bonds are imperfectly correlated. In these data, the correlation between the US$ returns on U.S. bonds and non-U.S. bonds is fairly low, averaging 0.38. And the correlation of returns across all eight markets is also low, averaging 0.55. Thus, the ingredients for gains through portfolio diversification are present.

The final three rows of Table 14.3 report the performance of a nondollar portfolio and two world portfolios, one with countries weighted proportionately to their market

[17]The measure $(R_i - R_F)/\sigma$ is often referred to as the Sharpe ratio, after William F. Sharpe.

TABLE 14.3 Performance of Unhedged National Bond Markets and World
Portfolios, January 1978–September 1989

Portfolio	Return	Risk	Return/Risk	(Return-R_F)/Risk
U.S. dollar	10.1%	11.0%	0.92	0.11
Canadian dollar	10.4	13.6	0.76	0.11
German mark	8.9	16.2	0.55	0.003
Japanese yen	13.6	17.3	0.79	0.27
British pound	11.3	18.3	0.62	0.13
Swiss franc	6.4	16.1	0.40	−0.15
Dutch guilder	9.4	15.3	0.61	0.04
French franc	9.5	14.2	0.67	0.05
Nondollar portfolio, Value weighted	11.3	13.8	0.82	0.18
World portfolio, Value weighted	10.6	10.2	1.04	0.16
World portfolio, Equal weighted	10.0	12.0	0.83	0.10

Source: Philippe Jorion, "International Bonds: The Asset Class," Chapter 7 in *Global Portfolios,* ed. R. Z. Aliber and B. R. Bruce (Homewood, IL: Business One Irwin, 1991), and author's calculations. Bond indexes are from Salomon Brothers, Inc. R_F is the US$ risk-free rate estimated as the average U.S. Treasury bill rate for the period, 8.85 percent.

value and another with countries equally weighted. The world portfolios reduce risk relative to any individual country's bond market. But the risk measures remain similar to the U.S. bond market. In the value-weighted portfolio case, both total-return and excess-return performance measures are superior to the U.S. market alone, but the margin of superiority is small.

Returns on Currency-Hedged Bonds

The risk associated with the returns on unhedged foreign bonds has two components: variability in foreign bond prices and variability in the foreign exchange rate. As an empirical matter, variability in the foreign exchange rate is usually a larger contributing factor to the overall risk of a foreign bond investment.[18] By currency-hedging a foreign bond investment, we hope to reduce the riskiness of foreign bond returns without sacrificing too much on our overall returns. As the reader can anticipate from earlier chapters, if the forward rate and the future spot exchange rate average out to the same value, then the return on currency-hedged and unhedged portfolios should be very similar.

In the data we report here, currency-hedged returns are calculated based on a "perfect" currency hedge—that is, selling the amount B_{t+1} forward at a price F_t. This hedge is repeated, or rolled over, every month, so this is a passive strategy of always hedging.

In Table 14.4 we report return and risk (again *measured in US$ terms*) for the same eight bond markets, but this time calculated on a currency-hedged basis. Note that the statistics for the US$ bonds are identical to those in Table 14.3 because no currency risk or currency hedging is required for the US$ bonds. For the seven non-US$ markets, we

---

[18]Referring to equation (14.2), the covariance between domestic bond returns and the exchange rate is not sufficiently large and negative to offset the impact of exchange rate volatility.

TABLE 14.4 Performance of Currency-Hedged National Bond Markets and World Portfolios, January 1978–September 1989

Portfolio	Return	Risk	Return/Risk	(Return-R_F)/Risk
U.S. dollar	10.1%	11.0%	0.92	0.11
Canadian dollar	9.9	11.5	0.86	0.09
German mark	11.3	5.8	1.95	0.42
Japanese yen	12.8	6.4	2.00	0.62
British pound	10.4	10.4	1.00	0.15
Swiss franc	9.9	4.1	2.41	0.26
Dutch guilder	11.2	5.7	1.96	0.41
French franc	9.8	5.9	1.66	0.16
Global portfolio, Equal-weighted	10.7	5.5	1.95	0.34

Source: Philippe Jorion, "International Bonds: The Asset Class," Chapter 7 in *Global Portfolios,* ed. R. Z. Aliber and B. R. Bruce (Homewood, IL: Business One Irwin, 1991), and author's calculations. Bond indexes are from Salomon Brothers, Inc. R_f is US$ risk-free rate estimated as average U.S. Treasury bill rate for the period, 8.85 percent.

FIGURE 14.4 Efficient Frontiers of Unhedged and Currency-Hedged Global Bond Portfolios, 1977–1990

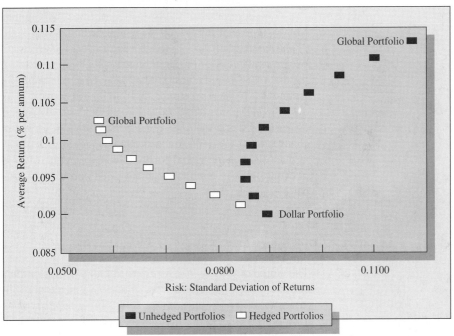

Note: The sample period is January 1977–December 1990, monthly data. Securities are 10-year government bonds issued by the United States, Canada, Germany, Japan, and the United Kingdom. The *unhedged* global portfolio is an equally weighted portfolio of non-U.S. securities. The *hedged* global portfolio is based on one-month forward currency contract, rolled over monthly. The end points of the frontier represent 100 percent in U.S. bonds or 100 percent in global bonds. Interior points on the frontier represent 90/10, 80/20, 70/30, etc. combinations.

Source: Richard Levich and Lee Thomas, "The Merits of Active Currency Risk Management: Evidence from International Bond Portfolios," *Financial Analysts Journal* 49, no. 5 (Sept.–Oct. 1993), pp. 63–70.

find that the currency-hedged returns in four markets (Germany, Switzerland, the Netherlands, and France) exceeded the returns in those markets on an unhedged basis. But in three of the non-US$ markets (Canada, Japan, and Britain) the currency-hedged returns fell short of the unhedged returns. Thus, in some countries the forward rate (F_t) tended to exceed the future spot rate S_{t+1} over the sample period, but in other countries the reverse was true.

While the impact of currency hedging on average returns appears ambiguous, the impact on risk is clear. In all cases, currency hedging lowers the total risk of investing in non-US$ bonds and in several cases the reduction is by more than 50 percent.

The impact of currency hedging on our performance measures is rather dramatic. The total return relative to risk measures and the excess return relative to risk measures rise substantially.[19] For the global portfolio of equally weighted markets, the total return divided by risk ratio is 1.95, or more than twice the magnitude of the US$ bond market. And the excess return divided by risk ratio is 0.34, or three times the magnitude for the US$ bond market.

The Efficient Frontier and Gains to International Bond Portfolios

The gains to diversification in international bond portfolios can be seen more easily by inspecting Figure 14.4, which shows combinations of return and risk for various portfolios. We assume (as is common) that investors are risk-averse utility maximizers. Therefore, investor utility is positively associated with higher returns (conditional on risk) and less risk (conditional on returns).

The curve labeled "Unhedged Portfolios" in Figure 14.4 depicts an investment frontier representing various weighted combinations of the U.S. bond portfolio and a global bond portfolio (unhedged against exchange risk). The graph suggests that a weight of about 30–40 percent on the global bond portfolio would minimize the overall risk for a US$-based investor. The higher available return for a given level of risk is consistent with a diversification gain from international investing.

The curve labeled "Hedged Portfolios" shows another investment frontier again constructed using the U.S. bond portfolio and a global portfolio hedged against exchange risk. This graph suggests a simultaneous increase in return and reduction in risk as the weight on the global portfolio increases toward 100 percent. The currency-hedged portfolios clearly dominate the unhedged portfolios by offering a higher rate of return per unit of risk.

Policy Matters—Private Investors and Institutions

The empirical evidence just reviewed paints a most attractive picture for portfolios of currency-hedged foreign bonds. In response, many portfolio managers have introduced international bond funds as a way to obtain superior investment performance for investors who otherwise would target a domestic bond portfolio or an unhedged international bond portfolio. However, some economists have questioned the interpretation of the empirical evidence. They have raised doubts about whether the results of past studies can be used to predict higher returns or lower risks from a currency-hedged strategy

---

[19]Canada is the single exception.

in the future. Still other economists have pointed out that the **passive strategies** of "never hedge anything" and "always hedge everything" are two extreme points on the continuum. **Active strategies** that allow for selective and partial hedging could have yet more desirable risk/return properties.

We now review some of these practical issues of implementing an international bond investment strategy.

Currency-Hedged Bonds: Is There a Free Lunch?

The empirical evidence we presented earlier showed the results of international bond portfolios for a US$-based investor on an unhedged and currency-hedged basis for the period from 1977 to 1990. The results show that some diversification gains were available in unhedged portfolios by holding 30–40 percent of the portfolio in foreign bonds. But substantially larger diversification gains were possible by currency hedging. Figure 14.4 even suggests that the optimal strategy for a US$-based investor over the sample period was an international bond portfolio *completely* currency-hedged. By simultaneously increasing return and reducing risk, currency-hedged bonds seem to offer investors a "free lunch."[20]

Michael Rosenberg (1990) was one of the first to seriously question the long-run benefits of currency-hedged bond portfolios. As Figure 14.4 shows, by holding foreign bonds on either an unhedged or a currency-hedged basis, US$-based investors added to their returns over the sample period. Rosenberg argued that this return pickup was an artifact of the sample period. As a long-run matter, the International Fisher Effect (uncovered interest parity) suggests that the interest differential should offset exchange rate movements, implying that any passive strategy should produce the same *level* of returns in the long run.

Another artifact of the sample period cited by Rosenberg is the unusually unstable monetary policy run by the United States compared with Germany and Japan, which exaggerated the volatility of returns in the U.S. bond market. At the same time, institutional rigidities kept capital from flowing into certain foreign markets, which may have artificially reduced the volatility of returns in foreign bond markets. Consequently, investments in foreign bonds helped US$-based investors to lower their exposure to interest rate risk over the sample period. Rosenberg contended that neither of these factors can be relied on in the future to support the free lunch claim for international bond portfolios. As a long-run matter, increased international capital mobility and coordination of domestic monetary policies should lead to convergence in the *volatility* of returns across national bond markets. Rosenberg concluded that this trend should limit the gains from international bond portfolio diversification both from the perspective of a US$-based investor or *any* non-US$-based investor.

Our analysis of risk and return lends some support to Rosenberg's analysis. On an unhedged basis, a substantial negative covariance between bond returns and currency returns is essential to offset the added effect of exchange rate risk on $\sigma^2(\tilde{R}_{\$,U})$ as shown in equation (14.2). Our matrix in Table 14.2 shows that Fisherian thinking results in a positive correlation of currency and bond market returns. Thus, large, negative correlations cannot be relied on.

On the other hand, our equations (14.5) and (14.6) show that a currency-hedged return is tantamount to a *US$ return with the interest rate risk of the foreign bond market*

---

[20]Perold and Shulman (1988) introduced the "free lunch" terminology into the discussion of international bond portfolios.

$[\sigma^2(\tilde{\epsilon}_{t+1})]$.[21] Consider the German government bond market as the foreign bond market. Prior to entering EMU in 1999, the interest rate risk of the German Bund market reflected two major forces:

1. Changes in nominal interest rates from variability in German monetary policy as practiced by the Bundesbank.
2. Changes in real interest rates from other factors that determine the real business cycle in Germany.

The interest rate risk of the currency-hedged German Bund reflects those determinants of the interest rate risk in the German Bund market. Because of this close correspondence between interest rate risk and central bank behavior, exposure to the interest rate risk of one market gives the investor an exposure to what we will call central bank risk.

Central banks play a key role in the delivery of interest rate risk by varying monetary policy in response to domestic economic activity. Some central banks have been adept at delivering a low inflation rate environment with a low volatility in domestic interest rates. While Germany and Switzerland have traditionally been associated with this prudent provision of monetary services, other countries are hoping to develop a similar reputation for delivering a stable monetary environment.[22] It seems unlikely that the investor's home country can be counted on *always* as the world's best provider of interest rate risk, so it makes sense for investors to diversify their exposure to home country interest rate risk and central bank risk by seeking other bond markets where synthetic US$-bonds (that is, currency-hedged bonds) can be constructed with different exposures to interest rate risk.

This reasoning offers a valid explanation for a permanent diversification gain from a diversified portfolio of currency-hedged bonds. If there are many providers of monetary and fiscal policy, investors may reduce their exposure to interest rate risks by holding assets that reflect a portfolio of exposures to interest rate risk. Diversification reduces investor reliance on one central bank to deliver a stable and predictable interest rate environment.

Note, however, that if the investor's home country itself provides a financial market with a low interest rate risk, then diversifying into foreign bonds will raise the investor's exposure to these risks.[23] Because investors may not be able to determine beforehand whether their home bond market is a high or low interest rate risk market, there can be a permanent advantage to diversifying these risks internationally.[24]

Investors could try to forecast which bond markets will have low volatility by using the implied volatility in interest rate options. But a strategy to select and overweight low volatility markets exposes the investor to extra, diversifiable risks.

---

[21]The currency hedge combines a long-term bond and a one-month currency forward contract. The mismatch in the duration of these two instruments leaves an exposure to interest rate risk in the foreign market.

[22]Research by Alesina and Summers (1993) shows that, over the 1958–88 period, countries with greater central bank independence tend to produce lower inflation results. See "There Was an Old Lady . . . ," *The Economist,* Nov. 20, 1993, pp. 94–95, for discussion on the trend toward greater central bank independence.

[23]Rosenberg and Marki (1988) show that Japanese investors would have fared worse over the sample period by holding a portfolio of hedged non-¥ bonds.

[24]The choice of individual stocks versus an index provides a good analogy. Ex post, investors would have been better off holding the stock with the highest Sharpe ratio. Ex ante, there is no way to identify this stock, so holding a diversified portfolio offers the best ex ante trade-off of risk and return.

Active versus Passive Currency-Hedging Strategies

The two international investment strategies we have explored—*unhedged,* meaning "never hedge currency risk" and *currency-hedged,* meaning "always hedge currency risk"—are extreme solutions to the problem of currency risk. They are also passive strategies, in the sense that the investor routinely follows the same policy toward currency risk month after month.

In this section, we consider several active strategies toward currency risk management in an international bond portfolio. An active strategy allows the investor to accept currency risk at some times but to hedge it at others.[25]

Currency and Bond Decisions Are Separable.   In a practical sense, investments in foreign bonds and foreign currency are often related. The same managers or investment funds are often pursuing both markets at the same time. But as our discussion suggests, investments in these two categories may be separated. An investor who trades in currency futures contracts is exposed only to foreign exchange risk. An investor who holds foreign bonds on a currency-hedged basis is exposed essentially only to foreign interest rate risk.[26] Or an investor may hold foreign bonds without currency hedging and face *both* foreign interest rate risk and foreign exchange risk. Some traditional approaches to international investment illustrate some common pitfalls from failing to observe this separation.[27]

"Currency-driven" investment places the central focus on finding high-performing currencies. According to this strategy, once the portfolio manager finds a high-performing currency, he or she should buy a relatively safe asset, such as a government bond, denominated in that currency. The problem with the currency-driven strategy is that it risks a loss on the government bond even if the currency decision is correct (see Table 14.2 and the column listing positive currency returns). The obvious way to speculate on a currency view is to take a position in foreign exchange spot, forward, or futures contracts. If the currency forecast is correct, the speculation will be profitable.

A second strategy is to "ignore currency" when making international investments, based on the premise that the currency effects cancel out over the long run. This sort of bottom-up approach to investing has merit. If the investor has expertise in picking good stocks or bonds, this expertise will be rewarded. However, if these stocks or bonds are denominated in a foreign currency, the investor bears an additional risk, which empirically could be large. If the forward rate and future spot rate are equal, on average, the investor can hedge this currency risk without sacrificing long-run return. Lowering risk without affecting return clearly improves investment performance.

A final strategy is the "ultraselective" approach, in which the investor picks only those situations where *both* positive foreign bond and currency returns are expected. This calls for either short positions in unhedged bonds (case A in Table 14.2), when both bonds and currency are expected to be weak, or long positions in unhedged bonds (case B), when both bonds and currency are expected to strengthen. While this approach may be successful, it is far too limiting. The investor passes up favorable bond markets when

---

[25]Black (1989, 1990) argued for adopting a universal hedge ratio—to hedge a fixed fraction, less than one, of currency exposure regardless of the investor's base country. Solnik (1993) refuted this result, showing that hedge ratios should vary systematically from country to country.

[26]This investor is also exposed to a small amount of foreign exchange risk on the unanticipated change in the price of bond, ϵ in equation (14.5).

[27]This section draws on Thomas (1990).

TABLE 14.5   The Expanded Opportunity Set of National Bond Markets
Currency Risk and Interest Rate Risk Dimensions

		Currency Risk		
		US$	*€*	*¥*
	United States	**U.S. Treasury bond**	U.S. Treasury bond: Currency-hedged to €	U.S. Treasury bond: Currency-hedged to ¥
Interest Rate Risk	*EMU*	German Bund: Currency-hedged to $	**German government bond (Bund)**	German Bund: Currency-hedged to ¥
	Japan	JGB: Currency-hedged to $	JGB: Currency-hedged to €	**Japanese government bond (JGB)**

the currency is expected to weaken (case D), and passes up favorable currency plays when profitable foreign stocks or bonds cannot be identified (case C).

Our analysis demonstrates that the currency and interest rate risk dimensions of an international bond portfolio are **separable investments.** We show this in Table 14.5 for a world with three countries and three currencies. The traditional assets are the U.S. Treasury bond, the German government bond (Bund), and the Japanese government bond (JGB) shown in bold on the main diagonal. The nontraditional assets (which we label currency-hedged or synthetic bonds) are the off-diagonal assets.

An investor (from the United States, Italy, Australia, or anywhere else) who wanted to invest in U.S. bonds but hold an exposure to ¥ currency risk would buy U.S. Treasuries and currency-hedge them into ¥ (cell A) by selling US$ forward for ¥. Another investor (again from anywhere) who wanted to invest in Japanese bonds but hold an exposure to € currency risk would buy JGBs and currency hedge them into € (cell B) by selling ¥ forward for €.

Some investors may be restricted from buying a foreign bond and/or trading in forward contracts. If this is the case, a securities firm or a bank can develop a **structured investment** that is a nonrestricted security priced in local currency, but with payoffs indexed to or proportionate to the desired cell in Table 14.5 (minus transaction costs, of course).

Timing the Currency-Hedge and Bond Market Decision.   While we have used Table 14.5 to argue that currency and interest rate dimensions of international investment are separable, there remains a sense in which they are related. These relationships were suggested in Table 14.2. The probabilities for cases A, B, C, and D may not be equal, and the two dimensions may be statistically dependent on each other rather than independent. If currency risk and interest rate risk depend on each other, then the performance of the currency will have implications for the performance of the foreign bond markets, and vice versa. In other words, currency risk may reflect some measure of interest rate risk, and interest rate risk may reflect some element of currency risk.[28]

---

[28]This occurs when the covariance term in equation (14.2) is nonzero.

Thus, our technique suggests that it is possible to hold currency risk *exclusively,* or hold interest rate risk *exclusively.* However, this is strictly the case only when the two risks are statistically independent of one another.[29]

For active investors, the currency hedging decision makes sense if we anticipate negative returns in the spot currency, cases A and D in Table 14.2. A hedging decision could be based on the probability that we expect to find negative currency returns. Active currency hedging requires a timing decision based on the probability of negative currency returns.

Empirical Evidence on Active Currency-Risk Management.   One technique for assessing the short-run advisability of hedging a currency position follows from the technical forecasting models we described in Chapter 7. Levich and Thomas (1993) use a set of 10 technical forecasts (7 filter rules and 3 moving average rules) to determine the currency position in an international bond portfolio.

The authors investigated two active currency risk management strategies. A **tactical hedging strategy** is one where the percentage of currency futures to sell for currency i ($P_{T,i}$) based on the 10 technical rules is determined by the formula:

$$P_{T,i} = [10 - (N_{L,i} - N_{S,i})] \times 10\%, \text{ for } N_{L,i} \geq 5$$
$$= 100\% \qquad\qquad\qquad \text{for } N_{L,i} \leq 4$$

where $N_{L,i}$ and $N_{S,i}$ are the number of technical rules advocating long and short currency positions. When all technical rules expect the value of FC to rise ($N_{L,i} = 10$), no hedging is recommended ($P_{T,i} = 0$). But when the trading rules are evenly split ($N_{L,i} = N_{S,i} = 5$), the tactical strategy results in a 100 percent hedge of the currency risk in a foreign bond portfolio. When most trading rules recommend a short foreign currency position, the tactical strategy also hedges fully. The return on the tactically hedged portfolio (R_T) is simply:

$$R_T = R_U (1 - P_T) + R_H (P_T)$$

where R_U is the return on the unhedged bond and R_H is the return on the currency-hedged bond.

The **currency overlay strategy** is actually a combination of two separate investments: (1) a foreign currency bond position that is always hedged against currency risk, and (2) a currency position governed by the trading rule [$P_i = (N_{L,i} - N_{S,i}) \times 10\%$]. At one extreme, if all trading rules recommend a long position the currency overlay strategy will be 100 percent unhedged, just like the tactical hedge. At the other extreme, if all trading rules recommend a short position the currency overlay strategy will "overhedge" to become net 100 percent *short* in the foreign currency. Recall that in this case, the tactical hedge resulted in a full hedge, yielding no net currency exposure. Because the range of currency positions is wider with the currency overlay strategy, it is more aggressive than the tactical hedge strategy.

The return on the currency overlay strategy (R_{CO}) is given by

$$R_{CO} = R_H + R_A$$

where R_A is the return on the active currency trading rule, or $R_A = \Sigma_t P_t \times \ln (S_{t+1}/F_t)$, and P_t, the percentage of futures contracts to buy, satisfies $-1.0 \leq P_t \leq +1.0$.

---

[29]Jorion (1994) examines the more general case where interactions between the underlying assets and exchange rates are explicitly considered.

TABLE 14.6   **Sharpe Ratios for International Portfolios with Alternative Currency Hedging Strategies, 1977–1990**

Strategy	DM	C$	£	¥	Global Portfolio
No hedge	0.12	0.06	0.35	0.29	0.29
Always hedge	0.35	0.04	0.30	0.49	0.38
Tactical hedge	0.50	0.12	0.67	0.69	0.75
Currency overlay	1.07	0.28	0.84	1.12	1.21

Note: The Sharpe ratio for US$ portfolio is 0.12.

Source: Richard M. Levich and Lee R. Thomas, "The Merits of Active Currency Risk Management: Evidence from International Bond Portfolios," *Financial Analysts Journal* 49, no. 5 (Sept.–Oct. 1993), pp. 63–70.

FIGURE 14.5   **Efficient Portfolio Frontiers with Active and Passive Hedges, 1977–1990**

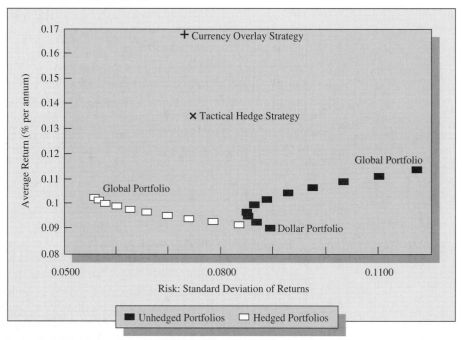

Note: The sample period is January 1977–December 1990, monthly data. Securities are 10-year government bonds issued by the United States, Canada, Germany, Japan, and the United Kingdom. The *unhedged* global portfolio is an equally weighted portfolio of non-U.S. securities. The *hedged* global portfolio based on one-month forward currency contract, rolled over monthly. The *tactical hedge* portfolio actively hedges a percentage of the global portfolio based on the signals from 10 technical trading rules. The *currency overlay* portfolio reflects the performance of the hedged global portfolio combined with a currency fund actively managed based on the signals from 10 technical trading rules.

Source: Richard M. Levich and Lee R. Thomas, "The Merits of Active Currency Risk Management: Evidence from International Bond Portfolios," *Financial Analysts Journal* 49, no. 5 (Sept.–Oct. 1993), pp. 63–70.

The results for the two active currency hedging strategies and our two passive strategies are summarized in Table 14.6 and Figure 14.5. The more conservative tactical currency hedging strategy beats the two passive approaches. The tactical strategy improves the realized Sharpe ratios for every currency compared to either passive strategy. The

FIGURE 14.6   Sharpe Ratios for Five Strategies in 1977–1990 and Five Subperiods

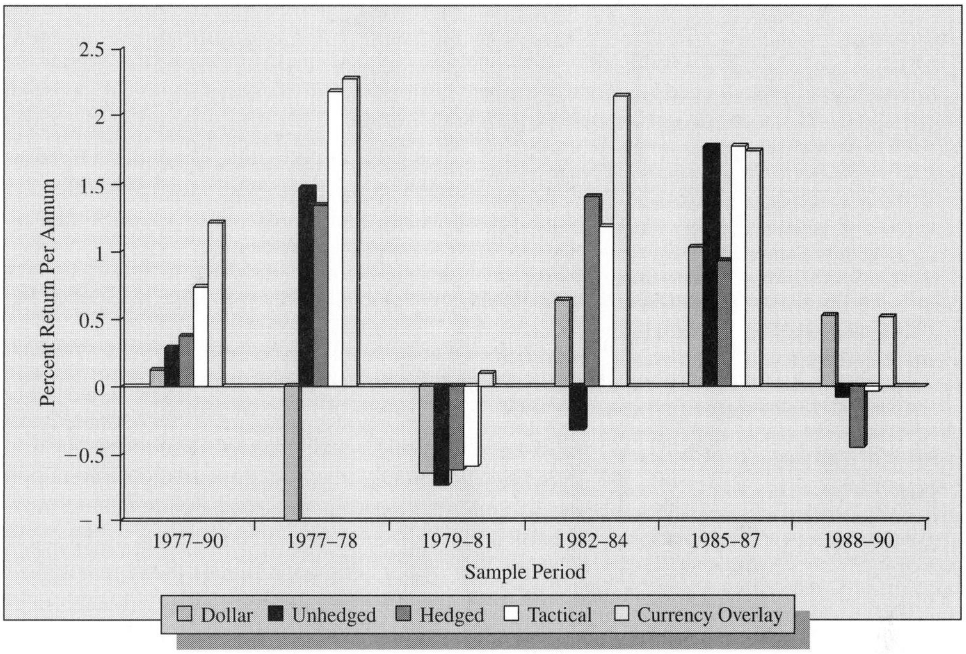

Note: The sample period is January 1977–December 1990, monthly data. Securities are 10-year government bonds issued by the United States, Canada, Germany, Japan, and the United Kingdom. The *unhedged* global portfolio is an equally weighted portfolio of non-U.S. securities. The *hedged* global portfolio is based on a one-month forward currency contract, rolled over monthly. The *tactical hedge* portfolio actively hedges a percentage of the global portfolio based on the signals from 10 technical trading rules. The *currency overlay* portfolio reflects the performance of the hedged global portfolio combined with a currency fund actively managed based on the signals from 10 technical trading rules.

Source: Richard M. Levich and Lee R. Thomas, "The Merits of Active Currency Risk Management: Evidence from International Bond Portfolios," *Financial Analysts Journal* 49, no. 5 (Sept.–Oct. 1993), pp. 63–70.

Sharpe ratio for the tactically managed global portfolio is 0.75, nearly twice that of the fully hedged global portfolio and more than six times that of the U.S. dollar portfolio.

The results for the currency overlay strategy are still more encouraging. Without exception, mean returns are higher than for the tactical hedging program, and volatility measures are about the same. The effect on the Sharpe ratio is unambiguous. For three currencies (DM, £, ¥) the return/risk ratios are substantially higher than for the pure U.S. dollar bond portfolio. For the global portfolio, the Sharpe ratio is 1.23, more than 10 times that for the U.S. dollar bond portfolio.

The results presented above are evidence that active hedging strategies (rather than always hedging or hedging a set percentage of exposure) would have been extremely beneficial to international bond portfolio managers.[30] However, in light of the wide swings in currencies over the sample period, it is possible that the results may largely reflect the events in a single year or two. To investigate this possibility, the authors broke the sample into five subperiods. These results are summarized in Figure 14.6. The active overlay strategy had the highest total return and the highest Sharpe ratio in four of the five subperiods. Moreover, in every subperiod, the currency overlay strategy produced a positive Sharpe ratio and a Sharpe ratio greater than the US$ portfolio. That is,

---

[30]Black (1989, 1990) proposed a fixed, universal hedge ratio. See note 25.

a foreign bond portfolio that includes an active currency risk management strategy based on a currency overlay approach dominated the performance of a passively held US$ bond portfolio.

The results presented here are ex post, and the usual caveat applies that an investor would need to identify the forecasting rules in advance. Technical models for short-term forecasting have been studied extensively and we discussed their limitations in Chapter 7. The use of the technical models here, in particular, assigning a fixed weight to each model in the tactical and currency overlay mode, was intended to offer a naive application of these technical forecasts rather than attempting to optimize their use.

Problems in Implementing an International Bond Portfolio

As this chapter has suggested, the argument for investing in an international portfolio of bonds has both theoretical support and compelling empirical evidence on data from the 1960s, 1970s, and 1980s. Early published research emphasized the diversification benefits—higher returns for a given level of risk or lower risks for a given level of return—that were possible with broadly diversified international bond portfolios.[31]

As the evidence accumulated, more institutional funds moved into international bond positions. Sales of publicly traded global bond funds accelerated in the early 1990s. However, the performance of global bond funds did not match the empirical expectation. In the five-year period ending December 1994, world bond funds averaged an annual return of 7.5 percent, compared with 8.2 percent for all categories of U.S. corporate bond funds (see Box 14.3).

It is unclear what conclusions we can draw from these two numbers. First, world bond funds are intended to deliver a lower risk, not necessarily a higher return. The newspaper article summarized in Box 14.3 says nothing about risk. Second, world bond funds invest primarily in government bonds. A comparison with the returns on corporate bond funds may not adequately control for credit risk. Finally, there is no information about the currency hedging strategies followed by these world bond funds. Some world bond funds *enhanced* their riskiness with currency bets—borrowing in one currency, say the DM, to buy higher yielding bonds in another currency, say the Italian lira—a good strategy when the DM/lira rate is stable, but a risky strategy that led to losses in the 1992 ERM collapse.

A recent study by Miranda Detzler (1999) analyzes the performance of 19 global bond mutual funds over the 1988–1995 period. Detzler reports that, overall, the funds do not demonstrate superior performance, net of expenses, to a variety of benchmarks. Indeed, these funds did not outperform a U.S. bond index, which suggests that management expenses may have outweighed potential diversification benefits over the sample period.

We will review some of the practical difficulties involved in implementing an international bond fund.

Additional Costs.   Most observers agree that the costs of operating an international bond fund are greater than those for a domestic bond fund. This is especially so for a US$-based investor. Bid-ask spreads in the U.S. government bond market are the narrowest in the world. J. P. Morgan (1989, p. 11) estimated the spread at only 3 basis

---

[31]Using data for the 1960–1980 period, Levy and Lerman (1988) showed that U.S. bond investors who earned 4.31 percent per annum over the period (with volatility of 5.53 percent) could have doubled their return at the same level of risk had they invested in a well-diversified international bond portfolio.

Box 14.3

Have Global Bond Funds Delivered?

After their introduction in the mid-1980s, sales of global bonds funds mounted, reaching their peak inflow in 1993. But in 1994, the U.S. bond market sold off sharply and many foreign bond funds followed suit. The sell-off extended to short-term global bond funds that often had been marketed under the guise of steady levels of current income and low volatility. In 1992 and 1993, many global bond funds fell victim to the breakup in the European Exchange Rate Mechanism. Reaching for extra returns by borrowing the low-interest-rate currency and holding the high-interest-rate currency, many funds sustained large losses when the high-interest-rate currencies devalued. In December 1994, other bond funds took large losses when the Mexican peso collapsed.

In *The Wall Street Journal* article cited as the source of this box, a manager from Putnam Investments defended global bond funds by claiming that these funds provide diversification benefits for investors. He added, however, that the funds were not well suited for conservative investors seeking a steady income stream.

It is true that short-term bond funds have lower exposure to interest rate risk. But global short-term bond funds also carry exposure to foreign exchange rate risk unless these risks are hedged. While the precise strategies of global bond funds vary, the record of the entire group is unimpressive. Morningstar Mutual Funds calculated that in the 1989–1994 period, U.S. corporate bond funds had average annual returns of 8.2 percent compared with only 7.5 percent for foreign bond funds. A Morningstar spokesperson summarized the theory of uncovered interest parity, arguing that any advantage of higher short-term interest rates would eventually be eaten up by a depreciating currency. "These funds are propagated on a free-lunch concept," he stated, that just isn't valid.

The performance record prompted John Bogle, chairman of the Vanguard Group, to say, "I think you're taking the added currency risk [with a foreign bond fund] without any payoff." Bogle predicted that with this kind of disappointing performance record, the short-term global fund was "on the way to vanishing."

While this prediction may be correct in the public arena, the currency overlay strategy continues to gain popularity among institutional investors who invest globally. Currency overlay managers who can limit the impact of exchange rate volatility, or take advantage of exchange rate changes, continue to be in strong demand among institutional investors.

Source: Adapted from "Analysts Question Need for Foreign-Bond Funds," *The Wall Street Journal,* Dec. 29, 1994, p. C1.

---

points for the "benchmark" most actively traded U.S. government bonds, and 6 basis points for traded but "less active" issues. In contrast, the spreads in non-U.S. markets average about 8 basis points for the benchmark issues and 20 basis points for traded but less active issues.

There is less agreement about the cost of continuously maintaining a currency-hedged international bond fund. Rosenberg (1990) cited estimates of 27–60 basis points (per annum) in additional costs for execution, settlement, and management of an always-hedged international bond fund.

Lee Thomas (1990) argued that the incremental costs of always hedging are lower than this. Whether hedged or unhedged, an international investor must buy spot foreign exchange and purchase the foreign bond, so these transaction costs are common. In the always-hedge strategy, managers sell a one-month forward contract at the same time they make their original spot currency purchase. At the end of each month, managers "roll forward" this contract—buying spot and selling forward. Thomas claimed that this transaction is inexpensive, and that the annual cost for 12 rollovers adds 20–25 basis points.

Managers of actual global bond funds exhibit similar differences of opinion, as reported in the article summarized in Box 14.4.

Box 14.4

To Hedge or Not to Hedge—A Global Bond Portfolio

The empirical evidence in the academic studies reviewed seemed to present a strong case in favor of currency hedging of either the passive or active variety. But these studies looked primarily at the world's major bond markets and from a US$-base currency perspective.

Hedging a portfolio of emerging market bonds could be more difficult (because dealer quotations on emerging market currencies are more scarce) or more costly, but the principles of hedging are identical. After the collapse of the Mexican peso in late 1994, it was clear that foreign bond investors *should* have hedged, and those who did not hedge suffered a large opportunity loss.

Yet, even after the peso's decline, professional investment managers disagreed about the proper role of currency hedging for global bond portfolios. These differences need not reflect a lack of sophistication among bond fund managers, but honest professional differences about the costs and benefits from hedging.

The managers of Edinburgh Latin America watched their fund decline by nearly 23 percent in one month (December 1994). They followed a policy of little or no hedging. Even after the fall, a spokesman for the firm said, "It is our experience that it is too expensive to hedge your currency exposure in emerging markets." He meant that the forward discount is high on Latin currencies, so hedging

locks in a substantial loss, which looks bad if the currency does not depreciate by still more than the forward discount.* A spokeswoman for Fidelity Investments made a similar comment: "We don't tend to hedge at all—in either stock or bond funds—on the basis that most of our investors are in it for the long haul . . . and it's very expensive."

In the same *Wall Street Journal* article, however, a bond manager at Norwich Unit Trust Managers Ltd. (UK) took an opposite point of view, arguing that even when the bonds are in a risky market such as Mexico, a bond manager can still hedge affordably by finding a bank that specializes in foreign exchange trading in that currency. The currency risks can be hedged in the usual way, using a short forward position or a currency swap. "You can't ignore the impact of currency on bonds," the manager commented. "You only have to look at the historic returns to tell you that."

---

*We examine the cost of hedging versus not hedging in Chapter 16.

Source: Adapted from "Following Emerging-Markets Tumble, Investors See Value of Hedging Foreign-Exchange Risks," *The Wall Street Journal,* Jan. 17, 1995, p. C17.

Other Sources of Risk.   Managers face other risks not mentioned in our review of international bond portfolios. In our review, portfolio allocations to the different national markets were determined in a naive fashion, such as equal allocations across markets or allocations proportional to market capitalization. These portfolio allocations were not *optimized* to find the portfolio with the best risk–return trade-off, and our allocations ruled out the possibility of a short position in any bond market.

In practice, bond managers may optimize their portfolio allocations to take advantage of anticipated price movements and the expected correlation of price movements (see Appendix 14.1). If these estimated price changes or correlations are incorrect, the "optimized" portfolio may have substantially worse performance (ex post) than a naive benchmark, such as an equally weighted portfolio. The error introduced by optimizing a portfolio on the basis of estimated returns and estimated variances (and covariances) of returns is referred to as **estimation risk.**[32]

For example, consider a case where a model predicts the expected rate of return on the € will be 3.2 percent and the expected rate of return on the SFr is 3.1 percent. An

---

[32]See Jorion (1985) for the first discussion of estimation risk in international asset portfolios. Annaert (1995) presents a recent application to international bond portfolios.

optimizing algorithm will indicate that profits are available if we short the SFr and take a long position in the €. If these forecasts are correct, we will make 0.1 percent on the magnitude of our position. As the historical correlation of the € and SFr increases, the optimizer will recommend larger and larger positions.

The reader will, hopefully, see that the above portfolio allocation is fraught with danger. Suppose that the *realized* return on the € is 3.0 percent and the *realized* return on the SFr is 3.5 percent (both fairly close to their forecasted values); then our position loses 0.5 percent. Leveraging this position (by borrowing as much SFr as possible) only makes things worse. This example shows the practical impact of estimation risk. Our € and SFr currency forecasts may have had enough precision to say that both currencies would strengthen, but they did not have enough precision to conclude which currency would appreciate by more.

This example is somewhat related to the second problem of running an international bond fund: the **peso problem,** which we introduced in Chapter 7. A peso problem refers to the situation where there is a small probability of a large, unexpected exchange rate change. A number of international bond funds may have followed the core strategy of diversification and currency hedging as described in this chapter. But some managers saw the European Monetary System as a way to enhance the returns of their funds. By borrowing in the low-interest-rate currency (the DM) and investing in a higher-interest-rate currency (like Italian lira, British £, Spanish peseta), managers attempted to pick up the extra yield on the interest differential—which they did until the ERM broke down in the summer of 1992 and again in 1993.

Some global bond managers repeated this strategy again in 1994 with investments in Mexican and Latin American debt. Mexican debt denominated in US$ fell in price because of the credit risks, and Mexican debt denominated in pesos fell because the interest differential favoring Mexico did not keep up with the depreciation of the peso.

Thus, while one can make a theoretical case for gains from international bond diversification, many global fund managers have been unable to deliver on this promise.

The Impact of the EMU on International Bond Markets

The arrival of the European Economic and Monetary Union (EMU) in 1999 changed the shape of international bond markets as we have known them for much of the 20th century. The fundamental change was the transfer of authority for making monetary policy from the central banks of 12 countries to a single central bank (the European Central Bank, ECB).[33] Prior to the EMU, European government bonds were risk-free (in nominal terms) because the national central banks could (if necessary) print domestic money to redeem their bonds in full. Now, government bonds of the 12 EMU nations bear credit risk, because money creation authority now rests solely within the ECB. In this respect, the EMU bond market resembles the state and municipal bond market in the United States, where the 50 states and various municipal government issue bonds in a single currency but none of these issuers may print money to repay their bonds.

Thus, all Euroland government bonds are not homogeneous in the same sense as all U.S. government bonds that are backed by the full faith and credit of a single entity— the U.S. Treasury. As a result, the market sets different prices and yields on different EMU government bonds. Table 14.7 shows a sample of yields for 10-year government

---

[33]The EMU began in 1999 with 11 countries—Austria, Belgium, Finland, France, Germany, Ireland, Italy, Luxembourg, Netherlands, Portugal, and Spain. In January 2001, Greece became the 12th member of EMU.

TABLE 14.7   Size and Pricing in the EMU Government Bond Market

Country	Government Bonds Outstanding, Year-End 1999 (US$ Billion)	% Share	Bid Yield, 10-Year Bond	Spread vs. Germany	S&P Long-Term Credit Rating for Local Currency Obligations
EMU Countries					
Austria	80.6	2.5%	5.59	0.27	AAA
Belgium	195.6	6.1%	5.59	0.27	AA+
Finland	44.6	1.4%	5.51	0.19	AA+
France	711.3	22.3%	5.42	0.10	AAA
Germany	767.8	24.0%	5.32	0.00	AAA
Ireland	23.8	0.7%	5.54	0.22	AA+
Italy	935.2	29.3%	5.62	0.30	AA
Luxembourg	NA	NA	NA	NA	AAA
Netherlands	174.5	5.5%	5.47	0.15	AAA
Portugal	36.2	1.1%	5.61	0.29	AA
Spain	223.5	7.0%	5.55	0.23	AA+
EMU Total	3193.1	100.0%			
Other EU Countries					
Denmark	82.5		5.65	0.33	AAA
Greece	NA		6.12	0.80	A−
Sweden	94.2		5.45	0.13	AAA
United Kingdom	466.3		5.32	0.00	AAA
Other EU Total	643.0				
EU Total	3836.1				

Source: Merrill Lynch, "Size and Structure of the World Bond Market: 2000," April 2000; *Financial Times,* June 21, 2000; Standard & Poor's Sovereign Ratings at <www.standardpoor.com/ratings/sovereigns/index.htm>.

Note: Greece is listed as an EU country to reflect its status on June 20, 2000 when the rates in this table were published. Greece was accepted by the EU Council on June 19 and is scheduled to join EMU effective January 1, 2001.

bonds on June 20, 2000. German bonds form the top, or benchmark, tier. France and the Netherlands make up a second tier, with yields 10–15 basis points (bp) higher. The remaining countries form a third tier, with yields 20–30 bp higher than German yields.

What this spread reflects is an open question. Liquidity differences may play a role. The German and French segments are large (implying high liquidity and low spread). But Italy has the largest outstanding supply of bonds of any Euroland country (a 29.3 percent share). This suggests that the outstanding supply of bonds may be a poor proxy for liquidity, which reflects an ability to trade large volumes quickly and at low transaction costs. Differences in credit quality may also be a factor. Only 5 of the 11 Euroland countries hold a AAA credit rating for long-term obligations denominated in local currency. Countries with lower ratings tend to have higher spreads relative to Germany.[34] However, Austria has a AAA credit rating but a large spread over German yields, which suggests that a lack of liquidity may contribute to higher Austrian yields.

The EMU affects international investors in one other way. With fewer central banks in the world exercising monetary policy, investors have fewer opportunities to diversify

[34] A related explanation is that investors may fear a breakup of the EMU, leading departing countries to repay their euro debts using new local currency. Investors assign higher yields to countries with a higher probability of leaving the EMU.

their exposure to central bank risk. Institutional investors who deal in large amounts will have three principal market places (the United States, the EMU, and Japan) to diversify their portfolios, plus a number of smaller bond markets including the United Kingdom, Switzerland, Australia, and Sweden.

Policy Matters—Public Policymakers

Certain public policy initiatives may affect the investment opportunities in international bond portfolios. In this section, we briefly examine the impact of the transition to European Monetary Union, and the developing market for bonds issued by emerging market governments.

The Impact of European Monetary Union

The transition to the European Economic and Monetary Union in January 1999 resolved many policy issues related to the planning for monetary union. With the EMU now in place, other policy issues are drawing greater attention.

By January 1, 1999, all fixed-income securities in EMU legacy currencies were redenominated into an equivalent number of euros using the conversion factors in Table 2.2. Thus, a German Bund with a 4 percent coupon and principal amount of DM1 million converted into a principal amount of €511,291.8812 at the conversion rate of 1.95583 DM/€. The 4 percent coupon remains the same but is now paid in € on the new principal amount. European financial markets themselves remain somewhat physically segmented, with most German bonds traded by German banks in Germany, and French bonds traded by French banks in France, but electronic trading systems and cross-border financial mergers are leading to some consolidation of trading activity.

Many pension funds and other institutional investors are constrained by law or by their charters to limit their exposure to foreign securities. Under the EMU, securities issued by German, French, and Italian firms are issued in separate national legal jurisdictions, but they all share the same currency. In some instances, Euroland investors are allowed to classify securities issued by EMU obligors as "domestic" for these purposes.

The EMU bond market will expand as more nations enter the EMU and issuers turn to the bond market to raise capital. Greece is the next country slated to join the EMU in January 2001. The Greek market will be a small addition to the overall Euroland bond market. The United Kingdom is the largest EU country remaining outside the EMU. British entry into EMU, should it occur, would add a large new segment to the EMU bond market.

One outcome that investors fear is excessive issuance of euro-denominated bonds, especially if they are the result of fiscal deficits. Excess supply of bonds drives down prices leading to capital losses for investors. The Maastricht Treaty still limits the size of national fiscal deficits and the Stability Agreement gives Brussels the right to impose penalties on countries that run excessive deficits, and potentially raise the cost of borrowing for other EMU nations. If EU policies clearly place the burden of debt repayment on the issuing country, ruling out the possibility for an ECB bailout or monetization of debt, then there should be few negative spillover effects onto other EMU borrowers. A heavy borrowing nation could see their credit rating fall and interest rate rise without affecting others. However, in the current market setting, it appears as if the government sector of the EMU bond market is shrinking, rather than expanding.

Brady Bonds and Emerging Market Debt Issues

The Brady Plan, named for U.S. Secretary of the Treasury Nicholas F. Brady and launched in 1989, represented a major building block in the recovery of many less-developed countries (LDCs) that were saddled with tremendous bank debt. After the 1982 Mexican debt crisis, commercial banks entered into extended negotiations with LDC central banks. These negotiations were tedious in the extreme, with hundreds of banks involved and thousands of separate bank loans, and terms and conditions more numerous than anyone could follow. An interbank market for these bank loans developed in the mid-1980s, which sent the secondary market value of these loans crashing because some banks wanted to eradicate these loans from their portfolios at almost any price.

The Brady Plan entailed a restructuring of nonperforming LDC bank debt into various uniform bond issues that could be sold to a wide spectrum of investors, not just banks. Trading in secondary markets would add further value to these securities.

A typical offering might be structured as follows: Suppose Mexico has $100 million in 15-year bank debt on which it has not been paying interest. Because the debt is non-performing, it has slumped to a price of $40 million in interbank trading. With only $13 million, Mexico can purchase U.S. Treasury zero-coupon bonds (yielding 5.78 percent) that will mature in 20 years with a value of $40 million. Once purchased, these U.S. Treasuries are placed in escrow outside Mexico to serve as collateral for the principal of $40 million worth of new 20-year bonds—so-called **Brady bonds**—that Mexico will swap with the banks to retire its $100 million bank debt. Mexico will service the interest payments on these Brady bonds at a lower rate, partly as a concession and partly to reflect that there is no principal at risk because the bonds are collateralized by U.S. Treasuries.

To benefit Mexico, the debt has been spread out over a longer term, and the interest rate is lower and on a smaller amount of principal. To benefit the investor, the Brady bond debt is serviced and the investor in addition has a liquid asset that can be sold if economic conditions change. The pioneering Brady deal with Mexico also included a rolling guarantee covering the first 18 months of interest obligations provided by international institutions, further encouraging banks to trade in their old loans.

Following Mexico, Brady bonds were issued by more than 20 countries. The common feature of Brady bonds is a swap of new debt for old, usually with the principal of the new debt collateralized or guaranteed in some manner, but numerous variations on this theme have been adopted. Sometimes certain interest payments were backed by Treasury bonds, and other sweeteners (such as value recovery rights linked to the price of oil) were part of some Brady issues. Examples of several Brady bonds, their terms and conditions, and recent prices and yields are shown in Table 14.8. By the mid-1990s, there were more than $170 billion of Brady bonds outstanding. Annual turnover in Brady bonds peaked at $2.5 trillion in 1997 before dropping off following the Asian and Russian financial crises.[35]

The combination of Brady Bonds, sovereign loans, and corporate bonds issued by firms in emerging markets comprise an emerging market for debt. The overall market for emerging market bonds totaled $1.2 trillion at year-end 1999.[36] Innovative contract design has allowed it to grow in popularity, even though these securities face substantial credit risk.

---

[35]Michael H. Chamberlin, "The Brady Plan—The First 10 Years and Beyond," *Latin Finance,* Spring 2000. Further information about Brady Bonds is available from BradyNet, Inc. at <www.bradynet.com> and the Emerging Markets Traders Association at <www.emta.org>.

[36]See Merrill Lynch, "Size and Structure of the World Bond Market: 2000," April 2000.

TABLE 14.8 **Characteristics of Individual Brady Bonds**

	Argentina Par Bond	Mexico Aztec Bond	Poland Discount Bond
Obligor	Republic of Argentina	United Mexican States	Republic of Poland
Guarantor	None	None	None
Form	Registered bonds	Registered bonds	Registered notes
Amount issued	US$ 12.7 billion	US$ 2.56 billion	US$ 3.0 billion
Denomination	$250,000	$250,000	$250,000
Currency	US$	US$	US$
Date issued	March 31, 1993	March 15, 1988	October 27, 1994
Maturity date	March 31, 2023	March 31, 2008	October 27, 2024
Coupon	Semiannual: Year 1: 4.0% Year 2: 4.25% Year 3: 5.0% Year 4: 5.25% Year 5: 5.5% Year 6: 5.75% Years 7–30: 6.0%	Semiannual: 6-month LIBOR + 1.625%	Semiannual: 6-month LIBOR + 0.8125%
Amortization	Bullet	Bullet	Bullet
Enhancements	U.S. Treasury zero-coupon in amount sufficient to collateralize principal payment and 12 months of rolling interest guarantees	U.S. Treasury zero-coupon in amount sufficient to collateralize principal payment	U.S. Treasury zero-coupon in amount sufficient to collateralize principal payment
S&P rating	BB–	BB	BB
Market prices of bond/collateral on 10/25/96	56.69 / 16.0	98.50 / 46.5	52.63 / 14.8
Stripped yield	15.40%	11.95%	8.92%
Stripped spread	8.74%	5.51%	2.11%

Notes: The market price of the bond is as a percentage of par (100). The market price of the collateral is market value of the zero-coupon U.S. Treasury collateral securing the principal. Stripped yield is the semiannual yield on the noncollateralized country cash flows. Stripped spread is the difference (in basis points) and the appropriate U.S. Treasury yield.

Source: BradyNet, Inc. at <www.bradynet.com>, in the pages titled Analysis (Bond Descriptions) and Prices.

Summary

In this chapter, we examined the return and risk properties of international bond portfolios from an investor's perspective. An investment in a foreign bond carries exposure to foreign interest rate risk as well as foreign currency risk. In general, there also is exposure to changes in credit risk, exchange controls, and the risk of default.

In terms of the investor's base currency, the unhedged return on a foreign bond equals the return on the bond in foreign currency terms plus the return on the foreign currency itself. The volatility of unhedged returns reflects the volatility of these two factors as well as the covariance between the returns on the foreign bond and the returns on spot foreign exchange. In theory, this covariance term could be either positive or negative. Investors can reduce their exposure to exchange rate risk by a strategy of hedging their currency position in the foreign bond. These hedging strategies leave investors exposed primarily to foreign interest rate risk (and to foreign exchange risk on the amount of the bond forecast error). The hedging approach demonstrates that exposure to foreign exchange risk and exposure to foreign interest rate risk is largely separable. Investors can synthetically construct securities with the interest rate risk of one market and the currency risk of another market.

Empirical evidence shows that international bond returns are weakly correlated, so international portfolios have produced superior performance in terms of risk and return compared with U.S. Treasury securities. These performance gains may reflect a diversification to central bank risk and the interest rate risk inherent in each national bond market. Bond portfolios that are passively hedged have outperformed unhedged portfolios; bond portfolios that are actively hedged have outperformed passively hedged portfolios.

The transition to monetary union has left the world bond markets heavily concentrated in only three markets: the United States, the European Monetary Union, and Japan. This development could reduce the potential diversification gains for international bond portfolios.

APPENDIX 14.1
GLOBAL ASSET ALLOCATION

Portfolio management calls on an investor to allocate his or her wealth (W) in proportions or weights (w_i) across a set of assets ($i = 1, \ldots N$). To determine an allocation, various inputs are required, including a set of expected returns on each asset [$E(R_i)$], volatility measures for each asset [$\sigma(R_i)$], and measures of the correlation of returns among assets [$\rho(R_i,R_j)$]. The set of assets may refer to a very fine grid of investments, such as individual stocks or bonds that will make N a large number in the thousands. In thinking about global asset allocation, N often refers to a smaller number of investments, possibly the overall stock index and bond index for each country—both on an unhedged and currency-hedged basis. In the limit, N may represent only six asset categories including the overall foreign bond market (unhedged and currency-hedged), the overall foreign stock market (unhedged and currency-hedged), and the domestic stock and bond markets.

To solve the allocation problem, the investor needs the following data inputs:

- Estimates of $E(R_i)$ for all $i = 1, \ldots N$ investments, using fundamental data on firms or macroeconomic data on countries, whichever is appropriate.
- Estimates of $\sigma(R_i)$ for all $i = 1, \ldots N$ investments, using historical data or implied volatilities from option prices.
- Estimates of $\rho(R_i,R_j)$ for all i,j pairs, using historical data or implied correlations from cross-rate option prices, where appropriate.

The definition of expected portfolio returns [$E(R_P)$] and portfolio risk [$\sigma^2(R_P)$] is:

$$E(R_P) = \sum_{i=1}^{N} w_i\, E(R_i)$$

$$\sigma^2(R_P) = \sum_{i=1}^{N} w_i^2\, \sigma^2(R_i) + 2 \sum_{i \neq j}^{N} w_i w_j\, \rho(R_i,R_j)\, \sigma(R_i)\, \sigma(R_j)$$

The asset allocation algorithm solves for a set of weights (w_i) that maximizes expected portfolio returns, conditional on a given level of portfolio risk. By allowing portfolio risk to vary, the asset allocation algorithm traces out an efficient frontier of investment opportunities. The weights are always constrained so that $\Sigma w_i = 1$ (all wealth is invested), and additional constraints, such as $w_i \geq 0$ (no short selling) are sometimes included.

Once the efficient frontier of expected portfolio returns and risk has been generated, the investor picks the allocation (the set of w_i) that produces the most desired combination of risk and return (See Figure 15.8, Chapter 15). The calculation of weights can often be made using spreadsheet software that contains features to solve for the maximum of a function subject to other constraints or conditions (such as the SOLVER routines in EXCEL).

Thomas (1990, pp. 303–15) has proposed a useful way to simplify and better understand the global asset allocation problem. Recognizing that some investors buy foreign stocks because they like the foreign currency, and that some investors avoid foreign stocks because they do not like the foreign currency, Thomas suggests that the investor try to separate these decisions to the extent possible using a three-step procedure. First, the "Asset Allocation Committee" assesses the return and risk of all global investments, but on a *currency-hedged basis*. Thus, the goal is to analyze how well investments in the various foreign markets will perform without taking any currency risk. The Asset Allocation Committee is permitted to reason: "We think the € will weaken and thus contribute to a stronger German bond and equity market, which still look good *after* we currency-hedge"; in this sense the asset and currency decisions are interdependent. But the Committee would *not* be permitted to say, "We feel the € will strengthen, and therefore we want to buy German bonds." The Asset Allocation Committee might (after running an optimization program) decide on the investment weights given in column 2 of the following table.

Country	Preferred Security Allocation	Preferred Currency Allocation	Reconciling Currency Transaction
U.S.	55%	70%	+15
Japan	20	0	−20
Germany	10	5	−5
U.K.	10	15	+5
New Zealand	5	5	0
Switzerland	0	5	+5
Total	100%	100%	0

The second phase of Thomas's approach is the "Currency Allocation Committee." This committee's job is to form estimates of the expected return and risk of currencies over the planning horizon. Again, the Currency Allocation Committee may use a formal portfolio optimization procedure, and it may constrain itself to hold only positive currency positions. The results of the Currency Allocation Committee analysis are shown in column 3 in the table. Notice that the Currency Allocation Committee has recommended positions in some currencies that the Asset Allocation Committee does not recommend; in this sense, the two committees function in an independent style.

The final stage of the process is to reconcile the decisions of the two committees. This is illustrated in the final column of the table, assuming a $100 million portfolio. After buying the Japanese bonds, our investor would sell $15 million worth of ¥ for US$, and $5 million worth of ¥ for £. After buying the $10 million in German bonds, our investor would sell $5 million worth of € in exchange for Swiss francs. The New Zealand bond position and the desired NZ$ currency position happen to be identical so no reconciling transactions are required. With this process, the investor hopes to profit from the committee's expertise in security selection and currency allocation.

Questions

1. What is home country bias in asset portfolios? How would you explain this phenomenon?

2. Compare central bank risk and interest rate risk.

3. Suppose you hold a SFr1 million Swiss long-term bond yielding 6 percent annually. The spot exchange rate is $0.60/SFr. The one-month forward exchange rate is $0.62/SFr. How would you protect your SFr investment from exchange rate fluctuations?

4. What are the obstacles you might face when trying to hedge a foreign bond portfolio?

5. Compare active hedging strategies to passive hedging strategies. What are the advantages of hedging actively instead of passively?

6. Define *rolling forward hedge*. Give an example for a five-year UK£ bond.

7. Describe a perfect currency hedge for an investor in a long-term foreign bond. Why is it difficult to implement a perfect currency hedge in the real world?

8. What are the key elements to take into consideration when investing in an international bond portfolio?

9. A report by the International Monetary Fund refers to "a secular rise in the correlation of long-term interest rates over time as a result of increasing capital market integration. The correlation of German and U.S. 10-year bond yields (based on monthly levels) has risen from an average of just 0.191 over the 1970–1979 period to 0.908 over the 1980–1989 period and to 0.934 over the 1990–1994 period. In the case of Japanese bonds, the correlation with U.S. bond yields has risen steadily from 0.182 in 1970–1979 to 0.826 in 1980–1989 and to 0.965 in 1990–1994. For all G-7 countries with the exception of Italy, the correlation of government bond yields with U.S. bond yields now exceeds 0.90." What are the implications of this trend for international bond portfolio managers? Would diversification gains still be present while investing abroad?

10. In 1989, two articles on international bond portfolio investments were published at about the same time with dramatically different conclusions. One article claimed that "currency hedging can substantially reduce volatility of foreign bonds and foreign bond portfolios, while having little effect on their returns." The other article, titled "Why There Is No Free Lunch in Currency Hedging," claimed that "the amount of risk reduction available from international bond diversification in the long run is independent of whether the currency risk is hedged or not." How would you explain the differing views of the two authors?

11. How would consideration of execution costs and settlement costs influence the claim that global, currency-hedged investment provides better return and risk characteristics than all-US$ investment?

Exercises

1. Suppose you can invest $1 million for 90 days. You are risk averse and want to invest in government issues. However, you have heard of theories claiming that international investing can enhance returns and are willing to give it a try. You have collected current three-month rates in Japan and Germany as well as current spot rates and current three-month forward rates. Also shown below are the actual spot exchange rates three months later.

	Interest Rates		*Spot*	*Forward*	*Actual*
Japan	3%	¥/$	100.00	100.50	98.00
Switzerland	6	SFr/$	1.50	1.4950	1.52
United States	5	$/$	1.00	1.00	1.00

   a. Calculate the unhedged returns (in US$ terms) at the end of the three months for a Japanese and a Swiss investment.
   b. Calculate the hedged returns for the same investments.
   c. Would you invest abroad? In which market? Would you hedge?

2. *You just inherited from your English aunt £1 million in three-year UK government bonds. The bonds are trading at par on the London bond market. The bonds have a coupon rate of 6 percent.
   a. Assuming a flat yield curve and stable interest rates over the life of the bond, what is your average monthly return at the end of the three years?
   b. The actual return (shown as a total return index) for the three-year UK bond over its life is shown in the table. (See spreadsheet file.) What is the average monthly return and risk for the three-year bond in £ terms? How does it compare to the previous return?
   c. As a US$-based investor, you are concerned about your returns in US$ terms. Using the spot rates from the disk, calculate your average monthly return and risk in US$ terms. How does it compare to £-based risk and return characteristics?

   d. How would you hedge your currency exposure? Calculate return and risk characteristics of your imperfectly hedged portfolio. (*Hint:* Use the forward rates shown in the table.) How does it compare to unhedged returns.
   e. Suppose you could forecast the monthly returns as shown in the table and hedge accordingly. Show the return and risk characteristics for your perfectly hedged portfolio. How does it compare to unhedged returns? How does it compare to the imperfectly hedged returns?

3. *This exercise relies on a spreadsheet file that shows a string of bond indexes from different countries: the United States, Germany, Japan, and the United Kingdom, as well as actual spot rates and forward rates for the DM, ¥, and £. The aim of this exercise is to help students understand the effect of hedging policies on bond portfolio returns.
   a. Calculate the monthly returns for each country's bond index. (*Hint:* Use a spreadsheet program to calculate returns.) What is the average return and the risk for each market, in local currency and in US$ terms? Calculate the return–risk ratio for each market. Which one is most risky? Calculate the correlation between the U.S. market and each of the three other markets. Is there any potential for a diversification gain?
   b. Create an international bond portfolio of the three markets (Germany, Japan, and the United Kingdom) using equal weights. Repeat the calculations of question *a* for this international portfolio. How does the international bond portfolio fare compared to individual markets?
   c. Repeat question *b* for a global bond fund, weighting equally all four markets including the U.S. market. Does the global fund have any superior characteristics when compared with the international bond portfolio?
   d. Calculate return and risk for the international bond portfolio and the global bond portfolio on a perfectly hedged basis. (*Hint:* Use the forward rates shown in the table.) How do the risk and return characteristics compare to those of the unhedged international bond portfolio? To the all-U.S. portfolio?

---

*Data from this exercise are provided at the author's website <www.stern.nyu.edu/~rlevich/book1/datafile.htm>.

References

Alesina, Alberto, and Lawrence H. Summers. "Central Bank Independence and Macroeconomic Performance: Some Comparative Evidence." *Journal of Money Credit and Banking* 25, no. 2 (May 1993); pp. 151–62.

Annaert, Jan. "Estimation Risk and International Bond Portfolio Selection." *Journal of Multinational Financial Management* 5, no. 2 (Jan. 1995): pp. 47–71.

Black, Fischer. "Equilibrium Exchange Rate Hedging." *Journal of Finance* 43 (1990), pp. 899–908.

———. "Universal Hedging: Optimizing Currency Risk and Reward in International Equity Portfolios." *Financial Analysts Journal* 45 (1989), pp. 16–22.

Detzler, Miranda Lam. "The Performance of Global Bond Mutual Funds." *Journal of Banking and Finance* 23 (1999), pp. 1195–1217.

Jorion, Philippe. "International Portfolio Diversification with Estimation Risk." *Journal of Business* 58 (July 1985), pp. 259–78.

———. "International Bonds: The Asset Class." Chapter 7 in *Global Portfolios,* ed. R. Z. Aliber and B. R. Bruce. Homewood, IL: Business One Irwin, 1991.

———. "Mean/Variance Analysis of Currency Overlays." *Financial Analysts Journal* 50, no. 3 (May–June 1994), pp. 48–56.

Kindleberger, Charles P. *A Financial History of Western Europe.* London: Allen and Unwin, 1984.

Levich, Richard M., and Lee R. Thomas. "The Merits of Active Currency Risk Management: Evidence from International Bond Portfolios." *Financial Analysts Journal* 49, no. 5 (Sept.–Oct. 1993), pp. 63–70.

Levy, Haim, and Zvi Lerman. "The Benefits of International Diversification in Bonds." *Financial Analysts Journal* 44, no. 5 (Sept.–Oct. 1988), pp. 56–64.

Lewis, Karen K. "Puzzles in International Financial Markets." In *Handbook of International Economics,* vol. 3, ed. G. Grossman and K. Rogoff. Amsterdam: North Holland, 1995.

Merrill Lynch & Company. "Size and Structure of the World Bond Market: 2000." Global Securities Research and Economics Group, April 2000.

J. P. Morgan, *World Financial Markets,* Nov. 22, 1989.

Perold, André F., and Evan C. Shulman. "The Free Lunch in Currency Hedging: Implications for Investment Policies and Performance Standards." *Financial Analysts Journal* (May–June 1988), pp. 45–50.

Putnam, Bluford. "False Bottom to the Holy Grail." In *The Currency-Hedging Debate,* ed. Lee R. Thomas. London: IFR Publishing, 1990.

Rosenberg, Michael R. "Why There Is No Free Lunch in Currency Hedging." In *The Currency-Hedging Debate,* ed. Lee R. Thomas. London: IFR Publishing, 1990.

Rosenberg, Michael R., and Frederick R. Marki. "How Strong Is the Case for Currency Hedged Foreign Bond Funds?" *Journal of International Securities Markets* (Winter 1988), pp. 269–75.

Tesar, Linda L., and Ingrid M. Werner. "Home Bias and High Turnover." *Journal of International Money and Finance* 14, no. 4 (August 1995), pp. 467–92.

Thomas, Lee R. "A Disciplined Approach to Global Asset Allocation." In *The Currency-Hedging Debate,* ed. Lee R. Thomas. London: IFR Publishing, 1990.

Solnik, Bruno. "Currency Hedging and Siegel's Paradox: On Black's Universal Hedging Rule." *Review of International Economics* 1, no. 2 (June 1993), pp. 180–87.

15 EQUITY PORTFOLIOS

"[T]he international diversification of portfolios is the source of an entirely new kind of world welfare gains from international economic relations, different from both the traditional 'gains from trade' and increased productivity flowing from the migration of the factors of production."

Grubel (1968)

Learning Objectives

After reading this chapter, students should

1. Be familiar with the overall composition of the global equity market, the relative importance of different locations, and institutional differences across markets.

2. Understand various techniques for making international portfolio investments including American Depositary Receipts, closed-end and open-end mutual funds, and direct share purchase.

3. Know how to calculate the unhedged return (in US$) on a foreign equity share.

4. Know how to calculate the hedged return (in US$) on a foreign equity share.

5. Be aware of the benefits from holding a global portfolio of equities (either hedged or unhedged) versus a portfolio of only US$ equities.

6. Recognize that investors typically overweight their home country portfolio (resulting in a home country bias) and that this is a puzzle that various theories try to address.

7. Be aware that emerging equity markets have grown in importance over the last 25 years, and that (as recent evidence suggests) price changes in these markets are more correlated with developed markets than in earlier years.

Equity markets, like bond markets, have been part of most market economies as long as private property rights have existed. The New York Stock Exchange was founded in 1792. The modern history of European stock exchanges dates back to the 1600s. The practice of international or cross-border equity investing has a longer history in Europe than in the United States. Private trusts and public investment funds based in London, Geneva, and Amsterdam have typified the international investor who constantly scans foreign markets for investment opportunities. In some cases, international investment followed the expansion of empire. In other cases, investors from small, wealthy nations were driven to consider foreign investment as a prudent complement to the limited menu of opportunities in domestic equity shares.

While they share a long history, equities and bonds are very different financial instruments. The owner of a £ bond is entitled to a set amount of £ at periodic intervals. All £ bonds (excluding those with equitylike features) are claims on some *nominal* amount of £. In comparison, the owner of an equity share in a British firm may receive dividends or distributions denominated in £. But what the shareholder truly owns is a claim on the *real assets* of the firm and all the cash flows that accrue to them once the firm has paid all of its creditors.

Both the £ bond and the British equity shares may be exposed to some similar market forces. If the £ bond was issued in London and trades in London, it will be subject to British exchange control risk, expropriation risks, and withholding taxes when viewed by non-British investors. These risks and the possibility of taxes on dividends and distributions will also concern a non-British investor assessing the value of equity shares in a British firm.

The fundamental difference between the £ bond and the British equity is this: The valuation of the £ bond is based on a stream of *nominal* £ cash flows that we can enumerate. The valuation of the British equity is linked to the firm's *real assets* (located in Britain and elsewhere) and the cash flows (in £ and possibly many other currencies) associated with the firm's operations.

The performance of equity investments is usually evaluated in two dimensions—expected return and risk—and it is useful to analyze international equity investment in this context as well. These dimensions describe the two basic incentives for international investment: (1) to enhance portfolio returns for the same level of risk, or (2) to reduce the riskiness of a portfolio without sacrificing expected return.

The first incentive for international investment, **expected value gains,** could occur in two situations. First, if foreign equity markets are *inefficient* (in the sense used in Chapter 7), then foreign equity prices do not reflect all available information. Pure profits are available to investors who spot these trading opportunities. Second, foreign equity markets may be *segmented* from other capital markets, meaning that investors in the foreign market receive a different compensation for bearing equity risk than in other markets. For example, suppose that a small, capital-scarce country must offer a 4 percent real rate of return to equity investors, while in a larger, capital-abundant country the real rate of return is only 2 percent for a project of similar risk. If these markets are kept segmented by an ocean or other barriers, these return differences can persist. But once the barrier is lifted, owners of capital in the large country receive a pure gain (associated with a more efficient worldwide allocation of capital) when they invest in the relatively capital scarce country.[1]

The second type of incentive for international investing is **diversification gains,** which we associate with the reduction in risk for a given level of investment return. Diversification gains result when a portfolio is extended to include new investments whose returns are imperfectly correlated with the original portfolio. Foreign equity markets have been an ideal candidate for diversification gains because the correlation of returns across countries is usually low.

Diversification gains are available even when domestic and foreign capital markets are *integrated,* so that risk bearing in different markets is rewarded in a similar fashion. When investors are risk averse, international equity investment offers an opportunity for

---

[1]See MacDougall (1960) for the classic exposition of this argument and its many variations.

FIGURE 15.1   **Return and Risk in World Equity Markets and Efficient Frontiers, 1959–1966**

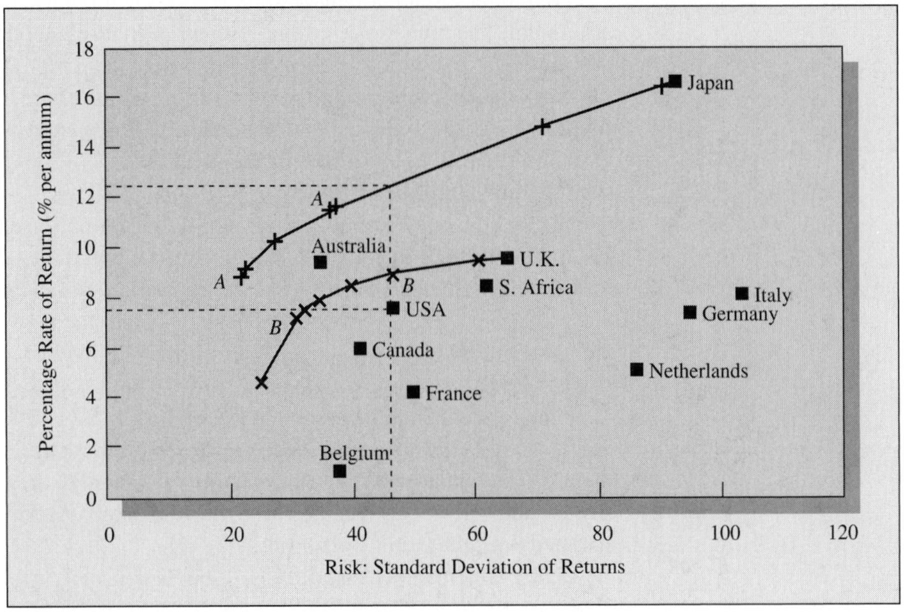

Note: Annualized data. Efficient frontier labeled *AA* includes all 11 industrial countries. Efficient frontier labeled *BB* includes only 8 European and North American countries.

Source: Adapted from Herbert G. Grubel, "Internationally Diversified Portfolios: Welfare Gains and Capital Flows," *American Economic Review* 58 (Dec. 1968), pp. 1299–1314.

welfare gains through superior "sharing" of international equity risks. To capture these diversification gains, large (gross) flows of capital may occur between countries, even when there is no apparent return incentive favoring either market.

Most studies have shown that the opportunities for diversification gains in international investment are greater than the diversification gains from domestic investment. This is especially true in smaller countries with a limited number of industries or firms to build a well-diversified portfolio. The pioneering study by Herbert Grubel (1968) showed that investors from 11 developed economies could have enjoyed substantially more favorable risk–return opportunities had they diversified their portfolios internationally in the 1960s. As Figure 15.1 shows, U.S. investors could have increased their returns from 7.5 percent to 12.6 percent per annum over this period, holding risk constant, by diversifying into international equities.

We now recognize that Grubel's analysis overstated the gains from international diversification. The efficient frontier derived in Figure 15.1 represents the ex post risk and return of these markets. Investors would have needed perfect foresight to select the ideal combination of country investment weights to reach the efficient frontier. Second, capital restrictions would have made some markets off-limits to foreign investors. Third, this efficient frontier could not have been obtained by *all* investors. The portfolios in segment *AA* of the efficient frontier call for roughly a 40 percent weight on Australia. Since Australia represents less than 1 percent of the world equity market, these portfolios were inconsistent with the overall valuation of equity markets.

Despite these shortcomings, Grubel's insight—that the principles of portfolio diversification can be applied in an international context—has been verified by many subsequent studies. And international diversification has been promoted by investment advisers as a prudent strategy for investors. Yet, as we saw in Table 14.1, most investor portfolios reflect a home country bias in equities as well as bonds.

This investment pattern is a puzzle that has rekindled research into international equity markets. Have home country investors been inexcusably slow to diversify their portfolios internationally? Or have important aspects of the international investment process been left out of the theoretical and empirical analysis thus far?

In this chapter, we will address a variety of topics linked to the operation and performance of international equities, including:

- The size and institutional features of major equity markets.
- Investment vehicles for accessing international equities.
- The historical record of risk and return in international equity markets.
- The determinants of international equity prices.
- The efficiency of international equity markets.
- Policy matters that affect private investors—the home country bias question, whether multinational firms are a close substitute for international investing, and whether investors can count on diversification gains in the future.
- Public policy issues—Policies governing national stock exchanges, rules governing accounting reports, and the harmonization of listing and new issue practices.

Size and Institutional Features of Global Equity Markets

Virtually every country that recognizes private property rights has a stock market. Data on equity markets in developed countries are tracked by many institutions, including Morgan Stanley Capital International (MSCI) and the International Finance Corporation (IFC).[2] The *Emerging Stock Markets Factbook 2000,* published by Standard & Poor's (S&P), presents detailed information on 54 emerging stock markets representing developing countries with growing private sectors, and summary information on another 36 national stock markets.[3] S&P prepares so-called investable indexes for 30 emerging markets to track the performance of stocks that are available to foreign institutional investors. In September 1996, the IFC began tracking a set of smaller emerging markets, so-called frontier markets, that now are 20 in number. Even Russia, where private property rights are tenuous, has a stock market. And Vietnam, which is on the road to a market-based economy, plans to introduce a stock market in the near future.

Market Capitalization Measures

The growth of global equity markets is depicted in Figure 15.2. The market capitalization of world equity markets reached $36.0 trillion in 1999, more than 10 times its value of $3.4 trillion in 1984. This increase in capitalization value represents several broad trends. First, worldwide expansion of GDP and productivity gains tends to increase the

---

[2]See *Capital International Perspectives* from MSCI, and *Emerging Stock Markets Factbook,* from IFC.

[3]S&P completed its acquisition of the International Finance Corporation's indices in December 1999. The IFC began its Emerging Markets Data Base project in 1981 and launched its set of emerging market indexes. The indexes are now known as S&P/IFC indexes.

FIGURE 15.2   World Equity Market Capitalization

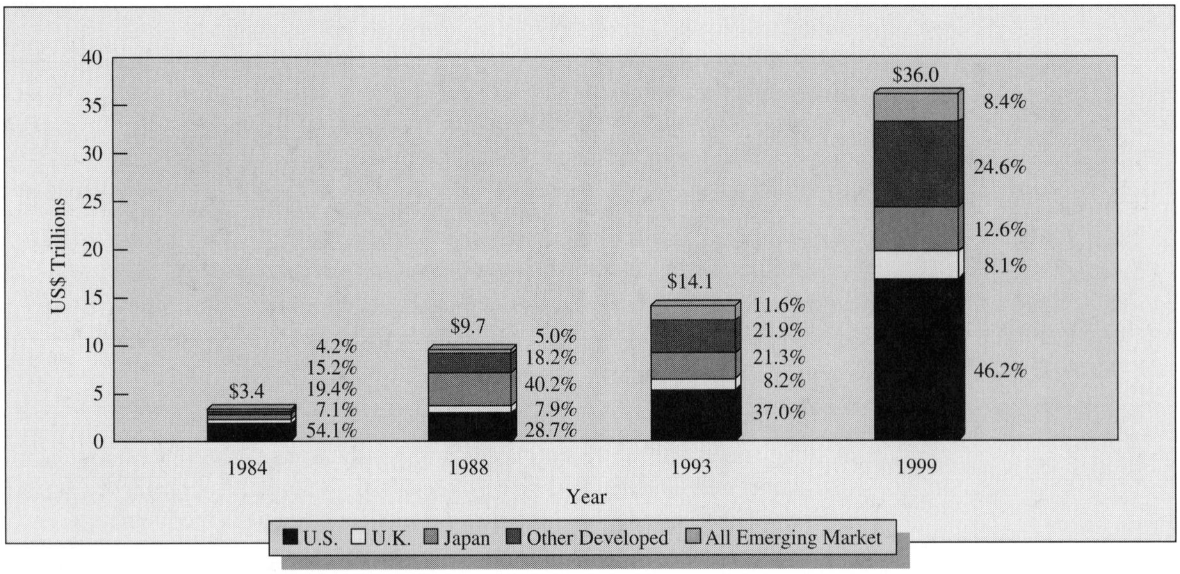

Note: Figures to the right of each bar are the percentage of the annual total accounted for by the United States, the United Kingdom, Japan, other developed, and all emerging markets, respectively.

Source: *Emerging Stock Market Factbook,* various issues.

valuation of existing equity shares. Second, new companies have been brought to market either through **privatization** of state-owned enterprises or public offerings of privately held companies. Privatization places more equity capital and real productive assets in public hands. Third, the depreciation of the US$ over parts of this period has increased the US$ valuation on foreign shares.

From Figure 15.2, we can see that U.S. market capitalization, while growing in absolute terms, fell in relative size from 54.1 percent of the world market in 1984 to 28.7 percent in 1988. In the 1960s, the U.S. market share was even higher, topping 70 percent.[4] One could have predicted that higher economic growth rates in smaller economies would lead to a long-term decline in the U.S. share of world equity market capitalization. However, faster U.S. growth over the 1990s, a bull market for U.S. equities, and new initial public offerings gave the United States a 46.2 percent market share in 1999.

Another trend is the faster growth of other developed country equity markets such as Hong Kong, Singapore, France, Germany, Italy, and Switzerland. The market share in these countries rose steadily from 15.2 percent in 1984 to 24.6 percent in 1999. Finally, we note the substantial growth of emerging markets, such as Brazil, Mexico, India, and the Philippines, from a 4.2 percent share in 1984 to a 11.6 percent share in 1993. Market capitalization in emerging markets actually fell between 1993 and 1999 as the Mexican (1995), Asian (1997), Russian (1998), and Latin American (1998) crises vaporized large fractions of the local equity market. For example, the market capitalization of the Mexican market (measured in US$) fell by more than 50 percent between 1993 and 1995. By 1999, the US$ value of the Mexican market was still 25 percent below its 1993 peak. Similarly, the Brazilian equity market fell by more than one-third (in US$ terms) between 1997 and 1998. The Russian stock market fell by more than 80

---

[4]See *Capital International Perspectives,* Geneva, Switzerland, Mar. 1976.

Box 15.1

How Large Is the Japanese Stock Market?

It should be a simple matter to calculate the size of a national equity market. However, **cross-holding** of securities is a practice that complicates the calculation of market capitalization values. Cross-holding is the practice of firm A owning equity shares in firm B. Cross-holding is common in Japan and in other countries (notably Germany) where banks are permitted to hold substantial and sometimes controlling interests in nonbanking firms, but cross-holding is fairly rare in the United States.

Consider the following example. Suppose that firm A has $100 of net productive assets and 100 shares outstanding, each valued at $1. Suppose that firm B is similar. The market value of these 200 shares of firms A and B is $200. Now, to introduce a cross-holding effect, let A issue 50 new shares at $1 each and use the proceeds to purchase shares in B. As conventionally measured (taking the number of shares outstanding and multiplying by the price per share) the market value of firms A and B is now $250. Yet the value of productive physical assets is unchanged at $200—and $200 is sufficient to purchase *all* of A's and B's stock.* To measure market value properly, we must adjust for the cross-holding effect by netting out the value of the cross-held shares.

In their paper, Kenneth French and James Poterba (1991) demonstrated that cross-holdings have a substantial effect on the estimated market value of Japanese shares relative to the value of the underlying productive assets of Japanese firms. For example, when the figures were adjusted for this cross-holding effect, French and Poterba showed that the estimated market capitalization of the Japanese market fell by about 50 percent in 1988 from $3.84 trillion to $1.99 trillion. This adjustment reduced the market capitalization weight for Japan from 44.0 percent to 29.5 percent, a figure very close to Japan's GDP weight in the world portfolio.

This is a startling and important result for institutional investors who attempt to track the world market. Using the commonly reported market capitalization figures, an investor would have needed a 44.0 percent weight on Japan to keep pace with the world index. Many investors felt that a 44.0 percent weight on a single country was too large, and so these investors underperformed the world index in the late 1980s as the Japanese market moved into record territory. The apparent underperformance of these investors would have been reduced if the world index had been corrected for the cross-holding effect.

In June 1996, the IFC began adjusting its own emerging market return indexes to eliminate the distortions caused by cross-holdings.[†]

---

*It takes $150 to buy all of A's stock, and only $50 to buy the remaining shares of B, not already acquired by purchasing A.
[†]*Emerging Stock Markets Factbook,* International Finance Corporation (1996), p. 292.

---

percent between 1997 and 1998. By 1999, the overall share of equities in emerging markets had fallen to 8.6 percent.

The pattern for Japan is unusual on two accounts. First, Japan's share of world stock market capitalization more than doubled between 1984 and 1988, and then dropped by half in 1993. This reflects the surge in Japanese equity prices in the late 1980s, which many label a speculative bubble, and the collapse of those prices in 1990. Second, Japan surpassed the United States in 1987 to become (for three years) the world's "largest" equity market in terms of the value of equities. Aside from granting "bragging rights" to Japan the rise of the Japanese market to the pinnacle of world stock market capitalization stood out as an oddity because the GNP of the United States *exceeds* that of Japan by about 75 percent. Thus, institutional investors whose positions in Japan were small (based on GNP weights) performed poorly when measured against *index benchmarks* constructed using market capitalization weights (see Box 15.1).

Over the 1990s, Japan experienced slow and at times negative economic growth. Bankruptcies, once exceedingly rare in Japan, occurred in the banking, securities, manufacturing, and retailing sectors. Since 1993, Japan's share of the world equity capital market has fallen further, to only 12.6 percent.

Institutional Aspects of Global Equity Markets

In addition to differences in capitalization values, global equity markets differ in other important dimensions, including numbers of listed firms, average firm size, market concentration, trading volume, transaction costs, and clearing and settlement conventions. These institutional features help determine whether and in what manner an investor enters a foreign market. A market with a large number of firms is inviting, but it may imply a large expense either to conduct fundamental investment analysis of a large number of companies or to identify a subset of firms that tracks the local market index. If the market concentration is high, investors may be able to mimic the market easily by owning a small number of firms. Investment is also facilitated by high trading volume, low transaction costs, and fast and efficient settlement of transactions.

Free capital inflows are a sufficient condition for attracting foreign investors. But free capital outflows are really a necessary condition. Investors are unlikely to invest abroad if restrictions and limitations affect the repatriation of their capital.[5]

Number of Firms Listed.   As we see in Table 15.1 (column 2a), more than 7,600 domestic firms have their shares listed in the United States. India, with a market capitalization only 1 percent as large as the United States, has nearly 6,000 listed firms. Other large equity markets—Japan, United Kingdom, Canada, and Australia—have more than 1,000 firms listed. Some emerging markets—Brazil, Korea, Malaysia, and South Africa—have more domestic firms listed than certain developed markets such as the Netherlands and Switzerland.

At year-end 1999, 835 foreign firms had their shares listed and traded on a U.S. exchange (see column 2b). This is up sharply from 541 foreign firms in 1995. As we will discuss later, requirements for listing shares are more stringent in the United States than elsewhere, which has acted as a deterrent. The United Kingdom (London) is a center for trading in foreign stocks, particularly shares of continental European firms.[6] Until recently, more foreign stocks were listed in London than in the United States. In several countries—Belgium, the Netherlands, and Switzerland—foreign stocks make up a large percentage of all listed securities. In emerging markets, however, we observe few if any foreign listings.

Average Firm Size.   Average firm size differs substantially around the world (column 3 in Table 15.1). The average market capitalization for a developed country firm is $1.4 billion, more than 10 times as large as the average market capitalization of an emerging market firm ($117 million). The New York Stock Exchange (NYSE) has an average firm size (as measured by market capitalization) in excess of $4.3 billion.[7] But the average market capitalization for a listed U.S. company is only about half as large ($2.17 billion).[8] The largest average market capitalization firms are in Italy ($3.0 billion) and Switzerland ($2.9 billion). Among emerging markets, the largest average market capitalization firms are in Mexico and Taiwan (both at $0.8 billion). This is a larger figure than for several developed country markets, such as those in Canada and New Zealand. However, in India, the average firm size is a mere $31 million.

---

[5]See Bartolini and Drazen (1996) for evidence that liberalization of capital *outflows* helps countries to attract inflows of foreign capital.

[6]Many foreign shares are traded in London through the Stock Exchange Automated Quotation System (SEAQ) International, even though the shares are not listed formally.

[7]As of December 1999. See NYSE *Fact Book*.

[8]The U.S. average includes firms listed on the NYSE, the American Stock Exchange, and NASDAQ.

TABLE 15.1   Market Statistics on U.S. and World Stock Markets, 1999

Country	(1) Market Capitalization[a]	(2a) Number of Listed Domestic Companies[b]	(2b) Number of Listed Foreign Companies[c]	(3) Average Company Size[d]	(4) Market Concentration[e]	(5) Market Turnover Ratio[f]
Developed Markets						
Australia	427,683	1,217	70	351	76.8	28.0
Belgium	184,942	172	122	1,075	59.0	27.5
Canada	800,914	3,767	48	213	72.7	54.2
France	1,475,457	968	176	1,524	80.8	62.4
Germany	1,432,190	933	234	1,535	79.2	107.5
Hong Kong	609,090	695	13	876	84.1	51.4
Italy	728,273	241	6	3,022	60.8	82.7
Japan	4,546,937	2,470	43	1,841	68.3	52.5
Netherlands	695,209	344	154	2,021	72.2	145.1
New Zealand	28,352	114	58	249	56.6	45.0
Singapore	198,407	355	45	559	64.9	66.9
Switzerland	693,127	239	173	2,900	79.1	78.0
United Kingdom	2,933,280	1,945	448	1,508	79.3	51.9
United States	16,635,114	7,651	835	2,174	70.8	123.5
Other developed	1,567,964	2,215	NA	708	NA	NA
Total	32,956,939	23,326	NA	1,413	NA	NA
Emerging Markets						
Brazil	227,962	478	2	477	32.6	44.9
Chile	68,228	285	0	239	42.3	11.4
China	330,703	950	0	348	30.3	134.2
India	184,605	5,963	0	31	31.2	84.4
Indonesia	64,087	277	0	231	47.6	46.2
Korea	308,534	725	0	426	59.1	346.7
Malaysia	145,445	757	3	192	33.4	39.8
Mexico	154,044	188	4	819	53.2	29.3
Philippines	48,105	226	1	213	42.2	47.2
Poland	29,577	221	0	134	59.0	44.6
South Africa	262,478	668	24	393	23.0	33.7
Taiwan	375,991	462	0	814	36.4	286.2
Thailand	58,365	392	0	149	46.8	89.2
Other emerging markets	815,747	14,722	NA	55	NA	NA
Total	3,073,871	26,314	NA	117	NA	NA
World Total	36,030,810	49,640	NA	726	NA	NA

[a]*Emerging Stock Markets Factbook 2000*, pp. 16–17; US$ millions.
[b]Ibid, pp. 22–23.
[c]International Federation of Stock Exchanges, Tables I.1 and V.1 at website <www.fibv.com>.
[d]In US$ millions; column (1)/column (2a).
[e]Data for developed countries represent the largest 5% of firms. Source: International Federation of Stock Exchanges, Table I.7.1 at website <www.fibv.com>. Data for emerging markets represent the 10 largest firms as percentage of market capitalization. Source: *Emerging Stock Markets Factbook 2000*, p. 46.
[f]Annual trading value / Market capitalization, *Emerging Stock Markets Factbook 2000*, p. 15.

Market Concentration.   Market concentration is another statistic with wide variation across countries. In emerging market countries, the S&P/IFC measures concentration as the percentage of market capitalization accounted for by the largest 10 firms. According to this measure, concentration in emerging markets varies from 30 to 60 percent. In developed countries, the International Federation of Stock Exchanges measures concentration as the percentage of market capitalization accounting for by the largest 5 percent of all firms. According to this measure, concentration in developed country markets varies from 55 to 85 percent.

Trading Volume.   Market turnover, measured as the annual volume of trading as a percentage of market capitalization, also varies substantially across countries (column 5 in Table 15.1). Among these countries, Korea has the highest turnover rate (347 percent in 1999) followed by Taiwan, with a 286 percent turnover rate. Several other countries (including the United States) had turnover near to or exceeding 100 percent. At the other extreme, some developed countries (such as Belgium) and emerging markets have turnover rates below 30 percent.

The statistics suggest that liquidity varies considerably across markets, as high trading volume tends to reduce liquidity risks and trading costs. But liquidity could vary as well within a market, with greater liquidity for a small number of high capitalization stocks, and much lower liquidity otherwise.

Transaction Taxes, Transaction Costs, Clearing and Settlement.   Other factors affect the overall cost of trading and, in turn, the volume of trading in a market. Many governments now impose **securities transaction taxes (STTs)** on the purchase or sale of certain financial instruments. A sample of STTs is shown in Table 15.2. In their study, John Campbell and Kenneth Froot (1994) concluded that in response to STTs, investors tend to shift their trading from taxed securities into nontaxed substitutes and to shift their trading from onshore to offshore locations to avoid taxation. Campbell and Froot found a trend toward lower transaction taxes. The authors cited Finland, Sweden, and Taiwan as recently lowering or eliminating their turnover taxes.[9]

Overall transaction costs vary considerably from country to country. Anthony Robinson (1989) estimated that transaction costs for a $500,000 trade in the United States average 0.20 percent, which is the lowest for any of the 15 countries in his sample.[10] The average cost in non-U.S. markets is 0.64 percent, ranging from 0.20 percent for sell orders in the U.K. to 1.30 percent for either buy or sell transactions in Sweden.

Standard and Poor's, *Emerging Stock Market Factbook 2000* (p. 404) reports the results of a study that regularly surveys the trading costs in both developed and emerging markets. Across 150 large global institutional investors surveyed, average round-trip trading costs in the fourth quarter of 1999 were estimated at 0.90 percent in developed country markets, and 1.80 percent in emerging markets. In developed country markets, round-trip trading costs were lowest in France (0.53 percent) and highest in Ireland (1.73 percent).[11] While in emerging markets, round-trip trading costs were lowest in Brazil (0.88 percent) and highest in the Czech Republic (3.59 percent).

A final characteristic that affects trading is the **settlement period** for making payment and obtaining delivery of securities (on the buy side) and delivering securities and obtaining cash settlement (on the sell side). Examples for selected countries are reported in Table 15.3. The United States reduced the settlement period to three business days in

---

[9]The United States is a counterexample. A general 0.5 percent tax on all security transactions was proposed during the 1990 budget negotiations. A flat fee for trading futures contracts was proposed again in 1994. Neither STT has been adopted.

[10]This is the cost for either a buy or a sell transaction, so round-trip transaction costs are 0.40 percent.

[11]In this study, estimated trading costs for institutional investors in the United States were 0.70 percent based on an average of NYSE and NASDAQ trading costs.

TABLE 15.2   Transaction Taxes around the World (through 1993)

Country	Tax Size 1991	Description	Notes; Changes since 1991
Australia	0.3%	Transaction tax	Additional stamp tax removed in 1991
Austria	0.15%	Transfer tax	May be avoided by trading off exchange
	0.06%	Arrangement fee	May be avoided by trading off exchange
	0.04%–0.09%	Courtage fee	
Belgium	0.17%	Stamp tax on buys and sells	No tax ex country; maximum of 10,000 Belgian francs
	0.025%	Stock market fee	No tax ex country; maximum of 2,500 Belgian francs
Canada		No taxes	
Denmark		No taxes for nonresidents	
Finland	0.5%	Transaction tax	Waived if both parties foreign, eliminated in 1992
France	0.15%	Trading tax	Tax on trades > 1 million francs, rate is doubled on smaller transactions, may be avoided by trading ex country
Germany	0.125%	Boersmumsatz Steuer	Residents only
	0.06%	Courtage tax (official broker fee)	Tax may be avoided by trading ex country
Hong Kong	0.25%	Stamp duty	
	0.006%	Special levy	May be avoided by trading off market
	0.050%	Exchange levy	May be avoided by trading off market
Italy	0.05%	Stamp duty tax	Tax may be avoided by trading ex country
Japan	0.30%	Sales tax	May be avoided by trading ex country
Malaysia	0.05%	Clearing fee	Maximum $100; may be avoided by trading off exchange
	0.3%	Transfer stamp duty on purchases and sales	Eliminated in 1992
Netherlands		No taxes	
New Zealand	0.0057% plus per trade fee	Transaction levy	May be avoided by trading off exchange; eliminated in 1992
Norway		No taxes	
Singapore	0.1%	Contract stamp duty	May be avoided by trading off exchange
	0.05%	Clearing fee	Maximum S$100, may be avoided by trading off exchange
	0.2%	Transfer stamp duty	Purchases only; eliminated in 1992
Sweden	0.5%	Turnover tax	Tax may be avoided by trading ex country; eliminated in 1991
Switzerland	0.0005%	Exchange fee	Tax may be avoided by trading ex country
	0.01%	State tax	Tax may be avoided by trading ex country
	0.075%	Stamp tax	Tax may be avoided by trading ex country
United States	0.0033%	SEC fee	
United Kingdom	£2	Levy	On trades over £5,000
	0.5%	Stamp duty tax	On purchases only

Source: John Y. Campbell and Kenneth A. Froot, "International Experience with Securities Transaction Taxes," in *The Internationalization of Equity Markets,* ed. J. Frankel (Chicago: Chicago University Press, 1994), p. 279.

June 1995. For many years, the standard U.S. settlement period had been five business days. In Germany, the settlement period is two business days. This feature attracted sellers after the October 1987 crash as a quick way to raise cash. As recently as 1995, other markets had settlement periods that extended out as long as 10 days to one month. A long settlement period is a deterrent to investment. Some securities firms have developed their

TABLE 15.3   Equity Trade Settlement Periods around the World

Country	Settlement Period	Country	Settlement Period
Argentina	$T + 3$	Korea	$T + 2$
Australia	$T + 3$ (was $T + 5$ in 1995)	Luxembourg	$T + 3$
Austria	$T + 3$ (was $T + 3$ weeks prior to 1997)	Malaysia	$T + 5$ (was $T + 6/7$ in 1995)
Belgium	$T + 3$, Forwards every two weeks	Mexico	$T + 2$
Brazil	$T + 3$	New Zealand	$T + 3$ (was $T + 5$ prior to 1995)
Canada	$T + 3$ (was $T + 5$ prior to June 1995)	Netherlands	$T + 3$ (was $T + 10$ prior to June 1995)
Chile	$T + 2$	Norway	$T + 3$
Colombia	$T + 3$	Pakistan	Weekly cycle (Mondays) $T + 7/13$
Czech Republic	$T + 3$	Peru	$T + 3$
Denmark	$T + 3$	Philippines	$T + 4$
Ecuador	$T + 3$ (was up to $T + 90$ in 1995)	Poland	$T + 0$ (book entry)
Egypt	$T + 4$ (was up to $T + 10$ in 1995)	Portugal	$T + 3$ (was $T + 4$ prior to 1995)
Finland	$T + 3$ (was $T + 4$ in 1995)	Singapore	$T + 5$
France	$T + 3$, Forwards monthly	South Africa	Weekly cycle (Tuesdays)
Germany	$T + 2$ (German counterparty)	Spain	$T + 3$ (was $T + 5$ prior to 1995)
	$T + 3$ (non-German counterparty)	Sri Lanka	$T + 7$
Greece	$T + 3$	Sweden	$T + 3$
Hong Kong	$T + 2$	Switzerland	$T + 3$
Hungary	$T + 5$	Thailand	$T + 3$
India	$T + 5$ (book entry) $T + 7$ otherwise	Taiwan	$T + 1$ (Citibank)
Indonesia	$T + 4$		$T + 2$ (International Federation)
Ireland	$T + 5$ (was $T + 10$ prior to June 1995)	Turkey	$T + 2$
Israel	$T + 1$	United Kingdom	$T + 5$ (was $T + 10$ prior to July 1995)
Italy	$T + 5$ (was monthly, 16th–19th	United States	$T + 3$ (was $T + 5$ prior to June 1995)
	day of month, in 1995)	Uruguay	$T + 1$
Japan	$T + 3$	Venezuela	$T + 5$
Jordan	$T + 3$		

Note: $T + n$ implies settlement in n business days after a transaction on date T, unless otherwise specified.
Source: Citibank Country Profiles, 4.0, Sept. 1, 1998, and spreadsheet of member's market information, supplied by the International Federation of Stock Exchange at their website <www.fibv.com/marketin.asp>.

own in-house settlement systems (collecting and delivering securities out of inventory) to facilitate trading in some foreign markets.[12]

International Investment Vehicles

Direct Purchase of Foreign Shares

The direct way to trade in foreign equity shares is on the foreign stock market itself. This route is usually reserved for large institutional investors because the purchase of foreign equity involves additional considerations: an initial foreign exchange purchase, a custodian to house the certificates, a bank account to collect and repatriate dividends

---

[12]Standard and Poor's, *Emerging Stock Market Factbook 2000* (pp. 402–3) provides survey information comparing settlement performance, safekeeping in regard to the collection of dividends, and operational risks across emerging market countries.

Box 15.2

The Russian ADRs Are Coming . . . The Russian ADRs Are Coming!

An American Depositary Receipt (ADR) is a simple, but highly useful, financial innovation that greatly increases American access to foreign equity securities and lowers the cost of transacting. Another element of the ADR issuing procedure can be especially important for emerging markets that lack an infrastructure for trading in equity securities.

Consider the Russian economy where state-owned firms are reaching broader ownership through privatization. Two problems exist for foreign investors who want to participate in the new, capitalistic Russian economy. First, there is often considerable uncertainty about who owns the shares of a firm. Many times, the firm, instead of an independent registration agency, keeps its own registry of shareholders and transactions. Second, there is uncertainty about how the shares are traded and how settlement occurs. No financial exchanges existed in the former Soviet Union, and current mechanisms for trading equity shares, in person or at a distance, are poorly developed.

The ADR addresses both of these problems. By certifying that valid shares are on deposit with the depositary, the ADR helps to circumvent problems of showing clear title and registration of shares. Since ADRs are traded in the U.S. market, trading mechanisms are well developed. As

one Russian banker commented, "In a typical emerging market, there is infrastructure but no stocks. In Russia, there are plenty of securities, but no infrastructure [for trading them]."*

At least one drawback to a surge in Russian issues remains. Most Russian companies have poor accounting records, with seldom more than one or two years of accounting statements. Even these are probably not audited.[†] This means that most Russian ADRs will trade over the counter on the "pink sheets." Russian firms can apply for a Level 1 ADR issue, using the same accounting information and disclosures in the United States as they do in Russia. Potentially, given the size of the economy, the Russian ADR market could be huge. As of 1996, there were only 13 Russian ADR issues from 5 firms. However, by 1999 the number had grown to 79 issues from 50 firms, including three firms (Vimpelcom, Rostlecom, and Tatneft) that meet the accounting and information disclosure requirements for NYSE listing.

---

*S. Liesman, "Russian Bank Blazes the Way to Wall Street with ADR Filing," *The Wall Street Journal,* Dec. 1, 1994.
[†]Ibid.

---

and distributions, and a capability to stay informed about rights offerings and other matters. These extra steps in addition to the higher transaction costs of foreign markets usually deter most small investors from direct purchases in foreign markets.

American Depositary Receipts

The **American Depositary Receipt (ADR)** was introduced in 1927 by the Morgan Guaranty Bank as a way to overcome many of the institutional barriers to foreign investment.[13] In order to issue an ADR, a U.S. bank takes custody of foreign shares in its foreign office. Then an ADR can be issued as a claim against these foreign shares. This can be especially valuable when there are doubts about the authenticity of foreign shares as in the recent issues of Russian ADR shares (see Box 15.2). Owners of the ADR have the right to redeem their ADR and obtain the true underlying foreign shares. Arbitrage of this sort ensures that the price of the ADR and the underlying shares will be nearly identical.[14]

---

[13]See Egly (1954) for a history of the development of the ADR at Guaranty Trust Company of New York, now Morgan Guaranty Bank.

[14]An ADR may represent a fraction of one foreign share or a multiple of one foreign share, depending on the conventional prices of foreign shares.

The issuing bank services the ADR by collecting all dividends, rights offerings, and so forth in foreign currency, and distributing the proceeds in US$ to the ADR owner. U.S. investors can trade ADRs with each other without recourse to the foreign equity market, without using the foreign exchange market, and without relying on foreign clearing and settlement. The underlying foreign shares remain with the custodian. Thus, the ADR dramatically reduces the cost of trading in foreign shares.

In a **sponsored ADR,** the foreign firm pays a fee to the depositary bank to cover the cost of the ADR program. In an **unsponsored ADR,** the issuance of the ADR is "demand driven" in response to a security firm's desire to facilitate trading in a popular foreign issue.

ADRs that are not listed on an exchange—a **Level 1 ADR**—trade on so-called pink sheets in the over-the-counter market and the company need only disclose the information in its home annual report. If the company meets the disclosure requirements of the U.S. exchange, the **Level 2 ADRs** may be listed for trading. If the firm complies fully with U.S. accounting principles and disclosure requirements, it may raise equity capital in the United States through a public offering of **Level 3 ADRs.**

In 1999, more than 2,000 ADRs were trading in the United States. The largest number of ADRs have been issued by U.K. firms (242), followed by Japan (163) and Australia (152). Altogether, firms from 80 countries have issued ADRs. Other characteristics of ADRs are listed in Table 15.4.

Usually, the *dominant market* for foreign shares in terms of trading volume and price determination is in the foreign country. The ADR market generally has lighter trading volume and functions as a *satellite market,* taking its "pricing cues" from the foreign market. In some instances (Telmex, for example), trading volume in the ADR may exceed volume in the foreign market. Thus, the ADR market becomes the dominant market for price-setting purposes. Nevertheless, it is important to stress that ADR securities bear the foreign exchange risk of the firm's cash flows even though the ADR shares are quoted, for convenience, in US$ terms. Any confusion on this point can perhaps be cleared up through the example of the slide in the US$ prices of Mexican shares along with the depreciation of the peso (see Box 15.3).

Closed-End and Open-End Mutual Funds

Mutual funds offer another vehicle for investing in foreign equity shares. As discussed, executing transactions on foreign stocks requires special expertise. A professionally managed mutual fund is a natural way for small investors to overcome these barriers and quickly obtain a broader portfolio of securities. Mutual funds that invest in foreign stocks can be grouped into several categories from a U.S. perspective:

1. Global—investing in U.S. and non-U.S. shares.
2. International—investing in non-U.S. shares only.
3. Regional—investing in a geographic area.
4. Country—investing in a single country.
5. Specialty—international investments in an industry group such as telecommunications, or special themes such as newly privatized firms.

In addition, foreign stock funds are classified as either *open-end* or *closed-end.* An **open-end fund** stands ready to issue and redeem shares at prices reflecting the net asset value of the underlying foreign shares. A **closed-end fund** issues a fixed number of shares against an initial capital offering. The shares of the closed-end fund then trade in

TABLE 15.4   Characteristics of American Depositary Receipts
As of January 7, 2000

Exchange Where Traded	Number of ADRs
NYSE	339
AMEX	7
NASDAQ	184
OTC ("pink sheets")	906
144a Issues	372
Other / NA	277
Total	2,085

Sponsorship	
Sponsored	1,821
Unsponsored	264
Total	2,085

Depository Institution	
Bank of New York	1,354
Citibank	539
Morgan Guaranty	370
Bankers Trust	178
Others	66
Total	Not Meaningful*

Parent Country	
United Kingdom	242
Japan	163
Australia	152
Hong Kong	106
India	98
Mexico	94
Brazil	91
South Africa	89
Russia	79
Taiwan	60
France	55
Germany	52
All others	804
Total	2,085

ADR Offerings in 1999	
Public	
Number of issues	67
Capital raised (Bn)	$16.00
Private	
Number of issues	45
Capital raised (Bn)	$ 5.90

Top 10 ADR Issues by Volume of Trading in 1999

Company	Country	US$ Share Volume (Bn)
1. Nokkia	Finland	70.64
2. Vodaphone Airtouch	U.K.	49.91
3. BP Amoco	U.K.	40.11
4. Telebras	Brazil	36.68
5. Ericsson Telephone	Sweden	34.80
6. Royal Dutch Petroleum	Netherlands	32.67
7. Telefonos de Mexico	Mexico	28.32
8. Elan Corporation	Ireland	15.66
9. ST Micro Electronics	Netherlands	13.54
10. Philips Electronics	Netherlands	12.33

*Some companies use multiple depositary institutions.

Source: Bank of New York, "1999 Year-End Market Review," and The Bank of New York listing of all ADRs at <www.bankofny.com/adr/index.htm>.

a secondary market (usually listed on an exchange) at prices reflecting a premium or discount relative to the net asset value of the underlying foreign shares.

Closed-end country funds were the fastest growing segment of the public investment funds during the late 1980s.[15] At the end of 1992, there were 42 closed-end country funds listed in the United States, representing $4.3 billion in equity. The progression of initial public offerings for these closed-end funds is illustrated in Figure 15.3. By

[15]See Hardouvelis et al. (1994), p. 345.

Box 15.3

ADRs: US$ Securities with Substantial Foreign Exchange Risk

An investor pays for an ADR with US$, receives dividends in US$, and may even trade the ADR over the New York Stock Exchange. Even so, the ADR bears all of the foreign exchange risk of the underlying security as if it were traded on a foreign stock exchange.

After the Mexican peso plunged in December 1994, an ADR analyst for Morningstar clearly summarized the essential points:

> You would hope that it's clear to U.S. investors that the same risks exist for the ADR as for the stock in the home market. But judging from what we have heard, some people were a

little surprised. Investors need to understand that the ADR is underpinned by the value of the stock itself in the home market. You take all the same risks as if you were investing in the home market.*

The Mexican case illustrated the worst possible combination: a depreciating peso and a falling local stock market, both working to reduce the US$ value of ADR shares associated with Mexican equities.

———

*D. Kansas, "ADR Holders Feel Heat from Crisis in Mexico," *The Wall Street Journal,* Jan. 12, 1995.

FIGURE 15.3   **Initial Public Offerings of Country Funds, 1981–1992**

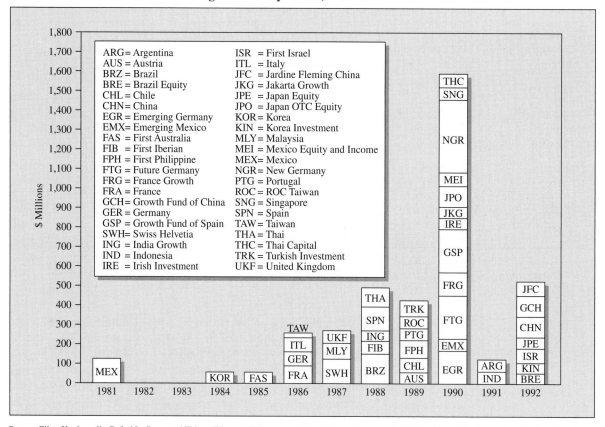

Source: Gikas Hardouvelis, Rafael La Porta, and Thierry Wizman, "What Moves the Discount on Country Equity Funds?" in *The Internationalization of Equity Markets,* ed. J. Frankel (Chicago: University of Chicago Press, 1994), p. 346.

year-end 1999, the number of closed-end country funds had increased to 69, with total net assets of $38.6 billion.[16]

To the extent that foreign equity markets lack liquidity, impose higher transaction costs, and restrict full liquidation and repatriation of positions, an open-end fund that stands ready to liquidate stock positions on demand is not a practical or cost-effective foreign investment vehicle. Where restrictions on the inflow and outflow of capital are present, a closed-end fund has clear advantages.[17] Catherine Bosner-Neal et al. (1990) showed that when investment restrictions are present, closed-end funds are likely to trade at a premium to net asset value. They also showed that the premium responds significantly to news announcements of changes in investment restrictions.

Closed-end funds are not forced to liquidate positions when shareholders wish to exit the fund. Purchases and sales, however, may affect the premium or discount on the fund shares. The owner of an open-end fund earns a return that equals the change in the net asset value on the fund's underlying assets (adjusted by management fees, sales charges, and so forth). The owner of a closed-end fund earns a return that equals the change in net asset value on the fund's underlying assets plus the change in the fund's discount (or premium) to net asset value. Thus, returns on the closed-end fund are related to returns in the foreign stock market *plus* other factors that impact the fund's discount.

Figures 15.4a and 15.4b show the discount or premium on the Mexico Fund and the Germany Fund. The discounts for the Mexico Fund show substantial variation, typically in a range of 0 to 40 percent. The data for the Germany Fund show a tremendous burst around the fall of the Berlin Wall when the premium over net asset value rose to 100 percent. During this period, other country funds as diverse as Switzerland and Taiwan also experienced increases in share price relative to net asset value.

A recent paper by Gikas Hardouvelis et al. (1994) analyzed the behavior of closed-end country fund discounts. The authors drew several important conclusions. Discounts and premiums on country funds have varied widely and are a significant factor in the variability of country fund returns. On average, the variance of country fund returns is three times larger than the variance on the underlying foreign assets. Discounts tend to be mean reverting, implying that unusually large discounts and premiums tend back toward their average value. Thus, by selecting a closed-end country fund, the investor also takes a position on an additional unobserved factor: call it local sentiment about world events and country-specific events.

In a related study, James Bodurtha et al. (1995) showed that premiums on closed-end country funds tend to move together, but not with the premiums on U.S. domestic closed-end funds. Because closed-end country funds are generally held by small domestic investors rather than institutional or foreign investors, the country fund premium could reflect the differential sentiment between domestic and foreign investors. Consistent with a market sentiment view, Bodurtha et al. found that country fund premiums are positively related to future domestic stock price changes.

World Equity Benchmark Shares (WEBS).   A new vehicle for international investing, **World Equity Benchmark Shares (WEBS),** was introduced in 1996. WEBS represent shares in an index fund that is intended to track the performance of a single

---

[16]Year-end 1999 figures from private correspondence, courtesy of Lipper Inc.

[17]Capital restrictions in Korea did not permit foreign ownership or export of securities. The Korea Fund, a closed-end U.S. fund traded on the NYSE, was granted a special permit to invest in Korean securities with Korean custodial arrangements.

FIGURE 15.4A   Weekly Percentage Discount or Premium of the Mexico Fund

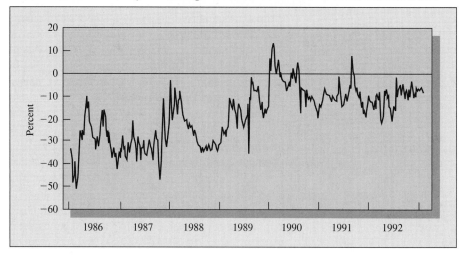

FIGURE 15.4B   Weekly Percentage Discount or Premium of the Germany Fund

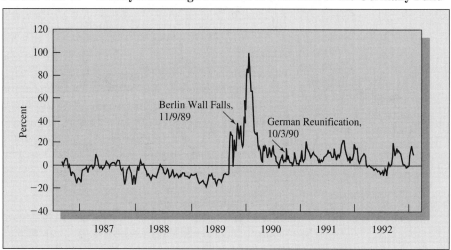

Source: Gikas Hardouvelis, Rafael La Porta, and Thierry Wizman, "What Moves the Discount on Country Equity Funds?" in *The Internationalization of Equity Markets,* ed. J. Frankel. (Chicago: University of Chicago Press, 1994), p. 347.

country index. Currently WEBS are available for 19 countries, with shares listed on the American Stock Exchange and designed to track the MSCI for that country.[18]

WEBS are innovations that combine features of closed-end and open-end funds, as well as ADRs. They rely on so-called **creation units** to initiate the fund's activities. In exchange for a large sum of money, roughly $500,000 or more, an investor purchases a

---

[18]A similar investment vehicle called Country Baskets (CB) was also introduced in 1996 by investment manager Deutsche Morgan Grenfell. CBs were designed to track the Financial Times/S&P Actuaries Index for various countries. In 1997, even though CBs were gaining some popularity, Deutsche Bank (the parent of Deutsche Morgan Grenfell) decided to abandon this product, and CBs were de-listed from the NYSE.

creation unit in one index fund. The fund manager (Barclays Global Investors) uses these funds to purchase shares whose performance will match that of the index. Each creation unit divides into a specified number of shares, which the investor can sell or transfer through the stock exchange that lists the shares. Thus, like an open-end fund, the size of the WEBS funds can grow without limit, but the shares are traded on an exchange throughout the day like a closed-end fund.[19] Because WEBS are run as passive index funds, their management expenses are expected to be lower than other international or country funds that operate active strategies and attempt to outperform an index.[20]

Prices of WEBS are kept close to the net asset value of the underlying securities through an arbitrage process that resembles ADR arbitrage. Suppose that the net asset value for the Japan WEBS is $16, but that Japan WEBS are quoted at $17 on the exchange. In this case, a large investor would purchase a creation unit for $9.6 million (representing 600,000 shares at $16) plus transaction costs. The investor could then sell the individual WEBS into the market at $17 per share, earning $10.2 million minus transaction costs.

Suppose instead that WEBS are quoted at $15 on the exchange. Now the investor arbitrages by purchasing 600,000 shares for $9 million plus transaction costs. The investor redeems one creation unit for which he or she receives a pro rata number of the underlying shares in the Japan index fund. The investor can then sell these shares to obtain the net asset value of $9.6 million less transaction costs. In this example, the WEBS shares are like "maxi-ADRs"; if the WEBS price is too low, the investor can claim the underlying securities represented by the WEBS and sell them for full market value. This arbitrage, however, is available only to large-scale investors and carries the risk of price changes in the underlying shares.

In May 2000, Barclays Global Investors (BGI) changed the name of its WEBS product to "iShares MSCI" to reflect a consistent brand name for all of the exchange-traded funds managed by BGI. The term *iShares* implies index shares of exchange-traded mutual funds.[21]

Risk and Return in International Equity Markets

Calculating the Unhedged Returns on Foreign Equity in US$ Terms

The calculation of returns on a foreign equity for a US$-based investor is analogous to the calculation of returns on a foreign bond. Let E_t represent the initial purchase price of the equity in foreign currency terms. And let S_t represent the spot exchange rate, in $/FC terms, on the purchase date. The product, $E_t S_t$, is the US$ purchase price of the foreign equity. After one period, the value of the equity is $\tilde{E}_{t+1}$, representing the initial equity

---

[19]Most open-end funds can only be purchased or sold at end-of-day prices. WEBS can be sold short, which is not possible for open-end funds.

[20]The annual expense ratio is estimated at 0.82 percent for WEBS and 1.53 percent for the average closed-end country fund. See "Investing Overseas Is Getting to Be a Snap," *Business Week,* Apr. 15, 1996, p. 118.

[21]More information about the composition and performance of iShares is available through Barclay's website <www.ishares.com>.

price plus the price change over the period ($\tilde{\Delta}_{t+1}$) plus dividends (D_{t+1}). So, the value of the equity after one period in US$ terms is $\tilde{E}_{t+1}\tilde{S}_{t+1}$, where:

$$\tilde{E}_{t+1} \equiv E_t + \tilde{\Delta}_{t+1} + D_{t+1}$$

The continuous rate of return on the foreign equity *measured in US$* and *on an unhedged basis* is:

$$\tilde{R}_{\$,U} = \ln\left(\frac{\tilde{E}_{t+1}\tilde{S}_{t+1}}{E_t S_t}\right) = \ln\left(\frac{\tilde{E}_{t+1}}{E_t}\right) + \ln\left(\frac{\tilde{S}_{t+1}}{S_t}\right) = \tilde{E}_{FC} + \tilde{S}_{US\$,FC} \quad (15.1)$$

Equation (15.1) shows that the unhedged US$ return on the foreign equity has two pieces: the return on the equity shares in foreign currency terms plus the return on the foreign currency used to buy the shares. Both terms in equation (15.1) may be greater than or less than zero. As with the foreign bond, the return on a foreign equity measured in US$ has an additional source of uncertainty, namely the foreign exchange gain or loss.[22]

The variance of the returns in equation (15.1) reflects the variance of each term and the covariance between the returns on the foreign equity and the returns on spot foreign exchange, or:

$$\sigma^2(\tilde{R}_{\$,U}) = \sigma^2(\tilde{E}_{FC}) + \sigma^2(\tilde{S}_{US\$,FC}) + 2\,\mathrm{Cov}\,(\tilde{E}_{FC}; \tilde{S}_{US\$,FC}) \quad (15.2)$$

As a theoretical matter, the covariance term can be either positive or negative.[23] A positive covariance implies that the value of foreign equity tends to fall or rise along with the value of foreign currency, as shown in cells *A* and *B* in Table 15.5. The Mexican peso devaluation in late 1994 and early 1995 is an example of cell *A,* where capital flight and a loss in confidence in the Mexican economy brought the Mexican stock market down as well. With the peso overvalued and the country running a large current account deficit, Mexican policymakers allowed the peso to depreciate. Interest rates rose dramatically, as did import prices; the Mexican stock market dropped sharply in anticipation of a fall in Mexican GDP and corporate profits.

A negative covariance implies that the value of foreign equity falls (rises) when foreign currency appreciates (depreciates), as shown in cells *C* and *D* in Table 15.5. The Venezuelan bolivar devaluation in the spring of 1996 is an example of cell *D,* where a massive devaluation (from 170 bolivar/US$ in mid-1995 to roughly 500 bolivar/US$ in April 1996) coincided with a relaxation of capital controls and a credible stabilization program. This policy change led to expectations that inflation in Venezuela would subside and investment and growth would return. As a result, the Venezuelan stock market rose over the same period by 36 percent in US$ terms.

As an empirical matter, the correlation of spot exchange rate changes and aggregate stock indexes is fairly small. For a sample of 19 industrial countries using monthly data from 1980 to 1995, we calculate that $\mathrm{Corr}(\tilde{E}_{FC}; \tilde{S}_{US\$,FC})$ generally has an absolute value of less than 0.25 and averages near zero across all countries.

Portfolio Risk in Domestic and International Stocks

The Fundamental Diversification Picture.   A fundamental result in portfolio theory is that the idiosyncratic risks of individual securities can be reduced by investing in a

---

[22]The construction of currency-hedged US$ returns on foreign equities is left as an exercise for the reader.

[23]This covariance represents the sensitivity of share returns to exchange rate changes, which we will adopt as a measure of corporate exposure to exchange risk in Chapter 16.

TABLE 15.5 Currency Market Return and Stock Market Return Combinations

		Currency Market Return	
		Negative	*Positive*
Stock Market Returns	*Negative*	Stock market prices ↓ Spot FX ↓ (A)	Stock market prices ↓ Spot FX ↑ (C)
	Positive	Stock market prices ↑ Spot FX ↓ (D)	Stock market prices ↑ Spot FX ↑ (B)

broadly diversified portfolio of many securities. To illustrate this point, consider two securities (A and B) with returns $\tilde{R}_A$ and $\tilde{R}_B$ and risk measures $\sigma(\tilde{R}_A)$ and $\sigma(\tilde{R}_B)$. The return and risk on a portfolio (P) combining both securities is calculated as:

$$\tilde{R}_P = w_A \tilde{R}_A + w_B \tilde{R}_B$$

$$\sigma^2(\tilde{R}_P) = w_A^2 \sigma^2(\tilde{R}_A) + w_B^2 \sigma^2(\tilde{R}_B) + 2\, w_A\, w_B\, \text{Cov}(\tilde{R}_A, \tilde{R}_B)$$

$$= w_A^2 \sigma^2(\tilde{R}_A) + w_B^2 \sigma^2(\tilde{R}_B) + 2\, w_A\, w_B\, \text{Corr}(\tilde{R}_A, \tilde{R}_B)\, \sigma(\tilde{R}_A)\, \sigma(\tilde{R}_B)$$

where w_A and w_B are the investment weights in securities A and B, and $w_A + w_B = 1$.

In Figure 15.5, we show an example of a two-asset portfolio with $\tilde{R}_A = 0.05$, $\tilde{R}_B = 0.10$, $\sigma(\tilde{R}_A) = 0.20$ and $\sigma(\tilde{R}_B) = 0.40$. The investor's opportunity set is constructed with portfolio weights specified as $(w_A, w_B) = (100$ percent, 0 percent$)$, $(w_A, w_B) = (90$ percent, 10 percent$)$, . . . $(w_A, w_B) = (10$ percent, 90 percent$)$, $(w_A, w_B) = (0$ percent, 100 percent$)$, and for several values of the correlation between $\tilde{R}_A$ and $\tilde{R}_B$. Figure 15.5 shows how a low correlation of returns can substantially reduce risks without reducing returns. For example, the $(w_A, w_B) = (40$ percent, 60 percent$)$ portfolio has a risk of 0.32 if the assets are perfectly correlated. It drops to 0.25 if the assets have zero correlation, and drops further to 0.17 if the assets have -0.9 correlation.

Diversification Gains Using International Stocks.   Figure 15.6 illustrates the impact of international diversification compared with other strategies. The graphs show the total risk for portfolios of N randomly selected securities expressed as a ratio relative to the risk for a single representative U.S. security.

Figure 15.6a shows this relative risk measure for portfolios sampled from only U.S. securities and for portfolios sampled from all international stocks, including U.S. securities. As portfolio size increases in the U.S. universe, portfolio risk levels off at about 27 percent compared with the risk of an individual U.S. stock. For the international curve, portfolio risk declines more quickly and levels off at only 11.7 percent. The remaining risk is the *nondiversifiable,* or *systematic,* component of portfolio risk. Figure 15.6a suggests that, for the same size portfolio, randomly selected portfolios of international stocks offer more diversification than randomly selected portfolios of U.S. stocks.[24]

Figure 15.6b shows a similar graph with an additional curve representing international stocks on a currency-hedged basis. Notice that currency hedging further reduces

---

[24]The same result applies if the comparison is between international stocks and stocks from any other individual country.

FIGURE 15.5   Return and Risk for a Portfolio with Two Securities

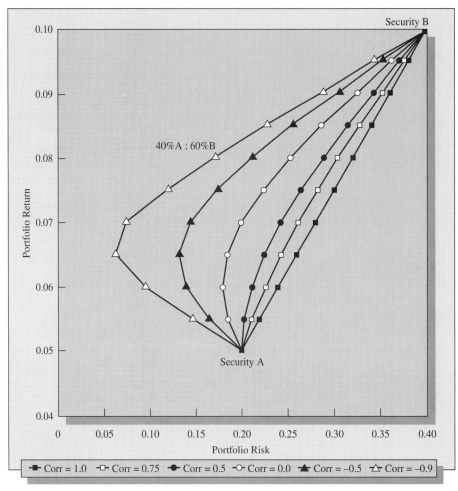

portfolio risks, but by a fairly small amount compared with the dramatic results we observed with foreign bonds. This happens because equity returns are considerably more variable than bond returns.

Figure 15.7 shows another comparison, this time between portfolios of size *N* sampled across seven industries from a single country and portfolios of size *N* (and similar returns) sampled across 12 European countries but from a single industry.[25] The graph shows that diversification across countries is a more powerful method of risk reduction than diversification across industries (within a single country). One implication of this result is that international diversification gains come more from differences in macroeconomic and market performance across countries than from differences in industrial structure.

---

[25]Based on monthly returns for 829 firms in 7 industries and 12 European Union countries. See Heston and Rouwenhorst (1994).

FIGURE 15.6A   **Risk Reduction through Domestic and International Diversification**

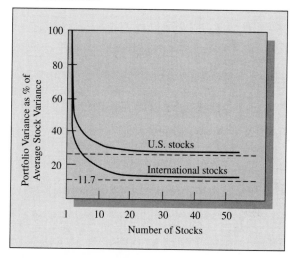

FIGURE 15.6B   **Risk Reduction through Domestic and International Diversification Hedged and Unhedged Results**

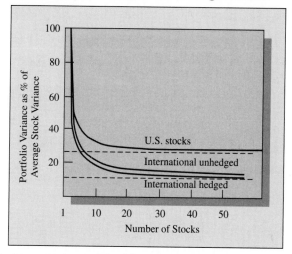

Note: The vertical axis of the graph is the ratio $\sigma^2(\tilde{R}_N)/\sigma^2(\tilde{R}_1)$ where N is the number of stocks in the portfolio.

Source: Bruno Solnik, "Why Not Diversify Internationally Rather Than Domestically?" *Financial Analysts Journal* 30, no. 4 (July–Aug. 1974), pp. 48–54.

An alternative way to illustrate the diversification effect of international securities is by graphing the mean and variance of domestic and international portfolios. Figure 15.8 shows the mean and variance of US$ returns for 16 foreign countries and the United States over the period 1970–1989. This chart updates the analysis by Grubel (Figure 15.1) on an earlier period. In Figure 15.8 we see that the World portfolio has a lower variance of returns than any single country. The World portfolio had returns equal to or superior to half of the countries, but with far less risk. It also appears that the World

FIGURE 15.7   Risk Reduction through Cross-Industry and Cross-Country Diversification

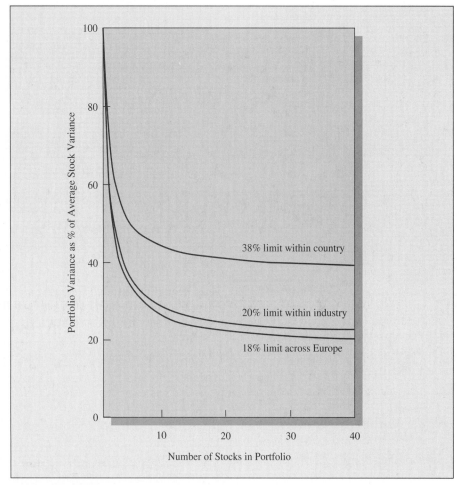

Source: Steven L. Heston and K. Geert Rouwenhorst, "Does Industrial Structure Explain the Benefits of International Diversification?" *Journal of Financial Economics* 36 (Aug. 1994), p. 20.

portfolio offered a risk/return trade-off at least as favorable—and often considerably more favorable—than any individual country.

These data suggest that the imperfect correlation of equity returns documented by Grubel in 1968 still exists. An important question for investors is whether this pattern of imperfect correlation of returns will persist. We return to this question at the end of this chapter.

Pricing Determinants

As this text has emphasized, understanding the determinants of prices is an important theme in any market. The analysis of international equity prices requires us to confront several challenging problems:

FIGURE 15.8   **Risk, Return, and the Minimum Variance Frontier for 17 Countries and the World Portfolio, 1970–1989**

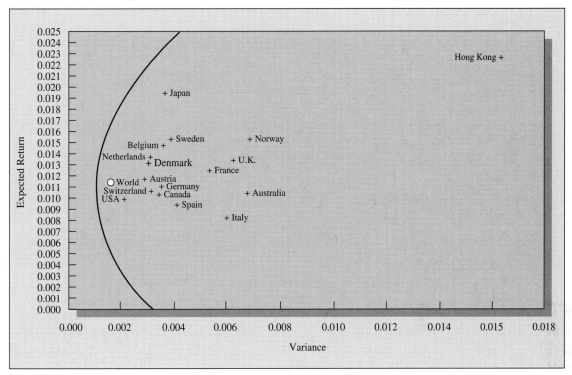

Note: Returns are in US$. Data are from Morgan Stanley Capital International. Data reflect 232 monthly observations, 1970:2–1989:5.

Source: Campbell R. Harvey, "The World Price of Covariance Risk," *Journal of Finance* 46 (Mar. 1991), pp. 111–58.

1. *Are national equity markets integrated or segmented?* If equity markets are integrated, then a similar formula is used in all markets for pricing a stream of cash flows. Expressed somewhat differently, in an integrated equity market, investors everywhere are rewarded with the same *per unit* compensation for bearing risk. In a segmented market, equity risks can be priced differently across markets. Barriers of various sorts limit the flow of capital to remove these pricing differences.

2. *Are national equity markets efficient or inefficient?* When equity markets are efficient, an equilibrium pricing model (such as the CAPM) may provide a reasonable explanation for equity prices. If markets are not efficient, then other factors play a role in asset pricing.

3. *Does purchasing power parity (PPP) hold or not?* If PPP holds, the exchange rate does not introduce a new element of risk that markets must price. To express this idea differently, imagine that each domestic equity market prices its own inflation risk. When PPP holds, exchange rates are perfectly correlated with inflation movements, so a separate source of risk is not introduced by virtue of each country using its own currency. Violations of PPP, however, would introduce a *new* element of risk, which if nondiversifiable would then be priced by equity markets.

4. *Do the assumptions of the capital asset pricing model (CAPM) apply or is arbitrage pricing theory (APT) more appropriate?* The traditional CAPM hypothesizes that

FIGURE 15.9 Traditional Capital Asset Pricing Model

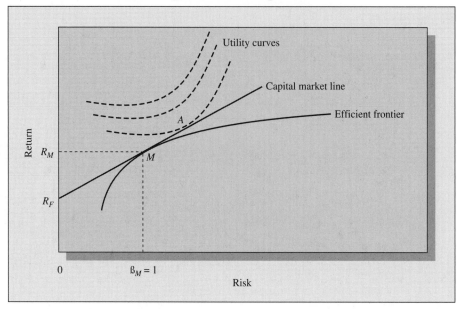

returns for an individual equity (R_i) in excess of the risk-free rate (R_F) are proportional to the systematic risk of the equity (β_{iM}) times the expected market risk premium, or:

$$R_i - R_F = \beta_{iM}\,[E(R_M) - R_F]$$

where $E(R_M)$ is the expected return on the market portfolio. The assumptions of the traditional CAPM are:

- Investors maximize their utility, which depends only on expected return (+) and risk (−).
- Investors have homogeneous expectations, agreeing about expected return and risk for all assets.
- Returns are expressed in nominal terms.
- A risk-free interest rate exists and unlimited borrowing and investing is possible at this rate.
- No transaction costs or taxes exist.

The CAPM leads to a *separation,* or *mutual fund theorem,* which claims that *all* investors will hold some combination of two assets: The risk-free asset and the market portfolio of *all* risky assets. As shown in Figure 15.9, investors select different combinations of the two assets to maximize their utility from investment.

The traditional CAPM is a useful paradigm for thinking about an individual capital market, but it does not incorporate the diversity of international markets with N countries each having its own risk-free rates. The CAPM can be made to "look" international with two additional assumptions:

- All investors have the same consumption patterns.
- Purchasing power parity holds continuously, keeping relative prices of consumption goods identical in all countries.

The CAPM formula then becomes:

$$R_i - R_F = \beta_{iW}\,[E(R_W) - R_F]$$

where $E(R_W)$ is the expected return on the *world* market portfolio and the systematic risk measure β_{iW} is computed as the covariance of returns on security i with the returns on the *world* market.[26]

Obviously, these assumptions are unrealistic.[27] Investors with different consumption patterns will each require their own portfolio of risky assets to hedge their particular stream of consumption expenditures.

A variation of the CAPM can be revived if inflation in the home country is not uncertain. In this case, the risk-free asset of each country is also risk free in real terms for home country investors. Exchange rate risk exists in foreign investments, but this can be hedged using forward contracts (or borrowing in foreign currencies). This CAPM can be described as an $N+1$ mutual fund theorem. Investors from all N countries hold their own risk-free asset (giving us N funds) plus the market portfolio (the $N+1$st fund) of all risky assets in the world hedged against exchange risk.

The strict assumptions of the CAPM have led some researchers to favor an arbitrage pricing theory (APT) framework. The APT begins with a descriptive, multifactor model where the returns on a security are related to a set of factors (γ_k) that are common to all securities, so that:

$$R_i = \beta_0 + \beta_1\gamma_1 + \beta_2\gamma_2 + \ldots + \beta_k\gamma_k + \epsilon_i$$

The coefficients ($\beta_1 \ldots \beta_k$) measure the sensitivity of security i to each factor, β_0 is a constant, and ϵ_i is the residual element representing the diversifiable risk of security i.

To transform the descriptive equation above into a pricing model, we assume that arbitrage is possible between securities. Investors sell those securities that pay a small premium on factor γ_k, and buy securities that pay a larger premium on the same factor. In equilibrium, the market arrives at an amount of compensation, a risk premium (RP_k), for each factor that is priced in the market. We can write this as:

$$E(R_i) = R_0 + \beta_1 RP_1 + \beta_2 RP_2 + \ldots + \beta_k RP_k$$

where R_0 is the risk-free rate and the coefficients ($\beta_1 \ldots \beta_k$) continue to measure the sensitivity of security i to each factor.

Empirical Evidence on Pricing

First Impressions.   To begin, it is useful to examine an overview of equity price relationships. In Figure 15.10, we show the price/book value, price/cash earnings, and price/earnings (P/E) ratios for 22 countries and the world as of April 28, 2000. The cross-country variation in each of these series is striking. The price/book value (Panel A) figure for Finland is nearly 10 times as great as that for New Zealand. The price/cash earnings figures (Panel B) vary by more than seven times from the first to the last

---

[26]This formulation would still suffer from the Roll (1977) critique. The world portfolio would have to include virtually *all* assets in the world, otherwise empirical estimates based on the formula could be unreliable.

[27]Even the traditional one-country CAPM assumes that all investors in the country have the same consumption bundle. This is also unrealistic. If the consumption patterns of investors living in the North or South, or urban or rural areas are very different, then the market portfolio provides varying degrees of inflation hedging protection for these different investors.

FIGURE 15.10   **Price/Book Value, Price/Cash Earnings, Price/Earnings Ratios**
Data as of April 28, 2000

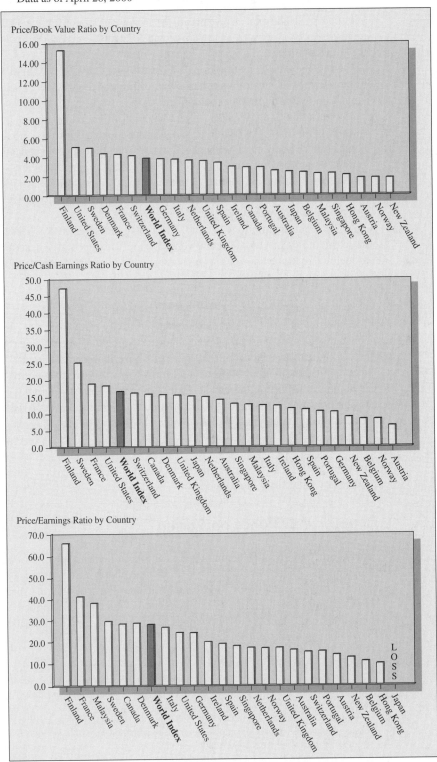

Source: *MSCI EAFE and World Perspective,* May 2000.

FIGURE 15.11   **Price/Earnings Ratios for Germany, Japan, United Kingdom, and United States**
January 1973–July 2000

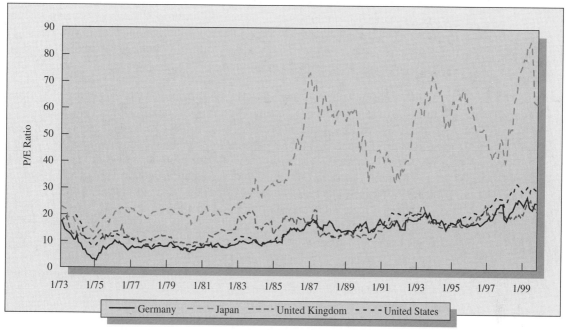

	Mean P/E Ratio	
	1973–1989	*1990–2000*
Japan	29.90	53.77
United Kingdom	9.70	17.24
Germany	13.90	18.25
United States	11.29	20.53

Source: Datastream and author's calculations.

country. The price/earnings ratio (Panel C) shows the most variation. Corporate earnings for Japan were negative, so a P/E ratio cannot be defined. There is considerable variation in the P/E for the remaining countries, with the ratio in Finland nearly five times the value in Hong Kong.[28]

The P/E ratios for Japan, the United Kingdom, Germany, and the United States over a 27-year period are plotted in Figure 15.11. The persistently higher P/E ratios for Japan are evident. The gradual increase of U.K. and U.S. P/E ratios, from single digits in the late 1970s to current values in the 25–30 range, is also shown in the figure.

On first glance, these figures may suggest that different markets pay substantially different prices for earnings, cash flows, or book values. These first impressions are inaccurate. Two reasons explain why.

First, the denominator of each statistic is an accounting figure that is calculated according to generally accepted accounting practices (GAAP) in each country. Wide differences exist in GAAP across countries, particularly in the treatment of consolidation

---

[28]Nokia, a fast-growing telecommunications company that accounts for about 65 percent of market capitalization on the Helsinki Stock Exchange, dominates the data for Finland.

across subsidiaries, depreciation rules for tangible and intangible assets, and provisions for bad debts and reserves. As a result, cross-country comparisons using raw accounting figures are not meaningful.

Second, the economic growth rates of different countries may vary. It is reasonable for markets to pay higher prices for similar accounting earnings when those earnings are expected to grow faster over time.[29] Thus, variability as observed in Figures 15.10 and 15.11 need not imply pricing inefficiency.

Evidence from Multicountry Models.   The traditional CAPM predicts that equity returns are related (through β_{iM}) to the excess returns on the domestic market portfolio. A strict, but unrealistic, international extension of the CAPM predicts that equity returns are related (through β_{iW}) to the excess returns on the world market portfolio. The APT framework takes a more agnostic view, claiming only that a set of "factors" (γ_k) drive equity returns. These factors could represent global economic conditions, national or industry influences, and currency factors to list the most intuitive categories.

Many tests of international asset pricing have been reported.[30] Recently, there has been a preference toward APT style tests, especially using financial variables as factors. Some researchers have criticized this approach, claiming that it is not very illuminating to use the variance of one set of financial variables to explain returns in another set of financial variables.[31] There is a need, the argument goes, to explain stock returns in terms of fundamental macroeconomic variables.[32]

Campbell Harvey (1994) took issue with this view, noting that the timing and measurement of financial variables is precise, and that financial variables incorporate the market's reaction to macroeconomic news. Data on macroeconomic fundamentals (for constructing APT factors) are released on an irregular basis, subject to news leaks and revisions, and subject to seasonal adjustment and smoothing—all of which make them less likely to produce meaningful results as factors. Perhaps the greatest problem is the tendency for researchers to sweep through hundreds of macroeconomic variables and then report the handful that "predicts" stock returns. Data mining of this sort is bound to produce spurious results.

The test results in Table 15.6 show the importance of several individual factors—representing world, industry, currency, and domestic financial market returns—for explaining the pattern of stock returns in 16 countries. The first four data columns report the average R^2 in a regression of stock returns against a single factor. The results show that, on average, the domestic market factor explains about 42 percent of the variation in individual stock returns, considerably more than the industry or world factors that explain only 23 percent and 18 percent. The impact of currency is negligible except for Hong Kong. When all four factors are pooled into a multifactor model, the average R^2 rises, but only slightly, to 46 percent.

Thus, while world, industry, and currency factors may affect stock returns, the domestic factor appears to matter the most. APT models are not able to explain much more by looking beyond the domestic factor, except for the United States and France. In these

---

[29]This conclusion is consistent with valuation based on the *dividend discount model* for a firm with growing dividends.

[30]See Cho, Eun, and Senbet (1986), and Korajczyk and Viallet (1989).

[31]Summers (1985) as discussed in Frankel (1994).

[32]For a recent empirical study using macroeconomic fundamentals, see Dumas (1994).

TABLE 15.6 Relative Importance of World, Industry, Currency, and Domestic Factors for Explaining Stock Returns: 1971–1984

	Average R^2 of Regression on Factors				
	Single-Factor Tests				
Locality	World	Industrial	Currency	Domestic	Joint Test All Four Factors
Switzerland	0.18	0.17	0.00	0.38	0.39
West Germany	0.08	0.10	0.00	0.41	0.42
Australia	0.24	0.26	0.01	0.72	0.72
Belgium	0.07	0.08	0.00	0.42	0.43
Canada	0.27	0.24	0.07	0.45	0.48
Spain	0.22	0.03	0.00	0.45	0.45
United States	0.26	0.47	0.01	0.35	0.55
France	0.13	0.08	0.01	0.45	0.60
United Kingdom	0.20	0.17	0.01	0.53	0.55
Hong Kong	0.06	0.25	0.17	0.79	0.81
Italy	0.05	0.03	0.00	0.35	0.35
Japan	0.09	0.16	0.01	0.26	0.33
Norway	0.17	0.28	0.00	0.84	0.85
Netherlands	0.12	0.07	0.01	0.34	0.31
Singapore	0.16	0.15	0.02	0.32	0.33
Sweden	0.19	0.06	0.01	0.42	0.43
All countries	0.18	0.23	0.01	0.42	0.46

Note: Results represent monthly data for December 1971–December 1984 for 279 firms. Domestic, industrial, and world indexes are from MSCI. Currency return is US$/FC except for the U.S. market, where the DM plays the role of the foreign currency.

Source: Bruno Solnik and A. de Freitas, "International Factors of Stock Price Behavior," in *Recent Developments in International Finance and Banking,* ed. S. Khoury and A. Ghosh (Lexington, MA: Lexington Books, 1988).

countries, the R^2s jump from 0.35 to 0.55 and from 0.45 to 0.60 when nondomestic factors are added.

Policy Matters—Private Investors

In this section, we reconsider the inconsistency between the theoretical case for international diversification and the revealed tendency for investors to hold portfolios with a home country bias. As we have seen, the U.S. share of world equity market capitalization has fallen from more than 70 percent in the 1960s to only 46 percent in 1999. The non-U.S. share has risen from less than 30 percent to 54 percent over the same period. But the percentage of foreign equities in U.S. investor portfolios remains small, perhaps only 10 percent, and a similar home country bias is found for investors in other markets.

As we have discussed, the world market portfolio—composed of equities from all nations in proportion to their market value—is an ideal portfolio for investors from the United States and other countries in only a very special case. Some of the requirements needed to render the global portfolio an optimal market portfolio make intuitive sense—such as no transaction costs, no taxes, and homogeneous expectations about the risk and return on assets.

Other assumptions, however, have a deeper purpose. Assuming a common consumption basket implies that every investor consumes the same goods and services produced by the world's real assets. Naturally, holding a portfolio of all the world's real assets is an ideal way to hedge every investor's future consumption risks. The PPP assumption implies that no group of investors faces a relative price risk that would tilt their portfolios toward a subset of special securities. And assuming that the world portfolio is efficient and includes *all* assets implies that no assets have been left out for any group of investors to add to their portfolios. Let us consider the impact of relaxing these assumptions.

Factors Favoring Overweighting Foreign Markets in Portfolios

Marianne Baxter and Urban Jermann (1997) pointed out that investors hold one nontraded asset: their *human capital*. The investor earns labor income in the domestic economy, and this return on human capital is highly correlated with the return on domestic assets. Stating this differently, when firms are performing well, investors (as laborers) have greater wage income and bonuses; when firms are performing poorly, there is a risk of lower wages, layoffs, or unemployment.[33] To hedge this risk, Baxter and Jermann argued that investors should short their own domestic equity shares—and hold a *substantial* short position since human capital represents a large portion of an investor's wealth. Thus, an optimal portfolio rule would lead investors to smaller or even short positions in their domestic stock market and larger, overweighted positions in foreign shares.[34] Factoring in human capital makes the home country bias puzzle worse.

Factors Favoring Overweighting Home Markets in Portfolios

The assumption that investors share a common consumption pattern is clearly incorrect. While investors may have some similarities in the consumption of traded goods (such as wheat, petroleum, and lumber), it is reasonable to assume that investors differ considerably in their consumption of nontraded goods (like personal care services, legal services, and medical services).[35] The production of nontraded goods may rely intensively on nontraded, domestic factors of production. As a hedge against planned consumption of nontraded (domestic) goods, Marianne Baxter, Urban Jermann, and Robert King (1998) argued that it is desirable for investors to overweight their holdings of domestic equities that represent the production of nontraded goods. Whether this change alone would fully explain home country bias is not clear.

Continuous purchasing power parity is another basic assumption in the benchmark international CAPM. When PPP is assumed, foreign investment does not entail the added risk of exchange rate changes. Allowing for deviations from PPP introduces an additional risk. How investors respond depends on the covariance of exchange rate returns and the investor's degree of risk aversion. Debra Glassman and Leigh Riddick

---

[33]Recently some examples of negative correlation have been observed: Stocks rise as labor-saving efficiencies permit layoffs and lower operating costs.

[34]This result is the international version of the maxim that, other things being equal, investors should not own shares in the firm they work for since their labor income (returns on human capital) already gives them a significant exposure to the firm.

[35]Some services such as legal, accounting, consulting, and others could be traded. Travel may render other services—leisure, education, and transportation itself—tradable.

(1996) showed that when the PPP assumption is dropped, they cannot reject the hypothesis that observed portfolio weights are equal to their optimal values. This result suggests that long positions in domestic securities are a better hedge than foreign securities against exchange rate uncertainty.[36]

Other factors, such as transactions costs and taxes, have been used in an anecdotal fashion to justify home country bias. Evidence reported by Kenneth French and James Poterba (1991) and Linda Tesar and Ingrid Werner (1995) shows that the gross volume of foreign portfolio transactions is large relative to the net flows of capital. This may represent a stock-adjustment phenomenon as investors from all countries attempt to make up for lost time and build diversified portfolios, or an ongoing flow of capital to maintain well-diversified portfolios. But the large magnitude of trading volume among foreign shares and foreign investors suggests that high transaction costs are probably *not* a barrier responsible for home country bias. French and Poterba also concluded that taxes, for which foreign investors usually receive a credit against their domestic taxes, are not large enough to account for the extent of home country bias.

Is Investment in MNCs a Close Substitute for International Investment?

If portfolios exhibit a home country bias, can investors argue that the shares of multinational corporations (MNCs) offer a close substitute for international diversification? The shares of an MNC could reflect real assets and/or cash flows from, say, 20 countries. The MNC could offer ready-made diversification and an inexpensive proxy for the purchase of 20 firms, each one based in a different country.

While this strategy sounds reasonable, the data reject the hypothesis that MNCs are a proxy for foreign markets or international diversification. A study by Bertrand Jacquillat and Bruno Solnik (1978) examined the returns of MNCs from nine countries by regressing their returns against all nine market indexes. In each case, the returns on MNCs were most closely connected with the domestic market index. In the case of U.S. and U.K. MNCs, the addition of foreign markets offered virtually no improved explanation of MNC share returns.

A later study by Andrew Senchack and William Beedles (1980) examined the diversification issue directly. The authors found that a portfolio of U.S. MNCs did not produce a smaller total risk than a portfolio of U.S. stocks with mostly domestic activities.

The results of these studies seem consistent with the evidence on home country bias and the importance of the "domestic" factor in explaining share prices. Even though the MNC has cash flows linked to various foreign economies, the large majority of shareholders are usually domestic. And these investors appear focused on domestic firms. Thus, investors are likely to evaluate the MNC in comparison with other domestic-headquartered firms. Thus, the share price of an MNC may behave more like a domestic firm than a collection of foreign firms, because its shareholder base is primarily domestic investors who have a bias toward home country equities. This explanation, however, suggests a segmented market where the valuation of a firm's cash flows depends on the nationality of the firm's owner. It also suggests that the market lacks a group of investors who arbitrage between markets and ensure that valuations are set consistently across markets.

---

[36]However, see Uppal (1992) for a differing view on PPP and home country bias.

Can Investors Create "Homemade" International Diversification?

In the most recent study related to the investment home bias puzzle, Vihang Errunza, Ked Hogan, and Mao-Wei Hung (1999) examine whether portfolios of domestically traded securities—including MNCs, country funds, ADR shares, and industry indexes—can mimic the returns on foreign indexes. Using data from 1973 to 1993 for seven developed and nine emerging markets, the authors find that a set of domestically traded assets (including market indexes, industry portfolios, MNCs, closed-end country funds, and ADRs) is successful at mimicking the gains from international portfolio diversification. These results support the view that investors may be able to re-create most of the international diversification benefits by holding domestically traded assets. In this view, "home bias" in investor portfolios need not be associated with lost international investment or diversification opportunities.

Furthermore, Errunza et al. show that incremental gains from creating true internationally diversified portfolios have been declining over time in relation to these homemade portfolios. The authors take this as evidence that barriers to international investment have been declining over time.

Can Investors Count on International Diversification Gains in the Future?

Another policy-related question is whether investors can expect diversification gains to continue into the future. Globalization in all aspects of economic activity—integration of production; international trade in goods, services, and technology; international capital movements; and so forth—has continued, raising the prospect that real business cycles are growing more synchronized and that the correlation of financial market returns is increasing, thus reducing the diversification gains from international investment.

In Grubel's (1968) study, the average correlation of returns between the United States and 10 other markets was 0.19 for the period 1959–1966. Calculations by Roger Ibbotson, Laurence Siegel, and Paul Kaplan (1991) for nine countries, 1970–1989, showed that the correlation of returns had increased to 0.51.[37] Over the 1990–1995 period, the IFC reported that the correlation between U.S. market returns (measured by the S&P 500) and returns on the Financial Times Euro-Pacific index was 0.38. And over the 1994–1999 period, Standard and Poor's *Emerging Stock Market Factbook 2000* (p. 72) reported that the same correlation between returns on the S&P 500 and returns on the Financial Times Euro-Pacific index had increased to 0.65. For a sample of seven countries over 1960–1990, François Longin and Bruno Solnik (1995) reported that the average correlation of the U.S. market with the other six markets has risen by about 0.36 in 30 years, or slightly more than 0.01 per year. Thus, there is some evidence that the average correlation of the U.S. market with other markets has risen over the last 30 years.[38]

Sang Bin Lee and Kwang Jung Kim (1993) tested whether the correlation of market returns changed in the 38-month subperiod before the October 1987 crash compared with the 38-month subperiod after the crash. The authors reported that for 12 major markets,

---

[37]The nine countries are Australia, Canada, France, Germany, Italy, Japan, the Netherlands, Switzerland, and the United Kingdom.

[38]Harvey (1991) measures the correlation of excess returns ($R_M - R_F$) and finds a slightly lower correlation. Excess returns in local currency are equal to the currency-hedged excess returns in any other currency unit, because of interest rate parity. See also Kaplanis (1988).

FIGURE 15.12   **S&P/IFC Global Total Return Index Correlations with U.S. S&P 500 Index**
Monthly US$ Returns, December 1994–December 1999

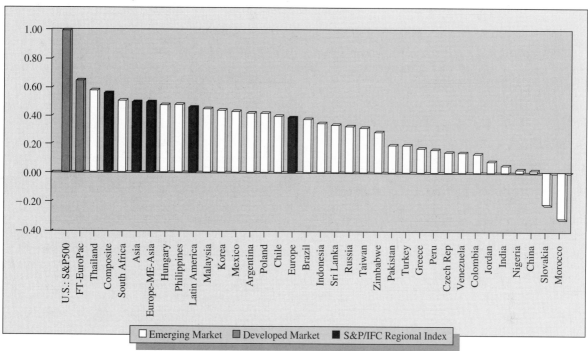

Source: Standard & Poor's, *Emerging Stock Markets Factbook 2000*, p. 72.

the correlation of weekly US$ returns increased from 0.23 before the crash to 0.39 afterward. The authors also showed that returns after the crash were more closely associated with international factors than prior to the crash. And finally, Lee and Kim showed that correlation among markets tends to increase when markets are more volatile.

This final result has particularly strong implications. It is precisely when markets are most volatile that investors would welcome the diversification associated with international portfolios. But when the United States or another major market experiences volatility, it appears that this volatility is experienced elsewhere. Richard Roll (1988) observed that all major world markets declined substantially in the October 1987 crash, an unusual event if the correlation among markets was indeed low. Longin and Solnik (1995) used time series econometrics to model the changing behavior of correlation among seven countries during 1960–1990. The authors also concluded that correlation tends to rise when market volatility increases.

While correlation among major markets appears to have risen, correlation of returns on major markets with returns on emerging markets remain relatively low. Figure 15.12 shows that for most emerging markets, the correlation is less than it is for developed markets and regions. In many cases the correlations are below 0.25 and in some cases less than zero.

Are Emerging Markets Integrated with World Capital Markets?

The weak correlation between emerging market returns and returns in developed country markets raises the issue of whether emerging market returns are driven by the same

FIGURE 15.13   **Risk and Return in S&P/IFC Total Return Indexes**
Monthly Figures, 1994–1999

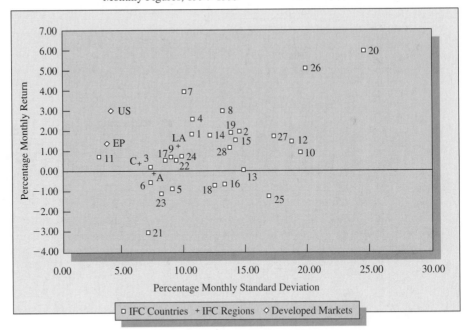

Note: IFC Emerging Market Countries are Argentina (1), Brazil (2), Chile (3), China (4), Columbia (5), Czech Republic (6), Greece (7), Hungary (8), India (9), Indonesia (10), Jordan (11), Korea (12), Malaysia (13), Mexico (14), Nigeria (15), Pakistan (16), Peru (17), Philippines (18), Poland (19), Russia (20), Slovakia (21), South Africa (22), Sri Lanka (23), Taiwan (24), Thailand (25), Turkey (26), Venezuela (27), Zimbabwe (28); IFC Regional Markets are Composite Emerging Market Index (C), Latin America (LA), Asia (A); Developed Markets are US-S&P500 (US) and FT-Euro-Pac Index (EP).

Source: Standard & Poor's, *Emerging Stock Markets Factbook 2000,* p. 70.

factors that drive the more developed financial markets. Recent research by Geert Bekaert et al. (1998) and by Bekaert and Harvey (1997) suggests that the pattern of returns in emerging markets is much different from that in developed markets. In particular, the evidence shows that emerging market returns are generally non-normally distributed, and that these deviations from normality appear to be time varying as well.

The presence of substantial skewness and kurtosis in returns suggests that the simple CAPM where returns are a linear function of systematic (beta) risk will fail. Indeed, the results in Bekaert et al. (1998) show that returns in emerging markets are related to volatility (total risk) and various other economic and country risk measures. Overall, this line of analysis shows that emerging markets are at best only partially integrated with world capital markets.[39]

Monthly return and risk measures for the 28 emerging market countries tracked by Standard & Poor's are plotted in Figure 15.13. Over the 1994–1999 period, the data show high risk in certain markets and substantial variation across markets. At one extreme the Russian market achieved average returns (in US$ terms) of 5.65 percent per month with a standard deviation of 24.8 percent per month. At another extreme, the Slovakia market declined at an average rate of −2.79 percent per month with a standard deviation of 7.2

---

[39]An excellent overview of the broad patterns of emerging market performance is provided in Mullin (1993).

percent per month. Across all 28 markets, the average volatility is 11.7 percent per month, almost five times as great as the figure for the S&P 500 Index in the United States over this period. The composite index of all 28 emerging markets (marked "C" in Figure 15.13), however, has a volatility of only 6.8 percent per month, which is roughly the same order of magnitude as that for the developed market and regional indexes.

Another issue that haunts the analysis of emerging market stock returns is **survivorship bias,** the tendency to analyze only markets where long series of data are available, and therefore to focus on markets that generally have survived and prospered. William Goetzmann and Philippe Jorion (1999) have documented some stock markets that were strong in the 19th and early 20th centuries, but war, political crisis, or economic collapse caused these markets to plunge in value.[40] Many of the returns in emerging stock markets would look considerably different if the period of analysis could be extended backward in time to match the long, uninterrupted history of the U.S. stock market.

Policy Matters—Public Policymakers

Like the other markets we have examined, equity markets bring together buyers and sellers in a regulatory climate shaped by policymakers. While most countries permit both inward and outward investment, certain barriers remain that inhibit the flow of portfolio investments across borders. Some of these barriers are economic:

- Exchange rate risk, transaction costs, transaction taxes.

Some are political:

- Expropriation risk, exchange controls and blocked funds, ownership and control restrictions on certain industries (defense contractors, telecommunications, airlines).

Others relate to rules and practices in the local markets:

- Procedures for clearing and settlement of transactions, corporate governance practices that allow concentrated ownership and limit investor control, restrictions on the outward investment of national pension funds, differences in accounting principles and disclosure practices.[41]

A study by Ben Steil et al. (1996) concludes that even though the European Union is *nominally* a **single market** (in that no legal restrictions exist to the movement of funds), numerous barriers, such as those listed above, remain and limit the extent of European capital market integration. Steil's study is instructive because in many ways the European situation is a microcosm for much of the world that shares many of the same barriers, although not the same stated objective of integrating distinct national capital markets.

---

[40]In the 1920s, for example, the market capitalization of Argentina exceeded that of the British stock market.

[41]See *Emerging Stock Markets Factbook* (2000), pp. 402–3, for the results of a survey that measures the risk of settlement as well as other safekeeping functions in emerging markets. See LaPorta et al. (1998) for a comparison of the legal and corporate governance differences across countries. The authors concluded that the legal setting and safeguards offered to investors can have a substantial impact on asset prices. For example, Russian firms might sell at very low P/E ratios, reflecting how little investors' rights in Russia are protected.

Many of these barriers to the flow of capital have their roots in public policy decisions. We will review two of these barriers and comment on possible policy changes.

Equity Market Trading Arrangements

Historical patterns of investment and equity financing have helped to fragment markets and raise barriers to international investing. In a closed economy, Ruthenian firms raise capital from Ruthenian investors who trade their shares on the Ruthenian Stock Exchange (RSE). The RSE is regulated by an agency of the Ruthenian government, ostensibly to protect Ruthenian investors, but with the side effect of protecting the RSE against competitors, foreign or domestic. Such protection tends to raise transaction costs and dampen innovative trading practices.

As Ruthenia's economic borders open up and foreign investors own shares in Ruthenian firms, these investors (as well as Ruthenian firms) may not feel well served by the RSE. Specifically, foreign investors may determine that the RSE does not promote deep markets that permit large transactions to trade at low costs, and domestic firms may be unable to tap their desired pool of equity capital if they rely only on the RSE. As a result, the RSE monopoly may foster a demand for alternative market trading arrangements.

Steil (1996, Chapters 1–4) analyzed the evolution of European stock exchanges and found that trading in European equities is fragmented across countries and not conducive to low cost trading, especially for institutional investors who are a growing force in European markets. The London Stock Exchange's **SEAQ-International (SEAQ-I)** began in 1986 as a screen-based, NASDAQ-style system whereby designated market makers disseminate quotes and execute trades. Initially, SEAQ-I enjoyed some success by diverting some transactions away from continental European exchanges and by creating new trading volume.

In response, some European exchanges (Paris and Frankfurt) introduced new electronic auction trading systems that drew liquidity back to the home markets.[42] Gradually, London dealers withdrew their commitment to the SEAQ-I system, and spreads in the market widened. Still, the impact of widening the market for European stocks had a measurable effect on transaction costs. Marco Pagano and Alisa Röell (1990, 1993) reported that the London spread on French stocks fell by half (from 3.0 percent to 1.5 percent) when the Paris Bourse was open, but then would shoot up (to nearly 3.0 percent) after the Bourse closed. Similar findings have been reported for German and Italian stocks.[43]

Steil (1996) argued that in the near future, proprietary trading systems that rely on high-tech telecommunication links will gain a larger share of trading volume. Reuters's **Instinet** now operates two electronic trading systems for NASDAQ stocks that have captured between 13 percent and 50 percent of NASDAQ activity. **Tradepoint** began a continuous electronic auction in 1995 on the 400 most active U.K. stocks. As a private, profit-seeking company, Tradepoint is considering the addition of non-U.K. stocks to its list. With a staff and budget only 4 percent the size of the London Stock Exchange, Tradepoint (and other computer-based systems) can compete on the basis of lower transaction costs for large institutional order flow.

Steil (1996, p. 45) concluded that "the commoditization of trading services is under way, and no European exchange will be immune from its effects." At the moment,

---

[42]Steil (1996), p. 8.
[43]Ibid., pp. 26–27.

public policymakers are unsure how to treat new trading systems. If an Italian investor (buyer) uses a broker in Spain to dial a computer in Luxembourg, which finds a broker in Frankfurt who has a client (seller) in Denmark for a transaction in a French stock—who regulates the transaction? Clearly, national stock exchanges dislike new forms of competition that cut into their traditional market share. But **regulatory arbitrage,** whereby some country permits these new forms of trading, will be an important force to widen the markets for European shares, reduce the cost of transacting, and help to internationalize investors' portfolios and firms' shareholder base.

The commoditization of trading discussed by Steil appears to be under way. In March 2000, the Paris, Amsterdam, and Brussels stock exchanges agreed to merge into a new entity known as EURONEXT, which expected to begin trading in the first quarter of 2001. If successful, EURONEXT would list about 1,360 firms with market capitalization of $2.4 trillion. In May 2000, the London Stock Exchange and Deutsche Börse announced their own merger to form iX, but the plan collapsed in September. Had it been successful, the new exchange could have boasted of more than 2,900 listings, with a market capitalization exceeding $4.3 trillion.

Diversity in Accounting Principles and Disclosure Practices

The term **accounting diversity** refers to cross-country differences in accounting principles and disclosure practices. Recently, more attention has been focused on accounting diversity to determine whether it is a significant barrier to international investment and whether public policy reforms are advisable.

While major financial markets are generally open to both investors and issuers, U.S. regulatory policies with respect to accounting principles and information disclosure are considerably more demanding than in other countries. U.S. policy could be described as a form of **national treatment;** that is, all foreign firms are invited to issue and list their equity shares on U.S. exchanges as long as they report and/or reconcile their accounting statements to U.S. GAAP. "Investor protection" is the driving force behind this policy decision by the U.S. Securities Exchange Commission (SEC). The SEC believes that U.S. GAAP offers investors the clearest picture of corporate performance, and that allowing investors to trade in foreign shares on U.S. exchanges without access to U.S. GAAP information would put investors at additional risk.

Outside the United States, regulators permit open markets by practicing **reciprocity.** Regulators in Switzerland, Germany, and the Netherlands do not require foreign companies to restate their accounting reports into local GAAP before shares may be listed or traded on their markets. As long as firms conform to their home country's GAAP, these exchanges permit listing and trading in foreign securities. The London Stock Exchange has a modified form of reciprocity; it retains the right to require additional accounting information in individual cases.

These regulatory differences raise related policy questions.

Does Accounting Diversity Adversely Affect Investors?   Two studies by Frederick Choi and Richard Levich (1990, 1996) showed that many investors feel that accounting diversity is a barrier and would welcome proposals to harmonize both accounting principles and disclosure standards. The 1996 survey by the authors confirmed that most European institutional investors regard accounting information as extremely important for their investment analysis, and that more than 80 percent make cross-country investment comparisons of individual firms. However, 45 percent of those surveyed indicated that they assign a higher risk rating to companies that disclose insufficient information, 35 percent avoid investing in such companies altogether, and 26 percent require higher returns from them. These answers suggest that accounting diversity may have some effect (of unknown magnitude) on capital market prices.

However, investors apply a range of reasonably effective coping strategies when faced with different accounting principles or less than the preferred amount of disclosure.[44] Moreover, most respondents indicate that accounting barriers to cross-border investment are relatively insignificant compared with those associated with liquidity and currency risks.

Is Harmonization of Accounting Standards a Useful Response?   Harmonization of accounting standards sounds like a useful idea, but it runs the risk of making firms that are different (similar) in real economic terms appear similar (different).

> There is a danger that international standards delude the unsophisticated into thinking that you've genuinely harmonized. It may in fact be healthy to have things look a little different because it makes people realize that there are some differences.[45]

Harmonization may be particularly misleading when firms make economic decisions and pay taxes on the basis of one set of accounting standards, and use another set of accounting principles for financial reporting. By virtue of its headquarters location, a firm has access to the local tax-accounting and regulatory-accounting provisions. For the firm, the right to use local tax and regulatory accounting rules is equivalent to a nontraded asset. Choi and Levich (1990) cited a foreign securities official who argues that it is more prudent to have investors see the original home country accounting statements:

> The merit of accepting the foreign-practice accounting statements is that the local investor will receive the same information as the foreign country's investor.[46]

Access to and understanding of home country accounting statements may be especially important when share ownership and trading are dominated by home country investors.

While efforts of the International Accounting Standards Committee (IASC) are in progress to further harmonize accounting principles across countries, it does not make sense to apply a harmonized set of accounting principles without first achieving harmonization of important components of the legal, tax, and social environment. An externally imposed accounting system that fails to communicate material cross-country differences in the economic environment would be unlikely to facilitate further equity market integration across borders.

Can Regulators Harmonize Issuing and Listing Standards?   In June 1991, the United States and Canada adopted the **Multijurisdictional Disclosure System (MJDS)** designed to enhance the opportunities for cross-border securities activities between the two countries. The MJDS reduces the costs of new issues by permitting the use of reciprocity (that is, home country accounting disclosures) for companies larger than C$300 million. In theory, the MJDS should allow the United States and Canada to function more like a single capital market. However, in the first two years of operation, Canadian firms have used the MJDS to launch securities issues in the U.S. market, but no U.S.

---

[44]For example, an investment firm may hire individuals who specialize in the analysis of foreign company accounting statements or it may schedule special meetings with company officials to better understand the firm's business strategy and performance.

[45]An unnamed survey participant quoted in Choi and Levich (1990), p. 91.

[46]Ibid., p. 66.

firms have used the MJDS for travel to the Canadian market.[47] Differences in accounting principles and underwriting practices keep the markets somewhat segmented.

If policymakers succeed in harmonizing accounting statements to a greater degree, then it may be possible to harmonize issuing and listing standards across countries. The International Organization of Securities Commissions (IOSCO) is at work with the International Accounting Standards Committee (IASC) to develop a set of accounting standards that can be accepted by securities exchanges worldwide. Such a "universal accounting code" would most likely focus on a core set of requirements that would then facilitate cross-border offering and listing of securities. The U.S. SEC appears to endorse the concept of a universal accounting code, but agreement on the exact accounting principles and disclosure rules, and whether the code would only apply to "large" firms, are details that must be worked out.

In February 2000, the SEC took a further step by issuing a "concept release" soliciting comments on the quality of IASC standards and concerns that would be raised by acceptance of IASC standards. Some members of the U.S. accounting and investment community maintain that investor protection will be best served by requiring reconciliation of IASC statements with U.S. GAAP. Others feel that IASC standards have reached a par with U.S. GAAP and that the SEC could acknowledge both standards.[48] For one, the New York Stock Exchange has long advocated some relaxation of SEC accounting and disclosure rules for foreign companies, so that the NYSE can more fully participate in the growth of issuing and trading in foreign equity shares.[49]

---

[47]See Fisher (1994) for a discussion of the MJDS.

[48]The full text of the SEC's concept release on international accounting standards is available at <www.sec.gov/news/intlacct.htm>. The comment letters can also be reviewed at <www.sec.gov/rules/s70400.htm>.

[49]The NYSE position is described in Cochrane (1994).

Summary

In this chapter, we have analyzed a range of issues that relate to the markets in equity shares around the world. Characteristics such as market capitalization, number of firms, trading activity, and market concentration vary considerably from country to country. While the United States has the largest equity market in terms of capitalization, other markets (especially emerging markets) have been growing more rapidly over the last decade. Investors can transact in foreign equity markets directly, but several innovations such as ADRs, closed-end funds, and more recently WEBS have significantly lowered the cost of foreign equity investing, particularly for small investors.

Diversification has been the central motive for international investment. Empirical evidence accumulated over the last 30 years shows that portfolios have smaller total risk when they are constructed from a universe of international firms instead of from a single country.

There is less agreement about the appropriate way to model the determinants of international equity prices. Empirical evidence shows that domestic factors are most important for explaining share prices, but industry factors and overall world factors also play a significant role.

The correlation of returns across national markets has increased relative to 30 years ago, which may decrease the opportunities for diversification gains through international investment. Moreover, the correlation of returns appears to increase when volatility increases. Emerging markets may offer a fresh opportunity for diversification, but individual emerging markets exhibit non-normal returns and high volatility.

One of the most robust, stylized observations about equity markets is that investors tend to overweight the proportion of home securities in their portfolios, or home country bias. Various explanations have been put forward to rationalize home country bias, including barriers to international investment and consumption preferences that tilt toward domestic and nontraded goods. However, a complete understanding of the home country bias in portfolios remains a puzzle.

Facing a wide array of equity markets, many of which are small and prone to higher trading costs, private companies have developed proprietary trading systems to compete with traditional national stock exchanges. Public policies here are evolving as policy-makers still must determine the regulatory jurisdiction and weigh the interests of investors, firms, and stock exchanges. While some investors believe they can cope successfully with international accounting diversity, many others report that accounting diversity is a barrier that raises their perceived risk or required rate of return on international investments. In response, public policy-makers are exploring ways to harmonize accounting standards for cross-border trading and listing of equity shares.

Questions

1. Compare ADRs traded in the United States with the underlying common shares traded in foreign markets. What are the main features and respective advantages of each investment?

2. Does investing in ADRs protect the U.S. investor from currency fluctuations?

3. Describe how cross-holding of securities distorts market capitalization comparison across countries.

4. What are the major hurdles faced by investors willing to invest in foreign equity markets?

5. Describe the limitations of the CAPM model in assessing expected returns and the level of risks in foreign markets.

6. Describe how multinational corporations could serve as a reasonable proxy for investing in foreign equity markets.

7. How would you explain differences in valuation (using such yardsticks as P/E or P/BV) across different markets? What factors influence these differences?

8. What kind of investors would be interested in investing in emerging markets stocks? What are the trade-offs for investing in emerging stock markets?

9. What alternative vehicles for international equity investment are available to an individual investor?

10. Describe the difference between a closed-end and open-end country fund. Why might fund managers decide to set up a closed-end country fund rather than an open-end country fund?

11. Define the terms *discount* and *premium* as they apply to closed-end country funds. Why might a closed-end fund trade at a discount or premium? Why might the discount or premium change over time?

12. On what basis could you argue that countries should adopt harmonized accounting standards for corporate financial reporting? On what basis could you argue for the status quo?

13. Do you think the benefits of international portfolio diversification are likely to be greater in the next decade than in the last decade? Explain why or why not.

Exercises

Cross-holding

1. Suppose firm A has 1,000 shares outstanding and firm B has 500 shares outstanding. Firms A and B each issue 100 new shares. Firm A purchases the shares from firm B and firm B purchases the shares from firm A.

   a. What is the net effect on the market capitalization of firms A and B? On overall market capitalization?

   b. What is the net effect on each firm's balance sheet?

c. If firms A and B are part of the overall market index, what will happen to their respective weights in the index?

d. How is the debt-to-equity ratio affected?

e. What is the number of shares now available for trading in the open market?

International Equity Investment

2. Suppose you have $100,000 to invest in the Swiss equity market. Nestlé is a major blue-chip firm and is trading at SFr 666. The current exchange rate is 1.50 SFr/$.

a. How many shares of Nestlé can you buy?

b. Suppose the share price rises to SFr 800 over one year. Calculate the percentage return on your investment in SFr terms. Calculate the dollar return in the following cases:
- The spot rate stays the same.
- The US$ appreciates to 1.70 SFr/$.
- The US$ depreciates to 1.35 SFr/$.

c. Make the same calculation as in b, but assume that the end-of-year share price is SFr666.

d. Make the same calculation as in b, but assume that the end-of-year share price is SFr600.

e. Suppose that at the beginning of the period, you could sell SFr150,000 forward (your initial SFr investment) for one-year delivery. Would this offer you a perfect hedge, an underhedge, or an overhedge?

f. Determine the dollar return in each scenario for questions b and c, assuming that you sell SFr150,000 forward at a one-year forward rate of 1.60 SFr/$.

g. Has currency hedging (in f) affected the exposure of US$ returns to foreign exchange changes?

3. Consider the case of a British investor. Suppose that the US$ is at a recent low against the pound, at $1.62/£.

a. What factors should the British investor take into consideration when assessing the opportunity to invest in the US$-denominated equities?

b. If the British investor forecasts that the fall of the US$ is over and a rebound is likely, should the investor hedge his or her exposure to U.S. equities?

c. Suppose the investor buys 1,000 shares of IBM at $80 a share. What is the cost of these shares in £ terms?

d. Suppose the price of IBM shares stays at $80 and the dollar subsequently rebounds to $1.55/£. What is the net gain for the British investor?

e. At $1.55/£, how far could IBM share prices fall before the British investor starts to lose money?

4. In the first quarter of 1995, the Mexican economic crisis resulted in the devaluation of the peso from 3.40 MP/$ to 7 MP/$. Stock prices on the Mexican Bolsa plummeted by 40 percent in peso terms.

a. Calculate the loss during the quarter for a U.S. investor in the Mexican stock market.

b. Shares of Telmex, traded in the U.S. market in the form of ADRs, plunged from $60 to $26. How much did Telmex lose in peso terms?

c. In the absence of an active futures market in the peso prior to the crisis, how would you hedge your Telmex shares?

5. In the mid-1990s, a large investment fund has invested in international equity markets using the following weights: 20 percent United Kingdom, 20 percent Germany, 15 percent France, 5 percent Italy, 5 percent Switzerland, 20 percent Japan, 10 percent Hong Kong, and 5 percent Mexico. The percentage returns (measured in logarithmic, continuous terms) for each country and for each currency gauged against the dollar are shown in the table below:

	Market	*Currency*
United Kingdom	+10%	− 2%
Germany	+ 7	+ 5
France	+ 6	+ 4
Italy	+10	− 5
Switzerland	+ 6	+ 5
Japan	−15	+10
Hong Kong	−25	+ 0
Mexico	−40	−50

a. Calculate the overall return for the portfolio in U.S. dollar terms.

b. Calculate the proportion of the overall return that was the result of rising share prices.

c. Calculate the proportion of the overall return that was the result of currency price changes.

References

Bartolini, Leonardo, and Allan Drazen. "Capital Account Liberalization as a Signal." *American Economic Review* 87, no. 1 (March 1997), pp. 138–54.

Baxter, Marianne, and Urban J. Jermann. "The International Diversification Puzzle Is Worse Than You Think." *American Economic Review* 87, no. 1 (March 1997), pp. 170–80.

Baxter, Marianne; Urban J. Jermann; and Robert G. King. "Nontraded Goods, Nontraded Factors, and International Non-Diversification." *Journal of International Economics* 44, no. 2 (April 1998), pp. 211–29.

Bekaert, Geert; Claude B. Erb; Campbell R. Harvey; and Tadas E. Viskanta. "The Behavior of Emerging Market Returns." In *Emerging Market Capital Flows,* ed. Richard M. Levich. Boston: Kluwer Academic Publishers, 1998.

Bekaert, Geert, and Campbell R. Harvey. "Emerging Market Equity Volatility." *Journal of Financial Economics* 43 (1997), pp. 29–77.

Bodurtha, James N.; Dong-Soon Kim; and Charles Lee. "Closed-end Country Funds and U.S. Market Sentiment." *The Review of Financial Studies* 8, no. 3 (Fall 1995), pp. 879–918.

Bosner-Neal, Catherine; Gregory Brauer; Robert Neal; and Simon Wheatly. "International Investment Restrictions and Closed-End Country Fund Prices." *Journal of Finance* 45, no. 2 (June 1990), pp. 523–47.

Campbell, John Y., and Kenneth A. Froot. "International Experience with Securities Transaction Taxes." In *The Internationalization of Equity Markets,* ed. J. Frankel. Chicago: University of Chicago Press, 1994.

Cho, D. Chinhyung; Cheol S. Eun; and Lemma W. Senbet. "International Arbitrage Pricing: An Empirical Investigation." *Journal of Finance* 41, no. 2 (1986), pp. 313–30.

Choi, Frederick D. S., and Richard M. Levich. "Accounting Diversity." Chapter 8 in *The European Equity Markets,* ed. Benn Steil et al. London: Royal Institute of International Affairs, 1996.

———. *The Capital Market Effects of International Accounting Diversity.* Homewood, IL: Dow Jones–Irwin, 1990.

Cochrane, James L. "Helping to Keep U.S. Capital Market Competitive: Listing World-Class Non-U.S. Firms on U.S. Exchanges." In *International Capital Markets in a World of Accounting Differences,* ed. Frederick D. S. Choi and Richard M. Levich. Burr Ridge, IL: Richard D. Irwin, 1994.

Dumas, Bernard. "A Test of the International CAPM Using Business Cycles Indicators as Instrumental Variables." In *The Internationalization of Equity Markets,* ed.

Jeffrey A. Frankel. Chicago: University of Chicago Press, 1994.

Egly, Dean W. "The American Depositary Receipt as an Instrument of International Finance." Master's thesis, New York University, Graduate School of Business Administration, 1954.

Errunza, Vihang; Ked Hogan; and Mao-Wei Hung. "Can the Gains from International Diversification Be Achieved without Trading Abroad?" *Journal of Finance* 54, no. 6 (Dec. 1999), pp. 2075–2107.

Fisher, Robert P. "The U.S.-Canada Multijurisdictional Disclosure System." In *International Capital Markets in a World of Accounting Differences,* ed. Frederick D. S. Choi and Richard M. Levich. Burr Ridge, IL: Richard D. Irwin, 1994.

Frankel, Jeffrey A., ed. *The Internationalization of Equity Markets.* Chicago: University of Chicago Press, 1994.

French, Kenneth, and James Poterba. "Are Japanese Stock Prices Too High?" *Journal of Financial Economics* 29 (Oct. 1991), pp. 337–63.

Glassman, Debra A., and Leigh A. Riddick. "Why Empirical International Portfolio Models Fail: Evidence That Model Misspecification Creates Home Asset Bias." *Journal of International Money and Finance* 15, no. 2 (Apr. 1996), pp. 275–312.

Goetzmann, William N., and Philippe Jorion. "Re-Emerging Markets." *Journal of Financial and Quantitative Analysis* 34, no. 1 (Mar. 1999), pp. 1–32.

Grubel, Herbert G. "Internationally Diversified Portfolios: Welfare Gains and Capital Flows." *American Economic Review* 58 (Dec. 1968), pp. 1299–1314.

Hardouvelis, Gikas; Rafael La Porta; and Thierry Wizman. "What Moves the Discount on Country Equity Funds?" In *The Internationalization of Equity Markets,* ed. J. Frankel. Chicago: University of Chicago Press, 1994.

Harvey, Campbell R. "Comment." In *The Internationalization of Equity Markets,* ed. J. Frankel. Chicago: University of Chicago Press, 1994.

———. "The World Price of Covariance Risk." *Journal of Finance* 46 (Mar. 1991), pp. 111–58.

Heston, Steven L., and K. Geert Rouwenhorst. "Does Industrial Structure Explain the Benefits of International Diversification?" *Journal of Financial Economics* 36 (Aug. 1994), pp. 3–27.

Ibbotson, Roger G.; Laurence B. Siegel; and Paul D. Kaplan. "World Equities: The Past and the Future." In *Global Portfolios.* ed. R. Aliber and B. Bruce. Homewood, IL: Business One Irwin, 1991.

Jacquillat, Bertrand, and Bruno Solnik. "Multinationals Are Poor Tools for International Diversification." *Journal of Portfolio Management,* Winter 1978, pp. 8–12.

Kaplanis, Evi C. "Stability and Forecasting of the Comovement Measures of International Stock Market Returns." *Journal of International Money and Finance* 7, no. 1 (Mar. 1988), pp. 63–76.

Korajczyk, Robert A., and Claude Viallet. "An Empirical Investigation of International Asset Pricing." *Review of Financial Studies* 2, no. 4 (1989), pp. 553–85.

La Porta, Rafael; Florencio Lopez-de-Silanes; Andrei Shleifer; and Robert W. Vishny. "Law and Finance." *Journal of Political Economy* 106, no. 6 (Dec. 1998), pp. 1113–55.

Lee, Sang Bin, and Kwang Jung Kim. "Does the October 1987 Crash Strengthen the Co-Movements Among National Stock Markets?" *Review of Financial Economics* 3, no. 1 (Fall 1993), pp. 89–102.

Longin, François, and Bruno Solnik. "Is the Correlation in International Equity Returns Constant: 1960–1990." *Journal of International Money and Finance* 14, no. 1 (Feb. 1995), pp. 3–26.

MacDougall, G. D. A. "The Benefits and Costs of Private Investment Abroad: A Theoretical Approach." *Economic Record,* Mar. 1960, pp. 13–35.

Mullin, John. "Emerging Equity Markets in the Global Economy." *Quarterly Review*. Federal Reserve Bank of New York, Summer 1993, pp. 54–83.

Pagano, Marco, and Alisa Röell. "Shifting Gears: An Economic Evaluation of the Reform of the Paris Bourse." In *Financial Market Liberalization and the Role of Banks,* ed. V. Conti and R. Hamaui. London: Cambridge University Press, 1993.

———. "Trading Systems in European Stock Exchanges: Current Performance and Policy Options." *Economic Policy* 10 (Apr. 1990), pp. 63–115.

Robinson, Anthony W. "Comparison of Fundamental Issues in International and Domestic Equity Investing." In

International Investing for U.S. Pension Funds. Institute for Fiduciary Education, May 1989.

Roll, Richard. "A Critique of the Asset Pricing Theory's Tests; Part I: On Past and Potential Testability of Theory." *Journal of Financial Economics* 4, no. 2 (1977), pp. 129–76.

———. "The International Crash of 1987." *Financial Analysts Journal* 44, no. 5 (Sept.–Oct. 1987), pp. 19–35.

Senchack, Andrew J., and William L. Beedles. "Is Indirect International Diversification Desirable?" *Journal of Portfolio Management* 6, no. 2 (Winter 1980), pp. 49–57.

Solnik, Bruno. "Why Not Diversify Internationally Rather Than Domestically?" *Financial Analysts Journal* 30, no. 4 (July–Aug. 1974), pp. 48–54.

Solnik, Bruno, and A. de Freitas. "International Factors of Stock Price Behavior." In *Recent Developments in International Finance and Banking,* ed. S. Khoury and A. Ghosh. Lexington, MA: Lexington Books, 1988.

Steil, Benn, et al. *The European Equity Markets*. London: Royal Institute of International Affairs, 1996.

Summers, Lawrence H. "On Economics and Finance." *Journal of Finance* 40, no. 3 (July 1985), pp. 633–35.

Tesar, Linda L., and Ingrid M. Werner. "Home Bias and High Turnover," *Journal of International Money and Finance* 14, no. 4 (Aug. 1995), pp. 467–92.

Tesar, Linda L., and Ingrid M. Werner. "The Internationalization of Securities Markets Since the 1987 Crash." In *Brookings-Wharton Papers on Financial Services,* ed. Robert E. Litan and Anthony M. Santamero. Washington, DC: Brookings Institution Press, 1998.

Uppal, Raman. "The Economic Determinants of the Home Country Bias in Investors' Portfolios: A Survey." *Journal of International Financial Management and Accounting* 4, no. 3 (Autumn 1992), pp. 171–89.

VI INTERNATIONAL ASSET PORTFOLIOS AND FINANCIAL RISK MANAGEMENT

16 Measuring and Managing the Risk in International Financial Positions 600

16 MEASURING AND MANAGING THE RISK IN INTERNATIONAL FINANCIAL POSITIONS

The Classic Trade-Off Between Greed and Fear

"UNHEDGED"

Vanity license plate observed on sparkling new Porsche 911 Carrera parked in front of posh restaurant in New York

"I used to sleep easy at night with my VAR model."

Allen Wheat, CEO of Credit Suisse First Boston, quoted in *The Economist,* Nov. 14, 1998, p. 82.

Learning Objectives

After reading this chapter, students should

1. Understand that exposure to risk can be viewed as a sensitivity measure relating changes in the market value of a firm or portfolio to changes in the price of another asset.

2. Realize that the sources of a firm's exposure can be direct (from actual positions) or indirect (because the firm competes with other firms).

3. Know basic accounting techniques for measuring currency exposure.

4. Be familiar with several techniques for measuring economic exposure to currency risk including the regression approach and the scenario approach.

5. Understand how a firm can select a financial hedging strategy based on its currency profile and cash flow characteristics.

6. Be familiar with the value-at-risk approach for measuring the risk of financial positions.

In this chapter, our focus shifts away from the characteristics and behavior of prices in international financial markets and turns to the question of how price variability in these markets affects two prominent decision makers: the corporate treasurer and the investment manager. Specifically, we will examine how variability in exchange rates and interest rates affects the market value of a firm. In Chapters 11, 12, and 13, on futures, options, and swaps, we showed how the market value of a position in one of these contracts varied as a function of the spot exchange rate, an interest rate, or some other variable. This demonstrated that open positions in futures, options, and swaps carry an **exposure** to financial risk. In this chapter, we use the same approach and evaluate the link between the market value (*MV*) of either a firm or a financial portfolio and a financial price (say, the spot exchange rate *S*). This produces another sensitivity measure, in this case $\partial MV/\partial S$, which we will define as a firm's or portfolio's **exposure to foreign exchange risk.**

A corporate treasurer is interested in $\partial MV/\partial S$ for clear reasons. If $\partial MV/\partial S$ is nonzero, an adverse change in the spot rate may reduce the market value of the firm. If $\partial MV/\partial S$ is nonzero, an increase in the volatility of exchange rates could result in an increase in the volatility of the firm's market value. In this chapter, we analyze the sources of a firm's exposure to financial risk and review several techniques for measuring exposure. We then propose various methods that the treasurer can adopt to eliminate, or at least soften, the impact of uncertainty emanating from international financial markets. We focus only on **financial hedging** techniques that involve financial market transactions. Another class of techniques, called **operating hedges,** is an important part of hedging exposure to real exchange rate changes. Operating hedges encompass a range of strategies that the manager can invoke in response to a real exchange rate change in order to lessen the impact on the market value of the firm. Having production facilities in several countries or having the flexibility to change the sourcing of product inputs or to change the sales price of the product are examples of operating hedges. Such strategies are usually outside the scope of the corporate treasurer, so we do not discuss operating hedges here.[1]

An investment manager who holds a portfolio of securities (such as those described in Chapters 14 and 15) is also interested in $\partial MV/\partial S$ for similar reasons. If $\partial MV/\partial S$ is nonzero, an investment in a portfolio of bonds and/or equities carries an exposure to foreign exchange risk. The investment manager then must determine whether to retain the risk or to hedge it. More generally, an investment manager (or trader) can assess the sensitivity of an entire portfolio to changes in exchange rates, interest rates, and other financial variables. We will show that an investment manager (or trader) can use similar techniques for measuring exposure to risks and managing them using financial instruments.

By their nature, the business operations of a firm are exposed to many kinds of uncertainties. International business operations and foreign exchange transactions have often been treated as a separate and perhaps different source of uncertainty when compared with business operations that are conducted only in the domestic country and in domestic currency. In this chapter, we will argue that the distinction is exaggerated. The risks facing firms with domestic operations and firms with foreign operations are similar in many respects.

A domestic firm operating in a single, closed economy is exposed to a variety of price risks. The firm faces *relative price risk* on its inputs. For example, an airline that uses jet fuel or a manufacturer of baseball bats is exposed to the risk that its raw material (input) prices may rise faster than the general price level. Similarly, the firm faces a relative price risk on its outputs. For example, a paperboard manufacturer is exposed to the risk that its product (output) prices may fall relative to the general price level, perhaps because of overbuilding and excess production capacity in the paperboard industry.

An international firm operating in an open economy faces these same price risks plus an important additional price risk. A change in the *real exchange rate* (defined in Chapter 5) can signify an *especially* important relative price change because it influences the relative cost of *all* inputs used by competitors and the relative price of *all*

---

[1]For a discussion of operating hedges, see Oxelheim and Wihlborg (1987).

outputs purchased by consumers around the world. Thus, a change in the real exchange rate can affect *all* firms that operate in an open economy in many subtle and, at times, significant ways. The sensitivity of a firm's cash flows, and hence its market value, to changes in real exchange rates is an example of foreign exchange exposure.

Our hypothetical domestic firm also faces *interest rate risk* if it holds a net asset (or liability) position in financial assets that differs from that of its competitors. For example, a firm that has raised long-term, floating-rate debt is exposed to the risk of higher interest rates as long as the firm does not hold financial assets that rise in value in response to the same interest rate move. A firm also faces interest rate risk if the cost of financing is an important component of the purchase price of its products. For example, an automobile or home appliance manufacturer may experience a fall in demand as interest rates rise, because many customers finance the purchase of these big-ticket items. By extension, a hypothetical international firm faces domestic and foreign currency interest rate risk when the values of the firm's financial assets, financial liabilities, or cash flows from operations change in response to interest rate changes.

A better understanding of a firm's foreign exchange exposure is possible if the reader recalls the interplay between exchange rate changes and macroeconomic activity from the standpoint of a nation. It is well known that changes in exchange rates have a predictable impact on the pattern of international trade and competition. A US$ depreciation improves the price competitiveness of U.S. products and increases the range of U.S. products that are exportable. Similarly, the US$ depreciation raises the price of imports and shrinks the range of foreign products that are importable—transforming some of them into domestically produced nontraded goods. Trade theory thus predicts that a US$ depreciation will lead to an expansion of the export goods sector, a transformation of the nontraded goods sector to include some goods that were formerly imported, and a contraction in those sectors that relied on imports as intermediate inputs.

Similarly, a real appreciation of the US$ has a predictable, but opposite, effect on trade patterns. By raising the price of U.S. goods over those produced in other countries, the appreciation shrinks the range of products that are exportable while expanding the range of imports that can compete on price terms with nontraded goods. Trade theory thus predicts that a US$ appreciation will lead to a contraction of the export goods sector, a transformation of the nontraded goods sector as imported goods supplant certain domestically produced goods, and an expansion in those sectors that rely on imports as intermediate inputs.

These effects of exchange rate changes on national trade patterns are well known. It is often overlooked, however, that the changes that occur at the national level are actually comprised of changes that occur in *individual firms.* The impact that exchange rate changes may have on patterns of employment, production, and corporate profitability at the national level actually reflects the impact that is felt on individual firms— what we call the firm's foreign exchange exposure.

We should also not omit the fact that a real depreciation (appreciation) of the US$ is tantamount to a real appreciation (depreciation) of foreign currencies. Thus, when a US$ depreciation (or appreciation) has an effect on firms located within the United States, an essentially opposite effect is felt by firms located abroad.

In this introduction, we have highlighted the role that exchange rates have on the composition of international trade. But current and prospective exchange rate changes also impact a nation's capital account transactions, which in turn affect the pricing and availability of financial capital. These effects could be felt across financial assets denominated in a particular currency (such as, when a prospective UK£ devaluation leads to a rise in all UK£ interest rates) or across financial claims for a particular country (such as, when a prospective Mexican peso devaluation reduces lending to all Mexican firms). These effects are also a part of the firm's foreign exchange exposure.

In this chapter, we will analyze the key ideas in formulating and implementing a strategy for financial risk management. Corporate treasurers are directly responsible for managing the firm's exposure to financial risk, but the risks that remain are then held by the investor, who can reduce these risks through a diversified portfolio of shares or by applying some of the same hedging techniques available to the corporate treasurer.

The Corporate Treasurer's Financial Risk Management Problem

While our definition of *exposure* applies equally to the market value of a portfolio of securities or a firm, in this section we focus on the firm's exposure to foreign exchange risk.

The Market Value of the Firm and Channels of Risk

Market Value and Cash Flows.   Earlier in this chapter we defined exchange rate exposure as the sensitivity of the firm's market value to exchange rate changes. Let us now examine the *channels* through which the impact of exchange rate changes are felt.

To begin, the **market value** of the firm at time t (MV_t) is defined in equation (16.1) as the summation of the firm's cash flows (CF) over time discounted back to their present value by an appropriate discount factor (i):

$$MV_t = \sum_{t=0}^{T} \frac{CF_t}{(1+i_t)^t} \tag{16.1}$$

Now consider that these cash flows are composed of flows from various currencies—US\$, £, €, ¥, and others. We can then rewrite the market value of the firm in US\$ as:

$$MV_t = \sum_{t=0}^{T} \frac{CF_{\$,t}}{(1+i_{\$,t})^t} + \sum_{t=0}^{T} \frac{CF_{£,t}S_{\$/£,t}}{(1+i_{£,t})^t} + \sum_{t=0}^{T} \frac{CF_{€,t}S_{\$/€,t}}{(1+i_{€,t})^t} + \sum_{t=0}^{T} \frac{CF_{¥,t}S_{\$/¥,t}}{(1+i_{¥,t})^t} \ldots \tag{16.2}$$

where cash flows in each currency are discounted at their own appropriate interest rate and multiplied by a spot exchange rate.

The decomposition of cash flows needs to go a bit further. Cash flows in any of the currencies can be divided into revenues and costs as in the following equation using, for example, € cash flows:

$$CF_{€,t} = \text{REVENUES}_{€,t} - \text{COSTS}_{€,t} \tag{16.3}$$

Revenues in € can be defined as the quantity of goods sold times the price per unit, or:

$$\text{REVENUES}_{€,t} = \text{PRICE}_{€,t} \times \text{QUANTITY}_{€,t} \tag{16.4}$$

Costs, also in € for the sake of illustration, can be defined as the sum of a fixed component plus a variable component times the number of goods produced, or:

$$\text{COSTS}_{€,t} = \text{FIXED}_{€,t} + \text{VARIABLE}_{€,t} \times \text{NUMBER}_{€,t} \tag{16.5}$$

Exchange Rate Exposure Is a Sensitivity Measure.   Now that we have broken the market value of the firm up into a large number of smaller pieces, how does that help us understand exchange rate exposure?

Our measure of exchange rate exposure, the sensitivity of the market value of the firm to a change in the \$/€ exchange rate, can be expressed in mathematical symbols as:

$$\frac{\partial MV}{\partial S_{\$/€}} \tag{16.6}$$

This expression is a *partial derivative* measuring the change in the market value of the firm in response to a small change in the \$/€ exchange rate *while holding other economic variables constant.* Thus, $\partial MV / \partial S_{\$/€}$ measures the marginal impact on the firm's market value associated with a change in the \$/€ exchange rate.[2]

A change in the exchange rate affects the market value of the firm to the extent that it affects each of the individual terms in equation (16.2)—either in the numerator through prices or quantities of inputs and outputs, or in the denominator through changes in the appropriate discount rate. The decomposition in equations (16.3), (16.4), and (16.5) shows in greater detail the channels through which an exchange rate change could affect the prices and quantities of inputs and outputs that underlie the firm's cash flows. These equations form a road map (albeit somewhat crude in our example) for the treasurer to think through how an exchange rate change could impact the firm, by thinking through how prices and quantities could change in response to an exchange rate change. This form of **scenario analysis** is an essential way for the firm to assess its exposure to foreign exchange risk.

To illustrate these linkages, first consider the revenue component of cash flows. Suppose that the firm's products are priced in US\$. A US\$ devaluation ($S_{\$/€}\uparrow$) could result in higher sales to German customers, and more so the greater the price elasticity of demand. But suppose that the firm's products are priced in €. Then, a US\$ devaluation might have no impact on prices or on German sales unless the firm decides to use the strong € as an opportunity to lower its € prices (keeping US\$ prices constant) and gain market share in Germany. Changing local € prices in response to an exchange rate change is defined as the **exchange rate pass-through effect.** It can be an important way for firms to counteract exchange rate changes—a subject we will discuss later in this chapter.

Now consider the cost component of cash flows. A US\$ devaluation will make production costs in Germany higher when expressed in US\$ terms. The firm could respond in two ways. First, it could take steps to raise production efficiency in Germany and lower its fixed or variable € production costs. On the other hand, the firm could reduce production in Germany and move it to an alternative, lower-cost country. If the firm uses inputs from Germany that are priced in €, it might try to negotiate a reduction in supply prices given the strong €.

Direct and Indirect Economic Exposure.   The discussion so far suggests that the firm's exposure to exchange rate risks depends heavily on the impact that the exchange rate has on prices and quantities of inputs and outputs. Some of these effects are the direct result of the firm's decisions on where to locate production, whether to alter its own output prices after an exchange rate change, and so on.

John Pringle and Robert Connolly (1993) argued that the overall impact on a firm from exchange rate changes depends not only on how the firm reacts, but also on how

---

[2]The partial derivative in equation (16.6) has the same meaning as a regression coefficient in a multiple regression equation. For an early discussion of the link between the exchange rate and the present discounted value of the firm, see Heckerman (1972).

TABLE 16.1 Channels of Exposure to Foreign Exchange Risk
Direct and Indirect Exposures

	Home Currency Strengthens	*Home Currency Weakens*
Direct Economic Exposure		
Sales abroad	Unfavorable—Revenue worth less in home currency terms	Favorable—Revenue worth more
Source abroad	Favorable—Inputs cheaper in home currency terms	Unfavorable—Inputs more expensive
Profits abroad	Unfavorable—Profits worth less	Favorable—Profits worth more
Indirect Economic Exposure		
Competitor that sources abroad	Unfavorable—Competitor's margins improve	Favorable—Competitor's margins decrease
Supplier that sources abroad	Favorable—Supplier's margins improve	Unfavorable—Supplier's margins decrease
Customer that sells abroad	Unfavorable—Customer's margins decrease	Favorable—Customer's margins improve
Customer that sources abroad	Favorable—Customer's margins improve	Unfavorable—Customer's margins decrease

Source: John J. Pringle and Robert A. Connolly, "The Nature and Causes of Foreign Currency Exposure," *Journal of Applied Corporate Finance* 6, no. 3 (Fall 1993), pp. 61–72.

the firm's competitors, customers, and suppliers react. The direct and indirect effects are summarized in Table 16.1.

The top part of Table 16.1 summarizes the direct effects of an exchange rate change on the firm. Others things being equal, the firm would prefer to draw sales and earn profits in markets with strong currencies. Also, it would prefer to incur sourcing and production costs in locales with weak currencies.

Moreover, the firm benefits when its competitors are under pressure, when its suppliers are enjoying healthy markets, and when its customers are prospering, as shown in the lower part of Table 16.1. The intuition behind these results is that in a market characterized by imperfect competition in which firms sell *differentiated products,* a firm's **price-over-cost margin** may vary. This price-over-cost margin, also known as a *profit margin,* may respond to market conditions in general and to the exchange rate in particular. So our firm gains a competitive edge when the US$ devalues and a competitor firm sources from Germany. This result occurs because the US$ devaluation raises our competitor's costs and lowers its profit margin. Similarly, our firm gains a potential edge when our suppliers source from abroad and the US$ appreciates. In an imperfectly competitive market, the supplier may be driven to pass along some benefit of the US$ appreciation to us. In the same spirit, our firm benefits when an exchange rate change acts to benefit our customers. In an imperfectly competitive market, customers may absorb higher prices rather than switching to another firm.

In these examples, we have illustrated that there are many channels through which an exchange rate change may affect the cash flows and market value of the firm. Therefore, a precise measure of the firm's exposure will depend on a rather detailed list of assumptions, or a **scenario,** regarding how the firm and its competitors, suppliers, and customers might respond to a given exchange rate change. The economic exposure of the firm to exchange rate changes represents the overall effect of these numerous responses.

The Range of Firms Facing Exchange Rate Exposure.   It is important to note that our definition of exposure to exchange rate changes, $\partial MV/\partial S$, extends to a wide range of firms. Clearly, firms with sales and production operations abroad or with assets and liabilities in foreign currencies are exposed to exchange rate risk. But domestic firms, meaning firms with only domestic operations and with assets and liabilities denominated in only domestic currency, could be exposed to exchange rate risk under our definition.

For example, a theme park situated in the United States staffed completely with American workers and financed completely in US$ could have a substantial currency exposure. A strong US$ would encourage American tourists to vacation abroad and discourage foreign tourists from visiting the United States. An American textile or auto parts manufacturer could have a similar exposure. A strong US$ would encourage foreign imports and therefore heighten competition and put pressure on the American firms' profit margins.

Taking this point to the extreme, virtually *any* domestic business could be exposed to exchange rate risk through a financial channel. For example, a weak US$ (weakened from inflationary fears) might lead the Federal Reserve to raise interest rates. And higher interest rates, *ceteris paribus,* lower the market valuation of firms.

The Time Dimension of Exposure.   Our definition of exposure, $\partial MV/\partial S$, suggests a focus on the very short run. Our definition measures the impact of a change in the spot rate over a time period when other variables are assumed not to change. However, over the longer run, two offsetting effects are possible. First, the firm can make changes in response to an unexpected exchange rate change. For example, the firm can change its suppliers, production locations, pricing policy, product design, and so forth. These actions can lessen the impact of an exchange rate change on the firm's market value.

Second, other economic events may follow the exchange rate change that lessen the impact on the firm. Recalling our discussion of exchange rate overshooting (Chapter 6) and the mean-reverting properties of the real exchange rate (Chapter 4), it is possible for the nominal and real exchange rates to reverse course after an initial shock. This again suggests that the firm's exposure may be less in the long run than in the short run.[3]

Nevertheless, the short-run exposure is critical since the firm must survive this shock to get to the long run. Consider Laker Airways, the British airline founded by Sir Freddie Laker in the mid-1970s to bring cut-rate fares to trans-Atlantic air travel. The product itself was well received and business expanded smartly. But Laker had a substantial currency exposure with sales in £ and many payables (for jet fuel and airplane leases) in US$. And, as a smaller, young, single-product firm, Laker Airways' situation was more precarious. After 1979, the fall in the £ left Laker unable to meet its US$ cash flow obligations. Laker declared bankruptcy and ceased operations a few years later.

Caterpillar Tractor, the manufacturer of heavy equipment based in Peoria, Illinois, faced a serious exposure during 1983–1985 when the strong US$ cut deeply into export sales. Caterpillar's market value sank. But as a larger, better capitalized, multiproduct firm, Caterpillar was able to weather this shock. By 1987, the US$ had weakened, in real terms, to its levels of the early 1980s. Caterpillar was once again able to export successfully from its U.S. base, aided by a weaker US$ and renewed demand for capital equipment abroad.

---

[3] See Froot (1993) for empirical evidence consistent with this assertion.

Accounting Measures of Foreign Exchange Exposure

Accounting principles offer a traditional measure of the firm's exposure to foreign exchange risk. The accounting approach is attractive because it provides a fairly unambiguous technique for measuring exposure. Accounting items are classified either as *exposed* or *not exposed.* Therefore, the accounting approach provides us with an exact numerical answer for the firm's exposure. One serious drawback, however, is that accounting measures of exposure often bear little relationship to economic measures of exposure.

The necessity for rules concerning foreign currency accounting items springs from the requirement that firms produce a single consolidated statement of accounts. Thus, for reporting purposes Coca-Cola (a U.S. company), which conducts business in nearly 200 countries, and Nestlé (a Swiss company), which operates in well over 100 countries, must report all of their foreign currency activities in their home currency. Hence, firms are required to **translate,** or convert, all foreign currency entries on the balance sheet or the income statement into a single numeraire currency. Accounting rules govern the translation of foreign currency amounts into their comparable home currency values.

For accounting purposes, the definition of **net exposure** is exposed assets minus exposed liabilities. A positive net exposure could be described as a **net asset exposure.** A negative net exposure could be noted as a **net liability exposure.** To measure the net exposure to risk in the ¥, for example, one would calculate:

$$\text{Net ¥ Exposure} = \text{Exposed ¥ Assets} - \text{Exposed ¥ Liabilities} \qquad (16.7)$$

Accounting exposure can be subdivided further into translation and transaction exposures, which we discuss next.

Exposure of the Balance Sheet: Translation Exposure

Translation exposure focuses on the book value of assets and liabilities as measured in the firm's balance sheet. As such, translation exposure is a static measure that emphasizes the past actions of the firm.

The rules for classifying balance sheet items as exposed or not exposed are summarized in Table 16.2.

Prior to 1976, U.S. firms could elect to measure their exposure by using either the **current/noncurrent approach** or the **monetary/nonmonetary approach.** The current/noncurrent approach classified all "current" balance sheet items (such as cash, short-term receivables, and short-term payables) as exposed, and "noncurrent" items (such as long-term receivables, fixed assets, and long-term payables) as not exposed. The monetary/nonmonetary approach classified all "monetary" balance sheet items (such as cash, accounts receivable, and short and long-term debt) as exposed, and "nonmonetary" items (such as inventories and fixed assets) as not exposed.

In Table 16.2, this classification is shown with the letter C to represent the current exchange rate and the letter H to represent the historical exchange rate. Using the current exchange rate implies that an accounting entry is exposed, since a new, current exchange rate is used each time a new balance sheet is constructed. Using the historical exchange rate implies that an accounting entry is not exposed, since the exchange rate used for translation purposes remains the same, always equal to its historical value.

Scanning the first two columns of Table 16.2, we can see that under these two translation methods, the treatment of long-term receivables and inventories differs. But the largest impact of the current/noncurrent versus monetary/nonmonetary approach will

TABLE 16.2   Balance Sheet Translation Rules for Various Accounting Standards

	Current/ Noncurrent	Monetary/ Nonmonetary	Temporal	All-Current (Closing Rate)
Assets				
Cash	C	C	C	C
Securities				
• Historical cost	C	C	H	C
• Market price	C	C	C	C
Receivables				
• Current	C	C	C	C
• Long-term	H	C	C	C
Inventory				
• Historical cost	C	H	H	C
• Market price	C	H	C	C
Fixed assets	H	H	H	C
Liabilities				
Current payables	C	C	C	C
Long-term debt	H	C	C	C
Equity	Residual	Residual	Residual	Residual

Notes: C ⇒ Item is translated at current exchange rate (i.e., exposed to exchange risk).

           H ⇒ Item is translated at historic exchange rate (i.e., not exposed to exchange risk).

Equity account may include translation gains and losses as required by the accounting standard-setting body.

likely come from the treatment of long-term debt, which for many companies is a large part of their capital structure.

Consider the situation of Marriott Hotels, a large, U.S.-based public corporation. Suppose that Marriott had purchased a hotel in Frankfurt, Germany, for DM100 million (equivalent to about $35 million) in 1973. Very likely, the hotel purchase would have been financed with DM. As the DM appreciated in the 1970s toward $0.40/DM, $0.45/DM, and so on, how would we assess the situation at the Frankfurt Marriott?

On the one hand, it is true that the cost of retiring the DM100 million long-term debt has increased when measured in US$ terms. A DM liability exposure represents an added cost when the DM strengthens. On the other hand, if the hotel remains profitable despite the strong DM, then it generates enough DM to service the DM debt. And the hotel is left with DM profits—a very favorable event given the greater US$ value of the DM. We expect that Marriott would have preferred the current/noncurrent approach for measuring the currency exposure in its German operation because the liability exposure associated with the monetary/nonmonetary approach does not correspond to the economic cash flows of the project.

After 1976, the Financial Accounting Standards Board (FASB) adopted Statement No. 8 (FASB-8), which eliminated choice and required firms to employ the **temporal method** for measuring balance sheet exposure. The temporal method instituted "time consistency": the valuation date of a balance sheet item determined the valuation date for an exchange rate.[4] Since monetary items are usually valued as of the balance sheet

---

[4]For example, on a December 31 balance sheet, inventories valued at their historical cost (as of June 30) would use the June 30 exchange rate. But inventories valued at a lower market price (as of December 31) would use the December 31 exchange rate.

date, the temporal method corresponded closely to the monetary/nonmonetary approach (see Table 16.2). Therefore, firms that had elected the current/noncurrent approach prior to 1976 saw a dramatic swing in the accounting measure of their foreign exchange exposure under the temporal method.

Dissatisfaction with FASB-8 (for reasons we will explore shortly) led to another revision in 1981. Under FASB-52, which remains the standard for U.S. accounting, all U.S. firms are required to adopt the **all-current, or closing-rate, method.** This system is the easiest to remember because it classifies all foreign currency denominated balance sheet items as exposed (see Table 16.2).

However, FASB-52 also introduced another feature into exposure measurement that addressed the situation described in our Marriott Hotel example. In that example, we assumed that the financing for the hotel was in DM. But other expenses for administration and operations were probably paid in DM, and hotel revenues also were collected in DM. When the bulk of the transactions related to the Frankfurt hotel are denominated in DM, Marriott must adopt the DM as the **functional currency** for its German operation.

Under the functional currency provisions, the U.S. parent prepares the accounting statements of the German subsidiary *in DM* using the temporal approach. The parent's equity stake in the German subsidiary is then translated at the current rate back into the parent's balance statement. So, if the Frankfurt Marriott were profitable, its owner's equity account tends to increase in terms of DM. The stronger DM then makes the Frankfurt hotel a more valuable asset to its U.S. parent. This treatment corresponds more closely with the economic advantage of holding income-producing assets in strong currency countries.

Along the same lines, FASB-52 also mandates a functional currency approach for countries with high inflation. In those locations, it is likely that many operations are conducted in a third currency (often the US$), or transactions in the home currency are indexed to changes in the local currency/US$ exchange rate.

Exposure of the Income Statement: Transaction Exposure

Transaction exposure focuses on the economic value of foreign currency denominated transactions that are planned or forecast to occur within the next reporting period and therefore will be realized in the firm's next income statement. As such, transaction exposure is more forward looking and cash flow oriented. However, it is still limited to those transactions within a planning period and is unlikely to take dynamic considerations into account.

In general, the rules for translating foreign currency transactions under FASB-52 and FASB-8 are similar. A foreign currency transaction (that is, a transaction in a currency other than the entity's functional currency) is recorded at the exchange rate in effect on the date of the transaction.[5] Any variation between the exchange rate on the transaction date and the exchange rate on (1) the settlement date or (2) the prior balance sheet date gives rise to transaction gains and losses. These gains and losses reflect realized amounts and are reported in current income.

For example, consider Gateway Computer, a U.S. company that has a manufacturing facility in Ireland. Suppose that Gateway pays its employees every two weeks in euros and that these payments are arranged two days in advance to coincide with settlement conditions in the foreign exchange market. Since the transaction date and the

---

[5]For transactions that take place continuously, such as receipts from foreign sales or payments to foreign employees, an average exchange rate may be used.

settlement date are identical, there is no foreign exchange gain or loss associated with this transaction.

Now assume that Gateway has signed a lease with a Danish firm to use a fleet of trucks in Europe for 350,000 Danish krone per month for three years.[6] The capitalized value of this lease is shown on the December 31 balance sheet of Gateway in € terms. As the monthly payments are made, any variation in the actual exchange rate (DKr/€) at time of the transaction and the rate on December 31 would be treated as a transaction gain or loss. The same approach would apply to a capitalized asset if Gateway, for example, had leased 100 personal computers to a British bank for £20,000 per month for three years. As the monthly payments are received by Gateway, any variation in the actual exchange rate (£/€) at the time of the transaction and the rate on December 31 is considered a transaction gain or loss.

U.S. Accounting Conventions: Reporting Accounting Gains and Losses

The method for *calculating* accounting gains and losses and the method for *reporting* them within the accounting statements have been treated as separate issues. Some of the major provisions of FASB-8 and FASB-52 are summarized in Table 16.3.

Translation Gains and Losses.   Perhaps the most controversial requirement of FASB-8 was the provision that *all* foreign exchange gains and losses, including *translation* gains and losses, had to be included in current income. Under FASB-8, long-term foreign currency debt became an exposed item. As the US$ depreciated against most currencies in 1976, 1977, and 1978, U.S. firms with debt denominated in foreign currency incurred substantial foreign exchange translation losses, all of which were carried to the bottom line and reported in current income. For some companies, the impact was especially dramatic. Exxon Corporation reported translation losses of $258 million for 1976 and more than $500 million in 1977.

However, as our discussion of the Marriott Hotel example showed, a company with foreign currency debt might actually be *favorably* affected by a weak US$. If the firm generates enough foreign currency income to service its debt and return a profit to the parent, in a cash flow sense the firm is really *long* foreign currency and benefits from a weak US$.

This was essentially the argument taken by Exxon and many other U.S. companies in this period. These companies declined to hedge their (short foreign currency) accounting exposure. Instead, they took the hit to accounting earnings, under the belief that they had a neutral, or perhaps long, cash flow exposure in foreign currencies. Clearly this stance required a careful explanation to financial analysts and investors. Exxon explained its decision in the company's 1977 annual report:

> The corporation recognizes that its reported earnings are susceptible to substantial volatility from the effects of currency changes under the prescribed translation procedures. However, it is Exxon's policy to base its financial decisions on fundamental long-term economic considerations rather than on the impact which short-term fluctuations have on reported earnings.[7]

---

[6]Recall that Denmark currently is not a member of the European Monetary Union and retains its own currency, the Danish krone (DKr).

[7]Exxon Corporation, 1977 annual report, p. 7.

TABLE 16.3 Comparison of Principle Provisions of FASB-8 and FASB-52

Provision	*FASB-8*	*FASB-52*
Translation method	Temporal method	Current rate method
Functional currency	Concept not used	The currency of the primary economic environment in which the entity operates
Translation in highly inflationary economies	Generally not a serious problem under temporal method	Requires remeasurement as if functional currency were the reporting currency (essentially, implies the temporal method)
Adjustments resulting from the translation of foreign currency statements	Reported currently in income	Accumulated as a separate component of equity (translation adjustment)
Realization of the separate component of equity	Not applicable	Upon sale or upon (substantially) complete liquidation of the investment
Gains and losses from foreign currency transactions	Reported currently in income	Reported currently in income
Conditions for a hedge of an identifiable foreign currency commitment	Forward exchange contract: • Extends from the commitment date to or beyond the transaction date • Denominated in the same currency as the foreign currency commitment • Commitment is firm and cannot be canceled	Forward exchange or other foreign currency transaction: • Designated as a hedge any time during commitment period • Denominated in the same currency as the foreign currency commitment, or a currency that moves "in tandem" • Commitment is firm
Gains and losses on transactions that hedge a net investment	Reported currently in income	Reported separately and included with translation adjustments in the separate component of equity
Gains and losses on intercompany transactions	Reported currently in income	Accumulated as a separate component of equity when deemed a long-term investment; otherwise reported in current income

Source: Adapted from Peat, Marwick Mitchell & Co. (1981).

Under FASB-52, translation gains and losses are not reported in current income. Instead, they are accumulated in a separate component of equity called the **translation adjustment account.** The change seems logical in that translation gains and losses have not been realized. Further, if translation gains and losses tend to balance out over time, it is sensible to exclude them from any measure of current income from ongoing operations.

Moreover, with the introduction of the functional currency approach, FASB-52 focuses on a parent's net investment in a foreign operation to measure the effect of exchange rate changes. Thus, when the DM appreciates, a profitable subsidiary in Germany adds to the parent's equity stake. Or if the £ depreciates, a profitable subsidiary in England could result in a lower US$ equity interest.[8]

With the treatment under FASB-52, a parent might elect to hedge its *net investment position* in a subsidiary. Net investment positions in profitable subsidiaries are positive

---

[8]In its 1992 annual report, Coca-Cola reported the use of "approximately (sic) 42 functional currencies" in the preparation of its accounts.

and increasing. Thus, a hedge transaction amounts to a sale of the foreign currency investment position. Gains and losses on the hedge transaction are also accumulated in the translation adjustment account.

Transaction Gains and Losses.   Transaction gains and losses represent *realized* exchanges. These have traditionally been reported in current income, but as a separate "unusual" item if they are significant.

FASB-52 introduced a more liberal definition of a hedging transaction (See Table 16.4). To return to our Gateway Computer example, suppose that Gateway decides to hedge its £20,000 per month receivable with a strip of 36 £/€ forward contracts. As time passes, the mark-to-market value of the remaining forward contracts changes. If each forward contract is a dedicated hedge to each monthly receivable, Gateway may defer the gain or loss on the forward contract until the monthly lease revenue is received.

Reporting Gains and Losses on Derivatives.   A new FASB Statement (No. 133, "Accounting for Derivative Instruments and Hedging Activities") becomes effective for corporations with fiscal years beginning after June 15, 2000. The simple purpose of this complex statement is to require companies to report the mark-to-market value of their derivative transactions, and to require them to allocate the unrealized gain or loss on derivatives into either current income, or a new category of deferred income called other comprehensive income (OCI).

To qualify for hedge accounting under FASB-133, a company must identify an exposure and link it with a clearly identified derivative instrument. FASB-133 allows for three types of hedges:

- Fair value hedges—designed to hedge the change in value of a recognized asset or liability.
- Cash flow hedges—designed to hedge changes in future cash flows of a recognized asset or liability.
- Net investment hedges—designed to hedge changes in the net investment value of a foreign operation.

The net investment hedge is a holdover from FASB-52, and is related only to currency exposure. Derivatives that do not qualify as hedges of underlying exposures must be marked to market, with gains or losses included in current income.

By requiring firms to report the current value of their derivatives positions at "fair value," FASB-133 attempts to introduce greater transparency into to a firm's use of derivatives. Furthermore, FASB-133 clarifies which transactions qualify as an acceptable hedge, and how to treat any unexpected gain or loss if the hedge is not "effective" (meaning that a $1 gain/loss on an exposure is *not* offset by precisely a $1 loss/gain on the associated derivative transaction). Under FASB-52, a company might have an ineffective or imprecise hedge but still be allowed to use hedge accounting and defer all gains or losses in the translation adjustment account. With FASB-133, a firm must document the effectiveness of its hedge transactions. "Small" gains or losses from lack of perfect hedging effectiveness are included in the firm's OCI. However, "large" gains or losses resulting from the unusual or ineffective portion of the hedge become part of current income.

When judging the prospective effectiveness of a hedge, FASB will give the firm wide latitude in its choice of statistical methods.[9] However, when judging the realized

---

[9]See International Treasurer, *FAS 133: The Final Countdown,* 2000, p. 8.

effectiveness of a hedge on an ongoing basis, companies must use the dollar-offset method, that is, measuring how much of the change in value of the underlying exposure was offset by the change in value of the hedge position. A hedge must be at least 80 percent effective to quality for hedge accounting treatment under FAS 133.[10]

Economic Logic of Accounting Conventions

Accounting conventions may appear ad hoc, but they can be consistent with economic relationships. Two of the parity conditions introduced earlier are useful to demonstrate this.[11]

Consider first the purchasing power parity (PPP) condition. When PPP holds, the real exchange rate is constant. The relative price of a firm's products is unchanged, so the firm's real revenues and real costs are also unchanged. It follows that the market value of real assets is unaffected by nominal exchange rate changes that leave the real rate unaffected.

Thus, when PPP holds, the real value of real assets is preserved and accounting rules should treat *nonmonetary* assets as not exposed. If PPP holds only in the long run, this supports a *current/noncurrent* classification on real assets.

Now consider the International Fisher Effect. When International Fisher holds, we observe that the extra cost of paying off debts in strong currencies is offset exactly by the lower interest cost on the debt, and the capital loss on holding assets in weak currencies is offset exactly by the higher interest paid on the asset. Foreign exchange gains and losses on monetary assets and liabilities are illusory in the sense that they ignore the impact of higher (or lower) interest payments on the foreign amounts.

When International Fisher holds, the value of monetary assets and liabilities is preserved whether they are held in domestic or foreign currency units. Thus, accounting rules should treat *monetary* assets as not exposed. If International Fisher holds only in the long run, then this supports a *current/noncurrent* classification on monetary assets.

Economic Measures of Foreign Exchange Exposure

An economic measure of foreign exchange exposure captures *more* than the combination of effects on balance sheet items (translation exposure) and on planned transactions (transaction exposure). Economic exposure captures the entire range of effects on the future cash flows of the firms, including the effects of exchange rate changes on customers, suppliers, and competitors. Our earlier definition of exposure, $\partial MV/\partial S$, reflects economic exposure. We first offer a discussion of the regression approach, followed by the scenario approach.

The Regression Approach: The Basic Model

The regression approach is the most appealing method for measuring economic exposure.[12] The regression approach directly measures the exposure of a firm to exchange

---

[10]See "Special Report on Financial Accounting Standard 133," *Risk,* May 2000, Supplement, p. 14.

[11]Aliber and Stickney (1975) develop the linkage between PPP, the Fisher International Effect, and accounting conventions.

[12]The regression approach was proposed by Adler and Dumas (1984). See also Hekman (1983) and Cornell and Shapiro (1983).

rate changes by estimating the relationship between the firm's market value at time t (MV_t) and the spot rate (S_t) using the equation:

$$MV_t = a + b\, S_t + e_t \tag{16.8}$$

To estimate the exposure of the firm to \$/€ rate changes, we would run the regression:

$$MV_t = a + b_1\, S_{\$/€,t} + e_t \tag{16.9}$$

The coefficient b_1 measures the sensitivity of the market value of the firm to the \$/€ exchange rate. Since the market value of our firm is denominated in US\$, it should be clear that the dimensions of b_1 must be in €. This coincides with the definition in Michael Adler and Bernard Dumas (1984) that *exposure is an amount of foreign currency* that represents the sensitivity of the real value of the firm to random variations in the exchange rate.

To interpret the regression analysis, we need to examine three results: the magnitude of b_1, the t-statistic of b_1, and the R^2 of the regression. First, a positive b_1 corresponds to an asset exposure in € since the market value of the firm rises with the €, while a negative b_1 implies a liability exposure. A zero value for b_1 implies that there is no exposure to the \$/€ rate.

Second, if b_1 is not statistically significant, then we have little confidence that the relationship between the market value and the exchange rate is systematic. Last but not least in importance, the R^2 measures the percentage of variation in market value explained by the exchange rate. Thus, b_1 might be large and significant, but if the R^2 is small (say, 1 percent or 3 percent) then variation in the \$/€ exchange rate is responsible for only a small part of variability in the firm's market value. In other words, other factors appear to explain the great bulk of market value variation.

Let us review an example using the regression approach. Suppose that we have data on the market value of firm XYZ and the \$/€ exchange rate for 19 months from January 1999 to July 2000 as shown in Figure 16.1. Using these data, we find that the estimated value of b_1 is 5,093 (and statistically significant) representing a €5,093 exposed asset position. The regression equation predicts that the market value of firm XYZ goes up and down with the exchange rate *as if* the firm held a €5,093 net asset position. The regression results also show that the \$/€ exchange rate explains about 41.6 percent of the variation in the market value of firm XYZ over this period.

These regression results are powerful because they have an immediate policy implication; namely, if firm XYZ had held a *short* €5,093 over this 19 month period, it would have reduced the variability in its market value in this example by 41.6 percent.[13] The market value of the firm would have varied considerably from month to month, but none of the variability would have been related (statistically) to the \$/€ exchange rate. Thus, the negative of the regression coefficient ($-b_1$) represents a **foreign exchange hedge position;** that is, a foreign exchange position that will eliminate the firm's exposure to foreign exchange risk.

The Regression Approach: An Application

In Table 16.4, we summarize the results of an analysis by Maurice Levi (1994) for the Canadian paper and forest products industry. This industry offers a good example because roughly 70 percent of Canada's paper output and more than 80 percent of lumber is exported. Overall, 80 percent of Canadian exports are to the United States.

---

[13]In Figure 16.1, we note that the variance of the firm's market value was 291,478. After taking account of the exchange rate, the variance of the residuals is 170,223, or 58.4 percent of the original amount.

FIGURE 16.1   **Market Value of Firm XYZ and $/Euro Rate**

Monthly Data: January 1999–July 2000

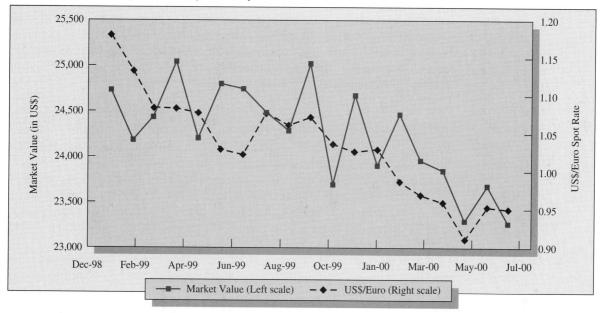

Regression results: Market value$_t = a + b\, S_{\$/€,t} + e_t$

	a	b
Coefficient	18,985	5,093
Standard error	1,516	1,464
T-value	12.5	3.5

Standard error of regression	424.5	Number of observations	19
R^2	0.416	Degrees of freedom	17

Variance of market value	291,478	100.0%
Variance of residuals (e)	170,223	58.4
Variance of fitted values	121,255	41.6

Source: Data on spot exchange rates are from Federal Reserve Board of Governors. Data on market values were simulated by the author.

TABLE 16.4   **The Regression Approach to Estimating Exposure to Foreign Exchange Risk**

An Example from the Canadian Forest Products Industry

Equation	Constant	Interest Rate	Market Return	Foreign Exchange Rates			R^2	Durbin-Watson
				C$/US$	C$/£	C$/¥		
A	−0.0052		1.1051	0.0002	−0.3081	0.5820	0.64	1.87
	(0.60)		(17.08)	(0.23)	(2.17)	(4.24)		
B	−0.0039	0.0001		0.2459	−0.2727	0.5841	0.11	1.83
	(0.44)	(0.16)		(0.74)	(1.93)	(4.23)		

Note: Results are based on 188 monthly observations from January 1970 to August 1985. The dependent variable is the return on the paper and forest products index of the Toronto Stock Exchange. Exchange rate changes are measured in real terms, adjusting for the relevant inflation differential. The interest rate is the three-month Canadian Treasury bill rate, and the market index is for the Toronto Stock Exchange. *T*-values are in parentheses.

Source: Maurice D. Levi, "Exchange Rates and the Valuation of Firms," in *Exchange Rates and Corporate Performance,* ed. Y. Amihud and R. Levich (Burr Ridge, IL: Richard D. Irwin, 1994), pp. 37–48.

Equation B reveals that shares of Canadian forest product companies are not exposed to the C\$/US\$ exchange rate. There is exposure to the C\$/£, but in an unexpected way—a 1.0 percent depreciation of the C\$ against the £ tends to lower returns by 0.27 percent. Exposure against the ¥ is significant and takes on the expected sign. Overall, foreign exchange rate changes explain about 11 percent of the variation in equity rates of return. Equation A shows essentially the same results for the exchange rate variables; the coefficient on the market return represents the "beta" for this industry group and captures much more variation in equity returns.

Levi notes that his results have several interpretations. The insignificant coefficient on the C\$/US\$ could imply that Canadian forest industry firms bear no exposure to the US\$. Alternatively, the result could be saying that Canadian forest industry firms have successfully hedged their exposure to the US\$, using financial or operational techniques. Still another interpretation is that currency exposure exists, but investors and stock analysts are unaware of it and do not efficiently adjust share prices in response to exchange rate changes. Levi observes that Canadian firms typically hedge their US\$ exposure, so that successful hedging could explain the insignificant US\$ coefficient. Similarly, Levi feels that hedging against the ¥ was uncommon during the sample period, which may account for the significant coefficient against the C\$/¥.

Levi's analysis shows the difficulty for outside analysts to draw conclusions about exposure and market behavior if we do not also have information about the firm's hedging activities. Equity returns may be insensitive to exchange rate changes because (1) there is no natural exposure or (2) firms have taken offsetting financial contracts to neutralize their currency exposure.

The Regression Approach: Three Extensions

In regression equation (16.9) we used a single exchange rate. To measure the firm's exposure to other exchange rates, a multiple regression could be estimated, such as:

$$MV_t = a + b_1 S_{\$/\unicode{x20AC},t} + b_2 S_{\$/\unicode{xA3},t} + b_3 S_{\$/\unicode{xA5},t} + e_t \qquad (16.10)$$

Each regression coefficient represents the firm's exposure in the respective currency unit. As before, the negative of each regression coefficient represents a foreign exchange hedge position.

If the firm has data on cash flows at the level of a subsidiary or project, the exposure of these smaller units could also be measured using regression analysis. The regression equation then becomes:

$$CF_t = a + b_1 S_{\$/\unicode{x20AC},t} + e_t \qquad (16.11)$$

where CF represents the cash flows. Managers may prefer this approach because it allows a direct analysis of exchange rate changes and corporate cash flows. Analyzing cash flows directly avoids having to assume that financial analysts correctly make the link between exchange rates and the market value of the firm, but it requires more detailed information that may not be available in all cases.

A third extension to the regression approach is measuring long-run exposure. By increasing the observation interval from one month, to one year, to five years, and so forth, we may find that exposure is lower in the long run. The intuition for this result follows from PPP (which tends to hold better in the longer run) and the ability for firms to make real operating adjustments in response to exchange rate changes. Recent evidence from Kenneth Froot (1993) seems to support the notion that exposure to real exchange rate changes is indeed lower at very long horizons.

The Scenario Approach

A scenario is a detailed set of assumptions concerning how the firm (and its suppliers, customers, and competitors) will respond conditional on a change in the path of an exchange rate. Given a scenario, we can estimate the firm's cash flows (and its market value) conditional on an exchange rate path. The scenario approach is well suited to a spreadsheet analysis where one is encouraged to ask a variety of "what-if" questions. The spreadsheet software then allows the user to estimate the value of the firm based on a particular scenario and conditional on an exchange rate path.

An example will help to illustrate the scenario approach. Assume that a U.S. firm manufactures kitchen food processors, half of which are sold in the United States and the remainder exported to Australia. Suppose that all fixed costs and 80 percent of variable costs are incurred in the United States and the remaining costs represent parts imported from Canada and Australia. Business has been very good—the firm sold 100,000 units in the United States at an average price of US$150 per unit and another 100,000 in Australia at an average price of A$240 per unit (with the average exchange rate at US$0.6250/A$).

The firm expects sales to grow at 5 percent per year, with price increases averaging 4 percent in the United States and 2 percent in Australia in line with inflation. The US$/A$ exchange rate is assumed to follow purchasing power parity, so the US$ is expected to depreciate at about 2 percent a year. The firm uses a 17.5 percent discount rate to value future cash flows. With these assumptions, we see in Figure 16.2 that the present value of future operating cash flows is US$39.577 million. These assumptions establish the *base case* scenario.[14]

To examine how the value of this firm is affected by an exchange rate change, consider the impact of a permanent 5 percent appreciation of the US$, *holding all other factors constant*. To implement this change, we divide the period zero exchange rate by 1.05.[15] The present value of cash flows falls to US$35.222 million, reflecting the fact that Australian sales now equate to fewer US$ revenues, although the cost of imported inputs has also declined somewhat. We can repeat the calculation with permanent US$ appreciations of 10 percent, 15 percent, 20 percent, and so on—each one corresponding to a lower present value of operating cash flows—and permanent US$ depreciation of 5 percent, 10 percent, 15 percent, and so on—each one corresponding to a higher present value of operating cash flows.

The solid curve in Figure 16.2 traces the present value of the firm's cash flows under the base case scenario (A) and different assumptions about the US$/A$ exchange rate. The curvature of the solid line (AOA^*) immediately indicates the presence of exchange rate exposure, since the present value of future cash flows varies along with the exchange rate *under scenario A*. To estimate the exposure of the firm, we rely on the definition of exposure, $\partial MV/\partial S$, replacing MV with the present value of cash flows. The slope of the solid line at point O in Figure 16.2 measures the exposure of the firm at the initial exchange rate.[16]

---

[14]For more details of the calculation, see Appendix 16.1.

[15]We multiply the US$/A$ exchange rate by $(1 + x)$ to show an x percent depreciation of the US$, and divide the US$/A$ exchange rate by $(1 + y)$ to show a y percent appreciation of the US$.

[16]To measure the slope in the context of a spreadsheet, allow the exchange rate to change by a small amount (say 1.0 percent) in either direction. The average change in present value divided by the exchange rate change (say 1.0 percent) measures the slope. Using this technique, the exposure is about A$144,560 (See Appendix 16.1).

FIGURE 16.2   The Scenario Approach to Estimating Exchange Rate Exposure: An Example

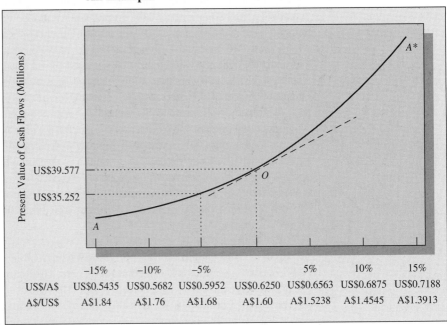

	−15%	−10%	−5%		5%	10%	15%
US$/A$	US$0.5435	US$0.5682	US$0.5952	US$0.6250	US$0.6563	US$0.6875	US$0.7188
A$/US$	A$1.84	A$1.76	A$1.68	A$1.60	A$1.5238	A$1.4545	A$1.3913

The Scenario Approach: Some Extensions

In our base case scenario (A), the firm suffers a decline in value as the US$ strengthens against the A$. Now consider a new scenario (B) where the firm is able to increase the A$ price of its food processors by 0.5 percent for every 1.0 percent decrease in the value of the A$. Suppose further that under scenario B the firm suffers no decline in sales volume following the decision to *pass through* 50 percent of the exchange rate change into the local sales price. Naturally, the firm is better off if the Australian customer bears some of the cost of the weak A$. We see this improvement in Figure 16.3 with the locus of cash flows marked *BO*.

How will the firm respond if the US$ weakens from the initial US$0.625 rate? For certain, the firm would like to keep its unit prices in Australia at the original A$240 level. If it succeeds, the line *BOA** traces the present value of cash flows. But as the US$ devalues, the firm may come under pressure to reduce its A$ prices. The reasoning is simple and takes us back to the **Law of One Price.**

If the US$ declines by 10 percent, an Australian tourist or importer could purchase a food processor in the United States for US$150, which equates to A$218.18 (=$150 × 1.4545 A$/US$). The firm must effectively *segment* the markets and successfully *price discriminate* to keep the U.S. price at US$150/unit and the Australian price at A$240/unit given the new exchange rate (recall Box 4.2). If the firm cannot maintain its A$240/unit price, it must pass through to consumers some of the benefits of a stronger A$, thus lowering the firm's value relative to the base case. Under scenario B with a 50 percent pass-through of both stronger and weaker exchange rates, the value of the firm is traced by the curve *BOB**.

Notice that the slope of *BOB** is flatter than *AOA** in the base case. This indicates that the firm has less exposure under scenario B than in scenario A. Under scenario B,

FIGURE 16.3   The Scenario Approach to Estimating Exchange Rate Exposure: Assuming 50 Percent Exchange Rate Pass-Through

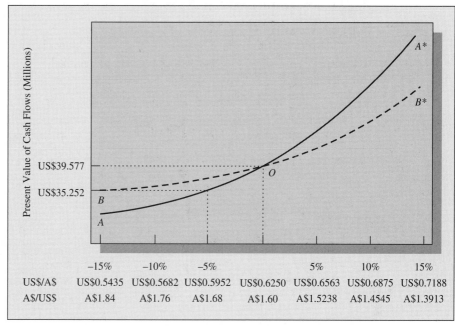

	–15%	–10%	–5%		5%	10%	15%
US$/A$	US$0.5435	US$0.5682	US$0.5952	US$0.6250	US$0.6563	US$0.6875	US$0.7188
A$/US$	A$1.84	A$1.76	A$1.68	A$1.60	A$1.5238	A$1.4545	A$1.3913

we assumed that the firm can pass along part of the exchange rate change to Australian customers, who now bear part of the exposure to exchange rate risk.

Imagine a final scenario (C) where *all* of the exchange rate change was passed along to the final customers, and the volume of sales is unaffected. If this were the case, then the value of the firm would flatten out still further as indicated in Figure 16.4 with curve *COC**. Under scenario C, the firm bears little exposure to exchange risk.[17] With full exchange rate pass-through, the firm is effectively using its domestic currency as the **invoice currency** for its product. In other words, the firm has set a price of US$150/unit and the Australian price is determined by taking US$150 times the A$/US$ exchange rate.

All of the scenarios we have discussed could be embellished further by allowing for nonzero price elasticity of demand, thereby permitting the quantity of goods sold to vary as a function of the change in local prices. Similar modifications could be made to the firm's cost structure of imported inputs.

These scenarios have shown that the ability to pass through adverse exchange rate movements onto local prices provides a **natural hedge,** in other words, a reduction in variability of cash flows that comes from the "normal way" the firm does business. We also have shown that if the firm can segment its market, and charge higher prices when the US$ weakens but pass through exchange rate changes when the US$ strengthens, its value curve develops a "kinked" shape resembling that of an option contract.

Empirical Evidence on Firm Profits, Share Prices, and Exchange Rates

The link between volatility in exchange rates and U.S. corporate profits in manufacturing was examined by Juann Hung (1993, 1995). Using data for the floating-rate period,

---

[17]The remaining exposure in this case is the variable cost of imported inputs.

FIGURE 16.4   The Scenario Approach to Estimating Exchange Rate Exposure:
Assuming Complete Exchange Rate Pass-Through

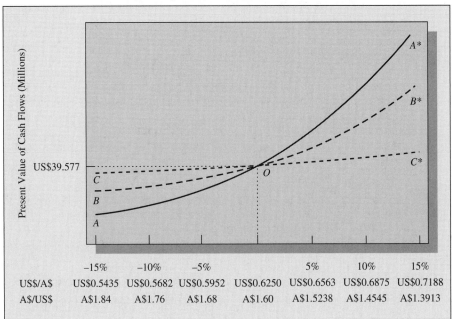

	−15%	−10%	−5%		5%	10%	15%
US$/A$	US$0.5435	US$0.5682	US$0.5952	US$0.6250	US$0.6563	US$0.6875	US$0.7188
A$/US$	A$1.84	A$1.76	A$1.68	A$1.60	A$1.5238	A$1.4545	A$1.3913

she found that a 1 percent US$ appreciation was associated with a 0.6 percent decline in
U.S. manufacturing profits and a 0.94 percent decline in the overseas profits of U.S.
firms. Hung (1993) estimated that over the decade of the 1980s, the strong US$ cost
U.S. firms $22.6 billion annually (or 10 percent of their manufacturing profits) and an-
other $5.5 billion annually in overseas profits. In the peak years of US$ appreciation
(1984–1986), Hung estimated that the exchange rate move cost U.S. firms $93 billion,
or 12 percent of their net corporate profits. These estimates suggest that exchange rate
changes can have a substantial impact on the overall U.S. economy, one that could be
more significant for individual firms and smaller countries.

An early analysis of exchange rate changes and share prices was prepared by Ian
Giddy (1974), who analyzed 18 official exchange rate changes during the Bretton
Woods pegged-rate period. Giddy found that the general stock market index tended to
move up (down) immediately after a devaluation (revaluation) of the local currency.
Export- and import-oriented industries showed more pronounced price changes follow-
ing the exchange rate announcement.

More recently, Philippe Jorion (1990) analyzed the exchange rate exposure of 287
U.S. multinational firms with large foreign operations.[18] Jorion estimated a regression
equation like:

$$R_{i,t} - R_{F,t} = \beta_{0,i} + \beta_{1,i}(R_{M,t} - R_{F,t}) + \beta_{2,i}PCXR_t + \epsilon_t \qquad (16.12)$$

---

[18]The basic notion of exposure as a sensitivity measure, $\partial MV/\partial S$ in equation 16.8, suggests that
researchers examine the relationship between changes in the firm's market value (a rate of return) and
changes in the exchange rate holding other factors constant. A regression of total returns on the stock versus
the exchange rate change captures this basic idea. A regression of excess returns on an individual firm ($R_{i,t}$
$- R_{F,t}$) against excess returns on the market ($R_{M,t} - R_{F,t}$) as well as the exchange rate change reflects the
desire to control for other common factors.

where $R_{i,t}$, $R_{M,t}$, and $R_{F,t}$ are the returns on the ith firm, the market and the risk-free rate at time t, respectively, and $PCXR_t$ is a variable representing the percentage change in the exchange rate. The coefficient $\beta_{2,i}$ measures the marginal impact of an exchange rate change on the firm's excess return. Jorion estimated this regression with data for 1971–1987 and found that only 15 firms had significant exposure coefficients. This is not strong evidence in favor of exposure because 15 is roughly the number of significant coefficients that one would expect by chance in a sample of 287.

Gordon Bodnar and William Gentry (1993) estimated an equation similar to equation (16.12) for industries in the United States, Canada, and Japan over the 1979–1988 period. The results show that $\beta_{2,i}$ is significant in 22 of the 78 industries examined. Even though $\beta_{2,i}$ is not significant in many individual industries, a joint test that *all* $\beta_{2,i}$ are zero is strongly rejected. Moreover, the average size of the $\beta_{2,i}$ coefficients tends to be larger for industries in Canada and Japan, which have smaller, more open economies than in the United States.

Two studies found little evidence of exposure at the individual firm level. Yakov Amihud (1994) examined the largest U.S. exporting firms and found no significant contemporaneous exposure. However, lagged exchange rate changes were sometimes significant. Eli Bartov and Gordon Bodnar (1994) examined a sample of U.S. firms with the largest accounting measures of exposure. Again, these authors found no contemporaneous relationship between exchange rate changes and excess equity market returns for these firms. But they confirmed that lagged exchange rate changes were significant. Indeed, the authors developed a trading rule whereby past changes in the dollar can be used to predict abnormal stock returns around the earnings announcement in the subsequent quarter. This finding implies that analysts do not fully use the information in past exchange rate changes when predicting a firm's future earnings.

More recently, George Allayannis (1996) has argued that several methodological problems may explain the failure to find significant contemporaneous correlation between exchange rate changes and excess returns at the firm level. For example, screening firms on the basis of their accounting exposure, level of export activity, or level of multinational operations may not isolate those firms that have the greatest *economic* exposure to exchange risk. Similarly, unless all firms within an industry or portfolio have similar exposures to exchange risk, analyzing industries or portfolios may mask the exposure of individual firms.

To address these issues, Allayannis investigated a sample of firms with the largest *net* exports-to-sales ratio and *net* imports-to-sales ratio. He found that significant exposure to exchange rate changes exists, but that exposure coefficients vary from firm to firm within the same industry and over time. Controlling for size, less mature firms in an industry appear more exposed to changes in exchange rates than mature firms. This may indicate that hedging procedures and effectiveness are enhanced as a firm gains experience in understanding its exposure.

Arguments for Hedging Risks at the Corporate Level

In the classical theory of finance, corporate managers run the firm as *agents* on behalf of shareholders, who are assumed to be risk averse. Managers, however, are directed by shareholders to manage the firm in a risk-neutral manner, seeking profit maximization without regard to risk. Shareholders prefer this system because they are assumed to operate in a perfect capital market without transaction costs or taxes. Shareholders, in this view, should not favor hedging because they can select well-diversified portfolios

---

Box 16.1

Why Debt Holders Prefer Hedging and Equity Holders Do Not

Consider a firm that is exposed to foreign exchange risk, so that the value of the firm depends on the spot US$/Swiss franc exchange rate. We show this in the figure below for a firm with $1.0 million in debt financing and a market value that depends positively on the spot rate in $/SFr terms. When the spot rate is $0.40, the value of the firm is $600,000; debt holders collect $600,000 ($D_0$) toward the face value of their debt and shareholders receive zero (E_0). When the spot rate is $0.60, the value of the firm is $1.4 million; debt holders collect $1 million ($D_1$) to retire their debt and shareholders receive $400,000 ($E_1$).

Assume that the value of the spot rate today is $0.50/SFr and with equal probability, the spot rate will be either $0.40/SFr or $0.60/SFr in the next period. Thus, the expected exchange rate, $E(S_{t+1})$, is $0.50/SFr and equal to the forward rate.

Let's examine the classical incentives to hedge or not hedge for debt holders and equity holders. If the firm does not hedge, debt holders will either receive $600,000 ($D_0$) if S_{t+1} is $0.40, or $1 million ($D_1$) if S_{t+1} is $0.60. For the debt holders, the expected value of not hedging is $800,000

(D_{NH}). On the other hand, if the firm hedges at the forward rate, debt holders are assured of $1 million ($D_H$). For risk-averse debt holders, it is clear that the cash flows associated with hedging (D_H) represent greater utility than the cash flows associated with not hedging (D_{NH}).

The incentives are the reverse for equity holders. If the firm does not hedge, equity holders receive zero (E_0) if S_{t+1} is $0.40, or $400,000 ($E_1$) if S_{t+1} is $0.60. For equity holders, the expected value of not hedging is $200,000 ($E_{NH}$). On the other hand, if the firm hedges and secures a forward rate equal to $0.50, equity holders are assured of zero (E_H). For equity holders (even those who are risk averse), it is clear that the cash flows associated with not hedging (E_{NH}) represent greater utility than the cash flows associated with hedging (E_H).

It is well known that the interests of debt holders and equity holders are in conflict. This example illustrates that risk-averse debt holders will generally prefer the firm to hedge its diversifiable foreign exchange risks, while equity holders will not.

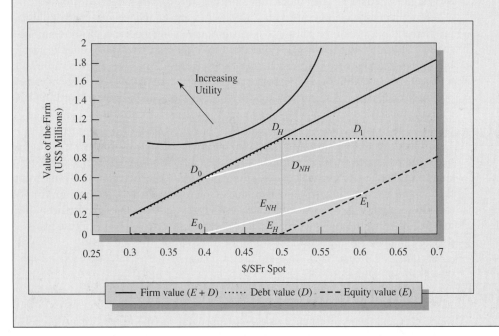

to rid themselves of firm-specific risks, and reach their desired level of exposure to corporate and currency risks. In contrast, risk-averse managers may prefer to hedge risks to maximize their own utility. And debt holders also may prefer corporate hedging to maximize their utility. We show the logic behind these conclusions in Box 16.1.

FIGURE 16.5   Variability of Cash Flows over Time with and without Hedging

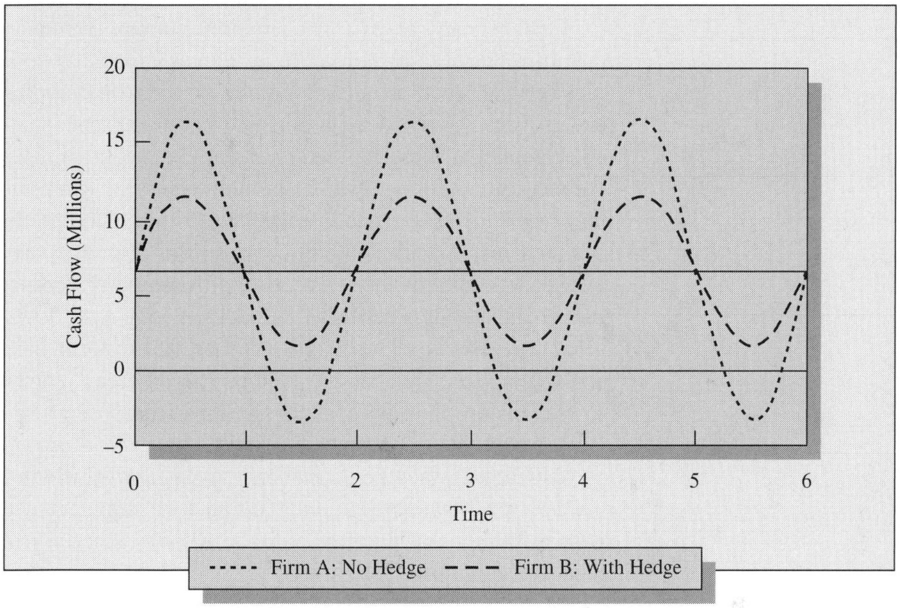

Note: Simulated data for firms with identical average cash flows.

In a perfect capital market, Modigliani and Miller showed that the financial policies of the firm are irrelevant because the shareholder can recreate or undo whatever financial decisions the firm has made.[19] Logically, corporate financial policy choices become important when transaction costs and taxes enter the analysis.[20]

In Figure 16.5, we show two firms with the same average cash flows ($\mu_A = \mu_B$) but different volatility of cash flows ($\sigma_A > \sigma_B$). The question is whether market values differ for firms A and B. In other words, can hedging that reduces the volatility of cash flows have an impact on the market value of a firm?

Corporate taxes offer one reason to prefer a less volatile pattern of earnings. Firms pay taxes when their earnings are positive and receive a tax credit (against future earnings) when they incur losses. However, if tax credits cannot be carried forward indefinitely, losses in the past will not be counted toward reducing a future tax bill. Firm A incurs losses over several successive periods. If the tax credits of firm A cannot be carried forward to reduce future tax payments, then firm B (which hedges) will enjoy greater after-tax cash flows and a higher market value.

Transaction costs, now implying the costs of starting up a new firm and the costs of entering into bankruptcy, are a key element favoring corporate hedging. Referring again to Figure 16.5, the greater volatility in firm A's cash flows leaves it open to the *costs of financial distress,* a term we use to summarize various additional costs that impact a firm with low or negative cash flows over part of its business cycle. The costs of financial distress represent the impact that volatile cash flows may have on the firm's relationships with its customers, employees, suppliers, bankers, bondholders, and other

---

[19]For a discussion of the Modigliani and Miller principles, see Brealey and Myers (1991, chap. 17).

[20]Smith and Stulz (1985) develop the case for hedging based on departures from the perfect capital market assumption.

constituencies. All of these costs may be reduced if the firm can reduce its cash flow volatility. A few examples will illustrate some of the costs of financial distress.

First, in many cases customers prefer to buy from companies that they expect will remain in business for a long time. This is especially so if the product requires after-sales service (such as, an automobile or electronic appliance), or is sold with an extended warranty (such as, a personal computer), or is subject to future revision and replacement (such as, computer software version 1.0). Clearly, the customer values the likelihood that the firm will be around to service, guarantee, or upgrade an expensive purchase. This preference is enhanced further if the product is of critical importance, such as using an automobile or computer for business purposes.

Second, employees often express the same preferences for long-term stability in cash flows. During a period of weak or negative cash flows, a firm may consider laying off employees, cutting back on amenities, and so forth. The best qualified employees of firm A may have an incentive to jump ship, thereby jeopardizing the firm's future cash flows. This problem is especially serious when future cash flows depend on research and development or accumulated know-how embodied in a few key employees.

Along the same lines, suppliers may also be reluctant to deal with firm A in periods of weak cash flows. If a supplier cuts back on shipments, cuts back on trade credits, and reduces its service commitment to the account, clearly firm A will be at a disadvantage in generating future cash flows.

In the classical theory of finance, firm A would be able to borrow (based on its future cash flows) from a perfect capital market in times of weak cash flows to avoid these adverse effects and pull it through into the recovery. But since future cash flows are uncertain in the real world, customers, employees, and suppliers may show a clear preference for dealing with less volatile firms.[21]

In the same way, banks and bondholders also show a preference for firms with less volatile cash flows (holding average cash flows equal). Costs of monitoring the firm's credit standing and costs associated with possible bankruptcy are high. Banks and bondholders will show a preference for firm B, and reward it with greater borrowing capacity and higher credit rating. Both of these factors open the way for firm B to earn greater cash flows and increase its value relative to firm A.

These arguments in favor of hedging at the corporate level also suggest the characteristics of those firms that, other things being equal, would be less likely to benefit by hedging. For example, firms that are large and well diversified across products and regions may not be concerned about tax losses from cyclical conditions. Firms that sell low-tech products that do not require after-sales service, such as food products or consumer nondurables, may not fear a consumer backlash in response to news about the firm's volatile performance in interest rates and currency markets. These firms also may not be concerned about the loss of key employees if the products are mature and R&D expenditures are low.

A stronger argument for hedging at the corporate level could be based on empirical evidence confirming a relationship between lower cash flow volatility and market value or equity returns. Unfortunately, no reliable empirical evidence exists on this point.[22]

---

[21]Froot, Scharfstein, and Stein (1993) developed a model in which information differences between the firm and its creditors make the cost of external finance greater than the cost of internal finance. For these firms, hedging offers a net benefit to shareholders.

[22]If nondiversifiable (σ) risk is priced in the market, this would suggest that hedging would *lower* the required rate of return for equity shareholders, thereby raising the market value of equity shares.

TABLE 16.5   Characteristics of Currency Exposure and Suitable Financial Hedging Instruments

Characteristics of Currency Exposure		*Financial Hedging Instruments*
Frequency of cash flows	Single period	Single contract (futures/options)
	Multiple periods	Sets ("strips") of contracts/swaps or present value hedge
Currency dimension	Single currency	Contracts on one currency
	Multiple currencies	Contracts on an index (ECU, US$) or synthetic hedge
Certainty about cash flows	Certain, contractual cash flows	Naive hedge matches contract size of financial instrument and exposure
	Uncertain, estimated cash flows	Option hedge or dynamic futures hedge to match probability of cash flows

Financial Strategies toward Risk Management

As we have discussed in this chapter, exchange rate changes may have complex and subtle effects on the firm's market value. Many financial instruments may be used to adjust the firm's exposure to exchange rate risk. As we will see, a hedging strategy may offset certain risks while leaving open or increasing other risks. We will offer a few examples suggesting that, at times, firms appeared to be unaware of the existence or magnitude of these additional risks. Let us now examine how the firm builds a strategy that matches an appropriate financial instrument to its currency exposure.

The Currency Profile and Suitable Financial Hedging Instruments

An important step in the process of determining the appropriate financial hedging instruments for a firm is to first analyze the nature of the firm's currency cash flows. Three aspects of the cash flows are critical: the frequency of foreign currency cash flows, the number of currencies, and the degree of certainty about the cash flows. These points are summarized in Table 16.5. For the time being, we consider only the issue of *how* to hedge and *what* financial instruments to use. The question of timing or *whether* or *when* to hedge is covered later.

Frequency of Cash Flows.   For some firms, foreign currency cash flows are a rare or infrequent event. If a foreign currency cash flow is expected in a single period, clearly a single futures or option contract will effectively offset the currency risk. This stylized single-period cash flow is the classic example for illustrating the use of futures and options as a hedging instrument.[23]

---

[23]See Chapters 11 and 12 for graphs showing the payoff profiles of futures and options to hedge a single-period cash flow.

TABLE 16.6   Two Strategies for Hedging a Five-Year £ Lease with
Semiannual Payments

Payment Number	Date Due	Strategy 1 Prices	Strategy 2 Prices
1	January 1, 1995	$F_{t,6}$	$F_{t,6}$
2	July 1, 1995	$F_{t,12}$	$F_{t,12}$
3	January 1, 1996	$F_{t,18}$	$F_{t + 12,6}$
4	July 1, 1996	$F_{t,24}$	$F_{t + 12,12}$
5	January 1, 1997	$F_{t,30}$	$F_{t + 24,6}$
6	July 1, 1997	$F_{t,36}$	$F_{t + 24,12}$
7	January 1, 1998	$F_{t,42}$	$F_{t + 36,6}$
8	July 1, 1998	$F_{t,48}$	$F_{t + 36,12}$
9	January 1, 1999	$F_{t,54}$	$F_{t + 48,6}$
10	July 1, 1999	$F_{t,60}$	$F_{t + 48,12}$

Note: The lease contract is signed on July 1, 1994, which is the initial hedging date (t) for both strategies. With strategy 1, all lease payments are hedged on July 1, 1994, by purchasing forward contracts five years into the future. With strategy 2, forward contracts are purchased on July 1, 1994, only 6 and 12 months ahead. Additional forward contracts are purchased on the yearly anniversary dates of the lease.

Long-term contracts such as property and equipment leases or royalty and licensing agreements may obligate a firm to pay or receive a set amount of foreign currency over many periods. Suppose our firm has leased office space in London for £10,000 a month (payable twice yearly) and that the lease runs for five years. The firm could hedge this amount payable in £ in several ways.

The firm could buy a strip of 10 forward contracts (each for £60,000) with maturities of 6, 12, 18, . . . 54, and 60 months. This naive hedge locks in a known US$ amount calculated from the current forward rates in the term structure of maturities ($F_{t,6}$, $F_{t,12}$, . . . , $F_{t,54}$, $F_{t,60}$). This technique eliminates exchange risk and leads to a US$ payment that varies from period to period.[24] Alternatively, the firm could engage in a five-year currency swap, agreeing to receive £60,000 every six months and to pay a fixed US$ amount in return. This technique also eliminates exchange risk and produces a constant US$ payment in each period. Finally, the firm could purchase a set of 10 call options on the £ with maturities ranging from 6 to 60 months. This technique places a cap on the US$ amount of the lease payments.

All of these techniques eliminate exchange risk at time t. But by covering all currency risks at time t, the firm runs the risk of obtaining a "bad draw" from prices quoted in the financial markets. In other words, buying a strip of futures contracts or option contracts today runs the risk that today's price of £ or of £ volatility is extraordinarily high. By hedging today at today's prices (labeled strategy 1 in Table 16.6), the firm gives up the alternative of hedging progressively over time. For example, the firm could elect to hedge by buying £ up to 12 months in advance at the start of each year in its five-year lease (shown as strategy 2 in Table 16.6). In strategy 2, the firm does not eliminate all currency exposure immediately, but hopes to gain a more diversified drawing on forward rates over the five-year period. See Box 16.2 for a case where several Japanese automakers lost windfall opportunities by hedging their cash flows over a long

---

[24]A money market hedge leads the firm to borrow an amount of US$ (at $i_{\$,m}$), buy spot £ (at S_t) and invest in £ (at $i_{£,m}$) for each maturity $m = 6, 12, . . . 60$ months in sufficient quantity to obtain £60,000. All transactions are completed at time t, so currency exposure is eliminated.

Box 16.2

How Hedging May Prevent Future Windfall Gains and Windfall Losses

In the 1990s, the Japanese yen appreciated more or less steadily against the US$. The ¥ broke below 110 ¥/US$ in April 1993, below 100 ¥/US$ in June 1994, below 90 ¥/US$ in March 1995, and even traded below 80 ¥/US$ in April 1995. Against this history, Japanese firms would have been wise to sell their US$ receivables forward and to do so as soon as possible before further appreciation whittled away more of their value. This is the logic underlying strategy 1 in Table 16.6.

The strategy of selling a weakening currency far forward is dangerous when there is exchange rate overshooting and the currency value is subject to mean reversion. If the exchange rate changes direction, the weakening currency will gain value and hedgers will regret that they rushed to sell it forward. They will wish that they had diversified their bets and sold some currency at a later time. This is the logic behind strategy 2 in Table 16.6.

In the spring of 1995, many Japanese companies sold six months to a year or more of their US$ receivables forward, apparently fearing that the ¥ would wind up at 75 ¥/US$, 70 ¥/US$ or stronger. But by July, the US$ had turned around. The ¥ surpassed 100 ¥/US$ by the fall and hit 110 ¥/US$ in the spring of 1996. The companies that hedged had to announce that there would be no windfall gain associated with the rising dollar.

In September 1995, Mitsubishi Motors announced that it had sold yen at rates near 90 for forward delivery through April 1996.* The hedge cost Mitsubishi as much as 10 percent of its fiscal year earnings. Later in the fall, Mazda Motor Corporation made a similar announcement.† As the US$ appreciated toward 110 ¥/US$, other companies (Honda Motor, Yamaha Motor, and Sony) announced that they too had hedged by selling almost all of their receivables forward through the end of the fiscal year (March 31, 1996).‡

The experience with strategy 1 made an impression on Yamaha Motor, which decided to hedge only some of its receivables for only the next quarter ahead. Feeling that currency markets are too difficult to forecast, Hitachi Limited stopped making exchange rate predictions and planned to hedge 50 percent of its expected receivables on a daily basis.

---

*"Mitsubishi Motors Stalls as Yen Falls," *The Wall Street Journal,* Sept. 12, 1995, p. C1.
†"Mazda Misses Much-Needed Windfall by Guessing Wrong on Weaker Yen," *The Wall Street Journal,* Nov. 1, 1995.
‡"As Yen Oscillates, Japanese Firms Mull Risks of Hedging Bets against Dollar," *The Wall Street Journal,* Feb. 8, 1996.

---

horizon. And see Box 16.3 for the case of a firm that hedged over the long term and wound up losing millions of dollars in the process.

The Net Present Value Hedge.   A situation with cash flows over multiple periods also raises the possibility of a **net present value (NPV) hedge,** in which the firm hedges the net present value of its exposed assets minus exposed liabilities evaluated at prevailing market interest rates. Consider the following example. Suppose our firm has a one-year receivable of €100 and a two-year payable of €108. Assume that € interest rates for one year and two years are 7.0 percent and 7.5 percent, respectively. The net present value of these cash flows $(100/1.07 - 108/1.075^2)$ is zero, indicating zero exposure. The economic logic behind the calculation is that the firm can invest its € 100 receivable for one year beginning one year from now at an interest rate of 8 percent.[25] Therefore, the cash flows represent no exposure to € currency risk.

---

[25]From the pure expectations version of the term structure of interest rates, the one-year interest rate one year from now is estimated as $(1.075)^2/1.07 - 1.0 = 0.08$. The firm could obtain a forward rate agreement to lock in a price close to 8 percent.

Box 16.3

Gold Bugs: The Costs of a Flawed Hedging Program

Gold is a beautiful commodity. But after hitting $800/ounce in 1980, its price declined more or less steadily, crossing below $300/ounce in December 1997. For most of the 1990s, Ashanti Goldfields Company Limited, one of Africa's largest gold producers, followed a gold-hedging operation designed to protect itself from declining gold prices. Ashanti is literally sitting on millions of ounces of gold, so a program to sell forward some of its future production might seem like a natural hedge, and not very risky. Indeed, Ashanti calculated that from 1994 to 1999, its hedging program had resulted in realized cash inflows of more than $700 million.* From January 1997 to July 1999, the price of gold fell almost continuously, from $400 to $250 per ounce. The price decline was aided by various central banks and international institutions that announced and began carrying out plans to dispose of much of their vast gold stocks. With the various, Latin, Asian, and Russian crises, central banks figured that gold sales were a good way to raise funds. After all, gold earns no interest, it is costly to store, and had been a very poor investment over the 1980s and 1990s.

In the summer of 1999, Ashanti continued its hedging program that prescribed a short position of approximately 10 million ounces of gold, the equivalent of about six years' production and 38 percent of the firm's known reserves.† Then something unexpected happened. On September 26, the 15 European central banks announced that they would limit their sales of gold. The price of gold shot up, by $90 per ounce in two weeks, and $75 per ounce in

the space of four trading days. Based on its 10-million-ounce short position, Ashanti lost about $600 million and faced cash margin calls of about $300 million, payable to creditor counterparties—*immediately*.‡ Ashanti owned 26 million ounces of gold, valued at roughly $8 billion. But gold buried in the ground cannot be used to meet a cash margin call due at the end of today's business.

Ashanti was forced to renegotiate its long-term credit agreements with 15 counterparties, granting them, among other concessions, warrants to purchase up to 15 percent of Ashanti's equity shares. Ashanti's share price tanked. Many on the board were forced to resign. Ashanti's plans for expanding production and growing its business were put on the shelf.

Among the many morals of this story, consider these: A hedging program designed to contain price risk may introduce new types of risks, such as liquidity or cash flow risks. A hedging program needs to be subjected to "stress testing," which includes the question, What happens if the price of gold suddenly changes by $20, $40 or $60? Risk managers have to imagine what will happen to the company if the unimaginable happens.

---

*Press release dated Nov. 1, 1999 from Ashanti Goldfields Company Limited. Available at <www.ashantigold.com/1november1999.htm>.
†Ibid.
‡"Gold Hedging—Bugs," *The Economist*, Oct. 16, 1999, and company press release, Nov. 1, 1999.

Along the same lines, if the firm has a €200 receivable in year 1 and a €108 payable in year 2, the NPV is €93.46. The firm can hedge this net asset position by selling €100 for delivery in one year. Finally, if the firm has a €100 receivable in year 1 and a €216 payable in year 2, the NPV is −€93.45. The firm can hedge this net liability position either by buying €100 for delivery in one year, or by immediately buying €93.45 and investing it at the two-year € interest rate.

Number of Currencies.   The classic examples for illustrating a financial hedge (see Figure 11.3 and Box 12.1) describe a single currency cash flow. In these stylized cases, clearly a single futures or option contract will effectively offset the currency risk.

Large multinational firms more commonly accumulate cash flow exposures in many currencies. These exposures can be hedged in a naive fashion by matching a currency futures or option contract to each currency cash flow. In the net present value approach, exposure can be hedged by constructing a hedge in each currency equal to the NPV of all positions in each currency.

A more efficient approach to hedging multiple currencies relies on the portfolio characteristics of the particular currencies. Suppose, for example, that in the early 1990s our firm held an asset position in each of the 12 currencies of the European currency unit (ECU).[26] If, in addition, these positions were in the same proportion as in the ECU, it is clear that selling an ECU futures or buying an ECU put option would effectively hedge our overall asset position. This strategy works because the ECU was *perfectly correlated* with the value of the firm's multicurrency asset position.

Consider another example. Suppose that the firm holds a one-year DKr740,000 receivable and a one-year €100,000 payable. Suppose further that the DKr/€ exchange rate is 7.4, exactly the ratio of our DKr-to-€ positions. If we posit that the DKr/€ exchange rate is likely to remain within a very narrow band around its present value, then this portfolio is not subject to much exposure from the perspective of a U.S. firm. With the cross-rate constant, any change in the $/DKr rate is also reflected in the $/€ rate—preserving the value of the firm.

Degree of Certainty.   A final issue to address is our confidence in the firm's expected cash flow positions. In our examples thus far, we have assumed (implicitly) that currency exposures reflected cash flows that were anticipated *with certainty*. Thus, a € futures or option in the notional amount of €100 represents a perfect naive hedge for an underlying €100 exposure. Cash flows that are contractual in nature (such as dividend, interest, and lease payments; royalty and licensing receipts) are usually considered as certain.

How should we treat uncertain foreign currency cash flows? Suppose that our firm expects to earn £250,000 in export sales each quarter next year, and we are 95 percent confident that sales will be in the £225,000–£275,000 range. Assume further that historically, our firm's sales are inversely correlated with the U.K. unemployment rate. If British unemployment, now at 9 percent, falls to 8 percent, sales should be at the high end of the range. But if unemployment rises toward 10 percent, our sales will slump toward the £225,000 level. Suppose our firm wants to sell its £ revenues forward to reduce its exposure. How much £ should it sell forward?[27]

To begin, it should be clear that if the firm sells its expected £ revenues (£250,000) forward, it will have underhedged if revenues are actually £275,000 and overhedged if revenues are only £225,000. These outcomes would leave the firm with residual risk, from having sold forward too many or too few £.

One strategy for dealing with cash uncertainty involves a mixture of forward and option contracts. In our example, this mixed strategy requires selling £225,000 forward (the lower bound on our sales) and buying a put option on £50,000. If sales exceed our lower bound of £225,000, we exercise the option for up to £50,000. And if sales are only £225,000, we do not exercise the put, but instead we collect its terminal option value.

While this strategy seems valid, it actually contains a flaw. Our firm needs the put option only if sales surpass £225,000. Ideally, we would like to own an option to sell only the actual £ revenues above £225,000, and no more.

An alternative strategy for handling our firm's sales uncertainty relies on a dynamic strategy for replicating the desired option, using the delta hedging principle discussed in Chapter 11.[28] Recall our assumption that the likelihood of high and low sales varies

---

[26]See Chapter 2 to review the composition of the ECU.

[27]Notice that in this example, the unemployment rate (*U*) is our proxy for the state of the economy. Changes in *U* are a source of risk as well as changes in *S*, the spot rate.

[28]See Kulatilaka and Marcus (1994) for a further explanation of this technique.

inversely with the unemployment rate. Assume that our initial expectation of unemployment is 9 percent and that this implies sales of £250,000—or the £225,000 base *plus* £25,000. We can create a synthetic put option for £25,000 by borrowing £25,000 and placing the proceeds (plus the fair put price) into a US$ interest-bearing account.[29] As our expectation of unemployment falls, we can dynamically increase the size of the synthetic put option (by borrowing additional £) toward a limit of £50,000. And as our expectation of unemployment rises, we decrease the size of the synthetic put option toward a limit of zero.

With this strategy, the firm always holds a position equivalent to an option on the *expected amount of extra £ sales* above the £225,000 floor. Clearly, however, the transaction costs of implementing the dynamic strategy could be high—perhaps higher than the cost of simply buying a put for the entire £50,000. Both strategies leave residual exposure for the 5 percent probability that revenues will be outside the £225,000–£275,000 range.

Cross-border mergers and acquisitions are another common example where a bidding firm may want to hedge by purchasing the foreign exchange needed to complete the purchase of a target firm. But the forward purchase is only a hedge if the planned merger or acquisition goes through. If not, the bidding firm has an exposure that could result in a substantial gain or loss, as described in Box 16.4.

Policy Issues—International Financial Managers

Problems in Estimating Economic Exposure

Our approach to modeling economic exposure focused on the sensitivity of the firm's market value or cash flows to exchange rate changes. To implement this approach, we suggested using regression analysis to estimate an exposure coefficient for one or more currencies. Application of this approach raises several difficult issues.

First, using market data to estimate the firm's exposure presumes that financial markets are efficient, and that share prices respond quickly and appropriately to exchange rate changes. As we have seen, there is some question whether securities markets respond contemporaneously to exchange rate shocks, or with a lag.

Second, there are the data requirements with the regression approach. Regression requires a sufficient number of observations on market values and exchange rates, making the approach unsuitable for newly organized firms, newly privatized firms, or newly merged or reorganized firms for which there is not a large sample of consistent observations. Regression also requires that the observations refer to a structurally consistent set of data—meaning that the firm followed the same hedging policies over the period and that the industry was characterized by a similar degree of international competition. By counterexample, if a firm followed a conservative hedging policy for several years and then an aggressive risk-taking policy, we would not expect that the share price response would be similar across the entire period.

Finally, once an exposure coefficient is estimated from historic data, we must assume that the relationship between exchange rate changes and market value remains

---

[29]The reader can think of this as a put on £50,000 with a delta of 0.50 representing the probability of reaching £50,000 in sales.

Box 16.4

Failed Marriages: When Hedging Becomes Speculation

When making a large transaction, the seller often requires the buyer to show that he has the financial means to make good on his bid. The United Kingdom Takeover Code formalizes this by requiring the bidder to demonstrate that it has both adequate committed financing and the appropriate amount of UK£ to eliminate the risk of exchange rate changes between the offer announcement date and the expected closing date.[a] A U.S. bidder for a U.K. firm might satisfy this requirement by purchasing call options or forwards on sterling for delivery at the expected date of the takeover. But suppose the bidder is unsuccessful? Then the bidder is left with a long UK£ position and no corresponding sterling liability or payable—in other words, a speculative position that exposes the bidding firm to loss.

This dire scenario recently befell two large American firms in their takeover bids for separate British firms. On June 13, 1997, PacifiCorp announced a $9.6 billion cash tender offer for The Energy Group PLC, one of Britain's leading electricity and gas companies and the owner of Peabody, the world's largest private producer of coal. PacifiCorp announced that they expected to consummate the offer, subject to shareholder approval, within a few months.[b] To satisfy the U.K. Takeover Code and as part of its financing for the deal, PacifiCorp purchased (for $9 million) call options on £1.45 billion at an effective strike price of $1.64/£.[c] Believing these out-of-pocket costs were high, PacifiCorp later converted their options to forward purchase commitments.

Trouble struck on August 1, 1997, when, because of concerns regarding how the new entity would be regulated, the deal was referred to Britain's monopolies and mergers commission. This temporarily terminated the deal and caused PacifiCorp to recognize any gains or losses on its currency contracts. Because UK£ had fallen to $1.58, PacifiCorp realized $65 million in after-tax losses, wiping out more than half the firm's anticipated third-quarter 1997 earnings.

In July 1999, Air Products & Chemicals (in concert with French firm Air Liquide) announced a £7.0 billion takeover bid for British industrial gases company BOC Group PLC. Prospects for the deal seemed uncertain at best. BOC had received five previous takeover bids in earlier months, and regulators in both Britain and the United States were looking into the anticompetitive aspects of the transaction.[d] In May 2000, the deal collapsed, partly because the parties failed to satisfy U.S. Federal Trade Commission regulator demands, and partly over concerns regarding the financial structure of the deal.

In connection with the prospective acquisition, Air Products had purchased sterling call options that they later converted to forward contracts. As the deal fell apart on May 11, the UK£ fell to $1.4932, a four-year low. Air Products' cumulative foreign exchange losses on the failed bid totaled over $500 million (pretax). To stop the bloodletting and cap its costs, Air Products purchased UK£ puts, at an additional cost of $79 million.[e]

Both of these traumatic episodes leave an important lesson. Both bidding firms purchased sterling call options, giving them the right to buy sterling if their takeover bids were successful. Believing that the call options were expensive, they switched their hedging technique to forward purchase contracts—contracts that place the owner fully exposed to a long sterling position, whether the takeover bid is successful or not. But in both cases, the takeover bid stood a low probability of success. Perhaps the bidder, or the bidder's adviser, thought the odds were higher. But in retrospect, we can surmise that the true odds were small. When the true odds of a successful cross-border takeover are low, an option contract is a better hedge than a forward contract that exposes the bidder to 100 percent of the currency price risk. To offset their currency exposure, both bidders could have taken a short position in some financial instrument closely linked to sterling, perhaps an FTSE equity futures, or a structured bond inversely linked to sterling. If the true odds of winning a takeover battle are low, bidders can attempt to lessen their exposure to currency risk by taking offsetting positions in other contracts.

---

[a]See 10-Q statement for June 30, 1997, of PacifiCorp, filed with the U.S. SEC on Aug. 12, 1997.

[b]Form S-3 filing of PacifiCorp, filed with the U.S. SEC on July 11, 1997.

[c]See "PacifiCorp to Take $65 Million Charge on Currency Deals," *The Wall Street Journal,* Aug. 8,1997.

[d]"Air Liquide, Air Products Join in BOC Bid," *Asian Wall Street Journal,* July 7, 1999.

[e]See 10-Q statement for Mar. 31, 2000, of Air Products, filed with the U.S. SEC on May 12, 2000.

stable in the future. If not, then we cannot apply the hedge coefficient for hedging decisions in the future.

Picking an Appropriate Hedge Ratio

Suppose we have performed a regression analysis and have estimated exposure coefficients—such as b_1, b_2, and b_3 in equation (16.10)—that are significant and meet all of the above statistical criteria. To use this analysis, the manager needs an objective function that summarizes what the firm is trying to maximize, minimize, or optimize.

If the manager does not hedge, the firm remains fully exposed to exchange rate changes. This may be the desired outcome if the manager forecasts that exchange rate changes will be in a favorable direction. The manager may hedge completely by taking offsetting positions, such as $-b_1$, $-b_2$, and $-b_3$ in equation (16.10). Taking these positions will eliminate any consistent relationship between exchange rate changes and the market value of the firm.

As an empirical matter, a firm's exposure measured using the regression approach may appear very large. Since the market value of the firm reflects all future cash flows, a small exchange rate change could portend a large change in market value. A manager may be reluctant to hedge using forward contracts in this situation, but the more direct approach is to restructure the firm's long-term financing to include a component of foreign currency assets or liabilities that permanently alter the firm's financial exposure.[30]

Otherwise, the manager may pick an intermediate solution, with hedge positions in between 0 and b_i. Intermediate positions presume some trade-off between the cost of financial hedging and the benefit of lower volatility in the firm's market value. The all-in cost of hedging is difficult to measure but would include the transaction costs of executing the hedging transactions and the administrative costs of monitoring the firm's current exposure. The benefit to the firm from hedging is also difficult to quantify, but would include the gain from avoiding cash flow shortfalls, not violating lending covenants, keeping an R&D and investment program on track, retaining all tax-loss carry-forwards, and so forth. Presumably, these costs would increase for more extreme exchange rate changes. These examples suggest that foreign exchange risk carries the risk of business disruption and ultimately the risk of ruin.

Tom Copeland, Yash Joshi, and Maggie Quinn (1996) argued that risk management at the firm level could be directed toward reducing the risk of ruin instead of simply reducing the overall volatility of a firm's cash flows and market value. Large firms with a high ratio of cash inflows to cash outflows may not need to hedge to remain safely above the boundary that entails disruption or risk of ruin.

The International Investor's Currency Risk Management Problem

A portfolio's exposure to foreign exchange risk can be measured using the regression approach in much the same way as the treasurer measures the firm's exposure. The investor can hedge foreign exchange risk using forward contracts or retain the risk using a risk–return decision criterion. Our corporate treasurer was led to hedging when costs of bankruptcy and financial distress could be reduced at low cost, thereby increasing the

---

[30]Bilson (1994) used the regression approach to measure the exposure of American Airlines to $/DM risk, market risk, and oil price risk. The estimated exposure to $/DM risk required a currency hedge of about $5.5 billion, a large number in absolute terms but consistent with American's other capital expenditures.

market value for shareholders. An investor who holds a well-diversified stock and bond portfolio also may hold some residual amount of foreign exchange risk that could be hedged with forward contracts.

In Chapters 14 and 15, we showed that currency hedging can significantly improve the performance of international bond and stock portfolios.[31] A study by Jack Glen and Philippe Jorion (1993) demonstrated again that currency hedging substantially improves the performance of international bond and mixed stock-and-bond portfolios. The authors reported this result even when portfolio positions were constrained and no short selling was permitted on stocks or bonds, and hedge positions were restricted to the size of the underlying exposure. Similar to the study by Richard Levich and Lee Thomas (1993) reviewed in Chapter 14, Glen and Jorion (1993) showed that selective hedging can significantly improve the performance of international stock and bond portfolios.

The Value-at-Risk Approach

Over the last few years, a new approach for measuring the exposure of financial assets has been developed. Known as **value-at-risk (VAR),** this approach can be applied to any portfolio of assets (and liabilities) whose market values are available on a periodic basis. In practice, this includes equities, bonds, currencies, futures, options, and swaps, and indexes built on these instruments.[32] To implement the VAR approach, we must know the probability distribution of price changes for each instrument (assume the normal distribution) and the price volatility (σ). Using our estimate of σ and the normal distribution, it is easy to calculate the size of a loss in value to our portfolio if an unlikely (say, 5 percent chance) adverse price movement occurs. The result of this calculation is the value at risk.

Consider the following example based on a portfolio with one asset valued at $12 million—namely, a €10 million position with the spot rate at $1.20/€. Suppose that our estimate (perhaps based on historical data) of exchange rate volatility is σ_ϵ = 6.0 percent per month and we are willing to assume that price changes are normally distributed. For the normal distribution, a 90 percent confidence band includes the range (-1.65σ; $+1.65\sigma$). With 90 percent confidence, we can say that the value of our position at the end of one month will be in the range ($10,812,000; $13,188,000). Thus, there is a 5 percent chance that we will lose at least $1,188,000 (= $1.65 \times 0.06 \times$ €10,000,000 $\times$ $1.20/€) over the next month.[33]

Using the same method, we could calculate the VAR associated with more extreme events. For example, there is a 2.5 percent chance that our €10 million position could lose $1,411,200 (= $1.96 \times 0.06 \times$ €10,000,000 $\times$ $1.20/€) in a month. A VAR could be estimated for a one-day or one-week period using the σ corresponding to that interval.

For a portfolio containing two or more currency positions (long or short) a gross measure of VAR for the portfolio can be measured by adding up the VAR for each individual currency position. This gross measure is an overestimate of the economic amount at risk in the portfolio, because there is less than perfect correlation in price changes across positions. In Box 16.5, we show an example for the VAR of a portfolio computed on a gross basis and on a net basis, taking correlations (ρ) in account.

---

[31]See Levich and Thomas (1993) for the evidence on currency-hedged bond portfolios, and Eun and Resnick (1988) for the evidence on currency-hedged stock portfolios.

[32]An asset such as "the rights to produce the Broadway show *Chorus Line*" would not be a good candidate because there is no active market for this asset. But a 1,000-acre forest might be appropriate for a VAR calculation if the forest represents a known quantity of lumber that has a known fluctuating market value.

[33]There is also a 5 percent chance of a *favorable* price move leading to a *gain* of at least $643,500 over the next month. This is not a threatening outcome in a VAR sense.

Box 16.5

An Example of the Value-at-Risk Approach
for Hedging Exchange Rate Exposure

Consider a firm or an investment manager with positions in five currencies as shown below. The overall position is $100,000 (long) comprised of long positions in four currencies and a short position in the British pound. This example applies to a firm, if we assume that these positions reflect the present value of anticipated accounts receivable (long positions) and accounts payable (short positions) from operations. This example also applies to an investment manager when the positions are cash balances held in the respective currencies.

To measure the value at risk, we need an estimate of the volatility for each currency. In this example, we use an estimate of σ based on historical volatility. Specifically, we use the 124 monthly observations on the spot exchange rate from January 1990 to April 2000 and compute σ based on 123 monthly rates of change.* The reader should understand that there are dozens of ways we could have chosen to estimate σ—for example, by using the past 20, 50, or 100 observations; by using daily or weekly observations; by weighting the observations unequally rather than equally, and so forth. Recall from Chapter 12 that there are other techniques for learning about volatility, such as implied volatility, or estimates based on the daily range of prices. Thus, our "estimate" of volatility is only one possible estimate.

To measure **gross value at risk,** multiply the absolute amount of the position in each currency times 1.65σ, and add the results across all currencies. Using 1.65σ yields a 95 percent (one-tailed) measure of the value at risk; that is, in 5 out of any 100 months, our portfolio is predicted to decline in value by as much (or more) than the gross VAR. The calculation is shown below.

Currency	Position (US$ equivalent)	Weight (%)
Canadian dollar	$ 60,000	60.0%
British pound	−20,000	−20.0
Euro	25,000	25.0
Japanese yen	25,000	25.0
Swiss franc	10,000	10.0
Total	$100,000	100.0%

Currency	Position (US$ equivalent)	Weight (%)	Volatility (%)	Amount at Risk
Canadian dollar	$ 60,000	60.0%	1.31	$1,297.05
British pound	−20,000	−20.0	2.85	937.51
Euro	25,000	25.0	2.97	1,220.88
Japanese yen	25,000	25/0	3.47	1,425.59
Swiss franc	10,000	10.0	3.32	545.67
Total	$100,000	100.0%	**Gross VAR** $\rightarrow$	**$5,426.71**

VAR is a general approach to the problem of risk measurement.[34] As such, VAR leaves several implementation issues unresolved. For example, a VAR calculation depends on values of σ and ρ, but it does not dictate how these values should be estimated. This is a key issue because there are so many ways to estimate σ and ρ. As we discussed in the

---

[34]One of the most well-known VAR models is RiskMetrics developed by Morgan Guaranty Trust Company. RiskMetrics datasets are available publicly at <www.riskmetrics.com>. See also Phelan (1995).

Notice that gross VAR is a conservative measure of exposure. Gross VAR measures the impact of an adverse 1.65σ move in all exchange rates, at once, against the US$. Note that in our example, *adverse* means a 1.65σ depreciation of the € versus the US$ and a 1.65σ appreciation of the UK£ versus the US$. However, this combination is not very likely given the links between Britain and eurozone countries.

Net VAR takes account of two types of portfolio diversification effects: the impact of short and long positions, and the impact of imperfect correlation among financial price changes. Net VAR is measured using the *volatility of the portfolio* (σ_p) instead of the volatility of each individual asset or liability. The formula for the volatility of portfolio returns is:

$$\sigma_P^2 = \sum_{i=1}^{n} \sum_{j=1}^{n} w_i w_j \sigma_i \sigma_j \rho_{ij} \qquad (16.13)$$

where w is the percentage weight of each asset in the portfolio, σ is the volatility of each asset in the portfolio, and ρ_{ij} is the correlation of price changes across assets i and j. It should be clear the ρ_{ij} constitutes another set of parameters that must be estimated, and the reader now appreciates that there are many ways to calculate such an estimate. In this example, we calculate the correlation of exchange rate changes using the monthly data from 1990–2000 we described earlier. The estimated correlations are in the following table.

The table shows only a weak correlation between the C$ and the other currencies in the portfolio. On the other hand, the correlation between the € and SFr exceeds 0.93.

Using equation (16.13), the estimated portfolio variance is 0.0002315; the square root of this number is $\sigma_P = 0.0152162$, or about 1.5 percent. A 95 percent net VAR calculation for the portfolio is computed by multiplying the portfolio's size ($100,000) times σ_P times 1.65 or $2,502.84. Note that the net VAR is smaller than the gross VAR. This relationship will always be the case because of the portfolio effects. In our example, net VAR is only 46 percent as large as gross VAR, primarily because the € and £ are highly correlated and the portfolio holds nearly equal and offsetting positions in these two currencies.

Many companies and consulting firms are in the business of providing ready-made and continuously updated estimates of σ and ρ for many financial assets. For example, RiskMetrics supplies both daily and monthly volatility and correlation estimates on more than 420 financial series, including foreign exchange, government bonds, swap and equity markets.[†] Industry specialists are aware that there are many ways to estimate the volatility and correlation parameters that underpin a VAR calculation. Consequently, estimates of value at risk should be treated as estimates of a portfolio's exposure, rather than hard facts.

---

[*]The data are line *ae* from *International Financial Statistics*. Exchange rates for the euro are proxied by the DM prior to January 1999.
[†]More than 88,000 volatility and correlation estimates are prepared. These data are available over at <www.riskmetrics.com>. Proprietary software has been developed to ease the staggering data requirements of a real-life VAR calculation.

Currency and Correlation (ρ) of price changes: 1990–2000	C$	UK£	€	J¥	SFr
C$	1.0	0.09	−0.03	−0.06	−0.07
UK£		1.0	0.71	0.32	0.65
€			1.0	0.47	0.93
J¥				1.0	0.51
SFr					1.0

chapter on options, σ could be estimated from historical data (using data from the past one month, six months, etc.) or using implied volatilities. Volatility could be estimated using scenario analysis (as we discussed earlier in this chapter) or statistical simulations.

Moreover, any VAR model relies on assumptions about statistical distributions that may not be fully supported by the data. For example, financial price changes could be non-normally distributed. If so, our calculations based on the normal distribution underestimate the VAR of any position.

Not surprisingly, different VAR models (built on different assumptions, data sets, and measurement methodologies) can produce significantly different measures of the value at risk.[35] More surprising, different computer software programs assigned to calculate the VAR for a given financial position using the same VAR model have been shown to produce different results.[36]

Despite these difficulties, the VAR approach has gained rapid acceptance. VAR is a useful technique for banks and other regulated financial firms to estimate their exposure to price changes in their financial positions and the necessary capital requirements for potential losses. VAR can be used to help determine whether or not to hedge and, if so, how much to hedge. The investment manager can compute directly how different hedges affect the probability of large losses (the VAR), and can act to keep VAR within desired limits.

The VAR approach also could be applied to measure the financial exposure of corporations. Because questions remain about the calculation and interpretation of any VAR figure, there is some concern about the usefulness of VAR information to investors and stock analysts. This subject is discussed in the next section.

Policy Issues—Public Policymakers

Disclosure of Financial Exposure

In this chapter, we have seen that individual firms may face substantial exposure to exchange rate changes. From earlier chapters, we know that exchange rates are prone to both short-term volatility and long-term swings. And we also know that trading in financial derivatives (futures, forward, options, and swaps) for both currencies and interest rates have soared in recent years. These factors create a genuine concern among investors and regulators regarding corporate exposure to financial risks.

In light of this, FASB Statement No. 105 mandated that all U.S. firms report information about their position in financial derivatives, including futures, forward, options, and swaps. Specifically, for fiscal years ending after June 15, 1990, firms were required to report the notional amounts of financial derivatives that they held, plus information about the credit risk and market risk of those instruments and the related accounting policy.

Both the SEC and the FASB have sought to mandate additional disclosure requirements, but reaching agreement on the specifics has been difficult. Some corporations have been reluctant to disclose many details of their derivatives transactions, for fear of disclosing their hedging strategy to competitors. Another concern was that by disclosing only derivative positions, and not the underlying business transactions to which they are linked, a firm might be creating confusion rather than clarifying its exposure to risk.

In January 1997, the SEC issued new rules for firms to report the market risk associated with derivatives positions.[37] These rules offer firms three alternative disclosure techniques: (1) a tabular presentation of expected cash flows, contract terms, and maturity dates, (2) a sensitivity analysis reporting possible losses in earnings or market

---

[35]See Beder (1995) and Hendricks (1996) for simulation analyses of alternative VAR models.

[36]See Marshall and Siegel (1996).

[37]See Jeffrey Taylor, "SEC Approves Rules on Disclosure of Derivatives Risk," *The Wall Street Journal*, Jan. 29, 1997, p. C24. For the complete text of Release No. 33-7386, see the SEC website <www.sec.gov/rules/finrindx.htm>.

values in response to changes in market prices, and (3) a value-at-risk disclosure designed to show the potential size and probability of losses over a stated time period. So far, most firms have adopted the sensitivity analysis method, although companies in the extractive industries tend to use a tabular presentation.

As discussed earlier in this chapter, FASB Statement 133 was accepted in 1998 for implementation in fiscal years beginning after June 15, 2000. FASB 133 requires companies to report the mark-to-market value of their derivative transactions, and requires them to allocate the unrealized gain or loss on derivatives into either current income, or to "other comprehensive income."

While these disclosures add to the information about the firm's financial exposures, they do not address the firm's operational exposure to currency and interest rate risk. As we have suggested, the firm's profit margins and ability to penetrate and compete in certain markets may be affected by changes in interest rates and exchange rates. Operational risk of this sort may be important for many firms and may vary from firm to firm even within the same industry. Thus, a firm without financial positions may still face a substantial currency and interest rate risk (related to its ongoing operations) while a firm with substantial financial positions may be using these to hedge its ongoing business operations. Therefore, disclosure of financial exposures alone could provide an incomplete or entirely misleading picture of the firm's economic exposure.

Financial Derivatives and Corporate Hedging Policies

Now that U.S. firms provide more detailed information about their use of currency derivatives, it is possible to examine the characteristics of firms that use derivatives and whether firms that use derivatives exhibit more or less exposure to foreign exchange risk. Christopher Géczy, Bernadette Minton, and Catherine Schrand (1997) analyzed a sample of 372 nonfinancial firms in the Fortune 500. The authors report that 41 percent of these firms used some type of currency derivative. But the likelihood of using currency derivatives increased for firms with higher growth opportunities and for firms that had tighter financial constraints. Thus, the findings were consistent with the notion that firms used derivatives to lower the variability in their cash flows or earnings. The likelihood of using derivatives was also positively related to foreign pretax income, foreign sales, and foreign-denominated debt.

George Allayannis and Eli Ofek (2001) estimated an equation like equation (16.12) for about 350 firms to measure each firm's exposure to currency risk. The authors then related this measure of exposure to the firm's use of currency derivatives, finding that the use of currency derivatives significantly reduces the firm's exposure to exchange rate risk. In related findings, Allayannis and Ofek also showed that larger firms and firms with greater R&D expenditures tend to have larger positions in currency derivatives, as previous theories predicted. However, exchange rate exposure seems to be the principal variable for explaining the use of currency derivatives in this sample of firms.

Summary

In this chapter, we have outlined the sources of economic exposure to foreign exchange risk and described several techniques for measuring it. Exposure can usefully be thought of as a sensitivity measure, $\partial MV/\partial S$, that gauges the change in market value of a firm or a financial portfolio with respect to a change in the exchange rate. In this context, a wide range of firms, even "domestic" firms, could face exchange rate exposure.

While various accounting techniques are used to measure exposure, these are often incomplete or inconsistent with economic measures. We highlighted the regression and scenario approaches for estimating economic exposure. Each approach assumes that the corporate treasurer has access to considerable data and insights about the firm and the competitive nature of the industry in which it operates.

Once the economic exposure of the firm is estimated, a financial strategy can be adopted to reduce risk. In theory, the negative of the exposure coefficient is the hedge amount that will eliminate the firm's exposure to foreign exchange risk. In practice, the exposure coefficient is estimated with error, so that foreign exchange risk cannot be completely eliminated. Even a naive strategy to hedge all exposures is difficult to implement because some future cash flows are uncertain, and the firm must decide whether to hedge its cash flows far into the future or on a rolling basis.

The financial exposure of pure financial positions can also be measured using the value-at-risk approach.

VAR is useful for estimating the likelihood of possible price changes in a portfolio at different horizons. However, the VAR approach depends critically on reasonable estimates of price volatility and correlations among financial assets as well as the assumed distribution of price changes.

Public policymakers have stepped up their disclosure requirements for firms to report their positions in financial derivatives. The SEC now requires firms to report one of three measures that will reveal the sensitivity of the firm's derivatives position to changes in market prices. And the FASB now mandates that firm's report the fair value of their derivatives positions, and account for any expected and unexpected gains or losses on these positions. While these disclosures will help to understand the exposure of the firms' financial positions, they do not address the inherent operational exposure that firms carry by virtue of doing business in an open world economy.

APPENDIX 16.1
A SCENARIO ANALYSIS OF ECONOMIC EXPOSURE TO FOREIGN EXCHANGE RISK

The following spreadsheet shows the elements needed for a scenario analysis of economic exposure to foreign exchange risk. From the text, recall that our hypothetical firm manufactures its products in the United States with 80 percent of the variable costs associated with the U.S. cost structure and 20 percent of variable costs associated with the foreign cost structure. We assume that sales are evenly divided between the U.S. and Australian markets. The entries in the spreadsheet detail the various prices and quantities that affect the firm's cash flows as in our equations (16.1) to (16.5).

In line 1 of the base case, we show the US$/A$ exchange rate, and the US$ depreciating at 2 percent per year. Lines 3 and 8 show U.S. and Australian sales volume of 100,000 units each, growing at 5 percent per year (lines 2 and 7). U.S. and Australian product prices (lines 5 and 10) are assumed to increase at the prospective rate of inflation (lines 4 and 9). With these assumptions, we can compute U.S. sales revenues (line 6), Australian sales revenues (line 12), and total revenues (line 16). Variable costs are shown in lines 13–15 and several types of fixed costs in lines 18–21. Earnings before interest and taxes appear in line 23. We assume that taxes are 35 percent, which leaves after-tax earnings in line 25.

Adding back depreciation (fixed values) and subtracting capital expenditures (at 115 percent of depreciation) we calculate free cash flows in line 30. The terminal value is the projection of the final free cash flow figure discounted as a perpetuity at the 17.5 percent cost of funds less the growth rate. The percent value of free cash flows (in line 33) is the sum of all entries in lines 31 and 32.

This discussion explains the base case. Scenario analysis is implemented by measuring the value of the firm, using various scenarios about exchange rates, product prices, input prices, sales figures, productions costs (assuming either continued or changed production patterns), and changing interest rates (cost of capital) in response to each exchange rate projection. A scenario could utilize a one-time exchange rate change (say, in 2000) or a permanent exchange rate change (that affects all years). A scenario could restrict exchange rates to follow purchasing power parity (by having the exchange rate change according to the inflation differential) or allow for deviations from PPP.

The company planner could assign probabilities to scenarios and focus on the most probable scenarios. The company planner could focus on the most costly or worst-case scenario and devise a hedging strategy to offset the impact on the firm if this scenario comes to pass. Strategies to deal with worst-case but unlikely scenarios resemble the case of catastrophic insurance. The company planner could focus on those scenarios that present the firm with a risk of ruin.

Base Case Scenario for a U.S. Kitchen Products Company

Base Case Line	(in 000s except for per unit or unit amounts) Category	2000	2001	2002	2003	2004	2005
1	US$/A$	0.625	0.638	0.650	0.663	0.667	0.690
United States							
2	U.S. growth, units %		5.0	5.0	5.0	5.0	5.0
3	U.S. volume, units	100,000	105,000	110,250	115,763	121,551	127,628
4	U.S. inflation (%)		4.0	4.0	4.0	4.0	4.0
5	U.S. $ price/unit	150.00	156.00	162.24	168.73	175.48	182.50
6	U.S. sales, US$	15,000	16,380	17,887	19,533	21,330	23,292
Australia							
7	Australian growth, units %		5.0	5.0	5.0	5.0	5.0
8	Australian volume, units	100,000	105,000	110,250	115,763	121,551	127,628
9	Australian inflation (%)		2.0	2.0	2.0	2.0	2.0
10	Australian A$ price/unit	240.00	244.80	249.70	254.69	259.78	264.98
11	Australian sales, A$	24,000	25,704	27,529	29,484	31,577	33,819
12	Australian sales, US$	15,000	16,386	17,901	19,555	21,362	23,337
13	U.S. Variable mfg. cost/unit in US$	40.00	41.60	43.26	44.99	46.79	48.67
14	Australian Variable mfg. cost/unit in A$	16.00	16.32	16.65	16.98	17.32	17.67
15	Australian Variable mfg. cost/unit in US$	10.00	10.40	10.82	11.26	11.72	12.19
16	Total revenues	$30,000	$32,766	$35,788	$39,088	$42,692	$46,629
17	Variable cost of sales	10,000	10,921	11,926	13,025	14,224	15,534
18	Depreciation	5,000	6,000	7,000	8,000	9,000	10,000
19	R & D	1,000	1,040	1,082	1,125	1,170	1,217
20	Distribution	2,500	2,600	2,704	2,812	2,925	3,042
21	Administration	4,500	4,680	4,867	5,062	5,264	5,475
22	Total costs	$23,000	$25,241	$27,579	$30,024	$32,583	$35,267
23	EBIT	7,000	7,525	8,208	9,064	10,109	11,361
24	Tax	2,450	2,634	2,873	3,172	3,538	3,977
25	EBIAT	4,550	4,892	5,335	5,892	6,571	7,385
26	Depreciation	5,000	6,000	7,000	8,000	9,000	10,000
27	Operating cash flow	9,550	10,892	12,335	13,892	15,571	17,385
28	Increase in NWC	0	0	0	0	0	0
29	Capital expenditures	5,750	6,900	8,050	9,200	10,350	11,500
30	Free cash flow	3,800	3,991	4,285	4,691	5,220	5,884
31	Terminal value						47,076
32	PV, free cash flow	3,800	3,397	3,104	2,892	2,739	23,646
33	Sum, PV of free cash flow	$39,577					

Questions

1. Define foreign exchange exposure for a firm. Is a purely domestic firm subject to some foreign exchange exposure? If yes, why?

2. If purchasing power parity holds, does the firm face any exchange rate risk?

3. When the International Fisher Effect holds in the long run, which accounting method for foreign exchange exposure is most appropriate?

4. What is the difference between translation risk and transaction risk? Define both.

5. What is the difference between accounting exposure and economic exposure? Define both. Which one is more accurate in describing the foreign exchange exposure of the firm?

6. Describe how the regression approach is used for measuring a firm's foreign exchange exposure.

7. Explain the limitations of the regression method for measuring a firm's foreign exchange exposure.

8. What are the advantages of the scenario approach for measuring a firm's foreign exchange exposure?

9. In this chapter, the Marriott Company was said to prefer using the current/noncurrent accounting method rather than the monetary/nonmonetary method for accounting for its investment in a hotel in Germany, financed by a loan in DM. Explain that choice. Define both methods and single out their main differences.

10. Under FASB-52, what method is required of U.S. companies for measuring their exposure to foreign exchange risk? What is the rationale behind the use of functional currencies for international operations of U.S. firms?

11. In the 1994 annual report for RJR Nabisco, a multinational food and tobacco company with headquarters in the United States, the translation adjustment account in the balance sheet showed a jump from $8.8 billion as of December 31, 1993, to $10 billion as of December 31, 1994. What is the translation adjustment account? What do you think are the likely reasons behind this change from 1993 to 1994?

12. In the annual reports of Nestlé, a large, diversified Swiss-based food company with operations in more than 100 countries, management states that it does not hedge foreign exchange exposure. What might be the rationale behind this policy?

13. Describe the costs of financial distress.

14. How would you hedge a three-year lease as opposed to a one-time export by a small firm? Explain.

15. Explain the difference between a net present value approach to hedging and hedging each cash flow separately using financial instruments.

16. Explain how to measure the gross VAR of a set of financial positions, and how to measure the net VAR. Why is net VAR always less than or equal to gross VAR?

17. Discuss how you would use the regression approach, the scenario approach, and the VAR approach to decide whether or not to hedge and how much to hedge.

18. Why might public disclosure of a firm's exposure to financial risks (say, using a VAR approach) create confusion about the firm's economic exposure?

Exercises

1. Suppose a U.S. firm decides to invest in Germany to produce its finished products for sale in Germany. The following is the stream of cash flows for the seven-year life of the investment and two interest rate scenarios:

Year	0	1	2	3	4	5	6	7
Cash flows (€)	−1,000	−100	100	200	300	400	400	2,000
Interest rates— Scenario 1	8%	9%	10%	10.5%	11%	11%	11%	11%
Interest rates— Scenario 2	8%	8%	8%	8%	8%	8%	8%	8%

a. Calculate the net present value in € for the project using both scenarios of interest rates.

b. Does this project give the firm a positive or negative foreign exchange exposure?

c. Describe how the firm could hedge this exposure using only a current spot € contract.

d. Describe how the firm could hedge this exposure using a group of seven € forward contracts.

e. Describe how the firm could hedge this exposure using only one forward € contract with a seven-year maturity.

f. Discuss the advantages and disadvantages of the approaches in exercises *c, d,* and *e.*

2. Suppose a U.S. auto parts manufacturer established a subsidiary in the *maquiladoras* on the U.S.–Mexican border. Parts are produced in

Mexico, shipped to the United States and Canada, and then assembled into more finished parts. These units are then sold to the U.S.-owned manufacturers located in Canada and the United States. No parts are sold in Mexico. The following is the balance sheet of the subsidiary, in thousands of Mexican pesos (MP):

Balance Sheet

Assets	
Cash	5,000
Securities	20,000
Receivables	100,000
Inventories	75,000
Plant & equipment	100,000
	300,000
Liabilities	
Payable	40,000
Accrued wages	10,000
Long-term debt	100,000
Equity	150,000
	300,000

Assumptions:

- To set up the subsidiary in Mexico, the U.S. parent has granted a long-term loan to its subsidiary. The loan is denominated in US$. The amount outstanding is MP50 million at the current exchange rate. The interest rate is 10 percent.

- The firm also obtained long-term funds from Mexican banks. Loans outstanding are MP50 million. The interest rate on these funds is 20 percent.

- The Mexican subsidiary imports its inputs from its U.S. parent, payable in US$. Inputs are 50 percent of total costs.

- Labor and overhead are incurred in MP and represent 50 percent of total cost.

- Receivables are denominated in US$ (80 percent) and Canadian dollars (20 percent).

- Budgeted sales for the current year are MP100 million. The gross profit margin is 20 percent.

- The firm has cash and securities totaling MP25 million: MP5 million in cash, MP10 million in Mexican bank CDs, and MP10 million worth of US$ CDs. Current exchange rates are MP3.40/$ and MP2.60/C$.

Answer the following questions:

a. Determine the cash flow statement for the firm.

b. Determine the translation exposure for the U.S. parent using the current/noncurrent method. Determine the translation gain or loss from a 100 percent devaluation of the Mexican peso.

c. Determine the translation exposure for the U.S. parent using the monetary/nonmonetary method. Determine the translation gain or loss from a 100 percent devaluation of the Mexican peso.

d. Determine the translation exposure for the U.S. parent using the all-current method. Determine the translation gain or loss from a 100 percent devaluation of the Mexican peso.

e. Determine the effect of a 100 percent devaluation of the Mexican peso against the U.S. dollar and the Canadian dollar on the income statement of the Mexican subsidiary.

f. How would you hedge your Mexican exposure?

g. What questions remain about the magnitude of the impact you calculated in part *e*?

3. The following questions use the financial positions, volatility measures, and correlations presented in Box 16.5.

a. Calculate the impact on gross VAR and net VAR if the manager fully hedges the Japanese yen exposure. By what percentages does this hedge lower the VAR compared with the figures in Box 16.5?

b. Calculate the impact on gross VAR and net VAR if the manager fully hedges the Swiss franc exposure. By what percentages does this hedge lower the VAR compared with the figures in Box 16.5?

c. What amount of hedging in Japanese yen would limit a 95 percent net VAR to no more than $2,000?

References

Adler, Michael, and Bernard Dumas. "Exposure to Currency Risk: Definition and Measurement." *Financial Management* 13, no. 2 (Summer 1984), pp. 41–50.

Aliber, Robert Z., and Clyde Stickney. "Accounting Measures of Foreign Exchange Exposure: The Long and Short of It." *Accounting Review* 50, no. 1 (Jan. 1975), pp. 44–57.

Allayannis, George. "Exchange Rates, Hedging, and the Value of the Firm." Ph.D. dissertation, New York University, Stern School of Business, 1996.

Allayannis, George, and Eli Ofek. "Exchange Rate Exposure, Hedging, and the Use of Foreign Currency Derivatives." *Journal of International Money and Finance,* forthcoming.

Amihud, Yakov. "Exchange Rates and the Valuation of Equity Shares." In *Exchange Rates and Corporate Performance,* ed. Y. Amihud and R. Levich. Burr Ridge, IL: Richard D. Irwin, 1994.

Bartov, Eli, and Gordon M. Bodnar. "Firm Valuation, Earnings Expectations, and the Exchange-Rate Exposure Effect." *Journal of Finance* 49, no. 5 (Dec. 1994), pp. 1755–85.

Beder, Tanya Styblo. "VAR: Seductive but Dangerous." *Financial Analysts Journal* 51, no. 5 (Sept.–Oct. 1995), pp. 12–24.

Bilson, John F. O. "Managing Economic Exposure to Foreign Exchange Risk: A Case Study of American Airlines." In *Exchange Rates and Corporate Performance,* ed. Y. Amihud and R. Levich. Burr Ridge, IL: Richard D. Irwin, 1994.

Bodnar, Gordon M., and William M. Gentry. "Exchange-Rate Exposure and Industry Characteristics: Evidence from Canada, Japan and the U.S." *Journal of International Money and Finance* 12, no. 1 (Feb. 1993), pp. 29–45.

Brealey, Richard A., and Stewart C. Myers. *Principles of Corporate Finance,* 4th ed. New York: McGraw-Hill, 1991.

Copeland, Tom; Yash Joshi; and Maggie Quinn. "How to Evaluate Corporate FX Risk Management Programs." Working Paper, McKinsey & Company, Apr. 22, 1996.

Cornell, Bradford, and Alan C. Shapiro. "Managing Foreign Exchange Risks." *Midland Corporate Finance Journal,* Fall 1983, pp. 16–31.

Eun, Cheol, and Bruce Resnick. "Exchange Rate Uncertainty, Forward Contracts, and International Portfolio Selection." *Journal of Finance* 43, no. 1 (Jan. 1988), pp. 197–216.

Financial Accounting Standards Board. "Disclosure of Information about Financial Instruments with Off-Balance-Sheet Risk and Financial Instruments with Concentrations of Credit Risk," Statement No. 105, FASB: Norwalk, CT, Mar. 1990.

Froot, Kenneth A. "Currency Hedging over Long Horizons." NBER Working Paper No. 4355, Cambridge, MA, May 1993.

Froot, Kenneth A; David S. Scharfstein; and Jeremy C. Stein. "Risk Management: Coordinating Corporate Investment and Financing Policies." *Journal of Finance* 48, no. 5 (Dec. 1993), pp. 1629–58.

Géczy, Christopher; Bernadette A. Minton; and Catherine Schrand. "Why Firms Use Derivatives." *Journal of Finance* 52, no. 4 (Sept. 1997), pp. 1323–54.

Giddy, Ian H. "Devaluations, Revaluations and Stock Market Prices." Ph.D. dissertation, University of Michigan, 1974.

Glen, Jack, and Philippe Jorion. "Currency Hedging for International Portfolios." *Journal of Finance* 48, no. 5 (Dec. 1993), pp. 1865–86.

Heckerman, Donald. "The Exchange Risks of Foreign Operations." *Journal of Business* 45, no. 1 (Jan. 1972), pp. 42–48.

Hendricks, Darryll. "Evaluation of Value-at-Risk Models Using Historical Data." *Economic Policy Review.* Federal Reserve Bank of New York, Apr. 1996, pp. 39–70.

Hekman, Christine R. "Measuring Foreign Exchange Exposure: A Practical Theory and Its Application." *Financial Analysts Journal,* Sept.–Oct. 1983, pp. 59–65.

Hung, Juann. "Assessing the Exchange Rate's Impact on U.S. Manufacturing Profits." *Quarterly Review.* Federal Reserve Bank of New York, Winter 1992–93, pp. 44–63.

———. "The Exchange Rate's Impact on Overseas Profits of U.S. Corporations." Working Paper, Federal Reserve Bank of New York, Apr. 1995.

Jorion, Philippe. "The Exchange-Rate Exposure of U.S. Multinationals." *Journal of Business* 63, no. 3 (July 1990), pp. 331–45.

Kulatilaka, Nalin, and Alan Marcus. "Hedging Foreign Project Risk." *Journal of International Financial Management and Accounting* 5, no. 2 (June 1994), pp. 142–56.

Levi, Maurice D. "Exchange Rates and the Valuation of Firms." In *Exchange Rates and Corporate Performance,* ed. Y. Amihud and R. Levich. Burr Ridge, IL: Richard D. Irwin, 1994.

Levich, Richard M., and Lee R. Thomas. "The Merits of Active Currency Risk Management: Evidence from International Bond Portfolios." *Financial Analysts Journal* 49, no. 5 (Sept.–Oct. 1993), pp. 63–70.

Marshall, Christopher, and Michael Siegel. "Value at Risk: Implementing a Risk Measurement Standard." MIT Working Paper No. 316-96R, July 1996.

Oxelheim, Lars, and Clas Wihlborg. *Macroeconomic Uncertainty.* Chichester England: John Wiley, 1987.

Phelan, Michael J. "Probability and Statistics Applied to the Practice of Financial Risk Management: The Case of J. P. Morgan's RiskMetrics." Working Paper No. 95-19, University of Pennsylvania Wharton School, Aug. 1995.

Pringle, John J., and Robert A. Connolly. "The Nature and Causes of Foreign Currency Exposure." *Journal of Applied Corporate Finance* 6, no. 3 (Fall 1993), pp. 61–72.

Smith, Clifford, and René Stulz. "The Determinants of Firm's Hedging Policies." *Journal of Financial and Quantitative Analysis* 20 (Dec. 1985), pp. 391–405.

P A R T

VII REGULATORY ISSUES

17 Giving Direction to International Financial Markets: Regulation and Intervention in the Competitive Marketplace 644

17 GIVING DIRECTION TO INTERNATIONAL FINANCIAL MARKETS:

Regulation and Intervention in the Competitive Marketplace

"The word 'intervention' . . . conjures up images of the government sending in the US Cavalry to impose order . . . Another analogy from the American West may be more appropriate than the arrival of the Cavalry. The foreign exchange market is a herd of steers, and central banks are herd dogs. They bark and nip at the heels of the steers, with the aim of moving the herd in the desired direction."

Dominguez and Frankel (1993)

Learning Objectives

After reading this chapter, students should

1. Better appreciate the problems facing public policymakers when deciding to regulate a market activity or intervene in some way, versus letting private market forces prevail.

2. Understand that regulation has both costs and benefits and that, in a world with many regulatory agencies, market participants may migrate to a country that better suits their needs, thus pitting regulators into competition with one another.

3. Understand the difference between sterilized and unsterilized foreign exchange market intervention, and why central banks have a preference for sterilized intervention.

4. Be familiar with evidence on the effectiveness and profitability of foreign exchange market intervention.

5. Be aware of the transaction tax argument as a way to slow down speculative behavior in the foreign exchange market.

The above quotation frames a fundamental dilemma facing today's policymakers: Have international financial markets grown so large and complex that policymakers can no longer effectively regulate and control them?

Throughout this book, we have seen how the range of products—foreign exchange, futures, options, swaps, international bonds, and equities, to name only the broad categories—has grown. Trading volume in these instruments has multiplied dramatically. Prices in underlying markets—for spot exchange, bonds, and equities—have been volatile and subject to sudden, sharp changes. Markets with this size, scope, and vitality represent a powerful force, like the herd of steers.

Can international financial markets take "direction" from any source? Or are competitive market forces the ultimate ruler of the market's direction?

In this chapter, we will focus on two types of direction, or policymaking. The first concerns the *regulation* of international financial markets. In an open economy, there are many financial market regulators, sometimes one and often more than one in each country. This sets the stage for competition among market regulators to provide a hospitable regulatory environment in addition to the typical competition among suppliers of financial services. What results is a dynamic process of regulation by one regulatory body, actions and innovations by market participants, reregulation by another regulatory body, further response by markets, and so forth until an equilibrium level of regulation is reached. We will examine this dynamic process in more detail and review its implications for the regulation of international financial markets.

The second type of direction is the more traditional type of **official,** or **central bank, intervention** to influence either the level or volatility of market prices. An important policy issue is whether intervention of this sort can be effective. The question applies to both a **floating exchange rate system,** where the central bank is under no obligation to set a price or to stabilize exchange rate fluctuations, and to a **pegged exchange rate system,** where the central bank stands ready to convert foreign exchange into home currency (and vice versa) at a rate that is maintained within a narrow range around a predetermined central rate.

The possibility that official intervention could correct exchange rate misalignments or quell excess exchange rate volatility has been debated for many years. We will review this debate, drawing attention to several new empirical studies based on recently released data on official intervention. We also review so-called securities transaction taxes (STTs) that have been proposed as an alternative form of official intervention to reduce exchange rate volatility.

Regulation of Financial Markets in an Open Economy

In this section, we use the word *regulation* in a broad sense, covering the rules that organize financial markets and the design of financial products; restrictions on ownership or trading in financial instruments; price ceilings, price floors, and limitations on price movements; transfer taxes, stamp duties, and fees imposed on trading; bank reserve requirements, capital adequacy requirements, and margin requirements; taxation of interest and dividends; information disclosure rules, accounting rules, and so on.

Financial Market Participants and Competitive Behavior

To analyze the dynamic effects of regulation on financial markets (and vice versa), it is convenient to consider three sets of market participants: (1) individuals and institutions that demand financial services, (2) firms that supply financial services, and (3) regulatory bodies that set the rules and monitor various aspects of financial transactions. Financial market regulations can entail costs and benefits for both users and suppliers of financial services; the net impact will depend on the specific regulations.

The Demand Side.   On the demand side, individuals benefit from regulations that reduce the negative externalities associated with a fully competitive banking and financial system. For example, rules that specify minimum capital requirements, monitoring of bank loan portfolios, and lender-of-last-resort responsibilities help support the integrity of individual banks and the safety and soundness of the financial system. Individuals acting alone would find it hard to accomplish these objectives. Individuals also benefit from regulations that provide a subsidy to the consumer of financial services. Deposit insurance priced below private cost, with an implicit government backup, is a common example.

Financial markets are often characterized by *imperfect information* or *asymmetric information*—where the sellers of securities have better information than the buyers. Small investors, in particular, gain to the extent that regulations produce higher quality information than the competitive market would provide. However, regulations that restrict the menu of financial products, raise transaction costs, or otherwise reduce financial efficiency or mobility reduce the welfare of individuals.

The Supply Side.   For institutions that supply financial services, a given regulatory regime bestows both benefits and costs on individual financial services firms. Regulations that (1) assure the stability and orderliness of the financial system over time and promote public confidence in financial institutions, (2) restrict entry into the industry and monitor anticompetitive pricing arrangements, and (3) provide ancillary services— such as deposit insurance or wire transfers—at below private cost and other transaction cost savings measures, all benefit private firms. Regulations may also result in revenue losses for these supplier institutions from (1) forgone interest on required reserves, (2) forgone earnings on excessive capital requirements, (3) cost of regulatory information and compliance, and (4) forgone revenues from limitations on geographic activity or product offerings as well as explicit charges. The difference between these costs and benefits defines the **net regulatory burden (NRB)** placed on private firms.[1]

In an individual, closed economy with a single regulatory body, competition will spark a dynamic interplay between demanders and suppliers of financial services, much as in any market situation. Users of financial services will vote with their feet, seeking similar or superior services if justified by considerations of cost and risk. Private firms will seek to reduce their NRB and increase their profitability. Product innovation and relocation of activities are two standard ways to lower the NRB.[2]

The Regulatory Side.   The familiar story of competitive equilibrium—based on private demand for services and private supply of services in a static regulatory setting— must be extended in two directions: (1) to include the case of multiple and sometimes overlapping domestic regulatory bodies, and (2) to the case of many countries with many suppliers of financial services and many regulatory bodies.

A single economy may have multiple regulatory bodies at the national level, complemented by a host of other regulatory groups at the state and local levels in countries organized politically along federal lines. At the federal level in the United States, financial activities could fall under the domain of the Federal Reserve Board, the Comptroller of the Currency, the Securities and Exchange Commission (SEC), and the Commodity Futures Trading Commission (CFTC), to name only the major regulatory

---

[1]Note that because some regulations may not generate revenues and some regulations entail externalities, the value of the net regulatory benefits received by firms need not equal the net regulatory costs collected by the regulatory authorities.

[2]Money-market mutual funds are an early example of product innovation designed to avoid reserve requirements on demand deposits while offering individuals liquid accounts that earned higher returns than bank deposits. An example of relocation is Citibank's decision to move its credit card operation to South Dakota after New York State usury ceilings on interest rates were breached in the early 1980s.

agencies. Each of the 50 states has its own regulatory bodies to deal with banking and insurance. In practice, the situation is complicated still further by ambiguity regarding the definitions of bank, security, exchange, and so forth, which may blur the categories of a financial service as well as raise questions about which regulatory agency holds jurisdiction.[3]

And financial innovation raises the competition among regulators yet another notch. If restrictions or transaction costs limit a market for futures, options, or swaps, it may be possible to design bank loans or marketable bonds with futureslike, optionlike, or swaplike features. **Structured finance** of this sort is encouraged when the market for bank loans or marketable bonds receives more favorable regulatory treatment than newer derivative instruments.

The twist to this story is that market regulators are not idle bystanders in this competitive market setting; regulators are themselves subject to competitive forces.[4] The footloose nature of financial transactions gives users of financial services strong incentives to seek product innovations and new trading locations that legally avoid cumbersome regulations. Regulators understand these incentives and have responded by adapting their regulations ("reregulating") to recover parts of their lost regulatory domain.

In the open international economy with many governments and regulatory authorities, we find a highly fertile ground for financial firms to reduce their NRB. National regulatory authorities may compete among themselves on the basis of NRB to preserve or reclaim their regulatory domain. Again, private firms benefit from such international competition, especially if financial innovation and technological change allow them to operate successfully at a distance from their home bases. Users of financial services also benefit to the extent that competition forces financial firms to pass through the lower NRB. An important question (to be discussed later) is whether society as a whole gains or loses as a result of the lower worldwide NRB brought about by regulatory competition.

Competition among Regulators

Compliance with regulations in onshore financial markets creates opportunities to develop a parallel offshore market for the delivery of similar services. As we noted in Chapters 9 and 10, barriers must exist to keep all activity from migrating offshore. In this case, political risk and fixed costs for entering offshore markets (leading to a minimum transaction size) temper the flow of deposits and investments offshore while size and credit quality perform a similar role for borrowers. In addition to traditional services such as bank deposits and loans, offshore markets can be used to replicate a variety of nonbank financial instruments (such as long-term forward contracts, short-term commercial paper, long-term bonds, and Eurocurrency interest rate futures), many of which also may be regulated by onshore financial authorities. Consequently, offshore markets raise a general competitive threat to onshore financial services activities.

---

[3]For example, most money-market mutual funds (MMMF) allow check writing and many investors use their money market funds as if they were a bank account. But MMMFs are regulated by the SEC, not the Fed. In the late 1970s, futures and options on currency could not be regulated by the CFTC on the grounds that foreign exchange is not a commodity. In the 1980s, disputes arose regarding whether futures and options on stock indexes were the domain of the SEC or the CFTC.

[4]See Kane (1987) for a detailed analysis of competition among financial regulators.

The rise of offshore markets underscores the fact that market participants can choose among several financial centers to execute their transactions. Consequently, if domestic regulators desire to have transactions conducted within their respective financial centers—driven by the regulators' desire to maintain an adequate level of prudential regulation, to sustain their revenues from the taxation of financial services, to support employment and output in the financial services industry and linked economic sectors, or simply to maximize their regulatory domain—then regulatory requirements cannot be set arbitrarily.

Indeed, as Edward Kane (1987) has argued, domestic financial regulations are determined competitively and endogenously after taking account of regulations (both present and prospective) in other financial centers. The essence of his analysis is that the market for suppliers of financial regulation is highly competitive. As such, the movement to liberalize regulations affecting financial institutions is not the result of a sudden outpouring of laissez-faire behavior, but the result of an endogenous process as national regulators vie for market share. The market for financial regulation is *contestable* in the sense that other national regulatory bodies offer (or threaten to offer) rules that may be more favorable than those of the domestic regulator. This actual or threatened competition serves to constrain the actions of financial regulators and tax authorities.

We have illustrated the process of competition in regulation previously in our discussion about the development of the Eurocurrency and Eurobond markets. Various policies such as Regulation Q interest rate ceilings, withholding taxes on interest payments to foreigners, and stringent U.S. GAAP reporting requirements gave private parties incentives to move offshore. In the 1960s, the United States adopted the Interest Rate Equalization Tax and Voluntary Foreign Credit Restraint programs. Instead of stopping the outflow of capital from the United States, these programs actually helped build the Eurocurrency and Eurobond markets.

In the 1980s, the United States revised its regulations rather than fight the market. International Banking Facilities were introduced in 1981, permitting a quasi-offshore Eurocurrency market in the United States. Withholding taxes were dropped on interest paid to foreigners in 1983 in an attempt to promote foreign demand for U.S. bonds and reduce U.S. borrowing costs. Rule 415 on shelf registration arrived in 1983 to reduce the administrative costs of U.S. registered bond offerings, which in a sense acknowledged the growth of the Eurobond market. The Rule 144a market began in 1990, as a more obvious competitor to the Eurobond market. In November 1999, the United States abolished the Depression-era Glass-Steagall Act, thus permitting "broad banking" and greater competition for securities underwriting in the U.S. market. And most recently, the SEC has put forward for public comment the possibility that foreign entities might use International Accounting Standards (rather than U.S. GAAP) for purposes of listing or offering securities in the United States. Each of these changes could be seen as an attempt to promote the efficiency and international competitiveness of U.S. capital markets, while balancing against possible adverse impacts on the safety and soundness of markets.

All of these regulatory changes illustrate what Kane (1987) has referred to as a "regulatory dialectic"—a dynamic interaction between the regulator and the regulated, where there is continuous action and reaction by all parties. The players in this strategic game may behave aggressively, with liberalization of rules and product innovations designed to attract business, or defensively, with restrictions on activities designed to contain markets. To the extent that the parties behave adaptively, even if underlying factors (such as communications technology and the level of financial transactions) remain constant, it will likely require considerable time for an equilibrium regulatory structure to emerge. But a harmonization of policies will evolve driven by market forces and competition among regulators.

In a changing environment, players adapt with varying speed and degrees of freedom. Kane (1987, p. 115) summarized the "average adaptive efficiencies" of various players as follows:

- Less-regulated players move faster and more freely than more tightly regulated ones.
- Private players move faster and more freely than governmental ones.
- Regulated players move faster and more freely than regulators.
- International regulatory bodies move more slowly and less freely than all other players.

Given this ordering of adaptive efficiencies, we expect the lag between a regulation and its avoidance is on average shorter than the lag between avoidance and reregulation. The lag in reregulation may be shorter for industry-based self-regulatory groups than for official government regulatory bodies. The lag before reregulation may be longest when international regulatory efforts are involved; this makes international financial regulation especially challenging to design.

Market regulators now fully recognize the challenges of domestic and international financial regulation. The European Union (EU) has designed a minimal core of regulation that seems to recognize the need for flexibility and the value of competition across EU countries. Recent statements from U.S. regulators also acknowledge the dynamic nature of financial markets and the regulatory process:

> We cannot escape the reality that the banking supervisors and regulators will have to innovate to continue to carry out their responsibilities. Bank, and more generally financial institution supervision, is, of necessity, a continually evolving process reflecting the continually changing structure and policies of the supervised institutions. We will eventually correct, for example, all, or most, of the anomalies we perceive in risk-based capital, only in a few years to be required to "correct" those corrections. This is not a fault, but a description of an appropriate regulatory process."[5]

This diagnosis leads to a prescription that "whenever possible, regulators should use approaches to regulation and supervision that include or simulate market techniques and signals."[6] We will present an example of this approach shortly with the new BIS proposals for capital adequacy and market risk.

The Net Regulatory Burden and Structural Arbitrage

Structural arbitrage is the transfer of financial activities into another regulatory domain when, *ceteris paribus,* the NRB on these activities can be reduced. In a perfect capital market with no entry or exit costs, no transaction costs, no barriers between countries, and no sovereign risk, all banking and securities activities will migrate to the country with the lowest NRB, inclusive of taxes. In the real world, a variety of imperfections exist that permit some dispersion of NRB across countries. For example, when the costs of operating at a distance are positive, firms will locate in those countries where they intend to sell financial services. Nevertheless, differences in the NRB across

---

[5]Alan Greenspan, "Remarks before the 32nd Annual Conference on Bank Structure and Competition," Federal Reserve Bank of Chicago, May 2, 1996, p. 10.

[6]Ibid.

countries cannot be too great; otherwise private firms will have an incentive to relocate their activities. Entry and exit costs, currency conversion costs, and distance-related delivery costs, plus the uncertainties surrounding these costs and other control measures, act as effective barriers to complete NRB equalization across countries. Technological change that has markedly lowered communications and information processing costs (combined with the rapid growth of international financial transactions) has cut the gap in the NRB needed to induce structural arbitrage.

In a similar fashion, regulators are more willing to compete on the basis of the net regulatory burden. Individual regulators must ensure that their regulatory revenues (including any supplementary budgetary support that comes willingly from informed taxpayers) are sufficient to produce a given set of regulatory services. If the revenues generated by regulation are insufficient to cover the costs of those same regulatory services, then the regulatory burden is not sustainable and reregulation will force it back into line. Similarly, if regulators are generating more revenues than their costs, they need to be concerned that private firms will migrate to lower NRB regions unless the associated transactions costs and information costs exceed the tax savings and/or regulatory savings. In this case, regulators could either lower their NRB or impose taxes and controls to stop the migration of financial activity.

Because taxes and controls are easily avoided, policymakers are likely to alter their NRB. In equilibrium, the NRB cannot be too high or too low. Assuming that regulators face structural arbitrage and a regulatory dialectic, it is interesting to ask: What is the long-run, equilibrium, sustainable value of the net regulatory burden?[7]

Richard Levich and Ingo Walter (1990) concluded that a long-run equilibrium can be maintained with a positive NRB. Financial transactions involve uncertainty—uncertainty about the monetary unit of account, the creditworthiness of the financial institutions and other counterparties, and the political stability of the financial center. Financial institutions value their access to lender-of-last-resort facilities, the opportunity to be headquartered in a stable political climate, and the like. Indeed, we observe that those markets that are largely unregulated, with an NRB approaching zero, have not completely dominated financial transactions subject to location shifting, such as the Eurocurrency markets. Financial institutions appear willing to pay some regulatory tax. The sustainable magnitude of this remains an open question. Exactly because the sustainable NRB is unknown, coordinated approaches to international financial regulation may impose additional costs and risks relative to retaining regulatory competition.

Coordinated versus Competitive Approaches to International Financial Regulation

We now return to the original theme of this chapter: Can international financial market regulation be directed in a coordinated fashion, or is the invisible hand of the competitive approach likely to produce a superior outcome? (See Box 17.1.)

On the surface, cooperation among governments to coordinate or harmonize policies seems like a laudable activity. National differences, whether in language, currency, electric voltage, or economic rules and regulations, create barriers that are costly

---

[7]A somewhat separate but related question involves social welfare and whether a reduction in the NRB that shifts the fiscal burden from financial market participants to other segments of society serves general welfare optimization goals. As any factor of production or economic activity gains mobility, it becomes increasingly difficult to subject it to tax. Of necessity, the fiscal burden will be redistributed onto less mobile factors or activities.

Box 17.1

Can We See the Invisible Hand?

When thinking about the regulation of giant multinational financial conglomerates, such as Citicorp, Deutsche Bank, Nomura, Barclays, and many others, it is natural to focus on the many regulatory agencies that supervise the operations of these firms in every country where they do business. Thomas Huertas (1992) suggests that another powerful supervisory force, which he calls "market supervision," is also at work.

Market supervision refers to the practice of market participants (including institutional investors, customers, companies, counterparties, and rating agencies) to monitor and control the exposure they have to financial firms. Whether the transaction is between swap counterparties, cash management clients, companies and their securities underwriters, or investors and their securities custodians, these market participants have strong incentives to scrutinize the business practices and credit standing of the firms with whom they deal.

Market supervision is "strict, and it is continuous," Huertas argues. As a result, financial firms that wish to deal with such clients have equally strong incentives to keep their business dealings as well as their credit rating in good standing. There is growing evidence that financial firms that let their business practices fall into ill repute suffer more than just a loss of reputation; they suffer a substantial decline in the market value of their shares and, in some cases, bankruptcy, loss of employment, and criminal punishment.*

The trick for making market supervision work, however, is to expose market participants to the risk of loss in order for them to take their market supervisory role seriously. Market scrutiny is of course imperfect, but it is an important complement to regulatory supervision, and even more so with the pace of financial innovation. Market supervision greatly increases the number of eyes watching over the safety and soundness of financial firms.

---

*Refer to Box 1.1 for a list of costly financial miscalculations. For an extended discussion of the market value of ethics and reputation in the financial services business, see Smith and Walter (1997).

---

to overcome. Uniformity eases these costs. National policies that are undisciplined or grossly out of line with those of their neighbors may transfer part of the cost of these policies to other countries. Coordination reduces the chance of these negative externalities.

In the context of financial markets, many factors favor harmonizing regulations. As world financial markets become more integrated, a bank loan, bond underwriting, or interest rate hedging product for a firm in Ohio is as likely to be supplied by a bank with headquarters in New York, London, or Tokyo. Harmonization would help to promote a level playing field across financial institutions worldwide. Also, the fear that an "under-regulated" bank in country X could produce contagion effects elsewhere is well founded. Harmonization could provide assurance that the safety net is cast wide.

However, regulatory harmonization itself is not without drawbacks. A common regulatory burden might be "too high," such as U.S. reserve requirements and Regulation Q interest rate ceilings in the 1960s, which inspired the Euromarkets. Certainly the regulatory burden could be "too low," a criticism levied against fixed-price federal deposit insurance and derivative securities that were classified as off-balance-sheet and without capital requirements in the 1980s. More likely, any set of harmonized rules may be simply poorly thought through, reflect gross compromises, be incapable of changing quickly with the times (especially as they are set by international bodies), and be exposed to unexpected events or produce unintended consequences.

A competitive approach, whereby each country or regulatory body sets its own regulations toward capital markets, sacrifices the gains of harmonization, but retains the ability to move swiftly in response to new financial products, changes in financial market risks, or new techniques for measuring risk. With many regulatory bodies in healthy competition, those setting the NRB too high or too low have incentives to modify their NRB toward a common sustainable level. Those bodies with NRB too high run the risk of losing market share to other locations. Those bodies with NRB too low run the risk of losing taxpayer money to compensate for financial losses not covered by the regulator's regulatory revenues. The risk to the system is from spillover effects; that is, if problems in a low NRB area spill over into other regions with more prudent NRB levels.

A New Twist to Financial Supervision

As we discussed in Chapter 16, banks have recently developed their own value-at-risk (VAR) techniques for measuring possible changes in value associated with an exposed trading position. These in-house techniques rely on estimates of the standard deviation of price changes (σ), correlation of price changes over time ($\rho_{i,\,t}$), and correlation of price changes across markets (ρ_{ij}). With these data, the manager can calculate the impact of an adverse 1.65σ move in prices for a position in one security or a portfolio. An adverse move of 1.65σ or larger measures the value-at-risk in the sense that on 19 of 20 trading days (that is, 95 percent of the time) the bank would not experience a one-day change in value greater than the calculated VAR.[8] The VAR for longer time intervals (length t) may be calculated in a similar way by replacing σ with $\sigma\sqrt{t}$.

For several reasons, such a calculation only approximates a "true VAR." First, measures of σ and ρ are commonly taken from historical data, which may understate their current values, especially during stressful market conditions. Second, the 1.65σ confidence band assumes normality, which understates the range of price movements when distributions are fat-tailed. Third, the calculation (based on 1.65σ) assumes that the portfolio's exposure can be liquidated in one trading day, which again may be optimistic during stressful times when trading is interrupted.

Against this background, the capital adequacy rules announced by the Bank for International Settlements (BIS) in April 1995 offer a surprising move toward a competitive approach.[9] Previously, banks were required to use standardized measures (summarized in Chapter 13) that banks criticized as crude and inconsistent with market practices. The new BIS proposal allows banks to use *their own* internal risk measurement systems as the basis for their statutory capital requirements for trading activity.

The new BIS proposal allows banks to use their own in-house system, *but* they must measure the impact of an adverse 2.327σ move in prices (implying only a 1 percent chance of a greater price swing), assuming that the portfolio cannot be liquidated for *10* trading days. The BIS system takes the highest VAR measured over the last 60 days and multiplies it by $\sqrt{10}$ to obtain the required capital amount.[10]

Box 17.2 provides an example of the BIS proposal compared with a particular in-house VAR system. This example points out substantial differences in the capital

---

[8]The σ in this discussion refers to the σ of daily price changes. In Box 16.5, we had used monthly data.

[9]See "Basle Model for Banking Safeguards," *Financial Times,* Apr. 13, 1995, and "Do-It-Yourself Regulation," *The Economist,* Apr. 15, 1995.

[10]The volatility for 10 days in $\sigma\sqrt{10}$ where σ is the one-day volatility. The BIS plan includes other details. Bank supervisors may impose a "plus factor" if the in-house models have been inaccurate in predicting their own performance. Banks will be permitted to use short-term subordinated debt as capital to support their trading activities.

TABLE 17.1   **Proposed Risk Weightings for Bank Claims**

Type of Obligor/ Creditor	Standard & Poor's Credit Rating					
	AAA to AA−	*A+ to A−*	*BBB+ to BBB−*	*BB+ to B−*	*Below B−*	*Unrated*
Sovereigns	0%	20%	50%	100%	150%	100%
Banks						
Option 1[a]	20	50	100	100	150	100
Option 2[b]	20	50[c]	50[c]	100[c]	150	50[c]
Corporates	20	100	100	100	150	100

[a]Risk weighting based on risk weighting of sovereign in which the bank is incorporated.

[b]Risk weighting based on the assessment of the individual bank.

[c]Claims on banks of a short original maturity, for example less than six months, would receive a weighting that is one category more favorable than the usual risk weighting on the bank's claims.

Source: Basle Committee on Banking Supervision, "A New Capital Adequacy Framework," BIS, June 1999, p. 31.

requirements for a position under the BIS proposal as opposed to a specific in-house method. Vigorous debate is likely to continue.

The details of the BIS plan are in some sense less critical than the philosophical change allowing banks to calculate their own value-at-risk based on their own methodology. Banks are still likely to argue that capital adequacy measures are too high given the BIS reliance on a 99 percent confidence limit, liquidation in 10 trading days, and limited use of cross-market correlations. Still, the BIS proposal signals that regulators do not own the perfect model for measuring trading risks. Rather than impose a uniform (but incorrect) model, the BIS is prepared to use market-determined measures of risk that should respond more quickly to changes in market conditions and changes in the trader's product list. This approach is thoroughly consistent with the remark quoted earlier that "whenever possible, regulators should use approaches to regulation and supervision that include or simulate market techniques and signals."[11]

Credit Ratings, Capital Requirements, and the BIS

Giving further validation to the theme that international financial regulation is an evolutionary process, in June 1999 the BIS proposed another modification to its capital adequacy requirements. In "A New Capital Adequacy Framework," the Basle Committee on Banking Supervision proposes to incorporate the credit rating of a bank's financial assets into its capital adequacy requirement.[12] In broad terms, the BIS proposal classifies bank assets in two dimensions—by credit rating and by type of obligor—as shown in Table 17.1. It then further divides the credit ratings (from say, AAA to B− and below) into five ranges (or "buckets") plus a sixth category for "unrated" claims.[13] And it

---

[11]Alan Greenspan, "Remarks before the 32nd Annual Conference on Bank Structure and Competition," Federal Reserve Bank of Chicago, May 2, 1996, p. 10.

[12]Basle Committee on Banking Supervision, "A New Capital Adequacy Framework," BIS, June 1999.

[13]To calculate the capital required for a given bank loan, multiply the notional value of the loan by the 8 percent requirement and by the risk weighting. Thus, a $1 million loan to a AAA-rated sovereign is considered risk-free and needs no capital backing, while a $1 million loan to a BBB-rated sovereign would require $40,000 (= $1,000,000 × 0.08 × 0.50) in capital backing.

Box 17.2

Estimating Value-at-Risk Using the BIS Guidelines versus the J. P. Morgan RiskMetrics™ Approach

The following example is based on a $100 position in a 10-year French government bond (*obligations assimilables du Trésor*, or *OATs*). A US$-based investor is exposed to both French interest rate risk and French franc/US$ exchange risk. The example shows the results for the value-at-risk estimate over rolling 10 business day periods.

The table shows the estimates of volatility (σ) that are the foundation of a VAR calculation. The BIS/Basle approach calls for the use of one year of historic data (equally weighted) to estimate σ. The J. P. Morgan RiskMetrics™ approach uses 90 days of historic data (with greater weights on more recent data) to estimate σ. These differences account for the varying estimates of σ and ρ shown in the table. These estimates are the values for May 5, 1995, and would change over time as the sample data change. The column marked "Additive" is the simple sum of the volatilities, not taking into account the correlation of French interest rates and the exchange rate. This column reflects portfolio risk as a gross VAR. The column marked "Diversified" shows the impact of the offsetting exchange risk and interest rate risk. This column reflects portfolio risk as a net VAR.

The graph on the next page shows the estimate of the amounts at risk from the three approaches (BIS additive, BIS diversified, and RiskMetrics™) along with the actual profit and loss from the initial $100 French bond position over the period from January 1994 to May 1995.

The black bars in the graph show the cumulative profit and loss (P&L) on the position realized over the following rolling 10-day periods. Note that most P&Ls are in the range of −$5 to +$5, and that the maximum loss is about $7.50 in spring 1994.

The dashed lines marked "Basle as proposed" represent the 10-day VAR estimated using $\sigma_{Additive}$, and a $2.327\sigma_{Additive}$ band—the amount expected to be exceeded only in 1 percent of the days on the positive side and 1 percent of the days on the negative side. Over the roughly 340-day period, the simulated P&Ls never reach these limits, indicating that these VAR estimates are overly conservative.

The solid lines marked "Basle diversified" represent the 10-day VAR estimated using $\sigma_{Diversified}$, and a $2.327\sigma_{Diversified}$ band—again to capture the 98 percent probability interval. This estimate appears more representative of the 1 percent risk criterion, as the simulated P&Ls meet or exceed the VAR limit on about 2 percent of the sample period days.

	10-year OATs Volatility	French Franc Volatility	Correlation	Additive	Diversified
BIS/Basle	5.26%	4.51%	−0.219	9.77%	6.13%
RiskMetrics™	5.62%	4.08%	−0.213	NA	6.20%

---

groups obligors into three categories—sovereigns, banks, and corporates. Claims on lower-related obligors require the bank to hold more capital to protect against the possibility of default. And for the top three credit ratings, claims on sovereigns require less capital banking than claims against banks or corporates.

The overall plan follows a clear logic, but there are several features that generated adverse reactions during the public comment period that ended March 31, 2000. For

The final set of dotted lines represent the 10-day VAR estimate using the standard RiskMetrics™ data from J. P. Morgan. Notice that this estimate, scaled to represent the same 98 percent probability interval, is more responsive to changing volatilities. Because the RiskMetrics™ calculation is based on only the past 90 days, the impact of the high market volatility during the 1993:Q1 is essentially ignored by 1994:Q3.

The estimated risk of this $100 French bond position illustrates an important issue, because a regulated financial institution would be required to hold some amount of capital to guard against the risk of an adverse price move. According to the BIS proposal, the capital charge on May 5, 1995, on this position would have been $29.40, representing the higher of (1) the current VAR estimate, $9.77, or

(2) three times the average VAR on each of the preceding 60 business days, $29.40. Because the VAR model had performed well in the past, there would be no penalty for the underestimation of risk—the so-called plus factor. Other approaches would naturally return different estimates of the underlying risk of the position. The large difference in the estimated risk of these techniques suggests that the proper method for setting capital requirements covering market risk should be a lively topic of research and debate in the future.

Source: The figures and calculations in this box are adapted from "RiskMetrics™/RD: A Regulatory Dataset," Morgan Guaranty Trust Company, New York, May 26, 1995. RiskMetrics was spun off from J. P. Morgan in 1998. Further information about RiskMetrics is available at its website <www.riskmetrics.com/>.

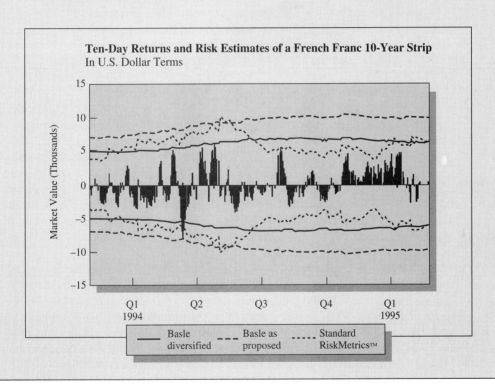

Ten-Day Returns and Risk Estimates of a French Franc 10-Year Strip
In U.S. Dollar Terms

example, while the typical sovereign borrower may be more creditworthy than the typical bank or corporate borrower, once we hold credit rating fixed it is unclear why a different capital requirement should result. This feature seems odd given the history of sovereign defaults and debt rescheduling associated with recent financial crises. Equally puzzling is the 100 percent risk weighting that applies to all corporate claims rated between A+ and B−. A recent study by Edward Altman and Anthony Saunders (2000) shows that the default experience of corporate loans varies substantially across these categories, making a constant risk weighting suspect. Finally, the "unrated" category is somewhat mysterious. If a bank obligor is unrated, it is unclear whether one should assume it to have a high credit rating or a low one. While this may be an accommodation by the BIS to the many countries where credit ratings are not common practice, it could well be argued that a bank should not lend to customers when the credit rating is unknown.

Building on its earlier capital adequacy standards to safeguard against market risk, the BIS proposal offers a "three-pillar" approach for dealing with credit risk. The pillars are (1) minimum regulatory capital requirements, (2) adequate supervisory review of each institution's capital adequacy and its internal assessment process, and (3) the importance of market discipline (discussed in Box 17.1), whereby sufficient disclosure of each bank's capital levels and risk exposures allows other market participants to gauge the adequacy of its counterparty institutions. The BIS proposal also continues the policy of permitting (under certain conditions) internal models of risk assessment, in this case when external (third-party) assessments are unavailable. The revised version of this BIS proposal may be released sometime in late 2000 or 2001.

Foreign Exchange Market Intervention

Intervention as a Policy Instrument

Many government actions (such as monetary policy, interest rate policy, fiscal spending, and taxation policies) could impact the foreign exchange rate in the short run and possibly in the long run. While such a broad view of the impact of official policy decisions is at times called for, official intervention (or central bank intervention) is usually defined as direct purchases and/or sales of foreign currency by the nation's central bank. Recalling Figure 2.2, we know that intervention is an essential part of a pegged exchange rate system. The central bank uses international reserves to buy its domestic currency at the lower intervention limit, and it stands ready to accumulate international reserves as it sells domestic currency at the upper intervention limit.

Under a floating exchange rate system, one might expect the demand by central banks for international reserves to be nil because, under a "pure" or freely floating system, exchange rates are determined only by private market forces.[14] However, after the breakup of Bretton Woods in 1973, central banks continued to safeguard and in some cases expand their stock of international reserves. The modern experience of floating exchange rates is better described as a period of **managed floating exchange rates.** Managed floating implies that from time to time and with greater or lesser amounts, central banks of the major industrial countries have intervened in the foreign exchange market—sometimes individually and sometimes in groups in a **coordinated intervention**—to influence either the level or variability of foreign exchange rates.

In theory, floating exchange rates need not be volatile exchange rates. If the fundamental determinants of foreign exchange rates are stable and predictable, and private speculation is **stabilizing** instead of **destabilizing** (terms we will define shortly), the

---

[14]Some demand for official reserves, say gold or the US$, could be associated with a nation's precautionary demand for funds. In case of a drought or war, the government might desire forms of international money to effect emergency purchases.

free market should produce a pattern of stable and predictable exchange rates just as policymakers and businesses desire. In practice, however, the underlying macro-economic determinants of exchange rates may be noisy and unpredictable, leading to volatile exchange rates—not necessarily more volatile than they *should* be based on economic fundamentals, but certainly more volatile than policymakers *would like* them to be. Moreover, private speculation could be destabilizing, leading either to excessive exchange rate volatility or temporary exchange rate misalignment.

Most policymakers have decided that exchange rates are too important to be left only to pure market forces. Richard Cooper (1984, p. 16) painted the policymaker's train of thought as follows:

> Governments everywhere are held responsible for the management of their national economies. For most countries, the exchange rate . . . [or] some appropriately weighted [combination of] exchange rates is the single most important price. Thus, it is inconceivable that a government held responsible for managing its economy could keep its hands off this particular price. And, sure enough, they have not left it alone.

Cooper's claim that the exchange rate is the single most important price is well known to policymakers in small, open economies. Typically, residents of small countries are *price takers.* They purchase much of what they buy on world markets at world prices and sell much of what they produce on world markets at world prices—and *world prices* commonly means US$ prices. Thus, an exchange rate change has an immediate impact on local currency denominated prices.

Prior to 1973, many economists and policymakers would have questioned whether foreign exchange rates were all that important to the United States. In the Bretton Woods period, the United States was somewhat insulated from exchange rate changes because it was a large country with low dependence on international trade. In addition, prices for many primary materials and manufactured products were denominated in US$.

Since the fall of Bretton Woods, most economists and policymakers have come to realize the far-reaching effects of exchange rate changes even for an economy as large and diverse as the United States. In part, the change of attitude reflects the increased openness of the U.S. economy. As we noted in Chapter 1, U.S. imports and exports (combined) as a percentage of GDP increased from only 6.8 percent in 1950 to nearly 20 percent in 1998. Exchange rate changes have dramatically affected the competitiveness of U.S. manufacturing firms over the floating-rate period and affected the US$ value of foreign direct investments. These effects could, in turn, trigger trade disputes and threaten to roll back the gains from expanding international trade.

The U.S. government itself has a direct interest in keeping foreign investors happy. The U.S. government had $5.6 trillion in debt outstanding at the end of September 1999, including $3.2 trillion in marketable securities. Remarkably, 40 percent of that (or $1.3 trillion) was held by foreign investors, up from only 20 percent in 1994.[15] If fear of foreign exchange changes were to reduce the foreign demand for U.S. government securities even by a small amount, a 10-basis-point (0.10 percent) increase in the cost of debt would raise the government's *annual* interest bill by $5.0 billion.

Acknowledging the importance of exchange rates and the potentially adverse effects of exchange rate misalignments or volatility does not automatically establish a

---

[15]See Michael M. Phillips, "Foreigners' Share of Treasurys Is Growing, Raising Some Fears," *The Wall Street Journal,* Dec. 20, 1999, and *Federal Reserve Bulletin,* Table 1.41, Gross Public Debt of U.S. Treasury, Oct. 1996, p. A27.

valid case for central bank intervention. Under floating exchange rates, an active intervention policy presumes that (1) markets are at times inefficient, thus permitting misaligned or excessively volatile rates, (2) policymakers can identify misaligned exchange rates and periods of excess price volatility, (3) intervention techniques can correct misalignments and excess volatility, and (4) the benefits from correcting misalignments and reducing volatility exceed the costs of conducting intervention.[16] Economists have questioned each of these four elements underpinning an active intervention policy.

As we saw in Chapter 7, the theory of market efficiency entails a joint hypothesis that often makes the interpretation of empirical evidence on efficiency ambiguous. Thus, claims of misaligned or overly volatile exchange rates are often disputed because of disagreement about the benchmark. Policymakers could (in their own self-interest) classify exchange rate behavior as "inefficient" to justify intervention or to blame markets if domestic economic goals are not reached. We also have seen many episodes where a central bank denounces the inefficiency of the market and announces its commitment to a particular exchange rate—only to find itself caving in and permitting an exchange rate change within a few days, weeks, or months.[17] In many of these instances, the central bank sets up a "one-way bet" for speculators, losing large sums of its wealth for the dubious good of postponing the inevitable rate change.

Given this background, many economists are cautious about the advisability or effectiveness of intervention as a policy instrument. We will examine more about the theory and empirical evidence regarding the effects of foreign exchange market intervention.

The Objectives of Central Bank Intervention

Throughout most of the 20th century, most governments sought some form of exchange rate stability, usually by pegging the value of their domestic currency to another currency—that of a neighboring country, a major trading partner, a former colonial parent, or a major international currency like the US$.

As we discussed in Chapter 2, the United States adopted the gold standard in 1879, following the practice of most other countries at that time. The classical gold standard resulted in stable exchange rates, but essentially made the workings of the internal economy subservient to balance in the external economy.[18] Government officials at the time were not happy about this ordering of priorities, and it remains true today that policymakers may forgo an international commitment for the sake of a national commitment.

The classical gold standard ended in 1914 on the eve of World War I and evolved into a gold exchange standard in which countries relied more on gold certificates to economize on scarce gold holdings. The U.S. Federal Reserve System was established in 1913 to supervise banking and "to furnish an elastic currency," unlike gold, which was added to the system largely by chance discoveries. At the conclusion of World War I, the industrial countries allowed their currencies to float until a gold exchange standard resumed in 1925.

---

[16]See Kohlhagen (1979) for an analysis of intervention as a cost-benefit decision.

[17]Central banks were notorious under Bretton Woods for committing to a central rate, only to abandon it under the pressure of economic fundamentals and speculative pressure. The same general description applies to the many instances of realignment within the EMS and with individual exchange regimes, such as Mexico in 1994.

[18]Recall our discussion in Chapter 2 at Figure 2.1.

FIGURE 17.1 Selected European Currencies as a Percentage of Their Pre–World War I Parities

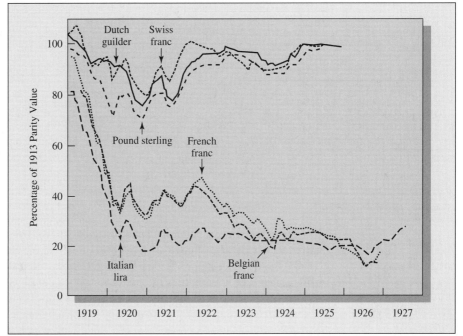

Source: Robert Z. Aliber, "Speculation in the Foreign Exchanges: The European Experience, 1919–1925," *Yale Economic Essays*, 1962.

This period warrants a brief discussion because of its impact on both economists and policymakers. Prices of six European exchange rates are shown in Figure 17.1. The series clearly reflect a volatile experience, with the prices of three currencies (Swiss, Dutch, and British) managing to recover their 1913 parities, and the prices of three others (French, Italian, and Belgian) settling at 15–25 percent of their 1913 parities.[19] Again, we know that fundamental factors could lay behind the paths of the exchange rates in Figure 17.1, making these "equilibrium paths." The alternative hypothesis is that market speculators created exchange rate volatility and misaligned prices, which in turn caused policymakers to reshape their fundamental policies.

Most analysts believed that "destabilizing" speculation was the reason for exchange rate misalignments and volatility. The experience of the 1920s left the strong impression that floating exchange rates were not a viable system. Writing just prior to the close of World War II and the meetings that would establish the Bretton Woods system, Ragnar Nurkse (1944, pp. 137–38) provided the classic interpretation of the 1920s experience:

> If there is anything that the inter-war experience has clearly demonstrated, it is that paper currency exchanges cannot be left free to fluctuate from day-to-day under the influences of market supply and demand . . . If currencies are left free to fluctuate, "speculation" in the widest sense is likely to play havoc with the exchange rate . . . Any considerable or continuous movement of the exchange rate is liable to generate anticipations of a further movement in the same direction.

---

[19]Recall (from Chapter 6) that Germany experienced its first hyperinflation during the early 1920s. The foreign exchange value of the German mark during this period became nearly worthless.

TABLE 17.2   Exchange Rate Arrangements for IFM Member Countries

Category	1984		1994		1998	
	Number	*Percentage*	*Number*	*Percentage*	*Number*	*Percentage*
Independently floating	12	8.1%	58	32.6%	54	29.7%
Managed floating	20	13.5	32	18.0	46	25.3
Subtotal	32	21.6	90	50.6	100	55.0
Pegged currencies	94	63.5	71	39.9	65	35.7
Other systems	22	14.9	17	9.5	17	9.3
Subtotal	116	78.4	88	49.4	82	45.0
Grand total	148	100.0%	178	100.0%	182	100.0%

Source: International Monetary Fund, *International Financial Statistics,* various issues.

Intervention was naturally a part of the pegged exchange rate system established at Bretton Woods. But shortly after the breakdown of the Bretton Woods Agreement in 1973, the International Monetary Fund (IMF) enacted a set of guidelines designed to limit the use of intervention and the potential for conflicts among nations.[20] Conflicts are possible because an exchange rate reflects the price of one currency in terms of another. Therefore, an exchange rate policy adopted by one country may have significant spillover effects in other countries. The guidelines, which are still in effect, specify that member nations of the IMF:

1. Have an obligation to intervene to prevent "disorderly conditions" in the foreign exchange market.
2. Should avoid manipulating exchange rates to prevent balance of payments adjustment or gain an unfair competitive advantage in trade.
3. Should take into account the interests and policies of other members when setting their own intervention policies.

While these guidelines are not binding, they show that the IMF sanctions intervention to promote orderly conditions in the foreign exchange market. In the name of maintaining "orderly market conditions," the IMF allows a broad range of intervention techniques from simple smoothing operations intended to limit short-run volatility in exchange rates, up to exchange rate targeting operations designed to peg the value of a currency at a specific level or range. Indeed, many countries continued to peg their currencies to the US$ or the currency of a major trading partner after 1973.

One illustration of the broad preference for currency stability is simply the large number of IMF member countries (78 percent in 1984) that adopted some form of pegged exchange rate compared with those that adopted a floating-rate system (see Table 17.2). By 1994, however, slightly more than half of the IMF members were following some form of floating regime. And the number of countries floating climbed even further by 1999. Even those listed as "independently floating," such as the United States, Japan, and Mexico, may actively intervene from time to time to manage the level or variability in their exchange rates.

---

[20]The guidelines are specified in the International Monetary Fund's 1974 annual report and the Second Amendment to the Articles of Agreement of the International Monetary Fund (1976).

The Mechanics of Intervention

Central bank intervention typically takes place in the spot foreign exchange market. If the domestic currency is stronger than desired, the central bank sells domestic currency (and buys foreign currency). This is a straightforward transaction because, after all, the central bank prints domestic currency and is well stocked. If the domestic currency is weaker than desired, the central bank buys domestic currency (and sells foreign currency). This is slightly more complicated than it sounds because the central bank does not print foreign currency. It obtains foreign currency from its existing foreign currency balances, from sales of its holdings of foreign government securities, or by borrowing from other central banks or the IMF.

The central bank's foreign exchange traders may buy and sell through a broker or call a trader directly at a major commercial bank (much as we discussed in Chapter 3). At times, a central bank may request that its transactions remain secret; that is, they are not disclosed to the trading community. Unless expressly forbidden, the Federal Reserve allows traders to disclose the Fed's presence in the market.

We now consider the mechanics of central bank intervention. To understand the full effect of official intervention on foreign exchange rates, it is important to consider both direct and indirect effects.

Direct Channels of Intervention.   The term **direct channel** suggests the direct effect associated with changing quantities of money and/or bonds that results from a central bank sale or purchase in the foreign exchange market. The magnitude of the direct effect depends on whether foreign exchange intervention is sterilized or unsterilized. An **unsterilized intervention** is simply a foreign exchange market sale or purchase which, as we will see, has a direct impact on the money supply in both countries. A **sterilized intervention** includes an offsetting transaction in the domestic money market that reverses, or sterilizes, the impact of the initial intervention transaction. As we will see, a sterilized intervention leaves the respective money supplies unchanged, but it affects both nations' bond supplies.

Unsterilized Intervention: An Example.   Suppose that the US$ is stronger than desired against the ¥, so that intervention to sell the dollar is called for. Assume that this intervention is conducted by the U.S. Federal Reserve. Four steps then take place.

1. The Fed writes an official check in US$ and places it on deposit in a U.S. commercial bank, which increases their holdings of US$ reserves at the Fed.
2. In return, the U.S. commercial bank issues a ¥ check payable to the Fed, which deposits the check at the Bank of Japan.
3. The Bank of Japan presents the check to a Japanese commercial bank for payment which reduces the Japanese commercial bank's ¥ reserves at the Bank of Japan.
4. The Japanese commercial bank deducts ¥ from the account of the U.S. commercial bank, and returns the check to the U.S. commercial bank, which makes a similar notation on their books (see Figure 17.2).[21]

---

[21]The Bank of Japan or another central bank also could intervene to support the ¥. This could add an additional step: The Bank of Japan would acquire US$ by selling U.S. Treasury securities or borrowing US$. See Batten and Ott (1984) for details.

FIGURE 17.2   **U.S. Intervention to Support the Japanese Yen**
An Unsterilized Intervention

Federal Reserve Banks (FRB)		U.S. Commercial Banks (USCB)	
+¥ deposits at BOJ (2)	+US$ Reserves of USCB (1)	+US$ Reserves at FRB (1)	
		−¥ deposits at JCB (4)	

Bank of Japan (BOJ)		Japanese Commercial Banks (JCB)	
	+¥ deposits of FRB (2)	−¥ Reserves at BOJ (3)	−¥ deposits at USCB (4)
	−¥ Reserves of JCB (3)		

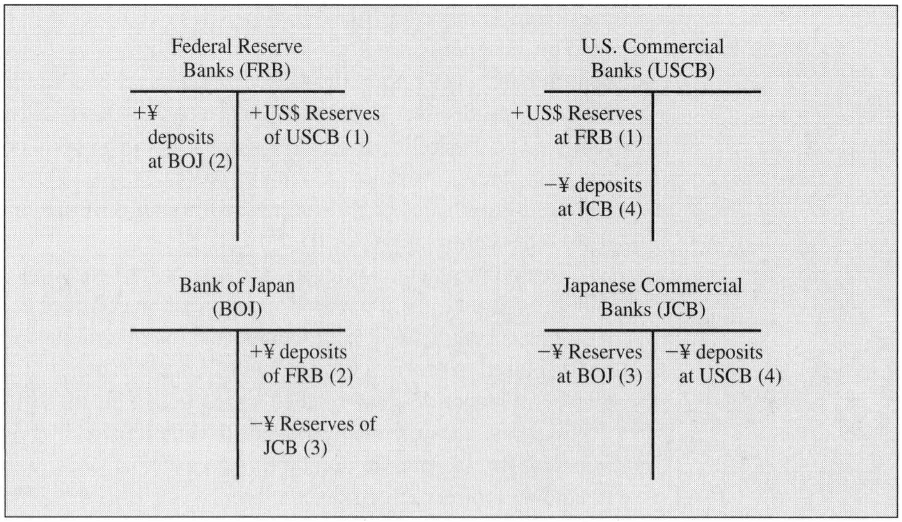

The impact of these steps is an increase in the US$ reserves of the Fed and U.S. commercial banks, and a decrease in the ¥ reserves of the Bank of Japan and Japanese commercial banks. Thus, unsterilized intervention to weaken the US$ is analogous to a monetary expansion in the United States and a monetary contraction in Japan—steps that we know from the monetary approach (see Chapter 6) ought to weaken the dollar. Thus, one could claim that unsterilized intervention is not really a new policy tool.

Sterilized Intervention: An Example.   In the above example, both money supply effects may be unwelcome by the central banks. The Fed may fear that expanding the U.S. money supply will stimulate inflation while the Bank of Japan may fear that a monetary contraction jeopardizes economic expansion. Both central banks can offset, or sterilize the foreign exchange intervention by using *open market operations*. The Fed can reduce the U.S. money supply by selling U.S. Treasury bills to drain reserves from U.S. commercial banks. The Bank of Japan can expand the Japanese money supply by buying Japanese government securities from Japanese commercial banks. These transactions are sketched in Figure 17.3 (below the dashed lines). By design, the money supplies in the United States and Japan are unaffected by a sterilized intervention.

The net effect of a sterilized intervention to weaken the US$ is an increase in the supply of U.S. Treasury securities in public hands, and a decrease in the supply of Japanese government securities in public hands. The impact of this change on the foreign exchange rate depends on the model we use to analyze it.

According to the monetary approach, government securities are assumed to be perfect substitutes with an interest differential equal to the expected exchange rate change. Taking the monetary approach, sterilized intervention therefore would have no *direct* impact on the exchange rate. However, using the portfolio-balance approach, the relative supply of government bonds helps to determine the exchange rate. At the margin, a

FIGURE 17.3 Open Market Operations to Sterilize Foreign Exchange Market Intervention

Federal Reserve Banks (FRB)		U.S. Commercial Banks (USCB)	
+¥ deposits at BOJ	+US$ Reserves of USCB	+US$ Reserves at FRB −¥ deposits at JCB	
	– – – – – – –	– – – – – – –	
	−US$ Reserves of USCB	−US$ Reserves at FRB	
	+U.S. Treasury bills	+U.S. Treasury bills	

Bank of Japan (BOJ)		Japanese Commercial Banks (JCB)	
	+¥ deposits of FRB	−¥ Reserves at BOJ	−¥ deposits at USCB
	−¥ Reserves of JCB		
	– – – – – – –	– – – – – – –	
	+¥ Reserves of JCB	+¥ Reserves at BOJ	
	−Japanese government securities	−Japanese government securities	

sterilized intervention contributes to an excess supply of U.S. Treasury securities. Through the portfolio-balance channel, this would weaken the US$.[22]

Indirect Channels of Intervention.   In addition to direct effects, central bank intervention may generate important indirect effects through the supplies of money and bonds. These **indirect channels** are potentially of greater importance given the huge size of the foreign exchange market and the relatively small size of intervention transactions.

First, foreign exchange intervention may serve as a technique for **signaling** the market about future monetary and fiscal policies. Central bank officials may be viewed as insiders who possess better knowledge of future policy intentions than private market participants. Central bankers could announce their policy intentions with press releases and statements that particular currencies are overvalued or undervalued. But private agents realize that governments face a credibility, or *moral hazard,* problem. The government could persuade people about their policy intentions, and then renege on their commitment.

---

[22]The portfolio-balance channel also includes the effect of the foreign exchange risk premium on the demand for government bonds. See the discussion of this model in Chapter 6.

Official intervention provides a stronger signal than a press release because the bank in essence "puts its money where its mouth is" in accordance with its announced policies. Mussa (1981, pp. 16–17) argued that the role of official intervention is particularly important when the credibility of government policy is in question:

> Official intervention provides a partial solution to the problem of moral hazard . . . when a central bank takes an official position . . . it is providing concrete evidence of the seriousness of [its] intentions by staking its capital in support of them . . . In effect, the central bank can purchase credibility by official intervention in the foreign exchange market.

The signaling channel sounds appealing, but it raises the question of why intervention is often kept secret from both traders and the general public. Dominguez and Frankel (1993, p. 60) argued that most traders are fairly well informed about the central bank's market presence, but other researchers found considerable errors in the public reports of intervention.[23]

A second indirect channel concerns the impact of central bank intervention on **noise trading.** Noise traders form their expectations of exchange rates by taking the recent history of prices (possibly representing only "noise") and extrapolating this into the future. Noise trading could therefore increase the volatility of currency markets and lead to prolonged misalignments. Intervention that interrupts a short-term pattern in rates could effectively reduce the profitability and incidence of noise trading.

Empirical Evidence on Intervention

Gathering evidence on the impact of central bank intervention has been difficult in large part because data on intervention activity are usually kept from the public or presented in summary form only. Data on *international reserves* are readily available for most countries on a quarterly and sometimes monthly basis. But the value of international reserves may change for many reasons, so reserve changes are a poor proxy for what we think of as intervention activity.

At the Versailles summit meeting in 1982, representatives of the G-7 countries agreed to share daily intervention with each other for a study of each country's intervention policy. Collectively, these studies were published in 1983 as the Jurgenson Report, which is summarized in Henderson and Sampson (1983).

More recently, the U.S. Treasury has allowed the Fed to release its daily intervention data to the public with a one-year lag. Some nongovernment researchers have obtained permission from the Bundesbank to use its daily intervention data from the 1980s. The Swiss National Bank has always made its intervention data available to the public.

Descriptive Data on Intervention.   Much of the available data on central bank intervention has been assembled and analyzed in a research monograph by Dominguez and Frankel (1993). We present several of their graphs and tables to summarize some of the general features of the data. Figure 17.4 shows the pattern of foreign exchange market intervention for three central banks: the U.S. Federal Reserve Bank, the German Bundesbank, and the Swiss National Bank. Positive figures indicate US$ purchases and negative figures represent US$ sales.

---

[23]By comparing press reports of intervention with official intervention data over the 1985–1989 period, Klein (1993) computed that there is a 72 percent chance that intervention will be reported (if it actually occurred), and an 88 percent chance that intervention has actually occurred (when we read a press report of intervention).

FIGURE 17.4   Time Patterns of Central Bank Intervention

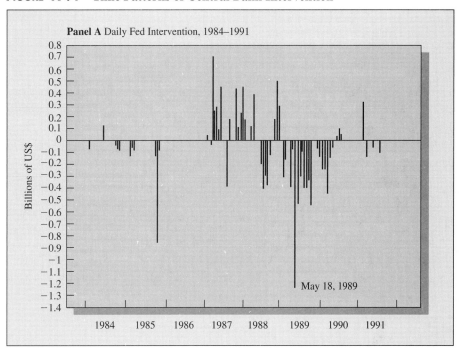

Panel A Daily Fed Intervention, 1984–1991

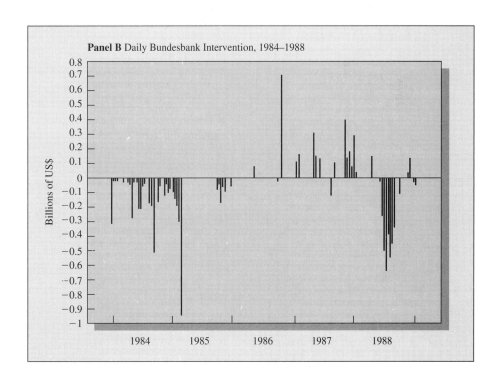

Panel B Daily Bundesbank Intervention, 1984–1988

FIGURE 17.4 (CONT.)   Time Patterns of Central Bank Intervention

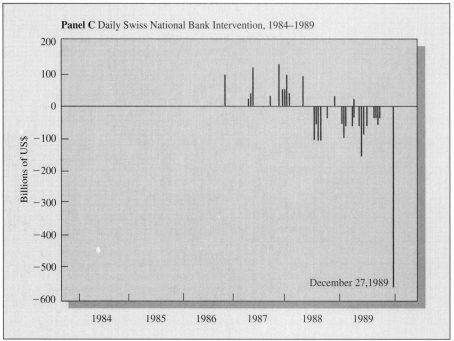

Panel C Daily Swiss National Bank Intervention, 1984–1989

Source: Kathryn Dominguez and Jeffrey A. Frankel, *Does Foreign Exchange Intervention Work?* (Washington, DC: Institute for International Economics, 1993).

The Fed was fairly inactive during the 1981–1984 period (Panel A), but it sold US$ heavily in September 1985 and then returned as a buyer of US$ on numerous dates in 1987. The Fed intervened on 286 days, out of 2,086 trading days from January 1984 to December 1991. On dates that the Fed intervened, its average daily purchase was $162 million and its average daily sale was $187 million over the whole sample. These are clearly small figures when compared with daily foreign exchange trading volume, which measured in the hundreds of billions of US$. Even the largest U.S. intervention, a sale of $1.25 billion against purchases of DM and ¥ on May 18, 1989, is small in comparison with daily transaction volume. Over the longer 1982–1991 period, the Fed was a net seller of US$, selling $35.8 billion and purchasing $15.8 billion.

In Panel B of Figure 17.4, we see that the Bundesbank was a frequent seller of US$ throughout 1984 and early 1985. Bundesbank intervention resumed in 1987 and 1988, very often coordinated with Fed or Swiss National Bank intervention. Bundesbank intervention was more frequent than Fed intervention, occurring on 457 days from January 1984 to December 1988. However, Bundesbank intervention was smaller than Fed intervention, averaging $126 million per day in US$ purchases and $109 million in US$ sales. Overall, however, the Bundesbank transacted net sales of US$ totaling $19.3 billion, about the same as the Fed.

Is Intervention Predictable?   A relevant question raised by Figure 17.4 is whether central bank intervention (I_t) can be related to other variables such as recent exchange rate changes (Δs_t), the deviation of the spot rate from a target level ($S_t - S_t^T$), or past

TABLE 17.3   Private Speculation and Official Intervention: Stabilizing or Destabilizing?

	Private Speculation	*Official Intervention*
Stabilizing	**A** Efficient markets view	**C** Official intervention smooths the market Credible signals of future policy remove uncertainty Encourages stabilizing private speculators
Destabilizing	**B** Inefficient markets: bandwagons, bubbles, noise traders	**D** Stabilization policy gamed by market and becomes destabilizing Intervention is inconsistent with underlying economic policies

interventions (I_{t-1}). The following regression equation illustrates an intervention **reaction function** designed to estimate the central bank's response to these key variables:

$$I_t = \beta_0 + \beta_1 \Delta s_t + \beta_2 (S_t - S_t^T) + \beta_3 I_{t-1} \qquad (17.1)$$

Dominguez and Frankel (1993) estimated several versions of equation (17.1) for both the Fed and the Bundesbank, using daily data for their sample period. In the pre-Plaza period (prior to September 1985), they found no evidence of predictability in the Fed's intervention, but in later subperiods the coefficients of deviations from the target rate (β_2) and previous Fed (and Bundesbank) intervention (β_3) were significant, explaining 30–40 percent of the variation in the Fed intervention.

The Effectiveness of Central Bank Intervention

A perennial debate about intervention is whether it has any effect—beneficial or detrimental—on the course of exchange rates and the ability of policymakers to achieve their larger macroeconomic goals. The debate hinges on whether a market failure has occurred and whether official intervention can correct this failure. Table 17.3 summarizes the key issues.

According to the efficient market theory, private speculators should have a stabilizing effect on market prices (cell A in Table 17.3). "Stabilizing" speculation *does not* mean reducing the variance of exchange rates to zero, but reducing the variance of exchange rates about their equilibrium value. "Destabilizing" private speculation has the opposite effect, driving the exchange rate farther away from its equilibrium value (cell B). Destabilizing speculation could be the result of private speculators who do not base their speculative decisions on fundamental information. Instead, these speculators could form their expectations by extrapolating recent trends (that is, noise trading) which leads to excessive volatility or possibly a speculative bubble.

In Figure 17.5, the solid line represents an equilibrium path of the US\$/DM exchange rate. The dotted line shows the exchange rate as it might appear if destabilizing

Figure 17.5   **Effect of Stabilizing and Destabilizing Speculation on Exchange Rates**

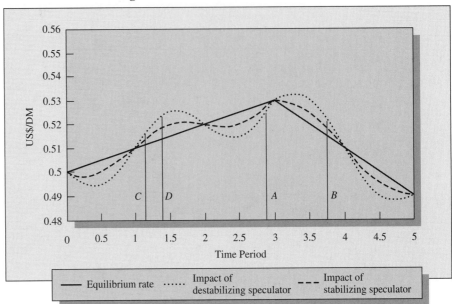

speculators joined the market. The dashed line shows the exchange rate as it would appear if stabilizing speculators were added. Notice that stabilizing speculators act to reduce the variability of the exchange rate around its equilibrium value.

Figure 17.5 also helps us to examine the profitability of these two types of speculation. Stabilizing speculators tend to buy when the exchange rate is undervalued (throughout the [0,1] interval) and sell when the exchange rate is overvalued (throughout the [1,2] interval). Thus, it is argued that stabilizing speculation tends to be profitable. This is not necessarily the case for every stabilizing speculator. If a purchase at point *A* is offset by a sale at point *B*, the two transactions generate a loss even though both transactions are stabilizing in nature.

In contrast, destabilizing speculators tend to buy at prices greater than the equilibrium and sell at prices lower than the equilibrium. This strategy would generally lead to losses for all destabilizing speculators combined. But clearly a few destabilizing speculators could profit by buying an overvalued currency and selling it to someone else at a still *more* overvalued price (say, between points *C* and *D* in Figure 17.5).

Referring back to Table 17.3, we can see that the relationship between official intervention and exchange rate stability also is questioned. Official intervention may be successful at stabilizing exchange rates (cell C). A central bank could use intervention to signal policy changes and reduce uncertainty, and to interrupt speculative bubbles and noise traders, thus reducing volatility in the process.

The connection between stabilizing speculation and profitable speculation has led some economists to assert that profitability is an appropriate criterion on which to evaluate the success of intervention. The earlier example (using points *A* and *B* in Figure 17.5) showed that stabilizing speculation need not be profitable. Moreover, central banks may claim that there are positive externalities associated with intervention. If lower exchange rate volatility promotes the gains from trade in goods and services and capital flows, welfare may still improve even if the central bank suffers a speculative loss.

The final box in Table 17.3 (cell D) raises the prospect that official intervention could actually destabilize the foreign exchange market. If official intervention is at all predictable, private speculators will "game the system" by taking positions in advance of anticipated intervention. More likely, official intervention may be politically motivated and leaving the central bank to support rates that are inconsistent with economic fundamentals. This sets up the classic one-way bet that destabilizes rates and transfers taxpayer resources to private speculators.

Empirical Evidence on the Effectiveness of Intervention.   Before daily intervention data were available, several studies examined whether sterilized intervention that changed the net supplies of bonds outstanding had any impact on exchange rates. These tests relied on portfolio balance models of the exchange rate. As intuition might suggest, intervention has been small relative to the net supplies of assets. Thus, the estimated impact of intervention is always quantitatively small and usually statistically insignificant.[24]

Profitabiliy is another way, although imperfect, for evaluating the effectiveness of intervention. In Chapter 3, we noted a study by Taylor (1982) which showed that central banks had lost considerable amounts in the 1973–1979 period. Published newspaper accounts suggested that European central banks lost billions in their attempt to defend the central rate in the European Exchange Rate Mechanism.[25]

A more recent study by Leahy (1995) used the daily intervention data from the Fed and incorporated interest cost and earnings on outstanding positions. His results show that the Fed made considerable profits during the 1980s. Figure 17.6 summarizes Leahy's results for U.S. intervention against the DM and the yen. Over the 1980s, Leahy estimated that the Fed earned more than $16.0 billion from its intervention activities. The explanation for these profits is not clear, but Leahy rejected chance or a currency risk premium as being responsible. The magnitude of this number may surprise the reader. But the sign of the number might be anticipated from the Fed's successful participation in an informal target zone of the US$ versus other currencies.

Several studies have examined the impact of intervention on the variance of exchange rates. In a model where volatility is allowed to fluctuate on a daily basis, Kathryn Dominguez (1993, 1998) found that in the post–Louvre Accord period, public announcements of Fed and Bundesbank intervention were associated with lower daily volatility. This evidence suggests that intervention may "work" to stabilize rates in certain circumstances.

Finally, studies have investigated the impact of intervention on the path of exchange rates. Dominguez and Frankel (1993) found that in 11 episodes of intervention, the exchange rate movement in the first month following the intervention was in the intended direction. In 6 of those 11 cases (see Table 17.4), this required the exchange rate to reverse its previous course.

---

[24]See Lewis (1988) for an example.

[25]European central banks lost an estimated $4–$6 billion during the month of September 1992. "Europe Central Banks Said to Have Lost Up to $6 Billion Trying to Help Currencies," *The Wall Street Journal,* Sept. 30, 1992.

FIGURE 17.6   **Cumulative Intervention Profits and Intervention Positions**
In the DM and Yen versus the US$

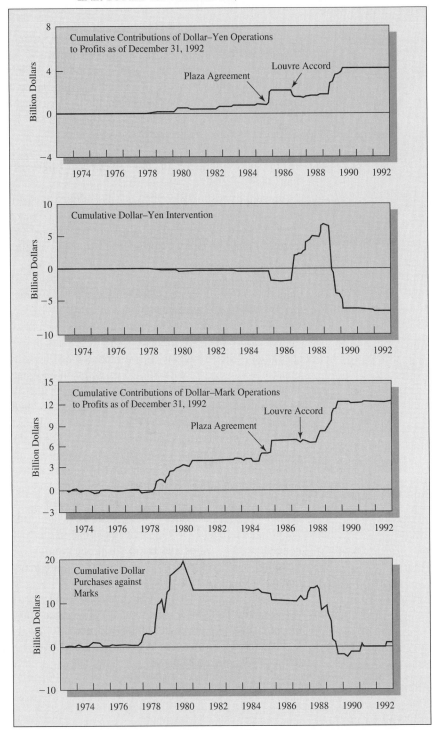

Source: Reprinted from Michael P. Leahy, "The Profitability of U.S. Intervention in the Foreign Exchange Market," *Journal of International Money and Finance* 14, no. 6 (Dec. 1995), pp. 832, 834, with kind permission from Elsevier Science Ltd., The Boulevard, Langford Lane, Kidlington OX5 IGB, UK.

TABLE 17.4 **Percentage Changes in the $/DM Exchange Rate**
One Month before and One Month after Frequent Concerted Intervention

Episode	Percent Change in DM/$ Month before Intervention	Federal Reserve Intervention	Bundesbank Intervention	Swiss National Bank Intervention	Percent Change in DM/$ Month after Intervention
Jan. 11–Mar. 4, 1985	2.3	−643	−3,470	0	−8.3
Sept. 23–Nov. 12, 1985	4.5	−3,301	−1,123	0	−3.5
Mar. 11–June 3, 1987	1.3	4,840	744	305	0.8
Oct. 19, 1987–Jan. 21, 1988	−0.5	4,600	3,130	935	2.0
May 31–Oct. 7, 1988	2.5	−5,066	−7,851	−730	−3.7
Oct. 31–Dec. 2, 1988	−5.8	2,600	359	70	3.0
Dec. 8, 1988–Feb. 6, 1989	−1.3	−2,230	−174	−415	−0.86
Mar. 3–Oct. 12, 1989	−0.86	−19,676	NA	−1,280	−1.5
Feb. 23–Apr. 9, 1990	−1.1	−1,780	NA	NA	−1.96
May 29–July 17, 1990	−0.16	1,000	NA	NA	−5.07
Feb. 4–Feb. 12, 1991	−2.59	1,336	NA	NA	7.98

Note: Intervention in millions of US$.

Source: Kathryn Dominguez and Jeffrey A. Frankel, *Does Foreign Exchange Intervention Work?* (Washington, DC: Institute for International Economics, 1993).

Dominguez and Frankel argued that intervention tends to work in these periods by changing traders' expectations; it tends to send the strongest signal and have the most chance of success when three conditions are met: surprise, publicity, and coordination with other central banks. The value of surprise is that unexpected events matter most in influencing exchange rates. This may sometimes mean that a central bank has to go against an earlier statement or promise. Publicity implies that public interventions have more impact than secret interventions. Coordination suggests that intervention is more likely to succeed when central banks act in unison, rather than as separate and smaller forces.

Security Transaction Taxes: Should We Throw Sand in the Gears of Financial Markets?

Finally, some economists have proposed securities transaction taxes (STTs) as an indirect technique for calming financial market volatility. For economists who view financial markets as prone to excessive volatility and pricing misalignments associated with a climate of short-run, speculative trading, it is an easy step to propose an STT. It is argued that taxing undesired short-run speculative behavior not only would discourage this behavior and make markets more efficient, but also could raise considerable tax revenue. James Tobin, the 1981 Nobel laureate in economics, was one of the first to endorse an STT; in some discussions an STT is called the "Tobin Tax."[26]

The case in favor of an STT rests on the argument that a transaction tax will reduce unwanted, destabilizing speculation without significantly affecting the ability of the market to channel long-term capital flows. By simple mathematics, a 0.5 percent transaction

---

[26]See Tobin (1978, 1984, 1992).

tax is a substantial disincentive to trade over a one-day horizon, but a far less important barrier for a one-year or five-year horizon.[27] This property, it is argued, would drive short-term, speculative traders out the market and reduce short-term exchange rate volatility. This in turn would reduce the risk premium associated with excess volatility, lower the cost of capital to firms, and raise investment spending.

The case against an STT has several components. Opponents of STTs argue that the jury is still out on the issue of excess volatility. As we concluded in Chapter 6, many fundamental explanations for exchange rate volatility can be offered without appealing to speculative bubbles. And empirical evidence can be offered that either favors or rejects the notion of excess volatility.[28] Moreover, as a theoretical matter we know that an STT will discourage both unwanted destabilizing speculation and desirable stabilizing speculation. Unless we can predict how an STT will affect both "good" and "bad" speculation, we cannot use theory to predict its impact on excess volatility.

This suggests that the relationship between an STT and excess volatility is an empirical matter. Many countries have some type of STT that applies to transaction in equity markets. The evidence shows that the presence of STTs in 23 countries did nothing to reduce the severity of the decline in stocks' prices at the time of the October 19, 1987, crash.[29] Analyzing longer periods before and after the crash, Roll (1989) found some evidence (albeit not significant) of inverse correlation between STTs and stock market volatility.

While there is a healthy controversy surrounding these technical issues, there is much broader agreement that the main obstacle to an STT is enforceability. Unless *all* countries in the world agree to a common STT with equal enforcement, it is clear that all (or nearly all) transactions would migrate to the abstaining countries, making the impact of the STT nil. Even if all countries were to commit to an STT, it is possible that markets could design a new security that is not taxed and/or a new means of clearing, settlement, and transfer that would effectively avoid the taxed transaction. Unless there is broad international political agreement, there is no incentive for an individual country to implement an STT and watch its financial transactions migrate to another country.

---

[27]See Hakkio (1994) for detailed examples.

[28]See MacDonald and Taylor (1992, pp. 11–16). Bartolini and Bodnar (1996) rejected the excess volatility interpretation.

[29]Hakkio (1994) looked at the period one week before to two weeks after the crash and found an insignificant 0.03 correlation between the STT rate and the size of the market decline.

Concluding Thoughts

In this chapter, we have argued that regulation can affect markets. But because of the dynamic nature of financial markets and competition among regulators there are constraints on what regulation can achieve and how international financial regulation can be implemented. Similarly, national policymakers can affect exchange rates and their volatility. But because of the size and speed of the market, there are constraints on what intervention can achieve and which intervention strategies are likely to succeed.

A central theme in this book has been the close connection between prices in financial markets and policies that private agents and public officials enact toward those markets.

We have covered many examples that have illustrated situations in which prices affect policies. Changes in exchange rates and other international financial market prices affect the risks and rewards facing institutional investors and corporate borrowers, large and small. Short- and long-term price volatility has forced fundamental changes onto these private agents—changing the currency, location, and terms on which to invest or borrow, and changing the way in which agents measure and manage risk. These price changes have also affected public policies and often in fundamental ways. Over the last 25 years, financial markets (not to mention entire economies) have opened up to international capital flows. Countries have changed their exchange rate arrangements, at times to permit greater flexibility in prices but often in attempts to reduce price volatility. The development of new markets for futures, options, and swaps has meant that public policies toward these markets often lagged behind market practices. The intent of policies often has been to dampen price movements and to be sure that players in the market have sufficient capital to withstand the risk of a sudden price change.

But there also are examples where policies affect prices and markets. Overregulation toward onshore markets was a key factor leading to the development of offshore markets. Official policies toward exchange rates, in particular pegging and targeting arrangements, have often been the source of exchange rate instability as speculators tested the credibility of those policies. Until recently, an absence of regulation allowed derivative securities to be treated as off-balance-sheet transactions without capital requirements, which increased the attractiveness of these instruments and the growth of the market.

In the lead quote to Chapter 1, Robert Aliber compared international finance to a game between politicians, who want to win elections and a revered place in their national history, and corporate treasurers who want to make money or at least avoid losses. The game has continued because the interests of national groups have been in conflict. Bureaucrats are chosen by domestic politicians who are elected by domestic voters who are largely focused on domestic, not international, issues. In the past, this has set the stage for profit opportunities in the private sector. Since the monetary and fiscal policies of the world's trading nations are often inconsistent, an adjustment eventually must take place, meaning a change in the exchange rate.

How does this natural tension among national economic policies end? A speculative answer is that harmonization will prevail. The markets we have analyzed in this text are truly global. They transcend national boundaries and are larger than most nation-states. Most markets operate on a 24-hour basis and technology is opening up access to wider groups that threaten the competitive advantage of existing players. This is not to say that international financial markets are beyond regulation. Indeed there is a growing effort to harmonize regulations across countries and to make regulation functional in that all institutions dealing in the same financial product will be regulated identically, thus creating a level international playing field. The ability of nation-states to safeguard their own national policies will decline.

A safer answer is that tension among national economic policies will persist. As long as there are nation-states with separately elected officials and national monies, conflict is inevitable. And as economic theory would predict, if national policymakers agree to a new set of rules about the exchange rate system, that will simply shift the conflict toward another area, such as industrial performance, unemployment, environmental considerations, or human rights. Market participants will always test the credibility of national policymakers and work to stay ahead of the game.

Questions

1. Describe two broad categories of policymaking that are available to give direction to international financial markets.

2. How do users of financial services benefit from a regulatory framework? Give some examples. Do users of financial services also incur costs from a regulatory framework?

3. What are the regulatory costs that might be incurred by suppliers of financial services? What is the net regulatory burden (NRB)?

4. What is structural arbitrage? How would you explain the discrepancy between what is implied by the theory of structural arbitrage and what we observe in the real world?

5. How do financial centers compete on NRB? Give some examples.

6. How does international competition among financial centers affect the users and suppliers of financial services?

7. List and explain Kane's "average adaptive efficiencies" of various players in the international financial markets.

8. What are the advantages of coordinated approaches to regulation in international financial markets? The disadvantages?

9. What is the BIS capital adequacy rule? What does it provide in terms of coordinated approaches to international financial markets?

10. Define the expression *value-at-risk (VAR)*. Describe several ways to measure VAR. What are some of the shortcomings?

11. What are the main goals of central bank intervention? What are its main channels?

12. Define the terms *stabilizing* and *destabilizing speculation*. Are these expressions synonymous with profitable and unprofitable speculation? Explain why or why not.

13. Define the terms *sterilized* and *unsterilized intervention*. Which one is likely to have more effect on exchange rates? Why do central banks often prefer to use sterilized intervention?

14. Describe the level of success in central bank intervention over the last 25 years. Suggest reasons why in some cases intervention was successful and in other cases it was not.

15. Summarize the main arguments for and against a securities transaction tax. Why is it difficult to enforce an STT?

Exercises

1. Suppose the differential in the net regulatory burden (NRB) between London and Singapore has traditionally been 10 basis points to the advantage of London.
   a. If London were to reduce reserve requirements and thus reduce its NRB by 10 basis points, what would you expect the Singaporean authorities to decide?
   b. What would happen if the authorities in Singapore did nothing? Under what conditions would Singapore's financial markets be relatively unaffected by the London move?

2. Suppose the A$ is overvalued against the euro.
   a. Describe how Australian authorities would proceed in an unsterilized intervention.
   b. According to the monetary approach, how will the intervention impact the exchange rate?

3. Suppose the Japanese ¥ is overvalued against the US$.
   a. Describe the process of sterilized intervention in this case.
   b. What would the monetary approach to exchange rates predict concerning the impact of the sterilized intervention? Why?

   c. What would the portfolio-balance approach to exchange rates predict concerning the impact of the sterilized intervention? Why?

4. In the early 1990s, the dollar continuously depreciated against major currencies, especially against the Japanese yen. Despite repeated interventions by the Federal Reserve and the Bank of Japan, the US$ depreciated from 125 ¥/$ at the beginning of 1993 to 85 ¥/$ at the beginning of 1995. During that time, the American economy boomed and the Japanese economy plunged into recession. The U.S. trade deficit stayed at record highs, especially against Japan. The U.S. budget deficit was reduced, but remained at a high level relative to the GDP. Inflation was moderate in the United States and low in Japan.
   a. Use the different frameworks developed in this book to explain why central bank intervention was not effective in halting the dollar slide against the yen.
   b. What kind of policy action could U.S. and Japanese authorities take to reverse the current trend?

References

Aliber, Robert Z. "Speculation in the Foreign Exchanges: The European Experience, 1919–1925." *Yale Economic Essays* 2, (1962), pp. 171–245.

Altman, Edward, and Anthony Saunders. "An Analysis and Critique of the BIS Proposal on Capital Adequacy Ratings." Working Paper, Stern School of Business, Feb. 2000.

Bartolini, Leonardo, and Gordon M. Bodnar. "Are Exchange Rates Excessively Volatile? And What Does 'Excessive Volatility' Mean, Anyway?" *IMF Staff papers* 43, no. 1 (Mar. 1996), pp. 72–96.

Batten, Dallas S., and Mack Ott. "What Can Central Banks Do about the Value of the Dollar?" *Monthly Review,* Federal Reserve Bank of St. Louis, May 1984.

Cooper, Richard N. "Recent History of World Monetary Problems." In *Future of the International Monetary System.* ed. T. Agmon, R. Hawkins, and R. Levich. Lexington, MA: D. C. Heath, 1984.

Dominguez, Kathryn. "Does Central Bank Intervention Increase the Volatility of Foreign Exchange Rates?" NBER Working Paper No. 4532, Cambridge, MA, Nov. 1993.

———. "Central Bank Intervention and Exchange Rate Volatility." *Journal of International Money and Finance* 17, no. 1 (Feb. 1998); pp. 161–90.

Dominguez, Kathryn, and Jeffrey A. Frankel. *Does Foreign Exchange Intervention Work?* Washington, DC: Institute for International Economics, 1993.

Hakkio, Craig S. "Should We Throw Sand in the Gears of Financial Markets?" Federal Reserve Bank of Kansas City. *Economic Review* 79, no. 2 (1994), pp. 17–30.

Henderson, Dale, and Stephanie Sampson. "Intervention in Foreign Exchange Markets: A Summary of Ten Staff Studies." *Federal Reserve Bulletin* 69 (Nov. 1983), pp. 830–36.

Huertas, Thomas F. "The Regulation of International Conglomerates: The Importance of Market Supervision." *Journal of International Financial Management and Accounting* 4, no. 3 (Autumn 1992), pp. 237–44.

Jurgensen, P. "Report of the Working Group on Exchange Market Intervention [Jurgensen Report]." Washington, DC: U.S. Treasury Department, 1983.

Kane, Edward J. "Competitive Financial Reregulation: An International Perspective." In *Threats to International Financial Stability.* ed. R. Portes and A. Swoboda, London: Cambridge University Press, 1987.

Klein, Michael W. "The Accuracy of Reports of Foreign Exchange Intervention." *Journal of International Money and Finance* 12, no. 6 (Dec. 1993), pp. 644–53.

Kohlhagen, Steven W. "The Identification of Destabilizing Foreign Exchange Speculation." *Journal of International Economics* 9, no. 3 (Aug. 1979), pp. 321–40.

Leahy, Michael P. "The Profitability of U.S. Intervention in the Foreign Exchange Market." *Journal of International Money and Finance* 14, no. 6 (Dec. 1995), pp. 823–44.

Levich, Richard M., and Ingo Walter. "Tax-Driven Regulatory Drag: European Financial Centers in the 1990s." In *Reforming Capital Income Taxation,* ed. Horst Siebert. Tübingen Germany: J. C. B. Mohr Publishing, 1990.

Lewis, Karen K. "Testing the Portfolio Balance Model: A Multi-Lateral Approach." *Journal of International Economics* 24 (1988), pp. 109–27.

MacDonald, Ronald, and Mark P. Taylor. "Exchange Rate Economics: A Survey." *IMF Staff Papers* 39, no. 1 (Mar. 1992), pp. 1–57.

Mussa, Michael. "The Role of Official Intervention." *Group of Thirty Occasional Papers,* No. 6. New York: Group of Thirty, 1981.

Nurkse, Ragnar. *International Currency Experience: Lessons of the Interwar Period.* Princeton, NJ: League of Nations, 1944.

Roll, Richard. "Price Volatility, International Market Links, and Their Implications for Regulatory Policies." *Journal of Financial Services Research* 3 (1989), pp. 211–46.

Smith, Roy C., and Ingo Walter. *Street Smarts.* Boston: Harvard University Press, 1997.

Taylor, Dean. "Official Intervention in the Foreign Exchange Market, or, Bet against the Central Bank," *Journal of Political Economy* 90, no. 2 (Apr. 1982), pp. 356–68.

Tobin, James. "On the Efficiency of the Financial System." *Lloyds Bank Review* 153 (July 1984), pp. 1–15.

——— . "A Proposal for International Monetary Reform." *Eastern Economic Journal* 4, no. 3–4 (1978), pp. 153–159.

——— . "Tax the Speculators." *Financial Times,* Dec. 22, 1992

APPENDIX A
PURCHASING POWER PARITY CALCULATIONS: UNITED STATES AND GERMANY

In this appendix, we show the method of calculation for the purchasing power parity (PPP) figures that appear in Figure 4.4. In the table that follows, data on the $/DM spot exchange rate, the German consumer price index (CPI) and the United States CPI appear in the three columns after the date. Note that the CPI takes the average of 1995 as an index value of 100. These are the only raw data needed to make the calculations for Figure 4.4.

In column 5, we show the ratio of the U.S. CPI relative to the German CPI. In column 6, we enter the PPP spot exchange rate for period $t+n$, defined in equation 4.7a as

$$S_{\text{PPP}, t+n} = S_{\text{\$/DM}, 0} \frac{P_{\text{US}, t+n} / P_{G, t+n}}{P_{\text{US}, 0} / P_{G, 0}} \qquad (4.7\text{a})$$

In our example, 1973 (quarter 1) is the base period that we selected arbitrarily to demonstrate the method of calculation.

In column 7, we calculate the real exchange rate defined from equation 4.9 as the ratio of the actual spot exchange rate relative to the PPP spot rate. Finally, in column 8 we show the percentage deviation from PPP measured as the natural logarithm of the real rate.

This technique measures the cumulative change in relative prices and the exchange rate starting from a base period. The real exchange rate measures the cumulative deviation from PPP starting from a base period. This technique allows us to measure the length of time required for exchange rates to revert back to their PPP level.

APPENDIX A Purchasing Power Parity Calculations
United States and Germany

Date: Year and Quarter	$/DM Spot, End of Period	Germany CPI	U.S. CPI	CPI (US)/ CPI (G)	PPP Spot	Ratio Actual/ PPP	Percent Deviation from PPP
1973Q1	0.3523	46.82	28.20	0.6023	0.3523	1.0000	0.0000
1973Q2	0.4124	47.73	28.82	0.6038	0.3532	1.1676	0.1549
1973Q3	0.4140	48.15	29.45	0.6116	0.3578	1.1572	0.1460
1973Q4	0.3700	49.10	30.14	0.6138	0.3591	1.0304	0.0299
1974Q1	0.3964	50.27	30.99	0.6165	0.3606	1.0992	0.0946
1974Q2	0.3914	51.08	31.86	0.6237	0.3648	1.0728	0.0703
1974Q3	0.3770	51.55	32.83	0.6369	0.3725	1.0120	0.0119
1974Q4	0.4150	52.25	33.79	0.6467	0.3783	1.0972	0.0927
1975Q1	0.4264	53.25	34.40	0.6460	0.3779	1.1286	0.1209
1975Q2	0.4247	54.26	34.94	0.6439	0.3766	1.1275	0.1200
1975Q3	0.3757	54.68	35.69	0.6527	0.3818	0.9842	−0.0160
1975Q4	0.3813	55.15	36.26	0.6575	0.3846	0.9916	−0.0084
1976Q1	0.3940	56.03	36.61	0.6534	0.3822	1.0308	0.0304
1976Q2	0.3885	56.67	37.06	0.6540	0.3825	1.0156	0.0155
1976Q3	0.4104	56.80	37.65	0.6629	0.3877	1.0586	0.0569
1976Q4	0.4233	57.18	38.08	0.6660	0.3895	1.0866	0.0831
1977Q1	0.4186	58.15	38.75	0.6664	0.3898	1.0740	0.0714
1977Q2	0.4277	58.77	39.58	0.6735	0.3939	1.0858	0.0823
1977Q3	0.4334	58.94	40.16	0.6814	0.3985	1.0874	0.0838
1977Q4	0.4751	59.19	40.60	0.6859	0.4012	1.1841	0.1690
1978Q1	0.4943	59.91	41.29	0.6892	0.4031	1.2262	0.2039
1978Q2	0.4819	60.44	42.36	0.7009	0.4099	1.1754	0.1616
1978Q3	0.5158	60.40	43.36	0.7179	0.4199	1.2285	0.2058
1978Q4	0.5470	60.60	44.24	0.7300	0.4270	1.2811	0.2477
1979Q1	0.5354	61.66	45.34	0.7353	0.4301	1.2449	0.2191
1979Q2	0.5411	62.50	46.90	0.7504	0.4389	1.2327	0.2092
1979Q3	0.5739	63.29	48.45	0.7655	0.4478	1.2817	0.2482
1979Q4	0.5775	63.84	49.86	0.7810	0.4568	1.2642	0.2345
1980Q1	0.5150	65.08	51.81	0.7961	0.4656	1.1059	0.1007
1980Q2	0.5688	66.14	53.68	0.8116	0.4747	1.1981	0.1807
1980Q3	0.5521	66.54	54.69	0.8219	0.4807	1.1484	0.1384
1980Q4	0.5105	67.16	56.12	0.8356	0.4888	1.0444	0.0434

Date: Year and Quarter	$/DM Spot, End of Period	Germany CPI	U.S. CPI	CPI (US)/ CPI (G)	PPP Spot	Ratio Actual/ PPP	Percent Deviation from PPP
1981Q1	0.4758	68.77	57.61	0.8377	0.4900	0.9710	−0.0294
1981Q2	0.4183	70.00	58.94	0.8420	0.4925	0.8492	−0.1634
1981Q3	0.4306	71.00	60.63	0.8539	0.4995	0.8620	−0.1485
1981Q4	0.4435	71.90	61.50	0.8554	0.5003	0.8864	−0.1205
1982Q1	0.4142	72.85	62.00	0.8511	0.4978	0.8321	−0.1838
1982Q2	0.4065	73.73	62.95	0.8538	0.4994	0.8141	−0.2057
1982Q3	0.3956	74.62	64.14	0.8596	0.5028	0.7869	−0.2396
1982Q4	0.4208	75.30	64.27	0.8535	0.4992	0.8429	−0.1710
1983Q1	0.4121	75.79	64.24	0.8476	0.4958	0.8313	−0.1848
1983Q2	0.3934	76.18	65.05	0.8539	0.4995	0.7877	−0.2387
1983Q3	0.3789	76.94	65.83	0.8556	0.5005	0.7571	−0.2782
1983Q4	0.3671	77.31	66.40	0.8589	0.5024	0.7308	−0.3136
1984Q1	0.3861	77.97	67.12	0.8608	0.5035	0.7668	−0.2655
1984Q2	0.3592	78.35	67.86	0.8661	0.5066	0.7090	−0.3439
1984Q3	0.3305	78.35	68.59	0.8754	0.5121	0.6455	−0.4377
1984Q4	0.3177	78.92	69.09	0.8754	0.5121	0.6204	−0.4775
1985Q1	0.3233	79.78	69.55	0.8718	0.5099	0.6341	−0.4556
1985Q2	0.3267	80.27	70.38	0.8768	0.5128	0.6371	−0.4509
1985Q3	0.3745	80.07	70.90	0.8855	0.5179	0.7232	−0.3241
1985Q4	0.4063	80.31	71.53	0.8907	0.5210	0.7799	−0.2486
1986Q1	0.4315	80.34	71.71	0.8926	0.5221	0.8265	−0.1906
1986Q2	0.4548	80.11	71.53	0.8929	0.5223	0.8709	−0.1382
1986Q3	0.4949	79.72	72.06	0.9039	0.5287	0.9360	−0.0661
1986Q4	0.5153	79.47	72.47	0.9119	0.5334	0.9660	−0.0346
1987Q1	0.5540	79.92	73.28	0.9169	0.5363	1.0329	0.0324
1987Q2	0.5465	80.22	74.23	0.9253	0.5412	1.0097	0.0096
1987Q3	0.5440	80.22	75.07	0.9358	0.5474	0.9938	−0.0062
1987Q4	0.6323	80.25	75.72	0.9436	0.5519	1.1457	0.1360
1988Q1	0.6027	80.62	76.17	0.9448	0.5526	1.0905	0.0867
1988Q2	0.5491	81.06	77.13	0.9515	0.5566	0.9866	−0.0135
1988Q3	0.5320	81.17	78.16	0.9629	0.5632	0.9445	−0.0571
1988Q4	0.5617	81.46	78.97	0.9694	0.5670	0.9906	−0.0095
1989Q1	0.5283	82.75	79.84	0.9648	0.5643	0.9362	−0.0659
1989Q2	0.5122	83.52	81.16	0.9717	0.5684	0.9011	−0.1042
1989Q3	0.5352	83.55	81.81	0.9792	0.5727	0.9345	−0.0677
1989Q4	0.5890	84.09	82.60	0.9823	0.5746	1.0251	0.0248
1990Q1	0.5902	85.01	84.02	0.9884	0.5781	1.0209	0.0207
1990Q2	0.5983	85.45	84.87	0.9932	0.5809	1.0298	0.0294
1990Q3	0.6393	85.83	86.34	1.0059	0.5884	1.0866	0.0831
1990Q4	0.6693	86.63	87.74	1.0128	0.5924	1.1299	0.1221
1991Q1	0.5824	85.47	88.46	1.0350	0.6054	0.9621	−0.0387
1991Q2	0.5519	86.24	88.99	1.0319	0.6036	0.9144	−0.0895
1991Q3	0.6013	87.71	89.69	1.0226	0.5981	1.0053	0.0053
1991Q4	0.6596	89.31	90.36	1.0118	0.5918	1.1146	0.1085
1992Q1	0.6088	90.51	91.00	1.0054	0.5881	1.0352	0.0345
1992Q2	0.6549	91.51	91.74	1.0025	0.5864	1.1168	0.1105
1992Q3	0.7096	92.04	92.46	1.0046	0.5876	1.2076	0.1886
1992Q4	0.6196	92.34	93.12	1.0084	0.5899	1.0504	0.0492
1993Q1	0.6195	94.67	93.91	0.9920	0.5802	1.0676	0.0654
1993Q2	0.5923	95.57	94.63	0.9902	0.5792	1.0228	0.0225
1993Q3	0.6173	96.17	95.00	0.9878	0.5778	1.0684	0.0662
1993Q4	0.5793	96.24	95.66	0.9940	0.5814	0.9964	−0.0036
1994Q1	0.5981	97.54	96.27	0.9870	0.5773	1.0360	0.0354
1994Q2	0.6268	98.17	96.88	0.9869	0.5772	1.0859	0.0824
1994Q3	0.6459	98.77	97.74	0.9896	0.5788	1.1158	0.1096
1994Q4	0.6457	98.74	98.20	0.9945	0.5817	1.1099	0.1043

Date: Year and Quarter	$/DM Spot, End of Period	Germany CPI	U.S. CPI	CPI (US)/ CPI (G)	PPP Spot	Ratio Actual/ PPP	Percent Deviation from PPP
1995Q1	0.7227	99.54	99.00	0.9946	0.5817	1.2423	0.2170
1995Q2	0.7227	99.94	99.88	0.9994	0.5846	1.2363	0.2121
1995Q3	0.7048	100.31	100.32	1.0001	0.5850	1.2049	0.1864
1995Q4	0.6976	100.21	100.80	1.0059	0.5884	1.1857	0.1703
1996Q1	0.6776	100.98	101.72	1.0073	0.5892	1.1501	0.1399
1996Q2	0.6571	101.38	102.72	1.0132	0.5926	1.1087	0.1032
1996Q3	0.6550	101.64	103.27	1.0160	0.5943	1.1021	0.0972
1996Q4	0.6432	101.68	104.01	1.0229	0.5983	1.0750	0.0723
1997Q1	0.5960	102.78	104.71	1.0188	0.5959	1.0002	0.0002
1997Q2	0.5734	102.91	105.13	1.0216	0.5975	0.9595	−0.0413
1997Q3	0.5664	103.91	105.55	1.0158	0.5941	0.9533	−0.0478
1997Q4	0.5580	103.78	105.96	1.0210	0.5972	0.9344	−0.0679
1998Q1	0.5415	104.01	106.25	1.0215	0.5975	0.9062	−0.0985
1998Q2	0.5529	104.34	106.81	1.0237	0.5988	0.9234	−0.0797
1998Q3	0.5967	104.61	107.23	1.0250	0.5996	0.9952	−0.0048
1998Q4	0.5977	104.24	107.60	1.0322	0.6038	0.9900	−0.0101
1999Q1	0.5492	104.28	108.02	1.0359	0.6059	0.9065	−0.0982
1999Q2	0.5281	104.84	109.07	1.0403	0.6085	0.8678	−0.1418
1999Q3	0.5453	105.28	109.75	1.0425	0.6098	0.8943	−0.1117
1999Q4	0.5136	105.24	110.42	1.0492	0.6137	0.8370	−0.1780

Average deviation from PPP $= -0.0067$

Standard deviation $=$ 0.1632

T-statistic $= -0.0067/(0.1632/\sqrt{107}) = -0.4254$

Source: Data source is *International Financial Statistics* for $/DM spot rate (line *ae*), Germany CPI (line 64), and U.S. CPI (line 64). Other figures are author's calculations. An electronic version of these data is available at the author's website <www.stern.nyu.edu/~rlevich/book1/datafile.htm>.

APPENDIX B
INTEREST RATE PARITY CALCULATIONS: $, £, AND DM EURORATES

In this appendix, we show the data and calculations for the interest rate parity (IRP) conditions that appear in Figure 5.4. Weekly data on the forward premium, $(F - S)/S$, expressed as a percent per annum and three-month interest rates on Eurocurrency deposits (all as a percentage per annum) are shown in the table that follows. The deviations from interest rate parity are computed using equation 5.2:

$$d_t = \frac{F_{t,1} - S_t}{S_t} - \frac{i_\$ - i_£}{(1 + i_£)} \qquad (5.2)$$

where the forward premium and both interest rates have been divided by four to account for their three-month term. The percentage deviation from IRP therefore reflects the overall incentive to engage in covered interest arbitrage before taking transaction costs into account. Notice that the deviations from IRP using Eurorates are quite small indicating that Eurocurrency instruments come close to being comparable in all dimensions of risk (except currency).

APPENDIX B   Interest Rate Parity Calculations

Date	3-Month Forward Premium: Percent per Annum		3-Month Eurorates: Percent per Annum			IRP Deviation: Percent	
	US$ vs. UK£	US$ vs. DM	US$	UK£	DM	US$ vs. UK£	US$ vs. DM
1/3/97	−0.90	2.41	5.4375	6.3750	3.0000	0.006%	−0.002%
1/10/97	−0.83	2.41	5.4375	6.3125	3.0000	0.008	−0.002
1/17/97	−0.74	2.40	5.4375	6.1875	3.0000	0.000	−0.005
1/24/97	−0.74	2.37	5.4375	6.1875	3.0625	0.000	0.003
1/31/97	−0.75	2.36	5.4375	6.1875	3.0000	−0.003	−0.015
2/7/97	−0.74	2.33	5.3750	6.1875	3.0000	0.015	−0.007
2/14/97	−0.78	2.31	5.3750	6.1875	3.0625	0.005	0.004
2/21/97	−0.77	2.19	5.3125	6.1250	3.1250	0.008	0.005
2/28/97	−0.69	2.31	5.3750	6.1250	3.1250	0.012	0.019
3/7/97	−0.65	2.32	5.4375	6.1250	3.1250	0.007	0.006
3/14/97	−0.62	2.39	5.4375	6.1250	3.1875	0.014	0.039
3/21/97	−0.65	2.48	5.5625	6.2500	3.2500	0.007	0.047
3/28/97	−0.61	2.38	5.6250	6.2500	3.1250	0.001	−0.025
4/4/97	−0.59	2.62	5.6875	6.3125	3.1250	0.006	0.019
4/11/97	−0.59	2.59	5.6875	6.3125	3.1250	0.006	0.012
4/18/97	−0.59	3.37	5.6875	6.3125	3.1250	0.006	0.207
4/25/97	−0.64	2.68	5.6875	6.3750	3.1250	0.009	0.034
5/2/97	−0.72	2.68	5.6875	6.4375	3.0625	0.005	0.019
5/9/97	−0.67	2.73	5.6875	6.3750	3.0625	0.002	0.031
5/16/97	−0.64	2.70	5.6875	6.3750	3.0625	0.009	0.024
5/23/97	−0.74	2.67	5.6875	6.4375	3.0625	0.000	0.016
5/30/97	−0.81	2.94	5.6875	6.5625	3.0625	0.013	0.084
6/6/97	−0.81	2.62	5.6875	6.5625	3.0625	0.013	0.004
6/13/97	−0.83	2.68	5.6875	6.5625	3.0000	0.008	0.003
6/20/97	−0.94	2.61	5.6250	6.6875	3.0000	0.026	0.001
6/27/97	−0.98	2.72	5.6250	6.7500	3.0000	0.032	0.029
7/3/97	−1.17	2.69	5.6875	6.9688	3.0313	0.022	0.013
7/11/97	−1.18	2.60	5.6250	7.0000	3.0625	0.043	0.014
7/18/97	−1.31	2.60	5.6250	6.9375	3.0625	−0.005	0.014
7/25/97	−1.28	2.54	5.6250	6.9375	3.0625	0.003	−0.001
8/1/97	−1.44	2.47	5.5625	7.0625	3.1250	0.008	0.013
8/8/97	−1.47	2.52	5.5625	7.0625	3.1250	0.001	0.025
8/15/97	−1.42	2.48	5.6250	7.1250	3.1875	0.013	0.015
8/22/97	−1.49	2.47	5.5625	7.1875	3.1875	0.027	0.028
8/29/97	−1.56	2.44	5.5625	7.1875	3.1875	0.009	0.021
9/5/97	−0.71	2.47	5.5625	7.1875	3.1875	0.222	0.028

	3-Month Forward Premium: Percent per Annum		3-Month Eurorates: Percent per Annum			IRP Deviation: Percent	
Date	*US$ vs. UK£*	*US$ vs. DM*	*US$*	*UK£*	*DM*	*US$ vs. UK£*	*US$ vs. DM*
9/12/97	−1.42	2.48	5.6250	7.1250	3.1875	0.013%	0.015%
9/19/97	−1.49	2.31	5.5625	7.1875	3.1875	0.027	−0.012
9/26/97	−0.50	2.40	5.5625	7.1875	3.1875	0.274	0.011
10/3/97	−1.52	2.39	5.6250	7.2500	3.3125	0.019	0.024
10/10/97	−1.51	2.18	5.6250	7.1875	3.5000	0.006	0.018
10/17/97	−1.48	2.11	5.6250	7.1875	3.5625	0.014	0.016
10/24/97	−1.47	2.14	5.6875	7.2500	3.5625	0.016	0.008
10/31/97	−1.50	2.10	5.6250	7.2500	3.5625	0.024	0.014
11/7/97	−1.73	2.10	5.6250	7.5000	3.5625	0.028	0.014
11/14/97	−1.70	2.16	5.7500	7.5625	3.6875	0.020	0.029
11/21/97	−1.68	2.14	5.7500	7.5625	3.6250	0.025	0.009
11/28/97	−1.67	2.12	5.7500	7.6563	3.7188	0.050	0.027
12/5/97	−1.65	2.12	5.7500	7.6250	3.6875	0.047	0.019
12/12/97	−1.67	2.14	5.7500	7.5625	3.6250	0.027	0.009
12/19/97	−1.63	2.14	5.7813	7.5625	3.6250	0.030	0.001
12/26/97	−1.60	2.20	5.8125	7.5625	3.5625	0.029	−0.008
1/2/98	−1.78	2.10	5.6875	7.5000	3.5625	0.000	−0.002
1/9/98	−1.78	2.07	5.5000	7.4375	3.3475	0.031	−0.016
1/16/98	−1.81	2.04	5.5000	7.4375	3.4375	0.023	−0.001
1/23/98	−1.76	2.06	5.5000	7.4375	3.4375	0.036	0.004
1/30/98	−1.78	2.05	5.5000	7.4375	3.4375	0.031	0.001
2/6/98	−1.75	2.13	5.5000	7.3750	3.4375	0.023	0.021
2/13/98	−1.79	2.09	5.5000	7.3750	3.4375	0.013	0.011
2/20/98	−1.76	2.05	5.5000	7.4375	3.3750	0.036	−0.014
2/27/98	−1.87	2.18	5.5620	7.4375	3.4375	−0.007	0.018
3/6/98	−1.76	2.19	5.5625	7.4375	3.3750	0.020	0.005
3/13/98	−1.76	2.17	5.5625	7.4375	3.4375	0.020	0.016
3/20/98	−1.75	2.15	5.5625	7.4375	3.4375	0.023	0.011
3/27/98	−1.76	2.14	5.5625	7.4375	3.4375	0.020	0.008
4/3/98	−1.75	2.07	5.5625	7.4375	3.5625	0.023	0.022
4/10/98	−1.75	2.03	5.5000	7.3750	3.5000	0.023	0.012
4/17/98	−1.78	2.03	5.5313	7.3750	3.5625	0.008	0.020
4/24/98	−1.63	2.06	5.5625	7.3750	3.5000	0.037	0.004
5/1/98	−1.68	2.04	5.5625	7.3125	3.5625	0.010	0.014
5/8/98	−1.69	2.09	5.5625	7.3750	3.5000	0.022	0.011
5/15/98	−1.69	2.10	5.5938	7.3750	3.5000	0.015	0.006
5/22/98	−1.71	2.15	5.5625	7.3750	3.5000	0.017	0.026
5/29/98	−1.70	2.11	5.5625	7.3750	3.4375	0.020	0.001
6/5/98	−1.90	2.18	5.5625	7.5625	3.4375	0.016	0.018
6/12/98	−1.89	2.13	5.5625	7.5625	3.4375	0.018	0.006
6/19/98	−1.94	2.16	5.5625	7.6250	3.4375	0.021	0.013
6/26/98	−2.04	2.18	5.5938	7.6875	3.4375	0.004	0.011
7/3/98	−2.06	2.19	5.5938	7.6875	3.4375	−0.001	0.013
7/10/98	−1.91	2.19	5.5625	7.7500	3.4375	0.059	0.021
7/17/98	−1.90	2.21	5.5625	7.6250	3.4375	0.031	0.026
7/24/98	−1.95	2.21	5.5625	7.6250	3.4375	0.018	0.026
7/31/98	−2.03	2.21	5.5625	7.6250	3.4375	−0.002	0.026
8/7/98	−1.98	2.22	5.5625	7.5625	3.4375	−0.004	0.028
8/14/98	−1.92	2.20	5.5625	7.5625	3.3750	0.011	0.008
8/21/98	−1.98	2.21	5.5625	7.5625	3.3750	−0.004	0.010
8/28/98	−1.86	2.18	5.5000	7.5000	3.3750	0.026	0.018
9/4/98	−1.87	2.15	5.5000	7.5000	3.3750	0.023	0.011
9/11/98	−1.80	2.08	5.3750	7.3125	3.3750	0.026	0.024
9/18/98	−1.78	2.07	5.3750	7.3125	3.3750	0.031	0.022

Date	3-Month Forward Premium: Percent per Annum		3-Month Eurorates: Percent per Annum			IRP Deviation: Percent	
	US$ vs. UK£	*US$ vs. DM*	*US$*	*UK£*	*DM*	*US$ vs. UK£*	*US$ vs. DM*
9/25/98	−1.92	1.78	5.1875	7.2500	3.3750	0.026%	−0.004%
10/2/98	−1.87	1.82	5.1875	7.1875	3.4375	0.024	0.021
10/9/98	−1.78	1.82	5.2813	7.1250	3.4375	0.008	−0.002
10/16/98	−1.79	1.69	5.0625	7.0000	3.4375	0.029	0.020
10/23/98	−1.79	1.72	5.1250	7.0000	3.4375	0.013	0.012
10/30/98	−1.76	1.68	5.1250	7.0625	3.5000	0.036	0.017
11/6/98	−1.42	1.82	5.2500	6.8125	3.5000	0.029	0.021
11/13/98	−1.49	1.78	5.2500	6.8750	3.5625	0.027	0.027
11/20/98	−1.62	1.64	5.1250	6.8125	3.5625	0.010	0.023
11/27/98	−1.42	1.67	5.1875	5.7500	3.5625	−0.216	0.015
12/4/98	−1.25	1.87	5.1250	6.5000	3.3125	0.026	0.018
12/11/98	−1.02	1.95	5.1250	6.2500	3.2500	0.022	0.023
12/18/98	−1.00	2.01	5.1250	6.2500	3.1875	0.027	0.022
12/31/98	−0.99	1.94	4.9375	6.0625	3.1250	0.030	0.035

Source: Harris Bank Data File, New York University. An electronic version of these data is available at the author's website <www.stern.nyu.edu/~rlevich/book1/datafile.htm>.

APPENDIX C
INTERNATIONAL FISHER EFFECT CALCULATIONS: UNITED STATES AND GERMANY

In this appendix, we show the data and calculations for the International Fisher Effect that appear in Figure 5.5. In the table that follows, quarterly data on the spot exchange rate (in $/DM) are in column 2. The future spot exchange rate (one quarter ahead) is shown in column 3. The percentage change in the spot rate is in column 4.

In columns 5 and 6, we show the three-month Eurocurrency interest rates for US$ and DM, respectively. The interest rate differential, $(i_\$ - i_{DM})/(1 + i_{DM})$, appears in column 7 where each interest rate has been divided by four to reflect its three-month term. The final column reports the difference between column 4 and column 7. The first number (0.1228) in column 7 implies that the interest differential (0.54%) at the start of the first quarter understated the actual exchange rate change over the first quarter (12.82%) by 12.28%.

Notice that the interest differential in column 7 stayed positive for many quarters, while the exchange rate change (in column 4) tended to alternate between positive and negative values. Thus the interest differential was a poor indicator of the actual exchange rate change on a quarter-by-quarter basis.

APPENDIX C International Fisher Effect Calculations
United States and Germany

Date mm/dd/yy	Current Spot Rate	Future Spot Rate	Percent Change Spot	$i_\$$ 3-month Euro	i_{DM} 3-month Euro	$(i_\$ - i_{DM})/(1 + i_{DM})$	Deviation from Fisher International
10573	0.3120	0.3520	0.1282	5.8750	3.6875	0.0054	0.1228
33073	0.3520	0.4117	0.1696	8.6250	2.5000	0.0152	0.1544
62873	0.4117	0.4142	0.0061	9.0625	6.1250	0.0072	−0.0012
92873	0.4142	0.3702	−0.1062	10.3750	6.1250	0.0105	−0.1167
122873	0.3702	0.3955	0.0683	10.1250	11.0000	−0.0021	0.0705
32974	0.3955	0.3919	−0.0091	9.8750	10.0000	−0.0003	−0.0088
62874	0.3919	0.3759	−0.0408	13.3750	10.8750	0.0061	−0.0469
92774	0.3759	0.4136	0.1003	12.1875	9.6250	0.0063	0.0940
122774	0.4136	0.4265	0.0312	10.4375	8.0000	0.0060	0.0252
32875	0.4265	0.4252	−0.0030	6.8750	4.5000	0.0059	−0.0089
62775	0.4252	0.3762	−0.1152	6.6875	4.8125	0.0046	−0.1199
92675	0.3762	0.3830	0.0181	7.5000	4.0000	0.0087	0.0094
122675	0.3830	0.3918	0.0230	6.1875	4.1250	0.0051	0.0179
32676	0.3918	0.3881	−0.0094	5.3750	3.1875	0.0054	−0.0149
62576	0.3881	0.4042	0.0415	5.9375	4.2500	0.0042	0.0373
92476	0.4042	0.4245	0.0502	5.5000	4.5000	0.0025	0.0478
123076	0.4245	0.4182	−0.0148	5.0625	4.8750	0.0005	−0.0153
32577	0.4182	0.4253	0.0170	5.1250	4.5000	0.0015	0.0154
62477	0.4253	0.4335	0.0193	5.8125	3.8750	0.0048	0.0145
93077	0.4335	0.4763	0.0987	6.8750	3.9375	0.0073	0.0915
123077	0.4763	0.5019	0.0537	7.2500	2.5000	0.0118	0.0419
33178	0.5019	0.4825	−0.0387	7.4375	3.3125	0.0102	−0.0489
63078	0.4825	0.5161	0.0696	8.6250	3.3750	0.0130	0.0566
92978	0.5161	0.5482	0.0622	9.5625	3.6875	0.0146	0.0476
122978	0.5482	0.5352	−0.0237	11.6875	3.4375	0.0204	−0.0442
33079	0.5352	0.5446	0.0176	10.6250	4.9375	0.0140	0.0035
62979	0.5446	0.5739	0.0538	10.4375	6.3750	0.0100	0.0438
92879	0.5739	0.5792	0.0092	12.7500	7.3750	0.0132	−0.0040
122879	0.5792	0.5184	−0.1050	14.9375	8.8750	0.0148	−0.1198
32880	0.5184	0.5667	0.0931	19.3750	9.7500	0.0235	0.0696
62780	0.5667	0.5544	−0.0216	9.4375	9.4375	0.0000	−0.0216
92680	0.5544	0.5135	−0.0738	13.1875	8.7500	0.0105	−0.0844
122680	0.5135	0.4689	−0.0868	18.0000	9.6875	0.0203	−0.1070
32781	0.4689	0.4162	−0.1124	14.3750	12.8750	0.0036	−0.1160
62681	0.4162	0.4292	0.0311	18.5000	12.0000	0.0158	0.0153
92581	0.4292	0.4444	0.0356	17.2500	11.9375	0.0129	0.0227

Date mm/dd/yy	Current Spot Rate	Future Spot Rate	Percent Change Spot	i_S 3-month Euro	i_{DM} 3-month Euro	$(i_S - i_{DM})/(1 + i_{DM})$	Deviation from Fisher International
123181	0.4444	0.4173	−0.0611	13.7500	10.5625	0.0078	−0.0688
32682	0.4173	0.4014	−0.0382	15.2500	9.1875	0.0148	−0.0530
62582	0.4014	0.3978	−0.0089	16.5000	9.1875	0.0179	−0.0268
92482	0.3978	0.4210	0.0583	11.8125	7.5625	0.0104	0.0479
123182	0.4210	0.4134	−0.0179	9.1900	5.8750	0.0082	−0.0260
32583	0.4134	0.3961	−0.0419	9.5625	4.8125	0.0117	−0.0536
62483	0.3961	0.3791	−0.0430	9.6875	5.1875	0.0111	−0.0541
93083	0.3791	0.3666	−0.0328	9.4375	5.7500	0.0091	−0.0419
123083	0.3666	0.3862	0.0533	9.8125	5.9375	0.0095	0.0437
33084	0.3862	0.3594	−0.0694	10.6250	5.6250	0.0123	−0.0817
62984	0.3594	0.3273	−0.0892	12.1250	5.8750	0.0154	−0.1046
92884	0.3273	0.3185	−0.0271	11.3750	5.7500	0.0139	−0.0409
122884	0.3185	0.3244	0.0185	8.6250	5.5625	0.0076	0.0109
32985	0.3244	0.3291	0.0145	8.9375	5.8750	0.0075	0.0069
62885	0.3291	0.3738	0.1361	7.7500	5.3750	0.0059	0.1302
92785	0.3738	0.4044	0.0817	8.0625	4.4375	0.0090	0.0727
122785	0.4044	0.4307	0.0650	7.9375	4.8125	0.0077	0.0573
32886	0.4307	0.4524	0.0504	7.2500	4.4375	0.0070	0.0435
62786	0.4524	0.4889	0.0808	6.8125	4.5000	0.0057	0.0751
92686	0.4889	0.5083	0.0396	5.9375	4.3750	0.0039	0.0358
122686	0.5083	0.5485	0.0791	6.4375	4.8750	0.0039	0.0752
32787	0.5485	0.5481	−0.0007	6.3125	3.8125	0.0062	−0.0069
62687	0.5481	0.5435	−0.0084	7.0625	3.6875	0.0084	−0.0168
100587	0.5435	0.6365	0.1711	8.1875	4.5000	0.0091	0.1620
123187	0.6365	0.6039	−0.0513	7.3125	3.3125	0.0099	−0.0612
40188	0.6039	0.5487	−0.0914	6.8750	3.2500	0.0090	−0.1003
70188	0.5487	0.5322	−0.0301	7.7500	4.3750	0.0083	−0.0384
93088	0.5322	0.5635	0.0589	8.5000	4.1250	0.0108	0.0481
123088	0.5635	0.5272	−0.0645	9.1875	5.3125	0.0096	−0.0740
33189	0.5272	0.5128	−0.0273	10.1875	6.3125	0.0095	−0.0368
63089	0.5128	0.5353	0.0439	9.1875	6.9375	0.0055	0.0384
92989	0.5353	0.5914	0.1047	9.1250	7.6875	0.0035	0.1011
122989	0.5914	0.5894	−0.0032	8.2500	8.2500	0.0000	−0.0032
33090	0.5894	0.6008	0.0192	8.3750	8.0000	0.0009	0.0183
62990	0.6008	0.6388	0.0632	8.2500	8.0625	0.0005	0.0628
92890	0.6388	0.6673	0.0447	8.2500	8.5000	−0.0006	0.0453
122890	0.6673	0.5858	−0.1221	7.4375	9.2500	−0.0044	−0.1177
32991	0.5858	0.5525	−0.0569	6.3125	9.1875	−0.0070	−0.0499
62891	0.5525	0.5967	0.0800	6.0625	9.0000	−0.0072	0.0871
92791	0.5967	0.6598	0.1059	5.5625	9.2500	−0.0090	0.1149
122791	0.6598	0.6064	−0.0810	4.2500	9.6875	−0.0133	−0.0677
32792	0.6064	0.6492	0.0705	4.2500	9.6250	−0.0131	0.0836
62692	0.6492	0.7020	0.0814	3.8125	9.6875	−0.0143	0.0957
100292	0.7020	0.6200	−0.1169	3.0625	8.8750	−0.0142	−0.1026
123192	0.6200	0.6231	0.0050	3.3125	8.6250	−0.0130	0.0180
40293	0.6231	0.5889	−0.0548	3.1250	7.9375	−0.0118	−0.0430
70293	0.5889	0.6094	0.0347	3.1875	7.3125	−0.0101	0.0449
100193	0.6094	0.5757	−0.0553	3.2500	6.6250	−0.0083	−0.0470
123193	0.5757	0.5900	0.0248	3.2500	5.8125	−0.0063	0.0311
40194	0.5900	0.6254	0.0600	3.8125	5.5625	−0.0043	0.0643
70194	0.6254	0.6461	0.0331	4.8125	4.8750	−0.0002	0.0333
93094	0.6461	0.6453	−0.0012	5.4375	5.0625	0.0009	−0.0022
123094	0.6453	0.7227	0.1199	6.3750	5.5188	0.0021	0.1178
33195	0.7227	0.7227	0.0000	6.1875	4.6875	0.0037	−0.0037
63095	0.7227	0.7048	−0.0248	5.9375	4.5625	0.0034	−0.0282
92995	0.7048	0.6976	−0.0102	5.8125	4.0625	0.0043	−0.0145

Date mm/dd/yy	Current Spot Rate	Future Spot Rate	Percent Change Spot	$i_\$$ 3-month Euro	i_{DM} 3-month Euro	$(i_\$ - i_{DM})/$ $(1 + i_{DM})$	Deviation from Fisher International
122995	0.6976	0.6785	−0.0274	5.5313	3.7500	0.0044	−0.0318
32996	0.6785	0.6565	−0.0324	5.0000	3.2500	0.0043	−0.0368
62896	0.6565	0.6572	0.0011	5.3750	3.2500	0.0053	−0.0042
92796	0.6572	0.6423	−0.0226	5.3125	3.0000	0.0057	−0.0283
122796	0.6423	0.5979	−0.0692	5.5625	4.0625	0.0037	−0.0729
32897	0.5979	0.5771	−0.0348	5.6250	3.1250	0.0062	−0.0410
62797	0.5771	0.5682	−0.0153	5.6250	3.0000	0.0065	−0.0219
92697	0.5682	0.5643	−0.0070	5.6250	3.3125	0.0057	−0.0127
122697	0.5643	0.5482	−0.0284	5.8125	3.5625	0.0056	−0.0340
32798	0.5482	0.5538	0.0102	5.5625	3.4375	0.0053	0.0049
62698	0.5538	0.6120	0.1050	5.5938	3.4375	0.0053	0.0997
100298	0.6120	0.5967	−0.0251	5.1875	3.4375	0.0043	−0.0294
123198	0.5967	0.5518	−0.0752	4.9375	3.1250	0.0045	−0.0797
40299	0.5518	0.5236	−0.0511	4.8750	2.8125	0.0051	−0.0562
70299	0.5236	0.5498	0.0500	5.1875	2.6250	0.0064	0.0436
100199	0.5498	0.5153	−0.0628	5.9375	3.1563	0.0069	−0.0697
123199	0.5153	0.4886	−0.0517	5.8750	3.2813	0.0064	−0.0581

Source: Harris Bank Data File, New York University. An electronic version of these data is available at the author's website
<www.stern.nyu.edu/~rlevich/book1/datafile.htm>.

Abuaf, Niso, 129, 130, 141, 282, 282n, 292
Adler, Michael, 613n, 614, 641
Alesina, Alberto, 536n, 553
Aliber, Robert, 1, 3, 17n, 22, 153, 181, 238, 258, 323n, 331, 613n, 641, 659, 673
Allayannis, George, 18n, 22, 621, 637, 642
Allen, Helen, 269, 293
Almeida, Alvaro, 216n, 225
Altman, Edward, 655, 675
Amihud, Yakov, 621, 642
Annaert, Jan, 544n, 553
Antl, Boris, 91n, 110

Bahamani-Oskoee, Mohsen, 153n, 181
Baillie, Richard, 206n, 225, 228n, 258
Balassa, Bela, 200n, 225
Bansal, Vipul, 487, 488, 515
Barth, James, 345n, 371
Bartolini, Leonardo, 218n, 225, 560n, 596, 672n, 675
Bartov, Eli, 18n, 22, 621, 642
Batten, Dallas, 661, 675
Baxter, Marianne, 584, 596
Beder, Tanya, 636n, 642
Beedles, William, 585, 597
Beidleman, Carl, 93, 110, 153, 181, 238, 259, 502n, 515
Bekaert Geert, 588, 596
Bennett, Adam, 67n, 75
Benston, George, 345n, 371
Berg, Andrew, 265n, 292
Bicksler, James, 515
Bilson, John, 205n, 207, 207n, 208, 225, 251, 252, 258, 264-266, 278, 280, 281, 281n, 292, 632n, 642
Black, Deborah, 407n, 416
Black, Fischer, 446n, 454, 473, 537n, 541n, 553
Bock, David, 484, 515
Bodnar, Gordon, 18n, 22, 218n, 225, 621, 642, 672n, 675

Bodurtha, James, 442n, 445n, 446n, 455, 456, 467n, 473, 569, 596
Bollerslev, Tim, 103n, 110
Borensztein, Eduardo, 457n, 457-459, 473
Borsy, Kristina, 364
Bosner-Neal, Catherine, 216n, 225, 569, 596
Boughton, James, 212, 225
Boyle, Glenn, 172, 181
Braas, Albéric, 83, 110
Bralver, Charles, 83, 110
Branson, William, 210n, 225
Brauer, Gegory, 596
Brealey, Richard, 623n, 642
Brumbough, Dan, 345n, 371
Burns, Arthur, 327n

Campa, José, 55n, 75, 265, 267, 292, 422n, 463, 473
Campbell, John, 412n, 416, 562, 563, 596
Carey, Mark, 366n, 367n, 371
Carter, E. Eugene, 375n, 417
Cassel, Gustav, 114n, 141
Chang, Carolyn, 399, 416
Chang, Jack, 399, 416
Chang, Kevin, 55n, 75, 265, 267, 292, 422n, 463, 473
Chang, Rosita, 171, 182
Chen, Andrew, 515
Cho, D. Chinhyung, 582n, 596
Choi, Frederick, 341n, 371, 591, 592, 592n, 596
Chrystal, K. Alec, 325n, 331
Claussen, A.W., 327n
Clements, Kenneth, 207
Clendenning, E. Wayne, 300n, 301, 331
Clinton, Kevin, 153n, 181
Cochrane, James, 593n, 596
Cody, Brian, 99n, 110
Connolly, Robert, 604, 605, 642
Coombs, Charles, 103n, 110
Cooper, Neil, 452, 474

Cooper, Richard, 28, 34, 75, 133n, 134, 141, 657, 675
Copeland, Tom, 632, 642
Cornell, W. Bradford, 245n, 258, 399, 416, 613n, 642
Corrigan, Gerald, 106n, 110
Coughlin, Cletus, 282n, 292
Courtadon, Georges, 442n, 445n, 446n, 455, 456, 467n, 473
Cox, John, 399n, 416
Crockett, Andrew, 322, 331
Crouhy, M., 141
Crouhy-Veyrac, L., 124, 141
Cumby, Robert, 173, 173n, 181, 275n, 292

Das, Satya, 153n, 181
Dam, Kenneth, 17n, 22, 325n, 331
Deardorff, Alan, 153, 181
deFreitas, A. 583, 597
Dermine, Jean, 369n, 371,
DeRosa, David, 465n, 467n, 468, 469n, 472, 474
Detzler, Miranda, 542, 553
Dietrich, J. Kimball, 245n, 258
Dominguez, Kathryn, 235n, 255, 258, 644, 664, 666, 667, 669, 671, 675
Domowitz, Ian, 103n, 110, 250n, 258
Dooley, Michael, 154, 181, 244, 245, 258, 300n, 331, 457n, 457-459, 473
Dornbusch, Rudiger, 111, 141, 200-202, 213, 215, 225
Drazen, Allan, 560n, 596
Dufey, Gunter, 227n, 259
Dumas, Bernard, 582n, 596, 613n, 614, 641

Edison, Hali, 84n, 110, 131n, 141
Egly, Dean, 565n, 596
Eichengreen, Barry, 26n, 75, 263n, 268n, 292

Einzig, Paul, 78, 110, 301, 322, 331
Eiteman, David, 477, 515
Elliott, Graham, 249, 258, 276, 276n, 293
Ellis, John, 323n, 331
Engel, Charles, 121, 141
Erb, Claude, 596
Errunza, Vihang, 586, 596
Eun, Cheol, 582n, 596, 633n, 642

Fama, Eugene, 111n, 113n, 141, 227n, 229, 234, 236, 236n, 258, 403n, 417
Farber, André, 403n, 417
Figlewski, Stephen, 236, 258, 411n, 417
Finnerty, John, 362, 371
Fisher, Frederick, 333, 335n, 342n, 343, 346n, 371
Fisher, Irving, 142, 155n, 158n, 181
Fisher, Robert, 593n, 596
Fletcher, Donna, 154, 181, 238, 258
Flood, Robert, 265n, 293
Frankel, Jeffrey, 35n, 75, 91n, 110, 161n, 177, 181, 197, 202, 208, 209, 210n, 218, 225, 235n, 238, 250n, 255, 258, 259, 261, 261n, 293, 404, 417, 463, 474, 582n, 596, 644, 664, 666, 667, 669, 671, 675
Fraser, Leon, 518
French, Kenneth, 559, 585, 596
Frenkel, Jacob, 129, 141, 144n, 152n, 153, 181, 185, 206, 207, 225, 238, 259
Friedman, Milton, 299n, 331
Froot, Kenneth, 123n, 141, 161n, 181, 249, 250n, 253n, 258, 259, 261, 261n, 293, 404, 412n, 416, 417, 562, 563, 596, 606n, 616, 624n, 642
Funabashi, Yoichi, 37n, 75

Garbade, Kenneth, 96, 110
Garber, Peter, 265n, 293
Garman, Mark, 446n, 474
Gastineau, Gary, 469n, 474
Géczy, Christopher, 637, 642
Gentry, William, 621, 642
Ghosh, Atish, 136, 141
Gibson, Rajna, 449n, 474
Giddy, Ian, 227n, 259, 620, 642
Glassman, Debra, 584, 596
Glen, Jack, 633, 642
Goetzmann, William, 589, 596
Goodhart, Charles, 216n, 225
Goodman, Stephen, 286n, 293
Grabbe, J. Orlin, 449n, 474
Gray, Robert, 410, 417
Greenleaf, James, 93, 110, 153, 181, 238, 259
Greenspan, Alan, 106n, 110,649n, 653n
Grossman, Sanford, 236, 259
Grubel, Herbert, 554, 556, 576, 586, 596

Hakkio, Craig, 214, 225, 250n, 258, 672n, 675
Halttunen, Hannu, 210n, 225
Hansen, Lars, 250, 259

Hardouvelis, Gikas, 567n, 568-570, 596
Harvey, Campbell, 577, 582, 586n, 588, 596
Harris, Ethan S., 214, 225
Hawkins, Robert, 310n, 331
Heckerman, Donald, 604n, 642
Hekman, Christine, 613n, 642
Helliwell, John, 128, 141
Henderson, Dale, 664, 675
Hendricks, Darryll, 510, 515, 636n, 642
Henriksson, Roy, 275n, 293
Herring, Richard, 296, 314n, 316n, 317, 331
Heston, Steven, 574n, 576, 596
Hiday, Jeffrey, 270n, 293
Hilley, John, 93, 110, 153, 181, 238, 259
Hinkle, Lawrence, 263n, 293
Hodrick, Robert, 228n, 237n, 250, 259
Hogan, Ked, 586n, 596
Howard, David, 221n, 225
Hsieh, David, 253n, 259
Huertas, Thomas, 651, 675
Hull, John, 465n, 474
Hung, Juann, 619, 642
Hung, Mao-Wei, 586, 596
Hutchinson, Michael, 192, 212, 225

Ibbotson, Roger, 586, 596
Ingersoll, Jonathan, 399n, 416
Isard, Peter, 123, 133, 141, 154, 181, 300n, 331
Ito, Takatoshi, 155n, 181, 249, 258, 276, 276n, 293

Jacquillat, Bertrand, 585, 596
Jagtiani, Julapa, 481n, 506n, 515
Jermann, Urban, 584, 596
Johnston, Elizabeth, 411n, 417
Jordon, J. 456, 474
Jorion, Philippe, 129, 130, 141, 282, 282n, 292, 293, 463, 474, 532, 533, 539n, 544n, 553, 589, 596, 620, 621, 633, 642
Joshi, Yash, 632, 642
Jurgensen, P., 664, 675

Kalter, Eliot, 332
Kamata, Sawaichiro, 107, 110
Kaminsky, Graciela, 265n, 293
Kane, Edward, 325n, 331, 647n, 648, 649, 675
Kaplan, Paul, 586, 596
Kaplanis, Evi, 586n, 597
Kapner, Kenneth, 502n, 515
Katseli-Papaefstratiou, Louka, 123n, 141
Keynes, John Maynard, 144n, 181
Kidwell, David, 360, 372
Kim, Dong-Soon, 596
Kim, Kuang-Jung, 586, 597
Kim, Yong Cheol, 363, 372
Kincaid, Russell, 332, 372
Kindleberger, Charles, 518, 519, 519n, 553
King, Robert, 584, 596
Klein, Michael, 214, 225, 265n, 293, 664n, 675

Koedijk, Kees, 282n, 292
Koeune, Jean-Claude, 38n, 76
Koh, Annie, 413n, 417
Kohlhagen, Steven, 87n, 110, 446n, 474, 658n, 675
Kolb, Robert, 407n, 417
Korajczyk, Robert, 582n, 597
Krieger, Andrew, 103n, 110
Krugman, Paul, 25n, 35n, 75, 111, 141, 159n, 181, 191n, 225, 265n, 293
Kübler, Friedrich, 314n, 316n, 317, 331
Kulantilaka, Nalin, 629n, 642
Kvasnicka, Joseph, 299n, 331
Kwok, Chuck, 269, 293

LaPorta, Rafael, 568, 570, 589n, 596
Leahy, Michael, 84n, 110, 669, 670, 675
LeBaron, Blake, 255, 259
Lee, Charles, 596
Lee, Sang-Bin, 586, 597
Leitch, Gordon, 276, 293
Lerman, Zvi, 542n, 553
Lessard, Donald, 128n, 141
Levi, Maurice, 149n, 182, 614-616, 642
Levich, Richard, 38n, 75, 82n, 110, 144n, 152n, 153, 169, 181, 196n, 202n, 225, 228n, 237n, 238, 246, 247, 259, 285, 286, 293, 306, 310n, 312, 325n, 331, 334n, 340, 341n, 349, 351, 352, 353n, 355n, 369n, 371, 372, 413n, 417, 511, 533, 539-541, 553, 591, 592, 592n, 596, 633, 633n, 642, 650, 675
Levy, Haim, 542n, 553
Lewis, Karen, 235n, 250, 259, 403n, 417, 550n, 553, 669n, 675
Lindert, Peter, 25n, 76, 135n, 141
Lizondo, Saul, 265n, 293
Longin, François, 586, 587, 597
Lopez-de-Silanes, Florencio, 597
Lothian, James, 282, 293
Lyons, Richard, 103, 103n, 105, 110, 253n, 259

MacArthur, Alan, 91n, 110, 177, 181, 238, 259
McConnell, John, 411n, 417
McCormick, Frank, 153n, 182
MacDonald, Ronald, 196n, 218n, 225, 672, 675
MacDougall, G. D. A., 555, 597
McKinnon, Ronald, 23, 26, 26n, 27, 27n, 29, 31, 32, 35, 36, 40, 40n, 41, 75, 114n, 123n, 141
McMahon, Patrick, 206n, 225, 228n, 258
Malz, Allan, 442n, 474
Marcus, Alan, 629n, 642
Marion, Nancy, 265n, 293
Mark, Nelson, 129n, 141, 212, 225, 283, 284, 293
Marki, Frederick, 536n, 553
Marr, M. Wayne, 360, 372
Marshall, Christopher, 636n, 642
Marshall, John, 502n, 515
Masson, Paul, 210n, 225

Masulis, Ronald, 104, 110
Mathieson, Donald, 332, 372
Meese, Richard, 129n, 141, 212n, 210-212, 226, 259, 261, 261n, 293
Melitz, J., 141
Mendelsohn, M.S. 335, 335n, 372
Merton, Robert, 275n, 293
Miller, Merton, 111n, 113n, 141, 374, 375n, 417, 623, 623n
Minton, Bernadette, 637, 642
Mizrach, Bruce, 214, 225
Modest, David, 275n, 292
Modigliani, Franco, 623, 623n
Moffett, Michael, 326n, 327, 331, 477, 515
Montiel, Peter, 263n, 293
Mueller, Gerhard, 341n, 371
Mullin, John, 588n, 597
Mundell, Robert, 71
Murphy, Robert 214, 225
Mussa, Michael, 65, 76, 183, 184, 219, 226, 235n, 259, 664, 675
Myers, Stewart, 623n, 642

Neal, Robert, 596
Neely, Christopher, 255, 259
Nurkse, Ragnar, 659, 675

Obstfeld, Maurice, 25n, 71, 71n, 72n, 75, 76, 131, 141, 173, 173n, 181
Ofek, Eli, 637, 642
Officer, Lawence, 123n, 141, 152n, 182
Ogden, J. 456, 474
Otani, Ichiro, 155n, 182
Ott, Mack, 661, 675
Oxelheim, Lars, 601n, 642

Pagano, Marco, 590, 597
Patillo, Catherine, 265n, 292
Payne, Richard, 216n, 225
Pearce, Douglas, 214, 255
Peek, Joe, 324, 331
Peel, David, 132, 141
Perold, André, 535n, 553
Phelan, Michael, 634n, 642
Poole, William, 227n, 259
Popper, Helen, 154, 182, 238, 259
Poterba, James, 559, 585, 596
Pringle, John, 604, 605, 642
Prowse, Stephen, 371
Pugel, Thomas, 25n, 76, 135n, 141
Putnam, Bluford, 526n, 553

Quinn, Maggie, 632, 642

Rea, John, 371
Reinganum, Mark, 399, 416
Reinhart, Carmen, 265, 293

Resnick, Bruce, 633n, 642
Rhee, S. Ghon, 171, 182
Riddick, Leigh, 584, 596
Riehl Heinz, 105n, 110
Ritter, Lawrence, 318n, 322n, 331
Robinson, Anthony, 562, 597
Rodriguez, Rita, 105n, 110, 375n, 417
Röell, Aliso, 590, 597
Rogers, John, 121, 141
Rogoff, Kenneth, 123n, 129n, 132, 141, 210-212, 212n, 226, 261
Roley, V. Vance, 216n, 225
Roll, Richard, 579, 587, 597, 672, 675
Rose, Andrew, 263n, 265n, 268n, 292, 293
Rosenberg, Michael, 478n, 515, 535, 536n, 543, 553
Rosengren, Eric, 324, 331
Ross, Stephen, 399n, 416
Rouwenhorst, Geert, 574n, 576, 596
Rungkasiri, Julapa, 481, 515
Ruttiens, Alain, 469n, 474

Sampson, Stephanie, 664, 675
Saudagaran, Shahrokh, 366n, 372
Saunders, Anthony, 655, 675
Scarlata, Jodi, 106n, 110
Scharfstein, David, 624n, 642
Scholes, Myron, 446n, 473
Schrand, Catherine, 637, 642
Schulmeister, Stephan, 245, 246, 259
Seale, W. 456, 474
Senbet, Lemma, 582n, 596
Senchack, Andrew, 585, 597
Sercu, Piet, 122n, 141
Shapiro, Alan, 613n, 642
Shafer, Jeffrey, 244, 245, 258
Shleifer, Andrei, 597
Shroff, Peter, 366n, 372
Shulman, Evan, 536n, 553
Siegel, Laurence, 586, 596
Siegel, Michael, 636n, 642
Silber, William, 96, 110, 255, 256, 259, 318, 322n, 331
Simons, Katerina, 495-497, 515
Smith, Clifford, 623n, 642
Smith, Roy, 356n, 372, 651, 675
Solnik, Bruno, 492n, 515, 537n, 553, 575, 583, 585-587, 596, 597
Somanath, V. S., 212, 226
Srivastava, Sanjay, 250, 259
Steil, Benn, 589, 590, 590n, 597
Stein, Jeremy, 624n, 642
Stickney, Clyde, 613n, 641
Stiglitz, Joseph, 236, 259
Stonehill, Arthur, 326n, 327, 331, 477, 515
Stulz, René, 363, 372, 623n, 642
Summers, Lawrence, 412n, 417, 536n, 553, 582n, 597
Summers, Victoria, 412n, 417
Svensson, Lars, 265n, 293
Sweeney, Richard 245, 245n, 259, 282, 293

Takagi, Shinji, 161n, 182
Talbot, James, 452, 474
Tandon, Kishore, 214n, 226
Tanner, J. Ernest, 276, 293
Taylor, Dean, 83n, 84, 110, 669, 675
Taylor, Larry, 154, 181, 238, 258
Taylor, Mark, 132, 141, 196n, 218n, 225, 226, 269, 282, 293, 672n, 675
Tesar, Linda, 521, 553, 585, 597
Thaler, Richard, 249, 253n, 259
Thomas, Jacob, 366n, 372
Thomas, Lee, 246, 247, 259, 533, 537, 539–541, 543, 550, 551, 553, 633, 633n, 642
Thompson, G. Rodney, 360, 372
Throop, Adrian, 192, 212, 225
Timberlake, Richard, 317n, 332
Titman, Sheridan, 503, 504, 504n, 515
Tiwari, Siddhart, 155n, 182
Tobin, James, 671, 671n, 675
Triffin, Robert, 32, 74
Tucker, A. 456, 474

Uchitelle, Louis, 173, 182
Udell, Gregory, 371
Umlauf, Steven, 412, 417
Uppal, Raman, 122n, 141, 585n, 597
Urich, Thomas, 214n, 226

Van de Gucht, Linda, 269, 293
Van Horne, James, 359n, 372
Van Hulle, Cynthia, 122n, 141
Viallet, Claude, 582n, 597
Vishny, Robert, 597
Viskanta, Tadas, 596

Walter, Ingo, 345n, 347n, 356n, 372, 650, 651, 675
Watson, Maxwell, 303n, 332, 340n, 372
Wei, Shang-Jin, 463, 474
Werner, Ingrid, 521, 553, 585, 597
Wheatly, Simon, 596
White, Alan, 465n, 474
White, Eugene, 345n, 372
Wihlborg, Clas, 601n, 642
Wilcox, James, 345n, 371
Willett, Thomas, 152n, 182
Williamson, John, 67n, 76, 118n, 141, 263n, 293
Wizman, Thierry, 568, 570, 596
Wolf, Holger, 136, 141
Working, Holbrook, 410, 417
Wyplosz, Charles, 263n, 268n, 292

Yao, Jian, 104, 110
Ypersele, Jacques van, 38n, 76

Zabka, Natasha, 214, 225

Absolute purchasing parity
  described, 114–117
  empirical evidence, 123, 124
  inflation, 116
  Law of One Price, 114–116
  market baskets, 116, 117
Accounting disclosure practices, 591–593,
  607–613, 637, 638
Accounting diversity, 591, 592
Accounting harmonization, 592, 593
Accounting practices
  generally accepted accounting practices
    (GAAP), 581, 648
  International Accounting Standards, 648
Active strategies, 537
Administered Prices, 121
Administered rate, 319
All Current method, 608
Allied Lyons, 8
American Depository Receipt (ADRs), 106,
  565–568, 570
American option, 421
American Stock Exchange, 342, 570
Amortization effect, 494
Arab Bank v. Barclays Bank, 314, 315
Arbitrage
  boundary conditions, 449–451, 455, 456
  covered interest arbitrage, 10, 89, 144,
    146–148, 170
  description, 10, 87
  efficiency, 237
  Fisher parity, 113
  interest rate parity, 89, 144–155, 313
  one-way arbitrage, 144, 170, 171
  onshore-offshore, 361–363
  purchasing power parity, 113–117,
    121, 122
  regulatory, 591
  round trip, 144, 170, 171
  spatial, 87, 88, 115, 237
  spot and forward foreign exchange,
    237, 238
  triangular, 88, 89

Arbitrage Pricing Theory (APT), 573,
  579, 582
Asset models; see Exchange rate models,
  Monetary approach
Average rate options, 469

Back-to-back loan; see Parallel loan
Balassa-Samuelson hypothesis, 131, 138
Bank of England, 14, 29, 30, 61, 322
Bank for International Settlements (BIS),
  capital adequacy rules, 6, 652–656
  capital requirements for swaps,
    506–508
  Eurocurrency, 325
  survey of trading, 81, 101, 385, 481
  VAR versus RiskMetricsTM, 654, 655
Bankers Trust
  and Gibson Greetings, 8, 504, 505
  and Manufacturers Hanover, 317
  and Proctor and Gamble, 8, 504, 505
Barings Bank, 9, 380, 381
Barrier options, 469
Base currency, 525
Basis risk, 487, 489
Basket options, 470
Basle Concordat, 323, 329, 369
Basle Committee on Banking Supervision,
  510, 653
Bearer securities, 344, 356
Big Mac Index, 124, 125, 134–137
Bilateral closeout netting agreement, 509
Black Scholes, 21, 457–461, 463
Bonds and bond markets (see Eurobond
  markets)
  active strategies, 537–542
  active versus passive strategies, 534–542
  central bank risk diversification, 522
  currency overlay strategy, 539–541
  description of global market, 519–522
  description of national markets, 522–524
  EMU, 545–549
  estimation risk, 544

Bonds and bond markets—Cont.
  global bond funds, 542–547
  history, 519–522
  prediction error, 527
  return and risk of global markets
    currency hedged, 532–534
    diversification, 534
    unhedged, 530–532
  return and risk of national markets
    currency hedged returns, 525,
      527–529
    unhedged returns, 525–527
  separable investments, 538
  structured investment, 538
  tactical hedging strategy, 539
Bought deal, 334, 343, 365
Brady bonds, 548, 549
Brady, Nicholas, 548
Braka v. Bancomer, 315
Bretton Woods agreement
  collapse of 6, 17, 20, 63, 65, 306,
    657, 660
  history, 20, 24, 26, 28–30, 32, 37, 38, 70
British Councils, 9, 506
Brokers, 96
Bulldog bonds, 334
Bundesbank
  clearing of bond issues, 342, 343
  intervention, 42, 664–666
  short-term treasury bills, 16
  US treasury, 85

Callable bond, 419
Call option, 420
Cap, 419
Capital adequacy rules, 652–656
Capital Asset Pricing Model (CAPM),
  577–579, 582–585
Capital crunch, 311
Capital Market Segmentation, 483
Capital market swap; see Swap
Carter Bonds, 47, 83, 84

Cash settlement, 379
Caterpillar Tractor, 606
Cedel, 339, 356
Central Bank intervention, 645
Central bank risk diversification, 522
Centralized exchanges, 377
Charles Fulton Holdings Ltd., 100
Chase Manhattan Bank 18, 82
    v. Garcia, 315
    v. Perez, 315
    v. Vishipco, 315, 316
Chicago Board of Trade, 376, 409, 419
Chicago Board Options Exchange, 376, 419
Chicago Mercantile Exchange (CME), 95,
    96, 408–410
    after hours trading introduced, 377
    foreign currency trading
        introduced, 375
    interest rate options introduced, 418
Citibank, 82
Clearinghouse, 96, 378
Clearinghouse Interbank Payments System
    (CHIPS), 317
Closed end fund, 566
Coca-Cola, 607, 611
Collar, 419, 438, 439
Commercial paper, 319
Commodity Futures Trading Commission
    (CFTC), 6, 646
Common Market; *see* European Economic
    Community
Comparative advantage, 194
Contagion, 8
Continuous rate of return, 139, 178
Convergence (EMS)
    criteria, 42
    defined, 48
Conversion factor, 390
Coordinated intervention, 37, 656
Cost-of-carry model, 395, 396
Counterparty, 475
Counterparty risk
    clearinghouse, 378
    defined, 6, 93
Country risk premium, 172
Covered interest parity; *see also* Interest rate
    parity
    description, 10, 59
Creation unit, defined, 570, 571
Credit exposure method (swaps), 507
Credit rationing, 342
Credit risk, 105, 172
Credit Suisse First Boston, 9, 82
Cross-border deposits, 314
Cross-rate
    definition, 88
    futures, 387
    growth, 422
    options, 422
    options prices on, 265
Currency appreciation, 47
Currency depreciation, 47
Currency boards, 24, 67–69
Currency Crisis, 7
Currency forward contract; *see also* Forward
    contracts

Currency forward contract—*Cont.*
    description, 374
    payoff profiles, 391–393
Currency futures; *see also* Futures contract
    description, 386–388
    payoff profiles, 391–393
Currency options; *see also* Options
    characteristics, 423–427
Currency risk premium; *see* Exchange risk
    premium
Currency swap; *see also* Swap
    description, 492–485
    IBM/World Bank, 484
    segmentation and scarcity, 483–485
Currency swap parity, description, 11
Currenex, 100, 101
Current/noncurrent approach, 607–613

Daiwa Bank
    Japan premium, 324
    unauthorized dealing, 9, 324
Default risk, 490
Delivery risk
    defined, 6, 106
    delivery versus payment, 107
Delta
    call delta, 441, 442, 448, 449
    delta hedge, 449, 464
    delta neutral, 449, 464
Delors, Jacques, 40, 42
Delors Plan, 41, 42
Derivative security, 91, 376
Deutsche Bank 82, 103
Diffusion effect, 493
Direct rate, 88
Divergence threshold, 39
Dodge Plan, 31
Dollarization, 69, 123, 129, 136
Domestic bonds, 334, 341
Dominant market, 566
Dow Jones Telerate, 98
Dual currency bond, 419
Duisenberg, William, 44
Dynamic adjustment path, 201
Dynamic hedging strategy, 464

EBS Partnership, 98
The Economist, 136
Effective Exchange Rate, 55
Electronic bond, 354, 355
Electronic Brokering Service, 98
Embedded option, 419
Emerging markets, 587–589
    Asian currency crisis, 9, 69
    currency boards, 67–69
    Russian currency crisis, 9, 70
Equilibrium benchmark, 229–230
Estimation risk, 544
Equity markets
    barriers, 589–591
    costs, 562–564
    description, 557–565
    disclosure practices, 591–593

Equity markets—*Cont.*
    diversification
        international market, 573–576
        multinationals, 585
        weighting of home and foreign,
            584–587
    investment indexes
        Morgan Stanley Capital
            International, 557
        International Finance
            Corporation, 557
    investment vehicles
        American Depository Receipt, 106,
            565–566
        mutual country funds, 566–569
        WEBS, 569–571
    performance
        expected diversification gains, 555
        expected value gains, 555
    portfolio risk, 572–576
    pricing determinants, 10
        evidence, 579–583
        theory, 576–579
    privatization, 558
    risk and return, 571–576
    settlement period, 562–564
    survivorship bias, 589
EUREX, 377, 408–410
Euro, 4, 24, 38, 73
Eurobond, 334, 335
Eurobond market, 333–370
    arbitrage opportunities, 359, 360,
        361–363
    bearer securities, 334, 356
    bought deal, 334, 343, 365
    characteristics, 340–344
    competition, 350–354
    conflict of interest, 347
    credit rationing, 342
    defined, 333
    and European Union, 368–370
    excessive competition, 348
    and Glass-Steagall Act, 345, 347
    gray market, 347–350
    issuing practices, 341–350
    origins and dimensions, 4, 5, 335–340
    pricing, 355–364
    queuing, 342, 343
    regulatory bodies, 340–344
    scarcity value, 359, 364, 365, 484
    syndicate tensions, 346, 347
    underwriting, 345, 346
    and value of the firm, 363, 364
Euroclear, 339, 356
Eurocurrency deposits, court cases
    Arab Bank v. Barclays Bank, 314, 315
    Braka v. Bancomer, 315
    Garcia v. Chase Manhattan Bank, 315
    Perez v. Chase Manhattan Bank, 315
    Sokoloff v. National City Bank, 315
    Vishipco v. Chase Manhattan Bank,
        315, 316
    Wells Fargo Asia Limited v. Citibank,
        316, 317
Eurocurrency interest rates; *see* LIBID,
LIBOR

Eurocurrency market, 296–332; also
  offshore market
  arbitrage, 313
  defined, 297, 322
  Eurocurrency deposits and loans
    Coexistence with onshore, 308–309
    costs, 307
    impact of capital controls, 310–311
    pricing, 305–313
    pricing across offshore centers,
      311, 312
  history, 299–305
  regulating, 321–325
  size and growth, 5, 301–305, 322
Eurodollar interest rate futures, 319–321
Eurodollars; *see also* Eurocurrency market
  creating, 302, 303
Euromoney magazine, 336
European central bank, 43, 44, 545
European Community (EC), 24, 368
European Council, 37, 42, 43
European Currency Unit (ECU)
  defined, 38
  history, 24, 40
  reserves, 40
European Economic and Monetary Union,
  see European Monetary Union
European Economic Community (EEC), 24
European Exchange Rate Mechanism, 14;
  see also Exchange Rate Mechanism
European Monetary Cooperation Fund
  (EMCF), 38–40
European Monetary System (EMS)
  capital controls, 368
  crisis of 1992–1993, 41, 42, 85
  Exchange Rate Mechanism, 265
  as a "greater DM" area, 26, 40–42
  history, 24, 26, 37–40
European Monetary Union (EMU)
  bonds, 545–549
  concerns, 70–73
  Delors Plan, 41, 42
  history, 4, 20, 38, 40–46
European option, 421, 450, 451
European Payments Union, 31
European System of Central Banks, 43
European Union (EU), 24, 38, 40, 42–44
  and Eurobond market, 368–370
  and regulation, 649
  as a single market, 328, 589
European Units of Account (EUA), 335
Eurorates, 297
Excess market return, 229
Exchange rate
  behavior, 193
  developments, 45–57
  news and, 184, 185, 191, 192
    current account news and,
      190–191
    empirical tests, 212–216
    interest rate news and, 187–190
    money supply news, 186, 187
  overshooting, 47
  purchasing parity, empirical evidence,
    123–136
  variability

Exchange rate—*Cont.*
  costs of, 66
  and financial decisions and
    hedging, 66
  and operating decisions and
    hedging, 66
  volatility
    post Bretton woods, 17
    spot exchange rates, 52–55
Exchange rate changes
  and inflation, 123–132
  floating exchange rate system, 265
  forward rate as a predictor, 164–167
  hybrid systems, 265
  pegged rate system, 263–265
Exchange rate forecasting
  composite, 283–287
  consumers of forecast, 287, 288
  evaluating
    accurate versus useful, 271–275
    cointegration testing, 282
    economic value, 275, 278
    percentage correct method, 276, 277
  exchange rate system, 263–267
  Exchange Rate Mechanism, 265–267
  forecast horizon, 263, 268–270
  foreign exchange units, 263, 270, 271
  International Fisher Effect, 157–159,
    175, 176
  international liquidity as an
    indicator, 265
  long run, 282–287
  magnitude of changes, 263
  market setting, 262–271
  problems, 288, 289
  pegged, 263
  producers of forecasts, 288
  short run, 278–281
Exchange Rate Mechanism (ERM)
  Crisis of 1992–1993, 41, 42
  definitions, 39
  forecasting 265–267
  part of EMS, 38, 40–43, 48–50
  United Kingdom, 12, 14
Exchange rate models
  asset approaches, 46, 194–205
  combined flow and stock, 196
  empirical evidence on, 205–216
  flexible-price monetary models,
    198–200
  flow approach, 193, 194
  monetary approach 196–202
  and overshooting, 47; *see also* sticky
    price *below*
  portfolio-balance approach, 197,
    203–205
  preferred local habitat model, 203, 204
  and role of news, 212–216
  sticky price (overshooting) monetary
    models, 200–202
  stock approach, 194–196
  uniform preference model, 203
Exchange rate pass-through effect, 136, 604
Exchange rate risk, 105
Exchange rate valuation; *see* Exchange rate
  models

Exchange risk premium
  definition, 59, 203
  empirical evidence, 403, 404
  in forwards, 402–404
  general efficiency hypothesis, 248
  International Fisher parity, 160
  portfolio theory, 403
  quality of money balances, 402–403
Exercise price, 421
Exotic options, 469, 470
Expected excess market return, 229
Expiration date, 421
Exxon Capital Corporation, 361, 362
Exxon Corporation, 610

Fair game, 230
Federal Reserve System
  established, 28, 658
  and intervention, 85, 661–663, 664–667
  regulation, 646
Fidelity Investments, 173
Filter rule
  defined, 239–242
  empirical evidence, 244–248
Financial Accounting Standards Board
  (FASB)
  FASB Statement #8, 608–610
  FASB Statement #52, 609–612
  FASB Statement #105, 636
  FASB Statement #133, 612, 613, 637
Financial engineering, 5
Financial losses, 8, 9
Financial markets
  competition among markets, 6–8
  competition among regulators, 7
  volatility, 5, 6
Fiscal budget deficit, 191
Fisher parities
  defined, 113, 114, 155
  Fisher Effect, 114, 155, 156, 402
  international Fisher effect
    and accounting conventions, 613
    currency risk premium, 402–404
    defined and derived, 114, 156–160,
      167, 214
    deviations from, 158, 160, 173, 174
    diversification possibilities, 174
    empirical evidence, 160–163
    and exchange rate predictions,
      157–159, 175, 176
    perfect substitutes, 196
    and policy matters, 167–169,
      173–177
    and real interest parity, 159, 160
    taxes, 160
    transaction costs, 160
    uncertainty, 160
Fixed-floating rate swap, 475
Fixed-price reoffering, 347
Fixed rate currency swap, 475
Fixed rate dollar standard, 26, 30–33
Floating exchange rate system
  central bank intervention, 645
  description, 33–37, 65, 66, 265
  history, 24

Floating rate dollar standard, Plaza-Louvre
  Intervention Accords, 26, 35–37
Floating-rate loan, 319
Floor, 419
Forecast bias, 402
Forecast error, 402
Foreign bonds, 334
Foreign Credit Restraint Program, 300
Foreign exchange; *see* Exchange rates
Foreign exchange broker, 96
Foreign exchange markets
  ability to customize, 96
  automated transactions, 98, 99
  concentration, 101–103
  corporate, 99, 100
  counterparties, 101–103
  CURRENEX, 100, 101
  description, 95, 96
  FXNET, 99
  interbank market, 97–99
  origins, 79, 80
  products, 86–95
Foreign exchange rates; *see* Exchange rate
  appreciation, defined, 47
  depreciation, defined, 47
  gains and losses, 18, 19
  importance in the U.S., 17–19
  importance outside the U.S., 15, 16
Foreign exchange risk exposure
  accounting measures
    approach, 607–609
    disclosure, 636–638
    reporting gains and losses,
      610–613
    transaction exposure, 609, 610
  all current method, 609
  defined, 601
  economic measures
    regression approach, 613–616
    scenario approach, 604, 605,
      617–619, 638, 639
  empirical evidence on firms, 619–621
  estimating, 630–637, 654, 655
  functional currency, 609
  hedging and management, 621–630
  market value and sources of risk,
    603–606
  temporal method, 609
Foreign exchange swaps, defined, 87
Foreign exchange trader, 80
  trader's calendar, 184, 185
Foreign exchange trading
  and brokers, 96
  controls, 105, 106
  direct dealing, 97, 98
  filter rules, 239–242, 244–248
  moving average rule, 239, 242, 243,
    245–247
  and news, 184–192
  technical trading, 239–247
  trading profits
    data, 80, 81
    reasons, 83–85
    speculative, 83
    role of central banks, 83–86
    valuing, 106

Foreign exchange trading—*Cont.*
  types, 87–89
  volume, 80–82
Forward contracts
  cash settlement, 379
  credit risk, 172
  customized, 377
  defined, 86, 87, 374
  descriptions, 374–377, 398
  versus futures, 377–395, 406
  payoff profile, 391–395
  pricing, 93, 94, 395–398
  redundant, 91, 376
  risk premium, 402–404
  variable counterparty risk, 378, 379
Forward currency rates
  pricing, 395–398
  term structure, 399, 400
Forward discount, 145
Forward interest rate
  description, 398
  term structure, 400–402
Forward premium
  across offshore centers, 313
  contemporaneous, 250, 251
  defined, 145
  tests of efficiency, 166, 167
Forward rate agreement, 398
Forward rate bias, 164
Forward rate forecast error, 402
Forward rate pricing, 164
Forward rate risk premium; *see also*
  Exchange risk premium
Forward rate unbiased parity condition
  defined, 113, 114, 163, 164
  empirical evidence on, 164–167
  policy matters, 169
Free-rider, 236
Friedman, Milton, 375
Ful-Tex Euro Services, Inc. 100
Functional currency, 609
Functions of money, 34
Fundamental disequilibrium, 29
Futures contract; *see also* Currency futures;
  Interest rate futures
  clearinghouse, 378, 379
  defined, 375
  description, 375–377, 384–390
  versus forwards, 377–395, 406
  marking to market, 379–384, 398, 399
  open interest, 386, 387
  internationalization, 408–410,
  Mutual Offset System, 409, 410,
  payoff profiles, 391–395
  redundant, 376
  standardized, 377, 378
  success and failure, 406–408
  taxes and transaction costs, 411, 412
  volatility, 410, 411
FXNET, 99

Garcia v. Chase Manhattan Bank, 315
Gateway, 609, 612
General efficiency hypothesis, 248
General Electric, 99

General Motors, 99
Gibson Greetings, 8, 504, 505
Glass-Steagall Act, 345, 347, 648
Global bonds, 354
Global equity markets; *see* Equity markets
Global master swap agreement, 509
Globex, 377, 409, 410
Goldman Sachs, 101
Gold Standard
  automatic adjustment, 27
  history, 24, 26–28, 658
  inflation, 27, 28
  mint parity, 26
  price-specie flow mechanism, 26
  purchasing power parity, 27
Gray markets, 134, 347–350

Hedge ratio, 449, 632; *see* Delta
Hedging
  debt versus equity, 622
  dynamic hedging strategy, 464
  financial, 601
  net present value hedge, 627
  and options, 437
  versus speculation, 631
Herstatt risk, 106
Historic forecast errors, 250
Historical volatility, 53, 460–463; *see also*
  Volatility
Home country bias, 522, 583
House of Lords, 506
Homogeneity postulate, 120
Hybrid exchange rate systems, 265
Hysteresis, 301

IBM/World Bank swap, 484
Implied volatility, 53; *see also* Volatility
Imperfect substitutes, 197
Implicit options, 419
Implied future spot rate, 157
Implied volatility
  defined, 53, 456
  as an estimate of future volatility, 463
Index of the real exchange rate, 120
Initial margin, 380, 383
In-sample results
  definition, 205
  spot exchange rate determination,
    205–210
Instinet, 590
Integrated capital market, 356, 483
Interbank Market, 378
Interest Equalization Tax (IET), 32, 300,
  335, 339, 648
Interest rate recent developments,
  57–65
Interest rate forward contracts,
  description, 385, 395, 400–402
  payoff profiles, 393–395
Interest Rate Equalization Tax; *see* Interest
  equalization tax
Interest rate futures; *see also* Futures contract
  description, 385, 388–390
  hedging, 319

Interest rate futures—*Cont.*
  payoff profiles, 393–395
  synthetic, 413, 414
Interest rate options; *see also* Options
  descriptions, 424, 425, 428–431
  prices at maturity, 434–439
Interest rate parity
  and arbitrage, 89, 144–155, 313
  and capital controls, 154, 155, 310, 311
  and country risk premium, 172
  covered and uncovered, 10, 59
  covered interest arbitrage, 59, 144,
    146–148
  and credit risk, 172
  description, 113, 114, 144–148, 167
  empirical evidence, 152–155
  and forward contracts, 172
  and longer-term securities, 153
  interest rate parity line, 146
  neutral band, 138, 153
  and offshore centers, 313
  and one-way arbitrage, 144, 170, 171
  in a perfect capital market, 144–148
  and policy matters, 167, 170–172
  taxes 148–151
  transaction costs, 148
  uncertainty, 151–152
Interest rate risk, 105, 602
Interest rate swaps; *see also* Swap
  description, 485–488
  interest rate volatility, 494, 495
  segmentation, 486
International Accounting Standards
  Committee (IASC), 593
International Banking Facilities (IBF)
  description, 297, 325
  rise of, 325–327
International bonds; *see* Eurobonds; Foreign
  bonds
International Finance Corporation, 557
International Monetary Market; *see* Chicago
  Mercantile Exchange
International Monetary Fund, 4, 28, 29, 32,
  34, 65
    Amendments to the Articles of
      Agreements, 34
    guidelines on exchange rates, 34, 660
International monetary systems
    Bretton Woods; *see* Bretton Woods
    currency boards, 24, 67–69
    European Monetary System, 24, 26,
      37–42, 85, 265, 368
    fixed-rate dollar standard, 26, 30–33
    floating-rate system, 24, 33–37,
      65, 66
    gold standard, 24, 26–28, 658
    hybrid, 265
    pegged rate system, 42, 263–265, 645
    target zones, 24, 37
International money markets sectors, 298
International Organization of Securities
  Commission (IOSCO), 593
International reserves, 29, 664
Intervention
    coordinated, 36, 37, 656
    direct channels, 661–663

Intervention—*Cont.*
    effectiveness, 667–669
    empirical evidence, 235, 664–667,
      669–671
    indirect channels, 663, 664
    mechanics, 661–664
    objectives, 658–661
    pegged, 263
    policy instrument, 656–658
    predictability, 666, 667
    profitability, 83, 84, 669
    as signaling, 663, 664
    sterilized, 37, 661–663
    unsterilized, 661, 662
Intrinsic value, 440
Investment dollar, 478
Investor heterogeneity, 236
Invoice currency, 619

Japan premium, 324
Japan stock market, 559
Johnson, Lyndon, 336

Kennedy, John, 335

L.L. Bean, 134
Laker Airways, 606
Law of one price,
    description, 114–116, 123, 133
    and price discrimination, 124
    foreign exchange exposure, 618
    gray market, 134
Lead management, 345–347
Leeson, Nicholas, 380, 381
Lehman Brothers, 103
LIBID, 308
LIBOR, 308
Liquidity risk, 6, 88
Loanable funds model, 305, 313
Logarithmic returns, 139, 178
London Stock Exchange, 590
Long-swings hypothesis, 48
Long Term Capital Management, 9
Louvre Accord, 37, 48

Maastricht Treaty, 41, 43, 547
Maintenance margin, 381
Managed Floating Exchange Rate, 656
Manufacturers Hanover, 316
Margin call, 381
Margin requirement, 375
Market-determined rate, 319
Market efficiency
    defined, 164, 229–233
    empirical evidence, 237–252
        certainty, 237, 238
        forward market, 248–252
        spot market, 239–247
        uncertainty, 238–252
    equilibrium benchmark, 229, 230
    and optimality, 228

Market efficiency—*Cont.*
    policy implications, 252–256
    predictions of exchange rates, 195, 196
    semistrong form, 234, 235
    strong form, 234–236
    theory, 229–237
    weak form, 234
Market inefficiency, forward rate
  bias, 164
Market makers, 95
Market risk, 490, 507
Market Value, 603
Marking to market
    defined, 375
    future pricing, 379–382, 398–402
Marriott Hotels, 608–610
Marshall Plan, 31
Master Swap Agreement, 509, 510
MATIF, 377, 409, 410
Mean reversion, 128
Medium of exchange, 79, 193
Mellon Bank, 82
Menu costs, 121
Merrill Lynch, 101, 103
Metallgesellschaft, 8
MINEX, 98
Mitsubishi Motors, 627
Modigliani and Miller, 623
Monetary approach to exchange rates,
  196–202
    flexible price model, 198–200
    sticky price (overshooting) model,
      200–202
Monetary/nonmonetary approach, 607, 613
Morgan, J.P., 82
Morgan Guaranty Bank, 565
Morgan Stanley Capital International
  (MSCI), 557
Morgan Stanley Dean Witter, 103
Moving-average cross-over rule
    defined, 239, 242, 243
    empirical evidence, 245–247
Multiple forward rates, 250
Multijurisdictional Disclosure System, 542
Mutual funds, 566–569
Mutual Offset System, 409

National City Bank of New York; *see*
  Citibank
Natural hedge, 619
NASDAQ, 590
Nestlé, 607
Net asset exposure, 607
Net exposure, 509, 607
Net liability exposure, 607
Net private savings, 190
Net public savings, 190
Net regulatory burden
    definition, 14, 646, 647
    and structural arbitrage, 649, 650
Netting agreements and systems, 99
Neutrality of money, 120
News and foreign exchange rates
    description, 184, 185, 190, 191
    examples of, 186–191

News and foreign exchange rates—*Cont.*
role of, 212–216
New York Stock Exchange
description, 95, 96, 342, 560
history, 554
Nixon, Richard, 33
No currency risk premium hypothesis, 248
Noise trader, 411, 664
Noise trading, 664
Nominal exchange rates
against the U.S. dollar, 45–48, 50–52
definition, 66
in the ERM, 48–50
Nominal interest rate,
differentials, 59–62
levels, 57–59
Non-callable bond, 419
Non-stationary time series, 129, 270, 272, 273
Noriega, Manuel, 316
Notional bonds, 360, 430
Notional yield, 430
Notional value, 476

Office of Foreign Direct Investment (OFDI), 33, 336, 339
Offshore markets, 297; *see also*
Eurocurrency; Eurobond markets
borrowers concerns, 318–321
competing offshore centers, 311, 312
description, 297–299
deposit concerns, 314–318
determination interest rates and market share, 311–313
European policies, 328, 329
growth, 300–305
impact of capital controls and taxes, 310, 311
Japanese Offshore Market, 324
limits to expansion, 322
macroeconomic stability, 321, 322
market share, 310, 311
parallel market, 298, 333
offshore and onshore coexistence, 308, 309
regulation of, 322–328
Offshore banking
description, 297–299
impact of onshore banking regulations, 300
origins, 299–301
Onshore markets, 297, 298
Open End Fund, 566
Open interest, 386, 387
Open outcry system, 377
Optimality, 228
Option futures 421
Option on spot, 421
Option premium, 421
Options
arbitrage boundary conditions, 449–451, 455, 456, 467, 468
Black–Scholes, 451–461, 463
capital requirements, 465
delta, 441, 442, 448, 449; *see* Delta

Options—*Cont.*
description, 420–431
exotic options, 469, 470
gamma risk, 460, 465
and hedging, 437
intrinsic value, 440
pricing, 431–455
arbitrage, 449–451
binomial model, 442–445, 466
continuous time lognormal approach, 445–449, 465
empirical evidence, 455–457
futures options, 451–455
at maturity, 432–440
payoff profiles, 431–435
prior to maturity, 440–442
pure jump model, 457, 459
replicating portfolio, 419, 443, 444
smile effect, 462
and speculation, 436, 437
time value, 440
volatility, 460–463
Options Clearing Corporation (OCC), 427
Orange County, 9
Orderly market conditions, 34, 660
Original exposure methods (swaps), 507
Overshooting, 202

Parallel loan, 478
Parallel market, 298, 333
Parity conditions
description, 10, 11, 113, 114, 167–169
Fisher parities; *see* Fisher parities
forward rate unbiased; *see* Forward rate unbiased parity condition
interest rate parities; *see* Interest rate parity
purchasing parity; *see* Purchasing power parity
role for management decisions, 132, 133
usefulness of, 112, 113, 143, 144
Par swap, 491
Path dependent options, *see* Exotic options
Passive strategies, 537
Payoff profiles
futures and forwards, 391–395
options, 431–442
Pegged exchange rate system
after Bretton Woods, 42
central bank intervention 263, 645
description, 263–265
forecasting, 263
Perez v. Chase Manhattan Bank, 315
Perfect capital market
assumptions, 111, 113
and interest rate parity, 144–155
and purchasing power parity, 114–122
Perfect capital mobility, 196
Perfect substitutability, 196
Peso problem, 254, 267, 268, 545, 568
Philadelphia Stock Exchange (PHLX), 418;
see also options
Plaza Accord, 36, 37
Plaza Hotel, 36, 48
Plaza-Louvre Intervention Accords, 26, 35–37

Post-sample results,
definition 205
spot exchange rate determination, 210–212
Predex, 251
Preferred local habitat model, 203–204
Price determinants, 10
Price discrimination, 124, 135
Price dispersion, 87, 88
Price discovery, 377
Price-over-cost margin, 605
Price relationships, 10, 11
Pricing efficiency, 11
Privatization, 558
Procter and Gamble, 8, 504, 505
Profit margin, 605
Profit maximizing, 133
Purchasing power parity (PPP), 111–138
absolute PPP; *see*
and the CAPM, 577–579, 582–585
causality, 118, 119
described, 113–119
deviations, 128
equities, 577–579, 582–585
in the gold standard, 27
neutral band, 122
perfect capital markets, 114–122
PPP spot rate, 118
real exchange rate and, 119–121
relative purchasing parity; *see*
taxes, 122
transaction costs, 121, 122
uncertainty, 122
usefulness, 112, 113
Pure expectations model, 395
Put-call-forward parity, 11, 450
Put-call parity, 11, 450
Put option, 421

Qualified institution buyer, 366
Queuing, 342, 343
Quotron, 98

Random walk, 11
with drift, 214
forecasting, 272, 273, 278–281
versus long-swings, 48
nonstationary time series, 129
and theory of market efficiency, 230–233
Rate risk, 105
Rational error, 402
Reaction function, 667
Real effective exchange rates, 55–57
Real exchange rate
definition, 66
index of, 120
and purchasing power parity, 119–121
Real income, 119
Real interest rates, 63–65
Reagan, Ronald, 35, 47,
Realignments in the EMS, 48
Reciprocity, 341
Redundancy problem, 31

Redundant security, 91, 376, 420
Regime shift, 46
Registered securities, 343, 356
Regulation
    competitive and coordinated approaches,
        647–652
    costs, 14
    domiciliary approach, 324, 325
    and European Union, 649
    of financial markets, 645–656
    harmonization of, 651
    market supervision as regulation, 651
    of offshore markets, 322–328
    and taxation, 14
Regulation Q, 300, 648, 651
Regulatory arbitrage, 591
Regulatory burden; *see* Net regulatory
    burden
Regulatory dialectic, 648
Regulatory differences, 3
Relative price risk, 601
Relative purchasing parity
    described, 114–119
    empirical evidence, 123–132
    hyperinflationary, 128, 129
    long run data, 129–131
Replicating portfolio
    and forward contracts, 90
    and options, 419, 443, 444, 447–449,
        466, 467
    and synthetic interest rate futures, 413
Reuters Dealing 2000–1, 98,99
Right of offset, 93, 490
Rights, 419
Risk managing, 133
Risk premium
    in forward, 402–404
Risk sharing, 3, 405, 555
Risk reversal, 452
RiskMetrics™, 635, 654, 655
Rollover risk, 6, 487, 489
Royal Dutch Shell 8
Rule 144a market, 366, 367, 648
Rule 415; *see also* shelf registration
Rules of the Game, 23–45; *see also*
    International monetary systems

SACOR, 335
Salomon Smith Barney, 82
Samurai bonds, 334
Satellite market, 566
Saturation effect, 484
Scarcity value, 359, 364, 365, 484
Scenario analysis, 604
SEAQ International, 590
Securities and Exchange Commission
    (SEC), 5, 340, 646
    and accounting diversity, 591, 592
Securities transaction taxes, 562, 645,
    671, 672
Segmented capital market, 356
Selling group, 346
Sentiment, 48
Settlement price, 380, 388
Settlement risk, 99

Shelf registration, 343, 365
Showa Shell, 8
Signaling, 85
Simple efficiency model, 229, 248
Simple returns, 178
Singapore International Monetary Exchange
    (SIMEX), 377, 409, 410
Smile effect, 462
Smithsonian Agreement, 33, 38
Snake in the tunnel, 38
Sokoloff v. National City Bank, 315
Soros, George, 174
Special Drawing Rights (SDR), 33
Speculation,
    description, 87
    destabilizing, 656, 659, 667–669,
        671, 672
    and options, 436, 437
    stabilizing, 656, 659, 667–669,
        671, 672
Speculative bubble, 35, 217, 672
Spot and forward contracts
    relationship between, 90–95
Spot contracts
    defined, 85, 86
Spot exchange rates; *see models of exchange
    rates*
Spot currency options; *see also* Options
State of Wisconsin, 9
State Street Bank, 82
Stationary time series, 129, 270, 272, 273
Sterilized intervention, 37, 661–663
Store of value, 80, 113
Straddles, 436, 437
Strike price, *see* Exercise price
Structural arbitrage, 649
Structured finance, 647
Sumitomo Corporation, 9
Survivorship bias, 589
Swap
    absolute advantage, 482
    amortization effect, 494
    applications 502–506
    BIS capital requirements, 506–508
    comparative advantage, 482
    description, 475, 481–488
    diffusion effect, 493
    exotic swaps, 469, 470
    expected exposure, 496–498
    formation of AAA subsidiaries, 505
    gross exposure, 481
    gross market value, 481
    and interest rate volatility, 494, 495
    and netting agreements, 508–510
    notional value, 475
    pricing, 498–501
    risks, 488–498
    simulation approach, 493
    stress testing, 505
Swap agreement, 475
Swap market
    defaults, 506
    dimension, 479–481
    origins, 477–481
    role of segmentation and saturation,
        483–485

Swap-driven loan, 94
Swiss National Bank, 85, 664
Synthetic interest rate futures, 413, 414
Synthetic fixed rate finance, 487
Synthetic forwards, 91, 172
Synthetic option, 420
Synthetic securities, 91, 94, 95
Systemic risk, 6
System of payments, 6

Target zones, 24, 37
Taxes, 122, 148, 149, 160, 411
Technical trading rules, 239–247
Temporal method, 608
Tequila effect, 9
Term structure of forward rates, 399–402
Term structure of implied forward interest
    rate, 401
Texaco, 100
Time value, 440
Tobin, James, 411, 671
Traders calendar, 184, 185
Trade-point, 590
Transaction costs, 121, 122
    and futures markets, 411
Transaction exposure, 609
Transamerica Inc., 100
Translation adjustment account, 611
Translation exposure, 607
Translation gains and losses, 610–612
Transparent, 96
Transport costs, 121
Triangular parity, 88
Trichet, Jean-Claude, 44
Triffin Dilemma, 32

Unbundling, 296, 301
Uncertainty, 122
Uncovered interest parity; *see*
    Fisher parities
Underwriting, 345, 346
Uniform Preference Model, 203
U.S. Treasury Specially Targeted Treasury
    Notes, 359
Units of the real exchange rate, 120
Unsterilized intervention, 661, 662

Value-at-risk (VAR), 106, 507, 633–636,
    652, 653
Variable-price reoffering, 347
Variation margin, 381
Vehicle contract, 414
Vehicle currency, 88
Vietnam War, 33, 315, 316
Vishipco v. Chase Manhattan Bank,
    315, 316
Volatility
    defined, 427, 428
    estimating volatility using historical and
        combined, 462, 463
    and financial performance, 5
    and firm performance, 17–19
    and future prices, 410, 411

Volatility—*Cont.*
    historical volatility, 53, 460–463
    implied volatility, 53, 456
    interest rate on swaps, 494, 495
    in spot exchange rates, 52–55
    in underlying markets, 464, 465
Voluntary Foreign Credit Restraint Program,
    32, 336, 648

Volcker, Paul, 35

Warburg Dillon Reed, 101
Warrants, 419
Wells Fargo Asia Limited v. Citibank, 316, 317
Werner Plan, 37, 38
World Bank, 4, 354, 355

World Equity Benchmark Shares (WEBS),
    569–571

Yankee bonds, 334

Zero-net supply, 420
Zero-sum game, 83, 420

SPOT EXCHANGE RATES
JANUARY 1970–DECEMBER 1999

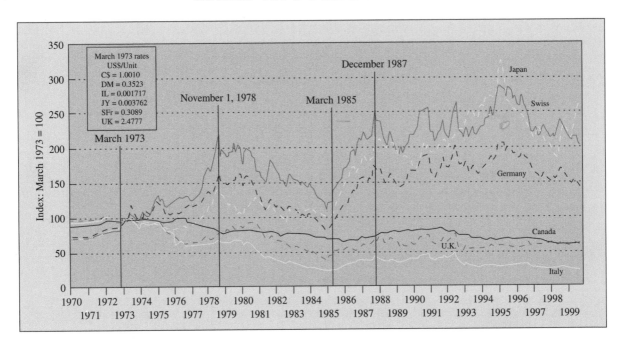